CORE
EU LEGISLATION 2021–22

Paul Drury

macmillan
international
HIGHER EDUCATION

RED GLOBE
PRESS

The *Macmillan Core Statutes* series

Macmillan Core Statutes

Core Statutes on Contract, Tort & Restitution — Graham Stephenson

Core Statutes on Criminal Law — Mark James

Core Statutes on Family Law — Frances Burton

Core Statutes on Property Law — Peter Luther & Alan Moran

Core Statutes on Company Law — Cowan Ervine

Core Statutes on Employment Law — Rachel Horton

Core Statutes on Commercial & Consumer Law — Graham Stephenson

Core EU Legislation — Paul Drury

Core Statutes on Conflict of Laws — Emmanuel Maganaris

Core Statutes on Criminal Justice & Sentencing — Martin Wasik

Core Statutes on Evidence — Jonathan McGahan

Core Documents on International Law — Karen Hulme

Core Documents on European & International Human Rights — Rhona Smith

Core Statutes on Intellectual Property — Margaret Dowie-Whybrow

The Macmillan Core Statutes series has been developed to meet the needs of today's law students. Compiled by experienced lecturers, each title contains the essential materials needed at LLB level and, where applicable, on GDL/CPE courses. They are specifically designed to be easy to use under exam conditions and in the lecture hall.

www.macmillanihe.com/corestatutes

macmillan international
HIGHER EDUCATION

RED GLOBE PRESS

This edition published 2021 by
RED GLOBE PRESS

Previous editions published under the imprint PALGRAVE

Red Globe Press in the UK is an imprint of Macmillan Education Limited, registered in England, company number 01755588, of 4 Crinan Street, London, N1 9XW.

Red Globe Press® is a registered trademark in the United States, the United Kingdom, Europe and other countries.

ISBN 978-1-352-01279-8 paperback

A catalogue record for this book is available from the British Library.

A catalog record for this book is available from the Library of Congress.

CONTENTS

Contents

PREFACE

Dear Reader,

Thank you for buying *EU Legislation 2021–22*, updated to reflect ongoing developments in EU law.

Since the last edition, the UK has withdrawn from the EU, and a Trade and Cooperation Agreement is now in effect.

As well as regular updates to exiting EU law, this edition includes the Ireland/Northern Ireland Protocol in the EU-UK Withdrawal Agreement.

This collection of EU treaty law and legislation will help you easily find the core legal texts of this international organisation. I have set out the law as it stands at the beginning of June 2021.

These materials are free from annotations and so are suitable for private study and for use in examinations. For more detailed study, recourse should be had to the full (unedited) text of the instruments, most of which can be located through links from the website of the European Union: http://europa.eu and from http://eur-lex.europa.eu.

I am grateful to receive any queries, comments or suggestions about the content and style of this book. If there are any suggestions for additional material you think should also be included, that will be interesting to hear about.

I hope this book helps you in your EU law related studies.

Paul Drury
June 2021

TABLES OF EQUIVALENCES

Treaty on the Functioning of the European Union

[Note. This table is extracted from the annex to the Treaty of Amsterdam and the Treaty of Lisbon. For reasons of space, only key provisions are replicated, primarily selected to aid understanding of older case law. Reference to the full text of each version of the Treaty may be required to identify the exact article or paragraph which is equivalent to any particular provision. Note also that the first article number is provided, though often the subject is addressed in immediately subsequent articles.]

TFEU (post Lisbon)	TEEC (post Amsterdam)	TEC (post Maastricht)
1 (principles of Union)	1	1
2 (tasks of Union)	2	2
8 (statement of equality)	3(2)	3
18 (non-discrimination and citizenship)	12	6
26 (internal market)	14	7a
28 (customs union)	23	9
34 (quantitative restrictions – goods)	28	30
38 (agriculture and fisheries)	32	38
45 (free movement of workers)	39	48
49 (right of establishment)	43	52
56 (freedom of services)	49	59
63 (free movement of capital)	56	73
67 (area of freedom, security and justice)	61	73i
77 (border checks, asylum and immigration)	62	73j
81 (judicial cooperation in civil matters)	65	73m
101 (rules on undertakings, competition law)	81	85
102 (dominant position, competition law)	82	86
107 (aids granted by States)	87	92
110 (tax provisions)	90	95
114 (approximation of laws)	95	100a
127 (monetary policy)	105	105
151 (social policy)	136	117
157 (equal pay for equal work)	141	119
162 (European Social Fund)	146	123
165 (education, vocational training, youth and sport)	149	126
167 (culture)	151	128
168 (public health)	152	129
169 (consumer protection)	153	129a
191 (environment)	174	130r
206 (common commercial policy)	131	110

TFEU (post Lisbon)	TEEC (post Amsterdam)	TEC (post Maastricht)
208 (development cooperation)	177	130u
223 (European Parliament)	189	137
235 (European Council)		
237 (Council (of Ministers))	202	145
244 (Commission)	211	155
251 (Court of Justice)	220	164
267 (preliminary rulings)	234	177
285 (Court of Auditors)	246	188a
288 (acts of the Union)	149	189
293 (procedures for adopting acts and other measures)	250	189a
301 (Economic and Social Committee)	257	193
305 (Committee of the Regions)	263	198a
308 (European Investment Bank)	266	198d

Treaty on European Union

Old numbering of the Treaty on European Union	New numbering of the Treaty on European Union	Old numbering of the Treaty on European Union	New numbering of the Treaty on European Union
Article 1	Article 1	Article 19	Article 34
Article 2	Article 3	Article 20	Article 35
Article 6	Article 6	Article 21	Article 36
Article 7	Article 7	Article 22	Article 30
Article 8	Article 9	Article 23	Article 31
Article 10	Article 20	Article 24	Article 37
Article 11	Article 24	Article 25	Article 38
Article 12	Article 25	Articles 43 to 45	Article 20
Article 13	Article 26	Article 47	Article 40
Article 14	Article 28	Article 48	Article 48
Article 15	Article 29	Article 49	Article 49
Article 16	Article 32	Article 51	Article 53
Article 17	Article 42	Article 52	Article 54
Article 18	Article 33	Article 53	Article 55

Treaty of Lisbon
EU Treaties Change Names

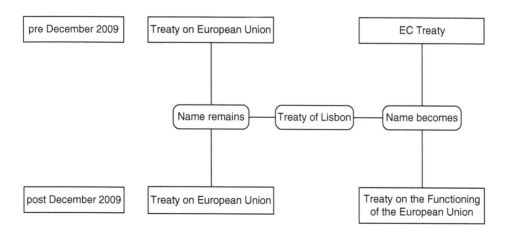

Figure 1   One of the EU Treaties changed its name in 2009 after amendment by the Treaty of Lisbon.

PRIMARY CONSTITUTIONAL LEGISLATION

CONSOLIDATED VERSION
OF THE TREATY ON EUROPEAN UNION

[THE CONTRACTING PARTIES]

RESOLVED to mark a new stage in the process of European integration undertaken with the establishment of the European Communities,

DRAWING INSPIRATION from the cultural, religious and humanist inheritance of Europe, from which have developed the universal values of the inviolable and inalienable rights of the human person, freedom, democracy, equality and the rule of law,

RECALLING the historic importance of the ending of the division of the European continent and the need to create firm bases for the construction of the future Europe,

CONFIRMING their attachment to the principles of liberty, democracy and respect for human rights and fundamental freedoms and of the rule of law,

CONFIRMING their attachment to fundamental social rights as defined in the European Social Charter signed at Turin on 18 October 1961 and in the 1989 Community Charter of the Fundamental Social Rights of Workers,

DESIRING to deepen the solidarity between their peoples while respecting their history, their culture and their traditions,

DESIRING to enhance further the democratic and efficient functioning of the institutions so as to enable them better to carry out, within a single institutional framework, the tasks entrusted to them,

RESOLVED to achieve the strengthening and the convergence of their economies and to establish an economic and monetary union including, in accordance with the provisions of this Treaty and of the Treaty on the Functioning of the European Union, a single and stable currency,

DETERMINED to promote economic and social progress for their peoples, taking into account the principle of sustainable development and within the context of the accomplishment of the internal market and of reinforced cohesion and environmental protection, and to implement policies ensuring that advances in economic integration are accompanied by parallel progress in other fields,

RESOLVED to establish a citizenship common to nationals of their countries,

RESOLVED to implement a common foreign and security policy including the progressive framing of a common defence policy, which might lead to a common defence in accordance with the provisions of Article 42, thereby reinforcing the European identity and its independence in order to promote peace, security and progress in Europe and in the world,

RESOLVED to facilitate the free movement of persons, while ensuring the safety and security of their peoples, by establishing an area of freedom, security and justice, in accordance with the provisions of this Treaty and of the Treaty on the Functioning of the European Union,

RESOLVED to continue the process of creating an ever closer union among the peoples of Europe, in which decisions are taken as closely as possible to the citizen in accordance with the principle of subsidiarity,

IN VIEW of further steps to be taken in order to advance European integration,

HAVE DECIDED to establish a European Union and to this end ... have agreed as follows.

TITLE I
COMMON PROVISIONS

Article 1

By this Treaty, the HIGH CONTRACTING PARTIES establish among themselves a EUROPEAN UNION, hereinafter called 'the Union' on which the Member States confer   to attain objectives they have in common.

This Treaty marks a new stage in the process of creating an ever closer union among the peoples of Europe, in which decisions are taken as openly as possible and as closely as possible to the citizen.

The Union shall be founded on the present Treaty and on the Treaty on the Functioning of the European Union (hereinafter referred to as 'the Treaties'). Those two Treaties shall have the same legal value. The Union shall replace and succeed the European Community.

Article 2

The Union is founded on the values of respect for human dignity, freedom, democracy, equality, the rule of law and respect for human rights, including the rights of persons belonging to minorities. These values are common to the Member States in a society in which pluralism, non-discrimination, tolerance, justice, solidarity and equality between women and men prevail.

Article 3

1. The Union's aim is to promote peace, its values and the well-being of its peoples.
2. The Union shall offer its citizens an area of freedom, security and justice without internal frontiers, in which the free movement of persons is ensured in conjunction with appropriate measures with respect to external border controls, asylum, immigration and the prevention and combating of crime.
3. The Union shall establish an internal market. It shall work for the sustainable development of Europe based on balanced economic growth and price stability, a highly competitive social market economy, aiming at full employment and social progress, and a high level of protection and improvement of the quality of the environment. It shall promote scientific and technological advance.

   It shall combat social exclusion and discrimination, and shall promote social justice and protection, equality between women and men, solidarity between generations and protection of the rights of the child.

   It shall promote economic, social and territorial cohesion, and solidarity among Member States.

   It shall respect its rich cultural and linguistic diversity, and shall ensure that Europe's cultural heritage is safeguarded and enhanced.
4. The Union shall establish an economic and monetary union whose currency is the euro.
5. In its relations with the wider world, the Union shall uphold and promote its values and contribute to the protection if its citizens. It shall contribute to peace, security, the sustainable development of the Earth, solidarity and mutual respect among peoples, free and fair trade, eradication of poverty and the protection of human rights, in particular the rights of the child, as well as to the strict observance and the development of international law , including respect for the principles of the United Nations Charter.
6. The Union shall pursue its objectives by appropriate means commensurate with the competences which are conferred upon it in the Treaties.

Article 4

1. In accordance with Article 5, competences not conferred upon the Union in the Treaties remain with the Member States.
2. The Union shall respect the equality of Member States before the Treaties as well as their national identities, inherent in their fundamental structures, political and constitutional, inclusive of regional and local self-government. it shall respect their essential State functions, including ensuring the territorial integrity of the State, maintaining law and order and safeguarding national security. In particular, national security remains the sole responsibility of each Member State.
3. Pursuant to the principle of sincere cooperation, the Union and the Member States shall, in full mutual respect, assist each other in carrying out tasks which flow from the Treaties. The Member States shall take any appropriate measure, general or particular, to ensure fulfilment of the obligations arising out of the Treaties or resulting from the acts of the institutions of the Union.

   The Member States shall facilitate the achievement of the Union's tasks and refrain from any measure which could jeopardise the attainment of the Union's objectives.

Article 5

1. The limits of Union competences are governed by the principle of conferral. The use of Union competences is governed by the principles of subsidiarity and proportionality.
2. Under the principle of conferral, the Union shall act only within the limits of the competences conferred upon it by the Member States in the Treaties to attain the objectives set out therein. Competences not conferred upon the Union in the Treaties remain with the Member States.

3. Under the principle of subsidiarity, in areas which do not fall within its exclusive competence, the Union shall act only if and insofar as the objectives of the proposed action cannot be sufficiently achieved by the Member States, either at central level or at regional and local level, but can rather, by reason of the scale or effects of the proposed action, be better achieved at Union level.
    The institutions of the Union shall apply the principle of subsidiarity as laid down in the Protocol on the application of the principles of subsidiarity and proportionality. National Parliaments ensure compliance with the principle of subsidiarity in accordance with the procedure set out in that Protocol.
4. Under the principle of proportionality, the content and form of Union action shall not exceed what is necessary to achieve the objectives of the Treaties.
    The institutions of the Union shall apply the principle of proportionality as laid down in the Protocol on the application of the principles of subsidiarity and proportionality.

Article 6

1. The Union recognises the rights, freedoms and principles set out in the Charter of Fundamental Rights of the European Union of 7 December 2000, as adapted at Strasbourg, on 12 December 2007, which shall have the same legal value as the Treaties. The provisions of the Charter shall not extend in any way the competences of the Union as defined in the Treaties.
    The rights, freedoms and principles in the Charter shall be interpreted in accordance with the general provisions in Title VII of the Charter governing its interpretation and application and with due regard to the explanations referred to in the Charter, that set out the sources of those provisions.
2. The Union shall accede to the European Convention for the Protection of Human Rights and Fundamental Freedoms. Such accession shall not affect the Union's competences as defined in the Treaties.
3. Fundamental rights, as guaranteed by the European Convention for the Protection of Human Rights and Fundamental Freedoms and as they result from the constitutional traditions common to the Member States, shall constitute general principles of the Union's law.

Article 7

1. On a reasoned proposal by one third of the Member States, by the European Parliament or by the European Commission, the Council, acting by a majority of four fifths of its members after obtaining the consent of the European Parliament, may determine that there is a clear risk of a serious breach by a Member State of the values referred to in Article 2. Before making such a determination, the Council shall hear the Member State in question and may address recommendations to it, acting in accordance with the same procedure.
    The Council shall regularly verify that the grounds on which such a determination was made continue to apply.
2. The European Council, acting by unanimity on a proposal by one third of the Member States or by the Commission and after obtaining the consent of the European Parliament, may determine the existence of a serious and persistent breach by a Member State of the values referred to in Article 2, after inviting the Member State in question to submit its observations.
3. Where a determination under paragraph 2 has been made, the Council, acting by a qualified majority, may decide to suspend certain of the rights deriving from the application of the Treaties to the Member State in question, including the voting rights of the representative of the government of that Member State in the Council. In doing so, the Council shall take into account the possible consequences of such a suspension on the rights and obligations of natural and legal persons.
    The obligations of the Member State in question under this Treaty shall in any case continue to be binding on that State.
4. The Council, acting by a qualified majority, may decide subsequently to vary or revoke measures taken under paragraph 3 in response to changes in the situation which led to their being imposed.

5.   The voting arrangements applying to the European Parliament, the European Council and the Council for the purposes of this Article are laid down in Article 354 of the Treaty on the Functioning of the European Union.

Article 8

1.   The Union shall develop a special relationship with neighbouring countries, aiming to establish an area of prosperity and good neighbourliness, founded on the values of the Union and characterised by close and peaceful relations based on cooperation.
2.   For the purposes of paragraph 1, the Union may conclude specific agreements with the countries concerned. These agreements may contain reciprocal rights and obligations as well as the possibility of undertaking activities jointly. Their implementation shall be the subject of periodic consultation.

TITLE II

PROVISIONS ON DEMOCRATIC PRINCIPLES

Article 9

In all its activities, the Union shall observe the principle of the equality of its citizens, who shall receive equal attention from its institutions, bodies, offices and agencies. Every national of a Member State shall be a citizen of the Union. Citizenship of the Union shall be additional to national citizenship and shall not replace it.

Article 10

1.   The functioning of the Union shall be founded on representative democracy.
2.   Citizens are directly represented at Union level in the European Parliament.
      Member States are represented in the European Council by their Heads of State or Government and in the Council by their governments, themselves democratically accountable either to their national Parliaments, or to their citizens.
3.   Every citizen shall have the right to participate in the democratic life of the Union. Decisions shall be taken as openly and as closely as possible to the citizen.
4.   Political parties at European level contribute to forming European political awareness and to expressing the will of citizens of the Union.

Article 11

1.   The institutions shall, by appropriate means, give citizens and representative associations the opportunity to make known and publicly exchange their views in all areas of Union action.
2.   The institutions shall maintain an open, transparent and regular dialogue with representative associations and civil society.
3.   The European Commission shall carry out broad consultations with parties concerned in order to ensure that the Union's actions are coherent and transparent.
4.   Not less than one million citizens who are nationals of a significant number of Member States may take the initiative of inviting the European Commission, within the framework of its powers, to submit any appropriate proposal on matters where citizens consider that a legal act of the Union is required for the purpose of implementing the Treaties.
      The procedures and conditions required for such a citizens' initiative shall be determined in accordance with the first paragraph of Article 24 of the Treaty on the Functioning of the European Union.

Article 12

National Parliaments contribute actively to the good functioning of the Union:

(a)   through being informed by the institutions of the Union and having draft legislative acts of the Union forwarded to them in accordance with the Protocol on the role of national Parliaments in the European Union;
(b)   by seeing to it that the principle of subsidiarity is respected in accordance with the procedures provided for in the Protocol on the application of the principles of subsidiarity and proportionality;
(c)   by taking part, within the framework of the area of freedom, security and justice, in the evaluation mechanisms for the implementation of the Union policies in that area, in accordance with Article 70 of the Treaty on the Functioning of

the European Union, and through being involved in the political monitoring of Europol and the evaluation of Eurojust's activities in accordance with Articles 88 and 85 of that Treaty;

(d) by taking part in the revision procedures of the Treaties, in accordance with Article 48 of this Treaty;

(e) by being notified of applications for accession to the Union, in accordance with Article 49 of this Treaty;

(f) by taking part in the interparliamentary cooperation between national Parliaments and with the European Parliament, in accordance with the Protocol on the role of national Parliaments in the European Union.

TITLE III
PROVISIONS ON THE INSTITUTIONS

Article 13

1. The Union shall have an institutional framework which shall aim to promote its values, advance its objectives, serve its interests, those of its citizens and those of the Member States, and ensure the consistency, effectiveness and continuity of its policies and actions. This institutional framework comprises:
   — The European Parliament,
   — The European Council,
   — The Council,
   — The European Commission (hereinafter referred to as 'the Commission'),
   — The Court of Justice of the European Union,
   — The European Central Bank,
   — The Court of Auditors.

2. Each institution shall act within the limits of the powers conferred on it in the Treaties, and in conformity with the procedures, conditions and objectives set out in them. The institutions shall practise mutual sincere cooperation.

3. The provisions relating to the European Central Bank and the Court of Auditors and detailed provisions on the other institutions are set out in the Treaty on the Functioning of the European Union.

4. The European Parliament, the Council and the Commission shall be assisted by an Economic and Social Committee and a Committee of the Regions acting in an advisory capacity.

Article 14

1. The European Parliament shall, jointly with the Council, exercise legislative and budgetary functions. It shall exercise functions of political control and consultation as laid down in the Treaties. It shall elect the President of the Commission.

2. The European Parliament shall be composed of representatives of the Union's citizens. They shall not exceed seven hundred and fifty in number, plus the President. Representation of citizens shall be degressively proportional, with a minimum threshold of six members per Member State. No Member State shall be allocated more than ninety-six seats.
   The European Council shall adopt by unanimity, on the initiative of the European Parliament and with its consent, a decision establishing the composition of the European Parliament, respecting the principles referred to in the first subparagraph.

3. The members of the European Parliament shall be elected for a term of five years by direct universal suffrage in a free and secret ballot.

4. The European Parliament shall elect its President and its officers from among its members.

Article 15

1. The European Council shall provide the Union with the necessary impetus for its development and shall define the general political directions and priorities thereof. It shall not exercise legislative functions.

2. The European Council shall consist of the Heads of State or Government of the Member States, together with its President and the President of the Commission. The High Representative of the Union for Foreign Affairs and Security Policy shall take part in its work.

3. The European Council shall meet twice every six months, convened by its President. When the agenda so requires, the members of the European Council may decide each to be assisted by a minister and, in the case of the President of the Commission, by a member of the Commission. When the situation so requires, the President shall convene a special meeting of the European Council.

4. Except where the Treaties provide otherwise, decisions of the European Council shall be taken by consensus.

5. The European Council shall elect its President, by a qualified majority, for a term of two and a half years, renewable once. In the event of an impediment or serious misconduct, the European Council can end the President's term of office in accordance with the same procedure.

6. The President of the European Council:
   (a) shall chair it and drive forward its work;
   (b) shall ensure the preparation and continuity of the work of the European Council in cooperation with the President of the Commission, and on the basis of the work of the General Affairs Council;
   (c) shall endeavour to facilitate cohesion and consensus within the European Council;
   (d) shall present a report to the European Parliament after each of the meetings of the European Council.

   The President of the European Council shall, at his or her level and in that capacity, ensure the external representation of the Union on issues concerning its common foreign and security policy, without prejudice to the powers of the High Representative of the Union for Foreign Affairs and Security Policy.

   The President of the European Council shall not hold a national office.

Article 16

1. The Council shall, jointly with the European Parliament, exercise legislative and budgetary functions. It shall carry out policy-making and coordinating functions as laid down in the Treaties.

2. The Council shall consist of a representative of each Member State at ministerial level, who may commit the government of the Member State in question and cast its vote.

3. The Council shall act by a qualified majority except where the Treaties provide otherwise.

4. As from 1 November 2014, a qualified majority shall be defined as at least 55% of the members of the Council, comprising at least fifteen of them and representing Member States comprising at least 65% of the population of the Union.

   A blocking minority must include at least four Council members, failing which the qualified majority shall be deemed attained.

   The other arrangements governing the qualified majority are laid down in Article 238(2) of the Treaty on the Functioning of the European Union.

5. The transitional provisions relating to the definition of the qualified majority which shall be applicable until 31 October 2014 and those which shall be applicable from 1 November 2014 to 31 March 2017 are laid down in the Protocol on transitional provisions.

6. The Council shall meet in different configurations, the list of which shall be adopted in accordance with Article 236 of the Treaty on the Functioning of the European Union.

   The General Affairs Council shall ensure consistency in the work of the different Council configurations. It shall prepare and ensure the follow-up to meetings of the European Council, in liaison with the President of the European Council and the Commission.

   The Foreign Affairs Council shall elaborate the Union's external action on the basis of strategic guidelines laid down by the European Council and ensure that the Union's action is consistent.

7. A Committee of Permanent Representatives of the Governments of the Member States shall be responsible for preparing the work of the Council.

8. The Council shall meet in public when it deliberates and votes on a draft legislative act. To this end, each Council meeting shall be divided into two parts, dealing respectively with deliberations on Union legislative acts and on non-legislative activities.

9. The Presidency of Council configurations, other than that of Foreign Affairs, shall be held by Member State representatives in the Council on the basis of equal rotation, in accordance with the conditions established in accordance with Article 236 of the Treaty on the Functioning of the European Union.

Article 17

1. The Commission shall promote the general interest of the Union and take appropriate initiatives to that end. It shall ensure the application of the Treaties, and of measures adopted by the institutions pursuant to the Treaties. It shall oversee the application of Union law under the control of the Court of Justice of the European Union. It shall execute the budget and manage programmes. It shall exercise coordinating, executive and management functions, as laid down in the Treaties. With the exception of the common foreign and security policy, and other cases provided for in the Treaties, it shall ensure the Union's external representation. It shall initiate the Union's annual and multiannual programming with a view to achieving interinstitutional agreements.

2. Union legislative acts may only be adopted on the basis of a Commission proposal, except where the Treaties provide otherwise. Other acts shall be adopted on the basis of a Commission proposal where the Treaties so provide.

3. The Commission's term of office shall be five years.

   The members of the Commission shall be chosen on the ground of their general competence and European commitment from persons whose independence is beyond doubt.

   In carrying out its responsibilities, the Commission shall be completely independent. Without prejudice to Article 18(2), the members of the Commission shall neither seek nor take instructions from any Government or other institution, body, office or entity. They shall refrain from any action incompatible with their duties or the performance of their tasks.

4. The Commission appointed between the date of entry into force of the Treaty of Lisbon and 31 October 2014, shall consist of one national of each Member State, including its President and the High Representative of the Union for Foreign Affairs and Security Policy who shall be one of its Vice-Presidents.

5. As from 1 November 2014, the Commission shall consist of a number of members, including its President and the High Representative of the Union for Foreign Affairs and Security Policy, corresponding to two thirds of the number of Member States, unless the European Council, acting unanimously, decides to alter this number.

   The members of the Commission shall be selected from among the nationals of the Member States on the basis of a system of strictly equal rotation between the Member States, reflecting the demographic and geographical range of all the Member States. This system shall be established unanimously by the European Council in accordance with Article 244 of the Treaty on the Functioning of the European Union.

6. The President of the Commission shall:
   (a) lay down guidelines within which the Commission is to work;
   (b) decide on the internal organisation of the Commission, ensuring that it acts consistently, efficiently and as a collegiate body;
   (c) appoint Vice-Presidents, other than the High Representative of the Union for Foreign Affairs and Security Policy, from among the members of the Commission.

   A member of the Commission shall resign if the President so requests. The High Representative of the Union for Foreign Affairs and Security Policy shall resign, in accordance with the procedure set out in Article 18(1), if the President so requests.

7. Taking into account the elections to the European Parliament and after having held the appropriate consultations, the European Council, acting by a qualified majority, shall propose to the European Parliament a candidate for President of the Commission. This candidate shall be elected by the European Parliament by a majority of its component members. If he does not obtain the required majority, the European Council, acting by a qualified majority, shall within one month propose a new candidate who shall be elected by the European Parliament following the same procedure.

   The Council, by common accord with the President-elect, shall adopt the list of the other persons whom it proposes for appointment as members of the Commission. They shall be selected, on the basis of the suggestions made by Member States, in accordance with the criteria set out in paragraph 3, second subparagraph, and paragraph 5, second subparagraph.

   The President, the High Representative of the Union for Foreign Affairs and Security Policy and the other members of the Commission shall be subject as a body to a vote of consent by the European Parliament. On the basis of this consent the Commission shall be appointed by the European Council, acting by a qualified majority.

8. The Commission, as a body, shall be responsible to the European Parliament. In accordance with Article 234 of the Treaty on the Functioning of the European Union, the European Parliament may vote on a motion of censure of the Commission. If such a motion is carried, the members of the Commission shall resign as a body and the High Representative of the Union for Foreign Affairs and Security Policy shall resign from the duties that he carries out in the Commission.

Article 18

1. The European Council, acting by a qualified majority, with the agreement of the President of the Commission, shall appoint the High Representative of the Union for Foreign Affairs and Security Policy. The European Council may end his term of office by the same procedure.

2. The High Representative shall conduct the Union's common foreign and security policy. He shall contribute by his proposals to the development of that policy, which he shall carry out as mandated by the Council. The same shall apply to the common security and defence policy.

3. The High Representative shall preside over the Foreign Affairs Council.

4. The High Representative shall be one of the Vice-Presidents of the Commission. He shall ensure the consistency of the Union's external action. He shall be responsible within the Commission for responsibilities incumbent on it in external relations and for coordinating other aspects of the Union's external action. In exercising these responsibilities within the Commission, and only for these responsibilities, the High Representative shall be bound by Commission procedures to the extent that this is consistent with paragraphs 2 and 3.

Article 19

1. The Court of Justice of the European Union shall include the Court of Justice, the General Court and specialised courts. It shall ensure that in the interpretation and application of the Treaties the law is observed.
    Member States shall provide remedies sufficient to ensure effective legal protection in the fields covered by Union law.

2. The Court of Justice shall consist of one judge from each Member State. It shall be assisted by Advocates-General.
    The General Court shall include at least one judge per Member State.
    The Judges and the Advocates-General of the Court of Justice and the Judges of the General Court shall be chosen from persons whose independence is beyond doubt and who satisfy the conditions set out in Articles 253 and 254 of the Treaty on the Functioning of the European Union. They shall be appointed by common accord of the governments of the Member States for six years. Retiring Judges and Advocates General may be reappointed.

3. The Court of Justice of the European Union shall, in accordance with the Treaties:
    (a) rule on actions brought by a Member State, an institution or a natural or legal person;
    (b) give preliminary rulings, at the request of courts or tribunals of the Member States, on the interpretation of Union law or the validity of acts adopted by the institutions;
    (c) rule in other cases provided for in the Treaties.

TITLE IV
PROVISIONS ON ENHANCED COOPERATION

Article 20

1. Member States which wish to establish enhanced cooperation between themselves within the framework of the Union's non-exclusive competences may make use of its institutions and exercise those competences by applying the relevant provisions of the Treaties, subject to the limits and in accordance with the detailed arrangements laid down in this Article and in Articles 326 to 334 of the Treaty on the Functioning of the European Union. Enhanced cooperation shall aim to further the objectives of the Union, protect its interests and reinforce its integration process. Such cooperation shall be open at any time to all Member States, in accordance with Article 328 of the Treaty on the Functioning of the European Union.

2. The decision authorising enhanced cooperation shall be adopted by the Council as a last resort, when it has established that the objectives of such cooperation cannot be attained within a reasonable period by the Union as a whole, and provided that at least nine Member States participate in it. The Council shall act in accordance with the procedure laid down in Article 329 of the Treaty on the Functioning of the European Union.

3. All members of the Council may participate in its deliberations, but only members of the Council representing the Member States participating in enhanced cooperation shall take part in the vote. The voting rules are set out in Article 330 of the Treaty on the Functioning of the European Union.

4. Acts adopted in the framework of enhanced cooperation shall bind only participating Member States. They shall not be regarded as part of the acquis which has to be accepted by candidate States for accession to the Union.

TITLE V
GENERAL PROVISIONS ON THE UNION'S EXTERNAL ACTION AND SPECIFIC PROVISIONS ON THE COMMON FOREIGN AND SECURITY POLICY

CHAPTER 1
GENERAL PROVISIONS ON THE UNION'S EXTERNAL ACTION

Article 21

1. The Union's action on the international scene shall be guided by the principles which have inspired its own creation, development and enlargement, and which it seeks to advance in the wider world: democracy, the rule of law, the universality and indivisibility of human rights and fundamental freedoms, respect for human dignity, the principles of equality and solidarity, and respect for the principles of the United Nations Charter and international law.
The Union shall seek to develop relations and build partnerships with third countries, and international, regional or global organisations which share the principles referred to in the first subparagraph. It shall promote multilateral solutions to common problems, in particular in the framework of the United Nations.

2. The Union shall define and pursue common policies and actions, and shall work for a high degree of cooperation in all fields of international relations, in order to:
   (a) safeguard its values, fundamental interests, security, independence and integrity;
   (b) consolidate and support democracy, the rule of law, human rights and the principles of international law;
   (c) preserve peace, prevent conflicts and strengthen international security, in accordance with the purposes and principles of the United Nations Charter, with the principles of the Helsinki Final Act and with the aims of the Charter of Paris, including those relating to external borders;
   (d) foster the sustainable economic, social and environmental development of developing countries, with the primary aim of eradicating poverty;
   (e) encourage the integration of all countries into the world economy, including through the progressive abolition of restrictions on international trade;
   (f) help develop international measures to preserve and improve the quality of the environment and the sustainable management of global natural resources, in order to ensure sustainable development;
   (g) assist populations, countries and regions confronting natural or man-made disasters; and
   (h) promote an international system based on stronger multilateral cooperation and good global governance.

3. The Union shall respect the principles and pursue the objectives set out in paragraphs 1 and 2 in the development and implementation of the different areas of the Union's external action covered by this Title and by Part Five of the Treaty on the Functioning of the European Union, and of the external aspects of its other policies.
The Union shall ensure consistency between the different areas of its external action and between these and its other policies. The Council and the Commission, assisted by the High Representative of the Union for Foreign Affairs and Security Policy, shall ensure that consistency and shall cooperate to that effect.

CHAPTER 2
SPECIFIC PROVISIONS CONCERNING THE COMMON FOREIGN AND SECURITY POLICY

SECTION 1
COMMON PROVISIONS

Article 23

The Union's action on the international scene, pursuant to this Chapter, shall be guided by the principles, shall pursue the objectives of, and be conducted in accordance with, the general provisions laid down in Chapter 1.

Article 24

1. The Union's competence in matters of common foreign and security policy shall cover all areas of foreign policy and all questions relating to the Union's security, including the progressive framing of a common defence policy that might lead to a common defence.

   The common foreign and security policy is subject to specific rules and procedures. It shall be defined and implemented by the European Council and the Council acting unanimously, except where the Treaties provide otherwise. The adoption of legislative acts shall be excluded. The common foreign and security policy shall be put into effect by the High Representative of the Union for Foreign Affairs and Security Policy and by Member States, in accordance with the Treaties. The specific role of the European Parliament and of the Commission in this area is defined by the Treaties. The Court of Justice of the European Union shall not have jurisdiction with respect to these provisions, with the exception of its jurisdiction to monitor compliance with Article 40 of this Treaty and to review the legality of certain decisions as provided for by the second paragraph of Article 275 of the Treaty on the Functioning of the European Union.

2. Within the framework of the principles and objectives of its external action, the Union shall conduct, define and implement a common foreign and security policy, based on the development of mutual political solidarity among Member States, the identification of questions of general interest and the achievement of an ever increasing degree of convergence of Member States' actions.

3. The Member States shall support the Union's external and security policy actively and unreservedly in a spirit of loyalty and mutual solidarity and shall comply with the Union's action in this area.

   The Member States shall work together to enhance and develop their mutual political solidarity. They shall refrain from any action which is contrary to the interests of the Union or likely to impair its effectiveness as a cohesive force in international relations. The Council and the High Representative shall ensure compliance with these principles.

Article 25

The Union shall conduct the common foreign and security policy by:

(a) defining the general guidelines,

(b) adopting decisions defining:

    (i) actions to be undertaken by the Union;

    (ii) positions to be taken by the Union;

    (iii) arrangements for the implementation of the decisions referred to in points (i) and (ii);

    and by

(c) strengthening systematic cooperation between Member States in the conduct of policy.

Article 26

1. The European Council shall identify the Union's strategic interests, determine the objectives of and define general guidelines for the common foreign and security policy, including for matters with defence implications. It shall adopt the necessary decisions.

If international developments so require, the President of the European Council shall convene an extraordinary meeting of the European Council in order to define the strategic lines of the Union's policy in the face of such developments.

2. The Council shall frame the common foreign and security policy and take the decisions necessary for defining and implementing it on the basis of the general guidelines and strategic lines defined by the European Council.

   The Council and the High Representative of the Union for Foreign Affairs and Security Policy shall ensure the unity, consistency and effectiveness of action by the Union.

3. The common foreign and security policy shall be put into effect by the High Representative and by the Member States, using national and Union resources.

Article 27

1. The High Representative of the Union for Foreign Affairs and Security Policy, who shall chair the Foreign Affairs Council, shall contribute through his proposals to the development of the common foreign and security policy and shall ensure implementation of the decisions adopted by the European Council and the Council.

2. The High Representative shall represent the Union for matters relating to the common foreign and security policy. He shall conduct political dialogue with third parties on the Union's behalf and shall express the Union's position in international organisations and at international conferences.

3. In fulfilling his mandate, the High Representative shall be assisted by a European External Action Service. This service shall work in cooperation with the diplomatic services of the Member States and shall comprise officials from relevant departments of the General Secretariat of the Council and of the Commission as well as staff seconded from national diplomatic services of the Member States. The organisation and functioning of the European External Action Service shall be established by a decision of the Council. The Council shall act on a proposal from the High Representative after consulting the European Parliament and after obtaining the consent of the Commission.

Article 28

1. Where the international situation requires operational action by the Union, the Council shall adopt the necessary decisions. They shall lay down their objectives, scope, the means to be made available to the Union, if necessary their duration, and the conditions for their implementation.

   If there is a change in circumstances having a substantial effect on a question subject to such a decision, the Council shall review the principles and objectives of that decision and take the necessary decisions.

2. Decisions referred to in paragraph 1 shall commit the Member States in the positions they adopt and in the conduct of their activity.

3. Whenever there is any plan to adopt a national position or take national action pursuant to a decision as referred to in paragraph I, information shall be provided by the Member State concerned in time to allow, if necessary, for prior consultations within the Council. The obligation to provide prior information shall not apply to measures which are merely a national transposition of Council decisions.

4. In cases of imperative need arising from changes in the situation and failing a review of the Council decision as referred to in paragraph 1, Member States may take the necessary measures as a matter of urgency having regard to the general objectives of that decision. The Member State concerned shall inform the Council immediately of any such measures.

5. Should there be any major difficulties in implementing a decision as referred to in this Article, a Member State shall refer them to the Council which shall discuss them and seek appropriate solutions. Such solutions shall not run counter to the objectives of the decision referred to in paragraph 1 or impair its effectiveness.

Article 29

The Council shall adopt decisions which shall define the approach of the Union to a particular matter of a geographical or thematic nature. Member States shall ensure that their national policies conform to the Union's positions.

Article 30

    1.   Any Member State, the High Representative of the Union for Foreign Affairs and Security Policy, or the High Representative with the Commission's support, may refer any question relating to the common foreign and security policy to the Council and may submit to it initiatives or proposals.

    2.   In cases requiring a rapid decision, the High Representative, of his own motion, or at the request of a Member State, shall convene an extraordinary Council meeting within 48 hours or, in an emergency, within a shorter period.

Article 31

    1.   Decisions under this Chapter shall be taken by the European Council and the Council acting unanimously, except where this Chapter provides otherwise. The adoption of legislative acts shall be excluded.

    ...

Article 37

The Union may conclude agreements with one or more States or international organisations in implementation of this Chapter.

Article 38

Without prejudice to Article 240 of the Treaty on the Functioning of the European Union, a Political and Security Committee shall monitor the international situation in the areas covered by the common foreign and security policy and contribute to the definition of policies by delivering opinions to the Council at the request of the Council or of the High Representative of the Union for Foreign Affairs and Security Policy or on its own initiative. It shall also monitor the implementation of agreed policies, without prejudice to the powers of the High Representative. Within the scope of this Chapter, the Political and Security Committee shall exercise, under the responsibility of the Council and of the High Representative, the political control and strategic direction of crisis management operations referred to in Article 43.

The Council may authorise the Committee, for the purpose and for the duration of a crisis management operation, as determined by the Council, to take the relevant decisions concerning the political control and strategic direction of the operation.

Article 39

In accordance with Article 16 of the Treaty on the Functioning of the European Union and by way of derogation from paragraph 2 thereof, the Council shall adopt a decision laying down the rules relating to the protection of individuals with regard to the processing of personal data by the Member States when carrying out activities which fall within the scope of this Chapter, and the rules relating to the free movement of such data. Compliance with these rules shall be subject to the control of independent authorities.

SECTION 2

PROVISIONS ON THE COMMON SECURITY AND DEFENCE POLICY

Article 42

    1.   The common security and defence policy shall be an integral part of the common foreign and security policy. It shall provide the Union with an operational capacity drawing on civilian and military assets. The Union may use them on missions outside the Union for peace-keeping, conflict prevention and strengthening international security in accordance with the principles of the United Nations Charter. The performance of these tasks shall be undertaken using capabilities provided by the Member States.

    2.   The common security and defence policy shall include the progressive framing of a common Union defence policy. This will lead to a common defence, when the European Council, acting unanimously, so decides. It shall in that case recommend to the Member States the adoption of such a decision in accordance with their respective constitutional requirements.

    The policy of the Union in accordance with this Section shall not prejudice the specific character of the security and defence policy of certain Member States and shall respect the obligations of certain Member States, which see their common defence realised in the North Atlantic Treaty Organisation (NATO), under the North Atlantic Treaty and be compatible with the common security and defence policy established within that framework.

3.   Member States shall make civilian and military capabilities available to the Union for the implementation of the common security and defence policy, to contribute to the objectives defined by the Council. Those Member States which together establish multinational forces may also make them available to the common security and defence policy.

Member States shall undertake progressively to improve their military capabilities. An Agency in the field of defence capabilities development, research, acquisition and armaments (hereinafter referred to as 'the European Defence Agency') shall identify operational requirements, shall promote measures to satisfy those requirements, shall contribute to identifying and, where appropriate, implementing any measure needed to strengthen the industrial and technological base of the defence sector, shall participate in defining a European capabilities and armaments policy, and shall assist the Council in evaluating the improvement of military capabilities.

4.   Decisions relating to the common security and defence policy, including those initiating a mission as referred to in this Article, shall be adopted by the Council acting unanimously on a proposal from the High Representative of the Union for Foreign Affairs and Security Policy or an initiative from a Member State. The High Representative may propose the use of both national resources and Union instruments, together with the Commission where appropriate.

5.   The Council may entrust the execution of a task, within the Union framework, to a group of Member States in order to protect the Union's values and serve its interests. The execution of such a task shall be governed by Article 44.

6.   Those Member States whose military capabilities fulfil higher criteria and which have made more binding commitments to one another in this area with a view to the most demanding missions shall establish permanent structured cooperation within the Union framework. Such cooperation shall be governed by Article 46. It shall not affect the provisions of Article 43.

7.   If a Member State is the victim of armed aggression on its territory, the other Member States shall have towards it an obligation of aid and assistance by all the means in their power, in accordance with Article 51 of the United Nations Charter. This shall not prejudice the specific character of the security and defence policy of certain Member States.

Commitments and cooperation in this area shall be consistent with commitments under the North Atlantic Treaty Organisation, which, for those States which are members of it, remains the foundation of their collective defence and the forum for its implementation.

Article 43

1.   The tasks referred to in Article 42(1), in the course of which the Union may use civilian and military means, shall include joint disarmament operations, humanitarian and rescue tasks, military advice and assistance tasks, conflict prevention and peacekeeping tasks, tasks of combat forces in crisis management, including peace-making and post-conflict stabilisation. All these tasks may contribute to the fight against terrorism, including by supporting third countries in combating terrorism in their territories.

2.   The Council shall adopt decisions relating to the tasks referred to in paragraph 1, defining their objectives and scope and the general conditions for their implementation. The High Representative of the Union for Foreign Affairs and Security Policy, acting under the authority of the Council and in close and constant contact with the Political and Security Committee, shall ensure coordination of the civilian and military aspects of such tasks.

Article 45

1.   The European Defence Agency referred to in Article 42(3), subject to the authority of the Council, shall have as its task to:

(a)   contribute to identifying the Member States' military capability objectives and evaluating observance of the capability commitments given by the Member States;

(b)   promote harmonisation of operational needs and adoption of effective, compatible procurement methods;

(c)   propose multilateral projects to fulfil the objectives in terms of military capabilities, ensure coordination of the programmes implemented by the Member States and management of specific cooperation programmes;

(d)   support defence technology research, and coordinate and plan joint research activities and the study of technical solutions meeting future operational needs;

(e)   contribute to identifying and, if necessary, implementing any useful measure for strengthening the industrial and technological base of the defence sector and for improving the effectiveness of military expenditure.

2.   The European Defence Agency shall be open to all Member States wishing to be part of it. The Council, acting by a qualified majority, shall adopt a decision defining the Agency's statute, seat and operational rules. That decision should take account of the level of effective participation in the Agency's activities. Specific groups shall be set up within the Agency bringing together Member States engaged in joint projects. The Agency shall carry out its tasks in liaison with the Commission where necessary.

TITLE VI
FINAL PROVISIONS

Article 47

The Union shall have legal personality.

Article 49

Any European State which respects the values referred to in Article 2 and is committed to promoting them may apply to become a member of the Union. The European Parliament and national Parliaments shall be notified of this application. The applicant State shall address its application to the Council, which shall act unanimously after consulting the Commission and after receiving the consent of the European Parliament, which shall act by a majority of its component members. The conditions of eligibility agreed upon by the European Council shall be taken into account.

The conditions of admission and the adjustments to the Treaties on which the Union is founded, which such admission entails, shall be the subject of an agreement between the Member States and the applicant State. This agreement shall be submitted for ratification by all the contracting States in accordance with their respective constitutional requirements.

Article 50

1.   Any Member State may decide to withdraw from the Union in accordance with its own constitutional requirements.

2.   A Member State which decides to withdraw shall notify the European Council of its intention. In the light of the guidelines provided by the European Council, the Union shall negotiate and conclude an agreement with that State, setting out the arrangements for its withdrawal, taking account of the framework for its future relationship with the Union. That agreement shall be negotiated in accordance with Article 218(3) of the Treaty on the Functioning of the European Union. It shall be concluded on behalf of the Union by the Council, acting by a qualified majority, after obtaining the consent of the European Parliament.

3.   The Treaties shall cease to apply to the State in question from the date of entry into force of the withdrawal agreement or, failing that, two years after the notification referred to in paragraph 2, unless the European Council, in agreement with the Member State concerned, unanimously decides to extend this period.

4.   For the purposes of paragraphs 2 and 3, the member of the European Council or of the Council representing the withdrawing Member State shall not participate in the discussions of the European Council or Council or in decisions concerning it.

A qualified majority shall be defined in accordance with Article 238(3)(b) of the Treaty on the Functioning of the European Union.

5.   If a State which has withdrawn from the Union asks to rejoin, its request shall be subject to the procedure referred to in Article 49.

CONSOLIDATED VERSION OF THE
TREATY ON THE FUNCTIONING OF THE EUROPEAN UNION

[THE CONTRACTING PARTIES]

DETERMINED to lay the foundations of an ever closer union among the peoples of Europe,

RESOLVED to ensure the economic and social progress of their States by common action to eliminate the barriers which divide Europe,

AFFIRMING as the essential objective of their efforts the constant improvements of the living and working conditions of their peoples,

RECOGNISING that the removal of existing obstacles calls for concerted action in order to guarantee steady expansion, balanced trade and fair competition,

ANXIOUS to strengthen the unity of their economies and to ensure their harmonious development by reducing the differences existing between the various regions and the backwardness of the less favoured regions,

DESIRING to contribute, by means of a common commercial policy, to the progressive abolition of restrictions on international trade,

INTENDING to confirm the solidarity which binds Europe and the overseas countries and desiring to ensure the development of their prosperity, in accordance with the principles of the Charter of the United Nations,

RESOLVED by thus pooling their resources to preserve and strengthen peace and liberty, and calling upon the other peoples of Europe who share their ideal to join in their efforts,

DETERMINED to promote the development of the highest possible level of knowledge for their peoples through a wide access to education and through its continuous updating,

and to this end ... have agreed as follows.

PART ONE
PRINCIPLES

Article 1

1.   This Treaty organises the functioning of the Union and determines the areas of, delimitation of, and arrangements for exercising its competences.
2.   This Treaty and the Treaty on European Union constitute the Treaties on which the Union is founded. These two Treaties, which have the same legal value, shall be referred to as 'the Treaties'.

TITLE I
CATEGORIES AND AREAS OF UNION COMPETENCE

Article 2

1.   When the Treaties confer on the Union exclusive competence in a specific area, only the Union may legislate and adopt legally binding acts, the Member States being able to do so themselves only if so empowered by the Union or for the implementation of acts of the Union.
2.   When the Treaties confer on the Union a competence shared with the Member States in a specific area, the Union and the Member States may legislate and adopt legally binding acts in that area. The Member States shall exercise their competence to the extent that the Union has not exercised its competence. The Member States shall exercise their competence again to the extent that the Union has decided to cease exercising its competence.
3.   The Member States shall coordinate their economic and employment policies within arrangements as determined by this Treaty, which the Union shall have competence to provide.
4.   The Union shall have competence, in accordance with the provisions of the Treaty on European Union, to define and implement a common foreign and security policy, including the progressive framing of a common defence policy.
5.   In certain areas and under the conditions laid down in the Treaties, the Union shall have competence to carry out actions to support, coordinate or supplement the actions of the Member States, without thereby superseding their competence in these areas.

Legally binding acts of the Union adopted on the basis of the provisions in the Treaties relating to these areas shall not entail harmonisation of Member States' laws or regulations.
6. The scope of and arrangements for exercising the Union's competences shall be determined by the provisions of the Treaties relating to each area.

Article 3

1. The Union shall have exclusive competence in the following areas:
    (a) customs union;
    (b) the establishing of the competition rules necessary for the functioning of the internal market;
    (c) monetary policy for the Member States whose currency is the euro;
    (d) the conservation of marine biological resources under the common fisheries policy;
    (e) common commercial policy.
2. The Union shall also have exclusive competence for the conclusion of an international agreement when its conclusion is provided for in a legislative act of the Union or is necessary to enable the Union to exercise its internal competence, or insofar as its conclusion may affect common rules or alter their scope.

Article 4

1. The Union shall share competence with the Member States where the Treaties confer on it a competence which does not relate to the areas referred to in Articles 3 and 6.
2. Shared competence between the Union and the Member States applies in the following principal areas:
    (a) internal market;
    (b) social policy, for the aspects defined in this Treaty;
    (c) economic, social and territorial cohesion;
    (d) agriculture and fisheries, excluding the conservation of marine biological resources;
    (e) environment;
    (f) consumer protection;
    (g) transport;
    (h) trans-European networks;
    (i) energy;
    (j) area of freedom, security and justice;
    (k) common safety concerns in public health matters, for the aspects defined in this Treaty.
3. In the areas of research, technological development and space, the Union shall have competence to carry out activities, in particular to define and implement programmes; however, the exercise of that competence shall not result in Member States being prevented from exercising theirs.
4. In the areas of development cooperation and humanitarian aid, the Union shall have competence to carry out activities and conduct a common policy; however, the exercise of that competence shall not result in Member States being prevented from exercising theirs.

Article 5

1. The Member States shall coordinate their economic policies within the Union. To this end, the Council shall adopt measures, in particular broad guidelines for these policies. Specific provisions shall apply to those Member States whose currency is the euro.
2. The Union shall take measures to ensure coordination of the employment policies of the Member States, in particular by defining guidelines for these policies.
3. The Union may take initiatives to ensure coordination of Member States' social policies.

Article 6

The Union shall have competence to carry out actions to support, coordinate or supplement the actions of the Member States. The areas of such action shall, at European level, be:
(a) protection and improvement of human health;
(b) industry;

(c)   culture;
(d)   tourism;
(e)   education, vocational training, youth and sport;
(f)   civil protection;
(g)   administrative cooperation.

TITLE II
PROVISIONS HAVING GENERAL APPLICATION

Article 7

The Union shall ensure consistency between its policies and activities, taking all of its objectives into account and in accordance with the principle of conferral of powers.

Article 8

In all its activities, the Union shall aim to eliminate inequalities, and to promote equality, between men and women.

Article 9

In defining and implementing its policies and actions, the Union shall take into account requirements linked to the promotion of a high level of employment, the guarantee of adequate social protection, the fight against social exclusion, and a high level of education, training and protection of human health.

Article 10

In defining and implementing its policies and activities, the Union shall aim to combat discrimination based on sex, racial or ethnic origin, religion or belief, disability, age or sexual orientation.

Article 11

Environmental protection requirements must be integrated into the definition and implementation of the Union policies and activities, in particular with a view to promoting sustainable development.

Article 12

Consumer protection requirements shall be taken into account in defining and implementing other Union policies and activities.

Article 13

In formulating and implementing the Union's agriculture, fisheries, transport, internal market, research and technological development and space policies, the Union and the Member States shall, since animals are sentient beings, pay full regard to the welfare requirements of animals, while respecting the legislative or administrative provisions and customs of the Member States relating in particular to religious rites, cultural traditions and regional heritage.

Article 14

Without prejudice to Article 4 of the Treaty on European Union or to Articles 93, 106 and 107 of this Treaty, and given the place occupied by services of general economic interest in the shared values of the Union as well as their role in promoting social and territorial cohesion, the Union and the Member States, each within their respective powers and within the scope of application of the Treaties, shall take care that such services operate on the basis of principles and conditions, particularly economic and financial conditions, which enable them to fulfil their missions. The European Parliament and the Council, acting by means of regulations in accordance with the ordinary legislative procedure, shall establish these principles and set these conditions without prejudice to the competence of Member States, in compliance with the Treaties, to provide, to commission and to fund such services.

Article 15

1.   In order to promote good governance and ensure the participation of civil society, the institutions, bodies, offices and agencies of the Union shall conduct their work as openly as possible.

2. The European Parliament shall meet in public, as shall the Council when considering and voting on a draft legislative act.

3. Any citizen of the Union, and any natural or legal person residing or having its registered office in a Member State, shall have a right of access to documents of the Union institutions, bodies, offices and agencies, whatever their medium, subject to the principles and the conditions to be defined in accordance with this paragraph.

General principles and limits on grounds of public or private interest governing this right of access to documents shall be determined by the European Parliament and the Council, acting by means of regulations in accordance with the ordinary legislative procedure. Each institution, body, office or agency shall ensure that its proceedings are transparent and shall elaborate in its own Rules of Procedure specific provisions regarding access to its documents, in accordance with the regulations referred to in the second subparagraph. The Court of Justice of the European Union, the European Central Bank and the European Investment Bank shall be subject to this paragraph only when exercising their administrative tasks.

The European Parliament and the Council shall ensure publication of the documents relating to the legislative procedures under the terms laid down by the regulation referred to in the second subparagraph.

Article 16

1. Everyone has the right to the protection of personal data concerning them.

2. The European Parliament and the Council, acting in accordance with the ordinary legislative procedure, shall lay down the rules relating to the protection of individuals with regard to the processing of personal data by Union institutions, bodies, offices and agencies, and by the Member States when carrying out activities which fall within the scope of Union law, and the rules relating to the free movement of such data. Compliance with these rules shall be subject to the control of independent authorities.

The rules adopted on the basis of this article shall be without prejudice to the specific rules laid down in Article 39 of the Treaty on European Union.

Article 17

1. The Union respects and does not prejudice the status under national law of churches and religious associations or communities in the Member States.

2. The Union equally respects the status under national law of philosophical and non-confessional organisations.

3. Recognising their identity and their specific contribution, the Union shall maintain an open, transparent and regular dialogue with these churches and organisations.

PART TWO
NON-DISCRIMINATION AND CITIZENSHIP OF THE UNION

Article 18

Within the scope of application of the Treaties, and without prejudice to any special provisions contained therein, any discrimination on grounds of nationality shall be prohibited.

The European Parliament and the Council, acting in accordance with the ordinary legislative procedure, may adopt rules designed to prohibit such discrimination.

Article 19

1. Without prejudice to the other provisions of the Treaties and within the limits of the powers conferred by them upon the Union, the Council, acting unanimously in accordance with a special legislative procedure and after obtaining the consent of the European Parliament, may take appropriate action to combat discrimination based on sex, racial or ethnic origin, religion or belief, disability, age or sexual orientation.

2. By way of derogation from paragraph 1, the European Parliament and the Council, acting in accordance with the ordinary legislative procedure, may adopt the basic principles of the Union's incentive measures, excluding any harmonisation of the laws and regulations of the Member States, to support action taken by the Member States in order to contribute to the achievement of the objectives referred to in paragraph 1.

Article 20

1.　Citizenship of the Union is hereby established. Every person holding the nationality of a Member State shall be a citizen of the Union. Citizenship of the Union shall be additional to and not replace national citizenship.

2.　Citizens of the Union shall enjoy the rights and be subject to the duties provided for in the Treaties. They shall have, *inter alia*:

　(a)　the right to move and reside freely within the territory of the Member States;

　(b)　the right to vote and to stand as candidates in elections to the European Parliament and in municipal elections in their Member State of residence, under the same conditions as nationals of that State;

　(c)　the right to enjoy, in the territory of a third country in which the Member State of which they are nationals is not represented, the protection of the diplomatic and consular authorities of any Member State on the same conditions as the nationals of that State;

　(d)　the right to petition the European Parliament, to apply to the European Ombudsman, and to address the institutions and advisory bodies of the Union in any of the Treaty languages and to obtain a reply in the same language.

　These rights shall be exercised in accordance with the conditions and limits defined by the Treaties and by the measures adopted thereunder.

Article 21

1.　Every citizen of the Union shall have the right to move and reside freely within the territory of the Member States, subject to the limitations and conditions laid down in the Treaties and by the measures adopted to give them effect.

2.　If action by the Union should prove necessary to attain this objective and the Treaties have not provided the necessary powers, the European Parliament and the Council, acting in accordance with the ordinary legislative procedure, may adopt provisions with a view to facilitating the exercise of the rights referred to in paragraph 1.

3.　For the same purposes as those referred to in paragraph 1 and if the Treaties have not provided the necessary powers, the Council, acting in accordance with a special legislative procedure, may adopt measures concerning social security or social protection. The Council shall act unanimously after consulting the European Parliament.

Article 22

1.　Every citizen of the Union residing in a Member State of which he is not a national shall have the right to vote and to stand as a candidate at municipal elections in the Member State in which he resides, under the same conditions as nationals of that State. This right shall be exercised subject to detailed arrangements adopted by the Council, acting unanimously in accordance with a special legislative procedure and after consulting the European Parliament; these arrangements may provide for derogations where warranted by problems specific to a Member State.

2.　Without prejudice to Article 223(1) and to the provisions adopted for its implementation, every citizen of the Union residing in a Member State of which he is not a national shall have the right to vote and to stand as a candidate in elections to the European Parliament in the Member State in which he resides, under the same conditions as nationals of that State. This right shall be exercised subject to detailed arrangements adopted by the Council, acting unanimously in accordance with a special legislative procedure and after consulting the European Parliament; these arrangements may provide for derogations where warranted by problems specific to a Member State.

Article 23

Every citizen of the Union shall, in the territory of a third country in which the Member State of which he is a national is not represented, be entitled to protection by the diplomatic or consular authorities of any Member State, on the same conditions as the nationals of that State. Member States shall adopt the necessary provisions and start the international negotiations required to secure this protection.

The Council, acting in accordance with a special legislative procedure and after consulting the European Parliament, may adopt directives establishing the coordination and cooperation measures necessary to facilitate such protection.

Article 24

The European Parliament and the Council, acting by means of regulations in accordance with the ordinary legislative procedure, shall adopt the provisions for the procedures and conditions required for a citizens' initiative within the meaning of Article 11 of the Treaty on European Union, including the minimum number of Member States from which such citizens must come. Every citizen of the Union shall have the right to petition the European Parliament in accordance with Article 227.

Every citizen of the Union may apply to the Ombudsman established in accordance with Article 228.

Every citizen of the Union may write to any of the institutions or bodies referred to in this Article or in Article 13 of the Treaty on European Union in one of the languages mentioned in Article 55(1) of the Treaty on European Union and have an answer in the same language.

PART THREE
UNION POLICIES AND INTERNAL ACTIONS

TITLE I
THE INTERNAL MARKET

Article 26

1. The Union shall adopt measures with the aim of establishing or ensuring the functioning of the internal market, in accordance with the relevant provisions of the Treaties.
2. The internal market shall comprise an area without internal frontiers in which the free movement of goods, persons, services and capital is ensured in accordance with the provisions of the Treaties.
3. The Council, on a proposal from the Commission, shall determine the guidelines and conditions necessary to ensure balanced progress in all the sectors concerned.

Article 27

When drawing up its proposals with a view to achieving the objectives set out in Article 26, the Commission shall take into account the extent of the effort that certain economies showing differences in development will have to sustain for the establishment of the internal market and it may propose appropriate provisions.

If these provisions take the form of derogations, they must be of a temporary nature and must cause the least possible disturbance to the functioning of the internal market.

TITLE II
FREE MOVEMENT OF GOODS

Article 28

1. The Union shall comprise a customs union which shall cover all trade in goods and which shall involve the prohibition between Member States of customs duties on imports and exports and of all charges having equivalent effect, and the adoption of a common customs tariff in their relations with third countries.
2. The provisions of Article 30 and of Chapter 3 of this Title shall apply to products originating in Member States and to products coming from third countries which are in free circulation in Member States.

Article 29

Products coming from a third country shall be considered to be in free circulation in a Member State if the import formalities have been complied with and any customs duties or charges having equivalent effect which are payable have been levied in that Member State, and if they have not benefited from a total or partial drawback of such duties or charges.

CHAPTER 1
THE CUSTOMS UNION

Article 30

Customs duties on imports and exports and charges having equivalent effect shall be prohibited between Member States. This prohibition shall also apply to customs duties of a fiscal nature.

Article 31

Common Customs Tariff duties shall be fixed by the Council on a proposal from the Commission.

Article 32

In carrying out the tasks entrusted to it under this chapter the Commission shall be guided by:
- (a) the need to promote trade between Member States and third countries;
- (b) developments in conditions of competition within the Union in so far as they lead to an improvement in the competitive capacity of undertakings;
- (c) the requirements of the Union as regards the supply of raw materials and semifinished goods; in this connection the Commission shall take care to avoid distorting conditions of competition between Member States in respect of finished goods;
- (d) the need to avoid serious disturbances in the economies of Member States and to ensure rational development of production and an expansion of consumption within the Union.

CHAPTER 2
CUSTOMS COOPERATION

Article 33

Within the scope of application of the Treaties, the European Parliament and the Council, acting in accordance with the ordinary legislative procedure, shall take measures in order to strengthen customs cooperation between Member States and between the latter and the Commission.

CHAPTER 3
PROHIBITION OF QUANTITATIVE RESTRICTIONS BETWEEN MEMBER STATES

Article 34

Quantitative restrictions on imports and all measures having equivalent effect shall be prohibited between Member States.

Article 35

Quantitative restrictions on exports, and all measures having equivalent effect, shall be prohibited between Member States.

Article 36

The provisions of Articles 34 and 35 shall not preclude prohibitions or restrictions on imports, exports or goods in transit justified on grounds of public morality, public policy or public security; the protection of health and life of humans, animals or plants; the protection of national treasures possessing artistic, historic or archaeological value; or the protection of industrial and commercial property. Such prohibitions or restrictions shall not, however, constitute a means of arbitrary discrimination or a disguised restriction on trade between Member States.

Article 37

1. Member States shall adjust any State monopolies of a commercial character so as to ensure that no discrimination regarding the conditions under which goods are procured and marketed exists between nationals of Member States.

The provisions of this Article shall apply to any body through which a Member State, in law or in fact, either directly or indirectly supervises, determines or appreciably influences imports or exports between Member States. These provisions shall likewise apply to monopolies delegated by the State to others.

2.   Member States shall refrain from introducing any new measure which is contrary to the principles laid down in paragraph 1 or which restricts the scope of the articles dealing with the prohibition of customs duties and quantitative restrictions between Member States.

3.   If a State monopoly of a commercial character has rules which are designed to make it easier to dispose of agricultural products or obtain for them the best return, steps should be taken in applying the rules contained in this article to ensure equivalent safeguards for the employment and standard of living of the producers concerned.

TITLE III
AGRICULTURE AND FISHERIES

Article 38

1.   The Union shall define and implement a common agriculture and fisheries policy. The internal market shall extend to agriculture, fisheries and trade in agricultural products. 'Agricultural products' means the products of the soil, of stock farming and of fisheries and products of first-stage processing directly related to these products. References to the common agricultural policy or to agriculture, and the use of the term 'agricultural', shall be understood as also referring to fisheries, having regard to the specific characteristics of this sector.

2.   Save as otherwise provided in Articles 39 to 44, the rules laid down for the establishment and functioning of the internal market shall apply to agricultural products.

3.   The products subject to the provisions of Articles 39 to 44 are listed in Annex I.

4.   The operation and development of the internal market for agricultural products must be accompanied by the establishment of a common agricultural policy.

Article 39

1.   The objectives of the common agricultural policy shall be:
   (a)   to increase agricultural productivity by promoting technical progress and by ensuring the rational development of agricultural production and the optimum utilisation of the factors of production, in particular labour;
   (b)   thus to ensure a fair standard of living for the agricultural community, in particular by increasing the individual earnings of persons engaged in agriculture;
   (c)   to stabilise markets;
   (d)   to assure the availability of supplies;
   (e)   to ensure that supplies reach consumers at reasonable prices.

2.   In working out the common agricultural policy and the special methods for its application, account shall be taken of:
   (a)   the particular nature of agricultural activity, which results from the social structure of agriculture and from structural and natural disparities between the various agricultural regions;
   (b)   the need to effect the appropriate adjustments by degrees;
   (c)   the fact that in the Member States agriculture constitutes a sector closely linked with the economy as a whole.

Article 40

1.   In order to attain the objectives set out in Article 39, a common organisation of agricultural markets shall be established.
This organisation shall take one of the following forms, depending on the product concerned:
   (a)   common rules on competition;
   (b)   compulsory coordination of the various national market organisations;
   (c)   a European market organisation.

2.   The common organisation established in accordance with paragraph 1 may include all measures required to attain the objectives set out in Article 39, in particular regulation

of prices, aids for the production and marketing of the various products, storage and carryover arrangements and common machinery for stabilising imports or exports.

The common organisation shall be limited to pursuit of the objectives set out in Article 39 and shall exclude any discrimination between producers or consumers within the Union. Any common price policy shall be based on common criteria and uniform methods of calculation.

3. In order to enable the common organisation referred to in paragraph 1 to attain its objectives, one or more agricultural guidance and guarantee funds may be set up.

Article 41

To enable the objectives set out in Article 39 to be attained, provision may be made within the framework of the common agricultural policy for measures such as:

(a) an effective coordination of efforts in the spheres of vocational training, of research and of the dissemination of agricultural knowledge; this may include joint financing of projects or institutions;

(b) joint measures to promote consumption of certain products.

Article 42

The provisions of the Chapter relating to rules on competition shall apply to production of and trade in agricultural products only to the extent determined by the European Parliament and the Council within the framework of Article 43(2) and in accordance with the procedure laid down therein, account being taken of the objectives set out in Article 39.

The Council, on a proposal from the Commission, may authorise the granting of aid:

(a) for the protection of enterprises handicapped by structural or natural conditions;

(b) within the framework of economic development programmes.

Article 43

1. The Commission shall submit proposals for working out and implementing the common agricultural policy, including the replacement of the national organisations by one of the forms of common organisation provided for in Article 40(1), and for implementing the measures specified in this title.

These proposals shall take account of the interdependence of the agricultural matters mentioned in this title.

...

Article 44

Where in a Member State a product is subject to a national market organisation or to internal rules having equivalent effect which affect the competitive position of similar production in another Member State, a countervailing charge shall be applied by Member States to imports of this product coming from the Member State where such organisation or rules exist, unless that State applies a countervailing charge on export.

The Commission shall fix the amount of these charges at the level required to redress the balance; it may also authorise other measures, the conditions and details of which it shall determine.

TITLE IV
FREE MOVEMENT OF PERSONS, SERVICES AND CAPITAL

CHAPTER 1
WORKERS

Article 45

1. Freedom of movement for workers shall be secured within the Union.

2. Such freedom of movement shall entail the abolition of any discrimination based on nationality between workers of the Member States as regards employment, remuneration and other conditions of work and employment.

3. It shall entail the right, subject to limitations justified on grounds of public policy, public security or public health:

(a) to accept offers of employment actually made;

(b) to move freely within the territory of Member States for this purpose;

(c) to stay in a Member State for the purpose of employment in accordance with the provisions governing the employment of nationals of that State laid down by law, regulation or administrative action;

(d) to remain in the territory of a Member State after having been employed in that State, subject to conditions which shall be embodied in regulations to be drawn up by the Commission.

4. The provisions of this article shall not apply to employment in the public service.

Article 46

The European Parliament and the Council shall, acting in accordance with the ordinary legislative procedure and after consulting the Economic and Social Committee, issue directives or make regulations setting out the measures required to bring about freedom of movement for workers, as defined in Article 45, in particular:

(a) by ensuring close cooperation between national employment services;

(b) by abolishing those administrative procedures and practices and those qualifying periods in respect of eligibility for available employment, whether resulting from national legislation or from agreements previously concluded between Member States, the maintenance of which would form an obstacle to liberalisation of the movement of workers;

(c) by abolishing all such qualifying periods and other restrictions provided for either under national legislation or under agreements previously concluded between Member States as imposed on workers of other Member States conditions regarding the free choice of employment other than those imposed on workers of the State concerned;

(d) by setting up appropriate machinery to bring offers of employment into touch with applications for employment and to facilitate the achievement of a balance between supply and demand in the employment market in such a way as to avoid serious threats to the standard of living and level of employment in the various regions and industries.

Article 47

Member States shall, within the framework of a joint programme, encourage the exchange of young workers.

Article 48

The European Parliament and the Council, acting in accordance with the ordinary legislative procedure, shall adopt such measures in the field of social security as are necessary to provide freedom of movement for workers; to this end, it shall make arrangements to secure for employed and self-employed migrant workers and their dependants:

(a) aggregation, for the purpose of acquiring and retaining the right to benefit and of calculating the amount of benefit, of all periods taken into account under the laws of the several countries;

(b) payment of benefits to persons resident in the territories of Member States.

Where a member of the Council declares that a draft legislative act referred to in the first subparagraph would affect important aspects of its social security system, including its scope, cost or financial structure, or would affect the financial balance of that system, it may request that the matter be referred to the European Council. In that case, the ordinary legislative procedure shall be suspended. After discussion, the European Council shall, within four months of this suspension, either:

(a) refer the draft back to the Council, which shall terminate the suspension of the ordinary legislative procedure, or

(b) take no action or request the Commission to submit a new proposal; in that case, the act originally proposed shall be deemed not to have been adopted.

CHAPTER 2

RIGHT OF ESTABLISHMENT

Article 49

Within the framework of the provisions set out below, restrictions on the freedom of establishment of nationals of a Member State in the territory of another Member State shall be prohibited. Such prohibition shall also apply to restrictions on the setting-up of agencies, branches or subsidiaries by nationals of any Member State established in the territory of any Member State.

Freedom of establishment shall include the right to take up and pursue activities as self-employed persons and to set up and manage undertakings, in particular companies or firms within the meaning of the second paragraph of Article 54, under the conditions laid down for its own nationals by the law of the country where such establishment is effected, subject to the provisions of the Chapter relating to capital.

Article 50

1. In order to attain freedom of establishment as regards a particular activity, the European Parliament and the Council, acting in accordance with the ordinary legislative procedure and after consulting the Economic and Social Committee, shall act by means of directives.

2. The European Parliament, the Council and the Commission shall carry out the duties devolving upon them under the preceding provisions, in particular:

   (a) by according, as a general rule, priority treatment to activities where freedom of establishment makes a particularly valuable contribution to the development of production and trade;

   (b) by ensuring close cooperation between the competent authorities in the Member States in order to ascertain the particular situation within the Union of the various activities concerned;

   (c) by abolishing those administrative procedures and practices, whether resulting from national legislation or from agreements previously concluded between Member States, the maintenance of which would form an obstacle to freedom of establishment;

   (d) by ensuring that workers of one Member State employed in the territory of another Member State may remain in that territory for the purpose of taking up activities therein as self-employed persons, where they satisfy the conditions which they would be required to satisfy if they were entering that State at the time when they intended to take up such activities;

   (e) by enabling a national of one Member State to acquire and use land and buildings situated in the territory of another Member State, in so far as this does not conflict with the principles laid down in Article 39(2);

   (f) by effecting the progressive abolition of restrictions on freedom of establishment in every branch of activity under consideration, both as regards the conditions for setting up agencies, branches or subsidiaries in the territory of a Member State and as regards the subsidiaries in the territory of a Member State and as regards the conditions governing the entry of personnel belonging to the main establishment into managerial or supervisory posts in such agencies, branches or subsidiaries;

   (g) by coordinating to the necessary extent the safeguards which, for the protection of the interests of members and other, are required by Member States of companies or firms within the meaning of the second paragraph of Article 54 with a view to making such safeguards equivalent throughout the Union;

   (h) by satisfying themselves that the conditions of establishment are not distorted by aids granted by Member States.

Article 51

The provisions of this Chapter shall not apply, so far as any given Member State is concerned, to activities which in that State are connected, even occasionally, with the exercise of official authority.

The European Parliament and the Council, acting in accordance with the ordinary legislative procedure, may rule that the provisions of this Chapter shall not apply to certain activities.

Article 52

1. The provisions of this Chapter and measures taken in pursuance thereof shall not prejudice the applicability of provisions laid down by law, regulation or administrative action providing for special treatment for foreign nationals on grounds of public policy, public security or public health.

2. The European Parliament and the Council, acting in accordance with the ordinary legislative procedure, shall issue directives for the coordination of the abovementioned provisions.

Article 53

1. In order to make it easier for persons to take up and pursue activities as self-employed persons, the European Parliament and the Council, acting in accordance with the ordinary legislative procedure, shall issue directives for the mutual recognition of diplomas, certificates and other evidence of formal qualifications and for the coordination of the provisions laid down by law, regulation or administrative action in Member States concerning the taking-up and pursuit of activities as self-employed persons.

2. In the case of the medical and allied and pharmaceutical professions, the progressive abolition of restrictions shall be dependent upon coordination of the conditions for their exercise in the various Member States.

Article 54

Companies or firms formed in accordance with the law of a Member State and having their registered office, central administration or principal place of business within the Union shall, for the purposes of this Chapter, be treated in the same way as natural persons who are nationals of Member States.

'Companies or firms' means companies or firms constituted under civil or commercial law, including cooperative societies, and other legal persons governed by public or private law, save for those which are non-profit-making.

Article 55

Member States shall accord nationals of the other Member States the same treatment as their own nationals as regards participation in the capital of companies or firms within the meaning of Article 54, without prejudice to the application of the other provisions of the Treaties.

CHAPTER 3
SERVICES

Article 56

Within the framework of the provisions set out below, restrictions on freedom to provide services within the Union shall be prohibited in respect of nationals of Member States who are established in a Member State other than that of the person for whom the services are intended.

The European Parliament and the Council, acting in the accordance with the ordinary legislative procedure, may extend the provisions of the Chapter to nationals of a third country who provide services and who are established within the Union.

Article 57

Services shall be considered to be 'services' within the meaning of the Treaties where they are normally provided for remuneration, in so far as they are not governed by the provisions relating to freedom of movement for goods, capital and persons.

'Services' shall in particular include:
(a) activities of an industrial character;
(b) activities of a commercial character;
(c) activities of craftsmen;
(d) activities of the professions.

Without prejudice to the provisions of the Chapter relating to the right of establishment, the person providing a service may, in order to do so, temporarily pursue his activity in the Member State where the service is provided, under the same conditions as are imposed by that State on its own nationals.

Article 58

1. Freedom to provide services in the field of transport shall be governed by the provisions of the title relating to transport.

2. The liberalisation of banking and insurance services connected with movements of capital shall be effected in step with the liberalisation of movement of capital.

Article 59

1. In order to achieve the liberalisation of a specific service, the European Parliament and the Council, acting in accordance with the ordinary legislative procedure and after consulting the Economic and Social Committee, shall issue directives.
2. As regards the directives referred to in paragraph 1, priority shall as a general rule be given to those services which directly affect production costs or the liberalisation of which helps to promote trade in goods.

Article 60

The Member States shall endeavour to undertake the liberalisation of services beyond the extent required by the directives issued pursuant to Article 59(1), if their general economic situation and the situation of the economic sector concerned so permit.

To this end, the Commission shall make recommendations to the Member States concerned.

Article 61

As long as restrictions on freedom to provide services have not been abolished, each Member State shall apply such restrictions without distinction on grounds of nationality or residence to all persons providing services within the meaning of the first paragraph of Article 56.

Article 62

The provisions of Articles 51 to 54 shall apply to the matters covered by this Chapter.

CHAPTER 4
CAPITAL AND PAYMENTS

Article 63

1. Within the framework of the provisions set out in this Chapter, all restrictions on the movement of capital between Member States and between Member States and third countries shall be prohibited.
2. Within the framework of the provisions set out in this Chapter, all restrictions on payments between Member States and between Member States and third countries shall be prohibited.

Article 64

1. The provisions of Article 63 shall be without prejudice to the application to third countries of any restrictions which exist on 31 December 1993 under national or Union law adopted in respect of the movement of capital to or from third countries involving direct investment — including in real estate — establishment, the provision of financial services or the admission of securities to capital markets. In respect of restrictions existing under national law in Bulgaria, Estonia and Hungary, the relevant date shall be 31 December 1999. In respect of restrictions existing under national law in Croatia, the relevant date shall be 31 December 2002.
2. Whilst endeavouring to achieve the objective of free movement of capital between Member States and third countries to the greatest extent possible and without prejudice to the other Chapters of the Treaties, the European Parliament and the Council, acting in accordance with the ordinary legislative procedure, shall adopt the measures on the movement of capital to or from third countries involving direct investment — including investment in real estate — establishment, the provision of financial services or the admission of securities to capital markets.
3. Notwithstanding paragraph 2, only the Council, acting in accordance with a special legislative procedure, may unanimously, and after consulting the European Parliament, adopt measures which constitute a step backwards in Union law as regards the liberalisation of the movement of capital to or from third countries.

Article 65

    1.   The provisions of Article 63 shall be without prejudice to the right of Member States:

        (a)   to apply the relevant provisions of their tax law which distinguish between taxpayers who are not in the same situation with regard to their place of residence or with regard to the place where their capital is invested;

        (b)   to take all requisite measures to prevent infringements of national law and regulations, in particular in the field of taxation and the prudential supervision of financial institutions, or to lay down procedures for the declaration of capital movements for purposes of administrative or statistical information, or to take measures which are justified on grounds of public policy or public security.

    2.   The provisions of this Chapter shall be without prejudice to the applicability of restrictions on the right of establishment which are compatible with the Treaties.

    3.   The measures and procedures referred to in paragraphs 1 and 2 shall not constitute a means of arbitrary discrimination or a disguised restriction on the free movement of capital and payments as defined in Article 63.

    4.   In the absence of measures pursuant to Article 64(3), the Commission or, in the absence of a Commission decision within three months from the request of the Member State concerned, the Council, may adopt a decision stating that restrictive tax measures adopted by a Member State concerning one or more third countries are to be considered compatible with the Treaties insofar as they are justified by one of the objectives of the Union and compatible with the proper functioning of the internal market. The Council shall act unanimously on application by a Member State.

Article 66

Where, in exceptional circumstances, movements of capital to or from third countries cause, or threaten to cause, serious difficulties for the operation of economic and monetary union, the Council, on a proposal from the Commission and after consulting the European Central Bank, may take safeguard measures with regard to third countries for a period not exceeding six months if such measures are strictly necessary.

TITLE V

AREA OF FREEDOM, SECURITY AND JUSTICE

CHAPTER 1

GENERAL PROVISIONS

Article 67

    1.   The Union shall constitute an area of freedom, security and justice with respect for fundamental rights and the different legal systems and traditions of the Member States.

    2.   It shall ensure the absence of internal border controls for persons and shall frame a common policy on asylum, immigration and external border control, based on solidarity between Member States, which is fair towards third-country nationals. For the purpose of this Title, stateless persons shall be treated as third-country nationals.

    3.   The Union shall endeavour to ensure a high level of security through measures to prevent and combat crime, racism and xenophobia, and through measures for coordination and cooperation between police and judicial authorities and other competent authorities, as well as through the mutual recognition of judgments in criminal matters and, if necessary, through the approximation of criminal laws.

    4.   The Union shall facilitate access to justice, in particular through the principle of mutual recognition of judicial and extrajudicial decisions in civil matters.

Article 68

The European Council shall define the strategic guidelines for legislative and operational planning within the area of freedom, security and justice.

Article 69

National Parliaments ensure that the proposals and legislative initiatives submitted under Chapters 4 and 5 comply with the principle of subsidiarity, in accordance with the arrangements laid down by the Protocol on the application of the principles of subsidiarity and proportionality.

Article 75

Where necessary to achieve the objectives set out in Article 67, as regards preventing and combating terrorism and related activities, the European Parliament and the Council, acting by means of regulations in accordance with the ordinary legislative procedure, shall define a framework for administrative measures with regard to capital movements and payments, such as the freezing of funds, financial assets or economic gains belonging to, or owned or held by, natural or legal persons, groups or non-State entities.

The Council, on a proposal from the Commission, shall adopt measures to implement the framework referred to in the first paragraph.

The acts referred to in this Article shall include necessary provisions on legal safeguards.

CHAPTER 2
POLICIES ON BORDER CHECKS, ASYLUM AND IMMIGRATION

Article 77

1. The Union shall develop a policy with a view to:
   (a) ensuring the absence of any controls on persons, whatever their nationality, when crossing internal borders;
   (b) carrying out checks on persons and efficient monitoring of the crossing of external borders;
   (c) the gradual introduction of an integrated management system for external borders.

2. For the purposes of paragraph I, the European Parliament and the Council, acting in accordance with the ordinary legislative procedure, shall adopt measures concerning:
   (a) the common policy on visas and other short-stay residence permits;
   (b) the checks to which persons crossing external borders are subject;
   (c) the conditions under which nationals of third countries shall have the freedom to travel within the Union for a short period;
   (d) any measure necessary for the gradual establishment of an integrated management system for external borders;
   (e) the absence of any controls on persons, whatever their nationality, when crossing internal borders.

3. If action by the Union should prove necessary to facilitate the exercise of the right referred to in Article 20(2)(a), and if the Treaties have not provided the necessary powers, the Council, acting in accordance with a special legislative procedure, may adopt provisions concerning passports, identity cards, residence permits or any other such document. The Council shall act unanimously after consulting the European Parliament.

4. This Article shall not affect the competence of the Member States concerning the geographical demarcation of their borders, in accordance with international law.

Article 78

1. The Union shall develop a common policy on asylum. subsidiary protection and temporary protection with a view to offering appropriate status to any third-country national requiring international protection and ensuring compliance with the principle of *non-refoulement*. This policy must be in accordance with the Geneva Convention of 28 July 1951 and the Protocol of 31 January 1967 relating to the status of refugees, and other relevant treaties.

2. For the purposes of paragraph 1. the European Parliament and the Council, acting in accordance with the ordinary legislative procedure. shall adopt measures for a common European asylum system comprising:
   (a) a uniform status of asylum for nationals of third countries, valid throughout the Union;
   (b) a uniform status of subsidiary protection for nationals of third countries who, without obtaining European asylum, are in need of international protection;
   (c) a common system of temporary protection for displaced persons in the event of a massive inflow;
   (d) common procedures for the granting and withdrawing of uniform asylum or subsidiary protection status;

     (e)   criteria and mechanisms for determining which Member State is responsible for considering an application for asylum or subsidiary protection;

     (f)   standards concerning the conditions for the reception of applicants for asylum or subsidiary protection;

     (g)   partnership and cooperation with third countries for the purpose of managing inflows of people applying for asylum or subsidiary or temporary protection.

3.   In the event of one or more Member States being confronted with an emergency situation characterised by a sudden inflow of nationals of third countries, the Council, on a proposal from the Commission, may adopt provisional measures for the benefit of the Member State(s) concerned. It shall act after consulting the European Parliament.

Article 79

1.   The Union shall develop a common immigration policy aimed at ensuring, at all stages, the efficient management of migration flows, fair treatment of third-country nationals residing legally in Member States, and the prevention of, and enhanced measures to combat, illegal immigration and trafficking in human beings.

2.   For the purposes of paragraph 1, the European Parliament and the Council, acting in accordance with the ordinary legislative procedure, shall adopt measures in the following areas:

     (a)   the conditions of entry and residence, and standards on the issue by Member States of long-term visas and residence permits, including those for the purpose of family reunification;

     (b)   the definition of the rights of third-country nationals residing legally in a Member State, including the conditions governing freedom of movement and of residence in other Member States;

     (c)   illegal immigration and unauthorised residence, including removal and repatriation of persons residing without authorisation;

     (d)   combating trafficking in persons, in particular women and children.

3.   The Union may conclude agreements with third countries for the readmission to their countries of origin or provenance of third-country nationals who do not or who no longer fulfil the conditions for entry, presence or residence in the territory of one of the Member States.

4.   The European Parliament and the Council, acting in accordance with the ordinary legislative procedure, may establish measures to provide incentives and support for the action of Member States with a view to promoting the integration of third-country nationals residing legally in their territories, excluding any harmonisation of the laws and regulations of the Member States.

5.   This Article shall not affect the right of Member States to determine volumes of admission of third-country nationals coming from third countries to their territory in order to seek work, whether employed or self-employed.

CHAPTER 3

JUDICIAL COOPERATION IN CIVIL MATTERS

Article 81

1.   The Union shall develop judicial cooperation in civil matters having cross-border implications, based on the principle of mutual recognition of judgments and of decisions in extrajudicial cases. Such cooperation may include the adoption of measures for the approximation of the laws and regulations of the Member States.

2.   For the purposes of paragraph 1, the European Parliament and the Council, acting in accordance with the ordinary legislative procedure, shall adopt measures, particularly when necessary for the proper functioning of the internal market, aimed at ensuring:

     (a)   the mutual recognition and enforcement between Member States of judgments and of decisions in extrajudicial cases;

     (b)   the cross-border service of judicial and extrajudicial documents;

     (c)   the compatibility of the rules applicable in the Member States concerning conflict of laws and of jurisdiction;

     (d)   cooperation in the taking of evidence;

     (e)   effective access to justice;

(f)   the elimination of obstacles to the proper functioning of civil proceedings, if necessary by promoting the compatibility of the rules on civil procedure applicable in the Member States;

(g)   the development of alternative methods of dispute settlement;

(h)   support for the training of the judiciary and judicial staff.

3.   Notwithstanding paragraph 2, measures concerning family law with cross-border implications shall be established by the Council, acting in accordance with a special legislative procedure. The Council shall act unanimously after consulting the European Parliament.

The Council, on a proposal from the Commission, may adopt a decision determining those aspects of family law with cross-border implications which may be the subject of acts adopted by the ordinary legislative procedure. The Council shall act unanimously after consulting the European Parliament.

The proposal referred to in the second subparagraph shall be notified to the national Parliaments. If a national Parliament makes known its opposition within six months of the date of such notification, the decision shall not be adopted. In the absence of opposition, the Council may adopt the decision.

CHAPTER 4
JUDICIAL COOPERATION IN CRIMINAL MATTERS

Article 82

1.   Judicial cooperation in criminal matters in the Union shall be based on the principle of mutual recognition of judgments and judicial decisions and shall include the approximation of the laws and regulations of the Member States in the areas referred to in paragraph 2 and in Article 83.

The European Parliament and the Council, acting in accordance with the ordinary legislative procedure, shall adopt measures to:

(a)   lay down rules and procedures for ensuring recognition throughout the Union of all forms of judgments and judicial decisions;

(b)   prevent and settle conflicts of jurisdiction between Member States;

(c)   support the training of the judiciary and judicial staff;

(d)   facilitate cooperation between judicial or equivalent authorities of the Member States in relation to proceedings in criminal matters and the enforcement of decisions.

2.   To the extent necessary to facilitate mutual recognition of judgments and judicial decisions and police and judicial cooperation in criminal matters having a cross-border dimension, the European Parliament and the Council may, by means of directives adopted in accordance with the ordinary legislative procedure, establish minimum rules. Such rules shall take into account the differences between the legal traditions and systems of the Member States.

They shall concern:

(a)   mutual admissibility of evidence between Member States;

(b)   the rights of individuals in criminal procedure;

(c)   the rights of victims of crime;

(d)   any other specific aspects of criminal procedure which the Council has identified in advance by a decision; for the adoption of such a decision, the Council shall act unanimously after obtaining the consent of the European Parliament.

Adoption of the minimum rules referred to in this paragraph shall not prevent Member States from maintaining or introducing a higher level of protection for individuals.

3.   Where a member of the Council considers that a draft directive as referred to in paragraph 2 would affect fundamental aspects of its criminal justice system, it may request that the draft directive be referred to the European Council. In that case, the ordinary legislative procedure shall be suspended. After discussion, and in case of a consensus, the European Council shall, within four months of this suspension, refer the draft back to the Council, which shall terminate the suspension of the ordinary legislative procedure.

Within the same timeframe, in case of disagreement, and if at least nine Member States wish to establish enhanced cooperation on the basis of the draft directive concerned, they shall notify the European Parliament, the Council and the

Commission accordingly. In such a case, the authorisation to proceed with enhanced cooperation referred to in Article 20(2) of the Treaty on European Union and Article 329(1) of this Treaty shall be deemed to be granted and the provisions on enhanced cooperation shall apply.

CHAPTER 5
POLICE COOPERATION

Article 87

1. The Union shall establish police cooperation involving all the Member States' competent authorities, including police, customs and other specialised law enforcement services in relation to the prevention, detection and investigation of criminal offences.

...

Article 88

1. Europol's mission shall be to support and strengthen action by the Member States' police authorities and other law enforcement services and their mutual cooperation in preventing and combating serious crime affecting two or more Member States, terrorism and forms of crime which affect a common interest covered by a Union policy.

...

TITLE VII
COMMON RULES ON COMPETITION, TAXATION AND APPROXIMATION OF LAWS

CHAPTER 1
RULES ON COMPETITION

SECTION 1
RULES APPLYING TO UNDERTAKINGS

Article 101

1. The following shall be prohibited as incompatible with the internal market: all agreements between undertakings, decisions by associations of undertakings and concerted practices which may affect trade between Member States and which have as their object or effect the prevention, restriction or distortion of competition within the internal market, and in particular those which:
    (a) directly or indirectly fix purchase or selling prices or any other trading conditions;
    (b) limit or control production, markets, technical development, or investment;
    (c) share markets or sources of supply;
    (d) apply dissimilar conditions to equivalent transactions with other trading parties, thereby placing them at a competitive disadvantage;
    (e) make the conclusion of contracts subject to acceptance by the other parties of supplementary obligations which, by their nature or according to commercial usage, have no connection with the subject of such contracts.
2. Any agreements or decisions prohibited pursuant to this Article shall be automatically void.
3. The provisions of paragraph 1 may, however, be declared inapplicable in the case of:
    — any agreement or category of agreements between undertakings,
    — any decision or category of decisions by associations of undertakings,
    — any concerted practice or category of concerted practices,
    which contributes to improving the production or distribution of goods or to promoting technical or economic progress, while allowing consumers a fair share of the resulting benefit, and which does not:
    (a) impose on the undertakings concerned restrictions which are not indispensable to the attainment of these objectives;
    (b) afford such undertakings the possibility of eliminating competition in respect of a substantial part of the products in question.

Article 102

Any abuse by one or more undertakings of a dominant position within the internal market or in a substantial part of it shall be prohibited as incompatible with the internal market in so far as it may affect trade between Member States.

Such abuse may, in particular, consist in:

(a) directly or indirectly imposing unfair purchase or selling prices or other unfair trading conditions;

(b) limiting production, markets or technical development to the prejudice of consumers;

(c) applying dissimilar conditions to equivalent transactions with other trading parties, thereby placing them at a competitive disadvantage;

(d) making the conclusion of contracts subject to acceptance by the other parties of supplementary obligations which, by their nature or according to commercial usage, have no connection with the subject of such contracts.

Article 103

1. The appropriate regulations or directives to give effect to the principles set out in Articles 101 and 102 shall be laid down by the Council, on a proposal from the Commission and after consulting the European Parliament.

2. The regulations or directives referred to in paragraph 1 shall be designed in particular:

(a) to ensure compliance with the prohibitions laid down in Article 101(1) and in Article 102 by making provision for fines and periodic penalty payments;

(b) to lay down detailed rules for the application of Article 101(3), taking into account the need to ensure effective supervision on the one hand, and to simplify administration to the greatest possible extent on the other;

(c) to define, if need be, in the various branches of the economy, the scope of the provisions of Articles 101 and 102;

(d) to define the respective functions of the Commission and of the Court of Justice of the European Union in applying the provisions laid down in this paragraph;

(e) to determine the relationship between national laws and the provisions contained in this Section or adopted pursuant to this Article.

Article 104

Until the entry into force of the provisions adopted in pursuance of Article 103, the authorities in Member States shall rule on the admissibility of agreements, decisions and concerted practices and on abuse of a dominant position in the internal market in accordance with the law of their country and with the provisions of Article 101, in particular paragraph 3, and of Article 102.

Article 105

1. Without prejudice to Article 104, the Commission shall ensure the application of the principles laid down in Articles 101 and 102. On application by a Member State or on its own initiative, and in cooperation with the competent authorities in the Member States, which shall give it their assistance, the Commission shall investigate cases of suspected infringement of these principles. If it finds that there has been an infringement, it shall propose appropriate measures to bring it to an end.

2. If the infringement is not brought to an end, the Commission shall record such infringement of the principles in a reasoned decision. The Commission may publish its decision and authorise Member States to take the measures, the conditions and details of which it shall determine, needed to remedy the situation.

3. The Commission may adopt regulations relating to the categories of agreement in respect of which the Council has adopted a regulation or a directive pursuant to Article 103(2)(b).

Article 106

1. In the case of public undertakings and undertakings to which Member States grant special or exclusive rights, Member States shall neither enact nor maintain in force any measure contrary to the rules contained in the Treaties, in particular to those rules provided for in Article 18 and Articles 101 to 109.

2. Undertakings entrusted with the operation of services of general economic interest or having the character of a revenue-producing monopoly shall be subject to the rules contained in the Treaties, in particular to the rules on competition, in so far as the application of such rules does not obstruct the performance, in law or in fact, of the particular tasks assigned to them. The development of trade must not be affected to such an extent as would be contrary to the interests of the Union.

3. The Commission shall ensure the application of the provisions of this Article and shall, where necessary, address appropriate directives or decisions to Member States.

SECTION 2
AIDS GRANTED BY STATES

Article 107

1. Save as otherwise provided in the Treaties, any aid granted by a Member State or through State resources in any form whatsoever which distorts or threatens to distort competition by favouring certain undertakings or the production of certain goods shall, in so far as it affects trade between Member States, be incompatible with the internal market.

2. The following shall be compatible with the internal market:
    (a) aid having a social character, granted to individual consumers, provided that such aid is granted without discrimination related to the origin of the products concerned;
    (b) aid to make good the damage caused by natural disasters or exceptional occurrences;
    (c) aid granted to the economy of certain areas of the Federal Republic of Germany affected by the division of Germany, in so far as such aid is required in order to compensate for the economic disadvantages caused by that division. Five years after the entry into force of the Treaty of Lisbon, the Council, acting on a proposal from the Commission, may adopt a decision repealing this point.

3. The following may be considered to be compatible with the internal market:
    (a) aid to promote the economic development of areas where the standard of living is abnormally low or where there is serious underemployment, and of the regions referred to in Article 349, in view of their structural, economic and social situation;
    (b) aid to promote the execution of an important project of common European interest or to remedy a serious disturbance in the economy of a Member State;
    (c) aid to facilitate the development of certain economic activities or of certain economic areas, where such aid does not adversely affect trading conditions to an extent contrary to the common interest;
    (d) aid to promote culture and heritage conservation where such aid does not affect trading conditions and competition in the Union to an extent that is contrary to the common interest;
    (e) such other categories of aid as may be specified by decision of the Council on a proposal from the Commission.

Article 108

1. The Commission shall, in cooperation with Member States, keep under constant review all systems of aid existing in those States. It shall propose to the latter any appropriate measures required by the progressive development or by the functioning of the internal market.

2. If, after giving notice to the parties concerned to submit their comments, the Commission finds that aid granted by a State or through State resources is not compatible with the internal market having regard to Article 107, or that such aid is being misused, it shall decide that the State concerned shall abolish or alter such aid within a period of time to be determined by the Commission.

    If the State concerned does not comply with this decision within the prescribed time, the Commission or any other interested State may, in derogation from the provisions of Articles 258 and 259, refer the matter to the Court of Justice of the European Union direct. On application by a Member State, the Council may, acting unanimously, decide that aid which that State is granting or intends to grant shall be considered to be compatible with the internal market, in derogation from the provisions of Article 107 or from the regulations provided for in Article 109, if such a decision is justified by exceptional circumstances. If, as regards the aid in question, the Commission has already initiated the procedure provided for in the first subparagraph of this paragraph, the fact that the State concerned has made its application to the Council shall have the effect of suspending that procedure until the Council has made its attitude known.

If, however, the Council has not made its attitude known within three months of the said application being made, the Commission shall give its decision on the case.

3. The Commission shall be informed, in sufficient time to enable it to submit its comments, of any plans to grant or alter aid. If it considers that any such plan is not compatible with the internal market having regard to Article 107, it shall without delay initiate the procedure provided for in paragraph 2. The Member State concerned shall not put its proposed measures into effect until this procedure has resulted in a final decision.

4. The Commission may adopt regulations relating to the categories of State aid that the Council has, pursuant to Article 109, determined may be exempted from the procedure provided for by paragraph 3 of this Article.

Article 109

The Council, on a proposal from the Commission and after consulting the European Parliament, may make any appropriate regulations for the application of Articles 107 and 108 and may in particular determine the conditions in which Article 108(3) shall apply and the categories of aid exempted from this procedure.

CHAPTER 2
TAX PROVISIONS

Article 110

No Member State shall impose, directly or indirectly, on the products of other Member States any internal taxation of any kind in excess of that imposed directly or indirectly on similar domestic products.

Furthermore, no Member State shall impose on the products of other Member States any internal taxation of such a nature as to afford indirect protection to other products.

Article 111

Where products are exported to the territory of any Member State, any repayment of internal taxation shall not exceed the internal taxation imposed on them whether directly or indirectly.

Article 112

In the case of charges other than turnover taxes, excise duties and other forms of indirect taxation, remissions and repayments in respect of exports to other Member States may not be granted and countervailing charges in respect of imports from Member States may not be imposed unless the measures contemplated have been previously approved for a limited period by the Council on a proposal from the Commission.

Article 113

The Council shall, acting unanimously in accordance with a special legislative procedure and after consulting the European Parliament and the Economic and Social Committee, adopt provisions for the harmonisation of legislation concerning turnover taxes, excise duties and other forms of indirect taxation to the extent that such harmonisation is necessary to ensure the establishment and the functioning of the internal market and to avoid distortion of competition.

CHAPTER 3
APPROXIMATION OF LAWS

Article 114

1. Save where otherwise provided in the Treaties, the following provisions shall apply for the achievement of the objectives set out in Article 26. The European Parliament

and the Council shall, acting in accordance with the ordinary legislative procedure and after consulting the Economic and Social Committee, adopt the measures for the approximation of the provisions laid down by law, regulation or administrative action in Member States which have as their object the establishment and functioning of the internal market.

2. Paragraph 1 shall not apply to fiscal provisions, to those relating to the free movement of persons nor to those relating to the rights and interests of employed persons.

3. The Commission, in its proposals envisaged in paragraph 1 concerning health, safety, environmental protection and consumer protection, will take as a base a high level of protection, taking account in particular of any new development based on scientific facts. Within their respective powers, the European Parliament and the Council will also seek to achieve this objective.

4. If, after the adoption of a harmonisation measure by the European Parliament and the Council, by the Council or by the Commission, a Member State deems it necessary to maintain national provisions on grounds of major needs referred to in Article 36, or relating to the protection of the environment or the working environment, it shall notify the Commission of these provisions as well as the grounds for maintaining them.

5. Moreover, without prejudice to paragraph 4, if, after the adoption of a harmonisation measure by the European Parliament and the Council, by the Council or by the Commission, a Member State deems it necessary to introduce national provisions based on new scientific evidence relating to the protection of the environment or the working environment on grounds of a problem specific to that Member State arising after the adoption of the harmonisation measure, it shall notify the Commission of the envisaged provisions as well as the grounds for introducing them.

6. The Commission shall, within six months of the notifications as referred to in paragraphs 4 and 5, approve or reject the national provisions involved after having verified whether or not they are a means of arbitrary discrimination or a disguised restriction on trade between Member States and whether or not they shall constitute an obstacle to the functioning of the internal market.

   In the absence of a decision by the Commission within this period the national provisions referred to in paragraphs 4 and 5 shall be deemed to have been approved. When justified by the complexity of the matter and in the absence of danger for human health, the Commission may notify the Member State concerned that the period referred to in this paragraph may be extended for a further period of up to six months.

7. When, pursuant to paragraph 6, a Member State is authorised to maintain or introduce national provisions derogating from a harmonisation measure, the Commission shall immediately examine whether to propose an adaptation to that measure.

8. When a Member State raises a specific problem on public health in a field which has been the subject of prior harmonisation measures, it shall bring it to the attention of the Commission which shall immediately examine whether to propose appropriate measures to the Council.

9. By way of derogation from the procedure laid down in Articles 258 and 259, the Commission and any Member State may bring the matter directly before the Court of Justice of the European Union if it considers that another Member State is making improper use of the powers provided for in this Article.

10. The harmonisation measures referred to above shall, in appropriate cases, include a safeguard clause authorising the Member States to take, for one or more of the non-economic reasons referred to in Article 36, provisional measures subject to a Union control procedure.

Article 115

Without prejudice to Article 114, the Council shall, acting unanimously in accordance with a special legislative procedure and after consulting the European Parliament and the Economic and Social Committee, issue directives for the approximation of such laws, regulations or administrative provisions of the Member States as directly affect the establishment or functioning of the internal market.

Article 116

Where the Commission finds that a difference between the provisions laid down by law, regulation or administrative action in Member States is distorting the conditions of competition in the internal market and that the resultant distortion needs to be eliminated, it shall consult the Member States concerned.

If such consultation does not result in an agreement eliminating the distortion in question, the European, Parliament and the Council, acting in accordance with the ordinary legislative procedure, shall issue the necessary directives. Any other appropriate measures provided for in the Treaties may be adopted.

Article 117

1. Where there is a reason to fear that the adoption or amendment of a provision laid down by law, regulation or administrative action may cause distortion within the meaning of Article 116, a Member State desiring to proceed therewith shall consult the Commission. After consulting the Member States, the Commission shall recommend to the States concerned such measures as may be appropriate to avoid the distortion in question.
2. If a State desiring to introduce or amend its own provisions does not comply with the recommendation addressed to it by the Commission, other Member States shall not be required, pursuant to Article 116, to amend their own provisions in order to eliminate such distortion. If the Member State which has ignored the recommendation of the Commission causes distortion detrimental only to itself, the provisions of Article 116 shall not apply.

Article 118

In the context of the establishment and functioning of the internal market, the European Parliament and the Council, acting in accordance with the ordinary legislative procedure, shall establish measures for the creation of European intellectual property rights to provide uniform protection of intellectual property rights throughout the Union and for the setting up of centralised Union-wide authorisation, coordination and supervision arrangements.

The Council, acting in accordance with a special legislative procedure, shall by means of regulations establish language arrangements for the European intellectual property rights. The Council shall act unanimously after consulting the European Parliament.

TITLE VIII
ECONOMIC AND MONETARY POLICY

CHAPTER 1
ECONOMIC POLICY

Article 119

1. For the purposes set out in Article 3 of the Treaty on European Union, the activities of the Member States and the Union shall include, as provided in the Treaties, the adoption of an economic policy which is based on the close coordination of Member States' economic policies, on the internal market and on the definition of common objectives, and conducted in accordance with the principle of an open market economy with free competition.
2. Concurrently with the foregoing, and as provided in the Treaties and in accordance with the procedures set out therein, these activities shall include a single currency, the euro, and the definition and conduct of a single monetary policy and exchange-rate policy the primary objective of both of which shall be to maintain price stability and, without prejudice to this objective, to support the general economic policies in the Union, in accordance with the principle of an open market economy with free competition.
3. These activities of the Member States and the Union shall entail compliance with the following guiding principles: stable prices, sound public finances and monetary conditions and a sustainable balance of payments.

CHAPTER 2
MONETARY POLICY

Article 127

1. The primary objective of the European System of Central Banks, hereinafter referred to as 'ESCB', shall be to maintain price stability. Without prejudice to the objective of price stability, the ESCB shall support the general economic policies in the Union with a view to contributing to the achievement of the objectives of the Union as laid down in Article 3 of the Treaty on European Union. The ESCB shall act in accordance with the principle of an open market economy with free competition, favouring an efficient allocation of resources, and in compliance with the principles set out in Article 119.
2. The basic tasks to be carried out through the ESCB shall be:
    — to define and implement the monetary policy of the Union,
    — to conduct foreign-exchange operations consistent with the provisions of Article 219;
    — to hold and manage the official foreign reserves of the Member States,
    — to promote the smooth operation of payment systems.

    ...

Article 128

1. The European Central Bank shall have the exclusive right to authorise the issue of euro banknotes within the Union. The European Central Bank and the national central banks may issue such notes. The banknotes issued by the European Central Bank and the national central banks shall be the only such notes to have the status of legal tender within the Union.
2. Member States may issue euro coins subject to approval by the European Central Bank of the volume of the issue. The Council, on a proposal from the Commission and after consulting the European Parliament and the European Central Bank, may, adopt measures to harmonise the denominations and technical specifications of all coins intended for circulation to the extent necessary to permit their smooth circulation within the Union.

CHAPTER 3
INSTITUTIONAL PROVISIONS

Article 134

1. In order to promote coordination of the policies of Member States to the full extent needed for the functioning of the internal market, an Economic and Financial Committee is hereby set up.
2. The Economic and Financial Committee shall have the following tasks:
    — to deliver opinions at the request of the Council or Commission, or on its own initiative for submission to those institutions,
    — to keep under review the economic and financial situation of the Member States and of the Union and to report regularly thereon to the Council and to the Commission, in particular on financial relations with third countries and international institutions,
    — without prejudice to Article 240, to contribute to the preparation of the work of the Council referred to in Articles 66, 75, 121(2), (3), (4) and (6), 122, 124, 125, 126, 127(6), 128(2), 129(3) and (4), 219, 138(1), 143, 144(2) and (3), and 140(2) and (3), and to carry out other advisory and preparatory tasks assigned to it by the Council,
    — to examine, at least once a year, the situation regarding the movement of capital and the freedom of payments, as they result from the application of the Treaties and of measures adopted by the Council; the examination shall cover all measures relating to capital movements and payments; the Committee shall report to the Commission and to the Council on the outcome of this examination.
    The Member States, the Commission and the European Central Bank shall each appoint no more than two members of the Committee.
3. The Council shall, on a proposal from the Commission and after consulting the European Central Bank and the Committee referred to in this Article, lay down detailed provisions concerning the composition of the Economic and Financial Committee. The President of the Council shall inform the European Parliament of such a decision.

4. In addition to the tasks set out in paragraph 2, if and as long as there are Member States with a derogation as referred to in Article 139, the Committee shall keep under review the monetary and financial situation and the general payments system of those Member States and report regularly thereon to the Council and to the Commission.

TITLE IX
EMPLOYMENT

Article 145

Member States and the Union shall, in accordance with this title, work towards developing a coordinated strategy for employment and particularly for promoting a skilled, trained and adaptable workforce and labour markets responsive to economic change with a view to achieving the objectives defined in Article 3 of the Treaty on European Union.

TITLE X
SOCIAL POLICY

Article 151

The Union and the Member States, having in mind fundamental social rights such as those set out in the European Social Charter signed at Turin on 21 October 1961 and in the 1989 Community Charter of the Fundamental Social Rights of Workers, shall have as their objectives the promotion of employment, improved living and working conditions, so as to make possible their harmonisation while the improvement is being maintained, proper social protection, dialogue between management and labour, the development of human resources with a view to lasting high employment and the combating of exclusion.

To this end the Union and the Member States shall implement measures which take account of the diverse forms of national practices, in particular in the field of contractual relations, and the need to maintain the competitiveness of the Union economy.

They believe that such a development will ensue not only from the functioning of the internal market, which will favour the harmonisation of social systems, but also from the procedures provided for in the Treaties and from the approximation of provisions laid down by law, regulation or administrative action.

Article 152

The Union recognises and promotes the role of the social partners at its level, taking into account the diversity of national systems. It shall facilitate dialogue between the social partners, respecting their autonomy.

The Tripartite Social Summit for Growth and Employment shall contribute to social dialogue.

Article 153

1. With a view to achieving the objectives of Article 151, the Union shall support and complement the activities of the Member States in the following fields:
   (a) improvement in particular of the working environment to protect workers' health and safety;
   (b) working conditions;
   (c) social security and social protection of workers;
   (d) protection of workers where their employment contract is terminated;
   (e) the information and consultation of workers;
   (f) representation and collective defence of the interests of workers and employers, including co-determination, subject to paragraph 5;
   (g) conditions of employment for third-country nationals legally residing in Union territory;
   (h) the integration of persons excluded from the labour market, without prejudice to Article 166;
   (i) equality between men and women with regard to labour market opportunities and treatment at work;
   (j) the combating of social exclusion;
   (k) the modernisation of social protection systems without prejudice to point (c).

2.   To this end, the European Parliament and the Council:

     (a)   may adopt measures designed to encourage cooperation between Member States through initiatives aimed at improving knowledge, developing exchanges of information and best practices, promoting innovative approaches and evaluating experiences, excluding any harmonisation of the laws and regulations of the Member States;

     (b)   may adopt, in the fields referred to in paragraph 1(a) to (i), by means of directives, minimum requirements for gradual implementation, having regard to the conditions and technical rules obtaining in each of the Member States. Such directives shall avoid imposing administrative, financial and legal constraints in a way which would hold back the creation and development of small and medium-sized undertakings.

     The European Parliament and the Council shall act in accordance with the ordinary legislative procedure after consulting the Economic and Social Committee and the Committee of the Regions.

     In the fields referred to in paragraph 1(c), (d), (f) and (g), the Council shall act unanimously, in accordance with a special legislative procedure, after consulting the European Parliament and the said Committees.

     The Council, acting unanimously on a proposal from the Commission, after consulting the European Parliament, may decide to render the ordinary legislative procedure applicable to paragraph 1(d), (f) and (g).

3.   A Member State may entrust management and labour, at their joint request, with the implementation of directives adopted pursuant to paragraph 2, or, where appropriate, with the implementation of a Council decision adopted in accordance with Article 155. In this case, it shall ensure that, no later than the date on which a directive or a decision must be transposed or implemented, management and labour have introduced the necessary measures by agreement, the Member State concerned being required to take any necessary measure enabling it at any time to be in a position to guarantee the results imposed by that directive or that decision.

4.   The provisions adopted pursuant to this Article:

     — shall not affect the right of Member States to define the fundamental principles of their social security systems and must not significantly affect the financial equilibrium thereof,

     — shall not prevent any Member State from maintaining or introducing more stringent protective measures compatible with the Treaties.

5.   The provisions of this Article shall not apply to pay, the right of association, the right to strike or the right to impose lock-outs.

Article 154

1.   The Commission shall have the task of promoting the consultation of management and labour at Union level and shall take any relevant measure to facilitate their dialogue by ensuring balanced support for the parties.

2.   To this end, before submitting proposals in the social policy field, the Commission shall consult management and labour on the possible direction of Union action.

3.   If, after such consultation, the Commission considers Union action advisable, it shall consult management and labour on the content of the envisaged proposal. Management and labour shall forward to the Commission an opinion or, where appropriate, a recommendation.

4.   On the occasion of such consultations set out in paragraphs 2 and 3, management and labour may inform the Commission of their wish to initiate the process provided for in Article 155. The duration of this process shall not exceed nine months, unless the management and labour concerned and the Commission decide jointly to extend it.

Article 155

1.   Should management and labour so desire, the dialogue between them at Union level may lead to contractual relations, including agreements.

2.   Agreements concluded at Union level shall be implemented either in accordance with the procedures and practices specific to management and labour and the Member

States or, in matters covered by Article 153, at the joint request of the signatory parties, by a Council decision on a proposal from the Commission. The European Parliament shall be informed. The Council shall act unanimously where the agreement in question contains one or more provisions relating to one of the areas for which unanimity is required pursuant to Article 153(2).

Article 156

With a view to achieving the objectives of Article 151 and without prejudice to the other provisions of the Treaties, the Commission shall encourage cooperation between the Member States and facilitate the coordination of their action in all social policy fields under this Chapter, particularly in matters relating to:
— employment,
— labour law and working conditions,
— basic and advanced vocational training,
— social security,
— prevention of occupational accidents and diseases, occupational hygiene,
— the right of association and collective bargaining between employers and workers.

To this end, the Commission shall act in close contact with Member States by making studies, delivering opinions and arranging consultations both on problems arising at national level and on those of concern to international organisations, in particular initiatives aiming at the establishment of guidelines and indicators, the organisation of exchange of best practice, and the preparation of the necessary elements for periodic monitoring and evaluation. The European Parliament shall be kept fully informed.

Before delivering the opinions provided for in this Article, the Commission shall consult the Economic and Social Committee.

Article 157

1. Each Member State shall ensure that the principle of equal pay for male and female workers for equal work or work of equal value is applied.
2. For the purpose of this article, 'pay' means the ordinary basic or minimum wage or salary and any other consideration, whether in cash or in kind, which the worker receives directly or indirectly, in respect of his employment, from his employer.
    Equal pay without discrimination based on sex means:
    (a) that pay for the same work at piece rates shall be calculated on the basis of the same unit of measurement;
    (b) that pay for work at time rates shall be the same for the same job.
3. The European Parliament and the Council, acting in accordance with the ordinary legislative procedure, and after consulting the Economic and Social Committee, shall adopt measures to ensure the application of the principle of equal opportunities and equal treatment of men and women in matters of employment and occupation, including the principle of equal pay for equal work or work of equal value.
4. With a view to ensuring full equality in practice between men and women in working life, the principle of equal treatment shall not prevent any Member State from maintaining or adopting measures providing for specific advantages in order to make it easier for the underrepresented sex to pursue a vocational activity or to prevent or compensate for disadvantages in professional careers.

Article 158

Member States shall endeavour to maintain the existing equivalence between paid holiday schemes.

Article 159

The Commission shall draw up a report each year on progress in achieving the objectives of Article 151, including the demographic situation in the Union. It shall forward the report to the European Parliament, the Council and the Economic and Social Committee.

Article 160

The Council, acting by a simple majority after consulting the European Parliament, shall establish a Social Protection Committee with advisory status to promote cooperation on

social protection policies between Member States and with the Commission. The tasks of the Committee shall be:
— to monitor the social situation and the development of social protection policies in the Member States and the Union,
— to promote exchanges of information, experience and good practice between Member States and with the Commission,
— without prejudice to Article 240, to prepare reports, formulate opinions or undertake other work within its fields of competence, at the request of either the Councilor the Commission or on its own initiative.

In fulfilling its mandate, the Committee shall establish appropriate contacts with management and labour.

Each Member State and the Commission shall appoint two members of the Committee.

Article 161

The Commission shall include a separate chapter on social developments within the Union in its annual report to the European Parliament.

The European Parliament may invite the Commission to draw up reports on any particular problems concerning social conditions.

TITLE XI
THE EUROPEAN SOCIAL FUND

Article 162

In order to improve employment opportunities for workers in the internal market and to contribute thereby to raising the standard of living, a European Social Fund is hereby established in accordance with the provisions set out below; it shall aim to render the employment of workers easier and to increase their geographical and occupational mobility within the Union, and to facilitate their adaptation to industrial changes and to changes in production systems, in particular through vocational training and retraining.

TITLE XII
EDUCATION, VOCATIONAL TRAINING, YOUTH AND SPORT

Article 165

1. The Union shall contribute to the development of quality education by encouraging cooperation between Member States and, if necessary, by supporting and supplementing their action, while fully respecting the responsibility of the Member States for the content of teaching and the organisation of education systems and their cultural and linguistic diversity.

    The Union shall contribute to the promotion of European sporting issues, while taking account of the specific nature of sport, its structures based on voluntary activity and its social and educational function.

2. Union action shall be aimed at:
    — developing the European dimension in education, particularly through the teaching and dissemination of the languages of the Member States,
    — encouraging mobility of students and teachers, by encouraging *inter alia*, the academic recognition of diplomas and periods of study,
    — promoting cooperation between educational establishments,
    — developing exchanges of information and experience on issues common to the education systems of the Member States,
    — encouraging the development of youth exchanges and of exchanges of socioeducational instructors, and encouraging the participation of young people in democratic life in Europe,
    — encouraging the development of distance education.
    — developing the European dimension in sport, by promoting fairness and openness in sporting competitions and cooperation between bodies responsible for sports, and by protecting the physical and moral integrity of sportsmen and sportswomen, especially the youngest sportsmen and sportswomen.

3. The Union and the Member States shall foster cooperation with third countries and the competent international organisations in the field of education and sport, in particular the Council of Europe.

4. In order to contribute to the achievement of the objectives referred to in this Article:
   — the European Parliament and the Council, acting in accordance with the ordinary legislative procedure, after consulting the Economic and Social Committee and the Committee of the Regions, shall adopt incentive measures, excluding any harmonisation of the laws and regulations of the Member States,
   — the Council, on a proposal from the Commission, shall adopt recommendations.

Article 166

1. The Union shall implement a vocational training policy which shall support and supplement the action of the Member States, while fully respecting the responsibility of the Member States for the content and organisation of vocational training.

2. Union action shall aim to:
   — facilitate adaptation to industrial changes, in particular through vocational training and retraining,
   — improve initial and continuing vocational training in order to facilitate vocational integration and reintegration into the labour market,
   — facilitate access to vocational training and encourage mobility of instructors and trainees and particularly young people,
   — stimulate cooperation on training between educational or training establishments and firms,
   — develop exchanges of information and experience on issues common to the training systems of the Member States.

3. The Union and the Member States shall foster cooperation with third countries and the competent international organisations in the sphere of vocational training.

4. The European Parliament and the Council, acting in accordance with the ordinary legislative procedure and after consulting the Economic and Social Committee and the Committee of the Regions, shall adopt measures to contribute to the achievement of the objectives referred to in this Article, excluding any harmonisation of the laws and regulations of the Member States, and the Council, on a proposal from the Commission, shall adopt recommendations.

TITLE XIII
CULTURE

Article 167

1. The Union shall contribute to the flowering of the cultures of the Member States, while respecting their national and regional diversity and at the same time bringing the common cultural heritage to the fore.

2. Action by the Union shall be aimed at encouraging cooperation between Member States and, if necessary, supporting and supplementing their action in the following areas:
   — improvement of the knowledge and dissemination of the culture and history of the European peoples,
   — conservation and safeguarding of cultural heritage of European significance,
   — non-commercial cultural exchanges,
   — artistic and literary creation, including in the audiovisual sector.

3. The Union and the Member States shall foster cooperation with third countries and the competent international organisations in the sphere of culture, in particular the Council of Europe.

4. The Union shall take cultural aspects into account in its action under other provisions of the Treaties, in particular in order to respect and to promote the diversity of its cultures.

5. In order to contribute to the achievement of the objectives referred to in this Article:
   — the European Parliament and the Council acting in accordance with the ordinary legislative procedure and after consulting the Committee of the Regions, shall adopt incentive measures, excluding any harmonisation of the laws and regulations of the Member States.
   — the Council, on a proposal from the Commission, shall adopt recommendations.

TITLE XIV
PUBLIC HEALTH

Article 168

1. A high level of human health protection shall be ensured in the definition and implementation of all the Union's policies and activities.

   Union action, which shall complement national policies, shall be directed towards improving public health, preventing human illness and diseases, and obviating sources of danger to physical and mental health. Such action shall cover the fight against the major health scourges, by promoting research into their causes, their transmission and their prevention, as well as health information and education, and monitoring, early warning of and combating serious cross-border threats to health.

   The Union shall complement the Member States' action in reducing drugs-related health damage, including information and prevention.

2. The Union shall encourage cooperation between the Member States in the areas referred to in this Article and, if necessary, lend support to their action. It shall in particular encourage cooperation between the Member States to improve the complementarity of their health services in cross-border areas.

   Member States shall, in liaison with the Commission, coordinate among themselves their policies and programmes in the areas referred to in paragraph 1. The Commission may, in close contact with the Member States, take any useful initiative to promote such coordination, in particular initiatives aiming at the establishment of guidelines and indicators, the organisation of exchange of best practice, and the preparation of the necessary elements for periodic monitoring and evaluation. The European Parliament shall be kept fully informed.

3. The Union and the Member States shall foster cooperation with third countries and the competent international organisations in the sphere of public health.

4. By way of derogation from Article 2(5) and Article 6(a) and in accordance with Article 4(2)(k), the European Parliament and the Council, acting in accordance with the ordinary legislative procedure and after consulting the Economic and Social Committee and the Committee of the Regions, shall contribute to the achievement of the objectives referred to in this Article through adopting, in order to meet common safety concerns:

   (a) measures setting high standards of quality and safety of organs and substances of human origin, blood and blood derivatives; these measures shall not prevent any Member State from maintaining or introducing more stringent protective measures;

   (b) measures in the veterinary and phytosanitary fields which have as their direct objective the protection of public health;

   (c) measures setting high standards of quality and safety for medicinal products and devices for medical use.

5. The European Parliament and the Council, acting in accordance with the ordinary legislative procedure and after consulting the Economic and Social Committee and the Committee of the Regions, may also adopt incentive measures designed to protect and improve human health and in particular to combat the major cross-border health scourges, measures concerning monitoring, early warning of and combating serious cross-border threats to health, and measures which have as their direct objective the protection of public health regarding tobacco and the abuse of alcohol, excluding any harmonisation of the laws and regulations of the Member States.

6. The Council, on a proposal from the Commission, may also adopt recommendations for the purposes set out in this Article.

7. Union action shall respect the responsibilities of the Member States for the definition of their health policy and for the organisation and delivery of health services and medical care. The responsibilities of the Member States shall include the management of health services and medical care and the allocation of the resources assigned to them. The measures referred to in paragraph 4(a) shall not affect national provisions on the donation or medical use of organs and blood.

TITLE XV
CONSUMER PROTECTION

Article 169

1. In order to promote the interests of consumers and to ensure a high level of consumer protection, the Union shall contribute to protecting the health, safety and economic interests of consumers, as well as to promoting their right to information, education and to organise themselves in order to safeguard their interests.

2. The Union shall contribute to the attainment of the objectives referred to in paragraph 1 through:
   (a) measures adopted pursuant to Article 114 in the context of the completion of the internal market;
   (b) measures which support, supplement and monitor the policy pursued by the Member States.

3. The European Parliament and the Council, acting in accordance with the ordinary legislative procedure and after consulting the Economic and Social Committee, shall adopt the measures referred to in paragraph 2(b).

4. Measures adopted pursuant to paragraph 3 shall not prevent any Member State from maintaining or introducing more stringent protective measures. Such measures must be compatible with the Treaties. The Commission shall be notified of them.

TITLE XVIII
ECONOMIC, SOCIAL AND TERRITORIAL COHESION

Article 174

In order to promote its overall harmonious development, the Union shall develop and pursue its actions leading to the strengthening of its economic, social and territorial cohesion.

In particular, the Union shall aim at reducing disparities between the levels of development of the various regions and the backwardness of the least favoured regions.

Among the regions concerned, particular attention shall be paid to rural areas, areas affected by industrial transition, and regions which suffer from severe and permanent natural or demographic handicaps such as the northernmost regions with very low population density and island, cross-border and mountain regions.

TITLE XX
ENVIRONMENT

Article 191

1. Union policy on the environment shall contribute to pursuit of the following objectives:
   — preserving, protecting and improving the quality of the environment,
   — protecting human health,
   — prudent and rational utilisation of natural resources,
   — promoting measures at international level to deal with regional or worldwide environmental problems, and in particular combating climate change.

2. Union policy on the environment shall aim at a high level of protection taking into account the diversity of situations in the various regions of the Union. It shall be based on the precautionary principle and on the principles that preventive action should be taken, that environmental damage should as a priority be rectified at source and that the polluter should pay.

   In this context, harmonisation measures answering environmental protection requirements shall include, where appropriate, a safeguard clause allowing Member States to take provisional measures, for non-economic environmental reasons, subject to a procedure of inspection by the Union.

3. In preparing its policy on the environment, the Union shall take account of:
   — available scientific and technical data,
   — environmental conditions in the various regions of the Union,
   — the potential benefits and costs of action or lack of action,
   — the economic and social development of the Union as a whole and the balanced development of its regions.

4. Within their respective spheres of competence, the Union and the Member States shall cooperate with third countries and with the competent international organisations. The arrangements for Union cooperation may be the subject of agreements between the Union and the third parties concerned.

    The previous subparagraph shall be without prejudice to Member States' competence to negotiate in international bodies and to conclude international agreements.

Article 192

1. The European Parliament and the Council, acting in accordance with the ordinary legislative procedure and after consulting the Economic and Social Committee and the Committee of the Regions, shall decide what action is to be taken by the Union in order to achieve the objectives referred to in Article 191.

    ...

TITLE XXI

ENERGY

Article 194

1. In the context of the establishment and functioning of the internal market and with regard for the need to preserve and improve the environment, the Union's policy on energy shall aim, in a spirit of solidarity between Member States, to:
    (a) ensure the functioning of the energy market;
    (b) ensure security of energy supply in the Union; and
    (c) promote energy efficiency and energy saving and the development of new and renewable forms of energy; and
    (d) promote the interconnection of energy networks.

    ...

TITLE XXII

TOURISM

Article 195

1. The Union shall complement the action of the Member States in the tourism sector, in particular by promoting the competitiveness of Union undertakings in that sector. To that end, Union action shall be aimed at:
    (a) encouraging the creation of a favourable environment for the development of undertakings in this sector;
    (b) promoting cooperation between the Member States, particularly by the exchange of good practice.
2. The European Parliament and the Council, acting in accordance with the ordinary legislative procedure, shall establish specific measures to complement actions within the Member States to achieve the objectives referred to in this Article, excluding any harmonisation of the laws and regulations of the Member States.

TITLE XXIII

CIVIL PROTECTION

Article 196

1. The Union shall encourage cooperation between Member States in order to improve the effectiveness of systems for preventing and protecting against natural or man-made disasters.

    The Union's action shall aim to:
    (a) support and complement Member States' action at national, regional and local level in risk prevention, in preparing their civil-protection personnel and in responding to natural or man-made disasters within the Union;
    (b) promote swift, effective operational cooperation within the Union between national civil-protection services;
    (c) promote consistency in international civil-protection work.

2. The European Parliament and Council, acting in accordance with the ordinary legislative procedure shall establish the measures necessary to help achieve the objectives referred to in paragraph 1, excluding any harmonisation of the laws and regulations of the Member States.

TITLE XXIV
ADMINISTRATIVE CO-OPERATION

Article 197

1. Effective implementation of Union law by the Member States, which is essential for the proper functioning of the Union, shall be regarded as a matter of common interest.
2. The Union may support the efforts of Member States to improve their administrative capacity to implement Union law. Such action may include facilitating the exchange of information and of civil servants as well as supporting training schemes. No Member State shall be obliged to avail itself of such support. The European Parliament and the Council, acting by means of regulations in accordance with the ordinary legislative procedure, shall establish the necessary measures to this end, excluding any harmonisation of the laws and regulations of the Member States.
3. This Article shall be without prejudice to the obligations of the Member States to implement Union law or to the prerogatives and duties of the Commission. It shall also be without prejudice to other provisions of the Treaties providing for administrative cooperation among the Member States and between them and the Union.

PART FIVE
THE UNION'S EXTERNAL ACTION

TITLE I
GENERAL PROVISIONS ON THE UNION'S EXTERNAL ACTION

Article 205

The Union's action on the international scene, pursuant to this Part, shall be guided by the principles, pursue the objectives and be conducted in accordance with the general provisions laid down in Chapter 1 of Title V of the Treaty on European Union.

TITLE II
COMMON COMMERCIAL POLICY

Article 206

By establishing a customs union in accordance with Articles 28 to 32, the Union shall contribute, in the common interest, to the harmonious development of world trade, the progressive abolition of restrictions on international trade and on foreign direct investment, and the lowering of customs and other barriers.

Article 207

1. The common commercial policy shall be based on uniform principles, particularly with regard to changes in tariff rates, the conclusion of tariff and trade agreements relating to trade in goods and services, and the commercial aspects of intellectual property, foreign direct investment, the achievement of uniformity in measures of liberalisation, export policy and measures to protect trade such as those to be taken in the event of dumping or subsidies. The common commercial policy shall be conducted in the context of the principles and objectives of the Union's external action.
2. The European Parliament and the Council, acting by means of regulations in accordance with the ordinary legislative procedure, shall adopt the measures defining the framework for implementing the common commercial policy.
3. Where agreements with one or more third countries or international organisations need to be negotiated and concluded, Article 218 shall apply, subject to the special provisions of this Article.

The Commission shall make recommendations to the Council, which shall authorise it to open the necessary negotiations. The Council and the Commission shall be responsible for ensuring that the agreements negotiated are compatible with internal Union policies and rules.

The Commission shall conduct these negotiations in consultation with a special committee appointed by the Council to assist the Commission in this task and within the framework of such directives as the Council may issue to it. The Commission shall report regularly to the special committee and to the European Parliament on the progress of negotiations.

4. For the negotiation and conclusion of the agreements referred to in paragraph 3, the Council shall act by a qualified majority.

For the negotiation and conclusion of agreements in the fields of trade in services and the commercial aspects of intellectual property, as well as foreign direct investment, the Council shall act unanimously where such agreements include provisions for which unanimity is required for the adoption of internal rules.

The Council shall also act unanimously for the negotiation and conclusion of agreements:

(a) in the field of trade in cultural and audiovisual services, where these agreements risk prejudicing the Union's cultural and linguistic diversity;

(b) in the field of trade in social, education and health services, where these agreements risk seriously disturbing the national organisation of such services and prejudicing the responsibility of Member States to deliver them.

5. The negotiation and conclusion of international agreements in the field of transport shall be subject to Title VI of Part Three and to Article 218.

6. The exercise of the competences conferred by this Article in the field of the common commercial policy shall not affect the delimitation of competences between the Union and the Member States, and shall not lead to harmonisation of legislative or regulatory provisions of the Member States insofar as the Treaties exclude such harmonisation.

TITLE III
COOPERATION WITH THIRD COUNTRIES AND HUMANITARIAN AID

CHAPTER 1
DEVELOPMENT COOPERATION

Article 208

1. Union policy in the field of development cooperation shall be conducted within the framework of the principles and objectives of the Union's external action. The Union's development cooperation policy and that of the Member States complement and reinforce each other.

The Union's development cooperation policy shall have as its primary objective the reduction and, in the long term, the eradication of poverty. The Union shall take account of the objectives of development cooperation in the policies that it implements which are likely to affect developing countries.

2. The Union and the Member States shall comply with the commitments and take account of the objectives they have approved in the context of the United Nations and other competent international organisations.

Article 209

1. The European Parliament and the Council, acting in accordance with the ordinary legislative procedure, shall adopt the measures necessary for the implementation of development cooperation policy, which may relate to multiannual cooperation programmes with developing countries or programmes with a thematic approach.

2. The Union may conclude with third countries and competent international organisations any agreement helping to achieve the objectives referred to in Article 21 of the Treaty on European Union and in Article 208 of this Treaty.

The first subparagraph shall be without prejudice to Member States' competence to negotiate in international bodies and to conclude agreements.

3. The European Investment Bank shall contribute, under the terms laid down in its Statute, to the implementation of the measures referred to in paragraph 1.

Article 210

1. In order to promote the complementarity and efficiency of their action, the Union and the Member States shall coordinate their policies on development cooperation and shall consult each other on their aid programmes, including in international organisations and during international conferences. They may undertake joint action. Member States shall contribute if necessary to the implementation of Union aid programmes.
2. The Commission may take any useful initiative to promote the coordination referred to in paragraph 1.

Article 211

Within their respective spheres of competence, the Union and the Member States shall cooperate with third countries and with the competent international organisations.

CHAPTER 2
ECONOMIC, FINANCIAL AND TECHNICAL COOPERATION WITH THIRD COUNTRIES

Article 212

1. Without prejudice to the other provisions of the Treaties, and in particular Articles 208 to 211, the Union shall carry out economic, financial and technical cooperation measures, including assistance, in particular financial assistance, with third countries other than developing countries. Such measures shall be consistent with the development policy of the Union and shall be carried out within the framework of the principles and objectives of its external action. The Union's measures and those of the Member States shall complement and reinforce each other.
2. The European Parliament and the Council, acting in accordance with the ordinary legislative procedure, shall adopt the measures necessary for the implementation of paragraph 1.
3. Within their respective spheres of competence, the Union and the Member States shall cooperate with third countries and the competent international organisations. The arrangements for Union cooperation may be the subject of agreements between the Union and the third parties concerned.

    The first subparagraph shall be without prejudice to the Member States' competence to negotiate in international bodies and to conclude international agreements.

Article 213

When the situation in a third country requires urgent financial assistance from the Union, the Council shall adopt the necessary decisions on a proposal from the Commission.

CHAPTER 3
HUMANITARIAN AID

Article 214

1. The Union's operations in the field of humanitarian aid shall be conducted within the framework of the principles and objectives of the external action of the Union. Such operations shall be intended to provide ad hoc assistance and relief and protection for people in third countries who are victims of natural or man-made disasters, in order to meet the humanitarian needs resulting from these different situations. The Union's operations and those of the Member States shall complement and reinforce each other.
2. Humanitarian aid operations shall be conducted in compliance with the principles of international law and with the principles of impartiality, neutrality and nondiscrimination.
3. The European Parliament and the Council, acting in accordance with the ordinary legislative procedure, shall establish the measures defining the framework within which the Union's humanitarian aid operations shall be implemented.
4. The Union may conclude with third countries and competent international organisations any agreement helping to achieve the objectives referred to in paragraph 1 and in Article 21 of the Treaty on European Union.

The first subparagraph shall be without prejudice to Member States' competence to negotiate in international bodies and to conclude agreements.

5. In order to establish a framework for joint contributions from young Europeans to the humanitarian aid operations of the Union, a European Voluntary Humanitarian Aid Corps shall be set up. The European Parliament and the Council, acting by means of regulations in accordance with the ordinary legislative procedure, shall determine the rules and procedures for the operation of the Corps.

6. The Commission may take any useful initiative to promote coordination between actions of the Union and those of the Member States, in order to enhance the efficiency and complementarity of Union and national humanitarian aid measures.

7. The Union shall ensure that its humanitarian aid operations are coordinated and consistent with those of international organisations and bodies, in particular those forming part of the United Nations system.

TITLE IV
RESTRICTIVE MEASURES

Article 215

1. Where a decision, adopted in accordance with Chapter 2 of Title V of the Treaty on European Union, provides for the interruption or reduction, in part or completely, of economic and financial relations with one or more third countries, the Council, acting by a qualified majority on a joint proposal from the High Representative of the Union for Foreign Affairs and Security Policy and the Commission, shall adopt the necessary measures. It shall inform the European Parliament thereof.

2. Where a decision adopted in accordance with Chapter 2 of Title V of the Treaty on European Union so provides, the Council may adopt restrictive measures under the procedure referred to in paragraph 1 against natural or legal persons and groups or non-State entities.

3. The acts referred to in this Article shall include necessary provisions on legal safeguards.

TITLE V
INTERNATIONAL AGREEMENTS

Article 216

1. The Union may conclude an agreement with one or more third countries or international organisations where the Treaties so provides or where the conclusion of an agreement is necessary in order to achieve, within the framework of the Union's policies, one of the objectives referred to in the Treaties, or is provided for in a legally binding act of the Union or is likely to affect common rules or alter their scope.

2. Agreements concluded by the Union are binding on the institutions of the Union and on its Member States.

Article 217

The Union may conclude with one or more third countries or international organisations agreements establishing an association involving reciprocal rights and obligations, common action and special procedure.

Article 218

1. Without prejudice to the specific provisions laid down in Article 207, agreements between the Union and third countries or international organisations shall be negotiated and concluded in accordance with the following procedure.

2. The Council shall authorise the opening of negotiations, adopt negotiating directives, authorise the signing of agreements and conclude them.

3. The Commission, or the High Representative of the Union for Foreign Affairs and Security Policy where the agreement envisaged relates exclusively or principally to the common foreign and security policy, shall submit recommendations to the Council, which shall adopt a decision authorising the opening of negotiations and, depending on the subject of the agreement envisaged, nominating the Union's negotiator or the head of the Union's negotiating team.

4. The Council may address directives to the negotiator and designate a special committee in consultation with which the negotiations must be conducted.

5. The Council, on a proposal by the negotiator, shall adopt a decision authorising the signing of the agreement and, if necessary, its provisional application before entry into force.

6. The Council, on a proposal by the negotiator, shall adopt a decision concluding the agreement.

   Except where agreements relate exclusively to the common foreign and security policy, the Council shall adopt the decision concluding the agreement:

   (a) after obtaining the consent of the European Parliament in the following cases:
       (i) association agreements;
       (ii) agreement on Union accession to the European Convention for the Protection of Human Rights and Fundamental Freedoms;
       (iii) agreements establishing a specific institutional framework by organising cooperation procedures;
       (iv) agreements with important budgetary implications for the Union;
       (v) agreements covering fields to which either the ordinary legislative procedure applies, or the special legislative procedure where consent by the European Parliament is required.

       The European Parliament and the Council may, in an urgent situation, agree upon a time-limit for consent.

   (b) after consulting the European Parliament in other cases. The European Parliament shall deliver its opinion within a time-limit which the Council may set depending on the urgency of the matter. In the absence of an opinion within that time-limit, the Council may act.

7. When concluding an agreement, the Council may, by way of derogation from paragraphs 5, 6 and 9, authorise the negotiator to approve on the Union's behalf modifications to the agreement where it provides for them to be adopted by a simplified procedure or by a body set up by the agreement. The Council may attach specific conditions to such authorisation.

8. The Council shall act by a qualified majority throughout the procedure.

   However, it shall act unanimously when the agreement covers a field for which unanimity is required for the adoption of an act of the Union as well as for association agreements and the agreements referred to in Article 212 with the States which are candidates for accession. The Council shall act unanimously for the agreement on accession of the Union to the European Convention for the Protection of Human Rights and Fundamental Freedoms; the decision concluding this agreement shall enter into force after it has been approved by the Member States in accordance with their respective constitutional requirements.

9. The Council, on a proposal from the Commission or the High Representative of the Union for Foreign Affairs and Security Policy, shall adopt a decision suspending application of an agreement and establishing the positions to be adopted on the Union's behalf in a body set up by an agreement, when that body is called upon to adopt acts having legal effects, with the exception of acts supplementing or amending the institutional framework of the agreement.

10. The European Parliament shall be immediately and fully informed at all stages of the procedure.

11. A Member State, the European Parliament, the Council or the Commission may obtain the opinion of the Court of Justice as to whether an agreement envisaged is compatible with the Treaties. Where the opinion of the Court is adverse, the agreement envisaged may not enter into force unless it is amended or the Treaties are revised.

Article 219

1. By way of derogation from Article 218(1), the Council, either on a recommendation from the European Central Bank or on a recommendation from the Commission and after consulting the European Central Bank, in an endeavour to reach a consensus consistent with the objective of price stability, may conclude formal agreements on an exchange-rate system for the euro in relation to currencies of third States. The Council shall act unanimously after consulting the European Parliament and in accordance with the procedure provided for in paragraph 3.

The Council may, either on a recommendation from the European Central Bank or on a recommendation from the Commission, and after consulting the European Central Bank, in an endeavour to reach a consensus consistent with the objective of price stability, adopt, adjust or abandon the central rates of the euro within the exchange rate system. The President of the Council shall inform the European Parliament of the adoption, adjustment or abandonment of the euro central rates.

2.   In the absence of an exchange-rate system in relation to one or more currencies of third States as referred to in paragraph 1, the Council, acting either on a recommendation from the Commission and after consulting the European Central Bank or on a recommendation from the European Central Bank, may formulate general orientations for exchange-rate policy in relation to these currencies. These general orientations shall be without prejudice to the primary objective of the ESCB to maintain price stability.

3.   By way of derogation from Article 218, where agreements concerning monetary or foreign exchange regime matters need to be negotiated by the Union with one or more third States or international organisations, the Council, acting on a recommendation from the Commission and after consulting the European Central Bank, shall decide the arrangements for the negotiation and for the conclusion of such agreements. These arrangements shall ensure that the Union expresses a single position. The Commission shall be fully associated with the negotiations.

4.   Without prejudice to Union competence and Union agreements as regards economic and monetary union, Member States may negotiate in international bodies and conclude international agreements.

TITLE VI

THE UNION'S RELATIONS WITH INTERNATIONAL ORGANISATIONS
AND THIRD COUNTRIES AND UNION DELEGATIONS

Article 220

1.   The Union shall establish all appropriate forms of cooperation with the organs of the United Nations and its specialised agencies, the Council of Europe, the Organisation for Security and Cooperation in Europe and the Organisation for Economic Cooperation and Development.

The Union shall also maintain such relations as are appropriate with other international organisations.

2.   The High Representative of the Union for Foreign Affairs and Security Policy shall be instructed to implement this Article.

Article 221

1.   Union delegations in third countries and at international organisations shall represent the Union.

2.   Union delegations shall be placed under the authority of the High Representative of the Union for Foreign Affairs and Security Policy. They shall act in close cooperation with Member States' diplomatic and consular missions.

TITLE VII

SOLIDARITY CLAUSE

Article 222

1.   The Union and its Member States shall act jointly in a spirit of solidarity if a Member State is the object of a terrorist attack or the victim of a natural or man-made disaster. The Union shall mobilise all the instruments at its disposal, including the military resources made available by the Member States, to:

(a)   — prevent the terrorist threat in the territory of the Member States;
       — protect democratic institutions and the civilian population from any terrorist attack;
       — assist a Member State in its territory, at the request of its political authorities, in the event of a terrorist attack;

(b)   assist a Member State in its territory, at the request of its political authorities, in the event of a natural or man-made disaster.

2. Should a Member State be the object of a terrorist attack or the victim of a natural or man-made disaster, the other Member States shall assist it at the request of its political authorities. To that end, the Member States shall coordinate between themselves in the Council.

3. The arrangements for the implementation by the Union of this solidarity clause shall be defined by a decision adopted by the Council acting on a joint proposal by the Commission and the High Representative of the Union for Foreign Affairs and Security Policy. The Council shall act in accordance with Article 31 (1) of the Treaty on European Union where this decision has defence implications. The European Parliament shall be informed.

   For the purposes of this paragraph and without prejudice to Article 240, the Council shall be assisted by the Political and Security Committee with the support of the structures developed in the context of the common security and defence policy and by the Committee referred to in Article 71; the two committees shall, if necessary, submit joint opinions.

4. The European Council shall regularly assess the threats facing the Union in order to enable the Union and its Member States to take effective action.

PART SIX
INSTITUTIONAL AND FINANCIAL PROVISIONS

TITLE I
PROVISIONS GOVERNING THE INSTITUTIONS

CHAPTER 1
THE INSTITUTIONS

SECTION 1
THE EUROPEAN PARLIAMENT

Article 223

1. The European Parliament shall draw up a proposal to lay down the provisions necessary for the election of its members by direct universal suffrage in accordance with a uniform procedure in all Member States or in accordance with principles common to all Member States.

   The Council, acting unanimously in accordance with a special legislative procedure and after obtaining the consent of the European Parliament, which shall act by a majority of its component members, shall lay down the necessary provisions. These provisions shall enter into force following their approval by the Member States in accordance with their respective constitutional requirements.

2. The European Parliament, acting by means of regulations on its own initiative in accordance with a special legislative procedure, after seeking an opinion from the Commission and with the consent of the Council, shall lay down the regulations and general conditions governing the performance of the duties of its Members. All rules or conditions relating to the taxation of Members or former Members shall require unanimity within the Council.

Article 224

The European Parliament and the Council, acting in accordance with the ordinary legislative procedure, by means of regulations, shall lay down the regulations governing political parties at European level referred to in Article 10(4) of the Treaty on European Union and in particular the rules regarding their funding.

Article 225

The European Parliament may, acting by a majority of its component members, request the Commission to submit any appropriate proposal on matters on which it considers that a Union act is required for the purpose of implementing the Treaties. If the Commission does not submit a proposal, it shall inform the European Parliament of the reasons.

Article 226

In the course of its duties, the European Parliament may, at the request of a quarter of its component Members, set up a temporary Committee of Inquiry to investigate, without prejudice to the powers conferred by the Treaties on other institutions or bodies, alleged contraventions or maladministration in the implementation of Union law, except where the alleged facts are being examined before a court and while the case is still subject to legal proceedings.

The temporary Committee of Inquiry shall cease to exist on the submission of its report.

The detailed provisions governing the exercise of the right of inquiry shall be determined by the European Parliament, acting by means of regulations on its own initiative in accordance with a special legislative procedure, after obtaining the consent of the Council and the Commission.

Article 227

Any citizen of the Union, and any natural or legal person residing or having its registered office in a Member State, shall have the right to address, individually or in association with other citizens or persons, a petition to the European Parliament on a matter which comes within the Union's fields of activity and which affects him, her or it directly.

Article 228

1. A European Ombudsman, elected by the European Parliament, shall be empowered to receive complaints from any citizen of the Union or any natural or legal person residing or having its registered office in a Member State concerning instances of maladministration in the activities of the Union institutions, bodies, offices or agencies, with the exception of the Court of Justice of the European Union acting in its judicial role. He or she shall examine such complaints and report on them.

    In accordance with his duties, the Ombudsman shall conduct inquiries for which he finds grounds, either on his own initiative or on the basis of complaints submitted to him direct or through a Member of the European Parliament, except where the alleged facts are or have been the subject of legal proceedings. Where the Ombudsman establishes an instance of maladministration, he shall refer the matter to the institution, body, office or agency concerned, which shall have a period of three months in which to inform him of its views. The Ombudsman shall then forward a report to the European Parliament and the institution, body, office or agency concerned. The person lodging the complaint shall be informed of the outcome of such inquiries.

    The Ombudsman shall submit an annual report to the European Parliament on the outcome of his inquiries.

2. The Ombudsman shall be elected after each election of the European Parliament for the duration of its term of office. The Ombudsman shall be eligible for reappointment.

    The Ombudsman may be dismissed by the Court of Justice at the request of the European Parliament if he no longer fulfils the conditions required for the performance of his duties or if he is guilty of serious misconduct.

3. The Ombudsman shall be completely independent in the performance of his duties. In the performance of those duties he shall neither seek nor take instructions from any Government, institution, body, office or entity. The Ombudsman may not, during his term of office, engage in any other occupation, whether gainful or not.

4. The European Parliament acting by means of regulations on its own initiative in accordance with a special legislative procedure shall, after seeking an opinion from the Commission and with the consent of the Council, lay down the regulations and general conditions governing the performance of the Ombudsman's duties.

Article 229

The European Parliament shall hold an annual session. It shall meet, without requiring to be convened, on the second Tuesday in March.

The European Parliament may meet in extraordinary part-session at the request of a majority of its component members or at the request of the Councilor of the Commission.

Article 230

The Commission may attend all the meetings and shall, at its request, be heard.

The Commission shall reply orally or in writing to questions put to it by the European Parliament or by its Members.

The European Council and the Council shall be heard by the European Parliament in accordance with the conditions laid down in the Rules of Procedure of the European Council and those of the Council.

Article 231

Save as otherwise provided in the Treaties, the European Parliament shall act by a majority of the votes cast.

The Rules of Procedure shall determine the quorum.

Article 232

The European Parliament shall adopt its Rules of Procedure, acting by a majority of its Members.

The proceedings of the European Parliament shall be published in the manner laid down in the Treaties and its Rules of Procedure.

Article 233

The European Parliament shall discuss in open session the annual general report submitted to it by the Commission.

Article 234

If a motion of censure on the activities of the Commission is tabled before it, the European Parliament shall not vote thereon until at least three days after the motion has been tabled and only by open vote.

If the motion of censure is carried by a two-thirds majority of the votes cast, representing a majority of the component members of the European Parliament, the members of the Commission shall resign as a body and the High Representative of the Union for Foreign Affairs and Security Policy shall resign from duties that he or she carries out in the Commission. They shall remain in office and continue to deal with current business until they are replaced in accordance with Article 17 of the Treaty on European Union. In this case, the term of office of the members of the Commission appointed to replace them shall expire on the date on which the term of office of the members of the Commission obliged to resign as a body would have expired.

SECTION 2

THE EUROPEAN COUNCIL

Article 235

1. Where a vote is taken, any member of the European Council may also act on behalf of not more than one other member.

 Article 16(4) of the Treaty on European Union and Article 238(2) of this Treaty shall apply to the European Council when it is acting by a qualified majority. Where the European Council decides by vote, its President and the President of the Commission shall not take part in the vote.

 Abstentions by members present in person or represented shall not prevent the adoption by the European Council of acts which require unanimity.

2. The President of the European Parliament may be invited to be heard by the European Council.

3. The European Council shall act by a simple majority for procedural questions and for the adoption of its Rules of Procedure.

4. The European Council shall be assisted by the General Secretariat of the Council.

Article 236

The European Council shall adopt by a qualified majority:

 (a) a decision establishing the list of Council configurations, other than those of the General Affairs Council and of the Foreign Affairs Council, in accordance with Article 16(6) of the Treaty on European Union;

 (b) a decision on the Presidency of Council configurations, other than that of Foreign Affairs, in accordance with Article 16(9) of the Treaty on European Union.

SECTION 3
THE COUNCIL

Article 237

The Council shall meet when convened by its President on his own initiative or at the request of one of its Members or of the Commission.

Article 238

1. Where it is required to act by a simple majority, the Council shall act by a majority of its component members.
2. By way of derogation from Article 16(4) of the Treaty on European Union, as from 1 November 2014 and subject to the provisions laid down in the Protocol on transitional provisions, where the Council does not act on a proposal from the Commission or from the High Representative of the Union for Foreign Affairs and Security Policy, the qualified majority shall be defined as at least 72% of the members of the Council, representing Member States comprising at least 65% of the population of the Union.
3. As from 1 November 2014 and subject to the provisions laid down in the Protocol on transitional provisions, in cases where, under the Treaties, not all the members of the Council participate in voting, a qualified majority shall be defined as follows:
   (a) A qualified majority shall be defined as at least 55% of the members of the Council representing the participating Member States, comprising at least 65% of the population of these States.
   A blocking minority must include at least the minimum number of Council members representing more than 35% of the population of the participating Member States, plus one member, failing which the qualified majority shall be deemed attained;
   (b) By way of derogation from point (a), when the Council does not act on a proposal from the Commission or from the High Representative of the Union for Foreign Affairs and Security Policy, the qualified majority shall be defined as at least 72% of the members of the Council representing Member States comprising at least 65% of the population of these States.
4. Abstentions by Members present in person or represented shall not prevent the adoption by the Council of acts which require unanimity.

Article 239

Where a vote is taken, any Member of the Council may also act on behalf of not more than one other member.

Article 240

1. A committee consisting of the Permanent Representatives of the Governments of the Member States shall be responsible for preparing the work of the Council and for carrying out the tasks assigned to it by the latter. The Committee may adopt procedural decisions in cases provided for in the Council's Rules of Procedure.
2. The Council shall be assisted by a General Secretariat, under the responsibility of a Secretary-General appointed by the Council.
   The Council shall decide on the organisation of the General Secretariat by a simple majority.
3. The Council shall act by a simple majority regarding procedural matters and for the adoption of its Rules of Procedure.

Article 241

The Council, acting by a simple majority, may request the Commission to undertake any studies the Council considers desirable for the attainment of the common objectives, and to submit to it any appropriate proposals. If the Commission does not submit a proposal, it shall inform the Council of the reasons.

Article 242

The Council acting by a simple majority shall, after consulting the Commission, determine the rules governing the committees provided for in the Treaties.

Article 243

The Council shall determine the salaries, allowances and pensions of the President of the European Council, the President of the Commission, the High Representative of the Union for Foreign Affairs and Security Policy, the members of the Commission, the Presidents, members and Registrars of the Court of Justice of the European Union, and the Secretary-General of the Council. It shall also determine any payment to be made instead of remuneration.

SECTION 4
THE COMMISSION

Article 244

In accordance with Article 17(5) of the Treaty on European Union, the members of the Commission shall be chosen on the basis of a system of rotation established unanimously by the European Council and on the basis of the following principles:

(a) Member States shall be treated on a strictly equal footing as regards determination of the sequence of, and the time spent by, their nationals as members of the Commission; consequently, the difference between the total number of terms of office held by nationals of any given pair of Member States may never be more than one;

(b) subject to point (a), each successive Commission shall be so composed as to reflect satisfactorily the demographic and geographical range of all the Member States.

Article 245

The Members of the Commission shall refrain from any action incompatible with their duties. Member States shall respect their independence and shall not seek to influence them in the performance of their tasks.

The Members of the Commission may not, during their term of office, engage in any other occupation, whether gainful or not. When entering upon their duties they shall give a solemn undertaking that, both during and after their term of office, they will respect the obligations arising therefrom and in particular their duty to behave with integrity and discretion as regards the acceptance, after they have ceased to hold office, of certain appointments or benefits. In the event of any breach of these obligations, the Court of Justice may, on application by the Council acting by a simple majority or the Commission, rule that the Member concerned be, according to the circumstances, either compulsorily retired in accordance with Article 247 or deprived of his right to a pension or other benefits in its stead.

Article 246

Apart from normal replacement, or death, the duties of a Member of the Commission shall end when he resigns or is compulsorily retired.

A vacancy caused by resignation, compulsory retirement or death shall be filled for the remainder of the member's term of office by a new member of the same nationality appointed by the Council, by common accord with the President of the Commission, after consulting the European Parliament and in accordance with the criteria set out in the second subparagraph of Article 17(3) of the Treaty on European Union.

The Council may, acting unanimously on a proposal from the President of the Commission, decide that such a vacancy need not be filled, in particular when the remainder of the member's term of office is short.

In the event of resignation, compulsory retirement or death, the President shall be replaced for the remainder of his term of office. The procedure laid down in Article 17(7), first subparagraph, of the Treaty on European Union shall be applicable for the replacement of the President.

In the event of resignation, compulsory retirement or death, the High Representative of the Union for Foreign Affairs and Security Policy shall be replaced, for the remainder of his or her term of office, in accordance with Article 18(l) of the Treaty on European Union.

In the case of the resignation of all the members of the Commission, they shall remain in office and continue to deal with current business until they have been replaced, for the remainder of their term of office, in accordance with Article 17 of the Treaty on European Union.

Article 247

If any Member of the Commission no longer fulfils the conditions required for the performance of his duties or if he has been guilty of serious misconduct, the Court of Justice may, on application by the Council acting by a simple majority or the Commission, compulsorily retire him.

Article 248

Without prejudice to Article 18(4) of the Treaty on European Union, the responsibilities incumbent upon the Commission shall be structured and allocated among its members by its President, in accordance with Article 17(6) of that Treaty. The President may reshuffle the allocation of those responsibilities during the Commission's term of office. The Members of the Commission shall carry out the duties devolved upon them by the President under his authority.

Article 249

1. The Commission shall adopt its Rules of Procedure so as to ensure that both it and its departments operate. It shall ensure that these Rules are published.
2. The Commission shall publish annually, not later than one month before the opening of the session of the European Parliament, a general report on the activities of the Union.

Article 250

The Commission shall act by a majority of its members.
Its Rules of Procedure shall determine the quorum.

SECTION 5
THE COURT OF JUSTICE OF THE EUROPEAN UNION

Article 251

The Court of Justice shall sit in chambers or in a Grand Chamber, in accordance with the rules laid down for that purpose in the Statute of the Court of Justice of the European Union.
When provided for in the Statute, the Court of Justice may also sit as a full Court.

Article 252

The Court of Justice shall be assisted by eight Advocates-General. Should the Court of Justice so request, the Council, acting unanimously, may increase the number of Advocates-General. It shall be the duty of the Advocate-General, acting with complete impartiality and independence, to make, in open court, reasoned submissions on cases which, in accordance with the Statute of the Court of Justice of the European Union, require his involvement.

Article 253

The Judges and Advocates-General of the Court of Justice shall be chosen from persons whose independence is beyond doubt and who possess the qualifications required for appointment to the highest judicial offices in their respective countries or who are jurisconsults of recognised competence; they shall be appointed by common accord of the governments of the Member States for a term of six years, after consultation of the panel provided for in Article 255.
Every three years there shall be a partial replacement of the Judges and Advocates-General, in accordance with the conditions laid down in the Statute of the Court of Justice of the European Union.
The Judges shall elect the President of the Court of Justice from among their number for a term of three years. He may be re-elected.
Retiring Judges and Advocates-General may be reappointed.
The Court of Justice shall appoint its Registrar and lay down the rules governing his service.
The Court of Justice shall establish its Rules of Procedure. Those Rules shall require the approval of the Council.

Article 254

The number of Judges of the General Court shall be determined by the Statute of the Court of Justice of the European Union. The Statute may provide for the General Court to be assisted by Advocates-General.

The members of the General Court shall be chosen from persons whose independence is beyond doubt and who possess the ability required for appointment to high judicial office. They shall be appointed by common accord of the governments of the Member States for a term of six years, after consultation of the panel provided for in Article 255. The membership shall be partially renewed every three years. Retiring members shall be eligible for reappointment. The Judges shall elect the President of the General Court from among their number for a term of three years. He may be re-elected.

The General Court shall appoint its Registrar and lay down the rules governing his service. The General Court shall establish its Rules of Procedure in agreement with the Court of Justice. Those Rules shall require the approval of the Council.

Unless the Statute of the Court of Justice of the European Union provides otherwise, the provisions of the Treaties relating to the Court of Justice shall apply to the General Court.

Article 255

A panel shall be set up in order to give an opinion on candidates' suitability to perform the duties of Judge and Advocate-General of the Court of Justice and the General Court before the governments of the Member States make the appointments referred to in Articles 253 and 254. The panel shall comprise seven persons chosen from among former members of the Court of Justice and the General Court, members of national supreme courts and lawyers of recognised competence, one of whom shall be proposed by the European Parliament. The Council shall adopt a decision establishing the panel's operating rules and a decision appointing its members. It shall act on the initiative of the President of the Court of Justice.

Article 256

1. The General Court shall have jurisdiction to hear and determine at first instance actions or proceedings referred to in Articles 263, 265, 268, 270 and 272, with the exception of those assigned to a specialised court set up under Article 257 and those reserved in the Statute for the Court of Justice. The Statute may provide for the General Court to have jurisdiction for other classes of action or proceeding.

    Decisions given by the General Court under this paragraph may be subject to a right of appeal to the Court of Justice on points of law only, under the conditions and within the limits laid down by the Statute.

2. The General Court shall have jurisdiction to hear and determine actions or proceedings brought against decisions of the specialised courts.

    Decisions given by the General Court under this paragraph may exceptionally be subject to review by the Court of Justice, under the conditions and within the limits laid down by the Statute, where there is a serious risk of the unity or consistency of Union law being affected.

3. The General Court shall have jurisdiction to hear and determine questions referred for a preliminary ruling under Article 267, in specific areas laid down by the Statute.

    Where the General Court considers that the case requires a decision of principle likely to affect the unity or consistency of Union law, it may refer the case to the Court of Justice for a ruling.

    Decisions given by the General Court on questions referred for a preliminary ruling may exceptionally be subject to review by the Court of Justice, under the conditions and within the limits laid down by the Statute, where there is a serious risk of the unity or consistency of Union law being affected.

Article 257

The European Parliament and the Council, acting in accordance with the ordinary legislative procedure, may establish specialised courts attached to the General Court to hear and determine at first instance certain classes of action or proceeding brought in specific areas.

The European Parliament and the Council shall act by means of regulations either on a proposal from the Commission after consultation of the Court of Justice or at the request of the Court of Justice after consultation of the Commission.

The regulation establishing a specialised court shall lay down the rules on the organisation of the court and the extent of the jurisdiction conferred upon it.

Decisions given by specialised courts may be subject to a right of appeal on points of law only or, when provided for in the regulation establishing the specialised court, a right of appeal also on matters of fact, before the General Court.

The members of the specialised courts shall be chosen from persons whose independence is beyond doubt and who possess the ability required for appointment to judicial office. They shall be appointed by the Council, acting unanimously.

The specialised courts shall establish their Rules of Procedure in agreement with the Court of Justice. Those Rules shall require the approval of the Council.

Unless the regulation establishing the specialised court provides otherwise, the provisions of the Treaties relating to the Court of Justice of the European Union and the provisions of the Statute of the Court of Justice of the European Union shall apply to the specialised courts. Title I of the Statute and Article 64 thereof shall in any case apply to the specialised courts.

Article 258

If the Commission considers that a Member State has failed to fulfil an obligation under the Treaties, it shall deliver a reasoned opinion on the matter after giving the State concerned the opportunity to submit its observations.

If the State concerned does not comply with the opinion within the period laid down by the Commission, the latter may bring the matter before the Court of Justice of the European Union.

Article 259

A Member State which considers that another Member State has failed to fulfil an obligation under the Treaties may bring the matter before the Court of Justice of the European Union. Before a Member State brings an action against another Member State for an alleged infringement of an obligation under the Treaties, it shall bring the matter before the Commission.

The Commission shall deliver a reasoned opinion after each of the States concerned has been given the opportunity to submit its own case and its observations on the other party's case both orally and in writing.

If the Commission has not delivered an opinion within three months of the date on which the matter was brought before it, the absence of such opinion shall not prevent the matter from being brought before the Court.

Article 260

1. If the Court of Justice of the European Union finds that a Member State has failed to fulfil an obligation under the Treaties, the State shall be required to take the necessary measures to comply with the judgment of the Court.

2. If the Commission considers that the Member State concerned has not taken the necessary measures to comply with the judgment of the Court, it may bring the case before the Court after giving that State the opportunity to submit its observations. It shall specify the amount of the lump sum or penalty payment to be paid by the Member State concerned which it considers appropriate in the circumstances.

    If the Court finds that the Member State concerned has not complied with its judgment it may impose a lump sum or penalty payment on it.

    This procedure shall be without prejudice to Article 259.

3. When the Commission brings a case before the Court pursuant to Article 258 on the grounds that the Member State concerned has failed to fulfil its obligation to notify measures transposing a directive adopted under a legislative procedure, it may, when it deems appropriate, specify the amount of the lump sum or penalty payment to be paid by the Member State concerned which it considers appropriate in the circumstances. If the Court finds that there is an infringement it may impose a lump sum or penalty payment on the Member State concerned not exceeding the amount specified by the Commission. The payment obligation shall take effect on the date set by the Court in its judgment.

Article 261

Regulations adopted jointly by the European Parliament and the Council, and by the Council, pursuant to the provisions of the Treaties, may give the Court of Justice of the European Union unlimited jurisdiction with regard to the penalties provided for in such regulations.

Article 262

Without prejudice to the other provisions of the Treaties, the Council, acting unanimously in accordance with a special legislative procedure and after consulting the European Parliament, may adopt provisions to confer jurisdiction, to the extent that it shall determine, on the Court of Justice of the European Union in disputes relating to the application of acts adopted on the basis of the Treaties which create European intellectual property rights. These provisions shall enter into force after their approval by the Member States in accordance with their respective constitutional requirements.

Article 263

The Court of Justice of the European Union shall review the legality of legislative acts, of acts of the Council, of the Commission and of the European Central Bank, other than recommendations and opinions, and of acts of the European Parliament and of the European Council intended to produce legal effects vis-à-vis third parties. It shall also review the legality of acts of bodies, offices or agencies of the Union intended to produce legal effects vis-à-vis third parties.

It shall for this purpose have jurisdiction in actions brought by a Member State, the European Parliament, the Council or the Commission on grounds of lack of competence, infringement of an essential procedural requirement, infringement of the Treaties or of any rule of law relating to their application, or misuse of powers.

The Court shall have jurisdiction under the same conditions in actions brought by the Court of Auditors, by the European Central Bank and by the Committee of the Regions for the purpose of protecting their prerogatives.

Any natural or legal person may, under the conditions referred to in the first and second subparagraphs, institute proceedings against an act addressed to that person or which is of direct and individual concern to them, and against a regulatory act which is of direct concern to them and does not entail implementing measures.

Acts setting up bodies, offices and agencies of the Union may lay down specific conditions and arrangements concerning actions brought by natural or legal persons against acts of these bodies, offices or agencies intended to produce legal effects in relation to them.

The proceedings provided for in this Article shall be instituted within two months of the publication of the measure, or of its notification to the plaintiff, or, in the absence thereof, of the day on which it came to the knowledge of the latter, as the case may be.

Article 264

If the action is well founded, the Court of Justice of the European Union shall declare the act
concerned to be void.

However, the Court shall, if it considers this necessary, state which of the effects of the act which it has declared void shall be considered as definitive.

Article 265

Should the European Parliament, the European Council, the Council, the Commission or the European Central Bank, in infringement of the Treaties, fail to act, the Member States and the other institutions of the Union may bring an action before the Court of Justice to have the infringement established. This Article shall apply, under the same conditions, to bodies, offices and agencies of the Union which fail to act.

The action shall be admissible only if the institution, body, office or agency concerned has first been called upon to act. If, within two months of being so called upon, the institution, body, office or agency concerned has not defined its position, the action may be brought within a further period of two months.

Any natural or legal person may, under the conditions laid down in the preceding paragraphs, complain to the Court that an institution, body, office or agency of the Union has failed to address to that person any act other than a recommendation or an opinion.

Article 266

The institution, body, office or agency whose act has been declared void or whose failure to act has been declared contrary to the Treaties shall be required to take the necessary measures to comply with the judgment of the Court of Justice.

This obligation shall not affect any obligation which may result from the application of the second paragraph of Article 340.

Article 267

The Court of Justice of the European Union shall have jurisdiction to give preliminary rulings concerning:

(a)   the interpretation of the Treaties;

(b)   the validity and interpretation of acts of the institutions, bodies, offices or agencies of the Union;

Where such a question is raised before any court or tribunal of a Member State, that court or tribunal may, if it considers that a decision on the question is necessary to enable it to give judgment, request the Court to give a ruling thereon.

Where any such question is raised in a case pending before a court or tribunal of a Member State against whose decisions there is no judicial remedy under national law, that court or tribunal shall bring the matter before the Court.

If such a question is raised in a case pending before a court or tribunal of a Member State with regard to a person in custody, the Court of Justice of the European Union shall act with the minimum of delay.

Article 268

The Court of Justice of the European Union shall have jurisdiction in disputes relating to compensation for damage provided for in the second and third paragraphs of Article 340.

Article 269

The Court of Justice shall have jurisdiction to decide on the legality of an act adopted by the European Councilor by the Council pursuant to Article 7 of the Treaty on European Union solely at the request of the Member State concerned by a determination of the European Council or of the Council and in respect solely of the procedural stipulations contained in that Article.

Such a request must be made within one month from the date of such determination. The Court shall rule within one month from the date of the request.

Article 270

The Court of Justice of the European Union shall have jurisdiction in any dispute between the Union and its servants within the limits and under the conditions laid down in the Staff Regulations of Officials and the Conditions of Employment of other servants of the Union.

Article 271

The Court of Justice of the European Union shall, within the limits hereinafter laid down, have jurisdiction in disputes concerning:

(a)   the fulfilment by Member States of obligations under the Statute of the European Investment Bank. In this connection, the Board of Directors of the Bank shall enjoy the powers conferred upon the Commission by Article 258;

(b)   measures adopted by the Board of Governors of the European Investment Bank. In this connection, any Member State, the Commission or the Board of Directors of the Bank may institute proceedings under the conditions laid down in Article 263;

(c)   measures adopted by the Board of Directors of the European Investment Bank. Proceedings against such measures may be instituted only by Member States or by the Commission, under the conditions laid down in Article 263, and solely on the grounds of non-compliance with the procedure provided for in Article 19(2), (5), (6) and (7) of the Statute of the Bank;

(d)   the fulfilment by national central banks of obligations under the Treaties and the Statute of the ESCB and of the ECB. In this connection the powers of the Governing Council of the European Central Bank in respect of national central banks shall be the same as those conferred upon the Commission in respect of Member States by Article 258. If the Court finds that a national central bank has failed to fulfil an obligation under the Treaties, that bank shall be required to take the necessary measures to comply with the judgment of the Court.

Article 272

The Court of Justice of the European Union shall have jurisdiction to give judgment pursuant to any arbitration clause contained in a contract concluded by or on behalf of the Union, whether that contract be governed by public or private law.

Article 273

The Court of Justice shall have jurisdiction in any dispute between Member States which relates to the subject matter of the Treaties if the dispute is submitted to it under a special agreement between the parties.

Article 274

Save where jurisdiction is conferred on the Court of Justice of the European Union by the Treaties, disputes to which the Union is a party shall not on that ground be excluded from the jurisdiction of the courts or tribunals of the Member States.

Article 275

The Court of Justice of the European Union shall not have jurisdiction with respect to the provisions relating to the common foreign and security policy nor with respect to acts adopted on the basis of those provisions.

However, the Court shall have jurisdiction to monitor compliance with Article 40 of the Treaty on European Union and to rule on proceedings, brought in accordance with the conditions laid down in the fourth paragraph of Article 263 of this Treaty, reviewing the legality of decisions providing for restrictive measures against natural or legal persons adopted by the Council on the basis of Chapter 2 of Title V of the Treaty on European Union.

Article 276

In exercising its powers regarding the provisions of Chapters 4 and 5 of Title V of Part Three relating to the area of freedom, security and justice, the Court of Justice of the European Union shall have no jurisdiction to review the validity or proportionality of operations carried out by the police or other law-enforcement services of a Member State or the exercise of the responsibilities incumbent upon Member States with regard to the maintenance of law and order and the safeguarding of internal security.

Article 277

Notwithstanding the expiry of the period laid down in Article 263, sixth paragraph, any party may, in proceedings in which an act of general application adopted by an institution, body, office or agency of the Union is at issue, plead the grounds specified in Article 263, second paragraph, in order to invoke before the Court of Justice of the European Union the inapplicability of that act.

Article 278

Actions brought before the Court of Justice of the European Union shall not have suspensory effect. The Court may, however, if it considers that circumstances so require, order that application of the contested act be suspended.

Article 279

The Court of Justice of the European Union may in any cases before it prescribe any necessary interim measures.

Article 280

The judgments of the Court of Justice of the European Union shall be enforceable under the conditions laid down in Article 299.

Article 281

The Statute of the Court of Justice of the European Union shall be laid down in a separate Protocol.

The European Parliament and the Council, acting in accordance with the ordinary legislative procedure, may amend the provisions of the Statute, with the exception of Title I and Article 64. The European Parliament and the Council shall act either at the request of the Court of Justice and after consultation of the Commission, or on a proposal from the Commission and after consultation of the Court of Justice.

SECTION 6

THE EUROPEAN CENTRAL BANK

Article 282

1. The European Central Bank, together with the national central banks, shall constitute the European System of Central Banks (ESCB). The European Central Bank, together with the national central banks of the Member States whose currency is the euro, which constitute the Eurosystem, shall conduct the monetary policy of the Union.
2. The ESCB shall be governed by the decision-making bodies of the European Central Bank. The primary objective of the ESCB shall be to maintain price stability. Without prejudice to that objective, it shall support the general economic policies in the Union in order to contribute to the achievement of the latter's objectives.
3. The European Central Bank shall have legal personality. It alone may authorise the issue of the euro. It shall be independent in the exercise of its powers and in the management of its finances. The institutions, bodies, offices and agencies of the Union and the governments of the Member States shall respect that independence.
4. The European Central Bank shall adopt such measures as are necessary to carry out its tasks in accordance with Articles 127 to 133, with Article 138, and with the conditions laid down in the Statute of the ECSB and of the ECB. In accordance with these same Articles, those Member States whose currency is not the euro, and their central banks, shall retain their powers in monetary matters.
5. Within the areas falling within its responsibilities, the European Central Bank shall be consulted on all proposed Union acts, and all proposals for regulation at national level, and may give an opinion.

SECTION 7

THE COURT OF AUDITORS

Article 285

The Court of Auditors shall carry out the Union's audit.

It shall consist of one national of each Member State. Its members shall be completely independent in the performance of their duties, in the Union's general interest.

Article 286

1. The Members of the Court of Auditors shall be chosen from among persons who belong or have belonged in their respective States to external audit bodies or who are especially qualified for this office. Their independence must be beyond doubt.
2. The Members of the Court of Auditors shall be appointed for a term of six years. The Council, after consulting the European Parliament, shall adopt the list of Members drawn up in accordance with the proposals made by each Member State. The term of office of the Members of the Court of Auditors shall be renewable.

   They shall elect the President of the Court of Auditors from among their number for a term of three years. The President may be re-elected.
3. In the performance of these duties, the Members of the Court of Auditors shall neither seek nor take instructions from any government or from any other body. The Members of the Court of Auditors shall refrain from any action incompatible with their duties.
4. The Members of the Court of Auditors may shall not, during their term of office, engage in any other occupation, whether gainful or not. When entering upon their duties they shall give a solemn undertaking that, both during and after their term of office, they

will respect the obligations arising therefrom and in particular their duty to behave with integrity and discretion as regards the acceptance, after they have ceased to hold office, of certain appointments or benefits.

5. Apart from normal replacement, or death, the duties of a Member of the Court of Auditors shall end when he resigns, or is compulsorily retired by a ruling of the Court of Justice pursuant to paragraph 6.

The vacancy thus caused shall be filled for the remainder of the Member's term of office. Save in the case of compulsory retirement, Members of the Court of Auditors shall remain in office until they have been replaced.

6. A Member of the Court of Auditors may be deprived of his office or of his right to a pension or other benefits in its stead only if the Court of Justice, at the request of the Court of Auditors, finds that he no longer fulfils the requisite conditions or meets the obligations arising from his office.

7. The Council shall determine the conditions of employment of the President and the Members of the Court of Auditors and in particular their salaries, allowances and pensions. It shall also, determine any payment to be made instead of remuneration.

8. The provisions of the Protocol on the privileges and immunities of the European Union applicable to the Judges of the Court of Justice of the European Union shall also apply to the Members of the Court of Auditors.

Article 287

1. The Court of Auditors shall examine the accounts of all revenue and expenditure of the Union. It shall also examine the accounts of all revenue and expenditure of all bodies, offices or agencies set up by the Union in so far as the relevant constituent instrument does not preclude such examination.

The Court of Auditors shall provide the European Parliament and the Council with a statement of assurance as to the reliability of the accounts and the legality and regularity of the underlying transactions which shall be published in the *Official Journal of the European Union*. This statement may be supplemented by specific assessments for each major area of Union activity.

2. The Court of Auditors shall examine whether all revenue has been received and all expenditure incurred in a lawful and regular manner and whether the financial management has been sound. In doing so, it shall report in particular on any cases of irregularity.

The audit of revenue shall be carried out on the basis both of the amounts established as due and the amounts actually paid to the Union.

The audit of expenditure shall be carried out on the basis both of commitments undertaken and payments made.

These audits may be carried out before the closure of accounts for the financial year in question.

3. The audit shall be based on records and, if necessary, performed on the spot in the other institutions, on the premises of any body, office or agency which manages revenue or expenditure on behalf of the Union and in the Member States, including on the premises of any natural or legal person in receipt of payments from the budget. In the Member States the audit shall be carried out in liaison with national audit bodies or, if these do not have the necessary powers, with the competent national departments. The Court of Auditors and the national audit bodies of the Member States shall cooperate in a spirit of trust while maintaining their independence. These bodies or departments shall inform the Court of Auditors whether they intend to take part in the audit.

The other institutions of the Union, any bodies, offices or agencies managing revenue or expenditure on behalf of the Union, any natural or legal person in receipt of payments from the budget, and the national audit bodies or, if these do not have the necessary powers, the competent national departments, shall forward to the Court of Auditors, at its request, any document or information necessary to carry out its task.

In respect of the European Investment Bank's activity in managing Union expenditure and revenue, the Court's rights of access to information held by the Bank shall be governed by an agreement between the Court, the Bank and the Commission. In the absence of an agreement, the Court shall nevertheless have access to information necessary for the audit of Union expenditure and revenue managed by the Bank.

4.   The Court of Auditors shall draw up an annual report after the close of each financial year. It shall be forwarded to the other institutions of the Union and shall be published, together with the replies of these institutions to the observations of the Court of Auditors, in the *Official Journal of the European Union*.

The Court of Auditors may also, at any time, submit observations, particularly in the form of special reports, on specific questions and deliver opinions at the request of one of the other institutions of the Union.

It shall adopt its annual reports, special reports or opinions by a majority of its component Members. However, it may establish internal chambers in order to adopt certain categories of reports or opinions under the conditions laid down by its Rules of Procedure.

It shall assist the European Parliament and the Council in exercising their powers of control over the implementation of the budget.

The Court of Auditors shall draw up its Rules of Procedure. Those rules shall require the approval of the Council.

CHAPTER 2
LEGAL ACTS OF THE UNION, ADOPTION PROCEDURES AND OTHER PROVISIONS

SECTION 1
THE LEGAL ACTS OF THE UNION

Article 288

To exercise the Union's competences, the institutions shall adopt regulations, directives, decisions, recommendations and opinions.

A regulation shall have general application. It shall be binding in its entirety and directly applicable in all Member States.

A directive shall be binding, as to the result to be achieved, upon each Member State to which it is addressed, but shall leave to the national authorities the choice of form and methods.

A decision shall be binding in its entirety. A decision which specifies those to whom it is addressed shall be binding only on them.

Recommendations and opinions shall have no binding force.

Article 289

1.   The ordinary legislative procedure shall consist in the joint adoption by the European Parliament and the Council of a regulation, directive or decision on a proposal from the Commission. This procedure is defined in Article 294.

2.   In the specific cases provided for by the Treaties, the adoption of a regulation, directive or decision by the European Parliament with the participation of the Council, or by the latter with the participation of the European Parliament, shall constitute a special legislative procedure.

3.   Legal acts adopted by legislative procedure shall constitute legislative acts.

4.   In the specific cases provided for by the Treaties, legislative acts may be adopted on the initiative of a group of Member States or of the European Parliament, on the recommendation of the European Central Bank or at the request of the Court of Justice or the European Investment Bank.

Article 290

1.   A legislative act may delegate to the Commission the power to adopt non-legislative acts to supplement or amend certain non-essential elements of the legislative act.

The objectives, content, scope and duration of the delegation of power shall be explicitly defined in the legislative acts. The essential elements of an area shall be reserved for the legislative act and accordingly shall not be the subject of a delegation of power.

2.   Legislative acts shall explicitly lay down the conditions to which the delegation is subject; these conditions may be as follows:

(a)   the European Parliament or the Council may decide to revoke the delegation;

(b)   the delegated act may enter into force only if no objection has been expressed by the European Parliament or the Council within a period set by the legislative act.
For the purposes of (a) and (b), the European Parliament shall act by a majority of its component members, and the Council by a qualified majority.

3.   The adjective 'delegated' shall be inserted in the title of delegated acts.

Article 291

1.   Member States shall adopt all measures of national law necessary to implement legally binding Union acts.

2.   Where uniform conditions for implementing legally binding Union acts are needed, those acts shall confer implementing powers on the Commission, or, in duly justified specific cases and in the cases provided for in Articles 24 and 26 of the Treaty on European Union, on the Council.

3.   For the purposes of paragraph 2, the European Parliament and the Council, acting by means of regulations in accordance with the ordinary legislative procedure, shall lay down in advance the rules and general principles concerning mechanisms for control by Member States of the Commission's exercise of implementing powers.

4.   The word 'implementing' shall be inserted in the title of implementing acts.

Article 292

The Council shall adopt recommendations. It shall act on a proposal from the Commission in all cases where the Treaties provide that it shall adopt acts on a proposal from the Commission. It shall act unanimously in those areas in which unanimity is required for the adoption of a Union act. The Commission, and the European Central Bank in the specific cases provided for in the Treaties, shall adopt recommendations.

SECTION 2

PROCEDURES FOR THE ADOPTION OF ACTS AND OTHER PROVISIONS

Article 293

1.   Where, pursuant to the Treaties, the Council acts on a proposal from the Commission, it may amend that proposal only by acting unanimously, except in the cases referred to in paragraphs 10 and 13 of Articles 294, in Articles 310, 312 and 314 and in the second paragraph of Article 315.

2.   As long as the Council has not acted, the Commission may alter its proposal at any time during the procedures leading to the adoption of a Union act.

Article 294

1.   Where reference is made in the Treaties to the ordinary legislative procedure for the adoption of an act, the following procedure shall apply.

2.   The Commission shall submit a proposal to the European Parliament and the Council.

First reading

3.   The European Parliament shall adopt its position at first reading and communicate it to the Council.

4.   If the Council approves the European Parliament's position, the act concerned shall be adopted in the wording which corresponds to the position of the European Parliament.

5.   If the Council does not approve the European Parliament's position, it shall adopt its position at first reading and communicate it to the European Parliament.

6.   The Council shall inform the European Parliament fully of the reasons which led it to adopt its position at first reading. The Commission shall inform the European Parliament fully of its position.

Second reading

7.   If, within three months of such communication, the European Parliament:

(a)   approves the Council's position at first reading or has not taken a decision, the act concerned shall be deemed to have been adopted in the wording which corresponds to the position of the Council;

(b)   rejects, by a majority of its component members, the Council's position at first reading, the proposed act shall be deemed not to have been adopted;

       (c)   proposes, by a majority of its component members, amendments to the Council's position at first reading, the text thus amended shall be forwarded to the Council and to the Commission, which shall deliver an opinion on those amendments.

8.   If, within three months of receiving the European Parliament's amendments, the Council, acting by a qualified majority:

       (a)   approves all those amendments, the act in question shall be deemed to have been adopted;

       (b)   does not approve all the amendments, the President of the Council, in agreement with the President of the European Parliament, shall within six weeks convene a meeting of the Conciliation Committee.

9.   The Council shall act unanimously on the amendments on which the Commission has delivered a negative opinion.

Conciliation

10.   The Conciliation Committee, which shall be composed of the members of the Councilor their representatives and an equal number of members representing the European Parliament, shall have the task of reaching agreement on a joint text, by a qualified majority of the members of the Councilor their representatives and by a majority of the members representing the European Parliament within six weeks of its being convened, on the basis of the positions of the European Parliament and the Council at second reading.

11.   The Commission shall take part in the Conciliation Committee's proceedings and shall take all necessary initiatives with a view to reconciling the positions of the European Parliament and the Council.

12.   If, within six weeks of its being convened, the Conciliation Committee does not approve the joint text, the proposed act shall be deemed not to have been adopted.

Third reading

13.   If, within that period, the Conciliation Committee approves a joint text, the European Parliament, acting by a majority of the votes cast, and the Council, acting by a qualified majority, shall each have a period of six weeks from that approval in which to adopt the act in question in accordance with the joint text. If they fail to do so, the proposed act shall be deemed not to have been adopted.

14.   The periods of three months and six weeks referred to in this Article shall be extended by a maximum of one month and two weeks respectively at the initiative of the European Parliament or the Council.

Special provisions

15.   Where, in the cases provided for in the Treaties, a legislative act is submitted to the ordinary legislative procedure on the initiative of a group of Member States, on a recommendation by the European Central Bank, or at the request of the Court of Justice, paragraph 2, the second sentence of paragraph 6, and paragraph 9 shall not apply.

In such cases, the European Parliament and the Council shall communicate the proposed act to the Commission with their positions at first and second readings. The European Parliament or the Council may request the opinion of the Commission throughout the procedure, which the Commission may also deliver on its own initiative. It may also, if it deems it necessary, take part in the Conciliation Committee in accordance with paragraph 11.

Article 295

The European Parliament, the Council and the Commission shall consult each other and by common agreement make arrangements for their cooperation. To that end, they may, in compliance with the Treaties, conclude interinstitutional agreements which may be of a binding nature.

Article 296

Where the Treaties do not specify the type of act to be adopted, the institutions shall select it on a case-by-case basis, in compliance with the applicable procedures and with the principle of proportionality.

Legal acts shall state the reasons on which they are based and shall refer to any proposals, initiatives, recommendations, requests or opinions required by the Treaties.

When considering draft legislative acts, the European Parliament and the Council shall refrain from adopting acts not provided for by the relevant legislative procedure in the area in question.

Article 297

1. Legislative acts adopted under the ordinary legislative procedure shall be signed by the President of the European Parliament and by the President of the Council.

   Legislative acts adopted under a special legislative procedure shall be signed by the President of the institution which adopted them.

   Legislative acts shall be published in the *Official Journal of the European Union*. They shall enter into force on the date specified in them or, in the absence thereof, on the twentieth day following that of their publication.

2. Non-legislative acts adopted in the form of regulations, directives or decisions which do not specify to whom they are addressed, shall be signed by the President of the institution which adopted them.

   Regulations and directives which are addressed to all Member States, as well as decisions which do not specify to whom they are addressed, shall be published in the *Official Journal of the European Union*. They shall enter into force on the date specified in them or, in the absence thereof, on the twentieth day following that of their publication.

   Other directives, and decisions which specify to whom they are addressed, shall be notified to those to whom they are addressed and shall take effect upon such notification.

Article 298

1. In carrying out their missions, the institutions, bodies, offices and agencies of the Union shall have the support of an open, efficient and independent European administration.

2. In compliance with the Staff Regulations and Conditions of Employment adopted on the basis of Article 336, the European Parliament and the Council, acting by means of regulations in accordance with the ordinary legislative procedure, shall establish provisions to that end.

Article 299

Acts of the Council, of the Commission or of the European Central Bank which impose a pecuniary obligation on persons other than States, shall be enforceable.

Enforcement shall be governed by the rules of civil procedure in force in the State in the territory of which it is carried out. The order for its enforcement shall be appended to the decision, without other formality than verification of the authenticity of the decision, by the national authority which the government of each Member State shall designate for this purpose and shall make known to the Commission and to the Court of Justice of the European Union.

When these formalities have been completed on application by the party concerned, the latter may proceed to enforcement in accordance with the national law, by bringing the matter directly before the competent authority.

Enforcement may be suspended only by a decision of the Court. However, the courts of the country concerned shall have jurisdiction over complaints that enforcement is being carried out in an irregular manner.

CHAPTER 3

THE UNION'S ADVISORY BODIES

Article 300

1. The European Parliament, the Council and the Commission shall be assisted by an Economic and Social Committee and a Committee of the Regions, exercising advisory functions.

2. The Economic and Social Committee shall consist of representatives of organisations of employers, of the employed, and of other parties representative of civil society, notably in socio-economic, civic, professional and cultural areas.

3. The Committee of the Regions shall consist of representatives of regional and local bodies who either hold a regional or local authority electoral mandate or are politically accountable to an elected assembly.
4. The members of the Economic and Social Committee and the Committee of the Regions shall not be bound by any mandatory instructions. They shall be completely independent in the performance of their duties, in the Union's general interest.
5. The rules referred to in paragraphs 2 and 3 governing the nature of their composition shall be reviewed at regular intervals by the Council to take account of economic, social and demographic developments within the Union. The Council, on a proposal from the Commission, shall adopt decisions to that end.

SECTION 1
THE ECONOMIC AND SOCIAL COMMITTEE

Article 301

The number of members of the Economic and Social Committee shall not exceed 350.
The Council, acting unanimously on a proposal from the Commission, shall adopt a decision determining the Committee's composition.

Article 302

1. The members of the Committee shall be appointed for five years The Council shall adopt the list of members drawn up in accordance with the proposals made by each Member State. The term of office of the members of the Committee shall be renewable.
2. The Council shall act after consulting the Commission. It may obtain the opinion of European bodies which are representative of the various economic and social sectors and of civil society to which the Union's activities are of concern.

Article 303

The Committee shall elect its chairman and officers from among its members for a term of two and a half years.
It shall adopt its Rules of Procedure.
The Committee shall be convened by its chairman at the request of the European Parliament, the Council or of the Commission. It may also meet on its own initiative.

Article 304

The Committee shall be consulted by the European Parliament, by the Councilor by the Commission where the Treaties so provide. The Committee may be consulted by these institutions in all cases in which they consider it appropriate. It may issue an opinion on its own initiative in cases in which it considers such action appropriate.
The European Parliament, the Councilor the Commission shall, if it considers it necessary, set the Committee, for the submission of its opinion, a time limit which may not be less than one month from the date on which the chairman receives notification to this effect. Upon expiry of the time limit, the absence of an opinion shall not prevent further action.
The opinion of the Committee, together with a record of the proceedings, shall be forwarded to the European Parliament, to the Council and to the Commission.

SECTION 2
THE COMMITTEE OF THE REGIONS

Article 305

The number of members of the Committee of the Regions shall not exceed 350.
The Council, acting unanimously on a proposal from the Commission, shall adopt a decision determining the Committee's composition.
The members of the Committee and an equal number of alternate members shall be appointed for five years. Their term of office shall be renewable. The Council shall adopt the list of members and alternate members drawn up in accordance with the proposals made by each Member State. When the mandate referred to in Article 300(3) on the basis of which they were proposed comes to an end, the term of office of members of the Committee shall terminate automatically and they shall then be replaced for the remainder of the said term

of office in accordance with the same procedure. No member of the Committee shall at the same time be a Member of the European Parliament.

Article 306

The Committee of the Regions shall elect its chairman and officers from among its members for a term of two and a half years.

It shall adopt its Rules of Procedure.

The Committee shall be convened by its chairman at the request of the European Parliament, the Councilor of the Commission. It may also meet on its own initiative.

Article 307

The Committee of the Regions shall be consulted by the European Parliament, by the Council or by the Commission where the Treaties so provide and in all other cases, in particular those which concern cross-border cooperation, in which one of these institutions considers it appropriate.

The European Parliament, the Councilor the Commission shall, if it considers it necessary, set the Committee, for the submission of its opinion, a time limit which may not be less than one month from the date on which the chairman receives notification to this effect. Upon expiry of the time limit, the absence of an opinion shall not prevent further action.

Where the Economic and Social Committee is consulted, the Committee of the Regions shall be informed by the European Parliament, the Councilor the Commission of the request for an opinion. Where it considers that specific regional interests are involved, the Committee of the Regions may issue an opinion on the matter.

It may issue an opinion on its own initiative in cases in which it considers such action appropriate. The opinion of the Committee, together with a record of the proceedings, shall be forwarded to the European Parliament, the Council and to the Commission.

CHAPTER 4
THE EUROPEAN INVESTMENT BANK

Article 308

The European Investment Bank shall have legal personality.

The members of the European Investment Bank shall be the Member States.

The Statute of the European Investment Bank is laid down in a Protocol annexed to the Treaties. The Council acting unanimously in accordance with a special legislative procedure, at the request of the European Investment Bank and after consulting the European Parliament and the Commission, or on a proposal from the Commission and after consulting the European Parliament and the European Investment Bank, may amend the Statute of the Bank.

TITLE II
FINANCIAL PROVISIONS

Article 310

1. All items of revenue and expenditure of the Union shall be included in estimates to be drawn up for each financial year and shall be shown in the budget.

    The Union's annual budget shall be established by the European Parliament and the Council in accordance with Article 314.

    The revenue and expenditure shown in the budget shall be in balance.

2. The expenditure shown in the budget shall be authorised for the annual budgetary period in accordance with the regulation referred to in Article 322.

3. The implementation of expenditure shown in the budget shall require the prior adoption of a legally binding act of the Union providing a legal basis for its action and for the implementation of the corresponding expenditure in accordance with the regulation referred to in Article 322, except in cases for which that law provides.

4. With a view to maintaining budgetary discipline, the Union shall not adopt any act which is likely to have appreciable implications for the budget without providing an assurance that the expenditure arising from such an act is capable of being financed within the limit of the Union's own resources and in compliance with the multiannual financial framework referred to in Article 312.

5. The budget shall be implemented in accordance with the principle of sound financial management. Member States shall cooperate with the Union to ensure that the appropriations entered in the budget are used in accordance with this principle.
6. The Union and the Member States, in accordance with Article 325, shall counter fraud and any other illegal activities affecting the financial interests of the Union.

CHAPTER 1
THE UNION'S OWN RESOURCES

Article 311

The Union shall provide itself with the means necessary to attain its objectives and carry through its policies.

Without prejudice to other revenue, the budget shall be financed wholly from own resources.

The Council, acting in accordance with a special legislative procedure, shall unanimously and after consulting the European Parliament adopt a decision laying down the provisions relating to the system of own resources of the Union. In this context it may establish new categories of own resources or abolish an existing category. That decision shall not enter into force until it is approved by the Member States in accordance with their respective constitutional requirements.

The Council, acting by means of regulations in accordance with a special legislative procedure, shall lay down implementing measures of the Union's own resources system insofar as this is provided for in the decision adopted on the basis of the third paragraph. The Council shall act after obtaining the consent of the European Parliament.

CHAPTER 2
THE MULTIANNUAL FINANCIAL FRAMEWORK

Article 312

1. The multiannual financial framework shall ensure that Union expenditure develops in an orderly manner and within the limits of its own resources. It shall be established for a period of at least five years.
    The annual budget of the Union shall comply with the multiannual financial framework.
2. The Council, acting in accordance with a special legislative procedure, shall adopt a regulation laying down the multi annual financial framework. The Council shall act unanimously after obtaining the consent of the European Parliament, which shall be given by a majority of its component members.
    The European Council may, unanimously, adopt a decision authorising the Council to act by a qualified majority when adopting the regulation of the Council referred to in the first subparagraph.
3. The financial framework shall determine the amounts of the annual ceilings on commitment appropriations by category of expenditure and of the annual ceiling on payment appropriations. The categories of expenditure, limited in number, shall correspond to the Union's major sectors of activity.
    The financial framework shall lay down any other provisions required for the annual budgetary procedure to run smoothly.
4. Where no Council regulation determining a new financial framework has been adopted by the end of the previous financial framework, the ceilings and other provisions corresponding to the last year of that framework shall be extended until such time as that act is adopted.
5. Throughout the procedure leading to the adoption of the financial framework, the European Parliament, the Council and the Commission shall take any measure necessary to facilitate its adoption.

CHAPTER 3
THE UNION'S ANNUAL BUDGET

Article 313

The financial year shall run from 1 January to 31 December.

Article 314

The European Parliament and the Council, acting in accordance with a special legislative procedure, shall establish the Union's annual budget in accordance with the following provisions.

1. With the exception of the European Central Bank, each institution shall, before 1 July, draw up estimates of its expenditure for the following financial year. The Commission shall consolidate these estimates in a draft budget. which may contain different estimates.

   The draft budget shall contain an estimate of revenue and an estimate of expenditure.

2. The Commission shall submit a proposal containing the draft budget to the European Parliament and to the Council not later than 1 September of the year preceding that in which the budget is to be implemented.

   The Commission may amend the draft budget during the procedure until such time as the Conciliation Committee, referred to in paragraph 5, is convened.

3. The Council shall adopt its position on the draft budget and forward it to the European Parliament not later than 1 October of the year preceding that in which the budget is to be implemented. The Council shall inform the European Parliament in full of the reasons which led it to adopt its position.

4. If, within forty-two days of such communication, the European Parliament:

   (a) approves the position of the Council, the budget shall be adopted;

   (b) has not taken a decision, the budget shall be deemed to have been adopted;

   (c) adopts amendments by a majority of its component members, the amended draft shall be forwarded to the Council and to the Commission. The President of the European Parliament, in agreement with the President of the Council, shall immediately convene a meeting of the Conciliation Committee. However, if within ten days of the draft being forwarded the Council informs the European Parliament that it has approved all its amendments, the Conciliation Committee shall not meet.

5. The Conciliation Committee, which shall be composed of the members of the Council or their representatives and an equal number of members representing the European Parliament, shall have the task of reaching agreement on a joint text, by a qualified majority of the members of the Council or their representatives and by a majority of the representatives of the European Parliament within twenty-one days of its being convened, on the basis of the positions of the European Parliament and the Council.

   The Commission shall take part in the Conciliation Committee's proceedings and shall take all the necessary initiatives with a view to reconciling the positions of the European Parliament and the Council.

6. If, within the twenty-one days referred to in paragraph 5, the Conciliation Committee agrees on a joint text, the European Parliament and the Council shall each have a period of fourteen days from the date of that agreement in which to approve the joint text.

7. If, within the period of fourteen days referred to in paragraph 6:

   (a) the European Parliament and the Council both approve the joint text or fail to take a decision, or if one of these institutions approves the joint text while the other one fails to take a decision, the budget shall be deemed to be definitively adopted in accordance with the joint text, or

   (b) the European Parliament, acting by a majority of its component members, and the Council both reject the joint text, or if one of these institutions rejects the joint text while the other one fails to take a decision, a new draft budget shall be submitted by the Commission, or

   (c) the European Parliament, acting by a majority of its component members, rejects the joint text while the Council approves it, a new draft budget shall be submitted by the Commission, or

   (d) the European Parliament approves the joint text whilst the Council rejects it, the European Parliament may, within fourteen days from the date of the rejection by the Council and acting by a majority of its component members and three-fifths of the votes cast, decide to confirm all or some of the amendments referred to in paragraph 4(c). Where a European Parliament amendment is not confirmed, the position agreed in the Conciliation Committee on the budget heading which is the subject of the amendment shall be retained. The budget shall be deemed to be definitively adopted on this basis.

8.   If, within the twenty-one days referred to in paragraph 5, the Conciliation Committee does not agree on a joint text, a new draft budget shall be submitted by the Commission.

9.   When the procedure provided for in this Article has been completed, the President of the European Parliament shall declare that the budget has been definitively adopted.

10.   Each institution shall exercise the powers conferred upon it under this Article in compliance with the Treaties and the acts adopted thereunder, with particular regard to the Union's own resources and the balance between revenue and expenditure.

Article 315

If, at the beginning of a financial year, the budget has not yet been definitively adopted, a sum equivalent to not more than one twelfth of the budget appropriations for the preceding financial year may be spent each month in respect of any chapter of the budget in accordance with the provisions of the Regulations made pursuant to Article 322; that sum shall not, however, exceed one twelfth of the appropriations provided for in the same chapter of the draft budget.

The Council on a proposal by the Commission may, provided that the other conditions laid down in the first paragraph are observed, authorise expenditure in excess of one twelfth, in accordance with the regulations made pursuant to Article 322. The Council shall forward the decision immediately to the European Parliament.

The decision referred to in the second subparagraph shall lay down the necessary measures relating to resources to ensure application of this Article, in accordance with the acts referred to in Article 311.

It shall enter into force thirty days following its adoption if the European Parliament, acting by a majority of its component members, has not decided to reduce this expenditure within that time-limit.

Article 316

In accordance with conditions to be laid down pursuant to Article 322, any appropriations, other than those relating to staff expenditure, that are unexpended at the end of the financial year may be carried forward to the next financial year only.

Appropriations shall be classified under different chapters grouping items of expenditure according to their nature or purpose and subdivided, in accordance with the regulations made pursuant to Article 322.

The expenditure of the European Parliament, the European Council and the Council, the Commission and the Court of Justice of the European Union shall be set out in separate parts of the budget, without prejudice to special arrangements for certain common items of expenditure.

CHAPTER 5
COMMON PROVISIONS

Article 320

The multiannual financial framework and the annual budget shall be drawn up in euro.

Article 321

The Commission may, provided it notifies the competent authorities of the Member States concerned, transfer into the currency of one of the Member States its holdings in the currency of another Member State, to the extent necessary to enable them to be used for purposes which come within the scope of the Treaties. The Commission shall as far as possible avoid making such transfers if it possesses cash or liquid assets in the currencies which it needs,

The Commission shall deal with each Member State through the authority designated by the State concerned, In carrying out financial operations the Commission shall employ the services of the bank of issue of the Member State concerned or of any other financial institution approved by that State,

Article 322

1.   The European Parliament and the Council, acting in accordance with the ordinary legislative procedure, and after consulting the Court of Auditors shall adopt by means of regulations:

     (a)   the financial rules which determine in particular the procedure to be adopted for establishing and implementing the budget and for presenting and auditing accounts;

     (b)   rules providing for checks on the responsibility of financial actors, in particular authorising officers and accounting officers.

2.   The Council, acting on a proposal from the Commission and after consulting the European Parliament and the Court of Auditors, shall determine methods and procedure whereby the budget revenue provided under the arrangements relating to the Union's own resources shall be made available to the Commission, and determine the measures to be applied, if need be, to meet cash requirements.

Article 323

The European Parliament, the Council and the Commission shall ensure that the financial means are made available to allow the Union to fulfil its legal obligations in respect of third parties.

Article 324

Regular meetings between the Presidents of the European Parliament, the Council and the Commission shall be convened, on the initiative of the Commission, under the budgetary procedures referred to in this Title. The Presidents shall take all the necessary steps to promote consultation and the reconciliation of the positions of the institutions over which they preside in order to facilitate the implementation of this Title.

CHAPTER 6
COMBATTING FRAUD

Article 325

1.   The Union and the Member States shall counter fraud and any other illegal activities affecting the financial interests of the Union through measures to be taken in accordance with this Article, which shall act as a deterrent and be such as to afford effective protection in the Member States, and in all the Union's institutions, bodies, offices and agencies.

...

TITLE III
ENHANCED COOPERATION

Article 326

Any enhanced cooperation shall comply with the Treaties and Union law.

Such cooperation shall not undermine the internal market or economic, social and territorial cohesion, It shall not constitute a barrier to or discrimination in trade between Member States, nor shall it distort competition between them.

Article 327

Any enhanced cooperation shall respect the competences, rights and obligations of those Member States which do not participate in it. Those Member States shall not impede its implementation by the participating Member States.

PART SEVEN
GENERAL AND FINAL PROVISIONS

Article 335

In each of the Member States, the Union shall enjoy the most extensive legal capacity accorded to legal persons under their laws; it may, in particular, acquire or dispose of movable and immovable property and may be a party to legal proceedings. To this end, the Union shall be represented by the Commission. However, the Union shall be represented by each of the institutions, by virtue of their administrative autonomy, in matters relating to their respective operation.

Article 336

The European Parliament and the Council shall, acting by means of regulations in accordance with the ordinary legislative procedure and after consulting the other institutions concerned, lay down the Staff Regulations of officials of the European Union and the Conditions of employment of other servants of the Union.

Article 337

The Commission may, within the limits and under conditions laid down by the Council, acting by a simple majority in accordance with the provisions of the Treaties, collect any information and carry out any checks required for the performance of the tasks entrusted to it.

Article 338

1. Without prejudice to Article 5 of the Protocol on the Statute of the European System of Central Banks and of the European Central Bank, the European Parliament and the Council, acting in accordance with the ordinary legislative procedure, shall adopt measures for the production of statistics where necessary for the performance of the activities of the Union.
2. The production of Union statistics shall conform to impartiality, reliability, objectivity, scientific independence, cost-effectiveness and statistical confidentiality; it shall not entail excessive burdens on economic operators.

Article 339

The members of the institutions of the Union, the members of committees, and the officials and other servants of the Union shall be required, even after their duties have ceased, not to disclose information of the kind covered by the obligation of professional secrecy, in particular information about undertakings, their business relations or their cost components.

Article 340

The contractual liability of the Union shall be governed by the law applicable to the contract in question.

In the case of non-contractual liability, the Union shall, in accordance with the general principles common to the laws of the Member States, make good any damage caused by its institutions or by its servants in the performance of their duties.

Notwithstanding the second paragraph, the European Central Bank shall, in accordance with the general principles common to the laws of the Member States, make good any damage caused by it or by its servants in the performance of their duties.

The personal liability of its servants towards the Union shall be governed by the provisions laid down in their Staff Regulations or in the Conditions of employment applicable to them.

Article 341

The seat of the institutions of the Union shall be determined by common accord of the governments of the Member States.

Article 342

The rules governing the languages of the institutions of the Union shall, without prejudice to the provisions contained in the Statute of the Court of Justice, be determined by the Council, acting unanimously by means of regulations.

Article 343

The Union shall enjoy in the territories of the Member States such privileges and immunities as are necessary for the performance of its tasks, under the conditions laid down in the Protocol of 8 April 1965 on the privileges and immunities of the European Union. The same shall apply to the European Central Bank and the European Investment Bank.

Article 344

Member States undertake not to submit a dispute concerning the interpretation or application of the Treaties to any method of settlement other than those provided for therein.

Article 345

The Treaties shall in no way prejudice the rules in Member States governing the system of property ownership.

Article 346

1. The provisions of the Treaties shall not preclude the application of the following rules:
   (a) no Member State shall be obliged to supply information the disclosure of which it considers contrary to the essential interests of its security;
   (b) any Member State may take such measures as it considers necessary for the protection of the essential interests of its security which are connected with the production of or trade in arms, munitions and war material; such measures shall not adversely affect the conditions of competition in the internal market regarding products which are not intended for specifically military purposes.
2. The Council may, acting unanimously on a proposal from the Commission, make changes to the list, which it drew up on 15 April 1958, of the products to which the provisions of paragraph 1(b) apply.

Article 347

Member States shall consult each other with a view to taking together the steps needed to prevent the functioning of the internal market being affected by measures which a Member State may be called upon to take in the event of serious internal disturbances affecting the maintenance of law and order, in the event of war, serious international tension constituting a threat of war, or in order to carry out obligations it has accepted for the purpose of maintaining peace and international security.

Article 348

If measures taken in the circumstances referred to in Articles 346 and 347 have the effect of distorting the conditions of competition in the internal market, the Commission shall, together with the State concerned, examine how these measures can be adjusted to the rules laid down in the Treaties.

By way of derogation from the procedure laid down in Articles 258 and 259, the Commission or any Member State may bring the matter directly before the Court of Justice if it considers that another Member State is making improper use of the powers provided for in Articles 346 and 347. The Court of Justice shall give its ruling in camera.

Article 349

Taking account of the structural social and economic situation of Guadeloupe, French Guiana, Martinique, Mayotte, Reunion, Saint Martin, the Azores, Madeira and the Canary Islands, which is compounded by their remoteness, insularity, small size, difficult topography and climate, economic dependence on a few products, the permanence and combination of which severely restrain their development, the Council, on a proposal from the Commission and after consulting the European Parliament, shall adopt specific measures aimed, in particular, at laying down the conditions of application of the Treaties to those regions, including common policies. Where the specific measures in question are adopted by the Council in accordance with a special legislative procedure, it shall also act on a proposal from the Commission and after consulting the European Parliament.

The measures referred to in the first paragraph concern in particular areas such as customs and trade policies, fiscal policy, free zones, agriculture and fisheries policies, conditions for supply of raw materials and essential consumer goods, State aids and conditions of access to structural funds and to horizontal Union programmes.

The Council shall adopt the measures referred to in the first subparagraph taking into account the special characteristics and constraints of the outermost regions without undermining the integrity and the coherence of the Union legal order, including the internal market and common policies.

Article 350

The provisions of the Treaties shall not preclude the existence or completion of regional unions between Belgium and Luxembourg, or between Belgium, Luxembourg and the Netherlands, to the extent that the objectives of these regional unions are not attained by application of the Treaties.

Article 351

The rights and obligations arising from agreements concluded before 1 January 1958 or, for acceding States, before the date of their accession, between one or more Member States on the one hand, and one or more third countries on the other, shall not be affected by the provisions of the Treaties.

To the extent that such agreements are not compatible with the Treaties, the Member State or States concerned shall take all appropriate steps to eliminate the incompatibilities established. Member States shall, where necessary, assist each other to this end and shall, where appropriate, adopt a common attitude.

In applying the agreements referred to in the first paragraph, Member States shall take into account the fact that the advantages accorded under the Treaties by each Member State form an integral part of the establishment of the Union and are thereby inseparably linked with the creation of common institutions, the conferring of powers upon them and the granting of the same advantages by all the other Member States.

Article 352

1. If action by the Union should prove necessary, within the framework of the policies defined by the Treaties, to attain one of the objectives set out in the Treaties, and the Treaties have not provided the necessary powers, the Council, acting unanimously on a proposal from the European Commission and after obtaining the consent of the European Parliament, shall adopt the appropriate measures. Where the measures in question are adopted by the Council in accordance with a special legislative procedure, it shall also act unanimously on a proposal from the Commission and after obtaining the consent of the European Parliament.

2. Using the procedure for monitoring the subsidiarity principle referred to in Article 5(3) of the Treaty on European Union, the Commission shall draw national Parliaments' attention to proposals based on this Article.

3. Measures based on this Article shall not entail harmonisation of Member States' laws or regulations in cases where the Treaties exclude such harmonisation.

4. This Article cannot serve as a basis for attaining objectives pertaining to the common foreign and security policy and any acts adopted pursuant to this Article shall respect the limits set out in Article 40, second paragraph, of the Treaty on European Union.

PROTOCOL (No 1)
on the Role of National Parliaments in the European Union

THE HIGH CONTRACTING PARTIES,

RECALLING that the way in which national Parliaments scrutinise their governments in relation to the activities of the Union is a matter for the particular constitutional organisation and practice of each Member State,

DESIRING to encourage greater involvement of national Parliaments in the activities of the European Union and to enhance their ability to express their views on draft legislative acts of the Union as well as on other matters which may be of particular interest to them,

HAVE AGREED UPON the following provisions, which shall be annexed to the Treaty on European Union, to the Treaty on the Functioning of the European Union and to the Treaty establishing the European Atomic Energy Community:

TITLE I
INFORMATION FOR NATIONAL PARLIAMENTS

Article 1

Commission consultation documents (green and white papers and communications) shall be forwarded directly by the Commission to national Parliaments upon publication. The

Commission shall also forward the annual legislative programme as well as any other instrument of legislative planning or policy to national Parliaments, at the same time as to the European Parliament and the Council.

Article 2

Draft legislative acts sent to the European Parliament and to the Council shall be forwarded to national Parliaments.

For the purposes of this Protocol, 'draft legislative acts' shall mean proposals from the Commission, initiatives from a group of Member States, initiatives from the European Parliament, requests from the Court of Justice, recommendations from the European Central Bank and requests from the European Investment Bank, for the adoption of a legislative act.

Draft legislative acts originating from the Commission shall be forwarded to national Parliaments directly by the Commission, at the same time as to the European Parliament and the Council.

Draft legislative acts originating from the European Parliament shall be forwarded to national Parliaments directly by the European Parliament.

Draft legislative acts originating from a group of Member States, the Court of Justice, the European Central Bank or the European Investment Bank shall be forwarded to national Parliaments by the Council.

Article 3

National Parliaments may send to the Presidents of the European Parliament, the Council and the Commission a reasoned opinion on whether a draft legislative act complies with the principle of subsidiarity, in accordance with the procedure laid down in the Protocol on the application of the principles of subsidiarity and proportionality.

If the draft legislative act originates from a group of Member States, the President of the Council shall forward the reasoned opinion or opinions to the governments of those Member States.

If the draft legislative act originates from the Court of Justice, the European Central Bank or the European Investment Bank, the President of the Council shall forward the reasoned opinion or opinions to the institution or body concerned.

Article 4

An eight-week period shall elapse between a draft legislative act being made available to national Parliaments in the official languages of the Union and the date when it is placed on a provisional agenda for the Council for its adoption or for adoption of a position under a legislative procedure.

Exceptions shall be possible in cases of urgency, the reasons for which shall be stated in the act or position of the Council. Save in urgent cases for which due reasons have been given, no agreement may be reached on a draft legislative act during those eight weeks. Save in urgent cases for which due reasons have been given, a ten-day period shall elapse between the placing of a draft legislative act on the provisional agenda for the Council and the adoption of a position.

Article 5

The agendas for and the outcome of meetings of the Council, including the minutes of meetings where the Council is deliberating on draft legislative acts, shall be forwarded directly to national Parliaments, at the same time as to Member States' governments.

Article 6

When the European Council intends to make use of the first or second subparagraphs of Article 48(7) of the Treaty on European Union, national Parliaments shall be informed of the initiative of the European Council at least six months before any decision is adopted.

Article 7

The Court of Auditors shall forward its annual report to national Parliaments, for information, at the same time as to the European Parliament and to the Council.

Article 8

Where the national Parliamentary system is not unicameral, Articles 1 to 7 shall apply to the component chambers.

TITLE II
INTERPARLIAMENTARY COOPERATION

Article 9

The European Parliament and national Parliaments shall together determine the organisation and promotion of effective and regular interparliamentary cooperation within the Union.

Article 10

A conference of Parliamentary Committees for Union Affairs may submit any contribution it deems appropriate for the attention of the European Parliament, the Council and the Commission. That conference shall in addition promote the exchange of information and best practice between national Parliaments and the European Parliament, including their special committees. It may also organise interparliamentary conferences on specific topics, in particular to debate matters of common foreign and security policy, including common security and defence policy. Contributions from the conference shall not bind national Parliaments and shall not prejudge their positions.

PROTOCOL (No 2)
on the Application of the Principles of Subsidiarity and Proportionality

THE HIGH CONTRACTING PARTIES,

WISHING to ensure that decisions are taken as closely as possible to the citizens of the Union, RESOLVED to establish the conditions for the application of the principles of subsidiarity and proportionality, as laid down in Article 5 of the Treaty on European Union, and to establish a system for monitoring the application of those principles,

HAVE AGREED UPON the following provisions, which shall be annexed to the Treaty on European Union and to the Treaty on the Functioning of the European Union:

Article 1

Each institution shall ensure constant respect for the principles of subsidiarity and proportionality, as laid down in Article 5 of the Treaty on European Union.

Article 2

Before proposing legislative acts, the Commission shall consult widely. Such consultations shall, where appropriate, take into account the regional and local dimension of the action envisaged. In cases of exceptional urgency, the Commission shall not conduct such consultations. It shall give reasons for its decision in its proposal.

Article 3

For the purposes of this Protocol, 'draft legislative acts' shall mean proposals from the Commission, initiatives from a group of Member States, initiatives from the European Parliament, requests from the Court of Justice, recommendations from the European Central Bank and requests from the European Investment Bank, for the adoption of a legislative act.

Article 4

The Commission shall forward its draft legislative acts and its amended drafts to national Parliaments at the same time as to the Union legislator.

The European Parliament shall forward its draft legislative acts and its amended drafts to national Parliaments.

The Council shall forward draft legislative acts originating from a group of Member States, the Court of Justice, the European Central Bank or the European Investment Bank and amended drafts to national Parliaments.

Upon adoption, legislative resolutions of the European Parliament and positions of the Council shall be forwarded by them to national Parliaments.

Article 5

Draft legislative acts shall be justified with regard to the principles of subsidiarity and proportionality. Any draft legislative act should contain a detailed statement making it possible to appraise compliance with the principles of subsidiarity and proportionality. This statement should contain some assessment of the proposal's financial impact and, in the case of a directive, of its implications for the rules to be put in place by Member States, including, where necessary, the regional legislation. The reasons for concluding that a Union objective can be better achieved at Union level shall be substantiated by qualitative and, wherever possible, quantitative indicators.

Draft legislative acts shall take account of the need for any burden, whether financial or administrative, falling upon the Union, national governments, regional or local authorities, economic operators and citizens, to be minimised and commensurate with the objective to be achieved.

Article 6

Any national Parliament or any chamber of a national Parliament may, within eight weeks from the date of transmission of a draft legislative act, in the official languages of the Union, send to the Presidents of the European Parliament, the Council and the Commission a reasoned opinion stating why it considers that the draft in question does not comply with the principle of subsidiarity. It will be for each national Parliament or each chamber of a national Parliament to consult, where appropriate, regional parliaments with legislative powers.

If the draft legislative act originates from a group of Member States, the President of the Council shall forward the opinion to the governments of those Member States.

If the draft legislative act originates from the Court of Justice, the European Central Bank or the European Investment Bank, the President of the Council shall forward the opinion to the institution or body concerned.

Article 7

1. The European Parliament, the Council and the Commission, and, where appropriate, the group of Member States, the Court of Justice, the European Central Bank or the European Investment Bank, if the draft legislative act originates from them, shall take account of the reasoned opinions issued by national Parliaments or by a chamber of a national Parliament.

    Each national Parliament shall have two votes, shared out on the basis of the national Parliamentary system. In the case of a bicameral Parliamentary system, each of the two chambers shall have one vote.

2. Where reasoned opinions on a draft legislative act's non-compliance with the principle of subsidiarity represent at least one third of all the votes allocated to the national Parliaments in accordance with the second subparagraph of paragraph 1, the draft must be reviewed. This threshold shall be a quarter in the case of a draft legislative act submitted on the basis of Article 76 of the Treaty on the Functioning of the European Union on the area of freedom, security and justice. After such review, the Commission or, where appropriate, the group of Member States, the European Parliament, the Court of Justice, the European Central Bank or the European Investment Bank, if the draft legislative act originates from them, may decide to maintain, amend or withdraw the draft. Reasons must be given for this decision.

3. Furthermore, under the ordinary legislative procedure, where reasoned opinions on the noncompliance of a proposal for a legislative act with the principle of subsidiarity represent at least a simple majority of the votes allocated to the national Parliaments in accordance with the second subparagraph of paragraph 1, the proposal must be reviewed. After such review, the Commission may decide to maintain, amend or withdraw the proposal.

    If it chooses to maintain the proposal, the Commission will have, in a reasoned opinion, to justify why it considers that the proposal complies with the principle of subsidiarity.

This reasoned opinion, as well as the reasoned opinions of the national Parliaments, will have to be submitted to the Union legislator, for consideration in the procedure:

(a) before concluding the first reading, the legislator (the European Parliament and the Council) shall consider whether the legislative proposal is compatible with the principle of subsidiarity, taking particular account of the reasons expressed and shared by the majority of national Parliaments as well as the reasoned opinion of the Commission;

(b) if, by a majority of 55% of the members of the Council or a majority of the votes cast in the European Parliament, the legislator is of the opinion that the proposal is not compatible with the principle of subsidiarity, the legislative proposal shall not be given further consideration.

Article 8

The Court of Justice of the European Union shall have jurisdiction in actions on grounds of infringement of the principle of subsidiarity by a legislative act, brought in accordance with the rules laid down in Article 263 of the Treaty on the Functioning of the European Union by Member States, or notified by them in accordance with their legal order on behalf of their national Parliament or a chamber thereof.

In accordance with the rules laid down in the said Article, the Committee of the Regions may also bring such actions against legislative acts for the adoption of which the Treaty on the Functioning of the European Union provides that it be consulted.

Article 9

The Commission shall submit each year to the European Council, the European Parliament, the Council and national Parliaments a report on the application of Article 5 of the Treaty on European Union. This annual report shall also be forwarded to the Economic and Social Committee and the Committee of the Regions.

PROTOCOL (No 3)
Statute of the Court of Justice of the European Union

THE HIGH CONTRACTING PARTIES

DESIRING to lay down the Statute of the Court of Justice of the European Union provided for in Article 281 of the Treaty on the Functioning of the European Union,

HAVE AGREED UPON the following provisions, which shall be annexed to the Treaty on European Union, the Treaty on the Functioning of the European Union and the Treaty establishing the European Atomic Energy Community

Article 1

The Court of Justice of the European Union shall be constituted and shall function in accordance with the provisions of the Treaties, of the Treaty establishing the European Atomic Energy Community (EAEC Treaty) and of this Statute.

TITLE I
JUDGES AND ADVOCATES-GENERAL

Article 2

Before taking up his duties each Judge shall, before the Court of Justice sitting in open court, take an oath to perform his duties impartially and conscientiously and to preserve the secrecy of the deliberations of the Court.

Article 3

The Judges shall be immune from legal proceedings. After they have ceased to hold office, they shall continue to enjoy immunity in respect of acts performed by them in their official capacity, including words spoken or written.

The Court of Justice, sitting as a full Court, may waive the immunity. If the decision concerns a member of the General Court or of a specialised court, the Court shall decide after consulting the court concerned.

Where immunity has been waived and criminal proceedings are instituted against a Judge, he shall be tried, in any of the Member States, only by the court competent to judge the members of the highest national judiciary.

Articles 11 to 14 and Article 17 of the Protocol on the privileges and immunities of the European Union shall apply to the Judges, Advocates-General, Registrar and Assistant Rapporteurs of the Court of Justice of the European Union, without prejudice to the provisions relating to immunity from legal proceedings of Judges which are set out in the preceding paragraphs.

Article 4

The Judges may not hold any political or administrative office.

They may not engage in any occupation, whether gainful or not, unless exemption is exceptionally granted by the Council, acting by a simple majority.

When taking up their duties, they shall give a solemn undertaking that, both during and after their term of office, they will respect the obligations arising therefrom, in particular the duty to behave with integrity and discretion as regards the acceptance, after they have ceased to hold office, of certain appointments or benefits.

Any doubt on this point shall be settled by decision of the Court of Justice. If the decision concerns a member of the General Court or of a specialised court, the Court shall decide after consulting the court concerned.

Article 5

Apart from normal replacement, or death, the duties of a Judge shall end when he resigns.

Where a Judge resigns, his letter of resignation shall be addressed to the President of the Court of Justice for transmission to the President of the Council. Upon this notification a vacancy shall arise on the bench.

Save where Article 6 applies, a Judge shall continue to hold office until his successor takes up his duties.

Article 6

A Judge may be deprived of his office or of his right to a pension or other benefits in its stead only if, in the unanimous opinion of the Judges and Advocates-General of the Court of Justice, he no longer fulfils the requisite conditions or meets the obligations arising from his office. The Judge concerned shall not take part in any such deliberations. If the person concerned is a member of the General Court or of a specialised court, the Court shall decide after consulting the court concerned.

The Registrar of the Court shall communicate the decision of the Court to the President of the European Parliament and to the President of the Commission and shall notify it to the President of the Council.

In the case of a decision depriving a Judge of his office, a vacancy shall arise on the bench upon this latter notification.

Article 7

A Judge who is to replace a member of the Court whose term of office has not expired shall be appointed for the remainder of his predecessor's term.

Article 8

The provisions of Articles 2 to 7 shall apply to the Advocates-General.

TITLE II

ORGANISATION OF THE COURT OF JUSTICE

Article 9

When, every three years, the Judges are partially replaced, one half of the number of Judges shall be replaced. If the number of Judges is an uneven number, the number of Judges who shall be replaced shall alternately be the number which is the next above one half of the number of Judges and the number which is next below one half.

The first paragraph shall also apply when the Advocates General are partially replaced, every three years.

Article 9a

The Judges shall elect the President and the Vice-President of the Court of Justice from among their number for a term of three years. They may be re-elected.

The Vice-President shall assist the President in accordance with the conditions laid down in the Rules of Procedure. He shall take the President's place when the latter is prevented from attending or when the office of President is vacant.

Article 10

The Registrar shall take an oath before the Court of Justice to perform his duties impartially and conscientiously and to preserve the secrecy of the deliberations of the Court of Justice.

Article 11

The Court of Justice shall arrange for replacement of the Registrar on occasions when he is prevented from attending the Court of Justice.

Article 12

Officials and other servants shall be attached to the Court of Justice to enable it to function. They shall be responsible to the Registrar under the authority of the President.

Article 13

At the request of the Court of Justice, the European Parliament and the Council may, acting in accordance with the ordinary legislative procedure, provide for the appointment of Assistant Rapporteurs and lay down the rules governing their service. The Assistant Rapporteurs may be required, under conditions laid down in the Rules of Procedure, to participate in preparatory inquiries in cases pending before the Court and to cooperate with the Judge who acts as Rapporteur.

The Assistant Rapporteurs shall be chosen from persons whose independence is beyond doubt and who possess the necessary legal qualifications; they shall be appointed by the Council, acting by a simple majority. They shall take an oath before the Court to perform their duties impartially and conscientiously and to preserve the secrecy of the deliberations of the Court.

Article 14

The Judges, the Advocates-General and the Registrar shall be required to reside at the place where the Court of Justice has its seat.

Article 15

The Court of Justice shall remain permanently in session. The duration of the judicial vacations shall be determined by the Court with due regard to the needs of its business.

Article 16

The Court of Justice shall form chambers consisting of three and five Judges. The Judges shall elect the Presidents of the chambers from among their number. The Presidents of the chambers of five Judges shall be elected for three years. They may be re-elected once.

The Grand Chamber shall consist of 15 Judges. It shall be presided over by the President of the Court. The Presidents of the chambers of five Judges and other Judges appointed in accordance with the conditions laid down in the Rules of Procedure shall also form part of the Grand Chamber.

The Court shall sit in a Grand Chamber when a Member State or an institution of the Union that is party to the proceedings so requests.

The Court shall sit as a full Court where cases are brought before it pursuant to Article 228(2), Article 245(2), Article 247 or Article 286(6) of the Treaty on the Functioning of the European Union.

Moreover, where it considers that a case before it is of exceptional importance, the Court may decide, after hearing the Advocate-General, to refer the case to the full Court.

Article 17

Decisions of the Court of Justice shall be valid only when an uneven number of its members is sitting in the deliberations.

Decisions of the chambers consisting of either three or five Judges shall be valid only if they are taken by three Judges.

Decisions of the Grand Chamber shall be valid only if 11 Judges are sitting.

Decisions of the full Court shall be valid only if 17 Judges are sitting.

In the event of one of the Judges of a chamber being prevented from attending, a Judge of another chamber may be called upon to sit in accordance with conditions laid down in the Rules of Procedure.

Article 18

No Judge or Advocate-General may take part in the disposal of any case in which he has previously taken part as agent or adviser or has acted for one of the parties, or in which he has been called upon to pronounce as a member of a court or tribunal, of a commission of inquiry or in any other capacity.

If, for some special reason, any Judge or Advocate-General considers that he should not take part in the judgment or examination of a particular case, he shall so inform the President.

If, for some special reason, the President considers that any Judge or Advocate-General should not sit or make submissions in a particular case, he shall notify him accordingly.

Any difficulty arising as to the application of this Article shall be settled by decision of the Court of Justice.

A party may not apply for a change in the composition of the Court or of one of its chambers on the grounds of either the nationality of a Judge or the absence from the Court or from the chamber of a Judge of the nationality of that party.

TITLE III
PROCEDURE BEFORE THE COURT OF JUSTICE

Article 19

The Member States and the institutions of the Union shall be represented before the Court of Justice by an agent appointed for each case; the agent may be assisted by an adviser or by a lawyer.

The States, other than the Member States, which are parties to the Agreement on the European Economic Area and also the EFTA Surveillance Authority referred to in that Agreement shall be represented in same manner.

Other parties must be represented by a lawyer.

Only a lawyer authorised to practise before a court of a Member State or of another State which is a party to the Agreement on the European Economic Area may represent or assist a party before the Court.

Such agents, advisers and lawyers shall, when they appear before the Court, enjoy the rights and immunities necessary to the independent exercise of their duties, under conditions laid down in the Rules of Procedure.

As regards such advisers and lawyers who appear before it, the Court shall have the powers normally accorded to courts of law, under conditions laid down in the Rules of Procedure.

University teachers being nationals of a Member State whose law accords them a right of audience shall have the same rights before the Court as are accorded by this Article to lawyers.

Article 20

The procedure before the Court of Justice shall consist of two parts: written and oral.

The written procedure shall consist of the communication to the parties and to the institutions of the Union whose decisions are in dispute, of applications, statements of case, defences and observations, and of replies, if any, as well as of all papers and documents in support or of certified copies of them.

Communications shall be made by the Registrar in the order and within the time laid down in the Rules of Procedure.

The oral procedure shall consist of the hearing by the Court of agents, advisers and lawyers and of the submissions of the Advocate-General, as well as the hearing, if any, of witnesses and experts.

Where it considers that the case raises no new point of law, the Court may decide, after hearing the Advocate-General, that the case shall be determined without a submission from the Advocate-General.

Article 21

A case shall be brought before the Court of Justice by a written application addressed to the Registrar. The application shall contain the applicant's name and permanent address and the description of the signatory, the name of the party or names of the parties against whom the application is made, the subject-matter of the dispute, the form of order sought and a brief statement of the pleas in law on which the application is based.

The application shall be accompanied, where appropriate, by the measure the annulment of which is sought or, in the circumstances referred to in Article 265 of the Treaty on the Functioning of the European Union, by documentary evidence of the date on which an institution was, in accordance with those Articles, requested to act. If the documents are not submitted with the application, the Registrar shall ask the party concerned to produce them within a reasonable period, but in that event the rights of the party shall not lapse even if such documents are produced after the time limit for bringing proceedings.

Article 23a

The Rules of Procedure may provide for an expedited or accelerated procedure and, for references for a preliminary ruling relating to the area of freedom, security and justice, an urgent procedure.

Those procedures may provide, in respect of the submission of statements of case or written observations, for a shorter period than that provided for by Article 23, and, in derogation from the fourth paragraph of Article 20, for the case to be determined without a submission from the Advocate General.

In addition, the urgent procedure may provide for restriction of the parties and other interested persons mentioned in Article 23, authorised to submit statements of case or written observations and, in cases of extreme urgency, for the written stage of the procedure to be omitted.

...

Article 31

The hearing in court shall be public, unless the Court of Justice, of its own motion or on application by the parties, decides otherwise for serious reasons.

...

Article 35

The deliberations of the Court of Justice shall be and shall remain secret.

Article 36

Judgments shall state the reasons on which they are based. They shall contain the names of the Judges who took part in the deliberations.

Article 37

Judgments shall be signed by the President and the Registrar. They shall be read in open court.

Article 38

The Court of Justice shall adjudicate upon costs.

...

Article 40

Member States and institutions of the Union may intervene in cases before the Court of Justice. The same right shall be open to the bodies, offices and agencies of the Union and to any other person which can establish an interest in the result of a case submitted to the Court. Natural or legal persons shall not intervene in cases between Member States, between institutions of the Union or between Member States and institutions of the Union. Without prejudice to the second paragraph, the States, other than the Member States, which are parties to the Agreement on the European Economic Area, and also the EFTA

Surveillance Authority referred to in that Agreement, may intervene in cases before the Court where one of the fields of application of that Agreement is concerned.

An application to intervene shall be limited to supporting the form of order sought by one of the parties.

Article 41

Where the defending party, after having been duly summoned, fails to file written submissions in defence, judgment shall be given against that party by default. An objection may be lodged against the judgment within one month of it being notified. The objection shall not have the effect of staying enforcement of the judgment by default unless the Court of Justice decides otherwise.

Article 42

Member States, institutions, bodies, offices and agencies of the Union and any other natural or legal persons may, in cases and under conditions to be determined by the Rules of Procedure, institute third-party proceedings to contest a judgment rendered without their being heard, where the judgment is prejudicial to their rights.

Article 43

If the meaning or scope of a judgment is in doubt, the Court of Justice shall construe it on application by any party or any institution of the Union establishing an interest therein.

Article 44

An application for revision of a judgment may be made to the Court of Justice only on discovery of a fact which is of such a nature as to be a decisive factor, and which, when the judgment was given, was unknown to the Court and to the party claiming the revision.

The revision shall be opened by a judgment of the Court expressly recording the existence of a new fact, recognising that it is of such a character as to lay the case open to revision and declaring the application admissible on this ground.

No application for revision may be made after the lapse of 10 years from the date of the judgment.

Article 45

Periods of grace based on considerations of distance shall be determined by the Rules of Procedure.

No right shall be prejudiced in consequence of the expiry of a time limit if the party concerned proves the existence of unforeseeable circumstances or of force majeure.

Article 46

Proceedings against the Union in matters arising from non-contractual liability shall be barred after a period of five years from the occurrence of the event giving rise thereto. The period of limitation shall be interrupted if proceedings are instituted before the Court of Justice or if prior to such proceedings an application is made by the aggrieved party to the relevant institution of the Union. In the latter event the proceedings must be instituted within the period of two months provided for in Article 263 of the Treaty on the Functioning of the European Union; the provisions of the second paragraph of Article 265 of the Treaty on the Functioning of the European Union shall apply where appropriate.

This Article shall also apply to proceedings against the European Central Bank regarding non-contractual liability.

...

TITLE IV

GENERAL COURT

Article 47

The first paragraph of Article 9, Article 9a, Articles 14 and 15, the first, second, fourth and fifth paragraphs of Article 17 and Article 18 shall apply to the General Court and its members. The fourth paragraph of Article 3 and Articles 10, 11 and 14 shall apply to the Registrar of the General Court *mutatis mutandis*.

Article 48
The General Court shall consist of:
(a)   40 Judges as from 25 December 2015;
(b)   47 Judges as from 1 September 2016;
(c)   two Judges per Member State as from 1 September 2019.

Article 49
The Members of the General Court may be called upon to perform the task of an Advocate-General.
It shall be the duty of the Advocate-General, acting with complete impartiality and independence, to make, in open court, reasoned submissions on certain cases brought before the General Court in order to assist the General Court in the performance of its task. The criteria for selecting such cases, as well as the procedures for designating the Advocates-General, shall be laid down in the Rules of Procedure of the General Court.
A Member called upon to perform the task of Advocate-General in a case may not take part in the judgment of the case.

Article 50
The General Court shall sit in chambers of three or five Judges. The Judges shall elect the Presidents of the chambers from among their number. The Presidents of the chambers of five Judges shall be elected for three years. They may be re-elected once.
The composition of the chambers and the assignment of cases to them shall be governed by the Rules of Procedure. In certain cases governed by the Rules of Procedure, the General Court may sit as a full court or be constituted by a single Judge.
The Rules of Procedure may also provide that the General Court may sit in a Grand Chamber in cases and under the conditions specified therein.

Article 50a
1.   The General Court shall exercise at first instance jurisdiction in disputes between the Union and its servants as referred to in Article 270 of the Treaty on the Functioning of the European Union, including disputes between all institutions, bodies, offices or agencies, on the one hand, and their servants, on the other, in respect of which jurisdiction is conferred on the Court of Justice of the European Union.
2.   At all stages of the procedure, including the time when the application is filed, the General Court may examine the possibilities of an amicable settlement of the dispute and may try to facilitate such settlement.

Article 51
By way of derogation from the rule laid down in Article 256(1) of the Treaty on the Functioning of the European Union, jurisdiction shall be reserved to the Court of Justice:
(a)   in actions referred to in Articles 263 and 265 of the Treaty on the Functioning of the European Union which are brought by a Member State against:
(i)   a legislative act, an act of the European Parliament, of the European Council or of the Council, or against a failure to act by one or more of those institutions, except for:
— decisions taken by the Council under the third subparagraph of Article 108(2) of the Treaty on the Functioning of the European Union,
— acts of the Council adopted pursuant to a Council regulation concerning measures to protect trade within the meaning of Article 207 of the Treaty on the Functioning of the European Union,
— acts of the Council by which the Council exercises implementing powers in accordance with Article 291(2) of the Treaty on the Functioning of the European Union;
(ii)   an act of, or a failure to act by, the Commission under Article 331(1) of the Treaty on the Functioning of the European Union;
(b)   in actions referred to in Articles 263 and 265 of the Treaty on the Functioning of the European Union which are brought by an institution of the Union against a legislative act, an act of the European Parliament, of the European Council, of

the Council, of the Commission or of the European Central Bank, or against a failure to act by one or more of those institutions;

(c) in actions referred to in Article 263 of the Treaty on the Functioning of the European Union which are brought by a Member State against an act of the Commission relating to a failure to comply with a judgment delivered by the Court under the second subparagraph of Article 260(2), or the second subparagraph of Article 260(3), of the Treaty on the Functioning of the European Union.';

Article 52

The President of the Court of Justice and the President of the General Court shall determine, by common accord, the conditions under which officials and other servants attached to the Court of Justice shall render their services to the General Court to enable it to function. Certain officials or other servants shall be responsible to the Registrar of the General Court under the authority of the President of the General Court.

Article 55

Final decisions of the General Court, decisions disposing of the substantive issues in part only or disposing of a procedural issue concerning a plea of lack of competence or inadmissibility, shall be notified by the Registrar of the General Court to all parties as well as all Member States and the institutions of the Union even if they did not intervene in the case before the General Court.

Article 56

An appeal may be brought before the Court of Justice, within two months of the notification of the decision appealed against, against final decisions of the General Court and decisions of that Court disposing of the substantive issues in part only or disposing of a procedural issue concerning a plea of lack of competence or inadmissibility.

Such an appeal may be brought by any party which has been unsuccessful, in whole or in part, in its submissions. However, interveners other than the Member States and the institutions of the Union may bring such an appeal only where the decision of the General Court directly affects them.

With the exception of cases relating to disputes between the Union and its servants, an appeal may also be brought by Member States and institutions of the Union which did not intervene in the proceedings before the General Court. Such Member States and institutions shall be in the same position as Member States or institutions which intervened at first instance.

Article 57

Any person whose application to intervene has been dismissed by the General Court may appeal to the Court of Justice within two weeks from the notification of the decision dismissing the application.

The parties to the proceedings may appeal to the Court of Justice against any decision of the General Court made pursuant to Article 278 or Article 279 or the fourth paragraph of Article 299 of the Treaty on the Functioning of the European Union or Article 157 or the third paragraph of Article 164 of the EAEC Treaty within two months from their notification.

The appeal referred to in the first two paragraphs of this Article shall be heard and determined under the procedure referred to in Article 39.

Article 58

An appeal to the Court of Justice shall be limited to points of law. It shall lie on the grounds of lack of competence of the General Court, a breach of procedure before it which adversely affects the interests of the appellant as well as the infringement of Union law by the General Court.

No appeal shall lie regarding only the amount of the costs or the party ordered to pay them.

Article 58a

An appeal brought against a decision of the General Court concerning a decision of an independent board of appeal of one of the following offices and agencies of the Union shall not proceed unless the Court of Justice first decides that it should be allowed to do so:

(a) the European Union Intellectual Property Office;

(b) the Community Plant Variety Office;

(c) the European Chemicals Agency;

(d) the European Union Aviation Safety Agency.

The procedure referred to in the first paragraph shall also apply to appeals brought against decisions of the General Court concerning a decision of an independent board of appeal, set up after 1 May 2019 within any other office or agency of the Union, which has to be seised before an action can be brought before the General Court.

An appeal shall be allowed to proceed, wholly or in part, in accordance with the detailed rules set out in the Rules of Procedure, where it raises an issue that is significant with respect to the unity, consistency or development of Union law.

The decision as to whether the appeal should be allowed to proceed or not shall be reasoned, and it shall be published.

Article 59

Where an appeal is brought against a decision of the General Court, the procedure before the Court of Justice shall consist of a written part and an oral part. In accordance with conditions laid down in the Rules of Procedure, the Court of Justice, having heard the Advocate-General and the parties, may dispense with the oral procedure.

Article 60

Without prejudice to Articles 278 and 279 of the Treaty on the Functioning of the European Union or Article 157 of the EAEC Treaty, an appeal shall not have suspensory effect.

By way of derogation from Article 280 of the Treaty on the Functioning of the European Union, decisions of the General Court declaring a regulation to be void shall take effect only as from the date of expiry of the period referred to in the first paragraph of Article 56 of this Statute or, if an appeal shall have been brought within that period, as from the date of dismissal of the appeal, without prejudice, however, to the right of a party to apply to the Court of Justice, pursuant to Articles 278 and 279 of the Treaty on the Functioning of the European Union or Article 157 of the EAEC Treaty, for the suspension of the effects of the regulation which has been declared void or for the prescription of any other interim measure.

Article 61

If the appeal is well founded, the Court of Justice shall quash the decision of the General Court. It may itself give final judgment in the matter, where the state of the proceedings so permits, or refer the case back to the General Court for judgment.

Where a case is referred back to the General Court, that Court shall be bound by the decision of the Court of Justice on points of law.

When an appeal brought by a Member State or an institution of the Union, which did not intervene in the proceedings before the General Court, is well founded, the Court of Justice may, if it considers this necessary, state which of the effects of the decision of the General Court which has been quashed shall be considered as definitive in respect of the parties to the litigation.

Article 62

In the cases provided for in Article 256(2) and (3) of the Treaty on the Functioning of the European Union, where the First Advocate-General considers that there is a serious risk of the unity or consistency of Union law being affected, he may propose that the Court of Justice review the decision of the General Court.

The proposal must be made within one month of delivery of the decision by the General Court. Within one month of receiving the proposal made by the First Advocate-General, the Court of Justice shall decide whether or not the decision should be reviewed.

Article 62a

The Court of Justice shall give a ruling on the questions which are subject to review by means of an urgent procedure on the basis of the file forwarded to it by the General Court.

Those referred to in Article 23 of this Statute and, in the cases provided for in Article 256(2) of the EC Treaty, the parties to the proceedings before the General Court shall be entitled to lodge statements or written observations with the Court of Justice relating to questions which are subject to review within a period prescribed for that purpose.

The Court of Justice may decide to open the oral procedure before giving a ruling.

Article 62b

In the cases provided for in Article 256(2) of the Treaty on the Functioning of the European Union, without prejudice to Articles 278 and 279 of the Treaty on the Functioning of the European Union, proposals for review and decisions to open the review procedure shall not have suspensory effect. If the Court of Justice finds that the decision of the General Court affects the unity or consistency of Union law, it shall refer the case back to the General Court which shall be bound by the points of law decided by the Court of Justice; the Court of Justice may state which of the effects of the decision of the General Court are to be considered as definitive in respect of the parties to the litigation. If, however, having regard to the result of the review, the outcome of the proceedings flows from the findings of fact on which the decision of the General Court was based, the Court of Justice shall give final judgment.

In the cases provided for in Article 256(3) of the Treaty on the Functioning of the European Union, in the absence of proposals for review or decisions to open the review procedure, the answer(s) given by the General Court to the questions submitted to it shall take effect upon expiry of the periods prescribed for that purpose in the second paragraph of Article 62. Should a review procedure be opened, the answer(s) subject to review shall take effect following that procedure, unless the Court of Justice decides otherwise. If the Court of Justice finds that the decision of the General Court affects the unity or consistency of Union law, the answer given by the Court of Justice to the questions subject to review shall be substituted for that given by the General Court.

TITLE IVa

SPECIALISED COURTS

Article 62c

The provisions relating to the jurisdiction, composition, organisation and procedure of any specialised court established under Article 257 of the Treaty on the Functioning of the European Union shall be contained in an Annex to this Statute.

TITLE V

FINAL PROVISIONS

Article 63

The Rules of Procedure of the Court of Justice and of the General Court shall contain any provisions necessary for applying and, where required, supplementing this Statute.

PROTOCOL (No 8)

relating to Article 6(2) of the Treaty on European Union of the Accession of the Union to the European Convention on the Protection of Human Rights and Fundamental Freedoms

Article 1

The agreement relating to the accession of the Union to the European Convention on the Protection of Human Rights and Fundamental Freedoms (hereinafter referred to as the 'European Convention') provided for in Article 6(2) of the Treaty on European Union shall make provision for preserving the specific characteristics of the Union and Union law, in particular with regard to:

(a) the specific arrangements for the Union's possible participation in the control bodies of the European Convention;

(b) the mechanisms necessary to ensure that proceedings by non-Member States and individual applications are correctly addressed to Member States and/or the Union as appropriate.

Article 2

The agreement referred to in Article 1 shall ensure that accession of the Union shall not affect the competences of the Union or the powers of its institutions. It shall ensure that nothing therein affects the situation of Member States in relation to the European Convention, in particular in relation to the Protocols thereto, measures taken by Member States derogating from the European Convention in accordance with Article 15 thereof and reservations to the European Convention made by Member States in accordance with Article 57 thereof.

Article 3

Nothing in the agreement referred to in Article 1 shall affect Article 292 of the Treaty on the Functioning of the European Union.

PROTOCOL (No 25)
on the Exercise of Shared Competence

THE HIGH CONTRACTING PARTIES,

HAVE AGREED UPON the following provisions, which shall be annexed to the Treaty on European Union and to the Treaty on the Functioning of the European Union:

Sole Article

With reference to Article 2(2) of the Treaty on the Functioning of the European Union on shared competence, when the Union has taken action in a certain area, the scope of this exercise of competence only covers those elements governed by the Union act in question and therefore does not cover the whole area

AGREEMENT
on the withdrawal of the United Kingdom of Great Britain and Northern Ireland from the European Union and the European Atomic Energy Community

[2020] OJ L29/7

PART ONE
COMMON PROVISIONS

Article 1   Objective

This Agreement sets out the arrangements for the withdrawal of the United Kingdom of Great Britain and Northern Ireland ("United Kingdom") from the European Union ("Union") and from the European Atomic Energy Community ("Euratom").

Article 2   Definitions

For the purposes of this Agreement, the following definitions shall apply:

(a) "Union law" means:

(i) the Treaty on European Union ("TEU"), the Treaty on the Functioning of the European Union ("TFEU") and the Treaty establishing the European Atomic Energy Community ("Euratom Treaty"), as amended or supplemented, as well as the Treaties of Accession and the Charter of Fundamental Rights of the European Union, together referred to as "the Treaties";

(ii) the general principles of the Union's law;

(iii) the acts adopted by the institutions, bodies, offices or agencies of the Union;

(iv) the international agreements to which the Union is party and the international agreements concluded by the Member States acting on behalf of the Union;

(v) the agreements between Member States entered into in their capacity as Member States of the Union;

(vi) acts of the Representatives of the Governments of the Member States meeting within the European Council or the Council of the European Union ("Council");

(vii) the declarations made in the context of intergovernmental conferences whichEU-UKdopted the Treaties;

(b) "Member States" means the Kingdom of Belgium, the Republic of Bulgaria, the Czech Republic, the Kingdom of Denmark, the Federal Republic of Germany, the Republic of Estonia, Ireland, the Hellenic Republic, the Kingdom of Spain, the French Republic, the Republic of Croatia, the Italian Republic, the Republic of Cyprus, the Republic of Latvia, the Republic of Lithuania, the Grand Duchy of Luxembourg, Hungary, the Republic of Malta, the Kingdom of the Netherlands, the Republic of Austria, the Republic of Poland, the Portuguese Republic, Romania, the Republic of Slovenia, the Slovak Republic, the Republic of Finland and the Kingdom of Sweden;

(c) "Union citizen" means any person holding the nationality of a Member State;

(d) "United Kingdom national" means a national of the United Kingdom, as defined in the New Declaration by the Government of the United Kingdom of Great Britain and Northern Ireland of 31 December 1982 on the definition of the term "nationals" [1] together with Declaration No 63 annexed to the Final Act of the intergovernmental conference which adopted the Treaty of Lisbon [2];

(e) "transition period" means the period provided in Article 126;

(f) "day" means a calendar day, unless otherwise provided in this Agreement or in provisions of Union law made applicable by this Agreement.

Article 3   Territorial scope

1. Unless otherwise provided in this Agreement or in Union law made applicable by this Agreement, any reference in this Agreement to the United Kingdom or its territory shall be understood as referring to:

(a) the United Kingdom;

(b) Gibraltar, to the extent that Union law was applicable to it before the date of entry into force of this Agreement;

(c) the Channel Islands and the Isle of Man, to the extent that Union law was applicable to them before the date of entry into force of this Agreement;

(d) the Sovereign Base Areas of Akrotiri and Dhekelia in Cyprus, to the extent necessary to ensure the implementation of the arrangements set out in the Protocol on the Sovereign Base Areas of the United Kingdom of Great Britain and Northern Ireland in Cyprus annexed to the Act concerning the conditions of accession of the Czech Republic, the Republic of Estonia, the Republic of Cyprus, the Republic of Latvia, the Republic of Lithuania, the Republic of Hungary, the Republic of Malta, the Republic of Poland, the Republic of Slovenia and the Slovak Republic to the European Union;

(e) the overseas countries and territories listed in Annex II to the TFEU having special relations with the United Kingdom [3], where the provisions of this Agreement relate to the special arrangements for the association of the overseas countries and territories with the Union.

2. Unless otherwise provided in this Agreement or in Union law made applicable by this Agreement, any reference in this Agreement to Member States, or their territory, shall be understood as covering the territories of the Member States to which the Treaties apply as provided in Article 355 TFEU.

Article 4   Methods and principles relating to the effect, the implementation and the application of this Agreement

1. The provisions of this Agreement and the provisions of Union law made applicable by this Agreement shall produce in respect of and in the United Kingdom the same legal effects as those which they produce within the Union and its Member States.

Accordingly, legal or natural persons shall in particular be able to rely directly on the provisions contained or referred to in this Agreement which meet the conditions for direct effect under Union law.

---

[1] OJ C 23, 28.1.1983, p. 1.

[2] OJ C 306, 17.12.2007, p. 270.

[3] Anguilla, Bermuda, British Antarctic Territory, British Indian Ocean Territory, British Virgin Islands, Cayman Islands, Falkland Islands, Montserrat, Pitcairn, Saint Helena, Ascension and Tristan da Cunha, South Georgia and the South Sandwich Islands, and Turks and Caicos Islands.

2.   The United Kingdom shall ensure compliance with paragraph 1, including as regards the required powers of its judicial and administrative authorities to disapply inconsistent or incompatible domestic provisions, through domestic primary legislation.

3.   The provisions of this Agreement referring to Union law or to concepts or provisions thereof shall be interpreted and applied in accordance with the methods and general principles of Union law.

4.   The provisions of this Agreement referring to Union law or to concepts or provisions thereof shall in their implementation and application be interpreted in conformity with the relevant case law of the Court of Justice of the European Union handed down before the end of the transition period.

5.   In the interpretation and application of this Agreement, the United Kingdom's judicial and administrative authorities shall have due regard to relevant case law of the Court of Justice of the European Union handed down after the end of the transition period.

Article 5   Good faith

The Union and the United Kingdom shall, in full mutual respect and good faith, assist each other in carrying out tasks which flow from this Agreement.

They shall take all appropriate measures, whether general or particular, to ensure fulfilment of the obligations arising from this Agreement and shall refrain from any measures which could jeopardise the attainment of the objectives of this Agreement.

This Article is without prejudice to the application of Union law pursuant to this Agreement, in particular the principle of sincere cooperation.

Article 6   References to Union law

1.   With the exception of Parts Four and Five, unless otherwise provided in this Agreement all references in this Agreement to Union law shall be understood as references to Union law, including as amended or replaced, as applicable on the last day of the transition period.

2.   Where in this Agreement reference is made to Union acts or provisions thereof, such reference shall, where relevant, be understood to include a reference to Union law or provisions thereof that, although replaced or superseded by the act referred to, continue to apply in accordance with that act.

3.   For the purposes of this Agreement, references to provisions of Union law made applicable by this Agreement shall be understood to include references to the relevant Union acts supplementing or implementing those provisions.

Article 7   References to the Union and to Member States

1.   For the purposes of this Agreement, all references to Member States and competent authorities of Member States in provisions of Union law made applicable by this Agreement shall be understood as including the United Kingdom and its competent authorities, except as regards:

     (a)   the nomination, appointment or election of members of the institutions, bodies, offices and agencies of the Union, as well as the participation in the decision-making and the attendance in the meetings of the institutions;

     (b)   the participation in the decision-making and governance of the bodies, offices and agencies of the Union;

     (c)   the attendance in the meetings of the committees referred to in Article 3(2) of Regulation (EU) No 182/2011 of the European Parliament and of the Council ([4]), of Commission expert groups or of other similar entities, or in the meetings of expert groups or similar entities of bodies, offices and agencies of the Union, unless otherwise provided in this Agreement.

2.   Unless otherwise provided in this Agreement, any reference to the Union shall be understood as including Euratom.

---

[4]   Regulation (EU) No 182/2011 of the European Parliament and of the Council of 16 February 2011 laying down the rules and general principles concerning mechanisms for control by Member States of the Commission's exercise of implementing powers (OJ L 55, 28.2.2011, p. 13).

Article 8   Access to networks, information systems and databases

Unless otherwise provided in this Agreement, at the end of the transition period the United Kingdom shall cease to be entitled to access any network, any information system and any database established on the basis of Union law. The United Kingdom shall take appropriate measures to ensure that it does not access a network, information system or database which it is no longer entitled to access.

PART TWO
CITIZENS' RIGHTS

TITLE I
GENERAL PROVISIONS

Article 9   Definitions

For the purposes of this Part, and without prejudice to Title III, the following definitions shall apply:

(a) "family members" means the following persons, irrespective of their nationality, who fall within the personal scope provided for in Article 10 of this Agreement:

   (i)   family members of Union citizens or family members of United Kingdom nationals as defined in point (2) of Article 2 of Directive 2004/38/EC of the European Parliament and of the Council [5];

   (ii)   persons other than those defined in Article 3(2) of Directive 2004/38/EC whose presence is required by Union citizens or United Kingdom nationals in order not to deprive those Union citizens or United Kingdom nationals of a right of residence granted by this Part;

(b) "frontier workers" means Union citizens or United Kingdom nationals who pursue an economic activity in accordance with Article 45 or 49 TFEU in one or more States in which they do not reside;

(c) "host State" means:

   (i)   in respect of Union citizens and their family members, the United Kingdom, if they exercised their right of residence there in accordance with Union law before the end of the transition period and continue to reside there thereafter;

   (ii)   in respect of United Kingdom nationals and their family members, the Member State in which they exercised their right of residence in accordance with Union law before the end of the transition period and in which they continue to reside thereafter;

(d) "State of work" means:

   (i)   in respect of Union citizens, the United Kingdom, if they pursued an economic activity as frontier workers there before the end of the transition period and continue to do so thereafter;

   (ii)   in respect of United Kingdom nationals, a Member State in which they pursued an economic activity as frontier workers before the end of the transition period and in which they continue to do so thereafter;

(e) "rights of custody" means rights of custody within the meaning of point (9) of Article 2 of Council Regulation (EC) No 2201/2003 [6], including rights of custody acquired by judgment, by operation of law or by an agreement having legal effect.

---

[5] Directive 2004/38/EC of the European Parliament and of the Council of 29 April 2004 on the right of citizens of the Union and their family members to move and reside freely within the territory of the Member States amending Regulation (EEC) No 1612/68 and repealing Directives 64/221/EEC, 68/360/EEC, 72/194/EEC, 73/148/EEC, 75/34/EEC, 75/35/EEC, 90/364/EEC, 90/365/EEC and 93/96/EEC (OJ L 158, 30.4.2004, p. 77).

[6] Council Regulation (EC) No 2201/2003 of 27 November 2003 concerning jurisdiction and the recognition and enforcement of judgments in matrimonial matters and the matters of parental responsibility, repealing Regulation (EC) No 1347/2000 (OJ L 338, 23.12.2003 p. 1).

Article 10   Personal scope

1. Without prejudice to Title III, this Part shall apply to the following persons:

    (a) Union citizens who exercised their right to reside in the United Kingdom in accordance with Union law before the end of the transition period and continue to reside there thereafter;

    (b) United Kingdom nationals who exercised their right to reside in a Member State in accordance with Union law before the end of the transition period and continue to reside there thereafter;

    (c) Union citizens who exercised their right as frontier workers in the United Kingdom in accordance with Union law before the end of the transition period and continue to do so thereafter;

    (d) United Kingdom nationals who exercised their right as frontier workers in one or more Member States in accordance with Union law before the end of the transition period and continue to do so thereafter;

    (e) family members of the persons referred to in points (a) to (d), provided that they fulfil one of the following conditions:

         (i)   they resided in the host State in accordance with Union law before the end of the transition period and continue to reside there thereafter;

         (ii) they were directly related to a person referred to in points (a) to (d) and resided outside the host State before the end of the transition period, provided that they fulfil the conditions set out in point (2) of Article 2 of Directive 2004/38/EC at the time they seek residence under this Part in order to join the person referred to in points (a) to (d) of this paragraph;

         (iii) they were born to, or legally adopted by, persons referred to in points (a) to (d) after the end of the transition period, whether inside or outside the host State, and fulfil the conditions set out in point (2)(c) of Article 2 of Directive 2004/38/EC at the time they seek residence under this Part in order to join the person referred to in points (a) to (d) of this paragraph and fulfil one of the following conditions:

               — both parents are persons referred to in points (a) to (d);

               — one parent is a person referred to in points (a) to (d) and the other is a national of the host State; or

               — one parent is a person referred to in points (a) to (d) and has sole or joint rights of custody of the child, in accordance with the applicable rules of family law of a Member State or of the United Kingdom, including applicable rules of private international law under which rights of custody established under the law of a third State are recognised in the Member State or in the United Kingdom, in particular as regards the best interests of the child, and without prejudice to the normal operation of such applicable rules of private international law [7];

    (f) family members who resided in the host State in accordance with Articles 12 and 13, Article 16(2) and Articles 17 and 18 of Directive 2004/38/EC before the end of the transition period and continue to reside there thereafter.

2. Persons falling under points (a) and (b) of Article 3(2) of Directive 2004/38/EC whose residence was facilitated by the host State in accordance with its national legislation before the end of the transition period in accordance with Article 3(2) of that Directive shall retain their right of residence in the host State in accordance with this Part, provided that they continue to reside in the host State thereafter.

3. Paragraph 2 shall also apply to persons falling under points (a) and (b) of Article 3(2) of Directive 2004/38/EC who have applied for facilitation of entry and residence before the end of the transition period, and whose residence is being facilitated by the host State in accordance with its national legislation thereafter.

4. Without prejudice to any right to residence which the persons concerned may have in their own right, the host State shall, in accordance with its national legislation and in accordance with point (b) of Article 3(2) of Directive 2004/38/EC, facilitate entry

---

[7] The notion of rights of custody is to be interpreted in accordance with point (9) of Article 2 of Regulation (EC) No 2201/2003. Therefore, it covers rights of custody acquired by judgment, by operation of law or by an agreement having legal effect.

and residence for the partner with whom the person referred to in points (a) to (d) of paragraph 1 of this Article has a durable relationship, duly attested, where that partner resided outside the host State before the end of the transition period, provided that the relationship was durable before the end of the transition period and continues at the time the partner seeks residence under this Part.

5. In the cases referred to in paragraphs 3 and 4, the host State shall undertake an extensive examination of the personal circumstances of the persons concerned and shall justify any denial of entry or residence to such persons.

Article 11   Continuity of residence

Continuity of residence for the purposes of Articles 9 and 10 shall not be affected by absences as referred to in Article 15(2).

The right of permanent residence acquired under Directive 2004/38/EC before the end of the transition period shall not be treated as lost through absence from the host State for a period specified in Article 15(3).

Article 12   Non-discrimination

Within the scope of this Part, and without prejudice to any special provisions contained therein, any discrimination on grounds of nationality within the meaning of the first subparagraph of Article 18 TFEU shall be prohibited in the host State and the State of work in respect of the persons referred to in Article 10 of this Agreement.

TITLE II

RIGHTS AND OBLIGATIONS

CHAPTER 1

RIGHTS RELATED TO RESIDENCE, RESIDENCE DOCUMENTS

Article 13   Residence rights

1. Union citizens and United Kingdom nationals shall have the right to reside in the host State under the limitations and conditions as set out in Articles 21, 45 or 49 TFEU and in Article 6(1), points (a), (b) or (c) of Article 7(1), Article 7(3), Article 14, Article 16(1) or Article 17(1) of Directive 2004/38/EC.

2. Family members who are either Union citizens or United Kingdom nationals shall have the right to reside in the host State as set out in Article 21 TFEU and in Article 6(1), point (d) of Article 7(1), Article 12(1) or (3), Article 13(1), Article 14, Article 16(1) or Article 17(3) and (4) of Directive 2004/38/EC, subject to the limitations and conditions set out in those provisions.

3. Family members who are neither Union citizens nor United Kingdom nationals shall have the right to reside in the host State under Article 21 TFEU and as set out in Article 6(2), Article 7(2), Article 12(2) or (3), Article 13(2), Article 14, Article 16(2), Article 17(3) or (4) or Article 18 of Directive 2004/38/EC, subject to the limitations and conditions set out in those provisions.

4. The host State may not impose any limitations or conditions for obtaining, retaining or losing residence rights on the persons referred to in paragraphs 1, 2 and 3, other than those provided for in this Title. There shall be no discretion in applying the limitations and conditions provided for in this Title, other than in favour of the person concerned.

Article 14   Right of exit and of entry

1. Union citizens and United Kingdom nationals, their respective family members, and other persons, who reside in the territory of the host State in accordance with the conditions set out in this Title shall have the right to leave the host State and the right to enter it, as set out in Article 4(1) and the first subparagraph of Article 5(1) of Directive 2004/38/EC, with a valid passport or national identity card in the case of Union citizens and United Kingdom nationals, and with a valid passport in the case of their respective family members and other persons who are not Union citizens or United Kingdom nationals.

Five years after the end of the transition period, the host State may decide no longer to accept national identity cards for the purposes of entry to or exit from its territory if such cards do not include a chip that complies with the applicable International Civil Aviation Organisation standards related to biometric identification.

2. No exit visa, entry visa or equivalent formality shall be required of holders of a valid document issued in accordance with Article 18 or 26.

3. Where the host State requires family members who join the Union citizen or United Kingdom national after the end of the transition period to have an entry visa, the host State shall grant such persons every facility to obtain the necessary visas. Such visas shall be issued free of charge as soon as possible, and on the basis of an accelerated procedure.

Article 15   Right of permanent residence

1. Union citizens and United Kingdom nationals, and their respective family members, who have resided legally in the host State in accordance with Union law for a continuous period of 5 years or for the period specified in Article 17 of Directive 2004/38/EC, shall have the right to reside permanently in the host State under the conditions set out in Articles 16, 17 and 18 of Directive 2004/38/EC. Periods of legal residence or work in accordance with Union law before and after the end of the transition period shall be included in the calculation of the qualifying period necessary for acquisition of the right of permanent residence.

2. Continuity of residence for the purposes of acquisition of the right of permanent residence shall be determined in accordance with Article 16(3) and Article 21 of Directive 2004/38/EC.

3. Once acquired, the right of permanent residence shall be lost only through absence from the host State for a period exceeding 5 consecutive years.

Article 16   Accumulation of periods

Union citizens and United Kingdom nationals, and their respective family members, who before the end of the transition period resided legally in the host State in accordance with the conditions of Article 7 of Directive 2004/38/EC for a period of less than 5 years, shall have the right to acquire the right to reside permanently under the conditions set out in Article 15 of this Agreement once they have completed the necessary periods of residence. Periods of legal residence or work in accordance with Union law before and after the end of the transition period shall be included in the calculation of the qualifying period necessary for acquisition of the right of permanent residence.

Article 17   Status and changes

1. The right of Union citizens and United Kingdom nationals, and their respective family members, to rely directly on this Part shall not be affected when they change status, for example between student, worker, self-employed person and economically inactive person. Persons who, at the end of the transition period, enjoy a right of residence in their capacity as family members of Union citizens or United Kingdom nationals, cannot become persons referred to in points (a) to (d) of Article 10(1).

2. The rights provided for in this Title for the family members who are dependants of Union citizens or United Kingdom nationals before the end of the transition period, shall be maintained even after they cease to be dependants.

Article 18   Issuance of residence documents

1. The host State may require Union citizens or United Kingdom nationals, their respective family members and other persons, who reside in its territory in accordance with the conditions set out in this Title, to apply for a new residence status which confers the rights under this Title and a document evidencing such status which may be in a digital form.

Applying for such a residence status shall be subject to the following conditions:

(a)   the purpose of the application procedure shall be to verify whether the applicant is entitled to the residence rights set out in this Title. Where that is the case, the applicant shall have a right to be granted the residence status and the document evidencing that status;

(b)   the deadline for submitting the application shall not be less than 6 months from the end of the transition period, for persons residing in the host State before the end of the transition period.

For persons who have the right to commence residence after the end of the transition period in the host State in accordance with this Title, the deadline for submitting the application shall be 3 months after their arrival or the expiry of the deadline referred to in the first subparagraph, whichever is later.

A certificate of application for the residence status shall be issued immediately;

(c)   the deadline for submitting the application referred to in point (b) shall be extended automatically by 1 year where the Union has notified the United Kingdom, or the United Kingdom has notified the Union, that technical problems prevent the host State either from registering the application or from issuing the certificate of application referred to in point (b). The host State shall publish that notification and shall provide appropriate public information for the persons concerned in good time;

(d)   where the deadline for submitting the application referred to in point (b) is not respected by the persons concerned, the competent authorities shall assess all the circumstances and reasons for not respecting the deadline and shall allow those persons to submit an application within a reasonable further period of time if there are reasonable grounds for the failure to respect the deadline;

(e)   the host State shall ensure that any administrative procedures for applications are smooth, transparent and simple, and that any unnecessary administrative burdens are avoided;

(f)   application forms shall be short, simple, user friendly and adapted to the context of this Agreement; applications made by families at the same time shall be considered together;

(g)   the document evidencing the status shall be issued free of charge or for a charge not exceeding that imposed on citizens or nationals of the host State for the issuing of similar documents;

(h)   persons who, before the end of the transition period, hold a valid permanent residence document issued under Article 19 or 20 of Directive 2004/38/EC or hold a valid domestic immigration document conferring a permanent right to reside in the host State, shall have the right to exchange that document within the period referred to in point (b) of this paragraph for a new residence document upon application after a verification of their identity, a criminality and security check in accordance with point (p) of this paragraph and confirmation of their ongoing residence; such new residence documents shall be issued free of charge;

(i)   the identity of the applicants shall be verified through the presentation of a valid passport or national identity card for Union citizens and United Kingdom nationals, and through the presentation of a valid passport for their respective family members and other persons who are not Union citizens or United Kingdom nationals; the acceptance of such identity documents shall not be made conditional upon any criteria other than that of the validity of the document. Where the identity document is retained by the competent authorities of the host State while the application is pending, the host State shall return that document upon application without delay, before the decision on the application has been taken;

(j)   supporting documents other than identity documents, such as civil status documents, may be submitted in copy. Originals of supporting documents may be required only in specific cases where there is a reasonable doubt as to the authenticity of the supporting documents submitted;

(k)   the host State may only require Union citizens and United Kingdom nationals to present, in addition to the identity documents referred to in point (i) of this paragraph, the following supporting documents as referred to in Article 8(3) of Directive 2004/38/EC:

(i)   where they reside in the host State in accordance with point (a) of Article 7(1) of Directive 2004/38/EC as workers or self-employed, a confirmation of engagement from the employer or a certificate of employment, or proof that they are self-employed;

(ii) where they reside in the host State in accordance with point (b) of Article 7(1) of Directive 2004/38/EC as economically inactive persons, evidence that they have sufficient resources for themselves and their family members not to become a burden on the social assistance system of the host State during their period of residence and that they have comprehensive sickness insurance cover in the host State; or

(iii) where they reside in the host State in accordance with point (c) of Article 7(1) of Directive 2004/38/EC as students, proof of enrolment at an establishment accredited or financed by the host State on the basis of its legislation or administrative practice, proof of comprehensive sickness insurance cover, and a declaration or equivalent means of proof, that they have sufficient resources for themselves and their family members not to become a burden on the social assistance system of the host State during their period of residence. The host State may not require such declarations to refer to any specific amount of resources.

With regard to the condition of sufficient resources, Article 8(4) of Directive 2004/38/EC shall apply;

(l) the host State may only require family members who fall under point (e)(i) of Article 10(1) or Article 10(2) or (3) of this Agreement and who reside in the host State in accordance with point (d) of Article 7(1) or Article 7(2) of Directive 2004/38/EC to present, in addition to the identity documents referred to in point (i) of this paragraph, the following supporting documents as referred to in Article 8(5) or 10(2) of Directive 2004/38/EC:

(i) a document attesting to the existence of a family relationship or registered partnership;

(ii) the registration certificate or, in the absence of a registration system, any other proof that the Union citizen or the United Kingdom national with whom they reside actually resides in the host State;

(iii) for direct descendants who are under the age of 21 or who are dependants and dependent direct relatives in the ascending line, and for those of the spouse or registered partner, documentary evidence that the conditions set out in point (c) or (d) of Article 2(2) of Directive 2004/38/EC are fulfilled;

(iv) for the persons referred to in Article 10(2) or (3) of this Agreement, a document issued by the relevant authority in the host State in accordance with Article 3(2) of Directive 2004/38/EC.

With regard to the condition of sufficient resources as concerns family members who are themselves Union citizens or United Kingdom nationals, Article 8(4) of Directive 2004/38/EC shall apply;

(m) the host State may only require family members who fall under point (e)(ii) of Article 10(1) or Article 10(4) of this Agreement to present, in addition to the identity documents referred to in point (i) of this paragraph, the following supporting documents as referred to in Articles 8(5) and 10(2) of Directive 2004/38/EC:

(i) a document attesting to the existence of a family relationship or of a registered partnership;

(ii) the registration certificate or, in the absence of a registration system, any other proof of residence in the host State of the Union citizen or of the United Kingdom nationals whom they are joining in the host State;

(iii) for spouses or registered partners, a document attesting to the existence of a family relationship or a registered partnership before the end of the transition period;

(iv) for direct descendants who are under the age of 21 or who are dependants and dependent direct relatives in the ascending line and those of the spouse or registered partner, documentary evidence that they were related to Union citizens or United Kingdom nationals before the end of the transition period and fulfil the conditions set out in point (c) or (d) of Article 2(2) of Directive 2004/38/EC relating to age or dependence;

(v)   for the persons referred to in Article 10(4) of this Agreement, proof that a durable relationship with Union citizens or United Kingdom nationals existed before the end of the transition period and continues to exist thereafter;

(n)   for cases other than those set out in points (k), (l) and (m), the host State shall not require applicants to present supporting documents that go beyond what is strictly necessary and proportionate to provide evidence that the conditions relating to the right of residence under this Title have been fulfilled;

(o)   the competent authorities of the host State shall help the applicants to prove their eligibility and to avoid any errors or omissions in their applications; they shall give the applicants the opportunity to furnish supplementary evidence and to correct any deficiencies, errors or omissions;

(p)   criminality and security checks may be carried out systematically on applicants, with the exclusive aim of verifying whether the restrictions set out in Article 20 of this Agreement may be applicable. For that purpose, applicants may be required to declare past criminal convictions which appear in their criminal record in accordance with the law of the State of conviction at the time of the application. The host State may, if it considers this essential, apply the procedure set out in Article 27(3) of Directive 2004/38/EC with respect to enquiries to other States regarding previous criminal records;

(q)   the new residence document shall include a statement that it has been issued in accordance with this Agreement;

(r)   the applicant shall have access to judicial and, where appropriate, administrative redress procedures in the host State against any decision refusing to grant the residence status. The redress procedures shall allow for an examination of the legality of the decision, as well as of the facts and circumstances on which the proposed decision is based. Such redress procedures shall ensure that the decision is not disproportionate.

2.   During the period referred to in point (b) of paragraph 1 of this Article and its possible one-year extension under point (c) of that paragraph, all rights provided for in this Part shall be deemed to apply to Union citizens or United Kingdom nationals, their respective family members, and other persons residing in the host State, in accordance with the conditions and subject to the restrictions set out in Article 20.

3.   Pending a final decision by the competent authorities on any application referred to in paragraph 1, and pending a final judgment handed down in case of judicial redress sought against any rejection of such application by the competent administrative authorities, all rights provided for in this Part shall be deemed to apply to the applicant, including Article 21 on safeguards and right of appeal, subject to the conditions set out in Article 20(4).

4.   Where a host State has chosen not to require Union citizens or United Kingdom nationals, their family members, and other persons, residing in its territory in accordance with the conditions set out in this Title, to apply for the new residence status referred to in paragraph 1 as a condition for legal residence, those eligible for residence rights under this Title shall have the right to receive, in accordance with the conditions set out in Directive 2004/38/EC, a residence document, which may be in a digital form, that includes a statement that it has been issued in accordance with this Agreement.

Article 19   Issuance of residence documents during the transition period

1.   During the transition period, a host State may allow applications for a residence status or residence document as referred to in Article 18(1) and (4) to be made voluntarily from the date of entry into force of this Agreement.

2.   Decisions to accept or refuse such applications shall be taken in accordance with Article 18(1) and (4). Decisions under Article 18(1) shall have no effect until after the end of the transition period.

3. If an application under Article 18(1) is accepted before the end of the transition period, the host State may not withdraw the decision granting the residence status before the end of the transition period on any grounds other than those set out in Chapter VI and Article 35 of Directive 2004/38/EC.

4. If an application is refused before the end of the transition period, the applicant may apply again at any time before the expiry of the period set out in point (b) of Article 18(1).

5. Without prejudice to paragraph 4, the redress procedures under point (r) of Article 18(1) shall be available from the date of any decision to refuse an application referred to in paragraph 2 of this Article.

Article 20   Restrictions of the rights of residence and entry

1. The conduct of Union citizens or United Kingdom nationals, their family members, and other persons, who exercise rights under this Title, where that conduct occurred before the end of the transition period, shall be considered in accordance with Chapter VI of Directive 2004/38/EC.

2. The conduct of Union citizens or United Kingdom nationals, their family members, and other persons, who exercise rights under this Title, where that conduct occurred after the end of the transition period, may constitute grounds for restricting the right of residence by the host State or the right of entry in the State of work in accordance with national legislation.

3. The host State or the State of work may adopt the necessary measures to refuse, terminate or withdraw any right conferred by this Title in the case of the abuse of those rights or fraud, as set out in Article 35 of Directive 2004/38/EC. Such measures shall be subject to the procedural safeguards provided for in Article 21 of this Agreement.

4. The host State or the State of work may remove applicants who submitted fraudulent or abusive applications from its territory under the conditions set out in Directive 2004/38/EC, in particular Articles 31 and 35 thereof, even before a final judgment has been handed down in the case of judicial redress sought against any rejection of such an application.

Article 21   Safeguards and right of appeal

The safeguards set out in Article 15 and Chapter VI of Directive 2004/38/EC shall apply in respect of any decision by the host State that restricts residence rights of the persons referred to in Article 10 of this Agreement.

Article 22   Related rights

In accordance with Article 23 of Directive 2004/38/EC, irrespective of nationality, the family members of a Union citizen or United Kingdom national who have the right of residence or the right of permanent residence in the host State or the State of work shall be entitled to take up employment or self-employment there.

Article 23   Equal treatment

1. In accordance with Article 24 of Directive 2004/38/EC, subject to the specific provisions provided for in this Title and Titles I and IV of this Part, all Union citizens or United Kingdom nationals residing on the basis of this Agreement in the territory of the host State shall enjoy equal treatment with the nationals of that State within the scope of this Part. The benefit of this right shall be extended to those family members of Union citizens or United Kingdom nationals who have the right of residence or permanent residence.

2. By way of derogation from paragraph 1, the host State shall not be obliged to confer entitlement to social assistance during periods of residence on the basis of Article 6 or point (b) of Article 14(4) of Directive 2004/38/EC, nor shall it be obliged, prior to a person's acquisition of the right of permanent residence in accordance with Article 15 of this Agreement, to grant maintenance aid for studies, including vocational training, consisting in student grants or student loans to persons other than workers, self-employed persons, persons who retain such status or to members of their families.

CHAPTER 2
RIGHTS OF WORKERS AND SELF-EMPLOYED PERSONS

Article 24 Rights of workers

1. Subject to the limitations set out in Article 45(3) and (4) TFEU, workers in the host State and frontier workers in the State or States of work shall enjoy the rights guaranteed by Article 45 TFEU and the rights granted by Regulation (EU) No 492/2011 of the European Parliament and of the Council ([8]). These rights include:

   (a) the right not to be discriminated against on grounds of nationality as regards employment, remuneration and other conditions of work and employment;

   (b) the right to take up and pursue an activity in accordance with the rules applicable to the nationals of the host State or the State of work;

   (c) the right to assistance afforded by the employment offices of the host State or the State of work as offered to own nationals;

   (d) the right to equal treatment in respect of conditions of employment and work, in particular as regards remuneration, dismissal and in case of unemployment, reinstatement or re-employment;

   (e) the right to social and tax advantages;

   (f) collective rights;

   (g) the rights and benefits accorded to national workers in matters of housing;

   (h) the right for their children to be admitted to the general educational, apprenticeship and vocational training courses under the same conditions as the nationals of the host State or the State of work, if such children are residing in the territory where the worker works.

2. Where a direct descendant of a worker who has ceased to reside in the host State is in education in that State, the primary carer for that descendant shall have the right to reside in that State until the descendant reaches the age of majority, and after the age of majority if that descendant continues to need the presence and care of the primary carer in order to pursue and complete his or her education.

3. Employed frontier workers shall enjoy the right to enter and exit the State of work in accordance with Article 14 of this Agreement and shall retain the rights they enjoyed as workers there, provided they are in one of the circumstances set out in points (a), (b), (c) and (d) of Article 7(3) of Directive 2004/38/EC, even where they do not move their residence to the State of work.

Article 25 Rights of self-employed persons

1. Subject to the limitations set out in Articles 51 and 52 TFEU, self-employed persons in the host State and self- employed frontier workers in the State or States of work shall enjoy the rights guaranteed by Articles 49 and 55 TFEU. These rights include:

   (a) the right to take up and pursue activities as self-employed persons and to set up and manage undertakings under the conditions laid down by the host State for its own nationals, as set out in Article 49 TFEU;

   (b) the rights as set out in points (c) to (h) of Article 24(1) of this Agreement.

2. Article 24(2) shall apply to direct descendants of self-employed workers.

3. Article 24(3) shall apply to self-employed frontier workers.

Article 26 Issuance of a document identifying frontier workers' rights

The State of work may require Union citizens and United Kingdom nationals who have rights as frontier workers under this Title to apply for a document certifying that they have such rights under this Title. Such Union citizens and United Kingdom nationals shall have the right to be issued with such a document.

---

[8] Regulation (EU) No 492/2011 of the European Parliament and of the Council of 5 April 2011 on freedom of movement for workers within the Union (OJ L 141, 27.5.2011, p. 1).

CHAPTER 3
PROFESSIONAL QUALIFICATIONS

Article 27   Recognised professional qualifications

1. The recognition, before the end of the transition period, of professional qualifications, as defined in point (b) of Article 3(1) of Directive 2005/36/EC of the European Parliament and of the Council [9], of Union citizens or United Kingdom nationals, and their family members, by their host State or their State of work shall maintain its effects in the respective State, including the right to pursue their profession under the same conditions as its nationals, where such recognition was made in accordance with any of the following provisions:
    (a) Title III of Directive 2005/36/EC in respect of the recognition of professional qualifications in the context of the exercise of the freedom of establishment, whether such recognition fell under the general system for the recognition of evidence of training, the system for the recognition of professional experience or the system for the recognition on the basis of coordination of minimum training conditions;
    (b) Article 10(1) and (3) of Directive 98/5/EC of the European Parliament and of the Council [10] in respect of gaining admission to the profession of lawyer in the host State or State of work;
    (c) Article 14 of Directive 2006/43/EC of the European Parliament and of the Council [11] in respect of the approval of statutory auditors from another Member State;
    (d) Council Directive 74/556/EEC [12] in respect of the acceptance of evidence of the knowledge and ability necessary to take up or pursue the activities of self-employed persons and of intermediaries engaging in the trade and distribution of toxic products or activities involving the professional use of toxic products.
2. Recognitions of professional qualifications for the purposes of point (a) of paragraph 1 of this Article shall include:
    (a) recognitions of professional qualifications which have benefited from Article 3(3) of Directive 2005/36/EC;
    (b) decisions granting partial access to a professional activity in accordance with Article 4f of Directive 2005/36/EC;
    (c) recognitions of professional qualifications for establishment purposes made under Article 4d of Directive 2005/36/EC.

Article 28   Ongoing procedures on the recognition of professional qualifications

Article 4, Article 4d in respect of recognitions of professional qualifications for establishment purposes, Article 4f and Title III of Directive 2005/36/EC, Article 10(1), (3) and (4) of Directive 98/5/EC, Article 14 of Directive 2006/43/EC and Directive 74/556/EEC shall apply in respect of the examination by a competent authority of the host State or State of work of any application for the recognition of professional qualifications introduced before the end of the transition period by Union citizens or United Kingdom nationals and in respect of the decision on any such application.

Articles 4a, 4b and 4e of Directive 2005/36/EC shall also apply to the extent relevant for the completion of the procedures for the recognitions of professional qualifications for establishment purposes under Article 4d of that Directive.

---

[9] Directive 2005/36/EC of the European Parliament and of the Council of 7 September 2005 on the recognition of professional qualifications (OJ L 255, 30.9.2005, p. 22).

[10] Directive 98/5/EC of the European Parliament and of the Council of 16 February 1998 to facilitate practice of the profession of lawyer on a permanent basis in a Member State other than that in which the qualification was obtained (OJ L 77, 14.3.1998, p. 36).

[11] Directive 2006/43/EC of the European Parliament and of the Council of 17 May 2006 on statutory audits of annual accounts and consolidated accounts, amending Council Directives 78/660/EEC and 83/349/EEC and repealing Council Directive 84/253/EEC (OJ L 157, 9.6.2006, p. 87).

[12] Council Directive 74/556/EEC of 4 June 1974 laying down detailed provisions concerning transitional measures relating to activities, trade in and distribution of toxic products and activities entailing the professional use of such products including activities of intermediaries (OJ L 307, 18.11.1974, p. 1).

Article 29 Administrative cooperation on recognition of professional qualifications

1. With regard to the pending applications referred to in Article 28, the United Kingdom and the Member States shall cooperate in order to facilitate the application of Article 28. Cooperation may include the exchange of information, including information on disciplinary action or criminal sanctions taken or any other serious and specific circumstances which are likely to have consequences for the pursuit of the activities falling under the Directives referred to in Article 28.

2. By way of derogation from Article 8, for a period not exceeding 9 months from the end of the transition period, the United Kingdom shall be entitled to use the internal market information system in respect of applications referred to in Article 28 insofar as they concern procedures for the recognition of professional qualifications for establishment purposes under Article 4d of Directive 2005/36/EC.

TITLE III
COORDINATION OF SOCIAL SECURITY SYSTEMS

Article 30 Persons covered

1. This Title shall apply to the following persons:
   (a) Union citizens who are subject to the legislation of the United Kingdom at the end of the transition period, as well as their family members and survivors;
   (b) United Kingdom nationals who are subject to the legislation of a Member State at the end of the transition period, as well as their family members and survivors;
   (c) Union citizens who reside in the United Kingdom and are subject to the legislation of a Member State at the end of the transition period, as well as their family members and survivors;
   (d) United Kingdom nationals who reside in a Member State, and are subject to the legislation of the United Kingdom at the end of the transition period, as well as their family members and survivors;
   (e) persons who do not fall within points (a) to (d) but are:
       (i) Union citizens who pursue an activity as an employed or self-employed person in the United Kingdom at the end of the transition period, and who, based on Title II of Regulation (EC) No 883/2004 of the European Parliament and of the Council [13], are subject to the legislation of a Member State, as well as their family members and survivors; or
       (ii) United Kingdom nationals who pursue an activity as an employed or self-employed person in one or more Member States at the end of the transition period, and who, based on Title II of Regulation (EC) No 883/2004, are subject to the legislation of the United Kingdom, as well as their family members and survivors;
   (f) stateless persons and refugees, residing in a Member State or in the United Kingdom, who are in one of the situations described in points (a) to (e), as well as their family members and survivors;
   (g) nationals of third countries, as well as members of their families and survivors, who are in one of the situations described in points (a) to (e), provided that they fulfil the conditions of Council Regulation (EC) No 859/2003 [14].

2. The persons referred to in paragraph 1 shall be covered for as long as they continue without interruption to be in one of the situations set out in that paragraph involving both a Member State and the United Kingdom at the same time.

3. This Title shall also apply to persons who do not, or who no longer, fall within points (a) to (e) of paragraph 1 of this Article but who fall within Article 10 of this Agreement, as well as their family members and survivors.

---

[13] Regulation (EC) No 883/2004 of the European Parliament and of the Council of 29 April 2004 on the coordination of social security systems (OJ L 166, 30.4.2004, p. 1).

[14] Council Regulation (EC) No 859/2003 of 14 May 2003 extending the provisions of Regulation (EEC) No 1408/71 and Regulation (EEC) No 574/72 to nationals of third countries who are not already covered by those provisions solely on the ground of their nationality (OJ L 124, 20.5.2003, p. 1).

4.   The persons referred to in paragraph 3 shall be covered for as long as they continue to have a right to reside in the host State under Article 13 of this Agreement, or a right to work in their State of work under Article 24 or 25 of this Agreement.

5.   Where this Article refers to family members and survivors, those persons shall be covered by this Title only to the extent that they derive rights and obligations in that capacity under Regulation (EC) No 883/2004.

Article 31   Social security coordination rules

1.   The rules and objectives set out in Article 48 TFEU, Regulation (EC) No 883/2004 and Regulation (EC) No 987/2009 of the European Parliament and of the Council ([15]) shall apply to the persons covered by this Title.

The Union and the United Kingdom shall take due account of the Decisions and Recommendations of the Administrative Commission for the Coordination of Social Security Systems attached to the European Commission, set up under Regulation (EC) No 883/2004 ("Administrative Commission") listed in Part I of Annex I to this Agreement.

2.   By way of derogation from Article 9 of this Agreement, for the purposes of this Title, the definitions in Article 1 of Regulation (EC) No 883/2004 shall apply.

3.   With regard to nationals of third countries who fulfil the conditions of Regulation (EC) No 859/2003, as well as their family members or survivors within the scope of this Title, the references to Regulation (EC) No 883/2004 and Regulation (EC) No 987/2009 in this Title shall be understood as references to Council Regulation (EEC) No 1408/71 ([16]) and Council Regulation (EEC) No 574/72 ([17]) respectively. References to specific provisions of Regulation (EC) No 883/2004 and Regulation (EC) No 987/2009 shall be understood as references to the corresponding provisions of Regulation (EEC) No 1408/71 and Regulation (EEC) No 574/72.

Article 32   Special situations covered

1.   The following rules shall apply in the following situations to the extent set out in this Article, insofar as they relate to persons not or no longer covered by Article 30:

(a)   the following persons shall be covered by this Title for the purposes of reliance on and aggregation of periods of insurance, employment, self-employment or residence, including rights and obligations deriving from such periods in accordance with Regulation (EC) No 883/2004:

   (i)   Union citizens, as well as stateless persons and refugees residing in a Member State and nationals of third countries who fulfil the conditions of Regulation (EC) No 859/2003, who have been subject to the legislation of the United Kingdom before the end of the transition period, as well as their family members and survivors;

   (ii)   United Kingdom nationals, as well as stateless persons and refugees residing in the United Kingdom and nationals of third countries who fulfil the conditions of Regulation (EC) No 859/2003, who have been subject to the legislation of a Member State before the end of the transition period, as well as their family members and survivors;

   for the purposes of the aggregation of periods, periods completed both before and after the end of the transition period shall be taken into account in accordance with Regulation (EC) No 883/2004;

(b)   the rules set out in Articles 20 and 27 of Regulation (EC) No 883/2004 shall continue to apply to persons who, before the end of the transition period, had requested authorisation to receive a course of planned health care treatment pursuant to Regulation (EC) No 883/2004, until the end of the treatment. The

---

[15] Regulation (EC) No 987/2009 of the European Parliament and of the Council of 16 September 2009 laying down the procedure for implementing Regulation (EC) No 883/2004 on the coordination of social security systems (OJ L 284, 30.10.2009, p. 1).

[16] Council Regulation (EEC) No 1408/71 of 14 June 1971 on the application of social security schemes to employed persons, to self- employed persons and to members of their families moving within the Community (OJ L 149, 5.7.1971, p. 2).

[17] Regulation (EEC) No 574/72 of the Council of 21 March 1972 fixing the procedure for implementing Regulation (EEC) No 1408/71 on the application of social security schemes to employed persons and their families moving within the Community (OJ L 74, 27.3.1972, p. 1).

corresponding reimbursement procedures shall also apply even after the treatment ends. Such persons and the accompanying persons shall enjoy the right to enter and exit the State of treatment in accordance with Article 14, *mutatis mutandis*;

(c) the rules set out in Articles 19 and 27 of Regulation (EC) No 883/2004 shall continue to apply to persons who are covered by Regulation (EC) No 883/2004 and who are on a stay at the end of the transition period in a Member State or the United Kingdom, until the end of their stay. The corresponding reimbursement procedures shall also apply even after the stay or treatment ends;

(d) the rules set out in Articles 67, 68 and 69 of Regulation (EC) No 883/2004 shall continue to apply, for as long as the conditions are fulfilled, to awards of family benefits to which there is entitlement at the end of the transition period for the following persons:

    (i) Union citizens, stateless persons and refugees residing in a Member State as well as nationals of third countries who fulfil the conditions of Regulation (EC) No 859/2003 and reside in a Member State, who are subject to the legislation of a Member State and have family members residing in the United Kingdom at the end of the transition period;

    (ii) United Kingdom nationals, as well as stateless persons and refugees residing in the United Kingdom and nationals of third countries who fulfil the conditions of Regulation (EC) No 859/2003 and reside in the United Kingdom, who are subject to the legislation of the United Kingdom and have family members residing in a Member State at the end of the transition period;

(e) in the situations set out in point (d)(i) and (ii) of this paragraph, for any persons who have rights as family members at the end of the transition period under Regulation (EC) No 883/2004, such as derived rights for sickness benefits in kind, that Regulation and the corresponding provisions of Regulation (EC) No 987/2009 shall continue to apply for as long as the conditions provided therein are fulfilled.

2. The provisions of Chapter 1 of Title III of Regulation (EC) No 883/2004 as regards sickness benefits shall apply to persons receiving benefits under point (a) of paragraph 1 of this Article.

This paragraph shall apply *mutatis mutandis* as regards family benefits based on Articles 67, 68 and 69 of Regulation (EC) No 883/2004.

Article 33   Nationals of Iceland, Liechtenstein, Norway and Switzerland

1. The provisions of this Title applicable to Union citizens shall apply to nationals of Iceland, the Principality of Liechtenstein, the Kingdom of Norway, and the Swiss Confederation provided that:

(a) Iceland, the Principality of Liechtenstein, the Kingdom of Norway, and the Swiss Confederation, as applicable, have concluded and apply corresponding agreements with the United Kingdom which apply to Union citizens; and

(b) Iceland, the Principality of Liechtenstein, the Kingdom of Norway, and the Swiss Confederation, as applicable, have concluded and apply corresponding agreements with the Union which apply to United Kingdom nationals.

2. Upon notification from the United Kingdom and from the Union of the date of entry into force of the agreements referred to in paragraph 1 of this Article, the Joint Committee established by Article 164 ("Joint Committee") shall set the date from which the provisions of this Title shall apply to the nationals of Iceland, the Principality of Liechtenstein, the Kingdom of Norway, and the Swiss Confederation, as applicable.

Article 34   Administrative cooperation

1. By way of derogation from Articles 7 and 128(1), as of the date of entry into force of this Agreement, the United Kingdom shall have the status of observer in the Administrative Commission. It may, where the items on the agenda relating to this Title concern the United Kingdom, send a representative, to be present in an advisory capacity, to the meetings of the Administrative Commission and to the meetings of the bodies referred to in Articles 73 and 74 of Regulation (EC) No 883/2004 where such items are discussed.

2.   By way of derogation from Article 8, the United Kingdom shall take part in the Electronic Exchange of Social Security Information (EESSI) and bear the related costs.

Article 35   Reimbursement, recovery and offsetting

The provisions of Regulations (EC) No 883/2004 and (EC) No 987/2009 on reimbursement, recovery and offsetting shall continue to apply in relation to events, insofar as they relate to persons not covered by Article 30, that:

(a)   occurred before the end of the transition period; or

(b)   occur after the end of the transition period and relate to persons who were covered by Articles 30 or 32 when the event occurred.

Article 36   Development of law and adaptations of Union acts

1.   Where Regulations (EC) No 883/2004 and (EC) No 987/2009 are amended or replaced after the end of the transition period, references to those Regulations in this Agreement shall be understood as referring to those Regulations as amended or replaced, in accordance with the acts listed in Part II of Annex I to this Agreement.

   The Joint Committee shall revise Part II of Annex I to this Agreement and align it to any act amending or replacing Regulations (EC) No 883/2004 and (EC) No 987/2009 as soon as such act is adopted by the Union. To that end, the Union shall, as soon as possible after adoption, inform the United Kingdom within the Joint Committee of any act amending or replacing those Regulations.

2.   By way of derogation from the second subparagraph of paragraph 1, the Joint Committee shall assess the effects of an act amending or replacing Regulations (EC) No 883/2004 and (EC) No 987/2009 where that act:

   (a)   amends or replaces the matters covered by Article 3 of Regulation (EC) No 883/2004; or

   (b)   makes a cash benefit exportable where that cash benefit was non-exportable under Regulation (EC) No 883/2004 at the end of the transition period, or makes a cash benefit non-exportable, where that cash benefit was exportable at the end of the transition period; or

   (c)   makes a cash benefit exportable for an unlimited period of time, where that cash benefit was exportable only for a limited period of time under Regulation (EC) No 883/2004 at the end of the transition period, or makes a cash benefit exportable only for a limited period of time, where that cash benefit was exportable for an unlimited period of time under that Regulation at the end of the transition period.

   In making its assessment, the Joint Committee shall consider in good faith the scale of the changes referred to in the first subparagraph of this paragraph, as well as the importance of the continued good functioning of Regulations (EC) No 883/2004 and (EC) No 987/2009 between the Union and the United Kingdom and the importance of there being a competent State in relation to individuals within the scope of Regulation (EC) No 883/2004.

   If the Joint Committee so decides within 6 months from receiving the information given by the Union pursuant to paragraph 1, Part II of Annex I to this Agreement shall not be aligned to the act referred to in the first subparagraph of this paragraph.

   For the purposes of this paragraph:

   (a)   "exportable" means payable under Regulation (EC) No 883/2004 to or in relation to a person residing in a Member State or in the United Kingdom if the institution responsible for providing the benefit is not situated there; "non- exportable" shall be interpreted accordingly; and

   (b)   "exportable for an unlimited period of time" means exportable for as long as the conditions giving rise to the entitlements are met.

3.   Regulations (EC) No 883/2004 and (EC) No 987/2009 shall, for the purposes of this Agreement, be understood as comprising the adaptations listed in Part III of Annex I to this Agreement. As soon as possible after the adoption of any changes in domestic provisions of relevance to Part III of Annex I to this Agreement, the United Kingdom shall inform the Union thereof within the Joint Committee.

4.   The Decisions and Recommendations of the Administrative Commission shall, for the purposes of this Agreement, be understood as comprising the decisions and

recommendations listed in Part I of Annex I. The Joint Committee shall amend Part I of Annex I to reflect any new Decision or Recommendation adopted by the Administrative Commission. To that end, as soon as possible after adoption of decisions and recommendations of the Administrative Commission, the Union shall inform the United Kingdom thereof within the Joint Committee. Such amendments shall be made by the Joint Committee on a proposal of the Union or the United Kingdom.

TITLE IV
OTHER PROVISIONS

Article 37   Publicity

The Member States and the United Kingdom shall disseminate information concerning the rights and obligations of persons covered by this Part, in particular by means of awareness-raising campaigns conducted, as appropriate, through national and local media and other means of communication.

Article 38   More favourable provisions

1.   This Part shall not affect any laws, regulations or administrative provisions applicable in a host State or a State of work which would be more favourable to the persons concerned. This paragraph shall not apply to Title III.
2.   Article 12 and Article 23(1) shall be without prejudice to the Common Travel Area arrangements between the United Kingdom and Ireland as regards more favourable treatment which may result from these arrangements for the persons concerned.

Article 39   Life-long protection

The persons covered by this Part shall enjoy the rights provided for in the relevant Titles of this Part for their lifetime, unless they cease to meet the conditions set out in those Titles.

PART THREE
SEPARATION PROVISIONS

TITLE I
GOODS PLACED ON THE MARKET

Article 40   Definitions

For the purposes of this Title, the following definitions shall apply:
(a)   "making available on the market" means any supply of a good for distribution, consumption or use on the market in the course of a commercial activity, whether in return for payment or free of charge;
(b)   "placing on the market" means the first making available of a good on the market in the Union or the United Kingdom;
(c)   "supply of a good for distribution, consumption or use" means that an existing and individually identifiable good, after the stage of manufacturing has taken place, is the subject matter of a written or verbal agreement between two or more legal or natural persons for the transfer of ownership, any other property right, or possession concerning the good in question, or is the subject matter of an offer to a legal or natural person or persons to conclude such an agreement;
(d)   "putting into service" means the first use of a good within the Union or the United Kingdom by the end user for the purposes for which it was intended or, in the case of marine equipment, placing on board;
(e)   "market surveillance" means the activities carried out and measures taken by market surveillance authorities to ensure that goods comply with the applicable requirements and do not endanger health, safety or any other aspect of public interest protection;
(f)   "market surveillance authority" means an authority of a Member State or of the United Kingdom responsible for carrying out market surveillance on its territory;
(g)   "conditions for the marketing of goods" means requirements concerning the characteristics of goods such as levels of quality, performance, safety or dimensions,

including on the composition of such goods or on the terminology, symbols, testing and testing methods, packaging, marking, labelling, and conformity assessment procedures used in relation to such goods; the term also covers requirements concerning production methods and processes, where these have an effect on product characteristics;

(h) "conformity assessment body" means a body that performs conformity assessment activities including calibration, testing, certification and inspection;

(i) "notified body" means a conformity assessment body authorised to carry out third-party conformity assessment tasks under Union law harmonising the conditions for the marketing of goods;

(j) "animal products" means products of animal origin, animal by-products and derived products, as referred to in points (29), (30) and (31) of Article 4 of Regulation (EU) 2016/429 of the European Parliament and of the Council ([18]), respectively, feed of animal origin, and food and feed containing products of animal origin.

Article 41   Continued circulation of goods placed on the market

1. Any good that was lawfully placed on the market in the Union or the United Kingdom before the end of the transition period may:

   (a) be further made available on the market of the Union or of the United Kingdom and circulate between these two markets until it reaches its end-user;

   (b) where provided in the applicable provisions of Union law, be put into service in the Union or in the United Kingdom.

2. The requirements set out in Articles 34 and 35 TFEU and the relevant Union law governing the marketing of goods, including the conditions for the marketing of goods, applicable to the goods concerned shall apply in respect of the goods referred to in paragraph 1.

3. Paragraph 1 shall apply to all existing and individually identifiable goods within the meaning of Title II of Part Three of the TFEU, with the exception of the circulation between the Union market and the United Kingdom's market or vice-versa of:

   (a) live animals and germinal products;

   (b) animal products.

4. In respect of a movement of live animals or of germinal products between a Member State and the United Kingdom, or vice-versa, the provisions of Union law listed in Annex II shall apply, provided that the date of departure was before the end of the transition period.

5. This Article shall be without prejudice to the possibility for the United Kingdom, a Member State or the Union to take measures to prohibit or restrict the making available on its market of a good referred to in paragraph 1, or a category of such goods, where and to the extent permitted by Union law.

6. The provisions of this Title shall be without prejudice to any applicable rules on modalities of sale, intellectual property, customs procedures, tariffs and taxes.

Article 42   Proof of placing on the market

Where an economic operator relies on Article 41(1) with respect to a specific good, that operator shall bear the burden of proof of demonstrating, on the basis of any relevant document, that the good was placed on the market in the Union or the United Kingdom before the end of the transition period.

Article 43   Market surveillance

1. The market surveillance authorities of the Member States and the market surveillance authorities of the United Kingdom shall exchange without delay any relevant information collected with regard to the goods referred to in Article 41(1) in the context of their respective market surveillance activities. They shall, in particular, communicate to each other and to the European Commission any information relating to those goods

---

[18] Regulation (EU) 2016/429 of the European Parliament and of the Council of 9 March 2016 on transmissible animal diseases and amending and repealing certain acts in the area of animal health ("Animal Health Law") (OJ L 84, 31.3.2016, p. 1).

presenting a serious risk, as well as any measures taken in relation to non-compliant goods, including relevant information drawn from networks, information systems and databases established under Union or United Kingdom law in relation to those goods.

2. The Member States and the United Kingdom shall transmit without delay any request from the market surveillance authorities of the United Kingdom or of a Member State, respectively, to a conformity assessment body established in their territory, where that request concerns a conformity assessment carried out by that body in its capacity as notified body before the end of the transition period. Member States and the United Kingdom shall ensure that any such request is promptly addressed by the conformity assessment body.

Article 44 Transfer of files and documents relating to ongoing procedures

The United Kingdom shall transfer without delay to the competent authority of a Member State designated in accordance with the procedures provided for in the applicable Union law all relevant files or documents in relation to assessments, approvals and authorisations ongoing on the day before the date of entry into force of this Agreement and led by a United Kingdom competent authority in accordance with Regulation (EU) No 528/2012 [19], Regulation (EC) No 1107/2009 [20], Directive 2001/83/EC [21] and Directive 2001/82/EC [22] of the European Parliament and of the Council.

Article 45 Making available of information in relation to past authorisation procedures for medicinal products

1. The United Kingdom shall, upon a reasoned request from a Member State or the European Medicines Agency, make available without delay the marketing authorisation dossier of a medicinal product authorised by a competent authority of the United Kingdom before the end of the transition period, where that dossier is necessary for the assessment of a marketing authorisation application in accordance with Articles 10 and 10a of Directive 2001/83/EC or Articles 13 and 13a of Directive 2001/82/EC.

2. A Member State shall, upon a reasoned request from the United Kingdom, make available without delay the marketing authorisation dossier of a medicinal product authorised by a competent authority of that Member State before the end of the transition period, where that dossier is necessary for the assessment of a marketing authorisation application in the United Kingdom in accordance with the United Kingdom's legislative requirements, to the extent that those legislative requirements replicate the circumstances of Articles 10 and 10a of Directive 2001/83/EC or Articles 13 and 13a of Directive 2001/82/EC.

Article 46 Making available of information held by notified bodies established in the United Kingdom or in a Member State

1. The United Kingdom shall ensure that information held by a conformity assessment body established in the United Kingdom in relation to its activities as a notified body under Union law before the end of the transition period is made available at the request of the certificate holder, without delay, to a notified body established in a Member State as indicated by the certificate holder.

2. Member States shall ensure that information held by a notified body established in the Member State concerned in relation to its activities before the end of the transition period is made available at the request of the certificate holder, without delay, to a conformity assessment body established in the United Kingdom as indicated by the certificate holder.

---

[19] Regulation (EU) No 528/2012 of the European Parliament and of the Council of 22 May 2012 concerning the making available on the market and use of biocidal products (OJ L 167, 27.6.2012, p. 1).
[20] Regulation (EC) No 1107/2009 of the European Parliament and of the Council of 21 October 2009 concerning the placing of plant protection products on the market (OJ L 309, 24.11.2009, p. 1).
[21] Directive 2001/83/EC of the European Parliament and of the Council of 6 November 2001 on the Community code relating to medicinal products for human use (OJ L 311, 28.11.2001, p. 67).
[22] Directive 2001/82/EC of the European Parliament and of the Council of 6 November 2001 on the Community code relating to veterinary medicinal products (OJ L 311, 28.11.2001, p. 1).

TITLE II

ONGOING CUSTOMS PROCEDURES

Article 47   Union status of goods

1.   Regulation (EU) No 952/2013 of the European Parliament and of the Council (23) shall apply in respect of Union goods referred to in point (^{23}) of Article 5 of that Regulation, where such goods move from the customs territory of the United Kingdom to the customs territory of the Union, or vice versa, provided that the movement started before the end of the transition period and ended thereafter. A movement of goods which has started before the end of the transition period and ends thereafter shall be treated as an intra-Union movement regarding importation and exportation licencing requirements in Union law.

2.   For the purposes of paragraph 1, the presumption of the customs status of Union goods as referred to in Article 153 (1) of Regulation (EU) No 952/2013 shall not apply. The customs status of those goods as Union goods, as well as the fact that the movement referred to in paragraph 1 started before the end of the transition period, shall need to be proven for every movement by the person concerned by any of the means referred to in Article 199 of Commission Implementing Regulation (EU) 2015/2447 (^{24}). The proof of the start of the movement shall be provided by means of a transport document relating to the goods.

3.   Paragraph 2 shall not apply in respect of Union goods that are carried by air and have been loaded or transhipped at an airport in the customs territory of the United Kingdom for consignment to the customs territory of the Union or have been loaded or transhipped at an airport in the customs territory of the Union for consignment to the customs territory of the United Kingdom, where such goods are carried under cover of a single transport document issued in either of the customs territories concerned, provided that the movement by air started before the end of the transition period and the movement ended thereafter.

4.   Paragraph 2 shall not apply in respect of Union goods that are carried by sea and have been shipped between ports in the customs territory of the United Kingdom and ports in the customs territory of the Union by a regular shipping service, as referred to in Article 120 of Commission Delegated Regulation (EU) 2015/2446 (^{25}), provided that:

    (a)   the voyage comprising the ports in the customs territory of the United Kingdom and ports in the customs territory of the Union started before the end of the transition period and ended thereafter; and

    (b)   the regular shipping service vessel called at one or several ports in the customs territory of the United Kingdom or in the customs territory of the Union before the end of the transition period.

5.   When during the voyage referred to in point (a) of paragraph 4 the regular shipping service vessel calls at one or several ports in the customs territory of the United Kingdom after the end of the transition period:

    (a)   for goods loaded before the end of the transition period and unloaded in those ports, the customs status of Union goods shall not be altered;

    (b)   for goods loaded in ports called after the end of the transition period, the customs status of Union goods shall not be altered provided that it is proven in accordance with paragraph 2.

(^{23}) Regulation (EU) No 952/2013 of the European Parliament and of the Council of 9 October 2013 laying down the Union Customs Code (OJ L 269, 10.10.2013, p. 1).

(^{24}) Commission Implementing Regulation (EU) 2015/2447 of 24 November 2015 laying down detailed rules for implementing certain provisions of Regulation (EU) No 952/2013 of the European Parliament and of the Council laying down the Union Customs Code (OJ L 343, 29.12.2015, p. 558).

(^{25}) Commission Delegated Regulation (EU) 2015/2446 of 28 July 2015 supplementing Regulation (EU) No 952/2013 of the European Parliament and of the Council as regards detailed rules concerning certain provisions of the Union Customs Code (OJ L 343, 29.12.2015, p. 1).

Article 48   Entry summary declaration and pre-departure declaration

1. Regulation (EU) No 952/2013 shall apply in respect of entry summary declarations that were lodged at a customs office of first entry in accordance with Chapter I of Title IV of that Regulation before the end of the transition period, and those declarations shall produce the same legal effects in the customs territory of the Union and the customs territory of the United Kingdom after the end of the transition period.

2. Regulation (EU) No 952/2013 shall apply in respect of pre-departure declarations that were lodged in accordance with Chapter I of Title VIII of that Regulation before the end of the transition period and, where applicable, where the goods were released in accordance with Article 194 of that Regulation before the end of the transition period. Those declarations shall produce the same legal effects in the customs territory of the Union and the customs territory of the United Kingdom after the end of the transition period.

Article 49   Ending of temporary storage or customs procedures

1. Regulation (EU) No 952/2013 shall apply in respect of non-Union goods that were in temporary storage referred to in point (17) of Article 5 of that Regulation at the end of the transition period and in respect of goods that were under any of the customs procedures referred to in point (16) of Article 5 of that Regulation in the customs territory of the United Kingdom at the end of the transition period, until such temporary storage is ended, until one of the special customs procedures is discharged, until the goods are released for free circulation, or until the goods are taken out of the territory, provided that such event occurs after the end of the transition period but not later than within the corresponding time limit referred to in Annex III.

   However, points (b) and (c) of Article 148(5) and Article 219 of Regulation (EU) No 952/2013 shall not apply in respect of movements of goods between the customs territory of the United Kingdom and the customs territory of the Union which end after the end of the transition period.

2. Regulation (EU) No 952/2013, Council Decision 2014/335/EU, Euratom (26), Council Regulation (EU, Euratom) No 608/2014 (27) and Council Regulation (EU, Euratom) No 609/2014 (28) shall apply in respect of any customs debt arising after the end of the transition period from the end of temporary storage or discharge referred to in paragraph 1.

3. Section 1 of Chapter 1 of Title II of Implementing Regulation (EU) 2015/2447 shall apply in respect of requests to benefit from tariff quotas which have been accepted by the customs authorities in the customs territory of the United Kingdom and where the required supporting documents have been provided in accordance with Article 50 of that Regulation by the customs authorities in the customs territory of the United Kingdom before the end of the transition period, and shall apply in respect of the cancellation of requests and returns of unused allocated quantities of such requests.

Article 50   Access to relevant networks, information systems and databases

By way of derogation from Article 8, the United Kingdom shall have access, to the extent strictly necessary to comply with its obligations under this Title, to the networks, information systems and databases listed in Annex IV. The United Kingdom shall reimburse the Union for the actual costs incurred by the Union as a consequence of facilitating that access. The Union shall communicate to the United Kingdom the amount of those costs by 31 March of each year until the end of the period referred to in Annex IV. In the event that the communicated amount of the actual costs incurred considerably diverges from the best estimates amount that was communicated by the Union to the United Kingdom before the signature of this Agreement, the United Kingdom shall pay without delay to the Union

---

(26) Council Decision 2014/335/EU, Euratom of 26 May 2014 on the system of own resources of the European Union (OJ L 168, 7.6.2014, p. 105).

(27) Council Regulation (EU, Euratom) No 608/2014 of 26 May 2014 laying down implementing measures for the system of own resources of the European Union (OJ L 168, 7.6.2014, p. 29).

(28) Council Regulation (EU, Euratom) No 609/2014 of 26 May 2014 on the methods and procedure for making available the traditional, VAT and GNI-based own resources and on the measures to meet cash requirements (OJ L 168, 7.6.2014, p. 39).

the best estimates amount and the Joint Committee shall determine the manner in which the difference between the actual costs incurred and the best estimates amount is to be addressed.

TITLE III

ONGOING VALUE ADDED TAX AND EXCISE DUTY MATTERS

Article 51   Value added tax (VAT)

1. Council Directive 2006/112/EC [29] shall apply in respect of goods dispatched or transported from the territory of the United Kingdom to the territory of a Member State, and vice versa, provided that the dispatch or transport started before the end of the transition period and ended thereafter.
2. Directive 2006/112/EC shall continue to apply until 5 years after the end of the transition period with regard to the taxable person's rights and obligations in relation to transactions with a cross-border element between the United Kingdom and a Member State that took place before the end of the transition period and with regard to transactions covered by paragraph 1.
3. By way of derogation from paragraph 2 and from Article 15 of Council Directive 2008/9/EC [30], refund applications that relate to VAT which was paid in a Member State by a taxable person established in the United Kingdom, or which was paid in the United Kingdom by a taxable person established in a Member State, shall be submitted under the conditions of that Directive at the latest on 31 March 2021.
4. By way of derogation from paragraph 2 and from Article 61(2) of Council Implementing Regulation (EU) No 282/2011 [31], amendments to VAT returns that were submitted in accordance with Article 364 or Article 369f of Directive 2006/112/EC either in the United Kingdom with regard to services supplied in Member States of consumption before the end of the transition period, or in a Member State with regard to services supplied in the United Kingdom before the end of the transition period, shall be submitted at the latest on 31 December 2021.

Article 52   Excise goods

Council Directive 2008/118/EC [32] shall apply in respect of movements of excise goods under a duty suspension arrangement and in respect of movements of excise goods after release for consumption from the territory of the United Kingdom to the territory of a Member State, or vice versa, provided that the movement started before the end of the transition period and ended thereafter.

Article 53   Access to relevant networks, information systems and databases

By way of derogation from Article 8, the United Kingdom shall have access, to the extent strictly necessary to comply with its obligations under this Title, to the networks, information systems and databases listed in Annex IV. The United Kingdom shall reimburse the Union for the actual costs incurred by the Union as a consequence of facilitating that access. The Union shall communicate to the United Kingdom the amount of those costs by 31 March of each year until the end of the period referred to in Annex IV. In the event that the communicated amount of the actual costs incurred considerably diverges from the best estimates amount that was communicated by the Union to the United Kingdom before the signature of this Agreement, the United Kingdom shall pay without delay to the Union the best estimates amount and the Joint Committee shall determine the manner in which the difference between the actual costs incurred and the best estimates amount is to be addressed.

---

[29] Council Directive 2006/112/EC of 28 November 2006 on the common system of value added tax (OJ L 347, 11.12.2006, p. 1).

[30] Council Directive 2008/9/EC of 12 February 2008 laying down detailed rules for the refund of value added tax, provided for in Directive 2006/112/EC, to taxable persons not established in the Member State of refund but established in another Member State (OJ L 44, 20.2.2008, p. 23).

[31] Council Implementing Regulation (EU) No 282/2011 of 15 March 2011 laying down implementing measures for Directive 2006/112/EC on the common system of value added tax (OJ L 77, 23.3.2011, p. 1).

[32] Council Directive 2008/118/EC of 16 December 2008 concerning the general arrangements for excise duty and repealing Directive 92/12/EEC (OJ L 9, 14.1.2009, p. 12).

TITLE IV
INTELLECTUAL PROPERTY

Article 54   Continued protection in the United Kingdom of registered or granted rights

1. The holder of any of the following intellectual property rights which have been registered or granted before the end of the transition period shall, without any re-examination, become the holder of a comparable registered and enforceable intellectual property right in the United Kingdom under the law of the United Kingdom:

    (a) the holder of a European Union trade mark registered in accordance with Regulation (EU) 2017/1001 of the European Parliament and of the Council [33] shall become the holder of a trade mark in the United Kingdom, consisting of the same sign, for the same goods or services;

    (b) the holder of a Community design registered and, where applicable, published following a deferral of publication in accordance with Council Regulation (EC) No 6/2002 [34] shall become the holder of a registered design right in the United Kingdom for the same design;

    (c) the holder of a Community plant variety right granted pursuant to Council Regulation (EC) No 2100/94 [35] shall become the holder of a plant variety right in the United Kingdom for the same plant variety.

2. Where a geographical indication, designation of origin or traditional speciality guaranteed within the meaning of Regulation (EU) No 1151/2012 of the European Parliament and of the Council [36], a geographical indication, designation of origin or traditional term for wine within the meaning of Regulation (EU) No 1308/2013 of the European Parliament and of the Council [37], a geographical indication within the meaning of Regulation (EC) No 110/2008 of the European Parliament and of the Council [38] or a geographical indication within the meaning of Regulation (EU) No 251/2014 of the European Parliament and of the Council [39], is protected in the Union on the last day of the transition period by virtue of those Regulations, those persons who are entitled to use the geographical indication, the designation of origin, the traditional speciality guaranteed or the traditional term for wine concerned shall be entitled, as from the end of the transition period, without any re-examination, to use the geographical indication, the designation of origin, the traditional speciality guaranteed or the traditional term for wine concerned in the United Kingdom, which shall be granted at least the same level of protection under the law of the United Kingdom as under the following provisions of Union law:

    (a) points (i), (j) and (k) of Article 4(1) of Directive (EU) 2015/2436 of the European Parliament and of the Council [40]; and

    (b) in view of the geographical indication, designation of origin, traditional speciality guaranteed or traditional term for wine concerned, Article 13, Article 14(1), Article 24, Article 36(3), Articles 38 and 44 and point (b) of Article 45(1) of

---

[33] Regulation (EU) 2017/1001 of the European Parliament and of the Council of 14 June 2017 on the European Union trade mark (OJ L 154, 16.6.2017, p. 1).

[34] Council Regulation (EC) No 6/2002 of 12 December 2001 on Community designs (OJ L 3, 5.1.2002, p. 1).

[35] Council Regulation (EC) No 2100/94 of 27 July 1994 on Community plant variety rights (OJ L 227, 1.9.1994, p. 1).

[36] Regulation (EU) No 1151/2012 of the European Parliament and of the Council of 21 November 2012 on quality schemes for agricultural products and foodstuffs (OJ L 343, 14.12.2012, p. 1).

[37] Regulation (EU) No 1308/2013 of the European Parliament and of the Council of 17 December 2013 establishing a common organisation of the markets in agricultural products and repealing Council Regulations (EEC) No 922/72, (EEC) No 234/79, (EC) No 1037/2001 and (EC) No 1234/2007 (OJ L 347, 20.12.2013, p. 671).

[38] Regulation (EC) No 110/2008 of the European Parliament and of the Council of 15 January 2008 on the definition, description, presentation, labelling and the protection of geographical indications of spirit drinks and repealing Council Regulation (EEC) No 1576/89 (OJ L 39, 13.2.2008, p. 16).

[39] Regulation (EU) No 251/2014 of the European Parliament and of the Council of 26 February 2014 on the definition, description, presentation, labelling and the protection of geographical indications of aromatised wine products and repealing Council Regulation (EEC) No 1601/91 (OJ L 84, 20.3.2014, p. 14).

[40] Directive (EU) 2015/2436 of the European Parliament and of the Council of 16 December 2015 to approximate the laws of the Member States relating to trade marks (OJ L 336, 23.12.2015, p. 1).

Regulation (EU) No 1151/2012; Article 90(1) of Regulation (EU) No 1306/2013 of the European Parliament and of the Council ([41]); Article 100(3), Article 102(1), Articles 103 and 113, and point (c)(x) of Article 157(1) of Regulation (EU) No 1308/2013; Article 62(3) and (4) of Commission Regulation (EC) No 607/2009 ([42]); the first subparagraph of Article 15(3), Article 16 and Article 23(1) of Regulation (EC) No 110/2008 and, insofar as to the extent related to compliance with those provisions of that Regulation, Article 24(1) of that Regulation; or Article 19(1) and Article 20 of Regulation (EU) No 251/2014.

Where a geographical indication, designation of origin, traditional speciality guaranteed or traditional term for wine referred to in the first subparagraph ceases to be protected in the Union after the end of the transition period, the first subparagraph shall cease to apply in respect of that geographical indication, designation of origin, traditional speciality guaranteed or traditional term for wine. The first subparagraph shall not apply where protection in the Union is derived from international agreements to which the Union is a party.

This paragraph shall apply unless and until an agreement as referred to in Article 184 that supersedes this paragraph enters into force or becomes applicable.

3. Notwithstanding paragraph 1, if an intellectual property right referred to in that paragraph is declared invalid or revoked, or, in the case of a Community plant variety right, is declared null and void or is cancelled, in the Union as the result of an administrative or judicial procedure which was ongoing on the last day of the transition period, the corresponding right in the United Kingdom shall also be declared invalid or revoked, or declared null and void, or be cancelled. The date of effect of the declaration or revocation or cancellation in the United Kingdom shall be the same as in the Union.

By way of derogation from the first subparagraph, the United Kingdom shall not be obliged to declare invalid or to revoke the corresponding right in the United Kingdom where the grounds for the invalidity or revocation of the European Union trade mark or registered Community design do not apply in the United Kingdom.

4. A trade mark or registered design right which arises in the United Kingdom in accordance with point (a) or (b) of paragraph 1 shall have as its first renewal date the renewal date of the corresponding intellectual property right registered in accordance with Union law.

5. In respect of trade marks in the United Kingdom referred to in point (a) of paragraph 1 of this Article, the following shall apply:

(a) the trade mark shall enjoy the date of filing or the date of priority of the European Union trade mark and, where appropriate, the seniority of a trade mark of the United Kingdom claimed under Article 39 or 40 of Regulation (EU) 2017/1001;

(b) the trade mark shall not be liable to revocation on the ground that the corresponding European Union trade mark had not been put into genuine use in the territory of the United Kingdom before the end of the transition period;

(c) the owner of a European Union trade mark that has acquired a reputation in the Union shall be entitled to exercise in the United Kingdom rights equivalent to those provided for in point (c) of Article 9(2) of Regulation (EU) 2017/1001 and point (a) of Article 5(3) of Directive (EU) 2015/2436 in respect of the corresponding trade mark on the basis of the reputation acquired in the Union by the end of the transition period and thereafter the continuing reputation of that trade mark shall be based on the use of the mark in the United Kingdom.

6. In respect of registered design rights and plant variety rights in the United Kingdom referred to in points (b) and (c) of paragraph 1, the following shall apply:

(a) the term of protection under the law of the United Kingdom shall be at least equal to the remaining period of protection under Union law of the corresponding registered Community design or Community plant variety right;

(b) the date of filing or date of priority shall be that of the corresponding registered Community design or Community plant variety right.

---

[41] Regulation (EU) No 1306/2013 of the European Parliament and of the Council of 17 December 2013 on the financing, management and monitoring of the common agricultural policy (OJ L 347, 20.12.2013, p. 549).

[42] Commission Regulation (EC) No 607/2009 of 14 July 2009 laying down certain detailed rules for the implementation of Council Regulation (EC) No 479/2008 as regards protected designations of origin and geographical indications, traditional terms, labelling and presentation of certain wine sector products (OJ L 193 24.7.2009, p. 60).

Article 55   Registration procedure

1.   The registration, grant or protection pursuant to Article 54(1) and (2) of this Agreement shall be carried out free of charge by the relevant entities in the United Kingdom, using the data available in the registries of the European Union Intellectual Property Office, the Community Plant Variety Office and the European Commission. Annex III to Regulation (EC) No 110/2008 shall be considered a registry for the purpose of this Article.

2.   For the purposes of paragraph 1, holders of the intellectual property rights referred to in Article 54(1) and those persons who are entitled to use a geographical indication, designation of origin, traditional speciality guaranteed or traditional term for wine referred to in Article 54(2) shall not be required to introduce an application or to undertake any particular administrative procedure. Holders of intellectual property rights referred to in Article 54(1) shall not be required to have a correspondence address in the United Kingdom in the 3 years following the end of the transition period.

3.   The European Union Intellectual Property Office, the Community Plant Variety Office and the European Commission shall provide to the relevant entities in the United Kingdom the information necessary for the registration, grant or protection in the United Kingdom pursuant to Article 54(1) or (2).

4.   This Article shall be without prejudice to renewal fees that may apply at the time of renewal of the rights, or the possibility for the holders concerned to surrender their intellectual property rights in the United Kingdom in accordance with the relevant procedure under the law of the United Kingdom.

Article 56   Continued protection in the United Kingdom of international registrations designating the Union

The United Kingdom shall take measures to ensure that natural or legal persons who have obtained protection before the end of the transition period for internationally registered trade marks or designs designating the Union pursuant to the Madrid system for the international registration of marks, or pursuant to the Hague system for the international deposit of industrial designs, enjoy protection in the United Kingdom for their trade marks or industrial designs in respect of those international registrations.

Article 57   Continued protection in the United Kingdom of unregistered Community designs

The holder of a right in relation to an unregistered Community design which arose before the end of the transition period in accordance with Regulation (EC) No 6/2002 shall in relation to that unregistered Community design ipso iure become the holder of an enforceable intellectual property right in the United Kingdom, under the law of the United Kingdom, that affords the same level of protection as that provided for in Regulation (EC) No 6/2002. The term of protection of that right under the law of the United Kingdom shall be at least equal to the remaining period of protection of the corresponding unregistered Community design under Article 11(1) of that Regulation.

Article 58   Continued protection of databases

1.   The holder of a right in relation to a database in respect of the United Kingdom in accordance with Article 7 of Directive 96/9/EC of the European Parliament and of the Council (⁴³) which arose before the end of the transition period shall, in relation to that database, maintain an enforceable intellectual property right in the United Kingdom, under the law of the United Kingdom, that affords the same level of protection as that provided for in Directive 96/9/EC, provided that the holder of that right continues to comply with the requirements of Article 11 of that Directive. The term of protection of that right under the law of the United Kingdom shall be at least equal to the remaining period of protection under Article 10 of Directive 96/9/EC.

2.   The following persons and undertakings shall be deemed to comply with the requirements of Article 11 of Directive 96/9/EC:

(⁴³) Directive 96/9/EC of the European Parliament and of the Council of 11 March 1996 on the legal protection of databases (OJ L 77, 27.3.1996, p. 20).

(a) United Kingdom nationals;
(b) natural persons with a habitual residence in the United Kingdom;
(c) undertakings established in the United Kingdom, provided that where such an undertaking has only its registered office in the United Kingdom, its operations are genuinely linked on an ongoing basis with the economy of the United Kingdom or of a Member State.

Article 59 Right of priority with respect to pending applications for European Union trade marks, Community designs and Community plant variety rights

1. Where a person has filed an application for a European Union trade mark or a Community design in accordance with Union law before the end of the transition period and where that application was accorded a date of filing, that person shall have, for the same trade mark in respect of goods or services which are identical with or contained within those for which the application has been filed in the Union or for the same design, the right to file an application in the United Kingdom within 9 months from the end of the transition period. An application made pursuant to this Article shall be deemed to have the same filing date and date of priority as the corresponding application filed in the Union and, where appropriate, the seniority of a trade mark of the United Kingdom claimed under Article 39 or 40 of Regulation (EU) 2017/1001.

2. Where a person has filed an application for a Community plant variety right in accordance with Union law before the end of the transition period, that person shall have, for the purpose of filing an application for the same plant variety right in the United Kingdom, an ad hoc right of priority in the United Kingdom during a period of 6 months from the end of the transition period. The right of priority shall cause the date of priority of the application for the Community plant variety right to be deemed to be the date of application for a plant variety right in the United Kingdom for the purpose of determining distinctness, novelty and entitlement to the right.

Article 60 Pending applications for supplementary protection certificates in the United Kingdom

1. Regulations (EC) No 1610/96 ([44]) and No 469/2009 ([45]) of the European Parliament and of the Council, respectively, shall apply in respect of applications for supplementary protection certificates for plant protection products and for medicinal products, as well as to applications for the extension of the duration of such certificates, where such applications were submitted to an authority in the United Kingdom before the end of the transition period in cases where the administrative procedure for the grant of the certificate concerned or of the extension of its duration was ongoing at the end of the transition period.

2. Any certificate granted pursuant to paragraph 1 shall provide for the same level of protection as that provided for in Regulation (EC) No 1610/96 or Regulation (EC) No 469/2009.

Article 61 Exhaustion of rights

Intellectual property rights which were exhausted both in the Union and in the United Kingdom before the end of the transition period under the conditions provided for by Union law shall remain exhausted both in the Union and in the United Kingdom.

TITLE V
ONGOING POLICE AND JUDICIAL COOPERATION IN CRIMINAL MATTERS

Article 62 Ongoing judicial cooperation proceedings in criminal matters

1. In the United Kingdom, as well as in the Member States in situations involving the United Kingdom, the following acts shall apply as follows:

---

[44] Regulation (EC) No 1610/96 of the European Parliament and of the Council of 23 July 1996 concerning the creation of a supplementary protection certificate for plant protection products (OJ L 198, 8.8.1996, p. 30).
[45] Regulation (EC) No 469/2009 of the European Parliament and of the Council of 6 May 2009 concerning the supplementary protection certificate for medicinal products (OJ L 152, 16.6.2009, p. 1).

(a)   the Convention, established by the Council in accordance with Article 34 of the Treaty on European Union on Mutual Assistance in Criminal Matters between the Member States of the European Union ([46]), and the Protocol established by the Council in accordance with Article 34 of the Treaty on European Union to the Convention on Mutual Assistance in Criminal Matters between the Member States of the European Union ([47]), shall apply in respect of mutual legal assistance requests received under the respective instrument before the end of the transition period by the central authority or judicial authority;

(b)   Council Framework Decision 2002/584/JHA ([48]) shall apply in respect of European arrest warrants where the requested person was arrested before the end of the transition period for the purposes of the execution of a European arrest warrant, irrespective of the decision of the executing judicial authority as to whether the requested person is to remain in detention or be provisionally released;

(c)   Council Framework Decision 2003/577/JHA ([49]) shall apply in respect of freezing orders received before the end of the transition period by the central authority or the competent judicial authority for execution, or by a judicial authority in the executing State with no jurisdiction to recognise or execute a freezing order, but which transmits the freezing order ex officio to the competent judicial authority for execution;

(d)   Council Framework Decision 2005/214/JHA ([50]) shall apply in respect of decisions received before the end of the transition period by the central authority or the competent authority in the executing State, or by an authority of the executing State with no jurisdiction to recognise or execute a decision, but which transmits the decision ex officio to the competent authority for execution;

(e)   Council Framework Decision 2006/783/JHA ([51]) shall apply in respect of confiscation orders received before the end of the transition period by the central authority or the competent authority of the executing State, or by an authority in the executing State with no jurisdiction to recognise or execute a confiscation order, but which transmits the confiscation order ex officio to the competent authority for execution;

(f)   Council Framework Decision 2008/909/JHA ([52]) shall apply:

    (i)   in respect of judgments received before the end of the transition period by the competent authority of the executing State, or by an authority of the executing State with no competence to recognise and enforce a judgment, but which transmits the judgment *ex officio* to the competent authority for execution;

    (ii)   for the purposes of Article 4(6) or Article 5(3) of Framework Decision 2002/584/JHA, where that Framework Decision is applicable by virtue of point (b) of this paragraph;

(g)   Council Framework Decision 2008/675/JHA ([53]) shall apply in respect of new criminal proceedings within the meaning of Article 3 of that Framework Decision that are initiated before the end of the transition period;

[46] OJ C 197, 12.7.2000, p. 3.

[47] OJ C 326, 21.11.2001, p. 2.

[48] Council Framework Decision 2002/584/JHA of 13 June 2002 on the European arrest warrant and the surrender procedures between Member States (OJ L 190, 18.7.2002, p. 1).

[49] Council Framework Decision 2003/577/JHA of 22 July 2003 on the execution in the European Union of orders freezing property or evidence (OJ L 196, 2.8.2003, p. 45).

[50] Council Framework Decision 2005/214/JHA of 24 February 2005 on the application of the principle of mutual recognition to financial penalties (OJ L 76, 22.3.2005, p. 16).

[51] Council Framework Decision 2006/783/JHA of 7 October 2006 on the application of the principle of mutual recognition to confiscation orders (OJ L 328, 24.11.2006, p. 54).

[52] Council Framework Decision 2008/909/JHA of 27 November 2008 on the application of the principle of mutual recognition to judgments in criminal matters imposing custodial sentences or measures involving deprivation of liberty for the purpose of their enforcement in the European Union (OJ L 327, 5.12.2008, p. 27).

[53] Council Framework Decision 2008/675/JHA of 24 July 2008 on taking account of convictions in the Member States of the European Union in the course of new criminal proceedings (OJ L 220, 15.8.2008, p. 32).

(h)　Council Framework Decision 2009/315/JHA ([54]) shall apply in respect of requests for information on conviction received before the end of the transition period by the central authority; however, after the end of the transition period, replies to such requests shall not be transmitted through the European Criminal Records Information System established pursuant to the Council Decision 2009/316/JHA ([55]);

(i)　Council Framework Decision 2009/829/JHA ([56]) shall apply in respect of decisions on supervision measures received before the end of the transition period by the central authority or the competent authority in the executing State, or by an authority of the executing State with no competence to recognise a decision, but which forwards it *ex officio* to the competent authority for execution;

(j)　Article 10(3) of Directive 2011/93/EU of the European Parliament and the Council ([57]) shall apply in respect of requests for information received before the end of the transition period by the central authority; however, after the end of the transition period, replies to such requests shall not be transmitted through the European Criminal Records Information System established pursuant to Decision 2009/316/JHA;

(k)　Directive 2011/99/EU of the European Parliament and of the Council ([58]) shall apply in respect of European protection orders received before the end of the transition period by the central authority or the competent authority of the executing State, or by an authority of the executing State with no competence to recognise a European protection order, but which forwards it *ex officio* to the competent authority for execution;

(l)　Directive 2014/41/EU of the European Parliament and of the Council ([59]) shall apply in respect of European Investigation Orders received before the end of the transition period by the central authority or the executing authority, or by an authority in the executing State with no competence to recognise or execute a European Investigation Order which forwards it *ex officio* to the executing authority for execution.

2.　The competent authorities of the United Kingdom may continue to participate in the joint investigation teams in which they were participating before the end of the transition period, where those investigation teams were set up either in accordance with Article 13 of the Convention established by the Council in accordance with Article 34 of the Treaty on European Union, on Mutual Assistance in Criminal Matters between the Member States of the European Union or in accordance with Council Framework Decision 2002/465/JHA ([60]).

By way of derogation from Article 8 of this Agreement, the United Kingdom shall be entitled to use, for no longer than one year after the end of the transition period, the Secure Information Exchange Network Application (SIENA) to the extent strictly necessary for the purpose of exchanging information within the joint investigation teams referred to in the first subparagraph of this paragraph. The United Kingdom shall reimburse the Union for the actual costs incurred by the Union as a consequence of facilitating the United Kingdom's use of SIENA. The Union shall communicate the

---

[54]　Council Framework Decision 2009/315/JHA of 26 February 2009 on the organisation and content of the exchange of information extracted from the criminal record between Member States (OJ L 93, 7.4.2009, p. 23).

[55]　Council Decision 2009/316/JHA of 6 April 2009 on the establishment of the European Criminal Records Information System (ECRIS) in application of Article 11 of Framework Decision 2009/315/JHA (OJ L 93, 7.4.2009, p. 33).

[56]　Council Framework Decision 2009/829/JHA of 23 October 2009 on the application, between Member States of the European Union, of the principle of mutual recognition to decisions on supervision measures as an alternative to provisional detention (OJ L 294, 11.11.2009, p. 20).

[57]　Directive 2011/93/EU of the European Parliament and the Council of 13 December 2011 on combatting the sexual abuse and sexual exploitation of children and child pornography, and replacing Council Framework Decision 2004/68/JHA (OJ L 335, 17.12.2011, p. 1).

[58]　Directive 2011/99/EU of the European Parliament and of the Council of 13 December 2011 on the European protection order (OJ L 338, 21.12.2011, p. 2).

[59]　Directive 2014/41/EU of the European Parliament and of the Council of 3 April 2014 regarding the European Investigation Order in criminal matters (OJ L 130, 1.5.2014, p. 1).

[60]　Council Framework Decision 2002/465/JHA of 13 June 2002 on joint investigation teams (OJ L 162, 20.6.2002, p. 1).

amount of those costs to the United Kingdom by 31 March 2021. In the event that the communicated amount of the actual costs incurred considerably diverges from the best estimates amount that was communicated by the Union to the United Kingdom before the signature of this Agreement, the United Kingdom shall pay without delay to the Union the best estimates amount and the Joint Committee shall determine the manner in which the difference between the actual costs incurred and the best estimates amount is to be addressed.

3.   Eurojust may, upon a request by the United Kingdom, subject to compliance with point (a) of Article 26a(7) and Article 27 of Council Decision 2002/187/JHA ([61]), provide information, including personal data, from its Case Management system, if necessary to complete the ongoing procedures referred to in points (a), (b) (c), (e) and (l) of paragraph 1 of this Article or the activities of the joint investigation teams referred to in paragraph 2 of this Article. The United Kingdom's competent authorities may, upon request, provide Eurojust with information in their possession if necessary to complete the ongoing procedures referred to in points (a), (b), (c), (e) and (l) of paragraph 1 of this Article or the activities of the joint investigation teams referred to in paragraph 2 of this Article. Where expenses of any extraordinary nature arise out of the application of this paragraph, the Joint Committee shall determine the manner in which such expenses are to be addressed.

Article 63 Ongoing law enforcement cooperation proceedings, police cooperation and exchange of information

1.   In the United Kingdom, as well as in the Member States in situations involving the United Kingdom, the following acts shall apply as follows:

(a)   Articles 39 and 40 of the Convention implementing the Schengen Agreement of 14 June 1985 ("Schengen Implementing Convention") ([62]), in conjunction with Articles 42 and 43 thereof, shall apply in respect of:

(i)   requests in accordance with Article 39 of the Schengen Implementing Convention that are received before the end of the transition period by the central body responsible in the Contracting Party for international police cooperation or by competent authorities of the requested Party, or by requested police authorities which do not have the power to deal with the request, but which forward the request to the competent authorities;

(ii)   requests for assistance in accordance with Article 40(1) of the Schengen Implementing Convention that are received before the end of the transition period by an authority designated by a Contracting Party;

(iii) cross-border surveillance that is carried out without prior authorisation in accordance with Article 40(2) of the Schengen Implementing Convention, where that surveillance started before the end of the transition period;

(b)   the Convention drawn up on the basis of Article K.3 of the Treaty on European Union, on mutual assistance and cooperation between customs administrations ([63]) shall apply in respect of:

(i)   requests for information that are received before the end of the transition period by the requested authority;

(ii)   requests for surveillance that are received before the end of the transition period by the requested authority;

(iii) requests for enquiries that are received before the end of the transition period by the requested authority;

(iv)   requests for notification that are received before the end of the transition period by the requested authority;

(v)   requests for authorisation of cross-border surveillance or for entrusting observation to the officers of the Member State in whose territory

---

[61] Council Decision 2002/187/JHA of 28 February 2002 setting up Eurojust with a view to reinforcing the fight against serious crime (OJ L 63, 6.3.2002, p. 1).

[62] Convention implementing the Schengen Agreement of 14 June 1985 between the Governments of the States of the Benelux Economic Union, the Federal Republic of Germany and the French Republic on the gradual abolition of checks at their common borders (OJ L 239, 22.9.2000, p. 19).

[63] OJ C 24, 23.1.1998, p. 2.

observation is carried out that are received before the end of the transition period by an authority designated by the requested Member State that is empowered to grant the requested authorisation or to pass on the request;

(vi)   cross-border surveillance that is carried out without prior authorisation in accordance with Article 40(2) of the Schengen Implementing Convention, where that surveillance started before the end of the transition period;

(vii)   requests to carry out controlled delivery that are received before the end of the transition period by the requested authority;

(viii) requests to authorise covert investigations that are received before the end of the transition period by the requested authority;

(ix)   joint special investigation teams that are set up pursuant to Article 24 of that Convention before the end of the transition period;

(c)   Council Decision 2000/642/JHA ([64]) shall apply in respect of requests that are received before the end of the transition period by the requested Financial Intelligence Unit;

(d)   Council Framework Decision 2006/960/JHA ([65]) shall apply in respect of requests that are received before the end of the transition period by the requested competent law enforcement authority;

(e)   Council Decision 2007/533/JHA ([66]) shall apply in respect of the exchange of supplementary information where there was a hit before the end of the transition period on an alert issued in the Schengen Information System, provided its provisions apply to the United Kingdom on the last day of the transition period. By way of derogation from Article 8 of this Agreement, the United Kingdom shall be entitled to use, for no longer than 3 months after the end of the transition period, the Communication Infrastructure as referred to in Article 8(1) of Decision 2007/533/JHA to the extent strictly necessary for the purpose of exchanging such supplementary information. The United Kingdom shall reimburse the Union for the actual costs incurred by the Union as a consequence of facilitating the United Kingdom's use of the Communication Infrastructure. The Union shall communicate to the United Kingdom the amount of those costs by 31 March 2021. In the event that the communicated amount of the actual costs incurred considerably diverges from the best estimates amount that was communicated by the Union to the United Kingdom before the signature of this Agreement, the United Kingdom shall pay without delay to the Union the best estimates amount and the Joint Committee shall determine the manner in which the difference between the actual costs incurred and the best estimates amount is to be addressed;

(f)   Council Decision 2007/845/JHA ([67]) shall apply in respect of requests received before the end of the transition period by an Asset Recovery Office;

(g)   Directive (EU) 2016/681 of the European Parliament and of the Council ([68]) shall apply in respect of requests received by the passenger information unit in accordance with Articles 9 and 10 of that Directive before the end of the transition period.

2.   By way of derogation from Article 8, the United Kingdom shall be entitled to use, for no longer than one year after the end of the transition period, the Secure Information Exchange Network Application (SIENA) to the extent strictly necessary to complete

---

[64] Council Decision 2000/642/JHA of 17 October 2000 concerning arrangements for cooperation between financial intelligence units of the Member States in respect of exchanging information (OJ L 271, 24.10.2000, p. 4).

[65] Council Framework Decision 2006/960/JHA of 18 December 2006 on simplifying the exchange of information and intelligence between law enforcement authorities of the Member States of the European Union (OJ L 386, 29.12.2006, p. 89).

[66] Council Decision 2007/533/JHA of 12 June 2007 on the establishment, operation and use of the second generation Schengen Information System (SIS II) (OJ L 205, 7.8.2007, p. 63).

[67] Council Decision 2007/845/JHA of 6 December 2007 concerning cooperation between Asset Recovery Offices of the Member States in the field of tracing and identification of proceeds from, or other property related to, crime (OJ L 332, 18.12.2007, p. 103).

[68] Directive (EU) 2016/681 of the European Parliament and of the Council of 27 April 2016 on the use of passenger name record (PNR) data for the prevention, detection, investigation and prosecution of terrorist offences and serious crime (OJ L 119, 4.5.2016, p. 132).

the ongoing procedures referred to in points (c), (d), (f) and (g) of paragraph 1 of this Article. The United Kingdom shall reimburse the Union for the actual costs incurred by the Union as a consequence of facilitating the United Kingdom's use of SIENA. The Union shall communicate to the United Kingdom the amount of those costs by 31 March 2021. In the event that the communicated amount of the actual costs incurred considerably diverges from the best estimates amount that was communicated by the Union to the United Kingdom before the signature of this Agreement, the United Kingdom shall pay without delay to the Union the best estimates amount and the Joint Committee shall determine the manner in which the difference between the actual costs incurred and the best estimates amount is to be addressed.

Article 64   Confirmation of receipt or arrest

1. The competent issuing or requesting authority may request an acknowledgement of the receipt of a judicial decision or request referred to in points (a), (c) to (e), (f)(i) and (h) to (l) of Article 62(1) and points (a)(i) and (ii), points (b)(i) to (v) and (vii), (viii) and (ix), and points (c), (d), (f) and (g) of Article 63(1) within 10 days after the end of the transition period where it has doubts as to whether such a judicial decision or request was received by the executing or requested authority before the end of the transition period.
2. In the cases referred to in point (b) of Article 62(1), where the competent issuing judicial authority has doubts as to whether the requested person was arrested pursuant to Article 11 of Framework Decision 2002/584/JHA before the end of the transition period, it may request from the competent executing judicial authority a confirmation of the arrest within 10 days after the end of the transition period.
3. Unless confirmation has already been provided pursuant to the applicable provisions of Union law, the executing or requested authority referred to in paragraphs 1 and 2 shall reply to a request for confirmation of receipt or arrest within 10 days after receiving the request.

Article 65   Other applicable Union acts

Directive 2010/64/EU of the European Parliament and of the Council ([69]) and Directive 2012/13/EU of the European Parliament and of the Council ([70]) shall apply in respect of the proceedings referred to in point (b) of Article 62(1) of this Agreement.

TITLE VI
ONGOING JUDICIAL COOPERATION IN CIVIL AND COMMERCIAL MATTERS

Article 66   Applicable law in contractual and non-contractual matters

In the United Kingdom, the following acts shall apply as follows:
(a) Regulation (EC) No 593/2008 of the European Parliament and of the Council ([71]) shall apply in respect of contracts concluded before the end of the transition period;
(b) Regulation (EC) No 864/2007 of the European Parliament and of the Council ([72]) shall apply in respect of events giving rise to damage, where such events occurred before the end of the transition period.

Article 67   Jurisdiction, recognition and enforcement of judicial decisions, and related cooperation between central authorities

1. In the United Kingdom, as well as in the Member States in situations involving the United Kingdom, in respect of legal proceedings instituted before the end of the transition period and in respect of proceedings or actions that are related to such legal proceedings pursuant to Articles 29, 30 and 31 of Regulation (EU) No 1215/2012 of the

---

[69] Directive 2010/64/EU of the European Parliament and of the Council of 20 October 2010 on the right to interpretation and translation in criminal proceedings (OJ L 280, 26.10.2010, p. 1).
[70] Directive 2012/13/EU of the European Parliament and of the Council of 22 May 2012 on the right to information in criminal proceedings (OJ L 142, 1.6.2012, p. 1).
[71] Regulation (EC) No 593/2008 of the European Parliament and of the Council of 17 June 2008 on the law applicable to contractual obligations (Rome I) (OJ L 177, 4.7.2008, p. 6).
[72] Regulation (EC) No 864/2007 of the European Parliament and of the Council of 11 July 2007 on the law applicable to non- contractual obligations (Rome II) (OJ L 199, 31.7.2007, p. 40).

European Parliament and of the Council ([73]), Article 19 of Regulation (EC) No 2201/2003 or Articles 12 and 13 of Council Regulation (EC) No 4/2009 ([74]), the following acts or provisions shall apply:

(a)   the provisions regarding jurisdiction of Regulation (EU) No 1215/2012;

(b)   the provisions regarding jurisdiction of Regulation (EU) 2017/1001, of Regulation (EC) No 6/2002, of Regulation (EC) No 2100/94, of Regulation (EU) 2016/679 of the European Parliament and of the Council ([75]) and of Directive 96/71/ EC of the European Parliament and of the Council ([76]);

(c)   the provisions of Regulation (EC) No 2201/2003 regarding jurisdiction;

(d)   the provisions of Regulation (EC) No 4/2009 regarding jurisdiction.

2.   In the United Kingdom, as well as in the Member States in situations involving the United Kingdom, the following acts or provisions shall apply as follows in respect of the recognition and enforcement of judgments, decisions, authentic instruments, court settlements and agreements:

(a)   Regulation (EU) No 1215/2012 shall apply to the recognition and enforcement of judgments given in legal proceedings instituted before the end of the transition period, and to authentic instruments formally drawn up or registered and court settlements approved or concluded before the end of the transition period;

(b)   the provisions of Regulation (EC) No 2201/2003 regarding recognition and enforcement shall apply to judgments given in legal proceedings instituted before the end of the transition period, and to documents formally drawn up or registered as authentic instruments, and agreements concluded before the end of the transition period;

(c)   the provisions of Regulation (EC) No 4/2009 regarding recognition and enforcement shall apply to decisions given in legal proceedings instituted before the end of the transition period, and to court settlements approved or concluded, and authentic instruments established before the end of the transition period;

(d)   Regulation (EC) No 805/2004 of the European Parliament and of the Council ([77]) shall apply to judgments given in legal proceedings instituted before the end of the transition period, and to court settlements approved or concluded and authentic instruments drawn up before the end of the transition period, provided that the certification as a European Enforcement Order was applied for before the end of the transition period.

3.   In the United Kingdom, as well as in the Member States in situations involving the United Kingdom, the following provisions shall apply as follows:

(a)   Chapter IV of Regulation (EC) No 2201/2003 shall apply to requests and applications received by the central authority or other competent authority of the requested State before the end of the transition period;

(b)   Chapter VII of Regulation (EC) No 4/2009 shall apply to applications for recognition or enforcement as referred to in point (c) of paragraph 2 of this Article and requests received by the central authority of the requested State before the end of the transition period;

(c)   Regulation (EU) 2015/848 of the European Parliament and of the Council ([78]) shall apply to insolvency proceedings, and actions referred to in Article 6(1) of that Regulation, provided that the main proceedings were opened before the end of the transition period;

---

[73] Regulation (EU) No 1215/2012 of the European Parliament and of the Council of 12 December 2012 on jurisdiction and the recognition and enforcement of judgments in civil and commercial matters (OJ L 351, 20.12.2012, p. 1).

[74] Council Regulation (EC) No 4/2009 of 18 December 2008 on jurisdiction, applicable law, recognition and enforcement of decisions and cooperation in matters relating to maintenance obligations (OJ L 7, 10.1.2009, p. 1).

[75] Regulation (EU) 2016/679 of the European Parliament and of the Council of 27 April 2016 on the protection of natural persons with regard to the processing of personal data and on the free movement of such data, and repealing Directive 95/46/EC (General Data Protection Regulation) (OJ L 119, 4.5.2016, p. 1).

[76] Directive 96/71/EC of the European Parliament and of the Council of 16 December 1996 concerning the posting of workers in the framework of the provision of services (OJ L 18, 21.1.1997, p. 1).

[77] Regulation (EC) No 805/2004 of the European Parliament and of the Council of 21 April 2004 creating a European Enforcement Order for uncontested claims (OJ L 143, 30.4.2004, p. 15).

[78] Regulation (EU) 2015/848 of the European Parliament and of the Council of 20 May 2015 on insolvency proceedings (OJ L 141, 5.6.2015, p. 19).

(d) Regulation (EC) No 1896/2006 of the European Parliament and of the Council ([79]) shall apply to European payment orders applied for before the end of the transition period; where, following such an application, the proceedings are transferred according to Article 17(1) of that Regulation, the proceedings shall be deemed to have been instituted before the end of the transition period;

(e) Regulation (EC) No 861/2007 of the European Parliament and of the Council ([80]) shall apply to small claims procedures for which the application was lodged before the end of the transition period;

(f) Regulation (EU) No 606/2013 of the European Parliament and of the Council ([81]) shall apply to certificates issued before the end of the transition period.

Article 68 Ongoing judicial cooperation procedures

In the United Kingdom, as well as in the Member States in situations involving the United Kingdom, the following acts shall apply as follows:

(a) Regulation (EC) No 1393/2007 of the European Parliament and of the Council ([82]) shall apply to judicial and extrajudicial documents which were received for the purposes of service before the end of the transition period by one of the following:
  (i) a receiving agency;
  (ii) a central body of the State where the service is to be effected; or
  (iii) diplomatic or consular agents, postal services or judicial officers, officials or other competent persons of the State addressed, as referred to in Articles 13, 14 and 15 of that Regulation;

(b) Council Regulation (EC) No 1206/2001 ([83]) shall apply to requests received before the end of the transition period by one of the following:
  (i) a requested court;
  (ii) a central body of the State where the taking of evidence is requested; or
  (iii) a central body or competent authority referred to in Article 17(1) of that Regulation;

(c) Council Decision 2001/470/EC ([84]) shall apply to requests that were received before the end of the transition period; the requesting contact point may request an acknowledgement of receipt within 7 days of the end of the transition period where it has doubts as to whether the request was received before the end of the transition period.

Article 69 Other applicable provisions

1. In the United Kingdom, as well as in the Member States in situations involving the United Kingdom, the following acts shall apply as follows:

   (a) Council Directive 2003/8/EC ([85]) shall apply to applications for legal aid that were received by the receiving authority before the end of the transition period. The requesting authority may request an acknowledgement of receipt within 7 days of the end of the transition period where it has doubts as to whether the request was received before that date;

   (b) Directive 2008/52/EC of the European Parliament and of the Council ([86]) shall apply where, before the end of the transition period:

---

[79] Regulation (EC) No 1896/2006 of the European Parliament and of the Council of 12 December 2006 creating a European order for payment procedure (OJ L 399, 30.12.2006, p. 1).

[80] Regulation (EC) No 861/2007 of the European Parliament and of the Council of 11 July 2007 establishing a European Small Claims Procedure (OJ L 199, 31.7.2007, p. 1).

[81] Regulation (EU) No 606/2013 of the European Parliament and of the Council of 12 June 2013 on mutual recognition of protection measures in civil matters (OJ L 181, 29.6.2013, p. 4).

[82] Regulation (EC) No 1393/2007 of the European Parliament and of the Council of 13 November 2007 on the service in the Member States of judicial and extrajudicial documents in civil or commercial matters (service of documents), and repealing Council Regulation (EC) No 1348/2000 (OJ L 324, 10.12.2007, p. 79).

[83] Council Regulation (EC) No 1206/2001 of 28 May 2001 on cooperation between the courts of the Member States in the taking of evidence in civil or commercial matters (OJ L 174, 27.6.2001, p. 1).

[84] Council Decision 2001/470/EC of 28 May 2001 establishing a European Judicial Network in civil and commercial matters (OJ L 174, 27.6.2001, p. 25).

[85] Council Directive 2003/8/EC of 27 January 2003 to improve access to justice in cross-border disputes by establishing minimum common rules relating to legal aid for such disputes (OJ L 26, 31.1.2003, p. 41).

[86] Directive 2008/52/EC of the European Parliament and of the Council of 21 May 2008 on certain aspects of mediation in civil and commercial matters (OJ L 136, 24.5.2008, p. 3).

        (i)   the parties agreed to use mediation after the dispute had arisen;

        (ii)   mediation was ordered by the court; or

        (iii)   a court invited the parties to use mediation;

   (c)   Council Directive 2004/80/EC ([87]) shall apply to applications received by the deciding authority before the end of the transition period.

2.   Point (a) of paragraph 1 and point (a) of paragraph 2 of Article 67 of this Agreement shall also apply in respect of the provisions of Regulation (EU) No 1215/2012 as applicable by virtue of the agreement between the European Community and the Kingdom of Denmark on jurisdiction and the recognition and enforcement of judgments in civil and commercial matters ([88]).

3.   Point (a) of Article 68 of this Agreement shall also apply with regard to the provisions of Regulation (EC) No 1393/2007 as applicable by virtue of the agreement between the European Community and the Kingdom of Denmark on the service of judicial and extrajudicial documents in civil and commercial matters ([89]).

TITLE VII

DATA AND INFORMATION PROCESSED OR OBTAINED BEFORE THE END OF THE TRANSITION PERIOD, OR ON THE BASIS OF THIS AGREEMENT

Article 70   Definition

For the purposes of this Title, "Union law on the protection of personal data" means:

(a)   Regulation (EU) 2016/679, with the exception of Chapter VII thereof;

(b)   Directive (EU) 2016/680 of the European Parliament and of the Council ([90]);

(c)   Directive 2002/58/EC of the European Parliament and of the Council ([91]);

(d)   any other provisions of Union law governing the protection of personal data.

Article 71   Protection of personal data

1.   Union law on the protection of personal data shall apply in the United Kingdom in respect of the processing of personal data of data subjects outside the United Kingdom, provided that the personal data:

   (a)   were processed under Union law in the United Kingdom before the end of the transition period; or

   (b)   are processed in the United Kingdom after the end of the transition period on the basis of this Agreement.

2.   Paragraph 1 shall not apply to the extent the processing of the personal data referred to therein is subject to an adequate level of protection as established in applicable decisions under Article 45(3) of Regulation (EU) 2016/679 or Article 36(3) of Directive (EU) 2016/680.

3.   To the extent that a decision referred to in paragraph 2 has ceased to be applicable, the United Kingdom shall ensure a level of protection of personal data essentially equivalent to that under Union law on the protection of personal data in respect of the processing of personal data of data subjects referred to in paragraph 1.

Article 72   Confidential treatment and restricted use of data and information in the United Kingdom

Without prejudice to Article 71, in addition to Union law on the protection of personal data, the provisions of Union law on confidential treatment, restriction of use, storage limitation and requirement to erase data and information shall apply in respect of data and information obtained by authorities or official bodies of or in the United Kingdom or by contracting

---

[87] Council Directive 2004/80/EC of 29 April 2004 relating to compensation to crime victims (OJ L 261, 6.8.2004, p. 15).

[88] OJ L 299, 16.11.2005, p. 62.

[89] OJ L 300 17.11.2005, p. 55.

[90] Directive (EU) 2016/680 of the European Parliament and of the Council of 27 April 2016 on the protection of natural persons with regard to the processing of personal data by competent authorities for the purposes of the prevention, investigation, detection or prosecution of criminal offences or the execution of criminal penalties, and on the free movement of such data, and repealing Council Framework Decision 2008/977/JHA (OJ L 119, 4.5.2016, p. 89).

[91] Directive 2002/58/EC of the European Parliament and of the Council of 12 July 2002 concerning the processing of personal data and the protection of privacy in the electronic communications sector (Directive on privacy and electronic communications) (OJ L 201, 31.7.2002, p. 37).

entities, as defined in Article 4 of Directive 2014/25/EU of the European Parliament and of the Council (⁹²), that are of or in the United Kingdom:

(a)   before the end of the transition period; or

(b)   on the basis of this Agreement.

Article 73   Treatment of data and information obtained from the United Kingdom

The Union shall not treat data and information obtained from the United Kingdom before the end of the transition period, or obtained after the end of the transition period on the basis of this Agreement, differently from data and information obtained from a Member State, on the sole ground of the United Kingdom having withdrawn from the Union.

Article 74   Information security

1.   The provisions of Union law on the protection of EU classified information and Euratom classified information shall apply in respect of classified information that was obtained by the United Kingdom either before the end of the transition period or on the basis of this Agreement or that was obtained from the United Kingdom by the Union or a Member State either before the end of the transition period or on the basis of this Agreement.

2.   The obligations resulting from Union law regarding industrial security shall apply to the United Kingdom in cases where the tendering, contracting or grant award procedure for the classified contract, classified subcontract or classified grant agreement was launched before the end of the transition period.

3.   The United Kingdom shall ensure that cryptographic products that use classified cryptographic algorithms developed under the control of, and evaluated and approved by the Crypto Approval Authority of a Member State or of the United Kingdom, which have been approved by the Union by the end of the transition period and that are present in the United Kingdom, are not transferred to a third country.

4.   Any requirements, limitations and conditions set out in the Union approval of cryptographic products shall apply to those products.

TITLE VIII

ONGOING PUBLIC PROCUREMENT AND SIMILAR PROCEDURES

Article 75   Definition

For the purposes of this Title, "relevant rules" means the general principles of Union law applicable to the award of public contracts, Directives 2009/81/EC (⁹³), 2014/23/EU (⁹⁴), 2014/24/EU (⁹⁵) and 2014/25/EU (⁹⁶) of the European Parliament and of the Council, Regulations (EC) No 2195/2002 (⁹⁷) and (EC) No 1370/2007 (⁹⁸) of the European Parliament and of the Council, Article 4 of Council Regulation (EEC) No 3577/92 (⁹⁹), Articles 11 and 12

[92]   Directive 2014/25/EU of the European Parliament and of the Council of 26 February 2014 on procurement by entities operating in the water, energy, transport and postal services sectors and repealing Directive 2004/17/EC (OJ L 94, 28.3.2014, p. 243).

[93]   Directive 2009/81/EC of the European Parliament and of the Council of 13 July 2009 on the coordination of procedures for the award of certain works contracts, supply contracts and service contracts by contracting authorities or entities in the fields of defence and security, and amending Directives 2004/17/EC and 2004/18/EC (OJ L 216, 20.8, 2009, p. 76).

[94]   Directive 2014/23/EU of the European Parliament and of the Council of 26 February 2014 on the award of concession contracts (OJ L 94, 28.3.2014, p. 1).

[95]   Directive 2014/24/EU of the European Parliament and of the Council of 26 February 2014 on public procurement and repealing Directive 2004/18/EC (OJ L 94, 28.3.2014, p. 65).

[96]   Directive 2014/25/EU of the European Parliament and of the Council of 26 February 2014 on procurement by entities operating in the water, energy, transport and postal services sectors and repealing Directive 2004/17/EC (OJ L 94, 28.3.2014, p. 243).

[97]   Regulation (EC) No 2195/2002 of the European Parliament and of the Council of 5 November 2002 on the Common Procurement Vocabulary (CPV) (OJ L 340, 16.12.2002, p. 1).

[98]   Regulation (EC) No 1370/2007 of the European Parliament and of the Council of 23 October 2007 on public passenger transport services by rail and by road and repealing Council Regulations (EEC) Nos 1191/69 and 1107/70 (OJ L 315, 3.12.2007, p. 1).

[99]   Council Regulation (EEC) No 3577/92 of 7 December 1992 applying the principle of freedom to provide services to maritime transport within Member States (maritime cabotage) (OJ L 364, 12.12.1992, p. 7).

of Council Directive 96/67/EC ($^{(100)}$), Articles 16, 17 and 18 of Regulation (EC) No 1008/2008 of the European Parliament and of the Council ($^{(101)}$), Articles 6 and 7 of Regulation (EU) 2017/352 of the European Parliament and of the Council ($^{(102)}$), and any other specific provisions of Union law governing public procurement procedures.

Article 76   Rules applicable to ongoing procedures

1.   The relevant rules shall apply:

(a)   without prejudice to point (b), in respect of procedures launched by contracting authorities or contracting entities from the Member States or the United Kingdom under those rules before the end of the transition period and not yet finalised on the last day of the transition period, including procedures using dynamic purchasing systems as well as procedures for which the call for competition takes the form of a prior information notice or periodic indicative notice or a notice on the existence of a qualification system; and

(b)   in respect of the procedures referred to in Article 29(2), (3) and (4) of Directive 2009/81/EC, Article 33(2) to (5) of Directive 2014/24/EU and Article 51(2) of Directive 2014/25/EU which relate to the performance of the following framework agreements concluded by contracting authorities or contracting entities from the Member States or the United Kingdom, including the award of contracts based on such framework agreements:

(i)   framework agreements concluded before the end of the transition period that have neither expired nor been terminated on the last day of the transition period; or

(ii)   framework agreements concluded after the end of the transition period in accordance with a procedure that falls under point (a) of this paragraph.

2.   Without prejudice to the application of any restriction in accordance with Union law, the non-discrimination principle shall be complied with by contracting authorities and contracting entities with regard to tenderers or, as applicable, persons who are otherwise entitled to submit applications, from the Member States and the United Kingdom in relation to the procedures referred to in paragraph 1.

3.   A procedure referred to in paragraph 1 shall be considered to have been launched when a call for competition or any other invitation to submit applications has been made in accordance with the relevant rules. Where the relevant rules allow for the use of procedures that do not require the use of a call for competition or other invitations to submit applications, the procedure shall be considered to have been launched when the contracting authority or contracting entity contacted economic operators in relation to the specific procedure.

4.   A procedure referred to in paragraph 1 shall be considered finalised:

(a)   upon publication of a contract award notice in accordance with the relevant rules or, where those rules do not require the publication of a contract award notice, upon conclusion of the relevant contract; or

(b)   upon informing tenderers or persons otherwise entitled to submit applications, as the case may be, of the reasons why the contract was not awarded, if the contracting authority or contracting entity decided not to award a contract.

5.   This Article shall not affect Union or United Kingdom rules on customs, the movement of goods, the provision of services, the recognition of professional qualifications or intellectual property.

$^{(100)}$ Council Directive 96/67/EC of 15 October 1996 on access to the groundhandling market at Community airports (OJ L 272, 25.10.1996, p. 36).
$^{(101)}$ Regulation (EC) No 1008/2008 of the European Parliament and of the Council of 24 September 2008 on common rules for the operation of air services in the Community (OJ L 293, 31.10.2008, p. 3).
$^{(102)}$ Regulation (EU) 2017/352 of the European Parliament and of the Council of 15 February 2017 establishing a framework for the provision of port services and common rules on the financial transparency of ports (OJ L 57, 3.3.2017, p. 1).

Article 77   Review procedures

Council Directives 89/665/EEC ([103]) and 92/13/EEC ([104]) shall apply in respect of the public procurement procedures referred to in Article 76 of this Agreement which fall within the scope of those Directives.

Article 78   Cooperation

By way of derogation from Article 8 of this Agreement, Article 61(2) of Directive 2014/24/EU shall apply for a period not exceeding 9 months from the end of the transition period in respect of the procedures under that Directive that were launched by contracting authorities from the United Kingdom before the end of the transition period and were not yet finalised on the last day of the transition period.

TITLE IX
EURATOM RELATED ISSUES

Article 79   Definitions

For the purposes of this Title, the following definitions shall apply:
(a)   "Community" means the European Atomic Energy Community;
(b)   "safeguards" means activities to verify that nuclear material and equipment are not diverted from their intended use as declared by the users and activities to verify that international legal obligations to use nuclear material and equipment for peaceful purposes are honoured;
(c)   "special fissile materials" means special fissile materials as defined in point (1) of Article 197 of the Euratom Treaty;
(d)   "ores" means ores as defined in point (4) of Article 197 of the Euratom Treaty;
(e)   "source materials" means source materials as defined in point (3) of Article 197 of the Euratom Treaty;
(f)   "nuclear material" means ores, source materials and special fissile materials;
(g)   "spent fuel" and "radioactive waste" mean spent fuel and radioactive waste as defined in points (7) and (11) of Article3 of Council Directive 2011/70/Euratom ([105]).

Article 80   End of Community responsibility for matters related to the United Kingdom

1.   The United Kingdom shall have sole responsibility for ensuring that all ores, source materials and special fissile materials covered by the Euratom Treaty and present on the territory of the United Kingdom at the end of the transition period are handled in accordance with relevant and applicable international treaties and conventions, including but not limited to international treaties and conventions on nuclear safety, safeguards, non-proliferation and physical protection of nuclear materials, and international treaties and conventions on safety of spent fuel management and the safety of radioactive waste management.
2.   The United Kingdom shall have sole responsibility for ensuring its compliance with international obligations arising as a consequence of its membership of the International Atomic Energy Agency or as a consequence of the Treaty on the Non-Proliferation of Nuclear Weapons or any other relevant international treaties or conventions to which the United Kingdom is a party.

Article 81   Safeguards

The United Kingdom shall implement a safeguards regime. This safeguards regime shall apply a system offering equivalent effectiveness and coverage as that provided by the Community in the territory of the United Kingdom in line with the Agreement between

---

[103] Council Directive 89/665/EEC of 21 December 1989 on the coordination of the laws, regulations and administrative provisions relating to the application of review procedures to the award of public supply and public works contracts (OJ L 395, 30.12.1989, p. 33).
[104] Council Directive 92/13/EEC of 25 February 1992 coordinating the laws, regulations and administrative provisions relating to the application of Community rules on the procurement procedures of entities operating in the water, energy, transport and telecommu- nications sectors (OJ L 76, 23.3.1992, p. 14).
[105] Council Directive 2011/70/Euratom of 19 July 2011 establishing a Community framework for the responsible and safe management of spent fuel and radioactive waste (OJ L 199, 2.8.2011, p. 48).

the United Kingdom of Great Britain and Northern Ireland, the European Atomic Energy Community and the International Atomic Energy Agency for the Application of Safeguards in the United Kingdom of Great Britain and Northern Ireland in Connection with the Treaty on the Non-Proliferation of Nuclear Weapons [INFCIRC/263], as amended.

Article 82   Specific obligations under international agreements

The United Kingdom shall ensure that any specific obligations under agreements concluded by the Community with third countries or international organisations in relation to any nuclear equipment, nuclear material or other nuclear items present on the territory of the United Kingdom at the end of the transition period are fulfilled, or otherwise identify appropriate arrangements in agreement with the third country or international organisation concerned.

Article 83   Ownership and rights of use and consumption of special fissile materials in the United Kingdom

1.   Special fissile materials present on the territory of the United Kingdom in respect of which Article 86 of the Euratom Treaty applied until the end of the transition period shall cease to be the property of the Community at the end of the transition period.

2.   Special fissile materials referred to in paragraph 1 shall become the property of the persons or undertakings that had unlimited right of use and consumption of those materials at the end of the transition period in accordance with Article 87 of the Euratom Treaty.

3.   Where the right of use and consumption of special fissile materials referred to in paragraph 2 ("materials concerned") is with a Member State, or with persons or undertakings established in the territory of a Member State, in order to protect the integrity of the common supply policy established under Chapter 6 of Title II of the Euratom Treaty and of the nuclear common market established under Chapter 9 of that Title, including with regard to the level of safeguards applicable to the materials concerned, the following shall apply:

(a)   having regard to Article 5 of this Agreement, the Community shall have the right to require that the materials concerned be deposited with the Agency established under point (b) of Article 52(2) of the Euratom Treaty or in other stores which are or can be supervised by the European Commission;

(b)   the Community shall have the right to conclude contracts relating to the supply of the materials concerned to any person or undertaking established in the territory of the United Kingdom or in a third country in accordance with Article 52(2) of the Euratom Treaty;

(c)   Article 20 of Commission Regulation (Euratom) No 302/2005 [106], with the exception of points (b) and (c) of paragraph 1, shall apply in respect of the materials concerned;

(d)   the export of the materials concerned to a third country shall be authorised by the competent authorities of the Member State in which the person or undertaking with the right to use and consume the materials concerned is established in accordance with Article 9(2) of Council Regulation (EC) No 428/2009 [107];

(e)   in respect of the materials concerned, the Community shall have the right to exert any other rights arising under the Euratom Treaty from ownership pursuant to Article 86 of that Treaty.

4.   Member States, persons or undertakings that have the unlimited right of use and consumption of special fissile materials present on the territory of the United Kingdom at the end of the transition period shall retain that right.

Article 84   Equipment and other property related to the provision of safeguards

1.   Community equipment and other property related to the provision of safeguards under the Euratom Treaty located in the United Kingdom at the end of the transition period,

---

[106] Commission Regulation (Euratom) No 302/2005 of 8 February 2005 on the application of Euratom safeguards (OJ L 54, 28.2.2005, p. 1).
[107] Council Regulation (EC) No 428/2009 of 5 May 2009 setting up a Community regime for the control of exports, transfer, brokering and transit of dual-use items (OJ L 134, 29.5.2009, p. 1).

as set out at Annex V, shall become the property of the United Kingdom. The United Kingdom shall reimburse to the Union the value of that equipment and other property, the calculation of which shall be based on the value assigned to that equipment and other property in the consolidated accounts for the year 2020.

2. The United Kingdom shall assume all of the Community's rights, liabilities and obligations associated with the equipment and other property referred to in paragraph 1.

Article 85   Spent fuel and radioactive waste

Article 4(1) and (2) and the first subparagraph of Article 4(4) of Directive 2011/70/Euratom shall apply in respect of the United Kingdom's ultimate responsibility for spent fuel and radioactive waste that was generated in the United Kingdom and is present on the territory of a Member State at the end of the transition period.

TITLE X
UNION JUDICIAL AND ADMINISTRATIVE PROCEDURES

CHAPTER 1
JUDICIAL PROCEDURES

Article 86   Pending cases before the Court of Justice of the European Union

1. The Court of Justice of the European Union shall continue to have jurisdiction in any proceedings brought by or against the United Kingdom before the end of the transition period. Such jurisdiction shall apply to all stages of proceedings, including appeal proceedings before the Court of Justice and proceedings before the General Court where the case is referred back to the General Court.

2. The Court of Justice of the European Union shall continue to have jurisdiction to give preliminary rulings on requests from courts and tribunals of the United Kingdom made before the end of the transition period.

3. For the purposes of this Chapter, proceedings shall be considered as having been brought before the Court of Justice of the European Union, and requests for preliminary rulings shall be considered as having been made, at the moment at which the document initiating the proceedings has been registered by the registry of the Court of Justice or the General Court, as the case may be.

Article 87   New cases before the Court of Justice

1. If the European Commission considers that the United Kingdom has failed to fulfil an obligation under the Treaties or under Part Four of this Agreement before the end of the transition period, the European Commission may, within 4 years after the end of the transition period, bring the matter before the Court of Justice of the European Union in accordance with the requirements laid down in Article 258 TFEU or the second subparagraph of Article 108(2) TFEU, as the case may be. The Court of Justice of the European Union shall have jurisdiction over such cases.

2. If the United Kingdom does not comply with a decision referred to in Article 95(1) of this Agreement, or fails to give legal effect in the United Kingdom's legal order to a decision, as referred to in that provision, that was addressed to a natural or legal person residing or established in the United Kingdom, the European Commission may, within 4 years from the date of the decision concerned, bring the matter to the Court of Justice of the European Union in accordance with the requirements laid down in Article 258 TFEU or the second subparagraph of Article 108(2) TFEU, as the case may be. The Court of Justice of the European Union shall have jurisdiction over such cases.

3. In deciding to bring matters under this Article, the European Commission shall apply the same principles in respect of the United Kingdom as in respect of any Member State.

Article 88   Procedural rules

The provisions of Union law governing the procedure before the Court of Justice of the European Union shall apply in respect of the proceedings and requests for preliminary rulings referred to in this Title.

Article 89   Binding force and enforceability of judgments and orders

1. Judgments and orders of the Court of Justice of the European Union handed down before the end of the transition period, as well as such judgments and orders handed down after the end of the transition period in proceedings referred to in Articles 86 and 87, shall have binding force in their entirety on and in the United Kingdom.
2. If, in a judgment referred to in paragraph 1, the Court of Justice of the European Union finds that the United Kingdom has failed to fulfil an obligation under the Treaties or this Agreement, the United Kingdom shall take the necessary measures to comply with that judgment.
3. Articles 280 and 299 TFEU shall apply in the United Kingdom in respect of the enforcement of the judgments and orders of the Court of Justice of the European Union referred to in paragraph 1 of this Article.

Article 90   Right to intervene and participate in the procedure

Until the judgments and orders of the Court of Justice of the European Union in all proceedings and requests for preliminary rulings referred to in Article 86 have become final, the United Kingdom may intervene in the same way as a Member State or, in the cases brought before the Court of Justice of the European Union in accordance with Article 267 TFEU, participate in the procedure before the Court of Justice of the European Union in the same way as a Member State. During that period, the Registrar of the Court of Justice of the European Union shall notify the United Kingdom, at the same time and in the same manner as the Member States, of any case referred to the Court of Justice of the European Union for a preliminary ruling by a court or tribunal of a Member State.

The United Kingdom may also intervene or participate in the procedure before the Court of Justice of the European Union in the same way as a Member State:

(a) in relation to cases which concern a failure to fulfil obligations under the Treaties, where the United Kingdom was subject to the same obligations before the end of the transition period, and where such cases are brought before the Court of Justice of the European Union in accordance with Articles 258 TFEU before the end of the period referred to in Article 87(1) or, as the case may be, until the moment, after the end of that period, at which the last judgment or order rendered by the Court of Justice of the European Union on the basis of Article 87(1) has become final;

(b) in relation to cases which concern acts or provisions of Union law which were applicable before the end of the transition period to and in the United Kingdom and which are brought before Court of Justice of the European Union in accordance with Article 267 TFEU before the end of the period referred to in Article 87(1) or, as the case may be, until the moment, after the end of that period, at which the last judgment or order rendered by the Court of Justice on the basis of Article 87(1) has become final; and

(c) in relation to the cases referred to in Article 95(3).

Article 91   Representation before the Court

1. Without prejudice to Article 88, where, before the end of the transition period, a lawyer authorised to practise before the courts or tribunals of the United Kingdom represented or assisted a party in proceedings before the Court of Justice of the European Union or in relation to requests for preliminary rulings made before the end of the transition period, that lawyer may continue to represent or assist that party in those proceedings or in relation to those requests. This right shall apply to all stages of proceedings, including appeal proceedings before the Court of Justice and proceedings before the General Court after a case has been referred back to it.
2. Without prejudice to Article 88, lawyers authorised to practise before the courts or tribunals of the United Kingdom may represent or assist a party before the Court of Justice of the European Union in the cases referred to in Article 87 and Article 95(3). Lawyers authorised to practise before the courts or tribunals of the United Kingdom may also represent or assist the United Kingdom in the proceedings covered by Article 90 in which the United Kingdom has decided to intervene or participate.
3. When representing or assisting a party before the Court of Justice of the European Union in the cases referred to in paragraphs 1 and 2, lawyers authorised to practise before the courts or tribunals of the United Kingdom shall in every respect be treated as lawyers authorised to practise before courts or tribunals of Member States representing or assisting a party before the Court of Justice of the European Union.

CHAPTER 2
ADMINISTRATIVE PROCEDURES

Article 92   Ongoing administrative procedures

1. The institutions, bodies, offices and agencies of the Union shall continue to be competent for administrative procedures which were initiated before the end of the transition period concerning:

    (a)   compliance with Union law by the United Kingdom, or by natural or legal persons residing or established in the United Kingdom; or

    (b)   compliance with Union law relating to competition in the United Kingdom.

2. Without prejudice to paragraph 3, for the purposes of this Chapter an administrative procedure shall be considered as having been initiated at the moment at which it has been formally registered with the Union institution, body, office or agency.

3. For the purposes of this Chapter:

    (a)   an administrative procedure on State aid governed by Council Regulation (EU) 2015/1589 ([108]) shall be considered as having been initiated at the moment at which the procedure has been allocated a case number;

    (b)   proceedings for the application of Article 101 or 102 TFEU conducted by the European Commission under Council Regulation (EC) No 1/2003 ([109]) shall be considered as having been initiated at the moment at which the European Commission has decided to initiate proceedings in accordance with Article 2(1) of Commission Regulation (EC) No 773/2004 ([110]);

    (c)   proceedings in connection with the control of concentrations between undertakings governed by Council Regulation (EC) No 139/2004 ([111]) shall be considered as having been initiated at the moment at which:

    (i)   a concentration of Union dimension has been notified to the European Commission in accordance with Articles 1, 3 and 4 of Regulation (EC) No 139/2004;

    (ii)   the time limit of 15 working days referred to in Article 4(5) of Regulation (EC) No 139/2004 has expired without any of the Member States competent to examine the concentration under their national competition law having expressed its disagreement as regards the request to refer the case to the European Commission; or

    (iii) the European Commission has decided, or is deemed to have decided, to examine the concentration in accordance with Article 22(3) of Regulation (EC) No 139/2004;

    (d)   an investigation by the European Securities and Markets Authority of an alleged infringement listed in Annex III to Regulation (EC) No 1060/2009 of the European Parliament and of the Council ([112]) or Annex I to Regulation (EU) No 648/2012 of the European Parliament and of the Council ([113]) shall be considered as having been initiated at the moment at which that Authority has appointed an independent investigating officer in accordance with Article 23e(1) of Regulation (EC) No 1060/2009 or Article 64(1) of Regulation (EU) No 648/2012.

4. The Union shall provide the United Kingdom with a list of all individual ongoing administrative procedures that fall within the scope of paragraph 1 within 3 months after the end of the transition period. By way of derogation from the first sentence,

---

[108] Council Regulation (EU) 2015/1589 of 13 July 2015 laying down detailed rules for the application of Article 108 of the Treaty on the Functioning of the European Union (OJ L 248, 24.9.2015, p. 9).

[109] Council Regulation (EC) No 1/2003 of 16 December 2002 on the implementation of the rules on competition laid down in Articles 81 and 82 of the Treaty (OJ L 1, 4.1.2003, p. 1).

[110] Commission Regulation (EC) No 773/2004 of 7 April 2004 relating to the conduct of proceedings by the Commission pursuant to Articles 81 and 82 of the EC Treaty (OJ L 123, 27.4.2004, p. 18).

[111] Council Regulation (EC) No 139/2004 of 20 January 2004 on the control of concentrations between undertakings (OJ L 24, 29.1.2004, p. 1).

[112] Regulation (EC) No 1060/2009 of the European Parliament and of the Council of 16 September 2009 on credit rating agencies (OJ L 302, 17.11.2009, p. 1).

[113] Regulation (EU) No 648/2012 of the European Parliament and of the Council of 4 July 2012 on OTC derivatives, central counterparties and trade repositories (OJ L 201, 27.7.2012, p. 1).

in the case of individual ongoing administrative procedures of the European Banking Authority, the European Securities and Markets Authority, and the European Insurance and Occupational Pensions Authority, the Union shall provide the United Kingdom with a list of such ongoing administrative procedures within 1 month after the end of the transition period.

5. In an administrative procedure on State aid governed by Regulation (EU) 2015/1589, the European Commission shall be bound in relation to the United Kingdom by the applicable case law and best practices, as if the United Kingdom were still a Member State. In particular, the European Commission shall, within a reasonable period of time, adopt one of the following decisions:

(a) a decision finding that the measure does not constitute aid pursuant to Article 4(2) of Regulation (EU) 2015/1589;

(b) a decision not to raise objections pursuant to Article 4(3) of Regulation (EU) 2015/1589;

(c) a decision to initiate formal investigation proceedings pursuant to Article 4(4) of Regulation (EU) 2015/1589.

Article 93   New State aid and European Anti-Fraud Office procedures

1. In respect of aid granted before the end of the transition period, for a period of 4 years after the end of the transition period, the European Commission shall be competent to initiate new administrative procedures on State aid governed by Regulation (EU) 2015/1589 concerning the United Kingdom.

The European Commission shall continue to be competent after the end of the 4-year period for procedures initiated before the end of that period.

Article 92(5) of this Agreement shall apply *mutatis mutandis*.

The European Commission shall inform the United Kingdom of any new administrative proceedings on State aid initiated under the first subparagraph of this paragraph within 3 months of initiating it.

2. Without prejudice to Articles 136 and 138 of this Agreement, for a period of 4 years after the end of the transition period, the European Anti-Fraud Office (OLAF) shall be competent to initiate new investigations governed by Regulation (EU, Euratom) No 883/2013 of the European Parliament and of the Council ([114]) in respect of:

(a) facts that occurred before the end of the transition period; or

(b) any customs debt arising after the end of the transition period from the discharge procedures referred to in Article 49(1) of this Agreement.

OLAF shall continue to be competent after the end of the 4-year period for procedures initiated before the end of that period.

OLAF shall inform the United Kingdom of any new investigation initiated under the first subparagraph of this paragraph within 3 months of initiating that investigation.

Article 94   Procedural rules

1. The provisions of Union law governing the different types of administrative procedures covered by this Chapter shall apply to the procedures referred to in Articles 92, 93 and 96.

2. When representing or assisting a party in relation to the administrative procedures referred to in Articles 92 and 93, the lawyers authorised to practise before the courts or tribunals of the United Kingdom shall in every respect be treated as lawyers authorised to practise before courts or tribunals of Member States who represent or assist a party in relation to such administrative procedures.

3. Article 128(5) shall apply to the extent necessary for any procedures referred to in Articles 92 and 93 after the end of the transition period.

---

[114] Regulation (EU, Euratom) No 883/2013 of the European Parliament and of the Council of 11 September 2013 concerning investigations conducted by the European Anti-Fraud Office (OLAF) and repealing Regulation (EC) No 1073/1999 of the European Parliament and of the Council and Council Regulation (Euratom) No 1074/1999 (OJ L 248, 18.9.2013, p. 1).

Article 95 Binding force and enforceability of decisions

1. Decisions adopted by institutions, bodies, offices and agencies of the Union before the end of the transition period, or adopted in the procedures referred to in Articles 92 and 93 after the end of the transition period, and addressed to the United Kingdom or to natural and legal persons residing or established in the United Kingdom, shall be binding on and in the United Kingdom.

2. Unless otherwise agreed between the European Commission and the designated national competition authority of the United Kingdom, the European Commission shall continue to be competent to monitor and enforce commitments given or remedies imposed in, or in relation to, the United Kingdom in connection with any proceedings for the application of Articles 101 or 102 TFEU conducted by the European Commission under Regulation (EC) No 1/2003 or proceedings conducted by the European Commission under Regulation (EC) No 139/2004 in connection with the control of concentrations between undertakings. If so agreed between the European Commission and the designated national competition authority of the United Kingdom, the European Commission shall transfer the monitoring and enforcement of such commitments or remedies in the United Kingdom to the designated national competition authority of the United Kingdom.

3. The legality of a decision referred to in paragraph 1 of this Article shall be reviewed exclusively by the Court of Justice of the European Union in accordance with Article 263 TFEU.

4. Article 299 TFEU shall apply in the United Kingdom in respect of the enforcement of decisions referred to in paragraph 1 of this Article that impose pecuniary obligations on natural and legal persons residing or established in the United Kingdom.

Article 96 Other ongoing procedures and reporting obligations

1. Technical examinations conducted by United Kingdom Examination Offices in cooperation with the Community Plant Variety Office pursuant to Regulation (EC) No 2100/94 which were ongoing on the day before the date of entry into force of this Agreement shall continue and be concluded in compliance with that Regulation.

2. Article 12(2a) and (3) and Articles 14, 15 and 16 of Directive 2003/87/EC of the European Parliament and of the Council ([115]) shall apply to and in the United Kingdom in respect of greenhouse gases emitted during the last year of the transition period.

3. Article 19 of Regulation (EU) No 517/2014 of the European Parliament and of the Council ([116]) and Articles 26 and 27 of Regulation (EC) No 1005/2009 of the European Parliament and of the Council ([117]) shall apply to and in the United Kingdom in respect of data reporting for the last year of the transition period.

4. Article 8(1), (2), (3) and (7) of Regulation (EC) 443/2009 of the European Parliament and of the Council ([118]), and Annex II to that Regulation, and Article 8(1), (2), (3), (8) and (10) of Regulation (EU) 510/2011 of the European Parliament and of the Council ([119]), and Annex II to that Regulation, as well as Articles 2 to 5, 7 and 8(2) and (3) of Commission Regulation (EU) No 1014/2010 and Articles 3 to 6 and 8 and Article 9(2) and (3) of Commission Implementing Regulation (EU) No 293/2012 ([120]) shall apply to and in the

---

[115] Directive 2003/87/EC of the European Parliament and of the Council of 13 October 2003 establishing a system for greenhouse gas emission allowance trading within the Union and amending Council Directive 96/61/EC (OJ L 275, 25.10.2003, p. 32).

[116] Regulation (EU) No 517/2014 of the European Parliament and of the Council of 16 April 2014 on fluorinated greenhouse gases and repealing Regulation (EC) No 842/2006 (OJ L 150, 20.5.2014, p. 195).

[117] Regulation (EC) No 1005/2009 of the European Parliament and of the Council of 16 September 2009 on substances that deplete the ozone layer (OJ L 286, 31.10.2009, p. 1).

[118] Regulation (EC) No 443/2009 of the European Parliament and of the Council of 23 April 2009 setting emission performance standards for new passenger cars as part of the Community's integrated approach to reduce CO_2 emissions from light-duty vehicles (OJ L 140, 5.6.2009, p. 1).

[119] Regulation (EU) No 510/2011 of the European Parliament and of the Council of 11 May 2011 setting emission performance standards for new light commercial vehicles as part of the Union's integrated approach to reduce CO_2 emissions from light-duty vehicles (OJ L 145, 31.5.2011, p. 1).

[120] Commission Implementing Regulation (EU) No 293/2012 of 3 April 2012 on monitoring and reporting of data on the registration of new light commercial vehicles pursuant to Regulation (EU) No 510/2011 of the European Parliament and of the Council (OJ L 98, 4.4.2012, p. 1).

United Kingdom in respect of the monitoring and reporting of relevant vehicle carbon dioxide emissions during the last year of the transition period.

5.   Articles 5, 7, 9 and 10, Article 11(3), points (a) and (d) of Article 17(1), and Articles 19, 22 and 23 of Regulation (EU) No 525/2013 of the European Parliament and of the Council ([121]) and Articles 3, 7 and 11 of Decision No 406/2009/EC of the European Parliament and of the Council ([122]) shall apply to the United Kingdom in respect of greenhouse gases emitted during 2019 and 2020, and Article 5 of Commission Regulation (EU) No 389/2013 ([123]) shall apply to the United Kingdom until the closure of the second commitment period of the Kyoto Protocol.

6.   By way of derogation from Article 8 of this Agreement:
    (a)   to the extent necessary to comply with paragraphs 2, 4 and 5 of this Article, the United Kingdom and operators in the United Kingdom shall have access to:
        (i)   the Union Registry and the United Kingdom's Kyoto Protocol Registry established by Regulation (EU) No 389/2013; and
        (ii)   the Central Data Repository of the European Environment Agency as provided for by Regulation (EU) No 1014/2010, Implementing Regulation (EU) No 293/2012 and Commission Implementing Regulation (EU) No 749/2014 ([124]);
    (b)   to the extent necessary to comply with paragraph 3 of this Article undertakings in the United Kingdom shall have access to:
        (i)   the reporting tool based on the format set out in the Annex to Commission Implementing Regulation (EU) No 1191/2014 ([125]) for the purposes of managing and reporting on fluorinated greenhouse gases; and
        (ii)   the Business Data Repository used for reporting by undertakings under Article 27 of Regulation (EC) No 1005/2009.

Upon a request from the United Kingdom, for a period ending one year after the end of the transition period, the Union shall provide the necessary information for the United Kingdom to:

(a)   comply with its reporting obligations under Article 7 of the Montreal Protocol on Substances that Deplete the Ozone Layer; and

(b)   apply penalties in accordance with Article 25 of Regulation (EU) No 517/2014 and Article 29 of Regulation (EC) No 1005/2009.

Article 97   Representation in ongoing proceedings before the European Union Intellectual Property Office

Where, before the end of the transition period, a person who is authorised to represent a natural or legal person before the European Union Intellectual Property Office in accordance with Union law was representing a party in a procedure brought before that Office, that representative may continue to represent that party in that procedure. This right shall apply to all stages of the procedure before that Office.

When representing a party before the European Union Intellectual Property Office in the proceedings referred to in the first subparagraph, such representative shall in every respect be treated as a professional representative authorised to represent a natural or legal person before the European Union Intellectual Property Office in accordance with Union law.

---

[121] Regulation (EU) No 525/2013 of the European Parliament and of the Council of 21 May 2013 on a mechanism for monitoring and reporting greenhouse gas emissions and for reporting other information at national and Union level relevant to climate change and repealing Decision No 280/2004/EC (OJ L 165, 18.6.2013, p. 13).

[122] Decision No 406/2009/EC of the European Parliament and of the Council of 23 April 2009 on the effort of Member States to reduce their greenhouse gas emissions to meet the Community's greenhouse gas emission reduction commitments up to 2020 (OJ L 140, 5.6.2009, p. 136).

[123] Commission Regulation (EU) No 389/2013 of 2 May 2013 establishing a Union Registry pursuant to Directive 2003/87/EC of the European Parliament and of the Council, Decisions No 280/2004/EC and No 406/2009/EC of the European Parliament and of the Council and repealing Commission Regulations (EU) No 920/2010 and No 1193/2011 (OJ L 122, 3.5.2013, p. 1).

[124] Commission Implementing Regulation (EU) No 749/2014 of 30 June 2014 on structure, format, submission processes and review of information reported by Member States pursuant to Regulation (EU) No 525/2013 of the European Parliament and of the Council (OJ L 203, 11.7.2014, p. 23).

[125] Commission Implementing Regulation (EU) No 1191/2014 of 30 October 2014 determining the format and means for submitting the report referred to in Article 19 of Regulation (EU) No 517/2014 of the European Parliament and of the Council on fluorinated greenhouse gases (OJ L 318, 5.11.2014, p. 5).

TITLE XI
ADMINISTRATIVE COOPERATION PROCEDURES BETWEEN MEMBER STATES AND THE
UNITED KINGDOM

Article 98   Administrative cooperation for customs

1.   Administrative cooperation procedures between a Member State and the United Kingdom set out in Annex VI that were launched in accordance with Union law before the end of the transition period shall be completed by that Member State and the United Kingdom in accordance with the relevant provisions of Union law.

2.   Administrative cooperation procedures between a Member State and the United Kingdom set out in Annex VI that are launched within a period of 3 years after the end of the transition period but concern facts that occurred before the end of the transition period shall be completed by that Member State and the United Kingdom in accordance with the relevant provisions of Union law.

Article 99   Administrative cooperation for matters related to indirect tax

1.   Council Regulation (EU) No 904/2010 ([126]) shall apply until 4 years after the end of the transition period in respect of cooperation between the competent authorities responsible for the application of the legislation on VAT in the Member States and the United Kingdom in relation to transactions that took place before the end of the transition period and in relation to transactions covered by Article 51(1) of this Agreement.

2.   Council Regulation (EU) No 389/2012 ([127]) shall apply until 4 years after the end of the transition period in respect of cooperation between the competent authorities responsible for the application of the legislation on excise duties in the Member States and the United Kingdom in relation to movements of excise goods that took place before the end of the transition period and in relation to movements of excise goods covered by Article 52 of this Agreement.

3.   By way of derogation from Article 8, the United Kingdom shall have access, to the extent strictly necessary to exercise its rights and comply with obligations under this Article, to the networks, information systems and databases listed in Annex IV. The United Kingdom shall reimburse the Union for the actual costs incurred by the Union as a consequence of facilitating that access. The Union shall communicate to the United Kingdom the amount of those costs by 31 March of each year until the end of the period referred to in Annex IV. In the event that the communicated amount of the actual costs incurred considerably diverges from the best estimates amount that was communicated by the Union to the United Kingdom before the signature of this Agreement, the United Kingdom shall pay without delay to the Union the best estimates amount and the Joint Committee shall determine the manner in which the difference between the actual costs incurred and the best estimates amount is to be addressed.

Article 100   Mutual assistance for the recovery of claims relating to taxes, duties and other measures

1.   Council Directive 2010/24/EU ([128]) shall apply until 5 years after the end of the transition period between the Member States and the United Kingdom in respect of claims relating to amounts that became due before the end of the transition period, claims relating to transactions that took place before the end of the transition period but where the amounts became due after that period, and claims relating to transactions

---

[126] Council Regulation (EU) No 904/2010 of 7 October 2010 on administrative cooperation and combating fraud in the field of value added tax (OJ L 268, 12.10.2010, p. 1).

[127] Council Regulation (EU) No 389/2012 of 2 May 2012 on administrative cooperation in the field of excise duties and repealing Regulation (EC) No 2073/2004 (OJ L 121, 8.5.2012, p. 1).

[128] Council Directive 2010/24/EU of 16 March 2010 concerning mutual assistance for the recovery of claims relating to taxes, duties and other measures (OJ L 84, 31.3.2010, p. 1).

covered by Article 51(1) of this Agreement or movements of excise goods covered by Article 52 of this Agreement.

2.   By way of derogation from Article 8, the United Kingdom shall have access, to the extent strictly necessary to exercise its rights and comply with obligations under this Article, to the networks, information systems and databases listed in Annex IV. The United Kingdom shall reimburse the Union for the actual costs incurred by the Union as a consequence of facilitating that access. The Union shall communicate to the United Kingdom the amount of those costs by 31 March of each year until the end of the period referred to in Annex IV. In the event that the communicated amount of the actual costs incurred considerably diverges from the best estimates amount that was communicated by the Union to the United Kingdom before the signature of this Agreement, the United Kingdom shall pay without delay to the Union the best estimates amount and the Joint Committee shall determine the manner in which the difference between the actual costs incurred and the best estimates amount is to be addressed.

TITLE XII
PRIVILEGES AND IMMUNITIES

Article 101   Definitions

1.   For the purposes of this Title, "members of the institutions" means, irrespective of their nationality, the President of the European Council, the members of the European Commission, the Judges, the Advocates-General, the Registrars and the Assistant Rapporteurs of the Court of Justice of the European Union, the members of the Court of Auditors, the members of the organs of the European Central Bank, the members of the organs of the European Investment Bank, as well as all other persons assimilated to any of those categories of persons under Union law for the purposes of Protocol (No 7) on the Privileges and Immunities of the European Union ("Protocol on the Privileges and Immunities"). The term "members of the institutions" does not include members of the European Parliament.

2.   Regulation (EURATOM, ECSC, EEC) No 549/69 of the Council ([129]) shall apply to determine the categories of officials and other servants covered by Articles 110 to 113 of this Agreement.

CHAPTER 1
PROPERTY, FUNDS, ASSETS AND OPERATIONS OF THE UNION

Article 102   Inviolability

Article 1 of the Protocol on the Privileges and Immunities shall apply in respect of premises, buildings, property and assets of the Union in the United Kingdom used by the Union before the end of the transition period, until they are no longer in official use or have been removed from the United Kingdom. The Union shall notify the United Kingdom when its premises, buildings, property or assets are no longer in such use or have been removed from the United Kingdom.

Article 103   Archives

Article 2 of the Protocol on the Privileges and Immunities shall apply in respect of all archives of the Union in the United Kingdom at the end of the transition period, until they have been removed from the United Kingdom. The Union shall notify the United Kingdom of the removal of any of its archives from the United Kingdom.

---

[129] Regulation (EURATOM, ECSC, EEC) No 549/69 of the Council of 25 March 1969 determining the categories of officials and other servants of the European Communities to whom the provisions of Article 12, the second paragraph of Article 13 and Article 14 of the Protocol on the Privileges and Immunities of the Communities apply (OJ L 74, 27.3.1969, p. 1).

Article 104   Taxation

Article 3 of the Protocol on the Privileges and Immunities shall apply in respect of the Union's assets, revenues and other property in the United Kingdom at the end of the transition period, until they are no longer in official use or have been removed from the United Kingdom.

CHAPTER 2
COMMUNICATIONS

Article 105   Communications

Article 5 of the Protocol on the Privileges and Immunities shall apply in the United Kingdom in respect of the official communications, official correspondence, and transmission of documents in relation to activities of the Union pursuant to this Agreement.

CHAPTER 3
MEMBERS OF THE EUROPEAN PARLIAMENT

Article 106   Immunity of members of the European Parliament

Article 8 of the Protocol on the Privileges and Immunities shall apply in the United Kingdom in respect of opinions expressed or votes cast before the end of the transition period by members of the European Parliament, including former members, irrespective of their nationality, in the performance of their duties.

Article 107   Social security

Former members of the European Parliament, irrespective of their nationality, who draw a pension in that capacity, as well as persons entitled to survivor's pensions as survivors of former members, irrespective of their nationality, shall be exempted from obligatory affiliation to and payment into national social security systems in the United Kingdom, under the same conditions as were applicable on the last day of the transition period, provided that the former members of the European Parliament were members of the European Parliament before the end of the transition period.

Article 108   Avoidance of double taxation on pensions and transitional allowances

Articles 12, 13 and 14 of Decision 2005/684/EC, Euratom of the European Parliament ([130]) shall apply in the United Kingdom in respect of pensions and transitional allowances paid to former members of the European Parliament, irrespective of their nationality, and Article 17 of that Decision shall apply in respect of persons entitled to survivor's pensions as survivors of former members, irrespective of their nationality, to the extent that the entitlement to a pension or transitional allowance was earned before the end of the transition period.

CHAPTER 4
REPRESENTATIVES OF MEMBER STATES AND OF THE UNITED KINGDOM
TAKING PART IN THE WORK OF THE INSTITUTIONS OF THE UNION

Article 109   Privileges, immunities and facilities

1.   Article 10 of the Protocol on the Privileges and Immunities shall apply in the United Kingdom in respect of representatives of Member States and of the United Kingdom who take part in the work of the institutions, bodies, offices and agencies of the Union, of their advisers and technical experts, and of members of the advisory bodies of the Union, irrespective of their nationality, as regards their participation in such work:
     (a)   that took place before the end of the transition period;
     (b)   that takes place after the end of the transition period in connection with activities of the Union pursuant to this Agreement.

---

[130] Decision 2005/684/EC, Euratom of the European Parliament of 28 September 2005 adopting the Statute for Members of the European Parliament (OJ L 262, 7.10.2005, p. 1).

2.   Article 10 of the Protocol on the Privileges and Immunities shall apply in the Union in respect of representatives of the United Kingdom who take part in the work of the institutions, bodies, offices and agencies of the Union, and of their advisers and technical experts, as regards their participation in such work:
(a)   that took place before the end of the transition period;
(b)   that takes place after the end of the transition period in connection with activities of the Union pursuant to this Agreement.

CHAPTER 5
MEMBERS OF THE INSTITUTIONS, OFFICIALS AND OTHER SERVANTS

Article 110   Privileges and Immunities

1.   Article 11(a) of the Protocol on the Privileges and Immunities shall apply in the United Kingdom in respect of acts performed, including in respect of their words spoken or written, by members of the institutions, officials and other servants of the Union, including former members, former officials and former other servants, of any nationality, in their official capacity:
(a)   before the end of the transition period;
(b)   after the end of the transition period in connection with activities of the Union pursuant to this Agreement.
2.   The first, second and third paragraphs of Article 3 of Protocol (No 3) on the Statute of the Court of Justice of the European Union shall apply in the United Kingdom in respect of the Judges of the Court of Justice of the European Union and the Advocates-General until the decisions of the Court of Justice of the European Union in all proceedings and requests for preliminary rulings referred to in Articles 86 and 87 of this Agreement have become final, and shall apply thereafter, including in respect of former Judges and former Advocates-General, as regards all acts performed by them in their official capacity, including words spoken or written, before the end of the transition period or in relation to the proceedings referred to in Articles 86 and 87.
3.   Article 11(b) to (e) of the Protocol on the Privileges and Immunities shall apply in the United Kingdom in respect of officials and other servants of the Union of any nationality, as well as in respect of their spouses and dependent members of their families, irrespective of their nationality, if those officials or other servants entered the service of the Union before the end of the transition period, until those persons have completed their relocation to the Union.

Article 111   Taxation

Article 12 of the Protocol on the Privileges and Immunities shall apply in the United Kingdom in respect of members of the institutions, officials and other servants of the Union of any nationality, including former members, former officials and former other servants, if those members, officials or other servants entered the service of the Union before the end of the transition period, provided that the persons concerned are liable to pay tax for the benefit of the Union on the salaries, wages, emoluments and pensions paid to them by the Union.

Article 112   Domicile for tax purposes

1.   Article 13 of the Protocol on the Privileges and Immunities shall apply in respect of members of the institutions, officials and other servants of the Union of any nationality, who entered the service of the Union before the end of the transition period, as well as, irrespective of their nationality, in respect of spouses not separately engaged in a gainful occupation and children who are dependent on and in the care of such members, officials or other servants.
2.   Paragraph 1 shall apply only in respect of persons who established their residence in a Member State solely by reason of the performance of their duties in the service of the Union and who had their domicile in the United Kingdom for tax purposes at the time of entering the service of the Union, and in respect of persons who established their residence in the United Kingdom solely by reason of the performance of their duties in the service of the Union and who had their domicile for tax purposes in a Member State at the time of entering the service of the Union.

Article 113   Social security contributions

Members of the institutions, officials and other servants of the Union of any nationality, including former members, former officials and former other servants, who entered the service of the Union before the end of the transition period and who reside in the United Kingdom, as well as, irrespective of their nationality, spouses not separately engaged in a gainful occupation and children who are dependent on and in the care of such members, officials or other servants, shall be exempted from obligatory affiliation to and payment into national social security systems in the United Kingdom, under the same conditions as were applicable on the last day of the transition period, provided that the persons concerned are affiliated to the social security scheme of the Union.

Article 114   Transfer of pension rights

In respect of officials and other servants of the Union of any nationality, including former officials and former other servants, who entered the service of the Union before the end of the transition period and who seek to transfer pension rights out of or into the United Kingdom pursuant to Article 11(1), (2) or (3) and Article 12 of Annex VIII to the Staff Regulations of Officials of the European Union ([131]) or Articles 39, 109 and 135 of the Conditions of Employment of Other Servants of the European Union, the obligations of the United Kingdom shall be the same as those existing before the end of the transition period.

Article 115   Unemployment insurance

Articles 28a, 96, and 136 of the Conditions of Employment of Other Servants of the European Union shall apply in respect of other servants of the Union of any nationality, including former other servants, who contributed to the Union's unemployment scheme before the end of the transition period if they reside in the United Kingdom and are registered with the unemployment authorities of the United Kingdom after the end of the transition period.

CHAPTER 6
OTHER PROVISIONS

Article 116   Waiver of immunities and cooperation

1. Articles 17 and 18 of the Protocol on the Privileges and Immunities shall apply in respect of privileges, immunities and facilities accorded by this Title.
2. When taking a decision under Article 17 of the Protocol on the Privileges and Immunities on whether to waive immunity upon the request of the authorities of the United Kingdom, the Union shall afford the same consideration as it affords to requests from the authorities of the Member States in comparable situations.
3. Upon the request of the authorities of the United Kingdom, the Union shall notify those authorities of the status of any person which is relevant to that person's entitlement to a privilege or immunity under this Title.

Article 117   European Central Bank

1. This Title shall apply in respect of the European Central Bank ("ECB"), the members of its organs, its staff, and the representatives of the national central banks in the European System of Central Banks ("ESCB") who take part in the activities of the ECB.
2. The second paragraph of Article 22 of the Protocol on the Privileges and Immunities shall apply in respect of the ECB, the members of its organs, its staff, the representatives of the national central banks in the ESCB who take part in the activities of the ECB, and any property, assets and operations of the ECB in the United Kingdom held, managed or conducted pursuant to Protocol (No 4) on the Statute of the European System of Central Banks and of the European Central Bank.
3. Paragraph 2 shall apply in respect of:
   (a)   such property and assets of the ECB that are held in the United Kingdom at the end of the transition period; and

---

[131] Staff Regulations of Officials of the European Union as laid down in Council Regulation (EEC, Euratom, ECSC) No 259/68 of 29 February 1968 laying down the Staff Regulations and the Conditions of Employment of Other Servants of the European Communities and instituting special measures temporarily applicable to officials of the Commission (OJ L 56, 4.3.1968, p. 1).

(b)   such operations of the ECB in the United Kingdom or with United Kingdom counterparts, and ancillary activities related thereto, that were ongoing at the end of the transition period, or that are initiated after the end of the transition period as part of its activities to sustain operations that were ongoing at the end of the transition period, until their final maturity, disposal or completion.

Article 118   European Investment Bank

1.   This Title shall apply in respect of the European Investment Bank ("EIB"), the members of its organs, its staff and the representatives of the Member States who take part in its activities, as well as to any subsidiaries or any other entities established by the EIB before the end of the transition period in accordance with Article 28(1) of Protocol (No 5) on the Statute of the European Investment Bank, in particular the European Investment Fund.

2.   The second paragraph of Article 21 of the Protocol on the Privileges and Immunities shall apply in respect of the EIB, the members of its organs, its staff and the representatives of the Member States who take part in its activities, as well as to any subsidiaries or any other entities established by the EIB before the end of the transition period in accordance with Article 28(1) of Protocol (No 5) on the Statute of the European Investment Bank, in particular the European Investment Fund.

3.   Paragraph 2 shall apply in respect of:

(a)   such property and assets of the EIB or of any subsidiaries and other entities established by the EIB before the end of the transition period in accordance with Article 28(1) of Protocol (No 5) on the Statute of the European Investment Bank, in particular the European Investment Fund, that are held in the United Kingdom at the end of the transition period; and

(b)   such borrowing, financing, guarantee, investment, treasury and technical assistance operations of the EIB and of any subsidiaries and other entities established by the EIB before the end of the transition period in accordance with Article 28(1) of Protocol (No 5) on the Statute of the European Investment Bank, in particular the European Investment Fund, in the United Kingdom or with United Kingdom counterparts, and ancillary activities related thereto, that were ongoing at the end of the transition period or that are initiated after the end of the transition period, as part of their activities to sustain operations that were ongoing at the end of the transition period until their final maturity, disposure, or completion.

Article 119   Host agreements

The Headquarters Agreement between the United Kingdom and the European Banking Authority of 8 May 2012, the Exchange of Letters concerning the Application in the United Kingdom of the Protocol on the Privileges and Immunities of the European Communities to the European Agency for the Evaluation of Medicinal Products of 24 June 1996, and the Agreement on the Hosting of the Galileo Security Monitoring Centre of 17 July 2013 shall apply, respectively, to the European Banking Authority, the European Medicines Agency and the Galileo Security Monitoring Centre, until their relocation to a Member State is completed. The date of notification by the Union of the completion date of the relocation shall constitute the termination date of those host agreements.

TITLE XIII
OTHER ISSUES RELATING TO THE FUNCTIONING OF THE INSTITUTIONS, BODIES, OFFICES AND AGENCIES OF THE UNION

Article 120   Obligation of professional secrecy

Article 339 TFEU and other provisions of Union law that impose an obligation of professional secrecy on certain individuals and institutions, bodies, offices and agencies of the Union shall apply in the United Kingdom in respect of any information of the kind covered by obligations of professional secrecy either obtained before the end of the transition period or obtained after the end of the transition period in connection with activities of the Union pursuant to this Agreement. The United Kingdom shall respect such obligations of individuals and institutions, bodies, offices and agencies and shall ensure that they are complied with in its territory.

Article 121   Obligation of professional discretion

Article 19 of the Staff Regulations of Officials of the European Union and other provisions of Union law that impose an obligation of professional discretion on certain individuals shall apply in the United Kingdom in respect of any information either obtained before the end of the transition period or obtained after the end of the transition period in connection with activities of the Union pursuant to this Agreement. The United Kingdom shall respect such obligations of individuals and shall ensure that they are complied with in its territory.

Article 122   Access to documents

1. For the purposes of the provisions of Union law on access to documents of the institutions, bodies, offices and agencies of the Union, all references to Member States and their authorities shall be understood as including the United Kingdom and its authorities in respect of documents drawn up by or obtained by the institutions, bodies, offices and agencies of the Union:
    (a) before the end of the transition period; or
    (b) after the end of the transition period in connection with activities of the Union pursuant to this Agreement.
2. Article 5 and Article 9(5) of Regulation (EC) No 1049/2001 of the European Parliament and of the Council ([132]) and Article 5 of Decision ECB/2004/3 of the European Central Bank ([133]) shall apply in the United Kingdom in respect of all documents falling within the scope of those provisions obtained by the United Kingdom:
    (a) before the end of the transition period; or
    (b) after the end of the transition period in connection with activities of the Union pursuant to this Agreement.

Article 123   European Central Bank

1. Articles 9.1, 17, 35.1, 35.2, and 35.4 of Protocol (No 4) on the Statute of the European System of Central Banks and of the European Central Bank, shall apply in respect of the ECB, the members of its organs, its staff, the representatives of the national central banks in the ESCB who take part in the activities of the ECB, and any property, assets and operations of the ECB in the United Kingdom held, managed or conducted pursuant to that Protocol. The ECB shall be exempt from requirements to register in the United Kingdom or to obtain any form of licence, permit or other authorisation or permission from the United Kingdom to carry out its operations.
2. Paragraph 1 shall apply in respect of:
    (a) such property and assets of the ECB that are held in the United Kingdom at the end of the transition period; and
    (b) such operations of the ECB in the United Kingdom or with United Kingdom counterparts, and ancillary activities related thereto, that were ongoing at the end of the transition period, or that are initiated after the end of the transition period as part of its activities to sustain operations that were ongoing at the end of the transition period, until their final maturity, disposal or completion.

Article 124   European Investment Bank

1. Article 13, Articles 20(2), 23(1), 23(4) and Article 26 and the first paragraph of Article 27 of Protocol (No 5) on the Statute of the European Investment Bank shall apply in respect of the EIB, the members of its organs, its staff and the representatives of the Member States who take part in its activities, as well as to any subsidiaries or any other entities established by the EIB before the end of the transition period in accordance with Article 28(1) of that Protocol, in particular the European Investment Fund. The EIB and the European Investment Fund shall be exempt from requirements to register in the United Kingdom or to obtain any form of licence, permit or other authorisation

---

[132] Regulation (EC) No 1049/2001 of the European Parliament and of the Council of 30 May 2001 regarding public access to European Parliament, Council and Commission documents (OJ L 145, 31.5.2001, p. 43).
[133] Decision of the European Central Bank of 4 March 2004 on public access to European Central Bank documents (ECB/2004/3) (2004/258/EC) (OJ L 80, 18.3.2004, p. 42).

or permission from the United Kingdom to carry out their operations. The currency of the United Kingdom shall remain freely transferable and convertible, subject to Article 23(2) of Protocol (No 5) on the Statute of the European Investment Bank in respect of the convertibility of the currency of the United Kingdom into a currency of a non-Member State, for the purposes of such operations.

2. Paragraph 1 shall apply in respect of:

   (a) such property and assets of the EIB or of any subsidiaries and other entities established by the EIB before the end of the transition period in accordance with Article 28(1) of Protocol (No 5) on the Statute of the European Investment Bank, in particular the European Investment Fund, that are held in the United Kingdom at the end of the transition period; and

   (b) such borrowing, financing, guarantee, investment, treasury and technical assistance operations of the EIB or of any subsidiaries and other entities established by the EIB before the end of the transition period in accordance with Article 28(1) of Protocol (No 5) on the Statute of the European Investment Bank, in particular the European Investment Fund, in the United Kingdom or with United Kingdom counterparts, and ancillary activities related thereto, that were ongoing at the end of the transition period or that are initiated after the end of the transition period, as part of their activities to sustain operations that were ongoing at the end of the transition period until their final maturity, disposure, or completion.

Article 125 European Schools

1. The United Kingdom shall be bound by the Convention defining the Statute of the European Schools ([134]), as well as by the Regulations on Accredited European Schools adopted by the Board of Governors of the European Schools, until the end of the school year that is ongoing at the end of the transition period.

2. The United Kingdom shall, with respect to pupils who before 31 August 2021 acquired a European baccalaureate and to pupils who are enrolled in a cycle of secondary studies in a European School before 31 August 2021 and acquire a European baccalaureate after that date, ensure that such pupils enjoy the rights provided for in Article 5(2) of the Convention defining the Statute of the European Schools.

PART FOUR
TRANSITION

Article 126 Transition period

There shall be a transition or implementation period, which shall start on the date of entry into force of this Agreement and end on 31 December 2020.

Article 127 Scope of the transition

1. Unless otherwise provided in this Agreement, Union law shall be applicable to and in the United Kingdom during the transition period.

   However, the following provisions of the Treaties, and acts adopted by the institutions, bodies, offices or agencies of the Union, shall not be applicable to and in the United Kingdom during the transition period:

   (a) provisions of the Treaties and acts which, pursuant to Protocol (No 15) on certain provisions relating to the United Kingdom of Great Britain and Northern Ireland, Protocol (No 19) on the Schengen acquis integrated into the framework of the European Union or Protocol (No 21) on the position of the United Kingdom and Ireland in respect of the area of freedom, security and justice, or pursuant to the provisions of the Treaties on enhanced cooperation, were not binding upon and in the United Kingdom before the date of entry into force of this Agreement as well as acts amending such acts;

   (b) Article 11(4) TEU, point (b) of Article 20(2), Article 22 and the first paragraph of Article 24 TFEU, Articles 39 and 40 of the Charter of Fundamental Rights of the European Union, and the acts adopted on the basis of those provisions.

---

[134] OJ L 212, 17.8.1994, p. 3.

2. In the event that the Union and the United Kingdom reach an agreement governing their future relationship in the areas of the Common Foreign and Security Policy and the Common Security and Defence Policy which becomes applicable during the transition period, Chapter 2 of Title V of the TEU and the acts adopted on the basis of those provisions shall cease to apply to the United Kingdom from the date of application of that agreement.

3. During the transition period, the Union law applicable pursuant to paragraph 1 shall produce in respect of and in the United Kingdom the same legal effects as those which it produces within the Union and its Member States, and shall be interpreted and applied in accordance with the same methods and general principles as those applicable within the Union.

4. The United Kingdom shall not participate in any enhanced cooperation:

   (a) in relation to which authorisation was granted after the date of entry into force of this Agreement; or

   (b) within the framework of which no acts were adopted before the date of entry into force of this Agreement.

5. During the transition period, in relation to measures which amend, build upon or replace an existing measure adopted pursuant to Title V of Part Three of the TFEU by which the United Kingdom is bound before the date of entry into force of this Agreement, Article 5 of Protocol (No 19) on the Schengen acquis integrated into the framework of the European Union and Article 4a of Protocol (No 21) on the position of the United Kingdom and Ireland in respect of the area of freedom, security and justice shall continue to apply *mutatis mutandis*. The United Kingdom shall not, however, have the right to notify its wish to take part in the application of new measures pursuant to Title V of Part Three of the TFEU other than those measures referred to in Article 4a of Protocol No 21.

   In order to support continuing cooperation between the Union and the United Kingdom, under the conditions set out for cooperation with third countries in the relevant measures, the Union may invite the United Kingdom to cooperate in relation to new measures adopted under Title V of Part III TFEU.

6. Unless otherwise provided in this Agreement, during the transition period, any reference to Member States in the Union law applicable pursuant to paragraph 1, including as implemented and applied by Member States, shall be understood as including the United Kingdom.

7. By way of derogation from paragraph 6:

   (a) for the purposes of Article 42(6) and Article 46 TEU and of Protocol (No 10) on permanent structured cooperation established by Article 42 TEU, any references to Member States shall be understood as not including the United Kingdom. This shall not preclude the possibility for the United Kingdom to be invited to participate as a third country in individual projects under the conditions set out in Council Decision (CFSP) 2017/2315 ([135]) on an exceptional basis, or in any other form of cooperation to the extent allowed and under the conditions set out by future Union acts adopted on the basis of Article 42(6) and Article 46 TEU;

   (b) where acts of the Union provide for the participation of Member States, nationals of Member States or natural or legal persons residing or established in a Member State in an information exchange, procedure or programme which continues to be implemented or which starts after the end of the transition period, and where such participation would grant access to security-related sensitive information that only Member States, nationals of Member States, or natural or legal persons residing or established in a Member State, are to have knowledge of, in such exceptional circumstances the references to Member States in such Union acts shall be understood as not including the United Kingdom. The Union shall notify the United Kingdom of the application of this derogation;

   (c) for the purposes of the recruitment of officials and other servants of the institutions, bodies, offices or agencies of the Union, any references to Member States in Articles 27 and 28(a) of the Staff Regulations and in Article 1 of Annex X

([135]) Council Decision (CFSP) 2017/2315 of 11 December 2017 establishing permanent structured cooperation (PESCO) and determining the list of participating Member States (OJ L 331, 14.12.2017, p. 57).

thereto and in Articles 12, 82 and 128 of the Conditions of Employment of Other Servants of the European Union, or in the relevant provisions of other staff rules applicable to those institutions, bodies, offices or agencies, shall be understood as not including the United Kingdom.

Article 128   Institutional arrangements

1. Notwithstanding Article 127, during the transition period Article 7 shall apply.
2. For the purposes of the Treaties, during the transition period, the parliament of the United Kingdom shall not be considered to be a national parliament of a Member State, except as regards Article 1 of Protocol (No 1) on the role of national parliaments in the European Union and, in respect of proposals which are in the public domain, Article 2 of that Protocol.
3. During the transition period, provisions of the Treaties which grant institutional rights to Member States enabling them to submit proposals, initiatives or requests to the institutions shall be understood as not including the United Kingdom ([136]).
4. For the purposes of participation in the institutional arrangements laid down in Articles 282 and 283 TFEU and in Protocol (No 4) on the Statute of the European system of central banks and of the European Central Bank, with the exception of Article 21(2) of that Protocol, during the transition period, the Bank of England shall not be considered to be a national central bank of a Member State.
5. By way of derogation from paragraph 1 of this Article and from Article 7, during the transition period, representatives or experts of the United Kingdom, or experts designated by the United Kingdom, may, upon invitation, exceptionally attend meetings or parts of meetings of the committees referred to in Article 3(2) of Regulation (EU) No 182/2011, meetings or parts of meetings of Commission expert groups, meetings or parts of meetings of other similar entities, and meetings or parts of meetings of bodies, offices or agencies, where and when representatives or experts of the Member States or experts designated by Member States take part, provided that one of the following conditions is fulfilled:
   (a)   the discussion concerns individual acts to be addressed during the transition period to the United Kingdom or to natural or legal persons residing or established in the United Kingdom;
   (b)   the presence of the United Kingdom is necessary and in the interest of the Union, in particular for the effective implementation of Union law during the transition period. During such meetings or parts of meetings, the representatives or experts of the United Kingdom or experts designated by the United Kingdom shall have no voting rights and their presence shall be limited to the specific agenda items that fulfil the conditions set out in point (a) or (b).
6. During the transition period, the United Kingdom shall not act as leading authority for risk assessments, examinations, approvals or authorisations at the level of the Union or at the level of Member States acting jointly as referred to in the acts and provisions listed in Annex VII.
7. During the transition period, where draft Union acts identify or refer directly to specific Member State authorities, procedures, or documents, the United Kingdom shall be consulted by the Union on such drafts, with a view to ensuring the proper implementation and application of those acts by and in the United Kingdom.

Article 129   Specific arrangements relating to the Union's external action

1. Without prejudice to Article 127(2), during the transition period, the United Kingdom shall be bound by the obligations stemming from the international agreements concluded by the Union, by Member States acting on its behalf, or by the Union and its Member States acting jointly, as referred to in point (a)(iv) of Article 2. (*)
2. During the transition period, representatives of the United Kingdom shall not participate in the work of any bodies set up by international agreements concluded by the Union,

---

[136] This should in particular concern Articles 7, 30, 42(4), 48(2) to (6) and 49 TEU and Articles 25, 76(b), 82(3), 83(3), 86(1), 87(3), 135, 218(8), 223(1), 262, 311 and 341 TFEU.

(*) The Union will notify the other parties to these agreements that during the transition period the United Kingdom is to be treated as a Member State for the purposes of these agreements.

or by Member States acting on its behalf, or by the Union and its Member States acting jointly, unless:

(a)   the United Kingdom participates in its own right; or

(b)   the Union exceptionally invites the United Kingdom to attend, as part of the Union's delegation, meetings or parts of meetings of such bodies, where the Union considers that the presence of the United Kingdom is necessary and in the interest of the Union, in particular for the effective implementation of those agreements during the transition period; such presence shall only be allowed where Member States participation is permitted under the applicable agreements.

3.   In accordance with the principle of sincere cooperation, the United Kingdom shall refrain, during the transition period, from any action or initiative which is likely to be prejudicial to the Union's interests, in particular in the framework of any international organisation, agency, conference or forum of which the United Kingdom is a party in its own right.

4.   Notwithstanding paragraph 3, during the transition period, the United Kingdom may negotiate, sign and ratify international agreements entered into in its own capacity in the areas of exclusive competence of the Union, provided those agreements do not enter into force or apply during the transition period, unless so authorised by the Union.

5.   Without prejudice to Article 127(2), whenever there is a need for coordination, the United Kingdom may be consulted, on a case-by-case basis.

6.   Following a decision of the Council falling under Chapter 2 of Title V TEU, the United Kingdom may make a formal declaration to the High Representative of the Union for Foreign Affairs and Security Policy, indicating that, for vital and stated reasons of national policy, in those exceptional cases it will not apply the decision. In a spirit of mutual solidarity, the United Kingdom shall refrain from any action likely to conflict with or impede Union action based on that decision, and the Member States shall respect the position of the United Kingdom.

7.   During the transition period, the United Kingdom shall not provide commanders of civilian operations, heads of mission, operation commanders or force commanders for missions or operations conducted under Articles 42, 43 and 44 TEU, nor shall it provide the operational headquarters for such missions or operations, or serve as framework nation for Union battlegroups. During the transition period, the United Kingdom shall not provide the head of any operational actions under Article 28 TEU.

Article 130   Specific arrangements relating to fishing opportunities

1.   As regards the fixing of fishing opportunities within the meaning of Article 43(3) TFEU for any period falling within the transition period, the United Kingdom shall be consulted in respect of the fishing opportunities related to the United Kingdom, including in the context of the preparation of relevant international consultations and negotiations.

2.   For the purposes of paragraph 1, the Union shall offer the opportunity to the United Kingdom to provide comments on the Annual Communication from the European Commission on fishing opportunities, the scientific advice from the relevant scientific bodies and the proposals from the European Commission for fishing opportunities for any period falling within the transition period.

3.   Notwithstanding point (b) of Article 129(2), with a view to allowing the United Kingdom to prepare its future membership in relevant international fora, the Union may exceptionally invite the United Kingdom to attend, as part of the Union's delegation, international consultations and negotiations referred to in paragraph 1 of this Article, to the extent allowed for Member States and permitted by the specific forum.

4.   Without prejudice to Article 127(1), the relative stability keys for the allocation of fishing opportunities referred to in paragraph 1 of this Article shall be maintained.

Article 131 Supervision and enforcement

During the transition period, the institutions, bodies, offices and agencies of the Union shall have the powers conferred upon them by Union law in relation to the United Kingdom and to natural and legal persons residing or established in the United Kingdom. In particular, the Court of Justice of the European Union shall have jurisdiction as provided for in the Treaties.

The first paragraph shall also apply during the transition period as regards the interpretation and application of this Agreement.

Article 132 Extension of the transition period

1.   Notwithstanding Article 126, the Joint Committee may, before 1 July 2020, adopt a single decision extending the transition period for up to 1 or 2 years. (**)

2.   In the event that the Joint Committee adopts a decision under paragraph 1, the following shall apply:

   (a)   by way of derogation from Article 127(6), the United Kingdom shall be considered as a third country for the purposes of the implementation of the Union programmes and activities committed under the multiannual financial framework applying as from the year 2021;

   (b)   by way of derogation from Article 127(1) and without prejudice to Part Five of this Agreement, the applicable Union law concerning the Union's own resources relating to the financial years covered by the extension of the transition period shall not apply to the United Kingdom after 31 December 2020;

   (c)   by way of derogation from Article 127(1) of this Agreement, Articles 107, 108 and 109 TFEU shall not apply to measures of the United Kingdom authorities, including on rural development, supporting the production of and trade in agricultural products in the United Kingdom up to an annual level of support which shall not be more than the total amount of expenditure incurred in the United Kingdom under the Common Agricultural Policy in 2019, and provided that a minimum percentage of that exempted support complies with the provisions of Annex 2 to the WTO Agreement on Agriculture. Such minimum percentage shall be determined on the basis of the last available percentage by which the overall expenditure under the Common Agricultural Policy in the Union complied with the provisions of Annex 2 to the WTO Agreement on Agriculture. In the event that the period by which the transition period is extended is not a multiple of 12 months, the maximum annual level of exempted support in the year for which the extended transition period covers less than 12 months shall be reduced pro rata;

   (d)   for the period from 1 January 2021 to the end of the transition period, the United Kingdom shall make a contribution to the Union budget, as determined in accordance with paragraph 3;

   (e)   subject to point (d) of paragraph 3, Part Five of this Agreement shall not be affected.

3.   A decision of the Joint Committee under paragraph 1 shall:

   (a)   establish the appropriate amount of the contribution of the United Kingdom to the Union budget for the period from 1 January 2021 to the end of the transition period, taking into account the status of the United Kingdom during that period, as well as the modalities of payment of that amount;

   (b)   specify the maximum level of exempted support, as well as the minimum percentage thereof that shall comply with the provisions of Annex 2 to the WTO Agreement on Agriculture, as referred to in point (c) of paragraph 2;

   (c)   lay down any other measure necessary for the implementation of paragraph 2;

   (d)   adapt the dates or periods referred to in Articles 51, 62, 63, 84, 96, 125, 141, 156, 157 and Annexes IV and V to reflect the extension of the transition period.

(**) In case of extension, the Union will notify other parties to international agreements thereof.

PART SIX
INSTITUTIONAL AND FINAL PROVISIONS

TITLE I
CONSISTENT INTERPRETATION AND APPLICATION

Article 158 References to the Court of Justice of the European Union concerning Part Two

1. Where, in a case which commenced at first instance within 8 years from the end of the transition period before a court or tribunal in the United Kingdom, a question is raised concerning the interpretation of Part Two of this Agreement, and where that court or tribunal considers that a decision on that question is necessary to enable it to give judgment in that case, that court or tribunal may request the Court of Justice of the European Union to give a preliminary ruling on that question.

    However, where the subject matter of the case before the court or tribunal in the United Kingdom is a decision on an application made pursuant to Article 18(1) or (4) or pursuant to Article 19, a request for a preliminary ruling may be made only where the case commenced at first instance within a period of 8 years from the date from which Article 19 applies.

2. The Court of Justice of the European Union shall have jurisdiction to give preliminary rulings on requests pursuant to paragraph 1. The legal effects in the United Kingdom of such preliminary rulings shall be the same as the legal effects of preliminary rulings given pursuant to Article 267 TFEU in the Union and its Member States.

3. In the event that the Joint Committee adopts a decision under Article 132(1), the period of eight years referred to in the second subparagraph of paragraph 1 shall be automatically extended by the corresponding number of months by which the transition period is extended.

Article 159 Monitoring of the implementation and application of Part Two

1. In the United Kingdom, the implementation and application of Part Two shall be monitored by an independent authority (the "Authority") which shall have powers equivalent to those of the European Commission acting under the Treaties to conduct inquiries on its own initiative concerning alleged breaches of Part Two by the administrative authorities of the United Kingdom and to receive complaints from Union citizens and their family members for the purposes of conducting such inquiries. The Authority shall also have the right, following such complaints, to bring a legal action before a competent court or tribunal in the United Kingdom in an appropriate judicial procedure with a view to seeking an adequate remedy.

2. The European Commission and the Authority shall each annually inform the specialised Committee on citizens' rights referred to in point (a) of Article 165(1) on the implementation and application of Part Two in the Union and in the United Kingdom, respectively. The information provided shall, in particular, cover measures taken to implement or comply with Part Two and the number and nature of complaints received.

3. The Joint Committee shall assess, no earlier than 8 years after the end of the transition period, the functioning of the Authority. Following such assessment, it may decide, in good faith, pursuant to point (f) of Article 164(4) and Article 166, that the United Kingdom may abolish the Authority.

Article 160 Jurisdiction of the Court of Justice of the European Union concerning certain provisions of Part Five

Without prejudice to Article 87 of this Agreement, Articles 258, 260 and 267 TFEU shall apply in respect of the interpretation and application of applicable Union law referred to in Article 136 and Article 138(1) or (2) of this Agreement. To this effect, any reference made in Articles 258, 260 and 267 TFEU to a Member State shall be understood as including the United Kingdom.

Article 161   Procedures before the Court of Justice of the European Union

1. Where a court or tribunal of a Member State refers a question concerning the interpretation of this Agreement to the Court of Justice of the European Union for a preliminary ruling, the decision of the national court or tribunal containing that question shall be notified to the United Kingdom.
2. The provisions of Union law governing procedures brought before the Court of Justice of the European Union in accordance with Article 267 TFEU shall apply *mutatis mutandis* to requests for a ruling of the Court of Justice of the European Union made pursuant to Article 158 of this Agreement.

    The provisions of Union law governing the procedure before the Court of Justice of the European Union shall apply in respect of the proceedings before the Court of Justice of the European Union and requests for preliminary rulings made in accordance with Article 160 of this Agreement.
3. In the cases brought before the Court of Justice of the European Union in accordance with paragraph 1 and Articles 158 and 160 of this Agreement and Article 12 of the Protocol on the Sovereign Base Areas:
    (a) the United Kingdom may participate in the proceedings before the Court of Justice of the European Union in the same way as a Member State;
    (b) lawyers authorised to practise before the courts or tribunals of the United Kingdom shall be entitled to represent or assist any parties to such proceedings before the Court of Justice of the European Union; in such cases those lawyers shall in every respect be treated as lawyers authorised to practise before courts of Member States representing or assisting a party before the Court of Justice of the European Union.

Article 162   Participation of the European Commission in cases pending in the United Kingdom

Where the consistent interpretation and application of this Agreement so requires, the European Commission may submit written observations to the courts and tribunals of the United Kingdom in pending cases where the interpretation of the Agreement is concerned. The European Commission may, with the permission of the court or tribunal in question, also make oral observations. The European Commission shall inform the United Kingdom of its intention to submit observations before formally making such submissions.

Article 163   Regular dialogue and exchange of information

In order to facilitate the consistent interpretation of this Agreement and in full deference to the independence of courts, the Court of Justice of the European Union and the United Kingdom's highest courts shall engage in regular dialogue, analogous to the dialogue in which the Court of Justice of the European Union engages with the highest courts of the Member States.

TITLE II

INSTITUTIONAL PROVISIONS

Article 164   Joint Committee

1. A Joint Committee, comprising representatives of the Union and of the United Kingdom, is hereby established. The Joint Committee shall be co-chaired by the Union and the United Kingdom.
2. The Joint Committee shall meet at the request of the Union or the United Kingdom, and in any event shall meet at least once a year. The Joint Committee shall set its meeting schedule and its agenda by mutual consent. The work of the Joint Committee shall be governed by the rules of procedure set out in Annex VIII to this Agreement.
3. The Joint Committee shall be responsible for the implementation and application of this Agreement. The Union and the United Kingdom may each refer to the Joint Committee any issue relating to the implementation, application and interpretation of this Agreement.
4. The Joint Committee shall:
    (a) supervise and facilitate the implementation and application of this Agreement;

      (b)   decide on the tasks of the specialised committees and supervise their work;

      (c)   seek appropriate ways and methods of preventing problems that might arise in areas covered by this Agreement or of resolving disputes that may arise regarding the interpretation and application of this Agreement;

      (d)   consider any matter of interest relating to an area covered by this Agreement;

      (e)   adopt decisions and make recommendations as set out in Article 166; and

      (f)   adopt amendments to this Agreement in the cases provided for in this Agreement.

5.   The Joint Committee may:

      (a)   delegate responsibilities to specialised committees, except those responsibilities referred to in points (b), (e) and (f) of paragraph 4;

      (b)   establish specialised committees other than those established by Article 165, in order to assist the Joint Committee in the performance of its tasks;

      (c)   change the tasks assigned to specialised committees and dissolve any of those committees;

      (d)   except in relation to Parts One, Four and Six, until the end of the fourth year following the end of the transition period, adopt decisions amending this Agreement, provided that such amendments are necessary to correct errors, to address omissions or other deficiencies, or to address situations unforeseen when this Agreement was signed, and provided that such decisions may not amend the essential elements of this Agreement;

      (e)   adopt amendments to the rules of procedure set out in Annex VIII; and

      (f)   take such other actions in the exercise of its functions as decided by the Union and the United Kingdom.

6.   The Joint Committee shall issue an annual report on the functioning of this Agreement.

Article 165   Specialised committees

1.   The following specialised committees are hereby established:

      (a)   the Committee on citizens' rights;

      (b)   the Committee on the other separation provisions;

      (c)   the Committee on issues related to the implementation of the Protocol on Ireland/Northern Ireland;

      (d)   the Committee on issues related to the implementation of the Protocol relating to the Sovereign Base Areas in Cyprus;

      (e)   the Committee on issues related to the implementation of the Protocol on Gibraltar; and

      (f)   the Committee on the financial provisions.

Those specialised committees shall comprise representatives of the Union and representatives of the United Kingdom.

2.   The work of the specialised committees shall be governed by the rules of procedure set out in Annex VIII to this Agreement.

Unless otherwise provided in this Agreement, or unless the co-chairs decide otherwise, the specialised committees shall meet at least once a year. Additional meetings may be held at the request of the Union, the United Kingdom, or of the Joint Committee. They shall be co-chaired by representatives of the Union and of the United Kingdom. The specialised committees shall set their meeting schedule and agenda by mutual consent. The specialised committees may draw up draft decisions and recommendations and refer them for adoption by the Joint Committee.

3.   The Union and the United Kingdom shall ensure that their respective representatives on the specialised committees have the appropriate expertise with respect to the issues under discussion.

4.   The specialised committees shall inform the Joint Committee of their meeting schedules and agenda sufficiently in advance of their meetings, and shall report to the Joint Committee on the results and conclusions of each of their meetings. The creation or existence of a specialised committee shall not prevent the Union or the United Kingdom from bringing any matter directly to the Joint Committee.

Article 166   Decisions and recommendations

1.   The Joint Committee shall, for the purposes of this Agreement, have the power to adopt decisions in respect of all matters for which this Agreement so provides and to make appropriate recommendations to the Union and the United Kingdom.

2. The decisions adopted by the Joint Committee shall be binding on the Union and the United Kingdom, and the Union and the United Kingdom shall implement those decisions. They shall have the same legal effect as this Agreement.

3. The Joint Committee shall adopt its decisions and make its recommendations by mutual consent.

TITLE III

DISPUTE SETTLEMENT

Article 167   Cooperation

The Union and the United Kingdom shall at all times endeavour to agree on the interpretation and application of this Agreement, and shall make every attempt, through cooperation and consultations, to arrive at a mutually satisfactory resolution of any matter that might affect its operation.

Article 168   Exclusivity

For any dispute between the Union and the United Kingdom arising under this Agreement, the Union and the United Kingdom shall only have recourse to the procedures provided for in this Agreement.

Article 169   Consultations and communications within the Joint Committee

1. The Union and the United Kingdom shall endeavour to resolve any dispute regarding the interpretation and application of the provisions of this Agreement by entering into consultations in the Joint Committee in good faith, with the aim of reaching a mutually agreed solution. A party wishing to commence consultations shall provide written notice to the Joint Committee.

2. Any communication or notification between the Union and the United Kingdom provided for in this Title shall be made within the Joint Committee.

Article 170   Initiation of the arbitration procedure

1. Without prejudice to Article 160, if no mutually agreed solution has been reached within 3 months after a written notice has been provided to the Joint Committee in accordance with Article 169(1), the Union or the United Kingdom may request the establishment of an arbitration panel. Such request shall be made in writing to the other party and to the International Bureau of the Permanent Court of Arbitration. The request shall identify the subject matter of the dispute to be brought before the arbitration panel and a summary of the legal arguments in support of the request.

2. The Union and the United Kingdom may agree that the establishment of an arbitration panel may be requested before the expiry of the time limit laid down in paragraph 1.

Article 171   Establishment of the arbitration panel

1. The Joint Committee shall, no later than by the end of the transition period, establish a list of 25 persons who are willing and able to serve as members of an arbitration panel. To that end, the Union and the United Kingdom shall each propose ten persons. The Union and the United Kingdom shall also jointly propose five persons to act as chairperson of the arbitration panel. The Joint Committee shall ensure that the list complies with these requirements at any moment in time.

2. The list established pursuant to paragraph 1 shall only comprise persons whose independence is beyond doubt, who possess the qualifications required for appointment to the highest judicial office in their respective countries or who are jurisconsults of recognised competence, and who possess specialised knowledge or experience of Union law and public international law. That list shall not comprise persons who are members, officials or other servants of the Union institutions, of the government of a Member State, or of the government of the United Kingdom.

3. An arbitration panel shall be composed of five members.

4. Within 15 days of the date of a request in accordance with Article 170, the panel shall be established in accordance with paragraphs 5 and 6.

5. The Union and the United Kingdom shall each nominate two members from among the persons on the list established under paragraph 1. The chairperson shall be selected

by consensus by the members of the panel from the persons jointly nominated by the Union and the United Kingdom to serve as a chairperson.

In the event that the members of the panel are unable to agree on the selection of the chairperson within the time limit laid down in paragraph 4, the Union or the United Kingdom may request the Secretary-General of the Permanent Court of Arbitration to select the chairperson by lot from among the persons jointly proposed by the Union and the United Kingdom to act as chairperson.

6. The Secretary-General of the Permanent Court of Arbitration shall make the selection referred to in second subparagraph of paragraph 5 within 5 days of the request referred to in paragraph 5. Representatives of the Union and of the United Kingdom shall be entitled to be present at the selection.

7. The date of establishment of the arbitration panel shall be the date on which the selection procedure is completed.

8. In the event that the list referred to in paragraph 1 has not been established by expiry of the time limit laid down in paragraph 4, the Union and the United Kingdom shall within 5 days each nominate two persons to serve as members of the panel. If persons have been proposed under paragraph 1, the nominations shall be made from among those persons. The chairperson shall then be appointed in accordance with the procedure set out in paragraph 5. In the event that the Union and the United Kingdom have not, within a further 5 days, jointly proposed at least one person to serve as chairperson, the Secretary-General of the Permanent Court of Arbitration shall within five days, after consultation with the Union and the United Kingdom, propose a chairperson who fulfils the requirements of paragraph 2. Unless either the Union or the United Kingdom objects to that proposal within 5 days, the person proposed by the Secretary-General of the Permanent Court of Arbitration shall be appointed.

9. In the event of failure to establish an arbitration panel within 3 months from the date of the request made pursuant to Article 170, the Secretary-General of the Permanent Court of Arbitration shall, upon request by either the Union or the United Kingdom, within 15 days of such request, after consultation with the Union and the United Kingdom, appoint persons who fulfil the requirements of paragraph 2 of this Article to constitute the arbitration panel.

Article 172   Rules of procedure

Dispute settlement procedures set out in this Title shall be governed by the rules of procedure set out in Part A of Annex IX ("Rules of Procedure"), the Joint Committee shall keep the functioning of those dispute settlement procedures under constant review and may amend the Rules of Procedure.

Article 173   Time-frame of the procedure before the arbitration panel

1. The arbitration panel shall notify its ruling to the Union, the United Kingdom and the Joint Committee within 12 months from the date of establishment of the arbitration panel. Where the arbitration panel considers that it cannot comply with this time limit, its chairperson shall notify the Union and the United Kingdom in writing, stating the reasons for the delay and the date on which the panel intends to conclude its work.

2. Within 10 days of the establishment of the arbitration panel the Union or the United Kingdom may submit a reasoned request to the effect that the case is urgent. In that case, the arbitration panel shall give a ruling on the urgency within 15 days from the receipt of such request. If it has determined the urgency of the case, the arbitration panel shall make every effort to notify its ruling to the Union and the United Kingdom within 6 months from the date of its establishment.

Article 174   Disputes raising questions of Union law

1. Where a dispute submitted to arbitration in accordance with this Title raises a question of interpretation of a concept of Union law, a question of interpretation of a provision of Union law referred to in this Agreement or a question of whether the United Kingdom has complied with its obligations under Article 89(2), the arbitration panel shall not decide on any such question. In such case, it shall request the Court of Justice of the European Union to give a ruling on the question. The Court of Justice of the

European Union shall have jurisdiction to give such a ruling which shall be binding on the arbitration panel.

The arbitration panel shall make the request referred to in the first subparagraph after having heard the parties.

2. Without prejudice to the first sentence of the first subparagraph of paragraph 1, if the Union or the United Kingdom considers that a request in accordance with paragraph 1 is to be made, it may make submissions to the arbitration panel to that effect. In such case, the arbitration panel shall submit the request in accordance with paragraph 1 unless the question raised does not concern the interpretation of a concept of Union law, interpretation of a provision of Union law referred to in this Agreement, or does not concern whether the United Kingdom has complied with its obligations under Article 89(2). The arbitration panel shall provide reasons for its assessment. Within 10 days following the assessment, either party may request the arbitration panel to review its assessment, and a hearing shall be organised within 15 days of the request for the parties to be heard on the matter. The arbitration panel shall provide reasons for its assessment.

3. In the cases referred to in paragraphs 1 and 2, the time limits laid down in Article 173 shall be suspended until the Court of Justice of the European Union has given its ruling. The arbitration panel shall not be required to give its ruling less than 60 days from the date on which the Court of Justice of the European Union has given its ruling.

4. The first subparagraph of Article 161(2) and Article 161(3) shall apply *mutatis mutandis* to the procedures brought before the Court of Justice of the European Union in accordance with this Article.

Article 175   Compliance with the arbitration panel ruling

The arbitration panel ruling shall be binding on the Union and the United Kingdom. The Union and the United Kingdom shall take any measures necessary to comply in good faith with the arbitration panel ruling and shall endeavour to agree on the period of time to comply with the ruling in accordance with the procedure in Article 176.

Article 176   Reasonable period of time for compliance

1. No later than 30 days after the notification of the arbitration panel ruling to the Union and the United Kingdom, the respondent shall, if the panel has ruled in favour of the complainant, notify the complainant of the time it considers it will require for compliance (the "reasonable period of time").

2. If there is disagreement between the Union and the United Kingdom on the reasonable period of time to comply with the arbitration panel ruling, the complainant shall, within 40 days of the notification by the respondent under paragraph 1, request the original arbitration panel in writing to determine the length of the reasonable period of time. Such request shall be notified simultaneously to the respondent. The arbitration panel shall notify its decision on the period for compliance to the Union and the United Kingdom within 40 days of the date of submission of the request.

3. In the event of the original arbitration panel, or some of its members, being unable to reconvene to consider a request under paragraph 2, a new arbitration panel shall be established as set out in Article 171. The time limit for notifying the decision shall be 60 days from the date of establishment of the new arbitration panel.

4. The respondent shall inform the complainant in writing of its progress in complying with the arbitration panel ruling referred to in Article 173 at least 1 month before the expiry of the reasonable period of time.

5. The reasonable period of time may be extended by mutual agreement of the Union and the United Kingdom.

Article 177   Review of any measure taken to comply with the arbitration panel ruling

1. The respondent shall notify the complainant before the end of the reasonable period of time of any measure that it has taken to comply with the arbitration panel ruling.

2. If, at the end of the reasonable period, the complainant considers that the respondent has failed to comply with the arbitration panel ruling referred to in Article 173, the

complainant may request the original arbitration panel in writing to rule on the matter. The arbitration panel shall notify its ruling to the Union and the United Kingdom within 90 days of the date of submission of the request.

3. In the event of the original arbitration panel, or some of its members, being unable to reconvene to consider a request under paragraph 2, a new arbitration panel shall be established as set out in Article 171. The time limit for notifying the ruling shall be 60 days from the date of establishment of the new arbitration panel.

4. Where a case referred to the arbitration panel pursuant to paragraph 2 raises a question of interpretation of a concept of Union law or a question of interpretation of a provision of Union law referred to in this Agreement, Article 174 shall apply *mutatis mutandis*.

Article 178   Temporary remedies in case of non-compliance

1. If the arbitration panel rules in accordance with Article 177(2) that the respondent has failed to comply with the arbitration panel ruling referred to in Article 173, at the request of the complainant it may impose a lump sum or penalty payment to be paid to the complainant. In determining the lump sum or penalty payment, the arbitration panel shall take into account the seriousness of the non-compliance and underlying breach of obligation, the duration of the non- compliance and underlying breach of obligation.

2. If, 1 month after the arbitration panel ruling referred to in paragraph 1, the respondent has failed to pay any lump sum or penalty payment imposed on it, or if, 6 months after the arbitration panel ruling referred to in Article 177(2), the respondent persists in not complying with the arbitration panel ruling referred to in Article 173, the complainant shall be entitled, upon notification to the respondent, to suspend obligations arising from:

   (a) any provision of this Agreement other than those contained in Part Two; or

   (b) parts of any other agreement between the Union and the United Kingdom under the conditions set out in that agreement.

   The notification shall specify the provisions which the complainant intends to suspend. Before deciding to suspend parts of an agreement referred to in point (b) the complainant shall first consider whether the suspension of the provision of this Agreement in accordance with point (a) would be an appropriate response to the breach. Any suspension shall be proportionate to the breach of obligation concerned, taking into account the gravity of the breach and the rights in question and, where the suspension is based on the fact that the respondent persists in not complying with the arbitration panel ruling referred to in Article 173, whether a penalty payment has been imposed on the respondent and has been paid or is still being paid by the latter.

   The complainant may implement the suspension at any moment but not earlier than 10 days after the date of the notification, unless the respondent has requested arbitration under paragraph 3.

3. If the respondent considers that the extent of the suspension set out in the notification referred to in paragraph 2 is not proportionate, it may request the original arbitration panel in writing to rule on the matter. Such request shall be notified to the complainant before the expiry of the 10-day period referred to in paragraph 2. The arbitration panel shall notify its ruling to the Union and the United Kingdom within 60 days of the date of submission of the request. Obligations shall not be suspended until the arbitration panel has notified its ruling, and any suspension shall be consistent with the arbitration panel ruling.

4. In the event of the original arbitration panel, or some of its members, being unable to reconvene to consider a request under paragraph 2, a new arbitration panel shall be established as set out in Article 171. In such cases, the period for notifying the ruling shall be 90 days from the date of establishment of the new arbitration panel.

5. The suspension of obligations shall be temporary and shall be applied only until any measure found to be inconsistent with the provisions of this Agreement has been withdrawn or amended, so as to achieve conformity with the provisions of this Agreement, or until the Union and the United Kingdom have agreed to otherwise settle the dispute.

Article 179   Review of any measure taken after temporary remedies

1. Where the complainant has suspended obligations in accordance with Article 178 or where the arbitration panel has imposed a penalty payment on the respondent in accordance with Article 178(1), the respondent shall notify the complainant of any measure it has taken to comply with the ruling of the arbitration panel and of its request for an end to the suspension of obligations applied by the complainant or to the penalty payment.

2. If the Union and the United Kingdom do not reach an agreement on whether the notified measure brings the respondent into conformity with the provisions of this Agreement within 45 days of the date of submission of the notification, either party may request the original arbitration panel in writing to rule on the matter. Such request shall be notified simultaneously to the other party. The arbitration panel ruling shall be notified to the Union and the United Kingdom and to the Joint Committee within 75 days of the date of submission of the request.

   If the arbitration panel rules that the respondent has brought itself into conformity with this Agreement, or if the complainant does not, within 45 days of the submission of the notification referred to in paragraph 1, request that the original arbitration panel rule on the matter:

   (a) the suspension of obligations shall be terminated within 15 days of either the ruling of the arbitration panel or the end of the 45-day period;

   (b) the penalty payment shall be terminated on the day after either the ruling of the arbitration panel or the end of the 45- day period.

3. In the event of the original arbitration panel, or some of its members, being unable to reconvene to consider a request under paragraph 2, a new arbitration panel shall be established as set out in Article 171. The period for notifying the ruling shall in that case be 90 days from the date of establishment of the new arbitration panel.

4. Where a case referred to the arbitration panel pursuant to paragraph 2 raises a question of interpretation of a concept of Union law or a question of interpretation of a provision of Union law referred to in this Agreement, Article 174 shall apply *mutatis mutandis*.

Article 180   Arbitration panel decisions and rulings

1. The arbitration panel shall make every effort to take decisions by consensus. Where, nevertheless, a decision cannot be arrived at by consensus, the matter at issue shall be decided by majority vote. However, in no case dissenting opinions of members of an arbitration panel shall be published.

2. Any ruling of the arbitration panel shall be binding on the Union and the United Kingdom. The ruling shall set out the findings of fact, the applicability of the relevant provisions of this Agreement, and the reasoning behind any findings and conclusions. The Union and the United Kingdom shall make the arbitration panel rulings and decisions publicly available in their entirety, subject to the protection of confidential information.

Article 181   Members of an arbitration panel

1. The members of an arbitration panel shall be independent, shall serve in their individual capacity and shall not take instructions from any organisation or government, and shall comply with the Code of Conduct set out in Part B of Annex IX. The Joint Committee may amend that Code of Conduct.

2. The members of an arbitration panel shall, as from the establishment thereof, enjoy immunity from legal proceedings in the Union and the United Kingdom with respect to acts performed by them in the exercise of their functions on that arbitration panel.

TITLE IV
FINAL PROVISIONS

Article 182   Protocols and Annexes

The Protocol on Ireland / Northern Ireland, the Protocol relating to the Sovereign Base Areas in Cyprus, the Protocol on Gibraltar, and Annexes I to IX shall form an integral part of this Agreement.

Article 183   Authentic texts and depositary

This Agreement is drawn up in a single original in the Bulgarian, Croatian, Czech, Danish, Dutch, English, Estonian, Finnish, French, German, Greek, Hungarian, Irish, Italian, Latvian, Lithuanian, Maltese, Polish, Portuguese, Romanian, Slovak, Slovenian, Spanish and Swedish languages, the texts in each of these languages being equally authentic.

The Secretary General of the Council shall be the depositary of this Agreement.

Article 184   Negotiations on the future relationship

The Union and the United Kingdom shall use their best endeavours, in good faith and in full respect of their respective legal orders, to take the necessary steps to negotiate expeditiously the agreements governing their future relationship referred to in the Political Declaration of 17 October 2019 and to conduct the relevant procedures for the ratification or conclusion of those agreements, with a view to ensuring that those agreements apply, to the extent possible, as from the end of the transition period.

Article 185   Entry into force and application

This Agreement shall enter into force on one of the following dates, whichever is the earliest:

(a)   the day following the end of the period provided for in Article 50(3) TEU, as extended by the European Council in agreement with the United Kingdom, provided that, prior to that date, the depositary of this Agreement has received the written notifications by the Union and the United Kingdom regarding the completion of the necessary internal procedures;

(b)   the first day of the month following the receipt by the depositary of this Agreement of the last of the written notifications referred to in point (a).

In the event that, prior to the end of the period provided for in Article 50(3) TEU, as extended by the European Council in agreement with the United Kingdom, the depositary of this Agreement has not received the written notifications referred to in point (a), this Agreement shall not enter into force.

When making the written notification referred to in the first paragraph, the Union, in respect of any Member State which has raised reasons related to fundamental principles of national law of that Member State, may declare that, during the transition period, in addition to the grounds for non-execution of a European arrest warrant referred to in Framework Decision 2002/584/JHA, the executing judicial authorities of that Member State may refuse to surrender its nationals to the United Kingdom pursuant to a European arrest warrant. In such a case, the United Kingdom may declare, no later than 1 month after the receipt of the Union's declaration, that its executing judicial authorities may refuse to surrender its nationals to that Member State.

Parts Two and Three, with the exception of Article 19, Article 34(1), Article 44, and Article 96(1), as well as Title I of Part Six and Articles 169 to 181, shall apply as from the end of the transition period.

The Protocol on Ireland/Northern Ireland shall apply as from the end of the transition period, with the exception of the following provisions of that Protocol, which shall apply as from the entry into force of this Agreement:

—   Article 1;
—   the third, fourth and sixth subparagraphs of Article 5 (2);
—   the second sentence of Article 5(3);
—   the last sentence of Article 10(2);
—   Article 12(3);
—   Article 13(8);
—   Article 14;
—   Article 15(1) to (4) and (6);
—   Article 19;
—   the first paragraph of Annex 6.

The Protocol relating to the Sovereign Base Areas of the United Kingdom of Great Britain and Northern Ireland in Cyprus, with the exception of Article 11 thereof, shall apply as from the end of the transition period.

The Protocol on Gibraltar, with the exception of Article 1 thereof, shall cease to apply at the end of the transition period.

PROTOCOL ON IRELAND/NORTHERN IRELAND

The Union and the United Kingdom,

HAVING REGARD to the historic ties and enduring nature of the bilateral relationship between Ireland and the United Kingdom,

RECALLING that the United Kingdom's withdrawal from the Union presents a significant and unique challenge to the island of Ireland, and reaffirming that the achievements, benefits and commitments of the peace process will remain of paramount importance to peace, stability and reconciliation there,

RECOGNISING that it is necessary to address the unique circumstances on the island of Ireland through a unique solution in order to ensure the orderly withdrawal of the United Kingdom from the Union,

AFFIRMING that the Good Friday or Belfast Agreement of 10 April 1998 between the Government of the United Kingdom, the Government of Ireland and the other participants in the multi-party negotiations (the "1998 Agreement"), which is annexed to the British-Irish Agreement of the same date (the "British-Irish Agreement"), including its subsequent implementation agreements and arrangements, should be protected in all its parts,

RECOGNISING that cooperation between Northern Ireland and Ireland is a central part of the 1998 Agreement and is essential for achieving reconciliation and the normalisation of relationships on the island of Ireland, and recalling the roles, functions and safeguards of the Northern Ireland Executive, the Northern Ireland Assembly and the North-South Ministerial Council (including cross-community provisions), as set out in the 1998 Agreement,

NOTING that Union law has provided a supporting framework for the provisions on Rights, Safeguards and Equality of Opportunity of the 1998 Agreement,

RECOGNISING that Irish citizens in Northern Ireland, by virtue of their Union citizenship, will continue to enjoy, exercise and have access to rights, opportunities and benefits, and that this Protocol should respect and be without prejudice to the rights, opportunities and identity that come with citizenship of the Union for the people of Northern Ireland who choose to assert their right to Irish citizenship, as defined in Annex 2 of the British-Irish Agreement "Declaration on the Provisions of Paragraph (vi) of Article 1 in Relation to Citizenship",

EMPHASISING that in order to ensure democratic legitimacy, there should be a process to ensure democratic consent in Northern Ireland to the application of Union law under this Protocol,

RECALLING the commitment of the United Kingdom to protect North-South cooperation and its guarantee of avoiding a hard border, including any physical infrastructure or related checks and controls,

NOTING that nothing in this Protocol prevents the United Kingdom from ensuring unfettered market access for goods moving from Northern Ireland to the rest of the United Kingdom's internal market,

UNDERLINING the Union's and the United Kingdom's shared aim of avoiding controls at the ports and airports of Northern Ireland, to the extent possible in accordance with applicable legislation and taking into account their respective regulatory regimes as well as the implementation thereof,

RECALLING the commitments of the Union and the United Kingdom reflected in the Joint Report from the negotiators of the European Union and the United Kingdom Government on progress during phase 1 of negotiations under Article 50 TEU on the United Kingdom's orderly withdrawal from the European Union of 8 December 2017,

RECALLING that the Union and the United Kingdom have carried out a mapping exercise which shows that North-South cooperation relies to a significant extent on a common Union legal and policy framework,

NOTING that therefore the United Kingdom's withdrawal from the Union gives rise to substantial challenges to the maintenance and development of North-South cooperation,

RECALLING that the United Kingdom remains committed to protecting and supporting continued North-South and East-West cooperation across the full range of political, economic, security, societal and agricultural contexts and frameworks for cooperation, including the continued operation of the North-South implementation bodies,

ACKNOWLEDGING the need for this Protocol to be implemented so as to maintain the necessary conditions for continued North-South cooperation, including for possible new arrangements in accordance with the 1998 Agreement,

RECALLING the Union's and the United Kingdom's commitments to the North South PEACE and INTERREG funding programmes under the current multi-annual financial framework and to the maintaining of the current funding proportions for the future programme,

AFFIRMING the commitment of the United Kingdom to facilitate the efficient and timely transit through its territory of goods moving from Ireland to another Member State or to a third country, and vice versa,

DETERMINED that the application of this Protocol should impact as little as possible on the everyday life of communities in both Ireland and Northern Ireland,

UNDERLINING their firm commitment to no customs and regulatory checks or controls and related physical infrastructure at the border between Ireland and Northern Ireland,

RECALLING that Northern Ireland is part of the customs territory of the United Kingdom and will benefit from participation in the United Kingdom's independent trade policy,

HAVING REGARD to the importance of maintaining the integral place of Northern Ireland in the United Kingdom's internal market,

MINDFUL that the rights and obligations of Ireland under the rules of the Union's internal market and customs union must be fully respected,

HAVE AGREED UPON the following provisions, which shall be annexed to the Withdrawal Agreement:

Article 1 Objectives

1. This Protocol is without prejudice to the provisions of the 1998 Agreement in respect of the constitutional status of Northern Ireland and the principle of consent, which provides that any change in that status can only be made with the consent of a majority of its people.
2. This Protocol respects the essential State functions and territorial integrity of the United Kingdom.
3. This Protocol sets out arrangements necessary to address the unique circumstances on the island of Ireland, to maintain the necessary conditions for continued North-South cooperation, to avoid a hard border and to protect the 1998 Agreement in all its dimensions.

Article 2 Rights of individuals

1. The United Kingdom shall ensure that no diminution of rights, safeguards or equality of opportunity, as set out in that part of the 1998 Agreement entitled Rights, Safeguards and Equality of Opportunity results from its withdrawal from the Union, including in the area of protection against discrimination, as enshrined in the provisions of Union law listed in Annex 1 to this Protocol, and shall implement this paragraph through dedicated mechanisms.
2. The United Kingdom shall continue to facilitate the related work of the institutions and bodies set up pursuant to the 1998 Agreement, including the Northern Ireland Human Rights Commission, the Equality Commission for Northern Ireland and the Joint Committee of representatives of the Human Rights Commissions of Northern Ireland and Ireland, in upholding human rights and equality standards.

Article 3 Common Travel Area

1. The United Kingdom and Ireland may continue to make arrangements between themselves relating to the movement of persons between their territories (the "Common Travel Area"), while fully respecting the rights of natural persons conferred by Union law.
2. The United Kingdom shall ensure that the Common Travel Area and the rights and privileges associated therewith can continue to apply without affecting the obligations

of Ireland under Union law, in particular with respect to free movement to, from and within Ireland for Union citizens and their family members, irrespective of their nationality.

Article 4   Customs territory of the United Kingdom

Northern Ireland is part of the customs territory of the United Kingdom.

Accordingly, nothing in this Protocol shall prevent the United Kingdom from including Northern Ireland in the territorial scope of any agreements it may conclude with third countries, provided that those agreements do not prejudice the application of this Protocol. In particular, nothing in this Protocol shall prevent the United Kingdom from concluding agreements with a third country that grant goods produced in Northern Ireland preferential access to that country's market on the same terms as goods produced in other parts of the United Kingdom.

Nothing in this Protocol shall prevent the United Kingdom from including Northern Ireland in the territorial scope of its Schedules of Concessions annexed to the General Agreement on Tariffs and Trade 1994.

Article 5   Customs, movement of goods

1. No customs duties shall be payable for a good brought into Northern Ireland from another part of the United Kingdom by direct transport, notwithstanding paragraph 3, unless that good is at risk of subsequently being moved into the Union, whether by itself or forming part of another good following processing.

   The customs duties in respect of a good being moved by direct transport to Northern Ireland other than from the Union or from another part of the United Kingdom shall be the duties applicable in the United Kingdom, notwithstanding paragraph 3, unless that good is at risk of subsequently being moved into the Union, whether by itself or forming part of another good following processing.

   No duties shall be payable by, as relief shall be granted to, residents of the United Kingdom for personal property, as defined in point (c) of Article 2(1) of Council Regulation (EC) No 1186/2009, brought into Northern Ireland from another part of the United Kingdom.

2. For the purposes of the first and second subparagraphs of paragraph 1, a good brought into Northern Ireland from outside the Union shall be considered to be at risk of subsequently being moved into the Union unless it is established that that good:

   (a) will not be subject to commercial processing in Northern Ireland; and

   (b) fulfils the criteria established by the Joint Committee in accordance with the fourth subparagraph of this paragraph.

   For the purposes of this paragraph, "processing" means any alteration of goods, any transformation of goods in any way, or any subjecting of goods to operations other than for the purpose of preserving them in good condition or for adding or affixing marks, labels, seals or any other documentation to ensure compliance with any specific requirements.

   Before the end of the transition period, the Joint Committee shall by decision establish the conditions under which processing is to be considered not to fall within point (a) of the first subparagraph, taking into account in particular the nature, scale and result of the processing.

   Before the end of the transition period, the Joint Committee shall by decision establish the criteria for considering that a good brought into Northern Ireland from outside the Union is not at risk of subsequently being moved into the Union. The Joint Committee shall take into consideration, inter alia:

   (a) the final destination and use of the good;

   (b) the nature and value of the good;

   (c) the nature of the movement; and

   (d) the incentive for undeclared onward-movement into the Union, in particular incentives resulting from the duties payable pursuant to paragraph 1.

   The Joint Committee may amend at any time its decisions adopted pursuant to this paragraph.

   In taking any decision pursuant to this paragraph, the Joint Committee shall have regard to the specific circumstances in Northern Ireland.

3. Legislation as defined in point (2) of Article 5 of Regulation (EU) No 952/2013 shall apply to and in the United Kingdom in respect of Northern Ireland (not including the territorial waters of the United Kingdom). However, the Joint Committee shall establish the conditions, including in quantitative terms, under which certain fishery and aquaculture products, as set out in Annex I to Regulation (EU) No 1379/2013 of the European Parliament and of the Council, brought into the customs territory of the Union defined in Article 4 of Regulation (EU) No 952/2013 by vessels flying the flag of the United Kingdom and having their port of registration in Northern Ireland are exempted from duties.

4. The provisions of Union law listed in Annex 2 to this Protocol shall also apply, under the conditions set out in that Annex, to and in the United Kingdom in respect of Northern Ireland.

5. Articles 30 and 110 TFEU shall apply to and in the United Kingdom in respect of Northern Ireland. Quantitative restrictions on exports and imports shall be prohibited between the Union and Northern Ireland.

6. Customs duties levied by the United Kingdom in accordance with paragraph 3 are not remitted to the Union.

    Subject to Article 10, the United Kingdom may in particular:

    (a) reimburse duties levied pursuant to the provisions of Union law made applicable by paragraph 3 in respect of goods brought into Northern Ireland;

    (b) provide for circumstances in which a customs debt which has arisen is to be waived in respect of goods brought into Northern Ireland;

    (c) provide for circumstances in which customs duties are to be reimbursed in respect of goods that can be shown not to have entered the Union; and

    (d) compensate undertakings to offset the impact of the application of paragraph 3.

    In taking decisions under Article 10, the European Commission shall take the circumstances in Northern Ireland into account as appropriate.

7. No duties shall be payable on consignments of negligible value, on consignments sent by one individual to another or on goods contained in travellers' personal baggage, under the conditions set out in the legislation referred to in paragraph 3.

Article 6 Protection of the UK internal market

1. Nothing in this Protocol shall prevent the United Kingdom from ensuring unfettered market access for goods moving from Northern Ireland to other parts of the United Kingdom's internal market. Provisions of Union law made applicable by this Protocol which prohibit or restrict the exportation of goods shall only be applied to trade between Northern Ireland and other parts of the United Kingdom to the extent strictly required by any international obligations of the Union. The United Kingdom shall ensure full protection under international requirements and commitments that are relevant to the prohibitions and restrictions on the exportation of goods from the Union to third countries as set out in Union law.

2. Having regard to Northern Ireland's integral place in the United Kingdom's internal market, the Union and the United Kingdom shall use their best endeavours to facilitate the trade between Northern Ireland and other parts of the United Kingdom, in accordance with applicable legislation and taking into account their respective regulatory regimes as well as the implementation thereof. The Joint Committee shall keep the application of this paragraph under constant review and shall adopt appropriate recommendations with a view to avoiding controls at the ports and airports of Northern Ireland to the extent possible.

3. Nothing in this Protocol shall prevent a product originating from Northern Ireland from being presented as originating from the United Kingdom when placed on the market in Great Britain.

4. Nothing in this Protocol shall affect the law of the United Kingdom regulating the placing on the market in other parts of the United Kingdom of goods from Northern Ireland that comply with or benefit from technical regulations, assessments, registrations, certificates, approvals or authorisations governed by provisions of Union law referred to in Annex 2 to this Protocol.

Article 7　Technical regulations, assessments, registrations, certificates, approvals and authorisations

1. Without prejudice to the provisions of Union law referred to in Annex 2 to this Protocol, the lawfulness of placing goods on the market in Northern Ireland shall be governed by the law of the United Kingdom as well as, as regards goods imported from the Union, by Articles 34 and 36 TFEU.

2. Where provisions of Union law made applicable by this Protocol provide for the indication of a Member State, including in abbreviated form, in markings, labelling, tags, or by any other means, the United Kingdom in respect of Northern Ireland shall be indicated as "UK(NI)" or "United Kingdom (Northern Ireland)". Where provisions of Union law made applicable by this Protocol provide for the indication in the form of a numeric code, the United Kingdom in respect of Northern Ireland shall be indicated with a distinguishable numeric code.

3. By way of derogation from Article 13(1) of this Protocol and from Article 7 of the Withdrawal Agreement, in respect of the recognition in one Member State of technical regulations, assessments, registrations, certificates, approvals and authorisations issued or carried out by the authorities of another Member State, or by a body established in another Member State, references to Member States in provisions of Union law made applicable by this Protocol shall not be read as including the United Kingdom in respect of Northern Ireland as regards technical regulations, assessments, registrations, certificates, approvals and authorisations issued or carried out by the authorities of the United Kingdom or by bodies established in the United Kingdom.

   The first subparagraph shall not apply to registrations, certifications, approvals and authorisations of sites, installations or premises in Northern Ireland issued or carried out by competent authorities of the United Kingdom, where the registration, certification, approval or authorisation may require an inspection of the sites, installations or premises. The first subparagraph shall not apply to veterinary certificates or official labels for plant reproductive material that are required by provisions of Union law made applicable by this Protocol.

   The first subparagraph is without prejudice to the validity, in Northern Ireland, of assessments, registrations, certificates, approvals and authorisations issued or carried out, on the basis of provisions of Union law made applicable by this Protocol, by the competent authorities of the United Kingdom or by bodies established in the United Kingdom. Any conformity marking, logo or similar required by the provisions of Union law made applicable by this Protocol which is affixed by economic operators based on the assessment, registration, certificate, approval or authorisation issued by competent authorities of the United Kingdom or by bodies established in the United Kingdom shall be accompanied by the indication "UK(NI)".

   The United Kingdom in respect of Northern Ireland may not initiate objection, safeguard or arbitration procedures provided for in provisions of Union law made applicable by this Protocol to the extent that those procedures concern the technical regulations, standards, assessments, registrations, certificates, approvals and authorisations issued or carried out by competent authorities of the Member States or by bodies established in Member States. The first subparagraph does not prevent the test and release by a qualified person in Northern Ireland of a batch of a medicinal product imported into or manufactured in Northern Ireland.

Article 8　VAT and excise

The provisions of Union law listed in Annex 3 to this Protocol concerning goods shall apply to and in the United Kingdom in respect of Northern Ireland.

In respect of Northern Ireland, the authorities of the United Kingdom shall be responsible for the application and the implementation of the provisions listed in Annex 3 to this Protocol, including the collection of VAT and excise duties. Under the conditions set out in those provisions, revenues resulting from transactions taxable in Northern Ireland shall not be remitted to the Union.

By way of derogation from the first paragraph, the United Kingdom may apply to supplies of goods taxable in Northern Ireland VAT exemptions and reduced rates that are applicable in Ireland in accordance with provisions listed in Annex 3 to this Protocol.

The Joint Committee shall regularly discuss the implementation of this Article, including as concerns the reductions and exemptions provided for in the provisions referred to in the first paragraph, and shall, where appropriate, adopt measures for its proper application, as necessary.

The Joint Committee may review the application of this Article, taking into account Northern Ireland's integral place in the United Kingdom's internal market, and may adopt appropriate measures as necessary.

Article 9   Single electricity market

The provisions of Union law governing wholesale electricity markets listed in Annex 4 to this Protocol shall apply, under the conditions set out in that Annex, to and in the United Kingdom in respect of Northern Ireland.

Article 10   State aid

1. The provisions of Union law listed in Annex 5 to this Protocol shall apply to the United Kingdom, including with regard to measures supporting the production of and trade in agricultural products in Northern Ireland, in respect of measures which affect that trade between Northern Ireland and the Union which is subject to this Protocol.

2. Notwithstanding paragraph 1, the provisions of Union law referred to in that paragraph shall not apply with respect to measures taken by the United Kingdom authorities to support the production of and trade in agricultural products in Northern Ireland up to a determined maximum overall annual level of support, and provided that a determined minimum percentage of that exempted support complies with the provisions of Annex 2 to the WTO Agreement on Agriculture. The determination of the maximum exempted overall annual level of support and the minimum percentage shall be governed by the procedures set out in Annex 6.

3. Where the European Commission examines information regarding a measure by the United Kingdom authorities that may constitute unlawful aid that is subject to paragraph 1, it shall ensure that the United Kingdom is kept fully and regularly informed of the progress and outcome of the examination of that measure.

Article 11   Other areas of North-South cooperation

1. Consistent with the arrangements set out in Articles 5 to 10, and in full respect of Union law, this Protocol shall be implemented and applied so as to maintain the necessary conditions for continued North-South cooperation, including in the areas of environment, health, agriculture, transport, education and tourism, as well as in the areas of energy, telecommunications, broadcasting, inland fisheries, justice and security, higher education and sport.

    In full respect of Union law, the United Kingdom and Ireland may continue to make new arrangements that build on the provisions of the 1998 Agreement in other areas of North-South cooperation on the island of Ireland.

2. The Joint Committee shall keep under constant review the extent to which the implementation and application of this Protocol maintains the necessary conditions for North-South cooperation. The Joint Committee may make appropriate recommendations to the Union and the United Kingdom in this respect, including on a recommendation from the Specialised Committee.

Article 12   Implementation, application, supervision and enforcement

1. Without prejudice to paragraph 4, the authorities of the United Kingdom shall be responsible for implementing and applying the provisions of Union law made applicable by this Protocol to and in the United Kingdom in respect of Northern Ireland.

2. Without prejudice to paragraph 4 of this Article, Union representatives shall have the right to be present during any activities of the authorities of the United Kingdom related to the implementation and application of provisions of Union law made applicable by this Protocol, as well as activities related to the implementation and application of Article 5, and the United Kingdom shall provide, upon request, all relevant information relating to such activities. The United Kingdom shall facilitate such presence of Union representatives and shall provide them with the information requested. Where the Union representative requests the authorities of the United Kingdom to carry out control measures in individual cases for duly stated reasons, the authorities of the United Kingdom shall carry out those control measures.

The Union and the United Kingdom shall exchange information on the application of Article 5 (1) and (2) on a monthly basis.

3.   The practical working arrangements relating to the exercise of the rights of Union representatives referred to in paragraph 2 shall be determined by the Joint Committee, upon proposal from the Specialised Committee.

4.   As regards the second subparagraph of paragraph 2 of this Article, Article 5 and Articles 7 to 10, the institutions, bodies, offices, and agencies of the Union shall in relation to the United Kingdom and natural and legal persons residing or established in the territory of the United Kingdom have the powers conferred upon them by Union law. In particular, the Court of Justice of the European Union shall have the jurisdiction provided for in the Treaties in this respect. The second and third paragraphs of Article 267 TFEU shall apply to and in the United Kingdom in this respect.

5.   Acts of the institutions, bodies, offices, and agencies of the Union adopted in accordance with paragraph 4 shall produce in respect of and in the United Kingdom the same legal effects as those which they produce within the Union and its Member States.

6.   When representing or assisting a party in relation to administrative procedures arising from the exercise of the powers of the institutions, bodies, offices, and agencies of the Union referred to in paragraph 4, lawyers authorised to practise before the courts or tribunals of the United Kingdom shall in every respect be treated as lawyers authorised to practise before courts or tribunals of Member States who represent or assist a party in relation to such administrative procedures.

7.   In cases brought before the Court of Justice of the European Union pursuant to paragraph 4:
      (a)   the United Kingdom may participate in the proceedings before the Court of Justice of the European Union in the same way as a Member State;
      (b)   lawyers authorised to practise before the courts or tribunals of the United Kingdom may represent or assist a party before the Court of Justice of the European Union in such proceedings and shall in every respect be treated as lawyers authorised to practise before courts or tribunals of Member States representing or assisting a party before the Court of Justice of the European Union.

Article 13   Common provisions

1.   For the purposes of this Protocol, any reference to the United Kingdom in the applicable provisions of the Withdrawal Agreement shall be read as referring to the United Kingdom or to the United Kingdom in respect of Northern Ireland, as the case may be.

Notwithstanding any other provisions of this Protocol, any reference to the territory defined in Article 4 of Regulation (EU) No 952/2013 in the applicable provisions of the Withdrawal Agreement and of this Protocol, as well as in the provisions of Union law made applicable to and in the United Kingdom in respect of Northern Ireland by this Protocol, shall be read as including the part of the territory of the United Kingdom to which Regulation (EU) No 952/2013 applies by virtue of Article 5(3) of this Protocol.

Titles I and III of Part Three and Part Six of the Withdrawal Agreement shall apply without prejudice to the provisions of this Protocol.

2.   Notwithstanding Article 4(4) and (5) of the Withdrawal Agreement, the provisions of this Protocol referring to Union law or to concepts or provisions thereof shall in their implementation and application be interpreted in conformity with the relevant case law of the Court of Justice of the European Union.

3.   Notwithstanding Article 6(1) of the Withdrawal Agreement, and unless otherwise provided, where this Protocol makes reference to a Union act, that reference shall be read as referring to that Union act as amended or replaced.

4.   Where the Union adopts a new act that falls within the scope of this Protocol, but which neither amends nor replaces a Union act listed in the Annexes to this Protocol, the Union shall inform the United Kingdom of the adoption of that act in the Joint Committee. Upon the request of the Union or the United Kingdom, the Joint Committee shall hold an exchange of views on the implications of the newly adopted act for the proper functioning of this Protocol, within 6 weeks after the request.

As soon as reasonably practical after the Union has informed the United Kingdom in the Joint Committee, the Joint Committee shall either:

(a)   adopt a decision adding the newly adopted act to the relevant Annex to this Protocol; or

(b)   where an agreement on adding the newly adopted act to the relevant Annex to this Protocol cannot be reached, examine all further possibilities to maintain the good functioning of this Protocol and take any decision necessary to this effect.

If the Joint Committee has not taken a decision referred to in the second subparagraph within a reasonable time, the Union shall be entitled, after giving notice to the United Kingdom, to take appropriate remedial measures. Such measures shall take effect at the earliest 6 months after the Union informed the United Kingdom in accordance with the first subparagraph, but in no event shall such measures take effect before the date on which the newly adopted act is implemented in the Union.

5.   By way of derogation from paragraph 1 of this Article and from Article 7 of the Withdrawal Agreement, unless the Union considers that full or partial access by the United Kingdom or the United Kingdom in respect of Northern Ireland, as the case may be, is strictly necessary to enable the United Kingdom to comply with its obligations under this Protocol, including where such access is necessary because access to the relevant information cannot be facilitated by the working group referred to in Article 15 of this Protocol or by any other practical means, in respect of access to any network, information system or database established on the basis of Union law, references to Member States and competent authorities of Member States in provisions of Union law made applicable by this Protocol shall not be read as including the United Kingdom or the United Kingdom in respect of Northern Ireland, as the case may be.

6.   Authorities of the United Kingdom shall not act as leading authority for risk assessments, examinations, approvals and authorisation procedures provided for in Union law made applicable by this Protocol.

7.   Articles 346 and 347 TFEU shall apply to this Protocol as regards measures taken by a Member State or by the United Kingdom in respect of Northern Ireland.

8.   Any subsequent agreement between the Union and the United Kingdom shall indicate the parts of this Protocol which it supersedes. Once a subsequent agreement between the Union and the United Kingdom becomes applicable after the entry into force of the Withdrawal Agreement, this Protocol shall then, from the date of application of such subsequent agreement and in accordance with the provisions of that agreement setting out the effect of that agreement on this Protocol, not apply or shall cease to apply, as the case may be, in whole or in part.

Article 14   Specialised Committee

The Committee on issues related to the implementation of the Protocol on Ireland/Northern Ireland established by Article 165 of the Withdrawal Agreement ("Specialised Committee") shall:

(a)   facilitate the implementation and application of this Protocol;

(b)   examine proposals concerning the implementation and application of this Protocol from the North-South Ministerial Council and North-South Implementation bodies set up under the 1998 Agreement;

(c)   consider any matter of relevance to Article 2 of this Protocol brought to its attention by the Northern Ireland Human Rights Commission, the Equality Commission for Northern Ireland, and the Joint Committee of representatives of the Human Rights Commissions of Northern Ireland and Ireland;

(d)   discuss any point raised by the Union or the United Kingdom that is of relevance to this Protocol and gives rise to a difficulty; and

(e)   make recommendations to the Joint Committee as regards the functioning of this Protocol.

Article 15   Joint consultative working group

1.   A joint consultative working group on the implementation of this Protocol ("working group") is hereby established. It shall serve as a forum for the exchange of information and mutual consultation.

2.   The working group shall be composed of representatives of the Union and the United Kingdom and shall carry out its functions under the supervision of the Specialised

Committee, to which it shall report. The working group shall have no power to take binding decisions other than the power to adopt its own rules of procedure referred to in paragraph 6.

3. Within the working group:
    (a) the Union and the United Kingdom shall, in a timely manner, exchange information about planned, ongoing and final relevant implementation measures in relation to the Union acts listed in the Annexes to this Protocol;
    (b) the Union shall inform the United Kingdom about planned Union acts within the scope of this Protocol, including Union acts that amend or replace the Union acts listed in the Annexes to this Protocol;
    (c) the Union shall provide to the United Kingdom all information the Union considers relevant to allow the United Kingdom to fully comply with its obligations under the Protocol; and
    (d) the United Kingdom shall provide to the Union all information that Member States are required to provide to one another or to the institutions, bodies, offices or agencies of the Union pursuant to the Union acts listed in the Annexes to this Protocol.

4. The working group shall be co-chaired by the Union and the United Kingdom.
5. The working group shall meet at least once a month, unless otherwise decided by the Union and the United Kingdom by mutual consent. Where necessary, the Union and the United Kingdom may exchange information referred to in points (c) and (d) of paragraph 3 between meetings.
6. The working group shall adopt its own rules of procedure by mutual consent.
7. The Union shall ensure that all views expressed by the United Kingdom in the working group and all information provided by the United Kingdom in the working group, including technical and scientific data, are communicated to the relevant institutions, bodies, offices and agencies of the Union without undue delay.

Article 16   Safeguards

1. If the application of this Protocol leads to serious economic, societal or environmental difficulties that are liable to persist, or to diversion of trade, the Union or the United Kingdom may unilaterally take appropriate safeguard measures. Such safeguard measures shall be restricted with regard to their scope and duration to what is strictly necessary in order to remedy the situation. Priority shall be given to such measures as will least disturb the functioning of this Protocol.
2. If a safeguard measure taken by the Union or the United Kingdom, as the case may be, in accordance with paragraph 1 creates an imbalance between the rights and obligations under this Protocol, the Union or the United Kingdom, as the case may be, may take such proportionate rebalancing measures as are strictly necessary to remedy the imbalance. Priority shall be given to such measures as will least disturb the functioning of this Protocol.
3. Safeguard and rebalancing measures taken in accordance with paragraphs 1 and 2 shall be governed by the procedures set out in Annex 7 to this Protocol.

Article 17   Protection of financial interests

The Union and the United Kingdom shall counter fraud and any other illegal activities affecting the financial interests of the Union or the financial interests of the United Kingdom.

Article 18   Democratic consent in Northern Ireland

1. Within 2 months before the end of both the initial period and any subsequent period, the United Kingdom shall provide the opportunity for democratic consent in Northern Ireland to the continued application of Articles 5 to 10.
2. For the purposes of paragraph 1, the United Kingdom shall seek democratic consent in Northern Ireland in a manner consistent with the 1998 Agreement. A decision expressing democratic consent shall be reached strictly in accordance with the unilateral declaration concerning the operation of the 'Democratic consent in Northern Ireland' provision of the Protocol on Ireland/Northern Ireland made by the United Kingdom on 17 October 2019, including with respect to the roles of the Northern Ireland Executive and Assembly.

3. The United Kingdom shall notify the Union before the end of the relevant period referred to in paragraph 5 of the outcome of the process referred to in paragraph 1.
4. Where the process referred to in paragraph 1 has been undertaken and a decision has been reached in accordance with paragraph 2, and the United Kingdom notifies the Union that the outcome of the process referred to in paragraph 1 is not a decision that the Articles of this Protocol referred to in that paragraph should continue to apply in Northern Ireland, then those Articles and other provisions of this Protocol, to the extent that those provisions depend on those Articles for their application, shall cease to apply 2 years after the end of the relevant period referred to in paragraph 5. In such a case the Joint Committee shall address recommendations to the Union and to the United Kingdom on the necessary measures, taking into account the obligations of the parties to the 1998 Agreement. Before doing so, the Joint Committee may seek an opinion from institutions created by the 1998 Agreement.
5. For the purposes of this Article, the initial period is the period ending 4 years after the end of the transition period. Where the decision reached in a given period was on the basis of a majority of Members of the Northern Ireland Assembly, present and voting, the subsequent period is the 4 year period following that period, for as long as Articles 5 to 10 continue to apply. Where the decision reached in a given period had cross-community support, the subsequent period is the 8-year period following that period, for as long as Articles 5 to 10 continue to apply.
6. For the purposes of paragraph 5, cross-community support means:
    (a) a majority of those Members of the Legislative Assembly present and voting, including a majority of the unionist and nationalist designations present and voting; or
    (b) a weighted majority (60 %) of Members of the Legislative Assembly present and voting, including at least 40 % of each of the nationalist and unionist designations present and voting.

ANNEXES
...
ANNEX 7
PROCEDURES REFERRED TO IN ARTICLE 16(3)

1. Where the Union or the United Kingdom is considering taking safeguard measures under Article 16(1) of this Protocol, it shall, without delay, notify the Union or the United Kingdom, as the case may be, through the Joint Committee and shall provide all relevant information.
2. The Union and the United Kingdom shall immediately enter into consultations in the Joint Committee with a view to finding a commonly acceptable solution.
3. The Union or the United Kingdom, as the case may be, may not take safeguard measures until 1 month has elapsed after the date of notification under point 1, unless the consultation procedure under point 2 has been concluded before the expiration of the state limit. When exceptional circumstances requiring immediate action exclude prior examination, the Union or the United Kingdom, as the case may be, may apply forthwith the protective measures strictly necessary to remedy the situation.
4. The Union or the United Kingdom, as the case may be, shall, without delay, notify the measures taken to the Joint Committee and shall provide all relevant information.
5. The safeguard measures taken shall be the subject of consultations in the Joint Committee every 3 months from the date of their adoption with a view to their abolition before the date of expiry envisaged, or to the limitation of their scope of application. The Union or the United Kingdom, as the case may be, may at any time request the Joint Committee to review such measures.
6. Points 1 to 5 shall apply, mutatis mutandis, to rebalancing measures referred to in Article 16(2) of this Protocol.

RULES OF PROCEDURE OF THE COURT OF JUSTICE 2012
[2012] OJ L265/1

INTRODUCTORY PROVISIONS

Article 1   Definitions

1. In these Rules:
   (a) provisions of the Treaty on European Union are referred to by the number of the article concerned followed by 'TEU',
   (b) provisions of the Treaty on the Functioning of the European Union are referred to by the number of the article concerned followed by 'TFEU',
   (c) provisions of the Treaty establishing the European Atomic Energy Community are referred to by the number of the article concerned followed by 'TEAEC',
   (d) 'Statute' means the Protocol on the Statute of the Court of Justice of the European Union,

   ...

   (f) 'Council Regulation No 1' means Council Regulation No 1 of 15 April 1958 determining the languages to be used by the European Economic Community.

2. For the purposes of these Rules:
   (a) 'institutions' means the institutions of the European Union referred to in Article 13(1) TEU and bodies, offices and agencies established by the Treaties, or by an act adopted in implementation thereof, which may be parties before the Court,
   (b) 'EFTA Surveillance Authority' means the surveillance authority referred to in the EEA Agreement,
   (c) 'interested persons referred to in Article 23 of the Statute' means all the parties, States, institutions, bodies, offices and agencies authorised, pursuant to that Article, to submit statements of case or observations in the context of a reference for a preliminary ruling.

Article 2   Purport of these Rules

These Rules implement and supplement, so far as necessary, the relevant provisions of the EU, FEU and EAEC Treaties, and the Statute.

TITLE I
ORGANISATION OF THE COURT

CHAPTER 1
JUDGES AND ADVOCATES GENERAL

Article 3   Commencement of the term of office of Judges and Advocates General

The term of office of a Judge or Advocate General shall begin on the date fixed for that purpose in the instrument of appointment. In the absence of any provisions in that instrument regarding the date of commencement of the term of office, that term shall begin on the date of publication of the instrument in the *Official Journal of the European Union*.

Article 4   Taking of the oath

Before taking up his duties, a Judge or Advocate General shall, at the first public sitting of the Court which he attends after his appointment, take the following oath provided for in Article 2 of the Statute:

'I swear that I will perform my duties impartially and conscientiously; I swear that I will preserve the secrecy of the deliberations of the Court.'

Article 5   Solemn undertaking

Immediately after taking the oath, a Judge or Advocate General shall sign a declaration by which he gives the solemn undertaking provided for in the third paragraph of Article 4 of the Statute.

Article 6 Depriving a Judge or Advocate General of his office

1. Where the Court is called upon, pursuant to Article 6 of the Statute, to decide whether a Judge or Advocate General no longer fulfils the requisite conditions or no longer meets the obligations arising from his office, the President shall invite the Judge or Advocate General concerned to make representations.
2. The Court shall give a decision in the absence of the Registrar.

Article 7 Order of seniority

1. The seniority of Judges and Advocates General shall be calculated without distinction according to the date on which they took up their duties.
2. Where there is equal seniority on that basis, the order of seniority shall be determined by age.
3. Judges and Advocates General whose terms of office are renewed shall retain their former seniority.

CHAPTER 2

PRESIDENCY OF THE COURT, CONSTITUTION OF THE CHAMBERS AND DESIGNATION OF THE FIRST ADVOCATE GENERAL

Article 8 Election of the President and of the Vice-President of the Court

1. The Judges shall, immediately after the partial replacement provided for in the second paragraph of Article 253 TFEU, elect one of their number as President of the Court for a term of three years.
2. If the office of the President falls vacant before the normal date of expiry of the term thereof, the Court shall elect a successor for the remainder of the term.
3. The elections provided for in this Article shall be by secret ballot. The Judge obtaining the votes of more than half the Judges of the Court shall be elected. If no Judge obtains that majority, further ballots shall be held until that majority is attained.
4. The Judges shall then elect one of their number as Vice-President of the Court for a term of three years, in accordance with the procedures laid down in the preceding paragraph. Paragraph 2 shall apply if the office of the Vice-President of the Court falls vacant before the normal date of expiry of the term thereof.
5. The names of the President and Vice-President elected in accordance with this Article shall be published in the *Official Journal of the European Union*.

Article 9 Responsibilities of the President of the Court

1. The President shall represent the Court.
2. The President shall direct the judicial business of the Court. He shall preside at general meetings of the Members of the Court and at hearings before and deliberations of the full Court and the Grand Chamber.
3. The President shall ensure the proper functioning of the services of the Court.

Article 10 Responsibilities of the Vice-President of the Court

1. The Vice-President shall assist the President of the Court in the performance of his duties and shall take the President's place when the latter is prevented from acting.
2. He shall take the President's place, at his request, in performing the duties referred to in Article 9(1) and (3) of these Rules.
3. The Court shall, by decision, specify the conditions under which the Vice-President shall take the place of the President of the Court in the performance of his judicial duties. That decision shall be published in the *Official Journal of the European Union*.

Article 11 Constitution of Chambers

1. The Court shall set up Chambers of five and three Judges in accordance with Article 16 of the Statute and shall decide which Judges shall be attached to them.
2. The Court shall designate the Chambers of five Judges which, for a period of one year, shall be responsible for cases of the kind referred to in Article 107 and Articles 193 and 194.
3. In respect of cases assigned to a formation of the Court in accordance with Article 60, the word 'Court' in these Rules shall mean that formation.

4. In respect of cases assigned to a Chamber of five or three Judges, the powers of the President of the Court shall be exercised by the President of the Chamber.
5. The composition of the Chambers and the designation of the Chambers responsible for cases of the kind referred to in Article 107 and Articles 193 and 194 shall be published in the *Official Journal of the European Union*.

Article 12 Election of Presidents of Chambers

1. The Judges shall, immediately after the election of the President and Vice-President of the Court, elect the Presidents of the Chambers of five Judges for a term of three years.
2. The Judges shall then elect the Presidents of the Chambers of three Judges for a term of one year.
3. The provisions of Article 8(2) and (3) shall apply.
4. The names of the Presidents of Chambers elected in accordance with this Article shall be published in the *Official Journal of the European Union*.

Article 13 Where the President and Vice-President of the Court are prevented from acting

When the President and the Vice-President of the Court are prevented from acting, the functions of President shall be exercised by one of the Presidents of the Chambers of five Judges or, failing that, by one of the Presidents of the Chambers of three Judges or, failing that, by one of the other Judges, according to the order of seniority laid down in Article 7.

Article 14 Designation of the First Advocate General

1. The Court shall, after hearing the Advocates General, designate a First Advocate General for a period of one year.
2. If the office of the First Advocate General falls vacant before the normal date of expiry of the term thereof, the Court shall designate a successor for the remainder of the term.
3. The name of the First Advocate General designated in accordance with this Article shall be published in the *Official Journal of the European Union.*

CHAPTER 3

ASSIGNMENT OF CASES TO JUDGE-RAPPORTEURS AND ADVOCATES GENERAL

Article 15 Designation of the Judge-Rapporteur

1. As soon as possible after the document initiating proceedings has been lodged, the President of the Court shall designate a Judge to act as Rapporteur in the case.
2. For cases of the kind referred to in Article 107 and Articles 193 and 194, the Judge-Rapporteur shall be selected from among the Judges of the Chamber designated in accordance with Article 11(2), on a proposal from the President of that Chamber. If, pursuant to Article 109, the Chamber decides that the reference is not to be dealt with under the urgent procedure, the President of the Court may reassign the case to a Judge-Rapporteur attached to another Chamber.
3. The President of the Court shall take the necessary steps if a Judge-Rapporteur is prevented from acting.

Article 16 Designation of the Advocate General

1. The First Advocate General shall assign each case to an Advocate General.
2. The First Advocate General shall take the necessary steps if an Advocate General is prevented from acting.

CHAPTER 4

ASSISTANT RAPPORTEURS

Article 17 Assistant Rapporteurs

1. Where the Court is of the opinion that the consideration of and preparatory inquiries in cases before it so require, it shall, pursuant to Article 13 of the Statute, propose the appointment of Assistant Rapporteurs.

2.   Assistant Rapporteurs shall in particular:
     (a)   assist the President of the Court in interim proceedings and
     (b)   assist the Judge-Rapporteurs in their work.
3.   In the performance of their duties the Assistant Rapporteurs shall be responsible to the President of the Court, the President of a Chamber or a Judge-Rapporteur, as the case may be.
4.   Before taking up his duties, an Assistant Rapporteur shall take before the Court the oath set out in Article 4 of these Rules.

CHAPTER 5
REGISTRY

Article 18 Appointment of the Registrar

1.   The Court shall appoint the Registrar.
2.   When the post of Registrar is vacant, an advertisement shall be published in the *Official Journal of the European Union*. Interested persons shall be invited to submit their applications within a time-limit of not less than three weeks, accompanied by full details of their nationality, university degrees, knowledge of languages, present and past occupations, and experience, if any, in judicial and international fields.
3.   The vote, in which the Judges and the Advocates General shall take part, shall take place in accordance with the procedure laid down in Article 8(3) of these Rules.
4.   The Registrar shall be appointed for a term of six years. He may be reappointed. The Court may decide to renew the term of office of the incumbent Registrar without availing itself of the procedure laid down in paragraph 2 of this Article.
5.   The Registrar shall take the oath set out in Article 4 and sign the declaration provided for in Article 5.
6.   The Registrar may be deprived of his office only if he no longer fulfils the requisite conditions or no longer meets the obligations arising from his office. The Court shall take its decision after giving the Registrar an opportunity to make representations.
7.   If the office of Registrar falls vacant before the normal date of expiry of the term thereof, the Court shall appoint a new Registrar for a term of six years.
8.   The name of the Registrar elected in accordance with this Article shall be published in the *Official Journal of the European Union*.

Article 19 Deputy Registrar

The Court may, in accordance with the procedure laid down in respect of the Registrar, appoint a Deputy Registrar to assist the Registrar and to take his place if he is prevented from acting.

Article 20 Responsibilities of the Registrar

1.   The Registrar shall be responsible, under the authority of the President of the Court, for the acceptance, transmission and custody of all documents and for effecting service as provided for by these Rules.
2.   The Registrar shall assist the Members of the Court in all their official functions.
3.   The Registrar shall have custody of the seals and shall be responsible for the records. He shall be in charge of the publications of the Court and, in particular, the European Court Reports.
4.   The Registrar shall direct the services of the Court under the authority of the President of the Court. He shall be responsible for the management of the staff and the administration, and for the preparation and implementation of the budget.

Article 21 Keeping of the register

1.   There shall be kept in the Registry, under the responsibility of the Registrar, a register in which all procedural documents and supporting items and documents lodged shall be entered in the order in which they are submitted.
2.   When a document has been registered, the Registrar shall make a note to that effect on the original and, if a party so requests, on any copy submitted for the purpose.
3.   Entries in the register and the notes provided for in the preceding paragraph shall be authentic.
4.   A notice shall be published in the *Official Journal of the European Union* indicating the date of registration of an application initiating proceedings, the names of the parties,

the form of order sought by the applicant and a summary of the pleas in law and of the main supporting arguments or, as the case may be, the date of lodging of a request for a preliminary ruling, the identity of the referring court or tribunal and the parties to the main proceedings, and the questions referred to the Court.

Article 22 Consultation of the register and of judgments and orders

1. Anyone may consult the register at the Registry and may obtain copies or extracts on payment of a charge on a scale fixed by the Court on a proposal from the Registrar.
2. The parties to a case may, on payment of the appropriate charge, obtain certified copies of procedural documents.
3. Anyone may, on payment of the appropriate charge, also obtain certified copies of judgments and orders.

CHAPTER 6
THE WORKING OF THE COURT

Article 23 Location of the sittings of the Court

The Court may choose to hold one or more specific sittings in a place other than that in which it has its seat.

Article 24 Calendar of the Court's judicial business

1. The judicial year shall begin on 7 October of each calendar year and end on 6 October of the following year.
2. The judicial vacations shall be determined by the Court.
3. In a case of urgency, the President may convene the Judges and the Advocates General during the judicial vacations.
4. The Court shall observe the official holidays of the place in which it has its seat.
5. The Court may, in proper circumstances, grant leave of absence to any Judge or Advocate General.
6. The dates of the judicial vacations and the list of official holidays shall be published annually in the *Official Journal of the European Union*.

Article 25 General meeting

Decisions concerning administrative issues or the action to be taken upon the proposals contained in the preliminary report referred to in Article 59 of these Rules shall be taken by the Court at the general meeting in which all the Judges and Advocates General shall take part and have a vote. The Registrar shall be present, unless the Court decides to the contrary.

Article 26 Drawing-up of minutes

Where the Court sits without the Registrar being present it shall, if necessary, instruct the most junior Judge for the purposes of Article 7 of these Rules to draw up minutes, which shall be signed by that Judge and by the President.

CHAPTER 7
FORMATIONS OF THE COURT

SECTION 1
COMPOSITION OF THE FORMATIONS OF THE COURT

Article 27 Composition of the Grand Chamber

1. The Grand Chamber shall, for each case, be composed of the President and the Vice-President of the Court, three Presidents of Chambers of five Judges, the Judge-Rapporteur and the number of Judges necessary to reach 15. The last-mentioned Judges and the three Presidents of Chambers of five Judges shall be designated from the lists referred to in paragraphs 3 and 4 of this Article, following the order laid down therein. The starting-point on each of those lists, in every case assigned to the Grand Chamber, shall be the name of the Judge immediately following the last Judge designated from the list concerned for the preceding case assigned to that formation of the Court.
2. After the election of the President and the Vice-President of the Court, and then of the Presidents of the Chambers of five Judges, a list of the Presidents of Chambers

of five Judges and a list of the other Judges shall be drawn up for the purposes of determining the composition of the Grand Chamber.

3. The list of the Presidents of Chambers of five Judges shall be drawn up according to the order laid down in Article 7 of these Rules.

4. The list of the other Judges shall be drawn up according to the order laid down in Article 7 of these Rules, alternating with the reverse order: the first Judge on that list shall be the first according to the order laid down in that Article, the second Judge shall be the last according to that order, the third Judge shall be the second according to that order, the fourth Judge the penultimate according to that order, and so on.

5. The lists referred to in paragraphs 3 and 4 shall be published in the *Official Journal of the European Union*.

6. In cases which are assigned to the Grand Chamber between the beginning of a calendar year in which there is a partial replacement of Judges and the moment when that replacement has taken place, two substitute Judges may be designated to complete the formation of the Court for so long as the attainment of the quorum referred to in the third paragraph of Article 17 of the Statute is in doubt. Those substitute Judges shall be the two Judges appearing on the list referred to in paragraph 4 immediately after the last Judge designated for the composition of the Grand Chamber in the case.

7. The substitute Judges shall replace, in the order of the list referred to in paragraph 4, such Judges as are unable to take part in the determination of the case.

Article 28 Composition of the Chambers of five and of three Judges

1. The Chambers of five Judges and of three Judges shall, for each case, be composed of the President of the Chamber, the Judge-Rapporteur and the number of Judges required to attain the number of five and three Judges respectively. Those last-mentioned Judges shall be designated from the lists referred to in paragraphs 2 and 3, following the order laid down therein. The starting-point on those lists, in every case assigned to a Chamber, shall be the name of the Judge immediately following the last Judge designated from the list for the preceding case assigned to the Chamber concerned.

2. For the composition of the Chambers of five Judges, after the election of the Presidents of those Chambers lists shall be drawn up including all the Judges attached to the Chamber concerned, with the exception of its President. The lists shall be drawn up in the same way as the list referred to in Article 27(4).

3. For the composition of the Chambers of three Judges, after the election of the Presidents of those Chambers lists shall be drawn up including all the Judges attached to the Chamber concerned, with the exception of its President. The lists shall be drawn up according to the order laid down in Article 7.

4. The lists referred to in paragraphs 2 and 3 shall be published in the *Official Journal of the European Union*.

Article 29 Composition of Chambers where cases are related or referred back

1. Where the Court considers that a number of cases must be heard and determined together by one and the same formation of the Court, the composition of that formation shall be that fixed for the case in respect of which the preliminary report was examined first.

2. Where a Chamber to which a case has been assigned requests the Court, pursuant to Article 60(3) of these Rules, to assign the case to a formation composed of a greater number of Judges, that formation shall include the members of the Chamber which has referred the case back.

Article 30 Where a President of a Chamber is prevented from acting

1. When the President of a Chamber of five Judges is prevented from acting, the functions of President of the Chamber shall be exercised by a President of a Chamber of three Judges, where necessary according to the order laid down in Article 7 of these Rules, or, if that formation of the Court does not include a President of a Chamber of three Judges, by one of the other Judges according to the order laid down in Article 7.

2. When the President of a Chamber of three Judges is prevented from acting, the functions of President of the Chamber shall be exercised by a Judge of that formation of the Court according to the order laid down in Article 7.

Article 31 Where a member of the formation of the Court is prevented from acting

1. When a member of the Grand Chamber is prevented from acting, he shall be replaced by another Judge according to the order of the list referred to in Article 27(4).
2. When a member of a Chamber of five Judges is prevented from acting, he shall be replaced by another Judge of that Chamber, according to the order of the list referred to in Article 28(2). If it is not possible to replace the Judge prevented from acting by a Judge of the same Chamber, the President of that Chamber shall so inform the President of the Court who may designate another Judge to complete the Chamber.
3. When a member of a Chamber of three Judges is prevented from acting, he shall be replaced by another Judge of that Chamber, according to the order of the list referred to in Article 28(3). If it is not possible to replace the Judge prevented from acting by a Judge of the same Chamber, the President of that Chamber shall so inform the President of the Court who may designate another Judge to complete the Chamber.

SECTION 2
DELIBERATIONS

Article 32 Procedures concerning deliberations

1. The deliberations of the Court shall be and shall remain secret.
2. When a hearing has taken place, only those Judges who participated in that hearing and, where relevant, the Assistant Rapporteur responsible for the consideration of the case shall take part in the deliberations.
3. Every Judge taking part in the deliberations shall state his opinion and the reasons for it.
4. The conclusions reached by the majority of the Judges after final discussion shall determine the decision of the Court.

Article 33 Number of Judges taking part in the deliberations

Where, by reason of a Judge being prevented from acting, there is an even number of Judges, the most junior Judge for the purposes of Article 7 of these Rules shall abstain from taking part in the deliberations unless he is the Judge-Rapporteur. In that case the Judge immediately senior to him shall abstain from taking part in the deliberations.

Article 34 Quorum of the Grand Chamber

1. If, for a case assigned to the Grand Chamber, it is not possible to attain the quorum referred to in the third paragraph of Article 17 of the Statute, the President of the Court shall designate one or more other Judges according to the order of the list referred to in Article 27(4) of these Rules.
2. If a hearing has taken place before that designation, the Court shall re-hear oral argument from the parties and the Opinion of the Advocate General.

Article 35 Quorum of the Chambers of five and of three Judges

1. If, for a case assigned to a Chamber of five or of three Judges, it is not possible to attain the quorum referred to in the second paragraph of Article 17 of the Statute, the President of the Court shall designate one or more other Judges according to the order of the list referred to in Article 28(2) or (3), respectively, of these Rules. If it is not possible to replace the Judge prevented from acting by a Judge of the same Chamber, the President of that Chamber shall so inform the President of the Court forthwith who shall designate another Judge to complete the Chamber.
2. Article 34(2) shall apply, *mutatis mutandis*, to the Chambers of five and of three Judges.

CHAPTER 8
LANGUAGES

Article 36 Language of a case

The language of a case shall be Bulgarian, Croatian, Czech, Danish, Dutch, English, Estonian, Finnish, French, German, Greek, Hungarian, Irish, Italian, Latvian, Lithuanian, Maltese, Polish, Portuguese, Romanian, Slovak, Slovenian, Spanish or Swedish.

Article 37 Determination of the language of a case

1. In direct actions, the language of a case shall be chosen by the applicant, except that:

   (a) where the defendant is a Member State, the language of the case shall be the official language of that State; where that State has more than one official language, the applicant may choose between them;

   (b) at the joint request of the parties, the use of another of the languages mentioned in Article 36 for all or part of the proceedings may be authorised;

   (c) at the request of one of the parties, and after the opposite party and the Advocate General have been heard, the use of another of the languages mentioned in Article 36 may be authorised as the language of the case for all or part of the proceedings by way of derogation from subparagraphs (a) and (b); such a request may not be submitted by one of the institutions of the European Union.

2. Without prejudice to the provisions of paragraph 1(b) and (c), and of Article 38(4) and (5) of these Rules,

   (a) in appeals against decisions of the General Court as referred to in Articles 56 and 57 of the Statute, the language of the case shall be the language of the decision of the General Court against which the appeal is brought;

   (b) where, in accordance with the second paragraph of Article 62 of the Statute, the Court decides to review a decision of the General Court, the language of the case shall be the language of the decision of the General Court which is the subject of review;

   (c) in the case of challenges concerning the costs to be recovered, applications to set aside judgments by default, third-party proceedings and applications for interpretation or revision of a judgment or for the Court to remedy a failure to adjudicate, the language of the case shall be the language of the decision to which those applications or challenges relate.

3. In preliminary ruling proceedings, the language of the case shall be the language of the referring court or tribunal. At the duly substantiated request of one of the parties to the main proceedings, and after the other party to the main proceedings and the Advocate General have been heard, the use of another of the languages mentioned in Article 36 may be authorised for the oral part of the procedure. Where granted, such authorisation shall apply in respect of all the interested persons referred to in Article 23 of the Statute.

4. Requests as above may be decided on by the President; the latter may, and where he wishes to accede to a request without the agreement of all the parties must, refer the request to the Court.

Article 38 Use of the language of the case

1. The language of the case shall in particular be used in the written and oral pleadings of the parties, including the items and documents produced or annexed to them, and also in the minutes and decisions of the Court.

2. Any item or document produced or annexed that is expressed in another language must be accompanied by a translation into the language of the case.

3. However, in the case of substantial items or lengthy documents, translations may be confined to extracts. At any time the Court may, of its own motion or at the request of one of the parties, call for a complete or fuller translation.

4. Notwithstanding the foregoing provisions, a Member State shall be entitled to use its official language when taking part in preliminary ruling proceedings, when intervening in a case before the Court or when bringing a matter before the Court pursuant to Article 259 TFEU. This provision shall apply both to written documents and to oral statements. The Registrar shall arrange in each instance for translation into the language of the case.

5. The States, other than the Member States, which are parties to the EEA Agreement, and also the EFTA Surveillance Authority, may be authorised to use one of the languages mentioned in Article 36, other than the language of the case, when they take part in preliminary ruling proceedings or intervene in a case before the Court. This provision shall apply both to written documents and to oral statements. The Registrar shall arrange in each instance for translation into the language of the case.

6.   Non-Member States taking part in preliminary ruling proceedings pursuant to the fourth paragraph of Article 23 of the Statute may be authorised to use one of the languages mentioned in Article 36 other than the language of the case. This provision shall apply both to written documents and to oral statements. The Registrar shall arrange in each instance for translation into the language of the case.

7.   Where a witness or expert states that he is unable adequately to express himself in one of the languages referred to in Article 36, the Court may authorise him to give his evidence in another language. The Registrar shall arrange for translation into the language of the case.

8.   The President and the Vice-President of the Court and also the Presidents of Chambers in conducting oral proceedings, Judges and Advocates General in putting questions and Advocates General in delivering their Opinions may use one of the languages referred to in Article 36 other than the language of the case. The Registrar shall arrange for translation into the language of the case.

Article 39 Responsibility of the Registrar concerning language arrangements

The Registrar shall, at the request of any Judge, of the Advocate General or of a party, arrange for anything said or written in the course of the proceedings before the Court to be translated into the languages chosen from those referred to in Article 36.

Article 40 Languages of the publications of the Court

Publications of the Court shall be issued in the languages referred to in Article 1 of Council Regulation No 1.

Article 41 Authentic texts

The texts of documents drawn up in the language of the case or, where applicable, in another language authorised pursuant to Articles 37 or 38 of these Rules shall be authentic.

Article 42 Language service of the Court

The Court shall set up a language service staffed by experts with adequate legal training and a thorough knowledge of several official languages of the European Union.

TITLE II

COMMON PROCEDURAL PROVISIONS

CHAPTER 1

RIGHTS AND OBLIGATIONS OF AGENTS, ADVISERS AND LAWYERS

Article 43 Privileges, immunities and facilities

1.   Agents, advisers and lawyers who appear before the Court or before any judicial authority to which the Court has addressed letters rogatory shall enjoy immunity in respect of words spoken or written by them concerning the case or the parties.

2.   Agents, advisers and lawyers shall also enjoy the following privileges and facilities:

     (a)   any papers and documents relating to the proceedings shall be exempt from both search and seizure. In the event of a dispute, the customs officials or police may seal those papers and documents; they shall then be immediately forwarded to the Court for inspection in the presence of the Registrar and of the person concerned;

     (b)   agents, advisers and lawyers shall be entitled to travel in the course of duty without hindrance.

Article 44 Status of the parties' representatives

1.   In order to qualify for the privileges, immunities and facilities specified in Article 43, persons entitled to them shall furnish proof of their status as follows:

     (a)   agents shall produce an official document issued by the party for whom they act, who shall immediately serve a copy thereof on the Registrar;

     (b)   lawyers shall produce a certificate that they are authorised to practise before a court of a Member State or of another State which is a party to the EEA Agreement, and, where the party which they represent is a legal person governed by private law, an authority to act issued by that person;

(c)   advisers shall produce an authority to act issued by the party whom they are assisting.

2.   The Registrar of the Court shall issue them with a certificate, as required. The validity of this certificate shall be limited to a specified period, which may be extended or curtailed according to the duration of the proceedings.

Article 45 Waiver of immunity

1.   The privileges, immunities and facilities specified in Article 43 of these Rules are granted exclusively in the interests of the proper conduct of proceedings.

2.   The Court may waive immunity where it considers that the proper conduct of proceedings will not be hindered thereby.

Article 46 Exclusion from the proceedings

1.   If the Court considers that the conduct of an agent, adviser or lawyer before the Court is incompatible with the dignity of the Court or with the requirements of the proper administration of justice, or that such agent, adviser or lawyer is using his rights for purposes other than those for which they were granted, it shall inform the person concerned. If the Court informs the competent authorities to whom the person concerned is answerable, a copy of the letter sent to those authorities shall be forwarded to the person concerned.

2.   On the same grounds, the Court may at any time, having heard the person concerned and the Advocate General, decide to exclude an agent, adviser or lawyer from the proceedings by reasoned order. That order shall have immediate effect.

3.   Where an agent, adviser or lawyer is excluded from the proceedings, the proceedings shall be suspended for a period fixed by the President in order to allow the party concerned to appoint another agent, adviser or lawyer.

4.   Decisions taken under this Article may be rescinded.

Article 47 University teachers and parties to the main proceedings

1.   The provisions of this Chapter shall apply to university teachers who have a right of audience before the Court in accordance with Article 19 of the Statute.

2.   They shall also apply, in the context of references for a preliminary ruling, to the parties to the main proceedings where, in accordance with the national rules of procedure applicable, those parties are permitted to bring or defend court proceedings without being represented by a lawyer, and to persons authorised under those rules to represent them.

CHAPTER 2
SERVICE

Article 48 Methods of service

1.   Where these Rules require that a document be served on a person, the Registrar shall ensure that service is effected at that person's address for service either by the dispatch of a copy of the document by registered post with a form for acknowledgement of receipt or by personal delivery of the copy against a receipt. The Registrar shall prepare and certify the copies of documents to be served, save where the parties themselves supply the copies in accordance with Article 57(2) of these Rules.

2.   Where the addressee has agreed that service is to be effected on him by telefax or any other technical means of communication, any procedural document, including a judgment or order of the Court, may be served by the transmission of a copy of the document by such means.

3.   Where, for technical reasons or on account of the nature or length of the document, such transmission is impossible or impracticable, the document shall be served, if the addressee has not specified an address for service, at his address in accordance with the procedures laid down in paragraph 1 of this Article. The addressee shall be so informed by telefax or any other technical means of communication. Service shall then be deemed to have been effected on the addressee by registered post on the 10th day following the lodging of the registered letter at the post office of the place in which the Court has its seat, unless it is shown by the acknowledgement of receipt that the letter

was received on a different date or the addressee informs the Registrar, within three weeks of being informed by telefax or any other technical means of communication, that the document to be served has not reached him.

4. The Court may, by decision, determine the criteria for a procedural document to be served by electronic means. That decision shall be published in the *Official Journal of the European Union*.

CHAPTER 3

TIME-LIMITS

Article 49 Calculation of time-limits

1. Any procedural time-limit prescribed by the Treaties, the Statute or these Rules shall be calculated as follows:
    (a) where a time-limit expressed in days, weeks, months or years is to be calculated from the moment at which an event occurs or an action takes place, the day during which that event occurs or that action takes place shall not be counted as falling within the time-limit in question;
    (b) a time-limit expressed in weeks, months or years shall end with the expiry of whichever day in the last week, month or year is the same day of the week, or falls on the same date, as the day during which the event or action from which the time-limit is to be calculated occurred or took place. If, in a time-limit expressed in months or years, the day on which it should expire does not occur in the last month, the time-limit shall end with the expiry of the last day of that month;
    (c) where a time-limit is expressed in months and days, it shall first be calculated in whole months, then in days;
    (d) time-limits shall include Saturdays, Sundays and the official holidays referred to in Article 24(6) of these Rules;
    (e) time-limits shall not be suspended during the judicial vacations.
2. If the time-limit would otherwise end on a Saturday, Sunday or an official holiday, it shall be extended until the end of the first subsequent working day.

Article 50 Proceedings against a measure adopted by an institution

Where the time-limit allowed for initiating proceedings against a measure adopted by an institution runs from the publication of that measure, that time-limit shall be calculated, for the purposes of Article 49(1)(a), from the end of the 14th day after publication of the measure in the *Official Journal of the European Union*.

Article 51 Extension on account of distance

The procedural time-limits shall be extended on account of distance by a single period of 10 days.

Article 52 Setting and extension of time-limits

1. Any time-limit prescribed by the Court pursuant to these Rules may be extended.
2. The President and the Presidents of Chambers may delegate to the Registrar power of signature for the purposes of setting certain time-limits which, pursuant to these Rules, it falls to them to prescribe, or of extending such time-limits.

CHAPTER 4

DIFFERENT PROCEDURES FOR DEALING WITH CASES

Article 53 Procedures for dealing with cases

1. Without prejudice to the special provisions laid down in the Statute or in these Rules, the procedure before the Court shall consist of a written part and an oral part.
2. Where it is clear that the Court has no jurisdiction to hear and determine a case or where a request or an application is manifestly inadmissible, the Court may, after hearing the Advocate General, at any time decide to give a decision by reasoned order without taking further steps in the proceedings.

3. The President may in special circumstances decide that a case be given priority over others.
4. A case may be dealt with under an expedited procedure in accordance with the conditions provided by these Rules.
5. A reference for a preliminary ruling may be dealt with under an urgent procedure in accordance with the conditions provided by these Rules.

Article 54 Joinder

1. Two or more cases of the same type concerning the same subject-matter may at any time be joined, on account of the connection between them, for the purposes of the written or oral part of the procedure or of the judgment which closes the proceedings.
2. A decision on whether cases should be joined shall be taken by the President after hearing the Judge-Rapporteur and the Advocate General, if the cases concerned have already been assigned, and, save in the case of references for a preliminary ruling, after also hearing the parties. The President may refer the decision on this matter to the Court.
3. Joined cases may be disjoined, in accordance with the provisions of paragraph 2.

Article 55 Stay of proceedings

1. The proceedings may be stayed:
   (a) in the circumstances specified in the third paragraph of Article 54 of the Statute, by order of the Court, made after hearing the Advocate General;
   (b) in all other cases, by decision of the President adopted after hearing the Judge-Rapporteur and the Advocate General and, save in the case of references for a preliminary ruling, the parties.
2. The proceedings may be resumed by order or decision, following the same procedure.
3. The orders or decisions referred to in paragraphs 1 and 2 shall be served on the parties or interested persons referred to in Article 23 of the Statute.
4. The stay of proceedings shall take effect on the date indicated in the order or decision of stay or, in the absence of such indication, on the date of that order or decision.
5. While proceedings are stayed time shall cease to run for the parties or interested persons referred to in Article 23 of the Statute for the purposes of procedural time-limits.
6. Where the order or decision of stay does not fix the length of stay, it shall end on the date indicated in the order or decision of resumption or, in the absence of such indication, on the date of the order or decision of resumption.
7. From the date of resumption of proceedings following a stay, the suspended procedural time-limits shall be replaced by new time-limits and time shall begin to run from the date of that resumption.

Article 56 Deferment of the determination of a case

After hearing the Judge-Rapporteur, the Advocate General and the parties, the President may in special circumstances, either of his own motion or at the request of one of the parties, defer a case to be dealt with at a later date.

CHAPTER 5
WRITTEN PART OF THE PROCEDURE

Article 57 Lodging of procedural documents

1. The original of every procedural document must bear the handwritten signature of the party's agent or lawyer or, in the case of observations submitted in the context of preliminary ruling proceedings, that of the party to the main proceedings or his representative, if the national rules of procedure applicable to those main proceedings so permit.
2. The original, accompanied by all annexes referred to therein, shall be submitted together with five copies for the Court and, in the case of proceedings other than preliminary ruling proceedings, a copy for every other party to the proceedings. Copies shall be certified by the party lodging them.

3. The institutions shall in addition produce, within time-limits laid down by the Court, translations of any procedural document into the other languages provided for by Article 1 of Council Regulation No 1. The preceding paragraph of this Article shall apply.

4. To every procedural document there shall be annexed a file containing the items and documents relied on in support of it, together with a schedule listing them.

5. Where in view of the length of an item or document only extracts from it are annexed to the procedural document, the whole item or document or a full copy of it shall be lodged at the Registry.

6. All procedural documents shall bear a date. In the calculation of procedural time-limits, only the date and time of lodgment of the original at the Registry shall be taken into account.

7. Without prejudice to the provisions of paragraphs 1 to 6, the date on and time at which a copy of the signed original of a procedural document, including the schedule of items and documents referred to in paragraph 4, is received at the Registry by telefax or any other technical means of communication available to the Court shall be deemed to be the date and time of lodgment for the purposes of compliance with the procedural time-limits, provided that the signed original of the procedural document, accompanied by the annexes and copies referred to in paragraph 2, is lodged at the Registry no later than 10 days thereafter.

8. Without prejudice to paragraphs 3 to 6, the Court may, by decision, determine the criteria for a procedural document sent to the Registry by electronic means to be deemed to be the original of that document. That decision shall be published in the *Official Journal of the European Union*.

Article 58 Length of procedural documents

Without prejudice to any special provisions laid down in these Rules, the Court may, by decision, set the maximum length of written pleadings or observations lodged before it. That decision shall be published in the *Official Journal of the European Union*.

CHAPTER 6
THE PRELIMINARY REPORT AND ASSIGNMENT OF CASES TO FORMATIONS OF THE COURT

Article 59 Preliminary report

1. When the written part of the procedure is closed, the President shall fix a date on which the Judge-Rapporteur is to present a preliminary report to the general meeting of the Court.

2. The preliminary report shall contain proposals as to whether particular measures of organisation of procedure, measures of inquiry or, if appropriate, requests to the referring court or tribunal for clarification should be undertaken, and as to the formation to which the case should be assigned. It shall also contain the Judge-Rapporteur's proposals, if any, as to whether to dispense with a hearing and as to whether to dispense with an Opinion of the Advocate General pursuant to the fifth paragraph of Article 20 of the Statute.

3. The Court shall decide, after hearing the Advocate General, what action to take on the proposals of the Judge-Rapporteur.

Article 60 Assignment of cases to formations of the Court

1. The Court shall assign to the Chambers of five and of three Judges any case brought before it in so far as the difficulty or importance of the case or particular circumstances are not such as to require that it should be assigned to the Grand Chamber, unless a Member State or an institution of the European Union participating in the proceedings has requested that the case be assigned to the Grand Chamber, pursuant to the third paragraph of Article 16 of the Statute.

2. The Court shall sit as a full Court where cases are brought before it pursuant to the provisions referred to in the fourth paragraph of Article 16 of the Statute. It may assign a case to the full Court where, in accordance with the fifth paragraph of Article 16 of the Statute, it considers that the case is of exceptional importance.

3.   The formation to which a case has been assigned may, at any stage of the proceedings, request the Court to assign the case to a formation composed of a greater number of Judges.

4.   Where the oral part of the procedure is opened without an inquiry, the President of the formation determining the case shall fix the opening date.

CHAPTER 7
MEASURES OF ORGANISATION OF PROCEDURE AND MEASURES OF INQUIRY

SECTION 1
MEASURES OF ORGANISATION OF PROCEDURE

Article 61 Measures of organisation prescribed by the Court

1.   In addition to the measures which may be prescribed in accordance with Article 24 of the Statute, the Court may invite the parties or the interested persons referred to in Article 23 of the Statute to answer certain questions in writing, within the time-limit laid down by the Court, or at the hearing. The written replies shall be communicated to the other parties or the interested persons referred to in Article 23 of the Statute.

2.   Where a hearing is organised, the Court shall, in so far as possible, invite the participants in that hearing to concentrate in their oral pleadings on one or more specified issues.

Article 62 Measures of organisation prescribed by the Judge-Rapporteur or the Advocate General

1.   The Judge-Rapporteur or the Advocate General may request the parties or the interested persons referred to in Article 23 of the Statute to submit within a specified time-limit all such information relating to the facts, and all such documents or other particulars, as they may consider relevant. The replies and documents provided shall be communicated to the other parties or the interested persons referred to in Article 23 of the Statute.

2.   The Judge-Rapporteur or the Advocate General may also send to the parties or the interested persons referred to in Article 23 of the Statute questions to be answered at the hearing.

SECTION 2
MEASURES OF INQUIRY

Article 63 Decision on measures of inquiry

1.   The Court shall decide in its general meeting whether a measure of inquiry is necessary.

2.   Where the case has already been assigned to a formation of the Court, the decision shall be taken by that formation.

Article 64 Determination of measures of inquiry

1.   The Court, after hearing the Advocate General, shall prescribe the measures of inquiry that it considers appropriate by means of an order setting out the facts to be proved.

2.   Without prejudice to Articles 24 and 25 of the Statute, the following measures of inquiry may be adopted:
     (a)   the personal appearance of the parties;
     (b)   a request for information and production of documents;
     (c)   oral testimony;
     (d)   the commissioning of an expert's report;
     (e)   an inspection of the place or thing in question.

3.   Evidence may be submitted in rebuttal and previous evidence may be amplified.

Article 65 Participation in measures of inquiry

1.   Where the formation of the Court does not undertake the inquiry itself, it shall entrust the task of so doing to the Judge-Rapporteur.

2.   The Advocate General shall take part in the measures of inquiry.

3.   The parties shall be entitled to attend the measures of inquiry.

Article 66 Oral testimony

1. The Court may, either of its own motion or at the request of one of the parties, and after hearing the Advocate General, order that certain facts be proved by witnesses.
2. A request by a party for the examination of a witness shall state precisely about what facts and for what reasons the witness should be examined.
3. The Court shall rule by reasoned order on the request referred to in the preceding paragraph. If the request is granted, the order shall set out the facts to be established and state which witnesses are to be heard in respect of each of those facts.
4. Witnesses shall be summoned by the Court, where appropriate after lodgment of the security provided for in Article 73(1) of these Rules.

Article 67 Examination of witnesses

1. After the identity of the witness has been established, the President shall inform him that he will be required to vouch the truth of his evidence in the manner laid down in these Rules.
2. The witness shall give his evidence to the Court, the parties having been given notice to attend. After the witness has given his evidence the President may, at the request of one of the parties or of his own motion, put questions to him.
3. The other Judges and the Advocate General may do likewise.
4. Subject to the control of the President, questions may be put to witnesses by the representatives of the parties.

Article 68 Witnesses' oath

1. After giving his evidence, the witness shall take the following oath:
   'I swear that I have spoken the truth, the whole truth and nothing but the truth.'
2. The Court may, after hearing the parties, exempt a witness from taking the oath.

Article 69 Pecuniary penalties

1. Witnesses who have been duly summoned shall obey the summons and attend for examination.
2. If, without good reason, a witness who has been duly summoned fails to appear before the Court, the Court may impose upon him a pecuniary penalty not exceeding EUR 5 000 and may order that a further summons be served on the witness at his own expense.
3. The same penalty may be imposed upon a witness who, without good reason, refuses to give evidence or to take the oath.

Article 70 Expert's report

1. The Court may order that an expert's report be obtained. The order appointing the expert shall define his task and set a time-limit within which he is to submit his report.
2. After the expert has submitted his report and that report has been served on the parties, the Court may order that the expert be examined, the parties having been given notice to attend. At the request of one of the parties or of his own motion, the President may put questions to the expert.
3. The other Judges and the Advocate General may do likewise.
4. Subject to the control of the President, questions may be put to the expert by the representatives of the parties.

Article 71 Expert's oath

1. After making his report, the expert shall take the following oath:
   'I swear that I have conscientiously and impartially carried out my task.'
2. The Court may, after hearing the parties, exempt the expert from taking the oath.

Article 72 Objection to a witness or expert

1. If one of the parties objects to a witness or an expert on the ground that he is not a competent or proper person to act as a witness or expert or for any other reason, or if a witness or expert refuses to give evidence or to take the oath, the matter shall be resolved by the Court.
2. An objection to a witness or an expert shall be raised within two weeks after service of the order summoning the witness or appointing the expert; the statement of objection must set out the grounds of objection and indicate the nature of any evidence offered.

Article 73 Witnesses' and experts' costs

1. Where the Court orders the examination of witnesses or an expert's report, it may request the parties or one of them to lodge security for the witnesses' costs or the costs of the expert's report.
2. Witnesses and experts shall be entitled to reimbursement of their travel and subsistence expenses. The cashier of the Court may make an advance payment towards these expenses.
3. Witnesses shall be entitled to compensation for loss of earnings, and experts to fees for their services. The cashier of the Court shall pay witnesses and experts these sums after they have carried out their respective duties or tasks.

Article 74 Minutes of inquiry hearings

1. The Registrar shall draw up minutes of every inquiry hearing. The minutes shall be signed by the President and by the Registrar. They shall constitute an official record.
2. In the case of the examination of witnesses or experts, the minutes shall be signed by the President or by the Judge-Rapporteur responsible for conducting the examination of the witness or expert, and by the Registrar. Before the minutes are thus signed, the witness or expert must be given an opportunity to check the content of the minutes and to sign them.
3. The minutes shall be served on the parties.

Article 75 Opening of the oral part of the procedure after the inquiry

1. Unless the Court decides to prescribe a time-limit within which the parties may submit written observations, the President shall fix the date for the opening of the oral part of the procedure after the measures of inquiry have been completed.
2. Where a time-limit has been prescribed for the submission of written observations, the President shall fix the date for the opening of the oral part of the procedure after that time-limit has expired.

CHAPTER 8
ORAL PART OF THE PROCEDURE

Article 76 Hearing

1. Any reasoned requests for a hearing shall be submitted within three weeks after service on the parties or the interested persons referred to in Article 23 of the Statute of notification of the close of the written part of the procedure. That time-limit may be extended by the President.
2. On a proposal from the Judge-Rapporteur and after hearing the Advocate General, the Court may decide not to hold a hearing if it considers, on reading the written pleadings or observations lodged during the written part of the procedure, that it has sufficient information to give a ruling.
3. The preceding paragraph shall not apply where a request for a hearing, stating reasons, has been submitted by an interested person referred to in Article 23 of the Statute who did not participate in the written part of the procedure.

Article 77 Joint hearing

If the similarities between two or more cases of the same type so permit, the Court may decide to organise a joint hearing of those cases.

Article 78 Conduct of oral proceedings

Oral proceedings shall be opened and directed by the President, who shall be responsible for the proper conduct of the hearing.

Article 79 Cases heard in camera

1. For serious reasons related, in particular, to the security of the Member States or to the protection of minors, the Court may decide to hear a case in camera.
2. The oral proceedings in cases heard in camera shall not be published.

Article 80 Questions

The members of the formation of the Court and the Advocate General may in the course of the hearing put questions to the agents, advisers or lawyers of the parties and, in the circumstances referred to in Article 47(2) of these Rules, to the parties to the main proceedings or to their representatives.

Article 81 Close of the hearing

After the parties or the interested persons referred to in Article 23 of the Statute have presented oral argument, the President shall declare the hearing closed.

Article 82 Delivery of the Opinion of the Advocate General

1. Where a hearing takes place, the Opinion of the Advocate General shall be delivered after the close of that hearing.
2. The President shall declare the oral part of the procedure closed after the Advocate General has delivered his Opinion.

Article 83 Opening or reopening of the oral part of the procedure

The Court may at any time, after hearing the Advocate General, order the opening or reopening of the oral part of the procedure, in particular if it considers that it lacks sufficient information or where a party has, after the close of that part of the procedure, submitted a new fact which is of such a nature as to be a decisive factor for the decision of the Court, or where the case must be decided on the basis of an argument which has not been debated between the parties or the interested persons referred to in Article 23 of the Statute.

Article 84 Minutes of hearings

1. The Registrar shall draw up minutes of every hearing. The minutes shall be signed by the President and by the Registrar. They shall constitute an official record.
2. The parties and interested persons referred to in Article 23 of the Statute may inspect the minutes at the Registry and obtain copies.

Article 85 Recording of the hearing

The President may, on a duly substantiated request, authorise a party or an interested person referred to in Article 23 of the Statute who has participated in the written or oral part of the proceedings to listen, on the Court's premises, to the soundtrack of the hearing in the language used by the speaker during that hearing.

CHAPTER 9
JUDGMENTS AND ORDERS

Article 86 Date of delivery of a judgment

The parties or interested persons referred to in Article 23 of the Statute shall be informed of the date of delivery of a judgment.

Article 87 Content of a judgment

A judgment shall contain:
- (a)   a statement that it is the judgment of the Court,
- (b)   an indication as to the formation of the Court,
- (c)   the date of delivery,
- (d)   the names of the President and of the Judges who took part in the deliberations, with an indication as to the name of the Judge-Rapporteur,
- (e)   the name of the Advocate General,
- (f)   the name of the Registrar,
- (g)   a description of the parties or of the interested persons referred to in Article 23 of the Statute who participated in the proceedings,
- (h)   the names of their representatives,
- (i)   in the case of direct actions and appeals, a statement of the forms of order sought by the parties,
- (j)   where applicable, the date of the hearing,
- (k)   a statement that the Advocate General has been heard and, where applicable, the date of his Opinion,
- (l)   a summary of the facts,

(m)   the grounds for the decision,
(n)   the operative part of the judgment, including, where appropriate, the decision as to costs.

Article 88 Delivery and service of the judgment

1.   The judgment shall be delivered in open court.
2.   The original of the judgment, signed by the President, by the Judges who took part in the deliberations and by the Registrar, shall be sealed and deposited at the Registry; certified copies of the judgment shall be served on the parties and, where applicable, the referring court or tribunal, the interested persons referred to in Article 23 of the Statute and the General Court.

Article 89 Content of an order

1.   An order shall contain:
   (a)   a statement that it is the order of the Court,
   (b)   an indication as to the formation of the Court,
   (c)   the date of its adoption,
   (d)   an indication as to the legal basis of the order,
   (e)   the names of the President and, where applicable, the Judges who took part in the deliberations, with an indication as to the name of the Judge-Rapporteur,
   (f)   the name of the Advocate General,
   (g)   the name of the Registrar,
   (h)   a description of the parties or of the parties to the main proceedings,
   (i)   the names of their representatives,
   (j)   a statement that the Advocate General has been heard,
   (k)   the operative part of the order, including, where appropriate, the decision as to costs.
2.   Where, in accordance with these Rules, an order must be reasoned, it shall in addition contain:
   (a)   in the case of direct actions and appeals, a statement of the forms of order sought by the parties,
   (b)   a summary of the facts,
   (c)   the grounds for the decision.

Article 90 Signature and service of the order

The original of the order, signed by the President and by the Registrar, shall be sealed and deposited at the Registry; certified copies of the order shall be served on the parties and, where applicable, the referring court or tribunal, the interested persons referred to in Article 23 of the Statute and the General Court.

Article 91 Binding nature of judgments and orders

1.   A judgment shall be binding from the date of its delivery.
2.   An order shall be binding from the date of its service.

Article 92 Publication in the *Official Journal of the European Union*

A notice containing the date and the operative part of the judgment or order of the Court which closes the proceedings shall be published in the *Official Journal of the European Union*.

TITLE III
REFERENCES FOR A PRELIMINARY RULING

CHAPTER 1
GENERAL PROVISIONS

Article 93 Scope

The procedure shall be governed by the provisions of this Title:
   (a)   in the cases covered by Article 23 of the Statute,
   (b)   as regards references for interpretation which may be provided for by agreements to which the European Union or the Member States are parties.

Article 94 Content of the request for a preliminary ruling

In addition to the text of the questions referred to the Court for a preliminary ruling, the request for a preliminary ruling shall contain:

    (a)   a summary of the subject-matter of the dispute and the relevant findings of fact as determined by the referring court or tribunal, or, at least, an account of the facts on which the questions are based;

    (b)   the tenor of any national provisions applicable in the case and, where appropriate, the relevant national case-law;

    (c)   a statement of the reasons which prompted the referring court or tribunal to inquire about the interpretation or validity of certain provisions of European Union law, and the relationship between those provisions and the national legislation applicable to the main proceedings.

Article 95 Anonymity

1.   Where anonymity has been granted by the referring court or tribunal, the Court shall respect that anonymity in the proceedings pending before it.

2.   At the request of the referring court or tribunal, at the duly reasoned request of a party to the main proceedings or of its own motion, the Court may also, if it considers it necessary, render anonymous one or more persons or entities concerned by the case.

Article 96 Participation in preliminary ruling proceedings

1.   Pursuant to Article 23 of the Statute, the following shall be authorised to submit observations to the Court:

    (a)   the parties to the main proceedings,

    (b)   the Member States,

    (c)   the European Commission,

    (d)   the institution which adopted the act the validity or interpretation of which is in dispute,

    (e)   the States, other than the Member States, which are parties to the EEA Agreement, and also the EFTA Surveillance Authority, where a question concerning one of the fields of application of that Agreement is referred to the Court for a preliminary ruling,

    (f)   non-Member States which are parties to an agreement relating to a specific subject-matter, concluded with the Council, where the agreement so provides and where a court or tribunal of a Member State refers to the Court of Justice for a preliminary ruling a question falling within the scope of that agreement.

2.   Non-participation in the written part of the procedure does not preclude participation in the oral part of the procedure.

Article 97 Parties to the main proceedings

1.   The parties to the main proceedings are those who are determined as such by the referring court or tribunal in accordance with national rules of procedure.

2.   Where the referring court or tribunal informs the Court that a new party has been admitted to the main proceedings, when the proceedings before the Court are already pending, that party must accept the case as he finds it at the time when the Court was so informed. That party shall receive a copy of every procedural document already served on the interested persons referred to in Article 23 of the Statute.

3.   As regards the representation and attendance of the parties to the main proceedings, the Court shall take account of the rules of procedure in force before the court or tribunal which made the reference. In the event of any doubt as to whether a person may under national law represent a party to the main proceedings, the Court may obtain information from the referring court or tribunal on the rules of procedure applicable.

Article 98 Translation and service of the request for a preliminary ruling

1.   The requests for a preliminary ruling referred to in this Title shall be served on the Member States in the original version, accompanied by a translation into the official language of the State to which they are being addressed. Where appropriate, on account of the length of the request, such translation shall be replaced by the translation into the official language of the State to which it is addressed of a summary

of that request, which will serve as a basis for the position to be adopted by that State. The summary shall include the full text of the question or questions referred for a preliminary ruling. That summary shall contain, in particular, in so far as that information appears in the request for a preliminary ruling, the subject-matter of the main proceedings, the essential arguments of the parties to those proceedings, a succinct presentation of the reasons for the reference for a preliminary ruling and the case-law and the provisions of national law and European Union law relied on.

2. In the cases covered by the third paragraph of Article 23 of the Statute, the requests for a preliminary ruling shall be served on the States, other than the Member States, which are parties to the EEA Agreement and also on the EFTA Surveillance Authority in the original version, accompanied by a translation of the request, or where appropriate of a summary, into one of the languages referred to in Article 36, to be chosen by the addressee.

3. Where a non-Member State has the right to take part in preliminary ruling proceedings pursuant to the fourth paragraph of Article 23 of the Statute, the original version of the request for a preliminary ruling shall be served on it accompanied by a translation of the request, or where appropriate of a summary, into one of the languages referred to in Article 36, to be chosen by the non-Member State concerned.

Article 99 Reply by reasoned order

Where a question referred to the Court for a preliminary ruling is identical to a question on which the Court has already ruled, where the reply to such a question may be clearly deduced from existing case-law or where the answer to the question referred for a preliminary ruling admits of no reasonable doubt, the Court may at any time, on a proposal from the Judge-Rapporteur and after hearing the Advocate General, decide to rule by reasoned order.

Article 100   Circumstances in which the Court remains seised

1. The Court shall remain seised of a request for a preliminary ruling for as long as it is not withdrawn by the court or tribunal which made that request to the Court. The withdrawal of a request may be taken into account until notice of the date of delivery of the judgment has been served on the interested persons referred to in Article 23 of the Statute.

2. However, the Court may at any time declare that the conditions of its jurisdiction are no longer fulfilled.

Article 101   Request for clarification

1. Without prejudice to the measures of organisation of procedure and measures of inquiry provided for in these Rules, the Court may, after hearing the Advocate General, request clarification from the referring court or tribunal within a time-limit prescribed by the Court.

2. The reply of the referring court or tribunal to that request shall be served on the interested persons referred to in Article 23 of the Statute.

Article 102   Costs of the preliminary ruling proceedings

It shall be for the referring court or tribunal to decide as to the costs of the preliminary ruling proceedings.

Article 103   Rectification of judgments and orders

1. Clerical mistakes, errors in calculation and obvious inaccuracies affecting judgments or orders may be rectified by the Court, of its own motion or at the request of an interested person referred to in Article 23 of the Statute made within two weeks after delivery of the judgment or service of the order.

2. The Court shall take its decision after hearing the Advocate General.

3. The original of the rectification order shall be annexed to the original of the rectified decision. A note of this order shall be made in the margin of the original of the rectified decision.

Article 104   Interpretation of preliminary rulings

1. Article 158 of these Rules relating to the interpretation of judgments and orders shall not apply to decisions given in reply to a request for a preliminary ruling.

2.   It shall be for the national courts or tribunals to assess whether they consider that sufficient guidance is given by a preliminary ruling, or whether it appears to them that a further reference to the Court is required.

CHAPTER 2
EXPEDITED PRELIMINARY RULING PROCEDURE

Article 105   Expedited procedure

1.   At the request of the referring court or tribunal or, exceptionally, of his own motion, the President of the Court may, where the nature of the case requires that it be dealt with within a short time, after hearing the Judge-Rapporteur and the Advocate General, decide that a reference for a preliminary ruling is to be determined pursuant to an expedited procedure derogating from the provisions of these Rules.

2.   In that event, the President shall immediately fix the date for the hearing, which shall be communicated to the interested persons referred to in Article 23 of the Statute when the request for a preliminary ruling is served.

3.   The interested persons referred to in the preceding paragraph may lodge statements of case or written observations within a time-limit prescribed by the President, which shall not be less than 15 days. The President may request those interested persons to restrict the matters addressed in their statement of case or written observations to the essential points of law raised by the request for a preliminary ruling.

4.   The statements of case or written observations, if any, shall be communicated to all the interested persons referred to in Article 23 of the Statute prior to the hearing.

5.   The Court shall rule after hearing the Advocate General.

Article 106   Transmission of procedural documents

1.   The procedural documents referred to in the preceding Article shall be deemed to have been lodged on the transmission to the Registry, by telefax or any other technical means of communication available to the Court, of a copy of the signed original and the items and documents relied on in support of it, together with the schedule referred to in Article 57(4). The original of the document and the annexes referred to above shall be sent to the Registry immediately.

2.   Where the preceding Article requires that a document be served on or communicated to a person, such service or communication may be effected by transmission of a copy of the document by telefax or any other technical means of communication available to the Court and the addressee.

CHAPTER 3
URGENT PRELIMINARY RULING PROCEDURE

Article 107   Scope of the urgent preliminary ruling procedure

1.   A reference for a preliminary ruling which raises one or more questions in the areas covered by Title V of Part Three of the Treaty on the Functioning of the European Union may, at the request of the referring court or tribunal or, exceptionally, of the Court's own motion, be dealt with under an urgent procedure derogating from the provisions of these Rules.

2.   The referring court or tribunal shall set out the matters of fact and law which establish the urgency and justify the application of that exceptional procedure and shall, in so far as possible, indicate the answer that it proposes to the questions referred.

3.   If the referring court or tribunal has not submitted a request for the urgent procedure to be applied, the President of the Court may, if the application of that procedure appears, prima facie, to be required, ask the Chamber referred to in Article 108 to consider whether it is necessary to deal with the reference under that procedure.

Article 108   Decision as to urgency

1.   The decision to deal with a reference for a preliminary ruling under the urgent procedure shall be taken by the designated Chamber, acting on a proposal from the

Judge-Rapporteur and after hearing the Advocate General. The composition of that Chamber shall be determined in accordance with Article 28(2) on the day on which the case is assigned to the Judge-Rapporteur if the application of the urgent procedure is requested by the referring court or tribunal, or, if the application of that procedure is considered at the request of the President of the Court, on the day on which that request is made.

2.   If the case is connected with a pending case assigned to a Judge-Rapporteur who is not a member of the designated Chamber, that Chamber may propose to the President of the Court that the case be assigned to that Judge-Rapporteur. Where the case is reassigned to that Judge-Rapporteur, the Chamber of five Judges which includes him shall carry out the duties of the designated Chamber in respect of that case. Article 29(1) shall apply.

Article 109   Written part of the urgent procedure

1.   A request for a preliminary ruling shall, where the referring court or tribunal has requested the application of the urgent procedure or where the President has requested the designated Chamber to consider whether it is necessary to deal with the reference under that procedure, be served forthwith by the Registrar on the parties to the main proceedings, on the Member State from which the reference is made, on the European Commission and on the institution which adopted the act the validity or interpretation of which is in dispute.

2.   The decision as to whether or not to deal with the reference for a preliminary ruling under the urgent procedure shall be served immediately on the referring court or tribunal and on the parties, Member State and institutions referred to in the preceding paragraph. The decision to deal with the reference under the urgent procedure shall prescribe the time-limit within which those parties or entities may lodge statements of case or written observations. The decision may specify the matters of law to which such statements of case or written observations must relate and may specify the maximum length of those documents.

3.   Where a request for a preliminary ruling refers to an administrative procedure or judicial proceedings conducted in a Member State other than that from which the reference is made, the Court may invite that first Member State to provide all relevant information in writing or at the hearing.

4.   As soon as the service referred to in paragraph 1 above has been effected, the request for a preliminary ruling shall also be communicated to the interested persons referred to in Article 23 of the Statute, other than the persons served, and the decision whether or not to deal with the reference for a preliminary ruling under the urgent procedure shall be communicated to those interested persons as soon as the service referred to in paragraph 2 has been effected.

5.   The interested persons referred to in Article 23 of the Statute shall be informed as soon as possible of the likely date of the hearing.

6.   Where the reference is not to be dealt with under the urgent procedure, the proceedings shall continue in accordance with the provisions of Article 23 of the Statute and the applicable provisions of these Rules.

Article 110   Service and information following the close of the written part of the procedure

1.   Where a reference for a preliminary ruling is to be dealt with under the urgent procedure, the request for a preliminary ruling and the statements of case or written observations which have been lodged shall be served on the interested persons referred to in Article 23 of the Statute other than the parties and entities referred to in Article 109(1). The request for a preliminary ruling shall be accompanied by a translation, where appropriate of a summary, in accordance with Article 98.

2.   The statements of case or written observations which have been lodged shall also be served on the parties and other interested persons referred to in Article 109(1).

3.   The date of the hearing shall be communicated to the interested persons referred to in Article 23 of the Statute at the same time as the documents referred to in the preceding paragraphs are served.

Article 111 Omission of the written part of the procedure
The designated Chamber may, in cases of extreme urgency, decide to omit the written part of the procedure referred to in Article 109(2).

Article 112 Decision on the substance
The designated Chamber shall rule after hearing the Advocate General.

Article 113 Formation of the Court
1. The designated Chamber may decide to sit in a formation of three Judges. In that event, it shall be composed of the President of the designated Chamber, the Judge-Rapporteur and the first Judge or, as the case may be, the first two Judges designated from the list referred to in Article 28(2) on the date on which the composition of the designated Chamber is determined in accordance with Article 108(1).
2. The designated Chamber may also request the Court to assign the case to a formation composed of a greater number of Judges. The urgent procedure shall continue before the new formation of the Court, where necessary after the reopening of the oral part of the procedure.

Article 114 Transmission of procedural documents
Procedural documents shall be transmitted in accordance with Article 106.

CHAPTER 4

LEGAL AID

Article 115 Application for legal aid
1. A party to the main proceedings who is wholly or in part unable to meet the costs of the proceedings before the Court may at any time apply for legal aid.
2. The application shall be accompanied by all information and supporting documents making it possible to assess the applicant's financial situation, such as a certificate issued by a competent national authority attesting to his financial situation.
3. If the applicant has already obtained legal aid before the referring court or tribunal, he shall produce the decision of that court or tribunal and specify what is covered by the sums already granted.

Article 116 Decision on the application for legal aid
1. As soon as the application for legal aid has been lodged it shall be assigned by the President to the Judge-Rapporteur responsible for the case in the context of which the application has been made.
2. The decision to grant legal aid, in full or in part, or to refuse it shall be taken, on a proposal from the Judge-Rapporteur and after hearing the Advocate General, by the Chamber of three Judges to which the Judge-Rapporteur is assigned. The formation of the Court shall, in that event, be composed of the President of that Chamber, the Judge-Rapporteur and the first Judge or, as the case may be, the first two Judges designated from the list referred to in Article 28(3) on the date on which the application for legal aid is brought before that Chamber by the Judge-Rapporteur.
3. If the Judge-Rapporteur is not a member of a Chamber of three Judges, the decision shall be taken, under the same conditions, by the Chamber of five Judges to which he is assigned. In addition to the Judge-Rapporteur, the formation of the Court shall be composed of four Judges designated from the list referred to in Article 28(2) on the date on which the application for legal aid is brought before that Chamber by the Judge-Rapporteur.
4. The formation of the Court shall give its decision by way of order. Where the application for legal aid is refused in whole or in part, the order shall state the reasons for that refusal.

Article 117 Sums to be advanced as legal aid
Where legal aid is granted, the cashier of the Court shall be responsible, where applicable within the limits set by the formation of the Court, for costs involved in the assistance and

representation of the applicant before the Court. At the request of the applicant or his representative, an advance on those costs may be paid.

Article 118   Withdrawal of legal aid

The formation of the Court which gave a decision on the application for legal aid may at any time, either of its own motion or on request, withdraw that legal aid if the circumstances which led to its being granted alter during the proceedings.

TITLE IV
DIRECT ACTIONS

CHAPTER 1
REPRESENTATION OF THE PARTIES

Article 119   Obligation to be represented

1. A party may be represented only by his agent or lawyer.
2. Agents and lawyers must lodge at the Registry an official document or an authority to act issued by the party whom they represent.
3. The lawyer acting for a party must also lodge at the Registry a certificate that he is authorised to practise before a court of a Member State or of another State which is a party to the EEA Agreement.
4. If those documents are not lodged, the Registrar shall prescribe a reasonable time-limit within which the party concerned is to produce them. If the applicant fails to produce the required documents within the time-limit prescribed, the Court shall, after hearing the Judge-Rapporteur and the Advocate General, decide whether the non-compliance with that procedural requirement renders the application or written pleading formally inadmissible.

CHAPTER 2
WRITTEN PART OF THE PROCEDURE

Article 120   Content of the application

An application of the kind referred to in Article 21 of the Statute shall state:
  (a) the name and address of the applicant;
  (b) the name of the party against whom the application is made;
  (c) the subject-matter of the proceedings, the pleas in law and arguments relied on and a summary of those pleas in law;
  (d) the form of order sought by the applicant;
  (e) where appropriate, any evidence produced or offered.

Article 121   Information relating to service

1. For the purpose of the proceedings, the application shall state an address for service. It shall indicate the name of the person who is authorised and has expressed willingness to accept service.
2. In addition to, or instead of, specifying an address for service as referred to in paragraph 1, the application may state that the lawyer or agent agrees that service is to be effected on him by telefax or any other technical means of communication.
3. If the application does not comply with the requirements referred to in paragraphs 1 or 2, all service on the party concerned for the purpose of the proceedings shall be effected, for so long as the defect has not been cured, by registered letter addressed to the agent or lawyer of that party. By way of derogation from Article 48, service shall then be deemed to be duly effected by the lodging of the registered letter at the post office of the place in which the Court has its seat.

Article 122   Annexes to the application

1. The application shall be accompanied, where appropriate, by the documents specified in the second paragraph of Article 21 of the Statute.

2. An application submitted under Article 273 TFEU shall be accompanied by a copy of the special agreement concluded between the Member States concerned.
3. If an application does not comply with the requirements set out in paragraphs 1 or 2 of this Article, the Registrar shall prescribe a reasonable time-limit within which the applicant is to produce the abovementioned documents. If the applicant fails to put the application in order, the Court shall, after hearing the Judge-Rapporteur and the Advocate General, decide whether the non-compliance with these conditions renders the application formally inadmissible.

Article 123   Service of the application

The application shall be served on the defendant. In cases where Article 119(4) or Article 122(3) applies, service shall be effected as soon as the application has been put in order or the Court has declared it admissible notwithstanding the failure to observe the requirements set out in those two Articles.

Article 124   Content of the defence

1. Within two months after service on him of the application, the defendant shall lodge a defence, stating:
    (a) the name and address of the defendant;
    (b) the pleas in law and arguments relied on;
    (c) the form of order sought by the defendant;
    (d) where appropriate, any evidence produced or offered.
2. Article 121 shall apply to the defence.
3. The time-limit laid down in paragraph 1 may exceptionally be extended by the President at the duly reasoned request of the defendant.

Article 125   Transmission of documents

Where the European Parliament, the Council or the European Commission is not a party to a case, the Court shall send to them copies of the application and of the defence, without the annexes thereto, to enable them to assess whether the inapplicability of one of their acts is being invoked under Article 277 TFEU.

Article 126   Reply and rejoinder

1. The application initiating proceedings and the defence may be supplemented by a reply from the applicant and by a rejoinder from the defendant.
2. The President shall prescribe the time-limits within which those procedural documents are to be produced. He may specify the matters to which the reply or the rejoinder should relate.

CHAPTER 3
PLEAS IN LAW AND EVIDENCE

Article 127   New pleas in law

1. No new plea in law may be introduced in the course of proceedings unless it is based on matters of law or of fact which come to light in the course of the procedure.
2. Without prejudice to the decision to be taken on the admissibility of the plea in law, the President may, on a proposal from the Judge-Rapporteur and after hearing the Advocate General, prescribe a time-limit within which the other party may respond to that plea.

Article 128   Evidence produced or offered

1. In reply or rejoinder a party may produce or offer further evidence in support of his arguments. The party must give reasons for the delay in submitting such evidence.
2. The parties may, exceptionally, produce or offer further evidence after the close of the written part of the procedure. They must give reasons for the delay in submitting such evidence. The President may, on a proposal from the Judge-Rapporteur and after hearing the Advocate General, prescribe a time-limit within which the other party may comment on such evidence.

CHAPTER 4
INTERVENTION

Article 129   Object and effects of the intervention
1.   The intervention shall be limited to supporting, in whole or in part, the form of order sought by one of the parties. It shall not confer the same procedural rights as those conferred on the parties and, in particular, shall not give rise to any right to request that a hearing be held.
2.   The intervention shall be ancillary to the main proceedings. It shall become devoid of purpose if the case is removed from the register of the Court as a result of a party's discontinuance or withdrawal from the proceedings or of an agreement between the parties, or where the application is declared inadmissible.
3.   The intervener must accept the case as he finds it at the time of his intervention.
4.   Consideration may be given to an application to intervene which is made after the expiry of the time-limit prescribed in Article 130 but before the decision to open the oral part of the procedure provided for in Article 60(4). In that event, if the President allows the intervention, the intervener may submit his observations during the hearing, if it takes place.

Article 130   Application to intervene
1.   An application to intervene must be submitted within six weeks of the publication of the notice referred to in Article 21(4).
2.   The application to intervene shall contain:
     (a)   a description of the case;
     (b)   a description of the main parties;
     (c)   the name and address of the intervener;
     (d)   the form of order sought, in support of which the intervener is applying for leave to intervene;
     (e)   a statement of the circumstances establishing the right to intervene, where the application is submitted pursuant to the second or third paragraph of Article 40 of the Statute.
3.   The intervener shall be represented in accordance with Article 19 of the Statute.
4.   Articles 119, 121 and 122 of these Rules shall apply.

Article 131   Decision on applications to intervene
1.   The application to intervene shall be served on the parties in order to obtain any written or oral observations they may wish to make on that application.
2.   Where the application is submitted pursuant to the first or third paragraph of Article 40 of the Statute, the intervention shall be allowed by decision of the President and the intervener shall receive a copy of every procedural document served on the parties, provided that those parties have not, within 10 days after the service referred to in paragraph 1 has been effected, put forward observations on the application to intervene or identified secret or confidential items or documents which, if communicated to the intervener, the parties claim would be prejudicial to them.
3.   In any other case, the President shall decide on the application to intervene by order or shall refer the application to the Court.
4.   If the application to intervene is granted, the intervener shall receive a copy of every procedural document served on the parties, save, where applicable, for the secret or confidential items or documents excluded from such communication pursuant to paragraph 3.

Article 132   Submission of statements
1.   The intervener may submit a statement in intervention within one month after communication of the procedural documents referred to in the preceding Article. That time-limit may be extended by the President at the duly reasoned request of the intervener.
2.   The statement in intervention shall contain:
     (a)   the form of order sought by the intervener in support, in whole or in part, of the form of order sought by one of the parties;

    (b)   the pleas in law and arguments relied on by the intervener;

    (c)   where appropriate, any evidence produced or offered.

3.   After the statement in intervention has been lodged, the President shall, where necessary, prescribe a time-limit within which the parties may reply to that statement.

CHAPTER 5
EXPEDITED PROCEDURE

Article 133   Decision relating to the expedited procedure

1.   At the request of the applicant or the defendant, the President of the Court may, where the nature of the case requires that it be dealt with within a short time, after hearing the other party, the Judge-Rapporteur and the Advocate General, decide that a case is to be determined pursuant to an expedited procedure derogating from the provisions of these Rules.

2.   The request for a case to be determined pursuant to an expedited procedure must be made by a separate document submitted at the same time as the application initiating proceedings or the defence, as the case may be, is lodged.

3.   Exceptionally the President may also take such a decision of his own motion, after hearing the parties, the Judge-Rapporteur and the Advocate General.

Article 134   Written part of the procedure

1.   Under the expedited procedure, the application initiating proceedings and the defence may be supplemented by a reply and a rejoinder only if the President, after hearing the Judge-Rapporteur and the Advocate General, considers this to be necessary.

2.   An intervener may submit a statement in intervention only if the President, after hearing the Judge-Rapporteur and the Advocate General, considers this to be necessary.

Article 135   Oral part of the procedure

1.   Once the defence has been submitted or, if the decision to determine the case pursuant to an expedited procedure is not made until after that pleading has been lodged, once that decision has been taken, the President shall fix a date for the hearing, which shall be communicated forthwith to the parties. He may postpone the date of the hearing where it is necessary to undertake measures of inquiry or where measures of organisation of procedure so require.

2.   Without prejudice to Articles 127 and 128, a party may supplement his arguments and produce or offer evidence during the oral part of the procedure. The party must, however, give reasons for the delay in producing such further arguments or evidence.

Article 136   Decision on the substance

The Court shall give its ruling after hearing the Advocate General.

CHAPTER 6
COSTS

Article 137   Decision as to costs

A decision as to costs shall be given in the judgment or order which closes the proceedings.

Article 138   General rules as to allocation of costs

1.   The unsuccessful party shall be ordered to pay the costs if they have been applied for in the successful party's pleadings.

2.   Where there is more than one unsuccessful party the Court shall decide how the costs are to be shared.

3.   Where each party succeeds on some and fails on other heads, the parties shall bear their own costs. However, if it appears justified in the circumstances of the case, the Court may order that one party, in addition to bearing its own costs, pay a proportion of the costs of the other party.

Article 139   Unreasonable or vexatious costs

The Court may order a party, even if successful, to pay costs which the Court considers that party to have unreasonably or vexatiously caused the opposite party to incur.

Article 140   Costs of interveners

1. The Member States and institutions which have intervened in the proceedings shall bear their own costs.
2. The States, other than the Member States, which are parties to the EEA Agreement, and also the EFTA Surveillance Authority, shall similarly bear their own costs if they have intervened in the proceedings.
3. The Court may order an intervener other than those referred to in the preceding paragraphs to bear his own costs.

Article 141   Costs in the event of discontinuance or withdrawal

1. A party who discontinues or withdraws from proceedings shall be ordered to pay the costs if they have been applied for in the other party's observations on the discontinuance.
2. However, at the request of the party who discontinues or withdraws from proceedings, the costs shall be borne by the other party if this appears justified by the conduct of that party.
3. Where the parties have come to an agreement on costs, the decision as to costs shall be in accordance with that agreement.
4. If costs are not claimed, the parties shall bear their own costs.

Article 142   Costs where a case does not proceed to judgment

Where a case does not proceed to judgment the costs shall be in the discretion of the Court.

Article 143   Costs of proceedings

Proceedings before the Court shall be free of charge, except that:
  (a) where a party has caused the Court to incur avoidable costs the Court may, after hearing the Advocate General, order that party to refund them;
  (b) where copying or translation work is carried out at the request of a party, the cost shall, in so far as the Registrar considers it excessive, be paid for by that party on the Registry's scale of charges referred to in Article 22.

Article 144   Recoverable costs

Without prejudice to the preceding Article, the following shall be regarded as recoverable costs:
  (a) sums payable to witnesses and experts under Article 73 of these Rules;
  (b) expenses necessarily incurred by the parties for the purpose of the proceedings, in particular the travel and subsistence expenses and the remuneration of agents, advisers or lawyers.

Article 145   Dispute concerning the costs to be recovered

1. If there is a dispute concerning the costs to be recovered, the Chamber of three Judges to which the Judge-Rapporteur who dealt with the case is assigned shall, on application by the party concerned and after hearing the opposite party and the Advocate General, make an order. In that event, the formation of the Court shall be composed of the President of that Chamber, the Judge-Rapporteur and the first Judge or, as the case may be, the first two Judges designated from the list referred to in Article 28(3) on the date on which the dispute is brought before that Chamber by the Judge-Rapporteur.
2. If the Judge-Rapporteur is not a member of a Chamber of three Judges, the decision shall be taken, under the same conditions, by the Chamber of five Judges to which he is assigned. In addition to the Judge-Rapporteur, the formation of the Court shall be composed of four Judges designated from the list referred to in Article 28(2) on the date on which the dispute is brought before that Chamber by the Judge-Rapporteur.
3. The parties may, for the purposes of enforcement, apply for an authenticated copy of the order.

Article 146   Procedure for payment

1. Sums due from the cashier of the Court and from its debtors shall be paid in euro.
2. Where costs to be recovered have been incurred in a currency other than the euro or where the steps in respect of which payment is due were taken in a country of which

the euro is not the currency, the conversion shall be effected at the European Central Bank's official rates of exchange on the day of payment.

CHAPTER 7

AMICABLE SETTLEMENT, DISCONTINUANCE, CASES THAT DO NOT PROCEED TO JUDGMENT AND PRELIMINARY ISSUES

Article 147   Amicable settlement

1.   If, before the Court has given its decision, the parties reach a settlement of their dispute and inform the Court of the abandonment of their claims, the President shall order the case to be removed from the register and shall give a decision as to costs in accordance with Article 141, having regard to any proposals made by the parties on the matter.
2.   This provision shall not apply to proceedings under Articles 263 TFEU and 265 TFEU.

Article 148   Discontinuance

If the applicant informs the Court in writing or at the hearing that he wishes to discontinue the proceedings, the President shall order the case to be removed from the register and shall give a decision as to costs in accordance with Article 141.

Article 149   Cases that do not proceed to judgment

If the Court declares that the action has become devoid of purpose and that there is no longer any need to adjudicate on it, the Court may at any time of its own motion, on a proposal from the Judge-Rapporteur and after hearing the parties and the Advocate General, decide to rule by reasoned order. It shall give a decision as to costs.

Article 150   Absolute bar to proceeding with a case

On a proposal from the Judge-Rapporteur, the Court may at any time of its own motion, after hearing the parties and the Advocate General, decide to rule by reasoned order on whether there exists any absolute bar to proceeding with a case.

Article 151   Preliminary objections and issues

1.   A party applying to the Court for a decision on a preliminary objection or issue not going to the substance of the case shall submit the application by a separate document.
2.   The application must state the pleas of law and arguments relied on and the form of order sought by the applicant; any supporting items and documents must be annexed to it.
3.   As soon as the application has been submitted, the President shall prescribe a time-limit within which the opposite party may submit in writing his pleas in law and the form of order which he seeks.
4.   Unless the Court decides otherwise, the remainder of the proceedings on the application shall be oral.
5.   The Court shall, after hearing the Advocate General, decide on the application as soon as possible or, where special circumstances so justify, reserve its decision until it rules on the substance of the case.
6.   If the Court refuses the application or reserves its decision, the President shall prescribe new time-limits for the further steps in the proceedings.

CHAPTER 8

JUDGMENTS BY DEFAULT

Article 152   Judgments by default

1.   If a defendant on whom an application initiating proceedings has been duly served fails to respond to the application in the proper form and within the time-limit prescribed, the applicant may apply to the Court for judgment by default.
2.   The application for judgment by default shall be served on the defendant. The Court may decide to open the oral part of the procedure on the application.
3.   Before giving judgment by default the Court shall, after hearing the Advocate General, consider whether the application initiating proceedings is admissible, whether the

appropriate formalities have been complied with, and whether the applicant's claims appear well founded. The Court may adopt measures of organisation of procedure or order measures of inquiry.

4.   A judgment by default shall be enforceable. The Court may, however, grant a stay of execution until the Court has given its decision on any application under Article 156 to set aside the judgment, or it may make execution subject to the provision of security of an amount and nature to be fixed in the light of the circumstances; this security shall be released if no such application is made or if the application fails.

CHAPTER 9
REQUESTS AND APPLICATIONS RELATING TO JUDGMENTS AND ORDERS

Article 153   Competent formation of the Court

1.   With the exception of applications referred to in Article 159, the requests and applications referred to in this Chapter shall be assigned to the Judge-Rapporteur who was responsible for the case to which the request or application relates, and shall be assigned to the formation of the Court which gave a decision in that case.

2.   If the Judge-Rapporteur is prevented from acting, the President of the Court shall assign the request or application referred to in this Chapter to a Judge who was a member of the formation of the Court which gave a decision in the case to which that request or application relates.

3.   If the quorum referred to in Article 17 of the Statute can no longer be attained, the Court shall, on a proposal from the Judge-Rapporteur and after hearing the Advocate General, assign the request or application to a new formation of the Court.

Article 154   Rectification

1.   Without prejudice to the provisions relating to the interpretation of judgments and orders, clerical mistakes, errors in calculation and obvious inaccuracies may be rectified by the Court, of its own motion or at the request of a party made within two weeks after delivery of the judgment or service of the order.

2.   Where the request for rectification concerns the operative part or one of the grounds constituting the necessary support for the operative part, the parties, whom the Registrar shall duly inform, may submit written observations within a time-limit prescribed by the President.

3.   The Court shall take its decision after hearing the Advocate General.

4.   The original of the rectification order shall be annexed to the original of the rectified decision. A note of this order shall be made in the margin of the original of the rectified decision.

Article 155   Failure to adjudicate

1.   If the Court has failed to adjudicate on a specific head of claim or on costs, any party wishing to rely on that may, within a month after service of the decision, apply to the Court to supplement its decision.

2.   The application shall be served on the opposite party and the President shall prescribe a time-limit within which that party may submit written observations.

3.   After these observations have been submitted, the Court shall, after hearing the Advocate General, decide both on the admissibility and on the substance of the application.

Article 156   Application to set aside

1.   Application may be made pursuant to Article 41 of the Statute to set aside a judgment delivered by default.

2.   The application to set aside the judgment must be made within one month from the date of service of the judgment and must be submitted in the form prescribed by Articles 120 to 122 of these Rules.

3.   After the application has been served, the President shall prescribe a time-limit within which the other party may submit his written observations.

4.   The proceedings shall be conducted in accordance with Articles 59 to 92 of these Rules.

5. The Court shall decide by way of a judgment which may not be set aside.

6. The original of this judgment shall be annexed to the original of the judgment by default. A note of the judgment on the application to set aside shall be made in the margin of the original of the judgment by default.

Article 157   Third-party proceedings

1. Articles 120 to 122 of these Rules shall apply to an application initiating third-party proceedings made pursuant to Article 42 of the Statute. In addition such an application shall:
   (a) specify the judgment or order contested;
   (b) state how the contested decision is prejudicial to the rights of the third party;
   (c) indicate the reasons for which the third party was unable to take part in the original case.

2. The application must be made against all the parties to the original case.

3. The application must be submitted within two months of publication of the decision in the *Official Journal of the European Union*.

4. The Court may, on application by the third party, order a stay of execution of the contested decision. The provisions of Chapter 10 of this Title shall apply.

5. The contested decision shall be varied on the points on which the submissions of the third party are upheld.

6. The original of the judgment in the third-party proceedings shall be annexed to the original of the contested decision. A note of the judgment in the third-party proceedings shall be made in the margin of the original of the contested decision.

Article 158   Interpretation

1. In accordance with Article 43 of the Statute, if the meaning or scope of a judgment or order is in doubt, the Court shall construe it on application by any party or any institution of the European Union establishing an interest therein.

2. An application for interpretation must be made within two years after the date of delivery of the judgment or service of the order.

3. An application for interpretation shall be made in accordance with Articles 120 to 122 of these Rules. In addition it shall specify:
   (a) the decision in question;
   (b) the passages of which interpretation is sought.

4. The application must be made against all the parties to the case in which the decision of which interpretation is sought was given.

5. The Court shall give its decision after having given the parties an opportunity to submit their observations and after hearing the Advocate General.

6. The original of the interpreting decision shall be annexed to the original of the decision interpreted. A note of the interpreting decision shall be made in the margin of the original of the decision interpreted.

Article 159   Revision

1. In accordance with Article 44 of the Statute, an application for revision of a decision of the Court may be made only on discovery of a fact which is of such a nature as to be a decisive factor and which, when the judgment was delivered or the order served, was unknown to the Court and to the party claiming the revision.

2. Without prejudice to the time-limit of 10 years prescribed in the third paragraph of Article 44 of the Statute, an application for revision shall be made within three months of the date on which the facts on which the application is founded came to the applicant's knowledge.

3. Articles 120 to 122 of these Rules shall apply to an application for revision. In addition such an application shall:
   (a) specify the judgment or order contested;
   (b) indicate the points on which the decision is contested;
   (c) set out the facts on which the application is founded;
   (d) indicate the nature of the evidence to show that there are facts justifying revision, and that the time-limits laid down in paragraph 2 have been observed.

4. The application for revision must be made against all parties to the case in which the contested decision was given.

5. Without prejudice to its decision on the substance, the Court shall, after hearing the Advocate General, give in the form of an order its decision on the admissibility of the application, having regard to the written observations of the parties.

6. If the Court declares the application admissible, it shall proceed to consider the substance of the application and shall give its decision in the form of a judgment in accordance with these Rules.

7. The original of the revising judgment shall be annexed to the original of the decision revised. A note of the revising judgment shall be made in the margin of the original of the decision revised.

CHAPTER 10
SUSPENSION OF OPERATION OR ENFORCEMENT AND OTHER INTERIM MEASURES

Article 160   Application for suspension or for interim measures

1. An application to suspend the operation of any measure adopted by an institution, made pursuant to Article 278 TFEU or Article 157 TEAEC, shall be admissible only if the applicant has challenged that measure in an action before the Court.

2. An application for the adoption of one of the other interim measures referred to in Article 279 TFEU shall be admissible only if it is made by a party to a case before the Court and relates to that case.

3. An application of a kind referred to in the preceding paragraphs shall state the subject-matter of the proceedings, the circumstances giving rise to urgency and the pleas of fact and law establishing a prima facie case for the interim measure applied for.

4. The application shall be made by a separate document and in accordance with the provisions of Articles 120 to 122 of these Rules.

5. The application shall be served on the opposite party, and the President shall prescribe a short time-limit within which that party may submit written or oral observations.

6. The President may order a preparatory inquiry.

7. The President may grant the application even before the observations of the opposite party have been submitted. This decision may be varied or cancelled even without any application being made by any party.

Article 161   Decision on the application

1. The President shall either decide on the application himself or refer it immediately to the Court.

2. If the President is prevented from acting, Articles 10 and 13 of these Rules shall apply.

3. Where the application is referred to it, the Court shall give a decision immediately, after hearing the Advocate General.

Article 162   Order for suspension of operation or for interim measures

1. The decision on the application shall take the form of a reasoned order, from which no appeal shall lie. The order shall be served on the parties forthwith.

2. The execution of the order may be made conditional on the lodging by the applicant of security, of an amount and nature to be fixed in the light of the circumstances.

3. Unless the order fixes the date on which the interim measure is to lapse, the measure shall lapse when the judgment which closes the proceedings is delivered.

4. The order shall have only an interim effect, and shall be without prejudice to the decision of the Court on the substance of the case.

Article 163   Change in circumstances

On application by a party, the order may at any time be varied or cancelled on account of a change in circumstances.

Article 164   New application

Rejection of an application for an interim measure shall not bar the party who made it from making a further application on the basis of new facts.

Article 165   Applications pursuant to Articles 280 TFEU and 299 TFEU and Article 164 TEAEC

1. The provisions of this Chapter shall apply to applications to suspend the enforcement of a decision of the Court or of any measure adopted by the Council, the European Commission or the European Central Bank, submitted pursuant to Articles 280 TFEU and 299 TFEU or Article 164 TEAEC.
2. The order granting the application shall fix, where appropriate, a date on which the interim measure is to lapse.

Article 166   Application pursuant to Article 81 TEAEC

1. An application of a kind referred to in the third and fourth paragraphs of Article 81 TEAEC shall contain:
    (a)   the names and addresses of the persons or undertakings to be inspected;
    (b)   an indication of what is to be inspected and of the purpose of the inspection.
2. The President shall give his decision in the form of an order. Article 162 of these Rules shall apply.
3. If the President is prevented from acting, Articles 10 and 13 of these Rules shall apply.

TITLE V
APPEALS AGAINST DECISIONS OF THE GENERAL COURT

CHAPTER 1
FORM AND CONTENT OF THE APPEAL, AND FORM OF ORDER SOUGHT

Article 167   Lodging of the appeal

1. An appeal shall be brought by lodging an application at the Registry of the Court of Justice or of the General Court.
2. The Registry of the General Court shall forthwith transmit to the Registry of the Court of Justice the file in the case at first instance and, where necessary, the appeal.

Article 168   Content of the appeal

1. An appeal shall contain:
    (a)   the name and address of the appellant;
    (b)   a reference to the decision of the General Court appealed against;
    (c)   the names of the other parties to the relevant case before the General Court;
    (d)   the pleas in law and legal arguments relied on, and a summary of those pleas in law;
    (e)   the form of order sought by the appellant.
2. Articles 119, 121 and 122(1) of these Rules shall apply to appeals.
3. The appeal shall state the date on which the decision appealed against was served on the appellant.
4. If an appeal does not comply with paragraphs 1 to 3 of this Article, the Registrar shall prescribe a reasonable time-limit within which the appellant is to put the appeal in order. If the appellant fails to put the appeal in order within the time-limit prescribed, the Court of Justice shall, after hearing the Judge-Rapporteur and the Advocate General, decide whether the non-compliance with that formal requirement renders the appeal formally inadmissible.

Article 169   Form of order sought, pleas in law and arguments of the appeal

1. An appeal shall seek to have set aside, in whole or in part, the decision of the General Court as set out in the operative part of that decision.
2. The pleas in law and legal arguments relied on shall identify precisely those points in the grounds of the decision of the General Court which are contested.

Article 170   Form of order sought in the event that the appeal is allowed

1. An appeal shall seek, in the event that it is declared well founded, the same form of order, in whole or in part, as that sought at first instance and shall not seek a different form of order. The subject-matter of the proceedings before the General Court may not be changed in the appeal.
2. Where the appellant requests that the case be referred back to the General Court if the decision appealed against is set aside, he shall set out the reasons why the state of the proceedings does not permit a decision by the Court of Justice.

CHAPTER 1A
PRIOR DETERMINATION AS TO WHETHER APPEALS UNDER ARTICLE 58a
OF THE STATUTE SHOULD BE ALLOWED TO PROCEED

Article 170a   Request that the appeal be allowed to proceed

1. In the situations referred to in the first and second paragraphs of Article 58a of the Statute, the appellant shall annex to the appeal a request that the appeal be allowed to proceed, setting out the issue raised by the appeal that is significant with respect to the unity, consistency or development of European Union law and containing all the information necessary to enable the Court of Justice to rule on that request. If there is no such request, the Vice-President of the Court shall declare the appeal inadmissible.
2. The request that the appeal be allowed to proceed shall not exceed seven pages and shall be drawn up taking into account all the formal requirements contained in the Practice Directions to parties concerning cases brought before the Court, adopted on the basis of these Rules.
3. If the request that the appeal be allowed to proceed does not comply with the requirements set out in the preceding paragraph, the Registrar shall prescribe a reasonable time limit within which the appellant is to put the request in order. If the appellant fails to put the request in order within the time limit prescribed, the Vice-President of the Court shall decide, on a proposal from the Judge-Rapporteur and after hearing the Advocate General, whether the non-compliance with that formal requirement renders the appeal formally inadmissible.

Article 170b   Decision on the request that the appeal be allowed to proceed

1. The Court of Justice shall rule as soon as possible on the request that the appeal be allowed to proceed.
2. The decision on that request shall be taken, on a proposal from the JudgeRapporteur and after hearing the Advocate General, by a Chamber specially established for that purpose, presided over by the Vice-President of the Court and including also the Judge-Rapporteur and the President of the Chamber of three Judges to which the Judge-Rapporteur is attached on the date on which the request is made.
3. The decision on the request that the appeal be allowed to proceed shall take the form of a reasoned order.
4. Where the Court of Justice decides that the appeal should be allowed to proceed, wholly or in part, having regard to the criteria set out in the third paragraph of Article 58a of the Statute, the proceedings shall continue in accordance with Articles 171 to 190a of these Rules. The order referred to in the preceding paragraph shall be served, together with the appeal, on the 70 parties to the relevant case before the General Court and shall specify, where the appeal is to be allowed to proceed in part, the pleas in law or parts of the appeal to which the response must relate.
5. The General Court and, if they were not parties to the proceedings before it, the Member States, the European Parliament, the Council and the European Commission shall forthwith be informed by the Registrar of the decision that the appeal should be allowed to proceed.

CHAPTER 2
RESPONSES, REPLIES AND REJOINDERS

Article 171   Service of the appeal

1. The appeal shall be served on the other parties to the relevant case before the General Court.
2. In a case where Article 168(4) of these Rules applies, service shall be effected as soon as the appeal has been put in order or the Court of Justice has declared it admissible notwithstanding the failure to observe the formal requirements laid down by that Article.

Article 172   Parties authorised to lodge a response

Any party to the relevant case before the General Court having an interest in the appeal being allowed or dismissed may submit a response within two months after service on him of the appeal. The time-limit for submitting a response shall not be extended.

Article 173   Content of the response

1.   A response shall contain:
      (a)   the name and address of the party submitting it;
      (b)   the date on which the appeal was served on him;
      (c)   the pleas in law and legal arguments relied on;
      (d)   the form of order sought.
2.   Articles 119 and 121 of these Rules shall apply to responses.

Article 174   Form of order sought in the response

A response shall seek to have the appeal allowed or dismissed, in whole or in part.

Article 175   Reply and rejoinder

1.   The appeal and the response may be supplemented by a reply and a rejoinder only where the President, on a duly reasoned application submitted by the appellant within seven days of service of the response, considers it necessary, after hearing the Judge-Rapporteur and the Advocate General, in particular to enable the appellant to present his views on a plea of inadmissibility or on new matters relied on in the response.
2.   The President shall fix the date by which the reply is to be produced and, upon service of that pleading, the date by which the rejoinder is to be produced. He may limit the number of pages and the subject-matter of those pleadings.

CHAPTER 3
FORM AND CONTENT OF THE CROSS-APPEAL, AND FORM OF ORDER SOUGHT

Article 176   Cross-appeal

1.   The parties referred to in Article 172 of these Rules may submit a cross-appeal within the same time-limit as that prescribed for the submission of a response.
2.   A cross-appeal must be introduced by a document separate from the response.

Article 177   Content of the cross-appeal

1.   A cross-appeal shall contain:
      (a)   the name and address of the party bringing the cross-appeal;
      (b)   the date on which the appeal was served on him;
      (c)   the pleas in law and legal arguments relied on;
      (d)   the form of order sought.
2.   Articles 119, 121 and 122(1) and (3) of these Rules shall apply to cross-appeals.

Article 178   Form of order sought, pleas in law and arguments of the cross-appeal

1.   A cross-appeal shall seek to have set aside, in whole or in part, the decision of the General Court.
2.   It may also seek to have set aside an express or implied decision relating to the admissibility of the action before the General Court.
3.   The pleas in law and legal arguments relied on shall identify precisely those points in the grounds of the decision of the General Court which are contested. The pleas in law and arguments must be separate from those relied on in the response.

CHAPTER 4
PLEADINGS CONSEQUENT ON THE CROSS-APPEAL

Article 179   Response to the cross-appeal

Where a cross-appeal is brought, the applicant at first instance or any other party to the relevant case before the General Court having an interest in the cross-appeal being allowed or dismissed may submit a response, which must be limited to the pleas in law relied on in that cross-appeal, within two months after its being served on him. That time-limit shall not be extended.

Article 180   Reply and rejoinder on a cross-appeal

1.   The cross-appeal and the response thereto may be supplemented by a reply and a rejoinder only where the President, on a duly reasoned application submitted by the party who brought the cross-appeal within seven days of service of the response to the cross-appeal, considers it necessary, after hearing the Judge-Rapporteur and the Advocate General, in particular to enable that party to present his views on a plea of inadmissibility or on new matters relied on in the response to the cross-appeal.
2.   The President shall fix the date by which that reply is to be produced and, upon service of that pleading, the date by which the rejoinder is to be produced. He may limit the number of pages and the subject-matter of those pleadings.

CHAPTER 5
APPEALS DETERMINED BY ORDER

Article 181   Manifestly inadmissible or manifestly unfounded appeal or cross-appeal

Where the appeal or cross-appeal is, in whole or in part, manifestly inadmissible or manifestly unfounded, the Court may at any time, acting on a proposal from the Judge-Rapporteur and after hearing the Advocate General, decide by reasoned order to dismiss that appeal or cross-appeal in whole or in part.

Article 182   Manifestly well-founded appeal or cross-appeal

Where the Court has already ruled on one or more questions of law identical to those raised by the pleas in law of the appeal or cross-appeal and considers the appeal or cross-appeal to be manifestly well founded, it may, acting on a proposal from the Judge-Rapporteur and after hearing the parties and the Advocate General, decide by reasoned order in which reference is made to the relevant case-law to declare the appeal or cross-appeal manifestly well founded.

CHAPTER 6
EFFECT ON A CROSS-APPEAL OF THE REMOVAL OF THE APPEAL FROM THE
REGISTER

Article 183   Effect on a cross-appeal of the discontinuance or manifest inadmissibility of the appeal

A cross-appeal shall be deemed to be devoid of purpose:
(a)   if the appellant discontinues his appeal;
(b)   if the appeal is declared manifestly inadmissible for non-compliance with the time-limit for lodging an appeal;
(c)   if the appeal is declared manifestly inadmissible on the sole ground that it is not directed against a final decision of the General Court or against a decision disposing of the substantive issues in part only or disposing of a procedural issue concerning a plea of lack of competence or inadmissibility within the meaning of the first paragraph of Article 56 of the Statute.

CHAPTER 7
COSTS AND LEGAL AID IN APPEALS

Article 184   Costs in appeals

1.   Subject to the following provisions, Articles 137 to 146 of these Rules shall apply, *mutatis mutandis*, to the procedure before the Court of Justice on an appeal against a decision of the General Court.
2.   Where the appeal is unfounded or where the appeal is well founded and the Court itself gives final judgment in the case, the Court shall make a decision as to the costs.
3.   When an appeal brought by a Member State or an institution of the European Union which did not intervene in the proceedings before the General Court is well founded,

the Court of Justice may order that the parties share the costs or that the successful appellant pay the costs which the appeal has caused an unsuccessful party to incur.

4.   Where the appeal has not been brought by an intervener at first instance, he may not be ordered to pay costs in the appeal proceedings unless he participated in the written or oral part of the proceedings before the Court of Justice. Where an intervener at first instance takes part in the proceedings, the Court may decide that he shall bear his own costs.

Article 185   Legal aid

1.   A party who is wholly or in part unable to meet the costs of the proceedings may at any time apply for legal aid.

2.   The application shall be accompanied by all information and supporting documents making it possible to assess the applicant's financial situation, such as a certificate issued by a competent national authority attesting to his financial situation.

Article 186   Prior application for legal aid

1.   If the application is made prior to the appeal which the applicant for legal aid intends to commence, it shall briefly state the subject of the appeal.

2.   The application for legal aid need not be made through a lawyer.

3.   The introduction of an application for legal aid shall, with regard to the person who made that application, suspend the time-limit prescribed for the bringing of the appeal until the date of service of the order making a decision on that application.

4.   The President shall assign the application for legal aid, as soon as it is lodged, to a Judge-Rapporteur who shall put forward, promptly, a proposal as to the action to be taken on it.

Article 187   Decision on the application for legal aid

1.   The decision to grant legal aid, in whole or in part, or to refuse it shall be taken, on a proposal from the Judge-Rapporteur and after hearing the Advocate General, by the Chamber of three Judges to which the Judge-Rapporteur is assigned. In that event, the formation of the Court shall be composed of the President of that Chamber, the Judge-Rapporteur and the first Judge or, as the case may be, the first two Judges designated from the list referred to in Article 28(3) on the date on which the application for legal aid is brought before that Chamber by the Judge-Rapporteur. It shall consider, if appropriate, whether the appeal is manifestly unfounded.

2.   If the Judge-Rapporteur is not a member of a Chamber of three Judges, the decision shall be taken, under the same conditions, by the Chamber of five Judges to which he is assigned. In addition to the Judge-Rapporteur, the formation of the Court shall be composed of four Judges designated from the list referred to in Article 28(2) on the date on which the application for legal aid is brought before that Chamber by the Judge-Rapporteur.

3.   The formation of the Court shall give its decision by way of order. Where the application for legal aid is refused in whole or in part, the order shall state the reasons for that refusal.

Article 188   Sums to be advanced as legal aid

1.   Where legal aid is granted, the cashier of the Court shall be responsible, where applicable within the limits set by the formation of the Court, for costs involved in the assistance and representation of the applicant before the Court. At the request of the applicant or his representative, an advance on those costs may be paid.

2.   In its decision as to costs the Court may order the payment to the cashier of the Court of sums advanced as legal aid.

3.   The Registrar shall take steps to obtain the recovery of these sums from the party ordered to pay them.

Article 189   Withdrawal of legal aid

The formation of the Court which gave a decision on the application for legal aid may at any time, either of its own motion or on request, withdraw that legal aid if the circumstances which led to its being granted alter during the proceedings.

CHAPTER 8
OTHER PROVISIONS APPLICABLE TO APPEALS

Article 190   Other provisions applicable to appeals

1. Articles 127, 129 to 136, 147 to 150, 153 to 155 and 157 to 166 of these Rules shall apply to the procedure before the Court of Justice on an appeal against decisions of the General Court.
2. By way of derogation from Article 130(1), an application to intervene shall, however, be made within one month of the publication of the notice referred to in Article 21(4).
3. Article 95 shall apply, *mutatis mutandis*, to the procedure before the Court of Justice on an appeal against decisions of the General Court.

Article 190a   Treatment of information or material produced before the General Court in accordance with Article 105 of its Rules of Procedure

1. Where an appeal is brought against a decision of the General Court adopted in proceedings in which information or material has been produced by a main party in accordance with Article 105 of the Rules of Procedure of the General Court and has not been communicated to the other main party, the Registry of the General Court shall make that information or material available to the Court of Justice, on the conditions laid down in the decision referred to in paragraph 11 of that Article.
2. The information or material referred to in paragraph 1 shall not be communicated to the parties to the proceedings before the Court of Justice.
3. The Court of Justice shall ensure that the confidential matters contained in the information or material referred to in paragraph 1 are not disclosed in the decision which closes the proceedings or in any Opinion of the Advocate General.
4. The information or material referred to in paragraph 1 shall be returned to the party that produced it before the General Court as soon as the decision closing the proceedings before the Court of Justice has been served, save where the case is referred back to the General Court. In the latter case, the information or material concerned shall again be made available to the General Court, on the conditions laid down in the decision referred to in paragraph 5.
5. The Court of Justice shall adopt, by decision, the security rules for protecting the information or material referred to in paragraph 1. That decision shall be published in the *Official Journal of the European Union*.

TITLE VI
REVIEW OF DECISIONS OF THE GENERAL COURT

Article 191   Reviewing Chamber

A Chamber of five Judges shall be designated for a period of one year for the purpose of deciding, in accordance with Articles 193 and 194 of these Rules, whether a decision of the General Court is to be reviewed in accordance with Article 62 of the Statute.

Article 192   Information and communication of decisions which may be reviewed

1. As soon as the date for the delivery or signature of a decision to be given under Article 256(2) or (3) TFEU is fixed, the Registry of the General Court shall inform the Registry of the Court of Justice.
2. The decision shall be communicated to the Registry of the Court of Justice immediately upon its delivery or signature, as shall the file in the case, which shall be made available forthwith to the First Advocate General.

Article 193   Review of decisions given on appeal

1. The proposal of the First Advocate General to review a decision of the General Court given under Article 256(2) TFEU shall be forwarded to the President of the Court of Justice and to the President of the reviewing Chamber. Notice of that transmission shall be given to the Registrar at the same time.
2. As soon as he is informed of the existence of a proposal, the Registrar shall communicate the file in the case before the General Court to the members of the reviewing Chamber.
3. As soon as the proposal to review has been received, the President of the Court shall designate the Judge-Rapporteur from among the Judges of the reviewing Chamber

      on a proposal from the President of that Chamber. The composition of the formation of the Court shall be determined in accordance with Article 28(2) of these Rules on the day on which the case is assigned to the Judge-Rapporteur.

4.   That Chamber, acting on a proposal from the Judge-Rapporteur, shall decide whether the decision of the General Court is to be reviewed. The decision to review the decision of the General Court shall indicate only the questions which are to be reviewed.

5.   The General Court, the parties to the proceedings before it and the other interested persons referred to in the second paragraph of Article 62a of the Statute shall forthwith be informed by the Registrar of the decision of the Court of Justice to review the decision of the General Court.

6.   Notice of the date of the decision to review the decision of the General Court and of the questions which are to be reviewed shall be published in the *Official Journal of the European Union*.

Article 194　Review of preliminary rulings

1.   The proposal of the First Advocate General to review a decision of the General Court given under Article 256(3) TFEU shall be forwarded to the President of the Court of Justice and to the President of the reviewing Chamber. Notice of that transmission shall be given to the Registrar at the same time.

2.   As soon as he is informed of the existence of a proposal, the Registrar shall communicate the file in the case before the General Court to the members of the reviewing Chamber.

3.   The Registrar shall also inform the General Court, the referring court or tribunal, the parties to the main proceedings and the other interested persons referred to in the second paragraph of Article 62a of the Statute of the existence of a proposal to review.

4.   As soon as the proposal to review has been received, the President of the Court shall designate the Judge-Rapporteur from among the Judges of the reviewing Chamber on a proposal from the President of that Chamber. The composition of the formation of the Court shall be determined in accordance with Article 28(2) of these Rules on the day on which the case is assigned to the Judge-Rapporteur.

5.   That Chamber, acting on a proposal from the Judge-Rapporteur, shall decide whether the decision of the General Court is to be reviewed. The decision to review the decision of the General Court shall indicate only the questions which are to be reviewed.

6.   The General Court, the referring court or tribunal, the parties to the main proceedings and the other interested persons referred to in the second paragraph of Article 62a of the Statute shall forthwith be informed by the Registrar of the decision of the Court of Justice as to whether or not the decision of the General Court is to be reviewed.

7.   Notice of the date of the decision to review the decision of the General Court and of the questions which are to be reviewed shall be published in the *Official Journal of the European Union*.

Article 195　Judgment on the substance of the case after a decision to review

1.   The decision to review a decision of the General Court shall be served on the parties and other interested persons referred to in the second paragraph of Article 62a of the Statute. The decision served on the Member States, and the States, other than the Member States, which are parties to the EEA Agreement, as well as the EFTA Surveillance Authority, shall be accompanied by a translation of the decision of the Court of Justice in accordance with the provisions of Article 98 of these Rules. The decision of the Court of Justice shall also be communicated to the General Court and, if applicable, to the referring court or tribunal.

2.   Within one month of the date of service referred to in paragraph 1, the parties and other interested persons on whom the decision of the Court of Justice has been served may lodge statements or written observations on the questions which are subject to review.

3.   As soon as a decision to review a decision of the General Court has been taken, the First Advocate General shall assign the review to an Advocate General.

4.   The reviewing Chamber shall rule on the substance of the case, after hearing the Advocate General.

5.   It may, however, request the Court of Justice to assign the case to a formation of the Court composed of a greater number of Judges.

6.   Where the decision of the General Court which is subject to review was given under Article 256(2) TFEU, the Court of Justice shall make a decision as to costs.

TITLE VII
OPINIONS

Article 196   Written part of the procedure

1. In accordance with Article 218(11) TFEU, a request for an Opinion may be made by a Member State, by the European Parliament, by the Council or by the European Commission.
2. A request for an Opinion may relate both to whether the envisaged agreement is compatible with the provisions of the Treaties and to whether the European Union or any institution of the European Union has the power to enter into that agreement.
3. It shall be served on the Member States and on the institutions referred to in paragraph 1, and the President shall prescribe a time-limit within which they may submit written observations.

Article 197   Designation of the Judge-Rapporteur and of the Advocate General

As soon as the request for an Opinion has been submitted, the President shall designate a Judge-Rapporteur and the First Advocate General shall assign the case to an Advocate General.

Article 198   Hearing

The Court may decide that the procedure before it shall also include a hearing.

Article 199   Time-limit for delivering the Opinion

The Court shall deliver its Opinion as soon as possible, after hearing the Advocate General.

Article 200   Delivery of the Opinion

The Opinion, signed by the President, the Judges who took part in the deliberations and the Registrar, shall be delivered in open court. It shall be served on all the Member States and on the institutions referred to in Article 196(1).

TITLE VIII
PARTICULAR FORMS OF PROCEDURE

Article 205   Settlement of the disputes referred to in Article 35 TEU in the version in force before the entry into force of the Treaty of Lisbon

1. In the case of disputes between Member States as referred to in Article 35(7) TEU in the version in force before the entry into force of the Treaty of Lisbon, as maintained in force by Protocol No 36 annexed to the Treaties, the matter shall be brought before the Court by an application by a party to the dispute. The application shall be served on the other Member States and on the European Commission.
2. In the case of disputes between Member States and the European Commission as referred to in Article 35(7) TEU in the version in force before the entry into force of the Treaty of Lisbon, as maintained in force by Protocol No 36 annexed to the Treaties, the matter shall be brought before the Court by an application by a party to the dispute. The application shall be served on the other Member States, the Council and the European Commission if it was submitted by a Member State. The application shall be served on the Member States and on the Council if it was submitted by the European Commission.
3. The President shall prescribe a time-limit within which the institutions and the Member States on which the application has been served may submit written observations.
4. As soon as the application referred to in paragraphs 1 and 2 has been submitted, the President shall designate a Judge-Rapporteur. The First Advocate General shall, immediately afterwards, assign the application to an Advocate General.
5. The Court may decide that the procedure before it shall also include a hearing.
6. The Court shall, after the Advocate General has delivered his Opinion, give its ruling on the dispute by way of judgment.
7. The same procedure as that laid down in the preceding paragraphs shall apply where an agreement concluded between the Member States confers jurisdiction on the Court to rule on a dispute between Member States or between Member States and an institution.

FINAL PROVISIONS

Article 207   Supplementary rules

Subject to the provisions of Article 253 TFEU and after consultation with the Governments concerned, the Court shall adopt supplementary rules concerning its practice in relation to:
- (a)   letters rogatory;
- (b)   applications for legal aid;
- (c)   reports by the Court of perjury by witnesses or experts, delivered pursuant to Article 30 of the Statute.

Article 208   Implementing rules

The Court may, by a separate act, adopt practice rules for the implementation of these Rules.

COMMUNITY CHARTER OF THE FUNDAMENTAL SOCIAL RIGHTS OF WORKERS

Having regard to the Resolutions of the European Parliament of 15 March 1989, 14 September 1989 and 22 November 1989, and to the Opinion of the Economic and Social Committee of 22 February 1989;

Whereas the completion of the internal market is the most effective means of creating employment and ensuring maximum well-being in the Community; whereas employment development and creation must be given first priority in the completion of the internal market; whereas it is for the Community to take up the challenges of the future with regard to economic competitiveness, taking into account, in particular, regional inbalances;

Whereas the social consensus contributes to the strengthening of the competitiveness of undertakings, of the economy as a whole and to the creation of employment; whereas in this respect it is an essential condition for ensuring sustained economic development;

Whereas the completion of the internal market must favour the approximation of improvements in living and working conditions, as well as economic and social cohesion within the European Community while avoiding distortions of competition;

Whereas the completion of the internal market must offer improvements in the social field for workers of the European Community, especially in terms of freedom of movement, living and working conditions, health and safety at work, social protection, education and training;

Whereas, in order to ensure equal treatment, it is important to combat every form of discrimination, including discrimination on grounds of sex, colour, race, opinions and beliefs, and whereas, in a spirit of solidarity, it is important to combat social exclusion;

Whereas it is for Member States to guarantee the workers from non-member countries and members of their families who are legally resident in a Member State of the European Community are able to enjoy, as regards their living and working conditions, treatment comparable to that enjoyed by workers who are nationals of the Member State concerned;

Whereas inspiration should be drawn from the Conventions of the International Labour Organisation and from the European Social Charter of Council of Europe;

Whereas the implementation of the Charter must not entail an extension of the Community's powers as defined by the Treaties;

Whereas the aim of the present Charter is on the one hand to consolidate the progress made in the social field, through action by the Member States, the two sides of industry and the Community;

Whereas its aim is on the other hand to declare solemnly that the implementation of the Single European Act must take full account of the social dimension of the Community and that it is necessary in this context to ensure at appropriate levels the development of the social rights of workers of the European Community, especially employed workers and self-employed persons; Whereas, in accordance with the conclusions of the Madrid European Council, the respective roles of Community rules, national legislation and collective agreements must be clearly established;

Whereas, by virtue of the principle of subsidiarity, responsibility for the initiatives to be taken with regard to the implementation of these social rights lies with the Member States or their constituent parts and, within the limits of its powers, with the European Community; whereas such implementation may take the form of laws, collective agreements or existing practices at the various appropriate levels and whereas it requires in many spheres the active involvement of the two sides of industry;

Whereas the solemn proclamation of fundamental social rights at European Community level may not, when implemented, provide grounds for any retrogression compared with the situation currently existing in each Member State;

Have adopted the following Declaration constituting the 'Community Charter of the Fundamental Social Rights of Workers':

TITLE I

FUNDAMENTAL SOCIAL RIGHTS OF WORKERS

Freedom of movement

1. Every worker of the European Community shall have the right to freedom of movement throughout the territory of the Community, subject to restrictions justified on grounds of public order, public safety or public health.
2. The right to freedom of movement shall enable any worker to engage in any occupation or profession in the Community in accordance with the principles of equal treatment as regards access to employment, working conditions and social protection in the host country.
3. The right of freedom of movement shall also imply:
    — harmonisation of conditions of residence in all Member States, particularly those concerning family reunification;
    — elimination of obstacles arising from the non-recognition of diplomas or equivalent occupational qualifications;
    — improvement of the living and working conditions of frontier workers.

Employment and remuneration

4. Every individual shall be free to choose and engage in an occupation according to the regulations governing each occupation.
5. All employment shall be fairly remunerated.
    To this end, in accordance with arrangements applying in each country:
    — workers shall be assured of an equitable wage, i.e., a wage sufficient to enable them to have a decent standard of living;
    — workers subject to terms of employment other than an open-ended full-time contract shall benefit from an equitable reference wage;
    — wages may be withheld, seized or transferred only in accordance with national law; such provisions should entail measures enabling the worker concerned to continue to enjoy the necessary means of subsistence for him or herself and his or her family.
6. Every individual must be able to have access to public placement services free of charge.

Improvement of living and working conditions

7. The completion of the internal market must lead to an improvement in the living and working conditions of workers in the European Community. This process must result from an approximation of these conditions while the improvement is being maintained, as regards in particular the duration and organisation of working time and forms of employment other than open-ended contracts, such as fixed-term contracts, part-time working, temporary-work and seasonal work.
    The improvement must cover, where necessary, the development of certain aspects of employment regulations such as procedures for collective redundancies and those regarding bankruptcies.
8. Every worker of the European Community shall have a right to a weekly rest period and to annual paid leave, the duration of which must be progressively harmonised in accordance with national practices.
9. The conditions of employment of every worker of the European Community shall be stipulated in laws, a collective agreement or a contract of employment, according to arrangements applying in each country.

Social protection

According to the arrangements applying in each country:

10. Every worker of the European Community shall have a right to adequate social protection and shall, whatever his status and whatever the size of the undertaking in which he is employed, enjoy an adequate level of social security benefits.

Persons who have been unable either to enter or re-enter the labour market and have no means of subsistence must be able to receive sufficient resources and social assistance in keeping with their particular situation.

Freedom of association and collective bargaining

11. Employers and workers of the European Community shall have the right of association in order to constitute professional organisations or trade unions of their choice for the defence of their economic and social interests.

Every employer and every worker shall have the freedom to join or not to join such organisations without any personal or occupational damage being thereby suffered by him.

12. Employers or employers' organisations, on the one hand, and workers' organisations, on the other, shall have the right to negotiate and conclude collective agreements under the conditions laid down by national legislation and practice.

The dialogue between the two sides of industry at European level which must be developed, may, if the parties deem it desirable, result in contractual relations in particular at inter-occupational and sectoral level.

13. The right to resort to collective action in the event of a conflict of interests shall include the right to strike, subject to the obligations arising under national regulations and collective agreements.

In order to facilitate the settlement of industrial disputes the establishment and utilisation at the appropriate levels of conciliation, mediation and arbitration procedures should be encouraged in accordance with national practice.

14. The internal legal order of the Member States shall determine under which conditions and to what extent the rights provided for in Articles 11 to 13 apply to the armed forces, the police and the civil service.

Vocational training

15. Every worker of the European Community must be able to have access to vocational training and to benefit therefrom throughout his working life. In the conditions governing access to such training there may be no discrimination on grounds of nationality.

The competent public authorities, undertakings or the two sides of industry, each within their own sphere of competence, should set up continuing and permanent training systems enabling every person to undergo retraining more especially through leave for training purposes, to improve his skills or to acquire new skills, particularly in the light of technical developments.

Equal treatment for men and women

16. Equal treatment for men and women must be assured. Equal opportunities for men and women must be developed.

To this end, action should be intensified to ensure the implementation of the principle of equality between men and women as regards in particular access to employment, remuneration, working conditions, social protection, education, vocational training and career development.

Measures should also be developed enabling men and women to reconcile their occupational and family obligations.

Information, consultation and participation for workers

17. Information, consultation and participation for workers must be developed along appropriate lines, taking account of the practices in force in the various Member States. This shall apply especially in companies or groups of companies having establishments or companies in two or more Member States of the European Community.

18. Such information, consultation and participation must be implemented in due time, particularly in the following cases:
    — when technological changes which, from the point of view of working conditions and work organisation, have major implications for the work-force, are introduced into undertakings;

- in connection with restructuring operations in undertakings or in cases of mergers having an impact on the employment of workers;
- in cases of collective redundancy procedures;
- when transfrontier workers in particular are affected by employment policies pursued by the undertaking where they are employed.

Health protection and safety at the workplace

19. Every worker must enjoy satisfactory health and safety conditions in his working environment. Appropriate measures must be taken in order to achieve further harmonisation of conditions in this area while maintaining the improvements made. These measures shall take account, in particular, of the need for the training, information, consultation and balanced participation of workers as regards the risks incurred and the steps taken to eliminate or reduce them.
The provisions regarding implementation of the internal market shall help to ensure such protection.

Protection of children and adolescents

20. Without prejudice to such rules as may be more favourable to young people, in particular those ensuring their preparation for work through vocational training, and subject to derogations limited to certain light work, the minimum employment age must not be lower than the minimum school-leaving age and, in any case, not lower than 15 years.
21. Young people who are in gainful employment must receive equitable remuneration in accordance with national practice.
22. Appropriate measures must be taken to adjust labour regulations applicable to young workers so that their specific development and vocational training and access to employment needs are met. The duration of work must, in particular, be limited – without it being possible to circumvent this limitation through recourse to overtime – and night work prohibited in the case of workers of under 18 years of age, save in the case of certain jobs laid down in national legislation or regulations.
23. Following the end of compulsory education, young people must be entitled to receive initial vocational training of a sufficient duration to enable them to adapt to the requirements of their future working life; for young workers, such training should take place during working hours.

Elderly persons

According to the arrangements applying in each country:
24. Every worker of the European Community must, at the time of retirement, be able to enjoy resources affording him or her a decent standard of living.
25. Any person who has reached retirement age but who is not entitled to a pension or who does not have other means of subsistence, must be entitled to sufficient resources and to medical and social assistance specifically suited to his needs.

Disabled persons

26. All disabled persons, whatever the origin and nature of their disablement, must be entitled to additional concrete measures aimed at improving their social and professional integration.
These measures must concern, in particular, according to the capacities of the beneficiaries, vocational training, ergonomics, accessibility, mobility, means of transport and housing.

TITLE II
IMPLEMENTATION OF THE CHARTER

27. It is more particularly the responsibility of the Member States, in accordance with national practices, notably through legislative measures or collective agreements, to guarantee the fundamental social rights in this Charter and to implement the social measures indispensable to the smooth operation of the internal market as part of a strategy of economic and social cohesion.
28. The European Council invites the Commission to submit as soon as possible initiatives which fall within its powers, as provided for in the Treaties, with a view to the adoption

of legal instruments for the effective implementation, as and when the internal market is completed, of those rights which come within the Community's area of competence.

29. The Commission shall establish each year, during the last three months, a report on the application of the Charter by the Member States and by the European Community.

30. The report of the Commission shall be forwarded to the European Council, the European Parliament and the Economic and Social Committee.

CHARTER OF FUNDAMENTAL RIGHTS OF THE EUROPEAN UNION (OJ 2016/C 202/02)

The European Parliament, the Council and the Commission solemnly proclaim the following text as the Charter of Fundamental Rights of the European Union.

TITLE I

DIGNITY

Article 1   Human dignity

Human dignity is inviolable. It must be respected and protected.

Article 2   Right to life

1. Everyone has the right to life.
2. No one shall be condemned to the death penalty, or executed.

Article 3   Right to the integrity of the person

1. Everyone has the right to respect for his or her physical and mental integrity.
2. In the fields of medicine and biology, the following must be respected in particular:
    (a) the free and informed consent of the person concerned, according to the procedures laid down by law;
    (b) the prohibition of eugenic practices, in particular those aiming at the selection of persons;
    (c) the prohibition on making the human body and its parts as such a source of financial gain;
    (d) the prohibition of the reproductive cloning of human beings.

Article 4   Prohibition of torture and inhuman or degrading treatment or punishment

No one shall be subjected to torture or to inhuman or degrading treatment or punishment.

Article 5   Prohibition of slavery and forced labour

1. No one shall be held in slavery or servitude.
2. No one shall be required to perform forced or compulsory labour.
3. Trafficking in human beings is prohibited.

TITLE II

FREEDOMS

Article 6   Right to liberty and security

Everyone has the right to liberty and security of person.

Article 7   Respect for private and family life

Everyone has the right to respect for his or her private and family life, home and communications.

Article 8   Protection of personal data

1. Everyone has the right to the protection of personal data concerning him or her.
2. Such data must be processed fairly for specified purposes and on the basis of the consent of the person concerned or some other legitimate basis laid down by law.

Everyone has the right of access to data which has been collected concerning him or her, and the right to have it rectified.

3. Compliance with these rules shall be subject to control by an independent authority.

Article 9 Right to marry and right to found a family

The right to marry and the right to found a family shall be guaranteed in accordance with the national laws governing the exercise of these rights.

Article 10 Freedom of thought, conscience and religion

1. Everyone has the right to freedom of thought, conscience and religion. This right includes freedom to change religion or belief and freedom, either alone or in community with others and in public or in private, to manifest religion or belief, in worship, teaching, practice and observance.
2. The right to conscientious objection is recognised, in accordance with the national laws governing the exercise of this right.

Article 11 Freedom of expression and information

1. Everyone has the right to freedom of expression. This right shall include freedom to hold opinions and to receive and impart information and ideas without interference by public authority and regardless of frontiers.
2. The freedom and pluralism of the media shall be respected.

Article 12 Freedom of assembly and of association

1. Everyone has the right to freedom of peaceful assembly and to freedom of association at all levels, in particular in political, trade union and civic matters, which implies the right of everyone to form and to join trade unions for the protection of his or her interests.
2. Political parties at Union level contribute to expressing the political will of the citizens of the Union.

Article 13 Freedom of the arts and sciences

The arts and scientific research shall be free of constraint. Academic freedom shall be respected.

Article 14 Right to education

1. Everyone has the right to education and to have access to vocational and continuing training.
2. This right includes the possibility to receive free compulsory education.
3. The freedom to found educational establishments with due respect for democratic principles and the right of parents to ensure the education and teaching of their children in conformity with their religious, philosophical and pedagogical convictions shall be respected, in accordance with the national laws governing the exercise of such freedom and right.

Article 15 Freedom to choose an occupation and right to engage in work

1. Everyone has the right to engage in work and to pursue a freely chosen or accepted occupation.
2. Every citizen of the Union has the freedom to seek employment, to work, to exercise the right of establishment and to provide services in any Member State.
3. Nationals of third countries who are authorised to work in the territories of the Member States are entitled to working conditions equivalent to those of citizens of the Union.

Article 16 Freedom to conduct a business

The freedom to conduct a business in accordance with Union law and national laws and practices is recognised.

Article 17 Right to property

1. Everyone has the right to own, use, dispose of and bequeath his or her lawfully acquired possessions. No one may be deprived of his or her possessions, except in the public interest and in the cases and under the conditions provided for by law,

subject to fair compensation being paid in good time for their loss. The use of property may be regulated by law in so far as is necessary for the general interest.

2. Intellectual property shall be protected.

Article 18 Right to asylum

The right to asylum shall be guaranteed with due respect for the rules of the Geneva Convention of 28 July 1951 and the Protocol of 31 January 1967 relating to the status of refugees and in accordance with the Treaty on European Union and the Treaty on the Functioning of the European Union (hereinafter referred to as 'the Treaties').

Article 19 Protection in the event of removal, expulsion or extradition

1. Collective expulsions are prohibited.
2. No one may be removed, expelled or extradited to a State where there is a serious risk that he or she would be subjected to the death penalty, torture or other inhuman or degrading treatment or punishment.

TITLE III
EQUALITY

Article 20 Equality before the law

Everyone is equal before the law.

Article 21 Non-discrimination

1. Any discrimination based on any ground such as sex, race, colour, ethnic or social origin, genetic features, language, religion or belief, political or any other opinion, membership of a national minority, property, birth, disability, age or sexual orientation shall be prohibited.
2. Within the scope of application of the Treaties and without prejudice to any of their specific provisions, any discrimination on grounds of nationality shall be prohibited.

Article 22 Cultural, religious and linguistic diversity

The Union shall respect cultural, religious and linguistic diversity.

Article 23 Equality between women and men

Equality between women and men must be ensured in all areas, including employment, work and pay.

The principle of equality shall not prevent the maintenance or adoption of measures providing for specific advantages in favour of the under-represented sex.

Article 24 The rights of the child

1. Children shall have the right to such protection and care as is necessary for their well-being. They may express their views freely. Such views shall be taken into consideration on matters which concern them in accordance with their age and maturity.
2. In all actions relating to children, whether taken by public authorities or private institutions, the child's best interests must be a primary consideration.
3. Every child shall have the right to maintain on a regular basis a personal relationship and direct contact with both his or her parents, unless that is contrary to his or her interests.

Article 25 The rights of the elderly

The Union recognises and respects the rights of the elderly to lead a life of dignity and independence and to participate in social and cultural life.

Article 26 Integration of persons with disabilities

The Union recognises and respects the right of persons with disabilities to benefit from measures designed to ensure their independence, social and occupational integration and participation in the life of the community.

TITLE IV
SOLIDARITY

Article 27 Workers' right to information and consultation within the undertaking

Workers or their representatives must, at the appropriate levels, be guaranteed information and consultation in good time in the cases and under the conditions provided for by Union law and national laws and practices.

Article 28 Right of collective bargaining and action

Workers and employers, or their respective organisations, have, in accordance with Union law and national laws and practices, the right to negotiate and conclude collective agreements at the appropriate levels and, in cases of conflicts of interest, to take collective action to defend their interests, including strike action.

Article 29 Right of access to placement services

Everyone has the right of access to a free placement service.

Article 30 Protection in the event of unjustified dismissal

Every worker has the right to protection against unjustified dismissal, in accordance with Union law and national laws and practices.

Article 31 Fair and just working conditions

1. Every worker has the right to working conditions which respect his or her health, safety and dignity.
2. Every worker has the right to limitation of maximum working hours, to daily and weekly rest periods and to an annual period of paid leave.

Article 32 Prohibition of child labour and protection of young people at work

The employment of children is prohibited. The minimum age of admission to employment may not be lower than the minimum school-leaving age, without prejudice to such rules as may be more favourable to young people and except for limited derogations.

Young people admitted to work must have working conditions appropriate to their age and be protected against economic exploitation and any work likely to harm their safety, health or physical, mental, moral or social development or to interfere with their education.

Article 33 Family and professional life

1. The family shall enjoy legal, economic and social protection.
2. To reconcile family and professional life, everyone shall have the right to protection from dismissal for a reason connected with maternity and the right to paid maternity leave and to parental leave following the birth or adoption of a child.

Article 34 Social security and social assistance

1. The Union recognises and respects the entitlement to social security benefits and social services providing protection in cases such as maternity, illness, industrial accidents, dependency or old age, and in the case of loss of employment, in accordance with the rules laid down by Union law and national laws and practices.
2. Everyone residing and moving legally within the European Union is entitled to social security benefits and social advantages in accordance with Union law and national laws and practices.
3. In order to combat social exclusion and poverty, the Union recognises and respects the right to social and housing assistance so as to ensure a decent existence for all those who lack sufficient resources, in accordance with the rules laid down by Union law and national laws and practices.

Article 35 Health care

Everyone has the right of access to preventive health care and the right to benefit from medical treatment under the conditions established by national laws and practices. A high level of human health protection shall be ensured in the definition and implementation of all the Union's policies and activities.

Article 36 Access to services of general economic interest

The Union recognises and respects access to services of general economic interest as provided for in national laws and practices, in accordance with the Treaties, in order to promote the social and territorial cohesion of the Union.

Article 37 Environmental protection

A high level of environmental protection and the improvement of the quality of the environment must be integrated into the policies of the Union and ensured in accordance with the principle of sustainable development.

Article 38 Consumer protection

Union policies shall ensure a high level of consumer protection.

TITLE V
CITIZENS' RIGHTS

Article 39 Right to vote and to stand as a candidate at elections to the European Parliament

1. Every citizen of the Union has the right to vote and to stand as a candidate at elections to the European Parliament in the Member State in which he or she resides, under the same conditions as nationals of that State.
2. Members of the European Parliament shall be elected by direct universal suffrage in a free and secret ballot.

Article 40 Right to vote and to stand as a candidate at municipal elections

Every citizen of the Union has the right to vote and to stand as a candidate at municipal elections in the Member State in which he or she resides under the same conditions as nationals of that State.

Article 41 Right to good administration

1. Every person has the right to have his or her affairs handled impartially, fairly and within a reasonable time by the institutions, bodies, offices and agencies of the Union.
2. This right includes:
    (a) the right of every person to be heard, before any individual measure which would affect him or her adversely is taken;
    (b) the right of every person to have access to his or her file, while respecting the legitimate interests of confidentiality and of professional and business secrecy;
    (c) the obligation of the administration to give reasons for its decisions.
3. Every person has the right to have the Union make good any damage caused by its institutions or by its servants in the performance of their duties, in accordance with the general principles common to the laws of the Member States.
4. Every person may write to the institutions of the Union in one of the languages of the Treaties and must have an answer in the same language.

Article 42 Right of access to documents

Any citizen of the Union, and any natural or legal person residing or having its registered office in a Member State, has a right of access to documents of the institutions, bodies, offices and agencies of the Union, whatever their medium.

Article 43 European Ombudsman

Any citizen of the Union and any natural or legal person residing or having its registered office in a Member State has the right to refer to the European Ombudsman cases of maladministration in the activities of the institutions, bodies, offices or agencies of the Union, with the exception of the Court of Justice of the European Union acting in its judicial role.

Article 44 Right to petition

Any citizen of the Union and any natural or legal person residing or having its registered office in a Member State has the right to petition the European Parliament.

Article 45 Freedom of movement and of residence
1. Every citizen of the Union has the right to move and reside freely within the territory of the Member States.
2. Freedom of movement and residence may be granted, in accordance with the Treaties, to nationals of third countries legally resident in the territory of a Member State.

Article 46 Diplomatic and consular protection
Every citizen of the Union shall, in the territory of a third country in which the Member State of which he or she is a national is not represented, be entitled to protection by the diplomatic or consular authorities of any Member State, on the same conditions as the nationals of that Member State.

TITLE VI
JUSTICE

Article 47 Right to an effective remedy and to a fair trial
Everyone whose rights and freedoms guaranteed by the law of the Union are violated has the right to an effective remedy before a tribunal in compliance with the conditions laid down in this Article.

Everyone is entitled to a fair and public hearing within a reasonable time by an independent and impartial tribunal previously established by law. Everyone shall have the possibility of being advised, defended and represented.

Legal aid shall be made available to those who lack sufficient resources in so far as such aid is necessary to ensure effective access to justice.

Article 48 Presumption of innocence and right of defence
1. Everyone who has been charged shall be presumed innocent until proved guilty according to law.
2. Respect for the rights of the defence of anyone who has been charged shall be guaranteed.

Article 49 Principles of legality and proportionality of criminal offences and penalties
1. No one shall be held guilty of any criminal offence on account of any act or omission which did not constitute a criminal offence under national law or international law at the time when it was committed. Nor shall a heavier penalty be imposed than the one that was applicable at the time the criminal offence was committed. If, subsequent to the commission of a criminal offence, the law provides for a lighter penalty, that penalty shall be applicable.
2. This Article shall not prejudice the trial and punishment of any person for any act or omission which, at the time when it was committed, was criminal according to the general principles recognised by the community of nations.
3. The severity of penalties must not be disproportionate to the criminal offence.

Article 50 Right not to be tried or punished twice in criminal proceedings for the same criminal offence
No one shall be liable to be tried or punished again in criminal proceedings for an offence for which he or she has already been finally acquitted or convicted within the Union in accordance with the law.

TITLE VII
GENERAL PROVISIONS GOVERNING THE INTERPRETATION AND APPLICATION
OF THE CHARTER

Article 51 Field of application
1. The provisions of this Charter are addressed to the institutions, bodies, offices and agencies of the Union with due regard for the principle of subsidiarity and to the Member States only when they are implementing Union law. They shall therefore respect the rights, observe the principles and promote the application thereof in accordance with their respective powers and respecting the limits of the powers of the Union as conferred on it in the Treaties.

2.   The Charter does not extend the field of application of Union law beyond the powers of the Union or establish any new power or task for the Union, or modify powers and tasks as defined in the Treaties.

Article 52 Scope and interpretation of rights and principles

1.   Any limitation on the exercise of the rights and freedoms recognised by this Charter must be provided for by law and respect the essence of those rights and freedoms. Subject to the principle of proportionality, limitations may be made only if they are necessary and genuinely meet objectives of general interest recognised by the Union or the need to protect the rights and freedoms of others.
2.   Rights recognised by this Charter for which provision is made in the Treaties shall be exercised under the conditions and within the limits defined by those Treaties.
3.   In so far as this Charter contains rights which correspond to rights guaranteed by the Convention for the Protection of Human Rights and Fundamental Freedoms, the meaning and scope of those rights shall be the same as those laid down by the said Convention. This provision shall not prevent Union law providing more extensive protection.
4.   In so far as this Charter recognises fundamental rights as they result from the constitutional traditions common to the Member States, those rights shall be interpreted in harmony with those traditions.
5.   The provisions of this Charter which contain principles may be implemented by legislative and executive acts taken by institutions, bodies, offices and agencies of the Union, and by acts of Member States when they are implementing Union law, in the exercise of their respective powers. They shall be judicially cognisable only in the interpretation of such acts and in the ruling on their legality.
6.   Full account shall be taken of national laws and practices as specified in this Charter.
7.   The explanations drawn up as a way of providing guidance in the interpretation of this Charter shall be given due regard by the courts of the Union and of the Member States.

Article 53 Level of protection

Nothing in this Charter shall be interpreted as restricting or adversely affecting human rights and fundamental freedoms as recognised, in their respective fields of application, by Union law and international law and by international agreements to which the Union or all the Member States are party, including the European Convention for the Protection of Human Rights and Fundamental Freedoms, and by the Member States' constitutions.

Article 54 Prohibition of abuse of rights

Nothing in this Charter shall be interpreted as implying any right to engage in any activity or to perform any act aimed at the destruction of any of the rights and freedoms recognised in this Charter or at their limitation to a greater extent than is provided for herein.

EU COMPETITION LAW

COUNCIL REGULATION (EC) No 1/2003
on the implementation of the rules on competition laid down in Articles 81 and 82 of the Treaty [now Articles 101 and 102 TFEU]
[2003] OJ L1/1

THE COUNCIL OF THE EUROPEAN UNION,

Having regard to the Treaty establishing the European Community, and in particular Article 83 thereof,

HAS ADOPTED THIS REGULATION:

CHAPTER I
PRINCIPLES

Article 1   Application of Articles 81 and 82 of the Treaty

1.   Agreements, decisions and concerted practices caught by Article 81(1) of the Treaty which do not satisfy the conditions of Article 81(3) of the Treaty shall be prohibited, no prior decision to that effect being required.

2.   Agreements, decisions and concerted practices caught by Article 81(1) of the Treaty which satisfy the conditions of Article 81(3) of the Treaty shall not be prohibited, no prior decision to that effect being required.

3.   The abuse of a dominant position referred to in Article 82 of the Treaty shall be prohibited, no prior decision to that effect being required.

Article 2   Burden of proof

In any national or Community proceedings for the application of Articles 81 and 82 of the Treaty, the burden of proving an infringement of Article 81(1) or of Article 82 of the Treaty shall rest on the party or the authority alleging the infringement. The undertaking or association of undertakings claiming the benefit of Article 81(3) of the Treaty shall bear the burden of proving that the conditions of that paragraph are fulfilled.

Article 3   Relationship between Articles 81 and 82 of the Treaty and national competition laws

1.   Where the competition authorities of the Member States or national courts apply national competition law to agreements, decisions by associations of undertakings or concerted practices within the meaning of Article 81(1) of the Treaty which may affect trade between Member States within the meaning of that provision, they shall also apply Article 81 of the Treaty to such agreements, decisions or concerted practices. Where the competition authorities of the Member States or national courts apply national competition law to any abuse prohibited by Article 82 of the Treaty, they shall also apply Article 82 of the Treaty.

2.   The application of national competition law may not lead to the prohibition of agreements, decisions by associations of undertakings or concerted practices which may affect trade between Member States but which do not restrict competition within the meaning of Article 81(1) of the Treaty, or which fulfil the conditions of Article 81(3) of the Treaty or which are covered by a Regulation for the application of Article 81(3) of the Treaty. Member States shall not under this Regulation be precluded from adopting and applying on their territory stricter national laws which prohibit or sanction unilateral conduct engaged in by undertakings.

3.   Without prejudice to general principles and other provisions of Community law, paragraphs 1 and 2 do not apply when the competition authorities and the courts of the Member States apply national merger control laws nor do they preclude the application of provisions of national law that predominantly pursue an objective different from that pursued by Articles 81 and 82 of the Treaty.

CHAPTER II
POWERS

Article 4   Powers of the Commission

For the purpose of applying Articles 81 and 82 of the Treaty, the Commission shall have the powers provided for by this Regulation.

Article 5   Powers of the competition authorities of the Member States

The competition authorities of the Member States shall have the power to apply Articles 81 and 82 of the Treaty in individual cases. For this purpose, acting on their own initiative or on a complaint, they may take the following decisions:

— requiring that an infringement be brought to an end,
— ordering interim measures,
— accepting commitments,
— imposing fines, periodic penalty payments or any other penalty provided for in their national law.

Where on the basis of the information in their possession the conditions for prohibition are not met they may likewise decide that there are no grounds for action on their part.

Article 6   Powers of the national courts

National courts shall have the power to apply Articles 81 and 82 of the Treaty.

CHAPTER III
COMMISSION DECISIONS

Article 7   Finding and termination of infringement

1. Where the Commission, acting on a complaint or on its own initiative, finds that there is an infringement of Article 81 or of Article 82 of the Treaty, it may by decision require the undertakings and associations of undertakings concerned to bring such infringement to an end. For this purpose, it may impose on them any behavioural or structural remedies which are proportionate to the infringement committed and necessary to bring the infringement effectively to an end. Structural remedies can only be imposed either where there is no equally effective behavioural remedy or where any equally effective behavioural remedy would be more burdensome for the undertaking concerned than the structural remedy. If the Commission has a legitimate interest in doing so, it may also find that an infringement has been committed in the past.

2. Those entitled to lodge a complaint for the purposes of paragraph 1 are natural or legal persons who can show a legitimate interest and Member States.

Article 8   Interim measures

1. In cases of urgency due to the risk of serious and irreparable damage to competition, the Commission, acting on its own initiative may by decision, on the basis of a prima facie finding of infringement, order interim measures.

2. A decision under paragraph 1 shall apply for a specified period of time and may be renewed in so far this is necessary and appropriate.

Article 9   Commitments

1. Where the Commission intends to adopt a decision requiring that an infringement be brought to an end and the undertakings concerned offer commitments to meet the concerns expressed to them by the Commission in its preliminary assessment, the Commission may by decision make those commitments binding on the undertakings. Such a decision may be adopted for a specified period and shall conclude that there are no longer grounds for action by the Commission.

2. The Commission may, upon request or on its own initiative, reopen the proceedings:
    (a)   where there has been a material change in any of the facts on which the decision was based;
    (b)   where the undertakings concerned act contrary to their commitments; or
    (c)   where the decision was based on incomplete, incorrect or misleading information provided by the parties.

Article 10 Finding of inapplicability

Where the Community public interest relating to the application of Articles 81 and 82 of the Treaty so requires, the Commission, acting on its own initiative, may by decision find that

Article 81 of the Treaty is not applicable to an agreement, a decision by an association of undertakings or a concerted practice, either because the conditions of Article 81(1) of the Treaty are not fulfilled, or because the conditions of Article 81(3) of the Treaty are satisfied. The Commission may likewise make such a finding with reference to Article 82 of the Treaty.

CHAPTER IV
COOPERATION

Article 11 Cooperation between the Commission and the competition authorities of the Member States

1. The Commission and the competition authorities of the Member States shall apply the Community competition rules in close cooperation.
2. The Commission shall transmit to the competition authorities of the Member States copies of the most important documents it has collected with a view to applying Articles 7, 8, 9, 10 and Article 29(1). At the request of the competition authority of a Member State, the Commission shall provide it with a copy of other existing documents necessary for the assessment of the case.
3. The competition authorities of the Member States shall, when acting under Article 81 or Article 82 of the Treaty, inform the Commission in writing before or without delay after commencing the first formal investigative measure. This information may also be made available to the competition authorities of the other Member States.
4. No later than 30 days before the adoption of a decision requiring that an infringement be brought to an end, accepting commitments or withdrawing the benefit of a block exemption Regulation, the competition authorities of the Member States shall inform the Commission. To that effect, they shall provide the Commission with a summary of the case, the envisaged decision or, in the absence thereof, any other document indicating the proposed course of action. This information may also be made available to the competition authorities of the other Member States. At the request of the Commission, the acting competition authority shall make available to the Commission other documents it holds which are necessary for the assessment of the case. The information supplied to the Commission may be made available to the competition authorities of the other Member States. National competition authorities may also exchange between themselves information necessary for the assessment of a case that they are dealing with under Article 81 or Article 82 of the Treaty.
5. The competition authorities of the Member States may consult the Commission on any case involving the application of Community law.
6. The initiation by the Commission of proceedings for the adoption of a decision under Chapter III shall relieve the competition authorities of the Member States of their competence to apply Articles 81 and 82 of the Treaty. If a competition authority of a Member State is already acting on a case, the Commission shall only initiate proceedings after consulting with that national competition authority.

Article 12 Exchange of information

1. For the purpose of applying Articles 81 and 82 of the Treaty the Commission and the competition authorities of the Member States shall have the power to provide one another with and use in evidence any matter of fact or of law, including confidential information.
2. Information exchanged shall only be used in evidence for the purpose of applying Article 81 or Article 82 of the Treaty and in respect of the subject-matter for which it was collected by the transmitting authority. However, where national competition law is applied in the same case and in parallel to Community competition law and does not lead to a different outcome, information exchanged under this Article may also be used for the application of national competition law.
3. Information exchanged pursuant to paragraph 1 can only be used in evidence to impose sanctions on natural persons where:
   - the law of the transmitting authority foresees sanctions of a similar kind in relation to an infringement of Article 81 or Article 82 of the Treaty or, in the absence thereof,
   - the information has been collected in a way which respects the same level of protection of the rights of defence of natural persons as provided for under the national rules of the receiving authority. However, in this case, the information exchanged cannot be used by the receiving authority to impose custodial sanctions.

Article 13 Suspension or termination of proceedings

1. Where competition authorities of two or more Member States have received a complaint or are acting on their own initiative under Article 81 or Article 82 of the Treaty against the same agreement, decision of an association or practice, the fact that one authority is dealing with the case shall be sufficient grounds for the others to suspend the proceedings before them or to reject the complaint. The Commission may likewise reject a complaint on the ground that a competition authority of a Member State is dealing with the case.

2. Where a competition authority of a Member State or the Commission has received a complaint against an agreement, decision of an association or practice which has already been dealt with by another competition authority, it may reject it.

Article 14 Advisory Committee

1. The Commission shall consult an Advisory Committee on Restrictive Practices and Dominant Positions prior to the taking of any decision under Articles 7, 8, 9, 10, 23, Article 24(2) and Article 29(1).

2. For the discussion of individual cases, the Advisory Committee shall be composed of representatives of the competition authorities of the Member States. For meetings in which issues other than individual cases are being discussed, an additional Member State representative competent in competition matters may be appointed. Representatives may, if unable to attend, be replaced by other representatives.

3. The consultation may take place at a meeting convened and chaired by the Commission, held not earlier than 14 days after dispatch of the notice convening it, together with a summary of the case, an indication of the most important documents and a preliminary draft decision. In respect of decisions pursuant to Article 8, the meeting may be held seven days after the dispatch of the operative part of a draft decision. Where the Commission dispatches a notice convening the meeting which gives a shorter period of notice than those specified above, the meeting may take place on the proposed date in the absence of an objection by any Member State. The Advisory Committee shall deliver a written opinion on the Commission's preliminary draft decision. It may deliver an opinion even if some members are absent and are not represented. At the request of one or several members, the positions stated in the opinion shall be reasoned.

4. Consultation may also take place by written procedure. However, if any Member State so requests, the Commission shall convene a meeting. In case of written procedure, the Commission shall determine a time-limit of not less than 14 days within which the Member States are to put forward their observations for circulation to all other Member States. In case of decisions to be taken pursuant to Article 8, the time-limit of 14 days is replaced by seven days. Where the Commission determines a time-limit for the written procedure which is shorter than those specified above, the proposed time-limit shall be applicable in the absence of an objection by any Member State.

5. The Commission shall take the utmost account of the opinion delivered by the Advisory Committee. It shall inform the Committee of the manner in which its opinion has been taken into account.

6. Where the Advisory Committee delivers a written opinion, this opinion shall be appended to the draft decision. If the Advisory Committee recommends publication of the opinion, the Commission shall carry out such publication taking into account the legitimate interest of undertakings in the protection of their business secrets.

7. At the request of a competition authority of a Member State, the Commission shall include on the agenda of the Advisory Committee cases that are being dealt with by a competition authority of a Member State under Article 81 or Article 82 of the Treaty. The Commission may also do so on its own initiative. In either case, the Commission shall inform the competition authority concerned.

   A request may in particular be made by a competition authority of a Member State in respect of a case where the Commission intends to initiate proceedings with the effect of Article 11(6).

   The Advisory Committee shall not issue opinions on cases dealt with by competition authorities of the Member States. The Advisory Committee may also discuss general issues of Community competition law.

Article 15 Cooperation with national courts

1. In proceedings for the application of Article 81 or Article 82 of the Treaty, courts of the Member States may ask the Commission to transmit to them information in its possession or its opinion on questions concerning the application of the Community competition rules.

2. Member States shall forward to the Commission a copy of any written judgment of national courts deciding on the application of Article 81 or Article 82 of the Treaty. Such copy shall be forwarded without delay after the full written judgment is notified to the parties.

3. Competition authorities of the Member States, acting on their own initiative, may submit written observations to the national courts of their Member State on issues relating to the application of Article 81 or Article 82 of the Treaty. With the permission of the court in question, they may also submit oral observations to the national courts of their Member State. Where the coherent application of Article 81 or Article 82 of the Treaty so requires, the Commission, acting on its own initiative, may submit written observations to courts of the Member States. With the permission of the court in question, it may also make oral observations.

   For the purpose of the preparation of their observations only, the competition authorities of the Member States and the Commission may request the relevant court of the Member State to transmit or ensure the transmission to them of any documents necessary for the assessment of the case.

4. This Article is without prejudice to wider powers to make observations before courts conferred on competition authorities of the Member States under the law of their Member State.

Article 16 Uniform application of Community competition law

1. When national courts rule on agreements, decisions or practices under Article 81 or Article 82 of the Treaty which are already the subject of a Commission decision, they cannot take decisions running counter to the decision adopted by the Commission. They must also avoid giving decisions which would conflict with a decision contemplated by the Commission in proceedings it has initiated. To that effect, the national court may assess whether it is necessary to stay its proceedings. This obligation is without prejudice to the rights and obligations under Article 234 of the Treaty.

2. When competition authorities of the Member States rule on agreements, decisions or practices under Article 81 or Article 82 of the Treaty which are already the subject of a Commission decision, they cannot take decisions which would run counter to the decision adopted by the Commission.

CHAPTER V

POWERS OF INVESTIGATION

Article 17 Investigations into sectors of the economy and into types of agreements

1. Where the trend of trade between Member States, the rigidity of prices or other circumstances suggest that competition may be restricted or distorted within the common market, the Commission may conduct its inquiry into a particular sector of the economy or into a particular type of agreements across various sectors. In the course of that inquiry, the Commission may request the undertakings or associations of undertakings concerned to supply the information necessary for giving effect to Articles 81 and 82 of the Treaty and may carry out any inspections necessary for that purpose.

   The Commission may in particular request the undertakings or associations of undertakings concerned to communicate to it all agreements, decisions and concerted practices.

   The Commission may publish a report on the results of its inquiry into particular sectors of the economy or particular types of agreements across various sectors and invite comments from interested parties.

2. Articles 14, 18, 19, 20, 22, 23 and 24 shall apply *mutatis mutandis*.

Article 18 Requests for information

1. In order to carry out the duties assigned to it by this Regulation, the Commission may, by simple request or by decision, require undertakings and associations of undertakings to provide all necessary information.

2. When sending a simple request for information to an undertaking or association of undertakings, the Commission shall state the legal basis and the purpose of the request, specify what information is required and fix the time-limit within which the information is to be provided, and the penalties provided for in Article 23 for supplying incorrect or misleading information.

3. Where the Commission requires undertakings and associations of undertakings to supply information by decision, it shall state the legal basis and the purpose of the request, specify what information is required and fix the time-limit within which it is to be provided. It shall also indicate the penalties provided for in Article 23 and indicate or impose the penalties provided for in Article 24. It shall further indicate the right to have the decision reviewed by the Court of Justice.

4. The owners of the undertakings or their representatives and, in the case of legal persons, companies or firms, or associations having no legal personality, the persons authorised to represent them by law or by their constitution shall supply the information requested on behalf of the undertaking or the association of undertakings concerned. Lawyers duly authorised to act may supply the information on behalf of their clients. The latter shall remain fully responsible if the information supplied is incomplete, incorrect or misleading.

5. The Commission shall without delay forward a copy of the simple request or of the decision to the competition authority of the Member State in whose territory the seat of the undertaking or association of undertakings is situated and the competition authority of the Member State whose territory is affected.

6. At the request of the Commission the governments and competition authorities of the Member States shall provide the Commission with all necessary information to carry out the duties assigned to it by this Regulation.

Article 19 Power to take statements

1. In order to carry out the duties assigned to it by this Regulation, the Commission may interview any natural or legal person who consents to be interviewed for the purpose of collecting information relating to the subject-matter of an investigation.

2. Where an interview pursuant to paragraph 1 is conducted in the premises of an undertaking, the Commission shall inform the competition authority of the Member State in whose territory the interview takes place. If so requested by the competition authority of that Member State, its officials may assist the officials and other accompanying persons authorised by the Commission to conduct the interview.

Article 20 The Commission's powers of inspection

1. In order to carry out the duties assigned to it by this Regulation, the Commission may conduct all necessary inspections of undertakings and associations of undertakings.

2. The officials and other accompanying persons authorised by the Commission to conduct an inspection are empowered:
    (a) to enter any premises, land and means of transport of undertakings and associations of undertakings;
    (b) to examine the books and other records related to the business, irrespective of the medium on which they are stored;
    (c) to take or obtain in any form copies of or extracts from such books or records;
    (d) to seal any business premises and books or records for the period and to the extent necessary for the inspection;
    (e) to ask any representative or member of staff of the undertaking or association of undertakings for explanations on facts or documents relating to the subject-matter and purpose of the inspection and to record the answers.

3. The officials and other accompanying persons authorised by the Commission to conduct an inspection shall exercise their powers upon production of a written authorisation specifying the subject matter and purpose of the inspection and the penalties provided for in Article 23 in case the production of the required books or other records related to the business is incomplete or where the answers to questions

asked under paragraph 2 of the present Article are incorrect or misleading. In good time before the inspection, the Commission shall give notice of the inspection to the competition authority of the Member State in whose territory it is to be conducted.

4. Undertakings and associations of undertakings are required to submit to inspections ordered by decision of the Commission. The decision shall specify the subject matter and purpose of the inspection, appoint the date on which it is to begin and indicate the penalties provided for in Articles 23 and 24 and the right to have the decision reviewed by the Court of Justice. The Commission shall take such decisions after consulting the competition authority of the Member State in whose territory the inspection is to be conducted.

5. Officials of as well as those authorised or appointed by the competition authority of the Member State in whose territory the inspection is to be conducted shall, at the request of that authority or of the Commission, actively assist the officials and other accompanying persons authorised by the Commission. To this end, they shall enjoy the powers specified in paragraph 2.

6. Where the officials and other accompanying persons authorised by the Commission find that an undertaking opposes an inspection ordered pursuant to this Article, the Member State concerned shall afford them the necessary assistance, requesting where appropriate the assistance of the police or of an equivalent enforcement authority, so as to enable them to conduct their inspection.

7. If the assistance provided for in paragraph 6 requires authorisation from a judicial authority according to national rules, such authorisation shall be applied for. Such authorisation may also be applied for as a precautionary measure.

8. Where authorisation as referred to in paragraph 7 is applied for, the national judicial authority shall control that the Commission decision is authentic and that the coercive measures envisaged are neither arbitrary nor excessive having regard to the subject matter of the inspection. In its control of the proportionality of the coercive measures, the national judicial authority may ask the Commission, directly or through the Member State competition authority, for detailed explanations in particular on the grounds the Commission has for suspecting infringement of Articles 81 and 82 of the Treaty, as well as on the seriousness of the suspected infringement and on the nature of the involvement of the undertaking concerned. However, the national judicial authority may not call into question the necessity for the inspection nor demand that it be provided with the information in the Commission's file. The lawfulness of the Commission decision shall be subject to review only by the Court of Justice.

Article 21 Inspection of other premises

1. If a reasonable suspicion exists that books or other records related to the business and to the subject-matter of the inspection, which may be relevant to prove a serious violation of Article 81 or Article 82 of the Treaty, are being kept in any other premises, land and means of transport, including the homes of directors, managers and other members of staff of the undertakings and associations of undertakings concerned, the Commission can by decision order an inspection to be conducted in such other premises, land and means of transport.

2. The decision shall specify the subject matter and purpose of the inspection, appoint the date on which it is to begin and indicate the right to have the decision reviewed by the Court of Justice. It shall in particular state the reasons that have led the Commission to conclude that a suspicion in the sense of paragraph 1 exists. The Commission shall take such decisions after consulting the competition authority of the Member State in whose territory the inspection is to be conducted.

3. A decision adopted pursuant to paragraph 1 cannot be executed without prior authorisation from the national judicial authority of the Member State concerned. The national judicial authority shall control that the Commission decision is authentic and that the coercive measures envisaged are neither arbitrary nor excessive having regard in particular to the seriousness of the suspected infringement, to the importance of the evidence sought, to the involvement of the undertaking concerned and to the reasonable likelihood that business books and records relating to the subject matter of the inspection are kept in the premises for which the authorisation is requested. The national judicial authority may ask the Commission, directly or through the Member

State competition authority, for detailed explanations on those elements which are necessary to allow its control of the proportionality of the coercive measures envisaged. However, the national judicial authority may not call into question the necessity for the inspection nor demand that it be provided with information in the Commission's file. The lawfulness of the Commission decision shall be subject to review only by the Court of Justice.

4.   The officials and other accompanying persons authorised by the Commission to conduct an inspection ordered in accordance with paragraph 1 of this Article shall have the powers set out in Article 20(2)(a), (b) and (c). Article 20(5) and (6) shall apply *mutatis mutandis*.

Article 22 Investigations by competition authorities of Member States

1.   The competition authority of a Member State may in its own territory carry out any inspection or other fact-finding measure under its national law on behalf and for the account of the competition authority of another Member State in order to establish whether there has been an infringement of Article 81 or Article 82 of the Treaty. Any exchange and use of the information collected shall be carried out in accordance with Article 12.

2.   At the request of the Commission, the competition authorities of the Member States shall undertake the inspections which the Commission considers to be necessary under Article 20(1) or which it has ordered by decision pursuant to Article 20(4). The officials of the competition authorities of the Member States who are responsible for conducting these inspections as well as those authorised or appointed by them shall exercise their   powers in accordance with their national law.

If so requested by the Commission or by the competition authority of the Member State in whose territory the inspection is to be conducted, officials and other accompanying persons authorised by the Commission may assist the officials of the authority concerned.

CHAPTER VI
PENALTIES

Article 23 Fines

1.   The Commission may by decision impose on undertakings and associations of undertakings fines not exceeding 1% of the total turnover in the preceding business year where, intentionally or negligently:

(a)   they supply incorrect or misleading information in response to a request made pursuant to Article 17 or Article 18(2);

(b)   in response to a request made by decision adopted pursuant to Article 17 or Article 18(3), they supply incorrect, incomplete or misleading information or do not supply information within the required time-limit;

(c)   they produce the required books or other records related to the business in incomplete form during inspections under Article 20 or refuse to submit to inspections ordered by a decision adopted pursuant to Article 20(4);

(d)   in response to a question asked in accordance with Article 20(2)(e),
    — they give an incorrect or misleading answer,
    — they fail to rectify within a time-limit set by the Commission an incorrect, incomplete or misleading answer given by a member of staff, or
    — they fail or refuse to provide a complete answer on facts relating to the subject-matter and purpose of an inspection ordered by a decision adopted pursuant to Article 20(4);

(e)   seals affixed in accordance with Article 20(2)(d) by officials or other accompanying persons authorised by the Commission have been broken.

2.   The Commission may by decision impose fines on undertakings and associations of undertakings where, either intentionally or negligently:

(a)   they infringe Article 81 or Article 82 of the Treaty; or

(b)   they contravene a decision ordering interim measures under Article 8; or

(c)   they fail to comply with a commitment made binding by a decision pursuant to Article 9.

For each undertaking and association of undertakings participating in the infringement, the fine shall not exceed 10% of its total turnover in the preceding business year.

Where the infringement of an association relates to the activities of its members, the fine shall not exceed 10% of the sum of the total turnover of each member active on the market affected by the infringement of the association.

3. In fixing the amount of the fine, regard shall be had both to the gravity and to the duration of the infringement.

4. When a fine is imposed on an association of undertakings taking account of the turnover of its members and the association is not solvent, the association is obliged to call for contributions from its members to cover the amount of the fine.

Where such contributions have not been made to the association within a time-limit fixed by the Commission, the Commission may require payment of the fine directly by any of the undertakings whose representatives were members of the decision-making bodies concerned of the association.

After the Commission has required payment under the second subparagraph, where necessary to ensure full payment of the fine, the Commission may require payment of the balance by any of the members of the association which were active on the market on which the infringement occurred.

However, the Commission shall not require payment under the second or the third subparagraph from undertakings which show that they have not implemented the infringing decision of the association and either were not aware of its existence or have actively distanced themselves from it before the Commission started investigating the case.

The financial liability of each undertaking in respect of the payment of the fine shall not exceed 10% of its total turnover in the preceding business year.

5. Decisions taken pursuant to paragraphs 1 and 2 shall not be of a criminal law nature.

Article 24 Periodic penalty payments

1. The Commission may, by decision, impose on undertakings or associations of undertakings periodic penalty payments not exceeding 5% of the average daily turnover in the preceding business year per day and calculated from the date appointed by the decision, in order to compel them:
    (a) to put an end to an infringement of Article 81 or Article 82 of the Treaty, in accordance with a decision taken pursuant to Article 7;
    (b) to comply with a decision ordering interim measures taken pursuant to Article 8;
    (c) to comply with a commitment made binding by a decision pursuant to Article 9;
    (d) to supply complete and correct information which it has requested by decision taken pursuant to Article 17 or Article 18(3);
    (e) to submit to an inspection which it has ordered by decision taken pursuant to Article 20(4).

2. Where the undertakings or associations of undertakings have satisfied the obligation which the periodic penalty payment was intended to enforce, the Commission may fix the definitive amount of the periodic penalty payment at a figure lower than that which would arise under the original decision. Article 23(4) shall apply correspondingly.

CHAPTER VII
LIMITATION PERIODS

Article 25 Limitation periods for the imposition of penalties

1. The powers conferred on the Commission by Articles 23 and 24 shall be subject to the following limitation periods:
    (a) three years in the case of infringements of provisions concerning requests for information or the conduct of inspections;
    (b) five years in the case of all other infringements.

2. Time shall begin to run on the day on which the infringement is committed. However, in the case of continuing or repeated infringements, time shall begin to run on the day on which the infringement ceases.

3. Any action taken by the Commission or by the competition authority of a Member State for the purpose of the investigation or proceedings in respect of an infringement shall interrupt the limitation period for the imposition of fines or periodic penalty payments. The limitation period shall be interrupted with effect from the date on which the action is notified to at least one undertaking or association of undertakings which

has participated in the infringement. Actions which interrupt the running of the period shall include in particular the following:

(a)   written requests for information by the Commission or by the competition authority of a Member State;

(b)   written authorisations to conduct inspections issued to its officials by the Commission or by the competition authority of a Member State;

(c)   the initiation of proceedings by the Commission or by the competition authority of a Member State;

(d)   notification of the statement of objections of the Commission or of the competition authority of a Member State.

4.   The interruption of the limitation period shall apply for all the undertakings or associations of undertakings which have participated in the infringement.

5.   Each interruption shall start time running afresh. However, the limitation period shall expire at the latest on the day on which a period equal to twice the limitation period has elapsed without the Commission having imposed a fine or a periodic penalty payment. That period shall be extended by the time during which limitation is suspended pursuant to paragraph 6.

6.   The limitation period for the imposition of fines or periodic penalty payments shall be suspended for as long as the decision of the Commission is the subject of proceedings pending before the Court of Justice.

Article 26 Limitation period for the enforcement of penalties

1.   The power of the Commission to enforce decisions taken pursuant to Articles 23 and 24 shall be subject to a limitation period of five years.

2.   Time shall begin to run on the day on which the decision becomes final.

3.   The limitation period for the enforcement of penalties shall be interrupted:

(a)   by notification of a decision varying the original amount of the fine or periodic penalty payment or refusing an application for variation;

(b)   by any action of the Commission or of a Member State, acting at the request of the Commission, designed to enforce payment of the fine or periodic penalty payment.

4.   Each interruption shall start time running afresh.

5.   The limitation period for the enforcement of penalties shall be suspended for so long as:

(a)   time to pay is allowed;

(b)   enforcement of payment is suspended pursuant to a decision of the Court of Justice.

CHAPTER VIII
HEARINGS AND PROFESSIONAL SECRECY

Article 27 Hearing of the parties, complainants and others

1.   Before taking decisions as provided for in Articles 7, 8, 23 and Article 24(2), the Commission shall give the undertakings or associations of undertakings which are the subject of the proceedings conducted by the Commission the opportunity of being heard on the matters to which the Commission has taken objection. The Commission shall base its decisions only on objections on which the parties concerned have been able to comment. Complainants shall be associated closely with the proceedings.

2.   The rights of defence of the parties concerned shall be fully respected in the proceedings. They shall be entitled to have access to the Commission's file, subject to the legitimate interest of undertakings in the protection of their business secrets. The right of access to the file shall not extend to confidential information and internal documents of the Commission or the competition authorities of the Member States. In particular, the right of access shall not extend to correspondence between the Commission and the competition authorities of the Member States, or between the latter, including documents drawn up pursuant to Articles 11 and 14. Nothing in this paragraph shall prevent the Commission from disclosing and using information necessary to prove an infringement.

3.   If the Commission considers it necessary, it may also hear other natural or legal persons. Applications to be heard on the part of such persons shall, where they show a sufficient interest, be granted. The competition authorities of the Member States may also ask the Commission to hear other natural or legal persons.

4. Where the Commission intends to adopt a decision pursuant to Article 9 or Article 10, it shall publish a concise summary of the case and the main content of the commitments or of the proposed course of action. Interested third parties may submit their observations within a time limit which is fixed by the Commission in its publication and which may not be less than one month. Publication shall have regard to the legitimate interest of undertakings in the protection of their business secrets.

Article 28 Professional secrecy

1. Without prejudice to Articles 12 and 15, information collected pursuant to Articles 17 to 22 shall be used only for the purpose for which it was acquired.
2. Without prejudice to the exchange and to the use of information foreseen in Articles 11, 12, 14, 15 and 27, the Commission and the competition authorities of the Member States, their officials, servants and other persons working under the supervision of these authorities as well as officials and civil servants of other authorities of the Member States shall not disclose information acquired or exchanged by them pursuant to this Regulation and of the kind covered by the obligation of professional secrecy. This obligation also applies to all representatives and experts of Member States attending meetings of the Advisory Committee pursuant to Article 14.

CHAPTER IX
EXEMPTION REGULATIONS

Article 29 Withdrawal in individual cases

1. Where the Commission, empowered by a Council Regulation, such as Regulations 19/65/EEC, (EEC) No 2821/71, (EEC) No 3976/ 87, (EEC) No 1534/91 or (EEC) No 479/92, to apply Article 81(3) of the Treaty by regulation, has declared Article 81(1) of the Treaty inapplicable to certain categories of agreements, decisions by associations of undertakings or concerted practices, it may, acting on its own initiative or on a complaint, withdraw the benefit of such an exemption Regulation when it finds that in any particular case an agreement, decision or concerted practice to which the exemption Regulation applies has certain effects which are incompatible with Article 81(3) of the Treaty.
2. Where, in any particular case, agreements, decisions by associations of undertakings or concerted practices to which a Commission Regulation referred to in paragraph 1 applies have effects which are incompatible with Article 81(3) of the Treaty in the territory of a Member State, or in a part thereof, which has all the characteristics of a distinct geographic market, the competition authority of that Member State may withdraw the benefit of the Regulation in question in respect of that territory.

CHAPTER X
GENERAL PROVISIONS

Article 30 Publication of decisions

1. The Commission shall publish the decisions, which it takes pursuant to Articles 7 to 10, 23 and 24.
2. The publication shall state the names of the parties and the main content of the decision, including any penalties imposed. It shall have regard to the legitimate interest of undertakings in the protection of their business secrets.

Article 31 Review by the Court of Justice

The Court of Justice shall have unlimited jurisdiction to review decisions whereby the Commission has fixed a fine or periodic penalty payment. It may cancel, reduce or increase the fine or periodic penalty payment imposed.

Article 32 Exclusions

This Regulation shall not apply to:
(a) international tramp vessel services as defined in Article 1(3)(a) of Regulation (EEC) No 4056/86;
(b) a maritime transport service that takes place exclusively between ports in one and the same Member State as foreseen in Article 1(2) of Regulation (EEC) No 4056/86.

Article 33 Implementing provisions

1. The Commission shall be authorised to take such measures as may be appropriate in order to apply this Regulation. The measures may concern, inter alia:
   (a) the form, content and other details of complaints lodged pursuant to Article 7 and the procedure for rejecting complaints;
   (b) the practical arrangements for the exchange of information and consultations provided for in Article 11;
   (c) the practical arrangements for the hearings provided for in Article 27.
2. Before the adoption of any measures pursuant to paragraph 1, the Commission shall publish a draft thereof and invite all interested parties to submit their comments within the time-limit it lays down, which may not be less than one month. Before publishing a draft measure and before adopting it, the Commission shall consult the Advisory Committee on Restrictive Practices and Dominant Positions.

Article 44 Report on the application of the present Regulation

Five years from the date of application of this Regulation, the Commission shall report to the European Parliament and the Council on the functioning of this Regulation, in particular on the application of Article 11(6) and Article 17.

On the basis of this report, the Commission shall assess whether it is appropriate to propose to the Council a revision of this Regulation.

Article 45 Entry into force

This Regulation shall enter into force on the 20th day following that of its publication in the *Official Journal of the European Communities*. It shall apply from 1 May 2004.

This Regulation shall be binding in its entirety and directly applicable in all Member States.

Regulation No 17
first regulation implementing Articles 81 and 82 of the Treaty
[1962] OJ L13/204

Article 8 Duration and revocation of decisions under Article 85(3)

...

3. The Commission may revoke or amend its decision or prohibit specified acts by the parties:
   (a) where there has been a change in any of the facts which were basic to the making of the decision;
   (b) where the parties commit a breach of any obligation attached to the decision;
   (c) where the decision is based on incorrect information or was induced by deceit;
   (d) where the parties abuse the exemption from the provisions of Article 85(1) of the Treaty granted to them by the decision.

   In cases to which subparagraphs (b), (c) or (d) apply, the decision may be revoked with retroactive effect.

COUNCIL REGULATION (EC) No 139/2004 of 20 JANUARY 2004
on the control of concentrations between undertakings (the EC Merger Regulation)
[2004] OJ L24/1

Article 1 Scope

1. Without prejudice to Article 4(5) and Article 22, this Regulation shall apply to all concentrations with a Community dimension as defined in this Article.
2. A concentration has a Community dimension where:
   (a) the combined aggregate worldwide turnover of all the undertakings concerned is more than EUR 5000 million; and
   (b) the aggregate Community-wide turnover of each of at least two of the undertakings concerned is more than EUR 250 million,

unless each of the undertakings concerned achieves more than two-thirds of its aggregate Community-wide turnover within one and the same Member State.

3. A concentration that does not meet the thresholds laid down in paragraph 2 has a Community dimension where:
   (a) the combined aggregate worldwide turnover of all the undertakings concerned is more than EUR 2 500 million;
   (b) in each of at least three Member States, the combined aggregate turnover of all the undertakings concerned is more than EUR 100 million;
   (c) in each of at least three Member States included for the purpose of point (b), the aggregate turnover of each of at least two of the undertakings concerned is more than EUR 25 million; and
   (d) the aggregate Community-wide turnover of each of at least two of the undertakings concerned is more than EUR 100 million,

   unless each of the undertakings concerned achieves more than two-thirds of its aggregate Community-wide turnover within one and the same Member State.

4. On the basis of statistical data that may be regularly provided by the Member States, the Commission shall report to the Council on the operation of the thresholds and criteria set out in paragraphs 2 and 3 by 1 July 2009 and may present proposals pursuant to paragraph 5.

5. Following the report referred to in paragraph 4 and on a proposal from the Commission, the Council, acting by a qualified majority, may revise the thresholds and criteria mentioned in paragraph 3.

Article 2 Appraisal of concentrations

1. Concentrations within the scope of this Regulation shall be appraised in accordance with the objectives of this Regulation and the following provisions with a view to establishing whether or not they are compatible with the common market.

   In making this appraisal, the Commission shall take into account:
   (a) the need to maintain and develop effective competition within the common market in view of, among other things, the structure of all the markets concerned and the actual or potential competition from undertakings located either within or out with the Community;
   (b) the market position of the undertakings concerned and their economic and financial power, the alternatives available to suppliers and users, their access to supplies or markets, any legal or other barriers to entry, supply and demand trends for the relevant goods and services, the interests of the intermediate and ultimate consumers, and the development of technical and economic progress provided that it is to consumers' advantage and does not form an obstacle to competition.

2. A concentration which would not significantly impede effective competition in the common market or in a substantial part of it, in particular as a result of the creation or strengthening of a dominant position, shall be declared compatible with the common market.

3. A concentration which would significantly impede effective competition, in the common market or in a substantial part of it, in particular as a result of the creation or strengthening of a dominant position, shall be declared incompatible with the common market.

4. To the extent that the creation of a joint venture constituting a concentration pursuant to Article 3 has as its object or effect the coordination of the competitive behaviour of undertakings that remain independent, such coordination shall be appraised in accordance with the criteria of Article 81(1) and (3) of the Treaty, with a view to establishing whether or not the operation is compatible with the common market.

5. In making this appraisal, the Commission shall take into account in particular:
   — whether two or more parent companies retain, to a significant extent, activities in the same market as the joint venture or in a market which is downstream or upstream from that of the joint venture or in a neighbouring market closely related to this market,
   — whether the coordination which is the direct consequence of the creation of the joint venture affords the undertakings concerned the possibility of eliminating competition in respect of a substantial part of the products or services in question.

Article 3 Definition of concentration

1. A concentration shall be deemed to arise where a change of control on a lasting basis results from:
   - (a) the merger of two or more previously independent undertakings or parts of undertakings, or
   - (b) the acquisition, by one or more persons already controlling at least one undertaking, or by one or more undertakings, whether by purchase of securities or assets, by contract or by any other means, of direct or indirect control of the whole or parts of one or more other undertakings.

2. Control shall be constituted by rights, contracts or any other means which, either separately or in combination and having regard to the considerations of fact or law involved, confer the possibility of exercising decisive influence on an undertaking, in particular by:
   - (a) ownership or the right to use all or part of the assets of an undertaking;
   - (b) rights or contracts which confer decisive influence on the composition, voting or decisions of the organs of an undertaking.

3. Control is acquired by persons or undertakings which:
   - (a) are holders of the rights or entitled to rights under the contracts concerned; or
   - (b) while not being holders of such rights or entitled to rights under such contracts, have the power to exercise the rights deriving therefrom.

4. The creation of a joint venture performing on a lasting basis all the functions of an autonomous economic entity shall constitute a concentration within the meaning of paragraph 1(b).

5. A concentration shall not be deemed to arise where:
   - (a) credit institutions or other financial institutions or insurance companies, the normal activities of which include transactions and dealing in securities for their own account or for the account of others, hold on a temporary basis securities which they have acquired in an undertaking with a view to reselling them, provided that they do not exercise voting rights in respect of those securities with a view to determining the competitive behaviour of that undertaking or provided that they exercise such voting rights only with a view to preparing the disposal of all or part of that undertaking or of its assets or the disposal of those securities and that any such disposal takes place within one year of the date of acquisition; that period may be extended by the Commission on request where such institutions or companies can show that the disposal was not reasonably possible within the period set;
   - (b) control is acquired by an office-holder according to the law of a Member State relating to liquidation, winding up, insolvency, cessation of payments, compositions or analogous proceedings;
   - (c) the operations referred to in paragraph 1(b) are carried out by the financial holding companies referred to in Article 5(3) of Fourth Council Directive 78/660/EEC of 25 July 1978 based on Article 54(3)(g) of the Treaty on the annual accounts of certain types of companies provided however that the voting rights in respect of the holding are exercised, in particular in relation to the appointment of members of the management and supervisory bodies of the undertakings in which they have holdings, only to maintain the full value of those investments and not to determine directly or indirectly the competitive conduct of those undertakings.

Article 4 Prior notification of concentrations and pre-notification referral at the request of the notifying parties

1. Concentrations with a Community dimension defined in this Regulation shall be notified to the Commission prior to their implementation and following the conclusion of the agreement, the announcement of the public bid, or the acquisition of a controlling interest. Notification may also be made where the undertakings concerned demonstrate to the Commission a good faith intention to conclude an agreement or, in the case of a public bid, where they have publicly announced an intention to make such a bid, provided that the intended agreement or bid would result in a concentration with a Community dimension.

For the purposes of this Regulation, the term 'notified concentration' shall also cover intended concentrations notified pursuant to the second subparagraph. For the purposes of paragraphs 4 and 5 of this Article, the term 'concentration' includes intended concentrations within the meaning of the second subparagraph.

2. A concentration which consists of a merger within the meaning of Article 3(1)(a) or in the acquisition of joint control within the meaning of Article 3(1)(b) shall be notified jointly by the parties to the merger or by those acquiring joint control as the case may be. In all other cases, the notification shall be effected by the person or undertaking acquiring control of the whole or parts of one or more undertakings.

3. Where the Commission finds that a notified concentration falls within the scope of this Regulation, it shall publish the fact of the notification, at the same time indicating the names of the undertakings concerned, their country of origin, the nature of the concentration and the economic sectors involved. The Commission shall take account of the legitimate interest of undertakings in the protection of their business secrets.

4. Prior to the notification of a concentration within the meaning of paragraph 1, the persons or undertakings referred to in paragraph 2 may inform the Commission, by means of a reasoned submission, that the concentration may significantly affect competition in a market within a Member State which presents all the characteristics of a distinct market and should therefore be examined, in whole or in part, by that Member State.

The Commission shall transmit this submission to all Member States without delay. The Member State referred to in the reasoned submission shall, within 15 working days of receiving the submission, express its agreement or disagreement as regards the request to refer the case. Where that Member State takes no such decision within this period, it shall be deemed to have agreed.

Unless that Member State disagrees, the Commission, where it considers that such a distinct market exists, and that competition in that market may be significantly affected by the concentration, may decide to refer the whole or part of the case to the competent authorities of that Member State with a view to the application of that State's national competition law.

The decision whether or not to refer the case in accordance with the third subparagraph shall be taken within 25 working days starting from the receipt of the reasoned submission by the Commission. The Commission shall inform the other Member States and the persons or undertakings concerned of its decision. If the Commission does not take a decision within this period, it shall be deemed to have adopted a decision to refer the case in accordance with the submission made by the persons or undertakings concerned.

If the Commission decides, or is deemed to have decided, pursuant to the third and fourth subparagraphs, to refer the whole of the case, no notification shall be made pursuant to paragraph 1 and national competition law shall apply. Article 9(6) to (9) shall apply *mutatis mutandis*.

5. With regard to a concentration as defined in Article 3 which does not have a Community dimension within the meaning of Article 1 and which is capable of being reviewed under the national competition laws of at least three Member States, the persons or undertakings referred to in paragraph 2 may, before any notification to the competent authorities, inform the Commission by means of a reasoned submission that the concentration should be examined by the Commission.

The Commission shall transmit this submission to all Member States without delay. Any Member State competent to examine the concentration under its national competition law may, within 15 working days of receiving the reasoned submission, express its disagreement as regards the request to refer the case.

Where at least one such Member State has expressed its disagreement in accordance with the third subparagraph within the period of 15 working days, the case shall not be referred. The Commission shall, without delay, inform all Member States and the persons or undertakings concerned of any such expression of disagreement.

Where no Member State has expressed its disagreement in accordance with the third subparagraph within the period of 15 working days, the concentration shall be deemed to have a Community dimension and shall be notified to the Commission in accordance with paragraphs 1 and 2. In such situations, no Member State shall apply its national competition law to the concentration.

6. The Commission shall report to the Council on the operation of paragraphs 4 and 5 by 1 July 2009. Following this report and on a proposal from the Commission, the Council, acting by a qualified majority, may revise paragraphs 4 and 5.

Article 5 Calculation of turnover

1. Aggregate turnover within the meaning of this Regulation shall comprise the amounts derived by the undertakings concerned in the preceding financial year from the sale of products and the provision of services falling within the undertakings' ordinary activities after deduction of sales rebates and of value added tax and other taxes directly related to turnover. The aggregate turnover of an undertaking concerned shall not include the sale of products or the provision of services between any of the undertakings referred to in paragraph 4.

    Turnover, in the Community or in a Member State, shall comprise products sold and services provided to undertakings or consumers, in the Community or in that Member State as the case may be.

2. By way of derogation from paragraph 1, where the concentration consists of the acquisition of parts, whether or not constituted as legal entities, of one or more undertakings, only the turnover relating to the parts which are the subject of the concentration shall be taken into account with regard to the seller or sellers.

    However, two or more transactions within the meaning of the first subparagraph which take place within a two-year period between the same persons or undertakings shall be treated as one and the same concentration arising on the date of the last transaction.

3. In place of turnover the following shall be used:

    (a) for credit institutions and other financial institutions, the sum of the following income items as defined in Council Directive 86/635/EEC, after deduction of value added tax and other taxes directly related to those items, where appropriate:

    (i) interest income and similar income;

    (ii) income from securities:
    — income from shares and other variable yield securities,
    — income from participating interests,
    — income from shares in affiliated undertakings;

    (iii) commissions receivable;

    (iv) net profit on financial operations;

    (v) other operating income.

    The turnover of a credit or financial institution in the Community or in a Member State shall comprise the income items, as defined above, which are received by the branch or division of that institution established in the Community or in the Member State in question, as the case may be;

    (b) for insurance undertakings, the value of gross premiums written which shall comprise all amounts received and receivable in respect of insurance contracts issued by or on behalf of the insurance undertakings, including also outgoing reinsurance premiums, and after deduction of taxes and parafiscal contributions or levies charged by reference to the amounts of individual premiums or the total volume of premiums; as regards Article 1(2)(b) and (3)(b), (c) and (d) and the final part of Article 1(2) and (3), gross premiums received from Community residents and from residents of one Member State respectively shall be taken into account.

4. Without prejudice to paragraph 2, the aggregate turnover of an undertaking concerned within the meaning of this Regulation shall be calculated by adding together the respective turnovers of the following:

    (a) the undertaking concerned;

    (b) those undertakings in which the undertaking concerned, directly or indirectly:

    (i) owns more than half the capital or business assets, or

    (ii) has the power to exercise more than half the voting rights, or

(iii)   has the power to appoint more than half the members of the supervisory board, the administrative board or bodies legally representing the undertakings, or

(iv)   has the right to manage the undertakings' affairs;

(c)   those undertakings which have in the undertaking concerned the rights or powers listed in (b);

(d)   those undertakings in which an undertaking as referred to in (c) has the rights or powers listed in (b);

(e)   those undertakings in which two or more undertakings as referred to in (a) to (d) jointly have the rights or powers listed in (b).

5.   Where undertakings concerned by the concentration jointly have the rights or powers listed in paragraph 4(b), in calculating the aggregate turnover of the undertakings concerned for the purposes of this Regulation:

(a)   no account shall be taken of the turnover resulting from the sale of products or the provision of services between the joint undertaking and each of the undertakings concerned or any other undertaking connected with any one of them, as set out in paragraph 4(b) to (e);

(b)   account shall be taken of the turnover resulting from the sale of products and the provision of services between the joint undertaking and any third undertakings. This turnover shall be apportioned equally amongst the undertakings concerned.

Article 6   Examination of the notification and initiation of proceedings

1.   The Commission shall examine the notification as soon as it is received.

(a)   Where it concludes that the concentration notified does not fall within the scope of this Regulation, it shall record that finding by means of a decision.

(b)   Where it finds that the concentration notified, although falling within the scope of this Regulation, does not raise serious doubts as to its compatibility with the common market, it shall decide not to oppose it and shall declare that it is compatible with the common market.

A decision declaring a concentration compatible shall be deemed to cover restrictions directly related and necessary to the implementation of the concentration.

(c)   Without prejudice to paragraph 2, where the Commission finds that the concentration notified falls within the scope of this Regulation and raises serious doubts as to its compatibility with the common market, it shall decide to initiate proceedings. Without prejudice to Article 9, such proceedings shall be closed by means of a decision as provided for in Article 8(1) to (4), unless the undertakings concerned have demonstrated to the satisfaction of the Commission that they have abandoned the concentration.

2.   Where the Commission finds that, following modification by the undertakings concerned, a notified concentration no longer raises serious doubts within the meaning of paragraph 1(c), it shall declare the concentration compatible with the common market pursuant to paragraph 1(b).

The Commission may attach to its decision under paragraph 1(b) conditions and obligations intended to ensure that the undertakings concerned comply with the commitments they have entered into vis-à-vis the Commission with a view to rendering the concentration compatible with the common market.

3.   The Commission may revoke the decision it took pursuant to paragraph 1(a) or (b) where:

(a)   the decision is based on incorrect information for which one of the undertakings is responsible or where it has been obtained by deceit, or

(b)   the undertakings concerned commit a breach of an obligation attached to the decision.

4.   In the cases referred to in paragraph 3, the Commission may take a decision under paragraph 1, without being bound by the time limits referred to in Article 10(1).

5.   The Commission shall notify its decision to the undertakings concerned and the competent authorities of the Member States without delay.

Article 7   Suspension of concentrations

1.   A concentration with a Community dimension as defined in Article 1, or which is to be examined by the Commission pursuant to Article 4(5), shall not be implemented either before its notification or until it has been declared compatible with the common market pursuant to a decision under Articles 6(1)(b), 8(1) or 8(2), or on the basis of a presumption according to Article 10(6).

2.   Paragraph 1 shall not prevent the implementation of a public bid or of a series of transactions in securities including those convertible into other securities admitted to trading on a market such as a stock exchange, by which control within the meaning of Article 3 is acquired from various sellers, provided that:

   (a)   the concentration is notified to the Commission pursuant to Article 4 without delay; and

   (b)   the acquirer does not exercise the voting rights attached to the securities in question or does so only to maintain the full value of its investments based on a derogation granted by the Commission under paragraph 3.

3.   The Commission may, on request, grant a derogation from the obligations imposed in paragraphs 1 or 2. The request to grant a derogation must be reasoned. In deciding on the request, the Commission shall take into account *inter alia* the effects of the suspension on one or more undertakings concerned by the concentration or on a third party and the threat to competition posed by the concentration. Such a derogation may be made subject to conditions and obligations in order to ensure conditions of effective competition. A derogation may be applied for and granted at any time, be it before notification or after the transaction.

4.   The validity of any transaction carried out in contravention of paragraph 1 shall be dependent on a decision pursuant to Article 6(1)(b) or Article 8(1), (2) or (3) or on a presumption pursuant to Article 10(6).

   This Article shall, however, have no effect on the validity of transactions in securities including those convertible into other securities admitted to trading on a market such as a stock exchange, unless the buyer and seller knew or ought to have known that the transaction was carried out in contravention of paragraph 1.

Article 8   Powers of decision of the Commission

1.   Where the Commission finds that a notified concentration fulfils the criterion laid down in Article 2(2) and, in the cases referred to in Article 2(4), the criteria laid down in Article 81(3) of the Treaty, it shall issue a decision declaring the concentration compatible with the common market.

   A decision declaring a concentration compatible shall be deemed to cover restrictions directly related and necessary to the implementation of the concentration.

2.   Where the Commission finds that, following modification by the undertakings concerned, a notified concentration fulfils the criterion laid down in Article 2(2) and, in the cases referred to in Article 2(4), the criteria laid down in Article 81(3) of the Treaty, it shall issue a decision declaring the concentration compatible with the common market. The Commission may attach to its decision conditions and obligations intended to ensure that the undertakings concerned comply with the commitments they have entered into vis-à-vis the Commission with a view to rendering the concentration compatible with the common market.

   A decision declaring a concentration compatible shall be deemed to cover restrictions directly related and necessary to the implementation of the concentration.

3.   Where the Commission finds that a concentration fulfils the criterion defined in Article 2(3) or, in the cases referred to in Article 2(4), does not fulfil the criteria laid down in Article 81(3) of the Treaty, it shall issue a decision declaring that the concentration is incompatible with the common market.

4.   Where the Commission finds that a concentration:

   (a)   has already been implemented and that concentration has been declared incompatible with the common market, or

   (b)   has been implemented in contravention of a condition attached to a decision taken under paragraph 2, which has found that, in the absence of the condition, the concentration would fulfil the criterion laid down in Article 2(3) or, in the cases referred to in Article 2(4), would not fulfil the criteria laid down in Article 81(3) of the Treaty, the Commission may:

— require the undertakings concerned to dissolve the concentration, in particular through the dissolution of the merger or the disposal of all the shares or assets acquired, so as to restore the situation prevailing prior to the implementation of the concentration; in circumstances where restoration of the situation prevailing before the implementation of the concentration is not possible through dissolution of the concentration, the Commission may take any other measure appropriate to achieve such restoration as far as possible,

— order any other appropriate measure to ensure that the undertakings concerned dissolve the concentration or take other restorative measures as required in its decision.

In cases falling within point (a) of the first subparagraph, the measures referred to in that subparagraph may be imposed either in a decision pursuant to paragraph 3 or by separate decision.

5. The Commission may take interim measures appropriate to restore or maintain conditions of effective competition where a concentration:

(a) has been implemented in contravention of Article 7, and a decision as to the compatibility of the concentration with the common market has not yet been taken;

(b) has been implemented in contravention of a condition attached to a decision under Article 6(1)(b) or paragraph 2 of this Article;

(c) has already been implemented and is declared incompatible with the common market.

6. The Commission may revoke the decision it has taken pursuant to paragraphs 1 or 2 where:

(a) the declaration of compatibility is based on incorrect information for which one of the undertakings is responsible or where it has been obtained by deceit; or

(b) the undertakings concerned commit a breach of an obligation attached to the decision.

7. The Commission may take a decision pursuant to paragraphs 1 to 3 without being bound by the time limits referred to in Article 10(3), in cases where:

(a) it finds that a concentration has been implemented

(i) in contravention of a condition attached to a decision under Article 6(1)(b), or

(ii) in contravention of a condition attached to a decision taken under paragraph 2 and in accordance with Article 10(2), which has found that, in the absence of the condition, the concentration would raise serious doubts as to its compatibility with the common market; or

(b) a decision has been revoked pursuant to paragraph 6.

8. The Commission shall notify its decision to the undertakings concerned and the competent authorities of the Member States without delay.

Article 9 Referral to the competent authorities of the Member States

1. The Commission may, by means of a decision notified without delay to the undertakings concerned and the competent authorities of the other Member States, refer a notified concentration to the competent authorities of the Member State concerned in the following circumstances.

2. Within 15 working days of the date of receipt of the copy of the notification, a Member State, on its own initiative or upon the invitation of the Commission, may inform the Commission, which shall inform the undertakings concerned, that:

(a) a concentration threatens to affect significantly competition in a market within that Member State, which presents all the characteristics of a distinct market, or

(b) a concentration affects competition in a market within that Member State, which presents all the characteristics of a distinct market and which does not constitute a substantial part of the common market.

3. If the Commission considers that, having regard to the market for the products or services in question and the geographical reference market within the meaning of paragraph 7, there is such a distinct market and that such a threat exists, either:

(a)   it shall itself deal with the case in accordance with this Regulation; or

(b)   it shall refer the whole or part of the case to the competent authorities of the Member State concerned with a view to the application of that State's national competition law.

If, however, the Commission considers that such a distinct market or threat does not exist, it shall adopt a decision to that effect which it shall address to the Member State concerned, and shall itself deal with the case in accordance with this Regulation.

In cases where a Member State informs the Commission pursuant to paragraph 2(b) that a concentration affects competition in a distinct market within its territory that does not form a substantial part of the common market, the Commission shall refer the whole or part of the case relating to the distinct market concerned, if it considers that such a distinct market is affected.

4.   A decision to refer or not to refer pursuant to paragraph 3 shall be taken:

(a)   as a general rule within the period provided for in Article 10(1), second subparagraph, where the Commission, pursuant to Article 6(1)(b), has not initiated proceedings; or

(b)   within 65 working days at most of the notification of the concentration concerned where the Commission has initiated proceedings under Article 6(1)(c), without taking the preparatory steps in order to adopt the necessary measures under Article 8(2), (3) or (4) to maintain or restore effective competition on the market concerned.

5.   If within the 65 working days referred to in paragraph 4(b) the Commission, despite a reminder from the Member State concerned, has not taken a decision on referral in accordance with paragraph 3 nor has taken the preparatory steps referred to in paragraph 4(b), it shall be deemed to have taken a decision to refer the case to the Member State concerned in accordance with paragraph 3(b).

6.   The competent authority of the Member State concerned shall decide upon the case without undue delay.

Within 45 working days after the Commission's referral, the competent authority of the Member State concerned shall inform the undertakings concerned of the result of the preliminary competition assessment and what further action, if any, it proposes to take. The Member State concerned may exceptionally suspend this time limit where necessary information has not been provided to it by the undertakings concerned as provided for by its national competition law.

Where a notification is requested under national law, the period of 45 working days shall begin on the working day following that of the receipt of a complete notification by the competent authority of that Member State.

7.   The geographical reference market shall consist of the area in which the undertakings concerned are involved in the supply and demand of products or services, in which the conditions of competition are sufficiently homogeneous and which can be distinguished from neighbouring areas because, in particular, conditions of competition are appreciably different in those areas. This assessment should take account in particular of the nature and characteristics of the products or services concerned, of the existence of entry barriers or of consumer preferences, of appreciable differences of the undertakings' market shares between the area concerned and neighbouring areas or of substantial price differences.

8.   In applying the provisions of this Article, the Member State concerned may take only the measures strictly necessary to safeguard or restore effective competition on the market concerned.

9.   In accordance with the relevant provisions of the Treaty, any Member State may appeal to the Court of Justice, and in particular request the application of Article 243 of the Treaty, for the purpose of applying its national competition law.

Article 10 Time limits for initiating proceedings and for decisions

1.   Without prejudice to Article 6(4), the decisions referred to in Article 6(1) shall be taken within 25 working days at most. That period shall begin on the working day following that of the receipt of a notification or, if the information to be supplied with the notification is incomplete, on the working day following that of the receipt of the

complete information. That period shall be increased to 35 working days where the Commission receives a request from a Member State in accordance with Article 9(2) or where, the undertakings concerned offer commitments pursuant to Article 6(2) with a view to rendering the concentration compatible with the common market.

2. Decisions pursuant to Article 8(1) or (2) concerning notified concentrations shall be taken as soon as it appears that the serious doubts referred to in Article 6(1)(c) have been removed, particularly as a result of modifications made by the undertakings concerned, and at the latest by the time limit laid down in paragraph 3.

3. Without prejudice to Article 8(7), decisions pursuant to Article 8(1) to (3) concerning notified concentrations shall be taken within not more than 90 working days of the date on which the proceedings are initiated. That period shall be increased to 105 working days where the undertakings concerned offer commitments pursuant to Article 8(2), second subparagraph, with a view to rendering the concentration compatible with the common market, unless these commitments have been offered less than 55 working days after the initiation of proceedings.

The periods set by the first subparagraph shall likewise be extended if the notifying parties make a request to that effect not later than 15 working days after the initiation of proceedings pursuant to Article 6(1)(c). The notifying parties may make only one such request. Likewise, at any time following the initiation of proceedings, the periods set by the first subparagraph may be extended by the Commission with the agreement of the notifying parties. The total duration of any extension or extensions effected pursuant to this subparagraph shall not exceed 20 working days.

4. The periods set by paragraphs 1 and 3 shall exceptionally be suspended where, owing to circumstances for which one of the undertakings involved in the concentration is responsible, the Commission has had to request information by decision pursuant to Article 11 or to order an inspection by decision pursuant to Article 13.

The first subparagraph shall also apply to the period referred to in Article 9(4)(b).

5. Where the Court of Justice gives a judgment which annuls the whole or part of a Commission decision which is subject to a time limit set by this Article, the concentration shall be reexamined by the Commission with a view to adopting a decision pursuant to Article 6(1).

The concentration shall be re-examined in the light of current market conditions.

The notifying parties shall submit a new notification or supplement the original notification, without delay, where the original notification becomes incomplete by reason of intervening changes in market conditions or in the information provided. Where there are no such changes, the parties shall certify this fact without delay.

The periods laid down in paragraph 1 shall start on the working day following that of the receipt of complete information in a new notification, a supplemented notification, or a certification within the meaning of the third subparagraph.

The second and third subparagraphs shall also apply in the cases referred to in Article 6(4) and Article 8(7).

6. Where the Commission has not taken a decision in accordance with Article 6(1)(b), (c), 8(1), (2) or (3) within the time limits set in paragraphs 1 and 3 respectively, the concentration shall be deemed to have been declared compatible with the common market, without prejudice to Article 9.

Article 11 Requests for information

1. In order to carry out the duties assigned to it by this Regulation, the Commission may, by simple request or by decision, require the persons referred to in Article 3(1)(b), as well as undertakings and associations of undertakings, to provide all necessary information.

2. When sending a simple request for information to a person, an undertaking or an association of undertakings, the Commission shall state the legal basis and the purpose of the request, specify what information is required and fix the time limit within which the information is to be provided, as well as the penalties provided for in Article 14 for supplying incorrect or misleading information.

3. Where the Commission requires a person, an undertaking or an association of undertakings to supply information by decision, it shall state the legal basis and the purpose of the request, specify what information is required and fix the time limit within

which it is to be provided. It shall also indicate the penalties provided for in Article 14 and indicate or impose the penalties provided for in Article 15. It shall further indicate the right to have the decision reviewed by the Court of Justice.

4.   The owners of the undertakings or their representatives and, in the case of legal persons, companies or firms, or associations having no legal personality, the persons authorised to represent them by law or by their constitution, shall supply the information requested on behalf of the undertaking concerned. Persons duly authorised to act may supply the information on behalf of their clients. The latter shall remain fully responsible if the information supplied is incomplete, incorrect or misleading.

5.   The Commission shall without delay forward a copy of any decision taken pursuant to paragraph 3 to the competent authorities of the Member State in whose territory the residence of the person or the seat of the undertaking or association of undertakings is situated, and to the competent authority of the Member State whose territory is affected. At the specific request of the competent authority of a Member State, the Commission shall also forward to that authority copies of simple requests for information relating to a notified concentration.

6.   At the request of the Commission, the governments and competent authorities of the Member States shall provide the Commission with all necessary information to carry out the duties assigned to it by this Regulation.

7.   In order to carry out the duties assigned to it by this Regulation, the Commission may interview any natural or legal person who consents to be interviewed for the purpose of collecting information relating to the subject matter of an investigation. At the beginning of the interview, which may be conducted by telephone or other electronic means, the Commission shall state the legal basis and the purpose of the interview.

Where an interview is not conducted on the premises of the Commission or by telephone or other electronic means, the Commission shall inform in advance the competent authority of the Member State in whose territory the interview takes place. If the competent authority of that Member State so requests, officials of that authority may assist the officials and other persons authorised by the Commission to conduct the interview.

Article 12 Inspections by the authorities of the Member States

1.   At the request of the Commission, the competent authorities of the Member States shall undertake the inspections which the Commission considers to be necessary under Article 13(1), or which it has ordered by decision pursuant to Article 13(4). The officials of the competent authorities of the Member States who are responsible for conducting these inspections as well as those authorised or appointed by them shall exercise their powers in accordance with their national law.

2.   If so requested by the Commission or by the competent authority of the Member State within whose territory the inspection is to be conducted, officials and other accompanying persons authorised by the Commission may assist the officials of the authority concerned.

Article 13 The Commission's powers of inspection

1.   In order to carry out the duties assigned to it by this Regulation, the Commission may conduct all necessary inspections of undertakings and associations of undertakings.

2.   The officials and other accompanying persons authorised by the Commission to conduct an inspection shall have the power:

(a)   to enter any premises, land and means of transport of undertakings and associations of undertakings;

(b)   to examine the books and other records related to the business, irrespective of the medium on which they are stored;

(c)   to take or obtain in any form copies of or extracts from such books or records;

(d)   to seal any business premises and books or records for the period and to the extent necessary for the inspection;

(e)   to ask any representative or member of staff of the undertaking or association of undertakings for explanations on facts or documents relating to the subject matter and purpose of the inspection and to record the answers.

3. Officials and other accompanying persons authorised by the Commission to conduct an inspection shall exercise their powers upon production of a written authorisation specifying the subject matter and purpose of the inspection and the penalties provided for in Article 14, in the production of the required books or other records related to the business which is incomplete or where answers to questions asked under paragraph 2 of this Article are incorrect or misleading. In good time before the inspection, the Commission shall give notice of the inspection to the competent authority of the Member State in whose territory the inspection is to be conducted.

4. Undertakings and associations of undertakings are required to submit to inspections ordered by decision of the Commission. The decision shall specify the subject matter and purpose of the inspection, appoint the date on which it is to begin and indicate the penalties provided for in Articles 14 and 15 and the right to have the decision reviewed by the Court of Justice. The Commission shall take such decisions after consulting the competent authority of the Member State in whose territory the inspection is to be conducted.

5. Officials of, and those authorised or appointed by, the competent authority of the Member State in whose territory the inspection is to be conducted shall, at the request of that authority or of the Commission, actively assist the officials and other accompanying persons authorised by the Commission. To this end, they shall enjoy the powers specified in paragraph 2.

6. Where the officials and other accompanying persons authorised by the Commission find that an undertaking opposes an inspection, including the sealing of business premises, books or records, ordered pursuant to this Article, the Member State concerned shall afford them the necessary assistance, requesting where appropriate the assistance of the police or of an equivalent enforcement authority, so as to enable them to conduct their inspection.

7. If the assistance provided for in paragraph 6 requires authorisation from a judicial authority according to national rules, such authorisation shall be applied for. Such authorisation may also be applied for as a precautionary measure.

8. Where authorisation as referred to in paragraph 7 is applied for, the national judicial authority shall ensure that the Commission decision is authentic and that the coercive measures envisaged are neither arbitrary nor excessive having regard to the subject matter of the inspection. In its control of proportionality of the coercive measures, the national judicial authority may ask the Commission, directly or through the competent authority of that Member State, for detailed explanations relating to the subject matter of the inspection. However, the national judicial authority may not call into question the necessity for the inspection nor demand that it be provided with the information in the Commission's file. The lawfulness of the Commission's decision shall be subject to review only by the Court of Justice.

Article 14 Fines

1. The Commission may by decision impose on the persons referred to in Article 3(1)b, undertakings or associations of undertakings, fines not exceeding 1% of the aggregate turnover of the undertaking or association of undertakings concerned within the meaning of Article 5 where, intentionally or negligently:
   (a) they supply incorrect or misleading information in a submission, certification, notification or supplement thereto, pursuant to Article 4, Article 10(5) or Article 22(3);
   (b) they supply incorrect or misleading information in response to a request made pursuant to Article 11(2);
   (c) in response to a request made by decision adopted pursuant to Article 11(3), they supply incorrect, incomplete or misleading information or do not supply information within the required time limit;
   (d) they produce the required books or other records related to the business in incomplete form during inspections under Article 13, or refuse to submit to an inspection ordered by decision taken pursuant to Article 13(4);
   (e) in response to a question asked in accordance with Article 13(2)(e),
      — they give an incorrect or misleading answer,
      — they fail to rectify within a time limit set by the Commission an incorrect, incomplete or misleading answer given by a member of staff, or

> — they fail or refuse to provide a complete answer on facts relating to the subject matter and purpose of an inspection ordered by a decision adopted pursuant to Article 13(4);

    (f)   seals affixed by officials or other accompanying persons authorised by the Commission in accordance with Article 13(2)(d) have been broken.

2. The Commission may by decision impose fines not exceeding 10% of the aggregate turnover of the undertaking concerned within the meaning of Article 5 on the persons referred to in Article 3(1)b or the undertakings concerned where, either intentionally or negligently, they:

    (a)   fail to notify a concentration in accordance with Articles 4 or 22(3) prior to its implementation, unless they are expressly authorised to do so by Article 7(2) or by a decision taken pursuant to Article 7(3);

    (b)   implement a concentration in breach of Article 7;

    (c)   implement a concentration declared incompatible with the common market by decision pursuant to Article 8(3) or do not comply with any measure ordered by decision pursuant to Article 8(4) or (5);

    (d)   fail to comply with a condition or an obligation imposed by decision pursuant to Articles 6(1)(b), Article 7(3) or Article 8(2), second subparagraph.

3. In fixing the amount of the fine, regard shall be had to the nature, gravity and duration of the infringement.

4. Decisions taken pursuant to paragraphs 1, 2 and 3 shall not be of a criminal law nature.

Article 15 Periodic penalty payments

1. The Commission may by decision impose on the persons referred to in Article 3(1) b, undertakings or associations of undertakings, periodic penalty payments not exceeding 5% of the average daily aggregate turnover of the undertaking or association of undertakings concerned within the meaning of Article 5 for each working day of delay, calculated from the date set in the decision, in order to compel them:

    (a)   to supply complete and correct information which it has requested by decision taken pursuant to Article 11(3);

    (b)   to submit to an inspection which it has ordered by decision taken pursuant to Article 13(4); (c) to comply with an obligation imposed by decision pursuant to Article 6(1)(b), Article 7(3) or Article 8(2), second subparagraph; or;

    (d)   to comply with any measures ordered by decision pursuant to Article 8(4) or (5).

2. Where the persons referred to in Article 3(1)(b), undertakings or associations of undertakings have satisfied the obligation which the periodic penalty payment was intended to enforce, the Commission may fix the definitive amount of the periodic penalty payments at a figure lower than that which would arise under the original decision.

Article 16 Review by the Court of Justice

The Court of Justice shall have unlimited jurisdiction within the meaning of Article 229 of the Treaty to review decisions whereby the Commission has fixed a fine or periodic penalty payments; it may cancel, reduce or increase the fine or periodic penalty payment imposed.

Article 17 Professional secrecy

1. Information acquired as a result of the application of this Regulation shall be used only for the purposes of the relevant request, investigation or hearing.

2. Without prejudice to Article 4(3), Articles 18 and 20, the Commission and the competent authorities of the Member States, their officials and other servants and other persons working under the supervision of these authorities as well as officials and civil servants of other authorities of the Member States shall not disclose information they have acquired through the application of this Regulation of the kind covered by the obligation of professional secrecy.

3. Paragraphs 1 and 2 shall not prevent publication of general information or of surveys which do not contain information relating to particular undertakings or associations of undertakings.

Article 18 Hearing of the parties and of third persons

1. Before taking any decision provided for in Article 6(3), Article 7(3), Article 8(2) to (6), and Articles 14 and 15, the Commission shall give the persons, undertakings and associations of undertakings concerned the opportunity, at every stage of the procedure up to the consultation of the Advisory Committee, of making known their views on the objections against them.

2. By way of derogation from paragraph 1, a decision pursuant to Articles 7(3) and 8(5) may be taken provisionally, without the persons, undertakings or associations of undertakings concerned being given the opportunity to make known their views beforehand, provided that the Commission gives them that opportunity as soon as possible after having taken its decision.

3. The Commission shall base its decision only on objections on which the parties have been able to submit their observations. The rights of the defence shall be fully respected in the proceedings. Access to the file shall be open at least to the parties directly involved, subject to the legitimate interest of undertakings in the protection of their business secrets.

4. In so far as the Commission or the competent authorities of the Member States deem it necessary, they may also hear other natural or legal persons. Natural or legal persons showing a sufficient interest and especially members of the administrative or management bodies of the undertakings concerned or the recognised representatives of their employees shall be entitled, upon application, to be heard.

Article 19 Liaison with the authorities of the Member States

1. The Commission shall transmit to the competent authorities of the Member States copies of notifications within three working days and, as soon as possible, copies of the most important documents lodged with or issued by the Commission pursuant to this Regulation. Such documents shall include commitments offered by the undertakings concerned vis-à-vis the Commission with a view to rendering the concentration compatible with the common market pursuant to Article 6(2) or Article 8(2), second subparagraph.

2. The Commission shall carry out the procedures set out in this Regulation in close and constant liaison with the competent authorities of the Member States, which may express their views upon those procedures. For the purposes of Article 9 it shall obtain information from the competent authority of the Member State as referred to in paragraph 2 of that Article and give it the opportunity to make known its views at every stage of the procedure up to the adoption of a decision pursuant to paragraph 3 of that Article; to that end it shall give it access to the file.

3. An Advisory Committee on concentrations shall be consulted before any decision is taken pursuant to Article 8(1) to (6), Articles 14 or 15 with the exception of provisional decisions taken in accordance with Article 18(2).

4. The Advisory Committee shall consist of representatives of the competent authorities of the Member States. Each Member State shall appoint one or two representatives; if unable to attend, they may be replaced by other representatives.
At least one of the representatives of a Member State shall be competent in matters of restrictive practices and dominant positions.

5. Consultation shall take place at a joint meeting convened at the invitation of and chaired by the Commission. A summary of the case, together with an indication of the most important documents and a preliminary draft of the decision to be taken for each case considered, shall be sent with the invitation. The meeting shall take place not less than 10 working days after the invitation has been sent. The Commission may in exceptional cases shorten that period as appropriate in order to avoid serious harm to one or more of the undertakings concerned by a concentration.

6. The Advisory Committee shall deliver an opinion on the Commission's draft decision, if necessary by taking a vote. The Advisory Committee may deliver an opinion even if some members are absent and unrepresented. The opinion shall be delivered in writing and appended to the draft decision. The Commission shall take the utmost account of the opinion delivered by the Committee. It shall inform the Committee of the manner in which its opinion has been taken into account.

7.   The Commission shall communicate the opinion of the Advisory Committee, together with the decision, to the addressees of the decision. It shall make the opinion public together with the decision, having regard to the legitimate interest of undertakings in the protection of their business secrets.

Article 20 Publication of decisions

1.   The Commission shall publish the decisions which it takes pursuant to Article 8(1) to (6), Articles 14 and 15 with the exception of provisional decisions taken in accordance with Article 18(2) together with the opinion of the Advisory Committee in the *Official Journal of the European Union*.
2.   The publication shall state the names of the parties and the main content of the decision; it shall have regard to the legitimate interest of undertakings in the protection of their business secrets.

Article 21 Application of the Regulation and jurisdiction

1.   This Regulation alone shall apply to concentrations as defined in Article 3, and Council Regulations (EC) No 1/2003, (EEC) No 1017/68, (EEC) No 4056/86 and (EEC) No 3975/87 shall not apply, except in relation to joint ventures that do not have a Community dimension and which have as their object or effect the coordination of the competitive behaviour of undertakings that remain independent.
2.   Subject to review by the Court of Justice, the Commission shall have sole jurisdiction to take the decisions provided for in this Regulation.
3.   No Member State shall apply its national legislation on competition to any concentration that has a Community dimension.
    The first subparagraph shall be without prejudice to any Member State's power to carry out any enquiries necessary for the application of Articles 4(4), 9(2) or after referral, pursuant to Article 9(3), first subparagraph, indent (b), or Article 9(5), to take the measures strictly necessary for the application of Article 9(8).
4.   Notwithstanding paragraphs 2 and 3, Member States may take appropriate measures to protect legitimate interests other than those taken into consideration by this Regulation and compatible with the general principles and other provisions of Community law.
    Public security, plurality of the media and prudential rules shall be regarded as legitimate interests within the meaning of the first subparagraph.
    Any other public interest must be communicated to the Commission by the Member State concerned and shall be recognised by the Commission after an assessment of its compatibility with the general principles and other provisions of Community law before the measures referred to above may be taken. The Commission shall inform the Member State concerned of its decision within 25 working days of that communication.

Article 22 Referral to the Commission

1.   One or more Member States may request the Commission to examine any concentration as defined in Article 3 that does not have a Community dimension within the meaning of Article 1 but affects trade between Member States and threatens to significantly affect competition within the territory of the Member State or States making the request.
    Such a request shall be made at most within 15 working days of the date on which the concentration was notified, or if no notification is required, otherwise made known to the Member State concerned.
2.   The Commission shall inform the competent authorities of the Member States and the undertakings concerned of any request received pursuant to paragraph 1 without delay. Any other Member State shall have the right to join the initial request within a period of 15 working days of being informed by the Commission of the initial request. All national time limits relating to the concentration shall be suspended until, in accordance with the procedure set out in this Article, it has been decided where the concentration shall be examined. As soon as a Member State has informed the Commission and the undertakings concerned that it does not wish to join the request, the suspension of its national time limits shall end.

3.   The Commission may, at the latest 10 working days after the expiry of the period set in paragraph 2, decide to examine, the concentration where it considers that it affects trade between Member States and threatens to significantly affect competition within the territory of the Member State or States making the request. If the Commission does not take a decision within this period, it shall be deemed to have adopted a decision to examine the concentration in accordance with the request.

The Commission shall inform all Member States and the undertakings concerned of its decision. It may request the submission of a notification pursuant to Article 4.

The Member State or States having made the request shall no longer apply their national legislation on competition to the concentration.

4.   Article 2, Article 4(2) to (3), Articles 5, 6, and 8 to 21 shall apply where the Commission examines a concentration pursuant to paragraph 3. Article 7 shall apply to the extent that the concentration has not been implemented on the date on which the Commission informs the undertakings concerned that a request has been made.

Where a notification pursuant to Article 4 is not required, the period set in Article 10(1) within which proceedings may be initiated shall begin on the working day following that on which the Commission informs the undertakings concerned that it has decided to examine the concentration pursuant to paragraph 3.

5.   The Commission may inform one or several Member States that it considers a concentration fulfils the criteria in paragraph 1. In such cases, the Commission may invite that Member State or those Member States to make a request pursuant to paragraph 1.

Article 23 Implementing provisions

1.   The Commission shall have the power to lay down in accordance with the procedure referred to in paragraph 2:

(a)   implementing provisions concerning the form, content and other details of notifications and submissions pursuant to Article 4;

(b)   implementing provisions concerning time limits pursuant to Article 4(4), (5) Articles 7, 9, 10 and 22;

(c)   the procedure and time limits for the submission and implementation of commitments pursuant to Article 6(2) and Article 8(2);

(d)   implementing provisions concerning hearings pursuant to Article 18.

2.   The Commission shall be assisted by an Advisory Committee, composed of representatives of the Member States.

(a)   Before publishing draft implementing provisions and before adopting such provisions, the Commission shall consult the Advisory Committee.

(b)   Consultation shall take place at a meeting convened at the invitation of and chaired by the Commission. A draft of the implementing provisions to be taken shall be sent with the invitation. The meeting shall take place not less than 10 working days after the invitation has been sent.

(c)   The Advisory Committee shall deliver an opinion on the draft implementing provisions, if necessary by taking a vote. The Commission shall take the utmost account of the opinion delivered by the Committee.

Article 24 Relations with third countries

1.   The Member States shall inform the Commission of any general difficulties encountered by their undertakings with concentrations as defined in Article 3 in a third country.

2.   Initially not more than one year after the entry into force of this Regulation and, thereafter periodically, the Commission shall draw up a report examining the treatment accorded to undertakings having their seat or their principal fields of activity in the Community, in the terms referred to in paragraphs 3 and 4, as regards concentrations in third countries. The Commission shall submit those reports to the Council, together with any recommendations.

3.   Whenever it appears to the Commission, either on the basis of the reports referred to in paragraph 2 or on the basis of other information, that a third country does not grant undertakings having their seat or their principal fields of activity in the Community, treatment comparable to that granted by the Community to undertakings from that country, the Commission may submit proposals to the Council for an appropriate mandate for negotiation with a view to obtaining comparable treatment for undertakings having their seat or their principal fields of activity in the Community.

4. Measures taken under this Article shall comply with the obligations of the Community or of the Member States, without prejudice to Article 307 of the Treaty, under international agreements, whether bilateral or multilateral.

Article 25 Repeal

1. Without prejudice to Article 26(2), Regulations (EEC) No 4064/89 and (EC) No 1310/97 shall be repealed with effect from 1 May 2004.
2. References to the repealed Regulations shall be construed as references to this Regulation and shall be read in accordance with the correlation table in the Annex.

Article 26 Entry into force and transitional provisions

1. This Regulation shall enter into force on the 20th day following that of its publication in the *Official Journal of the European Union*.
    It shall apply from 1 May 2004.
2. Regulation (EEC) No 4064/89 shall continue to apply to any concentration which was the subject of an agreement or announcement or where control was acquired within the meaning of Article 4(1) of that Regulation before the date of application of this Regulation, subject, in particular, to the provisions governing applicability set out in Article 25(2) and (3) of Regulation (EEC) No 4064/89 and Article 2 of Regulation (EEC) No 1310/97.
3. As regards concentrations to which this Regulation applies by virtue of accession, the date of accession shall be substituted for the date of application of this Regulation.

COMMISSION REGULATION (EU) No 330/2010
on the application of Article 101(3) of the Treaty on the Functioning of the European Union to categories of vertical agreements and concerted practices
[2010] OJ L102/1

THE EUROPEAN COMMISSION,

Having regard to the Treaty on the Functioning of the European Union,

Having regard to Regulation No 19/65/EEC of the Council of 2 March 1965 on the application of Article 85(3) of the Treaty to certain categories of agreements and concerted practices, and in particular Article 1 thereof,

Having published a draft of this Regulation,

After consulting the Advisory Committee on Restrictive Practices and Dominant Positions,

Whereas:

(1) Regulation No 19/65/EEC empowers the Commission to apply Article 101(3) of the Treaty on the Functioning of the European Union by regulation to certain categories of vertical agreements and corresponding concerted practices falling within Article 101(1) of the Treaty.

(2) Commission Regulation (EC) No 2790/1999 of 22 December 1999 on the application of Article 81(3) of the Treaty to categories of vertical agreements and concerted practices defines a category of vertical agreements which the Commission regarded as normally satisfying the conditions laid down in Article 101(3) of the Treaty. In view of the overall positive experience with the application of that Regulation, which expires on 31 May 2010, and taking into account further experience acquired since its adoption, it is appropriate to adopt a new block exemption regulation.

(3) The category of agreements which can be regarded as normally satisfying the conditions laid down in Article 101(3) of the Treaty includes vertical agreements for the purchase or sale of goods or services where those agreements are concluded between non-competing undertakings, between certain competitors or by certain associations of retailers of goods. It also includes vertical agreements containing ancillary provisions on the assignment or use of intellectual property rights. The term 'vertical agreements' should include the corresponding concerted practices.

(4) For the application of Article 101(3) of the Treaty by regulation, it is not necessary to define those vertical agreements which are capable of falling within Article 101(1) of the Treaty. In the individual assessment of agreements under Article 101(1) of the Treaty,

account has to be taken of several factors, and in particular the market structure on the supply and purchase side.

(5) The benefit of the block exemption established by this Regulation should be limited to vertical agreements for which it can be assumed with sufficient certainty that they satisfy the conditions of Article 101(3) of the Treaty.

(6) Certain types of vertical agreements can improve economic efficiency within a chain of production or distribution by facilitating better coordination between the participating undertakings. In particular, they can lead to a reduction in the transaction and distribution costs of the parties and to an optimisation of their sales and investment levels.

(7) The likelihood that such efficiency-enhancing effects will outweigh any anti-competitive effects due to restrictions contained in vertical agreements depends on the degree of market power of the parties to the agreement and, therefore, on the extent to which those undertakings face competition from other suppliers of goods or services regarded by their customers as interchangeable or substitutable for one another, by reason of the products' characteristics, their prices and their intended use.

(8) It can be presumed that, where the market share held by each of the undertakings party to the agreement on the relevant market does not exceed 30%, vertical agreements which do not contain certain types of severe restrictions of competition generally lead to an improvement in production or distribution and allow consumers a fair share of the resulting benefits.

(9) Above the market share threshold of 30%, there can be no presumption that vertical agreements falling within the scope of Article 101(1) of the Treaty will usually give rise to objective advantages of such a character and size as to compensate for the disadvantages which they create for competition. At the same time, there is no presumption that those vertical agreements are either caught by Article 101(1) of the Treaty or that they fail to satisfy the conditions of Article 101(3) of the Treaty.

(10) This Regulation should not exempt vertical agreements containing restrictions which are likely to restrict competition and harm consumers or which are not indispensable to the attainment of the efficiency-enhancing effects. In particular, vertical agreements containing certain types of severe restrictions of competition such as minimum and fixed resale-prices, as well as certain types of territorial protection, should be excluded from the benefit of the block exemption established by this Regulation irrespective of the market share of the undertakings concerned.

(11) In order to ensure access to or to prevent collusion on the relevant market, certain conditions should be attached to the block exemption. To this end, the exemption of non-compete obligations should be limited to obligations which do not exceed a defined duration. For the same reasons, any direct or indirect obligation causing the members of a selective distribution system not to sell the brands of particular competing suppliers should be excluded from the benefit of this Regulation.

(12) The market-share limitation, the non-exemption of certain vertical agreements and the conditions provided for in this Regulation normally ensure that the agreements to which the block exemption applies do not enable the participating undertakings to eliminate competition in respect of a substantial part of the products in question.

(13) The Commission may withdraw the benefit of this Regulation, pursuant to Article 29(1) of Council Regulation (EC) No 1/2003 of 16 December 2002 on the implementation of the rules on competition laid down in Articles 81 and 82 of the Treaty, where it finds in a particular case that an agreement to which the exemption provided for in this Regulation applies nevertheless has effects which are incompatible with Article 101(3) of the Treaty.

(14) The competition authority of a Member State may withdraw the benefit of this Regulation pursuant to Article 29(2) of Regulation (EC) No 1/2003 in respect of the territory of that Member State, or a part thereof where, in a particular case, an agreement to which the exemption provided for in this Regulation applies nevertheless has effects which are incompatible with Article 101(3) of the Treaty in the territory of that Member State, or in a part thereof, and where such territory has all the characteristics of a distinct geographic market.

(15) In determining whether the benefit of this Regulation should be withdrawn pursuant to Article 29 of Regulation (EC) No 1/2003, the anti-competitive effects that may derive

from the existence of parallel networks of vertical agreements that have similar effects which significantly restrict access to a relevant market or competition therein are of particular importance. Such cumulative effects may for example arise in the case of selective distribution or non compete obligations.

(16) In order to strengthen supervision of parallel networks of vertical agreements which have similar anti-competitive effects and which cover more than 50% of a given market, the Commission may by regulation declare this Regulation inapplicable to vertical agreements containing specific restraints relating to the market concerned, thereby restoring the full application of Article 101 of the Treaty to such agreements,

HAS ADOPTED THIS REGULATION:

Article 1   Definitions

1.   For the purposes of this Regulation, the following definitions shall apply:

(a)   'vertical agreement' means an agreement or concerted practice entered into between two or more undertakings each of which operates, for the purposes of the agreement or the concerted practice, at a different level of the production or distribution chain, and relating to the conditions under which the parties may purchase, sell or resell certain goods or services;

(b)   'vertical restraint' means a restriction of competition in a vertical agreement falling within the scope of Article 101(1) of the Treaty;

(c)   'competing undertaking' means an actual or potential competitor; 'actual competitor' means an undertaking that is active on the same relevant market; 'potential competitor' means an undertaking that, in the absence of the vertical agreement, would, on realistic grounds and not just as a mere theoretical possibility, in case of a small but permanent increase in relative prices be likely to undertake, within a short period of time, the necessary additional investments or other necessary switching costs to enter the relevant market;

(d)   'non-compete obligation' means any direct or indirect obligation causing the buyer not to manufacture, purchase, sell or resell goods or services which compete with the contract goods or services, or any direct or indirect obligation on the buyer to purchase from the supplier or from another undertaking designated by the supplier more than 80% of the buyer's total purchases of the contract goods or services and their substitutes on the relevant market, calculated on the basis of the value or, where such is standard industry practice, the volume of its purchases in the preceding calendar year;

(e)   'selective distribution system' means a distribution system where the supplier undertakes to sell the contract goods or services, either directly or indirectly, only to distributors selected on the basis of specified criteria and where these distributors undertake not to sell such goods or services to unauthorised distributors within the territory reserved by the supplier to operate that system;

(f)   'intellectual property rights' includes industrial property rights, know how, copyright and neighbouring rights;

(g)   'know-how' means a package of non-patented practical information, resulting from experience and testing by the supplier, which is secret, substantial and identified: in this context, 'secret' means that the know-how is not generally known or easily accessible; 'substantial' means that the know-how is significant and useful to the buyer for the use, sale or resale of the contract goods or services; 'identified' means that the know-how is described in a sufficiently comprehensive manner so as to make it possible to verify that it fulfils the criteria of secrecy and substantiality;

(h)   'buyer' includes an undertaking which, under an agreement falling within Article 101(1) of the Treaty, sells goods or services on behalf of another undertaking;

(i)   'customer of the buyer' means an undertaking not party to the agreement which purchases the contract goods or services from a buyer which is party to the agreement.

2.   For the purposes of this Regulation, the terms 'undertaking', 'supplier' and 'buyer' shall include their respective connected undertakings.

'Connected undertakings' means:
(a) undertakings in which a party to the agreement, directly or indirectly:
   (i) has the power to exercise more than half the voting rights, or
   (ii) has the power to appoint more than half the members of the supervisory board, board of management or bodies legally representing the undertaking, or
   (iii) has the right to manage the undertaking's affairs;
(b) undertakings which directly or indirectly have, over a party to the agreement, the rights or powers listed in point (a);
(c) undertakings in which an undertaking referred to in point (b) has, directly or indirectly, the rights or powers listed in point (a);
(d) undertakings in which a party to the agreement together with one or more of the undertakings referred to in points (a), (b) or (c), or in which two or more of the latter undertakings, jointly have the rights or powers listed in point (a);
(e) undertakings in which the rights or the powers listed in point (a) are jointly held by:
   (i) parties to the agreement or their respective connected undertakings referred to in points (a) to (d), or
   (ii) one or more of the parties to the agreement or one or more of their connected undertakings referred to in points (a) to (d) and one or more third parties.

Article 2 Exemption

1. Pursuant to Article 101(3) of the Treaty and subject to the provisions of this Regulation, it is hereby declared that Article 101(1) of the Treaty shall not apply to vertical agreements.
   This exemption shall apply to the extent that such agreements contain vertical restraints.

2. The exemption provided for in paragraph 1 shall apply to vertical agreements entered into between an association of undertakings and its members, or between such an association and its suppliers, only if all its members are retailers of goods and if no individual member of the association, together with its connected undertakings, has a total annual turnover exceeding EUR 50 million. Vertical agreements entered into by such associations shall be covered by this Regulation without prejudice to the application of Article 101 of the Treaty to horizontal agreements concluded between the members of the association or decisions adopted by the association.

3. The exemption provided for in paragraph 1 shall apply to vertical agreements containing provisions which relate to the assignment to the buyer or use by the buyer of intellectual property rights, provided that those provisions do not constitute the primary object of such agreements and are directly related to the use, sale or resale of goods or services by the buyer or its customers. The exemption applies on condition that, in relation to the contract goods or services, those provisions do not contain restrictions of competition having the same object as vertical restraints which are not exempted under this Regulation.

4. The exemption provided for in paragraph 1 shall not apply to vertical agreements entered into between competing undertakings. However, it shall apply where competing undertakings enter into a non-reciprocal vertical agreement and:
   (a) the supplier is a manufacturer and a distributor of goods, while the buyer is a distributor and not a competing undertaking at the manufacturing level; or
   (b) the supplier is a provider of services at several levels of trade, while the buyer provides its goods or services at the retail level and is not a competing undertaking at the level of trade where it purchases the contract services.

5. This Regulation shall not apply to vertical agreements the subject matter of which falls within the scope of any other block exemption regulation, unless otherwise provided for in such a regulation.

Article 3 Market share threshold

1. The exemption provided for in Article 2 shall apply on condition that the market share held by the supplier does not exceed 30% of the relevant market on which it sells the contract goods or services and the market share held by the buyer does not exceed 30% of the relevant market on which it purchases the contract goods or services.

2.   For the purposes of paragraph 1, where in a multi party agreement an undertaking buys the contract goods or services from one undertaking party to the agreement and sells the contract goods or services to another undertaking party to the agreement, the market share of the first undertaking must respect the market share threshold provided for in that paragraph both as a buyer and a supplier in order for the exemption provided for in Article 2 to apply.

Article 4   Restrictions that remove the benefit of the block exemption — hardcore restrictions

The exemption provided for in Article 2 shall not apply to vertical agreements which, directly or indirectly, in isolation or in combination with other factors under the control of the parties, have as their object:

(a)   the restriction of the buyer's ability to determine its sale price, without prejudice to the possibility of the supplier to impose a maximum sale price or recommend a sale price, provided that they do not amount to a fixed or minimum sale price as a result of pressure from, or incentives offered by, any of the parties;

(b)   the restriction of the territory into which, or of the customers to whom, a buyer party to the agreement, without prejudice to a restriction on its place of establishment, may sell the contract goods or services, except:

(i)   the restriction of active sales into the exclusive territory or to an exclusive customer group reserved to the supplier or allocated by the supplier to another buyer, where such a restriction does not limit sales by the customers of the buyer,

(ii)   the restriction of sales to end users by a buyer operating at the wholesale level of trade,

(iii)   the restriction of sales by the members of a selective distribution system to unauthorised distributors within the territory reserved by the supplier to operate that system, and

(iv)   the restriction of the buyer's ability to sell components, supplied for the purposes of incorporation, to customers who would use them to manufacture the same type of goods as those produced by the supplier;

(c)   the restriction of active or passive sales to end users by members of a selective distribution system operating at the retail level of trade, without prejudice to the possibility of prohibiting a member of the system from operating out of an unauthorised place of establishment;

(d)   the restriction of cross-supplies between distributors within a selective distribution system, including between distributors operating at different level of trade;

(e)   the restriction, agreed between a supplier of components and a buyer who incorporates those components, of the supplier's ability to sell the components as spare parts to end-users or to repairers or other service providers not entrusted by the buyer with the repair or servicing of its goods.

Article 5   Excluded restrictions

1.   The exemption provided for in Article 2 shall not apply to the following obligations contained in vertical agreements:

(a)   any direct or indirect non-compete obligation, the duration of which is indefinite or exceeds five years;

(b)   any direct or indirect obligation causing the buyer, after termination of the agreement, not to manufacture, purchase, sell or resell goods or services;

(c)   any direct or indirect obligation causing the members of a selective distribution system not to sell the brands of particular competing suppliers.

For the purposes of point (a) of the first subparagraph, a non-compete obligation which is tacitly renewable beyond a period of five years shall be deemed to have been concluded for an indefinite duration.

2.   By way of derogation from paragraph 1(a), the time limitation of five years shall not apply where the contract goods or services are sold by the buyer from premises and land owned by the supplier or leased by the supplier from third parties not connected with the buyer, provided that the duration of the non-compete obligation does not exceed the period of occupancy of the premises and land by the buyer.

3. By way of derogation from paragraph 1(b), the exemption provided for in Article 2 shall apply to any direct or indirect obligation causing the buyer, after termination of the agreement, not to manufacture, purchase, sell or resell goods or services where the following conditions are fulfilled:
   (a) the obligation relates to goods or services which compete with the contract goods or services;
   (b) the obligation is limited to the premises and land from which the buyer has operated during the contract period;
   (c) the obligation is indispensable to protect know-how transferred by the supplier to the buyer;
   (d) the duration of the obligation is limited to a period of one year after termination of the agreement.
   Paragraph 1(b) is without prejudice to the possibility of imposing a restriction which is unlimited in time on the use and disclosure of know-how which has not entered the public domain.

Article 6 Non-application of this Regulation

Pursuant to Article 1a of Regulation No 19/65/EEC, the Commission may by regulation declare that, where parallel networks of similar vertical restraints cover more than 50% of a relevant market, this Regulation shall not apply to vertical agreements containing specific restraints relating to that market.

Article 7 Application of the market share threshold

For the purposes of applying the market share thresholds provided for in Article 3 the following rules shall apply:
   (a) the market share of the supplier shall be calculated on the basis of market sales value data and the market share of the buyer shall be calculated on the basis of market purchase value data. If market sales value or market purchase value data are not available, estimates based on other reliable market information, including market sales and purchase volumes, may be used to establish the market share of the undertaking concerned;
   (b) the market shares shall be calculated on the basis of data relating to the preceding calendar year;
   (c) the market share of the supplier shall include any goods or services supplied to vertically integrated distributors for the purposes of sale;
   (d) if a market share is initially not more than 30% but subsequently rises above that level without exceeding 35%, the exemption provided for in Article 2 shall continue to apply for a period of two consecutive calendar years following the year in which the 30% market share threshold was first exceeded;
   (e) if a market share is initially not more than 30% but subsequently rises above 35%, the exemption provided for in Article 2 shall continue to apply for one calendar year following the year in which the level of 35% was first exceeded;
   (f) the benefit of points (d) and (e) may not be combined so as to exceed a period of two calendar years;
   (g) the market share held by the undertakings referred to in point (e) of the second subparagraph of Article 1(2) shall be apportioned equally to each undertaking having the rights or the powers listed in point (a) of the second subparagraph of Article 1(2).

Article 8 Application of the turnover threshold

1. For the purpose of calculating total annual turnover within the meaning of Article 2(2), the turnover achieved during the previous financial year by the relevant party to the vertical agreement and the turnover achieved by its connected undertakings in respect of all goods and services, excluding all taxes and other duties, shall be added together. For this purpose, no account shall be taken of dealings between the party to the vertical agreement and its connected undertakings or between its connected undertakings.

2. The exemption provided for in Article 2 shall remain applicable where, for any period of two consecutive financial years, the total annual turnover threshold is exceeded by no more than 10%.

Article 9 Transitional period

The prohibition laid down in Article 101(1) of the Treaty shall not apply during the period from 1 June 2010 to 31 May 2011 in respect of agreements already in force on 31 May 2010 which do not satisfy the conditions for exemption provided for in this Regulation but which, on 31 May 2010, satisfied the conditions for exemption provided for in Regulation (EC) No 2790/1999.

Article 10 Period of validity

This Regulation shall enter into force on 1 June 2010.

It shall expire on 31 May 2022.

This Regulation shall be binding in its entirety and directly applicable in all Member States.

COMMISSION NOTICE – GUIDELINES ON THE EFFECT ON TRADE CONCEPT CONTAINED IN ARTICLES 81 AND 82 OF THE TREATY [NOW ARTICLES 101 AND 102 TFEU] (2004/C101/07)

SUMMARY

Articles 101 and 102 of the Treaty on the Functioning of the European Union (TFEU) (ex-Articles 81 and 82 of the Treaty Establishing the European Community (TEC)) are applicable to horizontal and vertical agreements and practices on the part of undertakings which may affect trade between European Union (EU) countries.

The present guidelines spell out a rule indicating when agreements are in general unlikely to be capable of appreciably affecting trade between EU countries. They are not intended to be exhaustive. The aim is to set out the methodology for the application of the effect on trade concept and to provide guidance on its application in frequently occurring situations. Although not binding on them, these guidelines also intend to give guidance to the courts and authorities of the EU countries in their application of the effect on trade concept contained in Articles 101 and 102 TFEU.

The effect on trade criterion confines the scope of application of Articles 101 and 102 TFEU to agreements and practices that are capable of having a minimum level of cross-border effects within the EU.

In the case of Article 101 TFEU, it is the agreement that must be capable of affecting trade between EU countries. If the agreement as a whole is capable of affecting trade between EU countries, there is EU law jurisdiction in respect of the entire agreement, including any parts of the agreement that individually do not affect trade between EU countries. In cases where the contractual relations between the same parties cover several activities, these activities must, in order to form part of the same agreement, be directly linked and form an integral part of the same overall business arrangement. If not, each activity constitutes a separate agreement.

In the case of Article 102 TFEU, it is the abuse that must affect trade between EU countries. This does not imply, however, that each element of the behaviour must be assessed in isolation. Conduct that forms part of an overall strategy pursued by the dominant undertaking must be assessed in terms of its overall impact. Where a dominant undertaking adopts various practices in pursuit of the same aim, for instance practices that aim at eliminating or foreclosing competitors, in order for Article 102 TFEU to be applicable to all the practices forming part of this overall strategy, it is sufficient that at least one of these practices is capable of affecting trade between EU countries.

Analysis of the concept of affecting trade requires that three aspects in particular be addressed:

- the concept of 'trade between EU countries': the concept of 'trade' is not limited to traditional exchanges of goods and services across borders. It is a wider concept, covering all cross-border economic activity including establishment. This interpretation is consistent with the fundamental objective of the Treaty to promote free movement of goods, services, persons and capital. The requirement that there must be an effect on trade 'between EU countries' implies that there must be an impact on cross-border economic activity involving at least two EU countries;

— the notion 'may affect': the function of the notion 'may affect' is to define the nature of the required impact on trade between EU countries. According to the standard test developed by the Court of Justice, the notion 'may affect' implies that it must be possible to foresee with a sufficient degree of probability on the basis of a set of objective factors of law or fact that the agreement or practice may have an influence, direct or indirect, actual or potential, on the pattern of trade between EU countries. In cases where the agreement or practice is liable to affect the competitive structure inside the EU, EU law jurisdiction is established;

— the concept of 'appreciability': the effect on trade criterion incorporates a quantitative element, limiting EU law jurisdiction to agreements and practices that are capable of having effects of a certain magnitude. Appreciability can be appraised in particular by reference to the position and the importance of the relevant undertakings on the market for the products concerned. The assessment of appreciability depends on the circumstances of each individual case, in particular the nature of the agreement and practice, the nature of the products covered and the market position of the undertakings concerned. In its notice on agreements of minor importance, the Commission states that agreements between small and medium-sized enterprises rarely affect trade between EU countries to a significant degree. The Commission holds the view that in principle agreements are not capable of appreciably affecting trade between EU countries when the following cumulative conditions are met:

  — The threshold of EUR 40 million is calculated on the basis of total EU sales excluding tax during the previous financial year by the undertakings concerned, of the products covered by the agreement (the contract products). Sales between entities that form part of the same undertaking are excluded. In order to apply the market share threshold, it is necessary to determine the relevant market.

  — The Commission will apply the negative presumption to the application of the concept of affecting trade to all agreements, including agreements that by their very nature are capable of affecting trade between EU countries as well as agreements that involve trade with undertakings located in non-EU countries. Outside the scope of negative presumption, the Commission will take account of qualitative elements relating to the nature of the agreement or practice and the nature of the products that they concern.

  — The positive presumption relating to appreciability in the case of agreements also takes into account whether and how agreements and practices cover several EU countries, whether they are confined to a single EU country or to part of a single EU country. Agreements and practices involving non-EU countries are also dealt with. In the case of agreements and practices whose object is not to restrict competition inside the EU, it is normally necessary to proceed with a more detailed analysis of whether or not cross-border economic activity inside the EU, and thus patterns of trade between EU countries, are capable of being affected.

Editor's note: This is a summary of the full document which can be found here: https://eur-lex. europa.eu/legal-content/EN/TXT/?uri=celex%3A52004XC0427%2806%29 [Accessed 26 March 2018].

COMMUNICATION FROM THE COMMISSION
NOTICE ON AGREEMENTS OF MINOR IMPORTANCE WHICH DO NOT APPRECIABLY RESTRICT COMPETITION UNDER ARTICLE 101(1) OF THE TREATY ON THE FUNCTIONING OF THE EUROPEAN UNION (DE MINIMIS NOTICE)
(2014/C 291/01)

I.

1. Article 101(1) of the Treaty on the Functioning of the European Union prohibits agreements between undertakings which may affect trade between Member States and which have as their object or effect the prevention, restriction or distortion of competition within the internal market. The Court of Justice of the European Union has clarified that that provision

is not applicable where the impact of the agreement on trade between Member States or on competition is not appreciable.

2.   The Court of Justice has also clarified that an agreement which may affect trade between Member States and which has as its object the prevention, restriction or distortion of competition within the internal market constitutes, by its nature and independently of any concrete effects that it may have, an appreciable restriction of competition. This Notice therefore does not cover agreements which have as their object the prevention, restriction or distortion of competition within the internal market.

3.   In this Notice the Commission indicates, with the help of market share thresholds, the circumstances in which it considers that agreements which may have as their effect the prevention, restriction or distortion of competition within the internal market do not constitute an appreciable restriction of competition under Article 101 of the Treaty. This negative definition of appreciability does not imply that agreements between undertakings which exceed the thresholds set out in this Notice constitute an appreciable restriction of competition. Such agreements may still have only a negligible effect on competition and may therefore not be prohibited by Article 101(1) of the Treaty.

4.   Agreements may also fall outside Article 101(1) of the Treaty because they are not capable of appreciably affecting trade between Member States. This Notice does not indicate what constitutes an appreciable effect on trade between Member States. Guidance to that effect is to be found in the Commission's Notice on effect on trade, in which the Commission quantifies, with the help of the combination of a 5% market share threshold and a EUR 40 million turnover threshold, which agreements are in principle not capable of appreciably affecting trade between Member States. Such agreements normally fall outside Article 101(1) of the Treaty even if they have as their object the prevention, restriction or distortion of competition.

5.   In cases covered by this Notice, the Commission will not institute proceedings either upon a complaint or on its own initiative. In addition, where the Commission has instituted proceedings but undertakings can demonstrate that they have assumed in good faith that the market shares mentioned in points 8, 9, 10 and 11 were not exceeded, the Commission will not impose fines. Although not binding on them, this Notice is also intended to give guidance to the courts and competition authorities of the Member States in their application of Article 101 of the Treaty.

6.   The principles set out in this Notice also apply to decisions by associations of undertakings and to concerted practices.

7.   This Notice is without prejudice to any interpretation of Article 101 of the Treaty which may be given by the Court of Justice of the European Union.

II.

8.   The Commission holds the view that agreements between undertakings which may affect trade between Member States and which may have as their effect the prevention, restriction or distortion of competition within the internal market, do not appreciably restrict competition within the meaning of Article 101(1) of the Treaty:

(a)   if the aggregate market share held by the parties to the agreement does not exceed 10% on any of the relevant markets affected by the agreement, where the agreement is made between undertakings which are actual or potential competitors on any of those markets (agreements between competitors); or

(b)   if the market share held by each of the parties to the agreement does not exceed 15% on any of the relevant markets affected by the agreement, where the agreement is made between undertakings which are not actual or potential competitors on any of those markets (agreements between non-competitors).

9.   In cases where it is difficult to classify the agreement as either an agreement between competitors or an agreement between non-competitors the 10% threshold is applicable.

10.   Where, in a relevant market, competition is restricted by the cumulative effect of agreements for the sale of goods or services entered into by different suppliers or distributors (cumulative foreclosure effect of parallel networks of agreements having similar effects on the market), the market share thresholds set out in point 8 and 9 are reduced to 5%,

both for agreements between competitors and for agreements between non-competitors. Individual suppliers or distributors with a market share not exceeding 5%, are in general not considered to contribute significantly to a cumulative foreclosure effect. A cumulative foreclosure effect is unlikely to exist if less than 30% of the relevant market is covered by parallel (networks of) agreements having similar effects.

11. The Commission also holds the view that agreements do not appreciably restrict competition if the market shares of the parties to the agreement do not exceed the thresholds of respectively 10%, 15% and 5% set out in points 8, 9 and 10 during two successive calendar years by more than 2 percentage points.

12. In order to calculate the market share, it is necessary to determine the relevant market. This consists of the relevant product market and the relevant geographic market. When defining the relevant market, reference should be had to the Notice on the definition of the relevant market. The market shares are to be calculated on the basis of sales value data or, where appropriate, purchase value data. If value data are not available, estimates based on other reliable market information, including volume data, may be used.

13. In view of the clarification of the Court of Justice referred to in point 2, this Notice does not cover agreements which have as their object the prevention, restriction or distortion of competition within the internal market. The Commission will thus not apply the safe harbour created by the market share thresholds set out in points 8, 9, 10 and 11 to such agreements. For instance, as regards agreements between competitors, the Commission will not apply the principles set out in this Notice to, in particular, agreements containing restrictions which, directly or indirectly, have as their object: a) the fixing of prices when selling products to third parties; b) the limitation of output or sales; or c) the allocation of markets or customers. Likewise, the Commission will not apply the safe harbour created by those market share thresholds to agreements containing any of the restrictions that are listed as hardcore restrictions in any current or future Commission block exemption regulation, which are considered by the Commission to generally constitute restrictions by object.

14. The safe harbour created by the market share thresholds set out in points 8, 9, 10 and 11 is particularly relevant for categories of agreements not covered by any Commission block exemption regulation. The safe harbour is also relevant for agreements covered by a Commission block exemption regulation to the extent that those agreements contain a so-called excluded restriction, that is a restriction not listed as a hardcore restriction but nonetheless not covered by the Commission block exemption regulation.

15. For the purpose of this Notice, the terms 'undertaking', 'party to the agreement', 'distributor' and 'supplier' include their respective connected undertakings.

16. For the purpose of the Notice 'connected undertakings' are:
   (a) undertakings in which a party to the agreement, directly or indirectly:
      (i) has the power to exercise more than half the voting rights, or
      (ii) has the power to appoint more than half the members of the supervisory board, board of management or bodies legally representing the undertaking, or
      (iii) has the right to manage the undertaking's affairs;
   (b) undertakings which directly or indirectly have, over a party to the agreement, the rights or powers listed in (a);
   (c) undertakings in which an undertaking referred to in (b) has, directly or indirectly, the rights or powers listed in (a);
   (d) undertakings in which a party to the agreement together with one or more of the undertakings referred to in (a), (b) or (c), or in which two or more of the latter undertakings, jointly have the rights or powers listed in (a);
   (e) undertakings in which the rights or the powers listed in (a) are jointly held by:
      (i) parties to the agreement or their respective connected undertakings referred to in (a) to (d), or
      (ii) one or more of the parties to the agreement or one or more of their connected undertakings referred to in (a) to (d) and one or more third parties.

17. For the purposes of point (e) in point 16, the market share held by these jointly held undertakings is apportioned equally to each undertaking having the rights or the powers listed in point (a) in point 16.

COMMISSION NOTICE ON THE DEFINITION OF RELEVANT MARKET FOR THE PURPOSES OF COMMUNITY COMPETITION LAW [1997] OJ C372/03

I INTRODUCTION

1. The purpose of this notice is to provide guidance as to how the Commission applies the concept of relevant product and geographic market in its ongoing enforcement of Community competition law, in particular the application of Council Regulation No 17 and (EEC) No 4064/89, their equivalents in other sectoral applications such as transport, coal and steel, and agriculture, and the relevant provisions of the EEA Agreement. Throughout this notice, references to Articles 85 and 86 of the Treaty and to merger control are to be understood as referring to the equivalent provisions in the EEA Agreement and the ECSC Treaty.

2. Market definition is a tool to identify and define the boundaries of competition between firms. It serves to establish the framework within which competition policy is applied by the Commission. The main purpose of market definition is to identify in a systematic way the competitive constraints that the undertakings involved face. The objective of defining a market in both its product and geographic dimension is to identify those actual competitors of the undertakings involved that are capable of constraining those undertakings' behaviour and of preventing them from behaving independently of effective competitive pressure. It is from this perspective that the market definition makes it possible inter alia to calculate market shares that would convey meaningful information regarding market power for the purposes of assessing dominance or for the purposes of applying Article 85.

3. It follows from point 2 that the concept of 'relevant market' is different from other definitions of market often used in other contexts. For instance, companies often use the term 'market' to refer to the area where it sells its products or to refer broadly to the industry or sector where it belongs.

4. The definition of the relevant market in both its product and its geographic dimensions often has a decisive influence on the assessment of a competition case. By rendering public the procedures which the Commission follows when considering market definition and by indicating the criteria and evidence on which it relies to reach a decision, the Commission expects to increase the transparency of its policy and decision-making in the area of competition policy.

5. Increased transparency will also result in companies and their advisers being able to better anticipate the possibility that the Commission may raise competition concerns in an individual case. Companies could, therefore, take such a possibility into account in their own internal decision-making when contemplating, for instance, acquisitions, the creation of joint ventures, or the establishment of certain agreements. It is also intended that companies should be in a better position to understand what sort of information the Commission considers relevant for the purposes of market definition.

6. The Commission's interpretation of 'relevant market' is without prejudice to the interpretation which may be given by the Court of Justice or the Court of First Instance of the European Communities.

II DEFINITION OF RELEVANT MARKET

Definition of relevant product market and relevant geographic market

7. The Regulations based on Article 85 and 86 of the Treaty, in particular in section 6 of Form A/B with respect to Regulation No 17, as well as in section 6 of Form CO with respect to Regulation (EEC) No 4064/89 on the control of concentrations having a Community dimension have laid down the following definitions, 'Relevant product markets' are defined as follows:

'A relevant product market comprises all those products and/or services which are regarded as interchangeable or substitutable by the consumer, by reason of the products' characteristics, their prices and their intended use'.

8. 'Relevant geographic markets' are defined as follows:
    'The relevant geographic market comprises the area in which the undertakings concerned are involved in the supply and demand of products or services, in which the conditions of competition are sufficiently homogeneous and which can be distinguished from neighbouring areas because the conditions of competition are appreciably different in those area'.

9. The relevant market within which to assess a given competition issue is therefore established by the combination of the product and geographic markets. The Commission interprets the definitions in paragraphs 7 an 8 (which reflect the case-law of the Court of Justice and the Court of First Instance as well as its own decision-making practice) according to the orientations defined in this notice.

Concept of relevant market and objectives of Community competition policy

10. The concept of relevant market is closely related to the objectives pursued under Community competition policy. For example, under the Community's merger control, the objective in controlling structural changes in the supply of a product/service is to prevent the creation or reinforcement of a dominant position as a result of which effective competition would be significantly impeded in a substantial part of the common market. Under the Community's competition rules, a dominant position is such that a firm or group of firms would be in a position to behave to an appreciable extent independently of its competitors, customers and ultimately of its consumers. Such a position would usually arise when a firm or group of firms accounted for a large share of the supply in any given market, provided that other factors analysed in the assessment (such as entry barriers, customers' capacity to react, etc.) point in the same direction.

11. The same approach is followed by the Commission in its application of Article 86 of the Treaty to firms that enjoy a single or collective dominant position. Within the meaning of Regulation No 17, the Commission has the power to investigate and bring to an end abuses of such a dominant position, which must also be defined by reference to the relevant market. Markets may also need to be defined in the application of Article 85 of the Treaty, in particular, in determining whether an appreciable restriction of competition exists or in establishing if the condition pursuant to Article 85(3)(b) for an exemption from the application of Article 85(1) is met.

12. The criteria for defining the relevant market are applied generally for the analysis of certain types of behaviour in the market and for the analysis of structural changes in the supply of products. This methodology, though, might lead to different results depending on the nature of the competition issue being examined. For instance, the scope of the geographic market might be different when analysing a concentration, where the analysis is essentially prospective, from an analysis of past behaviour. The different time horizon considered in each case might lead to the result that different geographic markets are defined for the same products depending on whether the Commission is examining a change in the structure of supply, such as a concentration or a cooperative joint venture, or examining issues relating to certain past behaviour.

Basic principles for market definition

Competitive constraints

13. Firms are subject to three main sources or competitive constraints: demand substitutability, supply substitutability and potential competition. From an economic point of view, for the definition of the relevant market, demand substitution constitutes the most immediate and effective disciplinary force on the suppliers of a given product, in particular in relation to their pricing decisions. A firm or a group of firms cannot have a significant impact on the prevailing conditions of sale, such as prices, if its customers are in a position to switch easily to available substitute products or to suppliers located elsewhere. Basically, the exercise of market definition consists in identifying the effective alternative sources of supply for the customers of the undertakings involved, in terms both of products/services and of geographic location of suppliers.

14. The competitive constraints arising from supply side substitutability other than those described in paragraphs 20 to 23 and from potential competition are in general less immediate and in any case require an analysis of additional factors. As a result such constraints are taken into account at the assessment stage of competition analysis.

Demand substitution

15. The assessment of demand substitution entails a determination of the range of products which are viewed as substitutes by the consumer. One way of making this determination can be viewed as a speculative experiment, postulating a hypothetical small, lasting change in relative prices and evaluating the likely reactions of customers to that increase. The exercise of market definition focuses on prices for operational and practical purposes, and more precisely on demand substitution arising from small, permanent changes in relative prices. This concept can provide clear indications as to the evidence that is relevant in defining markets.

16. Conceptually, this approach means that, starting from the type of products that the undertakings involved sell and the area in which they sell them, additional products and areas will be included in, or excluded from, the market definition depending on whether competition from these other products and areas affect or restrain sufficiently the pricing of the parties' products in the short term.

17. The question to be answered is whether the parties' customers would switch to readily available substitutes or to suppliers located elsewhere in response to a hypothetical small (in the range 5% to 10%) but permanent relative price increase in the products and areas being considered. If substitution were enough to make the price increase unprofitable because of the resulting loss of sales, additional substitutes and areas are included in the relevant market. This would be done until the set of products and geographical areas is such that small, permanent increases in relative prices would be profitable. The equivalent analysis is applicable in cases concerning the concentration of buying power, where the starting point would then be the supplier and the price test serves to identify the alternative distribution channels or outlets for the supplier's products. In the application of these principles, careful account should be taken of certain particular situations as described within paragraphs 56 and 58.

18. A practical example of this test can be provided by its application to a merger of, for instance, soft-drink bottlers. An issue to examine in such a case would be to decide whether different flavours of soft drinks belong to the same market. In practice, the question to address would be whether consumers of flavour A would switch to other flavours when confronted with a permanent price increase of 5% to 10% for flavour A. If a sufficient number of consumers would switch to, say, flavour B, to such an extent that the price increase for flavour A would not be profitable owing to the resulting loss of sales, then the market would comprise at least flavours A and B. The process would have to be extended in addition to other available flavours until a set of products is identified for which a price rise would not induce a sufficient substitution in demand.

19. Generally, and in particular for the analysis of merger cases, the price to take into account will be the prevailing market price. This may not be the case where the prevailing price has been determined in the absence of sufficient competition. In particular for the investigation of abuses of dominant positions, the fact that the prevailing price might already have been substantially increased will be taken into account.

Supply substitution

20. Supply-side substitutability may also be taken into account when defining markets in those situations in which its effects are equivalent to those of demand substitution in terms of effectiveness and immediacy. This means that suppliers are able to switch production to the relevant products and market them in the short term without incurring significant additional costs or risks in response to small and permanent changes in relative prices. When these conditions are met, the additional production that is put on the market will have a disciplinary effect on the competitive behaviour of the companies involved. Such an impact in terms of effectiveness and immediacy is equivalent to the demand substitution effect.

21. These situations typically arise when companies market a wide range of qualities or grades of one product; even if, for a given final customer or group of consumers, the different qualities are not substitutable, the different qualities will be grouped into one product market, provided that most of the suppliers are able to offer and sell the various qualities immediately and without the significant increases in costs described above. In such cases, the relevant product market will encompass all products that are substitutable in demand and supply, and the current sales of those products will be

aggregated so as to give the total value or volume of the market. The same reasoning may lead to group different geographic areas.

22. A practical example of the approach to supply-side substitutability when defining product markets is to be found in the case of paper. Paper is usually supplied in a range of different qualities, from standard writing paper to high quality papers to be used, for instance, to publish art books. From a demand point of view, different qualities of paper cannot be used for any given use, i.e. an art book or a high quality publication cannot be based on lower quality papers. However, paper plants are prepared to manufacture the different qualities, and production can be adjusted with negligible costs and in a short time-frame. In the absence of particular difficulties in distribution, paper manufacturers are able therefore, to compete for orders of the various qualities, in particular if orders are placed with sufficient lead time to allow for modification of production plans. Under such circumstances, the Commission would not define a separate market for each quality of paper and its respective use. The various qualities of paper are included in the relevant market, and their sales added up to estimate total market value and volume.

23. When supply-side substitutability would entail the need to adjust significantly existing tangible and intangible assets, additional investments, strategic decisions or time delays, it will not be considered at the stage of market definition. Examples where supply-side substitution did not induce the Commission to enlarge the market are offered in the area of consumer products, in particular for branded beverages. Although bottling plants may in principle bottle different beverages, there are costs and lead times involved (in terms of advertising, product testing and distribution) before the products can actually be sold. In these cases, the effects of supply-side substitutability and other forms of potential competition would then be examined at a later stage.

Potential competition

24. The third source of competitive constraint, potential competition, is not taken into account when defining markets, since the conditions under which potential competition will actually represent an effective competitive constraint depend on the analysis of specific factors and circumstances related to the conditions of entry. If required, this analysis is only carried out at a subsequent stage, in general once the position of the companies involved in the relevant market has already been ascertained, and when such position gives rise to concerns from a competition point of view.

III EVIDENCE RELIED ON TO DEFINE RELEVANT MARKETS

The process of defining the relevant market in practice

Product dimension

25. There is a range of evidence permitting an assessment of the extent to which substitution would take place. In individual cases, certain types of evidence will be determinant, depending very much on the characteristics and specificity of the industry and products or services that are being examined. The same type of evidence may be of no importance in other cases. In most cases, a decision will have to be based on the consideration of a number of criteria and different items of evidence. The Commission follows an open approach to empirical evidence, aimed at making an effective use of all available information which may be relevant in individual cases. The Commission does not follow a rigid hierarchy of different sources of information or types of evidence.

26. The process of defining relevant markets may be summarised as follows: on the basis of the preliminary information available or information submitted by the undertakings involved, the Commission will usually be in a position to broadly establish the possible relevant markets within which, for instance, a concentration or a restriction of competition has to be assessed. In general, and for all practical purposes when handling individual cases, the question will usually be to decide on a few alternative possible relevant markets. For instance, with respect to the product market, the issue will often be to establish whether product A and product B belong or do not belong to the same product market. It is often the case that the inclusion of product B would be enough to remove any competition concerns.

27. In such situations it is not necessary to consider whether the market includes additional products, or to reach a definitive conclusion on the precise product market. If under the conceivable alternative market definitions the operation in question does not raise competition concerns, the question of market definition will be left open, reducing thereby the burden on companies to supply information.

Geographic dimension

28. The Commission's approach to geographic market definition might be summarised as follows: it will take a preliminary view of the scope of the geographic market on the basis of broad indications as to the distribution of market shares between the parties and their competitors, as well as a preliminary analysis of pricing and price differences at national and Community or EEA level. This initial view is used basically as a working hypothesis to focus the Commission's enquiries for the purposes of arriving at a precise geographic market definition.

29. The reasons behind any particular configuration of prices and market shares need to be explored. Companies might enjoy high market shares in their domestic markets just because of the weight of the past, and conversely, a homogeneous presence of companies throughout the EEA might be consistent with national or regional geographic markets. The initial working hypothesis will therefore be checked against an analysis of demand characteristics (importance of national or local preferences, current patterns of purchases of customers, product differentiation/brands, other) in order to establish whether companies in different areas do indeed constitute a real alternative source of supply for consumers. The theoretical experiment is again based on substitution arising from changes in relative prices, and the question to answer is again whether the customers of the parties would switch their orders to companies located elsewhere in the short term and at a negligible cost.

30. If necessary, a further check on supply factors will be carried out to ensure that those companies located in differing areas do not face impediments in developing their sales on competitive terms throughout the whole geographic market. This analysis will include an examination of requirements for a local presence in order to sell in that area the conditions of access to distribution channels, costs associated with setting up a distribution network, and the presence or absence of regulatory barriers arising from public procurement, price regulations, quotas and tariffs limiting trade or production, technical standards, monopolies, freedom of establishment, requirements for administrative authorisations, packaging regulations, etc. In short, the Commission will identify possible obstacles and barriers isolating companies located in a given area from the competitive pressure of companies located outside that area, so as to determine the precise degree of market interpenetration at national, European or global level.

31. The actual pattern and evolution of trade flows offers useful supplementary indications as to the economic importance of each demand or supply factor mentioned above, and the extent to which they may or may not constitute actual barriers creating different geographic markets. The analysis of trade flows will generally address the question of transport costs and the extent to which these may hinder trade between different areas, having regard to plant location, costs of production and relative price levels.

Market integration in the Community

32. Finally, the Commission also takes into account the continuing process of market integration, in particular in the Community, when defining geographic markets, especially in the area of concentrations and structural joint ventures. The measures adopted and implemented in the internal market programme to remove barriers to trade and further integrate the Community markets cannot be ignored when assessing the effects on competition of a concentration or a structural joint venture. A situation where national markets have been artificially isolated from each other because of the existence of legislative barriers that have now been removed will generally lead to a cautious assessment of past evidence regarding prices, market shares or trade patterns. A process of market integration that would, in the short term, lead to wider geographic markets may therefore be taken into consideration when defining the geographic market for the purposes of assessing concentrations and joint ventures.

The process of gathering evidence

33. When a precise market definition is deemed necessary, the Commission will often contact the main customers and the main companies in the industry to enquire into their views about the boundaries of product and geographic markets and to obtain the necessary factual evidence to reach a conclusion. The Commission might also contact the relevant professional associations, and companies active in upstream markets, so as to be able to define, in so far as necessary, separate product and geographic markets, for different levels of production or distribution of the products/services in question. It might also request additional information to the undertakings involved.

34. Where appropriate, the Commission will address written requests for information to the market players mentioned above. These requests will usually include questions relating to the perceptions of companies about reactions to hypothetical price increases and their views of the boundaries of the relevant market. They will also ask for provision of the factual information the Commission deems necessary to reach a conclusion on the extent of the relevant market. The Commission might also discuss with marketing directors or other officers of those companies to gain a better understanding on how negotiations between suppliers and customers take place and better understand issues relating to the definition of the relevant market. Where appropriate, they might also carry out visits or inspections to the premises of the parties, their customers and/or their competitors, in order to better understand how products are manufactured and sold.

35. The type of evidence relevant to reach a conclusion as to the product market can be categorised as follows:

Evidence to define markets — product dimension

36. An analysis of the product characteristics and its intended use allows the Commission, as a first step, to limit the field of investigation of possible substitutes. However, product characteristics and intended use are insufficient to show whether two products are demand substitutes. Functional interchangeability or similarity in characteristics may not, in themselves, provide sufficient criteria, because the responsiveness of customers to relative price changes may be determined by other considerations as well. For example, there may be different competitive constraints in the original equipment market for car components and in spare parts, thereby leading to a separate delineation of two relevant markets. Conversely, differences in product characteristics are not in themselves sufficient to exclude demand substitutability, since this will depend to a large extent on how customers value different characteristics.

37. The type of evidence the Commission considers relevant to assess whether two products are demand substitutes can be categorised as follows:

38. Evidence of substitution in the recent past. In certain cases, it is possible to analyse evidence relating to recent past events or shocks in the market that offer actual examples of substitution between two products. When available, this sort of information will normally be fundamental for market definition. If there have been changes in relative prices in the past (all else being equal), the reactions in terms of quantities demanded will be determinant in establishing substitutability. Launches of new products in the past can also offer useful information, when it is possible to precisely analyse which products have lost sales to the new product.

39. There are a number of quantitative tests that have specifically been designed for the purpose of delineating markets. These tests consist of various econometric and statistical approaches estimates of elasticities and cross-price elasticities for the demand of a product, tests based on similarity of price movements over time, the analysis of causality between price series and similarity of price levels and/or their convergence. The Commission takes into account the available quantitative evidence capable of withstanding rigorous scrutiny for the purposes of establishing patterns of substitution in the past.

40. Views of customers and competitors. The Commission often contacts the main customers and competitors of the companies involved in its enquiries, to gather their views on the boundaries of the product market as well as most of the factual information it requires to reach a conclusion on the scope of the market. Reasoned answers of customers and competitors as to what would happen if relative prices for the candidate products were to increase in the candidate geographic area by a small

amount (for instance of 5% to 10%) are taken into account when they are sufficiently backed by factual evidence.

41. Consumer preferences. In the case of consumer goods, it may be difficult for the Commission to gather the direct views of end consumers about substitute products. Marketing studies that companies have commissioned in the past and that are used by companies in their own decision-making as to pricing of their products and/or marketing actions may provide useful information for the Commission's delineation of the relevant market. Consumer surveys on usage patterns and attitudes, data from consumer's purchasing patterns, the views expressed by retailers and more generally, market research studies submitted by the parties and their competitors are taken into account to establish whether an economically significant proportion of consumers consider two products as substitutable, also taking into account the importance of brands for the products in question. The methodology followed in consumer surveys carried out ad hoc by the undertakings involved or their competitors for the purposes of a merger procedure or a procedure pursuant to Regulation No 17 will usually be scrutinised with utmost care. Unlike preexisting studies, they have not been prepared in the normal course of business for the adoption of business decisions.

42. Barriers and costs associated with switching demand to potential substitutes. There are a number of barriers and costs that might prevent the Commission from considering two prima facie demand substitutes as belonging to one single product market. It is not possible to provide an exhaustive list of all the possible barriers to substitution and of switching costs. These barriers or obstacles might have a wide range of origins, and in its decisions, the Commission has been confronted with regulatory barriers or other forms of State intervention, constraints arising in downstream markets, need to incur specific capital investment or loss in current output in order to switch to alternative inputs, the location of customers, specific investment in production process, learning and human capital investment, retooling costs or other investments, uncertainty about quality and reputation of unknown suppliers, and others.

43. Different categories of customers and price discrimination. The extent of the product market might be narrowed in the presence of distinct groups of customers. A distinct group of customers for the relevant product may constitute a narrower, distinct market when such ha group could be subject to price discrimination. This will usually be the case when two conditions are met: (a) it is possible to identify clearly which group an individual customer belongs to at the moment of selling the relevant products to him, and (b) trade among customers or arbitrage by third parties should not be feasible.

Evidence for defining markets — geographic dimension

44. The type of evidence the Commission considers relevant to reach a conclusion as to the geographic market can be categorised as follows:

45. Past evidence of diversion of orders to other areas. In certain cases, evidence on changes in prices between different areas and consequent reactions by customers might be available. Generally, the same quantitative tests used for product market definition might as well be used in geographic market definition, bearing in mind that international comparisons of prices might be more complex due to a number of factors such as exchange rate movements, taxation and product differentiation.

46. Basic demand characteristics. The nature of demand for the relevant product may in itself determine the scope of the geographical market. Factors such as national preferences or preferences for national brands, language, culture and life style, and the need for a local presence have a strong potential to limit the geographic scope of competition.

47. Views of customers and competitors. Where appropriate, the Commission will contact the main customers and competitors of the parties in its enquiries, to gather their views on the boundaries of the geographic market as well as most of the factual information it requires to reach a conclusion on the scope of the market when they are sufficiently backed by factual evidence.

48. Current geographic pattern of purchases. An examination of the customers' current geographic pattern of purchases provides useful evidence as to the possible scope of the geographic market. When customers purchase from companies located anywhere in the Community or the EEA on similar terms, or they procure their supplies through effective

tendering procedures in which companies from anywhere in the Community or the EEA submit bids, usually the geographic market will be considered to be Community-wide.

49. Trade flows/pattern of shipments. When the number of customers is so large that it is not possible to obtain through them a clear picture of geographic purchasing patterns, information on trade flows might be used alternatively, provided that the trade statistics are available with a sufficient degree of detail for the relevant products. Trade flows, and above all, the rationale behind trade flows provide useful insights and information for the purpose of establishing the scope of the geographic market but are not in themselves conclusive.

50. Barriers and switching costs associated to divert orders to companies located in other areas. The absence of trans-border purchases or trade flows, for instance, does not necessarily mean that the market is at most national in scope. Still, barriers isolating the national market have to identified before it is concluded that the relevant geographic market in such a case is national. Perhaps the clearest obstacle for a customer to divert its orders to other areas is the impact of transport costs and transport restrictions arising from legislation or from the nature of the relevant products. The impact of transport costs will usually limit the scope of the geographic market for bulky, low-value products, bearing in mind that a transport disadvantage might also be compensated by a comparative advantage in other costs (labour costs or raw materials). Access to distribution in a given area, regulatory barriers still existing in certain sectors, quotas and custom tariffs might also constitute barriers isolating a geographic area from the competitive pressure of companies located outside that area. Significant switching costs in procuring supplies from companies located in other countries constitute additional sources of such barriers.

51. On the basis of the evidence gathered, the Commission will then define a geographic market that could range from a local dimension to a global one, and there are examples of both local and global markets in past decisions of the Commission.

52. The paragraphs above describe the different factors which might be relevant to define markets. This does not imply that in each individual case it will be necessary to obtain evidence and assess each of these factors. Often in practice the evidence provided by a susbset of these factors will be sufficient to reach a conclusion, as shown in the past decisional practice of the Commission.

IV CALCULATION OF MARKET SHARE

53. The definition of the relevant market in both its product and geographic dimensions allows the identification the suppliers and the customers/consumers active on that market. On that basis, a total market size and market shares for each supplier can be calculated on the basis of their sales of the relevant products in the relevant area. In practice, the total market size and market shares are often available from market sources, i.e. companies' estimates, studies commissioned from industry consultants and/or trade associations. When this is not the case, or when available estimates are not reliable, the Commission will usually ask each supplier in the relevant market to provide its own sales in order to calculate total market size and market shares.

54. If sales are usually the reference to calculate market shares, there are nevertheless other indications that, depending on the specific products or industry in question, can offer useful information such as, in particular, capacity, the number of players in bidding markets, units of fleet as in aerospace, or the reserves held in the case of sectors such as mining.

55. As a rule of thumb, both volume sales and value sales provide useful information. In cases of differentiated products, sales in value and their associated market share will usually be considered to better reflect the relative position and strength of each supplier.

V ADDITIONAL CONSIDERATIONS

56. There are certain areas where the application of the principles above has to be undertaken with care. This is the case when considering primary and secondary markets, in particular, when the behaviour of undertakings at a point in time has to be analysed pursuant to Article 86. The method of defining markets in these cases is the

same, i.e. assessing the responses of customers based on their purchasing decisions to relative price changes, but taking into account as well, constraints on substitution imposed by conditions in the connected markets. A narrow definition of market for secondary products, for instance, spare parts, may result when compatibility with the primary product is important. Problems of finding compatible secondary products together with the existence of high prices and a long lifetime of the primary products may render relative price increases of secondary products profitable. A different market definition may result if significant substitution between secondary products is possible or if the characteristics of the primary products make quick and direct consumer responses to relative price increases of the secondary products feasible.

57. In certain cases, the existence of chains of substitution might lead to the definition of a relevant market where products or areas at the extreme of the market are not directly substitutable. An example might be provided by the geographic dimension of a product with significant transport costs. In such cases, deliveries from a given plant are limited to a certain area around each plant by the impact of transport costs. In principle, such an area could constitute the relevant geographic market. However, if the distribution of plants is such that there are considerable overlaps between the areas around different plants, it is possible that the pricing of those products will be constrained by a chain substitution effect, and lead to the definition of a broader geographic market. The same reasoning may apply if product B is a demand substitute for products A and C. Even if products A and C are not direct demand substitutes, they might be found to be in the same relevant product market since their respective pricing might be constrained by substitution to B.

58. From a practical perspective, the concept of chains of substitution has to be corroborated by actual evidence, for instance related to price interdependence at the extremes of the chains of substitution, in order to lead to an extension of the relevant market in an individual case. Price levels at the extremes of the chains would have to be of the same magnitude as well.

COMMISSION REGULATION (EC) No 773/2004
relating to the conduct of proceedings by the Commission pursuant to Articles 81 and 82 of the EC Treaty
[now Articles 101 and 102 TFEU]

[2004] OJ L123/18

CHAPTER I
SCOPE

Article 1 Subject-matter and scope

This regulation applies to proceedings conducted by the Commission for the application of Articles 81 and 82 of the Treaty.

CHAPTER II
INITIATION OF PROCEEDINGS

Article 2 Initiation of proceedings

1. The Commission may decide to initiate proceedings with a view to adopting a decision pursuant to Chapter III of Regulation (EC) No 1/2003 at any point in time, but no later than the date on which it issues a preliminary assessment as referred to in Article 9(1) of that Regulation, a statement of objections or a request for the parties to express their interest in engaging in settlement discussions, or the date on which a notice pursuant to Article 27(4) of that Regulation is published, whichever is the earlier.

2. The Commission may make public the initiation of proceedings, in any appropriate way. Before doing so, it shall inform the parties concerned.

3. The Commission may exercise its powers of investigation pursuant to Chapter V of Regulation (EC) No 1/2003 before initiating proceedings.

4. The Commission may reject a complaint pursuant to Article 7 of Regulation (EC) No 1/2003 without initiating proceedings.

CHAPTER III
INVESTIGATIONS BY THE COMMISSION

Article 3   Power to take statements

1.   Where the Commission interviews a person with his consent in accordance with Article 19 of Regulation (EC) No 1/2003, it shall, at the beginning of the interview, state the legal basis and the purpose of the interview, and recall its voluntary nature. It shall also inform the person interviewed of its intention to make a record of the interview.

2.   The interview may be conducted by any means including by telephone or electronic means.

3.   The Commission may record the statements made by the persons interviewed in any form. A copy of any recording shall be made available to the person interviewed for approval. Where necessary, the Commission shall set a time-limit within which the person interviewed may communicate to it any correction to be made to the statement.

Article 4   Oral questions during inspections

1.   When, pursuant to Article 20(2)(e) of Regulation (EC) No 1/2003, officials or other accompanying persons authorised by the Commission ask representatives or members of staff of an undertaking or of an association of undertakings for explanations, the explanations given may be recorded in any form.

2.   A copy of any recording made pursuant to paragraph 1 shall be made available to the undertaking or association of undertakings concerned after the inspection.

3.   In cases where a member of staff of an undertaking or of an association of undertakings who is not or was not authorised by the undertaking or by the association of undertakings to provide explanations on behalf of the undertaking or association of undertakings has been asked for explanations, the Commission shall set a time-limit within which the undertaking or the association of undertakings may communicate to the Commission any rectification, amendment or supplement to the explanations given by such member of staff. The rectification, amendment or supplement shall be added to the explanations as recorded pursuant to paragraph 1.

Article 4a   The Commission's Leniency Programme

1.   The Commission may set the requirements and cooperation conditions under which it may reward undertakings that are or have been party to secret cartels, for their cooperation in disclosing the cartel and facilitating the establishment of an infringement, with immunity from fines or a reduction in fines which would otherwise be imposed under Article 23(2) of Regulation (EC) No 1/2003 (the Commission leniency programme). Immunity from fines may be granted to the undertaking that is the first to submit evidence which in the Commission's view would enable it to carry out a targeted inspection or find an infringement of Article 101 of the Treaty in connection with the alleged cartel. A reduction in fines may be granted to undertakings which provide the Commission with evidence of the alleged infringement which represents significant added value with respect to the evidence already in the Commission's possession. The Commission will only grant immunity from or a reduction of the fine under its leniency programme if, at the end of the administrative proceedings, the undertaking has met the requirements and cooperation conditions set out in the leniency programme. Those may cover, among others, the type of information and evidence the undertakings are required to submit and the further cooperation expected from the undertakings during the administrative proceedings.

2.   In order to qualify for immunity from or reduction of the fine which would otherwise be imposed, undertakings shall provide the Commission with voluntary presentations of their knowledge of a secret cartel and their role therein, which may be also in the form of voluntary presentations of the knowledge of former or current employees or representatives of the undertaking (leniency corporate statements). Such leniency corporate statements shall be drawn up specifically for submission to the Commission with a view to obtaining immunity from or reduction of fines under the Commission's leniency programme.

3.   The Commission will offer parties appropriate methods of providing leniency corporate statements other than by written submission, including orally. Oral corporate statements may be recorded and transcribed at the Commission's premises. The undertaking shall

be granted an opportunity to check the technical accuracy of the recording of its oral statement at the Commission's premises, and, where necessary, to correct the substance of the statement without delay. The rules in this Regulation on leniency corporate statements shall apply to such statements irrespective of the medium on which they are stored. Pre-existing information, i.e. evidence that exists irrespective of the Commission proceedings and that is submitted to the Commission by an undertaking in the context of its application for immunity from or reduction of the fine, is not part of a leniency corporate statement.

CHAPTER IV

HANDLING OF COMPLAINTS

Article 5   Admissibility of complaints

1.   Natural and legal persons shall show a legitimate interest in order to be entitled to lodge a complaint for the purposes of Article 7 of Regulation (EC) No 1/2003.
     Such complaints shall contain the information required by Form C, as set out in the Annex. The Commission may dispense with this obligation as regards part of the information, including documents, required by Form C.
2.   Three paper copies as well as, if possible, an electronic copy of the complaint shall be submitted to the Commission. The complainant shall also submit a non-confidential version of the complaint, if confidentiality is claimed for any part of the complaint.
3.   Complaints shall be submitted in one of the official languages of the Community.

Article 6   Participation of complainants in proceedings

1.   Where the Commission issues a statement of objections relating to a matter in respect of which it has received a complaint, it shall provide the complainant with a copy of the non-confidential version of the statement of objections, except in cases where the settlement procedure applies, where it shall inform the complainant in writing of the nature and subject matter of the procedure. The Commission shall also set a time limit within which the complainant may make known its views in writing.
2.   The Commission may, where appropriate, afford complainants the opportunity of expressing their views at the oral hearing of the parties to which a statement of objections has been issued, if complainants so request in their written comments.

Article 7   Rejection of complaints

1.   Where the Commission considers that on the basis of the information in its possession there are insufficient grounds for acting on a complaint, it shall inform the complainant of its reasons and set a time-limit within which the complainant may make known its views in writing. The Commission shall not be obliged to take into account any further written submission received after the expiry of that time-limit.
2.   If the complainant makes known its views within the time-limit set by the Commission and the written submissions made by the complainant do not lead to a different assessment of the complaint, the Commission shall reject the complaint by decision.
3.   If the complainant fails to make known its views within the time-limit set by the Commission, the complaint shall be deemed to have been withdrawn.

Article 8   Access to information

1.   Where the Commission has informed the complainant of its intention to reject a complaint pursuant to Article 7(1) the complainant may request access to the documents on which the Commission bases its provisional assessment. For this purpose, the complainant may however not have access to business secrets and other confidential information belonging to other parties involved in the proceedings.

Article 9   Rejections of complaints pursuant to Article 13 of Regulation (EC) No 1/2003

Where the Commission rejects a complaint pursuant to Article 13 of Regulation (EC) No 1/2003, it shall inform the complainant without delay of the national competition authority which is dealing or has already dealt with the case.

CHAPTER V
EXERCISE OF THE RIGHT TO BE HEARD

Article 10 Statement of objections and reply

1. The Commission shall inform the parties concerned of the objections raised against them. The statement of objections shall be notified in writing to each of the parties against whom objections are raised.
2. The Commission shall, when notifying the statement of objections to the parties concerned, set a time-limit within which these parties may inform it in writing of their views. The Commission shall not be obliged to take into account written submissions received after the expiry of that time-limit.
3. The parties may, in their written submissions, set out all facts known to them which are relevant to their defence against the objections raised by the Commission. They shall attach any relevant documents as proof of the facts set out. They shall provide a paper original as well as an electronic copy or, where they do not provide an electronic copy, paper copies of their submission and of the documents attached to it. They may propose that the Commission hear persons who may corroborate the facts set out in their submission.

Article 10a Settlement procedure in cartel cases

1. After the initiation of proceedings pursuant to Article 11(6) of Regulation (EC) No 1/2003, the Commission may set a time limit within which the parties may indicate in writing that they are prepared to engage in settlement discussions with a view to possibly introducing settlement submissions. The Commission shall not be obliged to take into account replies received after the expiry of that time limit.

   If two or more parties within the same undertaking indicate their willingness to engage in settlement discussions pursuant to the first subparagraph, they shall appoint a joint representation to engage in discussions with the Commission on their behalf. When setting the time limit referred to in the first subparagraph, the Commission shall indicate to the relevant parties that they are identified within the same undertaking, for the sole purpose of enabling them to comply with this provision.
2. Parties taking part in settlement discussions may be informed by the Commission of:
   (a) the objections it envisages to raise against them;
   (b) the evidence used to determine the envisaged objections;
   (c) non-confidential versions of any specified accessible document listed in the case file at that point in time, in so far as a request by the party is justified for the purpose of enabling the party to ascertain its position regarding a time period or any other particular aspect of the cartel; and
   (d) the range of potential fines.

   This information shall be confidential vis-à-vis third parties, save where the Commission has given a prior explicit authorisation for disclosure.

   Should settlement discussions progress, the Commission may set a time limit within which the parties may commit to follow the settlement procedure by introducing settlement submissions reflecting the results of the settlement discussions and acknowledging their participation in an infringement of Article 101 of the Treaty as well as their liability. These settlement submissions shall be specifically drawn up by the undertakings concerned as a formal request to the Commission to adopt any decision in their case following the settlement procedure. Before the Commission sets a time limit for the introduction of settlement submissions, the parties concerned shall be entitled to have the information specified in the first subparagraph disclosed to them, upon request, in a timely manner. The Commission shall not be obliged to take into account settlement submissions received after the expiry of that time limit.
3. The Commission will offer parties appropriate methods of providing settlement submissions other than by written submission, including orally. Oral settlement submissions may be recorded and transcribed at the Commission's premises. The undertaking shall be granted an opportunity to check the technical accuracy of the recording of its oral submission at the Commission's premises, and, where necessary, to correct the substance of their submission without delay. The rules in this Regulation on settlement submissions shall apply to settlement submissions irrespective of the medium on which they are stored.

3.   When the statement of objections notified to the parties reflects the contents of their settlement submissions, the written reply to the statement of objections by the parties concerned shall, within a time limit set by the Commission, confirm that the statement of objections addressed to them reflects the contents of their settlement submissions. The Commission may then proceed to the adoption of a Decision pursuant to Article 7 and Article 23 of Regulation (EC) No 1/2003 after consultation of the Advisory Committee on Restrictive Practices and Dominant Positions pursuant to Article 14 of Regulation (EC) No 1/2003.

4.   The Commission may decide at any time during the procedure to discontinue settlement discussions altogether in a specific case or with respect to one or more of the parties involved, if it considers that procedural efficiencies are not likely to be achieved.

Article 11 Right to be heard

1.   The Commission shall give the parties to whom it addresses a statement of objections the opportunity to be heard before consulting the Advisory Committee referred to in Article 14(1) of Regulation (EC) No 1/2003.

2.   The Commission shall, in its decisions, deal only with objections in respect of which the parties referred to in paragraph 1 have been able to comment.

Article 12

1.   The Commission shall give the parties to whom it addresses a statement of objections the opportunity to develop their arguments at an oral hearing, if they so request in their written submissions.

2.   However, when introducing their settlement submissions the parties shall confirm to the Commission that they would only require having the opportunity to develop their arguments at an oral hearing, if the statement of objections does not reflect the contents of their settlement submissions.

Article 13 Hearing of other persons

1.   If natural or legal persons other than those referred to in Articles 5 and 11 apply to be heard and show a sufficient interest, the Commission shall inform them in writing of the nature and subject matter of the procedure and shall set a time-limit within which they may make known their views in writing.

2.   The Commission may, where appropriate, invite persons referred to in paragraph 1 to develop their arguments at the oral hearing of the parties to whom a statement of objections has been addressed, if the persons referred to in paragraph 1 so request in their written comments.

3.   The Commission may invite any other person to express its views in writing and to attend the oral hearing of the parties to whom a statement of objections has been addressed. The Commission may also invite such persons to express their views at that oral hearing.

Article 14 Conduct of oral hearings

1.   Hearings shall be conducted by a Hearing Officer in full independence.

2.   The Commission shall invite the persons to be heard to attend the oral hearing on such date as it shall determine.

3.   The Commission shall invite the competition authorities of the Member States to take part in the oral hearing. It may likewise invite officials and civil servants of other authorities of the Member States.

4.   Persons invited to attend shall either appear in person or be represented by legal representatives or by representatives authorised by their constitution as appropriate. Undertakings and associations of undertakings may also be represented by a duly authorised agent appointed from among their permanent staff.

5.   Persons heard by the Commission may be assisted by their lawyers or other qualified persons admitted by the Hearing Officer.

6.   Oral hearings shall not be public. Each person may be heard separately or in the presence of other persons invited to attend, having regard to the legitimate interest of the undertakings in the protection of their business secrets and other confidential information.

7. The Hearing Officer may allow the parties to whom a statement of objections has been addressed, the complainants, other persons invited to the hearing, the Commission services and the authorities of the Member States to ask questions during the hearing.

8. The statements made by each person heard shall be recorded. Upon request, the recording of the hearing shall be made available to the persons who attended the hearing. Regard shall be had to the legitimate interest of the parties in the protection of their business secrets and other confidential information.

CHAPTER VI
ACCESS TO THE FILE AND TREATMENT OF CONFIDENTIAL INFORMATION

Article 15 Access to the file

1. If so requested, the Commission shall grant access to the file to the parties to whom it has addressed a statement of objections. Access shall be granted after the notification of the statement of objections.

   1a. After the initiation of proceedings pursuant to Article 11(6) of Regulation (EC) No 1/2003 and in order to enable the parties to introduce settlement submissions, the Commission shall disclose to them the evidence and documents described in Article 10a(2) upon request and subject to the conditions established in the relevant subparagraphs. In view thereof, when introducing their settlement submissions, the parties shall confirm to the Commission that they will only require access to the file pursuant to paragraph 1 after the receipt of the statement of objections, if the statement of objections does not reflect the contents of their settlement submissions. Where settlement discussions have been discontinued with one or more of the parties, such party shall be granted access to the file pursuant to paragraph 1 when a statement of objections has been addressed to it.

   1b. Access pursuant to paragraph 1 or 1a to a leniency corporate statement within the meaning of Article 4a(2) or to a settlement submission within the meaning of Article 10a(2), shall only be granted at the premises of the Commission. The parties and their representatives shall not copy the leniency corporate statements or settlement submissions by any mechanical or electronic means.

2. The right of access to the file shall not extend to business secrets, other confidential information and internal documents of the Commission or of the competition authorities of the Member States. The right of access to the file shall also not extend to correspondence between the Commission and the competition authorities of the Member States or between the latter where such correspondence is contained in the file of the Commission.

3. Nothing in this Regulation prevents the Commission from disclosing and using information necessary to prove an infringement of Articles 81 or 82 of the Treaty.

Article 16 Identification and protection of confidential information

1. Information, including documents, shall not be communicated or made accessible by the Commission in so far as it contains business secrets or other confidential information of any person.

2. Any person which makes known its views pursuant to Article 6(1), Article 7(1), Article 10(2) and Article 13(1) and (3) or subsequently submits further information to the Commission in the course of the same procedure, shall clearly identify any material which it considers to be confidential, giving reasons, and provide a separate non-confidential version by the date set by the Commission for making its views known.

3. Without prejudice to paragraph 2 of this Article, the Commission may require undertakings and associations of undertakings which produce documents or statements pursuant to Regulation (EC) No 1/2003 to identify the documents or parts of documents which they consider to contain business secrets or other confidential information belonging to them and to identify the undertakings with regard to which such documents are to be considered confidential. The Commission may likewise require undertakings or associations of undertakings to identify any part of a statement of objections, a case summary drawn up pursuant to Article 27(4) of Regulation (EC) No 1/2003 or a decision adopted by the Commission which in their view contains business secrets. The Commission may set a time-limit within which the undertakings and associations of undertakings are to:

      (a)   substantiate their claim for confidentiality with regard to each individual document or part of document, statement or part of statement;

      (b)   provide the Commission with a non-confidential version of the documents or statements, in which the confidential passages are deleted;

      (c)   provide a concise description of each piece of deleted information.

4.   If undertakings or associations of undertakings fail to comply with paragraphs 2 and 3, the Commission may assume that the documents or statements concerned do not contain confidential information.

CHAPTER VIa
LIMITATIONS TO THE USE OF INFORMATION OBTAINED IN THE COURSE OF COMMISSION PROCEEDINGS

Article 16a

1.   Information obtained pursuant to this Regulation shall only be used for the purposes of judicial or administrative proceedings for the application of Articles 101 and 102 of the Treaty.

2.   Access to leniency corporate statements within the meaning of Article 4a(2) or to settlement submissions within the meaning of Article 10a(2) shall be granted only for the purposes of exercising the rights of defence in proceedings before the Commission. Information taken from such statements and submissions may be used by the party having obtained access to the file only where necessary for the exercise of its rights of defence in proceedings:

      (a)   before the European Union courts reviewing Commission decisions; or

      (b)   before the courts of the Member States in cases that are directly related to the case in which access has been granted, and which concern:

           (i)   the allocation between cartel participants of a fine imposed jointly and severally on them by the Commission; or

           (ii)   the review of a decision by which a competition authority of a Member State has found an infringement of Article 101 TFEU.

3.   The following categories of information obtained pursuant to this Regulation shall not be used in proceedings before national courts until the Commission has closed its proceedings against all parties under investigation by adopting a decision pursuant to Article 7, 9 or 10 of Regulation (EC) No 1/2003 or has otherwise terminated its proceedings:

      (a)   information that was prepared by other natural or legal persons specifically for the proceedings of the Commission; and

      (b)   information that the Commission has drawn up and sent to the parties in the course of its proceedings.

CHAPTER VII
GENERAL AND FINAL PROVISIONS

Article 17 Time-limits

1.   In setting the time limits provided for in Article 3(3), Article 4(3), Article 6(1), Article 7(1), Article 10(2), Article 10a(1), Article 10a(2), Article 10a(3) and Article 16(3), the Commission shall have regard both to the time required for preparation of the submission and to the urgency of the case.

2.   The time-limits referred to in Article 6(1), Article 7(1) and Article 10(2) shall be at least four weeks. However, for proceedings initiated with a view to adopting interim measures pursuant to Article 8 of Regulation (EC) No 1/2003, the time-limit may be shortened to one week.

3.   The time limits referred to in Article 4(3), Article 10a(1), Article 10a(2) and Article 16(3) shall be at least two weeks. The time limit referred to in Article 3(3) shall be at least two weeks, except for settlement submissions, for which corrections shall be made within one week. The time limit referred to in Article 10a(3) shall be at least two weeks.

4.   Where appropriate and upon reasoned request made before the expiry of the original time-limit, time-limits may be extended.

ANNEX

FORM C

COMPLAINT PURSUANT TO ARTICLE 7 OF REGULATION (EC) No 1/2003

I. Information regarding the complainant and the undertaking(s) or association of undertakings giving rise to the complaint

1.   Give full details on the identity of the legal or natural person submitting the complaint. Where the complainant is an undertaking, identify the corporate group to which it belongs and provide a concise overview of the nature and scope of its business activities. Provide a contact person (with telephone number, postal and e-mail-address) from which supplementary explanations can be obtained.

2.   Identify the undertaking(s) or association of undertakings whose conduct the complaint relates to, including, where applicable, all available information on the corporate group to which the undertaking(s) complained of belong and the nature and scope of the business activities pursued by them. Indicate the position of the complainant vis-à-vis the undertaking(s) or association of undertakings complained of (e.g. customer, competitor).

II. Details of the alleged infringement and evidence

3.   Set out in detail the facts from which, in your opinion, it appears that there exists an infringement of Article 81 or 82 of the Treaty and/or Article 53 or 54 of the EEA agreement. Indicate in particular the nature of the products (goods or services) affected by the alleged infringements and explain, where necessary, the commercial relationships concerning these products. Provide all available details on the agreements or practices of the undertakings or associations of undertakings to which this complaint relates. Indicate, to the extent possible, the relative market positions of the undertakings concerned by the complaint.

4.   Submit all documentation in your possession relating to or directly connected with the facts set out in the complaint (for example, texts of agreements, minutes of negotiations or meetings, terms of transactions, business documents, circulars, correspondence, notes of telephone conversations…). State the names and address of the persons able to testify to the facts set out in the complaint, and in particular of persons affected by the alleged infringement. Submit statistics or other data in your possession which relate to the facts set out, in particular where they show developments in the marketplace (for example information relating to prices and price trends, barriers to entry to the market for new suppliers etc.).

5.   Set out your view about the geographical scope of the alleged infringement and explain, where that is not obvious, to what extent trade between Member States or between the Community and one or more EFTA States that are contracting parties of the EEA Agreement may be affected by the conduct complained of.

III. Finding sought from the Commission and legitimate interest

6.   Explain what finding or action you are seeking as a result of proceedings brought by the Commission.

7.   Set out the grounds on which you claim a legitimate interest as complainant pursuant to Article 7 of Regulation (EC) No 1/2003. State in particular how the conduct complained of affects you and explain how, in your view, intervention by the Commission would be liable to remedy the alleged grievance.

IV. Proceedings before national competition authorities or national courts

8.   Provide full information about whether you have approached, concerning the same or closely related subject-matters, any other competition authority and/or whether a lawsuit has been brought before a national court. If so, provide full details about the administrative or judicial authority contacted and your submissions to such authority.

Declaration that the information given in this form and in the Annexes thereto is given entirely in good faith.

Date and signature.

DIRECTIVE 2014/104/EU OF THE EUROPEAN PARLIAMENT AND OF THE COUNCIL

of 26 November 2014

on certain rules governing actions for damages under national law for infringements of the competition law provisions of the Member States and of the European Union

[2014] OJ L349/1

CHAPTER I
SUBJECT MATTER, SCOPE AND DEFINITIONS

Article 1 Subject matter and scope

1. This Directive sets out certain rules necessary to ensure that anyone who has suffered harm caused by an infringement of competition law by an undertaking or by an association of undertakings can effectively exercise the right to claim full compensation for that harm from that undertaking or association. It sets out rules fostering undistorted competition in the internal market and removing obstacles to its proper functioning, by ensuring equivalent protection throughout the Union for anyone who has suffered such harm.

2. This Directive sets out rules coordinating the enforcement of the competition rules by competition authorities and the enforcement of those rules in damages actions before national courts.

Article 2 Definitions

For the purposes of this Directive, the following definitions apply:

1. 'infringement of competition law' means an infringement of Article 101 or 102 TFEU, or of national competition law;

2. 'infringer' means an undertaking or association of undertakings which has committed an infringement of competition law;

3. 'national competition law' means provisions of national law that predominantly pursue the same objective as Articles 101 and 102 TFEU and that are applied to the same case and in parallel to Union competition law pursuant to Article 3(1) of Regulation (EC) No 1/2003, excluding provisions of national law which impose criminal penalties on natural persons, except to the extent that such criminal penalties are the means whereby competition rules applying to undertakings are enforced;

4. 'action for damages' means an action under national law by which a claim for damages is brought before a national court by an alleged injured party, or by someone acting on behalf of one or more alleged injured parties where Union or national law provides for that possibility, or by a natural or legal person that succeeded in the right of the alleged injured party, including the person that acquired the claim;

5. 'claim for damages' means a claim for compensation for harm caused by an infringement of competition law;

6. 'injured party' means a person that has suffered harm caused by an infringement of competition law;

7. 'national competition authority' means an authority designated by a Member State pursuant to Article 35 of Regulation (EC) No 1/2003, as being responsible for the application of Articles 101 and 102 TFEU;

8. 'competition authority' means the Commission or a national competition authority or both, as the context may require;

9. 'national court' means a court or tribunal of a Member State within the meaning of Article 267 TFEU;

10. 'review court' means a national court that is empowered by ordinary means of appeal to review decisions of a national competition authority or to review judgments pronouncing on those decisions, irrespective of whether that court itself has the power to find an infringement of competition law;

11. 'infringement decision' means a decision of a competition authority or review court that finds an infringement of competition law;

12. 'final infringement decision' means an infringement decision that cannot be, or that can no longer be, appealed by ordinary means;

13. 'evidence' means all types of means of proof admissible before the national court seized, in partic ular documents and all other objects containing information, irrespective of the medium on which the information is stored;

14. 'cartel' means an agreement or concerted practice between two or more competitors aimed at coordinating their competitive behaviour on the market or influencing the relevant parameters of competition through practices such as, but not limited to, the fixing or coordination of purchase or selling prices or other trading conditions, including in relation to intellectual property rights, the allocation of production or sales quotas, the sharing of markets and customers, including bid-rigging, restrictions of imports or exports or anti-competitive actions against other competitors;

15. 'leniency programme' means a programme concerning the application of Article 101 TFEU or a corresponding provision under national law on the basis of which a participant in a secret cartel, independently of the other undertakings involved in the cartel, cooperates with an investigation of the competition authority, by voluntarily providing presentations regarding that participant's knowledge of, and role in, the cartel in return for which that participant receives, by decision or by a discontinuation of proceedings, immunity from, or a reduction in, fines for its involvement in the cartel;

16. 'leniency statement' means an oral or written presentation voluntarily provided by, or on behalf of, an undertaking or a natural person to a competition authority or a record thereof, describing the knowledge of that undertaking or natural person of a cartel and describing its role therein, which presentation was drawn up specifically for submission to the competition authority with a view to obtaining immunity or a reduction of fines under a leniency programme, not including pre-existing information;

17. 'pre-existing information' means evidence that exists irrespective of the proceedings of a competition authority, whether or not such information is in the file of a competition authority;

18. 'settlement submission' means a voluntary presentation by, or on behalf of, an undertaking to a competition authority describing the undertaking's acknowledgement of, or its renunciation to dispute, its participation in an infringement of competition law and its responsibility for that infringement of competition law, which was drawn up specifically to enable the competition authority to apply a simplified or expedited procedure;

19. 'immunity recipient' means an undertaking which, or a natural person who, has been granted immunity from fines by a competition authority under a leniency programme;

20. 'overcharge' means the difference between the price actually paid and the price that would otherwise have prevailed in the absence of an infringement of competition law;

21. 'consensual dispute resolution' means any mechanism enabling parties to reach the out-of-court resolution of a dispute concerning a claim for damages;

22. 'consensual settlement' means an agreement reached through consensual dispute resolution.

23. 'direct purchaser' means a natural or legal person who acquired, directly from an infringer, products or services that were the object of an infringement of competition law;

24. 'indirect purchaser' means a natural or legal person who acquired, not directly from an infringer, but from a direct purchaser or a subsequent purchaser, products or services that were the object of an infringement of competition law, or products or services containing them or derived therefrom.

Article 3   Right to full compensation

1. Member States shall ensure that any natural or legal person who has suffered harm caused by an infringement of competition law is able to claim and to obtain full compensation for that harm.

2. Full compensation shall place a person who has suffered harm in the position in which that person would have been had the infringement of competition law not been

committed. It shall therefore cover the right to compensation for actual loss and for loss of profit, plus the payment of interest.

3. Full compensation under this Directive shall not lead to overcompensation, whether by means of punitive, multiple or other types of damages.

Article 4   Principles of effectiveness and equivalence

In accordance with the principle of effectiveness, Member States shall ensure that all national rules and procedures relating to the exercise of claims for damages are designed and applied in such a way that they do not render practically impossible or excessively difficult the exercise of the Union right to full compensation for harm caused by an infringement of competition law. In accordance with the principle of equivalence, national rules and procedures relating to actions for damages resulting from infringements of Article 101 or 102 TFEU shall not be less favourable to the alleged injured parties than those governing similar actions for damages resulting from infringements of national law.

CHAPTER II

DISCLOSURE OF EVIDENCE

Article 5   Disclosure of evidence

1. Member States shall ensure that in proceedings relating to an action for damages in the Union, upon request of a claimant who has presented a reasoned justification containing reasonably available facts and evidence sufficient to support the plausibility of its claim for damages, national courts are able to order the defendant or a third party to disclose relevant evidence which lies in their control, subject to the conditions set out in this Chapter. Member States shall ensure that national courts are able, upon request of the defendant, to order the claimant or a third party to disclose relevant evidence.

   This paragraph is without prejudice to the rights and obligations of national courts under Regulation (EC) No 1206/2001.

2. Member States shall ensure that national courts are able to order the disclosure of specified items of evidence or relevant categories of evidence circumscribed as precisely and as narrowly as possible on the basis of reasonably available facts in the reasoned justification.

3. Member States shall ensure that national courts limit the disclosure of evidence to that which is proportionate. In determining whether any disclosure requested by a party is proportionate, national courts shall consider the legitimate interests of all parties and third parties concerned. They shall, in particular, consider:

   (a) the extent to which the claim or defence is supported by available facts and evidence justifying the request to disclose evidence;

   (b) the scope and cost of disclosure, especially for any third parties concerned, including preventing non-specific searches for information which is unlikely to be of relevance for the parties in the procedure;

   (c) whether the evidence the disclosure of which is sought contains confidential information, especially concerning any third parties, and what arrangements are in place for protecting such confidential information.

4. Member States shall ensure that national courts have the power to order the disclosure of evidence containing confidential information where they consider it relevant to the action for damages. Member States shall ensure that, when ordering the disclosure of such information, national courts have at their disposal effective measures to protect such information.

5. The interest of undertakings to avoid actions for damages following an infringement of competition law shall not constitute an interest that warrants protection.

6. Member States shall ensure that national courts give full effect to applicable legal professional privilege under Union or national law when ordering the disclosure of evidence.

7. Member States shall ensure that those from whom disclosure is sought are provided with an opportunity to be heard before a national court orders disclosure under this Article.

8. Without prejudice to paragraphs 4 and 7 and to Article 6, this Article shall not prevent Member States from maintaining or introducing rules which would lead to wider disclosure of evidence.

Article 6 Disclosure of evidence included in the file of a competition authority

1. Member States shall ensure that, for the purpose of actions for damages, where national courts order the disclosure of evidence included in the file of a competition authority, this Article applies in addition to Article 5.

2. This Article is without prejudice to the rules and practices on public access to documents under Regulation (EC) No 1049/2001.

3. This Article is without prejudice to the rules and practices under Union or national law on the protection of internal documents of competition authorities and of correspondence between competition authorities.

4. When assessing, in accordance with Article 5(3), the proportionality of an order to disclose information, national courts shall, in addition, consider the following:
    (a) whether the request has been formulated specifically with regard to the nature, subject matter or contents of documents submitted to a competition authority or held in the file thereof, rather than by a non-specific application concerning documents submitted to a competition authority;
    (b) whether the party requesting disclosure is doing so in relation to an action for damages before a national court; and
    (c) in relation to paragraphs 5 and 10, or upon request of a competition authority pursuant to paragraph 11, the need to safeguard the effectiveness of the public enforcement of competition law.

5. National courts may order the disclosure of the following categories of evidence only after a competition authority, by adopting a decision or otherwise, has closed its proceedings:
    (a) information that was prepared by a natural or legal person specifically for the proceedings of a competition authority;
    (b) information that the competition authority has drawn up and sent to the parties in the course of its proceedings; and
    (c) settlement submissions that have been withdrawn.

6. Member States shall ensure that, for the purpose of actions for damages, national courts cannot at any time order a party or a third party to disclose any of the following categories of evidence:
    (a) leniency statements; and
    (b) settlement submissions.

7. A claimant may present a reasoned request that a national court access the evidence referred to in point (a) or (b) of paragraph 6 for the sole purpose of ensuring that their contents correspond to the definitions in points (16) and (18) of Article 2. In that assessment, national courts may request assistance only from the competent competition authority. The authors of the evidence in question may also have the possibility to be heard. In no case shall the national court permit other parties or third parties access to that evidence.

8. If only parts of the evidence requested are covered by paragraph 6, the remaining parts thereof shall, depending on the category under which they fall, be released in accordance with the relevant paragraphs of this Article.

9. The disclosure of evidence in the file of a competition authority that does not fall into any of the categories listed in this Article may be ordered in actions for damages at any time, without prejudice to this Article.

10. Member States shall ensure that national courts request the disclosure from a competition authority of evidence included in its file only where no party or third party is reasonably able to provide that evidence.

11. To the extent that a competition authority is willing to state its views on the proportionality of disclosure requests, it may, acting on its own initiative, submit observations to the national court before which a disclosure order is sought.

Article 7 Limits on the use of evidence obtained solely through access to the file of a competition authority

1. Member States shall ensure that evidence in the categories listed in Article 6(6) which is obtained by a natural or legal person solely through access to the file of a competition authority is either deemed to be inadmissible in actions for damages or is otherwise protected under the applicable national rules to ensure the full effect of the limits on the disclosure of evidence set out in Article 6.

2. Member States shall ensure that, until a competition authority has closed its proceedings by adopting a decision or otherwise, evidence in the categories listed in Article 6(5) which is obtained by a natural or legal person solely through access to the file of that competition authority is either deemed to be inadmissible in actions for damages or is otherwise protected under the applicable national rules to ensure the full effect of the limits on the disclosure of evidence set out in Article 6.

3. Member States shall ensure that evidence which is obtained by a natural or legal person solely through access to the file of a competition authority and which does not fall under paragraph 1 or 2, can be used in an action for damages only by that person or by a natural or legal person that succeeded to that person's rights, including a person that acquired that person's claim.

Article 8 Penalties

1. Member States shall ensure that national courts are able effectively to impose penalties on parties, third parties and their legal representatives in the event of any of the following:
   (a) their failure or refusal to comply with the disclosure order of any national court;
   (b) their destruction of relevant evidence;
   (c) their failure or refusal to comply with the obligations imposed by a national court order protecting confidential information;
   (d) their breach of the limits on the use of evidence provided for in this Chapter.

2. Member States shall ensure that the penalties that can be imposed by national courts are effective, proportionate and dissuasive. The penalties available to national courts shall include, with regard to the behaviour of a party to proceedings for an action for damages, the possibility to draw adverse inferences, such as presuming the relevant issue to be proven or dismissing claims and defences in whole or in part, and the possibility to order the payment of costs.

CHAPTER III

EFFECT OF NATIONAL DECISIONS, LIMITATION PERIODS, JOINT AND SEVERAL LIABILITY

Article 9 Effect of national decisions

1. Member States shall ensure that an infringement of competition law found by a final decision of a national competition authority or by a review court is deemed to be irrefutably established for the purposes of an action for damages brought before their national courts under Article 101 or 102 TFEU or under national competition law.

2. Member States shall ensure that where a final decision referred to in paragraph 1 is taken in another Member State, that final decision may, in accordance with national law, be presented before their national courts as at least prima facie evidence that an infringement of competition law has occurred and, as appropriate, may be assessed along with any other evidence adduced by the parties.

3. This Article is without prejudice to the rights and obligations of national courts under Article 267 TFEU.

Article 10 Limitation periods

1. Member States shall, in accordance with this Article, lay down rules applicable to limitation periods for bringing actions for damages. Those rules shall determine when the limitation period begins to run, the duration thereof and the circumstances under which it is interrupted or suspended.

2. Limitation periods shall not begin to run before the infringement of competition law has ceased and the claimant knows, or can reasonably be expected to know:
    (a)   of the behaviour and the fact that it constitutes an infringement of competition law;
    (b)   of the fact that the infringement of competition law caused harm to it; and
    (c)   the identity of the infringer.
3. Member States shall ensure that the limitation periods for bringing actions for damages are at least five years.
4. Member States shall ensure that a limitation period is suspended or, depending on national law, interrupted, if a competition authority takes action for the purpose of the investigation or its proceedings in respect of an infringement of competition law to which the action for damages relates. The suspension shall end at the earliest one year after the infringement decision has become final or after the proceedings are otherwise terminated.

Article 11 Joint and several liability

1. Member States shall ensure that undertakings which have infringed competition law through joint behaviour are jointly and severally liable for the harm caused by the infringement of competition law; with the effect that each of those undertakings is bound to compensate for the harm in full, and the injured party has the right to require full compensation from any of them until he has been fully compensated.
2. By way of derogation from paragraph 1, Member States shall ensure that, without prejudice to the right of full compensation as laid down in Article 3, where the infringer is a small or medium-sized enterprise (SME) as defined in Commission Recommendation 2003/361/EC, the infringer is liable only to its own direct and indirect purchasers where:
    (a)   its market share in the relevant market was below 5% at any time during the infringement of competition law; and
    (b)   the application of the normal rules of joint and several liability would irretrievably jeopardise its economic viability and cause its assets to lose all their value.
3. The derogation laid down in paragraph 2 shall not apply where:
    (a)   the SME has led the infringement of competition law or has coerced other undertakings to participate therein; or
    (b)   the SME has previously been found to have infringed competition law.
4. By way of derogation from paragraph 1, Member States shall ensure that an immunity recipient is jointly and severally liable as follows:
    (a)   to its direct or indirect purchasers or providers; and
    (b)   to other injured parties only where full compensation cannot be obtained from the other undertakings that were involved in the same infringement of competition law.
    Member States shall ensure that any limitation period applicable to cases under this paragraph is reasonable and sufficient to allow injured parties to bring such actions.
5. Member States shall ensure that an infringer may recover a contribution from any other infringer, the amount of which shall be determined in the light of their relative responsibility for the harm caused by the infringement of competition law. The amount of contribution of an infringer which has been granted immunity from fines under a leniency programme shall not exceed the amount of the harm it caused to its own direct or indirect purchasers or providers.
6. Member States shall ensure that, to the extent the infringement of competition law caused harm to injured parties other than the direct or indirect purchasers or providers of the infringers, the amount of any contribution from an immunity recipient to other infringers shall be determined in the light of its relative responsibility for that harm.

CHAPTER IV
THE PASSING-ON OF OVERCHARGES

Article 12 Passing-on of overcharges and the right to full compensation

1. To ensure the full effectiveness of the right to full compensation as laid down in Article 3, Member States shall ensure that, in accordance with the rules laid down

in this Chapter, compensation of harm can be claimed by anyone who suffered it, irrespective of whether they are direct or indirect purchasers from an infringer, and that compensation of harm exceeding that caused by the infringement of competition law to the claimant, as well as the absence of liability of the infringer, are avoided.

2.   In order to avoid overcompensation, Member States shall lay down procedural rules appropriate to ensure that compensation for actual loss at any level of the supply chain does not exceed the overcharge harm suffered at that level.

3.   This Chapter shall be without prejudice to the right of an injured party to claim and obtain compensation for loss of profits due to a full or partial passing-on of the overcharge.

4.   Member States shall ensure that the rules laid down in this Chapter apply accordingly where the infringement of competition law relates to a supply to the infringer.

5.   Member States shall ensure that the national courts have the power to estimate, in accordance with national procedures, the share of any overcharge that was passed on.

Article 13 Passing-on defence

Member States shall ensure that the defendant in an action for damages can invoke as a defence against a claim for damages the fact that the claimant passed on the whole or part of the overcharge resulting from the infringement of competition law. The burden of proving that the overcharge was passed on shall be on the defendant, who may reasonably require disclosure from the claimant or from third parties.

Article 14 Indirect purchasers

1.   Member States shall ensure that, where in an action for damages the existence of a claim for damages or the amount of compensation to be awarded depends on whether, or to what degree, an overcharge was passed on to the claimant, taking into account the commercial practice that price increases are passed on down the supply chain, the burden of proving the existence and scope of such a passing-on shall rest with the claimant, who may reasonably require disclosure from the defendant or from third parties.

2.   In the situation referred to in paragraph 1, the indirect purchaser shall be deemed to have proven that a passing-on to that indirect purchaser occurred where that indirect purchaser has shown that:
     (a)   the defendant has committed an infringement of competition law;
     (b)   the infringement of competition law has resulted in an overcharge for the direct purchaser of the defendant; and
     (c)   the indirect purchaser has purchased the goods or services that were the object of the infringement of competition law, or has purchased goods or services derived from or containing them.

This paragraph shall not apply where the defendant can demonstrate credibly to the satisfaction of the court that the overcharge was not, or was not entirely, passed on to the indirect purchaser.

Article 15 Actions for damages by claimants from different levels in the supply chain

1.   To avoid that actions for damages by claimants from different levels in the supply chain lead to a multiple liability or to an absence of liability of the infringer, Member States shall ensure that in assessing whether the burden of proof resulting from the application of Articles 13 and 14 is satisfied, national courts seized of an action for damages are able, by means available under Union or national law, to take due account of any of the following:
     (a)   actions for damages that are related to the same infringement of competition law, but that are brought by claimants from other levels in the supply chain;
     (b)   judgments resulting from actions for damages as referred to in point (a);
     (c)   relevant information in the public domain resulting from the public enforcement of competition law.

2.   This Article shall be without prejudice to the rights and obligations of national courts under Article 30 of Regulation (EU) No 1215/2012.

Article 16 Guidelines for national courts

The Commission shall issue guidelines for national courts on how to estimate the share of the overcharge which was passed on to the indirect purchaser.

CHAPTER V

QUANTIFICATION OF HARM

Article 17 Quantification of harm

1.   Member States shall ensure that neither the burden nor the standard of proof required for the quantification of harm renders the exercise of the right to damages practically impossible or excessively difficult. Member States shall ensure that the national courts are empowered, in accordance with national procedures, to estimate the amount of harm if it is established that a claimant suffered harm but it is practically impossible or excessively difficult precisely to quantify the harm suffered on the basis of the evidence available.

2.   It shall be presumed that cartel infringements cause harm. The infringer shall have the right to rebut that presumption.

3.   Member States shall ensure that, in proceedings relating to an action for damages, a national competition authority may, upon request of a national court, assist that national court with respect to the determination of the quantum of damages where that national competition authority considers such assistance to be appropriate.

CHAPTER VI

CONSENSUAL DISPUTE RESOLUTION

Article 18 Suspensive and other effects of consensual dispute resolution

1.   Member States shall ensure that the limitation period for bringing an action for damages is suspended for the duration of any consensual dispute resolution process. The suspension of the limitation period shall apply only with regard to those parties that are or that were involved or represented in the consensual dispute resolution.

2.   Without prejudice to provisions of national law in matters of arbitration, Member States shall ensure that national courts seized of an action for damages may suspend their proceedings for up to two years where the parties thereto are involved in consensual dispute resolution concerning the claim covered by that action for damages.

3.   A competition authority may consider compensation paid as a result of a consensual settlement and prior to its decision imposing a fine to be a mitigating factor.

Article 19 Effect of consensual settlements on subsequent actions for damages

1.   Member States shall ensure that, following a consensual settlement, the claim of the settling injured party is reduced by the settling co-infringer's share of the harm that the infringement of competition law inflicted upon the injured party.

2.   Any remaining claim of the settling injured party shall be exercised only against non-settling co-infringers. Non-settling co-infringers shall not be permitted to recover contribution for the remaining claim from the settling co-infringer.

3.   By way of derogation from paragraph 2, Member States shall ensure that where the non-settling co-infringers cannot pay the damages that correspond to the remaining claim of the settling injured party, the settling injured party may exercise the remaining claim against the settling co-infringer.

The derogation referred to in the first subparagraph may be expressly excluded under the terms of the consensual settlement.

4.   When determining the amount of contribution that a co-infringer may recover from any other co-infringer in accordance with their relative responsibility for the harm caused by the infringement of competition law, national courts shall take due account of any damages paid pursuant to a prior consensual settlement involving the relevant co-infringer.

CHAPTER VII
FINAL PROVISIONS

Article 20 Review

1. The Commission shall review this Directive and shall submit a report thereon to the European Parliament and the Council by 27 December 2020.
2. The report referred to in paragraph 1 shall, inter alia, include information on all of the following:
   (a) the possible impact of financial constraints flowing from the payment of fines imposed by a competition authority for an infringement of competition law on the possibility for injured parties to obtain full compensation for the harm caused by that infringement of competition law;
   (b) the extent to which claimants for damages caused by an infringement of competition law established in an infringement decision adopted by a competition authority of a Member State are able to prove before the national court of another Member State that such an infringement of competition law has occurred;
   (c) the extent to which compensation for actual loss exceeds the overcharge harm caused by the infringement of competition law or suffered at any level of the supply chain.
3. If appropriate, the report referred to in paragraph 1 shall be accompanied by a legislative proposal.

Article 21 Transposition

1. Member States shall bring into force the laws, regulations and administrative provisions necessary to comply with this Directive by 27 December 2016. They shall forthwith communicate to the Commission the text thereof.
   When Member States adopt those measures, they shall contain a reference to this Directive or be accompanied by such a reference on the occasion of their official publication. Member States shall determine how such reference is to be made.
2. Member States shall communicate to the Commission the text of the main provisions of national law which they adopt in the field covered by this Directive.

Article 22 Temporal application

1. Member States shall ensure that the national measures adopted pursuant to Article 21 in order to comply with substantive provisions of this Directive do not apply retroactively.
2. Member States shall ensure that any national measures adopted pursuant to Article 21, other than those referred to in paragraph 1, do not apply to actions for damages of which a national court was seized prior to 26 December 2014.

Article 23 Entry into force

This Directive shall enter into force on the twentieth day following that of its publication in the *Official Journal of the European Union*.

Article 24 Addressees

This Directive is addressed to the Member States.
Done at Strasbourg, 26 November 2014.

COMMISSION NOTICE ON IMMUNITY FROM FINES AND REDUCTION OF FINES IN CARTEL CASES
[2006] C298/11

1   Introduction

(1) This notice sets out the framework for rewarding cooperation in the Commission investigation by undertakings which are or have been party to secret cartels affecting the Community. Cartels are agreements and/or concerted practices between two or

more competitors aimed at coordinating their competitive behaviour on the market and/or influencing the relevant parameters of competition through practices such as the fixing of purchase or selling prices or other trading conditions, the allocation of production or sales quotas, the sharing of markets including bid-rigging, restrictions of imports or exports and/or anti-competitive actions against other competitors. Such practices are among the most serious violations of Article 81 EC.

(2) By artificially limiting the competition that would normally prevail between them, undertakings avoid exactly those pressures that lead them to innovate, both in terms of product development and the introduction of more efficient production methods. Such practices also lead to more expensive raw materials and components for the Community companies that purchase from such producers. They ultimately result in artificial prices and reduced choice for the consumer. In the long term, they lead to a loss of competitiveness and reduced employment opportunities.

(3) By their very nature, secret cartels are often difficult to detect and investigate without the cooperation of undertakings or individuals implicated in them. Therefore, the Commission considers that it is in the Community interest to reward undertakings involved in this type of illegal practices which are willing to put an end to their participation and co-operate in the Commission's investigation, independently of the rest of the undertakings involved in the cartel. The interests of consumers and citizens in ensuring that secret cartels are detected and punished outweigh the interest in fining those undertakings that enable the Commission to detect and prohibit such practices.

(4) The Commission considers that the collaboration of an undertaking in the detection of the existence of a cartel has an intrinsic value. A decisive contribution to the opening of an investigation or to the finding of an infringement may justify the granting of immunity from any fine to the undertaking in question, on condition that certain additional requirements are fulfilled.

(5) Moreover, co-operation by one or more undertakings may justify a reduction of a fine by the Commission. Any reduction of a fine must reflect an undertaking's actual contribution, in terms of quality and timing, to the Commission's establishment of the infringement. Reductions are to be limited to those undertakings that provide the Commission with evidence that adds significant value to that already in the Commission's possession.

(6) In addition to submitting pre-existing documents, undertakings may provide the Commission with voluntary presentations of their knowledge of a cartel and their role therein prepared specially to be submitted under this leniency programme. These initiatives have proved to be useful for the effective investigation and termination of cartel infringements and they should not be discouraged by discovery orders issued in civil litigation. Potential leniency applicants might be dissuaded from cooperating with the Commission under this Notice if this could impair their position in civil proceedings, as compared to companies who do not cooperate. Such undesirable effect would significantly harm the public interest in ensuring effective public enforcement of Article 81 EC in cartel cases and thus its subsequent or parallel effective private enforcement.

(7) The supervisory task conferred on the Commission by the Treaty in competition matters does not only include the duty to investigate and punish individual infringements, but also encompasses the duty to pursue a general policy. The protection of corporate statements in the public interest is not a bar to their disclosure to other addressees of the statement of objections in order to safeguard their rights of defence in the procedure before the Commission, to the extent that it is technically possible to combine both interests by rendering corporate statements accessible only at the Commission premises and normally on a single occasion following the formal notification of the objections. Moreover, the Commission will process personal data in the context of this notice in conformity with its obligations under Regulation (EC) No 45/2001.

2 Immunity from fines
A. Requirements to qualify for immunity from fines

(8) The Commission will grant immunity from any fine which would otherwise have been imposed to an undertaking disclosing its participation in an alleged cartel affecting the

Community if that undertaking is the first to submit information and evidence which in the Commission's view will enable it to:

(a)   carry out a targeted inspection in connection with the alleged cartel; or

(b)   find an infringement of Article 81 EC in connection with the alleged cartel.

(9)   For the Commission to be able to carry out a targeted inspection within the meaning of point (8)(a), the undertaking must provide the Commission with the information and evidence listed below, to the extent that this, in the Commission's view, would not jeopardize the inspections:

     (a)   A corporate statement which includes, in so far as it is known to the applicant at the time of the submission:

            — A detailed description of the alleged cartel arrangement, including for instance its aims, activities and functioning; the product or service concerned, the geographic scope, the duration of and the estimated market volumes affected by the alleged cartel; the specific dates, locations, content of and participants in alleged cartel contacts, and all relevant explanations in connection with the pieces of evidence provided in support of the application.

            — The name and address of the legal entity submitting the immunity application as well as the names and addresses of all the other undertakings that participate(d) in the alleged cartel;

            — The names, positions, office locations and, where necessary, home addresses of all individuals who, to the applicant's knowledge, are or have been involved in the alleged cartel, including those individuals which have been involved on the applicant's behalf;

            — Information on which other competition authorities, inside or outside the EU, have been approached or are intended to be approached in relation to the alleged cartel; and

     (b)   Other evidence relating to the alleged cartel in possession of the applicant or available to it at the time of the submission, including in particular any evidence contemporaneous to the infringement.

(10)   Immunity pursuant to point (8)(a) will not be granted if, at the time of the submission, the Commission had already sufficient evidence to adopt a decision to carry out an inspection in connection with the alleged cartel or had already carried out such an inspection.

(11)   Immunity pursuant to point (8)(b) will only be granted on the cumulative conditions that the Commission did not have, at the time of the submission, sufficient evidence to find an infringement of Article 81 EC in connection with the alleged cartel and that no undertaking had been granted conditional immunity from fines under point (8)(a) in connection with the alleged cartel. In order to qualify, an undertaking must be the first to provide contemporaneous, incriminating evidence of the alleged cartel as well as a corporate statement containing the kind of information specified in point (9)(a), which would enable the Commission to find an infringement of Article 81 EC.

(12)   In addition to the conditions set out in points (8)(a), (9) and (10) or in points (8)(b) and 11, all the following conditions must be met in any case to qualify for any immunity from a fine:

     (a)   The undertaking cooperates genuinely, fully, on a continuous basis and expeditiously from the time it submits its application throughout the Commission's administrative procedure. This includes:

            — providing the Commission promptly with all relevant information and evidence relating to the alleged cartel that comes into its possession or is available to it;

            — remaining at the Commission's disposal to answer promptly to any request that may contribute to the establishment of the facts;

            — making current (and, if possible, former) employees and directors available for interviews with the Commission;

            — not destroying, falsifying or concealing relevant information or evidence relating to the alleged cartel; and

            — not disclosing the fact or any of the content of its application before the Commission has issued a statement of objections in the case, unless otherwise agreed;

    (b)   The undertaking ended its involvement in the alleged cartel immediately following its application, except for what would, in the Commission's view, be reasonably necessary to preserve the integrity of the inspections;

    (c)   When contemplating making its application to the Commission, the undertaking must not have destroyed, falsified or concealed evidence of the alleged cartel nor disclosed the fact or any of the content of its contemplated application, except to other competition authorities.

(13) An undertaking which took steps to coerce other undertakings to join the cartel or to remain in it is not eligible for immunity from fines. It may still qualify for a reduction of fines if it fulfils the relevant requirements and meets all the conditions therefor.

B. Procedure

(14) An undertaking wishing to apply for immunity from fines should contact the Commission's Directorate General for Competition. The undertaking may either initially apply for a marker or immediately proceed to make a formal application to the Commission for immunity from fines in order to meet the conditions in points (8)(a) or (8)(b), as appropriate. The Commission may disregard any application for immunity from fines on the ground that it has been submitted after the statement of objections has been issued.

(15) The Commission services may grant a marker protecting an immunity applicant's place in the queue for a period to be specified on a case-by-case basis in order to allow for the gathering of the necessary information and evidence. To be eligible to secure a marker, the applicant must provide the Commission with information concerning its name and address, the parties to the alleged cartel, the affected product(s) and territory(-ies), the estimated duration of the alleged cartel and the nature of the alleged cartel conduct. The applicant should also inform the Commission on other past or possible future leniency applications to other authorities in relation to the alleged cartel and justify its request for a marker. Where a marker is granted, the Commission services determine the period within which the applicant has to perfect the marker by submitting the information and evidence required to meet the relevant threshold for immunity. Undertakings which have been granted a marker cannot perfect it by making a formal application in hypothetical terms. If the applicant perfects the marker within the period set by the Commission services, the information and evidence provided will be deemed to have been submitted on the date when the marker was granted.

(16) An undertaking making a formal immunity application to the Commission must:

    (a)   provide the Commission with all information and evidence relating to the alleged cartel available to it, as specified in points (8) and (9), including corporate statements; or

    (b)   initially present this information and evidence in hypothetical terms, in which case the undertaking must present a detailed descriptive list of the evidence it proposes to disclose at a later agreed date. This list should accurately reflect the nature and content of the evidence, whilst safeguarding the hypothetical nature of its disclosure. Copies of documents, from which sensitive parts have been removed, may be used to illustrate the nature and content of the evidence. The name of the applying undertaking and of other undertakings involved in the alleged cartel need not be disclosed until the evidence described in its application is submitted. However, the product or service concerned by the alleged cartel, the geographic scope of the alleged cartel and the estimated duration must be clearly identified.

(17) If requested, the Directorate General for Competition will provide an acknowledgement of receipt of the undertaking's application for immunity from fines, confirming the date and, where appropriate, time of the application.

(18) Once the Commission has received the information and evidence submitted by the undertaking under point (16)(a) and has verified that it meets the conditions set out in points (8)(a) or (8)(b), as appropriate, it will grant the undertaking conditional immunity from fines in writing.

(19) If the undertaking has presented information and evidence in hypothetical terms, the Commission will verify that the nature and content of the evidence described in the detailed list referred to in point (16)(b) will meet the conditions set out in points (8) (a) or (8)(b), as appropriate, and inform the undertaking accordingly. Following the disclosure of the evidence no later than on the date agreed and having verified that it corresponds to the description made in the list, the Commission will grant the undertaking conditional immunity from fines in writing.

(20) If it becomes apparent that immunity is not available or that the undertaking failed to meet the conditions set out in points (8)(a) or (8)(b), as appropriate, the Commission will inform the undertaking in writing. In such case, the undertaking may withdraw the evidence disclosed for the purposes of its immunity application or request the Commission to consider it under section III of this notice. This does not prevent the Commission from using its normal powers of investigation in order to obtain the information.

(21) The Commission will not consider other applications for immunity from fines before it has taken a position on an existing application in relation to the same alleged infringement, irrespective of whether the immunity application is presented formally or by requesting a marker.

(22) If at the end of the administrative procedure, the undertaking has met the conditions set out in point (12), the Commission will grant it immunity from fines in the relevant decision. If at the end of the administrative procedure, the undertaking has not met the conditions set out in point (12), the undertaking will not benefit from any favorable treatment under this Notice. If the Commission, after having granted conditional immunity ultimately finds that the immunity applicant has acted as a coercer, it will withhold immunity.

3   Reduction of a fine

A. Requirements to qualify for reduction of a fine

(23) Undertakings disclosing their participation in an alleged cartel affecting the Community that do not meet the conditions under section II above may be eligible to benefit from a reduction of any fine that would otherwise have been imposed.

(24) In order to qualify, an undertaking must provide the Commission with evidence of the alleged infringement which represents significant added value with respect to the evidence already in the Commission's possession and must meet the cumulative conditions set out in points (12)(a) to (12)(c) above.

(25) The concept of 'added value' refers to the extent to which the evidence provided strengthens, by its very nature and/or its level of detail, the Commission's ability to prove the alleged cartel. In this assessment, the Commission will generally consider written evidence originating from the period of time to which the facts pertain to have a greater value than evidence subsequently established. Incriminating evidence directly relevant to the facts in question will generally be considered to have a greater value than that with only indirect relevance. Similarly, the degree of corroboration from other sources required for the evidence submitted to be relied upon against other undertakings involved in the case will have an impact on the value of that evidence, so that compelling evidence will be attributed a greater value than evidence such as statements which require corroboration if contested.

(26) The Commission will determine in any final decision adopted at the end of the administrative procedure the level of reduction an undertaking will benefit from, relative to the fine which would otherwise be imposed. For the:

- first undertaking to provide significant added value: a reduction of 30–50%,
- second undertaking to provide significant added value: a reduction of 20–30%,
- subsequent undertakings that provide significant added value: a reduction of up to 20%.

In order to determine the level of reduction within each of these bands, the Commission will take into account the time at which the evidence fulfilling the condition in point (24) was submitted and the extent to which it represents added value.

If the applicant for a reduction of a fine is the first to submit compelling evidence in the sense of point (25) which the Commission uses to establish additional facts increasing the gravity or the duration of the infringement, the Commission will not take such additional facts into account when setting any fine to be imposed on the undertaking which provided this evidence.

B. Procedure

(27) An undertaking wishing to benefit from a reduction of a fine must make a formal application to the Commission and it must present it with sufficient evidence of the alleged cartel to qualify for a reduction of a fine in accordance with point (24) of this Notice. Any voluntary submission of evidence to the Commission which the undertaking that submits it wishes to be considered for the beneficial treatment of section III of this Notice must be clearly identified at the time of its submission as being part of a formal application for a reduction of a fine.

(28) If requested, the Directorate General for Competition will provide an acknowledgement of receipt of the undertaking's application for a reduction of a fine and of any subsequent submissions of evidence, confirming the date and, where appropriate, time of each submission. The Commission will not take any position on an application for a reduction of a fine before it has taken a position on any existing applications for conditional immunity from fines in relation to the same alleged cartel.

(29) If the Commission comes to the preliminary conclusion that the evidence submitted by the undertaking constitutes significant added value within the meaning of points (24) and (25), and that the undertaking has met the conditions of points (12) and (27), it will inform the undertaking in writing, no later than the date on which a statement of objections is notified, of its intention to apply a reduction of a fine within a specified band as provided in point (26). The Commission will also, within the same time frame, inform the undertaking in writing if it comes to the preliminary conclusion that the undertaking does not qualify for a reduction of a fine. The Commission may disregard any application for a reduction of fines on the grounds that it has been submitted after the statement of objections has been issued.

(30) The Commission will evaluate the final position of each undertaking which filed an application for a reduction of a fine at the end of the administrative procedure in any decision adopted. The Commission will determine in any such final decision:
  (a)   whether the evidence provided by an undertaking represented significant added value with respect to the evidence in the Commission's possession at that same time;
  (b)   whether the conditions set out in points (12)(a) to (12)(c) above have been met;
  (c)   the exact level of reduction an undertaking will benefit from within the bands specified in point (26).
       If the Commission finds that the undertaking has not met the conditions set out in point (12), the undertaking will not benefit from any favourable treatment under this Notice.

4   Corporate statements made to qualify under this notice

(31) A corporate statement is a voluntary presentation by or on behalf of an undertaking to the Commission of the undertaking's knowledge of a cartel and its role therein prepared specially to be submitted under this Notice. Any statement made vis-à-vis the Commission in relation to this notice, forms part of the Commission's file and can thus be used in evidence.

(32) Upon the applicant's request, the Commission may accept that corporate statements be provided orally unless the applicant has already disclosed the content of the corporate statement to third parties. Oral corporate statements will be recorded and transcribed at the Commission's premises. In accordance with Article 19 of Council Regulation (EC) No 1/2003 and Articles 3 and 17 of Commission Regulation (EC) No 773/2004, undertakings making oral corporate statements will be granted the opportunity to check the technical accuracy of the recording, which will be available at the Commission's premises and to correct the substance of their oral statements within a given time limit. Undertakings may waive these rights within the said time-

limit, in which case the recording will from that moment on be deemed to have been approved. Following the explicit or implicit approval of the oral statement or the submission of any corrections to it, the undertaking shall listen to the recordings at the Commission's premises and check the accuracy of the transcript within a given time limit. Non-compliance with the last requirement may lead to the loss of any beneficial treatment under this Notice.

(33) Access to corporate statements is only granted to the addressees of a statement of objections, provided that they commit — together with the legal counsels getting access on their behalf — not to make any copy by mechanical or electronic means of any information in the corporate statement to which access is being granted and to ensure that the information to be obtained from the corporate statement will solely be used for the purposes mentioned below. Other parties such as complainants will not be granted access to corporate statements. The Commission considers that this specific protection of a corporate statement is not justified as from the moment when the applicant discloses to third parties the content thereof.

(34) In accordance with the Commission Notice on rules for access to the Commission file, access to the file is only granted to the addressees of a statement of objections on the condition that the information thereby obtained may only be used for the purposes of judicial or administrative proceedings for the application of the Community competition rules at issue in the related administrative proceedings. The use of such information for a different purpose during the proceeding may be regarded as lack of cooperation within the meaning of points (12) and (27) of this Notice. Moreover, if any such use is made after the Commission has already adopted a prohibition decision in the proceeding, the Commission may, in any legal proceedings before the Community Courts, ask the Court to increase the fine in respect of the responsible undertaking. Should the information be used for a different purpose, at any point in time, with the involvement of an outside counsel, the Commission may report the incident to the bar of that counsel, with a view to disciplinary action.

(35) Corporate statements made under the present Notice will only be transmitted to the competition authorities of the Member States pursuant to Article 12 of Regulation No 1/2003, provided that the conditions set out in the Network Notice are met and provided that the level of protection against disclosure awarded by the receiving competition authority is equivalent to the one conferred by the Commission.

5   General considerations

(36) The Commission will not take a position on whether or not to grant conditional immunity, or otherwise on whether or not to reward any application, if it becomes apparent that the application concerns infringements covered by the five years limitation period for the imposition of penalties stipulated in Article 25(1)(b) of Regulation 1/2003, as such applications would be devoid of purpose.

(37) From the date of its publication in the Official Journal, this notice replaces the 2002 Commission notice on immunity from fines and reduction of fines in cartel cases for all cases in which no undertaking has contacted the Commission in order to take advantage of the favourable treatment set out in that notice. However, points (31) to (35) of the current notice will be applied from the moment of its publication to all pending and new applications for immunity from fines or reduction of fines.

(38) The Commission is aware that this notice will create legitimate expectations on which undertakings may rely when disclosing the existence of a cartel to the Commission.

(39) In line with the Commission's practice, the fact that an undertaking cooperated with the Commission during its administrative procedure will be indicated in any decision, so as to explain the reason for the immunity or reduction of the fine. The fact that immunity or reduction in respect of fines is granted cannot protect an undertaking from the civil law consequences of its participation in an infringement of Article 81 EC.

(40) The Commission considers that normally public disclosure of documents and written or recorded statements received in the context of this notice would undermine certain public or private interests, for example the protection of the purpose of inspections and investigations, within the meaning of Article 4 of Regulation (EC) No 1049/2001, even after the decision has been taken.

FREE MOVEMENT OF GOODS

COMMISSION DIRECTIVE (EEC) No 70/50 of 22 DECEMBER 1969 based on the provisions of Article 33(7), on the abolition of measures which have an effect equivalent to quantitative restrictions on imports and are not covered by other provisions adopted in pursuance of the EEC Treaty
[1970] OJ L13/29, 17

Article 1

The purpose of this Directive is to abolish the measures referred to in Articles 2 and 3, which were operative at the date of entry into force of the EEC Treaty.

Article 2

1. This Directive covers measures, other than those applicable equally to domestic or imported products, which hinder imports which could otherwise take place, including measures which make importation more difficult or costly than the disposal of domestic production.

2. In particular, it covers measures which make imports or the disposal, at any marketing stage, of imported products subject to a condition — other than a formality — which is required in respect of imported products only, or a condition differing from that required for domestic products and more difficult to satisfy. Equally, it covers, in particular, measures which favour domestic products or grant them a preference, other than an aid, to which conditions may or may not be attached.

3. The measures referred to must be taken to include those measures which:

   (a) lay down, for imported products only, minimum or maximum prices below or above which imports are prohibited, reduced or made subject to conditions liable to hinder importation;

   (b) lay down less favourable prices for imported products than for domestic products;

   (c) fix profit margins or any other price components for imported products only or fix these differently for domestic products and for imported products, to the detriment of the latter;

   (d) preclude any increase in the price of the imported product corresponding to the supplementary costs and charges inherent in importation;

   (e) fix the prices of products solely on the basis of the cost price or the quality of domestic products at such a level as to create a hindrance to importation;

   (f) lower the value of an imported product, in particular by causing a reduction in its intrinsic value, or increase its costs;

   (g) make access of imported products to the domestic market conditional upon having an agent or representative in the territory of the importing Member State;

   (h) lay down conditions of payment in respect of imported products only, or subject imported products to conditions which are different from those laid down for domestic products and more difficult to satisfy;

   (i) require, for imports only, the giving of guarantees or making of payments on account;

   (j) subject imported products only to conditions, in respect, in particular of shape, size, weight, composition, presentation, identification or putting up, or subject imported products to conditions which are different from those for domestic products and more difficult to satisfy;

   (k) hinder the purchase by private individuals of imported products only, or encourage, require or give preference to the purchase of domestic products only;

   (l) totally or partially preclude the use of national facilities or equipment in respect of imported products only, or totally or partially confine the use of such facilities or equipment to domestic products only;

   (m) prohibit or limit publicity in respect of imported products only, or totally or partially confine publicity to domestic products only;

(n)   prohibit, limit or require stocking in respect of imported products only; totally or partially confine the use of stocking facilities to domestic products only, or make the stocking of imported products subject to conditions which are different from those required for domestic products and more difficult to satisfy;

(o)   make importation subject to the granting of reciprocity by one or more Member States;

(p)   prescribe that imported products are to conform, totally or partially, to rules other than those of the importing country;

(q)   specify time limits for imported products which are insufficient or excessive in relation to the normal course of the various transactions to which these time limits apply;

(r)   subject imported products to controls or, other than those inherent in the customs clearance procedure, to which domestic products are not subject or which are stricter in respect of imported products than they are in respect of domestic products, without this being necessary in order to ensure equivalent protection;

(s)   confine names which are not indicative of origin or source to domestic products only.

Article 3

This Directive also covers measures governing the marketing of products which deal, in particular, with shape, size, weight, composition, presentation, identification or putting up and which are equally applicable to domestic and imported products, where the restrictive effect of such measures on the free movement of goods exceeds the effects intrinsic to trade rules. This is the case, in particular, where:

— the restrictive effects on the free movement of goods are out of proportion to their purpose;

— the same objective can be attained by other means which are less of a hindrance to trade.

COMMISSION PRACTICE NOTE ON IMPORT PROHIBITIONS

Communication from the Commission concerning the consequences of the judgment given by the Court of Justice on 20 February 1979 in Case 120/78 ('Cassis De Dijon') [1980] OJ C256/2

The following is the text of a letter which has been sent to the Member States; the European Parliament and the Council have also been notified of it.

In the Commission's Communication of 6 November 1978 on 'Safeguarding free trade within the Community', it was emphasised that the free movement of goods is being affected by a growing number of restrictive measures.

The judgment delivered by the Court of Justice on 20 February 1979 in Case 120/78 (the 'Cassis de Dijon' case), and recently reaffirmed in the judgment of 26 June 1980 in Case 788/79, has given the Commission some interpretative guidance enabling it to monitor more strictly the application of the Treaty rules on the free movement of goods, particularly Articles 30 to 36 of the EEC Treaty.

The Court gives a very general definition of the barriers to free trade which are prohibited by the provisions of Article 30 et seq. of the EEC Treaty. These are taken to include 'any national measure capable of hindering, directly or indirectly, actually or potentially, intra-Community trade'.

In its judgment of 20 February 1979 the Court indicates the scope of this definition as it applies to technical and commercial rules.

Any product lawfully produced and marketed in one Member State must, in principle, be admitted to the market of any other Member State.

Technical and commercial rules, even those equally applicable to national and imported products, may create barriers to trade only where those rules are necessary to satisfy mandatory requirements and to serve a purpose which is in the general interest and for which they are an essential guarantee. This purpose must be such as to take precedence over the requirements of the free movement of goods, which constitutes one of the fundamental rules of the Community.

The conclusions in terms of policy which the Commission draws from this new guidance are set out below.

— Whereas Member States may, with respect to domestic products and in the absence of relevant Community provisions, regulate the terms on which such products are marketed, the case is different for products imported from other Member States.

Any product imported from another Member State must in principle be admitted to the territory of the importing Member State if it has been lawfully produced, that is, conforms to the rules and processes of manufacture that are customarily and traditionally accepted in the exporting country, and is marketed in the territory of the latter.

This principle implies that Member States, when drawing up commercial or technical rules liable to affect the free movement of goods, may not take an exclusively national viewpoint and take account only of requirements confined to domestic products. The proper functioning of the common market demands that each Member State also give consideration to the legitimate requirements of the other Member States.

— Only under very strict conditions does the Court accept exceptions to this principle; barriers to trade resulting from differences between commercial and technical rules are only admissible:

— if the rules are necessary, that is appropriate and not excessive, in order to satisfy mandatory requirements (public health, protection of consumers or the environment, the fairness of commercial transactions, etc.);

— if the rules serve a purpose in the general interest which is compelling enough to justify an exception to a fundamental rule of the Treaty such as the free movement of goods;

— if the rules are essential for such a purpose to be attained, i.e., are the means which are the most appropriate and at the same time least hinder trade. The Court's interpretation has induced the Commission to set out a number of guidelines.

— The principles deduced by the Court imply that a Member State may not in principle prohibit the sale in its territory of a product lawfully produced and marketed in another Member State even if the product is produced according to technical or quality requirements which differ from those imposed on its domestic products. Where a product 'suitably and satisfactorily' fulfils the legitimate objective of a Member State's own rules (public safety, protection of the consumer or the environment, etc.), the importing country cannot justify prohibiting its sale in its territory by claiming that the way it fulfils the objective is different from that imposed on domestic products.

In such a case, an absolute prohibition of sale could not be considered 'necessary' to satisfy a 'mandatory requirement' because it would not be an 'essential guarantee' in the sense defined in the Court's judgment.

The Commission will therefore have to tackle a whole body of commercial rules which lay down that products manufactured and marketed in one Member State must fulfil technical or qualitative conditions in order to be admitted to the market of another and specifically in all cases where the trade barriers occasioned by such rules are inadmissible according to the very strict criteria set out by the Court.

The Commission is referring in particular to rules covering the composition, designation, presentation and packaging of products as well as rules requiring compliance with certain technical standards.

— The Commission's work of harmonisation will henceforth have to be directed mainly at national laws having an impact on the functioning of the common market where barriers to trade to be removed arise from national provisions which are admissible under the criteria set by the Court.

The Commission will be concentrating on sectors deserving priority because of their economic relevance to the creation of a single internal market.

To forestall later difficulties, the Commission will be informing Member States of potential objections, under the terms of Community law, to provisions they may be considering introducing which come to the attention of the Commission.

It will be producing suggestions soon on the procedures to be followed in such cases.

The Commission is confident that this approach will secure greater freedom of trade for the Community's manufacturers, so strengthening the industrial base of the Community, while meeting the expectations of consumers.

COUNCIL REGULATION (EC) No 2679/98 of 7 DECEMBER 1998 on the functioning of the internal market in relation to the free movement of goods among the Member States
[1998] OJ L337/8

Article 1

For the purpose of this Regulation:

1. the term 'obstacle' shall mean an obstacle to the free movement of goods among Member States which is attributable to a Member State, whether it involves action or inaction on its part, which may constitute a breach of Articles 30 to 36 of the Treaty and which:
    (a) leads to serious disruption of the free movement of goods by physically or otherwise preventing, delaying or diverting their import into, export from or transport across a Member State,
    (b) causes serious loss to the individuals affected, and
    (c) requires immediate action in order to prevent any continuation, increase or intensification of the disruption or loss in question;
2. the term 'inaction' shall cover the case when the competent authorities of a Member State, in the presence of an obstacle caused by actions taken by private individuals, fail to take all necessary and proportionate measures within their powers with a view to removing the obstacle and ensuring the free movement of goods in their territory.

Article 2

This Regulation may not be interpreted as affecting in any way the exercise of fundamental rights as recognised in Member States, including the right or freedom to strike. These rights may also include the right or freedom to take other actions covered by the specific industrial relations systems in Member States.

Article 3

1. When an obstacle occurs or when there is a threat thereof
    (a) any Member State (whether or not it is the Member State concerned) which has relevant information shall immediately transmit it to the Commission, and
    (b) the Commission shall immediately transmit to the Member States that information and any information from any other source which it may consider relevant.
2. The Member State concerned shall respond as soon as possible to requests for information from the Commission and from other Member States concerning the nature of the obstacle or threat and the action which it has taken or proposes to take. Information exchange between Member States shall also be transmitted to the Commission.

Article 4

1. When an obstacle occurs, and subject to Article 2, the Member State concerned shall
    (a) take all necessary and proportionate measures so that the free movement of goods is assured in the territory of the Member State in accordance with the Treaty, and
    (b) inform the Commission of the actions which its authorities have taken or intend to take.
2. The Commission shall immediately transmit the information received under paragraph 1(b) to the other Member States.

Article 5

1. Where the Commission considers that an obstacle is occurring in a Member State, it shall notify the Member State concerned of the reasons that have led the Commission to such a conclusion and shall request the Member State to take all necessary and proportionate measures to remove the said obstacle within a period which it shall determine with reference to the urgency of the case.
2. In reaching its conclusion, the Commission shall have regard to Article 2.
3. The Commission may publish in the *Official Journal of the European Communities* the text of the notification which it has sent to the Member State concerned and shall immediately transmit the text to any party which requests it.
4. The Member State shall, within five working days of receipt of the text, either:

    — inform the Commission of the steps which it has taken or intends to take to implement paragraph 1, or

    — communicate a reasoned submission as to why there is no obstacle constituting a breach of Articles 30 to 36 of the Treaty.

5.   In exceptional cases, the Commission may allow an extension of the deadline mentioned in paragraph 4 if the Member State submits a duly substantiated request and the grounds cited are deemed acceptable.

REGULATION (EU) 2019/515 OF THE EUROPEAN PARLIAMENT AND OF THE COUNCIL of 19 March 2019
on the mutual recognition of goods lawfully marketed in another Member State and repealing Regulation (EC) No 764/2008
[2019] OJ L91/1

CHAPTER I
GENERAL PROVISIONS

Article 1   Subject matter

1.   The aim of this Regulation is to strengthen the functioning of the internal market by improving the application of the principle of mutual recognition and by removing unjustified barriers to trade.

2.   This Regulation lays down rules and procedures concerning the application by Member States of the principle of mutual recognition in individual cases in relation to goods which are subject to Article 34 TFEU and which are lawfully marketed in another Member State, having regard to Article 36 TFEU and the case-law of the Court of Justice of the European Union.

3.   This Regulation also provides for the establishment and maintenance of Product Contact Points in Member States and for cooperation and exchange of information in the context of the principle of mutual recognition.

Article 2   Scope

1.   This Regulation applies to goods of any type, including agricultural products within the meaning of the second subparagraph of Article 38(1) TFEU, and to administrative decisions that have been taken or are to be taken by a competent authority of a Member State of destination in relation to any such goods that are lawfully marketed in another Member State, where the administrative decision meets the following criteria:

    (a)   the basis for the administrative decision is a national technical rule applicable in the Member State of destination; and

    (b)   the direct or indirect effect of the administrative decision is to restrict or deny market access in the Member State of destination.

Administrative decision includes any administrative step that is based on a national technical rule and that has the same or substantially the same legal effect as the effect referred to in point (b).

2.   For the purposes of this Regulation, a 'national technical rule' is any provision of a law, regulation or other administrative provision of a Member State which has the following characteristics:

    (a)   it covers goods or aspects of goods that are not the subject of harmonisation at Union level;

    (b)   it either prohibits the making available of goods, or goods of a given type, on the market in that Member State, or it makes compliance with the provision compulsory, de facto or de jure, whenever goods, or goods of a given type, are made available on that market; and

    (c)   it does at least one of the following:

        (i)   it lays down the characteristics required of goods or of goods of a given type, such as their levels of quality, performance or safety, or their dimensions, including the requirements applicable to those goods as regards the names under which they are sold, terminology, symbols, testing and test methods, packaging, marking or labelling and conformity assessment procedures;

(ii)   for the purpose of protecting consumers or the environment, it imposes other requirements on goods or goods of a given type that affect the life-cycle of the goods after they have been made available on the market in that Member State, such as conditions of use, recycling, reuse or disposal, where such conditions can significantly influence either the composition or nature of those goods, or the making available of them on the market in that Member State.

3.   Point (c)(i) of paragraph 2 of this Article also covers production methods and processes used in respect of agricultural products as referred to in the second subparagraph of Article 38(1) TFEU, and in respect of products intended for human or animal consumption, as well as production methods and processes relating to other products, where these have an effect on their characteristics.

4.   A prior authorisation procedure does not itself constitute a national technical rule for the purposes of this Regulation, but a decision to refuse prior authorisation based on a national technical rule shall be considered to be an administrative decision to which this Regulation applies, if that decision fulfils the other requirements of the first subparagraph of paragraph 1.

5.   This Regulation does not apply to:

(a)   decisions of a judicial nature taken by national courts or tribunals;

(b)   decisions of a judicial nature taken by law enforcement authorities in the course of the investigation or prosecution of a criminal offence as regards the terminology, symbols or any material reference to unconstitutional or criminal organisations or offences of a racist, discriminatory or xenophobic nature.

6.   Articles 5 and 6 shall not affect the application of the following provisions:

(a)   points (b) to (f) of Article 8(1) and Article 8(3) of Directive 2001/95/EC;

(b)   point (a) of Article 50(3) and Article 54 of Regulation (EC) No 178/2002;

(c)   Article 90 of Regulation (EU) No 1306/2013; and

(d)   Article 138 of Regulation (EU) 2017/625.

7.   This Regulation does not affect the obligation under Directive (EU) 2015/1535 to notify draft national technical regulations to the Commission and the Member States prior to their adoption.

Article 3   Definitions

For the purposes of this Regulation, the following definitions apply:

(1)   'lawfully marketed in another Member State' means that goods or goods of that type comply with the relevant rules applicable in that Member State or are not subject to any such rules in that Member State, and are made available to end users in that Member State;

(2)   'making available on the market' means any supply of goods for distribution, consumption or use on the market within the territory of a Member State in the course of a commercial activity, whether in return for payment or free of charge;

(3)   'restricting market access' means imposing conditions to be fulfilled before goods can be made available on the market in the Member State of destination, or conditions for keeping goods on that market, which in either case require the modification of one or more of the characteristics of those goods, as referred to in point (c)(i) of Article 2(2), or require the performance of additional testing;

(4)   'denying market access' means any of the following:

(a)   prohibiting goods from being made available on the market in the Member State of destination or from being kept on that market; or

(b)   requiring the withdrawal or recall of those goods from that market;

(5)   'withdrawal' means any measure aimed at preventing goods in the supply chain from being made available on the market;

(6)   'recall' means any measure aimed at achieving the return of goods that have already been made available to the end user;

(7)   'prior authorisation procedure' means an administrative procedure under the law of a Member State whereby the competent authority of that Member State is required, on

the basis of an application by an economic operator, to give its formal approval before goods may be made available on the market in that Member State;

(8) 'producer' means:

 (a) any natural or legal person who manufactures goods or has goods designed or manufactured, or who produces goods which were not the result of a manufacturing process, including agricultural products, and markets them under that person's name or trademark,

 (b) any natural or legal person who modifies goods already lawfully marketed in a Member State in a way that might affect compliance with the relevant rules applicable in that Member State, or

 (c) any other natural or legal person who, by putting its name, trademark or other distinguishing feature on goods or on the documents that accompany those goods, presents itself as the producer of those goods;

(9) 'authorised representative' means any natural or legal person established within the Union who has received a written mandate from a producer to act on that producer's behalf with regard to the making available of goods on the market in question;

(10) 'importer' means any natural or legal person established within the Union who makes goods from a third country available on the Union market for the first time;

(11) 'distributor' means any natural or legal person in the supply chain, other than the producer or the importer, who makes goods available on the market in a Member State;

(12) 'economic operator' means any of the following in relation to goods: the producer, the authorised representative, the importer or the distributor;

(13) 'end user' means any natural or legal person residing or established in the Union, to whom the goods have been made available or are being made available, either as a consumer outside of any trade, business, craft or profession or as a professional end user in the course of its industrial or professional activities;

(14) 'legitimate public interest grounds' means any of the grounds set out in Article 36 TFEU or any other overriding reasons of public interest;

(15) 'conformity assessment body' means a conformity assessment body as defined in point 13 of Article 2 of Regulation (EC) No 765/2008.

CHAPTER II
PROCEDURES CONCERNING APPLICATION OF THE PRINCIPLE OF MUTUAL RECOGNITION IN INDIVIDUAL CASES

Article 4 Mutual recognition declaration

1. The producer of goods, or of goods of a given type, that are being made or are to be made available on the market in the Member State of destination may draw up a voluntary declaration of lawful marketing of goods for the purposes of mutual recognition ('mutual recognition declaration') in order to demonstrate to the competent authorities of the Member State of destination that the goods, or the goods of that type, are lawfully marketed in another Member State.

 The producer may mandate its authorised representative to draw up the mutual recognition declaration on its behalf.

 The mutual recognition declaration shall follow the structure set out in Part I and Part II of the Annex and shall contain all the information specified therein.

 The producer or its authorised representative, where mandated to do so, may fill in the mutual recognition declaration with only the information set out in Part I of the Annex. In such case the information set out in Part II of the Annex shall be filled in by the importer or by the distributor.

 Alternatively, both parts of the mutual recognition declaration may be drawn up by the importer or by the distributor, provided that the signatory can supply the evidence referred to in point (a) of Article 5(4).

 The mutual recognition declaration shall be drawn up in one of the official languages of the Union. Where that language is not the language required by the Member State of destination, the economic operator shall translate the mutual recognition declaration into a language required by the Member State of destination.

2. Economic operators who sign the mutual recognition declaration or a part of it shall be responsible for the content and accuracy of the information that they provide in

the mutual recognition declaration, including the correctness of the information they translate. For the purposes of this paragraph, economic operators shall be liable in accordance with national laws.

3. Economic operators shall ensure that the mutual recognition declaration is kept up to date at all times, reflecting any changes in the information that they have provided in the mutual recognition declaration.

4. The mutual recognition declaration may be supplied to the competent authority of the Member State of destination for the purposes of an assessment to be carried out under Article 5. It may be supplied either in paper form or by electronic means or be made available online in accordance with the requirements of the Member State of destination.

5. Where economic operators make the mutual recognition declaration available online, the following conditions apply:
    (a) the type of goods or the series to which the mutual recognition declaration applies shall be easily identifiable; and
    (b) the technical means used shall ensure easy navigation and shall be monitored to ensure the availability of, and access to, the mutual recognition declaration.

6. Where the goods for which the mutual recognition declaration is being supplied are also subject to a Union act requiring an EU declaration of conformity, the mutual recognition declaration may be attached to the EU declaration of conformity.

Article 5   Assessment of goods

1. Where a competent authority of the Member State of destination intends to assess goods subject to this Regulation to establish whether the goods or goods of that type are lawfully marketed in another Member State, and, if so, whether the legitimate public interests covered by the applicable national technical rule of the Member State of destination are adequately protected, having regard to the characteristics of the goods in question, it shall contact the economic operator concerned without delay.

2. When entering into contact with the economic operator concerned, the competent authority of the Member State of destination shall inform the economic operator of the assessment, indicating the goods that are subject to that assessment and specifying the applicable national technical rule or prior authorisation procedure. The competent authority of the Member State of destination shall also inform the economic operator of the possibility of supplying a mutual recognition declaration in accordance with Article 4 for the purposes of that assessment.

3. The economic operator shall be allowed to make the goods available on the market in the Member State of destination while the competent authority carries out the assessment under paragraph 1 of this Article, and may continue to do so unless the economic operator receives an administrative decision restricting or denying market access for those goods. This paragraph shall not apply where the assessment is carried out in the framework of a prior authorisation procedure, or where the competent authority temporary suspends the making available on the market of the goods that are subject to that assessment in accordance with Article 6.

4. If a mutual recognition declaration is supplied to a competent authority of the Member State of destination in accordance with Article 4, then for the purposes of the assessment under paragraph 1 of this Article:
    (a) the mutual recognition declaration, together with supporting evidence necessary to verify the information contained in it that was provided in response to a request by the competent authority, shall be accepted by the competent authority as sufficient to demonstrate that the goods are lawfully marketed in another Member State; and
    (b) the competent authority shall not require any other information or documentation from any economic operator for the purpose of demonstrating that the goods are lawfully marketed in another Member State.

5. If a mutual recognition declaration is not supplied to a competent authority of the Member State of destination in accordance with Article 4, then for the purposes of the assessment under paragraph 1 of this Article, the competent authority may request the economic operators concerned to provide documentation and information that is necessary for that assessment concerning the following:
    (a) the characteristics of the goods or type of goods in question; and
    (b) lawful marketing of the goods in another Member State.

6. The economic operator concerned shall be allowed at least 15 working days following the request of the competent authority of the Member State of destination in which to submit the documents and information referred to in point (a) of paragraph 4 or in paragraph 5, or to submit any arguments or comments that the economic operator might have.

7. For the purposes of the assessment under paragraph 1 of this Article, the competent authority of the Member State of destination, in accordance with Article 10(3), may contact the competent authorities or the Product Contact Points of the Member State in which an economic operator claims to be lawfully marketing its goods, if the competent authority needs to verify any information provided by the economic operator.

8. In carrying out the assessment under paragraph 1, the competent authorities of Member States of destination shall take due account of the content of test reports or certificates issued by a conformity assessment body that have been provided by any economic operator as part of the assessment. The competent authorities of Member States of destination shall not refuse test reports or certificates that were issued by a conformity assessment body accredited for the appropriate field of conformity assessment activity in accordance with Regulation (EC) No 765/2008 on grounds related to the competence of that body.

9. Where, on completion of an assessment under paragraph 1 of this Article, the competent authority of a Member State of destination takes an administrative decision with respect to the goods that it has assessed, it shall notify that administrative decision without delay to the economic operator referred to in paragraph 1 of this Article. The competent authority shall also notify that administrative decision to the Commission and to the other Member States no later than 20 working days after it took the decision. For that purpose, it shall use the system referred to in Article 11.

10. The administrative decision referred to in paragraph 9 shall set out the reasons for the decision in a manner that is sufficiently detailed and reasoned to facilitate an assessment of its compatibility with the principle of mutual recognition and with the requirements of this Regulation.

11. In particular, the following information shall be included in the administrative decision referred to in paragraph 9:
    (a) the national technical rule on which the administrative decision is based;
    (b) the legitimate public interest grounds justifying the application of the national technical rule on which the administrative decision is based;
    (c) the technical or scientific evidence that the competent authority of the Member State of destination considered, including, where applicable, any relevant changes in the state of the art that have occurred since the national technical rule came into force;
    (d) a summary of the arguments put forward by the economic operator concerned that are relevant for the assessment under paragraph 1, if any;
    (e) the evidence demonstrating that the administrative decision is appropriate for the purpose of achieving the objective pursued and that the administrative decision does not go beyond what is necessary in order to attain that objective.

12. The administrative decision referred to in paragraph 9 of this Article shall specify the remedies available under the national law of the Member State of destination and the time limits applicable to those remedies. It shall also include a reference to the possibility for economic operators to use SOLVIT and the procedure under Article 8.

13. The administrative decision referred to in paragraph 9 shall not take effect before it has been notified to the economic operator concerned under that paragraph.

Article 6 Temporary suspension of market access

1. When the competent authority of a Member State is carrying out an assessment of goods pursuant to Article 5, it may temporarily suspend the making available of those goods on the market in that Member State only if:
    (a) under normal or reasonably foreseeable conditions of use, the goods pose a serious risk to safety or health of persons or to the environment, including one where the effects are not immediate, which requires rapid intervention by the competent authority; or
    (b) the making available of the goods, or of goods of that type, on the market in that Member State is generally prohibited in that Member State on grounds of public morality or public security.

2. The competent authority of the Member State shall immediately notify the economic operator concerned, the Commission and the other Member States of any temporary suspension pursuant to paragraph 1 of this Article. The notification to the Commission and the other Member States shall be made by means of the system referred to in Article 11. In cases falling within point (a) of paragraph 1 of this Article, the notification shall be accompanied by a detailed technical or scientific justification demonstrating why the case falls within the scope of that point.

Article 7   Notification through RAPEX or RASFF

If the administrative decision referred to in Article 5 or the temporary suspension referred to in Article 6 is also a measure which is to be notified through the Rapid Information Exchange System (RAPEX) in accordance with Directive 2001/95/EC or through the Rapid Alert System for Food and Feed (RASFF) in accordance with Regulation (EC) No 178/2002, a separate notification to the Commission and the other Member States under this Regulation shall not be required, provided that the following conditions are met:

    (a) the RAPEX or RASFF notification indicates that the notification of the measure also serves as a notification under this Regulation; and

    (b) the supporting evidence required for the administrative decision under Article 5 or for the temporary suspension under Article 6 is included with the RAPEX or RASFF notification.

Article 8   Problem-solving procedure

1. Where an economic operator affected by an administrative decision has submitted it to SOLVIT and where, during the SOLVIT procedure, the Home Centre or the Lead Centre requests the Commission to give an opinion in order to assist in solving the case, the Home Centre and the Lead Centre shall provide the Commission with all relevant documents relating to the administrative decision concerned.

2. After receiving the request referred to in paragraph 1, the Commission shall assess whether the administrative decision is compatible with the principle of mutual recognition and with the requirements of this Regulation.

3. For the purposes of the assessment referred to in paragraph 2 of this Article, the Commission shall consider the administrative decision notified in accordance with Article 5(9) and the documents and information provided within the SOLVIT procedure. Where additional information or documents are needed for the purposes of the assessment referred to in paragraph 2 of this Article, the Commission shall, without undue delay, request the relevant SOLVIT Centre to enter into communication with the economic operator concerned or with the competent authorities which took the administrative decision, for the purpose of obtaining such additional information or documents.

4. Within 45 working days of receipt of the request referred to in paragraph 1, the Commission shall complete its assessment and issue an opinion. Where appropriate, the Commission's opinion shall identify any concerns that should be addressed in the SOLVIT case or shall make recommendations to assist in solving the case. The 45 working day period does not include the time necessary for the Commission to receive the additional information and documents as provided for in paragraph 3.

5. Where the Commission has been informed that the case is solved during the assessment referred to in paragraph 2, the Commission shall not be required to issue an opinion.

6. The Commission's opinion shall be communicated through the relevant SOLVIT Centre to the economic operator concerned and to the relevant competent authorities. That opinion shall be notified by the Commission to all Member States by means of the system referred to in Article 11. The opinion shall be taken into account during the SOLVIT procedure referred to in paragraph 1 of this Article.

CHAPTER III
ADMINISTRATIVE COOPERATION, MONITORING AND COMMUNICATION

Article 9   Tasks of the Product Contact Points

1 Member States shall designate and maintain Product Contact Points on their territory and shall ensure that their Product Contact Points have sufficient powers and adequate

resources for the proper performance of their tasks. They shall ensure that Product Contact Points deliver their services in accordance with Regulation (EU) 2018/1724.

2. Product Contact Points shall provide the following information online:

    (a) information on the principle of mutual recognition and the application of this Regulation in the territory of their Member State, including information on the procedure set out in Article 5;

    (b) the contact details, by means of which the competent authorities within that Member State may be contacted directly, including the particulars of the authorities responsible for supervising the implementation of the national technical rules applicable in the territory of their Member State;

    (c) the remedies and procedures available in the territory of their Member State in the event of a dispute between the competent authority and an economic operator, including the procedure set out in Article 8.

3. Where necessary to complement the information provided online under paragraph 2, Product Contact Points shall provide, at the request of an economic operator or a competent authority of another Member State, any useful information, such as electronic copies of, or online access to, the national technical rules and national administrative procedures applicable to specific goods or goods of a specific type in the territory in which the Product Contact Point is established or information on whether those goods or goods of that type are subject to prior authorisation under national law.

4. Product Contact Points shall respond within 15 working days of receiving any request under paragraph 3.

5. Product Contact Points shall not charge any fee for the provision of the information under paragraph 3.

Article 10   Administrative cooperation

1. The Commission shall provide for and ensure efficient cooperation among the competent authorities and the Product Contact Points of the various Member States through the following activities:

    (a) facilitating and coordinating the exchange and collection of information and best practices with regard to the application of the principle of mutual recognition;

    (b) supporting the functioning of the Product Contact Points and enhancing their cross-border cooperation;

    (c) facilitating and coordinating the exchange of officials among Member States and the organisation of common training and awareness raising programmes for authorities and businesses.

2. Member States shall ensure that their competent authorities and Product Contact Points participate in the activities referred to in paragraph 1.

3. Upon a request by a competent authority of the Member State of destination pursuant to Article 5(7), the competent authorities in the Member State in which an economic operator claims to be lawfully marketing its goods shall provide the competent authority of the Member State of destination within 15 working days with any information relevant for verifying data and documents supplied by the economic operator during the assessment under Article 5relating to those goods. The Product Contact Points may be used to facilitate contacts between the relevant competent authorities in accordance with the time limit for providing the requested information set out in Article 9(4).

Article 11   Information and communication system

1. For the purposes of Articles 5, 6 and 10 of this Regulation, the information and communication system set out in Article 23 of Regulation (EC) No 765/2008 shall be used, except as provided in Article 7 of this Regulation.

2. The Commission shall adopt implementing acts specifying the details and functionalities of the system referred to in paragraph 1 of this Article for the purposes of this Regulation. Those implementing acts shall be adopted in accordance with the examination procedure referred to in Article 15(2).

FREE MOVEMENT OF PERSONS

REGULATION (EU) No 492/2011 OF THE EUROPEAN PARLIAMENT AND OF THE COUNCIL
of 5 APRIL 2011
on freedom of movement for workers within the Union
[2011] OJ L141/1

CHAPTER I
EMPLOYMENT, EQUAL TREATMENT AND WORKERS' FAMILIES

SECTION 1

Eligibility for employment

Article 1

1. Any national of a Member State shall, irrespective of his place of residence, have the right to take up an activity as an employed person, and to pursue such activity, within the territory of another Member State in accordance with the provisions laid down by law, regulation or administrative action governing the employment of nationals of that State.
2. He shall, in particular, have the right to take up available employment in the territory of another Member State with the same priority as nationals of that State.

Article 2

Any national of a Member State and any employer pursuing an activity in the territory of a Member State may exchange their applications for and offers of employment, and may conclude and perform contracts of employment in accordance with the provisions in force laid down by law, regulation or administrative action, without any discrimination resulting therefrom.

Article 3

1. Under this Regulation, provisions laid down by law, regulation or administrative action or administrative practices of a Member State shall not apply:
    (a) where they limit application for and offers of employment, or the right of foreign nationals to take up and pursue employment or subject these to conditions not applicable in respect of their own nationals; or
    (b) where, though applicable irrespective of nationality, their exclusive or principal aim or effect is to keep nationals of other Member States away from the employment offered.
    The first subparagraph shall not apply to conditions relating to linguistic knowledge required by reason of the nature of the post to be filled.
2. There shall be included in particular among the provisions or practices of a Member State referred to in the first subparagraph of paragraph 1 those which:
    (a) prescribe a special recruitment procedure for foreign nationals;
    (b) limit or restrict the advertising of vacancies in the press or through any other medium or subject it to conditions other than those applicable in respect of employers pursuing their activities in the territory of that Member State;
    (c) subject eligibility for employment to conditions of registration with employment offices or impede recruitment of individual workers, where persons who do not reside in the territory of that State are concerned.

Article 4

1. Provisions laid down by law, regulation or administrative action of the Member States which restrict by number or percentage the employment of foreign nationals in any undertaking, branch of activity or region, or at a national level, shall not apply to nationals of the other Member States.
2. When in a Member State the granting of any benefit to undertakings is subject to a minimum percentage of national workers being employed, nationals of the other Member States shall be counted as national workers, subject to Directive 2005/36/EC of the European Parliament and of the Council of 7 September 2005 on the recognition of professional qualifications.

Article 5
A national of a Member State who seeks employment in the territory of another Member State shall receive the same assistance there as that afforded by the employment offices in that State to their own nationals seeking employment.

Article 6
1. The engagement and recruitment of a national of one Member State for a post in another Member State shall not depend on medical, vocational or other criteria which are discriminatory on grounds of nationality by comparison with those applied to nationals of the other Member State who wish to pursue the same activity.
2. A national who holds an offer in his name from an employer in a Member State other than that of which he is a national may have to undergo a vocational test, if the employer expressly requests this when making his offer of employment.

SECTION 2

Employment and equality of treatment

Article 7
1. A worker who is a national of a Member State may not, in the territory of another Member State, be treated differently from national workers by reason of his nationality in respect of any conditions of employment and work, in particular as regards remuneration, dismissal, and, should he become unemployed, reinstatement or re-employment.
2. He shall enjoy the same social and tax advantages as national workers.
3. He shall also, by virtue of the same right and under the same conditions as national workers, have access to training in vocational schools and retraining centres.
4. Any clause of a collective or individual agreement or of any other collective regulation concerning eligibility for employment, remuneration and other conditions of work or dismissal shall be null and void in so far as it lays down or authorises discriminatory conditions in respect of workers who are nationals of the other Member States.

Article 8
A worker who is a national of a Member State and who is employed in the territory of another Member State shall enjoy equality of treatment as regards membership of trade unions and the exercise of rights attaching thereto, including the right to vote and to be eligible for the administration or management posts of a trade union. He may be excluded from taking part in the management of bodies governed by public law and from holding an office governed by public law. Furthermore, he shall have the right of eligibility for workers' representative bodies in the undertaking.

The first paragraph of this Article shall not affect laws or regulations in certain Member States which grant more extensive rights to workers coming from the other Member States.

Article 9
1. A worker who is a national of a Member State and who is employed in the territory of another Member State shall enjoy all the rights and benefits accorded to national workers in matters of housing, including ownership of the housing he needs.
2. A worker referred to in paragraph 1 may, with the same right as nationals, put his name down on the housing lists in the region in which he is employed, where such lists exist, and shall enjoy the resultant benefits and priorities.

   If his family has remained in the country whence he came, they shall be considered for this purpose as residing in the said region, where national workers benefit from a similar presumption.

SECTION 3

Workers' families

Article 10
The children of a national of a Member State who is or has been employed in the territory of another Member State shall be admitted to that State's general educational, apprenticeship and vocational training courses under the same conditions as the nationals of that State, if such children are residing in its territory.

Member States shall encourage all efforts to enable such children to attend these courses under the best possible conditions.

CHAPTER II
CLEARANCE OF VACANCIES AND APPLICATIONS FOR EMPLOYMENT

SECTION 1

Cooperation between the Member States and with the Commission

...

SECTION 2

Machinery for vacancy clearance

...

SECTION 3

Measures for controlling the balance of the labour market

SECTION 4

European Coordination Office

CHAPTER III
COMMITTEES FOR ENSURING CLOSE COOPERATION BETWEEN THE MEMBER STATES IN MATTERS CONCERNING THE FREEDOM OF MOVEMENT OF WORKERS AND THEIR EMPLOYMENT

SECTION 1

The Advisory Committee

Article 21

The Advisory Committee shall be responsible for assisting the Commission in the examination of any questions arising from the application of the Treaty on the Functioning of the European Union and measures taken in pursuance thereof, in matters concerning the freedom of movement of workers and their employment.

Article 22

The Advisory Committee shall be responsible in particular for:
(a) examining problems concerning freedom of movement and employment within the framework of national manpower policies, with a view to coordinating the employment policies of the Member States at Union level, thus contributing to the development of the economies and to an improved balance of the labour market;
(b) making a general study of the effects of implementing this Regulation and any supplementary measures;
(c) submitting to the Commission any reasoned proposals for revising this Regulation;
(d) delivering, either at the request of the Commission or on its own initiative, reasoned opinions on general questions or on questions of principle, in particular on exchange of information concerning developments in the labour market, on the movement of workers between Member States, on programmes or measures to develop vocational guidance and vocational training which are likely to increase the possibilities of freedom of movement and employment, and on all forms of assistance to workers and their families, including social assistance and the housing of workers.

Article 23

1. The Advisory Committee shall be composed of six members for each Member State, two of whom shall represent the Government, two the trade unions and two the employers' associations.
2. For each of the categories referred to in paragraph 1, one alternate member shall be appointed by each Member State.
3. The term of office of the members and their alternates shall be 2 years. Their appointments shall be renewable.

   On expiry of their term of office, the members and their alternates shall remain in office until replaced or until their appointments are renewed.

Article 24

The members of the Advisory Committee and their alternates shall be appointed by the Council, which shall endeavour, when selecting representatives of trade unions and employers' associations, to achieve adequate representation on the Committee of the various economic sectors concerned.

The list of members and their alternates shall be published by the Council for information in the *Official Journal of the European Union*.

Article 25

The Advisory Committee shall be chaired by a member of the Commission or his representative. The Chairman shall not vote. The Committee shall meet at least twice a year. It shall be convened by its Chairman, either on his own initiative, or at the request of at least one third of the members.

Secretarial services shall be provided for the Committee by the Commission.

Article 26

The Chairman may invite individuals or representatives of bodies with wide experience in the field of employment or movement of workers to take part in meetings as observers or as experts. The Chairman may be assisted by expert advisers.

The European Labour Authority established by Regulation (EU) 2019/1149 of the European Parliament and of the Council shall participate in the meetings of the Advisory Committee as an observer, providing technical input and expertise as relevant.

Article 27

1. An opinion delivered by the Advisory Committee shall not be valid unless two thirds of the members are present.
2. Opinions shall state the reasons on which they are based; they shall be delivered by an absolute majority of the votes validly cast; they shall be accompanied by a written statement of the views expressed by the minority, when the latter so requests.

Article 28

The Advisory Committee shall establish its working methods by rules of procedure which shall enter into force after the Council, having received an opinion from the Commission, has given its approval. The entry into force of any amendment that the Committee decides to make thereto shall be subject to the same procedure.

SECTION 2

The Technical Committee

Article 29

The Technical Committee shall be responsible for assisting the Commission in the preparation, promotion and follow-up of all technical work and measures for giving effect to this Regulation and any supplementary measures.

Article 30

The Technical Committee shall be responsible in particular for:

(a) promoting and advancing cooperation between the public authorities concerned in the Member States on all technical questions relating to freedom of movement of workers and their employment;

(b) formulating procedures for the organisation of the joint activities of the public authorities concerned;

(c) facilitating the gathering of information likely to be of use to the Commission and the undertaking of the studies and research provided for in this Regulation, and encouraging exchange of information and experience between the administrative bodies concerned;

(d) investigating at a technical level the harmonisation of the criteria by which Member States assess the state of their labour markets.

Article 31

1. The Technical Committee shall be composed of representatives of the Governments of the Member States. Each Government shall appoint as member of the Technical Committee one of the members who represent it on the Advisory Committee.

2. Each Government shall appoint an alternate from among its other representatives — members or alternates — on the Advisory Committee.

Article 32

The Technical Committee shall be chaired by a member of the Commission or his representative. The Chairman shall not vote. The Chairman and the members of the Committee may be assisted by expert advisers.

Secretarial services shall be provided for the Committee by the Commission.

Article 33

The proposals and opinions formulated by the Technical Committee shall be submitted to the Commission, and the Advisory Committee shall be informed thereof. Any such proposals and opinions shall be accompanied by a written statement of the views expressed by the various members of the Technical Committee, when the latter so request.

Article 34

The Technical Committee shall establish its working methods by rules of procedure which shall enter into force after the Council, having received an opinion from the Commission, has given its approval. The entry into force of any amendment which the Committee decides to make thereto shall be subject to the same procedure.

CHAPTER IV

FINAL PROVISIONS

Article 35

The rules of procedure of the Advisory Committee in force on 8 November 1968 shall continue to apply.

Article 36

1. This Regulation shall not affect the provisions of the Treaty establishing the European Atomic Energy Community which deal with eligibility for skilled employment in the field of nuclear energy, nor any measures taken in pursuance of that Treaty.

   Nevertheless, this Regulation shall apply to the category of workers referred to in the first subparagraph and to members of their families in so far as their legal position is not governed by the above-mentioned Treaty or measures.

2. This Regulation shall not affect measures taken in accordance with Article 48 of the Treaty on the Functioning of the European Union.

3. This Regulation shall not affect the obligations of Member States arising out of special relations or future agreements with certain non-European countries or territories, based on institutional ties existing on 8 November 1968, or agreements in existence on 8 November 1968 with certain non-European countries or territories, based on institutional ties between them.

   Workers from such countries or territories who, in accordance with this provision, are pursuing activities as employed persons in the territory of one of those Member States may not invoke the benefit of the provisions of this Regulation in the territory of the other Member States.

Article 37

Member States shall, for information purposes, communicate to the Commission the texts of agreements, conventions or arrangements concluded between them in the manpower field between the date of their being signed and that of their entry into force.

Article 38

The Commission shall adopt measures pursuant to this Regulation for its implementation. To this end it shall act in close cooperation with the central public authorities of the Member States.

Article 39

The administrative expenditure of the Advisory Committee shall be included in the general budget of the European Union in the section relating to the Commission.

Article 40

This Regulation shall apply to the Member States and to their nationals, without prejudice to Articles 2 and 3.

Article 41

Regulation (EEC) No 1612/68 is hereby repealed.
References to the repealed Regulation shall be construed as references to this Regulation and shall be read in accordance with the correlation table in Annex II.

Article 42

This Regulation shall enter into force on the 20th day following its publication in the *Official Journal of the European Union*.
This Regulation shall be binding in its entirety and directly applicable in all Member States.

REGULATION (EU) 2016/589 OF THE EUROPEAN PARLIAMENT AND OF THE COUNCIL
of 13 April 2016
on a European network of employment services (EURES), workers' access to mobility services and the further integration of labour markets, and amending Regulations (EU) No 492/2011 and (EU) No 1296/2013
(Text with EEA relevance)

CHAPTER I
GENERAL PROVISIONS

Article 1 Subject matter

This Regulation establishes a framework for cooperation to facilitate the exercise of the freedom of movement for workers within the Union in accordance with Article 45 TFEU, by laying down principles and rules on:

(a) the organisation of the EURES network between the Commission, the European Labour Authority and the Member States;

(b) cooperation between the Commission, the European Labour Authority and the Member States on sharing relevant available data on job vacancies, job applications and CVs;

(c) actions by and between Member States to achieve a balance between supply and demand in the labour market, with a view to achieving a high level of quality employment;

(d) the functioning of the EURES network, including cooperation with the social partners and involvement of other actors;

(e) mobility support services related to the functioning of the EURES network to be provided to workers and employers, thereby also promoting mobility on a fair basis;

    (f)   promotion of the EURES network at Union level through effective communication measures taken by the Commission, the European Labour Authority and the Member States.

Article 2 Scope

This Regulation shall apply to the Member States and citizens of the Union without prejudice to Articles 2 and 3 of Regulation (EU) No 492/2011.

Article 3 Definitions

For the purpose of this Regulation, the following definitions apply:

(1) 'public employment services' or 'PES' means the organisations of the Member States, as part of relevant ministries, public bodies or corporations falling under public law, that are responsible for implementing active labour market policies and providing quality employment services in the public interest;

(2) 'employment services' means a legal entity lawfully operating in a Member State which provides services for workers seeking employment and for employers wishing to recruit workers;

(3) 'job vacancy' means an offer of employment which would allow the successful applicant to enter into an employment relationship that would qualify that applicant as a worker for the purposes of Article 45 TFEU;

(4) 'clearance' means the exchange of information and processing of job vacancies, job applications and CVs;

(5) 'common IT platform' means the IT infrastructure and related platforms set up at Union level for the purpose of transparency and clearance in accordance with this Regulation;

(6) 'frontier worker' means a worker pursuing an activity as an employed person in a Member State and who resides in another Member State to which that worker returns as a rule daily or at least once a week;

(7) 'EURES cross-border partnership' means a grouping of EURES Members or Partners and, where relevant, other stakeholders outside of the EURES network, with the intention of long-term cooperation in regional structures, set up in cross-border regions between: the employment services on regional, local and, where appropriate, national level; the social partners; and, where relevant, other stakeholders of at least two Member States or a Member State and another country participating in the Union instruments aiming to support the EURES network.

(8) 'European Labour Authority' means the body established pursuant to Regulation (EU) 2019/1149 of the European Parliament and of the Council.

Article 4 Accessibility

1. Services under this Regulation shall be available to all workers and employers across the Union and shall respect the principle of equal treatment.

2. Accessibility for persons with disabilities to the information provided on the EURES portal and to support services available at national level shall be ensured. The Commission, the European Coordination Office and EURES Members and Partners shall determine the means to ensure this with regard to their respective obligations.

CHAPTER II

RE-ESTABLISHMENT OF THE EURES NETWORK

Article 5 Re-establishment of the EURES network

1. The EURES network is hereby re-established.

2. This Regulation replaces the regulatory framework on EURES as set out in Chapter II of Regulation (EU) No 492/2011 and Implementing Decision 2012/733/EU adopted on the basis of Article 38 of that Regulation.

Article 6 Objectives of the EURES network

The EURES network shall, within the areas of its activities, contribute to the following objectives:

    (a)   facilitating the exercise of the rights conferred by Article 45 TFEU and by Regulation (EU) No 492/2011;

(b) implementing the coordinated strategy for employment and, in particular, for promoting a skilled, trained and adaptable workforce as referred to in Article 145 TFEU;

(c) improving the functioning, cohesion and integration of the labour markets in the Union, including at cross-border level;

(d) promoting voluntary geographical and occupational mobility in the Union, including in cross-border regions, on a fair basis and in compliance with Union and national law and practice;

(e) supporting transitions into the labour market, thereby promoting the social and employment objectives referred to in Article 3 TEU.

Article 7   Composition of the EURES network

1. The EURES network shall comprise the following categories of organisation:

(a) a European Coordination Office, which shall be established within the European Labour Authority and which shall be responsible for assisting the EURES network in carrying out its activities;

(b) national coordination offices (NCOs) responsible for the application of this Regulation in the respective Member State, which shall be designated by the Member States and which may be their PES;

(c) the EURES Members, namely:

(i) the PES appointed by the Member States in accordance with Article 10; and

(ii) organisations admitted in accordance with Article 11, or, for a transitional period in accordance with Article 40, to provide at national, regional or local level, including on a cross-border basis, support with clearance and support services to workers and employers;

(d) the EURES Partners, which are organisations admitted in accordance with Article 11, and in particular with paragraphs 2 and 4 thereof, or for a transitional period in accordance with Article 40, to provide at national, regional or local level, including on a cross-border basis, support with clearance or support services to workers and employers.

(e) the Commission.

2. Social partner organisations may become part of the EURES network as EURES Members or Partners in accordance with Article 11.

Article 8   Responsibilities of the European Coordination Office

1. The European Coordination Office shall assist the EURES network in carrying out its activities, in particular by developing and conducting, in close cooperation with the NCOs and the Commission, the following activities:

(a) the formulation of a coherent framework and the provision of horizontal support activities for the benefit of the EURES network, including:

(i) as the system owner for the EURES portal, and related IT services, the definition of user needs and business requirements to be transmitted to the Commission for the operation and development of the portal, including its systems and procedures for the exchange of job vacancies, job applications, CVs and supporting documents and other information, in cooperation with other relevant Union information and advisory services or networks, and initiatives;

(ii) information and communication activities regarding the EURES network;

(iii) a common training programme and continuing professional development for the staff of the EURES Members and Partners and of the NCOs, ensuring the necessary expertise;

(iv) a helpdesk function supporting the staff of the EURES Members and Partners and NCOs, in particular the staff in direct contact with workers and employers;

(v) the facilitation of networking, exchange of best practices and mutual learning within the EURES network;

(b) the analysis of geographic and occupational mobility, taking into account the different situations in the Member States;

(c) the development of an appropriate cooperation and clearance structure within the Union for apprenticeships and traineeships, in accordance with this Regulation.

2. The European Coordination Office shall be managed by the European Labour Authority. The European Coordination Office shall establish a regular dialogue with the representatives of the social partners at Union level.

3. The European Coordination Office shall, after consulting the Coordination Group referred to in Article 14 and the Commission, draw up its multiannual work programmes.

Article 9 Responsibilities of the NCOs

1. Member States shall designate NCOs in accordance with point (b) of Article 7(1). The Member States shall notify the European Coordination Office of those designations.

2. Each NCO shall be responsible for:
   (a) the organisation of work relating to the EURES network in the Member State, including ensuring a coordinated transfer to the EURES portal of information on job vacancies, job applications and CVs in accordance with Article 17 through a single coordinated channel;
   (b) cooperation with the Commission, the European Labour Authority and the Member States on the clearance within the framework set in Chapter III;
   (c) providing the European Coordination Office with any available information on discrepancies between the number of job vacancies notified and the total number of job vacancies at national level;
   (d) the coordination of actions within the Member State concerned and together with other Member States in accordance with Chapter V.

3. Each NCO shall organise the implementation at national level of the horizontal support activities provided by the European Coordination Office as referred to in Article 8, where appropriate in close cooperation with the European Coordination Office and other NCOs. Those horizontal support activities shall include in particular:
   (a) for the purpose of publication, in particular on the EURES portal, the collection and validation of up-to-date information on the EURES Members and Partners operating on the NCO's national territory, their activities and the scope of the support services that they provide to workers and employers;
   (b) the provision of pre-training activities relating to EURES activity and the selection of staff for participation in the common training programme and in mutual learning activities;
   (c) the collection and analysis of data relating to Articles 31 and 32.

4. For the purpose of publication, in particular on the EURES portal, in the interest of workers and employers, each NCO shall make available, regularly update and disseminate in a timely manner, information and guidance available at national level relating to the situation in the Member State concerning:
   (a) living and working conditions, including general information on social security and tax payments;
   (b) the relevant administrative procedures regarding employment, and the rules applicable to workers upon taking up employment;
   (c) its national regulatory framework for apprenticeships and traineeships and existing Union rules and instruments;
   (d) without prejudice to point (b) of Article 17(2), access to vocational education and training;
   (e) the situation of frontier workers in particular in cross-border regions;
   (f) post-recruitment assistance in general and information about where to obtain such assistance within and, if such information is available, outside the EURES network.

   Where appropriate, NCOs may make available and disseminate the information in cooperation with other information and advisory services and networks and appropriate bodies at national level, including those referred to in Article 4 of Directive 2014/54/EU.

5. NCOs shall exchange information on the mechanisms and standards referred to in Article 17(5) as well as on standards regarding data security and data protection of relevance for the common IT platform. They shall cooperate with each other and with the European Coordination Office, in particular with regard to complaints and job vacancies that are considered not to comply with those standards under national law.

6. Each NCO shall provide general support to the EURES Members and Partners regarding collaboration with their EURES counterparts in other Member States,

including advice to the EURES Members and Partners on how to handle complaints relating to EURES job vacancies and recruitments, as well as on cooperation with relevant public authorities. If the information is available to the NCO, the outcome of complaints procedures shall be transmitted to the European Coordination Office.

7.   The NCO shall promote collaboration with stakeholders such as the social partners, career guidance services, vocational training and higher education institutions, chambers of commerce, social services and organisations representing vulnerable groups on the labour market and organisations involved in apprenticeships and traineeships schemes.

Article 10 Appointment of PES as EURES Members

1.   Member States shall appoint the PES relevant for the activities in the EURES network as EURES Members. The Member States shall inform the European Coordination Office of those appointments. By virtue of their appointment, those PES shall enjoy a special status within the EURES network.

2.   Member States shall ensure that, in their role as EURES Members, PES fulfil all obligations laid down in this Regulation and meet at least the minimum common criteria set out in Annex I.

3.   PES may fulfil their obligations as EURES Members through organisations acting under the responsibility of the PES, on the basis of delegation, outsourcing or specific agreements.

Article 11 Admission as EURES Members (other than PES) and as EURES Partners

1.   Each Member State shall, without undue delay but at the latest by 13 May 2018, have in place a system to admit organisations to become EURES Members and Partners, to monitor their activities and their compliance with the applicable law when applying this Regulation and, where necessary, to revoke their admission. That system shall be transparent and proportionate, shall respect the principles of equal treatment for applicant organisations and due process of law and shall provide remedies sufficient to ensure effective legal protection.

2.   For the purposes of the system referred to in paragraph 1, Member States shall establish the requirements and criteria for admitting EURES Members and Partners. Those requirements and criteria shall at least contain the minimum common criteria laid down in Annex I. Member States may establish additional requirements or criteria which are necessary for the purpose of a correct application of the rules applicable to the activities of employment services and the effective management of labour-market policies on their territory.

3.   Organisations lawfully operating in a Member State may apply to become EURES Members, subject to the conditions laid down in this Regulation and to the system referred to in paragraph 1. An organisation applying to become a EURES Member shall, in its application, undertake to fulfil all the obligations addressed to Members under this Regulation, including to perform all tasks referred to in points (a), (b) and (c) of Article 12(2).

4.   An organisation lawfully operating in a Member State may apply to become a EURES Partner, subject to the conditions laid down in this Regulation and to the system referred to in paragraph 1, provided that it duly justifies that it can fulfil no more than two of the tasks listed in points (a), (b) and (c) of Article 12(2), on the grounds of the scale, financial resources and nature of the services normally provided by the organisation or organisational structure, including being a not-for-profit organisation. An organisation applying to become EURES Partner shall, in its application, undertake to fulfil all the requirements to which EURES Partners are subject under this Regulation and at least one of the tasks referred to in points (a), (b) and (c) of Article 12(2).

5.   Member States shall admit applicant organisations to become EURES Members or Partners if they fulfil the applicable criteria and requirements referred to in paragraphs 2, 3 and 4.

6.   The NCOs shall inform the European Coordination Office of the systems referred to in paragraph 1, including the additional criteria and requirements as referred to in paragraph 2, of the EURES Members and Partners admitted in accordance with that system and of any refusal of admittance on the grounds of non-compliance with point 1 of Section 1 of Annex I. The European Coordination Office shall forward that information to the other NCOs.

7.   Member States shall revoke the admission of EURES Members and Partners where they cease to fulfil the applicable criteria or requirements referred to in paragraphs 2, 3 and 4. The NCOs shall inform the European Coordination Office of any such revocation and the grounds therefor. The European Coordination Office shall forward that information to the other NCOs.

8.   The Commission may, by means of implementing acts, adopt a template for the description of the national system and procedures for sharing information between Member States about the systems referred to in paragraph 1. Those implementing acts shall be adopted in accordance with the advisory procedure referred to in Article 37(2).

Article 12 Responsibilities of the EURES Members and Partners

1.   The EURES Members and Partners shall contribute to the EURES network regarding the tasks for which they are appointed in accordance with Article 10 or for which they are admitted in accordance with Article 11(3) and (4), or, for a transitional period in accordance with Article 40, and they shall fulfil their other obligations under this Regulation.

2.   The EURES Members shall participate in the EURES network, including by fulfilling all of the following tasks and EURES Partners shall participate in the EURES network, including by fulfilling at least one of the following tasks:

(a)   contributing to the pool of job vacancies in accordance with point (a) of Article 17(1);

(b)   contributing to the pool of job applications and CVs in accordance with point (b) of Article 17(1);

(c)   providing support services to workers and employers in accordance with Articles 23 and 24, Article 25(1), Article 26 and, where relevant, Article 27.

3.   The EURES Members and, where applicable, the EURES Partners, shall provide, for the purposes of the EURES portal, all job vacancies made publicly available with them as well as all job applications and CVs where the worker has consented to making the information available also to the EURES portal in accordance with Article 17(3). The second subparagraph of Article 17(1) and Article 17(2) shall apply to job vacancies made publicly available through the EURES Members and, where applicable, the EURES Partners.

4.   The EURES Members and Partners shall designate one or more contact points, such as placement and recruitment offices, call centres and self-service tools in accordance with national criteria, where workers and employers can get support with clearance, access to support services, or both, in accordance with this Regulation. The contact points may also be based on staff exchange programmes, the detachment of liaison officers or involve common placement agencies.

5.   The EURES Members and, where relevant, the EURES Partners, shall ensure that the contact points they have designated clearly indicate the scope of the support services provided to workers and employers.

6.   In accordance with the principle of proportionality, Member States may, through their NCO, require the EURES Members and Partners to contribute to:

(a)   the collection of information and guidance to be published on the EURES portal referred to in Article 9(4);

(b)   the exchange of information as referred to in Article 30;

(c)   the programming cycle as referred to in Article 31;

(d)   the collection of data as referred to in Article 32.

Article 13 Joint responsibilities

In accordance with their respective roles and responsibilities, all organisations participating in the EURES network shall, in close cooperation with each other, seek to promote actively the opportunities that labour mobility in the Union offers and seek to enhance ways and means for workers and employers to enjoy mobility on a fair basis and to seize those opportunities at Union, national, regional and local level, including on a cross-border basis.

Article 14 Coordination Group

1. The Coordination Group shall be composed of representatives at the appropriate level of the Commission, the European Coordination Office and the NCOs.
2. The Coordination Group shall support the implementation of this Regulation by exchanging information and developing guidance. In particular, it shall advise the Commission on the templates referred to in Article 11(8) and Article 31(5), the draft technical standards and formats referred to in Article 17(8) and Article 19(6), and the uniform detailed specifications for data collection and analysis referred to in Article 32(3).
3. The Coordination Group may, inter alia, organise exchanges of best practices concerning the national admission systems referred to in Article 11(1) and the support services referred to in Articles 23 to 27.
4. The European Coordination Office shall organise the work of the Coordination Group and chair its meetings. It shall keep informed other relevant bodies or networks of the work of the Coordination Group.
    Representatives of the social partners at Union level shall have the right to attend the meetings of the Coordination Group.
5. The Coordination Group shall cooperate with the Board of the PES Network, in particular by informing it about the activities of the EURES network and exchanging best practices.

Article 15 Common identity and the trade mark

1. The name 'EURES' shall be used exclusively for activities within the EURES network in accordance with this Regulation. It shall be illustrated by a standard logo, the use of which is determined by a graphic design scheme adopted by the European Coordination Office.
2. The EURES service mark and logo shall be used by all organisations participating in the EURES network referred to in Article 7 in all their activities relating to the EURES network, to ensure a common visual identity.
3. Organisations participating in the EURES network shall ensure that the information and promotional material they provide is coherent with the overall communication activities, the common quality standards of the EURES network and the information coming from the European Coordination Office.
4. Organisations participating in the EURES network shall inform the European Coordination Office without delay of any abuse of the EURES service mark or logo by a third party or third country of which they become aware.

Article 16 Cooperation and other measures

1. The European Coordination Office shall facilitate the cooperation between the EURES network and other Union information and advisory services and networks.
2. The NCO shall cooperate with the services and networks referred to in paragraph 1 at Union, national, regional and local level to achieve synergies and avoid overlaps, and, where appropriate, shall involve the EURES Members and Partners.
3. The NCOs shall facilitate the cooperation of the EURES network with the social partners at national level by ensuring a regular dialogue with the social partners in accordance with national law and practice.
4. Member States shall encourage close cooperation at cross-border level between regional, local and, where relevant, national actors, such as practices and services delivered in the framework of EURES cross-border partnerships.
5. Member States shall seek to develop one-stop-shop solutions for communication, including online communication, with workers and employers with regard to the common areas of EURES activity and the services and networks referred to in paragraph 1.
6. Member States shall, together with the Commission and the European Coordination Office, examine every possibility of giving priority to citizens of the Union when filling job vacancies, in order to achieve a balance between labour supply and demand within the Union. Member States may adopt measures necessary for that purpose.

CHAPTER III
COMMON IT PLATFORM

Article 17 Organisation of the common IT platform

1. To bring together job vacancies and job applications each Member State shall make available to the EURES portal:

   (a) all job vacancies made publicly available through PES as well as those provided by the EURES Members and, where relevant, the EURES Partners in accordance with Article 12(3);

   (b) all job applications and CVs available through PES as well as those provided by the other EURES Members and, where relevant, the EURES Partners, in accordance with Article 12(3), provided that the workers concerned have consented to making the information available to the EURES portal under the terms defined in paragraph 3 of this Article.

   With regard to point (a) of the first subparagraph, Member States may introduce a mechanism allowing employers to opt not to have a vacancy published on the EURES portal if the request is duly justified on the basis of the skills and competence requirements relating to the job.

2. When making available job vacancy data to the EURES portal, Member States may exclude:

   (a) job vacancies which due to their nature or to national rules are open only to citizens of a specific country;

   (b) job vacancies relating to categories of apprenticeships and traineeships which, having mainly a learning component, are part of national education systems or which are funded publicly as part of a Member State's active labour market policies;

   (c) other job vacancies as part of a Member State's active labour market policies.

3. The consent of workers referred to in point (b) of paragraph 1 shall be explicit, unambiguous, freely given, specific and informed. Workers may, at any time, withdraw their consent and require the deletion or modification of any or all of the data made available. Workers may choose from a number of options to restrict access to their data or to certain attributes.

4. With regard to workers who are minors, their consent shall be provided together with that of their parents or legal guardians.

5. Member States shall have in place the appropriate mechanisms and standards necessary for ensuring the intrinsic and technical quality of job-vacancy, job-application and CV data.

6. Member States shall ensure that the sources of data can be traced for the purpose of monitoring the quality of those data.

7. To enable the matching of job vacancies with job applications and CVs each Member State shall ensure that the information referred to in paragraph 1 is provided in accordance with a uniform system and in a transparent manner.

8. The Commission shall adopt, by means of implementing acts, the necessary technical standards and formats aimed at reaching the uniform system referred to in paragraph 7. Those implementing acts shall be adopted in accordance with the examination procedure referred to in Article 37(3).

Article 18 Access at national level to the common IT platform

1. The EURES Members and Partners shall ensure that the EURES portal is clearly visible and easily searchable through all the job-search portals that they manage, whether at central, regional or local level, and that those portals are linked to the EURES portal.

2. The PES shall ensure that the organisations acting under their responsibility have a clearly visible link to the EURES portal on any web portals that they manage.

3. The EURES Members and Partners shall ensure that all job vacancies, job applications, and CVs made available on the EURES portal are easily accessible to their staff involved with the EURES network.

4. Member States shall ensure that the transfer of information on job vacancies, job applications and CVs referred to under Article 9(2)(a) is made through a single coordinated channel.

Article 19 Automated matching through the common IT platform

1. Member States shall cooperate with each other, with the Commission and with the European Coordination Office regarding interoperability between national systems and the European classification developed by the Commission. The Commission shall keep the Member States informed about the development of the European classification.

2. The Commission shall adopt and update, by means of implementing acts, the list of skills, competences and occupations of the European classification. Those implementing acts shall be adopted in accordance with the examination procedure referred to in Article 37(3). Where the committee delivers no opinion, the Commission shall not adopt the draft implementing act and the third subparagraph of Article 5(4) of Regulation (EU) No 182/2011 shall apply.

3. For the purpose of automated matching through the common IT platform, each Member State shall, without undue delay but no later than three years after the adoption of the list referred to in paragraph 2, establish an initial inventory to map its national, regional and sectoral classifications to and from that list and, following the introduction of the use of the inventory on the basis of an application made available by the European Coordination Office, regularly update the inventory to keep it updated with the evolution of recruitment services.

4. Member States may choose to replace their national classifications with the European classification, once completed, or maintain their interoperable national classification systems.

5. The Commission shall provide technical and, where possible, financial support to Member States when they establish the inventory pursuant to paragraph 3 and to the Member States which choose to replace national classifications with the European classification.

6. The Commission shall adopt, by means of implementing acts, the technical standards and formats necessary for the operation of the automated matching through the common IT platform using the European classification and the interoperability between national systems and the European classification. Those implementing acts shall be adopted in accordance with the examination procedure referred to in Article 37(3).

Article 20 Facilitated access mechanism for workers and employers

1. The EURES Members and Partners shall, upon request, assist workers and employers using their services with their registration on the EURES portal. That assistance shall be free of charge.

2. The EURES Members and Partners shall ensure that the workers and employers using their services have access to general information on how, when and where they can update, revise and withdraw the data concerned.

CHAPTER IV
SUPPORT SERVICES

Article 21 Principles

1. Member States shall ensure that workers and employers are able to gain access, without undue delay, whether online or offline, to support services at national level.

2. Member States shall support the development of a coordinated approach at national level to support services.
    Specific regional and local needs shall be taken into account.

3. Support services for workers and employers as referred to in Article 22, Article 25(1), Article 26 and, where relevant, Article 27 shall be free of charge.
    Support services for workers as referred to in Article 23 shall be free of charge.
    Support services for employers as referred to in Article 24 may be subject to a fee.

4. Any fee charged for services which the EURES Members and, where relevant, the EURES Partners offer under this chapter shall not be higher than those applicable to other comparable services provided by the EURES Members and Partners. Where applicable, the EURES Members and Partners shall inform workers and employers of any cost involved in a clear and precise manner.

5. The EURES Members and Partners concerned shall clearly indicate to workers and employers the range of support services they provide, where and how those services

are accessible and the conditions under which access is provided, using their information channels. That information shall be published on the EURES portal.

6. Without prejudice to Article 11(2), the EURES Members referred to in point (c)(ii) of Article 7(1) and EURES Partners may offer their services only online.

Article 22 Access to basic information

1. The EURES Members and, where relevant, the EURES Partners shall provide workers and employers with basic information concerning the EURES portal, including the job-application and CV database, and the EURES network, including contact details of relevant EURES Members and Partners at national level, information on the recruitment channels that they use (e-services, personalised services, location of contact points) and the relevant web links, in an easily accessible and user-friendly manner.

   The EURES Members and, where relevant, the EURES Partners shall, where appropriate, refer workers and employers to another EURES Member or Partner.

2. The European Coordination Office shall support the development of basic information under this Article and assist Member States in ensuring adequate language coverage, taking into account the demands of the Member States' labour markets.

Article 23 Support services for workers

1. The EURES Members and, where relevant, the EURES Partners shall offer, without undue delay, workers seeking employment the opportunity to access the services referred to in paragraphs 2 and 3.

2. Upon a worker's request, the EURES Members and, where relevant, the EURES Partners shall provide information and guidance on individual employment opportunities and, in particular, offer the worker the following services:

   (a) providing or referring to general information on living and working conditions in the country of destination;

   (b) giving assistance and guidance on obtaining the information referred to in Article 9(4);

   (c) where appropriate, providing assistance with the drawing up of job applications and CVs to ensure conformity with the European technical standards and formats referred to in Article 17(8) and Article 19(6), and with the uploading of such job applications and CVs on the EURES portal;

   (d) where appropriate, considering a possible placement within the Union as part of an individual action plan or supporting the drafting of an individual mobility plan as a means to reach a placement within the Union;

   (e) where appropriate, referring the worker to another EURES Member or Partner.

3. Upon a worker's reasonable request, the EURES Members and, where relevant, the EURES Partners shall provide further job-search assistance and other additional services, taking into account the worker's needs.

Article 24 Support services for employers

1. The EURES Members and, where relevant, the EURES Partners shall offer, without undue delay, employers interested in recruiting workers from other Member States the opportunity to access the services referred to in paragraphs 2 and 3.

2. Upon an employer's request, the EURES Members and, where relevant, the EURES Partners shall provide information and guidance on recruitment opportunities and, in particular, offer them the following services:

   (a) providing information on specific rules relating to recruitment from another Member State and on factors which can facilitate such recruitment;

   (b) where appropriate, providing information on and assistance with the formulation of individual job requirements in a job vacancy and with ensuring its conformity with the European technical standards and formats referred to in Article 17(8) and Article 19(6).

3. Where an employer requests further assistance and there is a reasonable likelihood of recruitment within the Union, the EURES Members or, where relevant, the EURES Partners, shall provide further assistance and additional services, taking into account the employer's needs.

Where requested, the EURES Members or, where relevant, the EURES Partners shall provide individual guidance on formulating requirements for vacancies.

Article 25 Post-recruitment assistance

1. The EURES Members and, where relevant, the EURES Partners shall, upon the request of a worker or of an employer, provide:

   (a) general information on post-recruitment assistance such as training on intercultural communication, language courses and support with integration, including general information on employment opportunities for the members of a worker's family;

   (b) where possible, the contact details of organisations which offer post-recruitment assistance.

2. Without prejudice to Article 21(4), the EURES Members and Partners which directly provide post-recruitment assistance to workers or employers may do so for a fee.

Article 26 Facilitated access to information on taxation, issues relating to work contracts, pension entitlement, health insurance, social security and active labour market measures

1. Upon the request of a worker or of an employer, the EURES Members and, where relevant, the EURES Partners shall refer requests for specific information on the rights relating to social security, active labour market measures, taxation, issues relating to work contracts, pension entitlement and health insurance to the national competent authorities and, if applicable, other appropriate bodies at national level supporting workers exercising their rights in the framework of the freedom of movement, including those referred to in Article 4 of Directive 2014/54/EU.

2. For the purpose of paragraph 1, the NCOs shall cooperate with the competent authorities at national level referred to in paragraph 1.

Article 27 Support services in cross-border regions

1. Where, in cross-border regions, the EURES Members or Partners participate in specific cooperation and service structures, such as cross-border partnerships, they shall provide frontier workers and employers with information relating to the specific situation of frontier workers and of relevance for employers in such regions.

2. The tasks of the cross-border partnerships may include placement and recruitment services, the coordination of cooperation between the participating organisations and the carrying out of activities relevant for cross-border mobility, including information and guidance to frontier workers, with a specific focus on multilingual services.

3. Organisations other than the EURES Members and Partners participating in structures referred to in paragraph 1 shall not be considered to be part of the EURES network for reasons of their participation therein.

4. In the cross-border regions referred to in paragraph 1, Member States shall seek to develop one-stop-shop solutions for providing information to frontier workers and employers.

Article 28 Access to active labour market measures

A Member State shall not limit access to national active labour market measures providing workers with job-search assistance solely on the ground that a worker seeks that assistance in order to find employment on the territory of another Member State.

CHAPTER V
EXCHANGE OF INFORMATION AND PROGRAMMING CYCLE

Article 29 Exchange of information on flows and patterns

The Commission and the Member States shall monitor and make public labour-mobility flows and patterns in the Union on the basis of reports by the European Labour Authority, using Eurostat statistics and available national data.

Article 30 Exchange of information between Member States

1. Each Member State shall, in particular, collect and analyse gender-disaggregated information on:
   (a) labour shortages and labour surpluses on national and sectoral labour markets, paying particular attention to the most vulnerable groups in the labour market and the regions most affected by unemployment;
   (b) EURES activities at national and, where appropriate, cross-border level.
2. The NCOs shall be responsible for sharing the available information within the EURES network and contributing to the joint analysis.
3. Member States shall carry out the programming referred to in Article 31, taking into account the exchange of information and the joint analysis referred to in paragraphs 1 and 2 of this Article.
4. The European Coordination Office shall make practical arrangements to facilitate the exchange of information between the NCOs and the development of joint analysis.

Article 31 Programming

1. The NCOs shall draw up annual national work programmes for the activities of the EURES network in their Member States.
2. The annual national work programmes shall specify:
   (a) the main activities to be carried out within the EURES network, at national level as a whole, and, where appropriate, at cross-border level;
   (b) the overall human and financial resources allocated for their implementation;
   (c) the arrangements for the monitoring and evaluation of the activities planned, and, where necessary, for updating them.
3. The NCOs and the European Coordination Office shall be given the opportunity to review together all draft national work programmes. Upon finalisation of that review, the national work programmes shall be adopted by the respective NCOs.
4. The representatives of the social partners at Union level participating in the Coordination Group shall be given the opportunity to comment on the draft national work programmes.
5. The Commission shall establish, by means of implementing acts, the necessary templates and procedures for the exchange of information on the national work programmes at Union level. Those implementing acts shall be adopted in accordance with the advisory procedure referred to in Article 37(2).

Article 32 Data collection and analysis

1. Member States shall ensure that procedures are in place to collect data on the following areas of EURES activity carried out at national level:
   (a) information and guidance by the EURES network, on the basis of the number of contacts that the case handlers of the EURES Members and Partners have with workers and employers;
   (b) employment performance, including placement and recruitment resulting from EURES activity, on the basis of the number of vacancies, job applications, CVs handled and processed by case handlers of the EURES Members and Partners and the number of workers recruited in another Member State accordingly, as known to those case handlers or, where available, on the basis of surveys;
   (c) customer satisfaction with the EURES network, obtained, inter alia, through the use of surveys.
2. The European Coordination Office shall be responsible for collecting data about the EURES portal and the development of the cooperation on the clearance under this Regulation.
3. On the basis of the information referred to in paragraph 1 and within the areas of EURES activity specified in that paragraph, the Commission shall adopt, by means of implementing acts, the uniform detailed specifications for data collection and analysis to monitor and evaluate the functioning of the EURES network. Those implementing acts shall be adopted in accordance with the examination procedure referred to in Article 37(3).

4. The Commission shall be empowered to adopt delegated acts in accordance with the procedure referred to in Article 36 to modify the areas specified in paragraph 1 of this Article or add to that paragraph other areas of EURES activity undertaken at national level within the framework of this Regulation.

Article 33 Reports on EURES activity

Taking into account the information gathered as referred to in this Chapter, the Commission shall, every two years, submit a report on EURES activity to the European Parliament, the Council, the European Economic and Social Committee and the Committee of the Regions. Until submission of the report referred to in Article 35, the report referred to in the first subparagraph of this Article shall include a description on the state of play of the application of this Regulation.

CHAPTER VI
FINAL PROVISIONS

Article 34 Protection of personal data

The measures provided for in this Regulation shall be carried out in accordance with Union law on the protection of personal data, in particular Directive 95/46/EC and the national implementing measures in relation thereto, as well as Regulation (EC) No 45/2001.

Article 35 Ex post *evaluation*

By 13 May 2021, the Commission shall submit to the European Parliament, the Council, the European Economic and Social Committee and the Committee of the Regions an *ex post* evaluation report of the operation and effects of this Regulation.

That report may be accompanied by legislative proposals amending this Regulation.

Article 36 Exercise of the delegation

1. The power to adopt delegated acts is conferred on the Commission subject to the conditions laid down in this Article. It is of particular importance that the Commission follow its usual practice and carry out consultations with experts, including Member States' experts, before adopting those delegated acts.
2. The power to adopt delegated acts referred to in Article 32(4) shall be conferred on the Commission for a period of five years from 12 May 2016. The Commission shall draw up a report in respect of the delegation of power not later than nine months before the end of the five-year period. The delegation of power shall be tacitly extended for periods of an identical duration, unless the European Parliament or the Council opposes such an extension not later than three months before the end of each period.
3. The delegation of power referred to in Article 32(4) may be revoked at any time by the European Parliament or by the Council. A decision of revocation shall put an end to the delegation of the power specified in that decision. It shall take effect on the day following the publication of the decision in the *Official Journal of the European Union* or at a later date specified therein. It shall not affect the validity of any delegated acts already in force.
4. As soon as it adopts a delegated act, the Commission shall notify it simultaneously to the European Parliament and to the Council.
5. A delegated act adopted pursuant to Article 32(4) shall enter into force only if no objection has been expressed either by the European Parliament or the Council within a period of two months of notification of that act to the European Parliament and the Council or if, before the expiry of that period, the European Parliament and the Council have both informed the Commission that they will not object. That period shall be extended by two months at the initiative of the European Parliament or the Council.

Article 37 Committee procedure

1. The Commission shall be assisted by the Committee 'EURES' established by this Regulation. That Committee shall be a committee within the meaning of Regulation (EU) No 182/2011.

2. Where reference is made to this paragraph, Article 4 of Regulation (EU) No 182/2011 shall apply.
3. Where reference is made to this paragraph, Article 5 of Regulation (EU) No 182/2011 shall apply.

Article 38 Amendments to Regulation (EU) No 1296/2013

1. Regulation (EU) No 1296/2013 is amended as follows:
    (a) Article 23 is deleted.
    (b) In Article 24, paragraph 2 is replaced by the following:
         '2. The EURES axis shall be open to all bodies, actors and institutions designated by a Member State or by the Commission which fulfil the conditions for participating in EURES, as set out in Regulation (EU) 2016/589 of the European Parliament and of the Council. Such bodies, actors and institutions shall include in particular:
         (a) national, regional and local authorities;
         (b) employment services;
         (c) social partner organisations and other interested parties.'
2. References to the deleted provision, as referred to in point (1)(a), shall be construed as references to Article 29 of this Regulation.
3. Point (1)(b) of this Article shall be without prejudice to applications submitted for financing under Regulation (EU) No 1296/2013 before 12 May 2016.

Article 39 Amendments to Regulation (EU) No 492/2011

1. Regulation (EU) No 492/2011 is amended as follows:
    (a) Articles 11 and 12, Article 13(2), Articles 14 to 20 and Article 38 are deleted.
    (b) Article 13(1) is deleted with effect from 13 May 2018.
2. References to the deleted provisions shall be construed as references to this Regulation and shall be read in accordance with the correlation table set out in Annex II.

Article 40 Transitional provisions

Organisations which are designated as 'EURES Partners' in accordance with Article 3(c) of Implementing Decision 2012/733/EU or which provide limited services as the 'Associated EURES Partners' in accordance with Article 3(d) of that Decision on 12 May 2016 may, by way of derogation from Article 11 of this Regulation, participate as EURES Members referred to in Article 7(1)(c)(ii) of this Regulation or as EURES Partners referred to in Article 7(1)(d) of this Regulation, until 13 May 2019, provided that they undertake to fulfil the relevant obligations under this Regulation. Where one of those organisations wishes to participate as a EURES Partner, it shall notify the NCO of the tasks that it will perform pursuant to Article 11(4) of this Regulation. The relevant NCO shall inform the European Coordination Office thereof. After expiry of the transitional period, the organisations concerned may, in order to remain within the EURES network, submit an application to that effect in accordance with Article 11 of this Regulation.

Article 41 Entry into force

1. This Regulation shall enter into force on the twentieth day following that of its publication in the *Official Journal of the European Union*.
2. Article 12(3) and Article 17(1) to (7) shall apply from 13 May 2018.

This Regulation shall be binding in its entirety and directly applicable in all Member States.

ANNEX I
MINIMUM COMMON CRITERIA
(AS REFERRED TO IN ARTICLES 10(2) AND 11(2))

Section 1 SERVICE DELIVERY

1. Commitment to have in place adequate mechanisms and procedures to verify and ensure full compliance with applicable labour standards and legal requirements, taking into account any existing licensing systems and authorisation schemes for

employment services other than PES when delivering the services, including applicable data protection law and, where applicable, requirements and standards on quality of job vacancy data.

2. Ability and demonstrated capacity to offer services on clearance, support services, or both, as referred to in this Regulation.

3. Ability to provide services through one or more easily accessible channels, with at least an internet/website of the organisation accessible.

4. Ability and capacity to refer workers and employers to other EURES Members and Partners and/or bodies with expertise on free movement for workers.

5. Confirmation to adhere to the principle of free support services for workers in accordance with the second subparagraph of Article 21(3).

Section 2 PARTICIPATION IN THE EURES NETWORK

1. Ability and commitment to ensure timely and reliable delivery of the data as referred to in Article 12(6).

2. Commitment to comply with the technical standards and formats for clearance and exchange of information under this Regulation.

3. Ability and commitment to contribute to the programming and reporting to the NCO as well as to provide information to the NCO on the service delivery and performance in accordance with this Regulation.

4. Existence of or commitment to ensuring the allocation of appropriate human resources for the respective tasks to be fulfilled.

5. Commitment to ensuring quality standards on staff and to register the staff for the relevant modules of the common training programme as referred to in point (a)(iii) of Article 8(1).

6. Commitment to use the EURES trade mark only for services and activities relating to the EURES network.

ANNEX II

CORRELATION TABLE

Regulation (EU) No 492/2011	This Regulation
Article 11(1), first subparagraph	Article 30(1), point (a)
Article 11(1), second subparagraph	Article 9(2), points (b) and (d), and 9(3) and Article 13
Article 11(2)	Articles 9 and 10
Article 12(1)	—
Article 12(2)	—
Article 12(3), first subparagraph	Article 9(4)
Article 12(3), second subparagraph	Article 18(1) and (2)
Article 13(1)	Article 12(3) and Article 17(1) to 17(6)
Article 13(2)	Article 17(7) to 17(8)
Article 14(1)	—
Article 14(2)	—
Article 14(3)	—
Article 15(1)	Article 10(1) and 10(2), Article 12(1) to 12(3) and Article 13
Article 15(2)	Article 9(3), point (a), and Article10(1)
Article 16	—
Article 17(1)	Article 30
Article 17(2)	Article 16(6)
Article 17(3)	Article 33
Article 18	Article 7(1), point (a)
Article 19(1)	Article 8
Article 19(2)	—
Article 20	Article 8(1), point (a)(iii) and (v), and Article 9(3), point (b)
Article 38	—

COUNCIL DIRECTIVE (EEC) No 77/249 OF 22 MARCH 1977
to facilitate the effective exercise by lawyers of freedom to provide services
[1977] OJ L78/17

Article 1

1. This Directive shall apply, within the limits and under the conditions laid down herein, to the activities of lawyers pursued by way of provision of services.

   Notwithstanding anything contained in this Directive, Member States may reserve to prescribed categories of lawyers the preparation of formal documents for obtaining title to administer estates of deceased persons, and the drafting of formal documents creating or transferring interests in land.

2. 'Lawyers' means any person entitled to pursue his professional activities under one of the following designations:

Austria:	Rechtsanwalt
Belgium:	Avocat/Advocaat
Denmark:	Advokat
Germany:	Rechtsanwalt
Greece:	Δικηγο'ρος
Finland:	Asianajaja/Advokat
France:	Avocat
Ireland:	Barrister
	Solicitor
Italy:	Avvocato
Luxembourg:	Avocat-avoué
Netherlands:	Advocaat
Portugal:	Advogado
Spain:	Abogado
Sweden:	Advokat
United Kingdom:	Advocate
	Barrister
	Solicitor
Czech Republic:	Advokát
Estonia:	Vandeadvokaat
Cyprus:	Δικηγο'ρος
Latvia:	Zverinats advokats
Lithuania:	Advokatas
Hungary:	Ügyvéd
Malta:	Avukat/Prokuratur Legali
Poland:	Adwokat/Radca prawny
Slovenia:	Odvetnik/Odvetnica
Slovakia:	Advokát/Komercny právnik.
Bulgaria:	Απbοκаt
Romania:	Avocat
Croatia:	Odvjetnik/Odvjetnica

Article 2

Each Member State shall recognise as a lawyer for the purpose of pursuing the activities specified in Article 1(1) any person listed in paragraph 2 of that Article.

Article 3

A person referred to in Article 1 shall adopt the professional title used in the Member State from which he comes, expressed in the language or one of the languages, of that State, with an indication of the professional organisation by which he is authorised to practise or the court of law before which he is entitled to practise pursuant to the laws of that State.

Article 4

1. Activities relating to the representation of a client in legal proceedings or before public authorities shall be pursued in each host Member State under the conditions laid down for lawyers established in that State, with the exception of any conditions requiring residence, or registration with a professional organisation, in that State.

2. A lawyer pursuing these activities shall observe the rules of professional conduct of the host Member State, without prejudice to his obligations in the Member State from which he comes.

3. When these activities are pursued in the United Kingdom, 'rules of professional conduct of the host Member State' means the rules of professional conduct applicable to solicitors, where such activities are not reserved for barristers and advocates. Otherwise the rules of professional conduct applicable to the latter shall apply. However, barristers from Ireland shall always be subject to the rules of professional conduct applicable in the United Kingdom to barristers and advocates.

   When these activities are pursued in Ireland 'rules of professional conduct of the host Member State' means, in so far as they govern the oral presentation of a case in court, the rules of professional conduct applicable to barristers. In all other cases the rules of professional conduct applicable to solicitors shall apply. However, barristers and advocates from the United Kingdom shall always be subject to the rules of professional conduct applicable in Ireland to barristers.

4. A lawyer pursuing activities other than those referred to in paragraph 1 shall remain subject to the conditions and rules of professional conduct of the Member State from which he comes without prejudice to respect for the rules, whatever their source, which govern the profession in the host Member State, especially those concerning the incompatibility of the exercise of the activities of a lawyer with the exercise of other activities in that State, professional secrecy, relation with other lawyers, the prohibition on the same lawyer acting for parties with mutually conflicting interests, and publicity. The latter rules are applicable only if they are capable of being observed by a lawyer who is not established in the host Member State and to the extent to which their observance is objectively justified to ensure, in that State, the proper exercise of a lawyer's activities, the standing of the profession and respect for the rules concerning incompatibility.

Article 5

For the pursuit of activities relating to the representation of a client in legal proceedings, a Member State may require lawyers to whom Article 1 applies:

— to be introduced, in accordance with local rules or customs, to the presiding judge and, where appropriate, to the President of the relevant Bar in the host Member State;

— to work in conjunction with a lawyer who practises before the judicial authority in question and who would, where necessary, be answerable to that authority, or with an 'avoué' or 'procuratore' practising before it.

Article 6

Any Member State may exclude lawyers who are in the salaried employment of a public or private undertaking from pursuing activities relating to the representation of that undertaking in legal proceedings in so far as lawyers established in that State are not permitted to pursue those activities.

Article 7

1. The competent authority of the host Member State may request the person providing the services to establish his qualifications as a lawyer.

2. In the event of non-compliance with the obligations referred to in Article 4 and in force in the host Member State, the competent authority of the latter shall determine in accordance with its own rules and procedures the consequences of such noncompliance, and to this end may obtain an appropriate professional information concerning the person providing services. It shall notify the competent authority of the Member State from which the person comes of any decision taken. Such exchanges shall not affect the confidential nature of the information supplied.

DIRECTIVE 98/5/EC OF THE EUROPEAN PARLIAMENT AND OF THE COUNCIL of 16 FEBRUARY 1998

to facilitate practice of the profession of lawyer on a permanent basis in a Member State other than that in which the qualification was obtained [1998] OJ L77/36

Article 1   Object, scope and definitions

1. The purpose of this Directive is to facilitate practice of the profession of lawyer on a permanent basis in a self-employed or salaried capacity in a Member State other than that in which the professional qualification was obtained.

2. For the purposes of this Directive:

   (a) *'lawyer'* means any person who is a national of a Member State and who is authorised to pursue his professional activities under one of the following professional titles:

Belgium	Avocat/Advocaat/Rechtsanwalt
Bulgaria	Аπbbкаτ
Czech Republic	Advokát
Croatia	Odvjetnik/Odvjetnica
Denmark	Advokat
Germany	Rechtsanwalt
Estonia	Vandeadvokaat
Greece	Δικηγο'ρος
Spain	Abogado/Advocat/Avogado/Abokatu
France	Avocat
Ireland	Barrister/Solicitor
Italy	Avvocato
Cyprus	Δικηγο'ρος
Latvia	Zverinats advokats
Lithuania	Advokatas
Luxembourg	Avocat
Hungary	Ügyvéd
Malta	Avukat/Prokuratur Legali
Netherlands	Advocaat
Austria	Rechtsanwalt
Poland	Adwokat/Radca prawny
Portugal	Advogado
Romania	Avocat
Slovenia	Odvetnik/Odvetnica
Slovakia	Advokát/Komercny právnik
Finland	Asianajaja/Advokat
Sweden	Advokat
United Kingdom	Advocate/Barrister/Solicitor

   (b) *'home Member State'* means the Member State in which a lawyer acquired the right to use one of the professional titles referred to in (a) before practising the profession of lawyer in another Member State;

   (c) *'host Member State'* means the Member State in which a lawyer practises pursuant to this Directive;

   (d) *'home-country professional title'* means the professional title used in the Member State in which a lawyer acquired the right to use that title before practising the profession of lawyer in the host Member State;

   (e) *'grouping'* means any entity, with or without legal personality, formed under the law of a Member State, within which lawyers pursue their professional activities jointly under a joint name;

   (f) *'relevant professional title'* or *'relevant profession'* means the professional title or profession governed by the competent authority with whom a lawyer has registered under Article 3, and 'competent authority' means that authority.

3. This Directive shall apply both to lawyers practising in a self-employed capacity and to lawyers practising in a salarial capacity in the home Member State and, subject to Article 8, in the host Member State.

4. Practice of the profession of lawyer within the meaning of this Directive shall not include the provision of services, which is covered by Directive 77/249/EEC.

Article 2   Right to practise under the home-country professional title

Any lawyer shall be entitled to pursue on a permanent basis, in any other Member State under his home-country professional title, the activities specified in Article 5.

Integration into the profession of lawyer in the host Member State shall be subject to Article 10.

Article 3   Registration with the competent authority

1. A lawyer who wishes to practise in a Member State other than that in which he obtained his professional qualification shall register with the competent authority in that State.

2. The competent authority in the host Member State shall register the lawyer upon presentation of a certificate attesting to his registration with the competent authority in the home Member State. It may require that, when presented by the competent authority of the home Member State, the certificate be not more than three months old. It shall inform the competent authority in the home Member State of the registration.

3. For the purpose of applying paragraph 1:
    — in the United Kingdom and Ireland, lawyers practising under a professional title other than those used in the United Kingdom or Ireland shall register either with the authority responsible for the profession of barrister or advocate or with the authority responsible for the profession of solicitor,
    — in the United Kingdom, the authority responsible for a barrister from Ireland shall be that responsible for the profession of barrister or advocate, and the authority responsible for a solicitor from Ireland shall be that responsible for the profession of solicitor,
    — in Ireland, the authority responsible for a barrister or an advocate from the United Kingdom shall be that responsible for the profession of barrister, and the authority responsible for a solicitor from the United Kingdom shall be that responsible for the profession of solicitor.

4. Where the relevant competent authority in a host Member State publishes the names of lawyers registered with it, it shall also publish the names of lawyers registered pursuant to this Directive.

Article 4   Practice under the home-country professional title

1. A lawyer practising in a host Member State under his home-country professional title shall do so under that title, which must be expressed in the official language or one of the official languages of his home Member State, in an intelligible manner and in such a way as to avoid confusion with the professional title of the host Member State.

2. For the purpose of applying paragraph 1, a host Member State may require a lawyer practising under his home-country professional title to indicate the professional body of which he is a member in his home Member State or the judicial authority before which he is entitled to practise pursuant to the laws of his home Member State. A host Member State may also require a lawyer practising under his home-country professional title to include a reference to his registration with the competent authority in that State.

Article 5   Area of activity

1. Subject to paragraphs 2 and 3, a lawyer practising under his home-country professional title carries on the same professional activities as a lawyer practising under the relevant professional title used in the host Member State and may, inter alia, give advice on the law of his home Member State, on Community law, on international law and on the law of the host Member State. He shall in any event comply with the rules of procedure applicable in the national courts.

2. Member States which authorise in their territory a prescribed category of lawyers to prepare deeds for obtaining title to administer estates of deceased persons and for creating or transferring interests in land which, in other Member States, are reserved

for professions other than that of lawyer may exclude from such activities lawyers practising under a home-country professional title conferred in one of the latter Member States.

3. For the pursuit of activities relating to the representation or defence of a client in legal proceedings and insofar as the law of the host Member State reserves such activities to lawyers practising under the professional title of that State, the latter may require lawyers practising under their home-country professional titles to work in conjunction with a lawyer who practises before the judicial authority in question and who would, where necessary, be answerable to that authority or with an 'avoué' practising before it.

    Nevertheless, in order to ensure the smooth operation of the justice system, Member States may lay down specific rules for access to supreme courts, such as the use of specialist lawyers.

Article 6   Rules of professional conduct applicable

1. Irrespective of the rules of professional conduct to which he is subject in his home Member State, a lawyer practising under his home-country professional title shall be subject to the same rules of professional conduct as lawyers practising under the relevant professional title of the host Member State in respect of all the activities he pursues in its territory.

2. Lawyers practising under their home-country professional titles shall be granted appropriate representation in the professional associations of the host Member State. Such representation shall involve at least the right to vote in elections to those associations' governing bodies.

3. The host Member State may require a lawyer practising under his home-country professional title either to take out professional indemnity insurance or to become a member of a professional guarantee fund in accordance with the rules which that State lays down for professional activities pursued in its territory. Nevertheless, a lawyer practising under his home-country professional title shall be exempted from that requirement if he can prove that he is covered by insurance taken out or a guarantee provided in accordance with the rules of his home Member State, insofar as such insurance or guarantee is equivalent in terms of the conditions and extent of cover.

    Where the equivalence is only partial, the competent authority in the host Member State may require that additional insurance or an additional guarantee be contracted to cover the elements which are not already covered by the insurance or guarantee contracted in accordance with the rules of the home Member State.

Article 7   Disciplinary proceedings

1. In the event of failure by a lawyer practising under his home-country professional title to fulfil the obligations in force in the host Member State, the rules of procedure, penalties and remedies provided for in the host Member State shall apply.

2. Before initiating disciplinary proceedings against a lawyer practising under his home-country professional title, the competent authority in the host Member State shall inform the competent authority in the home Member State as soon as possible, furnishing it with all the relevant details.

    The first subparagraph shall apply *mutatis mutandis* where disciplinary proceedings are initiated by the competent authority of the home Member State, which shall inform the competent authority of the host Member State(s) accordingly.

3. Without prejudice to the decision-making power of the competent authority in the host Member State, that authority shall cooperate throughout the disciplinary proceedings with the competent authority in the home Member State. In particular, the host Member State shall take the measures necessary to ensure that the competent authority in the home Member State can make submissions to the bodies responsible for hearing any appeal.

4. The competent authority in the home Member State shall decide what action to take, under its own procedural and substantive rules, in the light of a decision of the competent authority in the host Member State concerning a lawyer practising under his home-country professional title.

5. Although it is not a prerequisite for the decision of the competent authority in the host Member State, the temporary or permanent withdrawal by the competent authority in the home Member State of the authorisation to practise the profession shall automatically lead to the lawyer concerned being temporarily or permanently prohibited from practising under his home-country professional title in the host Member State.

Article 8 Salaried practice

A lawyer registered in a host Member State under his home-country professional title may practise as a salaried lawyer in the employ of another lawyer, an association or firm of lawyers, or a public or private enterprise to the extent that the host Member State so permits for lawyers registered under the professional title used in that State.

Article 9 Statement of reasons and remedies

Decisions not to effect the registration referred to in Article 3 or to cancel such registration and decisions imposing disciplinary measures shall state the reasons on which they are based.

A remedy shall be available against such decisions before a court or tribunal in accordance with the provisions of domestic law.

Article 10 Like treatment as a lawyer of the host Member State

1. A lawyer practising under his home-country professional title who has effectively and regularly pursued for a period of at least three years an activity in the host Member State in the law of that State including Community law shall, with a view to gaining admission to the profession of lawyer in the host Member State, be exempted from the conditions set out in Article 4(1)(b) of Directive 89/48/EEC, '*Effective and regular pursuit*' means actual exercise of the activity without any interruption other than that resulting from the events of everyday life.

   It shall be for the lawyer concerned to furnish the competent authority in the host Member State with proof of such effective regular pursuit for a period of at least three years of an activity in the law of the host Member State. To that end:
   (a) the lawyer shall provide the competent authority in the host Member State with any relevant information and documentation, notably on the number of matters he has dealt with and their nature;
   (b) the competent authority of the host Member State may verify the effective and regular nature of the activity pursued and may, if need be, request the lawyer to provide, orally or in writing, clarification of or further details on the information and documentation mentioned in point (a).

   Reasons shall be given for a decision by the competent authority in the host Member State not to grant an exemption where proof is not provided that the requirements laid down in the first subparagraph have been fulfilled, and the decision shall be subject to appeal under domestic law.

2. A lawyer practising under his home-country professional title in a host Member State may, at any time, apply to have his diploma recognised in accordance with Directive 89/48/EEC with a view to gaining admission to the profession of lawyer in the host Member State and practising it under the professional title corresponding to the profession in that Member State.

3. A lawyer practising under his home-country professional title who has effectively and regularly pursued a professional activity in the host Member State for a period of at least three years but for a lesser period in the law of that Member State may obtain from the competent authority of that State admission to the profession of lawyer in the host Member State and the right to practise it under the professional title corresponding to the profession in that Member State, without having to meet the conditions referred to in Article 4(1)(b) of Directive 89/ 48/EEC, under the conditions and in accordance with the procedures set out below:
   (a) The competent authority of the host Member State shall take into account the effective and regular professional activity pursued during the abovementioned period and any knowledge and professional experience of the law of the host Member State, and any attendance at lectures or seminars on the law of the host Member State, including the rules regulating professional practice and conduct.

(b)   The lawyer shall provide the competent authority of the host Member State with any relevant information and documentation, in particular on the matters he has dealt with. Assessment of the lawyer's effective and regular activity in the host Member State and assessment of his capacity to continue the activity he has pursued there shall be carried out by means of an interview with the competent authority of the host Member State in order to verify the regular and effective nature of the activity pursued.

Reasons shall be given for a decision by the competent authority in the host Member State not to grant authorisation where proof is not provided that the requirements laid down in the first subparagraph have been fulfilled, and the decision shall be subject to appeal under domestic law.

4.   The competent authority of the host Member State may, by reasoned decision subject to appeal under domestic law, refuse to allow the lawyer the benefit of the provisions of this Article if it considers that this would be against public policy, in a particular because of disciplinary proceedings, complaints or incidents of any kind.

5.   The representatives of the competent authority entrusted with consideration of the application shall preserve the confidentiality of any information received.

6.   A lawyer who gains admission to the profession of lawyer in the host Member State in accordance with paragraphs 1, 2 and 3 shall be entitled to use his home-country professional title, expressed in the official language or one of the official languages of his home Member State, alongside the professional title corresponding to the profession of lawyer in the host Member State.

Article 11 Joint practice

Where joint practise is authorised in respect of lawyers carrying on their activities under the relevant professional title in the host Member State, the following provisions shall apply in respect of lawyers wishing to carry on activities under that title or registering with the competent authority:

(1)   One or more lawyers who belong to the same grouping in their home Member State and who practise under their home-country professional title in a host Member State may pursue their professional activities in a branch or agency of their grouping in the host Member State. However, where the fundamental rules governing that grouping in the home Member State are incompatible with the fundamental rules laid down by law, regulation or administrative action in the host Member State, the latter rules shall prevail insofar as compliance therewith is justified by the public interest in protecting clients and third parties.

(2)   Each Member State shall afford two or more lawyers from the same grouping or the same home Member State who practise in its territory under their home-country professional titles access to a form of joint practice. If the host Member State gives its lawyers a choice between several forms of joint practice, those same forms shall also be made available to the aforementioned lawyers. The manner in which such lawyers practise jointly in the host Member State shall be governed by the laws, regulations and administrative provisions of that State.

(3)   The host Member State shall take the measures necessary to permit joint practice also between:

(a)   several lawyers from different Member States practising under their home-country professional titles;

(b)   one or more lawyers covered by point (a) and one or more lawyers from the host Member State.

The manner in which such lawyers practice jointly in the host Member State shall be governed by the laws, regulations and administrative provisions of that State.

(4)   A lawyer who wishes to practise under his home-country professional title shall inform the competent authority in the host Member State of the fact that he is a member of a grouping in his home Member State and furnish any relevant information on that grouping.

(5)   Notwithstanding points 1 to 4, a host Member State, insofar as it prohibits lawyers practising under its own relevant professional title from practising the profession of lawyer within a grouping in which some persons are not members of the profession,

may refuse to allow a lawyer registered under his home-country professional title to practice in its territory in his capacity as a member of his grouping. The grouping is deemed to include persons who are not members of the profession if
— the capital of the grouping is held entirely or partly, or
— the name under which it practises is used, or
— the decision-making power in that grouping is exercised, *de facto or de jure*,
by persons who do not have the status of lawyer within the meaning of Article 1(2).
Where the fundamental rules governing a grouping of lawyers in the home Member State are incompatible with the rules in force in the host Member State or with the provisions of the first subparagraph, the host Member State may oppose the opening of a branch or agency within its territory without the restrictions laid down in point (1).

Article 12 Name of the grouping
Whatever the manner in which lawyers practise under their home-country professional titles in the host Member State, they may employ the name of any grouping to which they belong in their home Member State.
The host Member State may require that, in addition to the name referred to in the first subparagraph, mention be made of the legal form of the grouping in the home Member State and/or of the names of any members of the grouping practising in the host Member State.

Article 13 Cooperation between the competent authorities in the home and host Member States and confidentiality
In order to facilitate the application of this Directive and to prevent its provisions from being misapplied for the sole purpose of circumventing the rules applicable in the host Member State, the competent authority in the host Member State and the competent authority in the home Member State shall collaborate closely and afford each other mutual assistance. They shall preserve the confidentiality of the information they exchange.

Article 14 Designation of the competent authorities
Member States shall designate the competent authorities empowered to receive the applications and to take the decisions referred to in this Directive by 14 March 2000.
They shall communicate this information to the other Member States and to the Commission.

Article 15 Report by the Commission
Ten years at the latest from the entry into force of this Directive, the Commission shall report to the European Parliament and to the Council on progress in the implementation of the Directive. After having held all the necessary consultations, it shall on that occasion present its conclusions and any amendments which could be made to the existing system.

Article 16 Implementation
1. Member States shall bring into force the laws, regulations and administrative provisions necessary to comply with this Directive by 14 March 2000. They shall forthwith inform the Commission thereof.
   When Member States adopt these measures, they shall contain a reference to this Directive or shall be accompanied by such reference on the occasion of their official publication. The methods of making such reference shall be adopted by Member States.
2. Member States shall communicate to the Commission the texts of the main provisions of domestic law which they adopt in the field covered by this Directive.

Article 17
This Directive shall enter into force on the date of its publication in the *Official Journal of the European Communities*.

Article 18
This Directive is addressed to the Member States.

COUNCIL AND PARLIAMENT DIRECTIVE (EC) No 2004/38
of 29 APRIL 2004

on the right of citizens of the Union and their family members to move and reside freely within the territory of the Member States amending Regulation (EEC) No 1612/68 and repealing Directives 64/221/EEC, 68/360/EEC, 72/194/EEC, 73/148/EEC, 75/34/EEC, 75/35/EEC, 90/364/EEC, 90/365/EEC and 93/96/EEC
[2004] OJ L158/77

THE EUROPEAN PARLIAMENT AND THE COUNCIL OF THE EUROPEAN UNION,

Having regard to the Treaty establishing the European Community, and in particular Articles 12, 18, 40, 44 and 52 thereof,

Having regard to the proposal from the Commission,

Having regard to the Opinion of the European Economic and Social Committee,

Having regard to the Opinion of the Committee of the Regions,

Acting in accordance with the procedure laid down in Article 251 of the Treaty, Whereas:

(1) Citizenship of the Union confers on every citizen of the Union a primary and individual right to move and reside freely within the territory of the Member States, subject to the limitations and conditions laid down in the Treaty and to the measures adopted to give it effect.

(2) The free movement of persons constitutes one of the fundamental freedoms of the internal market, which comprises an area without internal frontiers, in which freedom is ensured in accordance with the provisions of the Treaty.

(3) Union citizenship should be the fundamental status of nationals of the Member States when they exercise their right of free movement and residence. It is therefore necessary to codify and review the existing Community instruments dealing separately with workers, self-employed persons, as well as students and other inactive persons in order to simplify and strengthen the right of free movement and residence of all Union citizens.

(4) With a view to remedying this sector-by-sector, piecemeal approach to the right of free movement and residence and facilitating the exercise of this right, there needs to be a single legislative act to amend Council Regulation (EEC) No 1612/68 of 15 October 1968 on freedom of movement for workers within the Community, and to repeal the following acts:

Council Directive 68/360/EEC of 15 October 1968 on the abolition of restrictions on movement and residence within the Community for workers of Member States and their families, Council Directive 73/148/EEC of 21 May 1973 on the abolition of restrictions on movement and residence within the Community for nationals of Member States with regard to establishment and the provision of services, Council Directive 90/364/EEC of 28 June 1990 on the right of residence, Council Directive 90/365/EEC of 28 June 1990 on the right of residence for employees and self-employed persons who have ceased their occupational activity and Council Directive 93/96/EEC of 29 October 1993 on the right of residence for students.

(5) The right of all Union citizens to move and reside freely within the territory of the Member States should, if it is to be exercised under objective conditions of freedom and dignity, be also granted to their family members, irrespective of nationality. For the purposes of this Directive, the definition of 'family member' should also include the registered partner if the legislation of the host Member State treats registered partnership as equivalent to marriage.

(6) In order to maintain the unity of the family in a broader sense and without prejudice to the prohibition of discrimination on grounds of nationality, the situation of those persons who are not included in the definition of family members under this Directive, and who therefore do not enjoy an automatic right of entry and residence in the host Member State, should be examined by the host Member State on the basis of its own national legislation, in order to decide whether entry and residence could be granted to such persons, taking into consideration their relationship with the Union

citizen or any other circumstances, such as their financial or physical dependence on the Union citizen.

(7) The formalities connected with the free movement of Union citizens within the territory of Member States should be clearly defined, without prejudice to the provisions applicable to national border controls.

(8) With a view to facilitating the free movement of family members who are not nationals of a Member State, those who have already obtained a residence card should be exempted from the requirement to obtain an entry visa within the meaning of Council Regulation (EC) No 539/2001 of 15 March 2001 listing the third countries whose nationals must be in possession of visas when crossing the external borders and those whose nationals are exempt from that requirement or, where appropriate, of the applicable national legislation.

(9) Union citizens should have the right of residence in the host Member State for a period not exceeding three months without being subject to any conditions or any formalities other than the requirement to hold a valid identity card or passport, without prejudice to a more favourable treatment applicable to job-seekers as recognised by the case-law of the Court of Justice.

(10) Persons exercising their right of residence should not, however, become an unreasonable burden on the social assistance system of the host Member State during an initial period of residence. Therefore, the right of residence for Union citizens and their family members for periods in excess of three months should be subject to conditions.

(11) The fundamental and personal right of residence in another Member State is conferred directly on Union citizens by the Treaty and is not dependent upon their having fulfilled administrative procedures.

(12) For periods of residence of longer than three months, Member States should have the possibility to require Union citizens to register with the competent authorities in the place of residence, attested by a registration certificate issued to that effect.

(13) The residence card requirement should be restricted to family members of Union citizens who are not nationals of a Member State for periods of residence of longer than three months.

(14) The supporting documents required by the competent authorities for the issuing of a registration certificate or of a residence card should be comprehensively specified in order to avoid divergent administrative practices or interpretations constituting an undue obstacle to the exercise of the right of residence by Union citizens and their family members.

(15) Family members should be legally safeguarded in the event of the death of the Union citizen, divorce, annulment of marriage or termination of a registered partnership. With due regard for family life and human dignity, and in certain conditions to guard against abuse, measures should therefore be taken to ensure that in such circumstances family members already residing within the territory of the host Member State retain their right of residence exclusively on a personal basis.

(16) As long as the beneficiaries of the right of residence do not become an unreasonable burden on the social assistance system of the host Member State they should not be expelled. Therefore, an expulsion measure should not be the automatic consequence of recourse to the social assistance system. The host Member State should examine whether it is a case of temporary difficulties and take into account the duration of residence, the personal circumstances and the amount of aid granted in order to consider whether the beneficiary has become an unreasonable burden on its social assistance system and to proceed to his expulsion. In no case should an expulsion measure be adopted against workers, self-employed persons or job-seekers as defined by the Court of Justice save on grounds of public policy or public security.

(17) Enjoyment of permanent residence by Union citizens who have chosen to settle long term in the host Member State would strengthen the feeling of Union citizenship and is a key element in promoting social cohesion, which is one of the fundamental objectives of the Union. A right of permanent residence should therefore be laid down for all Union citizens and their family members who have resided in the host Member State in compliance with the conditions laid down in this Directive during a continuous period of five years without becoming subject to an expulsion measure.

(18) In order to be a genuine vehicle for integration into the society of the host Member State in which the Union citizen resides, the right of permanent residence, once obtained, should not be subject to any conditions.

(19) Certain advantages specific to Union citizens who are workers or self-employed persons and to their family members, which may allow these persons to acquire a right of permanent residence before they have resided five years in the host Member State, should be maintained, as these constitute acquired rights, conferred by Commission Regulation (EEC) No 1251/70 of 29 June 1970 on the right of workers to remain in the territory of a Member State after having been employed in that State and Council Directive 75/34/EEC of 17 December 1974 concerning the right of nationals of a Member State to remain in the territory of another Member State after having pursued therein an activity in a self-employed capacity.

(20) In accordance with the prohibition of discrimination on grounds of nationality, all Union citizens and their family members residing in a Member State on the basis of this Directive should enjoy, in that Member State, equal treatment with nationals in areas covered by the Treaty, subject to such specific provisions as are expressly provided for in the Treaty and secondary law.

(21) However, it should be left to the host Member State to decide whether it will grant social assistance during the first three months of residence, or for a longer period in the case of job-seekers, to Union citizens other than those who are workers or self-employed persons or who retain that status or their family members, or maintenance assistance for studies, including vocational training, prior to acquisition of the right of permanent residence, to these same persons.

(22) The Treaty allows restrictions to be placed on the right of free movement and residence on grounds of public policy, public security or public health. In order to ensure a tighter definition of the circumstances and procedural safeguards subject to which Union citizens and their family members may be denied leave to enter or may be expelled, this Directive should replace Council Directive 64/221/EEC of 25 February 1964 on the coordination of special measures concerning the movement and residence of foreign nationals, which are justified on grounds of public policy, public security or public health.

(23) Expulsion of Union citizens and their family members on grounds of public policy or public security is a measure that can seriously harm persons who, having availed themselves of the rights and freedoms conferred on them by the Treaty, have become genuinely integrated into the host Member State. The scope for such measures should therefore be limited in accordance with the principle of proportionality to take account of the degree of integration of the persons concerned, the length of their residence in the host Member State, their age, state of health, family and economic situation and the links with their country of origin.

(24) Accordingly, the greater the degree of integration of Union citizens and their family members in the host Member State, the greater the degree of protection against expulsion should be. Only in exceptional circumstances, where there are imperative grounds of public security, should an expulsion measure be taken against Union citizens who have resided for many years in the territory of the host Member State, in particular when they were born and have resided there throughout their life. In addition, such exceptional circumstances should also apply to an expulsion measure taken against minors, in order to protect their links with their family, in accordance with the United Nations Convention on the Rights of the Child, of 20 November 1989.

(25) Procedural safeguards should also be specified in detail in order to ensure a high level of protection of the rights of Union citizens and their family members in the event of their being denied leave to enter or reside in another Member State, as well as to uphold the principle that any action taken by the authorities must be properly justified.

(26) In all events, judicial redress procedures should be available to Union citizens and their family members who have been refused leave to enter or reside in another Member State.

(27) In line with the case-law of the Court of Justice prohibiting Member States from issuing orders excluding for life persons covered by this Directive from their territory, the right

of Union citizens and their family members who have been excluded from the territory of a Member State to submit a fresh application after a reasonable period, and in any event after a three year period from enforcement of the final exclusion order, should be confirmed.

(28) To guard against abuse of rights or fraud, notably marriages of convenience or any other form of relationships contracted for the sole purpose of enjoying the right of free movement and residence, Member States should have the possibility to adopt the necessary measures.

(29) This Directive should not affect more favourable national provisions.

(30) With a view to examining how further to facilitate the exercise of the right of free movement and residence, a report should be prepared by the Commission in order to evaluate the opportunity to present any necessary proposals to this effect, notably on the extension of the period of residence with no conditions.

(31) This Directive respects the fundamental rights and freedoms and observes the principles recognised in particular by the Charter of Fundamental Rights of the European Union. In accordance with the prohibition of discrimination contained in the Charter, Member States should implement this Directive without discrimination between the beneficiaries of this Directive on grounds such as sex, race, colour, ethnic or social origin, genetic characteristics, language, religion or beliefs, political or other opinion, membership of an ethnic minority, property, birth, disability, age or sexual orientation,

HAVE ADOPTED THIS DIRECTIVE:

CHAPTER I
GENERAL PROVISIONS

Article 1 Subject

This Directive lays down:

(a) the conditions governing the exercise of the right of free movement and residence within the territory of the Member States by Union citizens and their family members;

(b) the right of permanent residence in the territory of the Member States for Union citizens and their family members;

(c) the limits placed on the rights set out in (a) and (b) on grounds of public policy, public security or public health.

Article 2 Definitions

For the purposes of this Directive:

(1) 'Union citizen' means any person having the nationality of a Member State;

(2) 'Family member' means:

(a) the spouse;

(b) the partner with whom the Union citizen has contracted a registered partnership, on the basis of the legislation of a Member State, if the legislation of the host Member State treats registered partnerships as equivalent to marriage and in accordance with the conditions laid down in the relevant legislation of the host Member State;

(c) the direct descendants who are under the age of 21 or are dependants and those of the spouse or partner as defined in point (b);

(d) the dependent direct relatives in the ascending line and those of the spouse or partner as defined in point (b);

(3) 'Host Member State' means the Member State to which a Union citizen moves in order to exercise his/her right of free movement and residence.

Article 3 Beneficiaries

1. This Directive shall apply to all Union citizens who move to or reside in a Member State other than that of which they are a national, and to their family members as defined in point 2 of Article 2 who accompany or join them.

2. Without prejudice to any right to free movement and residence the persons concerned may have in their own right, the host Member State shall, in accordance with its national legislation, facilitate entry and residence for the following persons:

(a) any other family members, irrespective of their nationality, not falling under the definition in point 2 of Article 2 who, in the country from which they have come, are dependants or members of the household of the Union citizen having the primary right of residence, or where serious health grounds strictly require the personal care of the family member by the Union citizen;

(b) the partner with whom the Union citizen has a durable relationship, duly attested.

The host Member State shall undertake an extensive examination of the personal circumstances and shall justify any denial of entry or residence to these people.

CHAPTER II
RIGHT OF EXIT AND ENTRY

Article 4 Right of exit

1. Without prejudice to the provisions on travel documents applicable to national border controls, all Union citizens with a valid identity card or passport and their family members who are not nationals of a Member State and who hold a valid passport shall have the right to leave the territory of a Member State to travel to another Member State.

2. No exit visa or equivalent formality may be imposed on the persons to whom paragraph 1 applies.

3. Member States shall, acting in accordance with their laws, issue to their own nationals, and renew, an identity card or passport stating their nationality.

4. The passport shall be valid at least for all Member States and for countries through which the holder must pass when travelling between Member States. Where the law of a Member State does not provide for identity cards to be issued, the period of validity of any passport on being issued or renewed shall be not less than five years.

Article 5 Right of entry

1. Without prejudice to the provisions on travel documents applicable to national border controls, Member States shall grant Union citizens leave to enter their territory with a valid identity card or passport and shall grant family members who are not nationals of a Member State leave to enter their territory with a valid passport.

No entry visa or equivalent formality may be imposed on Union citizens.

2. Family members who are not nationals of a Member State shall only be required to have an entry visa in accordance with Regulation (EC) No 539/2001 or, where appropriate, with national law. For the purposes of this Directive, possession of the valid residence card referred to in Article 10 shall exempt such family members from the visa requirement. Member States shall grant such persons every facility to obtain the necessary visas. Such visas shall be issued free of charge as soon as possible and on the basis of an accelerated procedure.

3. The host Member State shall not place an entry or exit stamp in the passport of family members who are not nationals of a Member State provided that they present the residence card provided for in Article 10.

4. Where a Union citizen, or a family member who is not a national of a Member State, does not have the necessary travel documents or, if required, the necessary visas, the Member State concerned shall, before turning them back, give such persons every reasonable opportunity to obtain the necessary documents or have them brought to them within a reasonable period of time or to corroborate or prove by other means that they are covered by the right of free movement and residence.

5. The Member State may require the person concerned to report his/her presence within its territory within a reasonable and non-discriminatory period of time. Failure to comply with this requirement may make the person concerned liable to proportionate and non-discriminatory sanctions.

CHAPTER III
RIGHT OF RESIDENCE

Article 6　Right of residence for up to three months

1. Union citizens shall have the right of residence on the territory of another Member State for a period of up to three months without any conditions or any formalities other than the requirement to hold a valid identity card or passport.

2. The provisions of paragraph 1 shall also apply to family members in possession of a valid passport who are not nationals of a Member State, accompanying or joining the Union citizen.

Article 7　Right of residence for more than three months

1. All Union citizens shall have the right of residence on the territory of another Member State for a period of longer than three months if they:
   (a) are workers or self-employed persons in the host Member State; or
   (b) have sufficient resources for themselves and their family members not to become a burden on the social assistance system of the host Member State during their period of residence and have comprehensive sickness insurance cover in the host Member State; or
   (c) — are enrolled at a private or public establishment, accredited or financed by the host Member State on the basis of its legislation or administrative practice, for the principal purpose of following a course of study, including vocational training; and
   — have comprehensive sickness insurance cover in the host Member State and assure the relevant national authority, by means of a declaration or by such equivalent means as they may choose, that they have sufficient resources for themselves and their family members not to become a burden on the social assistance system of the host Member State during their period of residence; or
   (d) are family members accompanying or joining a Union citizen who satisfies the conditions referred to in points (a), (b) or (c).

2. The right of residence provided for in paragraph 1 shall extend to family members who are not nationals of a Member State, accompanying or joining the Union citizen in the host Member State, provided that such Union citizen satisfies the conditions referred to in paragraph 1(a), (b) or (c).

3. For the purposes of paragraph 1(a), a Union citizen who is no longer a worker or self-employed person shall retain the status of worker or self-employed person in the following circumstances:
   (a) he/she is temporarily unable to work as the result of an illness or accident;
   (b) he/she is in duly recorded involuntary unemployment after having been employed for more than one year and has registered as a job-seeker with the relevant employment office;
   (c) he/she is in duly recorded involuntary unemployment after completing a fixed-term employment contract of less than a year or after having become involuntarily unemployed during the first twelve months and has registered as a job-seeker with the relevant employment office. In this case, the status of worker shall be retained for no less than six months;
   (d) he/she embarks on vocational training. Unless he/she is involuntarily unemployed, the retention of the status of worker shall require the training to be related to the previous employment.

4. By way of derogation from paragraphs 1(d) and 2 above, only the spouse, the registered partner provided for in Article 2(2)(b) and dependent children shall have the right of residence as family members of a Union citizen meeting the conditions under 1(c) above. Article 3(2) shall apply to his/her dependent direct relatives in the ascending lines and those of his/her spouse or registered partner.

Article 8 Administrative formalities for Union citizens

1. Without prejudice to Article 5(5), for periods of residence longer than three months, the host Member State may require Union citizens to register with the relevant authorities.

2. The deadline for registration may not be less than three months from the date of arrival. A registration certificate shall be issued immediately, stating the name and address of the person registering and the date of the registration. Failure to comply with the registration requirement may render the person concerned liable to proportionate and non-discriminatory sanctions.

3. For the registration certificate to be issued, Member States may only require that
   — Union citizens to whom point (a) of Article 7(1) applies present a valid identity card or passport, a confirmation of engagement from the employer or a certificate of employment, or proof that they are self-employed persons;
   — Union citizens to whom point (b) of Article 7(1) applies present a valid identity card or passport and provide proof that they satisfy the conditions laid down therein;
   — Union citizens to whom point (c) of Article 7(1) applies present a valid identity card or passport, provide proof of enrolment at an accredited establishment and of comprehensive sickness insurance cover and the declaration or equivalent means referred to in point (c) of Article 7(1). Member States may not require this declaration to refer to any specific amount of resources.

4. Member States may not lay down a fixed amount which they regard as 'sufficient resources', but they must take into account the personal situation of the person concerned. In all cases this amount shall not be higher than the threshold below which nationals of the host Member State become eligible for social assistance, or, where this criterion is not applicable, higher than the minimum social security pension paid by the host Member State.

5. For the registration certificate to be issued to family members of Union citizens, who are themselves Union citizens, Member States may require the following documents to be presented:
   (a) a valid identity card or passport;
   (b) a document attesting to the existence of a family relationship or of a registered partnership;
   (c) where appropriate, the registration certificate of the Union citizen whom they are accompanying or joining;
   (d) in cases falling under points (c) and (d) of Article 2(2), documentary evidence that the conditions laid down therein are met;
   (e) in cases falling under Article 3(2)(a), a document issued by the relevant authority in the country of origin or country from which they are arriving certifying that they are dependants or members of the household of the Union citizen, or proof of the existence of serious health grounds which strictly require the personal care of the family member by the Union citizen;
   (f) in cases falling under Article 3(2)(b), proof of the existence of a durable relationship with the Union citizen.

Article 9 Administrative formalities for family members who are not nationals of a Member State

1. Member States shall issue a residence card to family members of a Union citizen who are not nationals of a Member State, where the planned period of residence is for more than three months.

2. The deadline for submitting the residence card application may not be less than three months from the date of arrival.

3. Failure to comply with the requirement to apply for a residence card may make the person concerned liable to proportionate and non-discriminatory sanctions.

Article 10 Issue of residence cards

1. The right of residence of family members of a Union citizen who are not nationals of a Member State shall be evidenced by the issuing of a document called 'Residence card of a family member of a Union citizen' no later than six months from the date on which they submit the application. A certificate of application for the residence card shall be issued immediately.

2. For the residence card to be issued, Member States shall require presentation of the following documents:
    (a)   a valid passport;
    (b)   a document attesting to the existence of a family relationship or of a registered partnership;
    (c)   the registration certificate or, in the absence of a registration system, any other proof of residence in the host Member State of the Union citizen whom they are accompanying or joining;
    (d)   in cases falling under points (c) and (d) of Article 2(2), documentary evidence that the conditions laid down therein are met;
    (e)   in cases falling under Article 3(2)(a), a document issued by the relevant authority in the country of origin or country from which they are arriving certifying that they are dependants or members of the household of the Union citizen, or proof of the existence of serious health grounds which strictly require the personal care of the family member by the Union citizen;
    (f)   in cases falling under Article 3(2)(b), proof of the existence of a durable relationship with the Union citizen.

Article 11 Validity of the residence card
1. The residence card provided for by Article 10(1) shall be valid for five years from the date of issue or for the envisaged period of residence of the Union citizen, if this period is less than five years.
2. The validity of the residence card shall not be affected by temporary absences not exceeding six months a year, or by absences of a longer duration for compulsory military service or by one absence of a maximum of twelve consecutive months for important reasons such as pregnancy and childbirth, serious illness, study or vocational training, or a posting in another Member State or a third country.

Article 12 Retention of the right of residence by family members in the event of death or departure of the Union citizen
1. Without prejudice to the second subparagraph, the Union citizen's death or departure from the host Member State shall not affect the right of residence of his/her family members who are nationals of a Member State.
    Before acquiring the right of permanent residence, the persons concerned must meet the conditions laid down in points (a), (b), (c) or (d) of Article 7(1).
2. Without prejudice to the second subparagraph, the Union citizen's death shall not entail loss of the right of residence of his/her family members who are not nationals of a Member State and who have been residing in the host Member State as family members for at least one year before the Union citizen's death.
    Before acquiring the right of permanent residence, the right of residence of the persons concerned shall remain subject to the requirement that they are able to show that they are workers or self-employed persons or that they have sufficient resources for themselves and their family members not to become a burden on the social assistance system of the host Member State during their period of residence and have comprehensive sickness insurance cover in the host Member State, or that they are members of the family, already constituted in the host Member State, of a person satisfying these requirements. 'Sufficient resources' shall be as defined in Article 8(4). Such family members shall retain their right of residence exclusively on a personal basis.
3. The Union citizen's departure from the host Member State or his/her death shall not entail loss of the right of residence of his/her children or of the parent who has actual custody of the children, irrespective of nationality, if the children reside in the host Member State and are enrolled at an educational establishment, for the purpose of studying there, until the completion of their studies.

Article 13 Retention of the right of residence by family members in the event of divorce, annulment of marriage or termination of registered partnership
1. Without prejudice to the second subparagraph, divorce, annulment of the Union citizen's marriage or termination of his/her registered partnership, as referred to in

point 2(b) of Article 2 shall not affect the right of residence of his/her family members who are nationals of a Member State.

2. Without prejudice to the second subparagraph, divorce, annulment of marriage or termination of the registered partnership referred to in point 2(b) of Article 2 shall not entail loss of the right of residence of a Union citizen's family members who are not nationals of a Member State where:

(a) prior to initiation of the divorce or annulment proceedings or termination of the registered partnership referred to in point 2(b) of Article 2, the marriage or registered partnership has lasted at least three years, including one year in the host Member State; or

(b) by agreement between the spouses or the partners referred to in point 2(b) of Article 2 or by court order, the spouse or partner who is not a national of a Member State has custody of the Union citizen's children; or

(c) this is warranted by particularly difficult circumstances, such as having been a victim of domestic violence while the marriage or registered partnership was subsisting; or

(d) by agreement between the spouses or partners referred to in point 2(b) of Article 2 or by court order, the spouse or partner who is not a national of a Member State has the right of access to a minor child, provided that the court has ruled that such access must be in the host Member State, and for as long as is required.

Before acquiring the right of permanent residence, the right of residence of the persons concerned shall remain subject to the requirement that they are able to show that they are workers or self-employed persons or that they have sufficient resources for themselves and their family members not to become a burden on the social assistance system of the host Member State during their period of residence and have comprehensive sickness insurance cover in the host Member State, or that they are members of the family, already constituted in the host Member State, of a person satisfying these requirements. 'Sufficient resources' shall be as defined in Article 8(4). Such family members shall retain their right of residence exclusively on personal basis.

Article 14 Retention of the right of residence

1. Union citizens and their family members shall have the right of residence provided for in Article 6, as long as they do not become an unreasonable burden on the social assistance system of the host Member State.

2. Union citizens and their family members shall have the right of residence provided for in Articles 7, 12 and 13 as long as they meet the conditions set out therein.

In specific cases where there is a reasonable doubt as to whether a Union citizen or his/her family members satisfies the conditions set out in Articles 7, 12 and 13, Member States may verify if these conditions are fulfilled. This verification shall not be carried out systematically.

3. An expulsion measure shall not be the automatic consequence of a Union citizen's or his or her family member's recourse to the social assistance system of the host Member State.

4. By way of derogation from paragraphs 1 and 2 and without prejudice to the provisions of Chapter VI, an expulsion measure may in no case be adopted against Union citizens or their family members if:

(a) the Union citizens are workers or self-employed persons, or

(b) the Union citizens entered the territory of the host Member State in order to seek employment. In this case, the Union citizens and their family members may not be expelled for as long as the Union citizens can provide evidence that they are continuing to seek employment and that they have a genuine chance of being engaged.

Article 15 Procedural safeguards

1. The procedures provided for by Articles 30 and 31 shall apply by analogy to all decisions restricting free movement of Union citizens and their family members on grounds other than public policy, public security or public health.

2. Expiry of the identity card or passport on the basis of which the person concerned entered the host Member State and was issued with a registration certificate or residence card shall not constitute a ground for expulsion from the host Member State.
3. The host Member State may not impose a ban on entry in the context of an expulsion decision to which paragraph 1 applies.

CHAPTER IV
RIGHT OF PERMANENT RESIDENCE

SECTION I
ELIGIBILITY

Article 16 General rule for Union citizens and their family members

1. Union citizens who have resided legally for a continuous period of five years in the host Member State shall have the right of permanent residence there. This right shall not be subject to the conditions provided for in Chapter III.
2. Paragraph 1 shall apply also to family members who are not nationals of a Member State and have legally resided with the Union citizen in the host Member State for a continuous period of five years.
3. Continuity of residence shall not be affected by temporary absences not exceeding a total of six months a year, or by absences of a longer duration for compulsory military service, or by one absence of a maximum of twelve consecutive months for important reasons such as pregnancy and childbirth, serious illness, study or vocational training, or a posting in another Member State or a third country.
4. Once acquired, the right of permanent residence shall be lost only through absence from the host Member State for a period exceeding two consecutive years.

Article 17 Exemptions for persons no longer working in the host Member State and their family members

1. By way of derogation from Article 16, the right of permanent residence in the host Member State shall be enjoyed before completion of a continuous period of five years of residence by:
    (a) workers or self-employed persons who, at the time they stop working, have reached the age laid down by the law of that Member State for entitlement to an old age pension or workers who cease paid employment to take early retirement, provided that they have been working in that Member State for at least the preceding twelve months and have resided there continuously for more than three years.
    If the law of the host Member State does not grant the right to an old age pension to certain categories of self-employed persons, the age condition shall be deemed to have been met once the person concerned has reached the age of 60;
    (b) workers or self-employed persons who have resided continuously in the host Member State for more than two years and stop working there as a result of permanent incapacity to work.
    If such incapacity is the result of an accident at work or an occupational disease entitling the person concerned to a benefit payable in full or in part by an institution in the host Member State, no condition shall be imposed as to length of residence;
    (c) workers or self-employed persons who, after three years of continuous employment and residence in the host Member State, work in an employed or self-employed capacity in another Member State, while retaining their place of residence in the host Member State, to which they return, as a rule, each day or at least once a week.
    For the purposes of entitlement to the rights referred to in points (a) and (b), periods of employment spent in the Member State in which the person concerned is working shall be regarded as having been spent in the host Member State.

Periods of involuntary unemployment duly recorded by the relevant employment office, periods not worked for reasons not of the person's own making and absences from work or cessation of work due to illness or accident shall be regarded as periods of employment.

2. The conditions as to length of residence and employment laid down in point (a) of paragraph 1 and the condition as to length of residence laid down in point (b) of paragraph 1 shall not apply if the worker's or the self-employed person's spouse or partner as referred to in point 2(b) of Article 2 is a national of the host Member State or has lost the nationality of that Member State by marriage to that worker or self-employed person.

3. Irrespective of nationality, the family members of a worker or a self-employed person who are residing with him in the territory of the host Member State shall have the right of permanent residence in that Member State, if the worker or self-employed person has acquired himself the right of permanent residence in that Member State on the basis of paragraph 1.

4. If, however, the worker or self-employed person dies while still working but before acquiring permanent residence status in the host Member State on the basis of paragraph 1, his family members who are residing with him in the host Member State shall acquire the right of permanent residence there, on condition that:

    (a) the worker or self-employed person had, at the time of death, resided continuously on the territory of that Member State for two years; or

    (b) the death resulted from an accident at work or an occupational disease; or

    (c) the surviving spouse lost the nationality of that Member State following marriage to the worker or self-employed person.

Article 18 Acquisition of the right of permanent residence by certain family members who are not nationals of a Member State

Without prejudice to Article 17, the family members of a Union citizen to whom Articles 12(2) and 13(2) apply, who satisfy the conditions laid down therein, shall acquire the right of permanent residence after residing legally for a period of five consecutive years in the host Member State.

SECTION II
ADMINISTRATIVE FORMALITIES

Article 19 Document certifying permanent residence for Union citizens

1. Upon application Member States shall issue Union citizens entitled to permanent residence, after having verified duration of residence, with a document certifying permanent residence.

2. The document certifying permanent residence shall be issued as soon as possible.

Article 20 Permanent residence card for family members who are not nationals of a Member State

1. Member States shall issue family members who are not nationals of a Member State entitled to permanent residence with a permanent residence card within six months of the submission of the application. The permanent residence card shall be renewable automatically every ten years.

2. The application for a permanent residence card shall be submitted before the residence card expires. Failure to comply with the requirement to apply for a permanent residence card may render the person concerned liable to proportionate and non-discriminatory sanctions.

3. Interruption in residence not exceeding two consecutive years shall not affect the validity of the permanent residence card.

Article 21 Continuity of residence

For the purposes of this Directive, continuity of residence may be attested by any means of proof in use in the host Member State. Continuity of residence is broken by any expulsion decision duly enforced against the person concerned.

CHAPTER V

PROVISIONS COMMON TO THE RIGHT OF RESIDENCE AND THE RIGHT OF PERMANENT RESIDENCE

Article 22 Territorial scope

The right of residence and the right of permanent residence shall cover the whole territory of the host Member State. Member States may impose territorial restrictions on the right of residence and the right of permanent residence only where the same restrictions apply to their own nationals.

Article 23 Related rights

Irrespective of nationality, the family members of a Union citizen who have the right of residence or the right of permanent residence in a Member State shall be entitled to take up employment or self-employment there.

Article 24 Equal treatment

1. Subject to such specific provisions as are expressly provided for in the Treaty and secondary law, all Union citizens residing on the basis of this Directive in the territory of the host Member State shall enjoy equal treatment with the nationals of that Member State within the scope of the Treaty. The benefit of this right shall be extended to family members who are not nationals of a Member State and who have the right of residence or permanent residence.
2. By way of derogation from paragraph 1, the host Member State shall not be obliged to confer entitlement to social assistance during the first three months of residence or, where appropriate, the longer period provided for in Article 14(4)(b), nor shall it be obliged, prior to acquisition of the right of permanent residence, to grant maintenance aid for studies, including vocational training, consisting in student grants or student loans to persons other than workers, self-employed persons, persons who retain such status and members of their families.

Article 25 General provisions concerning residence documents

1. Possession of a registration certificate as referred to in Article 8, of a document certifying permanent residence, of a certificate attesting submission of an application for a family member residence card, of a residence card or of a permanent residence card, may under no circumstances be made a precondition for the exercise of a right or the completion of an administrative formality, as entitlement to rights may be attested by any other means of proof.
2. All documents mentioned in paragraph 1 shall be issued free of charge or for a charge not exceeding that imposed on nationals for the issuing of similar documents.

Article 26 Checks

Member States may carry out checks on compliance with any requirement deriving from their national legislation for non-nationals always to carry their registration certificate or residence card, provided that the same requirement applies to their own nationals as regards their identity card. In the event of failure to comply with this requirement, Member States may impose the same sanctions as those imposed on their own nationals for failure to carry their identity card.

CHAPTER VI

RESTRICTIONS ON THE RIGHT OF ENTRY AND THE RIGHT OF RESIDENCE ON GROUNDS OF PUBLIC POLICY, PUBLIC SECURITY OR PUBLIC HEALTH

Article 27 General principles

1. Subject to the provisions of this Chapter, Member States may restrict the freedom of movement and residence of Union citizens and their family members, irrespective of nationality, on grounds of public policy, public security or public health. These grounds shall not be invoked to serve economic ends.
2. Measures taken on grounds of public policy or public security shall comply with the principle of proportionality and shall be based exclusively on the personal conduct

of the individual concerned. Previous criminal convictions shall not in themselves constitute grounds for taking such measures.

The personal conduct of the individual concerned must represent a genuine, present and sufficiently serious threat affecting one of the fundamental interests of society. Justifications that are isolated from the particulars of the case or that rely on considerations of general prevention shall not be accepted.

3.   In order to ascertain whether the person concerned represents a danger for public policy or public security, when issuing the registration certificate or, in the absence of a registration system, not later than three months from the date of arrival of the person concerned on its territory or from the date of reporting his/her presence within the territory, as provided for in Article 5(5), or when issuing the residence card, the host Member State may, should it consider this essential, request the Member State of origin and, if need be, other Member States to provide information concerning any previous police record the person concerned may have. Such enquiries shall not be made as a matter of routine. The Member State consulted shall give its reply within two months.

4.   The Member State which issued the passport or identity card shall allow the holder of the document who has been expelled on grounds of public policy, public security, or public health from another Member State to re-enter its territory without any formality even if the document is no longer valid or the nationality of the holder is in dispute.

Article 28 Protection against expulsion

1.   Before taking an expulsion decision on grounds of public policy or public security, the host Member State shall take account of considerations such as how long the individual concerned has resided on its territory, his/her age, state of health, family and economic situation, social and cultural integration into the host Member State and the extent of his/her links with the country of origin.

2.   The host Member State may not take an expulsion decision against Union citizens or their family members, irrespective of nationality, who have the right of permanent residence on its territory, except on serious grounds of public policy or public security.

3.   An expulsion decision may not be taken against Union citizens, except if the decision is based on imperative grounds of public security, as defined by Member States, if they:
     (a)   have resided in the host Member State for the previous ten years; or
     (b)   are a minor, except if the expulsion is necessary for the best interests of the child, as provided for in the United Nations Convention on the Rights of the Child of 20 November 1989.

Article 29 Public health

1.   The only diseases justifying measures restricting freedom of movement shall be the diseases with epidemic potential as defined by the relevant instruments of the World Health Organisation and other infectious diseases or contagious parasitic diseases if they are the subject of protection provisions applying to nationals of the host Member State.

2.   Diseases occurring after a three-month period from the date of arrival shall not constitute grounds for expulsion from the territory.

3.   Where there are serious indications that it is necessary, Member States may, within three months of the date of arrival, require persons entitled to the right of residence to undergo, free of charge, a medical examination to certify that they are not suffering from any of the conditions referred to in paragraph 1. Such medical examinations may not be required as a matter of routine.

Article 30 Notification of decisions

1.   The persons concerned shall be notified in writing of any decision taken under Article 27(1), in such a way that they are able to comprehend its content and the implications for them.

2.   The persons concerned shall be informed, precisely and in full, of the public policy, public security or public health grounds on which the decision taken in their case is based, unless this is contrary to the interests of State security.

3. The notification shall specify the court or administrative authority with which the person concerned may lodge an appeal, the time limit for the appeal and, where applicable, the time allowed for the person to leave the territory of the Member State. Save in duly substantiated cases of urgency, the time allowed to leave the territory shall be not less than one month from the date of notification.

Article 31 Procedural safeguards

1. The persons concerned shall have access to judicial and, where appropriate, administrative redress procedures in the host Member State to appeal against or seek review of any decision taken against them on the grounds of public policy, public security or public health.

2. Where the application for appeal against or judicial review of the expulsion decision is accompanied by an application for an interim order to suspend enforcement of that decision, actual removal from the territory may not take place until such time as the decision on the interim order has been taken, except:
   — where the expulsion decision is based on a previous judicial decision; or
   — where the persons concerned have had previous access to judicial review; or
   — where the expulsion decision is based on imperative grounds of public security under Article 28(3).

3. The redress procedures shall allow for an examination of the legality of the decision, as well as of the facts and circumstances on which the proposed measure is based. They shall ensure that the decision is not disproportionate, particularly in view of the requirements laid down in Article 28.

4. Member States may exclude the individual concerned from their territory pending the redress procedure, but they may not prevent the individual from submitting his/her defence in person, except when his/her appearance may cause serious troubles to public policy or public security or when the appeal or judicial review concerns a denial of entry to the territory.

Article 32 Duration of exclusion orders

1. Persons excluded on grounds of public policy or public security may submit an application for lifting of the exclusion order after a reasonable period, depending on the circumstances, and in any event after three years from enforcement of the final exclusion order which has been validly adopted in accordance with Community law, by putting forward arguments to establish that there has been a material change in the circumstances which justified the decision ordering their exclusion.
   The Member State concerned shall reach a decision on this application within six months of its submission.

2. The persons referred to in paragraph 1 shall have no right of entry to the territory of the Member State concerned while their application is being considered.

Article 33 Expulsion as a penalty or legal consequence

1. Expulsion orders may not be issued by the host Member State as a penalty or legal consequence of a custodial penalty, unless they conform to the requirements of Articles 27, 28 and 29.

2. If an expulsion order, as provided for in paragraph 1, is enforced more than two years after it was issued, the Member State shall check that the individual concerned is currently and genuinely a threat to public policy or public security and shall assess whether there has been any material change in the circumstances since the expulsion order was issued.

CHAPTER VII
FINAL PROVISIONS

Article 34 Publicity

Member States shall disseminate information concerning the rights and obligations of Union citizens and their family members on the subjects covered by this Directive, particularly by means of awareness-raising campaigns conducted through national and local media and other means of communication.

Article 35 Abuse of rights

Member States may adopt the necessary measures to refuse, terminate or withdraw any right

conferred by this Directive in the case of abuse of rights or fraud, such as marriages of convenience. Any such measure shall be proportionate and subject to the procedural safeguards provided for in Articles 30 and 31.

Article 36 Sanctions

Member States shall lay down provisions on the sanctions applicable to breaches of national rules adopted for the implementation of this Directive and shall take the measures required for their application. The sanctions laid down shall be effective and proportionate. Member States shall notify the Commission of these provisions not later than [30 April 2006] and as promptly as possible in the case of any subsequent changes.

Article 37 More favourable national provisions

The provisions of this Directive shall not affect any laws, regulations or administrative provisions laid down by a Member State which would be more favourable to the persons covered by this Directive.

Article 38 Repeals

1. ...
2. Directives 64/221/EEC, 68/360/EEC, 72/194/EEC, 73/148/EEC, 75/34/EEC, 75/35/EEC, 90/364/EEC, 90/365/EEC and 93/96/EEC shall be repealed with effect from [30 April 2006].
3. References made to the repealed provisions and Directives shall be construed as being made to this Directive.

Article 39 Report

No later than [30 April 2008] the Commission shall submit a report on the application of this Directive to the European Parliament and the Council, together with any necessary proposals, notably on the opportunity to extend the period of time during which Union citizens and their family members may reside in the territory of the host Member State without any conditions. The Member States shall provide the Commission with the information needed to produce the report.

Article 40 Transposition

1. Member States shall bring into force the laws, regulations and administrative provisions necessary to comply with this Directive by [30 April 2006].
    When Member States adopt those measures, they shall contain a reference to this Directive or shall be accompanied by such a reference on the occasion of their official publication. The methods of making such reference shall be laid down by the Member States.
2. Member States shall communicate to the Commission the text of the provisions of national law which they adopt in the field covered by this Directive together with a table showing how the provisions of this Directive correspond to the national provisions adopted.

Article 41 Entry into force

This Directive shall enter into force on the day of its publication in the *Official Journal of the European Union*.

Article 42 Addressees

This Directive is addressed to the Member States.

DIRECTIVE 2005/36/EC OF THE EUROPEAN PARLIAMENT AND OF THE COUNCIL of 7 SEPTEMBER 2005

on the recognition of professional qualifications
[2005] OJ L255/22

TITLE I
GENERAL PROVISIONS

Article 1   Purpose

This Directive establishes rules according to which a Member State which makes access to or pursuit of a regulated profession in its territory contingent upon possession of specific professional qualifications (referred to hereinafter as the host Member State) shall recognise professional qualifications obtained in one or more other Member States (referred to hereinafter as the home Member State) and which allow the holder of the said qualifications to pursue the same profession there, for access to and pursuit of that profession.

This Directive also establishes rules concerning partial access to a regulated profession and recognition of professional traineeships pursued in another Member State.

Article 2   Scope

1. This Directive shall apply to all nationals of a Member State wishing to pursue a regulated profession in a Member State, including those belonging to the liberal professions, other than that in which they obtained their professional qualifications, on either a self-employed or employed basis.

   This Directive shall also apply to all nationals of a Member State who have pursued a professional traineeship outside the home Member State.

2. Each Member State may permit Member State nationals in possession of evidence of professional qualifications not obtained in a Member State to pursue a regulated profession within the meaning of Article 3(1)(a) on its territory in accordance with its rules. In the case of professions covered by Title III, Chapter III, this initial recognition shall respect the minimum training conditions laid down in that Chapter.

3. Where, for a given regulated profession, other specific arrangements directly related to the recognition of professional qualifications are established in a separate instrument of Community law, the corresponding provisions of this Directive shall not apply.

4. This Directive shall not apply to notaries who are appointed by an official act of government.

Article 3   Definitions

1. For the purposes of this Directive, the following definitions apply:

   (a) 'regulated profession': a professional activity or group of professional activities, access to which, the pursuit of which, or one of the modes of pursuit of which is subject, directly or indirectly, by virtue of legislative, regulatory or administrative provisions to the possession of specific professional qualifications; in particular, the use of a professional title limited by legislative, regulatory or administrative provisions to holders of a given professional qualification shall constitute a mode of pursuit. Where the first sentence of this definition does not apply, a profession referred to in paragraph 2 shall be treated as a regulated profession;

   (b) 'professional qualifications': qualifications attested by evidence of formal qualifications, an attestation of competence referred to in Article 11, point (a)(i) and/or professional experience;

   (c) 'evidence of formal qualifications': diplomas, certificates and other evidence issued by an authority in a Member State designated pursuant to legislative, regulatory or administrative provisions of that Member State and certifying successful completion of professional training obtained mainly in the Community. Where the first sentence of this definition does not apply, evidence of formal qualifications referred to in paragraph 3 shall be treated as evidence of formal qualifications;

(d) 'competent authority': any authority or body empowered by a Member State specifically to issue or receive training diplomas and other documents or information and to receive the applications, and take the decisions, referred to in this Directive;

(e) 'regulated education and training': any training which is specifically geared to the pursuit of a given profession and which comprises a course or courses complemented, where appropriate, by professional training, or probationary or professional practice.

The structure and level of the professional training, probationary or professional practice shall be determined by the laws, regulations or administrative provisions of the Member State concerned or monitored or approved by the authority designated for that purpose;

(f) 'professional experience': the actual and lawful full-time or equivalent part-time pursuit of the profession concerned in a Member State;

(g) 'adaptation period': the pursuit of a regulated profession in the host Member State under the responsibility of a qualified member of that profession, such period of supervised practice possibly being accompanied by further training. This period of supervised practice shall be the subject of an assessment. The detailed rules governing the adaptation period and its assessment as well as the status of a migrant under supervision shall be laid down by the competent authority in the host Member State.

The status enjoyed in the host Member State by the person undergoing the period of supervised practice, in particular in the matter of right of residence as well as obligations, social rights and benefits, allowances and remuneration, shall be established by the competent authorities in that Member State in accordance with applicable Community law;

(h) 'aptitude test': a test of the professional knowledge, skills and competences of the applicant, carried out or recognised by the competent authorities of the host Member State with the aim of assessing the ability of the applicant to pursue a regulated profession in that Member State.

In order to permit this test to be carried out, the competent authorities shall draw up a list of subjects which, on the basis of a comparison of the education and training required in the host Member State and that received by the applicant, are not covered by the diploma or other evidence of formal qualifications possessed by the applicant.

The aptitude test must take account of the fact that the applicant is a qualified professional in the home Member State or the Member State from which the applicant comes. It shall cover subjects to be selected from those on the list, knowledge of which is essential in order to be able to pursue the profession in question in the host Member State. The test may also cover knowledge of the professional rules applicable to the activities in question in the host Member State. The detailed application of the aptitude test and the status, in the host Member State, of the applicant who wishes to prepare himself for the aptitude test in that Member State shall be determined by the competent authorities in that Member State;

(i) 'manager of an undertaking': any person who in an undertaking in the occupational field in question has pursued an activity:

    (i) as a manager of an undertaking or a manager of a branch of an undertaking; or

    (ii) as a deputy to the proprietor or the manager of an undertaking where that post involves responsibility equivalent to that of the proprietor or manager represented; or

    (iii) in a managerial post with duties of a commercial and/or technical nature and with responsibility for one or more departments of the undertaking.

(j) 'professional traineeship': without prejudice to Article 46(4), a period of professional practice carried out under supervision provided it constitutes a condition for access to a regulated profession, and which can take place either during or after completion of an education leading to a diploma;

(k) 'European Professional Card': an electronic certificate proving either that the professional has met all the necessary conditions to provide services in a host Member State on a temporary and occasional basis or the recognition of professional qualifications for establishment in a host Member State;

(l) 'lifelong learning': all general education, vocational education and training, non-formal education and informal learning undertaken throughout life, resulting in an improvement in knowledge, skills and competences, which may include professional ethics;

(m) 'overriding reasons of general interest': reasons recognised as such in the case-law of the Court of Justice of the European Union;

(n) 'European Credit Transfer and Accumulation System or ECTS credits': the credit system for higher education used in the European Higher Education Area.

2. A profession practised by the members of an association or organisation listed in Annex I shall be treated as a regulated profession.

The purpose of the associations or organisations referred to in the first subparagraph is, in particular, to promote and maintain a high standard in the professional field concerned. To that end they are recognised in a special form by a Member State and award evidence of formal qualifications to their members, ensure that their members respect the rules of professional conduct which they prescribe, and confer on them the right to use a title or designatory letters or to benefit from a status corresponding to those formal qualifications.

On each occasion that a Member State grants recognition to an association or organisation referred to in the first subparagraph, it shall inform the Commission. The Commission shall examine whether that association or organisation fulfils the conditions provided for in the second subparagraph. In order to take due account of regulatory developments in Member States, the Commission shall be empowered to adopt delegated acts in accordance with Article 57c in order to update Annex I where the conditions provided for in the second subparagraph are satisfied.

Where the conditions provided for in the second subparagraph are not satisfied, the Commission shall adopt an implementing act in order to reject the requested update of Annex I.

3. Evidence of formal qualifications issued by a third country shall be regarded as evidence of formal qualifications if the holder has three years' professional experience in the profession concerned on the territory of the Member State which recognised that evidence of formal qualifications in accordance with Article 2(2), certified by that Member State.

Article 4 Effects of recognition

1. The recognition of professional qualifications by the host Member State shall allow beneficiaries to gain access in that Member State to the same profession as that for which they are qualified in the home Member State and to pursue it in the host Member State under the same conditions as its nationals.

2. For the purposes of this Directive, the profession which the applicant wishes to pursue in the host Member State is the same as that for which he is qualified in his home Member State if the activities covered are comparable.

3. By way of derogation from paragraph 1, partial access to a profession in the host Member State shall be granted under the conditions laid down in Article 4f.

Article 4a European Professional Card

1. Member States shall issue holders of a professional qualification with a European Professional Card upon their request and on condition that the Commission has adopted the relevant implementing acts provided for in paragraph 7.

2. When a European Professional Card has been introduced for a particular profession by means of relevant implementing acts adopted pursuant to paragraph 7, the holder of a professional qualification concerned may choose to apply for such a Card or to make use of the procedures provided for in Titles II and III.

3. Member States shall ensure that the holder of a European Professional Card benefits from all the rights conferred by Articles 4b to 4e.

4. Where the holder of a professional qualification intends to provide services under Title II other than those covered by Article 7(4), the competent authority of the home Member State shall issue the European Professional Card in accordance with Articles 4b and 4c. The European Professional Card shall, where applicable, constitute the declaration under Article 7.

5. Where the holder of a professional qualification intends to establish himself in another Member State under Chapters I to IIIa of Title III or to provide services under Article 7(4), the competent authority of the home Member State shall complete all preparatory steps with regard to the individual file of the applicant created within the Internal Market Information System (IMI) (IMI file) as provided for in Articles 4b and 4d. The competent authority of the host Member State shall issue the European Professional Card in accordance with Articles 4b and 4d.

For the purpose of establishment, the issuance of a European Professional Card shall not provide an automatic right to practise a particular profession if there are registration requirements or other control procedures already in place in the host Member State before a European Professional Card is introduced for that profession.

6. Member States shall designate competent authorities for dealing with IMI files and issuing European Professional Cards. Those authorities shall ensure an impartial, objective and timely processing of applications for European Professional Cards. The assistance centres referred to in Article 57b may also act in the capacity of a competent authority. Member States shall ensure that competent authorities and assistance centres inform citizens, including prospective applicants, about the functioning and the added value of a European Professional Card for the professions for which it is available.

7. The Commission shall, by means of implementing acts, adopt measures necessary to ensure the uniform application of the provisions on the European Professional Cards for those professions that meet the conditions laid down in the second subparagraph of this paragraph, including measures concerning the format of the European Professional Card, the processing of written applications, the translations to be provided by the applicant to support any application for a European Professional Card, details of the documents required pursuant to Article 7(2) or Annex VII to present a complete application and procedures for making and processing payments for a European Professional Card, taking into account the particularities of the profession concerned. The Commission shall also specify, by means of implementing acts, how, when and for which documents competent authorities may request certified copies in accordance with the second subparagraph of Article 4b(3), Articles 4d(2) and 4d(3) for the profession concerned.

The introduction of a European Professional Card for a particular profession by means of the adoption of relevant implementing acts referred to in the first subparagraph shall be subject to all of the following conditions:

(a) there is significant mobility or potential for significant mobility in the profession concerned;

(b) there is sufficient interest expressed by the relevant stakeholders;

(c) the profession or the education and training geared to the pursuit of the profession is regulated in a significant number of Member States.

Those implementing acts shall be adopted in accordance with the examination procedure referred to in Article 58(2).

8. Any fees which applicants may incur in relation to administrative procedures to issue a European Professional Card shall be reasonable, proportionate and commensurate with the costs incurred by the home and the host Member States and shall not act as a disincentive to apply for a European Professional Card.

Article 4b Application for a European Professional Card and creation of an IMI file

1. The home Member State shall enable a holder of a professional qualification to apply for a European Professional Card through an on-line tool, provided by the Commission, that automatically creates an IMI file for the particular applicant. Where a home Member State allows also for written applications, it shall put in place all necessary arrangements for the creation of the IMI file, any information to be sent to the applicant and the issuance of the European Professional Card.

2. Applications shall be supported by the documents required in the implementing acts to be adopted pursuant to Article 4a(7).

3. Within one week of receipt of the application, the competent authority of the home Member State shall acknowledge receipt of the application and inform the applicant of any missing document.

   Where applicable, the competent authority of the home Member State shall issue any supporting certificate required under this Directive. The competent authority of the home Member State shall verify whether the applicant is legally established in the home Member State and whether all the necessary documents which have been issued in the home Member State are valid and authentic. In the event of duly justified doubts, the competent authority of the home Member State shall consult the relevant body and may request from the applicant certified copies of documents. In case of subsequent applications by the same applicant, the competent authorities of the home and the host Member States may not request the re-submission of documents which are already contained in the IMI file and which are still valid.

4. The Commission may, by means of implementing acts, adopt the technical specifications, the measures necessary to ensure integrity, confidentiality and accuracy of information contained in the European Professional Card and in the IMI file, and the conditions and the procedures for issuing a European Professional Card to its holder, including the possibility of downloading it or submitting updates for the IMI file. Those implementing acts shall be adopted in accordance with the examination procedure referred to in Article 58(2).

Article 4c European Professional Card for the temporary and occasional provision of services other than those covered by Article 7(4)

1. The competent authority of the home Member State shall verify the application and the supporting documents in the IMI file and issue the European Professional Card for the temporary and occasional provision of services other than those covered by Article 7(4) within three weeks. That time period shall start upon receipt of the missing documents referred to in the first subparagraph of Article 4b(3) or, if no further documents were requested, upon the expiry of the one-week period referred to in that subparagraph. It shall then transmit the European Professional Card immediately to the competent authority of each host Member State concerned and shall inform the applicant accordingly. The host Member State may not require any further declaration under Article 7 for the following 18 months.

2. The decision of the competent authority of the home Member State, or the absence of a decision within the period of three weeks referred to in paragraph 1, shall be subject to appeal under national law.

3. If a holder of a European Professional Card wishes to provide services in Member States other than those initially mentioned in the application referred to in paragraph 1 that holder may apply for such extension. If the holder wishes to continue providing services beyond the period of 18 months referred to in paragraph 1, that holder shall inform the competent authority accordingly. In either case, that holder shall also provide any information on material changes in the situation substantiated in the IMI file that may be required by the competent authority in the home Member State in accordance with the implementing acts to be adopted pursuant to Article 4a(7). The competent authority of the home Member State shall transmit the updated European Professional Card to the host Member States concerned.

4. The European Professional Card shall be valid in the entire territory of all the host Member States concerned for as long as its holder maintains the right to practice on the basis of the documents and information contained in the IMI file.

Article 4d European Professional Card for establishment and for the temporary and occasional provision of services under Article 7(4)

1. The competent authority of the home Member State shall, within one month, verify the authenticity and validity of the supporting documents in the IMI file for the purpose of issuing a European Professional Card for establishment or for the temporary and occasional provision of services under Article 7(4). That time period shall start upon

receipt of the missing documents referred to in the first subparagraph of Article 4b(3) or, if no further documents were requested, upon the expiry of the one-week period referred to in that subparagraph. It shall then transmit the application immediately to the competent authority of the host Member State. The home Member State shall inform the applicant of the status of the application at the same time as it transmits the application to the host Member State.

2. In the cases referred to in Articles 16, 21, 49a and 49b, a host Member State shall decide whether to issue a European Professional Card under paragraph 1 within one month of receipt of the application transmitted by the home Member State. In the event of duly justified doubts, the host Member State may request additional information from, or the inclusion of a certified copy of a document by, the home Member State, which the latter shall provide no later than two weeks after the submission of the request. Subject to the second subparagraph of paragraph 5, the period of one month shall apply, notwithstanding any such request.

3. In the cases referred to in Articles 7(4) and 14, a host Member State shall decide whether to issue a European Professional Card or to subject the holder of a professional qualification to compensation measures within two months of receipt of the application transmitted by the home Member State. In the event of duly justified doubts, the host Member State may request additional information from, or the inclusion of a certified copy of a document by, the home Member State which the latter shall provide no later than two weeks after the submission of the request. Subject to the second subparagraph of paragraph 5, the period of two months shall apply, notwithstanding any such request.

4. In the event that the host Member State does not receive the necessary information which it may require in accordance with this Directive for taking a decision on the issuance of the European Professional Card from either the home Member State or the applicant, it may refuse to issue the Card. Such refusal shall be duly justified.

5. Where the host Member State fails to take a decision within the time limits set out in paragraphs 2 and 3 of this Article or fails to organise an aptitude test in accordance with Article 7(4), the European Professional Card shall be deemed to be issued and shall be sent automatically, through IMI, to the holder of a professional qualification.

    The host Member State shall have the possibility to extend by two weeks the deadlines set out in paragraphs 2 and 3 for the automatic issuance of the European Professional Card. It shall explain the reason for the extension and inform the applicant accordingly. Such an extension may be repeated once and only where it is strictly necessary, in · particular for reasons relating to public health or the safety of the service recipients.

6. The actions taken by the home Member State in accordance with paragraph 1 shall replace any application for recognition of professional qualifications under the national law of the host Member State.

7. The decisions of the home and the host Member State adopted under paragraphs 1 to 5 or the absence of decision by the home Member State shall be subject to appeal under the national law of the Member State concerned.

Article 4e Processing and access to data regarding the European Professional Card

1. Without prejudice to the presumption of innocence, the competent authorities of the home and the host Member States shall update, in a timely manner, the corresponding IMI file with information regarding disciplinary actions or criminal sanctions which relate to a prohibition or restriction and which have consequences for the pursuit of activities by the holder of a European Professional Card under this Directive. In so doing they shall respect personal data protection rules provided for in Directive 95/46/EC of the European Parliament and of the Council of 24 October 1995 on the protection of individuals with regard to the processing of personal data and on the free movement of such data and Directive 2002/58/EC of the European Parliament and of the Council of 12 July 2002 concerning the processing of personal data and the protection of privacy in the electronic communications sector (Directive on privacy and electronic communications). Such updates shall include the deletion of information

which is no longer required. The holder of the European Professional Card as well as the competent authorities that have access to the corresponding IMI file shall be informed immediately of any updates. That obligation shall be without prejudice to the alert obligations for Member States under Article 56a.

2. The content of the information updates referred to in paragraph 1 shall be limited to the following:

(a) the identity of the professional;

(b) the profession concerned;

(c) information about the national authority or court which has adopted the decision on restriction or prohibition;

(d) the scope of the restriction or the prohibition; and

(e) the period for which the restriction or the prohibition applies.

3. Access to the information in the IMI file shall be limited to the competent authorities of the home and the host Member States, in accordance with Directive 95/46/EC. The competent authorities shall inform the holder of the European Professional Card of the content of the IMI file upon that holder's request.

4. The information included in the European Professional Card shall be limited to the information that is necessary to ascertain its holder's right to exercise the profession for which it has been issued, namely the holder's name, surname, date and place of birth, profession, formal qualifications, and the applicable regime, competent authorities involved, Card number, security features and reference to a valid proof of identity. Information relating to professional experience acquired, or compensation measures passed, by the holder of the European Professional Card shall be included in the IMI file.

5. The personal data included in the IMI file may be processed for as long as it is needed for the purpose of the recognition procedure as such and as evidence of the recognition or of the transmission of the declaration required under Article 7. Member States shall ensure that the holder of a European Professional Card has the right at any time, and at no cost to that holder, to request the rectification of inaccurate or incomplete data, or the deletion or blocking of the IMI file concerned. The holder shall be informed of this right at the time the European Professional Card is issued, and reminded of it every two years thereafter. The reminder shall be sent automatically via IMI where the initial application for the European Professional Card was submitted online.

In the event of a request for deletion of an IMI file linked to a European Professional Card issued for the purpose of establishment or temporary and occasional provision of services under Article 7(4), the competent authorities of the host Member State concerned shall issue the holder of professional qualifications with evidence attesting to the recognition of his professional qualifications.

6. In relation to the processing of personal data in the European Professional Card and all IMI files, the relevant competent authorities of the Member States shall be regarded as controllers within the meaning of point (d) of Article 2 of Directive 95/46/EC. In relation to its responsibilities under paragraphs 1 to 4 of this Article and the processing of personal data involved therein, the Commission shall be regarded as a controller within the meaning of point (d) of Article 2 of Regulation (EC) No 45/2001 of the European Parliament and of the Council of 18 December 2000 on the protection of individuals with regard to the processing of personal data by the Community institutions and bodies and on the free movement of such data.

7. Without prejudice to paragraph 3, host Member States shall provide that employers, customers, patients, public authorities and other interested parties may verify the authenticity and validity of a European Professional Card presented to them by the Card holder.

The Commission shall, by means of implementing acts, lay down rules concerning access to the IMI file, and the technical means and the procedures for the verification referred to in the first subparagraph. Those implementing acts shall be adopted in accordance with the examination procedure referred to in Article 58(2).

Article 4f Partial access

1. The competent authority of the host Member State shall grant partial access, on a case-by-case basis, to a professional activity in its territory only when all the following conditions are fulfilled:

    (a) the professional is fully qualified to exercise in the home Member State the professional activity for which partial access is sought in the host Member State;

    (b) differences between the professional activity legally exercised in the home Member State and the regulated profession in the host Member State as such are so large that the application of compensation measures would amount to requiring the applicant to complete the full programme of education and training required in the host Member State to have access to the full regulated profession in the host Member State;

    (c) the professional activity can objectively be separated from other activities falling under the regulated profession in the host Member State.

    For the purpose of point (c), the competent authority of the host Member State shall take into account whether the professional activity can be pursued autonomously in the home Member State.

2. Partial access may be rejected if such rejection is justified by overriding reasons of general interest, suitable for securing the attainment of the objective pursued, and does not go beyond what is necessary to attain that objective.

3. Applications for the purpose of establishment in a host Member State shall be examined in accordance with Chapters I and IV of Title III.

4. Applications for the purpose of providing temporary and occasional services in the host Member State concerning professional activities that have public health or safety implications shall be examined in accordance with Title II.

5. By derogation from the sixth subparagraph of Article 7(4) and Article 52(1), the professional activity shall be exercised under the professional title of the home Member State once partial access has been granted. The host Member State may require use of that professional title in the languages of the host Member State. Professionals benefiting from partial access shall clearly indicate to the service recipients the scope of their professional activities.

6. This Article shall not apply to professionals benefiting from automatic recognition of their professional qualifications under Chapters II, III and IIIa of Title III.

TITLE II
FREE PROVISION OF SERVICES

Article 5 Principle of the free provision of services

1. Without prejudice to specific provisions of Community law, as well as to Articles 6 and 7 of this Directive, Member States shall not restrict, for any reason relating to professional qualifications, the free provision of services in another Member State:

    (a) if the service provider is legally established in a Member State for the purpose of pursuing the same profession there (hereinafter referred to as the Member State of establishment), and

    (b) where the service provider moves, if he has pursued that profession in one or several Member States for at least one year during the last 10 years preceding the provision of services when the profession is not regulated in the Member State of establishment. The condition of one year's pursuit shall not apply if the profession or the education and training leading to the profession is regulated.

2. The provisions of this title shall only apply where the service provider moves to the territory of the host Member State to pursue, on a temporary and occasional basis, the profession referred to in paragraph 1.

    The temporary and occasional nature of the provision of services shall be assessed case by case, in particular in relation to its duration, its frequency, its regularity and its continuity.

3. Where a service provider moves, he shall be subject to professional rules of a professional, statutory or administrative nature which are directly linked to professional qualifications, such as the definition of the profession, the use of titles and serious

professional malpractice which is directly and specifically linked to consumer protection and safety, as well as disciplinary provisions which are applicable in the host Member State to professionals who pursue the same profession in that Member State.

Article 6   Exemptions

Pursuant to Article 5(1), the host Member State shall exempt service providers established in another Member State from the requirements which it places on professionals established in its territory relating to:

(a)   authorisation by, registration with or membership of a professional organisation or body. In order to facilitate the application of disciplinary provisions in force on their territory according to Article 5(3), Member States may provide either for automatic temporary registration with or for pro forma membership of such a professional organisation or body, provided that such registration or membership does not delay or complicate in any way the provision of services and does not entail any additional costs for the service provider. A copy of the declaration and, where applicable, of the renewal referred to in Article 7(1), accompanied, for professions which have implications for public health and safety referred to in Article 7(4) or which benefit from automatic recognition under Title III Chapter III, by a copy of the documents referred to in
Article 7(2) shall be sent by the competent authority to the relevant professional organisation or body, and this shall constitute automatic temporary registration or pro forma membership for this purpose;

(b)   registration with a public social security body for the purpose of settling accounts with an insurer relating to activities pursued for the benefit of insured persons.
The service provider shall, however, inform in advance or, in an urgent case, afterwards, the body referred to in point (b) of the services which he has provided.

Article 7   Declaration to be made in advance, if the service provider moves

1.   Member States may require that, where the service provider first moves from one Member State to another in order to provide services, he shall inform the competent authority in the host Member State in a written declaration to be made in advance including the details of any insurance cover or other means of personal or collective protection with regard to professional liability. Such declaration shall be renewed once a year if the service provider intends to provide temporary or occasional services in that Member State during that year. The service provider may supply the declaration by any means.

2.   Moreover, for the first provision of services or if there is a material change in the situation substantiated by the documents, Member States may require that the declaration be accompanied by the following documents:

(a)   proof of the nationality of the service provider;

(b)   an attestation certifying that the holder is legally established in a Member State for the purpose of pursuing the activities concerned and that he is not prohibited from practising, even temporarily, at the moment of delivering the attestation;

(c)   evidence of professional qualifications;

(d)   for cases referred to in point (b) of Article 5(1), any means of proof that the service provider has pursued the activity concerned for at least one year during the previous 10 years;

(e)   for professions in the security sector, in the health sector and professions related to the education of minors, including in childcare and early childhood education, where the Member State so requires for its own nationals, an attestation confirming the absence of temporary or final suspensions from exercising the profession or of criminal convictions;

(f)   for professions that have patient safety implications, a declaration about the applicant's knowledge of the language necessary for practising the profession in the host Member State;

(g)   for professions covering the activities referred to in Article 16 and which were notified by a Member State in accordance with Article 59(2), a certificate concerning the nature and duration of the activity issued by the competent authority or body of the Member State where the service provider is established.

2a.   Submission of a required declaration by the service provider in accordance with paragraph 1 shall entitle that service provider to have access to the service activity or to exercise that activity in the entire territory of the Member State concerned. A Member State may require additional information listed in paragraph 2 concerning the professional qualifications of the service provider if:

   (a)   the profession is regulated in parts of that Member State's territory in a different manner;

   (b)   such regulation is applicable also to all nationals of that Member State;

   (c)   the differences in such regulation are justified by overriding reasons of general interest relating to public health or safety of service recipients; and

   (d)   the Member State has no other means of obtaining such information.

3.   The service shall be provided under the professional title of the Member State of establishment, in so far as such a title exists in that Member State for the professional activity in question. That title shall be indicated in the official language or one of the official languages of the Member State of establishment in such a way as to avoid any confusion with the professional title of the host Member State. Where no such professional title exists in the Member State of establishment, the service provider shall indicate his formal qualification in the official language or one of the official languages of that Member State. By way of exception, the service shall be provided under the professional title of the host Member State for cases referred to in Title III Chapter III.

4.   For the first provision of services, in the case of regulated professions that have public health or safety implications which do not benefit from automatic recognition under Chapter II, III or IIIa of Title III, the competent authority of the host Member State may check the professional qualifications of the service provider prior to the first provision of services. Such a prior check shall be possible only where the purpose of the check is to avoid serious damage to the health or safety of the service recipient due to a lack of professional qualification of the service provider and where the check does not go beyond what is necessary for that purpose.

   No later than one month after receipt of the declaration and accompanying documents, referred to in paragraphs 1 and 2, the competent authority shall inform the service provider of its decision:

   (a)   not to check his professional qualifications;

   (b)   having checked his professional qualifications:

      (i)   to require the service provider to take an aptitude test; or

      (ii)   to allow the provision of services.

   Where there is a difficulty which would result in delay in taking a decision under the second subparagraph, the competent authority shall notify the service provider of the reason for the delay within the same deadline. The difficulty shall be solved within one month of that notification and the decision finalised within two months of resolution of the difficulty.

   Where there is a substantial difference between the professional qualifications of the service provider and the training required in the host Member State, to the extent that that difference is such as to be harmful to public health or safety, and that it cannot be compensated by the service provider's professional experience or by knowledge, skills and competences acquired through lifelong learning formally validated to that end by a relevant body, the host Member State shall give that service provider the opportunity to show, by means of an aptitude test, as referred to in point (b) of the second subparagraph, that they have acquired the knowledge, skills or competence that were lacking. The host Member State shall take a decision on that basis on whether to allow the provision of services. In any case, it must be possible to provide the service within one month of the decision taken in accordance with the second subparagraph.

   In the absence of a reaction of the competent authority within the deadlines set out in the second and third subparagraphs, the service may be provided.

   In cases where professional qualifications have been verified under this paragraph, the service shall be provided under the professional title of the host Member State.

In the absence of a reaction of the competent authority within the deadlines set in the previous subparagraphs, the service may be provided.

In cases where qualifications have been verified under this paragraph, the service shall be provided under the professional title of the host Member State.

Article 8   Administrative cooperation

1. The competent authorities of the host Member State may ask the competent authorities of the Member State of establishment, in the event of justified doubts, to provide any information relevant to the legality of the service provider's establishment and good conduct, as well as the absence of any disciplinary or criminal sanctions of a professional nature. In the event that the competent authorities of the host Member State decide to check the service provider's professional qualifications, they may ask the competent authorities of the Member State of establishment for information about the service provider's training courses to the extent necessary to assess substantial differences likely to be harmful to public health or safety. The competent authorities of the Member State of establishment shall provide that information in accordance with Article 56. In the case of non-regulated professions in the home Member State, the assistance centres referred to in Article 57b may also provide such information.

2. The competent authorities shall ensure the exchange of all information necessary for complaints by a recipient of a service against a service provider to be correctly pursued. Recipients shall be informed of the outcome of the complaint.

Article 9   Information to be given to the recipients of the service

In cases where the service is provided under the professional title of the Member State of establishment or under the formal qualification of the service provider, in addition to the other requirements relating to information contained in Community law, the competent authorities of the host Member State may require the service provider to furnish the recipient of the service with any or all of the following information:

(a) if the service provider is registered in a commercial register or similar public register, the register in which he is registered, his registration number, or equivalent means of identification contained in that register;

(b) if the activity is subject to authorisation in the Member State of establishment, the name and address of the competent supervisory authority;

(c) any professional association or similar body with which the service provider is registered;

(d) the professional title or, where no such title exists, the formal qualification of the service provider and the Member State in which it was awarded;

(e) if the service provider performs an activity which is subject to VAT, the VAT identification number referred to in Article 22(1) of the sixth Council Directive 77/388/EEC of 17 May 1977 on the harmonisation of the laws of the Member States relating to turnover taxes – Common system of value added tax: uniform basis of assessment;

(f) details of any insurance cover or other means of personal or collective protection with regard to professional liability.

TITLE III
FREEDOM OF ESTABLISHMENT

CHAPTER I
GENERAL SYSTEM FOR THE RECOGNITION OF EVIDENCE OF TRAINING

Article 10 Scope

This Chapter applies to all professions which are not covered by Chapters II and III of this Title and in the following cases in which the applicant, for specific and exceptional reasons, does not satisfy the conditions laid down in those Chapters:

(a) for activities listed in Annex IV, when the migrant does not meet the requirements set out in Articles 17, 18 and 19;

(b)   for doctors with basic training, specialised doctors, nurses responsible for general care, dental practitioners, specialised dental practitioners, veterinary surgeons, midwives, pharmacists and architects, when the migrant does not meet the requirements of effective and lawful professional practice referred to in Articles 23, 27, 33, 37, 39, 43 and 49;

(c)   for architects, when the migrant holds evidence of formal qualification not listed in Annex V, point 5.7;

(d)   without prejudice to Articles 21(1), 23 and 27, for doctors, nurses, dental practitioners, veterinary surgeons, midwives, pharmacists and architects holding evidence of formal qualifications as a specialist, which must follow the training leading to the possession of a title listed in Annex V, points 5.1.1, 5.2.2, 5.3.2, 5.4.2, 5.5.2, 5.6.2 and 5.7.1, and solely for the purpose of the recognition of the relevant specialty;

(e)   for nurses responsible for general care and specialised nurses holding evidence of formal qualifications as a specialist which follows the training leading to the possession of a title listed in Annex V, point 5.2.2, when the migrant seeks recognition in another Member State where the relevant professional activities are pursued by specialised nurses without training as general care nurse;

(f)   for specialised nurses without training as general care nurse, when the migrant seeks recognition in another Member State where the relevant professional activities are pursued by nurses responsible for general care, specialised nurses without training as general care nurse or specialised nurses holding evidence of formal qualifications as a specialist which follows the training leading to the possession of the titles listed in Annex V, point 5.2.2;

(g)   for migrants meeting the requirements set out in Article 3(3).

Article 11 Levels of qualification

For the purposes of Article 13 and Article 14(6), professional qualifications shall be grouped under the following levels:

(a)   an attestation of competence issued by a competent authority in the home Member State designated pursuant to legislative, regulatory or administrative provisions of that Member State, on the basis of:

(i)   either a training course not forming part of a certificate or diploma within the meaning of points (b), (c), (d) or (e), or a specific examination without prior training, or full-time pursuit of the profession in a Member State for three consecutive years or for an equivalent duration on a part-time basis during the previous 10 years,

(ii)   or general primary or secondary education, attesting that the holder has acquired general knowledge;

(b)   a certificate attesting to a successful completion of a secondary course,

(i)   either general in character, supplemented by a course of study or professional training other than those referred to in point (c) and/or by the probationary or professional practice required in addition to that course,

(ii)   or technical or professional in character, supplemented where appropriate by a course of study or professional training as referred to in point (i), and/or by the probationary or professional practice required in addition to that course;

(c)   a diploma certifying successful completion of

(i)   either training at post-secondary level other than that referred to in points (d) and (e) of a duration of at least one year or of an equivalent duration on a part-time basis, one of the conditions of entry of which is, as a general rule, the successful completion of the secondary course required to obtain entry to university or higher education or the completion of equivalent school education of the second secondary level, as well as the professional training which may be required in addition to that post-secondary course; or

(ii)   regulated education and training or, in the case of regulated professions, vocational training with a special structure, with competences going beyond what is provided for in level b, equivalent to the level of training provided for under point (i), if such training provides a comparable professional standard and prepares the trainee for a comparable level of responsibilities and functions provided that the diploma is accompanied by a certificate from the home Member State;

(d)   a diploma certifying that the holder has successfully completed training at post-secondary level of at least three and not more than four years' duration, or of an equivalent duration on a part-time basis, which may in addition be expressed with an equivalent number of ECTS credits, at a university or establishment of higher education or another establishment of equivalent level and, where appropriate, that he has successfully completed the professional training required in addition to the post-secondary course;

(e)   a diploma certifying that the holder has successfully completed a post-secondary course of at least four years' duration, or of an equivalent duration on a part-time basis, which may in addition be expressed with an equivalent number of ECTS credits, at a university or establishment of higher education or another establishment of equivalent level and, where appropriate, that he has successfully completed the professional training required in addition to the post-secondary course.

Article 12 Equal treatment of qualifications

Any evidence of formal qualifications or set of evidence of formal qualifications issued by a competent authority in a Member State, certifying successful completion of training in the Union, on a full or part-time basis, within or outside formal programmes, which is recognised by that Member State as being of an equivalent level and which confers on the holder the same rights of access to or pursuit of a profession or prepares for the pursuit of that profession, shall be treated as evidence of formal qualifications referred to in Article 11, including the level in question.

Any professional qualification which, although not satisfying the requirements contained in the legislative, regulatory or administrative provisions in force in the home Member State for access to or the pursuit of a profession, confers on the holder acquired rights by virtue of these provisions, shall also be treated as such evidence of formal qualifications under the same conditions as set out in the first subparagraph. This applies in particular if the home Member State raises the level of training required for admission to a profession and for its exercise, and if an individual who has undergone former training, which does not meet the requirements of the new qualification, benefits from acquired rights by virtue of national legislative, regulatory or administrative provisions; in such case this former training is considered by the host Member State, for the purposes of the application of Article 13, as corresponding to the level of the new training.

Article 13 Conditions for recognition

1.   If access to or pursuit of a regulated profession in a host Member State is contingent upon possession of specific professional qualifications, the competent authority of that Member State shall permit applicants to access and pursue that profession, under the same conditions as apply to its nationals, if they possess an attestation of competence or evidence of formal qualifications referred to in Article 11, required by another Member State in order to gain access to and pursue that profession on its territory.

Attestations of competence or evidence of formal qualifications shall be issued by a competent authority in a Member State, designated in accordance with the laws, regulations or administrative provisions of that Member State.

2.   Access to, and pursuit of, a profession as described in paragraph 1 shall also be granted to applicants who have pursued the profession in question on a full-time basis for one year or for an equivalent overall duration on a part-time basis during the previous 10 years in another Member State which does not regulate that profession, and who possess one or more attestations of competence or evidence of formal qualifications issued by another Member State which does not regulate the profession.

Attestations of competence and evidence of formal qualifications shall satisfy the following conditions:

(a)   they are issued by a competent authority in a Member State, designated in accordance with the laws, regulations or administrative provisions of that Member State;

(b)   they attest that the holder has been prepared for the pursuit of the profession in question.

The one year of professional experience referred to in the first subparagraph may not, however, be required if the evidence of formal qualifications which the applicant possesses certifies regulated education and training.

3.   The host Member State shall accept the level attested under Article 11 by the home Member State, as well as the certificate by which the home Member State certifies that regulated education and training or vocational training with a special structure referred to in point (c)(ii) of Article 11 is equivalent to the level provided for in point (c)(i) of Article 11.

4.   By way of derogation from paragraphs 1 and 2 of this Article and from Article 14, the competent authority of the host Member State may refuse access to, and pursuit of, the profession to holders of an attestation of competence classified under point (a) of Article 11 where the national professional qualification required to exercise the profession on its territory is classified under point (e) of Article 11.

Article 14 Compensation measures

1.   Article 13 shall not preclude the host Member State from requiring the applicant to complete an adaptation period of up to three years or to take an aptitude test if:

(a)   the training the applicant has received covers substantially different matters than those covered by the evidence of formal qualifications required in the host Member State;

(b)   the regulated profession in the host Member State comprises one or more regulated professional activities which do not exist in the corresponding profession in the applicant's home Member State, and the training required in the host Member State covers substantially different matters from those covered by the applicant's attestation of competence or evidence of formal qualifications.

2.   If the host Member State makes use of the option provided for in paragraph 1, it must offer the applicant the choice between an adaptation period and an aptitude test.

Where a Member State considers, with respect to a given profession, that it is necessary to derogate from the requirement, set out in the previous subparagraph, that it give the applicant a choice between an adaptation period and an aptitude test, it shall inform the other Member States and the Commission in advance and provide sufficient justification for the derogation.

Where the Commission considers that the derogation referred to in the second subparagraph is inappropriate or that it is not in accordance with Union law, it shall adopt an implementing act, within three months of receiving all necessary information, to ask the relevant Member State to refrain from taking the envisaged measure. In the absence of a response from the Commission within that deadline, the derogation may be applied.

3.   By way of derogation from the principle of the right of the applicant to choose, as laid down in paragraph 2, for professions whose pursuit requires precise knowledge of national law and in respect of which the provision of advice and/or assistance concerning national law is an essential and constant aspect of the professional activity, the host Member State may stipulate either an adaptation period or an aptitude test.

This applies also to the cases provided for in Article 10 points (b) and (c), in Article 10 point

(d) concerning doctors and dental practitioners, in Article 10 point (f) when the migrant seeks recognition in another Member State where the relevant professional activities are pursued by nurses responsible for general care or specialised nurses holding evidence of formal qualifications as a specialist which follows the training leading to the possession of the titles listed in Annex V, point 5.2.2 and in Article 10 point (g).

In the cases covered by Article 10 point (a), the host Member State may require an adaptation period or an aptitude test if the migrant envisages pursuing professional activities in a self-employed capacity or as a manager of an undertaking which require the knowledge and the application of the specific national rules in force, provided that knowledge and application of those rules are required by the competent authorities of the host Member State for access to such activities by its own nationals.

By way of derogation from the principle of the right of the applicant to choose, as laid down in paragraph 2, the host Member State may stipulate either an adaptation period or an aptitude test in the case of:

(a)   a holder of a professional qualification referred to in point (a) of Article 11, who applies for recognition of his professional qualifications where the national professional qualification required is classified under point (c) of Article 11; or

(b)   a holder of a professional qualification referred to in point (b) of Article 11, who applies for recognition of his professional qualifications where the national professional qualification required is classified under point (d) or (e) of Article 11.

In the case of a holder of a professional qualification referred to in point (a) of Article 11 who applies for recognition of his professional qualifications where the national professional qualification required is classified under point (d) of Article 11, the host Member State may impose both an adaptation period and an aptitude test.

4.   For the purposes of paragraphs 1 and 5, 'substantially different matters' means matters in respect of which knowledge, skills and competences acquired are essential for pursuing the profession and with regard to which the training received by the migrant shows significant differences in terms of content from the training required by the host Member State.

5.   Paragraph 1 shall be applied with due regard to the principle of proportionality. In particular, if the host Member State intends to require the applicant to complete an adaptation period or take an aptitude test, it must first ascertain whether the knowledge, skills and competences acquired by the applicant in the course of his professional experience or through lifelong learning, and formally validated to that end by a relevant body, in any Member State or in a third country, is of such nature as to cover, in full or in part, the substantially different matters defined in paragraph 4.

6.   The decision imposing an adaptation period or an aptitude test shall be duly justified. In particular, the applicant shall be provided with the following information:

(a)   the level of the professional qualification required in the host Member State and the level of the professional qualification held by the applicant in accordance with the classification set out in Article 11; and

(b)   the substantial differences referred to in paragraph 4 and the reasons for which those differences cannot be compensated by knowledge, skills and competences acquired in the course of professional experience or through lifelong learning formally validated to that end by a relevant body.

7.   Member States shall ensure that an applicant has the possibility of taking the aptitude test referred to in paragraph 1 not later than six months after the initial decision imposing an aptitude test on the applicant.

CHAPTER II
RECOGNITION OF PROFESSIONAL EXPERIENCE

Article 16 Requirements regarding professional experience

If, in a Member State, access to or pursuit of one of the activities listed in Annex IV is contingent upon possession of general, commercial or professional knowledge and aptitudes, that Member State shall recognise previous pursuit of the activity in another Member State as sufficient proof of such knowledge and aptitudes. The activity must have been pursued in accordance with Articles 17, 18 and 19.

Article 17 Activities referred to in list I of Annex IV

1.   For the activities in list I of Annex IV, the activity in question must have been previously pursued:

(a)   for six consecutive years on a self-employed basis or as a manager of an undertaking; or

(b)   for three consecutive years on a self-employed basis or as a manager of an undertaking, where the beneficiary proves that he has received previous training of at least three years for the activity in question, evidenced by a certificate recognised by the Member State or judged by a competent professional body to be fully valid; or

    (c)   for four consecutive years on a self-employed basis or as a manager of an undertaking, where the beneficiary can prove that he has received, for the activity in question, previous training of at least two years' duration, attested by a certificate recognised by the Member State or judged by a competent professional body to be fully valid; or

    (d)   for three consecutive years on a self-employed basis, if the beneficiary can prove that he has pursued the activity in question on an employed basis for at least five years; or

    (e)   for five consecutive years in an executive position, of which at least three years involved technical duties and responsibility for at least one department of the company, if the beneficiary can prove that he has received, for the activity in question, previous training of at least three years' duration, as attested by a certificate recognised by the Member State or judged by a competent professional body to be fully valid.

2.   In cases (a) and (d), the activity must not have finished more than 10 years before the date on which the complete application was submitted by the person concerned to the competent authority referred to in Article 56.

3.   Paragraph 1(e) shall not apply to activities in Group ex 855, hairdressing establishments, of the ISIC Nomenclature.

Article 18 Activities referred to in list II of Annex IV

1.   For the activities in list II of Annex IV, the activity in question must have been previously pursued:

    (a)   for five consecutive years on a self-employed basis or as a manager of an undertaking, or

    (b)   for three consecutive years on a self-employed basis or as a manager of an undertaking, where the beneficiary proves that he has received previous training of at least three years for the activity in question, evidenced by a certificate recognised by the Member State or judged by a competent professional body to be fully valid, or

    (c)   for four consecutive years on a self-employed basis or as a manager of an undertaking, where the beneficiary can prove that he has received, for the activity in question, previous training of at least two years' duration, attested by a certificate recognised by the Member State or judged by a competent professional body to be fully valid, or

    (d)   for three consecutive years on a self-employed basis or as a manager of an undertaking, if the beneficiary can prove that he has pursued the activity in question on an employed basis for at least five years, or

    (e)   for five consecutive years on an employed basis, if the beneficiary can prove that he has received, for the activity in question, previous training of at least three years' duration, as attested by a certificate recognised by the Member State or judged by a competent professional body to be fully valid, or

    (f)   for six consecutive years on an employed basis, if the beneficiary can prove that he has received previous training in the activity in question of at least two years' duration, as attested by a certificate recognised by the Member State or judged by a competent professional body to be fully valid.

2.   In cases (a) and (d), the activity must not have finished more than 10 years before the date on which the complete application was submitted by the person concerned to the competent authority referred to in Article 56.

Article 19 Activities referred to in list III of Annex IV

1.   For the activities in list III of Annex IV, the activity in question must have been previously pursued:

    (a)   for three consecutive years, either on a self-employed basis or as a manager of an undertaking, or

    (b)   for two consecutive years, either on a self-employed basis or as a manager of an undertaking, if the beneficiary can prove that he has received previous training for the activity in question, as attested by a certificate recognised by the Member State or judged by a competent professional body to be fully valid, or

(c)   for two consecutive years, either on a self-employed basis or as a manager of an undertaking, if the beneficiary can prove that he has pursued the activity in question on an employed basis for at least three years, or

(d)   for three consecutive years, on an employed basis, if the beneficiary can prove that he has received previous training for the activity in question, as attested by a certificate recognised by the Member State or judged by a competent professional body to be fully valid.

2.   In cases (a) and (c), the activity must not have finished more than 10 years before the date on which the complete application was submitted by the person concerned to the competent authority referred to in Article 56.

Article 20 Adaptation of the lists of activities in Annex IV

The Commission shall be empowered to adopt delegated acts in accordance with Article 57c concerning the adaptation of the lists of activities set out in Annex IV which are the subject of recognition of professional experience pursuant to Article 16, with a view to updating or clarifying the activities listed in Annex IV in particular in order to further specify their scope and to take due account of the latest developments in the field of activity-based nomenclatures, provided that this does not involve any narrowing of the scope of the activities related to the individual categories and that there is no shift of activities between the existing lists I, II and III of Annex IV.

CHAPTER III
RECOGNITION ON THE BASIS OF COORDINATION OF MINIMUM TRAINING CONDITIONS

SECTION 1
GENERAL PROVISIONS

Article 21 Principle of automatic recognition

1.   Each Member State shall recognise evidence of formal qualifications as doctor giving access to the professional activities of doctor with basic training and specialised doctor, as nurse responsible for general care, as dental practitioner, as specialised dental practitioner, as veterinary surgeon, as pharmacist and as architect, listed in Annex V, points 5.1.1, 5.1.2, 5.2.2, 5.3.2, 5.3.3, 5.4.2, 5.6.2 and 5.7.1 respectively, which satisfy the minimum training conditions referred to in Articles 24, 25, 31, 34, 35, 38, 44 and 46 respectively, and shall, for the purposes of access to and pursuit of the professional activities, give such evidence the same effect on its territory as the evidence of formal qualifications which it itself issues.

Such evidence of formal qualifications must be issued by the competent bodies in the Member States and accompanied, where appropriate, by the certificates listed in Annex V, points 5.1.1, 5.1.2, 5.2.2, 5.3.2, 5.3.3, 5.4.2, 5.6.2 and 5.7.1 respectively.

The provisions of the first and second subparagraphs do not affect the acquired rights referred to in Articles 23, 27, 33, 37, 39 and 49.

2.   Each Member State shall recognise, for the purpose of pursuing general medical practice in the framework of its national social security system, evidence of formal qualifications listed in Annex V, point 5.1.4 and issued to nationals of the Member States by the other Member States in accordance with the minimum training conditions laid down in Article 28. The provisions of the previous subparagraph do not affect the acquired rights referred to in Article 30.

3.   Each Member State shall recognise evidence of formal qualifications as a midwife, awarded to nationals of Member States by the other Member States, listed in Annex V, point 5.5.2, which complies with the minimum training conditions referred to in Article 40 and satisfies the criteria set out in Article 41, and shall, for the purposes of access to and pursuit of the professional activities, give such evidence the same effect on its territory as the evidence of formal qualifications which it itself issues. This provision does not affect the acquired rights referred to in Articles 23 and 43.

4.   In respect of the operation of pharmacies that are not subject to territorial restrictions, a Member State may, by way of derogation, decide not to give effect to evidence of formal qualifications referred to in point 5.6.2 of Annex V, for the setting up of new

pharmacies open to the public. For the purposes of this paragraph, pharmacies which have been open for less than three years shall also be considered as new pharmacies. That derogation may not be applied in respect of pharmacists whose formal qualifications have already been recognised by the competent authorities of the host Member State for other purposes and who have been effectively and lawfully engaged in the professional activities of a pharmacist for at least three consecutive years in that Member State.

5. Evidence of formal qualifications as an architect referred to in Annex V, point 5.7.1, which is subject to automatic recognition pursuant to paragraph 1, proves completion of a course of training which began not earlier than during the academic reference year referred to in that Annex.

6. Each Member State shall make access to, and pursuit of, the professional activities of doctors, nurses responsible for general care, dental practitioners, veterinary surgeons, midwives and pharmacists subject to possession of evidence of formal qualifications referred to in points 5.1.1, 5.1.2, 5.1.4, 5.2.2, 5.3.2, 5.3.3, 5.4.2, 5.5.2 and 5.6.2 of Annex V respectively, attesting that the professional concerned, over the duration of his training, has acquired, as appropriate, the knowledge, skills and competences referred to in Articles 24(3), 31(6), 31(7), 34(3), 38(3), 40(3) and 44(3).

In order to take account of generally acknowledged scientific and technical progress, the Commission shall be empowered to adopt delegated acts in accordance with Article 57c to update the knowledge and skills referred to in Articles 24(3), 31(6), 34(3), 38(3), 40(3), 44(3) and 46(4) to reflect the evolution of Union law directly affecting the professionals concerned.

Such updates shall not entail an amendment of existing essential legislative principles in Member States regarding the structure of professions as regards training and conditions of access by natural persons. Such updates shall respect the responsibility of the Member States for the organisation of education systems, as set out in Article 165(1) of the Treaty on the Functioning of the European Union (TFEU).

Article 21a Notification procedure

1. Each Member State shall notify the Commission of the laws, regulations and administrative provisions which it adopts with regard to the issuing of evidence of formal qualifications in the professions covered by this Chapter.

In the case of evidence of formal qualifications referred to in Section 8, notification in accordance with the first subparagraph shall also be addressed to the other Member States.

2. The notification referred to in paragraph 1 shall include information about the duration and content of the training programmes.

3. The notification referred to in paragraph 1 shall be transmitted via IMI.

4. In order to take due account of legislative and administrative developments in the Member States, and on condition that the laws, regulations and administrative provisions notified pursuant to paragraph 1 of this Article are in conformity with the conditions set out in this Chapter, the Commission shall be empowered to adopt delegated acts in accordance with Article 57c in order to amend points 5.1.1 to 5.1.4, 5.2.2, 5.3.2, 5.3.3, 5.4.2, 5.5.2, 5.6.2 and 5.7.1 of Annex V, concerning the updating of the titles adopted by the Member States for evidence of formal qualifications and, where appropriate, the body which issues the evidence of formal qualifications, the certificate which accompanies it and the corresponding professional title.

5. Where the legislative, regulatory and administrative provisions notified pursuant to paragraph 1 are not in conformity with the conditions set out in this Chapter, the Commission shall adopt an implementing act in order to reject the requested amendment of points 5.1.1 to 5.1.4, 5.2.2, 5.3.2, 5.3.3, 5.4.2, 5.5.2, 5.6.2 or 5.7.1 of Annex V.

Article 22 Common provisions on training

With regard to the training referred to in Articles 24, 25, 28, 31, 34, 35, 38, 40, 44 and 46:

(a) Member States may authorise part-time training under conditions laid down by the competent authorities; those authorities shall ensure that the overall duration, level and quality of such training is not lower than that of continuous full-time training;

(b)   Member States shall, in accordance with the procedures specific to each Member State, ensure, by encouraging continuous professional development, that professionals whose professional qualification is covered by Chapter III of this Title are able to update their knowledge, skills and competences in order to maintain a safe and effective practice and keep abreast of professional developments.

Member States shall communicate to the Commission the measures taken pursuant to point (b) of the first paragraph by 18 January 2016.

Article 23 Acquired rights

1.   Without prejudice to the acquired rights specific to the professions concerned, in cases where the evidence of formal qualifications as doctor giving access to the professional activities of doctor with basic training and specialised doctor, as nurse responsible for general care, as dental practitioner, as specialised dental practitioner, as veterinary surgeon, as midwife and as pharmacist held by Member States nationals does not satisfy all the training requirements referred to in Articles 24, 25, 31, 34, 35, 38, 40 and 44, each Member State shall recognise as sufficient proof evidence of formal qualifications issued by those Member States insofar as such evidence attests successful completion of training which began before the reference dates laid down in Annex V, points 5.1.1, 5.1.2, 5.2.2, 5.3.2, 5.3.3, 5.4.2, 5.5.2 and 5.6.2 and is accompanied by a certificate stating that the holders have been effectively and lawfully engaged in the activities in question for at least three consecutive years during the five years preceding the award of the certificate.

2.   The same provisions shall apply to evidence of formal qualifications as doctor giving access to the professional activities of doctor with basic training and specialised doctor, as nurse responsible for general care, as dental practitioner, as specialised dental practitioner, as veterinary surgeon, as midwife and as pharmacist, obtained in the territory of the former German Democratic Republic, which does not satisfy all the minimum training requirements laid down in Articles 24, 25, 31, 34, 35, 38, 40 and 44 if such evidence certifies successful completion of training which began before:

(a)   3 October 1990 for doctors with basic training, nurses responsible for general care, dental practitioners with basic training, specialised dental practitioners, veterinary surgeons, midwives and pharmacists, and

(b)   3 April 1992 for specialised doctors.

The evidence of formal qualifications referred to in the first subparagraph confers on the holder the right to pursue professional activities throughout German territory under the same conditions as evidence of formal qualifications issued by the competent German authorities referred to in Annex V, points 5.1.1, 5.1.2, 5.2.2, 5.3.2, 5.3.3, 5.4.2, 5.5.2 and 5.6.2.

3.   Without prejudice to the provisions of Article 37(1), each Member State shall recognise evidence of formal qualifications as doctor giving access to the professional activities of doctor with basic training and specialised doctor, as nurse responsible for general care, as veterinary surgeon, as midwife, as pharmacist and as architect held by Member States nationals and issued by the former Czechoslovakia, or whose training commenced, for the Czech Republic and Slovakia, before 1 January 1993, where the authorities of either of the two aforementioned Member States attest that such evidence of formal qualifications has the same legal validity within their territory as the evidence of formal qualifications which they issue and, with respect to architects, as the evidence of formal qualifications specified for those Member States in Annex VI, point 6, as regards access to the professional activities of doctor with basic training, specialised doctor, nurse responsible for general care, veterinary surgeon, midwife, pharmacist with respect to the activities referred to in Article 45(2), and architect with respect to the activities referred to in Article 48, and the pursuit of such activities.

Such an attestation must be accompanied by a certificate issued by those same authorities stating that such persons have effectively and lawfully been engaged in the activities in question within their territory for at least three consecutive years during the five years prior to the date of issue of the certificate.

4.   Each Member State shall recognise evidence of formal qualifications as doctor giving access to the professional activities of doctor with basic training and specialised doctor, as nurse responsible for general care, as dental practitioner, as specialised dental practitioner, as veterinary surgeon, as midwife, as pharmacist and as architect held by nationals of the Member States and issued by the former Soviet Union, or whose training commenced

(a)   for Estonia, before 20 August 1991,

(b)   for Latvia, before 21 August 1991,

(c)   for Lithuania, before 11 March 1990,

where the authorities of any of the three aforementioned Member States attest that such evidence has the same legal validity within their territory as the evidence which they issue and, with respect to architects, as the evidence of formal qualifications specified for those Member States in Annex VI, point 6, as regards access to the professional activities of doctor with basic training, specialised doctor, nurse responsible for general care, dental practitioner, specialised dental practitioner, veterinary surgeon, midwife, pharmacist with respect to the activities referred to in Article 45(2), and architect with respect to the activities referred to in Article 48, and the pursuit of such activities.

Such an attestation must be accompanied by a certificate issued by those same authorities stating that such persons have effectively and lawfully been engaged in the activities in question within their territory for at least three consecutive years during the five years prior to the date of issue of the certificate.

With regard to evidence of formal qualifications as veterinary surgeons issued by the former Soviet Union or in respect of which training commenced, for Estonia, before 20 August 1991, the attestation referred to in the preceding subparagraph must be accompanied by a certificate issued by the Estonian authorities stating that such persons have effectively and lawfully been engaged in the activities in question within their territory for at least five consecutive years during the seven years prior to the date of issue of the certificate.

5.   Without prejudice to Article 43b, each Member State shall recognise evidence of formal qualifications as doctor giving access to the professional activities of doctor with basic training and specialised doctor, as nurse responsible for general care, as dental practitioner, as specialised dental practitioner, as veterinary surgeon, as midwife, as pharmacist and as architect held by nationals of the Member States and issued by the former Yugoslavia, or whose training commenced,

(a)   for Slovenia, before 25 June 1991; and

(b)   for Croatia, before 8 October 1991;

where the authorities of the aforementioned Member States attest that such evidence has the same legal validity within their territory as the evidence which they issue and, with respect to architects, as the evidence of formal qualifications specified for those Member States in Annex VI, point 6, as regards access to the professional activities of doctor with basic training, specialised doctor, nurse responsible for general care, dental practitioner, specialised dental practitioner, veterinary surgeon, midwife, pharmacist with respect to the activities referred to in Article 45(2), and architect with respect to the activities referred to in Article 48, and the pursuit of such activities.

Such an attestation must be accompanied by a certificate issued by those same authorities stating that such persons have effectively and lawfully been engaged in the activities in question within their territory for at least three consecutive years during the five years prior to the date of issue of the certificate.

6.   Each Member State shall recognise as sufficient proof for Member State nationals whose evidence of formal qualifications as a doctor, nurse responsible for general care, dental practitioner, veterinary surgeon, midwife and pharmacist does not correspond to the titles given for that Member State in Annex V, points 5.1.1, 5.1.2, 5.1.3, 5.1.4, 5.2.2, 5.3.2, 5.3.3, 5.4.2, 5.5.2 and 5.6.2, evidence of formal qualifications issued by those Member States accompanied by a certificate issued by the competent authorities or bodies.

The certificate referred to in the first subparagraph shall state that the evidence of formal qualifications certifies successful completion of training in accordance with Articles 24, 25, 28, 31, 34, 35, 38, 40 and 44 respectively and is treated by the Member State which issued it in the same way as the qualifications whose titles are listed in Annex V, points 5.1.1, 5.1.2, 5.1.3, 5.1.4, 5.2.2, 5.3.2, 5.3.3, 5.4.2, 5.5.2 and 5.6.2.

Article 23a Specific circumstances

1. By way of derogation from the present Directive, Bulgaria may authorise the holders of the qualification of [feldsher] awarded in Bulgaria before 31 December 1999 and exercising this profession under the Bulgarian national social security scheme on 1 January 2000 to continue to exercise the said profession, even if parts of their activity fall under the provisions of the present Directive concerning doctors of medicine and nurses responsible for general care respectively.

2. The holders of the Bulgarian qualification of [feldsher] referred to in paragraph 1 are not entitled to obtain professional recognition in other Member States as doctors of medicine nor as nurses responsible for general care under this Directive.

SECTION 2

DOCTORS OF MEDICINE

Article 24 Basic medical training

1. Admission to basic medical training shall be contingent upon possession of a diploma or certificate providing access, for the studies in question, to universities.

2. Basic medical training shall comprise a total of at least five years of study, which may in addition be expressed with the equivalent ECTS credits, and shall consist of at least 5 500 hours of theoretical and practical training provided by, or under the supervision of, a university.

   For professionals who began their studies before 1 January 1972, the course of training referred to in the first subparagraph may comprise six months of full-time practical training at university level under the supervision of the competent authorities.

3. Basic medical training shall provide an assurance that the person in question has acquired the following knowledge and skills:

   (a) adequate knowledge of the sciences on which medicine is based and a good understanding of the scientific methods including the principles of measuring biological functions, the evaluation of scientifically established facts and the analysis of data;

   (b) sufficient understanding of the structure, functions and behaviour of healthy and sick persons, as well as relations between the state of health and physical and social surroundings of the human being;

   (c) adequate knowledge of clinical disciplines and practices, providing him with a coherent picture of mental and physical diseases, of medicine from the points of view of prophylaxis, diagnosis and therapy and of human reproduction;

   (d) suitable clinical experience in hospitals under appropriate supervision.

Article 25 Specialist medical training

1. Admission to specialist medical training shall be contingent upon completion and validation of a basic medical training programme as referred to in Article 24(2) in the course of which the trainee has acquired the relevant knowledge of basic medicine.

2. Specialist medical training shall comprise theoretical and practical training at a university or medical teaching hospital or, where appropriate, a medical care establishment approved for that purpose by the competent authorities or bodies.

   The Member States shall ensure that the minimum duration of specialist medical training courses referred to in Annex V, point 5.1.3 is not less than the duration provided for in that point. Training shall be given under the supervision of the competent authorities or bodies. It shall include personal participation of the trainee specialised doctor in the activity and responsibilities entailed by the services in question.

3. Training shall be given on a full-time basis at specific establishments which are recognised by the competent authorities. It shall entail participation in the full range of medical activities of the department where the training is given, including duty on call, in such a way that the trainee specialist devotes all his professional activity to his practical and theoretical training throughout the entire working week and throughout the year, in accordance with the procedures laid down by the competent authorities. Accordingly, these posts shall be the subject of appropriate remuneration.

3a. Member States may provide, in national legislation, for partial exemptions from parts of the specialist medical training courses listed in point 5.1.3 of Annex V, to be applied on a case-by-case basis provided that that part of the training has been followed already during another specialist training course listed in point 5.1.3 of Annex V, for which the professional has already obtained the professional qualification in a Member State. Member States shall ensure that the granted exemption equates to not more than half of the minimum duration of the specialist medical training course in question. Each Member State shall notify the Commission and the other Member States of the national legislation concerned for any such partial exemptions.

4. The Member States shall make the issuance of evidence of specialist medical training contingent upon possession of evidence of basic medical training referred to in Annex V, point 5.1.1.

5. The Commission shall be empowered to adopt delegated acts in accordance with Article 57c concerning the adaptation of the minimum periods of training referred to in point 5.1.3 of Annex V to scientific and technical progress.

Article 26 Types of specialist medical training

Evidence of formal qualifications as a specialised doctor referred to in Article 21 is such evidence awarded by the competent authorities or bodies referred to in Annex V, point 5.1.2 as corresponds, for the specialised training in question, to the titles in use in the various Member States and referred to in Annex V, point 5.1.3.

In order to take due account of changes in national legislation and with a view to updating this Directive, the Commission shall be empowered to adopt delegated acts in accordance with Article 57c concerning the inclusion in point 5.1.3 of Annex V of new medical specialties common to at least two-fifths of the Member States.

Article 27 Acquired rights specific to specialised doctors

1. A host Member State may require of specialised doctors whose part-time specialist medical training was governed by legislative, regulatory and administrative provisions in force as of 20 June 1975 and who began their specialist training no later than 31 December 1983 that their evidence of formal qualifications be accompanied by a certificate stating that they have been effectively and lawfully engaged in the relevant activities for at least three consecutive years during the five years preceding the award of that certificate.

2. Every Member State shall recognise the qualification of specialised doctors awarded in Spain to doctors who completed their specialist training before 1 January 1995, even if that training does not satisfy the minimum training requirements provided for in Article 25, in so far as that qualification is accompanied by a certificate issued by the competent Spanish authorities and attesting that the person concerned has passed the examination in specific professional competence held in the context of exceptional measures concerning recognition laid down in Royal Decree 1497/99, with a view to ascertaining that the person concerned possesses a level of knowledge and skill comparable to that of doctors who possess a qualification as a specialised doctor defined for Spain in Annex V, points 5.1.2 and 5.1.3.

2a. Member States shall recognise the qualifications of specialised doctors awarded in Italy, and listed in points 5.1.2 and 5.1.3 of Annex V, to doctors who started their specialist training after 31 December 1983 and before 1 January 1991, despite the training concerned not satisfying all the training requirements set out in Article 25, if the qualification is accompanied by a certificate issued by the competent Italian authorities stating that the doctor concerned has effectively and lawfully been engaged, in Italy, in the activities of a medical specialist in the same specialist area concerned, for at least seven consecutive years during the 10 years preceding the award of the certificate.

3. Every Member State which has repealed its legislative, regulatory or administrative provisions relating to the award of evidence of formal qualifications as a specialised doctor referred to in Annex V, points 5.1.2 and 5.1.3 and which has adopted measures relating to acquired rights benefiting its nationals, shall grant nationals of other Member States the right to benefit from those measures, in so far as such evidence of formal

qualifications was issued before the date on which the host Member State ceased to issue such evidence for the specialty in question.

The dates on which these provisions were repealed are set out in Annex V, point 5.1.3.

Article 28 Specific training in general medical practice

1. Admission to specific training in general medical practice shall be contingent upon completion and validation of a basic medical training programme as referred to in Article 24(2) in the course of which the trainee has acquired the relevant knowledge of basic medicine.

2. The specific training in general medical practice leading to the award of evidence of formal qualifications issued before 1 January 2006 shall be of a duration of at least two years on a full-time basis. In the case of evidence of formal qualifications issued after that date, the training shall be of a duration of at least three years on a full-time basis. Where the training programme referred to in Article 24 comprises practical training given by an approved hospital possessing appropriate general medical equipment and services or as part of an approved general medical practice or an approved centre in which doctors provide primary medical care, the duration of that practical training may, up to a maximum of one year, be included in the duration provided for in the first subparagraph for certificates of training issued on or after 1 January 2006.

   The option provided for in the second subparagraph shall be available only for Member States in which the specific training in general medical practice lasted two years as of 1 January 2001.

3. The specific training in general medical practice shall be carried out on a full-time basis, under the supervision of the competent authorities or bodies. It shall be more practical than theoretical.

   The practical training shall be given, on the one hand, for at least six months in an approved hospital possessing appropriate equipment and services and, on the other hand, for at least six months as part of an approved general medical practice or an approved centre at which doctors provide primary health care.

   The practical training shall take place in conjunction with other health establishments or structures concerned with general medicine. Without prejudice to the minimum periods laid down in the second subparagraph, however, the practical training may be given during a period of not more than six months in other approved establishments or health structures concerned with general medicine.

   The training shall require the personal participation of the trainee in the professional activity and responsibilities of the persons with whom he is working.

4. Member States shall make the issuance of evidence of formal qualifications in general medical practice subject to possession of evidence of formal qualifications in basic medical training referred to in Annex V, point 5.1.1.

5. Member States may issue evidence of formal qualifications referred to in Annex V, point 5.1.4 to a doctor who has not completed the training provided for in this Article but who has completed a different, supplementary training, as attested by evidence of formal qualifications issued by the competent authorities in a Member State. They may not, however, award evidence of formal qualifications unless it attests knowledge of a level qualitatively equivalent to the knowledge acquired from the training provided for in this Article.

   Member States shall determine, inter alia, the extent to which the complementary training and professional experience already acquired by the applicant may replace the training provided for in this Article.

   The Member States may only issue the evidence of formal qualifications referred to in Annex V, point 5.1.4 if the applicant has acquired at least six months' experience of general medicine in a general medical practice or a centre in which doctors provide primary health care of the types referred to in paragraph 3.

Article 29 Pursuit of the professional activities of general practitioners

Each Member State shall, subject to the provisions relating to acquired rights, make the pursuit of the activities of a general practitioner in the framework of its national social security system contingent upon possession of evidence of formal qualifications referred to in Annex V, point 5.1.4.

Member States may exempt persons who are currently undergoing specific training in general medicine from this condition.

Article 30 Acquired rights specific to general practitioners

1.   Each Member State shall determine the acquired rights. It shall, however, confer as an acquired right the right to pursue the activities of a general practitioner in the framework of its national social security system, without the evidence of formal qualifications referred to in Annex V, point 5.1.4, on all doctors who enjoy this right as of the reference date stated in that point by virtue of provisions applicable to the medical profession giving access to the professional activities of doctor with basic training and who are established as of that date on its territory, having benefited from the provisions of Articles 21 or 23.

The competent authorities of each Member State shall, on demand, issue a certificate stating the holder's right to pursue the activities of general practitioner in the framework of their national social security systems, without the evidence of formal qualifications referred to in Annex V, point 5.1.4, to doctors who enjoy acquired rights pursuant to the first subparagraph.

2.   Every Member State shall recognise the certificates referred to in paragraph 1, second subparagraph, awarded to nationals of Member States by the other Member States, and shall give such certificates the same effect on its territory as evidence of formal qualifications which it awards and which permit the pursuit of the activities of a general practitioner in the framework of its national social security system.

SECTION 3
NURSES RESPONSIBLE FOR GENERAL CARE

Article 31 Training of nurses responsible for general care

1.   Admission to training for nurses responsible for general care shall be contingent upon either:

(a)   completion of general education of 12 years, as attested by a diploma, certificate or other evidence issued by the competent authorities or bodies in a Member State or a certificate attesting success in an examination of an equivalent level and giving access to universities or to higher education institutions of a level recognised as equivalent; or

(b)   completion of general education of at least 10 years, as attested by a diploma, certificate or other evidence issued by the competent authorities or bodies in a Member State or a certificate attesting success in an examination of an equivalent level and giving access to a vocational school or vocational training programme for nursing.

2.   Training of nurses responsible for general care shall be given on a full-time basis and shall include at least the programme described in Annex V, point 5.2.1.

The Commission shall be empowered to adopt delegated acts in accordance with Article 57c concerning amendments to the list set out in point 5.2.1 of Annex V with a view to adapting it to scientific and technical progress.

The amendments referred to in the second subparagraph shall not entail an amendment of existing essential legislative principles in Member States regarding the structure of professions as regards training and conditions of access by natural persons. Such amendments shall respect the responsibility of the Member States for the organisation of education systems, as set out in Article 165(1) TFEU.

3.   The training of nurses responsible for general care shall comprise a total of at least three years of study, which may in addition be expressed with the equivalent ECTS credits, and shall consist of at least 4,600 hours of theoretical and clinical training, the duration of the theoretical training representing at least one third and the duration of the clinical training at least one half of the minimum duration of the training. Member States may grant partial exemptions to professionals who have received part of their training on courses which are of at least an equivalent level.

The Member States shall ensure that institutions providing nursing training are responsible for the coordination of theoretical and clinical training throughout the entire study programme.

4.   Theoretical education is that part of nurse training from which trainee nurses acquire the professional knowledge, skills and competences required under paragraphs 6 and 7. The training shall be given by teachers of nursing care and by other competent persons, at universities, higher education institutions of a level recognised as equivalent or at vocational schools or through vocational training programmes for nursing.

5.   Clinical training is that part of nurse training in which trainee nurses learn, as part of a team and in direct contact with a healthy or sick individual and/or community, to organise, dispense and evaluate the required comprehensive nursing care, on the basis of the knowledge, skills and competences which they have acquired. The trainee nurse shall learn not only how to work in a team, but also how to lead a team and organise overall nursing care, including health education for individuals and small groups, within health institutes or in the community.

This training shall take place in hospitals and other health institutions and in the community, under the responsibility of nursing teachers, in cooperation with and assisted by other qualified nurses. Other qualified personnel may also take part in the teaching process.

Trainee nurses shall participate in the activities of the department in question insofar as those activities are appropriate to their training, enabling them to learn to assume the responsibilities involved in nursing care.

6.   Training for nurses responsible for general care shall provide an assurance that the professional in question has acquired the following knowledge and skills:

(a)   comprehensive knowledge of the sciences on which general nursing is based, including sufficient understanding of the structure, physiological functions and behaviour of healthy and sick persons, and of the relationship between the state of health and the physical and social environment of the human being;

(b)   knowledge of the nature and ethics of the profession and of the general principles of health and nursing;

(c)   adequate clinical experience; such experience, which should be selected for its training value, should be gained under the supervision of qualified nursing staff and in places where the number of qualified staff and equipment are appropriate for the nursing care of the patient;

(d)   the ability to participate in the practical training of health personnel and experience of working with such personnel;

(e)   experience of working together with members of other professions in the health sector.

7.   Formal qualifications as a nurse responsible for general care shall provide evidence that the professional in question is able to apply at least the following competences regardless of whether the training took place at universities, higher education institutions of a level recognised as equivalent or at vocational schools or through vocational training programmes for nursing:

(a)   competence to independently diagnose the nursing care required using current theoretical and clinical knowledge and to plan, organise and implement nursing care when treating patients on the basis of the knowledge and skills acquired in accordance with points (a), (b) and (c) of paragraph 6 in order to improve professional practice;

(b)   competence to work together effectively with other actors in the health sector, including participation in the practical training of health personnel on the basis of the knowledge and skills acquired in accordance with points (d) and (e) of paragraph 6;

(c)   competence to empower individuals, families and groups towards healthy lifestyles and self-care on the basis of the knowledge and skills acquired in accordance with points (a) and (b) of paragraph 6;

(d)   competence to independently initiate life-preserving immediate measures and to carry out measures in crises and disaster situations;

(e)   competence to independently give advice to, instruct and support persons needing care and their attachment figures;

(f)   competence to independently assure the quality of, and to evaluate, nursing care;

(g)   competence to comprehensively communicate professionally and to cooperate with members of other professions in the health sector;

(h)   competence to analyse the care quality to improve his own professional practice as a nurse responsible for general care.

Article 32 Pursuit of the professional activities of nurses responsible for general care

For the purposes of this Directive, the professional activities of nurses responsible for general care are the activities pursued on a professional basis and referred to in Annex V, point 5.2.2.

Article 33 Acquired rights specific to nurses responsible for general care

1.   Where the general rules of acquired rights apply to nurses responsible for general care, the activities referred to in Article 23 must have included full responsibility for the planning, organisation and administration of nursing care delivered to the patient.

3.   Member States shall recognise evidence of formal qualifications in nursing that:

(a)   were awarded in Poland, to nurses who completed training before 1 May 2004, which did not comply with the minimum training requirements laid down in Article 31; and

(b)   are attested by the diploma 'bachelor' which was obtained on the basis of a special upgrading programme contained in:

(i)   Article 11 of the Act of 20 April 2004 on the amendment of the Act on professions of nurse and midwife and on some other legal acts (*Official Journal of the Republic of Poland* of 2004 No 92, pos. 885 and of 2007, No 176, pos. 1237) and the Regulation of the Minister of Health of 11 May 2004 on the detailed conditions of delivering studies for nurses and midwives, who hold a certificate of secondary school (final examination – matura) and are graduates of medical lyceum and medical vocational schools teaching in a profession of a nurse and a midwife (*Official Journal of the Republic of Poland* of 2004 No 110, pos. 1170 and of 2010 No 65, pos. 420); or

(ii)   Article 52.3 point 2 of the Act of 15 July 2011 on professions of nurse and midwife (*Official Journal of the Republic of Poland* of 2011 No 174, pos. 1039) and the Regulation of the Minister of Health of 14 June 2012 on the detailed conditions of delivering higher education courses for nurses and midwives who hold a certificate of secondary school (final examination – matura) and are graduates of a medical secondary school or a post-secondary school teaching in a profession of a nurse and a midwife (*Official Journal of the Republic of Poland* of 2012, pos. 770), for the purpose of verifying that the nurse concerned has a level of knowledge and competence comparable to that of nurses holding the qualifications listed for Poland in point 5.2.2 of Annex V.

Article 33(a)

As regards the Romanian qualification of nurse responsible for general care, only the following acquired rights provisions shall apply:

In the case of nationals of Member States who were trained as a nurse responsible for general care in Romania and whose training does not satisfy the minimum training requirements laid down in Article 31, Member States shall recognise the following evidence of formal qualifications as a nurse responsible for general care as being sufficient proof, provided that that evidence is accompanied by a certificate stating that those Member State nationals have effectively and lawfully been engaged in the activities of a nurse responsible for general care in Romania, including taking full responsibility for the planning, organisation and carrying out of the nursing care of patients, for a period of at least three consecutive years during the five years prior to the date of issue of the certificate:

(a)   Certificat de competente profesionale de asistent medical generalist with post-secondary education obtained from a şcoală postliceală, attesting to training started before 1 January 2007;

(b)   Diplomă de absolvire de asistent medical generalist with short-time higher education studies, attesting to training started before 1 October 2003;

(c)   Diplomă de licență de asistent medical generalist with long-time higher education studies, attesting to training started before 1 October 2003.

SECTION 4
DENTAL PRACTITIONERS

Article 34 Basic dental training

1.   Admission to basic dental training presupposes possession of a diploma or certificate giving access, for the studies in question, to universities or higher institutes of a level recognised as equivalent, in a Member State.

2.   Basic dental training shall comprise a total of at least five years of study, which may in addition be expressed with the equivalent ECTS credits, and shall consist of at least 5 000 hours of full-time theoretical and practical training that comprises at least the programme described in point 5.3.1 of Annex V and that is provided in a university, in a higher institute providing training recognised as being of an equivalent level or under the supervision of a university.

The Commission shall be empowered to adopt delegated acts in accordance with Article 57c concerning the amendment of the list set out in point 5.3.1 of Annex V with a view to adapting it to scientific and technical progress.

The amendments referred to in the second subparagraph shall not entail an amendment of existing essential legislative principles in Member States regarding the structure of professions as regards training and conditions of access by natural persons. Such amendments shall respect the responsibility of the Member States for the organisation of education systems, as set out in Article 165(1) TFEU.

3.   Basic dental training shall provide an assurance that the person in question has acquired the following knowledge and skills:

(a)   adequate knowledge of the sciences on which dentistry is based and a good understanding of scientific methods, including the principles of measuring biological functions, the evaluation of scientifically established facts and the analysis of data;

(b)   adequate knowledge of the constitution, physiology and behaviour of healthy and sick persons as well as the influence of the natural and social environment on the state of health of the human being, in so far as these factors affect dentistry;

(c)   adequate knowledge of the structure and function of the teeth, mouth, jaws and associated tissues, both healthy and diseased, and their relationship to the general state of health and to the physical and social well-being of the patient;

(d)   adequate knowledge of clinical disciplines and methods, providing the dentist with a coherent picture of anomalies, lesions and diseases of the teeth, mouth, jaws and associated tissues and of preventive, diagnostic and therapeutic dentistry;

(e)   suitable clinical experience under appropriate supervision.

This training shall provide him with the skills necessary for carrying out all activities involving the prevention, diagnosis and treatment of anomalies and diseases of the teeth, mouth, jaws and associated tissues.

Article 35 Specialist dental training

1.   Admission to specialist dental training shall be contingent upon completion and validation of basic dental training referred to in Article 34, or possession of the documents referred to in Articles 23 and 37.

2.   Specialist dental training shall comprise theoretical and practical instruction in a university centre, in a treatment teaching and research centre or, where appropriate, in a health establishment approved for that purpose by the competent authorities or bodies.

Full-time specialist dental courses shall be of a minimum of three years' duration and shall be supervised by the competent authorities or bodies. They shall involve the personal participation of the dental practitioner training to be a specialist in the activity and in the responsibilities of the establishment concerned.

3.   The Member States shall make the issuance of evidence of specialist dental training contingent upon possession of evidence of basic dental training referred to in Annex V, point 5.3.2.

4.   The Commission shall be empowered to adopt delegated acts in accordance with Article 57c concerning the adaptation of the minimum period of training referred to in paragraph 2 to scientific and technical progress.

5.   In order to take due account of changes in national legislation, and with a view to updating this Directive, the Commission shall be empowered to adopt delegated acts in accordance with Article 57c concerning the inclusion in point 5.3.3 of Annex V of new dental specialties common to at least two-fifths of the Member States.

Article 36 Pursuit of the professional activities of dental practitioners

1.   For the purposes of this Directive, the professional activities of dental practitioners are the activities defined in paragraph 3 and pursued under the professional qualifications listed in Annex V, point 5.3.2.

2.   The profession of dental practitioner shall be based on dental training referred to in Article 34 and shall constitute a specific profession which is distinct from other general or specialised medical professions. Pursuit of the activities of a dental practitioner requires the possession of evidence of formal qualifications referred to in Annex V, point 5.3.2. Holders of such evidence of formal qualifications shall be treated in the same way as those to whom Articles 23 or 37 apply.

3.   The Member States shall ensure that dental practitioners are generally able to gain access to and pursue the activities of prevention, diagnosis and treatment of anomalies and diseases affecting the teeth, mouth, jaws and adjoining tissue, having due regard to the regulatory provisions and rules of professional ethics on the reference dates referred to in Annex V, point 5.3.2.

Article 37 Acquired rights specific to dental practitioners

1.   Every Member State shall, for the purposes of the pursuit of the professional activities of dental practitioners under the qualifications listed in Annex V, point 5.3.2, recognise evidence of formal qualifications as a doctor issued in Italy, Spain, Austria, the Czech Republic and Slovakia and Romania to persons who began their medical training on or before the reference date stated in that Annex for the Member State concerned, accompanied by a certificate issued by the competent authorities of that Member State. The certificate must show that the two following conditions are met:

(a)   that the persons in question have been effectively, lawfully and principally engaged in that Member State in the activities referred to in Article 36 for at least three consecutive years during the five years preceding the award of the certificate;

(b)   that those persons are authorised to pursue the said activities under the same conditions as holders of evidence of formal qualifications listed for that Member State in Annex V, point 5.3.2.

Persons who have successfully completed at least three years of study, certified by the competent authorities in the Member State concerned as being equivalent to the training referred to in Article 34, shall be exempt from the three-year practical work experience referred to in the second subparagraph, point (a).

With regard to the Czech Republic and Slovakia, evidence of formal qualifications obtained in the former Czechoslovakia shall be accorded the same level of recognition as Czech and Slovak evidence of formal qualifications and under the same conditions as set out in the preceding subparagraphs.

2.   Each Member State shall recognise evidence of formal qualifications as a doctor issued in Italy to persons who began their university medical training after 28 January 1980 and no later than 31 December 1984, accompanied by a certificate issued by the competent Italian authorities.

The certificate must show that the three following conditions are met:

(a)   that the persons in question passed the relevant aptitude test held by the competent Italian authorities with a view to establishing that those persons possess a level of knowledge and skills comparable to that of persons possessing evidence of formal qualifications listed for Italy in Annex V, point 5.3.2;

(b)   that they have been effectively, lawfully and principally engaged in the activities referred to in Article 36 in Italy for at least three consecutive years during the five years preceding the award of the certificate;

(c)   that they are authorised to engage in or are effectively, lawfully and principally engaged in the activities referred to in Article 36, under the same conditions as the holders of evidence of formal qualifications listed for Italy in Annex V, point 5.3.2.

Persons who have successfully completed at least three years of study certified by the competent authorities as being equivalent to the training referred to in Article 34 shall be exempt from the aptitude test referred to in the second subparagraph, point (a).

Persons who began their university medical training after 31 December 1984 shall be treated in the same way as those referred to above, provided that the abovementioned three years of study began before 31 December 1994.

3.   As regards evidence of formal qualifications of dental practitioners, Member States shall recognise such evidence pursuant to Article 21 in cases where the applicants began their training on or before 18 January 2016.

4.   Each Member State shall recognise evidence of formal qualifications as a doctor issued in Spain to professionals who began their university medical training between 1 January 1986 and 31 December 1997, accompanied by a certificate issued by the Spanish competent authorities.

The certificate shall confirm that the following conditions have been met:

(a)   the professional in question has successfully completed at least three years of study, certified by the Spanish competent authorities as being equivalent to the training referred to in Article 34;

(b)   the professional in question was effectively, lawfully and principally engaged in the activities referred to in Article 36 in Spain for at least three consecutive years during the five years preceding the award of the certificate;

(c)   the professional in question is authorised to engage in or is effectively, lawfully and principally engaged in the activities referred to in Article 36, under the same conditions as the holders of evidence of formal qualifications listed for Spain in point 5.3.2 of Annex V.

SECTION 5
VETERINARY SURGEONS

Article 38 The training of veterinary surgeons

1.   The training of veterinary surgeons shall comprise a total of at least five years of full-time theoretical and practical study, which may in addition be expressed with the equivalent ECTS credits, at a university or at a higher institute providing training recognised as being of an equivalent level, or under the supervision of a university, covering at least the study programme referred to in point 5.4.1 of Annex V.

The Commission shall be empowered to adopt delegated acts in accordance with Article 57c concerning the amendment of the list set out in point 5.4.1 of Annex V with a view to adapting it to scientific and technical progress.

The amendments referred to in the second subparagraph shall not entail an amendment of existing essential legislative principles in Member States regarding the structure of professions as regards training and conditions of access by natural persons. Such amendments shall respect the responsibility of the Member States for the organisation of education systems, as set out in Article 165(1) TFEU.

2.   Admission to veterinary training shall be contingent upon possession of a diploma or certificate entitling the holder to enter, for the studies in question, university establishments or institutes of higher education recognised by a Member State to be of an equivalent level for the purpose of the relevant study.

3.   Training as a veterinary surgeon shall provide an assurance that the professional in question has acquired the following knowledge and skills:

(a)   adequate knowledge of the sciences on which the activities of a veterinary surgeon are based and of the Union law relating to those activities;

(b)   adequate knowledge of the structure, functions, behaviour and physiological needs of animals, as well as the skills and competences needed for their husbandry, feeding, welfare, reproduction and hygiene in general;

(c) the clinical, epidemiological and analytical skills and competences required for the prevention, diagnosis and treatment of the diseases of animals, including anaesthesia, aseptic surgery and painless death, whether considered individually or in groups, including specific knowledge of the diseases which may be transmitted to humans;

(d) adequate knowledge, skills and competences for preventive medicine, including competences relating to inquiries and certification;

(e) adequate knowledge of the hygiene and technology involved in the production, manufacture and putting into circulation of animal feedstuffs or foodstuffs of animal origin intended for human consumption, including the skills and competences required to understand and explain good practice in this regard;

(f) the knowledge, skills and competences required for the responsible and sensible use of veterinary medicinal products, in order to treat the animals and to ensure the safety of the food chain and the protection of the environment.

Article 39 Acquired rights specific to veterinary surgeons

Without prejudice to Article 23(4), with regard to nationals of Member States whose evidence of formal qualifications as a veterinary surgeon was issued by, or whose training commenced in, Estonia before 1 May 2004, Member States shall recognise such evidence of formal qualifications as a veterinary surgeon if it is accompanied by a certificate stating that such persons have effectively and lawfully been engaged in the activities in question in Estonia for at least five consecutive years during the seven years prior to the date of issue of the certificate.

SECTION 6
MIDWIVES

Article 40　The training of midwives

1. The training of midwives shall comprise a total of at least:

   (a) specific full-time training as a midwife comprising at least three years of theoretical and practical study (route I) comprising at least the programme described in Annex V, point 5.5.1, or

   (b) specific full-time training as a midwife of 18 months' duration (route II), comprising at least the study programme described in Annex V, point 5.5.1, which was not the subject of equivalent training of nurses responsible for general care.

   The Member States shall ensure that institutions providing midwife training are responsible for coordinating theory and practice throughout the programme of study.

   The Commission shall be empowered to adopt delegated acts in accordance with Article 57c concerning the amendment of the list set out in point 5.5.1 of Annex V with a view to adapting it to scientific and technical progress.

   The amendments referred to in the third subparagraph shall not entail an amendment of existing essential legislative principles in Member States regarding the structure of professions as regards training and conditions of access by natural persons. Such amendments shall respect the responsibility of the Member States for the organisation of education systems, as set out in Article 165(1) TFEU.

2. Admission to training as a midwife shall be contingent upon one of the following conditions:

   (a) completion of at least 12 years of general school education or possession of a certificate attesting success in an examination, of an equivalent level, for admission to a midwifery school for route I;

   (b) possession of evidence of formal qualifications as a nurse responsible for general care referred to in point 5.2.2 of Annex V for route II.

3. Training as a midwife shall provide an assurance that the professional in question has acquired the following knowledge and skills:

   (a) detailed knowledge of the sciences on which the activities of midwives are based, particularly midwifery, obstetrics and gynaecology;

   (b) adequate knowledge of the ethics of the profession and the legislation relevant for the practice of the profession;

(c) adequate knowledge of general medical knowledge (biological functions, anatomy and physiology) and of pharmacology in the field of obstetrics and of the newly born, and also knowledge of the relationship between the state of health and the physical and social environment of the human being, and of his behaviour;

(d) adequate clinical experience gained in approved institutions allowing the midwife to be able, independently and under his own responsibility, to the extent necessary and excluding pathological situations, to manage the antenatal care, to conduct the delivery and its consequences in approved institutions, and to supervise labour and birth, postnatal care and neonatal resuscitation while awaiting a medical practitioner;

(e) adequate understanding of the training of health personnel and experience of working with such personnel.

Article 41 Procedures for the recognition of evidence of formal qualifications as a midwife

1. The evidence of formal qualifications as a midwife referred to in point 5.5.2 of Annex V shall be subject to automatic recognition pursuant to Article 21 in so far as they satisfy one of the following criteria:

(a) full-time training of at least three years as a midwife, which may in addition be expressed with the equivalent ECTS credits, consisting of at least 4 600 hours of theoretical and practical training, with at least one third of the minimum duration representing clinical training;

(b) full-time training as a midwife of at least two years, which may in addition be expressed with the equivalent ECTS credits, consisting of at least 3 600 hours, contingent upon possession of evidence of formal qualifications as a nurse responsible for general care referred to in point 5.2.2 of Annex V;

(c) full-time training as a midwife of at least 18 months, which may in addition be expressed with the equivalent ECTS credits, consisting of at least 3 000 hours, contingent upon possession of evidence of formal qualifications as a nurse responsible for general care referred to in point 5.2.2 of Annex V, and followed by one year's professional practice for which a certificate has been issued in accordance with paragraph 2.

2. The certificate referred to in paragraph 1 shall be issued by the competent authorities in the home Member State. It shall certify that the holder, after obtaining evidence of formal qualifications as a midwife, has satisfactorily pursued all the activities of a midwife for a corresponding period in a hospital or a health care establishment approved for that purpose.

Article 42 Pursuit of the professional activities of a midwife

1. The provisions of this section shall apply to the activities of midwives as defined by each Member State, without prejudice to paragraph 2, and pursued under the professional titles set out in Annex V, point 5.5.2.

2. The Member States shall ensure that midwives are able to gain access to and pursue at least the following activities:

(a) provision of sound family planning information and advice;

(b) diagnosis of pregnancies and monitoring normal pregnancies; carrying out the examinations necessary for the monitoring of the development of normal pregnancies;

(c) prescribing or advising on the examinations necessary for the earliest possible diagnosis of pregnancies at risk;

(d) provision of programmes of parenthood preparation and complete preparation for childbirth including advice on hygiene and nutrition;

(e) caring for and assisting the mother during labour and monitoring the condition of the foetus in utero by the appropriate clinical and technical means;

(f) conducting spontaneous deliveries including where required episiotomies and in urgent cases breech deliveries;

(g)   recognising the warning signs of abnormality in the mother or infant which necessitate referral to a doctor and assisting the latter where appropriate; taking the necessary emergency measures in the doctor's absence, in particular the manual removal of the placenta, possibly followed by manual examination of the uterus;

(h)   examining and caring for the new-born infant; taking all initiatives which are necessary in case of need and carrying out where necessary immediate resuscitation;

(i)   caring for and monitoring the progress of the mother in the post-natal period and giving all necessary advice to the mother on infant care to enable her to ensure the optimum progress of the new-born infant;

(j)   carrying out treatment prescribed by doctors;

(k)   drawing up the necessary written reports.

Article 43 Acquired rights specific to midwives

1.   Every Member State shall, in the case of Member State nationals whose evidence of formal qualifications as a midwife satisfies all the minimum training requirements laid down in Article 40 but, by virtue of Article 41, is not recognised unless it is accompanied by a certificate of professional practice referred to in Article 41(2), recognise as sufficient proof evidence of formal qualifications issued by those Member States before the reference date referred to in Annex V, point 5.5.2, accompanied by a certificate stating that those nationals have been effectively and lawfully engaged in the activities in question for at least two consecutive years during the five years preceding the award of the certificate.

1a.   As regards evidence of formal qualifications of midwives, Member States shall recognise automatically those qualifications where the applicant started the training before 18 January 2016, and the admission requirement for such training was 10 years of general education or an equivalent level for route I, or completed training as a nurse responsible for general care as attested by evidence of formal qualification referred to in point 5.2.2 of Annex V before starting a midwifery training falling under route II.

2.   The conditions laid down in paragraph 1 shall apply to the nationals of Member States whose evidence of formal qualifications as a midwife certifies completion of training received in the territory of the former German Democratic Republic and satisfying all the minimum training requirements laid down in Article 40 but where the evidence of formal qualifications, by virtue of Article 41, is not recognised unless it is accompanied by the certificate of professional experience referred to in Article 41(2), where it attests a course of training which began before 3 October 1990.

4.   Member States shall recognise evidence of formal qualifications in midwifery that:

(a)   were awarded in Poland, to midwives who completed training before 1 May 2004, which did not comply with the minimum training requirements laid down in Article 40; and

(b)   are attested by the diploma 'bachelor' which was obtained on the basis of a special upgrading programme contained in:

(i)   Article 11 of the Act of 20 April 2004 on the amendment of the Act on professions of nurse and midwife and on some other legal acts (*Official Journal of the Republic of Poland* of 2004 No 92, pos. 885 and of 2007 No 176, pos. 1237) and the Regulation of the Minister of Health of 11 May 2004 on the detailed conditions of delivering studies for nurses and midwives, who hold a certificate of secondary school (final examination – matura) and are graduates of medical lyceum and medical vocational schools teaching in a profession of a nurse and a midwife (*Official Journal of the Republic of Poland* of 2004 No 110, pos. 1170 and of 2010 No 65, pos. 420); or

(ii)   Article 53.3 point 3 of the Act of 15 July 2011 on professions of nurse and midwife (*Official Journal of the Republic of Poland* of 2011 No 174, pos. 1039) and the Regulation of the Minister of Health of 14 June 2012 on the detailed conditions of delivering higher education courses for nurses and midwives who hold a certificate of secondary school (final examination – matura) and are graduates of a medical secondary school or a post-secondary school teaching in a profession of a nurse and a midwife (*Official Journal of the*

Republic of Poland of 2012, pos. 770), for the purpose of verifying that the midwife concerned has a level of knowledge and competence comparable to that of midwives holding the qualifications listed for Poland in point 5.5.2 of Annex V.

Article 43a

As regards the Romanian qualifications in midwifery, only the following acquired rights provisions will apply:

In the case of nationals of the Member States whose evidence of formal qualifications as a midwife (*asistent medical obstetrica-ginecologie*/obstetrics-gynecology nurse) were awarded by Romania before the date of accession and which do not satisfy the minimum training requirements laid down in Article 40, Member States shall recognise the said evidence of formal qualifications as being sufficient proof for the purposes of carrying out the activities of midwife, if they are accompanied by a certificate stating that those Member State nationals have effectively and lawfully been engaged in the activities of midwife in Romania, for at least five consecutive years during the seven years prior to the issue of the certificate.

Article 43b

Acquired rights in midwifery shall not apply to the following qualifications which were obtained in Croatia before 1 July 2013: viša medicinska sestra ginekološko-opstetričkog smjera (High Gynaecology-Obstetrical Nurse), medicinska sestra ginekološko-opstetričkog smjera (Gynaecology-Obstetrical Nurse), viša medicinska sestra primaljskog smjera (High Nurse with Midwifery Degree), medicinska sestra primaljskog smjera (Nurse with Midwifery Degree), ginekološko-opstetrička primalja (Gynaecology-Obstetrical Midwife) and primalja (Midwife).

SECTION 7
PHARMACIST

Article 44 Training as a pharmacist

1. Admission to a course of training as a pharmacist shall be contingent upon possession of a diploma or certificate giving access, in a Member State, to the studies in question, at universities or higher institutes of a level recognised as equivalent.
2. Evidence of formal qualifications as a pharmacist shall attest to training of at least five years' duration, which may in addition be expressed with the equivalent ECTS credits, comprising at least:
   (a) four years of full-time theoretical and practical training at a university or at a higher institute of a level recognised as equivalent, or under the supervision of a university;
   (b) during or at the end of the theoretical and practical training, six-month traineeship in a pharmacy which is open to the public or in a hospital under the supervision of that hospital's pharmaceutical department.

   The training cycle referred to in this paragraph shall include at least the programme described in point 5.6.1 of Annex V. The Commission shall be empowered to adopt delegated acts in accordance with Article 57c concerning the amendment of the list set out in point 5.6.1 of Annex V with a view to adapting it to scientific and technical progress, including the evolution of pharmacological practice.

   The amendments referred to in the second subparagraph shall not entail an amendment of existing essential legislative principles in Member States regarding the structure of professions as regards training and conditions of access by natural persons. Such amendments shall respect the responsibility of the Member States for the organisation of education systems, as set out in Article 165(1) TFEU.
3. Training for pharmacists shall provide an assurance that the person concerned has acquired the following knowledge and skills:
   (a) adequate knowledge of medicines and the substances used in the manufacture of medicines;
   (b) adequate knowledge of pharmaceutical technology and the physical, chemical, biological and microbiological testing of medicinal products;

(c)   adequate knowledge of the metabolism and the effects of medicinal products and of the action of toxic substances, and of the use of medicinal products;

(d)   adequate knowledge to evaluate scientific data concerning medicines in order to be able to supply appropriate information on the basis of this knowledge;

(e)   adequate knowledge of the legal and other requirements associated with the pursuit of pharmacy.

Article 45 Pursuit of the professional activities of a pharmacist

1.   For the purposes of this Directive, the activities of a pharmacist are those, access to which and pursuit of which are contingent, in one or more Member States, upon professional qualifications and which are open to holders of evidence of formal qualifications of the types listed in Annex V, point 5.6.2.

2.   The Member States shall ensure that the holders of evidence of formal qualifications in pharmacy at university level or a level recognised as equivalent, which satisfies the requirements of Article 44, are able to gain access to and pursue at least the following activities, subject to the requirement, where appropriate, of supplementary professional experience:

(a)   preparation of the pharmaceutical form of medicinal products;

(b)   manufacture and testing of medicinal products;

(c)   testing of medicinal products in a laboratory for the testing of medicinal products;

(d)   storage, preservation and distribution of medicinal products at the wholesale stage;

(e)   supply, preparation, testing, storage, distribution and dispensing of safe and efficacious medicinal products of the required quality in pharmacies open to the public;

(f)   preparation, testing, storage and dispensing of safe and efficacious medicinal products of the required quality in hospitals;

(g)   provision of information and advice on medicinal products as such, including on their appropriate use;

(h)   reporting of adverse reactions of pharmaceutical products to the competent authorities;

(i)   personalised support for patients who administer their medication;

(j)   contribution to local or national public health campaigns.

3.   If a Member State makes access to or pursuit of one of the activities of a pharmacist contingent upon supplementary professional experience, in addition to possession of evidence of formal qualifications referred to in Annex V, point 5.6.2, that Member State shall recognise as sufficient proof in this regard a certificate issued by the competent authorities in the home Member State stating that the person concerned has been engaged in those activities in the home Member State for a similar period.

4.   The recognition referred to in paragraph 3 shall not apply with regard to the two-year period of professional experience required by the Grand Duchy of Luxembourg for the grant of a State public pharmacy concession.

5.   If, on 16 September 1985, a Member State had a competitive examination in place designed to select from among the holders referred to in paragraph 2, those who are to be authorised to become owners of new pharmacies whose creation has been decided on as part of a national system of geographical division, that Member State may, by way of derogation from paragraph 1, proceed with that examination and require nationals of Member States who possess evidence of formal qualifications as a pharmacist referred to in Annex V, point 5.6.2 or who benefit from the provisions of Article 23 to take part in it.

SECTION 8
ARCHITECT

Article 46 Training of architects

1.   Training as an architect shall comprise:

(a)   a total of at least five years of full-time study at a university or a comparable teaching institution, leading to successful completion of a university-level examination; or

    (b)   not less than four years of full-time study at a university or a comparable teaching institution leading to successful completion of a university-level examination, accompanied by a certificate attesting to the completion of two years of professional traineeship in accordance with paragraph 4.

2.   Architecture must be the principal component of the study referred to in paragraph 1. The study shall maintain a balance between theoretical and practical aspects of architectural training and shall guarantee at least the acquisition of the following knowledge, skills and competences:

    (a)   the ability to create architectural designs that satisfy both aesthetic and technical requirements;

    (b)   adequate knowledge of the history and theories of architecture and the related arts, technologies and human sciences;

    (c)   knowledge of the fine arts as an influence on the quality of architectural design;

    (d)   adequate knowledge of urban design, planning and the skills involved in the planning process;

    (e)   understanding of the relationship between people and buildings, and between buildings and their environment, and of the need to relate buildings and the spaces between them to human needs and scale;

    (f)   understanding of the profession of architect and the role of the architect in society, in particular in preparing briefs that take account of social factors;

    (g)   understanding of the methods of investigation and preparation of the brief for a design project;

    (h)   understanding of the structural design, and constructional and engineering problems associated with building design;

    (i)   adequate knowledge of physical problems and technologies and of the function of buildings so as to provide them with internal conditions of comfort and protection against the climate, in the framework of sustainable development;

    (j)   the necessary design skills to meet building users' requirements within the constraints imposed by cost factors and building regulations;

    (k)   adequate knowledge of the industries, organisations, regulations and procedures involved in translating design concepts into buildings and integrating plans into overall planning.

3.   The number of years of academic study referred to in paragraphs 1 and 2 may in addition be expressed with the equivalent ECTS credits.

4.   The professional traineeship referred to in point (b) of paragraph 1 shall take place only after completion of the first three years of the study. At least one year of the professional traineeship shall build upon knowledge, skills and competences acquired during the study referred to in paragraph 2. To that end, the professional traineeship shall be carried out under the supervision of a person or body that has been authorised by the competent authority in the home Member State. Such supervised traineeship may take place in any country. The professional traineeship shall be evaluated by the competent authority in the home Member State.

Article 47 Derogations from the conditions for the training of architects

By way of derogation from Article 46, the following shall also be recognised as complying with Article 21: training as part of social betterment schemes or part-time university studies which satisfies the requirements set out in Article 46(2), as attested by an examination in architecture passed by a professional who has been working for seven years or more in the field of architecture under the supervision of an architect or architectural bureau. The examination must be of university level and be equivalent to the final examination referred to in point (b) of Article 46(1).

Article 48 Pursuit of the professional activities of architects

1.   For the purposes of this Directive, the professional activities of an architect are the activities regularly carried out under the professional title of 'architect'.

2.   Nationals of a Member State who are authorised to use that title pursuant to a law which gives the competent authority of a Member State the power to award that title to Member States nationals who are especially distinguished by the quality of their work in the field of architecture shall be deemed to satisfy the conditions required for

the pursuit of the activities of an architect, under the professional title of 'architect'. The architectural nature of the activities of the persons concerned shall be attested by a certificate awarded by their home Member State.

Article 49 Acquired rights specific to architects

1. Each Member State shall accept evidence of formal qualifications as an architect listed in Annex VI, awarded by the other Member States, and attesting a course of training which began no later than the reference academic year referred to in that Annex, even if they do not satisfy the minimum requirements laid down in Article 46, and shall, for the purposes of access to and pursuit of the professional activities of an architect, give such evidence the same effect on its territory as evidence of formal qualifications as an architect which it itself issues.

   Under these circumstances, certificates issued by the competent authorities of the Federal Republic of Germany attesting that evidence of formal qualifications issued on or after 8 May 1945 by the competent authorities of the German Democratic Republic is equivalent to such evidence listed in that Annex, shall be recognised.

1a. Paragraph 1 shall also apply to evidence of formal qualifications as an architect listed in Annex V, where the training started before 18 January 2016.

2. Without prejudice to paragraph 1, every Member State shall recognise the following evidence of formal qualifications and shall, for the purposes of access to and pursuit of the professional activities of an architect performed, give them the same effect on its territory as evidence of formal qualifications which it itself issues: certificates issued to nationals of Member States by the Member States which have enacted rules governing the access to and pursuit of the activities of an architect as of the following dates:
   (a) 1 January 1995 for Austria, Finland and Sweden;
   (b) 1 May 2004 for the Czech Republic, Estonia, Cyprus, Latvia, Lithuania, Hungary, Malta, Poland, Slovenia and Slovakia;
   (ba) 1 July 2013 for Croatia;
   (c) 5 August 1987 for the other Member States.

   The certificates referred to in the first subparagraph shall certify that the holder was authorised, no later than the respective date, to use the professional title of architect, and that he has been effectively engaged, in the context of those rules, in the activities in question for at least three consecutive years during the five years preceding the award of the certificate.

3. Each Member State shall give the following evidence the same effect on its territory as evidence of formal qualifications it itself issues for the purposes of access to and pursuit of the professional activities of an architect: evidence of completion of training existing as of 5 August 1985 and commenced no later than 17 January 2014, provided by 'Fachhochschulen' in the Federal Republic of Germany over a period of three years, satisfying the requirements set out in Article 46(2) and giving access to the activities referred to in Article 48 in that Member State under the professional title of 'architect', in so far as the training was followed by a four-year period of professional experience in the Federal Republic of Germany, as attested by a certificate issued by the competent authority in whose roll the name of the architect wishing to benefit from the provisions of this Directive appears.

CHAPTER IIIA
AUTOMATIC RECOGNITION ON THE BASIS OF COMMON TRAINING PRINCIPLES

Article 49a Common training framework

1. For the purpose of this Article, 'common training framework' means a common set of minimum knowledge, skills and competences necessary for the pursuit of a specific profession. A common training framework shall not replace national training programmes unless a Member State decides otherwise under national law. For the purpose of access to and pursuit of a profession in Member States which regulate that profession, a Member State shall give evidence of professional qualifications acquired on the basis of such a framework the same effect in its territory as the evidence of

formal qualifications which it itself issues, on condition that such framework fulfils the conditions laid down in paragraph 2.

2.   A common training framework shall comply with the following conditions:

   (a)   the common training framework enables more professionals to move across Member States;

   (b)   the profession to which the common training framework applies is regulated, or the education and training leading to the profession is regulated in at least one third of the Member States;

   (c)   the common set of knowledge, skills and competences combines the knowledge, skills and competences required in the systems of education and training applicable in at least one third of the Member States; it shall be irrelevant whether the knowledge, skills and competences have been acquired as part of a general training course at a university or higher education institution or as part of a vocational training course;

   (d)   the common training framework shall be based on levels of the EQF, as defined in Annex II of the Recommendation of the European Parliament and of the Council of 23 April 2008 on the establishment of the European Qualifications Framework for lifelong learning;

   (e)   the profession concerned is neither covered by another common training framework nor subject to automatic recognition under Chapter III of Title III;

   (f)   the common training framework has been prepared following a transparent due process, including the relevant stakeholders from Member States where the profession is not regulated;

   (g)   the common training framework permits nationals from any Member State to be eligible for acquiring the professional qualification under such framework without first being required to be a member of any professional organisation or to be registered with such organisation.

3.   Representative professional organisations at Union level, as well as national professional organisations or competent authorities from at least one third of the Member States, may submit to the Commission suggestions for common training frameworks which meet the conditions laid down in paragraph 2.

4.   The Commission shall be empowered to adopt delegated acts in accordance with Article 57c to establish a common training framework for a given profession based on the conditions laid down in paragraph 2 of this Article.

5.   A Member State shall be exempted from the obligation of introducing the common training framework referred to in paragraph 4 on its territory and from the obligation of granting automatic recognition to the professional qualifications acquired under that common training framework if one of the following conditions is fulfilled:

   (a)   there are no education or training institutions available in its territory to offer such training for the profession concerned;

   (b)   the introduction of the common training framework would adversely affect the organisation of its system of education and professional training;

   (c)   there are substantial differences between the common training framework and the training required in its territory, which entail serious risks for public policy, public security, public health or for the safety of the service recipients or the protection of the environment.

6.   Member States shall, within six months of the entry into force of the delegated act referred to in paragraph 4, notify to the Commission and to the other Member States:

   (a)   the national qualifications, and where applicable the national professional titles, that comply with the common training framework; or

   (b)   any use of the exemption referred to in paragraph 5, along with a justification of which conditions under that paragraph were fulfilled. The Commission may, within three months, request further clarification if it considers that a Member State has provided no or insufficient justification that one of these conditions has been fulfilled. The Member State shall reply within three months of any such request.

The Commission may adopt an implementing act to list the national professional qualifications and national professional titles benefiting from automatic recognition under the common training framework adopted in accordance with paragraph 4.

7. This Article also applies to specialties of a profession, provided such specialties concern professional activities the access to and the pursuit of which are regulated in Member States, where the profession is already subject to automatic recognition under Chapter III of Title III, but not the specialty concerned.

Article 49b Common training tests

1. For the purpose of this Article, a 'common training test' means a standardised aptitude test available across participating Member States and reserved to holders of a particular professional qualification. Passing such a test in a Member State shall entitle the holder of a particular professional qualification to pursue the profession in any host Member State concerned under the same conditions as the holders of professional qualifications acquired in that Member State.

2. The common training test shall comply with the following conditions:
    (a) the common training test enables more professionals to move across Member States;
    (b) the profession to which the common training test applies is regulated, or the education and training leading to the profession concerned is regulated in at least one third of the Member States;
    (c) the common training test has been prepared following a transparent due process, including the relevant stakeholders from Member States where the profession is not regulated;
    (d) the common training test permits nationals from any Member State to participate in such a test and in the practical organisation of such tests in Member States without first being required to be a member of any professional organisation or to be registered with such organisation.

3. Representative professional organisations at Union level, as well as national professional organisations or competent authorities from at least one third of the Member States, may submit to the Commission suggestions for common training tests which meet the conditions laid down in paragraph 2.

4. The Commission shall be empowered to adopt delegated acts in accordance with Article 57c to establish the contents of a common training test, and the conditions required for taking and passing the test.

5. A Member State shall be exempted from the obligation of organising the common training test referred to in paragraph 4 on its territory and from the obligation of granting automatic recognition to professionals who have passed the common training test if one of the following conditions is fulfilled:
    (a) the profession concerned is not regulated on its territory;
    (b) the contents of the common training test will not sufficiently mitigate serious risks for public health or the safety of the service recipients, which are relevant on its territory;
    (c) the contents of the common training test would render access to the profession significantly less attractive compared to national requirements.

6. Member States shall, within six months of the entry into force of the delegated act referred to in paragraph 4, notify to the Commission and to the other Member States:
    (a) the available capacity for organising such tests; or
    (b) any use of the exemption referred to in paragraph 5, along with the justification of which conditions under that paragraph were fulfilled. The Commission may, within three months, request further clarification, if it considers that a Member State has provided no or insufficient justification that one of these conditions has been fulfilled. The Member State shall reply within three months of any such request.

The Commission may adopt an implementing act to list the Member States in which the common training tests adopted in accordance with paragraph 4 are to be organised, the frequency during a calendar year and other arrangements necessary for organising common training tests across Member States.

CHAPTER IV
COMMON PROVISIONS ON ESTABLISHMENT

Article 50 Documentation and formalities

1. Where the competent authorities of the host Member State decide on an application for authorisation to pursue the regulated profession in question by virtue of this Title, those authorities may demand the documents and certificates listed in Annex VII.

   The documents referred to in Annex VII, point 1(d), (e) and (f), shall not be more than three months old by the date on which they are submitted.

   The Member States, bodies and other legal persons shall guarantee the confidentiality of the information which they receive.

2. In the event of justified doubts, the host Member State may require from the competent authorities of a Member State confirmation of the authenticity of the attestations and evidence of formal qualifications awarded in that other Member State, as well as, where applicable, confirmation of the fact that the beneficiary fulfils, for the professions referred to in Chapter III of this Title, the minimum training conditions set out respectively in Articles 24, 25, 28, 31, 34, 35, 38, 40, 44 and 46.

3. In cases of justified doubt, where evidence of formal qualifications, as defined in Article 3(1)(c), has been issued by a competent authority in a Member State and includes training received in whole or in part in an establishment legally established in the territory of another Member State, the host Member State shall be entitled to verify with the competent body in the Member State of origin of the award:

   (a) whether the training course at the establishment which gave the training has been formally certified by the educational establishment based in the Member State of origin of the award;

   (b) whether the evidence of formal qualifications issued is the same as that which would have been awarded if the course had been followed entirely in the Member State of origin of the award; and

   (c) whether the evidence of formal qualifications confers the same professional rights in the territory of the Member State of origin of the award.

3a. In the event of justified doubts, the host Member State may require from the competent authorities of a Member State confirmation of the fact that the applicant is not suspended or prohibited from the pursuit of the profession as a result of serious professional misconduct or conviction of criminal offences relating to the pursuit of any of his professional activities.

3b. Exchange of information between competent authorities of different Member States under this Article shall take place via IMI.

4. Where a host Member State requires its nationals to swear a solemn oath or make a sworn statement in order to gain access to a regulated profession, and where the wording of that oath or statement cannot be used by nationals of the other Member States, the host Member State shall ensure that the persons concerned can use an appropriate equivalent wording.

Article 51 Procedure for the mutual recognition of professional qualifications

1. The competent authority of the host Member State shall acknowledge receipt of the application within one month of receipt and inform the applicant of any missing document.

2. The procedure for examining an application for authorisation to practise a regulated profession must be completed as quickly as possible and lead to a duly substantiated decision by the competent authority in the host Member State in any case within three months after the date on which the applicant's complete file was submitted. However, this deadline may be extended by one month in cases falling under Chapters I and II of this Title.

3. The decision, or failure to reach a decision within the deadline, shall be subject to appeal under national law.

Article 52 Use of professional titles

1. If, in a host Member State, the use of a professional title relating to one of the activities of the profession in question is regulated, nationals of the other Member States who are authorised to practise a regulated profession on the basis of Title III shall use the professional title of the host Member State, which corresponds to that profession in that Member State, and make use of any associated initials.

2. Where a profession is regulated in the host Member State by an association or organisation within the meaning of Article 3(2), nationals of Member States shall not be authorised to use the professional title issued by that organisation or association, or its abbreviated form, unless they furnish proof that they are members of that association or organisation.

    If the association or organisation makes membership contingent upon certain qualifications, it may do so, only under the conditions laid down in this Directive, in respect of nationals of other Member States who possess professional qualifications.

3. A Member State may not reserve the use of the professional title to the holders of professional qualifications if it has not notified the association or organisation to the Commission and to the other Member States in accordance with Article 3(2).

TITLE IV
DETAILED RULES FOR PURSUING THE PROFESSION

Article 53 Knowledge of languages

1. Professionals benefiting from the recognition of professional qualifications shall have a knowledge of languages necessary for practising the profession in the host Member State.

2. A Member State shall ensure that any controls carried out by, or under the supervision of, the competent authority for controlling compliance with the obligation under paragraph 1 shall be limited to the knowledge of one official language of the host Member State, or one administrative language of the host Member State provided that it is also an official language of the Union.

3. Controls carried out in accordance with paragraph 2 may be imposed if the profession to be practised has patient safety implications. Controls may be imposed in respect of other professions in cases where there is a serious and concrete doubt about the sufficiency of the professional's language knowledge in respect of the professional activities that that professional intends to pursue.

    Controls may be carried out only after the issuance of a European Professional Card in accordance with Article 4d or after the recognition of a professional qualification, as the case may be.

4. Any language controls shall be proportionate to the activity to be pursued. The professional concerned shall be allowed to appeal such controls under national law.

Article 54 Use of academic titles

Without prejudice to Articles 7 and 52, the host Member State shall ensure that the right shall be conferred on the persons concerned to use academic titles conferred on them in the home Member State, and possibly an abbreviated form thereof, in the language of the home Member State. The host Member State may require that title to be followed by the name and address of the establishment or examining board which awarded it. Where an academic title of the home Member State is liable to be confused in the host Member State with a title which, in the latter Member State, requires supplementary training not acquired by the beneficiary, the host Member State may require the beneficiary to use the academic title of the home Member State in an appropriate form, to be laid down by the host Member State.

Article 55 Approval by health insurance funds

Without prejudice to Article 5(1) and Article 6, first subparagraph, point (b), Member States which require persons who acquired their professional qualifications in their territory to complete a preparatory period of in-service training and/or a period of professional experience in order to be approved by a health insurance fund, shall waive this obligation for the holders of evidence of professional qualifications of doctor and dental practitioner acquired in other Member States.

Article 55a Recognition of professional traineeship

1. If access to a regulated profession in the home Member State is contingent upon completion of a professional traineeship, the competent authority of the home Member State shall, when considering a request for authorisation to exercise the regulated profession, recognise professional traineeships carried out in another Member State provided the traineeship is in accordance with the published guidelines referred to in paragraph 2, and shall take into account professional traineeships carried out in a third country. However, Member States may, in national legislation, set a reasonable limit on the duration of the part of the professional traineeship which can be carried out abroad.

2. Recognition of the professional traineeship shall not replace any requirements in place to pass an examination in order to gain access to the profession in question. The competent authorities shall publish guidelines on the organisation and recognition of professional traineeships carried out in another Member State or in a third country, in particular on the role of the supervisor of the professional traineeship.

TITLE V

ADMINISTRATIVE COOPERATION AND RESPONSIBILITY TOWARDS CITIZENS FOR IMPLEMENTATION

Article 56 Competent authorities

1. The competent authorities of the host Member State and of the home Member State shall work in close collaboration and shall provide mutual assistance in order to facilitate application of this Directive. They shall ensure the confidentiality of the information which they exchange.

2. The competent authorities of the host and home Member States shall exchange information regarding disciplinary action or criminal sanctions taken or any other serious, specific circumstances which are likely to have consequences for the pursuit of activities under this Directive. In so doing, they shall respect personal data protection rules provided for in Directives 95/46/EC and 2002/58/EC.

    The home Member State shall examine the veracity of the circumstances and its authorities shall decide on the nature and scope of the investigations which need to be carried out and shall inform the host Member State of the conclusions which it draws from the information available to it.

2a. For the purposes of paragraphs 1 and 2, the competent authorities shall use IMI.

3. Each Member State shall, no later than 20 October 2007, designate the authorities and bodies competent to award or receive evidence of formal qualifications and other documents or information, and those competent to receive applications and take the decisions referred to in this Directive, and shall forthwith inform the other Member States and the Commission thereof.

4. Each Member State shall designate a coordinator for the activities of the competent authorities referred to in paragraph 1 and shall inform other Member States and the Commission thereof.

    The coordinators' tasks shall be:

    (a) to promote uniform application of this Directive;

    (b) to collect all the information which is relevant for application of this Directive, such as on the conditions for access to regulated professions in the Member States;

    (c) to examine suggestions for common training frameworks and common training tests;

    (d) to exchange information and best practice for the purpose of optimising continuous professional development in Member States;

    (e) to exchange information and best practice on the application of compensation measures referred to in Article 14.

    For the purpose of carrying out the task set out in point (b) of this paragraph, the coordinators may solicit the help of the assistance centres referred to in Article 57b.

Article 56a Alert mechanism

1. The competent authorities of a Member State shall inform the competent authorities of all other Member States about a professional whose pursuit on the territory of that Member State of the following professional activities in their entirety or parts thereof has been restricted or prohibited, even temporarily, by national authorities or courts:

   (a) doctor of medicine and of general practice possessing evidence of a formal qualification referred to in points 5.1.1 and 5.1.4 of Annex V;

   (b) specialist doctor of medicine possessing a title referred to in point 5.1.3 of Annex V;

   (c) nurse responsible for general care possessing evidence of a formal qualification referred to in point 5.2.2 of Annex V;

   (d) dental practitioner possessing evidence of a formal qualification referred to in point 5.3.2 of Annex V;

   (e) specialist dentists possessing evidence of a formal qualification referred to in point 5.3.3 of Annex V;

   (f) veterinary surgeon possessing evidence of a formal qualification referred to in point 5.4.2 of Annex V;

   (g) midwife possessing evidence of a formal qualification referred to in point 5.5.2 of Annex V;

   (h) pharmacist possessing evidence of a formal qualification listed in point 5.6.2 of Annex V;

   (i) holders of certificates mentioned in point 2 of Annex VII attesting that the holder completed a training which satisfies the minimum requirements listed in Articles 24, 25, 31, 34, 35, 38, 40, or 44 respectively, but which started earlier than the reference dates of the qualifications listed in points 5.1.3, 5.1.4, 5.2.2, 5.3.2, 5.3.3, 5.4.2, 5.5.2, 5.6.2 of Annex V;

   (j) holders of certificates of acquired rights as referred to in Articles 23, 27, 29, 33, 33a, 37, 43 and 43a;

   (k) other professionals exercising activities that have patient safety implications, where the professional is pursuing a profession regulated in that Member State;

   (l) professionals exercising activities relating to the education of minors, including in childcare and early childhood education, where the professional is pursuing a profession regulated in that Member State.

2. Competent authorities shall send the information referred to in paragraph 1 by way of alert via IMI at the latest within three days from the date of adoption of the decision restricting or prohibiting pursuit of the professional activity in its entirety or in part by the professional concerned. That information shall be limited to the following:

   (a) the identity of the professional;

   (b) the profession concerned;

   (c) information about the national authority or court adopting the decision on restriction or prohibition;

   (d) the scope of the restriction or the prohibition; and

   (e) the period during which the restriction or the prohibition applies.

3. The competent authorities of a Member State concerned shall, at the latest within three days from the date of adoption of the court decision, inform the competent authorities of all other Member States, by way of alert via IMI, about the identity of professionals who have applied for the recognition of a qualification under this Directive and who have subsequently been found by courts to have used falsified evidence of professional qualifications in this context.

4. The processing of personal data for the purpose of the exchange of information referred to in paragraphs 1 and 3 shall be carried out in accordance with Directives 95/46/EC and 2002/58/EC. The processing of personal data by the Commission shall be carried out in accordance with Regulation (EC) No 45/2001.

5. The competent authorities of all Member States shall be informed without delay when a prohibition or a restriction referred to in paragraph 1 has expired. For that purpose, the competent authority of the Member State which provides the information in accordance with paragraph 1 shall also be required to provide the date of expiry as well as any subsequent change to that date.

6. Member States shall provide that professionals, in respect of whom alerts are sent to other Member States, are informed in writing of decisions on alerts at the same time as the alert itself, may appeal under national law against the decision or apply for rectification of such decisions and shall have access to remedies in respect of any damage caused by false alerts sent to other Member States, and in such cases the decision on the alert shall be qualified to indicate that it is subject to proceedings by the professional.

7. Data regarding alerts may be processed within IMI for as long as they are valid. Alerts shall be deleted within three days from the date of adoption of the revoking decision or from the expiry of the prohibition or the restriction referred to in paragraph 1.

8. The Commission shall adopt implementing acts for the application of the alert mechanism.

Those implementing acts shall include provisions on the authorities entitled to send or receive alerts and on the withdrawal and closure of alerts, and measures to ensure the security of processing. Those implementing acts shall be adopted in accordance with the examination procedure referred to in Article 58(2).

Article 57 Central online access to information

1. Member States shall ensure that the following information is available online through the points of single contact, referred to in Article 6 of Directive 2006/123/EC of the European Parliament and of the Council of 12 December 2006 on services in the internal market, and regularly updated:

    (a) a list of all regulated professions in the Member State including contact details of the competent authorities for each regulated profession and the assistance centres referred to in Article 57b;

    (b) a list of the professions for which a European Professional Card is available, the functioning of that Card, including all related fees to be paid by professionals, and the competent authorities for issuing that Card;

    (c) a list of all professions for which the Member State applies Article 7(4) under national laws, regulations and administrative provisions;

    (d) a list of regulated education and training, and training with a special structure, referred to in point (c)(ii) of Article 11;

    (e) the requirements and procedures referred to in Articles 7, 50, 51 and 53 for the professions regulated in the Member State, including all related fees to be paid by citizens and documents to be submitted by citizens to competent authorities;

    (f) details on how to appeal, under national laws, regulations and administrative provisions, decisions of competent authorities adopted under this Directive.

2. Member States shall ensure that the information referred to in paragraph 1 is provided in a clear and comprehensive way for users, that it is easily accessible remotely and by electronic means and that it is kept up to date.

3. Member States shall ensure that any request for information addressed to the point of single contact is replied to as soon as possible.

4. Member States and the Commission shall take accompanying measures in order to encourage points of single contact to make the information provided for in paragraph 1 available in other official languages of the Union. This shall not affect the legislation of Member States on the use of languages in their territory.

5. Member States shall cooperate with each other and the Commission for the purpose of implementing paragraphs 1, 2 and 4.

Article 57a Procedures by electronic means

1. Member States shall ensure that all requirements, procedures and formalities relating to matters covered by this Directive may be easily completed, remotely and by electronic means, through the relevant point of single contact or the relevant competent authorities. This shall not prevent competent authorities of Member States from requesting certified copies at a later stage in the event of justified doubts and where strictly necessary.

2. Paragraph 1 shall not apply to the carrying out of an adaptation period or aptitude test.

3. Where it is justified for Member States to ask for advanced electronic signatures, as defined in point 2 of Article 2 of Directive 1999/93/EC of the European Parliament

and of the Council of 13 December 1999 on a Community framework for electronic signatures, for the completion of procedures referred to in paragraph 1 of this Article, Member States shall accept electronic signatures in compliance with Commission Decision 2009/767/EC of 16 October 2009 setting out measures facilitating the use of procedures by electronic means through the points of single contact under Directive 2006/123/EC of the European Parliament and of the Council on services in the internal market and provide for technical means to process documents with advanced electronic signature in formats defined by Commission Decision 2011/130/EU of 25 February 2011 establishing minimum requirements for the cross-border processing of documents signed electronically by competent authorities under Directive 2006/123/EC of the European Parliament and of the Council on services in the internal market.

4.   All procedures shall be carried out in accordance with Article 8 of Directive 2006/123/EC relating to the points of single contact. The procedural time limits set out in Article 7(4) and Article 51 of this Directive shall commence at the point when an application or any missing document has been submitted by a citizen to a point of single contact or directly to the relevant competent authority. Any request for certified copies referred to in paragraph 1 of this Article shall not be considered as a request for missing documents.

Article 57b Assistance centres

1.   Each Member State shall designate, no later than 18 January 2016, an assistance centre whose remit shall be to provide citizens, as well as assistance centres of the other Member States, with assistance concerning the recognition of professional qualifications provided for in this Directive, including information on the national legislation governing the professions and the pursuit of those professions, social legislation, and, where appropriate, the rules of ethics.

2.   The assistance centres in host Member States shall assist citizens in exercising the rights conferred on them by this Directive, in cooperation, where appropriate, with the assistance centre in the home Member State and the competent authorities and the points of single contact in the host Member State.

3.   Any competent authority in the home or host Member State shall be required to fully cooperate with the assistance centre in the host Member State and where appropriate the home Member State, and provide all relevant information about individual cases to such assistance centres upon their request and subject to data protection rules in accordance with Directives 95/46/EC and 2002/58/EC.

4.   At the Commission's request, the assistance centres shall inform the Commission of the result of enquiries with which they are dealing within two months after receiving such a request.

Article 57c Exercise of the delegation

1.   The power to adopt delegated acts is conferred on the Commission subject to the conditions laid down in this Article.

2.   The power to adopt delegated acts referred to in the third subparagraph of Article 3(2), Article 20, the second subparagraph of Article 21(6), Article 21a(4), Article 25(5), the second paragraph of Article 26, the second subparagraph of Article 31(2), the second subparagraph of Article 34(2), Article 35(4) and (5), the second subparagraph of Article 38(1), the third subparagraph of Article 40(1), the second subparagraph of Article 44(2), Article 49a(4) and Article 49b(4) shall be conferred on the Commission for a period of five years from 17 January 2014. The Commission shall draw up a report in respect of the delegation of power not later than nine months before the end of the five-year period. The delegation of power shall be tacitly extended for periods of an identical duration, unless the European Parliament or the Council opposes such extension not later than three months before the end of each period.

3.   The power to adopt delegated acts referred to in the third subparagraph of Article 3(2), Article 20, the second subparagraph of Article 21(6), Article 21a(4), Article 25(5), the second paragraph of Article 26, the second subparagraph of Article 31(2), the second subparagraph of Article 34(2), Article 35(4) and (5), the second subparagraph of Article 38(1), the third subparagraph of Article 40(1), the second subparagraph

of Article 44(2), Article 49a(4) and Article 49b(4) may be revoked at any time by the European Parliament or by the Council. A decision to revoke shall put an end to the delegation of the power specified in that decision. It shall take effect the day following the publication of the decision in the *Official Journal of the European Union* or at a later date specified therein. It shall not affect the validity of any delegated acts already in force.

4. As soon as it adopts a delegated act, the Commission shall notify it simultaneously to the European Parliament and to the Council.

5. A delegated act adopted pursuant to the third subparagraph of Article 3(2), Article 20, the second subparagraph of Article 21(6), Article 21a(4), Article 25(5), the second paragraph of Article 26, the second subparagraph of Article 31(2), the second subparagraph of Article 34(2), Article 35(4) and (5), the second subparagraph of Article 38(1), the third subparagraph of Article 40(1), the second subparagraph of Article 44(2), Article 49a(4) and Article 49b(4) shall enter into force only if no objection has been expressed either by the European Parliament or the Council within a period of two months of notification of that act to the European Parliament and the Council or if, before the expiry of that period, the European Parliament and the Council have both informed the Commission that they will not object. That period shall be extended by two months at the initiative of the European Parliament or of the Council.

Article 58 Committee procedure

1. The Commission shall be assisted by a Committee on the recognition of professional qualifications. That committee shall be a committee within the meaning of Regulation (EU) No 182/2011.

2. Where reference is made to this paragraph, Article 5 of Regulation (EU) No 182/2011 shall apply.

Article 59 Transparency

1. Member States shall notify to the Commission a list of existing regulated professions, specifying the activities covered by each profession, and a list of regulated education and training, and training with a special structure, referred to in point (c)(ii) of Article 11, in their territory by 18 January 2016. Any change to those lists shall also be notified to the Commission without undue delay. The Commission shall set up and maintain a publicly available database of regulated professions, including a general description of activities covered by each profession.

2. By 18 January 2016, Member States shall notify to the Commission the list of professions for which a prior check of qualifications is necessary under Article 7(4). Member States shall provide the Commission with a specific justification for the inclusion of each of those professions on that list.

3. Member States shall examine whether requirements under their legal system restricting the access to a profession or its pursuit to the holders of a specific professional qualification, including the use of professional titles and the professional activities allowed under such title, referred to in this Article as 'requirements' are compatible with the following principles:
   (a) requirements must be neither directly nor indirectly discriminatory on the basis of nationality or residence;
   (b) requirements must be justified by overriding reasons of general interest;
   (c) requirements must be suitable for securing the attainment of the objective pursued and must not go beyond what is necessary to attain that objective.

4. Paragraph 1 shall also apply to professions regulated in a Member State by an association or organisation within the meaning of Article 3(2) and any requirements for membership of those associations or organisations.

5. By 18 January 2016, Member States shall provide the Commission with information on the requirements they intend to maintain and the reasons for considering that those requirements comply with paragraph 3. Member States shall provide information on the requirements they subsequently introduced, and the reasons for considering that those requirements comply with paragraph 3, within six months of the adoption of the measure.

6. By 18 January 2016, and every two years thereafter, Member States shall also submit a report to the Commission about the requirements which have been removed or made less stringent.
7. The Commission shall forward the reports referred to in paragraph 6 to the other Member States which shall submit their observations within six months. Within the same period of six months, the Commission shall consult interested parties, including the professions concerned.
8. The Commission shall provide a summary report based on the information provided by Member States to the Group of Coordinators established under Commission Decision 2007/172/EC of 19 March 2007 setting up the group of coordinators for the recognition of professional qualifications (*), which may make observations.
9. In light of the observations provided for in paragraphs 7 and 8, the Commission shall, by 18 January 2017, submit its final findings to the European Parliament and the Council, accompanied where appropriate by proposals for further initiatives.

TITLE VI
OTHER PROVISIONS

Article 60 Reports

1. As from 20 October 2007, Member States shall, every two years, send a report to the Commission on the application of the system. In addition to general observations, the report shall contain a statistical summary of decisions taken and a description of the main problems arising from the application of this Directive.

   As from 18 January 2016 the statistical summary of decisions taken referred to in the first subparagraph shall contain detailed information on the number and types of decisions taken in accordance with this Directive, including the types of decisions on partial access taken by competent authorities in accordance with Article 4f, and a description of the main problems arising from application of this Directive.
2. By 18 January 2019, and every five years thereafter, the Commission shall publish a report on the implementation of this Directive.

   The first such report shall focus in particular on the new elements introduced in this Directive and consider in particular the following issues:
   (a) the functioning of the European Professional Card;
   (b) the modernisation of the knowledge, skills and competences for the professions covered by Chapter III of Title III, including the list of competences referred to in Article 31(7);
   (c) the functioning of the common training frameworks and common training tests;
   (d) the results of the special upgrading programme laid down under Romanian laws, regulations and administrative provisions for holders of the evidence of formal qualifications mentioned in Article 33a, as well as for holders of evidence of formal qualifications of post-secondary level, with a view to assessing the need to review the current provisions governing the acquired rights regime applicable to the Romanian evidence of formal qualifications as nurse responsible for general care.

Member States shall provide all necessary information for the preparation of that report.

Article 61 Derogation clause

If, for the application of one of the provisions of this Directive, a Member State encounters major difficulties in a particular area, the Commission shall examine those difficulties in collaboration with the Member State concerned.

Where appropriate, the Commission shall adopt an implementing act to permit the Member State in question to derogate from the relevant provision for a limited period of time.

Article 62 Repeal

Directives 77/452/EEC, 77/453/EEC, 78/686/EEC, 78/687/EEC, 78/1026/EEC, 78/1027/EEC, 80/154/EEC, 80/155/EEC, 85/384/EEC, 85/432/EEC, 85/433/EEC, 89/48/EEC, 92/51/EEC, 93/16/EEC and 1999/42/EC are repealed with effect from 20 October 2007. References to the repealed Directives shall be understood as references to this Directive and the acts adopted on the basis of those Directives shall not be affected by the repeal.

Article 63 Transposition

Member States shall bring into force the laws, regulations and administrative provisions necessary to comply with this Directive by 20 October 2007 at the latest. They shall forthwith inform the Commission thereof.

When Member States adopt these measures, they shall contain a reference to this Directive or be accompanied by such a reference on the occasion of their official publication. Member States shall determine how such reference is to be made.

Article 64 Entry into force

This Directive shall enter into force on the 20th day following its publication in the *Official Journal of the European Union*.

Article 65 Addressees

This Directive is addressed to the Member States.

ANNEX I

LIST OF PROFESSIONAL ASSOCIATIONS OR ORGANISATIONS FULFILLING THE CONDITIONS OF ARTICLE 3(2)

IRELAND
1. The Institute of Chartered Accountants in Ireland
2. The Institute of Certified Public Accountants in Ireland
3. The Association of Certified Accountants
4. Institution of Engineers of Ireland
5. Irish Planning Institute

UNITED KINGDOM
1. Institute of Chartered Accountants in England and Wales
2. Institute of Chartered Accountants of Scotland
3. Institute of Chartered Accountants in Ireland
4. Chartered Association of Certified Accountants
5. Chartered Institute of Loss Adjusters
6. Chartered Institute of Management Accountants
7. Institute of Chartered Secretaries and Administrators
8. Chartered Insurance Institute
9. Institute of Actuaries
10. Faculty of Actuaries
11. Chartered Institute of Bankers
12. Institute of Bankers in Scotland
13. Royal Institution of Chartered Surveyors
14. Royal Town Planning Institute
15. Chartered Society of Physiotherapy
16. Royal Society of Chemistry
17. British Psychological Society
18. Library Association
19. Institute of Chartered Foresters
20. Chartered Institute of Building
21. Engineering Council
22. Institute of Energy
23. Institution of Structural Engineers
24. Institution of Civil Engineers
25. Institution of Mining Engineers
26. Institution of Mining and Metallurgy
27. Institution of Electrical Engineers
28. Institution of Gas Engineers
29. Institution of Mechanical Engineers

30. Institution of Chemical Engineers
31. Institution of Production Engineers
32. Institution of Marine Engineers
33. Royal Institution of Naval Architects
34. Royal Aeronautical Society
35. Institute of Metals
36. Chartered Institution of Building Services Engineers
37. Institute of Measurement and Control
38. British Computer Society

COUNCIL DIRECTIVE 2003/109/EC
of 25 NOVEMBER 2003

concerning the status of third-country nationals who are long-term residents

THE COUNCIL OF THE EUROPEAN UNION,

Having regard to the Treaty establishing the European Community, and in particular Article 63(3) and (4) thereof,

Having regard to the proposal from the Commission,

Having regard to the opinion of the European Parliament,

Having regard to the opinion of the European Economic and Social Committee,

Having regard to the opinion of the Committee of the Regions,

Whereas:

(1) With a view to the progressive establishment of an area of freedom, security and justice, the Treaty establishing the European Community provides both for the adoption of measures aimed at ensuring the free movement of persons, in conjunction with flanking measures relating to external border controls, asylum and immigration, and for the adoption of measures relating to asylum, immigration and safeguarding the rights of third-country nationals.

(2) The European Council, at its special meeting in Tampere on 15 and 16 October 1999, stated that the legal status of third-country nationals should be approximated to that of Member States' nationals and that a person who has resided legally in a Member State for a period of time to be determined and who holds a long-term residence permit should be granted in that Member State a set of uniform rights which are as near as possible to those enjoyed by citizens of the European Union.

(3) This Directive respects the fundamental rights and observes the principles recognised in particular by the European Convention for the Protection of Human Rights and Fundamental Freedoms and by the Charter of Fundamental Rights of the European Union.

(4) The integration of third-country nationals who are long-term residents in the Member States is a key element in promoting economic and social cohesion, a fundamental objective of the Community stated in the Treaty.

(5) Member States should give effect to the provisions of this Directive without discrimination on the basis of sex, race, colour, ethnic or social origin, genetic characteristics, language, religion or beliefs, political or other opinions, membership of a national minority, fortune, birth, disabilities, age or sexual orientation.

(6) The main criterion for acquiring the status of long-term resident should be the duration of residence in the territory of a Member State. Residence should be both legal and continuous in order to show that the person has put down roots in the country. Provision should be made for a degree of flexibility so that account can be taken of circumstances in which a person might have to leave the territory on a temporary basis.

(7) To acquire long-term resident status, third-country nationals should prove that they have adequate resources and sickness insurance, to avoid becoming a burden for the Member State. Member States, when making an assessment of the possession of stable and regular resources may take into account factors such as contributions to the pension system and fulfilment of tax obligations.

(8) Moreover, third-country nationals who wish to acquire and maintain long-term resident status should not constitute a threat to public policy or public security. The notion of public policy may cover a conviction for committing a serious crime.

(9) Economic considerations should not be a ground for refusing to grant long-term resident status and shall not be considered as interfering with the relevant conditions.

(10) A set of rules governing the procedures for the examination of application for long-term resident status should be laid down. Those procedures should be effective and manageable, taking account of the normal workload of the Member States' administrations, as well as being transparent and fair, in order to offer appropriate legal certainty to those concerned. They should not constitute a means of hindering the exercise of the right of residence.

(11) The acquisition of long-term resident status should be certified by residence permits enabling those concerned to prove their legal status easily and immediately. Such residence permits should also satisfy high-level technical standards, notably as regards protection against falsification and counterfeiting, in order to avoid abuses in the Member State in which the status is acquired and in Member States in which the right of residence is exercised.

(12) In order to constitute a genuine instrument for the integration of long-term residents into society in which they live, long-term residents should enjoy equality of treatment with citizens of the Member State in a wide range of economic and social matters, under the relevant conditions defined by this Directive.

(13) With regard to social assistance, the possibility of limiting the benefits for long-term residents to core benefits is to be understood in the sense that this notion covers at least minimum income support, assistance in case of illness, pregnancy, parental assistance and long-term care. The modalities for granting such benefits should be determined by national law.

(14) The Member States should remain subject to the obligation to afford access for minors to the educational system under conditions similar to those laid down for their nationals.

(15) The notion of study grants in the field of vocational training does not cover measures which are financed under social assistance schemes. Moreover, access to study grants may be dependent on the fact that the person who applies for such grants fulfils on his/her own the conditions for acquiring long-term resident status. As regards the issuing of study grants, Member States may take into account the fact that Union citizens may benefit from this same advantage in the country of origin.

(16) Long-term residents should enjoy reinforced protection against expulsion. This protection is based on the criteria determined by the decisions of the European Court of Human Rights. In order to ensure protection against expulsion Member States should provide for effective legal redress.

(17) Harmonisation of the terms for acquisition of long-term resident status promotes mutual confidence between Member States. Certain Member States issue permits with a permanent or unlimited validity on conditions that are more favourable than those provided for by this Directive. The possibility of applying more favourable national provisions is not excluded by the Treaty. However, for the purposes of this Directive, it should be provided that permits issued on more favourable terms do not confer the right to reside in other Member States.

(18) Establishing the conditions subject to which the right to reside in another Member State may be acquired by third-country nationals who are long-term residents should contribute to the effective attainment of an internal market as an area in which the free movement of persons is ensured. It could also constitute a major factor of mobility, notably on the Union's employment market.

(19) Provision should be made that the right of residence in another Member State may be exercised in order to work in an employed or self-employed capacity, to study or even to settle without exercising any form of economic activity.

(20) Family members should also be able to settle in another Member State with a long-term resident in order to preserve family unity and to avoid hindering the exercise of the long-term resident's right of residence. With regard to the family members who may be authorised to accompany or to join the long-term residents, Member States should pay special attention to the situation of disabled adult children and of first-degree relatives in the direct ascending line who are dependent on them.

(21) The Member State in which a long-term resident intends to exercise his/her right of residence should be able to check that the person concerned meets the conditions for residing in its territory. It should also be able to check that the person concerned does not constitute a threat to public policy, public security or public health.

(22) To avoid rendering the right of residence nugatory, long-term residents should enjoy in the second Member State the same treatment, under the conditions defined by this Directive, they enjoy in the Member State in which they acquired the status. The granting of benefits under social assistance is without prejudice to the possibility for the Member States to withdraw the residence permit if the person concerned no longer fulfils the requirements set by this Directive.

(23) Third-country nationals should be granted the possibility of acquiring long-term resident status in the Member State where they have moved and have decided to settle under comparable conditions to those required for its acquisition in the first Member State.

(24) Since the objectives of the proposed action, namely the determination of terms for granting and withdrawing long-term resident status and the rights pertaining thereto and terms for the exercise of rights of residence by long-term residents in other Member States, cannot be sufficiently achieved by the Member States and can therefore, by reason of the scale and effects of the action, be better achieved by the Community, the Community may adopt measures, in accordance with the principle of subsidiarity as set out in Article 5 of the Treaty. In accordance with the principle of proportionality, as set out in that Article, this Directive does not go beyond what is necessary to achieve those objectives.

(25) In accordance with Articles 1 and 2 of the Protocol on the position of the United Kingdom and Ireland, annexed to the Treaty on European Union and to the Treaty establishing the European Community, and without prejudice to Article 4 of the said Protocol, these Member States are not participating in the adoption of this Directive and are not bound by or subject to its application.

(28) In accordance with Articles 1 and 2 of the Protocol on the position of Denmark, annexed to the Treaty on European Union and the Treaty establishing the European Community, Denmark does not take part in the adoption of this Directive, and is not bound by it or subject to its application,

HAS ADOPTED THIS DIRECTIVE:

CHAPTER I
GENERAL PROVISIONS

Article 1   Subject matter

This Directive determines:

(a) the terms for conferring and withdrawing long-term resident status granted by a Member State in relation to third-country nationals legally residing in its territory, and the rights pertaining thereto; and

(b) the terms of residence in Member States other than the one which conferred long-term status on them for third-country nationals enjoying that status.

Article 2   Definitions

For the purposes of this Directive:

(a) 'third-country national' means any person who is not a citizen of the Union within the meaning of Article 17(1) of the Treaty;

(b) 'long-term resident' means any third-country national who has long-term resident status as provided for under Articles 4 to 7;

(c) 'first Member State' means the Member State which for the first time granted long-term resident status to a third-country national;

(d) 'second Member State' means any Member State other than the one which for the first time granted long-term resident status to a third-country national and in which that long-term resident exercises the right of residence;

(e) 'family members' means the third-country nationals who reside in the Member State concerned in accordance with Council Directive 2003/86/EC of 22 September 2003 on the right to family reunification; (¹)

(f) 'international protection' means international protection as defined in Article 2(a) of Council Directive 2004/83/EC of 29 April 2004 on minimum standards for the qualification and status of third-country nationals or stateless persons as refugees or as persons who otherwise need international protection and the content of the protection granted

(g) 'long-term resident's EC residence permit' means a residence permit issued by the Member State concerned upon the acquisition of long-term resident status.

Article 3 Scope

1. This Directive applies to third-country nationals residing legally in the territory of a Member State.

2. This Directive does not apply to third-country nationals who:

(a) reside in order to pursue studies or vocational training;

(b) are authorised to reside in a Member State on the basis of temporary protection or have applied for authorisation to reside on that basis and are awaiting a decision on their status;

(c) are authorised to reside in a Member State on the basis of a form of protection other than international protection or have applied for authorisation to reside on that basis and are awaiting a decision on their status;

(d) have applied for international protection and whose application has not yet given rise to a final decision;

(e) reside solely on temporary grounds such as au pair or seasonal worker, or as workers posted by a service provider for the purposes of cross-border provision of services, or as cross-border providers of services or in cases where their residence permit has been formally limited;

(f) enjoy a legal status governed by the Vienna Convention on Diplomatic Relations of 1961, the Vienna Convention on Consular Relations of 1963, the Convention of 1969 on Special Missions or the Vienna Convention on the Representation of States in their Relations with International Organisations of a Universal Character of 1975.

3. This Directive shall apply without prejudice to more favourable provisions of:

(a) bilateral and multilateral agreements between the Community or the Community and its Member States, on the one hand, and third countries, on the other;

(b) bilateral agreements already concluded between a Member State and a third country before the date of entry into force of this Directive;

(c) the European Convention on Establishment of 13 December 1955, the European Social Charter of 18 October 1961, the amended European Social Charter of 3 May 1987, the European Convention on the Legal Status of Migrant Workers of 24 November 1977, paragraph 11 of the Schedule to the Convention Relating to the Status of Refugees of 28 July 1951, as amended by the Protocol signed in New York on 31 January 1967, and the European Agreement on Transfer of Responsibility for Refugees of 16 October 1980.

CHAPTER II
LONG-TERM RESIDENT STATUS IN A MEMBER STATE

Article 4   Duration of residence

1. Member States shall grant long-term resident status to third-country nationals who have resided legally and continuously within its territory for five years immediately prior to the submission of the relevant application.

(¹) OJ L 251, 3.10.2003, p. 12.

1a. Member States shall not grant long-term resident status on the basis of international protection in the event of the revocation of, ending of or refusal to renew international protection as laid down in Articles 14(3) and 19(3) of Directive 2004/83/EC.

2. Periods of residence for the reasons referred to in Article 3(2)(e) and (f) shall not be taken into account for the purposes of calculating the period referred to in paragraph 1. Regarding persons to whom international protection has been granted, at least half of the period between the date of the lodging of the application for international protection on the basis of which that international protection was granted and the date of the grant of the residence permit referred to in Article 24 of Directive 2004/83/EC, or the whole of that period if it exceeds 18 months, shall be taken into account in the calculation of the period referred to in paragraph 1.

3. Periods of absence from the territory of the Member State concerned shall not interrupt the period referred to in paragraph 1 and shall be taken into account for its calculation where they are shorter than six consecutive months and do not exceed in total 10 months within the period referred to in paragraph 1.

In cases of specific or exceptional reasons of a temporary nature and in accordance with their national law, Member States may accept that a longer period of absence than that which is referred to in the first subparagraph shall not interrupt the period referred to in paragraph 1. In such cases Member States shall not take into account the relevant period of absence in the calculation of the period referred to in paragraph 1.

By way of derogation from the second subparagraph, Member States may take into account in the calculation of the total period referred to in paragraph 1 periods of absence relating to secondment for employment purposes, including the provision of cross-border services.

Article 5   Conditions for acquiring long-term resident status

1. Member States shall require third-country nationals to provide evidence that they have, for themselves and for dependent family members:

   (a) stable and regular resources which are sufficient to maintain himself/herself and the members of his/her family, without recourse to the social assistance system of the Member State concerned. Member States shall evaluate these resources by reference to their nature and regularity and may take into account the level of minimum wages and pensions prior to the application for long-term resident status;

   (b) sickness insurance in respect of all risks normally covered for his/her own nationals in the Member State concerned.

2. Member States may require third-country nationals to comply with integration conditions, in accordance with national law.

Article 6   Public policy and public security

1. Member States may refuse to grant long-term resident status on grounds of public policy or public security.

   When taking the relevant decision, the Member State shall consider the severity or type of offence against public policy or public security, or the danger that emanates from the person concerned, while also having proper regard to the duration of residence and to the existence of links with the country of residence.

2. The refusal referred to in paragraph 1 shall not be founded on economic considerations.

Article 7   Acquisition of long-term resident status

1. To acquire long-term resident status, the third-country national concerned shall lodge an application with the competent authorities of the Member State in which he/she resides. The application shall be accompanied by documentary evidence to be determined by national law that he/she meets the conditions set out in Articles 4 and 5 as well as, if required, by a valid travel document or its certified copy.

   The evidence referred to in the first subparagraph may also include documentation with regard to appropriate accommodation.

2. The competent national authorities shall give the applicant written notification of the decision as soon as possible and in any event no later than six months from the date on which the application was lodged. Any such decision shall be notified to the third-country national concerned in accordance with the notification procedures under the relevant national legislation.

    In exceptional circumstances linked to the complexity of the examination of the application, the time limit referred to in the first subparagraph may be extended.

    In addition, the person concerned shall be informed about his/her rights and obligations under this Directive.

    Any consequences of no decision being taken by the end of the period provided for in this provision shall be determined by national legislation of the relevant Member State.

3. If the conditions provided for by Articles 4 and 5 are met, and the person does not represent a threat within the meaning of Article 6, the Member State concerned shall grant the third-country national concerned long-term resident status.

Article 8 Long-term resident's EC residence permit

1. The status as long-term resident shall be permanent, subject to Article 9.

2. Member States shall issue a long-term resident's EC residence permit to long-term residents. The permit shall be valid at least for five years; it shall, upon application if required, be automatically renewable on expiry.

3. A long-term resident's EC residence permit may be issued in the form of a sticker or of a separate document. It shall be issued in accordance with the rules and standard model as set out in Council Regulation (EC) No 1030/2002 of 13 June 2002 laying down a uniform format for residence permits for third-country nationals[1]. Under the heading 'type of permit', the Member States shall enter 'long-term resident − EC'.

4. Where a Member State issues a long-term resident's EU residence permit to a third-country national to whom it granted international protection, it shall enter the following remark in that long-term resident's EU residence permit, under the heading 'Remarks': 'International protection granted by [name of the Member State] on [date]'.

5. Where a long-term resident's EU residence permit is issued by a second Member State to a third-country national who already has a long-term resident's EU residence permit issued by another Member State which contains the remark referred to in paragraph 4, the second Member State shall enter the same remark in the long-term resident's EU residence permit.

    Before the second Member State enters the remark referred to in paragraph 4, it shall request the Member State mentioned in that remark to provide information as to whether the long-term resident is still a beneficiary of international protection. The Member State mentioned in the remark shall reply no later than 1 month after receiving the request for information. Where international protection has been withdrawn by a final decision, the second Member State shall not enter that remark.

6. Where, in accordance with the relevant international instruments or national law, responsibility for the international protection of the long-term resident was transferred to the second Member State after the long-term resident's EU residence permit referred to in paragraph 5 was issued, the second Member State shall amend accordingly the remark referred to in paragraph 4 no later than 3 months after the transfer.

Article 9 Withdrawal or loss of status

1. Long-term residents shall no longer be entitled to maintain long-term resident status in the following cases:

    (a) detection of fraudulent acquisition of long-term resident status;

    (b) adoption of an expulsion measure under the conditions provided for in Article 12;

    (c) in the event of absence from the territory of the Community for a period of 12 consecutive months.

2. By way of derogation from paragraph 1(c), Member States may provide that absences exceeding 12 consecutive months or for specific or exceptional reasons shall not entail withdrawal or loss of status.

---

[1] OJ L 157, 15.6.2002, p. 1.

3. Member States may provide that the long-term resident shall no longer be entitled to maintain his/her long-term resident status in cases where he/she constitutes a threat to public policy, in consideration of the seriousness of the offences he/ she committed, but such threat is not a reason for expulsion within the meaning of Article 12.

3a. Member States may withdraw the long-term resident status in the event of the revocation of, ending of or refusal to renew international protection as laid down in Articles 14(3) and 19(3) of Directive 2004/83/EC if the long-term resident status was obtained on the basis of international protection.

4. The long-term resident who has resided in another Member State in accordance with Chapter III shall no longer be entitled to maintain his/her long-term resident status acquired in the first Member State when such a status is granted in another Member State pursuant to Article 23.

In any case after six years of absence from the territory of the Member State that granted long-term resident status the person concerned shall no longer be entitled to maintain his/her long term resident status in the said Member State.

By way of derogation from the second subparagraph the Member State concerned may provide that for specific reasons the long-term resident shall maintain his/her status in the said Member State in case of absences for a period exceeding six years.

5. With regard to the cases referred to in paragraph 1(c) and in paragraph 4, Member States who have granted the status shall provide for a facilitated procedure for the re-acquisition of long-term resident status.

The said procedure shall apply in particular to the cases of persons that have resided in a second Member State on grounds of pursuit of studies.

The conditions and the procedure for the re-acquisition of long-term resident status shall be determined by national law.

6. The expiry of a long-term resident's EC residence permit shall in no case entail withdrawal or loss of long-term resident status.

7. Where the withdrawal or loss of long-term resident status does not lead to removal, the Member State shall authorise the person concerned to remain in its territory if he/she fulfils the conditions provided for in its national legislation and/or if he/she does not constitute a threat to public policy or public security.

Article 10 Procedural guarantees

1. Reasons shall be given for any decision rejecting an application for long-term resident status or withdrawing that status. Any such decision shall be notified to the third-country national concerned in accordance with the notification procedures under the relevant national legislation. The notification shall specify the redress procedures available and the time within which he/she may act.

2. Where an application for long-term resident status is rejected or that status is withdrawn or lost or the residence permit is not renewed, the person concerned shall have the right to mount a legal challenge in the Member State concerned.

Article 11 Equal treatment

1. Long-term residents shall enjoy equal treatment with nationals as regards:
   (a) access to employment and self-employed activity, provided such activities do not entail even occasional involvement in the exercise of public authority, and conditions of employment and working conditions, including conditions regarding dismissal and remuneration;
   (b) education and vocational training, including study grants in accordance with national law;
   (c) recognition of professional diplomas, certificates and other qualifications, in accordance with the relevant national procedures;
   (d) social security, social assistance and social protection as defined by national law;
   (e) tax benefits;
   (f) access to goods and services and the supply of goods and services made available to the public and to procedures for obtaining housing;
   (g) freedom of association and affiliation and membership of an organisation representing workers or employers or of any organisation whose members are engaged in a specific occupation, including the benefits conferred by such organisations, without prejudice to the national provisions on public policy and public security;

(h)   free access to the entire territory of the Member State concerned, within the limits provided for by the national legislation for reasons of security.

2.   With respect to the provisions of paragraph 1, points (b), (d), (e), (f) and (g), the Member State concerned may restrict equal treatment to cases where the registered or usual place of residence of the long-term resident, or that of family members for whom he/she claims benefits, lies within the territory of the Member State concerned.

3.   Member States may restrict equal treatment with nationals in the following cases:

(a)   Member States may retain restrictions to access to employment or self-employed activities in cases where, in accordance with existing national or Community legislation, these activities are reserved to nationals, EU or EEA citizens;

(b)   Member States may require proof of appropriate language proficiency for access to education and training. Access to university may be subject to the fulfilment of specific educational prerequisites.

4.   Member States may limit equal treatment in respect of social assistance and social protection to core benefits.

4a.   As far as the Member State which granted international protection is concerned, paragraphs 3 and 4 shall be without prejudice to Directive 2004/83/EC.

5.   Member States may decide to grant access to additional benefits in the areas referred to in paragraph 1.

Member States may also decide to grant equal treatment with regard to areas not covered in paragraph 1.

Article 12 Protection against expulsion

1.   Member States may take a decision to expel a long-term resident solely where he/she constitutes an actual and sufficiently serious threat to public policy or public security.

2.   The decision referred to in paragraph 1 shall not be founded on economic considerations.

3.   Before taking a decision to expel a long-term resident, Member States shall have regard to the following factors:

(a)   the duration of residence in their territory;

(b)   the age of the person concerned;

(c)   the consequences for the person concerned and family members;

(d)   links with the country of residence or the absence of links with the country of origin.

3a.   Where a Member State decides to expel a long-term resident whose long-term resident's EU residence permit contains the remark referred to in Article 8(4), it shall request the Member State mentioned in that remark to confirm whether the person concerned is still a beneficiary of international protection in that Member State. The Member State mentioned in the remark shall reply no later than 1 month after receiving the request for information.

3b.   If the long-term resident is still a beneficiary of international protection in the Member State mentioned in the remark, that person shall be expelled to that Member State, which shall, without prejudice to the applicable Union or national law and to the principle of family unity, immediately readmit, without formalities, that beneficiary and his/her family members.

3c.   By way of derogation from paragraph 3b, the Member State which adopted the expulsion decision shall retain the right to remove, in accordance with its international obligations, the long-term resident to a country other than the Member State which granted international protection where that person fulfils the conditions specified in Article 21(2) of Directive 2004/83/EC.

4.   Where an expulsion decision has been adopted, a judicial redress procedure shall be available to the long-term resident in the Member State concerned.

5.   Legal aid shall be given to long-term residents lacking adequate resources, on the same terms as apply to nationals of the State where they reside.

6.   This Article shall be without prejudice to Article 21(1) of Directive 2004/83/EC.

Article 13 More favourable national provisions

Member States may issue residence permits of permanent or unlimited validity on terms that are more favourable than those laid down by this Directive. Such residence permits shall not confer the right of residence in the other Member States as provided by Chapter III of this Directive.

DIRECTIVE 96/71/EC OF THE EUROPEAN PARLIAMENT AND OF THE COUNCIL OF 16 DECEMBER 1996
concerning the posting of workers in the framework of the provision of services
[1996] OJ L18/1

Article 1　Subject-matter and scope

-1.　This Directive shall ensure the protection of posted workers during their posting in relation to the freedom to provide services, by laying down mandatory provisions regarding working conditions and the protection of workers' health and safety that must be respected.

-1a.　This Directive shall not in any way affect the exercise of fundamental rights as recognised in the Member States and at Union level, including the right or freedom to strike or to take other action covered by the specific industrial relations systems in Member States, in accordance with national law and/or practice. Nor does it affect the right to negotiate, to conclude and enforce collective agreements, or to take collective action in accordance with national law and/or practice.

1.　This Directive shall apply to undertakings established in a Member State which, in the framework of the transnational provision of services, post workers, in accordance with paragraph 3, to the territory of a Member State.

2.　This Directive shall not apply to merchant navy undertakings as regards seagoing personnel.

3.　This Directive shall apply to the extent that the undertakings referred to in paragraph 1 take one of the following transnational measures:

(a)　post workers to the territory of a Member State on their account and under their direction, under a contract concluded between the undertaking making the posting and the party for whom the services are intended, operating in that Member State, provided there is an employment relationship between the undertaking making the posting and the worker during the period of posting; or

(b)　post workers to an establishment or to an undertaking owned by the group in the territory of a Member State, provided there is an employment relationship between the undertaking making the posting and the worker during the period of posting; or

(c)　being a temporary employment undertaking or placement agency, hire out a worker to a user undertaking established or operating in the territory of a Member State, provided that there is an employment relationship between the temporary employment undertaking or placement agency and the worker during the period of posting.

Where a worker who has been hired out by a temporary employment undertaking or placement agency to a user undertaking as referred to in point (c) is to carry out work in the framework of the transnational provision of services within the meaning of point (a), (b) or (c) by the user undertaking in the territory of a Member State other than where the worker normally works for the temporary employment undertaking or placement agency, or for the user undertaking, the worker shall be considered to be posted to the territory of that Member State by the temporary employment undertaking or placement agency with which the worker is in an employment relationship. The temporary employment undertaking or placement agency shall be considered to be an undertaking as referred to in paragraph 1 and shall fully comply with the relevant provisions of this Directive and Directive 2014/67/EU of the European Parliament and of the Council (1).

---

(1) Directive 2014/67/EU of the European Parliament and of the Council of 15 May 2014 on the enforcement of Directive 96/71/EC concerning the posting of workers in the framework of the provision of services and amending Regulation (EU) No 1024/2012 on administrative cooperation through the Internal Market Information System ('the IMI Regulation') (OJ L 159, 28.5.2014, p. 11).

The user undertaking shall inform the temporary employment undertaking or placement agency which hired out the worker in due time before commencement of the work referred to in the second subparagraph.

4. Undertakings established in a non-member State must not be given more favourable treatment than undertakings established in a Member State.

Article 2   Definition

1. For the purposes of this Directive, 'posted worker' means a worker who, for a limited period, carries out his work in the territory of a Member State other than the State in which he normally works.

2. For the purposes of this Directive, the definition of a worker is that which applies in the law of the Member State to whose territory the worker is posted.

Article 3   Terms and conditions of employment

1. Member States shall ensure, irrespective of which law applies to the employment relationship, that undertakings as referred to in Article 1(1) guarantee, on the basis of equality of treatment, workers who are posted to their territory the terms and conditions of employment covering the following matters which are laid down in the Member State where the work is carried out:

   — by law, regulation or administrative provision, and/or
   — by collective agreements or arbitration awards which have been declared universally applicable or otherwise apply in accordance with paragraph 8:

   (a) maximum work periods and minimum rest periods;
   (b) minimum paid annual leave;
   (c) remuneration, including overtime rates; this point does not apply to supplementary occupational retirement pension schemes;
   (d) the conditions of hiring-out of workers, in particular the supply of workers by temporary employment undertakings;
   (e) health, safety and hygiene at work;
   (f) protective measures with regard to the terms and conditions of employment of pregnant women or women who have recently given birth, of children and of young people;
   (g) equality of treatment between men and women and other provisions on non-discrimination;
   (h) the conditions of workers' accommodation where provided by the employer to workers away from their regular place of work;
   (i) allowances or reimbursement of expenditure to cover travel, board and lodging expenses for workers away from home for professional reasons.

   Point (i) shall apply exclusively to travel, board and lodging expenditure incurred by posted workers where they are required to travel to and from their regular place of work in the Member State to whose territory they are posted, or where they are temporarily sent by their employer from that regular place of work to another place of work.

   For the purposes of this Directive, the concept of remuneration shall be determined by the national law and/or practice of the Member State to whose territory the worker is posted and means all the constituent elements of remuneration rendered mandatory by national law, regulation or administrative provision, or by collective agreements or arbitration awards which, in that Member State, have been declared universally applicable or otherwise apply in accordance with paragraph 8.

   Without prejudice to Article 5 of Directive 2014/67/EU, Member States shall publish the information on the terms and conditions of employment, in accordance with national law and/or practice, without undue delay and in a transparent manner, on the single official national website referred to in that Article, including the constituent elements of remuneration as referred to in the third subparagraph of this paragraph and all the terms and conditions of employment in accordance with paragraph 1a of this Article.

Member States shall ensure that the information provided on the single official national website is accurate and up to date. The Commission shall publish on its website the addresses of the single official national websites.

Where, contrary to Article 5 of Directive 2014/67/EU, the information on the single official national website does not indicate which terms and conditions of employment are to be applied, that circumstance shall be taken into account, in accordance with national law and/or practice, in determining penalties in the event of infringements of the national provisions adopted pursuant to this Directive, to the extent necessary to ensure the proportionality thereof.

1a.   Where the effective duration of a posting exceeds 12 months, Member States shall ensure, irrespective of which law applies to the employment relationship, that undertakings as referred to in Article 1(1) guarantee, on the basis of equality of treatment, workers who are posted to their territory, in addition to the terms and conditions of employment referred to in paragraph 1 of this Article, all the applicable terms and conditions of employment which are laid down in the Member State where the work is carried out:

—   by law, regulation or administrative provision, and/or

—   by collective agreements or arbitration awards which have been declared universally applicable or otherwise apply in accordance with paragraph 8.

The first subparagraph of this paragraph shall not apply to the following matters:

(a)   procedures, formalities and conditions of the conclusion and termination of the employment contract, including non-competition clauses;

(b)   supplementary occupational retirement pension schemes.

Where the service provider submits a motivated notification, the Member State where the service is provided shall extend the period referred to in the first subparagraph to 18 months.

Where an undertaking as referred to in Article 1(1) replaces a posted worker by another posted worker performing the same task at the same place, the duration of the posting shall, for the purposes of this paragraph, be the cumulative duration of the posting periods of the individual posted workers concerned.

The concept of 'the same task at the same place' referred to in the fourth subparagraph of this paragraph shall be determined taking into consideration, inter alia, the nature of the service to be provided, the work to be performed and the address(es) of the workplace.

1b.   Member States shall provide that the undertakings referred to in point (c) of Article 1(3) guarantee posted workers the terms and conditions of employment which apply pursuant to Article 5 of Directive 2008/104/EC of the European Parliament and of the Council (¹) to temporary agency workers hired-out by temporary-work agencies established in the Member State where the work is carried out.

The user undertaking shall inform the undertakings referred to in point (c) of Article 1(3) of the terms and conditions of employment that it applies regarding the working conditions and remuneration to the extent covered by the first subparagraph of this paragraph.

2.   In the case of initial assembly and/or first installation of goods where this is an integral part of a contract for the supply of goods and necessary for taking the goods supplied into use and carried out by the skilled and/or specialist workers of the supplying undertaking, the first subparagraph of paragraph 1 (b) and (c) shall not apply, if the period of posting does not exceed eight days.

This provision shall not apply to activities in the field of building work listed in the Annex.

3.   Member States may, after consulting employers and labour, in accordance with the traditions and practices of each Member State, decide not to apply the first subparagraph of paragraph 1 (c) in the cases referred to in Article 1 (3) (a) and (b) when the length of the posting does not exceed one month.

4.   Member States may, in accordance with national laws and/or practices, provide that exemptions may be made from the first subparagraph of paragraph 1 (c) in the cases

---

(¹) Directive 2008/104/EC of the European Parliament and of the Council of 19 November 2008 on temporary agency work (OJ L 327, 5.12.2008, p. 9).

referred to in Article 1 (3) (a) and (b) and from a decision by a Member State within the meaning of paragraph 3 of this Article, by means of collective agreements within the meaning of paragraph 8 of this Article, concerning one or more sectors of activity, where the length of the posting does not exceed one month.

5. Member States may provide for exemptions to be granted from the first subparagraph of paragraph 1 (b) and (c) in the cases referred to in Article 1 (3) (a) and (b) on the grounds that the amount of work to be done is not significant.

   Member States availing themselves of the option referred to in the first subparagraph shall lay down the criteria which the work to be performed must meet in order to be considered as 'non-significant'.

6. The length of the posting shall be calculated on the basis of a reference period of one year from the beginning of the posting.

   For the purpose of such calculations, account shall be taken of any previous periods for which the post has been filled by a posted worker.

7. Paragraphs 1 to 6 shall not prevent the application of terms and conditions of employment which are more favourable to workers.

   Allowances specific to the posting shall be considered to be part of remuneration, unless they are paid in reimbursement of expenditure actually incurred on account of the posting, such as expenditure on travel, board and lodging. The employer shall, without prejudice to point (i) of the first subparagraph of paragraph 1, reimburse the posted worker for such expenditure in accordance with the national law and/or practice applicable to the employment relationship.

   Where the terms and conditions of employment applicable to the employment relationship do not determine whether and, if so, which elements of the allowance specific to the posting are paid in reimbursement of expenditure actually incurred on account of the posting or which are part of remuneration, then the entire allowance shall be considered to be paid in reimbursement of expenditure.

8. 'Collective agreements or arbitration awards which have been declared universally applicable' means collective agreements or arbitration awards which must be observed by all undertakings in the geographical area and in the profession or industry concerned.

   In the absence of, or in addition to, a system for declaring collective agreements or arbitration awards to be of universal application within the meaning of the first subparagraph, Member States may, if they so decide, base themselves on:

   — collective agreements or arbitration awards which are generally applicable to all similar undertakings in the geographical area and in the profession or industry concerned, and/or

   — collective agreements which have been concluded by the most representative employers' and labour organisations at national level and which are applied throughout national territory,

   Provided that their application to undertakings as referred to in Article 1(1) ensures equality of treatment on matters listed in the first subparagraph of paragraph 1 of this Article and, where applicable, with regard to the terms and conditions of employment to be guaranteed posted workers in accordance with paragraph 1a of this Article, between those undertakings and the other undertakings referred to in this subparagraph which are in a similar position. Equality of treatment, within the meaning of this Article, shall be deemed to exist where national undertakings in a similar position:

   — are subject, in the place in question or in the sector concerned, to the same obligations as undertakings as referred to in Article 1(1) as regards the matters listed in the first subparagraph of paragraph 1 of this Article and, where applicable, as regards the terms and conditions of employment to be guaranteed posted workers in accordance with paragraph 1a of this Article, and

   — are required to fulfil such obligations with the same effects.

9. Member States may require undertakings as referred to in Article 1(1) to guarantee workers referred to in point (c) of Article 1(3), in addition to the terms and conditions of employment referred to in paragraph 1b of this Article, other terms and conditions that apply to temporary agency workers in the Member State where the work is carried out.

10. This Directive shall not preclude the application by Member States, in compliance with the Treaties, to national undertakings and to the undertakings of other Member States, on the basis of equality of treatment, of terms and conditions of employment on matters other than those referred to in the first subparagraph of paragraph 1 in the case of public policy provisions.

Article 4 Cooperation on information

1. For the purposes of implementing this Directive, Member States shall, in accordance with national legislation and/or practice, designate one or more liaison offices or one or more competent national bodies.

2. Member States shall make provision for cooperation between the competent authorities or bodies, including public authorities, which, in accordance with national law, are responsible for monitoring the terms and conditions of employment referred to in Article 3, including at Union level. Such cooperation shall in particular consist in replying to reasoned requests from those authorities or bodies for information on the transnational hiring-out of workers, and in tackling manifest abuses or possible cases of unlawful activities, such as transnational cases of undeclared work and bogus self-employment linked to the posting of workers. Where the competent authority or body in the Member State from which the worker is posted does not possess the information requested by the competent authority or body of the Member State to whose territory the worker is posted, it shall seek to obtain that information from other authorities or bodies in that Member State. In the event of persistent delays in the provision of such information to the Member State to whose territory the worker is posted, the Commission shall be informed and shall take appropriate measures.

   The Commission and the public authorities referred to in the first subparagraph shall cooperate closely in order to examine any difficulties which might arise in the application of Article 3 (10).

   Mutual administrative assistance shall be provided free of charge.

3. Each Member State shall take the appropriate measures to make the information on the terms and conditions of employment referred to in Article 3 generally available.

4. Each Member State shall notify the other Member States and the Commission of the liaison offices and/or competent bodies referred to in paragraph 1.

Article 5 Monitoring, control and enforcement

The Member State to whose territory the worker is posted and the Member State from which the worker is posted shall be responsible for the monitoring, control and enforcement of the obligations laid down in this Directive and in Directive 2014/67/EU and shall take appropriate measures in the event of failure to comply with this Directive.

Member States shall lay down the rules on penalties applicable to infringements of national provisions adopted pursuant to this Directive and shall take all measures necessary to ensure that they are implemented. The penalties provided for shall be effective, proportionate and dissuasive.

Member States shall in particular ensure that adequate procedures are available to workers and/or workers' representatives for the enforcement of obligations under this Directive.

Where, following an overall assessment made pursuant to Article 4 of Directive 2014/67/EU by a Member State, it is established that an undertaking is improperly or fraudulently creating the impression that the situation of a worker falls within the scope of this Directive, that Member State shall ensure that the worker benefits from relevant law and practice.

Member States shall ensure that this Article does not lead to the worker concerned being subject to less favourable conditions than those applicable to posted workers.

Article 6 Jurisdiction

In order to enforce the right to the terms and conditions of employment guaranteed in Article 3, judicial proceedings may be instituted in the Member State in whose territory the worker is or was posted, without prejudice, where applicable, to the right, under existing international conventions on jurisdiction, to institute proceedings in another State.

Article 7   Implementation

Member States shall adopt the laws, regulations and administrative provisions necessary to comply with this Directive by 16 December 1999 at the latest. They shall forthwith inform the Commission thereof.

When Member States adopt these provisions, they shall contain a reference to this Directive or shall be accompanied by such reference on the occasion of their official publication. The methods of making such reference shall be laid down by Member States.

Article 8   Commission review

By 16 December 2001 at the latest, the Commission shall review the operation of this Directive with a view to proposing the necessary amendments to the Council where appropriate.

Article 9

This Directive is addressed to the Member States.

ANNEX

The activities referred to in Article 3(2) include all building work related to the construction, repair, upkeep, alteration or demolition of buildings, and in particular the following work:

1. excavation
2. earthmoving
3. actual building work
4. assembly and dismantling of prefabricated elements
5. fitting out or installation
6. alterations
7. renovation
8. repairs
9. dismantling
10. demolition
11. maintenance
12. upkeep, painting and cleaning work
13. improvements.

FREE MOVEMENT OF SERVICES

DIRECTIVE 2006/123/EC OF THE EUROPEAN PARLIAMENT AND OF THE COUNCIL of 12 DECEMBER 2006
on services in the internal market
[2006] OJ L376/36

CHAPTER I
GENERAL PROVISIONS

Article 1 Subject matter

1. This Directive establishes general provisions facilitating the exercise of the freedom of establishment for service providers and the free movement of services, while maintaining a high quality of services.
2. This Directive does not deal with the liberalisation of services of general economic interest, reserved to public or private entities, nor with the privatisation of public entities providing services.
3. This Directive does not deal with the abolition of monopolies providing services nor with aids granted by Member States which are covered by Community rules on competition. This Directive does not affect the freedom of Member States to define, in conformity with Community law, what they consider to be services of general economic interest, how those services should be organised and financed, in compliance with the State aid rules, and what specific obligations they should be subject to.
4. This Directive does not affect measures taken at Community level or at national level, in conformity with Community law, to protect or promote cultural or linguistic diversity or media pluralism.
5. This Directive does not affect Member States' rules of criminal law. However, Member States may not restrict the freedom to provide services by applying criminal law provisions which specifically regulate or affect access to or exercise of a service activity in circumvention of the rules laid down in this Directive.
6. This Directive does not affect labour law, that is any legal or contractual provision concerning employment conditions, working conditions, including health and safety at work and the relationship between employers and workers, which Member States apply in accordance with national law which respects Community law. Equally, this Directive does not affect the social security legislation of the Member States.
7. This Directive does not affect the exercise of fundamental rights as recognised in the Member States and by Community law. Nor does it affect the right to negotiate, conclude and enforce collective agreements and to take industrial action in accordance with national law and practices which respect Community law.

Article 2 Scope

1. This Directive shall apply to services supplied by providers established in a Member State.
2. This Directive shall not apply to the following activities:
   (a) non-economic services of general interest;
   (b) financial services, such as banking, credit, insurance and re-insurance, occupational or personal pensions, securities, investment funds, payment and investment advice, including the services listed in Annex I to Directive 2006/48/EC;
   (c) electronic communications services and networks, and associated facilities and services, with respect to matters covered by Directives 2002/19/EC, 2002/20/EC, 2002/21/EC, 2002/22/EC and 2002/58/EC;
   (d) services in the field of transport, including port services, falling within the scope of Title V of the Treaty;
   (e) services of temporary-work agencies;
   (f) healthcare services whether or not they are provided via healthcare facilities, and regardless of the ways in which they are organised and financed at national level or whether they are public or private;
   (g) audiovisual services, including cinematographic services, whatever their mode of production, distribution and transmission, and radio broadcasting;

(h)   gambling activities which involve wagering a stake with pecuniary value in games of chance, including lotteries, gambling in casinos and betting transactions;

(i)   activities which are connected with the exercise of official authority as set out in Article 45 of the Treaty;

(j)   social services relating to social housing, childcare and support of families and persons permanently or temporarily in need which are provided by the State, by providers mandated by the State or by charities recognised as such by the State;

(k)   private security services;

(l)   services provided by notaries and bailiffs, who are appointed by an official act of government.

3.   This Directive shall not apply to the field of taxation.

Article 3   Relationship with other provisions of Community law

1.   If the provisions of this Directive conflict with a provision of another Community act governing specific aspects of access to or exercise of a service activity in specific sectors or for specific professions, the provision of the other Community act shall prevail and shall apply to those specific sectors or professions. These include:

(a)   Directive 96/71/EC;

(b)   Regulation (EEC) No 1408/71;

(c)   Council Directive 89/552/EEC of 3 October 1989 on the coordination of certain provisions laid down by law, regulation or administrative action in Member States concerning the pursuit of television broadcasting activities;

(d)   Directive 2005/36/EC.

2.   This Directive does not concern rules of private international law, in particular rules governing the law applicable to contractual and non contractual obligations, including those which guarantee that consumers benefit from the protection granted to them by the consumer protection rules laid down in the consumer legislation in force in their Member State.

3.   Member States shall apply the provisions of this Directive in compliance with the rules of the Treaty on the right of establishment and the free movement of services.

Article 4   Definitions

For the purposes of this Directive, the following definitions shall apply:

(1)   'service' means any self-employed economic activity, normally provided for remuneration, as referred to in Article 50 of the Treaty;

(2)   'provider' means any natural person who is a national of a Member State, or any legal person as referred to in Article 48 of the Treaty and established in a Member State, who offers or provides a service;

(3)   'recipient' means any natural person who is a national of a Member State or who benefits from rights conferred upon him by Community acts, or any legal person as referred to in Article 48 of the Treaty and established in a Member State, who, for professional or non-professional purposes, uses, or wishes to use, a service;

(4)   'Member State of establishment' means the Member State in whose territory the provider of the service concerned is established;

(5)   'establishment' means the actual pursuit of an economic activity, as referred to in Article 43 of the Treaty, by the provider for an indefinite period and through a stable infrastructure from where the business of providing services is actually carried out;

(6)   'authorisation scheme' means any procedure under which a provider or recipient is in effect required to take steps in order to obtain from a competent authority a formal decision, or an implied decision, concerning access to a service activity or the exercise thereof;

(7)   'requirement' means any obligation, prohibition, condition or limit provided for in the laws, regulations or administrative provisions of the Member States or in consequence of case-law, administrative practice, the rules of professional bodies, or the collective rules of professional associations or other professional organisations, adopted in the exercise of their legal autonomy; rules laid down in collective agreements negotiated by the social partners shall not as such be seen as requirements within the meaning of this Directive;

(8)   'overriding reasons relating to the public interest' means reasons recognised as such in the case law of the Court of Justice, including the following grounds: public policy; public security; public safety; public health; preserving the financial equilibrium of the social security system; the protection of consumers, recipients of services and workers;

fairness of trade transactions; combating fraud; the protection of the environment and the urban environment; the health of animals; intellectual property; the conservation of the national historic and artistic heritage; social policy objectives and cultural policy objectives;

(9) 'competent authority' means any body or authority which has a supervisory or regulatory role in a Member State in relation to service activities, including, in particular, administrative authorities, including courts acting as such, professional bodies, and those professional associations or other professional organisations which, in the exercise of their legal autonomy, regulate in a collective manner access to service activities or the exercise thereof;

(10) 'Member State where the service is provided' means the Member State where the service is supplied by a provider established in another Member State;

(11) 'regulated profession' means a professional activity or a group of professional activities as referred to in Article 3(1)(a) of Directive 2005/36/EC;

(12) 'commercial communication' means any form of communication designed to promote, directly or indirectly, the goods, services or image of an undertaking, organisation or person engaged in commercial, industrial or craft activity or practising a regulated profession. The following do not in themselves constitute commercial communications:

(a) information enabling direct access to the activity of the undertaking, organisation or person, including in particular a domain name or an electronic-mailing address;

(b) communications relating to the goods, services or image of the undertaking, organisation or person, compiled in an independent manner, particularly when provided for no financial consideration.

CHAPTER II
ADMINISTRATIVE SIMPLIFICATION

Article 5   Simplification of procedures

1. Member States shall examine the procedures and formalities applicable to access to a service activity and to the exercise thereof. Where procedures and formalities examined under this paragraph are not sufficiently simple, Member States shall simplify them.

2. The Commission may introduce harmonised forms at Community level, in accordance with the procedure referred to in Article 40(2). These forms shall be equivalent to certificates, attestations and any other documents required of a provider.

3. Where Member States require a provider or recipient to supply a certificate, attestation or any other document proving that a requirement has been satisfied, they shall accept any document from another Member State which serves an equivalent purpose or from which it is clear that the requirement in question has been satisfied. They may not require a document from another Member State to be produced in its original form, or as a certified copy or as a certified translation, save in the cases provided for in other Community instruments or where such a requirement is justified by an overriding reason relating to the public interest, including public order and security.
   The first subparagraph shall not affect the right of Member States to require non-certified translations of documents in one of their official languages.

4. Paragraph 3 shall not apply to the documents referred to in Article 7(2) and 50 of Directive 2005/36/EC, in Articles 45(3), 46, 49 and 50 of Directive 2004/18/EC of the European Parliament and of the Council of 31 March 2004 on the coordination of procedures for the award of public works contracts, public supply contracts and public service contracts, in Article 3(2) of Directive 98/5/EC of the European Parliament and of the Council of 16 February 1998 to facilitate practice of the profession of lawyer on a permanent basis in a Member State other than that in which the qualification was obtained, in the First Council Directive 68/151/EEC of 9 March 1968 on coordination of safeguards which, for the protection of the interests of members and others, are required by Member States of companies within the meaning of the second paragraph of Article 58 of the Treaty, with a view to making such safeguards equivalent throughout the Community and in the Eleventh Council Directive 89/666/EEC of 21 December 1989 concerning disclosure requirements in respect of branches opened in a Member State by certain types of company governed by the law of another State.

Article 6 Points of single contact

1. Member States shall ensure that it is possible for providers to complete the following procedures and formalities through points of single contact:

    (a) all procedures and formalities needed for access to his service activities, in particular, all declarations, notifications or applications necessary for authorisation from the competent authorities, including applications for inclusion in a register, a roll or a database, or for registration with a professional body or association;

    (b) any applications for authorisation needed to exercise his service activities.

2. The establishment of points of single contact shall be without prejudice to the allocation of functions and powers among the authorities within national systems.

Article 7 Right to information

1. Member States shall ensure that the following information is easily accessible to providers and recipients through the points of single contact:

    (a) requirements applicable to providers established in their territory, in particular those requirements concerning the procedures and formalities to be completed in order to access and to exercise service activities;

    (b) the contact details of the competent authorities enabling the latter to be contacted directly, including the details of those authorities responsible for matters concerning the exercise of service activities;

    (c) the means of, and conditions for, accessing public registers and databases on providers and services;

    (d) the means of redress which are generally available in the event of dispute between the competent authorities and the provider or the recipient, or between a provider and a recipient or between providers;

    (e) the contact details of the associations or organisations, other than the competent authorities, from which providers or recipients may obtain practical assistance.

2. Member States shall ensure that it is possible for providers and recipients to receive, at their request, assistance from the competent authorities, consisting in information on the way in which the requirements referred to in point (a) of paragraph 1 are generally interpreted and applied. Where appropriate, such advice shall include a simple step-by-step guide. The information shall be provided in plain and intelligible language.

3. Member States shall ensure that the information and assistance referred to in paragraphs 1 and 2 are provided in a clear and unambiguous manner, that they are easily accessible at a distance and by electronic means and that they are kept up to date.

4. Member States shall ensure that the points of single contact and the competent authorities respond as quickly as possible to any request for information or assistance as referred to in paragraphs 1 and 2 and, in cases where the request is faulty or unfounded, inform the applicant accordingly without delay.

5. Member States and the Commission shall take accompanying measures in order to encourage points of single contact to make the information provided for in this Article available in other Community languages. This does not interfere with Member States' legislation on the use of languages.

6. The obligation for competent authorities to assist providers and recipients does not require those authorities to provide legal advice in individual cases but concerns only general information on the way in which requirements are usually interpreted or applied.

Article 8 Procedures by electronic means

1. Member States shall ensure that all procedures and formalities relating to access to a service activity and to the exercise thereof may be easily completed, at a distance and by electronic means, through the relevant point of single contact and with the relevant competent authorities.

2. Paragraph 1 shall not apply to the inspection of premises on which the service is provided or of equipment used by the provider or to physical examination of the capability or of the personal integrity of the provider or of his responsible staff.

3. The Commission shall, in accordance with the procedure referred to in Article 40(2), adopt detailed rules for the implementation of paragraph 1 of this Article with a view to facilitating the interoperability of information systems and use of procedures by electronic means between Member States, taking into account common standards developed at Community level.

CHAPTER III
FREEDOM OF ESTABLISHMENT FOR PROVIDERS

SECTION 1
AUTHORISATIONS

Article 9 Authorisation schemes

1. Member States shall not make access to a service activity or the exercise thereof subject
    to an authorisation scheme unless the following conditions are satisfied:
    (a) the authorisation scheme does not discriminate against the provider in question;
    (b) the need for an authorisation scheme is justified by an overriding reason relating to the public interest;
    (c) the objective pursued cannot be attained by means of a less restrictive measure, in particular because an a posteriori inspection would take place too late to be genuinely effective.
2. In the report referred to in Article 39(1), Member States shall identify their authorisation schemes and give reasons showing their compatibility with paragraph 1 of this Article.
3. This section shall not apply to those aspects of authorisation schemes which are governed directly or indirectly by other Community instruments.

Article 10 Conditions for the granting of authorisation

1. Authorisation schemes shall be based on criteria which preclude the competent authorities from exercising their power of assessment in an arbitrary manner.
2. The criteria referred to in paragraph 1 shall be:
    (a) non-discriminatory;
    (b) justified by an overriding reason relating to the public interest;
    (c) proportionate to that public interest objective;
    (d) clear and unambiguous;
    (e) objective;
    (f) made public in advance;
    (g) transparent and accessible.
3. The conditions for granting authorisation for a new establishment shall not duplicate requirements and controls which are equivalent or essentially comparable as regards their purpose to which the provider is already subject in another Member State or in the same Member State. The liaison points referred to in Article 28(2) and the provider shall assist the competent authority by providing any necessary information regarding those requirements.
4. The authorisation shall enable the provider to have access to the service activity, or to exercise that activity, throughout the national territory, including by means of setting up agencies, subsidiaries, branches or offices, except where an authorisation for each individual establishment or a limitation of the authorisation to a certain part of the territory is justified by an overriding reason relating to the public interest.
5. The authorisation shall be granted as soon as it is established, in the light of an appropriate examination, that the conditions for authorisation have been met.
6. Except in the case of the granting of an authorisation, any decision from the competent authorities, including refusal or withdrawal of an authorisation, shall be fully reasoned and shall be open to challenge before the courts or other instances of appeal.
7. This Article shall not call into question the allocation of the competences, at local or regional level, of the Member States' authorities granting authorisations.

Article 11 Duration of authorisation

1. An authorisation granted to a provider shall not be for a limited period, except where:
    (a) the authorisation is being automatically renewed or is subject only to the continued fulfilment of requirements;
    (b) the number of available authorisations is limited by an overriding reason relating to the public interest; or
    (c) a limited authorisation period can be justified by an overriding reason relating to the public interest.

2. Paragraph 1 shall not concern the maximum period before the end of which the provider must actually commence his activity after receiving authorisation.

3. Member States shall require a provider to inform the relevant point of single contact provided for in Article 6 of the following changes:
   (a) the creation of subsidiaries whose activities fall within the scope of the authorisation scheme;
   (b) changes in his situation which result in the conditions for authorisation no longer being met.

4. This Article shall be without prejudice to the Member States' ability to revoke authorisations, when the conditions for authorisation are no longer met.

Article 12 Selection from among several candidates

1. Where the number of authorisations available for a given activity is limited because of the scarcity of available natural resources or technical capacity, Member States shall apply a selection procedure to potential candidates which provides full guarantees of impartiality and transparency, including, in particular, adequate publicity about the launch, conduct and completion of the procedure.

2. In the cases referred to in paragraph 1, authorisation shall be granted for an appropriate limited period and may not be open to automatic renewal nor confer any other advantage on the provider whose authorisation has just expired or on any person having any particular links with that provider.

3. Subject to paragraph 1 and to Articles 9 and 10, Member States may take into account, in establishing the rules for the selection procedure, considerations of public health, social policy objectives, the health and safety of employees or self-employed persons, the protection of the environment, the preservation of cultural heritage and other overriding reasons relating to the public interest, in conformity with Community law.

Article 13 Authorisation procedures

1. Authorisation procedures and formalities shall be clear, made public in advance and be such as to provide the applicants with a guarantee that their application will be dealt with objectively and impartially.

2. Authorisation procedures and formalities shall not be dissuasive and shall not unduly complicate or delay the provision of the service. They shall be easily accessible and any charges which the applicants may incur from their application shall be reasonable and proportionate to the cost of the authorisation procedures in question and shall not exceed the cost of the procedures.

3. Authorisation procedures and formalities shall provide applicants with a guarantee that their application will be processed as quickly as possible and, in any event, within a reasonable period which is fixed and made public in advance. The period shall run only from the time when all documentation has been submitted. When justified by the complexity of the issue, the time period may be extended once, by the competent authority, for a limited time. The extension and its duration shall be duly motivated and shall be notified to the applicant before the original period has expired.

4. Failing a response within the time period set or extended in accordance with paragraph 3, authorisation shall be deemed to have been granted. Different arrangements may nevertheless be put in place, where justified by overriding reasons relating to the public interest, including a legitimate interest of third parties.

5. All applications for authorisation shall be acknowledged as quickly as possible. The acknowledgement must specify the following:
   (a) the period referred to in paragraph 3;
   (b) the available means of redress;
   (c) where applicable, a statement that in the absence of a response within the period specified, the authorisation shall be deemed to have been granted.

6. In the case of an incomplete application, the applicant shall be informed as quickly as possible of the need to supply any additional documentation, as well as of any possible effects on the period referred to in paragraph 3.

7. When a request is rejected because it fails to comply with the required procedures or formalities, the applicant shall be informed of the rejection as quickly as possible.

SECTION 2
REQUIREMENTS PROHIBITED OR SUBJECT TO EVALUATION

Article 14 Prohibited requirements

Member States shall not make access to, or the exercise of, a service activity in their territory subject to compliance with any of the following:

(1) discriminatory requirements based directly or indirectly on nationality or, in the case of companies, the location of the registered office, including in particular:

(a) nationality requirements for the provider, his staff, persons holding the share capital or members of the provider's management or supervisory bodies;

(b) a requirement that the provider, his staff, persons holding the share capital or members of the provider's management or supervisory bodies be resident within the territory;

(2) a prohibition on having an establishment in more than one Member State or on being entered in the registers or enrolled with professional bodies or associations of more than one Member State;

(3) restrictions on the freedom of a provider to choose between a principal or a secondary establishment, in particular an obligation on the provider to have its principal establishment in their territory, or restrictions on the freedom to choose between establishment in the form of an agency, branch or subsidiary;

(4) conditions of reciprocity with the Member State in which the provider already has an establishment, save in the case of conditions of reciprocity provided for in Community instruments concerning energy;

(5) the case-by-case application of an economic test making the granting of authorisation subject to proof of the existence of an economic need or market demand, an assessment of the potential or current economic effects of the activity or an assessment of the appropriateness of the activity in relation to the economic planning objectives set by the competent authority; this prohibition shall not concern planning requirements which do not pursue economic aims but serve overriding reasons relating to the public interest;

(6) the direct or indirect involvement of competing operators, including within consultative bodies, in the granting of authorisations or in the adoption of other decisions of the competent authorities, with the exception of professional bodies and associations or other organisations acting as the competent authority; this prohibition shall not concern the consultation of organisations, such as chambers of commerce or social partners, on matters other than individual applications for authorisation, or a consultation of the public at large;

(7) an obligation to provide or participate in a financial guarantee or to take out insurance from a provider or body established in their territory. This shall not affect the possibility for Member States to require insurance or financial guarantees as such, nor shall it affect requirements relating to the participation in a collective compensation fund, for instance for members of professional bodies or organisations;

(8) an obligation to have been pre-registered, for a given period, in the registers held in their territory or to have previously exercised the activity for a given period in their territory.

Article 15 Requirements to be evaluated

1. Member States shall examine whether, under their legal system, any of the requirements listed in paragraph 2 are imposed and shall ensure that any such requirements are compatible with the conditions laid down in paragraph 3. Member States shall adapt their laws, regulations or administrative provisions so as to make them compatible with those conditions.

2. Member States shall examine whether their legal system makes access to a service activity or the exercise of it subject to compliance with any of the following non-discriminatory requirements:

(a) quantitative or territorial restrictions, in particular in the form of limits fixed according to population or of a minimum geographical distance between providers;

(b) an obligation on a provider to take a specific legal form;

(c) requirements which relate to the shareholding of a company;

(d)　requirements, other than those concerning matters covered by Directive 2005/36/EC or provided for in other Community instruments, which reserve access to the service activity in question to particular providers by virtue of the specific nature of the activity;

(e)　a ban on having more than one establishment in the territory of the same State;

(f)　requirements fixing a minimum number of employees;

(g)　fixed minimum and/or maximum tariffs with which the provider must comply;

(h)　an obligation on the provider to supply other specific services jointly with his service.

3.　Member States shall verify that the requirements referred to in paragraph 2 satisfy the following conditions:

(a)　non-discrimination: requirements must be neither directly nor indirectly discriminatory according to nationality nor, with regard to companies, according to the location of the registered office;

(b)　necessity: requirements must be justified by an overriding reason relating to the public interest;

(c)　proportionality: requirements must be suitable for securing the attainment of the objective pursued; they must not go beyond what is necessary to attain that objective and it must not be possible to replace those requirements with other, less restrictive measures which attain the same result.

4.　Paragraphs 1, 2 and 3 shall apply to legislation in the field of services of general economic interest only insofar as the application of these paragraphs does not obstruct the performance, in law or in fact, of the particular task assigned to them.

5.　In the mutual evaluation report provided for in Article 39(1), Member States shall specify the following:

(a)　the requirements that they intend to maintain and the reasons why they consider that those requirements comply with the conditions set out in paragraph 3;

(b)　the requirements which have been abolished or made less stringent.

6.　From 28 December 2006 Member States shall not introduce any new requirement of a kind listed in paragraph 2, unless that requirement satisfies the conditions laid down in paragraph 3.

7.　Member States shall notify the Commission of any new laws, regulations or administrative provisions which set requirements as referred to in paragraph 6, together with the reasons for those requirements. The Commission shall communicate the provisions concerned to the other Member States. Such notification shall not prevent Member States from adopting the provisions in question.

Within a period of 3 months from the date of receipt of the notification, the Commission shall examine the compatibility of any new requirements with Community law and, where appropriate, shall adopt a decision requesting the Member State in question to refrain from adopting them or to abolish them.

The notification of a draft national law in accordance with Directive 98/34/EC shall fulfil the obligation of notification provided for in this Directive.

CHAPTER IV
FREE MOVEMENT OF SERVICES

SECTION 1
FREEDOM TO PROVIDE SERVICES AND RELATED DEROGATIONS

Article 16 Freedom to provide services

1.　Member States shall respect the right of providers to provide services in a Member State other than that in which they are established.

The Member State in which the service is provided shall ensure free access to and free exercise of a service activity within its territory.

Member States shall not make access to or exercise of a service activity in their territory subject to compliance with any requirements which do not respect the following principles:

(a)　non-discrimination: the requirement may be neither directly nor indirectly discriminatory with regard to nationality or, in the case of legal persons, with regard to the Member State in which they are established;

(b)   necessity: the requirement must be justified for reasons of public policy, public security, public health or the protection of the environment;

(c)   proportionality: the requirement must be suitable for attaining the objective pursued, and must not go beyond what is necessary to attain that objective.

2.   Member States may not restrict the freedom to provide services in the case of a provider established in another Member State by imposing any of the following requirements:

(a)   an obligation on the provider to have an establishment in their territory;

(b)   an obligation on the provider to obtain an authorisation from their competent authorities including entry in a register or registration with a professional body or association in their territory, except where provided for in this Directive or other instruments of Community law;

(c)   a ban on the provider setting up a certain form or type of infrastructure in their territory, including an office or chambers, which the provider needs in order to supply the services in question;

(d)   the application of specific contractual arrangements between the provider and the recipient which prevent or restrict service provision by the self-employed;

(e)   an obligation on the provider to possess an identity document issued by its competent authorities specific to the exercise of a service activity;

(f)   requirements, except for those necessary for health and safety at work, which affect the use of equipment and material which are an integral part of the service provided;

(g)   restrictions on the freedom to provide the services referred to in Article 19.

3.   The Member State to which the provider moves shall not be prevented from imposing requirements with regard to the provision of a service activity, where they are justified for reasons of public policy, public security, public health or the protection of the environment and in accordance with paragraph 1. Nor shall that Member State be prevented from applying, in accordance with Community law, its rules on employment conditions, including those laid down in collective agreements.

4.   By 28 December 2011 the Commission shall, after consultation of the Member States and the social partners at Community level, submit to the European Parliament and the Council a report on the application of this Article, in which it shall consider the need to propose harmonisation measures regarding service activities covered by this Directive.

Article 17 Additional derogations from the freedom to provide services

Article 16 shall not apply to:

(1)   services of general economic interest which are provided in another Member State, inter alia:

(a)   in the postal sector, services covered by Directive 97/67/EC of the European Parliament and of the Council of 15 December 1997 on common rules for the development of the internal market of Community postal services and the improvement of quality of service;

(b)   in the electricity sector, services covered by Directive 2003/54/EC of the European Parliament and of the Council of 26 June 2003 concerning common rules for the internal market in electricity;

(c)   in the gas sector, services covered by Directive 2003/55/EC of the European Parliament and of the Council of 26 June 2003 concerning common rules for the internal market in natural gas;

(d)   water distribution and supply services and waste water services;

(e)   treatment of waste;

(2)   matters covered by Directive 96/71/EC;

(3)   matters covered by Directive 95/46/EC of the European Parliament and of the Council of 24 October 1995 on the protection of individuals with regard to the processing of personal data and on the free movement of such data;

(4)   matters covered by Council Directive 77/249/EEC of 22 March 1977to facilitate the effective exercise by lawyers of freedom to provide services;

(5)   the activity of judicial recovery of debts;

(6)   matters covered by Title II of Directive 2005/36/EC, as well as requirements in the Member State where the service is provided which reserve an activity to a particular profession;

(7)   matters covered by Regulation (EEC) No 1408/71;

(8)   as regards administrative formalities concerning the free movement of persons and their residence, matters covered by the provisions of Directive 2004/38/EC that lay down administrative formalities of the competent authorities of the Member State where the service is provided with which beneficiaries must comply;

(9)   as regards third country nationals who move to another Member State in the context of the provision of a service, the possibility for Member States to require visa or residence permits for third country nationals who are not covered by the mutual recognition regime provided for in Article 21 of the Convention implementing the Schengen Agreement of 14 June 1985 on the gradual abolition of checks at the common borders or the possibility to oblige third country nationals to report to the competent authorities of the Member State in which the service is provided on or after their entry;

(10)   as regards the shipment of waste, matters covered by Council Regulation (EEC) No 259/93 of 1 February 1993 on the supervision and control of shipments of waste within, into and out of the European Community;

(11)   copyright, neighbouring rights and rights covered by Council Directive 87/54/EEC of 16 December 1986 on the legal protection of topographies of semiconductor products and by Directive 96/9/EC of the European Parliament and of the Council of 11 March 1996 on the legal protection of databases, as well as industrial property rights;

(12)   acts requiring by law the involvement of a notary;

(13)   matters covered by Directive 2006/43/EC of the European Parliament and of the Council of 17 May 2006 on statutory audit of annual accounts and consolidated accounts;

(14)   the registration of vehicles leased in another Member State;

(15)   provisions regarding contractual and non-contractual obligations, including the form of contracts, determined pursuant to the rules of private international law.

Article 18 Case-by-case derogations

1.   By way of derogation from Article 16, and in exceptional circumstances only, a Member State may, in respect of a provider established in another Member State, take measures relating to the safety of services.

2.   The measures provided for in paragraph 1 may be taken only if the mutual assistance procedure laid down in Article 35 is complied with and the following conditions are fulfilled:

   (a)   the national provisions in accordance with which the measure is taken have not been subject to Community harmonisation in the field of the safety of services;

   (b)   the measures provide for a higher level of protection of the recipient than would be the case in a measure taken by the Member State of establishment in accordance with its national provisions;

   (c)   the Member State of establishment has not taken any measures or has taken measures which are insufficient as compared with those referred to in Article 35(2);

   (d)   the measures are proportionate.

3.   Paragraphs 1 and 2 shall be without prejudice to provisions, laid down in Community instruments, which guarantee the freedom to provide services or which allow derogations therefrom.

SECTION 2
RIGHTS OF RECIPIENTS OF SERVICES

Article 19 Prohibited restrictions

Member States may not impose on a recipient requirements which restrict the use of a service supplied by a provider established in another Member State, in particular the following requirements:

   (a)   an obligation to obtain authorisation from or to make a declaration to their competent authorities;

   (b)   discriminatory limits on the grant of financial assistance by reason of the fact that the provider is established in another Member State or by reason of the location of the place at which the service is provided.

Article 20 Non-discrimination

1. Member States shall ensure that the recipient is not made subject to discriminatory requirements based on his nationality or place of residence.

2. Member States shall ensure that the general conditions of access to a service, which are made available to the public at large by the provider, do not contain discriminatory provisions relating to the nationality or place of residence of the recipient, but without precluding the possibility of providing for differences in the conditions of access where those differences are directly justified by objective criteria.

Article 21 Assistance for recipients

1. Member States shall ensure that recipients can obtain, in their Member State of residence, the following information:

   (a) general information on the requirements applicable in other Member States relating to access to, and exercise of, service activities, in particular those relating to consumer protection;

   (b) general information on the means of redress available in the case of a dispute between a provider and a recipient;

   (c) the contact details of associations or organisations, including the centres of the European Consumer Centres Network, from which providers or recipients may obtain practical assistance.

   Where appropriate, advice from the competent authorities shall include a simple step-by-step guide. Information and assistance shall be provided in a clear and unambiguous manner, shall be easily accessible at a distance, including by electronic means, and shall be kept up to date.

2. Member States may confer responsibility for the task referred to in paragraph 1 on points of single contact or on any other body, such as the centres of the European Consumer Centres Network, consumer associations or Euro Info Centres.

   Member States shall communicate to the Commission the names and contact details of the designated bodies. The Commission shall transmit them to all Member States.

3. In fulfilment of the requirements set out in paragraphs 1 and 2, the body approached by the recipient shall, if necessary, contact the relevant body for the Member State concerned. The latter shall send the information requested as soon as possible to the requesting body which shall forward the information to the recipient. Member States shall ensure that those bodies give each other mutual assistance and shall put in place all possible measures for effective cooperation. Together with the Commission, Member States shall put in place practical arrangements necessary for the implementation of paragraph 1.

4. The Commission shall, in accordance with the procedure referred to in Article 40(2), adopt measures for the implementation of paragraphs 1, 2 and 3 of this Article, specifying the technical mechanisms for the exchange of information between the bodies of the various Member States and, in particular, the interoperability of information systems, taking into account common standards.

CHAPTER V

QUALITY OF SERVICES

Article 22 Information on providers and their services

1. Member States shall ensure that providers make the following information available to the recipient:

   (a) the name of the provider, his legal status and form, the geographic address at which he is established and details enabling him to be contacted rapidly and communicated with directly and, as the case may be, by electronic means;

   (b) where the provider is registered in a trade or other similar public register, the name of that register and the provider's registration number, or equivalent means of identification in that register;

   (c) where the activity is subject to an authorisation scheme, the particulars of the relevant competent authority or the single point of contact;

   (d) where the provider exercises an activity which is subject to VAT, the identification number referred to in Article 22(1) of Sixth Council Directive 77/388/EEC of 17 May

1977 on the harmonisation of the laws of the Member States relating to turnover taxes – Common system of value added tax: uniform basis of assessment;

(e)   in the case of the regulated professions, any professional body or similar institution with which the provider is registered, the professional title and the Member State in which that title has been granted;

(f)   the general conditions and clauses, if any, used by the provider;

(g)   the existence of contractual clauses, if any, used by the provider concerning the law applicable to the contract and/or the competent courts;

(h)   the existence of an after-sales guarantee, if any, not imposed by law;

(i)   the price of the service, where a price is pre-determined by the provider for a given type of service;

(j)   the main features of the service, if not already apparent from the context;

(k)   the insurance or guarantees referred to in Article 23(1), and in particular the contact details of the insurer or guarantor and the territorial coverage.

2.   Member States shall ensure that the information referred to in paragraph 1, according to the provider's preference:

(a)   is supplied by the provider on his own initiative;

(b)   is easily accessible to the recipient at the place where the service is provided or the contract concluded;

(c)   can be easily accessed by the recipient electronically by means of an address supplied by the provider;

(d)   appears in any information documents supplied to the recipient by the provider which set out a detailed description of the service he provides.

3.   Member States shall ensure that, at the recipient's request, providers supply the following additional information:

(a)   where the price is not pre-determined by the provider for a given type of service, the price of the service or, if an exact price cannot be given, the method for calculating the price so that it can be checked by the recipient, or a sufficiently detailed estimate;

(b)   as regards the regulated professions, a reference to the professional rules applicable in the Member State of establishment and how to access them;

(c)   information on their multidisciplinary activities and partnerships which are directly linked to the service in question and on the measures taken to avoid conflicts of interest. That information shall be included in any information document in which providers give a detailed description of their services;

(d)   any codes of conduct to which the provider is subject and the address at which these codes may be consulted by electronic means, specifying the language version available;

(e)   where a provider is subject to a code of conduct, or member of a trade association or professional body which provides for recourse to a non-judicial means of dispute settlement, information in this respect. The provider shall specify how to access detailed information on the characteristics of, and conditions for, the use of non-judicial means of dispute settlement.

4.   Member States shall ensure that the information which a provider must supply in accordance with this Chapter is made available or communicated in a clear and unambiguous manner, and in good time before conclusion of the contract or, where there is no written contract, before the service is provided.

5.   The information requirements laid down in this Chapter are in addition to requirements already provided for in Community law and do not prevent Member States from imposing additional information requirements applicable to providers established in their territory.

6.   The Commission may, in accordance with the procedure referred to in Article 40(2), specify the content of the information provided for in paragraphs 1 and 3 of this Article according to the specific nature of certain activities and may specify the practical means of implementing paragraph 2 of this Article.

Article 23 Professional liability insurance and guarantees

1.   Member States may ensure that providers whose services present a direct and particular risk to the health or safety of the recipient or a third person, or to the financial

security of the recipient, subscribe to professional liability insurance appropriate to the nature and extent of the risk, or provide a guarantee or similar arrangement which is equivalent or essentially comparable as regards its purpose.

2.   When a provider establishes himself in their territory, Member States may not require professional liability insurance or a guarantee from the provider where he is already covered by a guarantee which is equivalent, or essentially comparable as regards its purpose and the cover it provides in terms of the insured risk, the insured sum or a ceiling for the guarantee and possible exclusions from the cover, in another Member State in which the provider is already established. Where equivalence is only partial, Member States may require a supplementary guarantee to cover those aspects not already covered.

When a Member State requires a provider established in its territory to subscribe to professional liability insurance or to provide another guarantee, that Member State shall accept as sufficient evidence attestations of such insurance cover issued by credit institutions and insurers established in other Member States.

3.   Paragraphs 1 and 2 shall not affect professional insurance or guarantee arrangements provided for in other Community instruments.

4.   For the implementation of paragraph 1, the Commission may, in accordance with the regulatory procedure referred to in Article 40(2), establish a list of services which exhibit the characteristics referred to in paragraph 1 of this Article. The Commission may also, in accordance with the procedure referred to in Article 40(3), adopt measures designed to amend non-essential elements of this Directive by supplementing it by establishing common criteria for defining, for the purposes of the insurance or guarantees referred to in paragraph 1 of this Article, what is appropriate to the nature and extent of the risk.

5.   For the purpose of this Article
   — 'direct and particular risk' means a risk arising directly from the provision of the service,
   — 'health and safety' means, in relation to a recipient or a third person, the prevention of death or serious personal injury,
   — 'financial security' means, in relation to a recipient, the prevention of substantial losses of money or of value of property,
   — 'professional liability insurance' means insurance taken out by a provider in respect of potential liabilities to recipients and, where applicable, third parties arising out of the provision of the service.

Article 24 Commercial communications by the regulated professions

1.   Member States shall remove all total prohibitions on commercial communications by the regulated professions.

2.   Member States shall ensure that commercial communications by the regulated professions comply with professional rules, in conformity with Community law, which relate, in particular, to the independence, dignity and integrity of the profession, as well as to professional secrecy, in a manner consistent with the specific nature of each profession. Professional rules on commercial communications shall be non-discriminatory, justified by an overriding reason relating to the public interest and proportionate.

Article 25 Multidisciplinary activities

1.   Member States shall ensure that providers are not made subject to requirements which oblige them to exercise a given specific activity exclusively or which restrict the exercise jointly or in partnership of different activities.

However, the following providers may be made subject to such requirements:
   (a)   the regulated professions, in so far as is justified in order to guarantee compliance with the rules governing professional ethics and conduct, which vary according to the specific nature of each profession, and is necessary in order to ensure their independence and impartiality;
   (b)   providers of certification, accreditation, technical monitoring, test or trial services, in so far as is justified in order to ensure their independence and impartiality.

2.   Where multidisciplinary activities between providers referred to in points (a) and (b) of paragraph 1 are authorised, Member States shall ensure the following:
   (a)   that conflicts of interest and incompatibilities between certain activities are prevented;
   (b)   that the independence and impartiality required for certain activities is secured;

(c)   that the rules governing professional ethics and conduct for different activities are compatible with one another, especially as regards matters of professional secrecy.

3.   In the report referred to in Article 39(1), Member States shall indicate which providers are subject to the requirements laid down in paragraph 1 of this Article, the content of those requirements and the reasons for which they consider them to be justified.

Article 26 Policy on quality of services

1.   Member States shall, in cooperation with the Commission, take accompanying measures to encourage providers to take action on a voluntary basis in order to ensure the quality of service provision, in particular through use of one of the following methods:

(a)   certification or assessment of their activities by independent or accredited bodies;

(b)   drawing up their own quality charter or participation in quality charters or labels drawn up by professional bodies at Community level.

2.   Member States shall ensure that information on the significance of certain labels and the criteria for applying labels and other quality marks relating to services can be easily accessed by providers and recipients.

3.   Member States shall, in cooperation with the Commission, take accompanying measures to encourage professional bodies, as well as chambers of commerce and craft associations and consumer associations, in their territory to cooperate at Community level in order to promote the quality of service provision, especially by making it easier to assess the competence of a provider.

4.   Member States shall, in cooperation with the Commission, take accompanying measures to encourage the development of independent assessments, notably by consumer associations, in relation to the quality and defects of service provision, and, in particular, the development at Community level of comparative trials or testing and the communication of the results.

5.   Member States, in cooperation with the Commission, shall encourage the development of voluntary European standards with the aim of facilitating compatibility between services supplied by providers in different Member States, information to the recipient and the quality of service provision.

Article 27 Settlement of disputes

1.   Member States shall take the general measures necessary to ensure that providers supply contact details, in particular a postal address, fax number or e-mail address and telephone number to which all recipients, including those resident in another Member State, can send a complaint or a request for information about the service provided. Providers shall supply their legal address if this is not their usual address for correspondence. Member States shall take the general measures necessary to ensure that providers respond to the complaints referred to in the first subparagraph in the shortest possible time and make their best efforts to find a satisfactory solution.

2.   Member States shall take the general measures necessary to ensure that providers are obliged to demonstrate compliance with the obligations laid down in this Directive as to the provision of information and to demonstrate that the information is accurate.

3.   Where a financial guarantee is required for compliance with a judicial decision, Member States shall recognise equivalent guarantees lodged with a credit institution or insurer established in another Member State. Such credit institutions must be authorised in a Member State in accordance with Directive 2006/48/EC and such insurers in accordance, as appropriate, with First Council Directive 73/239/EEC of 24 July 1973 on the coordination of laws, regulations and administrative provisions relating to the taking-up and pursuit of the business of direct insurance other than life assurance and Directive 2002/83/EC of the European Parliament and of the Council of 5 November 2002 concerning life assurance.

4.   Member States shall take the general measures necessary to ensure that providers who are subject to a code of conduct, or are members of a trade association or professional body, which provides for recourse to a non-judicial means of dispute settlement inform the recipient thereof and mention that fact in any document which presents their services in detail, specifying how to access detailed information on the characteristics of, and conditions for, the use of such a mechanism.

CHAPTER VI
ADMINISTRATIVE COOPERATION

Article 28 Mutual assistance – general obligations

1. Member States shall give each other mutual assistance, and shall put in place measures for effective cooperation with one another, in order to ensure the supervision of providers and the services they provide.
2. For the purposes of this Chapter, Member States shall designate one or more liaison points, the contact details of which shall be communicated to the other Member States and the Commission. The Commission shall publish and regularly update the list of liaison points.
3. Information requests and requests to carry out any checks, inspections and investigations under this Chapter shall be duly motivated, in particular by specifying the reason for the request. Information exchanged shall be used only in respect of the matter for which it was requested.
4. In the event of receiving a request for assistance from competent authorities in another Member State, Member States shall ensure that providers established in their territory supply their competent authorities with all the information necessary for supervising their activities in compliance with their national laws.
5. In the event of difficulty in meeting a request for information or in carrying out checks, inspections or investigations, the Member State in question shall rapidly inform the requesting Member State with a view to finding a solution.
6. Member States shall supply the information requested by other Member States or the Commission by electronic means and within the shortest possible period of time.
7. Member States shall ensure that registers in which providers have been entered, and which may be consulted by the competent authorities in their territory, may also be consulted, in accordance with the same conditions, by the equivalent competent authorities of the other Member States.
8. Member States shall communicate to the Commission information on cases where other Member States do not fulfil their obligation of mutual assistance. Where necessary, the Commission shall take appropriate steps, including proceedings provided for in Article 226 of the Treaty, in order to ensure that the Member States concerned comply with their obligation of mutual assistance. The Commission shall periodically inform Member States about the functioning of the mutual assistance provisions.

Article 29 Mutual assistance – general obligations for the Member State of establishment

1. With respect to providers providing services in another Member State, the Member State of establishment shall supply information on providers established in its territory when requested to do so by another Member State and, in particular, confirmation that a provider is established in its territory and, to its knowledge, is not exercising his activities in an unlawful manner.
2. The Member State of establishment shall undertake the checks, inspections and investigations requested by another Member State and shall inform the latter of the results and, as the case may be, of the measures taken. In so doing, the competent authorities shall act to the extent permitted by the powers vested in them in their Member State. The competent authorities can decide on the most appropriate measures to be taken in each individual case in order to meet the request by another Member State.
3. Upon gaining actual knowledge of any conduct or specific acts by a provider established in its territory which provides services in other Member States, that, to its knowledge, could cause serious damage to the health or safety of persons or to the environment, the Member State of establishment shall inform all other Member States and the Commission within the shortest possible period of time.

Article 30 Supervision by the Member State of establishment in the event of the temporary movement of a provider to another Member State

1. With respect to cases not covered by Article 31(1), the Member State of establishment shall ensure that compliance with its requirements is supervised in conformity with the

powers of supervision provided for in its national law, in particular through supervisory measures at the place of establishment of the provider.

2. The Member State of establishment shall not refrain from taking supervisory or enforcement measures in its territory on the grounds that the service has been provided or caused damage in another Member State.

3. The obligation laid down in paragraph 1 shall not entail a duty on the part of the Member State of establishment to carry out factual checks and controls in the territory of the Member State where the service is provided. Such checks and controls shall be carried out by the authorities of the Member State where the provider is temporarily operating at the request of the authorities of the Member State of establishment, in accordance with Article 31.

Article 31 Supervision by the Member State where the service is provided in the event of the temporary movement of the provider

1. With respect to national requirements which may be imposed pursuant to Articles 16 or 17, the Member State where the service is provided is responsible for the supervision of the activity of the provider in its territory. In conformity with Community law, the Member State where the service is provided:

   (a) shall take all measures necessary to ensure the provider complies with those requirements as regards the access to and the exercise of the activity;

   (b) shall carry out the checks, inspections and investigations necessary to supervise the service provided.

2. With respect to requirements other than those referred to in paragraph 1, where a provider moves temporarily to another Member State in order to provide a service without being established there, the competent authorities of that Member State shall participate in the supervision of the provider in accordance with paragraphs 3 and 4.

3. At the request of the Member State of establishment, the competent authorities of the Member State where the service is provided shall carry out any checks, inspections and investigations necessary for ensuring the effective supervision by the Member State of establishment. In so doing, the competent authorities shall act to the extent permitted by the powers vested in them in their Member State. The competent authorities may decide on the most appropriate measures to be taken in each individual case in order to meet the request by the Member State of establishment.

4. On their own initiative, the competent authorities of the Member State where the service is provided may conduct checks, inspections and investigations on the spot, provided that those checks, inspections or investigations are not discriminatory, are not motivated by the fact that the provider is established in another Member State and are proportionate.

Article 32 Alert mechanism

1. Where a Member State becomes aware of serious specific acts or circumstances relating to a service activity that could cause serious damage to the health or safety of persons or to the environment in its territory or in the territory of other Member States, that Member State shall inform the Member State of establishment, the other Member States concerned and the Commission within the shortest possible period of time.

2. The Commission shall promote and take part in the operation of a European network of Member States' authorities in order to implement paragraph 1.

3. The Commission shall adopt and regularly update, in accordance with the procedure referred to in Article 40(2), detailed rules concerning the management of the network referred to in paragraph 2 of this Article.

Article 33 Information on the good repute of providers

1. Member States shall, at the request of a competent authority in another Member State, supply information, in conformity with their national law, on disciplinary or administrative actions or criminal sanctions and decisions concerning insolvency or bankruptcy involving fraud taken by their competent authorities in respect of the provider which are directly relevant to the provider's competence or professional reliability. The Member State which supplies the information shall inform the provider thereof. A request made pursuant to the first subparagraph must be duly substantiated, in particular as regards the reasons for the request for information.

2. Sanctions and actions referred to in paragraph 1 shall only be communicated if a final decision has been taken. With regard to other enforceable decisions referred to in paragraph 1, the Member State which supplies the information shall specify whether a particular decision is final or whether an appeal has been lodged in respect of it, in which case the Member State in question should provide an indication of the date when the decision on appeal is expected.
    Moreover, that Member State shall specify the provisions of national law pursuant to which the provider was found guilty or penalised.
3. Implementation of paragraphs 1 and 2 must comply with rules on the provision of personal data and with rights guaranteed to persons found guilty or penalised in the Member States concerned, including by professional bodies. Any information in question which is public shall be accessible to consumers.

Article 34 Accompanying measures

1. The Commission, in cooperation with Member States, shall establish an electronic system for the exchange of information between Member States, taking into account existing information systems.
2. Member States shall, with the assistance of the Commission, take accompanying measures to facilitate the exchange of officials in charge of the implementation of mutual assistance and training of such officials, including language and computer training.
3. The Commission shall assess the need to establish a multiannual programme in order to organise relevant exchanges of officials and training.

Article 35 Mutual assistance in the event of case-by-case derogations

1. Where a Member State intends to take a measure pursuant to Article 18, the procedure laid down in paragraphs 2 to 6 of this Article shall apply without prejudice to court proceedings, including preliminary proceedings and acts carried out in the framework of a criminal investigation.
2. The Member State referred to in paragraph 1 shall ask the Member State of establishment to take measures with regard to the provider, supplying all relevant information on the service in question and the circumstances of the case.
    The Member State of establishment shall check, within the shortest possible period of time, whether the provider is operating lawfully and verify the facts underlying the request. It shall inform the requesting Member State within the shortest possible period of time of the measures taken or envisaged or, as the case may be, the reasons why it has not taken any measures.
3. Following communication by the Member State of establishment as provided for in the second subparagraph of paragraph 2, the requesting Member State shall notify the Commission and the Member State of establishment of its intention to take measures, stating the following:
    (a) the reasons why it believes the measures taken or envisaged by the Member State of establishment are inadequate;
    (b) the reasons why it believes the measures it intends to take fulfil the conditions laid down in Article 18.
4. The measures may not be taken until fifteen working days after the date of notification provided for in paragraph 3.
5. Without prejudice to the possibility for the requesting Member State to take the measures in question upon expiry of the period specified in paragraph 4, the Commission shall, within the shortest possible period of time, examine the compatibility with Community law of the measures notified.
    Where the Commission concludes that the measure is incompatible with Community law, it shall adopt a decision asking the Member State concerned to refrain from taking the proposed measures or to put an end to the measures in question as a matter of urgency.
6. In the case of urgency, a Member State which intends to take a measure may derogate from paragraphs 2, 3 and 4. In such cases, the measures shall be notified within the shortest possible period of time to the Commission and the Member State of establishment, stating the reasons for which the Member State considers that there is urgency.

Article 36 Implementing measures

In accordance with the procedure referred to in Article 40(3), the Commission shall adopt the implementing measures designed to amend non-essential elements of this Chapter by supplementing it by specifying the time-limits provided for in Articles 28 and 35. The Commission shall also adopt, in accordance with the procedure referred to in Article 40(2), the practical arrangements for the exchange of information by electronic means between Member States, and in particular the interoperability provisions for information systems.

CHAPTER VII
CONVERGENCE PROGRAMME

Article 37 Codes of conduct at Community level

1.   Member States shall, in cooperation with the Commission, take accompanying measures to encourage the drawing up at Community level, particularly by professional bodies, organisations and associations, of codes of conduct aimed at facilitating the provision of services or the establishment of a provider in another Member State, in conformity with Community law.
2.   Member States shall ensure that the codes of conduct referred to in paragraph 1 are accessible at a distance, by electronic means.

Article 38 Additional harmonisation

The Commission shall assess, by 28 December 2010 the possibility of presenting proposals for harmonisation instruments on the following subjects:
   (a)   access to the activity of judicial recovery of debts;
   (b)   private security services and transport of cash and valuables.

Article 39 Mutual evaluation

1.   By 28 December 2009 at the latest, Member States shall present a report to the Commission, containing the information specified in the following provisions:
   (a)   Article 9(2), on authorisation schemes;
   (b)   Article 15(5), on requirements to be evaluated;
   (c)   Article 25(3), on multidisciplinary activities.
2.   The Commission shall forward the reports provided for in paragraph 1 to the Member States, which shall submit their observations on each of the reports within six months of receipt. Within the same period, the Commission shall consult interested parties on those reports.
3.   The Commission shall present the reports and the Member States' observations to the Committee referred to in Article 40(1), which may make observations.
4.   In the light of the observations provided for in paragraphs 2 and 3, the Commission shall, by 28 December 2010 at the latest, present a summary report to the European Parliament and to the Council, accompanied where appropriate by proposals for additional initiatives.
5.   By 28 December 2009 at the latest, Member States shall present a report to the Commission on the national requirements whose application could fall under the third subparagraph of Article 16(1) and the first sentence of Article 16(3), providing reasons why they consider that the application of those requirements fulfil the criteria referred to in the third subparagraph of Article 16(1) and the first sentence of Article 16(3).
   Thereafter, Member States shall transmit to the Commission any changes in their requirements, including new requirements, as referred to above, together with the reasons for them.
   The Commission shall communicate the transmitted requirements to other Member States. Such transmission shall not prevent the adoption by Member States of the provisions in question. The Commission shall on an annual basis thereafter provide analyses and orientations on the application of these provisions in the context of this Directive.

Article 40 Committee procedure

1.   The Commission shall be assisted by a Committee.
2.   Where reference is made to this paragraph, Articles 5 and 7 of Decision 1999/468/EC shall apply, having regard to the provisions of Article 8 thereof. The period laid down in Article 5(6) of Decision 1999/468/EC shall be set at three months.

3. Where reference is made to this paragraph, Article 5a(1) to (4), and Article 7 of Decision 1999/468/EC shall apply, having regard to the provisions of Article 8 thereof.

Article 41 Review clause

The Commission, by 28 December 2011 and every three years thereafter, shall present to the European Parliament and to the Council a comprehensive report on the application of this Directive. This report shall, in accordance with Article 16(4), address in particular the application of Article 16. It shall also consider the need for additional measures for matters excluded from the scope of application of this Directive. It shall be accompanied, where appropriate, by proposals for amendment of this Directive with a view to completing the Internal Market for services.

Article 42 Amendment of Directive 98/27/EC

In the Annex to Directive 98/27/EC of the European Parliament and of the Council of 19 May 1998 on injunctions for the protection of consumers' interests, the following point shall be added: '13. Directive 2006/123/EC of the European Parliament and of the Council of 12 December 2006 on services in the internal market (OJ L 376, 27.12.2006, p. 36)'.

Article 43 Protection of personal data

The implementation and application of this Directive and, in particular, the provisions on supervision shall respect the rules on the protection of personal data as provided for in Directives 95/46/EC and 2002/58/EC.

CHAPTER VIII
FINAL PROVISIONS

Article 44 Transposition

1. Member States shall bring into force the laws, regulations and administrative provisions necessary to comply with this Directive before 28 December 2009. They shall forthwith communicate to the Commission the text of those measures.
When Member States adopt these measures, they shall contain a reference to this Directive or shall be accompanied by such a reference on the occasion of their official publication. The methods of making such reference shall be laid down by Member States.
2. Member States shall communicate to the Commission the text of the main provisions of national law which they adopt in the field covered by this Directive.

Article 45 Entry into force

This Directive shall enter into force on the day following that of its publication in the *Official Journal of the European Union*.

Article 46 Addressees

This Directive is addressed to the Member States.

SOCIAL SECURITY

REGULATION (EC) No 883/2004 OF THE EUROPEAN PARLIAMENT AND OF THE COUNCIL of 29 APRIL 2004
on the coordination of social security systems
[2004] OJ L166/1

TITLE I
GENERAL PROVISIONS

Article 1   Definitions

For the purposes of this Regulation:

(a) 'activity as an employed person' means any activity or equivalent situation treated as such for the purposes of the social security legislation of the Member State in which such activity or equivalent situation exists;

(b) 'activity as a self-employed person' means any activity or equivalent situation treated as such for the purposes of the social security legislation of the Member State in which such activity or equivalent situation exists;

(c) 'insured person', in relation to the social security branches covered by Title III, Chapters 1 and 3, means any person satisfying the conditions required under the legislation of the Member State competent under Title II to have the right to benefits, taking into account the provisions of this Regulation;

(d) 'civil servant' means a person considered to be such or treated as such by the Member State to which the administration employing him/her is subject;

(e) 'special scheme for civil servants' means any social security scheme which is different from the general social security scheme applicable to employed persons in the Member State concerned and to which all, or certain categories of, civil servants are directly subject;

(f) 'frontier worker' means any person pursuing an activity as an employed or self-employed person in a Member State and who resides in another Member State to which he/she returns as a rule daily or at least once a week;

(g) 'refugee' shall have the meaning assigned to it in Article 1 of the Convention relating to the Status of Refugees, signed in Geneva on 28 July 1951;

(h) 'stateless person' shall have the meaning assigned to it in Article 1 of the Convention relating to the Status of Stateless Persons, signed in New York on 28 September 1954;

(i) 'member of the family' means:

   1. (i) any person defined or recognised as a member of the family or designated as a member of the household by the legislation under which benefits are provided;

      (ii) with regard to benefits in kind pursuant to Title III, Chapter 1 on sickness, maternity and equivalent paternity benefits, any person defined or recognised as a member of the family or designated as a member of the household by the legislation of the Member State in which he/she resides;

   2. if the legislation of a Member State which is applicable under subparagraph 1 does not make a distinction between the members of the family and other persons to whom it is applicable, the spouse, minor children, and dependent children who have reached the age of majority shall be considered members of the family;

   3. if, under the legislation which is applicable under subparagraphs 1 and 2, a person is considered a member of the family or member of the household only if he/she lives in the same household as the insured person or pensioner, this condition shall be considered satisfied if the person in question is mainly dependent on the insured person or pensioner;

(j) 'residence' means the place where a person habitually resides;

(k) 'stay' means temporary residence;

(l) 'legislation' means, in respect of each Member State, laws, regulations and other statutory provisions and all other implementing measures relating to the social security branches covered by Article 3(1);

This term excludes contractual provisions other than those which serve to implement an insurance obligation arising from the laws and regulations referred to in the preceding subparagraph or which have been the subject of a decision by the public authorities which makes them obligatory or extends their scope, provided that the Member State concerned makes a declaration to that effect, notified to the President of the European Parliament and the President of the Council of the European Union. Such declaration shall be published in the *Official Journal of the European Union*;

(m) 'competent authority' means, in respect of each Member State, the Minister, Ministers or other equivalent authority responsible for social security schemes throughout or in any part of the Member State in question;

(n) 'Administrative Commission' means the commission referred to in Article 71;

(na) 'European Labour Authority' means the body established by Regulation (EU) 2019/1149 of the European Parliament and of the Council and referred to in Article 74a;

(o) 'Implementing Regulation' means the Regulation referred to in Article 89;

(p) 'institution' means, in respect of each Member State, the body or authority responsible for applying all or part of the legislation;

(q) 'competent institution' means:
  (i) the institution with which the person concerned is insured at the time of the application for benefit; or
  (ii) the institution from which the person concerned is or would be entitled to benefits if he/she or a member or members of his/her family resided in the Member State in which the institution is situated; or
  (iii) the institution designated by the competent authority of the Member State concerned; or
  (iv) in the case of a scheme relating to an employer's obligations in respect of the benefits set out in Article 3(1), either the employer or the insurer involved or, in default thereof, the body or authority designated by the competent authority of the Member State concerned;

(r) 'institution of the place of residence' and 'institution of the place of stay' mean respectively the institution which is competent to provide benefits in the place where the person concerned resides and the institution which is competent to provide benefits in the place where the person concerned is staying, in accordance with the legislation administered by that institution or, where no such institution exists, the institution designated by the competent authority of the Member State concerned;

(s) 'competent Member State' means the Member State in which the competent institution is situated;

(t) 'period of insurance' means periods of contribution, employment or self-employment as defined or recognised as periods of insurance by the legislation under which they were completed or considered as completed, and all periods treated as such, where they are regarded by the said legislation as equivalent to periods of insurance;

(u) 'period of employment' or 'period of self-employment' mean periods so defined or recognised by the legislation under which they were completed, and all periods treated as such, where they are regarded by the said legislation as equivalent to periods of employment or to periods of self-employment;

(v) 'period of residence' means periods so defined or recognised by the legislation under which they were completed or considered as completed;

(va) 'Benefits in kind' means:
  (i) for the purposes of Title III, Chapter 1 (sickness, maternity and equivalent paternity benefits), benefits in kind provided for under the legislation of a Member State which are intended to supply, make available, pay directly or reimburse the cost of medical care and products and services ancillary to that care. This includes long-term care benefits in kind;
  (ii) for the purposes of Title III, Chapter 2 (accidents at work and occupational diseases), all benefits in kind relating to accidents at work and occupational diseases as defined in point (i) above and provided for under the Member States' accidents at work and occupational diseases schemes;

(w) 'pension' covers not only pensions but also lump-sum benefits which can be substituted for them and payments in the form of reimbursement of contributions and, subject to the provisions of Title III, revaluation increases or supplementary allowances;

(x) 'pre-retirement benefit' means: all cash benefits, other than an unemployment benefit or an early old-age benefit, provided from a specified age to workers who have reduced, ceased or suspended their remunerative activities until the age at which they qualify for an old-age pension or an early retirement pension, the receipt of which is not conditional upon the person concerned being available to the employment services of the competent State; 'early old-age benefit' means a benefit provided before the normal pension entitlement age is reached and which either continues to be provided once the said age is reached or is replaced by another old-age benefit;

(y) 'death grant' means any one-off payment in the event of death excluding the lump-sum benefits referred to in subparagraph w;

(z) 'family benefit' means all benefits in kind or in cash intended to meet family expenses, excluding advances of maintenance payments and special childbirth and adoption allowances mentioned in Annex I.

Article 2 Persons covered

1. This Regulation shall apply to nationals of a Member State, stateless persons and refugees residing in a Member State who are or have been subject to the legislation of one or more Member States, as well as to the members of their families and to their survivors.

2. It shall also apply to the survivors of persons who have been subject to the legislation of one or more Member States, irrespective of the nationality of such persons, where their survivors are nationals of a Member State or stateless persons or refugees residing in one of the Member States.

Article 3 Matters covered

1. This Regulation shall apply to all legislation concerning the following branches of social security:
   (a) sickness benefits;
   (b) maternity and equivalent paternity benefits;
   (c) invalidity benefits;
   (d) old-age benefits;
   (e) survivors' benefits;
   (f) benefits in respect of accidents at work and occupational diseases;
   (g) death grants;
   (h) unemployment benefits;
   (i) pre-retirement benefits;
   (j) family benefits.

2. Unless otherwise provided for in Annex XI, this Regulation shall apply to general and special social security schemes, whether contributory or non-contributory, and to schemes relating to the obligations of an employer or shipowner.

3. This Regulation shall also apply to the special non-contributory cash benefits covered by Article 70.

4. The provisions of Title III of this Regulation shall not, however, affect the legislative provisions of any Member State concerning a shipowner's obligations.

5. This Regulation shall not apply to:
   (a) social and medical assistance or
   (b) benefits in relation to which a Member State assumes the liability for damages to persons and provides for compensation, such as those for victims of war and military action or their consequences; victims of crime, assassination or terrorist acts; victims of damage occasioned by agents of the Member State in the course of their duties; or victims who have suffered a disadvantage for political or religious reasons or for reasons of descent.

Article 4 Equality of treatment

Unless otherwise provided for by this Regulation, persons to whom this Regulation applies shall enjoy the same benefits and be subject to the same obligations under the legislation of any Member State as the nationals thereof.

Article 5 Equal treatment of benefits, income, facts or events

Unless otherwise provided for by this Regulation and in the light of the special implementing provisions laid down, the following shall apply:

(a) where, under the legislation of the competent Member State, the receipt of social security benefits and other income has certain legal effects, the relevant provisions of that legislation shall also apply to the receipt of equivalent benefits acquired under the legislation of another Member State or to income acquired in another Member State;

(b) where, under the legislation of the competent Member State, legal effects are attributed to the occurrence of certain facts or events, that Member State shall take account of like facts or events occurring in any Member State as though they had taken place in its own territory.

Article 6 Aggregation of periods

Unless otherwise provided for by this Regulation, the competent institution of a Member State whose legislation makes:

— the acquisition, retention, duration or recovery of the right to benefits,

— the coverage by legislation, or

— the access to or the exemption from compulsory, optional continued or voluntary insurance,

conditional upon the completion of periods of insurance, employment, self-employment or residence shall, to the extent necessary, take into account periods of insurance, employment, self-employment or residence completed under the legislation of any other Member State as though they were periods completed under the legislation which it applies.

Article 7 Waiving of residence rules

Unless otherwise provided for by this Regulation, cash benefits payable under the legislation of one or more Member States or under this Regulation shall not be subject to any reduction, amendment, suspension, withdrawal or confiscation on account of the fact that the beneficiary or the members of his/her family reside in a Member State other than that in which the institution responsible for providing benefits is situated.

Article 8 Relations between this Regulation and other coordination instruments

1. This Regulation shall replace any social security convention applicable between Member States falling under its scope. Certain provisions of social security conventions entered into by the Member States before the date of application of this Regulation shall, however, continue to apply provided that they are more favourable to the beneficiaries or if they arise from specific historical circumstances and their effect is limited in time. For these provisions to remain applicable, they shall be included in Annex II. If, on objective grounds, it is not possible to extend some of these provisions to all persons to whom the Regulation applies this shall be specified.

2. Two or more Member States may, as the need arises, conclude conventions with each other based on the principles of this Regulation and in keeping with the spirit thereof.

Article 9 Declarations by the Member States on the scope of this Regulation

1. The Member States shall notify the European Commission in writing of the declarations made in accordance with point (l) of Article 1, the legislation and schemes referred to in Article 3, the conventions entered into as referred to in Article 8(2), the minimum benefits referred to in Article 58, and the lack of an insurance system as referred to in Article 65a(1), as well as substantive amendments. Such notifications shall indicate the date from which this Regulation will apply to the schemes specified by the Member States therein.

2. These notifications shall be submitted to the European Commission every year and shall be given the necessary publicity.

Article 10 Prevention of overlapping of benefits

Unless otherwise specified, this Regulation shall neither confer nor maintain the right to several benefits of the same kind for one and the same period of compulsory insurance.

TITLE II
DETERMINATION OF THE LEGISLATION APPLICABLE

Article 11 General rules

1. Persons to whom this Regulation applies shall be subject to the legislation of a single Member State only. Such legislation shall be determined in accordance with this Title.

2. For the purposes of this Title, persons receiving cash benefits because or as a consequence of their activity as an employed or self-employed person shall be considered to be pursuing the said activity. This shall not apply to invalidity, old-age or survivors' pensions or to pensions in respect of accidents at work or occupational diseases or to sickness benefits in cash covering treatment for an unlimited period.

3. Subject to Articles 12 to 16:
   (a) a person pursuing an activity as an employed or self-employed person in a Member State shall be subject to the legislation of that Member State;
   (b) a civil servant shall be subject to the legislation of the Member State to which the administration employing him/her is subject;
   (c) a person receiving unemployment benefits in accordance with Article 65 under the legislation of the Member State of residence shall be subject to the legislation of that Member State;
   (d) a person called up or recalled for service in the armed forces or for civilian service in a Member State shall be subject to the legislation of that Member State;
   (e) any other person to whom subparagraphs (a) to (d) do not apply shall be subject to the legislation of the Member State of residence, without prejudice to other provisions of this Regulation guaranteeing him/her benefits under the legislation of one or more other Member States.

4. For the purposes of this Title, an activity as an employed or self-employed person normally pursued on board a vessel at sea flying the flag of a Member State shall be deemed to be an activity pursued in the said Member State. However, a person employed on board a vessel flying the flag of a Member State and remunerated for such activity by an undertaking or a person whose registered office or place of business is in another Member State shall be subject to the legislation of the latter Member State if he/she resides in that State. The undertaking or person paying the remuneration shall be considered as the employer for the purposes of the said legislation.

5. An activity as a flight crew or cabin crew member performing air passenger or freight services shall be deemed to be an activity pursued in the Member State where the home base, as defined in Annex III to Regulation (EEC) No 3922/91, is located.

Article 12 Special rules

1. A person who pursues an activity as an employed person in a Member State on behalf of an employer which normally carries out its activities there and who is posted by that employer to another Member State to perform work on that employer's behalf shall continue to be subject to the legislation of the first Member State, provided that the anticipated duration of such work does not exceed 24 months and that he/she is not sent to replace another person.

2. A person who normally pursues an activity as a self-employed person in a Member State who goes to pursue a similar activity in another Member State shall continue to be subject to the legislation of the first Member State, provided that the anticipated duration of such activity does not exceed 24 months.

Article 13 Pursuit of activities in two or more Member States

1. A person who normally pursues an activity as an employed person in two or more Member
   States shall be subject:
   (a) to the legislation of the Member State of residence if he/she pursues a substantial part of his/her activity in that Member State; or
   (b) if he/she does not pursue a substantial part of his/her activity in the Member State of residence:
      (i) to the legislation of the Member State in which the registered office or place of business of the undertaking or employer is situated if he/she is employed by one undertaking or employer; or

      (ii)   to the legislation of the Member State in which the registered office or place of business of the undertakings or employers is situated if he/she is employed by two or more undertakings or employers which have their registered office or place of business in only one Member State; or

      (iii)   to the legislation of the Member State in which the registered office or place of business of the undertaking or employer is situated other than the Member State of residence if he/she is employed by two or more undertakings or employers, which have their registered office or place of business in two Member States, one of which is the Member State of residence; or

      (iv)   to the legislation of the Member State of residence if he/she is employed by two or more undertakings or employers, at least two of which have their registered office or place of business in different Member States other than the Member State of residence.

2.   A person who normally pursues an activity as a self-employed person in two or more Member States shall be subject to:

    (a)   the legislation of the Member State of residence if he/she pursues a substantial part of his/her activity in that Member State; or

    (b)   the legislation of the Member State in which the centre of interest of his/her activities is situated, if he/she does not reside in one of the Member States in which he/she pursues a substantial part of his/her activity.

3.   A person who normally pursues an activity as an employed person and an activity as a self-employed person in different Member States shall be subject to the legislation of the Member State in which he/she pursues an activity as an employed person or, if he/she pursues such an activity in two or more Member States, to the legislation determined in accordance with paragraph 1.

4.   A person who is employed as a civil servant by one Member State and who pursues an activity as an employed person and/or as a self-employed person in one or more other Member States shall be subject to the legislation of the Member State to which the administration employing him/her is subject.

5.   Persons referred to in paragraphs 1 to 4 shall be treated, for the purposes of the legislation determined in accordance with these provisions, as though they were pursuing all their activities as employed or self-employed persons and were receiving all their income in the Member State concerned.

Article 14 Voluntary insurance or optional continued insurance

1.   Articles 11 to 13 shall not apply to voluntary insurance or to optional continued insurance unless, in respect of one of the branches referred to in Article 3(1), only a voluntary scheme of insurance exists in a Member State.

2.   Where, by virtue of the legislation of a Member State, the person concerned is subject to compulsory insurance in that Member State, he/she may not be subject to a voluntary insurance scheme or an optional continued insurance scheme in another Member State. In all other cases in which, for a given branch, there is a choice between several voluntary insurance schemes or optional continued insurance schemes, the person concerned shall join only the scheme of his/her choice.

3.   However, in respect of invalidity, old age and survivors' benefits, the person concerned may join the voluntary or optional continued insurance scheme of a Member State, even if he/she is compulsorily subject to the legislation of another Member State, provided that he/she has been subject, at some stage in his/her career, to the legislation of the first Member State because or as a consequence of an activity as an employed or self-employed person and if such overlapping is explicitly or implicitly allowed under the legislation of the first Member State.

4.   Where the legislation of a Member State makes admission to voluntary insurance or optional continued insurance conditional upon residence in that Member State or upon previous activity as an employed or self-employed person, Article 5(b) shall apply only to persons who have been subject, at some earlier stage, to the legislation of that Member State on the basis of an activity as an employed or self-employed person.

Article 15 Contract staff of the European Communities

Contract staff of the European Communities may opt to be subject to the legislation of the Member State in which they are employed, to the legislation of the Member State to which they were last subject or to the legislation of the Member State whose nationals they are, in respect of provisions other than those relating to family allowances, provided under the scheme applicable to such staff. This right of option, which may be exercised once only, shall take effect from the date of entry into employment.

Article 16 Exceptions to Articles 11 to 15

1. Two or more Member States, the competent authorities of these Member States or the bodies designated by these authorities may by common agreement provide for exceptions to Articles 11 to 15 in the interest of certain persons or categories of persons.
2. A person who receives a pension or pensions under the legislation of one or more Member States and who resides in another Member State may at his/her request be exempted from application of the legislation of the latter State provided that he/she is not subject to that legislation on account of pursuing an activity as an employed or self-employed person.

TITLE III
SPECIAL PROVISIONS CONCERNING THE VARIOUS CATEGORIES OF BENEFITS

CHAPTER 1
SICKNESS, MATERNITY AND EQUIVALENT PATERNITY BENEFITS

SECTION 1
INSURED PERSONS AND MEMBERS OF THEIR FAMILIES, EXCEPT PENSIONERS AND MEMBERS OF THEIR FAMILIES

Article 17 Residence in a Member State other than the competent Member State

An insured person or members of his/her family who reside in a Member State other than the competent Member State shall receive in the Member State of residence benefits in kind provided, on behalf of the competent institution, by the institution of the place of residence, in accordance with the provisions of the legislation it applies, as though they were insured under the said legislation.

Article 18 Stay in the competent Member State when residence is in another Member State – Special rules for the members of the families of frontier workers

1. Unless otherwise provided for by paragraph 2, the insured person and the members of his/her family referred to in Article 17 shall also be entitled to benefits in kind while staying in the competent Member State. The benefits in kind shall be provided by the competent institution and at its own expense, in accordance with the provisions of the legislation it applies, as though the persons concerned resided in that Member State.
2. The members of the family of a frontier worker shall be entitled to benefits in kind during their stay in the competent Member State.
   Where the competent Member State is listed in Annex III however, the members of the family of a frontier worker who reside in the same Member State as the frontier worker shall be entitled to benefits in kind in the competent Member State only under the conditions laid down in Article 19(1).

Article 19 Stay outside the competent Member State

1. Unless otherwise provided for by paragraph 2, an insured person and the members of his/her family staying in a Member State other than the competent Member State shall be entitled to the benefits in kind which become necessary on medical grounds during their stay, taking into account the nature of the benefits and the expected length of the stay. These benefits shall be provided on behalf of the competent institution by the institution of the place of stay, in accordance with the provisions of the legislation it applies, as though the persons concerned were insured under the said legislation.

2.   The Administrative Commission shall establish a list of benefits in kind which, in order to be provided during a stay in another Member State, require for practical reasons a prior agreement between the person concerned and the institution providing the care.

Article 20 Travel with the purpose of receiving benefits in kind — authorisation to receive appropriate treatment outside the Member State of residence

1.   Unless otherwise provided for by this Regulation, an insured person travelling to another Member State with the purpose of receiving benefits in kind during the stay shall seek authorisation from the competent institution.

2.   An insured person who is authorised by the competent institution to go to another Member State with the purpose of receiving the treatment appropriate to his/her condition shall receive the benefits in kind provided, on behalf of the competent institution, by the institution of the place of stay, in accordance with the provisions of the legislation it applies, as though he/she were insured under the said legislation. The authorisation shall be accorded where the treatment in question is among the benefits provided for by the legislation in the Member State where the person concerned resides and where he/she cannot be given such treatment within a time limit which is medically justifiable, taking into account his/her current state of health and the probable course of his/her illness.

3.   Paragraphs 1 and 2 shall apply *mutatis mutandis* to the members of the family of an insured person.

4.   If the members of the family of an insured person reside in a Member State other than the Member State in which the insured person resides, and this Member State has opted for reimbursement on the basis of fixed amounts, the cost of the benefits in kind referred to in paragraph 2 shall be borne by the institution of the place of residence of the members of the family. In this case, for the purposes of paragraph 1, the institution of the place of residence of the members of the family shall be considered to be the competent institution.

Article 21 Cash benefits

1.   An insured person and members of his/her family residing or staying in a Member State other than the competent Member State shall be entitled to cash benefits provided by the competent institution in accordance with the legislation it applies. By agreement between the competent institution and the institution of the place of residence or stay, such benefits may, however, be provided by the institution of the place of residence or stay at the expense of the competent institution in accordance with the legislation of the competent Member State.

2.   The competent institution of a Member State whose legislation stipulates that the calculation of cash benefits shall be based on average income or on an average contribution basis shall determine such average income or average contribution basis exclusively by reference to the incomes confirmed as having been paid, or contribution bases applied, during the periods completed under the said legislation.

3.   The competent institution of a Member State whose legislation provides that the calculation of cash benefits shall be based on standard income shall take into account exclusively the standard income or, where appropriate, the average of standard incomes for the periods completed under the said legislation.

4.   Paragraphs 2 and 3 shall apply *mutatis mutandis* to cases where the legislation applied by the competent institution lays down a specific reference period which corresponds in the case in question either wholly or partly to the periods which the person concerned has completed under the legislation of one or more other Member States.

Article 22 Pension claimants

1.   An insured person who, on making a claim for a pension, or during the investigation thereof, ceases to be entitled to benefits in kind under the legislation of the Member State last competent, shall remain entitled to benefits in kind under the legislation of the Member State in which he/she resides, provided that the pension claimant satisfies the insurance conditions of the legislation of the Member State referred to in paragraph 2. The right to benefits in kind in the Member State of residence shall also apply to the members of the family of the pension claimant.

2. The benefits in kind shall be chargeable to the institution of the Member State which, in the event of a pension being awarded, would become competent under Articles 23 to 25.

SECTION 2
PENSIONERS AND MEMBERS OF THEIR FAMILIES

Article 23 Right to benefits in kind under the legislation of the Member State of residence

A person who receives a pension or pensions under the legislation of two or more Member States, of which one is the Member State of residence, and who is entitled to benefits in kind under the legislation of that Member State, shall, with the members of his/her family, receive such benefits in kind from and at the expense of the institution of the place of residence, as though he/she were a pensioner whose pension was payable solely under the legislation of that Member State.

Article 24 No right to benefits in kind under the legislation of the Member State of residence

1. A person who receives a pension or pensions under the legislation of one or more Member States and who is not entitled to benefits in kind under the legislation of the Member State of residence shall nevertheless receive such benefits for himself/herself and the members of his/her family, in so far as he/she would be entitled thereto under the legislation of the Member State or of at least one of the Member States competent in respect of his/her pensions, if he/she resided in that Member State. The benefits in kind shall be provided at the expense of the institution referred to in paragraph 2 by the institution of the place of residence, as though the person concerned were entitled to a pension and benefits in kind under the legislation of that Member State.

2. In the cases covered by paragraph 1, the cost of benefits in kind shall be borne by the institution as determined in accordance with the following rules:

    (a) where the pensioner is entitled to benefits in kind under the legislation of a single Member State, the cost shall be borne by the competent institution of that Member State;

    (b) where the pensioner is entitled to benefits in kind under the legislation of two or more Member States, the cost thereof shall be borne by the competent institution of the Member State to whose legislation the person has been subject for the longest period of time; should the application of this rule result in several institutions being responsible for the cost of benefits, the cost shall be borne by the institution applying the legislation to which the pensioner was last subject.

Article 25 Pensions under the legislation of one or more Member States other than the Member State of residence, where there is a right to benefits in kind in the latter Member State

Where the person receiving a pension or pensions under the legislation of one or more Member States resides in a Member State under whose legislation the right to receive benefits in kind is not subject to conditions of insurance, or of activity as an employed or self-employed person, and no pension is received from that Member State, the cost of benefits in kind provided to him/her and to members of his/her family shall be borne by the institution of one of the Member States competent in respect of his/her pensions determined in accordance with Article 24(2), to the extent that the pensioner and the members of his/her family would be entitled to such benefits if they resided in that Member State.

Article 26 Residence of members of the family in a Member State other than the one in which the pensioner resides

Members of the family of a person receiving a pension or pensions under the legislation of one or more Member States who reside in a Member State other than the one in which the pensioner resides shall be entitled to receive benefits in kind from the institution of the place of their residence in accordance with the provisions of the legislation it applies, in so far as the pensioner is entitled to benefits in kind under the legislation of a Member

State. The costs shall be borne by the competent institution responsible for the costs of the benefits in kind provided to the pensioner in his/her Member State of residence.

Article 27 Stay of the pensioner or the members of his/her family in a Member State other than the Member State in which they reside — stay in the competent Member State — authorisation for appropriate treatment outside the Member State of residence

1. Article 19 shall apply *mutatis mutandis* to a person receiving a pension or pensions under the legislation of one or more Member States and entitled to benefits in kind under the legislation of one of the Member States which provide his/her pension(s) or to the members of his/her family who are staying in a Member State other than the one in which they reside.

2. Article 18(1) shall apply *mutatis mutandis* to the persons described in paragraph 1 when they stay in the Member State in which is situated the competent institution responsible for the cost of the benefits in kind provided to the pensioner in his/her Member State of residence and the said Member State has opted for this and is listed in Annex IV.

3. Article 20 shall apply *mutatis mutandis* to a pensioner and/or the members of his/her family who are staying in a Member State other than the one in which they reside with the purpose of receiving there the treatment appropriate to their condition.

4. Unless otherwise provided for by paragraph 5, the cost of the benefits in kind referred to in paragraphs 1 to 3 shall be borne by the competent institution responsible for the cost of benefits in kind provided to the pensioner in his/her Member State of residence.

5. The cost of the benefits in kind referred to in paragraph 3 shall be borne by the institution of the place of residence of the pensioner or of the members of his/her family, if these persons reside in a Member State which has opted for reimbursement on the basis of fixed amounts. In these cases, for the purposes of paragraph 3, the institution of the place of residence of the pensioner or of the members of his/her family shall be considered to be the competent institution.

Article 28 Special rules for retired frontier workers

1. A frontier worker who has retired because of old-age or invalidity is entitled in the event of sickness to continue to receive benefits in kind in the Member State where he/she last pursued his/her activity as an employed or self-employed person, in so far as this is a continuation of treatment which began in that Member State. 'Continuation of treatment' means the continued investigation, diagnosis and treatment of an illness for its entire duration.
   The first subparagraph shall apply *mutatis mutandis* to the members of the family of the former frontier worker unless the Member State where the frontier worker last pursued his/her activity is listed in Annex III.

2. A pensioner who, in the five years preceding the effective date of an old-age or invalidity pension has been pursuing an activity as an employed or self-employed person for at least two years as a frontier worker shall be entitled to benefits in kind in the Member State in which he/she pursued such an activity as a frontier worker, if this Member State and the Member State in which the competent institution responsible for the costs of the benefits in kind provided to the pensioner in his/her Member State of residence is situated have opted for this and are both listed in Annex V.

3. Paragraph 2 shall apply *mutatis mutandis* to the members of the family of a former frontier worker or his/her survivors if, during the periods referred to in paragraph 2, they were entitled to benefits in kind under Article 18(2), even if the frontier worker died before his/her pension commenced, provided he/she had been pursuing an activity as an employed or self-employed person as a frontier worker for at least two years in the five years preceding his/her death.

4. Paragraphs 2 and 3 shall be applicable until the person concerned becomes subject to the legislation of a Member State on the basis of an activity as an employed or self-employed person.

5.   The cost of the benefits in kind referred to in paragraphs 1 to 3 shall be borne by the competent institution responsible for the cost of benefits in kind provided to the pensioner or to his/her survivors in their respective Member States of residence.

Article 29 Cash benefits for pensioners

1.   Cash benefits shall be paid to a person receiving a pension or pensions under the legislation of one or more Member States by the competent institution of the Member State in which is situated the competent institution responsible for the cost of benefits in kind provided to the pensioner in his/her Member State of residence. Article 21 shall apply *mutatis mutandis.*
2.   Paragraph 1 shall also apply to the members of a pensioner's family.

Article 30 Contributions by pensioners

1.   The institution of a Member State which is responsible under the legislation it applies for making deductions in respect of contributions for sickness, maternity and equivalent paternity benefits, may request and recover such deductions, calculated in accordance with the legislation it applies, only to the extent that the cost of the benefits pursuant to Articles 23 to 26 is to be borne by an institution of the said Member State.
2.   Where, in the cases referred to in Article 25, the acquisition of sickness, maternity and equivalent paternity benefits is subject to the payment of contributions or similar payments
      under the legislation of a Member State in which the pensioner concerned resides, these contributions shall not be payable by virtue of such residence.

SECTION 3
COMMON PROVISIONS

Article 31 General provision

Articles 23 to 30 shall not apply to a pensioner or the members of his/her family who are entitled to benefits under the legislation of a Member State on the basis of an activity as an employed or self-employed person. In such a case, the person concerned shall be subject, for the purposes of this Chapter, to Articles 17 to 21.

Article 32 Prioritising of the right to benefits in kind — special rule for the right of members of the family to benefits in the Member State of residence

1.   An independent right to benefits in kind based on the legislation of a Member State or on this Chapter shall take priority over a derivative right to benefits for members of a family. A derivative right to benefits in kind shall, however, take priority over independent rights, where the independent right in the Member State of residence exists directly and solely on the basis of the residence of the person concerned in that Member State.
2.   Where the members of the family of an insured person reside in a Member State under whose legislation the right to benefits in kind is not subject to conditions of insurance or activity as an employed or self-employed person, benefits in kind shall be provided at the expense of the competent institution in the Member State in which they reside, if the spouse or the person caring for the children of the insured person pursues an activity as an employed or self-employed person in the said Member State or receives a pension from that Member State on the basis of an activity as an employed or self-employed person.

Article 33 Substantial benefits in kind

1.   An insured person or a member of his/her family who has had a right to a prosthesis, a major appliance or other substantial benefits in kind recognised by the institution of a Member State, before he/she became insured under the legislation applied by the institution of another Member State, shall receive such benefits at the expense of the first institution, even if they are awarded after the said person has already become insured under the legislation applied by the second institution.
2.   The Administrative Commission shall draw up the list of benefits covered by paragraph 1.

Article 34 Overlapping of long-term care benefits

1.   If a recipient of long-term care benefits in cash, which have to be treated as sickness benefits and are therefore provided by the Member State competent for cash benefits under Articles 21 or 29, is, at the same time and under this Chapter, entitled to claim benefits in kind intended for the same purpose from the institution of the place of residence or stay in another Member State, and an institution in the first Member State is also required to reimburse the cost of these benefits in kind under Article 35, the general provision on prevention of overlapping of benefits laid down in Article 10 shall be applicable, with the following restriction only: if the person concerned claims and receives the benefit in kind, the amount of the benefit in cash shall be reduced by the amount of the benefit in kind which is or could be claimed from the institution of the first Member State required to reimburse the cost.

2.   The Administrative Commission shall draw up the list of the cash benefits and benefits in kind covered by paragraph 1.

3.   Two or more Member States, or their competent authorities, may agree on other or supplementary measures which shall not be less advantageous for the persons concerned than the principles laid down in paragraph 1.

Article 35 Reimbursements between institutions

1.   The benefits in kind provided by the institution of a Member State on behalf of the institution of another Member State under this Chapter shall give rise to full reimbursement.

2.   The reimbursements referred to in paragraph 1 shall be determined and effected in accordance with the arrangements set out in the Implementing Regulation, either on production of proof of actual expenditure, or on the basis of fixed amounts for Member States the legal or administrative structures of which are such that the use of reimbursement on the basis of actual expenditure is not appropriate.

3.   Two or more Member States, and their competent authorities, may provide for other methods of reimbursement or waive all reimbursement between the institutions coming under their jurisdiction.

CHAPTER 2

BENEFITS IN RESPECT OF ACCIDENTS AT WORK AND OCCUPATIONAL DISEASES

Article 36 Right to benefits in kind and in cash

1.   Without prejudice to any more favourable provisions in paragraphs 2 and 2a of this Article, Articles 17, 18(1), 19(1) and 20(1) shall also apply to benefits relating to accidents at work or occupational diseases.

2.   A person who has sustained an accident at work or has contracted an occupational disease and who resides or stays in a Member State other than the competent Member State shall be entitled to the special benefits in kind of the scheme covering accidents at work and occupational diseases provided, on behalf of the competent institution, by the institution of the place of residence or stay in accordance with the legislation which it applies, as though he/she were insured under the said legislation.

2a.   The competent institution may not refuse to grant the authorisation provided for in Article 20(1) to a person who has sustained an accident at work or who has contracted an occupational disease and who is entitled to benefits chargeable to that institution, where the treatment appropriate to his/her condition cannot be given in the Member State in which he/she resides within a time-limit which is medically justifiable, taking into account his/her current state of health and the probable course of the illness.

3.   Article 21 shall also apply to benefits falling within this Chapter.

Article 37 Costs of transport

1.   The competent institution of a Member State whose legislation provides for meeting the costs of transporting a person who has sustained an accident at work or is suffering from an occupational disease, either to his/her place of residence or to a hospital, shall meet such costs to the corresponding place in another Member State where the person resides, provided that that institution gives prior authorisation for

such transport, duly taking into account the reasons justifying it. Such authorisation shall not be required in the case of a frontier worker.

2. The competent institution of a Member State whose legislation provides for meeting the costs of transporting the body of a person killed in an accident at work to the place of burial shall, in accordance with the legislation it applies, meet such costs to the corresponding place in another Member State where the person was residing at the time of the accident.

Article 38 Benefits for an occupational disease where the person suffering from such a disease has been exposed to the same risk in several Member States

When a person who has contracted an occupational disease has, under the legislation of two or more Member States, pursued an activity which by its nature is likely to cause the said disease, the benefits that he/she or his/her survivors may claim shall be provided exclusively under the legislation of the last of those States whose conditions are satisfied.

Article 39 Aggravation of an occupational disease

In the event of aggravation of an occupational disease for which a person suffering from such a disease has received or is receiving benefits under the legislation of a Member State, the following rules shall apply:

(a) if the person concerned, while in receipt of benefits, has not pursued, under the legislation of another Member State, an activity as an employed or self-employed person likely to cause or aggravate the disease in question, the competent institution of the first Member State shall bear the cost of the benefits under the provisions of the legislation which it applies, taking into account the aggravation;

(b) if the person concerned, while in receipt of benefits, has pursued such an activity under the legislation of another Member State, the competent institution of the first

Member State shall bear the cost of the benefits under the legislation it applies without taking the aggravation into account. The competent institution of the second Member State shall grant a supplement to the person concerned, the amount of which shall be equal to the difference between the amount of benefits due after the aggravation and the amount which would have been due prior to the aggravation under the legislation it applies, if the disease in question had occurred under the legislation of that Member State;

(c) the rules concerning reduction, suspension or withdrawal laid down by the legislation of a Member State shall not be invoked against persons receiving benefits provided by institutions of two Member States in accordance with subparagraph (b).

Article 40 Rules for taking into account the special features of certain legislation

1. If there is no insurance against accidents at work or occupational diseases in the Member State in which the person concerned resides or stays, or if such insurance exists but there is no institution responsible for providing benefits in kind, those benefits shall be provided by the institution of the place of residence or stay responsible for providing benefits in kind in the event of sickness.

2. If there is no insurance against accidents at work or occupational diseases in the competent Member State, the provisions of this Chapter concerning benefits in kind shall nevertheless be applied to a person who is entitled to those benefits in the event of sickness, maternity or equivalent paternity under the legislation of that Member State if that person sustains an accident at work or suffers from an occupational disease during a residence or stay in another Member State. Costs shall be borne by the institution which is competent for the benefits in kind under the legislation of the competent Member State.

3. Article 5 shall apply to the competent institution in a Member State as regards the equivalence of accidents at work and occupational diseases which either have occurred or have been confirmed subsequently under the legislation of another

Member State when assessing the degree of incapacity, the right to benefits or the amount thereof, on condition that:

(a)   no compensation is due in respect of an accident at work or an occupational disease which had occurred or had been confirmed previously under the legislation it applies; and

(b)   no compensation is due in respect of an accident at work or an occupational disease which had occurred or had been confirmed subsequently, under the legislation of the other Member State under which the accident at work or the occupational disease had occurred or been confirmed.

Article 41 Reimbursements between institutions

1.   Article 35 shall also apply to benefits falling within this Chapter, and reimbursement shall be made on the basis of actual costs.

2.   Two or more Member States, or their competent authorities, may provide for other methods of reimbursement or waive all reimbursement between the institutions under their jurisdiction.

CHAPTER 3
DEATH GRANTS

Article 42 Right to grants where death occurs in, or where the person entitled resides in, a Member State other than the competent Member State

1.   When an insured person or a member of his/her family dies in a Member State other than the competent Member State, the death shall be deemed to have occurred in the competent Member State.

2.   The competent institution shall be obliged to provide death grants payable under the legislation it applies, even if the person entitled resides in a Member State other than the competent Member State.

3.   Paragraphs 1 and 2 shall also apply when the death is the result of an accident at work or an occupational disease.

Article 43 Provision of benefits in the event of the death of a pensioner

1.   In the event of the death of a pensioner who was entitled to a pension under the legislation of one Member State, or to pensions under the legislations of two or more Member States, when that pensioner was residing in a Member State other than that of the institution responsible for the cost of benefits in kind provided under Articles 24 and 25, the death grants payable under the legislation administered by that institution shall be provided at its own expense as though the pensioner had been residing at the time of his/her death in the Member State in which that institution is situated.

2.   Paragraph 1 shall apply *mutatis mutandis* to the members of the family of a pensioner.

CHAPTER 4
INVALIDITY BENEFITS

Article 44 Persons subject only to type A legislation

1.   For the purposes of this Chapter, 'type A legislation' means any legislation under which the amount of invalidity benefits is independent of the duration of the periods of insurance or residence and which is expressly included by the competent Member State in Annex VI, and 'type B legislation' means any other legislation.

2.   A person who h.as been successively or alternately subject to the legislation of two or more Member States and who has completed periods of insurance or residence exclusively under type A legislations shall be entitled to benefits only from the institution of the Member State whose legislation was applicable at the time when the incapacity for work followed by invalidity occurred, taking into account, where appropriate, Article 45, and shall receive such benefits in accordance with that legislation.

3.   A person who is not entitled to benefits under paragraph 2 shall receive the benefits to which he/she is still entitled under the legislation of another Member State, taking into account, where appropriate, Article 45.

4.   If the legislation referred to in paragraph 2 or 3 contains rules for the reduction, suspension or withdrawal of invalidity benefits in the case of overlapping with other income or with benefits of a different kind within the meaning of Article 53(2), Articles 53(3) and 55(3) shall apply *mutatis mutandis*.

Article 45 Special provisions on aggregation of periods

The competent institution of a Member State whose legislation makes the acquisition, retention or recovery of the right to benefits conditional upon the completion of periods of insurance or residence shall, where necessary, apply Article 51(1) *mutatis mutandis*.

Article 46 Persons subject either only to type B legislation or to type A and B legislation

1.   A person who has been successively or alternately subject to the legislation of two or more Member States, of which at least one is not a type A legislation, shall be entitled to benefits under Chapter 5, which shall apply *mutatis mutandis* taking into account paragraph 3.

2.   However, if the person concerned has been previously subject to a type B legislation and suffers incapacity for work leading to invalidity while subject to a type A legislation, he/she shall receive benefits in accordance with Article 44, provided that:
   − he satisfies the conditions of that legislation exclusively or of others of the same type, taking into account, where appropriate, Article 45, but without having recourse to periods of insurance or residence completed under a type B legislation, and
   − he does not assert any claims to old-age benefits, taking into account Article 50(1).

3.   A decision taken by an institution of a Member State concerning the degree of invalidity of a claimant shall be binding on the institution of any other Member State concerned, provided that the concordance between the legislation of these Member States on conditions relating to the degree of invalidity is acknowledged in Annex VII.

Article 47 Aggravation of invalidity

1.   In the case of aggravation of an invalidity for which a person is receiving benefits under the legislation of one or more Member States, the following provisions shall apply, taking the aggravation into account:
   (a)   the benefits shall be provided in accordance with Chapter 5, applied *mutatis mutandis;*
   (b)   however, where the person concerned has been subject to two or more type A legislations and since receiving benefit has not been subject to the legislation of another Member State, the benefit shall be provided in accordance with Article 44(2).

2.   If the total amount of the benefit or benefits payable under paragraph 1 is lower than the amount of the benefit which the person concerned was receiving at the expense of the institution previously competent for payment, that institution shall pay him/her a supplement equal to the difference between the two amounts.

3.   If the person concerned is not entitled to benefits at the expense of an institution of another Member State, the competent institution of the Member State previously competent shall provide the benefits in accordance with the legislation it applies, taking into account the aggravation and, where appropriate, Article 45.

Article 48 Conversion of invalidity benefits into old-age benefits

1.   Invalidity benefits shall be converted into old-age benefits, where appropriate, under the conditions laid down by the legislation or legislations under which they are provided and in accordance with Chapter 5.

2.   Where a person receiving invalidity benefits can establish a claim to old-age benefits under the legislation of one or more other Member States, in accordance with Article 50, any institution which is responsible for providing invalidity benefits under the legislation of a Member State shall continue to provide such a person with the invalidity benefits to which he/she is entitled under the legislation it applies until paragraph 1 becomes applicable in respect of that institution, or otherwise for as long as the person concerned satisfies the conditions for such benefits.

3. Where invalidity benefits provided under the legislation of a Member State, in accordance with Article 44, are converted into old-age benefits and where the person concerned does not yet satisfy the conditions laid down by the legislation of one or more of the other Member States for receiving those benefits, the person concerned shall receive, from that or those Member States, invalidity benefits from the date of the conversion.

Those invalidity benefits shall be provided in accordance with Chapter 5 as if that Chapter had been applicable at the time when the incapacity for work leading to invalidity occurred, until the person concerned satisfies the qualifying conditions for old-age benefit laid down by the national legislations concerned or, where such conversion is not provided for, for as long as he/she is entitled to invalidity benefits under the latter legislation or legislations.

4. The invalidity benefits provided under Article 44 shall be recalculated in accordance with Chapter 5 as soon as the beneficiary satisfies the qualifying conditions for invalidity benefits laid down by a type B legislation, or as soon as he/she receives old-age benefits under the legislation of another Member State.

Article 49 Special provisions for civil servants

Articles 6, 44, 46, 47 and 48 and Article 60(2) and (3) shall apply *mutatis mutandis* to persons covered by a special scheme for civil servants.

CHAPTER 5

OLD-AGE AND SURVIVORS' PENSIONS

Article 50 General provisions

1. All the competent institutions shall determine entitlement to benefit, under all the legislations of the Member States to which the person concerned has been subject, when a request for award has been submitted, unless the person concerned expressly requests deferment of the award of old-age benefits under the legislation of one or more Member States.

2. If at a given moment the person concerned does not satisfy, or no longer satisfies, the conditions laid down by all the legislations of the Member States to which he/she has been subject, the institutions applying legislation the conditions of which have been satisfied shall not take into account, when performing the calculation in accordance with Article 52(1) (a) or (b), the periods completed under the legislations the conditions of which have not been satisfied, or are no longer satisfied, where this gives rise to a lower amount of benefit.

3. Paragraph 2 shall apply *mutatis mutandis* when the person concerned has expressly requested deferment of the award of old-age benefits.

4. A new calculation shall be performed automatically as and when the conditions to be fulfilled under the other legislations are satisfied or when a person requests the award of an old-age benefit deferred in accordance with paragraph 1, unless the periods completed under the other legislations have already been taken into account by virtue of paragraph 2 or 3.

Article 51 Special provisions on aggregation of periods

1. Where the legislation of a Member State makes the granting of certain benefits conditional upon the periods of insurance having been completed only in a specific activity as an employed or self-employed person or in an occupation which is subject to a special scheme for employed or self-employed persons, the competent institution of that Member State shall take into account periods completed under the legislation of other Member States only if completed under a corresponding scheme or, failing that, in the same occupation, or where appropriate, in the same activity as an employed or self-employed person.

If, account having been taken of the periods thus completed, the person concerned does not satisfy the conditions for receipt of the benefits of a special scheme, these periods shall be taken into account for the purposes of providing the benefits of the general scheme or, failing that, of the scheme applicable to manual or clerical workers, as the case may be, provided that the person concerned had been affiliated to one or other of those schemes.

2. The periods of insurance completed under a special scheme of a Member State shall be taken into account for the purposes of providing the benefits of the general scheme or, failing that, of the scheme applicable to manual or clerical workers, as the case may be, of another Member State, provided that the person concerned had been affiliated to one or other of those schemes, even if those periods have already been taken into account in the latter Member State under a special scheme.

3. Where the legislation or specific scheme of a Member State makes the acquisition, retention or recovery of the right to benefits conditional upon the person concerned being insured at the time of the materialisation of the risk, this condition shall be regarded as having been satisfied if that person has been previously insured under the legislation or specific scheme of that Member State and is, at the time of the materialisation of the risk, insured under the legislation of another Member State for the same risk or, failing that, if a benefit is due under the legislation of another Member State for the same risk. The latter condition shall, however, be deemed to be fulfilled in the cases referred to in Article 57.

Article 52 Award of benefits

1. The competent institution shall calculate the amount of the benefit that would be due:
    (a) under the legislation it applies, only where the conditions for entitlement to benefits have been satisfied exclusively under national law (independent benefit);
    (b) by calculating a theoretical amount and subsequently an actual amount (pro rata benefit), as follows:
        (i) the theoretical amount of the benefit is equal to the benefit which the person concerned could claim if all the periods of insurance and/or of residence which have been completed under the legislations of the other Member States had been completed under the legislation it applies on the date of the award of the benefit. If, under this legislation, the amount does not depend on the duration of the periods completed, that amount shall be regarded as being the theoretical amount;
        (ii) the competent institution shall then establish the actual amount of the pro rata benefit by applying to the theoretical amount the ratio between the duration of the periods completed before materialisation of the risk under the legislation it applies and the total duration of the periods completed before materialisation of the risk under the legislations of all the Member States concerned.

2. Where appropriate, the competent institution shall apply, to the amount calculated in accordance with subparagraphs 1(a) and (b), all the rules relating to reduction, suspension or withdrawal, under the legislation it applies, within the limits provided for by Articles 53 to 55.

3. The person concerned shall be entitled to receive from the competent institution of each Member State the higher of the amounts calculated in accordance with subparagraphs 1(a) and (b).

4. Where the calculation pursuant to paragraph 1(a) in one Member State invariably results in the independent benefit being equal to or higher than the pro rata benefit, calculated in accordance with paragraph 1(b), the competent institution shall waive the pro rata calculation, provided that:
    (i) such a situation is set out in Part 1 of Annex VIII;
    (ii) no legislation containing rules against overlapping, as referred to in Articles 54 and 55, is applicable unless the conditions laid down in Article 55(2) are fulfilled; and
    (iii) Article 57 is not applicable in relation to periods completed under the legislation of another Member State in the specific circumstances of the case.

5. Notwithstanding the provisions of paragraphs 1, 2 and 3, the pro rata calculation shall not apply to schemes providing benefits in respect of which periods of time are of no relevance to the calculation, subject to such schemes being listed in part 2 of Annex VIII. In such cases, the person concerned shall be entitled to the benefit calculated in accordance with the legislation of the Member State concerned.

Article 53 Rules to prevent overlapping

1. Any overlapping of invalidity, old age and survivors' benefits calculated or provided on the basis of periods of insurance and/or residence completed by the same person shall be considered to be overlapping of benefits of the same kind.
2. Overlapping of benefits which cannot be considered to be of the same kind within the meaning of paragraph 1 shall be considered to be overlapping of benefits of a different kind.
3. The following provisions shall be applicable for the purposes of rules to prevent overlapping laid down by the legislation of a Member State in the case of overlapping of a benefit in respect of invalidity, old age or survivors with a benefit of the same kind or a benefit of a different kind or with other income:
    (a) the competent institution shall take into account the benefits or incomes acquired in another Member State only where the legislation it applies provides for benefits or income acquired abroad to be taken into account;
    (b) the competent institution shall take into account the amount of benefits to be paid by another Member State before deduction of tax, social security contributions and other individual levies or deductions, unless the legislation it applies provides for the application of rules to prevent overlapping after such deductions, under the conditions and the procedures laid down in the Implementing Regulation;
    (c) the competent institution shall not take into account the amount of benefits acquired under the legislation of another Member State on the basis of voluntary insurance or continued optional insurance;
    (d) if a single Member State applies rules to prevent overlapping because the person concerned receives benefits of the same or of a different kind under the legislation of other Member States or income acquired in other Member States, the benefit due may be reduced solely by the amount of such benefits or such income.

Article 54 Overlapping of benefits of the same kind

1. Where benefits of the same kind due under the legislation of two or more Member States overlap, the rules to prevent overlapping laid down by the legislation of a Member State shall not be applicable to a pro rata benefit.
2. The rules to prevent overlapping shall apply to an independent benefit only if the benefit concerned is:
    (a) a benefit the amount of which does not depend on the duration of periods of insurance or residence, or
    (b) a benefit the amount of which is determined on the basis of a credited period deemed to have been completed between the date on which the risk materialised and a later date, overlapping with:
        (i) a benefit of the same type, except where an agreement has been concluded between two or more Member States to avoid the same credited period being taken into account more than once, or
        (ii) a benefit referred to in subparagraph (a).
        The benefits and agreements referred to in subparagraphs (a) and (b) are listed in Annex IX.

Article 55 Overlapping of benefits of a different kind

1. If the receipt of benefits of a different kind or other income requires the application of the provided for by the legislation of the Member States concerned regarding:
    (a) two or more independent benefits, the competent institutions shall divide the amounts of the benefit or benefits or other income, as they have been taken into account, by the number of benefits subject to the said rules;
        however, the application of this subparagraph cannot deprive the person concerned of his/her status as a pensioner for the purposes of the other chapters of this Title under the conditions and the procedures laid down in the Implementing Regulation;
    (b) one or more pro rata benefits, the competent institutions shall take into account the benefit or benefits or other income and all the elements stipulated for applying the rules to prevent overlapping as a function of the ratio between the periods of insurance and/or residence established for the calculation referred to in Article 52(1)(b)(ii);

    (c)   one or more independent benefits and one or more pro-rata benefits, the competent institutions shall apply *mutatis mutandis* subparagraph (a) as regards independent benefits and subparagraph (b) as regards pro rata benefits.

2.   The competent institution shall not apply the division stipulated in respect of independent benefits, if the legislation it applies provides for account to be taken of benefits of a different kind and/or other income and all other elements for calculating part of their amount determined as a function of the ratio between periods of insurance and/or residence referred to in Article 52(1)(b)(ii).

3.   Paragraphs 1 and 2 shall apply *mutatis mutandis* where the legislation of one or more Member States provides that a right to a benefit cannot be acquired in the case where the person concerned is in receipt of a benefit of a different kind, payable under the legislation of another Member State, or of other income.

Article 56 Additional provisions for the calculation of benefits

1.   For the calculation of the theoretical and pro rata amounts referred to in Article 52(1)(b), the following rules shall apply:

    (a)   where the total length of the periods of insurance and/or residence completed before the risk materialised under the legislations of all the Member States concerned is longer than the maximum period required by the legislation of one of these Member States for receipt of full benefit, the competent institution of that Member State shall take into account this maximum period instead of the total length of the periods completed; this method of calculation shall not result in the imposition on that institution of the cost of a benefit greater than the full benefit provided for by the legislation it applies. This provision shall not apply to benefits the amount of which does not depend on the length of insurance;

    (b)   the procedure for taking into account overlapping periods is laid down in the Implementing Regulation;

    (c)   if the legislation of a Member State provides that the benefits are to be calculated on the basis of incomes, contributions, bases of contributions, increases, earnings, other amounts or a combination of more than one of them (average, proportional, fixed or credited), the competent institution shall:

        (i)   determine the basis for calculation of the benefits in accordance only with periods of insurance completed under the legislation it applies;

        (ii)   use, in order to determine the amount to be calculated in accordance with the periods of insurance and/or residence completed under the legislation of the other Member States, the same elements determined or recorded for the periods of insurance completed under the legislation it applies; where necessary in accordance with the procedures laid down in Annex XI for the Member State concerned;

    (d)   In the event that point(c) is not applicable because the legislation of a Member State provides for the benefit to be calculated on the basis of elements other than periods of insurance or residence which are not linked to time, the competent institution shall take into account, in respect of each period of insurance or residence completed under the legislation of any other Member State, the amount of the capital accrued, the capital which is considered as having been accrued or any other element for the calculation under the legislation it administers divided by the corresponding units of periods in the pension scheme concerned.

2.   The provisions of the legislation of a Member State concerning the revalorisation of the elements taken into account for the calculation of benefits shall apply, as appropriate, to the elements to be taken into account by the competent institution of that Member State, in accordance with paragraph 1, in respect of the periods of insurance or residence completed under the legislation of other Member States.

Article 57 Periods of insurance or residence of less than one year

1.   Notwithstanding Article 52(1)(b), the institution of a Member State shall not be required to provide benefits in respect of periods completed under the legislation it applies which are taken into account when the risk materialises, if:

    — the duration of the said periods is less than one year, and

    — taking only these periods into account no right to benefit is acquired under that legislation.

For the purposes of this Article, 'periods' shall mean all periods of insurance, employment, self-employment or residence which either qualify for, or directly increase, the benefit concerned.

2. The competent institution of each of the Member States concerned shall take into account the periods referred to in paragraph 1, for the purposes of Article 52(1)(b)(i).

3. If the effect of applying paragraph 1 would be to relieve all the institutions of the Member States concerned of their obligations, benefits shall be provided exclusively under the legislation of the last of those Member States whose conditions are satisfied, as if all the periods of insurance and residence completed and taken into account in accordance with Articles 6 and 51(1) and (2) had been completed under the legislation of that Member State.

4. This Article shall not apply to schemes listed in Part 2 of Annex VIII.

Article 58 Award of a supplement

1. A recipient of benefits to whom this chapter applies may not, in the Member State of residence and under whose legislation a benefit is payable to him/her, be provided with a benefit which is less than the minimum benefit fixed by that legislation for a period of insurance or residence equal to all the periods taken into account for the payment in accordance with this chapter.

2. The competent institution of that Member State shall pay him/her throughout the period of his/her residence in its territory a supplement equal to the difference between the total of the benefits due under this chapter and the amount of the minimum benefit.

Article 59 Recalculation and revaluation of benefits

1. If the method for determining benefits or the rules for calculating benefits are altered under the legislation of a Member State, or if the personal situation of the person concerned undergoes a relevant change which, under that legislation, would lead to an adjustment of the amount of the benefit, a recalculation shall be carried out in accordance with Article 52.

2. On the other hand, if, by reason of an increase in the cost of living or changes in the level of income or other grounds for adjustment, the benefits of the Member State concerned are altered by a percentage or fixed amount, such percentage or fixed amount shall be applied directly to the benefits determined in accordance with Article 52, without the need for a recalculation.

Article 60 Special provisions for civil servants

1. Articles 6, 50, 51(3) and 52 to 59 shall apply *mutatis mutandis* to persons covered by a special scheme for civil servants.

2. However, if the legislation of a competent Member State makes the acquisition, liquidation, retention or recovery of the right to benefits under a special scheme for civil servants subject to the condition that all periods of insurance be completed under one or more special schemes for civil servants in that Member State, or be regarded by the legislation of that Member State as equivalent to such periods, the competent institution of that State shall take into account only the periods which can be recognised under the legislation it applies.

   If, account having been taken of the periods thus completed, the person concerned does not satisfy the conditions for the receipt of these benefits, these periods shall be taken into account for the award of benefits under the general scheme or, failing that, the scheme applicable to manual or clerical workers, as the case may be.

3. Where, under the legislation of a Member State, benefits under a special scheme for civil servants are calculated on the basis of the last salary or salaries received during a reference period, the competent institution of that State shall take into account, for the purposes of the calculation, only those salaries, duly revalued, which were received during the period or periods for which the person concerned was subject to that legislation.

CHAPTER 6
UNEMPLOYMENT BENEFITS

Article 61 Special rules on aggregation of periods of insurance, employment or self-employment

1. The competent institution of a Member State whose legislation makes the acquisition, retention, recovery or duration of the right to benefits conditional upon the completion of either periods of insurance, employment or self-employment shall, to the extent necessary, take into account periods of insurance, employment or self-employment completed under the legislation of any other Member State as though they were completed under the legislation it applies.

    However, when the applicable legislation makes the right to benefits conditional on the completion of periods of insurance, the periods of employment or self-employment completed under the legislation of another Member State shall not be taken into account unless such periods would have been considered to be periods of insurance had they been completed in accordance with the applicable legislation.

2. Except in the cases referred to in Article 65(5)(a), the application of paragraph 1 of this Article shall be conditional on the person concerned having the most recently completed, in accordance with the legislation under which the benefits are claimed:
    — periods of insurance, if that legislation requires periods of insurance,
    — periods of employment, if that legislation requires periods of employment, or
    — periods of self-employment, if that legislation requires periods of self-employment.

Article 62 Calculation of benefits

1. The competent institution of a Member State whose legislation provides for the calculation of benefits on the basis of the amount of the previous salary or professional income shall take into account exclusively the salary or professional income received by the person concerned in respect of his/her last activity as an employed or self-employed person under the said legislation.

2. Paragraph 1 shall also apply where the legislation administered by the competent institution provides for a specific reference period for the determination of the salary which serves as a basis for the calculation of benefits and where, for all or part of that period, the person concerned was subject to the legislation of another Member State.

3. By way of derogation from paragraphs 1 and 2, as far as the unemployed persons covered by Article 65(5)(a) are concerned, the institution of the place of residence shall take into account the salary or professional income received by the person concerned in the Member State to whose legislation he/she was subject during his/her last activity as an employed or self-employed person, in accordance with the Implementing Regulation.

Article 63 Special provisions for the waiving of residence rules

For the purposes of this Chapter, Article 7 shall apply only in the cases provided for by Articles 64, 65 and 65a and within the limits prescribed therein.

Article 64 Unemployed persons going to another Member State

1. A wholly unemployed person who satisfies the conditions of the legislation of the competent Member State for entitlement to benefits, and who goes to another Member State in order to seek work there, shall retain his/her entitlement to unemployment benefits in cash under the following conditions and within the following limits:

    (a) before his/her departure, the unemployed person must have been registered as a person seeking work and have remained available to the employment services of the competent Member State for at least four weeks after becoming unemployed. However, the competent services or institutions may authorise his/her departure before such time has expired;

    (b) the unemployed person must register as a person seeking work with the employment services of the Member State to which he/she has gone, be subject to the control procedure organised there and adhere to the conditions laid down under the legislation of that Member State. This condition shall be considered satisfied for the period before registration if the person concerned registers within seven days of the date on which he/she ceased to be available to the employment services of the Member State which he/she left. In exceptional cases, the competent services or institutions may extend this period;

(c) entitlement to benefits shall be retained for a period of three months from the date when the unemployed person ceased to be available to the employment services of the Member State which he/she left, provided that the total duration for which the benefits are provided does not exceed the total duration of the period of his/her entitlement to benefits under the legislation of that Member State; the competent services or institutions may extend the period of three months up to a maximum of six months;

(d) the benefits shall be provided by the competent institution in accordance with the legislation it applies and at its own expense.

2. If the person concerned returns to the competent Member State on or before the expiry of the period during which he/she is entitled to benefits under paragraph 1(c), he/she shall continue to be entitled to benefits under the legislation of that Member State. He/she shall lose all entitlement to benefits under the legislation of the competent Member State if he/she does not return there on or before the expiry of the said period, unless the provisions of that legislation are more favourable. In exceptional cases the competent services or institutions may allow the person concerned to return at a later date without loss of his/her entitlement.

3. Unless the legislation of the competent Member State is more favourable, between two periods of employment the maximum total period for which entitlement to benefits shall be retained under paragraph 1 shall be three months; the competent services or institutions may extend that period up to a maximum of six months.

4. The arrangements for exchanges of information, cooperation and mutual assistance between the institutions and services of the competent Member State and the Member State to which the person goes in order to seek work shall be laid down in the Implementing Regulation.

Article 65 Unemployed persons who resided in a Member State other than the competent State

1. A person who is partially or intermittently unemployed and who, during his/her last activity as an employed or self-employed person, resided in a Member State other than the competent Member State shall make himself/herself available to his/her employer or to the employment services in the competent Member State. He/she shall receive benefits in accordance with the legislation of the competent Member State as if he/she were residing in that Member State. These benefits shall be provided by the institution of the competent Member State.

2. A wholly unemployed person who, during his/her last activity as an employed or self-employed person, resided in a Member State other than the competent Member State and who continues to reside in that Member State or returns to that Member State shall make himself/ herself available to the employment services in the Member State of residence. Without prejudice to Article 64, a wholly unemployed person may, as a supplementary step, make himself/herself available to the employment services of the Member State in which he/she pursued his/her last activity as an employed or self-employed person.

   An unemployed person, other than a frontier worker, who does not return to his/her Member State of residence, shall make himself/herself available to the employment services in the Member State to whose legislation he/she was last subject.

3. The unemployed person referred to in the first sentence of paragraph 2 shall register as a person seeking work with the competent employment services of the Member State in which he/she resides, shall be subject to the control procedure organised there and shall adhere to the conditions laid down under the legislation of that Member State. If he/she chooses also to register as a person seeking work in the Member State in which he/she pursued his/her last activity as an employed or self-employed person, he/she shall comply with the obligations applicable in that State.

4.   The implementation of the second sentence of paragraph 2 and of the second sentence of paragraph 3, as well as the arrangements for exchanges of information, cooperation and mutual assistance between the institutions and services of the Member State of residence and the Member State in which he/she pursued his/her last occupation, shall be laid down in the Implementing Regulation.

5.   (a)   The unemployed person referred to in the first and second sentences of paragraph 2 shall receive benefits in accordance with the legislation of the Member State of residence as if he/she had been subject to that legislation during his/her last activity as an employed or self-employed person. Those benefits shall be provided by the institution of the place of residence.

(b)   However, a worker other than a frontier worker who has been provided benefits at the expense of the competent institution of the Member State to whose legislation he/she was last subject shall firstly receive, on his/her return to the Member State of residence, benefits in accordance with Article 64, receipt of the benefits in accordance with (a) being suspended for the period during which he/she receives benefits under the legislation to which he/she was last subject.

6.   The benefits provided by the institution of the place of residence under paragraph 5 shall continue to be at its own expense. However, subject to paragraph 7, the competent institution of the Member State to whose legislation he/she was last subject shall reimburse to the institution of the place of residence the full amount of the benefits provided by the latter institution during the first three months. The amount of the reimbursement during this period may not be higher than the amount payable, in the case of unemployment, under the legislation of the competent Member State. In the case referred to in paragraph 5(b), the period during which benefits are provided under Article 64 shall be deducted from the period referred to in the second sentence of this paragraph. The arrangements for reimbursement shall be laid down in the Implementing Regulation.

7.   However, the period of reimbursement referred to in paragraph 6 shall be extended to five months when the person concerned has, during the preceding 24 months, completed periods of employment or self-employment of at least 12 months in the Member State to whose legislation he/she was last subject, where such periods would qualify for the purposes of establishing entitlement to unemployment benefits.

8.   For the purposes of paragraphs 6 and 7, two or more Member States, or their competent authorities, may provide for other methods of reimbursement or waive all reimbursement between the institutions falling under their jurisdiction.

Article 65a Special provisions for wholly unemployed self-employed frontier workers where no unemployment benefits system covering self-employed persons exists in the Member State of residence

1.   By way of derogation from Article 65, a wholly unemployed person who, as a frontier worker, has most recently completed periods of insurance as a self-employed person or periods of self-employment recognised for the purposes of granting unemployment benefits in a Member State other than his/her Member State of residence and whose Member State of residence has submitted notification that there is no possibility for any category of self-employed persons to be covered by an unemployment benefits system of that Member State, shall register with and make himself/herself available to the employment services in the Member State in which he/she pursued his/her last activity as a self-employed person and, when he/she applies for benefits, shall continuously adhere to the conditions laid down under the legislation of the latter Member State. The wholly unemployed person may, as a supplementary step, make himself/herself available to the employment services of the Member State of residence.

2.   Benefits shall be provided to the wholly unemployed person referred to in paragraph 1 by the Member State to whose legislation he/she was last subject in accordance with the legislation which that Member State applies.

3.   If the wholly unemployed person referred to in paragraph 1 does not wish to become or remain available to the employment services of the Member State of last activity after having been registered there, and wishes to seek work in the Member State of residence, Article 64 shall apply *mutatis mutandis*, except Article 64(1)(a). The competent institution may extend the period referred to in the first sentence of Article 64(1)(c) up to the end of the period of entitlement to benefits.

CHAPTER 7
PRE-RETIREMENT BENEFITS

Article 66 Benefits

When the applicable legislation makes the right to pre-retirement benefits conditional on the completion of periods of insurance, of employment or of self-employment, Article 6 shall not apply.

CHAPTER 8
FAMILY BENEFITS

Article 67 Members of the family residing in another Member State

A person shall be entitled to family benefits in accordance with the legislation of the competent Member State, including for his/her family members residing in another Member State, as if they were residing in the former Member State. However, a pensioner shall be entitled to family benefits in accordance with the legislation of the Member State competent for his/her pension.

Article 68 Priority rules in the event of overlapping

1. Where, during the same period and for the same family members, benefits are provided for under the legislation of more than one Member State the following priority rules shall apply:
    (a)   in the case of benefits payable by more than one Member State on different bases, the order of priority shall be as follows: firstly, rights available on the basis of an activity as an employed or self-employed person, secondly, rights available on the basis of receipt of a pension and finally, rights obtained on the basis of residence;
    (b)   in the case of benefits payable by more than one Member State on the same basis, the order of priority shall be established by referring to the following subsidiary criteria:
        (i)   in the case of rights available on the basis of an activity as an employed or self-employed person: the place of residence of the children, provided that there is such activity, and additionally, where appropriate, the highest amount of the benefits provided for by the conflicting legislations. In the latter case, the cost of benefits shall be shared in accordance with criteria laid down in the Implementing Regulation;
        (ii)   in the case of rights available on the basis of receipt of pensions: the place of residence of the children, provided that a pension is payable under its legislation, and additionally, where appropriate, the longest period of insurance or residence under the conflicting legislations;
        (iii) in the case of rights available on the basis of residence: the place of residence of the children.
2. In the case of overlapping entitlements, family benefits shall be provided in accordance with the legislation designated as having priority in accordance with paragraph 1. Entitlements to family benefits by virtue of other conflicting legislation or legislations shall be suspended up to the amount provided for by the first legislation and a differential supplement shall be provided, if necessary, for the sum which exceeds this amount. However, such a differential supplement does not need to be provided for children residing in another Member State when entitlement to the benefit in question is based on residence only.
3. If, under Article 67, an application for family benefits is submitted to the competent institution of a Member State whose legislation is applicable, but not by priority right in accordance with paragraphs 1 and 2 of this Article:
    (a)   that institution shall forward the application without delay to the competent institution of the Member State whose legislation is applicable by priority, inform the person concerned and, without prejudice to the provisions of the Implementing Regulation concerning the provisional award of benefits, provide, if necessary, the differential supplement mentioned in paragraph 2;

(b)		the competent institution of the Member State whose legislation is applicable by priority shall deal with this application as though it were submitted directly to itself, and the date on which such an application was submitted to the first institution shall be considered as the date of its claim to the institution with priority.

Article 68a Provision of benefits

In the event that family benefits are not used by the person to whom they should be provided for the maintenance of the members of the family, the competent institution shall discharge its legal obligations by providing those benefits to the natural or legal person in fact maintaining the members of the family, at the request and through the agency of the institution in their Member State of residence or of the designated institution or body appointed for that purpose by the competent authority of their Member State of residence.

Article 69 Additional provisions

1.		If, under the legislation designated by virtue of Articles 67 and 68, no right is acquired to the payment of additional or special family benefits for orphans, such benefits shall be paid by default, and in addition to the other family benefits acquired in accordance with the abovementioned legislation, under the legislation of the Member State to which the deceased worker was subject for the longest period of time, in so far as the right was acquired under that legislation. If no right was acquired under that legislation, the conditions for the acquisition of such right under the legislations of the other Member States shall be examined and benefits provided in decreasing order of the length of periods of insurance or residence completed under the legislation of those Member States.

2.		Benefits paid in the form of pensions or supplements to pensions shall be provided and calculated in accordance with Chapter 5.

CHAPTER 9
SPECIAL NON-CONTRIBUTORY CASH BENEFITS

Article 70 General provision

1.		This Article shall apply to special non-contributory cash benefits which are provided under legislation which, because of its personal scope, objectives and/or conditions for entitlement, has characteristics both of the social security legislation referred to in Article 3(1) and of social assistance.

2.		For the purposes of this Chapter, 'special non-contributory cash benefits' means those which:

(a)		are intended to provide either:

(i)		supplementary, substitute or ancillary cover against the risks covered by the branches of social security referred to in Article 3(1), and which guarantee the persons concerned a minimum subsistence income having regard to the economic and social situation in the Member State concerned; or

(ii)		solely specific protection for the disabled, closely linked to the said person's social environment in the Member State concerned, and

(b)		where the financing exclusively derives from compulsory taxation intended to cover general public expenditure and the conditions for providing and for calculating the benefits are not dependent on any contribution in respect of the beneficiary. However, benefits provided to supplement a contributory benefit shall not be considered to be contributory benefits for this reason alone, and

(c)		are listed in Annex X.

3.		Article 7 and the other chapters of this Title shall not apply to the benefits referred to in paragraph 2 of this Article.

4.		The benefits referred to in paragraph 2 shall be provided exclusively in the Member State in which the persons concerned reside, in accordance with its legislation. Such benefits shall be provided by and at the expense of the institution of the place of residence.

TITLE IV
ADMINISTRATIVE COMMISSION AND ADVISORY COMMITTEE

Article 71 Composition and working methods of the Administrative Commission

1. The Administrative Commission for the Coordination of Social Security Systems (hereinafter called the Administrative Commission) attached to the European Commission shall be made up of a government representative from each of the Member States, assisted, where necessary, by expert advisers. A representative of the European Commission shall attend the meetings of the Administrative Commission in an advisory capacity.

2. The Administrative Commission shall act by a qualified majority as defined by the Treaties, except when adopting its rules which shall be drawn up by mutual agreement among its members.

    Decisions on questions of interpretation referred to in Article 72(a) shall be given the necessary publicity.

3. Secretarial services for the Administrative Commission shall be provided by the Commission of the European Communities.

Article 72 Tasks of the Administrative Commission

The Administrative Commission shall:

(a) deal with all administrative questions and questions of interpretation arising from the provisions of this Regulation or those of the Implementing Regulation, or from any agreement concluded or arrangement made thereunder, without prejudice to the right of the authorities, institutions and persons concerned to have recourse to the procedures and tribunals provided for by the legislation of the Member States, by this Regulation or by the Treaty;

(b) facilitate the uniform application of Community law, especially by promoting exchange of experience and best administrative practices;

(c) foster and develop cooperation between Member States and their institutions in social security matters in order, inter alia, to take into account particular questions regarding certain categories of persons; facilitate realisation of actions of cross-border cooperation activities in the area of the coordination of social security systems;

(d) encourage as far as possible the use of new technologies in order to facilitate the free movement of persons, in particular by modernising procedures for exchanging information and adapting the information flow between institutions for the purposes of exchange by electronic means, taking account of the development of data processing in each Member State; the Administrative Commission shall adopt the common structural rules for data processing services, in particular on security and the use of standards, and shall lay down provisions for the operation of the common part of those services;

(e) undertake any other function falling within its competence under this Regulation and the Implementing Regulation or any agreement or arrangement concluded thereunder;

(f) make any relevant proposals to the European Commission concerning the coordination of social security schemes, with a view to improving and modernising the Community acquis by drafting subsequent Regulations or by means of other instruments provided for by the Treaty;

(g) establish the factors to be taken into account for drawing up accounts relating to the costs to be borne by the institutions of the Member States under this Regulation and to adopt the annual accounts between those institutions, based on the report of the Audit Board referred to in Article 74.

Article 73 Technical Commission for Data Processing

1. A Technical Commission for Data Processing (hereinafter called the Technical Commission) shall be attached to the Administrative Commission. The Technical Commission shall propose to the Administrative Commission common architecture rules for the operation of data-processing services, in particular on security and the use of standards; it shall deliver reports and a reasoned opinion before decisions are

taken by the Administrative Commission pursuant to Article 72(d). The composition and working methods of the Technical Commission shall be determined by the Administrative Commission.

2.   To this end, the Technical Commission shall:
   (a)   gather together the relevant technical documents and undertake the studies and other work required to accomplish its tasks;
   (b)   submit to the Administrative Commission the reports and reasoned opinions referred to in paragraph 1;
   (c)   carry out all other tasks and studies on matters referred to it by the Administrative Commission;
   (d)   ensure the management of Community pilot projects using data-processing services and, for the Community part, operational systems using data-processing services.

Article 74 Audit Board

1.   An Audit Board shall be attached to the Administrative Commission. The composition and working methods of the Audit Board shall be determined by the Administrative Commission.

   The Audit Board shall:
   (a)   verify the method of determining and calculating the annual average costs presented by Member States;
   (b)   collect the necessary data and carry out the calculations required for establishing the annual statement of claims of each Member State;
   (c)   give the Administrative Commission periodic accounts of the results of the implementation of this Regulation and of the Implementing Regulation, in particular as regards the financial aspect;
   (d)   provide the data and reports necessary for decisions to be taken by the Administrative Commission pursuant to Article 72(g);
   (e)   make any relevant suggestions it may have to the Administrative Commission, including those concerning this Regulation, in connection with subparagraphs (a), (b) and (c);
   (f)   carry out all work, studies or assignments on matters referred to it by the Administrative Commission.

Article 74a The European Labour Authority

1.   Without prejudice to the tasks and activities of the Administrative Commission, the European Labour Authority shall support the application of this Regulation in accordance with its tasks set out in Regulation (EU) 2019/1149. The Administrative Commission shall cooperate with the European Labour Authority in order to coordinate the activities in mutual agreement and avoid any duplication. To that end, it shall conclude a cooperation agreement with the European Labour Authority.

2.   The Administrative Commission may request the European Labour Authority to refer an issue concerning social security under mediation in accordance with the third subparagraph of Article 13(11) of Regulation (EU) 2019/1149.

Article 75 Advisory Committee for the Coordination of Social Security Systems

1.   An Advisory Committee for the Coordination of Social Security Systems (hereinafter referred to as Advisory Committee) is hereby established, comprising, from each Member State:
   (a)   one government representative;
   (b)   one representative from the trade unions;
   (c)   one representative from the employers' organisations.

   For each of the categories referred to above, an alternate member shall be appointed for each Member State.

   The members and alternate members of the Advisory Committee shall be appointed by the Council. The Advisory Committee shall be chaired by a representative of the European Commission. The Advisory Committee shall draw up its Rules of Procedure.

2.   The Advisory Committee shall be empowered, at the request of the European Commission, the Administrative Commission or on its own initiative:

(a)   to examine general questions or questions of principle and problems arising from the implementation of the Community provisions on the coordination of social security systems, especially regarding certain categories of persons;

(b)   to formulate opinions on such matters for the Administrative Commission and proposals for any revisions of the said provisions.

TITLE V

MISCELLANEOUS PROVISIONS

Article 76 Cooperation

1.   The competent authorities of the Member States shall communicate to each other all information regarding:

     (a)   measures taken to implement this Regulation;

     (b)   changes in their legislation which may affect the implementation of this Regulation.

2.   For the purposes of this Regulation, the authorities and institutions of the Member States shall lend one another their good offices and act as though implementing their own legislation. The administrative assistance given by the said authorities and institutions shall, as a rule, be free of charge. However, the Administrative Commission shall establish the nature of reimbursable expenses and the limits above which their reimbursement is due.

3.   The authorities and institutions of the Member States may, for the purposes of this Regulation, communicate directly with one another and with the persons involved or their representatives.

4.   The institutions and persons covered by this Regulation shall have a duty of mutual information and cooperation to ensure the correct implementation of this Regulation. The institutions, in accordance with the principle of good administration, shall respond to all queries within a reasonable period of time and shall in this connection provide the persons concerned with any information required for exercising the rights conferred on them by this Regulation.

The persons concerned must inform the institutions of the competent Member State and of the Member State of residence as soon as possible of any change in their personal or family situation which affects their right to benefits under this Regulation.

5.   Failure to respect the obligation of information referred to in the third subparagraph of paragraph 4 may result in the application of proportionate measures in accordance with national law. Nevertheless, these measures shall be equivalent to those applicable to similar situations under domestic law and shall not make it impossible or excessively difficult in practice for claimants to exercise the rights conferred on them by this Regulation.

6.   In the event of difficulties in the interpretation or application of this Regulation which could jeopardise the rights of a person covered by it, the institution of the competent Member State or of the Member State of residence of the person concerned shall contact the institution(s) of the Member State(s) concerned. If a solution cannot be found within a reasonable period, the authorities concerned may call on the Administrative Commission to intervene.

7.   The authorities, institutions and tribunals of one Member State may not reject applications or other documents submitted to them on the grounds that they are written in an official language of another Member State, recognised as an official language of the Community institutions in accordance with Article 290 of the Treaty.

Article 77 Protection of personal data

1.   Where, according to this Regulation or to the Implementing Regulation, the authorities or institutions of a Member State communicate personal data to the authorities or institutions of another Member State, such communication shall be subject to the data protection legislation of the Member State transmitting them. Any communication from the authority or institution of the receiving Member State as well as the storage, alteration and destruction of the data provided by that Member State shall be subject to the data protection legislation of the receiving Member State.

2.   Data required for the application of this Regulation and the Implementing Regulation shall be transmitted by one Member State to another Member State in accordance with Community provisions on the protection of natural persons with regard to the processing and free movement of personal data.

Article 78 Data processing

1.   Member States shall progressively use new technologies for the exchange, access and processing of the data required to apply this Regulation and the Implementing Regulation. The European Commission shall lend its support to activities of common interest as soon as the Member States have established such data-processing services.

2.   Each Member State shall be responsible for managing its own part of the data-processing services in accordance with the Community provisions on the protection of natural persons with regard to the processing and the free movement of personal data.

3.   An electronic document sent or issued by an institution in conformity with this Regulation and the Implementing Regulation may not be rejected by any authority or institution of another Member State on the grounds that it was received by electronic means, once the receiving institution has declared that it can receive electronic documents. Reproduction and recording of such documents shall be presumed to be a correct and accurate reproduction of the original document or representation of the information it relates to, unless there is proof to the contrary.

4.   An electronic document shall be considered valid if the computer system on which the document is recorded contains the safeguards necessary in order to prevent any alteration, disclosure or unauthorised access to the recording. It shall at any time be possible to reproduce the recorded information in an immediately readable form. When an electronic document is transferred from one social security institution to another, appropriate security measures shall be taken in accordance with the Community provisions on the protection of natural persons with regard to the processing and the free movement of personal data.

Article 79 Funding of activities in the social security field

In connection with this Regulation and the Implementing Regulation, the European Commission may fund in full or in part:

(a)   activities aimed at improving exchanges of information between the social security authorities and institutions of the Member States, particularly the electronic exchange of data;

(b)   any other activity aimed at providing information to the persons covered by this Regulation and their representatives about the rights and obligations deriving from this Regulation, using the most appropriate means.

Article 80 Exemptions

1.   Any exemption from or reduction of taxes, stamp duty, notarial or registration fees provided for under the legislation of one Member State in respect of certificates or documents required to be produced in application of the legislation of that Member State shall be extended to similar certificates or documents required to be produced in application of the legislation of another Member State or of this Regulation.

2.   All statements, documents and certificates of any kind whatsoever required to be produced in application of this Regulation shall be exempt from authentication by diplomatic or consular authorities.

Article 81 Claims, declarations or appeals

Any claim, declaration or appeal which should have been submitted, in application of the legislation of one Member State, within a specified period to an authority, institution or tribunal of that Member State shall be admissible if it is submitted within the same period to a corresponding authority, institution or tribunal of another Member State. In such a case the authority, institution or tribunal receiving the claim, declaration or appeal shall forward it without delay to the competent authority, institution or tribunal of the former Member State either directly or through the competent authorities of the Member States concerned. The date on which such claims, declarations or appeals were submitted to the authority, institution or tribunal of the second Member State shall be considered as the date of their submission to the competent authority, institution or tribunal.

Article 82 Medical examinations

Medical examinations provided for by the legislation of one Member State may be carried out at the request of the competent institution, in another Member State, by the institution of the place of residence or stay of the claimant or the person entitled to benefits, under the conditions laid down in the Implementing Regulation or agreed between the competent authorities of the Member States concerned.

Article 83 Implementation of legislation

Special provisions for implementing the legislation of certain Member States are referred to in Annex XI.

Article 84 Collection of contributions and recovery of benefits

1. Collection of contributions due to an institution of one Member State and recovery of benefits provided by the institution of one Member State but not due may be effected in another Member State in accordance with the procedures and with the guarantees and privileges applicable to the collection of contributions due to the corresponding institution of the latter Member State and the recovery of benefits provided by it but not due.
2. Enforceable decisions of the judicial and administrative authorities relating to the collection of contributions, interest and any other charges or to the recovery of benefits provided but not due under the legislation of one Member State shall be recognised and enforced at the request of the competent institution in another Member State within the limits and in accordance with the procedures laid down by the legislation and any other procedures applicable to similar decisions of the latter Member State. Such decisions shall be declared enforceable in that Member State in so far as the legislation and any other procedures of that Member State so require.
3. Claims of an institution of one Member State shall in enforcement, bankruptcy or settlement proceedings in another Member State enjoy the same privileges as the legislation of the latter Member State accords to claims of the same kind.
4. The procedure for implementing this Article, including costs reimbursement, shall be governed by the Implementing Regulation or, where necessary and as a complementary measure, by means of agreements between Member States.

Article 85 Rights of institutions

1. If a person receives benefits under the legislation of one Member State in respect of an injury resulting from events occurring in another Member State, any rights of the institution responsible for providing benefits against a third party liable to provide compensation for the injury shall be governed by the following rules:
    (a) where the institution responsible for providing benefits is, under the legislation it applies, subrogated to the rights which the beneficiary has against the third party, such subrogation shall be recognised by each Member State;
    (b) where the institution responsible for providing benefits has a direct right against the third party, each Member State shall recognise such rights.
2. If a person receives benefits under the legislation of one Member State in respect of an injury resulting from events occurring in another Member State, the provisions of the said legislation which determine the cases in which the civil liability of employers or of their employees is to be excluded shall apply with regard to the said person or to the competent institution.
    Paragraph 1 shall also apply to any rights of the institution responsible for providing benefits against employers or their employees in cases where their liability is not excluded.
3. Where, in accordance with Article 35(3) and/or Article 41(2), two or more Member States or their competent authorities have concluded an agreement to waive reimbursement between institutions under their jurisdiction, or, where reimbursement does not depend on the amount of benefits actually provided, any rights arising against a liable third party shall be governed by the following rules:
    (a) where the institution of the Member State of residence or stay accords benefits to a person in respect of an injury sustained in its territory, that institution, in

accordance with the provisions of the legislation it applies, shall exercise the right to subrogation or direct action against the third party liable to provide compensation for the injury;

(b)   for the application of (a):

    (i)   the person receiving benefits shall be deemed to be insured with the institution of the place of residence or stay, and

    (ii)   that institution shall be deemed to be the institution responsible for providing benefits;

(c)   paragraphs 1 and 2 shall remain applicable in respect of any benefits not covered by the waiver agreement or a reimbursement which does not depend on the amount of benefits actually provided.

Article 86 Bilateral agreements

As far as relations between, on the one hand, Luxembourg and, on the other hand, France, Germany and Belgium are concerned, the application and the duration of the period referred to in Article 65(7) shall be subject to the conclusion of bilateral agreements.

TITLE VI

TRANSITIONAL AND FINAL PROVISIONS

Article 87 Transitional provisions

1.   No rights shall be acquired pursuant to this Regulation for the period before its date of application.

2.   Any period of insurance and, where appropriate, any period of employment, self-employment or residence completed under the legislation of a Member State prior to the date of application of this Regulation in the Member State concerned shall be taken into consideration for the determination of rights acquired under this Regulation.

3.   Subject to paragraph 1, a right shall be acquired under this Regulation even if it relates to a contingency arising before its date of application in the Member State concerned.

4.   Any benefit which has not been awarded or which has been suspended by reason of the nationality or place of residence of the person concerned shall, at the request of that person, be provided or resumed with effect from the date of application of this Regulation in the Member State concerned, provided that the rights for which benefits were previously provided have not given rise to a lump-sum payment.

5.   The rights of a person to whom a pension was provided prior to the date of application of this Regulation in a Member State may, at the request of the person concerned, be reviewed, taking into account this Regulation.

6.   If a request referred to in paragraph 4 or 5 is submitted within two years from the date of application of this Regulation in a Member State, the rights acquired in accordance with this Regulation shall have effect from that date, and the legislation of any Member State concerning the forfeiture or limitation of rights may not be invoked against the persons concerned.

7.   If a request referred to in paragraph 4 or 5 is submitted after the expiry of the two-year period following the date of application of this Regulation in the Member State concerned, rights not forfeited or not time-barred shall have effect from the date on which the request was submitted, subject to any more favourable provisions under the legislation of any Member State.

8.   If, as a result of this Regulation, a person is subject to the legislation of a Member State other than that determined in accordance with Title II of Regulation (EEC) No 1408/71, that legislation shall continue to apply while the relevant situation remains unchanged and in any case for no longer than 10 years from the date of application of this Regulation unless the person concerned requests that he/she be subject to the legislation applicable under this Regulation. The request shall be submitted within 3 months after the date of application of this Regulation to the competent institution of the Member State whose legislation is applicable under this Regulation if the person concerned is to be subject to the legislation of that Member State as of the date of application of this Regulation. If the request is made after the time limit indicated, the change of applicable legislation shall take place on the first day of the following month.

9. Article 55 of this Regulation shall apply only to pensions not subject to Article 46c of Regulation (EEC) No 1408/71 on the date of application of this Regulation.

10. The provisions of the second sentences of Article 65(2) and (3) shall be applicable to Luxembourg at the latest two years after the date of application of this Regulation.

10a. The entries in Annex III corresponding to Estonia, Spain, Italy, Lithuania, Hungary and the Netherlands shall cease to have effect 4 years after the date of application of this Regulation.

10b. The list contained in Annex III shall be reviewed no later than 31 October 2014 on the basis of a report by the Administrative Commission. That report shall include an impact assessment of the significance, frequency, scale and costs, both in absolute and in relative terms, of the application of the provisions of Annex III. That report shall also include the possible effects of repealing those provisions for those Member States which continue to be listed in that Annex after the date referred to in paragraph 10a. In the light of that report, the Commission shall decide whether to submit a proposal concerning a review of the list, with the aim in principle of repealing the list unless the report of the Administrative Commission provides compelling reasons not to do so.

11. Member States shall ensure that appropriate information is provided regarding the changes in rights and obligations introduced by this Regulation and the Implementing Regulation.

Article 87a Transitional provision for application of Regulation (EU) No 465/2012

1. If as a result of the entry into force of Regulation (EU) No 465/2012, a person is subject, in accordance with Title II of this Regulation, to the legislation of a different Member State than that to which he/she was subject before that entry into force, the legislation of the Member State applicable before that date shall continue to apply to him/her for a transitional period lasting for as long as the relevant situation remains unchanged and, in any case, for no longer than 10 years from the date of entry into force of Regulation (EU) No 465/2012. Such a person may request that the transitional period no longer applies to him/her. Such request shall be submitted to the institution designated by the competent authority of the Member State of residence. Requests submitted by 29 September 2012 shall be deemed to take effect on 28 June 2012. Requests submitted after 29 September 2012 shall take effect on the first day of the month following that of their submission.

2. No later than 29 June 2014, the Administrative Commission shall evaluate the implementation of the provisions laid down in Article 65a of this Regulation and present a report on their application. On the basis of this report, the European Commission may, as appropriate, submit proposals to amend those provisions.

Article 88 Updating of the Annexes

The Annexes of this Regulation shall be revised periodically.

Article 89 Implementing Regulation

A further Regulation shall lay down the procedure for implementing this Regulation.

Article 90 Repeal

1. Council Regulation (EEC) No 1408/71 shall be repealed from the date of application of this Regulation.

However, Regulation (EEC) No 1408/71 shall remain in force and shall continue to have legal effect for the purposes of:

(a) Council Regulation (EC) No 859/2003 of 14 May 2003 extending the provisions of Regulation (EEC) No 1408/71 and Regulation (EEC) No 574/72 to nationals of third countries who are not already covered by those provisions solely on the ground of their nationality, for as long as that Regulation has not been repealed or modified;

(b) Council Regulation (EEC) No 1661/85 of 13 June 1985 laying down the technical adaptations to the Community rules on social security for migrant workers with regard to Greenland, for as long as that Regulation has not been repealed or modified;

(c)   the Agreement on the European Economic Area and the Agreement between the European Community and its Member States, of the one part, and the Swiss Confederation, of the other part, on the free movement of persons and other agreements which contain a reference to Regulation (EEC) No 1408/71, for as long as those agreements have not been modified in the light of this Regulation.

2.   References to Regulation (EEC) No 1408/71 in Council Directive 98/49/EC of 29 June 1998 on safeguarding the supplementary pension rights of employed and self-employed persons moving within the Community are to be read as referring to this Regulation.

Article 91 Entry into force

This Regulation shall enter into force on the 20th day after its publication in the *Official Journal of the European Union*.

It shall apply from the date of entry into force of the Implementing Regulation.

This Regulation shall be binding in its entirety and directly applicable in all Member States

EMPLOYMENT: EQUALITY

COUNCIL DIRECTIVE (EEC) No 79/7 of 19 DECEMBER 1978
on the progressive implementation of the principle of equal treatment
for men and women in matters of social security
[1979] OJ L6/24

Article 1

The purpose of this Directive is the progressive implementation, in the field of social security and other elements of social protection provided for in Article 3, of the principle of equal treatment for men and women in matters of social security, hereinafter referred to as 'the principle of equal treatment'.

Article 2

This Directive shall apply to the working population—including self-employed persons, workers and self-employed persons whose activity is interrupted by illness, accident or involuntary unemployment and persons seeking employment—and to retired or invalided workers and self-employed persons.

Article 3

1. This Directive shall apply to:
    (a) statutory schemes which provide protection against the following risks:
        — sickness,
        — invalidity,
        — old age,
        — accidents at work and occupational diseases,
        — unemployment;
    (b) social assistance, in so far as it is intended to supplement or replace the schemes referred to in (a).
2. This Directive shall not apply to the provisions concerning survivors' benefits nor to those concerning family benefits, except in the case of family benefits granted by way of increases of benefits due in respect of the risks referred to in paragraph 1(a).
3. With a view to ensuring implementation of the principle of equal treatment in occupational schemes, the Council, acting on a proposal from the Commission, will adopt provisions defining its substance, its scope and the arrangements for its application.

Article 4

1. The principle of equal treatment means that there shall be no discrimination whatsoever on ground of sex either directly, or indirectly by reference in particular to marital or family status, in particular as concerns:
    — the scope of the schemes and the conditions of access thereto,
    — the obligation to contribute and the calculation of contributions,
    — the calculation of benefits including increases due in respect of a spouse and for dependants and the conditions governing the duration and retention of entitlement to benefits.
2. The principle of equal treatment shall be without prejudice to the provisions relating to the protection of women on the grounds of maternity.

Article 5

Member States shall take the measures necessary to ensure that any laws, regulations and administrative provisions contrary to the principle of equal treatment are abolished.

Article 6

Member States shall introduce into their national legal systems such measures as are necessary to enable all persons who consider themselves wronged by failure to apply the principle of equal treatment to pursue their claims by judicial process, possibly after recourse to other competent authorities.

Article 7

1. This Directive shall be without prejudice to the right of Member States to exclude from its scope:
    (a) the determination of pensionable age for the purposes of granting old-age and retirement pensions and the possible consequences thereof for other benefits;
    (b) advantages in respect of old-age pension schemes granted to persons who have brought up children; the acquisition of benefit entitlements following periods of interruption of employment due to the bringing up of children;
    (c) the granting of old-age or invalidity benefit entitlements by virtue of the derived entitlements of a wife;
    (d) the granting of increases of long-term invalidity, old-age, accidents at work and occupational disease benefits for a dependent wife;
    (e) the consequences of the exercise, before the adoption of this Directive, of a right of option not to acquire rights or incur obligations under a statutory scheme.
2. Member States shall periodically examine matters excluded under paragraph 1 in order to ascertain, in the light of social developments in the matter concerned, whether there is justification for maintaining the exclusions concerned.

Article 8

1. Member States shall bring into force the laws, regulations and administrative provisions necessary to comply with this Directive within six years of its notification. They shall immediately inform the Commission thereof.
2. Member States shall communicate to the Commission the text of laws, regulations and administrative provisions which they adopt in the field covered by this Directive, including measures adopted pursuant to Article 7(2).
    They shall inform the Commission of their reasons for maintaining any existing provisions on the matters referred to in Article 7(1) and of the possibilities for reviewing them at a later date.

Article 9

Within seven years of notification of this Directive, Member States shall forward all information necessary to the Commission to enable it to draw up a report on the application of this Directive for submission to the Council and to propose such further measures as may be required for the implementation of the principle of equal treatment.

Article 10

This Directive is addressed to the Member States.

COUNCIL DIRECTIVE (EC) No 2000/43 of 29 JUNE 2000 implementing the principle of equal treatment between persons irrespective of racial or ethnic origin [2000] OJ L180/22

THE COUNCIL OF THE EUROPEAN UNION,
Having regard to the Treaty establishing the European Community and in particular Article 13 thereof,
Having regard to the proposal from the Commission,
Having regard to the opinion of the European Parliament,
Having regard to the opinion of the Economic and Social Committee,
Having regard to the opinion of the Committee of the Regions,
Whereas:
(1) The Treaty on European Union marks a new stage in the process of creating an ever closer union among the peoples of Europe.
(2) In accordance with Article 6 of the Treaty on European Union, the European Union is founded on the principles of liberty, democracy, respect for human rights and fundamental freedoms, and the rule of law, principles which are common to the Member States, and should respect fundamental rights as guaranteed by the European Convention for the protection of Human Rights and Fundamental Freedoms and as they result from the constitutional traditions common to the Member States, as general principles of Community Law.

(3) The right to equality before the law and protection against discrimination for all persons constitutes a universal right recognised by the Universal Declaration of Human Rights, the United Nations Convention on the Elimination of all forms of Discrimination Against Women, the International Convention on the Elimination of all forms of Racial Discrimination and the United Nations Covenants on Civil and Political Rights and on Economic, Social and Cultural Rights and by the European Convention for the Protection of Human Rights and Fundamental Freedoms, to which all Member States are signatories.

(4) It is important to respect such fundamental rights and freedoms, including the right to freedom of association. It is also important, in the context of the access to and provision of goods and services, to respect the protection of private and family life and transactions carried out in this context.

(5) The European Parliament has adopted a number of Resolutions on the fight against racism in the European Union.

(6) The European Union rejects theories which attempt to determine the existence of separate human races. The use of the term 'racial origin' in this Directive does not imply an acceptance of such theories.

(7) The European Council in Tampere, on 15 and 16 October 1999, invited the Commission to come forward as soon as possible with proposals implementing Article 13 of the EC Treaty as regards the fight against racism and xenophobia.

(8) The Employment Guidelines 2000 agreed by the European Council in Helsinki, on 10 and 11 December 1999, stress the need to foster conditions for a socially inclusive labour market by formulating a coherent set of policies aimed at combating discrimination against groups such as ethnic minorities.

(9) Discrimination based on racial or ethnic origin may undermine the achievement of the objectives of the EC Treaty, in particular the attainment of a high level of employment and of social protection, the raising of the standard of living and quality of life, economic and social cohesion and solidarity. It may also undermine the objective of developing the European Union as an area of freedom, security and justice.

(10) The Commission presented a communication on racism, xenophobia and anti-Semitism in December 1995.

(11) The Council adopted on 15 July 1996 Joint Action (96/443/JHA) concerning action to combat racism and xenophobia under which the Member States undertake to ensure effective judicial cooperation in respect of offences based on racist or xenophobic behaviour.

(12) To ensure the development of democratic and tolerant societies which allow the participation of all persons irrespective of racial or ethnic origin, specific action in the field of discrimination based on racial or ethnic origin should go beyond access to employed and self-employed activities and cover areas such as education, social protection including social security and health-care, social advantages and access to and supply of goods and services.

(13) To this end, any direct or indirect discrimination based on racial or ethnic origin as regards the areas covered by this Directive should be prohibited throughout the Community. This prohibition of discrimination should also apply to nationals of third countries, but does not cover differences of treatment based on nationality and is without prejudice to provisions governing the entry and residence of third-country nationals and their access to employment and to occupation.

(14) In implementing the principle of equal treatment irrespective of racial or ethnic origin, the Community should, in accordance with Article 3(2) of the EC Treaty, aim to eliminate inequalities, and to promote equality between men and women, especially since women are often the victims of multiple discrimination.

(15) The appreciation of the facts from which it may be inferred that there has been direct or indirect discrimination is a matter for national judicial or other competent bodies, in accordance with rules of national law or practice. Such rules may provide in particular for indirect discrimination to be established by any means including on the basis of statistical evidence.

(16) It is important to protect all natural persons against discrimination on grounds of racial or ethnic origin. Member States should also provide, where appropriate and in accordance with their national traditions and practice, protection for legal persons where they suffer discrimination on grounds of the racial or ethnic origin of their members.

(17) The prohibition of discrimination should be without prejudice to the maintenance or adoption of measures intended to prevent or compensate for disadvantages suffered by a group of persons of a particular racial or ethnic origin, and such measures may permit organisations of persons of a particular racial or ethnic origin where their main object is the promotion of the special needs of those persons.

(18) In very limited circumstances, a difference of treatment may be justified where a characteristic related to racial or ethnic origin constitutes a genuine and determining occupational requirement, when the objective is legitimate and the requirement is proportionate. Such circumstances should be included in the information provided by the Member States to the Commission.

(19) Persons who have been subject to discrimination based on racial and ethnic origin should have adequate means of legal protection. To provide a more effective level of protection, associations or legal entities should also be empowered to engage, as the Member States so determine, either on behalf or in support of any victim, in proceedings, without prejudice to national rules of procedure concerning representation and defence before the courts.

(20) The effective implementation of the principle of equality requires adequate judicial protection against victimisation.

(21) The rules on the burden of proof must be adapted when there is a prima facie case of discrimination and, for the principle of equal treatment to be applied effectively, the burden of proof must shift back to the respondent when evidence of such discrimination is brought.

(22) Member States need not apply the rules on the burden of proof to proceedings in which it is for the court or other competent body to investigate the facts of the case. The procedures thus referred to are those in which the plaintiff is not required to prove the facts, which it is for the court or competent body to investigate.

(23) Member States should promote dialogue between the social partners and with non-governmental organisations to address different forms of discrimination and to combat them.

(24) Protection against discrimination based on racial or ethnic origin would itself be strengthened by the existence of a body or bodies in each Member State, with competence to analyse the problems involved, to study possible solutions and to provide concrete assistance for the victims.

(25) This Directive lays down minimum requirements, thus giving the Member States the option of introducing or maintaining more favourable provisions. The implementation of this Directive should not serve to justify any regression in relation to the situation which already prevails in each Member State.

(26) Member States should provide for effective, proportionate and dissuasive sanctions in case of breaches of the obligations under this Directive.

(27) The Member States may entrust management and labour, at their joint request, with the implementation of this Directive as regards provisions falling within the scope of collective agreements, provided that the Member States take all the necessary steps to ensure that they can at all times guarantee the results imposed by this Directive.

(28) In accordance with the principles of subsidiarity and proportionality as set out in Article 5 of the EC Treaty, the objective of this Directive, namely ensuring a common high level of protection against discrimination in all the Member States, cannot be sufficiently achieved by the Member States and can therefore, by reason of the scale and impact of the proposed action, be better achieved by the Community. This Directive does not go beyond what is necessary in order to achieve those objectives,

HAS ADOPTED THIS DIRECTIVE:

CHAPTER I
GENERAL PROVISIONS

Article 1   Purpose

The purpose of this Directive is to lay down a framework for combating discrimination on the grounds of racial or ethnic origin, with a view to putting into effect in the Member States the principle of equal treatment.

Article 2   Concept of discrimination

1. For the purposes of this Directive, the principle of equal treatment shall mean that there shall be no direct or indirect discrimination based on racial or ethnic origin.
2. For the purposes of paragraph 1:
    (a) direct discrimination shall be taken to occur where one person is treated less favourably than another is, has been or would be treated in a comparable situation on grounds of racial or ethnic origin;
    (b) indirect discrimination shall be taken to occur where an apparently neutral provision, criterion or practice would put persons of a racial or ethnic origin at a particular disadvantage compared with other persons, unless that provision, criterion or practice is objectively justified by a legitimate aim and the means of achieving that aim are appropriate and necessary.
3. Harassment shall be deemed to be discrimination within the meaning of paragraph 1, when an unwanted conduct related to racial or ethnic origin takes place with the purpose or effect of violating the dignity of a person and of creating an intimidating, hostile, degrading, humiliating or offensive environment. In this context, the concept of harassment may be defined in accordance with the national laws and practice of the Member States.
4. An instruction to discriminate against persons on grounds of racial or ethnic origin shall be deemed to be discrimination within the meaning of paragraph 1.

Article 3   Scope

1. Within the limits of the powers conferred upon the Community, this Directive shall apply to all persons, as regards both the public and private sectors, including public bodies, in relation to:
    (a) conditions for access to employment, to self-employment and to occupation, including selection criteria and recruitment conditions, whatever the branch of activity and at all levels of the professional hierarchy, including promotion;
    (b) access to all types and to all levels of vocational guidance, vocational training, advanced vocational training and retraining, including practical work experience;
    (c) employment and working conditions, including dismissals and pay;
    (d) membership of and involvement in an organisation of workers or employers, or any organisation whose members carry on a particular profession, including the benefits provided for by such organisations;
    (e) social protection, including social security and healthcare;
    (f) social advantages;
    (g) education;
    (h) access to and supply of goods and services which are available to the public, including housing.
2. This Directive does not cover difference of treatment based on nationality and is without prejudice to provisions and conditions relating to the entry into and residence of third-country nationals and stateless persons on the territory of Member States, and to any treatment which arises from the legal status of the third-country nationals and stateless persons concerned.

Article 4   Genuine and determining occupational requirements

Notwithstanding Article 2(1) and (2), Member States may provide that a difference of treatment which is based on a characteristic related to racial or ethnic origin shall not constitute discrimination where, by reason of the nature of the particular occupational activities concerned or of the context in which they are carried out, such a characteristic constitutes a genuine and determining occupational requirement, provided that the objective is legitimate and the requirement is proportionate.

Article 5   Positive action

With a view to ensuring full equality in practice, the principle of equal treatment shall not prevent any Member State from maintaining or adopting specific measures to prevent or compensate for disadvantages linked to racial or ethnic origin.

Article 6   Minimum requirements
1.   Member States may introduce or maintain provisions which are more favourable to the protection of the principle of equal treatment than those laid down in this Directive.
2.   The implementation of this Directive shall under no circumstances constitute grounds for a reduction in the level of protection against discrimination already afforded by Member States in the fields covered by this Directive.

CHAPTER II
REMEDIES AND ENFORCEMENT

Article 7   Defence of rights
1.   Member States shall ensure that judicial and/or administrative procedures, including where they deem it appropriate conciliation procedures, for the enforcement of obligations under this Directive are available to all persons who consider themselves wronged by failure to apply the principle of equal treatment to them, even after the relationship in which the discrimination is alleged to have occurred has ended.
2.   Member States shall ensure that associations, organisations or other legal entities, which have, in accordance with the criteria laid down by their national law, a legitimate interest in ensuring that the provisions of this Directive are complied with, may engage, either on behalf or in support of the complainant, with his or her approval, in any judicial and/or administrative procedure provided for the enforcement of obligations under this Directive.
3.   Paragraphs 1 and 2 are without prejudice to national rules relating to time limits for bringing actions as regards the principle of equality of treatment.

Article 8   Burden of proof
1.   Member States shall take such measures as are necessary, in accordance with their national judicial systems, to ensure that, when persons who consider themselves wronged because the principle of equal treatment has not been applied to them establish, before a court or other competent authority, facts from which it may be presumed that there has been direct or indirect discrimination, it shall be for the respondent to prove that there has been no breach of the principle of equal treatment.
2.   Paragraph 1 shall not prevent Member States from introducing rules of evidence which are more favourable to plaintiffs.
3.   Paragraph 1 shall not apply to criminal procedures.
4.   Paragraphs 1, 2 and 3 shall also apply to any proceedings brought in accordance with Article 7(2).
5.   Member States need not apply paragraph 1 to proceedings in which it is for the court or competent body to investigate the facts of the case.

Article 9   Victimisation
Member States shall introduce into their national legal systems such measures as are necessary to protect individuals from any adverse treatment or adverse consequence as a reaction to a complaint or to proceedings aimed at enforcing compliance with the principle of equal treatment.

Article 10   Dissemination of information
Member States shall take care that the provisions adopted pursuant to this Directive, together with the relevant provisions already in force, are brought to the attention of the persons concerned by all appropriate means throughout their territory.

Article 11   Social dialogue
1.   Member States shall, in accordance with national traditions and practice, take adequate measures to promote the social dialogue between the two sides of industry with a view to fostering equal treatment, including through the monitoring of workplace practices, collective agreements, codes of conduct, research or exchange of experiences and good practices.
2.   Where consistent with national traditions and practice, Member States shall encourage the two sides of the industry without prejudice to their autonomy to conclude, at the appropriate level, agreements laying down anti-discrimination rules in the fields

referred to in Article 3 which fall within the scope of collective bargaining. These agreements shall respect the minimum requirements laid down by this Directive and the relevant national implementing measures.

Article 12 Dialogue with non-governmental organisations

Member States shall encourage dialogue with appropriate non-governmental organisations which have, in accordance with their national law and practice, a legitimate interest in contributing to the fight against discrimination on grounds of racial and ethnic origin with a view to promoting the principle of equal treatment.

CHAPTER III
BODIES FOR THE PROMOTION OF EQUAL TREATMENT

Article 13

1. Member States shall designate a body or bodies for the promotion of equal treatment of all persons without discrimination on the grounds of racial or ethnic origin. These bodies may form part of agencies charged at national level with the defence of human rights or the safeguard of individuals' rights.
2. Member States shall ensure that the competences of these bodies include:
    — without prejudice to the right of victims and of associations, organisations or other legal entities referred to in Article 7(2), providing independent assistance to victims of discrimination in pursuing their complaints about discrimination,
    — conducting independent surveys concerning discrimination,
    — publishing independent reports and making recommendations on any issue relating to such discrimination.

CHAPTER IV
FINAL PROVISIONS

Article 14 Compliance

Member States shall take the necessary measures to ensure that:
(a) any laws, regulations and administrative provisions contrary to the principle of equal treatment are abolished;
(b) any provisions contrary to the principle of equal treatment which are included in individual or collective contracts or agreements, internal rules of undertakings, rules governing profit-making or non-profit-making associations, and rules governing the independent professions and workers' and employers' organisations, are or may be declared, null and void or are amended.

Article 15 Sanctions

Member States shall lay down the rules on sanctions applicable to infringements of the national provisions adopted pursuant to this Directive and shall take all measures necessary to ensure that they are applied. The sanctions, which may comprise the payment of compensation to the victim, must be effective, proportionate and dissuasive. The Member States shall notify those provisions to the Commission by 19 July 2003 at the latest and shall notify it without delay of any subsequent amendment affecting them.

Article 16 Implementation

Member States shall adopt the laws, regulations and administrative provisions necessary to comply with this Directive by 19 July 2003 or may entrust management and labour, at their joint request, with the implementation of this Directive as regards provisions falling within the scope of collective agreements. In such cases, Member States shall ensure that by 19 July 2003, management and labour introduce the necessary measures by agreement, Member States being required to take any necessary measures to enable them at any time to be in a position to guarantee the results imposed by this Directive. They shall forthwith inform the Commission thereof.

When Member States adopt these measures, they shall contain a reference to this Directive or be accompanied by such a reference on the occasion of their official publication. The methods of making such a reference shall be laid down by the Member States.

Article 17 Report

1. Member States shall communicate to the Commission by 19 July 2005, and every five years thereafter, all the information necessary for the Commission to draw up a report to the European Parliament and the Council on the application of this Directive.

2. The Commission's report shall take into account, as appropriate, the views of the European Monitoring Centre on Racism and Xenophobia, as well as the viewpoints of the social partners and relevant non-governmental organisations. In accordance with the principle of gender mainstreaming, this report shall, inter alia, provide an assessment of the impact of the measures taken on women and men. In the light of the information received, this report shall include, if necessary, proposals to revise and update this Directive.

Article 18 Entry into force

This Directive shall enter into force on the day of its publication in the *Official Journal of the European Communities*.

Article 19 Addressees

This Directive is addressed to the Member States.

COUNCIL DIRECTIVE (EC) No 2000/78 of 27 NOVEMBER 2000
establishing a general framework for equal treatment in employment and occupation
[2000] OJ L303/16

THE COUNCIL OF THE EUROPEAN UNION,

Having regard to the Treaty establishing the European Community, and in particular Article 13 thereof,

Having regard to the proposal from the Commission,

Having regard to the Opinion of the European Parliament,

Having regard to the Opinion of the Economic and Social Committee,

Having regard to the Opinion of the Committee of the Regions,

Whereas:

(1) In accordance with Article 6 of the Treaty on European Union, the European Union is founded on the principles of liberty, democracy, respect for human rights and fundamental freedoms, and the rule of law, principles which are common to all Member States and it respects fundamental rights, as guaranteed by the European Convention for the Protection of Human Rights and Fundamental Freedoms and as they result from the constitutional traditions common to the Member States, as general principles of Community law.

(2) The principle of equal treatment between women and men is well established by an important body of Community law, in particular in Council Directive 76/207/EEC of 9 February 1976 on the implementation of the principle of equal treatment for men and women as regards access to employment, vocational training and promotion, and working conditions.

(3) In implementing the principle of equal treatment, the Community should, in accordance with Article 3(2) of the EC Treaty, aim to eliminate inequalities, and to promote equality between men and women, especially since women are often the victims of multiple discrimination.

(4) The right of all persons to equality before the law and protection against discrimination constitutes a universal right recognised by the Universal Declaration of Human Rights, the United Nations Convention on the Elimination of All Forms of Discrimination against Women, United Nations Covenants on Civil and Political Rights and on Economic, Social and Cultural Rights and by the European Convention for the Protection of Human Rights and Fundamental Freedoms, to which all Member States are signatories. Convention No 111 of the International Labour Organisation (ILO) prohibits discrimination in the field of employment and occupation.

(5) It is important to respect such fundamental rights and freedoms. This Directive does not prejudice freedom of association, including the right to establish unions with others and to join unions to defend one's interests.

(6) The Community Charter of the Fundamental Social Rights of Workers recognises the importance of combating every form of discrimination, including the need to take appropriate action for the social and economic integration of elderly and disabled people.

(7) The EC Treaty includes among its objectives the promotion of coordination between employment policies of the Member States. To this end, a new employment chapter was incorporated in the EC Treaty as a means of developing a coordinated European strategy for employment to promote a skilled, trained and adaptable workforce.

(8) The Employment Guidelines for 2000 agreed by the European Council at Helsinki on 10 and 11 December 1999 stress the need to foster a labour market favourable to social integration by formulating a coherent set of policies aimed at combating discrimination against groups such as persons with disability. They also emphasise the need to pay particular attention to supporting older workers, in order to increase their participation in the labour force.

(9) Employment and occupation are key elements in guaranteeing equal opportunities for all and contribute strongly to the full participation of citizens in economic, cultural and social life and to realising their potential.

(10) On 29 June 2000 the Council adopted Directive 2000/43/EC implementing the principle of equal treatment between persons irrespective of racial or ethnic origin. That Directive already provides protection against such discrimination in the field of employment and occupation.

(11) Discrimination based on religion or belief, disability, age or sexual orientation may undermine the achievement of the objectives of the EC Treaty, in particular the attainment of a high level of employment and social protection, raising the standard of living and the quality of life, economic and social cohesion and solidarity, and the free movement of persons.

(12) To this end, any direct or indirect discrimination based on religion or belief, disability, age or sexual orientation as regards the areas covered by this Directive should be prohibited throughout the Community. This prohibition of discrimination should also apply to nationals of third countries but does not cover differences of treatment based on nationality and is without prejudice to provisions governing the entry and residence of third-country nationals and their access to employment and occupation.

(13) This Directive does not apply to social security and social protection schemes whose benefits are not treated as income within the meaning given to that term for the purpose of applying Article 141 of the EC Treaty, nor to any kind of payment by the State aimed at providing access to employment or maintaining employment.

(14) This Directive shall be without prejudice to national provisions laying down retirement ages.

(15) The appreciation of the facts from which it may be inferred that there has been direct or indirect discrimination is a matter for national judicial or other competent bodies, in accordance with rules of national law or practice. Such rules may provide, in particular, for indirect discrimination to be established by any means including on the basis of statistical evidence.

(16) The provision of measures to accommodate the needs of disabled people at the workplace plays an important role in combating discrimination on grounds of disability.

(17) This Directive does not require the recruitment, promotion, maintenance in employment or training of an individual who is not competent, capable and available to perform the essential functions of the post concerned or to undergo the relevant training, without prejudice to the obligation to provide reasonable accommodation for people with disabilities.

(18) This Directive does not require, in particular, the armed forces and the police, prison or emergency services to recruit or maintain in employment persons who do not have the required capacity to carry out the range of functions that they may be called upon to perform with regard to the legitimate objective of preserving the operational capacity of those services.

(19) Moreover, in order that the Member States may continue to safeguard the combat effectiveness of their armed forces, they may choose not to apply the provisions of this Directive concerning disability and age to all or part of their armed forces. The Member States which make that choice must define the scope of that derogation.

(20) Appropriate measures should be provided, i.e. effective and practical measures to adapt the workplace to the disability, for example adapting premises and equipment, patterns of working time, the distribution of tasks or the provision of training or integration resources.

(21) To determine whether the measures in question give rise to a disproportionate burden, account should be taken in particular of the financial and other costs entailed, the scale and financial resources of the organisation or undertaking and the possibility of obtaining public funding or any other assistance.

(22) This Directive is without prejudice to national laws on marital status and the benefits dependent thereon.

(23) In very limited circumstances, a difference of treatment may be justified where a characteristic related to religion or belief, disability, age or sexual orientation constitutes a genuine and determining occupational requirement, when the objective is legitimate and the requirement is proportionate. Such circumstances should be included in the information provided by the Member States to the Commission.

(24) The European Union in its Declaration No 11 on the status of churches and non-confessional organisations, annexed to the Final Act of the Amsterdam Treaty, has explicitly recognised that it respects and does not prejudice the status under national law of churches and religious associations or communities in the Member States and that it equally respects the status of philosophical and non-confessional organisations. With this in view, Member States may maintain or lay down specific provisions on genuine, legitimate and justified occupational requirements which might be required for carrying out an occupational activity.

(25) The prohibition of age discrimination is an essential part of meeting the aims set out in the Employment Guidelines and encouraging diversity in the workforce. However, differences in treatment in connection with age may be justified under certain circumstances and therefore require specific provisions which may vary in accordance with the situation in Member States. It is therefore essential to distinguish between differences in treatment which are justified, in particular by legitimate employment policy, labour market and vocational training objectives, and discrimination which must be prohibited.

(26) The prohibition of discrimination should be without prejudice to the maintenance or adoption of measures intended to prevent or compensate for disadvantages suffered by a group of persons of a particular religion or belief, disability, age or sexual orientation, and such measures may permit organisations of persons of a particular religion or belief, disability, age or sexual orientation where their main object is the promotion of the special needs of those persons.

(27) In its Recommendation 86/379/EEC of 24 July 1986 on the employment of disabled people in the Community, the Council established a guideline framework setting out examples of positive action to promote the employment and training of disabled people, and in its Resolution of 17 June 1999 on equal employment opportunities for people with disabilities, affirmed the importance of giving specific attention inter alia to recruitment, retention, training and lifelong learning with regard to disabled persons.

(28) This Directive lays down minimum requirements, thus giving the Member States the option of introducing or maintaining more favourable provisions. The implementation of this Directive should not serve to justify any regression in relation to the situation which already prevails in each Member State.

(29) Persons who have been subject to discrimination based on religion or belief, disability, age or sexual orientation should have adequate means of legal protection. To provide a more effective level of protection, associations or legal entities should also be empowered to engage in proceedings, as the Member States so determine, either on behalf or in support of any victim, without prejudice to national rules of procedure concerning representation and defence before the courts.

(30) The effective implementation of the principle of equality requires adequate judicial protection against victimisation.

(31) The rules on the burden of proof must be adapted when there is a prima facie case of discrimination and, for the principle of equal treatment to be applied effectively, the burden of proof must shift back to the respondent when evidence of such discrimination is brought. However, it is not for the respondent to prove that the plaintiff adheres to a particular religion or belief, has a particular disability, is of a particular age or has a particular sexual orientation.

(32) Member States need not apply the rules on the burden of proof to proceedings in which it is for the court or other competent body to investigate the facts of the case. The procedures thus referred to are those in which the plaintiff is not required to prove the facts, which it is for the court or competent body to investigate.

(33) Member States should promote dialogue between the social partners and, within the framework of national practice, with non-governmental organisations to address different forms of discrimination at the workplace and to combat them.

(34) The need to promote peace and reconciliation between the major communities in Northern Ireland necessitates the incorporation of particular provisions into this Directive.

(35) Member States should provide for effective, proportionate and dissuasive sanctions in case of breaches of the obligations under this Directive.

(36) Member States may entrust the social partners, at their joint request, with the implementation of this Directive, as regards the provisions concerning collective agreements, provided they take any necessary steps to ensure that they are at all times able to guarantee the results required by this Directive.

(37) In accordance with the principle of subsidiarity set out in Article 5 of the EC Treaty, the objective of this Directive, namely the creation within the Community of a level playing-field as regards equality in employment and occupation, cannot be sufficiently achieved by the Member States and can therefore, by reason of the scale and impact of the action, be better achieved at Community level. In accordance with the principle of proportionality, as set out in that Article, this Directive does not go beyond what is necessary in order to achieve that objective,

HAS ADOPTED THIS DIRECTIVE:

CHAPTER I
GENERAL PROVISIONS

Article 1   Purpose

The purpose of this Directive is to lay down a general framework for combating discrimination on the grounds of religion or belief, disability, age or sexual orientation as regards employment and occupation, with a view to putting into effect in the Member States the principle of equal treatment.

Article 2   Concept of discrimination

1. For the purposes of this Directive, the 'principle of equal treatment' shall mean that there shall be no direct or indirect discrimination whatsoever on any of the grounds referred to in Article 1.

2. For the purposes of paragraph 1:
   (a) direct discrimination shall be taken to occur where one person is treated less favourably than another is, has been or would be treated in a comparable situation, on any of the grounds referred to in Article 1;
   (b) indirect discrimination shall be taken to occur where an apparently neutral provision, criterion or practice would put persons having a particular religion or belief, a particular disability, a particular age, or a particular sexual orientation at a particular disadvantage compared with other persons unless:
      (i) that provision, criterion or practice is objectively justified by a legitimate aim and the means of achieving that aim are appropriate and necessary, or
      (ii) as regards persons with a particular disability, the employer or any person or organisation to whom this Directive applies, is obliged, under national legislation, to take appropriate measures in line with the principles contained in Article 5 in order to eliminate disadvantages entailed by such provision, criterion or practice.

3. Harassment shall be deemed to be a form of discrimination within the meaning of paragraph 1, when unwanted conduct related to any of the grounds referred to in Article 1 takes place with the purpose or effect of violating the dignity of a person and of creating an intimidating, hostile, degrading, humiliating or offensive environment. In this context, the concept of harassment may be defined in accordance with the national laws and practice of the Member States.

4. An instruction to discriminate against persons on any of the grounds referred to in Article 1 shall be deemed to be discrimination within the meaning of paragraph 1.

5. This Directive shall be without prejudice to measures laid down by national law which, in a democratic society, are necessary for public security, for the maintenance of

public order and the prevention of criminal offences, for the protection of health and for the protection of the rights and freedoms of others.

Article 3 Scope

1. Within the limits of the areas of competence conferred on the Community, this Directive shall apply to all persons, as regards both the public and private sectors, including public bodies, in relation to:
   (a) conditions for access to employment, to self-employment or to occupation, including selection criteria and recruitment conditions, whatever the branch of activity and at all levels of the professional hierarchy, including promotion;
   (b) access to all types and to all levels of vocational guidance, vocational training, advanced vocational training and retraining, including practical work experience;
   (c) employment and working conditions, including dismissals and pay;
   (d) membership of, and involvement in, an organisation of workers or employers, or any organisation whose members carry on a particular profession, including the benefits provided for by such organisations.
2. This Directive does not cover differences of treatment based on nationality and is without prejudice to provisions and conditions relating to the entry into and residence of third-country nationals and stateless persons in the territory of Member States, and to any treatment which arises from the legal status of the third-country nationals and stateless persons concerned.
3. This Directive does not apply to payments of any kind made by state schemes or similar, including state social security or social protection schemes.
4. Member States may provide that this Directive, in so far as it relates to discrimination on the grounds of disability and age, shall not apply to the armed forces.

Article 4 Occupational requirements

1. Notwithstanding Article 2(1) and (2), Member States may provide that a difference of treatment which is based on a characteristic related to any of the grounds referred to in Article 1 shall not constitute discrimination where, by reason of the nature of the particular occupational activities concerned or of the context in which they are carried out, such a characteristic constitutes a genuine and determining occupational requirement, provided that the objective is legitimate and the requirement is proportionate.
2. Member States may maintain national legislation in force at the date of adoption of this Directive or provide for future legislation incorporating national practices existing at the date of adoption of this Directive pursuant to which, in the case of occupational activities within churches and other public or private organisations the ethos of which is based on religion or belief, a difference of treatment based on a person's religion or belief shall not constitute discrimination where, by reason of the nature of these activities or of the context in which they are carried out, a person's religion or belief constitute a genuine, legitimate and justified occupational requirement, having regard to the organisation's ethos. This difference of treatment shall be implemented taking account of Member States' constitutional provisions and principles, as well as the general principles of Community law, and should not justify discrimination on another ground.
   Provided that its provisions are otherwise complied with, this Directive shall thus not prejudice the right of churches and other public or private organisations, the ethos of which is based on religion or belief, acting in conformity with national constitutions and laws, to require individuals working for them to act in good faith and with loyalty to the organisation's ethos.

Article 5 Reasonable accommodation for disabled persons

In order to guarantee compliance with the principle of equal treatment in relation to persons with disabilities, reasonable accommodation shall be provided. This means that employers shall take appropriate measures, where needed in a particular case, to enable a person with a disability to have access to, participate in, or advance in employment, or to undergo training, unless such measures would impose a disproportionate burden on the employer. This burden shall not be disproportionate when it is sufficiently remedied by measures existing within the framework of the disability policy of the Member State concerned.

Article 6   Justification of differences of treatment on grounds of age

1. Notwithstanding Article 2(2), Member States may provide that differences of treatment on grounds of age shall not constitute discrimination, if, within the context of national law, they are objectively and reasonably justified by a legitimate aim, including legitimate employment policy, labour market and vocational training objectives, and if the means of achieving that aim are appropriate and necessary. Such differences of treatment may include, among others:
    (a)   the setting of special conditions on access to employment and vocational training, employment and occupation, including dismissal and remuneration conditions, for young people, older workers and persons with caring responsibilities in order to promote their vocational integration or ensure their protection;
    (b)   the fixing of minimum conditions of age, professional experience or seniority in service for access to employment or to certain advantages linked to employment;
    (c)   the fixing of a maximum age for recruitment which is based on the training requirements of the post in question or the need for a reasonable period of employment before retirement.
2. Notwithstanding Article 2(2), Member States may provide that the fixing for occupational social security schemes of ages for admission or entitlement to retirement or invalidity benefits, including the fixing under those schemes of different ages for employees or groups or categories of employees, and the use, in the context of such schemes, of age criteria in actuarial calculations, does not constitute discrimination on the grounds of age, provided this does not result in discrimination on the grounds of sex.

Article 7   Positive action

1. With a view to ensuring full equality in practice, the principle of equal treatment shall not prevent any Member State from maintaining or adopting specific measures to prevent or compensate for disadvantages linked to any of the grounds referred to in Article 1.
2. With regard to disabled persons, the principle of equal treatment shall be without prejudice to the right of Member States to maintain or adopt provisions on the protection of health and safety at work or to measures aimed at creating or maintaining provisions or facilities for safeguarding or promoting their integration into the working environment.

Article 8   Minimum requirements

1. Member States may introduce or maintain provisions which are more favourable to the protection of the principle of equal treatment than those laid down in this Directive.
2. The implementation of this Directive shall under no circumstances constitute grounds for a reduction in the level of protection against discrimination already afforded by Member States in the fields covered by this Directive.

CHAPTER II
REMEDIES AND ENFORCEMENT

Article 9   Defence of rights

1. Member States shall ensure that judicial and/or administrative procedures, including where they deem it appropriate conciliation procedures, for the enforcement of obligations under this Directive are available to all persons who consider themselves wronged by failure to apply the principle of equal treatment to them, even after the relationship in which the discrimination is alleged to have occurred has ended.
2. Member States shall ensure that associations, organisations or other legal entities which have, in accordance with the criteria laid down by their national law, a legitimate interest in ensuring that the provisions of this Directive are complied with, may engage, either on behalf or in support of the complainant, with his or her approval, in any judicial and/or administrative procedure provided for the enforcement of obligations under this Directive.
3. Paragraphs 1 and 2 are without prejudice to national rules relating to time limits for bringing actions as regards the principle of equality of treatment.

Article 10 Burden of proof

1. Member States shall take such measures as are necessary, in accordance with their national judicial systems, to ensure that, when persons who consider themselves wronged because the principle of equal treatment has not been applied to them establish, before a court or other competent authority, facts from which it may be presumed that there has been direct or indirect discrimination, it shall be for the respondent to prove that there has been no breach of the principle of equal treatment.
2. Paragraph 1 shall not prevent Member States from introducing rules of evidence which are more favourable to plaintiffs.
3. Paragraph 1 shall not apply to criminal procedures.
4. Paragraphs 1, 2 and 3 shall also apply to any legal proceedings commenced in accordance with Article 9(2).
5. Member States need not apply paragraph 1 to proceedings in which it is for the court or competent body to investigate the facts of the case.

Article 11 Victimisation

Member States shall introduce into their national legal systems such measures as are necessary to protect employees against dismissal or other adverse treatment by the employer as a reaction to a complaint within the undertaking or to any legal proceedings aimed at enforcing compliance with the principle of equal treatment.

Article 12 Dissemination of information

Member States shall take care that the provisions adopted pursuant to this Directive, together with the relevant provisions already in force in this field, are brought to the attention of the persons concerned by all appropriate means, for example at the workplace, throughout their territory.

Article 13 Social dialogue

1. Member States shall, in accordance with their national traditions and practice, take adequate measures to promote dialogue between the social partners with a view to fostering equal treatment, including through the monitoring of workplace practices, collective agreements, codes of conduct and through research or exchange of experiences and good practices.
2. Where consistent with their national traditions and practice, Member States shall encourage the social partners, without prejudice to their autonomy, to conclude at the appropriate level agreements laying down anti-discrimination rules in the fields referred to in Article 3 which fall within the scope of collective bargaining. These agreements shall respect the minimum requirements laid down by this Directive and by the relevant national implementing measures.

Article 14 Dialogue with non-governmental organisations

Member States shall encourage dialogue with appropriate non-governmental organisations which have, in accordance with their national law and practice, a legitimate interest in contributing to the fight against discrimination on any of the grounds referred to in Article 1 with a view to promoting the principle of equal treatment.

CHAPTER III
PARTICULAR PROVISIONS

Article 15 Northern Ireland

1. In order to tackle the under-representation of one of the major religious communities in the police service of Northern Ireland, differences in treatment regarding recruitment into that service, including its support staff, shall not constitute discrimination insofar as those differences in treatment are expressly authorised by national legislation.
2. In order to maintain a balance of opportunity in employment for teachers in Northern Ireland while furthering the reconciliation of historical divisions between the major religious communities there, the provisions on religion or belief in this Directive shall not apply to the recruitment of teachers in schools in Northern Ireland in so far as this is expressly authorised by national legislation.

CHAPTER IV
FINAL PROVISIONS

Article 16 Compliance

Member States shall take the necessary measures to ensure that:
   (a)   any laws, regulations and administrative provisions contrary to the principle of equal treatment are abolished;
   (b)   any provisions contrary to the principle of equal treatment which are included in contracts or collective agreements, internal rules of undertakings or rules governing the independent occupations and professions and workers' and employers' organisations are, or may be, declared null and void or are amended.

Article 17 Sanctions

Member States shall lay down the rules on sanctions applicable to infringements of the national provisions adopted pursuant to this Directive and shall take all measures necessary to ensure that they are applied. The sanctions, which may comprise the payment of compensation to the victim, must be effective, proportionate and dissuasive. Member States shall notify those provisions to the Commission by 2 December 2003 at the latest and shall notify it without delay of any subsequent amendment affecting them.

Article 18 Implementation

Member States shall adopt the laws, regulations and administrative provisions necessary to comply with this Directive by 2 December 2003 at the latest or may entrust the social partners, at their joint request, with the implementation of this Directive as regards provisions concerning collective agreements. In such cases, Member States shall ensure that, no later than 2 December 2003, the social partners introduce the necessary measures by agreement, the Member States concerned being required to take any necessary measures to enable them at any time to be in a position to guarantee the results imposed by this Directive. They shall forthwith inform the Commission thereof.

In order to take account of particular conditions, Member States may, if necessary, have an additional period of 3 years from 2 December 2003, that is to say a total of 6 years, to implement the provisions of this Directive on age and disability discrimination. In that event they shall inform the Commission forthwith. Any Member State which chooses to use this additional period shall report annually to the Commission on the steps it is taking to tackle age and disability discrimination and on the progress it is making towards implementation. The Commission shall report annually to the Council.

When Member States adopt these measures, they shall contain a reference to this Directive or be accompanied by such reference on the occasion of their official publication. The methods of making such reference shall be laid down by Member States.

Article 19 Report

   1.   Member States shall communicate to the Commission, by 2 December 2005 at the latest and every five years thereafter, all the information necessary for the Commission to draw up a report to the European Parliament and the Council on the application of this Directive.
   2.   The Commission's report shall take into account, as appropriate, the viewpoints of the social partners and relevant non-governmental organisations. In accordance with the principle of gender mainstreaming, this report shall, inter alia, provide an assessment of the impact of the measures taken on women and men. In the light of the information received, this report shall include, if necessary, proposals to revise and update this Directive.

Article 20 Entry into force

This Directive shall enter into force on the day of its publication in the *Official Journal of the European Communities*.

Article 21 Addressees

This Directive is addressed to the Member States.

DIRECTIVE 2006/54/EC OF THE EUROPEAN PARLIAMENT AND OF THE COUNCIL of 5 JULY 2006
on the implementation of the principle of equal opportunities and equal treatment of men and women in matters of employment and occupation (recast)
[2006] OJ L204/23

THE EUROPEAN PARLIAMENT AND THE COUNCIL OF THE EUROPEAN UNION,

Having regard to the Treaty establishing the European Community, and in particular Article 141(3) thereof,

Having regard to the proposal from the Commission,

Having regard to the opinion of the European Economic and Social Committee,

Acting in accordance with the procedure laid down in Article 251 of the Treaty,

Whereas:

(1)   Council Directive 76/207/EEC of 9 February 1976 on the implementation of the principle of equal treatment for men and women as regards access to employment, vocational training and promotion, and working conditions and Council Directive 86/378/EEC of 24 July 1986 on the implementation of the principle of equal treatment for men and women in occupational social security schemes have been significantly amended. Council Directive 75/117/EEC of 10 February 1975 on the approximation of the laws of the Member States relating to the application of the principle of equal pay for men and women and Council Directive 97/80/EC of 15 December 1997 on the burden of proof in cases of discrimination based on sex also contain provisions which have as their purpose the implementation of the principle of equal treatment between men and women. Now that new amendments are being made to the said Directives, it is desirable, for reasons of clarity, that the provisions in question should be recast by bringing together in a single text the main provisions existing in this field as well as certain developments arising out of the case-law of the Court of Justice of the European Communities (hereinafter referred to as the Court of Justice).

(2)   Equality between men and women is a fundamental principle of Community law under Article 2 and Article 3(2) of the Treaty and the case-law of the Court of Justice. Those Treaty provisions proclaim equality between men and women as a 'task' and an 'aim' of the Community and impose a positive obligation to promote it in all its activities.

(3)   The Court of Justice has held that the scope of the principle of equal treatment for men and women cannot be confined to the prohibition of discrimination based on the fact that a person is of one or other sex. In view of its purpose and the nature of the rights which it seeks to safeguard, it also applies to discrimination arising from the gender reassignment of a person.

(4)   Article 141(3) of the Treaty now provides a specific legal basis for the adoption of Community measures to ensure the application of the principle of equal opportunities and equal treatment in matters of employment and occupation, including the principle of equal pay for equal work or work of equal value.

(5)   Articles 21 and 23 of the Charter of Fundamental Rights of the European Union also prohibit any discrimination on grounds of sex and enshrine the right to equal treatment between men and women in all areas, including employment, work and pay.

(6)   Harassment and sexual harassment are contrary to the principle of equal treatment between men and women and constitute discrimination on grounds of sex for the purposes of this Directive. These forms of discrimination occur not only in the workplace, but also in the context of access to employment, vocational training and promotion. They should therefore be prohibited and should be subject to effective, proportionate and dissuasive penalties.

(7)   In this context, employers and those responsible for vocational training should be encouraged to take measures to combat all forms of discrimination on grounds of sex and, in particular, to take preventive measures against harassment and sexual harassment in the workplace and in access to employment, vocational training and promotion, in accordance with national law and practice.

(8)   The principle of equal pay for equal work or work of equal value as laid down by Article 141 of the Treaty and consistently upheld in the case-law of the Court of Justice

constitutes an important aspect of the principle of equal treatment between men and women and an essential and indispensable part of the acquis communautaire, including the case-law of the Court concerning sex discrimination. It is therefore appropriate to make further provision for its implementation.

(9) In accordance with settled case-law of the Court of Justice, in order to assess whether workers are performing the same work or work of equal value, it should be determined whether, having regard to a range of factors including the nature of the work and training and working conditions, those workers may be considered to be in a comparable situation.

(10) The Court of Justice has established that, in certain circumstances, the principle of equal pay is not limited to situations in which men and women work for the same employer.

(11) The Member States, in collaboration with the social partners, should continue to address the problem of the continuing gender-based wage differentials and marked gender segregation on the labour market by means such as flexible working time arrangements which enable both men and women to combine family and work commitments more successfully. This could also include appropriate parental leave arrangements which could be taken up by either parent as well as the provision of accessible and affordable child-care facilities and care for dependent persons.

(12) Specific measures should be adopted to ensure the implementation of the principle of equal treatment in occupational social security schemes and to define its scope more clearly.

(13) In its judgment of 17 May 1990 in Case C-262/88, the Court of Justice determined that all forms of occupational pension constitute an element of pay within the meaning of Article 141 of the Treaty.

(14) Although the concept of pay within the meaning of Article 141 of the Treaty does not encompass social security benefits, it is now clearly established that a pension scheme for public servants falls within the scope of the principle of equal pay if the benefits payable under the scheme are paid to the worker by reason of his/her employment relationship with the public employer, notwithstanding the fact that such scheme forms part of a general statutory scheme. According to the judgments of the Court of Justice in Cases C-7/93 and C-351/00, that condition will be satisfied if the pension scheme concerns a particular category of workers and its benefits are directly related to the period of service and calculated by reference to the public servant's final salary. For reasons of clarity, it is therefore appropriate to make specific provision to that effect.

(15) The Court of Justice has confirmed that whilst the contributions of male and female workers to a defined-benefit pension scheme are covered by Article 141 of the Treaty, any inequality in employers' contributions paid under funded defined-benefit schemes which is due to the use of actuarial factors differing according to sex is not to be assessed in the light of that same provision.

(16) By way of example, in the case of funded defined-benefit schemes, certain elements, such as conversion into a capital sum of part of a periodic pension, transfer of pension rights, a reversionary pension payable to a dependant in return for the surrender of part of a pension or a reduced pension where the worker opts to take earlier retirement, may be unequal where the inequality of the amounts results from the effects of the use of actuarial factors differing according to sex at the time when the scheme's funding is implemented.

(17) It is well established that benefits payable under occupational social security schemes are not to be considered as remuneration insofar as they are attributable to periods of employment prior to 17 May 1990, except in the case of workers or those claiming under them who initiated legal proceedings or brought an equivalent claim under the applicable national law before that date. It is therefore necessary to limit the implementation of the principle of equal treatment accordingly.

(18) The Court of Justice has consistently held that the Barber Protocol does not affect the right to join an occupational pension scheme and that the limitation of the effects in time of the judgment in Case C-262/88 does not apply to the right to join an occupational pension scheme. The Court of Justice also ruled that the national rules relating to time limits for bringing actions under national law may be relied on against workers who assert their right to join an occupational pension scheme, provided that they are not less favourable for that type of action than for similar actions of a domestic nature and that they do not render the exercise of rights conferred by Community law impossible

in practice. The Court of Justice has also pointed out that the fact that a worker can claim retroactively to join an occupational pension scheme does not allow the worker to avoid paying the contributions relating to the period of membership concerned.

(19) Ensuring equal access to employment and the vocational training leading thereto is fundamental to the application of the principle of equal treatment of men and women in matters of employment and occupation. Any exception to this principle should therefore be limited to those occupational activities which necessitate the employment of a person of a particular sex by reason of their nature or the context in which they are carried out, provided that the objective sought is legitimate and complies with the principle of proportionality.

(20) This Directive does not prejudice freedom of association, including the right to establish unions with others and to join unions to defend one's interests. Measures within the meaning of Article 141(4) of the Treaty may include membership or the continuation of the activity of organisations or unions whose main objective is the promotion, in practice, of the principle of equal treatment between men and women.

(21) The prohibition of discrimination should be without prejudice to the maintenance or adoption of measures intended to prevent or compensate for disadvantages suffered by a group of persons of one sex. Such measures permit organisations of persons of one sex where their main object is the promotion of the special needs of those persons and the promotion of equality between men and women.

(22) In accordance with Article 141(4) of the Treaty, with a view to ensuring full equality in practice between men and women in working life, the principle of equal treatment does not prevent Member States from maintaining or adopting measures providing for specific advantages in order to make it easier for the under-represented sex to pursue a vocational activity or to prevent or compensate for disadvantages in professional careers. Given the current situation and bearing in mind Declaration No 28 to the Amsterdam Treaty, Member States should, in the first instance, aim at improving the situation of women in working life.

(23) It is clear from the case-law of the Court of Justice that unfavourable treatment of a woman related to pregnancy or maternity constitutes direct discrimination on grounds of sex. Such treatment should therefore be expressly covered by this Directive.

(24) The Court of Justice has consistently recognised the legitimacy, as regards the principle of equal treatment, of protecting a woman's biological condition during pregnancy and maternity and of introducing maternity protection measures as a means to achieve substantive equality. This Directive should therefore be without prejudice to Council Directive 92/85/EEC of 19 October 1992 on the introduction of measures to encourage improvements in the safety and health at work of pregnant workers and workers who have recently given birth or are breastfeeding. This Directive should further be without prejudice to Council Directive 96/34/EC of 3 June 1996 on the framework agreement on parental leave concluded by UNICE, CEEP and the ETUC.

(25) For reasons of clarity, it is also appropriate to make express provision for the protection of the employment rights of women on maternity leave and in particular their right to return to the same or an equivalent post, to suffer no detriment in their terms and conditions as a result of taking such leave and to benefit from any improvement in working conditions to which they would have been entitled during their absence.

(26) In the Resolution of the Council and of the Ministers for Employment and Social Policy, meeting within the Council, of 29 June 2000 on the balanced participation of women and men in family and working life, Member States were encouraged to consider examining the scope for their respective legal systems to grant working men an individual and non-transferable right to paternity leave, while maintaining their rights relating to employment.

(27) Similar considerations apply to the granting by Member States to men and women of an individual and nontransferable right to leave subsequent to the adoption of a child. It is for the Member States to determine whether or not to grant such a right to paternity and/or adoption leave and also to determine any conditions, other than dismissal and return to work, which are outside the scope of this Directive.

(28) The effective implementation of the principle of equal treatment requires appropriate procedures to be put in place by the Member States.

(29) The provision of adequate judicial or administrative procedures for the enforcement of the obligations imposed by this Directive is essential to the effective implementation of the principle of equal treatment.

(30) The adoption of rules on the burden of proof plays a significant role in ensuring that the principle of equal treatment can be effectively enforced. As the Court of Justice has held, provision should therefore be made to ensure that the burden of proof shifts to the respondent when there is a prima facie case of discrimination, except in relation to proceedings in which it is for the court or other competent national body to investigate the facts. It is however necessary to clarify that the appreciation of the facts from which it may be presumed that there has been direct or indirect discrimination remains a matter for the relevant national body in accordance with national law or practice. Further, it is for the Member States to introduce, at any appropriate stage of the proceedings, rules of evidence which are more favourable to plaintiffs.

(31) With a view to further improving the level of protection offered by this Directive, associations, organisations and other legal entities should also be empowered to engage in proceedings, as the Member States so determine, either on behalf or in support of a complainant, without prejudice to national rules of procedure concerning representation and defence.

(32) Having regard to the fundamental nature of the right to effective legal protection, it is appropriate to ensure that workers continue to enjoy such protection even after the relationship giving rise to an alleged breach of the principle of equal treatment has ended. An employee defending or giving evidence on behalf of a person protected under this Directive should be entitled to the same protection.

(33) It has been clearly established by the Court of Justice that in order to be effective, the principle of equal treatment implies that the compensation awarded for any breach must be adequate in relation to the damage sustained. It is therefore appropriate to exclude the fixing of any prior upper limit for such compensation, except where the employer can prove that the only damage suffered by an applicant as a result of discrimination within the meaning of this Directive was the refusal to take his/her job application into consideration.

(34) In order to enhance the effective implementation of the principle of equal treatment, Member States should promote dialogue between the social partners and, within the framework of national practice, with non-governmental organisations.

(35) Member States should provide for effective, proportionate and dissuasive penalties for breaches of the obligations under this Directive.

(36) Since the objectives of this Directive cannot be sufficiently achieved by the Member States and can therefore be better achieved at Community level, the Community may adopt measures in accordance with the principle of subsidiarity as set out in Article 5 of the Treaty. In accordance with the principle of proportionality, as set out in that Article, this Directive does not go beyond what is necessary in order to achieve those objectives.

(37) For the sake of a better understanding of the different treatment of men and women in matters of employment and occupation, comparable statistics disaggregated by sex should continue to be developed, analysed and made available at the appropriate levels.

(38) Equal treatment of men and women in matters of employment and occupation cannot be restricted to legislative measures. Instead, the European Union and the Member States should continue to promote the raising of public awareness of wage discrimination and the changing of public attitudes, involving all parties concerned at public and private level to the greatest possible extent. The dialogue between the social partners could play an important role in this process.

(39) The obligation to transpose this Directive into national law should be confined to those provisions which represent a substantive change as compared with the earlier Directives. The obligation to transpose the provisions which are substantially unchanged arises under the earlier Directives.

(40) This Directive should be without prejudice to the obligations of the Member States relating to the time limits for transposition into national law and application of the Directives set out in Annex I, Part B.

(41) In accordance with paragraph 34 of the Interinstitutional agreement on better law-making, Member States are encouraged to draw up, for themselves and in the interest of the Community, their own tables, which will, as far as possible, illustrate the correlation between this Directive and the transposition measures and to make them public,

HAVE ADOPTED THIS DIRECTIVE:

TITLE I
GENERAL PROVISIONS

Article 1 Purpose

The purpose of this Directive is to ensure the implementation of the principle of equal opportunities and equal treatment of men and women in matters of employment and occupation.

To that end, it contains provisions to implement the principle of equal treatment in relation to:

(a)   access to employment, including promotion, and to vocational training;
(b)   working conditions, including pay;
(c)   occupational social security schemes.

It also contains provisions to ensure that such implementation is made more effective by the establishment of appropriate procedures.

Article 2 Definitions

1.   For the purposes of this Directive, the following definitions shall apply:

(a)   'direct discrimination': where one person is treated less favourably on grounds of sex than another is, has been or would be treated in a comparable situation;

(b)   'indirect discrimination': where an apparently neutral provision, criterion or practice would put persons of one sex at a particular disadvantage compared with persons of the other sex, unless that provision, criterion or practice is objectively justified by a legitimate aim, and the means of achieving that aim are appropriate and necessary;

(c)   'harassment': where unwanted conduct related to the sex of a person occurs with the purpose or effect of violating the dignity of a person, and of creating an intimidating, hostile, degrading, humiliating or offensive environment;

(d)   'sexual harassment': where any form of unwanted verbal, non-verbal or physical conduct of a sexual nature occurs, with the purpose or effect of violating the dignity of a person, in particular when creating an intimidating, hostile, degrading, humiliating or offensive environment;

(e)   'pay': the ordinary basic or minimum wage or salary and any other consideration, whether in cash or in kind, which the worker receives directly or indirectly, in respect of his/ her employment from his/her employer;

(f)   'occupational social security schemes': schemes not governed by Council Directive 79/7/EEC of 19 December 1978 on the progressive implementation of the principle of equal treatment for men and women in matters of social security whose purpose is to provide workers, whether employees or self-employed, in an undertaking or group of undertakings, area of economic activity, occupational sector or group of sectors with benefits intended to supplement the benefits provided by statutory social security schemes or to replace them, whether membership of such schemes is compulsory or optional.

2.   For the purposes of this Directive, discrimination includes:

(a)   harassment and sexual harassment, as well as any less favourable treatment based on a person's rejection of or submission to such conduct;

(b)   instruction to discriminate against persons on grounds of sex;

(c)   any less favourable treatment of a woman related to pregnancy or maternity leave within the meaning of Directive 92/85/EEC.

Article 3 Positive action

Member States may maintain or adopt measures within the meaning of Article 141(4) of the Treaty with a view to ensuring full equality in practice between men and women in working life.

TITLE II
SPECIFIC PROVISIONS

CHAPTER 1
EQUAL PAY

Article 4 Prohibition of discrimination

For the same work or for work to which equal value is attributed, direct and indirect discrimination on grounds of sex with regard to all aspects and conditions of remuneration shall be eliminated.

In particular, where a job classification system is used for determining pay, it shall be based on the same criteria for both men and women and so drawn up as to exclude any discrimination on grounds of sex.

CHAPTER 2

EQUAL TREATMENT IN OCCUPATIONAL SOCIAL SECURITY SCHEMES

Article 5   Prohibition of discrimination

Without prejudice to Article 4, there shall be no direct or indirect discrimination on grounds of sex in occupational social security schemes, in particular as regards:

    (a)   the scope of such schemes and the conditions of access to them;

    (b)   the obligation to contribute and the calculation of contributions;

    (c)   the calculation of benefits, including supplementary benefits due in respect of a spouse or dependants, and the conditions governing the duration and retention of entitlement to benefits.

Article 6   Personal scope

This Chapter shall apply to members of the working population, including self-employed persons, persons whose activity is interrupted by illness, maternity, accident or involuntary unemployment and persons seeking employment and to retired and disabled workers, and to those claiming under them, in accordance with national law and/or practice.

Article 7   Material scope

1.   This Chapter applies to:

    (a)   occupational social security schemes which provide protection against the following risks:

        (i)   sickness,

        (ii)   invalidity,

        (iii)   old age, including early retirement,

        (iv)   industrial accidents and occupational diseases,

        (v)   unemployment;

    (b)   occupational social security schemes which provide for other social benefits, in cash or in kind, and in particular survivors' benefits and family allowances, if such benefits constitute a consideration paid by the employer to the worker by reason of the latter's employment.

2.   This Chapter also applies to pension schemes for a particular category of worker such as that of public servants if the benefits payable under the scheme are paid by reason of the employment relationship with the public employer. The fact that such a scheme forms part of a general statutory scheme shall be without prejudice in that respect.

Article 8   Exclusions from the material scope

1.   This Chapter does not apply to:

    (a)   individual contracts for self-employed persons;

    (b)   single-member schemes for self-employed persons;

    (c)   insurance contracts to which the employer is not a party, in the case of workers;

    (d)   optional provisions of occupational social security schemes offered to participants individually to guarantee them:

        (i)   either additional benefits,

        (ii)   or a choice of date on which the normal benefits for self-employed persons will start, or a choice between several benefits;

    (e)   occupational social security schemes in so far as benefits are financed by contributions paid by workers on a voluntary basis.

2.   This Chapter does not preclude an employer granting to persons who have already reached the retirement age for the purposes of granting a pension by virtue of an occupational social security scheme, but who have not yet reached the retirement age for the purposes of granting a statutory retirement pension, a pension supplement, the aim of which is to make equal or more nearly equal the overall amount of benefit paid to these persons in relation to the amount paid to persons of the other sex in the same situation who have already reached the statutory retirement age, until the persons benefiting from the supplement reach the statutory retirement age.

Article 9 Examples of discrimination

1. Provisions contrary to the principle of equal treatment shall include those based on sex, either directly or indirectly, for:
   (a) determining the persons who may participate in an occupational social security scheme;
   (b) fixing the compulsory or optional nature of participation in an occupational social security scheme;
   (c) laying down different rules as regards the age of entry into the scheme or the minimum period of employment or membership of the scheme required to obtain the benefits thereof;
   (d) laying down different rules, except as provided for in points (h) and (j), for the reimbursement of contributions when a worker leaves a scheme without having fulfilled the conditions guaranteeing a deferred right to long-term benefits;
   (e) setting different conditions for the granting of benefits or restricting such benefits to workers of one or other of the sexes;
   (f) fixing different retirement ages;
   (g) suspending the retention or acquisition of rights during periods of maternity leave or leave for family reasons which are granted by law or agreement and are paid by the employer;
   (h) setting different levels of benefit, except in so far as may be necessary to take account of actuarial calculation factors which differ according to sex in the case of defined contribution schemes; in the case of funded defined-benefit schemes, certain elements may be unequal where the inequality of the amounts results from the effects of the use of actuarial factors differing according to sex at the time when the scheme's funding is implemented;
   (i) setting different levels for workers' contributions;
   (j) setting different levels for employers' contributions, except:
      (i) in the case of defined-contribution schemes if the aim is to equalise the amount of the final benefits or to make them more nearly equal for both sexes,
      (ii) in the case of funded defined-benefit schemes where the employer's contributions are intended to ensure the adequacy of the funds necessary to cover the cost of the benefits defined;
   (k) laying down different standards or standards applicable only to workers of a specified sex, except as provided for in points (h) and (j), as regards the guarantee or retention of entitlement to deferred benefits when a worker leaves a scheme.
2. Where the granting of benefits within the scope of this Chapter is left to the discretion of the scheme's management bodies, the latter shall comply with the principle of equal treatment.

Article 10 Implementation as regards self-employed persons

1. Member States shall take the necessary steps to ensure that the provisions of occupational social security schemes for self-employed persons contrary to the principle of equal treatment are revised with effect from 1 January 1993 at the latest or for Member States whose accession took place after that date, at the date that Directive 86/378/EEC became applicable in their territory.
2. This Chapter shall not preclude rights and obligations relating to a period of membership of an occupational social security scheme for self-employed persons prior to revision of that scheme from remaining subject to the provisions of the scheme in force during that period.

Article 11 Possibility of deferral as regards self-employed persons

As regards occupational social security schemes for self-employed persons, Member States may defer compulsory application of the principle of equal treatment with regard to:
   (a) determination of pensionable age for the granting of old age or retirement pensions, and the possible implications for other benefits:
      (i) either until the date on which such equality is achieved in statutory schemes,
      (ii) or, at the latest, until such equality is prescribed by a directive;

    (b)   survivors' pensions until Community law establishes the principle of equal treatment in statutory social security schemes in that regard;

    (c)   the application of Article 9(1)(i) in relation to the use of actuarial calculation factors, until 1 January 1999 or for Member States whose accession took place after that date until the date that Directive 86/378/EEC became applicable in their territory.

Article 12 Retroactive effect

1.   Any measure implementing this Chapter, as regards workers, shall cover all benefits under occupational social security schemes derived from periods of employment subsequent to 17 May 1990 and shall apply retroactively to that date, without prejudice to workers or those claiming under them who have, before that date, initiated legal proceedings or raised an equivalent claim under national law. In that event, the implementation measures shall apply retroactively to 8 April 1976 and shall cover all the benefits derived from periods of employment after that date. For Member States which acceded to the Community after 8 April 1976, and before 17 May 1990, that date shall be replaced by the date on which Article 141 of the Treaty became applicable in their territory.

2.   The second sentence of paragraph 1 shall not prevent national rules relating to time limits for bringing actions under national law from being relied on against workers or those claiming under them who initiated legal proceedings or raised an equivalent claim under national law before 17 May 1990, provided that they are not less favourable for that type of action than for similar actions of a domestic nature and that they do not render the exercise of rights conferred by Community law impossible in practice.

3.   For Member States whose accession took place after 17 May 1990 and which were on 1 January 1994 Contracting Parties to the Agreement on the European Economic Area, the date of 17 May 1990 in the first sentence of paragraph 1 shall be replaced by 1 January 1994.

4.   For other Member States whose accession took place after 17 May 1990, the date of 17 May 1990 in paragraphs 1 and 2 shall be replaced by the date on which Article 141 of the Treaty became applicable in their territory.

Article 13 Flexible pensionable age

Where men and women may claim a flexible pensionable age under the same conditions, this shall not be deemed to be incompatible with this Chapter.

CHAPTER 3
EQUAL TREATMENT AS REGARDS ACCESS TO EMPLOYMENT, VOCATIONAL TRAINING AND PROMOTION AND WORKING CONDITIONS

Article 14 Prohibition of discrimination

1.   There shall be no direct or indirect discrimination on grounds of sex in the public or private sectors, including public bodies, in relation to:

    (a)   conditions for access to employment, to self-employment or to occupation, including selection criteria and recruitment conditions, whatever the branch of activity and at all levels of the professional hierarchy, including promotion;

    (b)   access to all types and to all levels of vocational guidance, vocational training, advanced vocational training and retraining, including practical work experience;

    (c)   employment and working conditions, including dismissals, as well as pay as provided for in Article 141 of the Treaty;

    (d)   membership of, and involvement in, an organisation of workers or employers, or any organisation whose members carry on a particular profession, including the benefits provided for by such organisations.

2.   Member States may provide, as regards access to employment including the training leading thereto, that a difference of treatment which is based on a characteristic related to sex shall not constitute discrimination where, by reason of the nature of the particular occupational activities concerned or of the context in which they are carried out, such a characteristic constitutes a genuine and determining occupational requirement, provided that its objective is legitimate and the requirement is proportionate.

Article 15 Return from maternity leave

A woman on maternity leave shall be entitled, after the end of her period of maternity leave, to return to her job or to an equivalent post on terms and conditions which are no less favourable to her and to benefit from any improvement in working conditions to which she would have been entitled during her absence.

Article 16 Paternity and adoption leave

This Directive is without prejudice to the right of Member States to recognise distinct rights to paternity and/or adoption leave. Those Member States which recognise such rights shall take the necessary measures to protect working men and women against dismissal due to exercising those rights and ensure that, at the end of such leave, they are entitled to return to their jobs or to equivalent posts on terms and conditions which are no less favourable to them, and to benefit from any improvement in working conditions to which they would have been entitled during their absence.

TITLE III
HORIZONTAL PROVISIONS

CHAPTER 1
REMEDIES AND ENFORCEMENT

SECTION 1
REMEDIES

Article 17 Defence of rights

1. Member States shall ensure that, after possible recourse to other competent authorities including where they deem it appropriate conciliation procedures, judicial procedures for the enforcement of obligations under this Directive are available to all persons who consider themselves wronged by failure to apply the principle of equal treatment to them, even after the relationship in which the discrimination is alleged to have occurred has ended.
2. Member States shall ensure that associations, organisations or other legal entities which have, in accordance with the criteria laid down by their national law, a legitimate interest in ensuring that the provisions of this Directive are complied with, may engage, either on behalf or in support of the complainant, with his/her approval, in any judicial and/or administrative procedure provided for the enforcement of obligations under this Directive.
3. Paragraphs 1 and 2 are without prejudice to national rules relating to time limits for bringing actions as regards the principle of equal treatment.

Article 18 Compensation or reparation

Member States shall introduce into their national legal systems such measures as are necessary to ensure real and effective compensation or reparation as the Member States so determine for the loss and damage sustained by a person injured as a result of discrimination on grounds of sex, in a way which is dissuasive and proportionate to the damage suffered. Such compensation or reparation may not be restricted by the fixing of a prior upper limit, except in cases where the employer can prove that the only damage suffered by an applicant as a result of discrimination within the meaning of this Directive is the refusal to take his/her job application into consideration.

SECTION 2
BURDEN OF PROOF

Article 19 Burden of proof

1. Member States shall take such measures as are necessary, in accordance with their national judicial systems, to ensure that, when persons who consider themselves wronged because the principle of equal treatment has not been applied to them

establish, before a court or other competent authority, facts from which it may be presumed that there has been direct or indirect discrimination, it shall be for the respondent to prove that there has been no breach of the principle of equal treatment.

2. Paragraph 1 shall not prevent Member States from introducing rules of evidence which are more favourable to plaintiffs.

3. Member States need not apply paragraph 1 to proceedings in which it is for the court or competent body to investigate the facts of the case.

4. Paragraphs 1, 2 and 3 shall also apply to:
   (a) the situations covered by Article 141 of the Treaty and, insofar as discrimination based on sex is concerned, by Directives 92/85/EEC and 96/34/EC;
   (b) any civil or administrative procedure concerning the public or private sector which provides for means of redress under national law pursuant to the measures referred to in (a) with the exception of out-of-court procedures of a voluntary nature or provided for in national law.

5. This Article shall not apply to criminal procedures, unless otherwise provided by the Member States.

CHAPTER 2
PROMOTION OF EQUAL TREATMENT — DIALOGUE

Article 20 Equality bodies

1. Member States shall designate and make the necessary arrangements for a body or bodies for the promotion, analysis, monitoring and support of equal treatment of all persons without discrimination on grounds of sex. These bodies may form part of agencies with responsibility at national level for the defence of human rights or the safeguard of individuals' rights.

2. Member States shall ensure that the competences of these bodies include:
   (a) without prejudice to the right of victims and of associations, organisations or other legal entities referred to in Article 17(2), providing independent assistance to victims of discrimination in pursuing their complaints about discrimination;
   (b) conducting independent surveys concerning discrimination;
   (c) publishing independent reports and making recommendations on any issue relating to such discrimination;
   (d) at the appropriate level exchanging available information with corresponding European bodies such as any future European Institute for Gender Equality.

Article 21 Social dialogue

1. Member States shall, in accordance with national traditions and practice, take adequate measures to promote social dialogue between the social partners with a view to fostering equal treatment, including, for example, through the monitoring of practices in the workplace, in access to employment, vocational training and promotion, as well as through the monitoring of collective agreements, codes of conduct, research or exchange of experience and good practice.

2. Where consistent with national traditions and practice, Member States shall encourage the social partners, without prejudice to their autonomy, to promote equality between men and women, and flexible working arrangements, with the aim of facilitating the reconciliation of work and private life, and to conclude, at the appropriate level, agreements laying down antidiscrimination rules in the fields referred to in Article 1 which fall within the scope of collective bargaining. These agreements shall respect the provisions of this Directive and the relevant national implementing measures.

3. Member States shall, in accordance with national law, collective agreements or practice, encourage employers to promote equal treatment for men and women in a planned and systematic way in the workplace, in access to employment, vocational training and promotion.

4. To this end, employers shall be encouraged to provide at appropriate regular intervals employees and/or their representatives with appropriate information on equal treatment for men and women in the undertaking.

Such information may include an overview of the proportions of men and women at different levels of the organisation; their pay and pay differentials; and possible measures to improve the situation in cooperation with employees' representatives.

Article 22 Dialogue with non-governmental organisations

Member States shall encourage dialogue with appropriate non-governmental organisations which have, in accordance with their national law and practice, a legitimate interest in contributing to the fight against discrimination on grounds of sex with a view to promoting the principle of equal treatment.

CHAPTER 3
GENERAL HORIZONTAL PROVISIONS

Article 23 Compliance

Member States shall take all necessary measures to ensure that:

(a) any laws, regulations and administrative provisions contrary to the principle of equal treatment are abolished;

(b) provisions contrary to the principle of equal treatment in individual or collective contracts or agreements, internal rules of undertakings or rules governing the independent occupations and professions and workers' and employers' organisations or any other arrangements shall be, or may be, declared null and void or are amended;

(c) occupational social security schemes containing such provisions may not be approved or extended by administrative measures.

Article 24 Victimisation

Member States shall introduce into their national legal systems such measures as are necessary to protect employees, including those who are employees' representatives provided for by national laws and/or practices, against dismissal or other adverse treatment by the employer as a reaction to a complaint within the undertaking or to any legal proceedings aimed at enforcing compliance with the principle of equal treatment.

Article 25 Penalties

Member States shall lay down the rules on penalties applicable to infringements of the national provisions adopted pursuant to this Directive, and shall take all measures necessary to ensure that they are applied. The penalties, which may comprise the payment of compensation to the victim, must be effective, proportionate and dissuasive. The Member States shall notify those provisions to the Commission by 5 October 2005 at the latest and shall notify it without delay of any subsequent amendment affecting them.

Article 26 Prevention of discrimination

Member States shall encourage, in accordance with national law, collective agreements or practice, employers and those responsible for access to vocational training to take effective measures to prevent all forms of discrimination on grounds of sex, in particular harassment and sexual harassment in the workplace, in access to employment, vocational training and promotion.

Article 27 Minimum requirements

1. Member States may introduce or maintain provisions which are more favourable to the protection of the principle of equal treatment than those laid down in this Directive.

2. Implementation of this Directive shall under no circumstances be sufficient grounds for a reduction in the level of protection of workers in the areas to which it applies, without prejudice to the Member States' right to respond to changes in the situation by introducing laws, regulations and administrative provisions which differ from those in force on the notification of this Directive, provided that the provisions of this Directive are complied with.

Article 28 Relationship to Community and national provisions

1. This Directive shall be without prejudice to provisions concerning the protection of women, particularly as regards pregnancy and maternity.

2.   This Directive shall be without prejudice to the provisions of Directive 96/34/EC and Directive 92/85/EEC.

Article 29 Gender mainstreaming

Member States shall actively take into account the objective of equality between men and women when formulating and implementing laws, regulations, administrative provisions, policies and activities in the areas referred to in this Directive.

Article 30 Dissemination of information

Member States shall ensure that measures taken pursuant to this Directive, together with the provisions already in force, are brought to the attention of all the persons concerned by all suitable means and, where appropriate, at the workplace.

TITLE IV
FINAL PROVISIONS

Article 31 Reports

1.   By 15 February 2011, the Member States shall communicate to the Commission all the information necessary for the Commission to draw up a report to the European Parliament and the Council on the application of this Directive.

2.   Without prejudice to paragraph 1, Member States shall communicate to the Commission, every four years, the texts of any measures adopted pursuant to Article 141(4) of the Treaty, as well as reports on these measures and their implementation. On the basis of that information, the Commission will adopt and publish every four years a report establishing a comparative assessment of any measures in the light of Declaration No 28 annexed to the Final Act of the Treaty of Amsterdam.

3.   Member States shall assess the occupational activities referred to in Article 14(2), in order to decide, in the light of social developments, whether there is justification for maintaining the exclusions concerned. They shall notify the Commission of the results of this assessment periodically, but at least every 8 years.

Article 32 Review

By 15 February 2011 at the latest, the Commission shall review the operation of this Directive and if appropriate, propose any amendments it deems necessary.

Article 33 Implementation

Member States shall bring into force the laws, regulations and administrative provisions necessary to comply with this Directive by 15 August 2008 at the latest or shall ensure, by that date, that management and labour introduce the requisite provisions by way of agreement. Member States may, if necessary to take account of particular difficulties, have up to one additional year to comply with this Directive. Member States shall take all necessary steps to be able to guarantee the results imposed by this Directive. They shall forthwith communicate to the Commission the texts of those measures.

When Member States adopt these measures, they shall contain a reference to this Directive or be accompanied by such reference on the occasion of their official publication. They shall also include a statement that references in existing laws, regulations and administrative provisions to the Directives repealed by this Directive shall be construed as references to this Directive. Member States shall determine how such reference is to be made and how that statement is to be formulated.

The obligation to transpose this Directive into national law shall be confined to those provisions which represent a substantive change as compared with the earlier Directives. The obligation to transpose the provisions which are substantially unchanged arises under the earlier Directives.

Member States shall communicate to the Commission the text of the main provisions of national law which they adopt in the field covered by this Directive.

Article 34 Repeal

1. With effect from 15 August 2009 Directives 75/117/EEC, 76/207/EEC, 86/378/EEC and 97/80/EC shall be repealed without prejudice to the obligations of the Member States relating to the time-limits for transposition into national law and application of the Directives set out in Annex I, Part B.

2. References made to the repealed Directives shall be construed as being made to this Directive and should be read in accordance with the correlation table in Annex II.

Article 35 Entry into force

This Directive shall enter into force on the 20th day following its publication in the *Official Journal of the European Union*.

Article 36 Addressees

This Directive is addressed to the Member States.

DIRECTIVE (EU) 2019/1158 OF THE EUROPEAN PARLIAMENT AND OF THE COUNCIL of 20 JUNE 2019
on work-life balance for parents and carers and repealing Council Directive 2010/18/EU
[2019] OJ L188/79

Article 1   Subject matter

This Directive lays down minimum requirements designed to achieve equality between men and women with regard to labour market opportunities and treatment at work, by facilitating the reconciliation of work and family life for workers who are parents, or carers. To that end, this Directive provides for individual rights related to the following:

(a) paternity leave, parental leave and carers' leave;

(b) flexible working arrangements for workers who are parents, or carers.

Article 2   Scope

This Directive applies to all workers, men and women, who have an employment contract or employment relationship as defined by the law, collective agreements or practice in force in each Member State, taking into account the case-law of the Court of Justice.

Article 3   Definitions

1. For the purposes of this Directive, the following definitions apply:

    (a) 'paternity leave' means leave from work for fathers or, where and insofar as recognised by national law, for equivalent second parents, on the occasion of the birth of a child for the purposes of providing care;

    (b) 'parental leave' means leave from work for parents on the grounds of the birth or adoption of a child to take care of that child;

    (c) 'carers' leave' means leave from work for workers in order to provide personal care or support to a relative, or to a person who lives in the same household as the worker, and who is in need of significant care or support for a serious medical reason, as defined by each Member State;

    (d) 'carer' means a worker providing personal care or support to a relative, or to a person who lives in the same household as the worker, and who is in need of significant care or support for a serious medical reason, as defined by each Member State;

    (e) 'relative' means a worker's son, daughter, mother, father, spouse or, where such partnerships are recognised by national law, partner in civil partnership;

    (f) 'flexible working arrangements' means the possibility for workers to adjust their working patterns, including through the use of remote working arrangements, flexible working schedules, or reduced working hours.

2. The reference to working days in Articles 4 and 6 shall be understood as referring to the full-time working pattern, as defined in the Member State in question.

    A worker's entitlement to leave may be calculated proportionally to the worker's working time, in accordance with the working pattern specified in the worker's contract of employment or employment relationship.

Article 4   Paternity leave

1. Member States shall take the necessary measures to ensure that fathers or, where and insofar as recognised by national law, equivalent second parents, have the right to paternity leave of 10 working days that is to be taken on the occasion of the birth of the worker's child. Member States may determine whether to allow paternity leave to be taken partly before or only after the birth of the child and whether to allow such leave to be taken in flexible ways.
2. The right to paternity leave shall not be made subject to a period of work qualification or to a length of service qualification.
3. The right to paternity leave shall be granted irrespective of the worker's marital or family status, as defined by national law.

Article 5   Parental leave

1. Member States shall take the necessary measures to ensure that each worker has an individual right to parental leave of four months that is to be taken before the child reaches a specified age, up to the age of eight, to be specified by each Member State or by collective agreement. That age shall be determined with a view to ensuring that each parent is able to exercise their right to parental leave effectively and on an equal basis.
2. Member States shall ensure that two months of parental leave cannot be transferred.
3. Member States shall establish a reasonable period of notice that is to be given by workers to employers where they exercise their right to parental leave. In doing so, Member States shall take into account the needs of both the employers and the workers.
    Member States shall ensure that the worker's request for parental leave specifies the intended beginning and end of the period of leave.
4. Member States may make the right to parental leave subject to a period of work qualification or to a length of service qualification, which shall not exceed one year. In the case of successive fixed-term contracts within the meaning of Council Directive 1999/70/EC with the same employer, the sum of those contracts shall be taken into account for the purpose of calculating the qualifying period.
5. Member States may establish the circumstances in which an employer, following consultation in accordance with national law, collective agreements or practice, is allowed to postpone the granting of parental leave for a reasonable period of time on the grounds that the taking of parental leave at the time requested would seriously disrupt the good functioning of the employer. Employers shall provide reasons for such a postponement of parental leave in writing.
6. Member States shall take the necessary measures to ensure that workers have the right to request that they take parental leave in flexible ways. Member States may specify the modalities of application thereof. The employer shall consider and respond to such requests, taking into account the needs of both the employer and the worker. The employer shall provide reasons for any refusal to accede to such a request in writing within a reasonable period after the request.
7. Member States shall take the necessary measures to ensure that when considering requests for full-time parental leave, employers shall, prior to any postponement in accordance with paragraph 5, offer, to the extent possible, flexible ways of taking parental leave pursuant to paragraph 6.
8. Member States shall assess the need for the conditions of access to and the detailed arrangements for the application of parental leave to be adapted to the needs of adoptive parents, parents with a disability and parents with children with a disability or a long-term illness.

Article 6   Carers' leave

1. Member States shall take the necessary measures to ensure that each worker has the right to carers' leave of five working days per year. Member States may determine additional details regarding the scope and conditions of carers' leave in accordance with national law or practice. The use of that right may be subject to appropriate substantiation, in accordance with national law or practice.

2. Member States may allocate carers' leave on the basis of a reference period other than a year, per person in need of care or support, or per case.

Article 7   Time off from work on grounds of force majeure

Member States shall take the necessary measures to ensure that each worker has the right to time off from work on grounds of *force majeure* for urgent family reasons in the case of illness or accident making the immediate attendance of the worker indispensable. Member States may limit the right of each worker to time off from work on grounds of *force majeure* to a certain amount of time each year or by case, or both.

Article 8   Payment or allowance

1. In accordance with national circumstances, such as national law, collective agreements or practice, and taking into account the powers delegated to the social partners, Member States shall ensure that workers who exercise their right to leave provided for in Article 4(1) or Article 5(2) receive a payment or an allowance in accordance with paragraphs 2 and 3 of this Article.
2. With regard to paternity leave as referred to in Article 4(1), such payment or allowance shall guarantee an income at least equivalent to that which the worker concerned would receive in the event of a break in the worker's activities on grounds connected with the worker's state of health, subject to any ceiling laid down in national law. Member States may make the right to a payment or an allowance subject to periods of previous employment, which shall not exceed six months immediately prior to the expected date of the birth of the child.
3. With regard to parental leave as referred to in Article 5(2), such payment or allowance shall be defined by the Member State or the social partners and shall be set in such a way as to facilitate the take-up of parental leave by both parents.

Article 9   Flexible working arrangements

1. Member States shall take the necessary measures to ensure that workers with children up to a specified age, which shall be at least eight years, and carers, have the right to request flexible working arrangements for caring purposes. The duration of such flexible working arrangements may be subject to a reasonable limitation.
2. Employers shall consider and respond to requests for flexible working arrangements as referred to in paragraph 1 within a reasonable period of time, taking into account the needs of both the employer and the worker. Employers shall provide reasons for any refusal of such a request or for any postponement of such arrangements.
3. When flexible working arrangements as referred to in paragraph 1 are limited in duration, the worker shall have the right to return to the original working pattern at the end of the agreed period. The worker shall also have the right to request to return to the original working pattern before the end of the agreed period where justified on the basis of a change of circumstances. The employer shall consider and respond to a request for an early return to the original working pattern, taking into account the needs of both the employer and the worker.
4. Member States may make the right to request flexible working arrangements subject to a period of work qualification or to a length of service qualification, which shall not exceed six months. In the case of successive fixed-term contracts within the meaning of Directive 1999/70/EC with the same employer, the sum of those contracts shall be taken into account for the purpose of calculating the qualifying period.

Article 10   Employment rights

1. Rights that have been acquired or that are in the process of being acquired by workers on the date on which leave provided for in Articles 4, 5 and 6 or time off from work provided for in Article 7 starts shall be maintained until the end of such leave or time off from work. At the end of such leave or time off from work, those rights, including any changes arising from national law, collective agreements or practice, shall apply.
2. Member States shall ensure that, at the end of leave provided for in Articles 4, 5 and 6, workers are entitled to return to their jobs or to equivalent posts on terms and conditions which are no less favourable to them, and to benefit from any improvement in working conditions to which they would have been entitled had they not taken the leave.

3.   Member States shall define the status of the employment contract or employment relationship for the period of leave provided for in Articles 4, 5 and 6, or time off from work provided for in Article 7, including as regards entitlements to social security, including pension contributions, while ensuring that the employment relationship is maintained during that period.

Article 11   Discrimination

Member States shall take the necessary measures to prohibit less favourable treatment of workers on the ground that they have applied for, or have taken, leave provided for in Articles 4, 5 and 6 or time off from work provided for in Article 7, or that they have exercised the rights provided for in Article 9.

Article 12   Protection from dismissal and burden of proof

1.   Member States shall take the necessary measures to prohibit the dismissal and all preparations for the dismissal of workers, on the grounds that they have applied for, or have taken, leave provided for in Articles 4, 5 and 6, or have exercised the right to request flexible working arrangements referred to in Article 9.
2.   Workers who consider that they have been dismissed on the grounds that they have applied for, or have taken, leave provided for in Articles 4, 5 and 6, or have exercised the right to request flexible working arrangements as referred to in Article 9, may request the employer to provide duly substantiated reasons for their dismissal. With respect to the dismissal of a worker who has applied for, or has taken, leave provided for in Article 4, 5 or 6, the employer shall provide reasons for the dismissal in writing.
3.   Member States shall take the measures necessary to ensure that where workers who consider that they have been dismissed on the grounds that they have applied for, or have taken, leave provided for in Articles 4, 5 and 6 establish, before a court or other competent authority, facts capable of giving rise to a presumption that they have been dismissed on such grounds, it shall be for the employer to prove that the dismissal was based on other grounds.
4.   Paragraph 3 shall not prevent Member States from introducing rules of evidence which are more favourable to workers.
5.   Member States shall not be required to apply paragraph 3 to proceedings in which it is for the court or competent body to investigate the facts of the case.
6.   Paragraph 3 shall not apply to criminal proceedings, unless otherwise provided by the Member States.

Article 13   Penalties

Member States shall lay down the rules on penalties applicable to infringements of national provisions adopted pursuant to this Directive, or the relevant provisions already in force concerning the rights which are within the scope of this Directive, and shall take all measures necessary to ensure that they are implemented. The penalties provided for shall be effective, proportionate and dissuasive.

Article 14   Protection against adverse treatment or consequences

Member States shall introduce measures necessary to protect workers, including workers who are employees' represen tatives, from any adverse treatment by the employer or adverse consequences resulting from a complaint lodged within the undertaking or any legal proceedings for the purpose of enforcing compliance with the requirements laid down in this Directive.

Article 15   Equality bodies

Without prejudice to the competence of labour inspectorates or other bodies that enforce the rights of workers, including the social partners, Member States shall ensure that the body or bodies designated, pursuant to Article 20 of Directive 2006/54/EC, for the promotion, analysis, monitoring and support of equal treatment of all persons without discrimination on grounds of sex, are competent with regard to issues relating to discrimination falling within the scope of this Directive.

Article 16   Level of protection

1.   Member States may introduce or maintain provisions that are more favourable to workers than those laid down in this Directive.

2.   The implementation of this Directive shall not constitute grounds for justifying a reduction in the general level of protection of workers in the areas covered by this Directive. The prohibition of such a reduction in the level of protection shall be without prejudice to the right of Member States and the social partners to lay down, in light of changing circumstances, legislative, regulatory or contractual arrangements other than those in force on 1 August 2019, provided that the minimum requirements laid down in this Directive are complied with.

Article 17   Dissemination of information

Member States shall ensure that the national measures transposing this Directive, together with the relevant provisions already in force relating to the subject matter as set out in Article 1, are brought to the attention of workers and employers, including employers that are SMEs, by all appropriate means throughout their territory.

Article 18   Reporting and review

1.   By 2 August 2027, Member States shall communicate to the Commission all information concerning the implementation of this Directive that is necessary for the Commission to draw up a report. That information shall include available aggregated data on the take-up of different types of leave and flexible working arrangements, by men and women pursuant to this Directive, for the purposes of allowing the proper monitoring and assessment of the implementation of this Directive, in particular with regard to gender equality.

2.   The Commission shall submit the report referred to in paragraph 1 to the European Parliament and to the Council. The report shall, if appropriate, be accompanied by a legislative proposal.

The report shall also be accompanied by:

(a)   a study of the interaction between the different types of leave provided for in this Directive as well as other types of family-related leave, such as adoption leave; and

(b)   a study of the rights to family-related leave that are granted to self-employed persons.

Article 19   Repeal

1.   Directive 2010/18/EU is repealed with effect from 2 August 2022. References to the repealed Directive shall be construed as references to this Directive and shall be read in accordance with the correlation table set out in the Annex.

2.   Notwithstanding the repeal of Directive 2010/18/EU pursuant to paragraph 1 of this Article, any period or separate cumulative periods of parental leave taken or transferred by a worker pursuant to that Directive before 2 August 2022 may be deducted from that worker's parental leave entitlement under Article 5 of this Directive.

Article 20   Transposition

1.   Member States shall bring into force the laws, regulations and administrative provisions necessary to comply with this Directive by 2 August 2022. They shall immediately inform the Commission thereof.

2.   Notwithstanding paragraph 1 of this Article, for the payment or allowance corresponding to the last two weeks of parental leave as provided for in Article 8(3), Member States shall bring into force the laws, regulations and administrative provisions necessary to comply with this Directive by 2 August 2024. They shall immediately inform the Commission thereof.

3.   When Member States adopt the measures referred to in paragraphs 1 and 2, they shall contain a reference to this Directive or shall be accompanied by such a reference on the occasion of their official publication. The methods of making such reference shall be laid down by Member States.

4.   Member States shall communicate to the Commission the text of the main measures of national law which they adopt in the areas covered by this Directive.

5. The detailed rules and modalities for applying this Directive shall be established in accordance with national law, collective agreements or practice, as long as the minimum requirements and the objectives of this Directive are respected.

6. For the purposes of complying with Articles 4, 5, 6 and 8 of this Directive and with Directive 92/85/EEC, Member States may take into account any period of, and payment or allowance with respect to, family-related time off work, in particular maternity leave, paternity leave, parental leave and carers' leave, available at national level which is above the minimum standards provided for in this Directive or in Directive 92/85/EEC, provided that the minimum requirements for such leave are met and that the general level of protection provided to workers in the areas covered by those Directives is not reduced.

7. Where Member States ensure a payment or an allowance of at least 65% of the worker's net wage, which may be subject to a ceiling, for at least six months of parental leave for each parent, they may decide to maintain such system rather than provide for the payment or allowance referred to in Article 8(2).

8. Member States may entrust the social partners with the implementation of this Directive, where the social partners jointly request to do so, provided that Member States take all the necessary steps to ensure that the results sought by this Directive are guaranteed at all times.

Article 21   Entry into force

This Directive shall enter into force on the twentieth day following that of its publication in the *Official Journal of the European Union*.

Article 22   Addressees

This Directive is addressed to the Member States.
Done at Brussels, 20 June 2019.

DIRECTIVE 2010/41/EU OF THE EUROPEAN PARLIAMENT AND OF THE COUNCIL
of 7 JULY 2010
on the application of the principle of equal treatment between men and women engaged in an activity in a self-employed capacity and repealing Council Directive 86/613/EEC
[2010] OJ L180/1

Article 1   Subject matter

1. This Directive lays down a framework for putting into effect in the Member States the principle of equal treatment between men and women engaged in an activity in a self-employed capacity, or contributing to the pursuit of such an activity, as regards those aspects not covered by Directives 2006/54/EC and 79/7/EEC.

2. The implementation of the principle of equal treatment between men and women in the access to and supply of goods and services remains covered by Directive 2004/113/EC.

Article 2   Scope

This Directive covers:

(a) self-employed workers, namely all persons pursuing a gainful activity for their own account, under the conditions laid down by national law;

(b) the spouses of self-employed workers or, when and in so far as recognised by national law, the life partners of self-employed workers, not being employees or business partners, where they habitually, under the conditions laid down by national law, participate in the activities of the self-employed worker and perform the same tasks or ancillary tasks.

Article 3 Definitions

For the purposes of this Directive, the following definitions shall apply:

(a) 'direct discrimination': where one person is treated less favourably on grounds of sex than another is, has been or would be, treated in a comparable situation;

(b) 'indirect discrimination': where an apparently neutral provision, criterion or practice would put persons of one sex at a particular disadvantage compared with persons of the other sex, unless that provision, criterion or practice is objectively justified by a legitimate aim, and the means of achieving that aim are appropriate and necessary;

(c) 'harassment': where unwanted conduct related to the sex of a person occurs with the purpose, or effect, of violating the dignity of that person, and of creating an intimidating, hostile, degrading, humiliating or offensive environment;

(d) 'sexual harassment': where any form of unwanted verbal, non-verbal, or physical, conduct of a sexual nature occurs, with the purpose or effect of violating the dignity of a person, in particular when creating an intimidating, hostile, degrading, humiliating or offensive environment.

Article 4 Principle of equal treatment

1. The principle of equal treatment means that there shall be no discrimination whatsoever on grounds of sex in the public or private sectors, either directly or indirectly, for instance in relation to the establishment, equipment or extension of a business or the launching or extension of any other form of self-employed activity.

2. In the areas covered by paragraph 1, harassment and sexual harassment shall be deemed to be discrimination on grounds of sex and therefore prohibited. A person's rejection of, or submission to, such conduct may not be used as a basis for a decision affecting that person.

3. In the areas covered by paragraph 1, an instruction to discriminate against persons on grounds of sex shall be deemed to be discrimination.

Article 5 Positive action

Member States may maintain or adopt measures within the meaning of Article 157(4) of the Treaty on the Functioning of the European Union with a view to ensuring full equality in practice between men and women in working life, for instance aimed at promoting entrepreneurship initiatives among women.

Article 6 Establishment of a company

Without prejudice to the specific conditions for access to certain activities which apply equally to both sexes, the Member States shall take the measures necessary to ensure that the conditions for the establishment of a company between spouses, or between life partners when and in so far as recognised by national law, are not more restrictive than the conditions for the establishment of a company between other persons.

Article 7 Social protection

1. Where a system for social protection for self-employed workers exists in a Member State, that Member State shall take the necessary measures to ensure that spouses and life partners referred to in Article 2(b) can benefit from a social protection in accordance with national law.

2. The Member States may decide whether the social protection referred to in paragraph 1 is implemented on a mandatory or voluntary basis.

Article 8 Maternity benefits

1. The Member States shall take the necessary measures to ensure that female self-employed workers and female spouses and life partners referred to in Article 2 may, in accordance with national law, be granted a sufficient maternity allowance enabling interruptions in their occupational activity owing to pregnancy or motherhood for at least 14 weeks.

2. The Member States may decide whether the maternity allowance referred to in paragraph 1 is granted on a mandatory or voluntary basis.

3. The allowance referred to in paragraph 1 shall be deemed sufficient if it guarantees an income at least equivalent to:

(a) the allowance which the person concerned would receive in the event of a break in her activities on grounds connected with her state of health and/or;

(b) the average loss of income or profit in relation to a comparable preceding period subject to any ceiling laid down under national law and/or;

(c) any other family related allowance established by national law, subject to any ceiling laid down under national law.

4. The Member States shall take the necessary measures to ensure that female self-employed workers and female spouses and life partners referred to in Article 2 have access to any existing services supplying temporary replacements or to any existing national social services. The Member States may provide that access to those services is an alternative to or a part of the allowance referred to in paragraph 1 of this Article.

Article 9 Defence of rights

1. The Member States shall ensure that judicial or administrative proceedings, including, where Member States consider it appropriate, conciliation procedures, for the enforcement of the obligations under this Directive are available to all persons who consider they have sustained loss or damage as a result of a failure to apply the principle of equal treatment to them, even after the relationship in which the discrimination is alleged to have occurred has ended.

2. The Member States shall ensure that associations, organisations and other legal entities which have, in accordance with the criteria laid down by their national law, a legitimate interest in ensuring that this Directive is complied with may engage, either on behalf or in support of the complainant, with his or her approval, in any judicial or administrative proceedings provided for the enforcement of obligations under this Directive.

3. Paragraphs 1 and 2 shall be without prejudice to national rules on time limits for bringing actions relating to the principle of equal treatment.

Article 10 Compensation or reparation

The Member States shall introduce such measures into their national legal systems as are necessary to ensure real and effective compensation or reparation, as Member States so determine, for the loss or damage sustained by a person as a result of discrimination on grounds of sex, such compensation or reparation being dissuasive and proportionate to the loss or damage suffered. Such compensation or reparation shall not be limited by the fixing of a prior upper limit.

Article 11 Equality bodies

1. The Member States shall take the necessary measures to ensure that the body or bodies designated in accordance with Article 20 of Directive 2006/54/EC are also competent for the promotion, analysis, monitoring and support of equal treatment of all persons covered by this Directive without discrimination on grounds of sex.

2. The Member States shall ensure that the tasks of the bodies referred to in paragraph 1 include:

(a) providing independent assistance to victims of discrimination in pursuing their complaints of discrimination, without prejudice to the rights of victims and of associations, organisations and other legal entities referred to in Article 9(2);

(b) conducting independent surveys on discrimination;

(c) publishing independent reports and making recommendations on any issue relating to such discrimination;

(d) exchanging, at the appropriate level, the information available with the corresponding European bodies, such as the European Institute for Gender Equality.

Article 12 Gender mainstreaming

The Member States shall actively take into account the objective of equality between men and women when formulating and implementing laws, regulations, administrative provisions, policies and activities in the areas referred to in this Directive.

Article 13 Dissemination of information

The Member States shall ensure that the provisions adopted pursuant to this Directive, together with the relevant provisions already in force, are brought by all appropriate means to the attention of the persons concerned throughout their territory.

Article 14 Level of protection

The Member States may introduce or maintain provisions which are more favourable to the protection of the principle of equal treatment between men and women than those laid down in this Directive.

The implementation of this Directive shall under no circumstances constitute grounds for a reduction in the level of protection against discrimination already afforded by Member States in the fields covered by this Directive.

Article 15 Reports

1. Member States shall communicate all available information concerning the application of this Directive to the Commission by 5 August 2015.

   The Commission shall draw up a summary report for submission to the European Parliament and to the Council no later than 5 August 2016. That report should take into account any legal change concerning the duration of maternity leave for employees. Where appropriate, that report shall be accompanied by proposals for amending this Directive.

2. The Commission's report shall take the viewpoints of the stakeholders into account.

Article 16 Implementation

1. The Member States shall bring into force the laws, regulations and administrative provisions necessary to comply with this Directive by 5 August 2012 at the latest. They shall forthwith communicate to the Commission the text of those provisions.

   When the Member States adopt those provisions, they shall contain a reference to this Directive or be accompanied by such a reference on the occasion of their official publication. Member States shall determine how such reference is to be made.

2. Where justified by particular difficulties, the Member States may, if necessary, have an additional period of two years until 5 August 2014 in order to comply with Article 7, and in order to comply with Article 8 as regards female spouses and life partners referred to in Article 2(b).

3. The Member States shall communicate to the Commission the text of the main provisions of national law which they adopt in the field covered by this Directive.

Article 17 Repeal

Directive 86/613/EEC shall be repealed, with effect from 5 August 2012.

References to the repealed Directive shall be construed as references to this Directive.

Article 18 Entry into force

This Directive shall enter into force on the 20th day following its publication in the *Official Journal of the European Union*.

Article 19 Addressees

This Directive is addressed to the Member States.

EMPLOYMENT: WORKER PROTECTION

COUNCIL DIRECTIVE (EC) No 2001/23 of 12 MARCH 2001
on the approximation of the laws of the Member States relating to the safeguarding of employees' rights in the event of transfers of undertakings, businesses or parts of undertakings or businesses
[2001] OJ L82/16

THE COUNCIL OF THE EUROPEAN UNION,

Having regard to the Treaty establishing the European Community, and in particular Article 94 thereof,

Having regard to the proposal from the Commission,

Having regard to the opinion of the European Parliament,

Having regard to the opinion of the Economic and Social Committee,

Whereas:

(1) Council Directive 77/187/EEC of 14 February 1977 on the approximation of the laws of the Member States relating to the safeguarding of employees' rights in the event of transfers of undertakings, businesses or parts of undertakings or businesses has been substantially amended. In the interests of clarity and rationality, it should therefore be codified.

(2) Economic trends are bringing in their wake, at both national and Community level, changes in the structure of undertakings, through transfers of undertakings, businesses or parts of undertakings or businesses to other employers as a result of legal transfers or mergers.

(3) It is necessary to provide for the protection of employees in the event of a change of employer, in particular, to ensure that their rights are safeguarded.

(4) Differences still remain in the Member States as regards the extent of the protection of employees in this respect and these differences should be reduced.

(5) The Community Charter of the Fundamental Social Rights of Workers adopted on 9 December 1989 ('Social Charter') states, in points 7, 17 and 18 in particular that: 'The completion of the internal market must lead to an improvement in the living and working conditions of workers in the European Community. The improvement must cover, where necessary, the development of certain aspects of employment regulations such as procedures for collective redundancies and those regarding bankruptcies. Information, consultation and participation for workers must be developed along appropriate lines, taking account of the practice in force in the various Member States. Such information, consultation and participation must be implemented in due time, particularly in connection with restructuring operations in undertakings or in cases of mergers having an impact on the employment of workers'.

(6) In 1977 the Council adopted Directive 77/187/EEC to promote the harmonisation of the relevant national laws ensuring the safeguarding of the rights of employees and requiring transferors and transferees to inform and consult employees' representatives in good time.

(7) That Directive was subsequently amended in the light of the impact of the internal market, the legislative tendencies of the Member States with regard to the rescue of undertakings in economic difficulties, the case-law of the Court of Justice of the European Communities, Council Directive 75/129/EEC of 17 February 1975 on the approximation of the laws of the Member States relating to collective redundancies and the legislation already in force in most Member States.

(8) Considerations of legal security and transparency required that the legal concept of transfer be clarified in the light of the case-law of the Court of Justice. Such clarification has not altered the scope of Directive 77/187/EEC as interpreted by the Court of Justice.

(9) The Social Charter recognises the importance of the fight against all forms of discrimination, especially based on sex, colour, race, opinion and creed.

(10) This Directive should be without prejudice to the time limits set out in Annex I Part B within which the Member States are to comply with Directive 77/187/EEC, and the act amending it,

HAS ADOPTED THIS DIRECTIVE:

CHAPTER I
SCOPE AND DEFINITIONS

Article 1

1. (a)   This Directive shall apply to any transfer of an undertaking, business, or part of an undertaking or business to another employer as a result of a legal transfer or merger.

    (b)   Subject to subparagraph (a) and the following provisions of this Article, there is a transfer within the meaning of this Directive where there is a transfer of an economic entity which retains its identity, meaning an organised grouping of resources which has the objective of pursuing an economic activity, whether or not that activity is central or ancillary.

    (c)   This Directive shall apply to public and private undertakings engaged in economic activities whether or not they are operating for gain. An administrative reorganisation of public administrative authorities, or the transfer of administrative functions between public administrative authorities, is not a transfer within the meaning of this Directive.

2. This Directive shall apply where and in so far as the undertaking, business or part of the undertaking or business to be transferred is situated within the territorial scope of the Treaty.

3. This Directive shall apply to a transfer of a seagoing vessel that is part of a transfer of an undertaking, business or part of an undertaking or business within the meaning of paragraphs 1 and 2, provided that the transferee is situated, or the transferred undertaking, business, or part of an undertaking or business remains, within the territorial scope of the Treaty.
    This Directive shall not apply where the object of the transfer consists exclusively of one or more seagoing vessels.

Article 2

1. For the purposes of this Directive:
    (a)   'transferor' shall mean any natural or legal person who, by reason of a transfer within the meaning of Article 1(1), ceases to be the employer in respect of the undertaking, business or part of the undertaking or business;

    (b)   'transferee' shall mean any natural or legal person who, by reason of a transfer within the meaning of Article 1(1), becomes the employer in respect of the undertaking, business or part of the undertaking or business;

    (c)   'representatives of employees' and related expressions shall mean the representatives of the employees provided for by the laws or practices of the Member States;

    (d)   'employee' shall mean any person who, in the Member State concerned, is protected as an employee under national employment law.

2. This Directive shall be without prejudice to national law as regards the definition of contract of employment or employment relationship. However, Member States shall not exclude from the scope of this Directive contracts of employment or employment relationships solely because:
    (a)   of the number of working hours performed or to be performed,
    (b)   they are employment relationships governed by a fixed-duration contract of employment within the meaning of Article 1(1) of Council Directive 91/383/EEC of 25 June 1991 supplementing the measures to encourage improvements in the safety and health at work of workers with a fixed-duration employment relationship or a temporary employment relationship, or

(c)   they are temporary employment relationships within the meaning of Article 1(2) of Directive 91/383/EEC, and the undertaking, business or part of the undertaking or business transferred is, or is part of, the temporary employment business which is the employer.

CHAPTER II

SAFEGUARDING OF EMPLOYEES' RIGHTS

Article 3

1.   The transferor's rights and obligations arising from a contract of employment or from an employment relationship existing on the date of a transfer shall, by reason of such transfer, be transferred to the transferee.

   Member States may provide that, after the date of transfer, the transferor and the transferee shall be jointly and severally liable in respect of obligations which arose before the date of transfer from a contract of employment or an employment relationship existing on the date of the transfer.

2.   Member States may adopt appropriate measures to ensure that the transferor notifies the transferee of all the rights and obligations which will be transferred to the transferee under this Article, so far as those rights and obligations are or ought to have been known to the transferor at the time of the transfer. A failure by the transferor to notify the transferee of any such right or obligation shall not affect the transfer of that right or obligation and the rights of any employees against the transferee and/or transferor in respect of that right or obligation.

3.   Following the transfer, the transferee shall continue to observe the terms and conditions agreed in any collective agreement on the same terms applicable to the transferor under that agreement, until the date of termination or expiry of the collective agreement or the entry into force or application of another collective agreement. Member States may limit the period for observing such terms and conditions with the proviso that it shall not be less than one year.

4.   (a)   Unless Member States provide otherwise, paragraphs 1 and 3 shall not apply in relation to employees' rights to old-age, invalidity or survivors' benefits under supplementary company or intercompany pension schemes outside the statutory social security schemes in Member States.

   (b)   Even where they do not provide in accordance with subparagraph (a) that paragraphs 1 and 3 apply in relation to such rights, Member States shall adopt the measures necessary to protect the interests of employees and of persons no longer employed in the transferor's business at the time of the transfer in respect of rights conferring on them immediate or prospective entitlement to old age benefits, including survivors' benefits, under supplementary schemes referred to in subparagraph (a).

Article 4

1.   The transfer of the undertaking, business or part of the undertaking or business shall not in itself constitute grounds for dismissal by the transferor or the transferee. This provision shall not stand in the way of dismissals that may take place for economic, technical or organisational reasons entailing changes in the workforce. Member States may provide that the first subparagraph shall not apply to certain specific categories of employees who are not covered by the laws or practice of the Member States in respect of protection against dismissal.

2.   If the contract of employment or the employment relationship is terminated because the transfer involves a substantial change in working conditions to the detriment of the employee, the employer shall be regarded as having been responsible for termination of the contract of employment or of the employment relationship.

Article 5

1.   Unless Member States provide otherwise, Articles 3 and 4 shall not apply to any transfer of an undertaking, business or part of an undertaking or business where the transferor is the subject of bankruptcy proceedings or any analogous insolvency

proceedings which have been instituted with a view to the liquidation of the assets of the transferor and are under the supervision of a competent public authority (which may be an insolvency practitioner authorised by a competent public authority).

2. Where Articles 3 and 4 apply to a transfer during insolvency proceedings which have been opened in relation to a transferor (whether or not those proceedings have been instituted with a view to the liquidation of the assets of the transferor) and provided that such proceedings are under the supervision of a competent public authority (which may be an insolvency practitioner determined by national law) a Member State may provide that:

(a) notwithstanding Article 3(1), the transferor's debts arising from any contracts of employment or employment relationships and payable before the transfer or before the opening of the insolvency proceedings shall not be transferred to the transferee, provided that such proceedings give rise, under the law of that Member State, to protection at least equivalent to that provided for in situations covered by Council Directive 80/987/EEC of 20 October 1980 on the approximation of the laws of the Member States relating to the protection of employees in the event of the insolvency of their employer, and, or alternatively, that,

(b) the transferee, transferor or person or persons exercising the transferor's functions, on the one hand, and the representatives of the employees on the other hand may agree alterations, in so far as current law or practice permits, to the employees' terms and conditions of employment designed to safeguard employment opportunities by ensuring the survival of the undertaking, business or part of the undertaking or business.

3. A Member State may apply paragraph 20(b) to any transfers where the transferor is in a situation of serious economic crisis, as defined by national law, provided that the situation is declared by a competent public authority and open to judicial supervision, on condition that such provisions already existed in national law on 17 July 1998.

The Commission shall present a report on the effects of this provision before 17 July 2003 and shall submit any appropriate proposals to the Council.

4. Member States shall take appropriate measures with a view to preventing misuse of insolvency proceedings in such a way as to deprive employees of the rights provided for in this Directive.

Article 6

1. If the undertaking, business or part of an undertaking or business preserves its autonomy, the status and function of the representatives or of the representation of the employees affected by the transfer shall be preserved on the same terms and subject to the same conditions as existed before the date of the transfer by virtue of law, regulation, administrative provision or agreement, provided that the conditions necessary for the constitution of the employee's representation are fulfilled.

The first subparagraph shall not apply if, under the laws, regulations, administrative provisions or practice in the Member States, or by agreement with the representatives of the employees, the conditions necessary for the reappointment of the representatives of the employees or for the reconstitution of the representation of the employees are fulfilled. Where the transferor is the subject of bankruptcy proceedings or any analogous insolvency proceedings which have been instituted with a view to the liquidation of the assets of the transferor and are under the supervision of a competent public authority (which may be an insolvency practitioner authorised by a competent public authority), Member States may take the necessary measures to ensure that the transferred employees are properly represented until the new election or designation of representatives of the employees.

If the undertaking, business or part of an undertaking or business does not preserve its autonomy, the Member States shall take the necessary measures to ensure that the employees transferred who were represented before the transfer continue to be properly represented during the period necessary for the reconstitution or reappointment of the representation of employees in accordance with national law or practice.

2. If the term of office of the representatives of the employees affected by the transfer expires as a result of the transfer, the representatives shall continue to enjoy the protection provided by the laws, regulations, administrative provisions or practice of the Member States.

CHAPTER III
INFORMATION AND CONSULTATION

Article 7

1. The transferor and transferee shall be required to inform the representatives of their respective employees affected by the transfer of the following:
   — the date or proposed date of the transfer,
   — the reasons for the transfer,
   — the legal, economic and social implications of the transfer for the employees,
   — any measures envisaged in relation to the employees. The transferor must give such information to the representatives of his employees in good time, before the transfer is carried out.
   The transferee must give such information to the representatives of his employees in good time, and in any event before his employees are directly affected by the transfer as regards their conditions of work and employment.

2. Where the transferor or the transferee envisages measures in relation to his employees, he shall consult the representatives of his employees in good time on such measures with a view to reaching an agreement.

3. Member States whose laws, regulations or administrative provisions provide that representatives of the employees may have recourse to an arbitration board to obtain a decision on the measures to be taken in relation to employees may limit the obligations laid down in paragraphs 1 and 2 to cases where the transfer carried out gives rise to a change in the business likely to entail serious disadvantages for a considerable number of the employees. The information and consultations shall cover at least the measures envisaged in relation to the employees.
   The information must be provided and consultations take place in good time before the change in the business as referred to in the first subparagraph is effected.

4. The obligations laid down in this Article shall apply irrespective of whether the decision resulting in the transfer is taken by the employer or an undertaking controlling the employer. In considering alleged breaches of the information and consultation requirements laid down by this Directive, the argument that such a breach occurred because the information was not provided by an undertaking controlling the employer shall not be accepted as an excuse.

5. Member States may limit the obligations laid down in paragraphs 1, 2 and 3 to undertakings or businesses which, in terms of the number of employees, meet the conditions for the election or nomination of a collegiate body representing the employees.

6. Member States shall provide that, where there are no representatives of the employees in an undertaking or business through no fault of their own, the employees concerned must be informed in advance of:
   — the date or proposed date of the transfer,
   — the reason for the transfer,
   — the legal, economic and social implications of the transfer for the employees,
   — any measures envisaged in relation to the employees.

CHAPTER IV
FINAL PROVISIONS

Article 8

This Directive shall not affect the right of Member States to apply or introduce laws, regulations or administrative provisions which are more favourable to employees or to promote or permit collective agreements or agreements between social partners more favourable to employees.

Article 9

Member States shall introduce into their national legal systems such measures as are necessary to enable all employees and representatives of employees who consider themselves wronged by failure to comply with the obligations arising from this Directive to pursue their claims by judicial process after possible recourse to other competent authorities.

Article 10

The Commission shall submit to the Council an analysis of the effect of the provisions of this Directive before 17 July 2006. It shall propose any amendment which may seem necessary.

Article 11

Member States shall communicate to the Commission the texts of the laws, regulations and administrative provisions which they adopt in the field covered by this Directive.

Article 12

Directive 77/187/EEC, as amended by the Directive referred to in Annex I, Part A, is repealed, without prejudice to the obligations of the Member States concerning the time limits for implementation set out in Annex I, Part B.

References to the repealed Directive shall be construed as references to this Directive and shall be read in accordance with the correlation table in Annex II.

Article 13

This Directive shall enter into force on the 20th day following its publication in the *Official Journal of the European Communities*.

Article 14

This Directive is addressed to the Member States.

ANNEX I

PART A

Repealed Directive and its amending Directive (referred to in Article 12)
Council Directive 77/187/EEC (OJ L61, 5.3.1977, p. 26)
Council Directive 98/50/EC (OJ L201, 17.7.1998, p. 88)

PART B

Deadlines for transposition into national law (referred to in Article 12)

Directive	Deadline for transposition
77/187/EEC	16 February 1979
98/50/EC 17	July 2001

ANNEX II
CORRELATION TABLE

Directive 77/187/EEC	This Directive
Article 1	Article 1
Article 2	Article 2
Article 3	Article 3
Article 4	Article 4
Article 4a	Article 5
Article 5	Article 6
Article 6	Article 7

COUNCIL DIRECTIVE (EEC) No 89/391 of 12 JUNE 1989
on the introduction of measures to encourage improvements in the safety and health of workers at work
[1989] OJ L183/1

SECTION I
GENERAL PROVISIONS

Article 1 Object

1. The object of this Directive is to introduce measures to encourage improvements in the safety and health of workers at work.
2. To that end it contains general principles concerning the prevention of occupational risks, the protection of safety and health, the elimination of risk and accident factors, the informing, consultation, balanced participation in accordance with national laws and/or practices and training of workers and their representatives, as well as general guidelines for the implementation of the said principles.
3. This Directive shall be without prejudice to existing or future national and Community provisions which are more favourable to protection of the safety and health of workers at work.

Article 2 Scope

1. This Directive shall apply to all sectors of activity, both public and private (industrial, agricultural, commercial, administrative, service, educational, cultural, leisure, etc.).
2. This Directive shall not be applicable where characteristics peculiar to certain specific public service activities, such as the armed forces or the police, or to certain specific activities in the civil protection services inevitably conflict with it.
    In that event, the safety and health of workers must be ensured as far as possible in the light of the objectives of this Directive.

Article 3 Definitions

For the purposes of this Directive, the following terms shall have the following meanings:

(a) worker: any person employed by an employer, including trainees and apprentices but excluding domestic servants;
(b) employer: any natural or legal person who has an employment relationship with the worker and has responsibility for the undertaking and/or establishment;
(c) workers' representative with specific responsibility for the safety and health of workers: any person elected, chosen or designated in accordance with national laws and/or practices to represent workers where problems arise relating to the safety and health protection of workers at work;

(d)   prevention: all the steps or measures taken or planned at all stages of work in the undertaking to prevent or reduce occupational risks.

Article 4

1.   Member States shall take the necessary steps to ensure that employers, workers and workers' representatives are subject to the legal provisions necessary for the implementation of this Directive.

2.   In particular, Member States shall ensure adequate controls and supervision.

SECTION II
EMPLOYERS' OBLIGATIONS

Article 5   General provision

1.   The employer shall have a duty to ensure the safety and health of workers in every aspect related to the work.

2.   Where, pursuant to Article 7(3), an employer enlists competent external services or persons, this shall not discharge him from his responsibilities in this area.

3.   The workers' obligations in the field of safety and health at work shall not affect the principle of the responsibility of the employer.

4.   This Directive shall not restrict the option of Member States to provide for the exclusion or the limitation of employers' responsibility where occurrences are due to unusual and unforeseeable circumstances, beyond the employers' control, or to exceptional events, the consequences of which could not have been avoided despite the exercise of all due care. Member States need not exercise the option referred to in the first subparagraph.

Article 6   General obligations on employers

1.   Within the context of his responsibilities, the employer shall take the measures necessary for the safety and health protection of workers, including prevention of occupational risks and provision of information and training, as well as provision of the necessary organisation and means. The employer shall be alert to the need to adjust these measures to take account of changing circumstances and aim to improve existing situations.

2.   The employer shall implement the measures referred to in the first subparagraph of paragraph 1 on the basis of the following general principles of prevention:
(a)   avoiding risks;
(b)   evaluating the risks which cannot be avoided:
(c)   combating the risks at source;
(d)   adapting the work to the individual, especially as regards the design of work places, the choice of work equipment and the choice of working and production methods, with a view, in particular, to alleviating monotonous work and work at a predetermined work-rate and to reducing their effect on health.
(e)   adapting to technical progress;
(f)   replacing the dangerous by the non-dangerous or the less dangerous;
(g)   developing a coherent overall prevention policy which covers technology, organisation of work, working conditions, social relationships and the influence of factors related to the working environment;
(h)   giving collective protective measures priority over individual protective measures;
(i)   giving appropriate instructions to the workers.

3.   Without prejudice to the other provisions of this Directive, the employer shall, taking into account the nature of the activities of the enterprise and/or establishment:
(a)   evaluate the risks to the safety and health of workers, inter alia in the choice of work equipment, the chemical substances or preparations used, and the fitting-out of work places.

Subsequent to this evaluation and as necessary, the preventive measures and the working and production methods implemented by the employer must:
- assure an improvement in the level of protection afforded to workers with regard to safety and health,
- be integrated into all the activities of the undertaking and/or establishment and at all hierarchical levels;

(b) where he entrusts tasks to a worker, take into consideration the worker's capabilities as regards health and safety;

(c) ensure that the planning and introduction of new technologies are the subject of consultation with the workers and/or their representatives, as regards the consequences of the choice of equipment, the working conditions and the working environment for the safety and health of workers;

(d) take appropriate steps to ensure that only workers who have received adequate instructions may have access to areas where there is serious and specific danger.

4. Without prejudice to the other provisions of this Directive, where several undertakings share a work place, the employers shall cooperate in implementing the safety, health and occupational hygiene provisions and, taking into account the nature of the activities, shall coordinate their actions in matters of the protection and prevention of occupational risks, and shall inform one another and their respective workers and/or workers' representatives of these risks.

5. Measures related to safety, hygiene and health at work may in no circumstances involve the workers in financial cost.

Article 7 Protective and preventive services

1. Without prejudice to the obligations referred to in Articles 5 and 6, the employer shall designate one or more workers to carry out activities related to the protection and prevention of occupational risks for the undertaking and/or establishment.

2. Designated workers may not be placed at any disadvantage because of their activities related to the protection and prevention of occupational risks. Designated workers shall be allowed adequate time to enable them to fulfil their obligations arising from this Directive.

3. If such protective and preventive measures cannot be organised for lack of competent personnel in the undertaking and/or establishment, the employer shall enlist competent external services or persons.

4. Where the employer enlists such services or persons, he shall inform them of the factors known to affect, or suspected of affecting, the safety and health of the workers and they must have access to the information referred to in Article 10(2).

5. In all cases:
- the workers designated must have the necessary capabilities and the necessary means,
- the external services or persons consulted must have the necessary aptitudes and the necessary personal and professional means, and
- the workers designated and the external services or persons consulted must be sufficient in number

to deal with the organisation of protective and preventive measures, taking into account the size of the undertaking and/or establishment and/or the hazards to which the workers are exposed and their distribution throughout the entire undertaking and/or establishment.

6. The protection from, and prevention of, the health and safety risks which form the subject of this Article shall be the responsibility of one or more workers, of one service or of separate services whether from inside or outside the undertaking and/or establishment. The worker(s) and/or agency(ies) must work together whenever necessary.

7. Member States may define, in the light of the nature of the activities and size of the undertakings, the categories of undertakings in which the employer, provided he is competent, may himself take responsibility for the measures referred to in paragraph 1.

8. Member States shall define the necessary capabilities and aptitudes referred to in paragraph 5.
    They may determine the sufficient number referred to in paragraph 5.

Article 8 First aid, fire-fighting and evacuation of workers, serious and imminent danger

1. The employer shall:
    — take the necessary measures for first aid, fire-fighting and evacuation of workers, adapted to the nature of the activities and the size of the undertaking and/or establishment and taking into account other persons present,
    — arrange any necessary contacts with external services, particularly as regards first aid, emergency medical care, rescue work and fire-fighting.

2. Pursuant to paragraph 1, the employer shall, inter alia, for first aid, fire-fighting and the evacuation of workers, designate the workers required to implement such measures. The number of such workers, their training and the equipment available to them shall be adequate, taking account of the size and/or specific hazards of the undertaking and/or establishment.

3. The employer shall:
    (a) as soon as possible, inform all workers who are, or may be, exposed to serious and imminent danger of the risk involved and of the steps taken or to be taken as regards protection;
    (b) take action and give instructions to enable workers in the event of serious, imminent and unavoidable danger to stop work and/or immediately to leave the work place and proceed to a place of safety;
    (c) save in exceptional cases for reasons duly substantiated, refrain from asking workers to resume work in a working situation where there is still a serious and imminent danger.

4. Workers who, in the event of serious, imminent and unavoidable danger, leave their workstation and/or a dangerous area may not be placed at any disadvantage because of their action and must be protected against any harmful and unjustified consequences, in accordance with national laws and/or practices.

5. The employer shall ensure that all workers are able, in the event of serious and imminent danger to their own safety and/or that of other persons, and where the immediate superior responsible cannot be contacted, to take the appropriate steps in the light of their knowledge and the technical means at their disposal, to avoid the consequences of such danger.
    Their actions shall not place them at any disadvantage, unless they acted carelessly or there was negligence on their part.

Article 9 Various obligations on employers

1. The employer shall:
    (a) be in possession of an assessment of the risks to safety and health at work, including those facing groups of workers exposed to particular risks;
    (b) decide on the protective measures to be taken and, if necessary, the protective equipment to be used;
    (c) keep a list of occupational accidents resulting in a worker being unfit for work for more than three working days;
    (d) draw up, for the responsible authorities and in accordance with national laws and/or practices, reports on occupational accidents suffered by his workers.

2. Member States shall define, in the light of the nature of the activities and size of the undertakings, the obligations to be met by the different categories of undertakings in respect of the drawing-up of the documents provided for in paragraph 1(a) and (b) and when preparing the documents provided for in paragraph 1(c) and (d).

Article 10 Worker information

1. The employer shall take appropriate measures so that workers and/or their representatives in the undertaking and/or establishment receive, in accordance with national laws and/or practices which may take account, *inter alia*, of the size of the undertaking and/or establishment, all the necessary information concerning:
    (a)   the safety and health risks and protective and preventive measures and activities in respect of both the undertaking and/or establishment in general and each type of workstation and/or job;
    (b)   the measures taken pursuant to Article 8(2).
2. The employer shall take appropriate measures so that employers of workers from any outside undertakings and/or establishments engaged in work in his undertaking and/or establishment receive, in accordance with national laws and/or practices, adequate information concerning the points referred to in paragraph 1(a) and (b) which is to be provided to the workers in question.
3. The employer shall take appropriate measures so that workers with specific functions in protecting the safety and health of workers, or workers' representatives with specific responsibility for the safety and health of workers shall have access, to carry out their functions and in accordance with national laws and/or practices, to:
    (a)   the risk assessment and protective measures referred to in Article 9(1)(a) and (b);
    (b)   the list and reports referred to in Article 9(1)(c) and (d);
    (c)   the information yielded by protective and preventive measures, inspection agencies and bodies responsible for safety and health.

Article 11 Consultation and participation of workers

1. Employers shall consult workers and/or their representatives and allow them to take part in discussions on all questions relating to safety and health at work. This presupposes:
    — the consultation of workers,
    — the right of workers and/or their representatives to make proposals,
    — balanced participation in accordance with national laws and/or practices.
2. Workers or workers' representatives with specific responsibility for the safety and health of workers shall take part in a balanced way, in accordance with national laws and/or practices, or shall be consulted in advance and in good time by the employer with regard to:
    (a)   any measure which may substantially affect safety and health;
    (b)   the designation of workers referred to in Articles 7(1) and 8(2) and the activities referred to in Article 7(1);
    (c)   the information referred to in Articles 9(1) and 10;
    (d)   the enlistment, where appropriate, of the competent services or persons outside the undertaking and/or establishment, as referred to in Article 7(3);
    (e)   the planning and organisation of the training referred to in Article 12.
3. Workers' representatives with specific responsibility for the safety and health of workers shall have the right to ask the employer to take appropriate measures and to submit proposals to him to that end to mitigate hazards for workers and/or to remove sources of danger.
4. The workers referred to in paragraph 2 and the workers' representatives referred to in paragraphs 2 and 3 may not be placed at a disadvantage because of their respective activities referred to in paragraphs 2 and 3.
5. Employers must allow workers' representatives with specific responsibility for the safety and health of workers adequate time off work, without loss of pay, and provide them with the necessary means to enable such representatives to exercise their rights and functions deriving from this Directive.
6. Workers and/or their representatives are entitled to appeal, in accordance with national law and/or practice, to the authority responsible for safety and health protection at work if they consider that the measures taken and the means employed by the employer are inadequate for the purposes of ensuring safety and health at work.
    Workers' representatives must be given the opportunity to submit their observations during inspection visits by the competent authority.

Article 12 Training of workers

1.   The employer shall ensure that each worker receives adequate safety and health training, in particular in the form of information and instructions specific to his workstation or job:
     — on recruitment,
     — in the event of a transfer or a change of job,
     — in the event of the introduction of new work equipment or a change in equipment
     — in the event of the introduction of any new technology.
     The training shall be:
     — adapted to take account of new or changed risks, and
     — repeated periodically if necessary.
2.   The employer shall ensure that workers from outside undertakings and/or establishments engaged in work in his undertaking and/or establishment have in fact received appropriate instructions regarding health and safety risks during their activities in his undertaking and/or establishment.
3.   Workers' representatives with a specific role in protecting the safety and health of workers shall be entitled to appropriate training.
4.   The training referred to in paragraphs 1 and 3 may not be at the workers' expense or at that of the workers' representatives.
     The training referred to in paragraph 1 must take place during working hours.
     The training referred to in paragraph 3 must take place during working hours or in accordance with national practice either within or outside the undertaking and/or the establishment.

SECTION III
WORKERS' OBLIGATIONS

Article 13

1.   It shall be the responsibility of each worker to take care as far as possible of his own safety and health and that of other persons affected by his acts or omissions at work in accordance with his training and the instructions given by his employer.
2.   To this end, workers must in particular, in accordance with their training and the instructions given by their employer:
     (a)   make correct use of machinery, apparatus, tools, dangerous substances, transport equipment and other means of production;
     (b)   make correct use of the personal protective equipment supplied to them and, after use, return it to its proper place;
     (c)   refrain from disconnecting, changing or removing arbitrarily safety devices fitted, e.g. to machinery, apparatus, tools, plant and buildings, and use such safety devices correctly;
     (d)   immediately inform the employer and/or the workers with specific responsibility for the safety and health of workers of any work situation they have reasonable grounds for considering represents a serious and immediate danger to safety and health and of any shortcomings in the protection arrangements;
     (e)   cooperate, in accordance with national practice, with the employer and/or workers with specific responsibility for the safety and health of workers, for as long as may be necessary to enable any tasks or requirements imposed by the competent authority to protect the safety and health of workers at work to be carried out;
     (f)   cooperate, in accordance with national practice, with the employer and/or workers with specific responsibility for the safety and health of workers, for as long as may be necessary to enable the employer to ensure that the working environment and working conditions are safe and pose no risk to safety and health within their field of activity.

SECTION IV
MISCELLANEOUS PROVISIONS

Article 14 Health surveillance

1. To ensure that workers receive health surveillance appropriate to the health and safety risks they incur at work, measures shall be introduced in accordance with national law and/or practices.
2. The measures referred to in paragraph 1 shall be such that each worker, if he so wishes, may receive health surveillance at regular intervals.
3. Health surveillance may be provided as part of a national health system.

Article 15 Risk groups

Particularly sensitive risk groups must be protected against the dangers which specifically affect them.

Article 16 Individual Directives — Amendments — General scope of this Directive

1. The Council, acting on a proposal from the Commission based on Article 118a of the Treaty, shall adopt individual Directives, *inter alia*, in the areas listed in the Annex.
2. This Directive and, without prejudice to the procedure referred to in Article 17 concerning technical adjustments, the individual Directives may be amended in accordance with the procedure provided for in Article 118a of the Treaty.
3. The provisions of this Directive shall apply in full to all the areas covered by the individual Directives, without prejudice to more stringent and/or specific provisions contained in these individual Directives.

Article 17 Committee procedure

1. The Commission shall be assisted by a committee to make purely technical adjustments to the individual directives provided for in Article 16(1) in order to take account of:
   (a) the adoption of directives in the field of technical harmonisation and standardisation;
   (b) technical progress, changes in international regulations or specifications and new findings.

   Those measures, designed to amend non-essential elements of the individual directives, shall be adopted in accordance with the regulatory procedure with scrutiny referred to in paragraph 2. On imperative grounds of urgency, the Commission may have recourse to the urgency procedure referred to in paragraph 3.
2. Where reference is made to this paragraph, Article 5a(1) to (4) and Article 7 of Decision 1999/468/EC shall apply, having regard to the provisions of Article 8 thereof.
3. Where reference is made to this paragraph, Article 5a(1), (2), (4) and (6) and Article 7 of Decision 1999/468/EC shall apply, having regard to the provisions of Article 8 thereof.

Article 17a Implementation reports

1. Every five years, the Member States shall submit a single report to the Commission on the practical implementation of this Directive and individual Directives within the meaning of Article 16(1), indicating the points of view of the social partners. The report shall assess the various points related to the practical implementation of the different Directives and, where appropriate and available, provide data disaggregated by gender.
2. The structure of the report, together with a questionnaire specifying its content, shall be defined by the Commission, in cooperation with the Advisory Committee on Safety and Health at Work.

   The report shall include a general part on the provisions of this Directive relating to the common principles and points applicable to all of the Directives referred to in paragraph 1. To complement the general part, specific chapters shall deal with implementation of the particular aspects of each Directive, including specific indicators, where available.

3.   The Commission shall submit the structure of the report, together with the above-mentioned questionnaire specifying its content, to the Member States at least six months before the end of the period covered by the report. The report shall be transmitted to the Commission within 12 months of the end of the five-year period that it covers.

4.   Using these reports as a basis, the Commission shall evaluate the implementation of the Directives concerned in terms of their relevance, of research and of new scientific knowledge in the various fields in question. It shall, within 36 months of the end of the five-year period, inform the European Parliament, the Council, the European Economic and Social Committee and the Advisory Committee on Safety and Health at Work of the results of this evaluation and, if necessary, of any initiatives to improve the operation of the regulatory framework.

5.   The first report shall cover the period 2007 to 2012.

Article 18 Final provisions

1.   Member States shall bring into force the laws, regulations and administrative provisions necessary to comply with this Directive by 31 December 1992. They shall forthwith inform the Commission thereof.

2.   Member States shall communicate to the Commission the texts of the provisions of national law which they have already adopted or adopt in the field covered by this Directive.

Article 19

This Directive is addressed to the Member States.

ANNEX

List of areas referred to in Article 16 (1)

— Work places
— Work equipment
— Personal protective equipment
— Work with visual display units
— Handling of heavy loads involving risk of back injury
— Temporary or mobile work sites
— Fisheries and agriculture

COUNCIL DIRECTIVE (EEC) No 92/85 of 19 OCTOBER 1992
on the introduction of measures to encourage improvements in the safety and health at work of pregnant workers and workers who have recently given birth or are breastfeeding (tenth individual Directive within the meaning of Article 16(1) of Directive 89/391/EEC)
[1992] OJ L348/1

SECTION I
PURPOSE AND DEFINITIONS

Article 1   Purpose

1.   The purpose of this Directive, which is the tenth individual Directive within the meaning of Article 16(1) of Directive 89/391/EEC, is to implement measures to encourage improvements in the safety and health at work of pregnant workers and workers who have recently given birth or who are breastfeeding.

2.   The provisions of Directive 89/391/EEC, except for Article 2(2) thereof, shall apply in full to the whole area covered by paragraph 1, without prejudice to any more stringent and/or specific provisions contained in this Directive.

3. This Directive may not have the effect of reducing the level of protection afforded to pregnant workers, workers who have recently given birth or who are breastfeeding as compared with the situation which exists in each Member State on the date on which this Directive is adopted.

Article 2 Definitions

For the purposes of this Directive:
(a) pregnant worker shall mean a pregnant worker who informs her employer of her condition, in accordance with national legislation and/or national practice;
(b) worker who has recently given birth shall mean a worker who has recently given birth within the meaning of national legislation and/or national practice and who informs her employer of her condition, in accordance with that legislation and/or practice;
(c) worker who is breastfeeding shall mean a worker who is breastfeeding within the meaning of national legislation and/or national practice and who informs her employer of her condition, in accordance with that legislation and/or practice.

SECTION II
GENERAL PROVISIONS

Article 3 Guidelines

1. In consultation with the Member States and assisted by the Advisory Committee on Safety, Hygiene and Health Protection at Work, the Commission shall draw up guidelines on the assessment of the chemical, physical and biological agents and industrial processes considered hazardous for the safety or health of workers within the meaning of Article 2.
   The guidelines referred to in the first subparagraph shall also cover movements and postures, mental and physical fatigue and other types of physical and mental stress connected with the work done by workers within the meaning of Article 2.
2. The purpose of the guidelines referred to in paragraph 1 is to serve as a basis for the assessment referred to in Article 4(1).
   To this end, Member States shall bring these guidelines to the attention of all employers and all female workers and/or their representatives in the respective Member State.

Article 4 Assessment and information

1. For all activities liable to involve a specific risk of exposure to the agents, processes or working conditions of which a non-exhaustive list is given in Annex I, the employer shall assess the nature, degree and duration of exposure, in the undertaking and/or establishment concerned, of workers within the meaning of Article 2, either directly or by way of the protective and preventive services referred to in Article 7 of Directive 89/391/EEC, in order to:
   — assess any risks to the safety or health and any possible effect on the pregnancy or breastfeeding of workers within the meaning of Article 2,
   — decide what measures should be taken.
2. Without prejudice to Article 10 of Directive 89/391/EEC, workers within the meaning of Article 2 and workers likely to be in one of the situations referred to in Article 2 in the undertaking and/or establishment concerned and/or their representatives shall be informed of the results of the assessment referred to in paragraph 1 and of all measures to be taken concerning health and safety at work.

Article 5 Action further to the results of the assessment

1. Without prejudice to Article 6 of Directive 89/391/EEC, if the results of the assessment referred to in Article 4(1) reveal a risk to the safety or health or an effect on the pregnancy or breastfeeding of a worker within the meaning of Article 2, the employer shall take the necessary measures to ensure that, by temporarily adjusting the working conditions and/or the working hours of the worker concerned, the exposure of that worker to such risks is avoided.

2.   If the adjustment of her working conditions and/or working hours is not technically and/or objectively feasible, or cannot reasonably be required on duly substantiated grounds, the employer shall take the necessary measures to move the worker concerned to another job.

3.   If moving her to another job is not technically and/or objectively feasible or cannot reasonably be required on duly substantiated grounds, the worker concerned shall be granted leave in accordance with national legislation and/or national practice for the whole of the period necessary to protect her safety or health.

4.   The provisions of this Article shall apply *mutatis mutandis* to the case where a worker pursuing an activity which is forbidden pursuant to Article 6 becomes pregnant or starts breastfeeding and informs her employer thereof.

Article 6   Cases in which exposure is prohibited

In addition to the general provisions concerning the protection of workers, in particular those relating to the limit values for occupational exposure:

1.   pregnant workers within the meaning of Article 2(a) may under no circumstances be obliged to perform duties for which the assessment has revealed a risk of exposure, which would jeopardise safety or health, to the agents and working conditions listed in Annex II, Section A;

2.   workers who are breastfeeding, within the meaning of Article 2(c), may under no circumstances be obliged to perform duties for which the assessment has revealed a risk of exposure, which would jeopardise safety or health, to the agents and working conditions listed in Annex II, Section B.

Article 7   Night work

1.   Member States shall take the necessary measures to ensure that workers referred to in Article 2 are not obliged to perform night work during their pregnancy and for a period following childbirth which shall be determined by the national authority competent for safety and health, subject to submission, in accordance with the procedures laid down by the Member States, of a medical certificate stating that this is necessary for the safety or health of the worker concerned.

2.   The measures referred to in paragraph 1 must entail the possibility, in accordance with national legislation and/or national practice, of:
(a)   transfer to daytime work; or
(b)   leave from work or extension of maternity leave where such a transfer is not technically and/or objectively feasible or cannot reasonably by required on duly substantiated grounds.

Article 8   Maternity leave

1.   Member States shall take the necessary measures to ensure that workers within the meaning of Article 2 are entitled to a continuous period of maternity leave of a least 14 weeks allocated before and/or after confinement in accordance with national legislation and/or practice.

2.   The maternity leave stipulated in paragraph 1 must include compulsory maternity leave of at least two weeks allocated before and/or after confinement in accordance with national legislation and/or practice.

Article 9   Time off for ante-natal examinations

Member States shall take the necessary measures to ensure that pregnant workers within the meaning of Article 2(a) are entitled to, in accordance with national legislation and/or practice, time off, without loss of pay, in order to attend ante-natal examinations, if such examinations have to take place during working hours.

Article 10   Prohibition of dismissal

In order to guarantee workers, within the meaning of Article 2, the exercise of their health and safety protection rights as recognised under this Article, it shall be provided that:

1.   Member States shall take the necessary measures to prohibit the dismissal of workers, within the meaning of Article 2, during the period from the beginning of their pregnancy to the end of the maternity leave referred to in Article 8(1), save in exceptional cases

not connected with their condition which are permitted under national legislation and/or practice and, where applicable, provided that the competent authority has given its consent;

2. if a worker, within the meaning of Article 2, is dismissed during the period referred to in point 1, the employer must cite duly substantiated grounds for her dismissal in writing;

3. Member States shall take the necessary measures to protect workers, within the meaning of Article 2, from consequences of dismissal which is unlawful by virtue of point 1.

Article 11 Employment rights

In order to guarantee workers within the meaning of Article 2 the exercise of their health and safety protection rights as recognised in this Article, it shall be provided that:

1. in the cases referred to in Articles 5, 6 and 7, the employment rights relating to the employment contract, including the maintenance of a payment to, and/or entitlement to an adequate allowance for, workers within the meaning of Article 2, must be ensured in accordance with national legislation and/or national practice;

2. in the case referred to in Article 8, the following must be ensured:
   (a) the rights connected with the employment contract of workers within the meaning of Article 2, other than those referred to in point (b) below;
   (b) maintenance of a payment to, and/or entitlement to an adequate allowance for, workers within the meaning of Article 2;

3. the allowance referred to in point 2(b) shall be deemed adequate if it guarantees income at least equivalent to that which the worker concerned would receive in the event of a break in her activities on grounds connected with her state of health, subject to any ceiling laid down under national legislation;

4. Member States may make entitlement to pay or the allowance referred to in points 1 and 2(b) conditional upon the worker concerned fulfilling the conditions of eligibility for such benefits laid down under national legislation.

   These conditions may under no circumstances provide for periods of previous employment in excess of 12 months immediately prior to the presumed date of confinement.

Article 12 Defence of rights

Member States shall introduce into their national legal systems such measures as are necessary to enable all workers who should themselves wronged by failure to comply with the obligations arising from this Directive to pursue their claims by judicial process (and/or, in accordance with national laws and/or practices) by recourse to other competent authorities.

Article 13 Amendments to the Annexes

1. Strictly technical adjustments to Annex I as a result of technical progress, changes in international regulations or specifications and new findings in the area covered by this Directive shall be adopted in accordance with the procedure laid down in Article 17 of Directive 89/391/EEC.

2. Annex II may be amended only in accordance with the procedure laid down in Article 118a of the Treaty.

Article 14 Final provisions

1. Member States shall bring into force the laws, regulations and administrative provisions necessary to comply with this Directive not later than two years after the adoption thereof or ensure, at the latest two years after adoption of this Directive, that the two sides of industry introduce the requisite provisions by means of collective agreements, with Member States being required to make all the necessary provisions to enable them at all times to guarantee the results laid down by this Directive. They shall forthwith inform the Commission thereof.

2. When Member States adopt the measures referred to in paragraph 1, they shall contain a reference of this Directive or shall be accompanied by such reference on the occasion of their official publication. The methods of making such a reference shall be laid down by the Member States.

3.   Member States shall communicate to the Commission the texts of the essential provisions of national law which they have already adopted or adopt in the field governed by this Directive.

Article 15

This Directive is addressed to the Member States.

ANNEX I

NON-EXHAUSTIVE LIST OF AGENTS, PROCESSES AND WORKING CONDITIONS

referred to in Article 4 (1)

A.   Agents

1.   Physical agents where these are regarded as agents causing foetal lesions and/or likely to disrupt placental attachment, and in particular:
(a)   shocks, vibration or movement;
(b)   handling of loads entailing risks, particularly of a dorsolumbar nature;
(c)   noise;
(d)   ionizing radiation (6);
(e)   non-ionizing radiation;
(f)   extremes of cold or heat;
(g)   movements and postures, travelling — either inside or outside the establishment — mental and physical fatigue and other physical burdens connected with the activity of the worker within the meaning of Article 2 of the Directive.
2.   Biological agents
Biological agents of risk groups 2, 3 and 4 within the meaning of points 2, 3 and 4 of second paragraph of Article 2 of Directive 2000/54/EC of the European Parliament and of the Council (7), in so far as it is known that such agents or the therapeutic measures necessitated by them endanger the health of pregnant women and the unborn child, and in so far as they do not yet appear in Annex II.
3.   Chemical agents
The following chemical agents in so far as it is known that they endanger the health of pregnant women and the unborn child and in so far as they do not yet appear in Annex II:
(a)   substances and mixtures which meet the criteria for classification under Regulation (EC) No 1272/2008 of the European Parliament and of the Council (8) in one or more of the following hazard classes and hazard categories with one or more of the following hazard statements, in so far as they do not yet appear in Annex II:
— germ cell mutagenicity, category 1A, 1B or 2 (H340, H341);
— carcinogenicity, category 1A, 1B or 2 (H350, H350i, H351);
— reproductive toxicity, category 1A, 1B or 2 or the additional category for effects on or via lactation (H360, H360D, H360FD, H360Fd, H360Df, H361, H361d, H361fd, H362);
— specific target organ toxicity after single exposure, category 1 or 2 (H370, H371);
(b)   chemical agents in Annex I to Directive 2004/37/EC of the European Parliament and of the Council (9);
(c)   mercury and mercury derivatives;
(d)   antimitotic drugs;
(e)   carbon monoxide;
(f)   chemical agents of known and dangerous percutaneous absorption.

B.   Processes

Industrial processes listed in Annex I to Directive 2004/37/EC.

C.   Working conditions

Underground mining work.

ANNEX II
NON-EXHAUSTIVE LIST OF AGENTS AND WORKING CONDITIONS

referred to in Article 6

A. **Pregnant workers within the meaning of Article 2(a)**
   1. Agents
      (a) Physical agents
          Work in hyperbaric atmosphere, e.g. pressurised enclosures and underwater diving.
      (b) Biological agents
          The following biological agents:
          — toxoplasma,
          — rubella virus, unless the pregnant workers are proved to be adequately protected against such agents by immunisation.
      (c) Chemical agents
          Lead and lead derivatives in so far as these agents are capable of being absorbed by the human organism.
   2. Working conditions
      Underground mining work.

B. **Workers who are breastfeeding within the meaning of Article 2(c)**
   1. Agents
      (a) Chemical agents
          Lead and lead derivatives in so far as these agents are capable of being absorbed by the human organism.
   2. Working conditions
      Underground mining work.

Statement of the Council and the Commission concerning Article 11(3) of Directive 92/85/EEC, entered in the minutes of the 1608th meeting of the Council (Luxembourg, 19 October 1992)

THE COUNCIL AND THE COMMISSION stated that:
'In determining the level of the allowances referred to in Article 11(2)(b) and (3), reference shall be made, for purely technical reasons, to the allowance which a worker would receive in the event of a break in her activities on grounds connected with her state of health. Such a reference is not intended in any way to imply that pregnancy and childbirth be equated with sickness. The national social security legislation of all Member States provides for an allowance to be paid during an absence from work due to sickness. The link with such allowance in the chosen formulation is simply intended to serve as a concrete, fixed reference amount in all Member States for the determination of the minimum amount of maternity allowance payable. In so far as allowances are paid in individual Member States which exceed those provided for in the Directive, such allowances are, of course, retained. This is clear from Article 1(3) of the Directive.'

COUNCIL DIRECTIVE (EC) No 94/33 of 22 JUNE 1994
on the protection of young people at work
[1994] OJ L216/12

SECTION I

Article 1 Purpose
   1. Member States shall take the necessary measures to prohibit work by children.
      They shall ensure, under the conditions laid down by this Directive, that the minimum working or employment age is not lower than the minimum age at which compulsory full-time schooling as imposed by national law ends or 15 years in any event.
   2. Member States ensure that work by adolescents is strictly regulated and protected under the conditions laid down in this Directive.

3. Member States shall ensure in general that employers guarantee that young people have working conditions which suit their age.
    They shall ensure that young people are protected against economic exploitation and against any work likely to harm their safety, health or physical, mental, moral or social development or to jeopardise their education.

Article 2   Scope

1. This Directive shall apply to any person under 18 years of age having an employment contract or an employment relationship defined by the law in force in a Member State and/or governed by the law in force in a Member State.
2. Member States may make legislative or regulatory provision for this Directive not to apply, within the limits and under the conditions which they set by legislative or regulatory provision, to occasional work or short-term work involving:
    (a)   domestic service in a private household, or
    (b)   work regarded as not being harmful, damaging or dangerous to young people in a family undertaking.

Article 3   Definitions

For the purposes of this Directive:
(a)   'young person' shall mean any person under 18 years of age referred to in Article 2(1);
(b)   'child' shall mean any young person of less than 15 years of age or who is still subject to compulsory full-time schooling under national law;
(c)   'adolescent' shall mean any young person of at least 15 years of age but less than 18 years of age who is no longer subject to compulsory full-time schooling under national law;
(d)   'light work' shall mean all work which, on account of the inherent nature of the tasks which it involves and the particular conditions under which they are performed:
    (i)   is not likely to be harmful to the safety, health or development of children, and
    (ii) is not such as to be harmful to their attendance at school, their participation in vocational guidance or training programmes approved by the competent authority or their capacity to benefit from the instruction received;
(e)   'working time' shall mean any period during which the young person is at work, at the employer's disposal and carrying out his activity or duties in accordance with national legislation and/or practice;
(f)   'rest period' shall mean any period which is not working time.

Article 4   Prohibition of work by children

1. Member States shall adopt the measures necessary to prohibit work by children.
2. Taking into account the objectives set out in Article 1, Member States may make legislative or regulatory provision for the prohibition of work by children not to apply to:
    (a)   children pursuing the activities set out in Article 5;
    (b)   children of at least 14 years of age working under a combined work/training scheme or an in-plant work-experience scheme, provided that such work is done in accordance with the conditions laid down by the competent authority;
    (c)   children of at least 14 years of age performing light work other than that covered by Article 5; light work other than that covered by Article 5 may, however, be performed by children of 13 years of age for a limited number of hours per week in the case of categories of work determined by national legislation.
3. Member States that make use of the opinion referred to in paragraph 2(c) shall determine, subject to the provisions of this Directive, the working conditions relating to the light work in question.

Article 5   Cultural or similar activities

1. The employment of children for the purposes of performance in cultural, artistic, sports or advertising activities shall be subject to prior authorisation to be given by the competent authority in individual cases.

2.   Member States shall by legislative or regulatory provision lay down the working conditions for children in the cases referred to in paragraph 1 and the details of the prior authorisation procedure, on condition that the activities:
    (i)   are not likely to be harmful to the safety, health or development of children, and
    (ii)   are not such as to be harmful to their attendance at school, their participation in vocational guidance or training programmes approved by the competent authority or their capacity to benefit from the instruction received.

3.   By way of derogation from the procedure laid down in paragraph 1, in the case of children of at least 13 years of age, Member States may authorise, by legislative or regulatory provision, in accordance with conditions which they shall determine, the employment of children for the purposes of performance in cultural, artistic, sports or advertising activities.

4.   The Member States which have a specific authorisation system for modelling agencies with regard to the activities of children may retain that system.

SECTION II

Article 6 General obligations on employers

1.   Without prejudice to Article 4(1), the employer shall adopt the measures necessary to protect the safety and health of young people, taking particular account of the specific risks referred to in Article 7(1).

2.   The employer shall implement the measures provided for in paragraph 1 on the basis of an assessment of the hazards to young people in connection with their work. The assessment must be made before young people begin work and when there is any major change in working conditions and must pay particular attention to the following points:
    (a)   the fitting-out and layout of the workplace and the workstation;
    (b)   the nature, degree and duration of exposure to physical, biological and chemical agents;
    (c)   the form, range and use of work equipment, in particular agents, machines, apparatus and devices, and the way in which they are handled;
    (d)   the arrangement of work processes and operations and the way in which these are combined (organisation of work);
    (e)   the level of training and instruction given to young people.
Where this assessment shows that there is a risk to the safety, the physical or mental health or development of young people, an appropriate free assessment and monitoring of their health shall be provided at regular intervals without prejudice to Directive 89/391/ EEC. The free health assessment and monitoring may form part of a national health system.

3.   The employer shall inform young people of possible risks and of all measures adopted concerning their safety and health.
Furthermore, he shall inform the legal representatives of children of possible risks and of all measures adopted concerning children's safety and health.

4.   The employer shall involve the protective and preventive services referred to in Article 7 of Directive 89/391/EEC in the planning, implementation and monitoring of the safety and health conditions applicable to young people.

Article 7 Vulnerability of young people — Prohibition of work

1.   Member States shall ensure that young people are protected from any specific risks to their safety, health and development which are a consequence of their lack of experience, of absence of awareness of existing or potential risks or of the fact that young people have not yet fully matured.

2.   Without prejudice to Article 4(1), Member States shall to this end prohibit the employment of young people for:
    (a)   work which is objectively beyond their physical or psychological capacity;
    (b)   work involving harmful exposure to agents which are toxic, carcinogenic, cause heritable genetic damage, or harm to the unborn child or which in any other way chronically affect human health;

(c)   work involving harmful exposure to radiation;

(d)   work involving the risk of accidents which it may be assumed cannot be recognised or avoided by young persons owing to their insufficient attention to safety or lack of experience or training; or

(e)   work in which there is a risk to health from extreme cold or heat, or from noise or vibration. Work which is likely to entail specific risks for young people within the meaning of paragraph 1 includes:

— work involving harmful exposure to the physical, biological and chemical agents referred to in point I of the Annex, and

— processes and work referred to in point II of the Annex.

3.   Member States may, by legislative or regulatory provision, authorise derogations from paragraph 2 in the case of adolescents where such derogations are indispensable for their vocational training, provided that protection of their safety and health is ensured by the fact that the work is performed under the supervision of a competent person within the meaning of Article 7 of Directive 89/391/EEC and provided that the protection afforded by that Directive is guaranteed.

SECTION III

Article 8 Working time

1.   Member States which make use of the option in Article 4(2)(b) or (c) shall adopt the measures necessary to limit the working time of children to:

(a)   eight hours a day and 40 hours a week for work performed under a combined work/training scheme or an in-plant work-experience scheme;

(b)   two hours on a school day and 12 hours a week for work performed in term-time outside the hours fixed for school attendance, provided that this is not prohibited by national legislation and/or practice; in no circumstances may the daily working time exceed seven hours; this limit may be raised to eight hours in the case of children who have reached the age of 15;

(c)   seven hours a day and 35 hours a week for work performed during a period of at least a week when school is not operating; these limits may be raised to eight hours a day and 40 hours a week in the case of children who have reached the age of 15;

(d)   seven hours a day and 35 hours a week for light work performed by children no longer subject to compulsory full-time schooling under national law.

2.   Member States shall adopt the measures necessary to limit the working time of adolescents to eight hours a day and 40 hours a week.

3.   The time spent on training by a young person working under a theoretical and/or practical combined work/training scheme or an in-plant work-experience scheme shall be counted as working time.

4.   Where a young person is employed by more than one employer, working days and working time shall be cumulative.

5.   Member States may, by legislative or regulatory provision, authorise derogations from paragraph 1(a) and paragraph 2 either by way of exception or where there are objective grounds for so doing. Member States shall, by legislative or regulatory provision, determine the conditions, limits and procedure for implementing such derogations.

Article 9 Night work

1. (a)   Member States which make use of the option in Article 4(2)(b) or (c) shall adopt the measures necessary to prohibit work by children between 8 p.m. and 6 a.m.

(b)   Member States shall adopt the measures necessary to prohibit work by adolescents either between 10 p.m. and 6 a.m. or between 11 p.m. and 7 a.m.

2. (a)   Member States may, by legislative or regulatory provision, authorise work by adolescents in specific areas of activity during the period in which night work is prohibited as referred to in paragraph 1(b). In that event, Member States shall take appropriate measures to ensure that the adolescent is supervised by an adult where such supervision is necessary for the adolescent's protection.

(b)   If point (a) is applied, work shall continue to be prohibited between midnight and 4 a.m.

However, Member States may, by legislative or regulatory provision, authorise work by adolescents during the period in which night work is prohibited in the following cases, where there are objective grounds for so doing and provided that adolescents are allowed suitable compensatory rest time and that the objectives set out in Article 1 are not called into question:
— work performed in the shipping or fisheries sectors;
— work performed in the context of the armed forces or the police;
— work performed in hospitals or similar establishments;
— cultural, artistic, sports or advertising activities.

3.   Prior to any assignment to night work and at regular intervals thereafter, adolescents shall be entitled to a free assessment of their health and capacities, unless the work they do during the period during which work is prohibited is of an exceptional nature.

Article 10 Rest period

1.   (a)   Member States which make use of the option in Article 4(2)(b) or (c) shall adopt the measures necessary to ensure that, for each 24-hour period, children are entitled to a minimum rest period of 14 consecutive hours.

       (b)   Member States shall adopt the measures necessary to ensure that, for each 24-hour period, adolescents are entitled to a minimum rest period of 12 consecutive hours.

2.   Member States shall adopt the measures necessary to ensure that, for each seven-day period:
— children in respect of whom they have made use of the option in Article 4(2)(b) or (c), and
— adolescents

are entitled to a minimum rest period of two days, which shall be consecutive if possible. Where justified by technical or organisation reasons, the minimum rest period may be reduced, but may in no circumstances be less than 36 consecutive hours. The minimum rest period referred to in the first and second subparagraphs shall in principle include Sunday.

3.   Member States may, by legislative or regulatory provision, provide for the minimum rest periods referred to in paragraphs 1 and 2 to be interrupted in the case of activities involving periods of work that are split up over the day or are of short duration.

4.   Member States may make legislative or regulatory provision for derogations from paragraph 1(b) and paragraph 2 in respect of adolescents in the following cases, where there are objective grounds for so doing and provided that they are granted appropriate compensatory rest time and that the objectives set out in Article 1 are not called into question:
   (a)   work performed in the shipping or fisheries sectors;
   (b)   work performed in the context of the armed forces or the police;
   (c)   work performed in hospitals or similar establishments;
   (d)   work performed in agriculture;
   (e)   work performed in the tourism industry or in the hotel, restaurant and café sector;
   (f)   activities involving periods of work split up over the day.

Article 11 Annual rest

Member States which make use of the option referred to in Article 4(2)(b) or (c) shall see to it that a period free of any work is included, as far as possible, in the school holidays of children subject to compulsory full-time schooling under national law.

Article 12 Breaks

Member States shall adopt the measures necessary to ensure that, where daily working time is more than four and a half hours, young people are entitled to a break of at least 30 minutes, which shall be consecutive if possible.

Article 13 Work by adolescents in the event of force majeure

Member States may, by legislative or regulatory provision, authorise derogations from Article 8(2), Article 9(1)(b), Article 10(1)(b) and, in the case of adolescents, Article 12, for work in the circumstances referred to in Article 5(4) of Directive 89/391/EEC, provided that such work is of a temporary nature and must be performed immediately, that adult workers are not available and that the adolescents are allowed equivalent compensatory rest time within the following three weeks.

SECTION IV

Article 14 Measures

Each Member State shall lay down any necessary measures to be applied in the event of failure to comply with the provisions adopted in order to implement this Directive; such measures must be effective and proportionate.

Article 15 Amendments to the Annex

The Commission is empowered to adopt delegated acts in accordance with Article 15a to make strictly technical amendments to the Annex, in the light of technical progress, changes in international rules or specifications and advances in knowledge concerning the protection of young people at work.

Article 15a Exercise of the delegation

1. The power to adopt delegated acts is conferred on the Commission subject to the conditions laid down in this Article.
2. The power to adopt delegated acts referred to in Article 15 shall be conferred on the Commission for a period of five years from 26 July 2019. The Commission shall draw up a report in respect of the delegation of power not later than nine months before the end of the five-year period. The delegation of power shall be tacitly extended for periods of an identical duration, unless the European Parliament or the Council opposes such extension not later than three months before the end of each period.
3. The delegation of power referred to in Article 15 may be revoked at any time by the European Parliament or by the Council. A decision to revoke shall put an end to the delegation of the power specified in that decision. It shall take effect the day following the publication of the decision in the Official Journal of the European Union or at a later date specified therein. It shall not affect the validity of any delegated acts already in force.
4. Before adopting a delegated act, the Commission shall consult experts designated by each Member State in accordance with the principles laid down in the Interinstitutional Agreement of 13 April 2016 on Better Law-Making.
5. As soon as it adopts a delegated act, the Commission shall notify it simultaneously to the European Parliament and to the Council.
6. A delegated act adopted pursuant to Article 15 shall enter into force only if no objection has been expressed either by the European Parliament or the Council within a period of two months of notification of that act to the European Parliament and the Council or if, before the expiry of that period, the European Parliament and the Council have both informed the Commission that they will not object. That period shall be extended by two months at the initiative of the European Parliament or of the Council.

Article 16 Non-reducing clause

Without prejudice to the right of Member States to develop, in the light of changing circumstances, different provisions on the protection of young people, as long as the minimum requirements provided for by this Directive are complied with, the implementation of this Directive shall not constitute valid grounds for reducing the general level of protection afforded to young people.

Article 17 Final provisions

1. (a) Member States shall bring into force the laws, regulations and administrative provisions necessary to comply with this Directive not later than 22 June 1996 or ensure, by that date at the latest, that the two sides of industry introduce the requisite provisions by means of collective agreements, with Member States being required to make all the necessary provisions to enable them at all times to guarantee the results laid down by this Directive.

(b)   The United Kingdom may refrain from implementing the first subparagraph of Article 8(1)(b) with regard to the provision relating to the maximum weekly working time, and also Article 8(2) and Article 9(1)(b) and (2) for a period of four years from the date specified in subparagraph (a).

The Commission shall submit a report on the effects of this provision.

The Council, acting in accordance with the conditions laid down by the Treaty, shall decide whether this period should be extended.

(c)   Member States shall forthwith inform the Commission thereof.

2.   When Member States adopt the measures referred to in paragraph 1, such measures shall contain a reference to this Directive or shall be accompanied by such reference on the occasion of their official publication. The methods of making such reference shall be laid down by Member States.

3.   Member States shall communicate to the Commission the texts of the main provisions of national law which they have already adopted or adopt in the field governed by this Directive.

Article 17a Implementation report

Every five years, the Member States shall submit to the Commission a report on the practical implementation of this Directive in the form of a specific chapter of the single report referred to in Article 17a(1), (2) and (3) of Directive 89/391/EEC, which serves as a basis for the Commission's evaluation, in accordance with Article 17a(4) of that Directive.

Article 18

This Directive is addressed to the Member States.

ANNEX

NON-EXHAUSTIVE LIST OF AGENTS, PROCESSES AND WORK

(Article 7(2), second subparagraph)

I.   Agents

1.   Physical agents

(a)   Ionizing radiation;

(b)   Work in a high-pressure atmosphere, e. g. in pressurized containers, diving.

2.   Biological agents

(a)   Biological agents of risk groups 3 and 4 within the meaning of points 3 and 4 of second paragraph of Article 2 of Directive 2000/54/EC of the European Parliament and of the Council.

3.   Chemical agents

(a)   Substances and mixtures which meet the criteria for classification under Regulation (EC) No 1272/2008 of the European Parliament and of the Council (7) in one or more of the following hazard classes and hazard categories with one or more of the following hazard statements:

— acute toxicity, category 1, 2 or 3 (H300, H310, H330, H301, H311, H331);

— skin corrosion, category 1A, 1B or 1C (H314);

— flammable gas, category 1 or 2 (H220, H221);

— flammable aerosols, category 1 (H222);

— flammable liquid, category 1 or 2 (H224, H225);

— explosives, categories 'Unstable explosive', or explosives of Divisions 1.1, 1.2, 1.3, 1.4, 1.5 (H200, H201, H202, H203, H204, H205);

— self-reactive substances and mixtures, type A, B, C or D (H240, H241, H242);

— organic peroxides, type A or B (H240, H241);

— specific target organ toxicity after single exposure, category 1 or 2 (H370, H371);

— specific target organ toxicity after repeated exposure, category 1 or 2 (H372, H373);

— respiratory sensitisation, category 1, subcategory 1A or 1B (H334);

— skin sensitisation, category 1, subcategory 1A or 1B (H317);

— carcinogenicity, category 1A, 1B or 2 (H350, H350i, H351);

    — germ cell mutagenicity, category 1A, 1B or 2 (H340, H341);
    — reproductive toxicity, category 1A or 1B (H360, H360F, H360FD, H360Fd, H360D, H360Df).

...

(d)   Substances and mixtures referred to in point (ii) of point (a) of Article 2 of Directive 2004/37/EC of the European Parliament and of the Council (8);

(e)   Lead and compounds thereof, inasmuch as the agents in question are absorbable by the human organism;

(f)   Asbestos.

II.   Processes and work

1.   Processes at work referred to in Annex I to Directive 2004/37/EC.
2.   Manufacture and handling of devices, fireworks or other objects containing explosives.
3.   Work with fierce of poisonous animals.
4.   Animal slaughtering on an industrial scale.
5.   Work involving the handling of equipment for the production, storage or application of compressed, liquefied or dissolved gases.
6.   Work with vats, tanks, reservoirs or carboys containing chemical agents referred to in 1.3.
7.   Work involving a risk of structural collapse.
8.   Work involving high-voltage electrical hazards.
9.   Work the pace of which is determined by machinery and involving payment by results.

COUNCIL DIRECTIVE 2009/38/EC OF THE EUROPEAN PARLIAMENT AND OF THE COUNCIL of 6 MAY 2009
on the establishment of a European Works Council or a procedure in Community-scale undertakings and Community-scale groups of undertakings for the purposes of informing and consulting employees (Recast)
[2009] OJ L122/28

THE EUROPEAN PARLIAMENT AND THE COUNCIL OF THE EUROPEAN UNION,

Having regard to the Treaty establishing the European Community, and in particular Article 137 thereof,

Having regard to the proposal from the Commission,

Having regard to the opinion of the European Economic and Social Committee,

Having consulted the Committee of the Regions,

Acting in accordance with the procedure referred to in Article 251 of the Treaty,

Whereas:

(1)   A number of substantive changes are to be made to Council Directive 94/45/EC of 22 September 1994 on the establishment of a European Works Council or a procedure in Community-scale undertakings and Community-scale groups of undertakings for the purposes of informing and consulting employees. In the interests of clarity, that Directive should be recast.

(2)   Pursuant to Article 15 of Directive 94/45/EC, the Commission has, in consultation with the Member States and with management and labour at European level, reviewed the operation of that Directive and, in particular, examined whether the workforce size thresholds are appropriate, with a view to proposing suitable amendments where necessary.

(3)   Having consulted the Member States and management and labour at European level, the Commission submitted, on 4 April 2000, a report on the application of Directive 94/45/EC to the European Parliament and to the Council.

(4)   Pursuant to Article 138(2) of the Treaty, the Commission consulted management and labour at Community level on the possible direction of Community action in this area.

(5)   Following this consultation, the Commission considered that Community action was advisable and again consulted management and labour at Community level on the content of the planned proposal, pursuant to Article 138(3) of the Treaty.

(6) Following this second phase of consultation, management and labour have not informed the Commission of their shared wish to initiate the process which might lead to the conclusion of an agreement, as provided for in Article 138(4) of the Treaty.

(7) It is necessary to modernise Community legislation on transnational information and consultation of employees with a view to ensuring the effectiveness of employees' transnational information and consultation rights, increasing the proportion of European Works Councils established while enabling the continuous functioning of existing agreements, resolving the problems encountered in the practical application of Directive 94/45/EC and remedying the lack of legal certainty resulting from some of its provisions or the absence of certain provisions, and ensuring that Community legislative instruments on information and consultation of employees are better linked.

(8) Pursuant to Article 136 of the Treaty, one particular objective of the Community and the Member States is to promote dialogue between management and labour.

(9) This Directive is part of the Community framework intended to support and complement the action taken by Member States in the field of information and consultation of employees. This framework should keep to a minimum the burden on undertakings or establishments while ensuring the effective exercise of the rights granted.

(10) The functioning of the internal market involves a process of concentrations of undertakings, cross-border mergers, take-overs, joint ventures and, consequently, a transnationalisation of undertakings and groups of undertakings. If economic activities are to develop in a harmonious fashion, undertakings and groups of undertakings operating in two or more Member States must inform and consult the representatives of those of their employees who are affected by their decisions.

(11) Procedures for informing and consulting employees as embodied in legislation or practice in the Member States are often not geared to the transnational structure of the entity which takes the decisions affecting those employees. This may lead to the unequal treatment of employees affected by decisions within one and the same undertaking or group of undertakings.

(12) Appropriate provisions must be adopted to ensure that the employees of Community-scale undertakings or Community-scale groups of undertakings are properly informed and consulted when decisions which affect them are taken in a Member State other than that in which they are employed.

(13) In order to guarantee that the employees of undertakings or groups of undertakings operating in two or more Member States are properly informed and consulted, it is necessary to set up European Works Councils or to create other suitable procedures for the transnational information and consultation of employees.

(14) The arrangements for informing and consulting employees need to be defined and implemented in such a way as to ensure their effectiveness with regard to the provisions of this Directive. To that end, informing and consulting the European Works Council should make it possible for it to give an opinion to the undertaking in a timely fashion, without calling into question the ability of undertakings to adapt. Only dialogue at the level where directions are prepared and effective involvement of employees' representatives make it possible to anticipate and manage change.

(15) Workers and their representatives must be guaranteed information and consultation at the relevant level of management and representation, according to the subject under discussion. To achieve this, the competence and scope of action of a European Works Council must be distinct from that of national representative bodies and must be limited to transnational matters.

(16) The transnational character of a matter should be determined by taking account of both the scope of its potential effects, and the level of management and representation that it involves. For this purpose, matters which concern the entire undertaking or group or at least two Member States are considered to be transnational. These include matters which, regardless of the number of Member States involved, are of importance for the European workforce in terms of the scope of their potential effects or which involve transfers of activities between Member States.

(17) It is necessary to have a definition of 'controlling undertaking' relating solely to this Directive, without prejudice to the definitions of 'group' or 'control' in other acts.

(18) The mechanisms for informing and consulting employees in undertakings or groups of undertakings operating in two or more Member States must encompass all of the

establishments or, as the case may be, the group's undertakings located within the Member States, regardless of whether the undertaking or the group's controlling undertaking has its central management inside or outside the territory of the Member States.

(19) In accordance with the principle of autonomy of the parties, it is for the representatives of employees and the management of the undertaking or the group's controlling undertaking to determine by agreement the nature, composition, the function, mode of operation, procedures and financial resources of European Works Councils or other information and consultation procedures so as to suit their own particular circumstances.

(20) In accordance with the principle of subsidiarity, it is for the Member States to determine who the employees' representatives are and in particular to provide, if they consider appropriate, for a balanced representation of different categories of employees.

(21) It is necessary to clarify the concepts of information and consultation of employees, in accordance with the definitions in the most recent Directives on this subject and those which apply within a national framework, with the objectives of reinforcing the effectiveness of dialogue at transnational level, permitting suitable linkage between the national and transnational levels of dialogue and ensuring the legal certainty required for the application of this Directive.

(22) The definition of 'information' needs to take account of the goal of allowing employees representatives to carry out an appropriate examination, which implies that the information be provided at such time, in such fashion and with such content as are appropriate without slowing down the decision-making process in undertakings.

(23) The definition of 'consultation' needs to take account of the goal of allowing for the expression of an opinion which will be useful to the decision-making process, which implies that the consultation must take place at such time, in such fashion and with such content as are appropriate.

(24) The information and consultation provisions laid down in this Directive must be implemented in the case of an undertaking or a group's controlling undertaking which has its central management outside the territory of the Member States by its representative agent, to be designated if necessary, in one of the Member States or, in the absence of such an agent, by the establishment or controlled undertaking employing the greatest number of employees in the Member States.

(25) The responsibility of undertakings or groups of undertakings in the transmission of the information required to commence negotiations must be specified in a way that enables employees to determine whether the undertaking or group of undertakings where they work is a Community-scale undertaking or group of undertakings and to make the necessary contacts to draw up a request to commence negotiations.

(26) The special negotiating body must represent employees from the various Member States in a balanced fashion. Employees' representatives must be able to cooperate to define their positions in relation to negotiations with the central management.

(27) Recognition must be given to the role that recognised trade union organisations can play in negotiating and renegotiating the constituent agreements of European Works Councils, providing support to employees' representatives who express a need for such support. In order to enable them to monitor the establishment of new European Works Councils and promote best practice, competent trade union and employers' organisations recognised as European social partners shall be informed of the commencement of negotiations. Recognised competent European trade union and employers' organisations are those social partner organisations that are consulted by the Commission under Article 138 of the Treaty. The list of those organisations is updated and published by the Commission.

(28) The agreements governing the establishment and operation of European Works Councils must include the methods for modifying, terminating, or renegotiating them when necessary, particularly where the make-up or structure of the undertaking or group of undertakings is modified.

(29) Such agreements must lay down the arrangements for linking the national and transnational levels of information and consultation of employees appropriate for the particular conditions of the undertaking or group of undertakings. The arrangements must be defined in such a way that they respect the competences and areas of action of the employee representation bodies, in particular with regard to anticipating and managing change.

(30) Those agreements must provide, where necessary, for the establishment and operation of a select committee in order to permit coordination and greater effectiveness of the regular activities of the European Works Council, together with information and consultation at the earliest opportunity where exceptional circumstances arise.

(31) Employees' representatives may decide not to seek the setting-up of a European Works Council or the parties concerned may decide on other procedures for the transnational information and consultation of employees.

(32) Provision should be made for certain subsidiary requirements to apply should the parties so decide or in the event of the central management refusing to initiate negotiations or in the absence of agreement subsequent to such negotiations.

(33) In order to perform their representative role fully and to ensure that the European Works Council is useful, employees' representatives must report to the employees whom they represent and must be able to receive the training they require.

(34) Provision should be made for the employees' representatives acting within the framework of this Directive to enjoy, when exercising their functions, the same protection and guarantees as those provided to employees' representatives by the legislation and/or practice of the country of employment. They must not be subject to any discrimination as a result of the lawful exercise of their activities and must enjoy adequate protection as regards dismissal and other sanctions.

(35) The Member States must take appropriate measures in the event of failure to comply with the obligations laid down in this Directive.

(36) In accordance with the general principles of Community law, administrative or judicial procedures, as well as sanctions that are effective, dissuasive and proportionate in relation to the seriousness of the offence, should be applicable in cases of infringement of the obligations arising from this Directive.

(37) For reasons of effectiveness, consistency and legal certainty, there is a need for linkage between the Directives and the levels of informing and consulting employees established by Community and national law and/or practice. Priority must be given to negotiations on these procedures for linking information within each undertaking or group of undertakings. If there are no agreements on this subject and where decisions likely to lead to substantial changes in work organisation or contractual relations are envisaged, the process must be conducted at both national and European level in such a way that it respects the competences and areas of action of the employee representation bodies. Opinions expressed by the European Works Council should be without prejudice to the competence of the central management to carry out the necessary consultations in accordance with the schedules provided for in national legislation and/or practice. National legislation and/or practice may have to be adapted to ensure that the European Works Council can, where applicable, receive information earlier or at the same time as the national employee representation bodies, but must not reduce the general level of protection of employees.

(38) This Directive should be without prejudice to the information and consultation procedures referred to in Directive 2002/14/EC of the European Parliament and of the Council of 11 March 2002 establishing a general framework for informing and consulting employees in the European Community and to the specific procedures referred to in Article 2 of Council Directive 98/59/EC of 20 July 1998 on the approximation of the laws of the Member States relating to collective redundancies and Article 7 of Council Directive 2001/23/EC of 12 March 2001 on the approximation of the laws of the Member States relating to the safeguarding of employees' rights in the event of transfers of undertakings, businesses or parts of undertakings or businesses.

(39) Special treatment should be accorded to Community-scale undertakings and groups of undertakings in which there existed, on 22 September 1996, an agreement, covering the entire workforce, providing for the transnational information and consultation of employees.

(40) Where the structure of the undertaking or group of undertakings changes significantly, for example, due to a merger, acquisition or division, the existing European Works Council(s) must be adapted. This adaptation must be carried out as a priority pursuant to the clauses of the applicable agreement, if such clauses permit the required adaptation to be carried out. If this is not the case and a request establishing the need is made, negotiations, in which the members of the existing European Works Council(s) must be involved, will commence on a new agreement. In order to permit the information and consultation of

employees during the often decisive period when the structure is changed, the existing European Works Council(s) must be able to continue to operate, possibly with adaptations, until a new agreement is concluded. Once a new agreement is signed, the previously established councils must be dissolved, and the agreements instituting them must be terminated, regardless of their provisions on validity or termination.

(41) Unless this adaptation clause is applied, the agreements in force should be allowed to continue in order to avoid their obligatory renegotiation when this would be unnecessary. Provision should be made so that, as long as agreements concluded prior to 22 September 1996 under Article 13(1) of Directive 94/45/EC or under Article 3(1) of Directive 97/74/EC remain in force, the obligations arising from this Directive should not apply to them. Furthermore, this Directive does not establish a general obligation to renegotiate agreements concluded pursuant to Article 6 of Directive 94/45/EC between 22 September 1996 and 5 June 2011.

(42) Without prejudice to the possibility of the parties to decide otherwise, a European Works Council set up in the absence of agreement between the parties must, in order to fulfil the objective of this Directive, be kept informed and consulted on the activities of the undertaking or group of undertakings so that it may assess the possible impact on employees' interests in at least two different Member States. To that end, the undertaking or controlling undertaking must be required to communicate to the employees' appointed representatives general information concerning the interests of employees and information relating more specifically to those aspects of the activities of the undertaking or group of undertakings which affect employees' interests. The European Works Council must be able to deliver an opinion at the end of the meeting.

(43) Certain decisions having a significant effect on the interests of employees must be the subject of information and consultation of the employees' appointed representatives as soon as possible.

(44) The content of the subsidiary requirements which apply in the absence of an agreement and serve as a reference in the negotiations must be clarified and adapted to developments in the needs and practices relating to transnational information and consultation. A distinction should be made between fields where information must be provided and fields where the European Works Council must also be consulted, which involves the possibility of obtaining a reasoned response to any opinions expressed. To enable the select committee to play the necessary coordinating role and to deal effectively with exceptional circumstances, that committee must be able to have up to five members and be able to consult regularly.

(45) Since the objective of this Directive, namely the improvement of the right to information and to consultation of employees in Community-scale undertakings and Community-scale groups of undertakings, cannot be sufficiently achieved by the Member States and can therefore be better achieved at Community level, the Community may adopt measures, in accordance with the principle of subsidiarity as set out in Article 5 of the Treaty. In accordance with the principle of proportionality as set out in that Article, this Directive does not go beyond what is necessary in order to achieve that objective.

(46) This Directive respects fundamental rights and observes in particular the principles recognised by the Charter of Fundamental Rights of the European Union. In particular, this Directive seeks to ensure full respect for the right of workers or their representatives to be guaranteed information and consultation in good time at the appropriate levels in the cases and under the conditions provided for by Community law and national laws and practices (Article 27 of the Charter of Fundamental Rights of the European Union).

(47) The obligation to transpose this Directive into national law should be confined to those provisions which represent a substantive change as compared with the earlier Directives. The obligation to transpose the provisions which are unchanged arises under the earlier Directives.

(48) In accordance with point 34 of the Interinstitutional Agreement on better law-making, Member States are encouraged to draw up, for themselves and in the interests of the Community, tables illustrating, as far as possible, the correlation between this Directive and the transposition measures, and to make them public.

(49) This Directive should be without prejudice to the obligations of the Member States relating to the time limits set out in Annex II, Part B for transposition into national law and application of the Directives,

HAVE ADOPTED THIS DIRECTIVE:

SECTION I
GENERAL

Article 1   Objective

1. The purpose of this Directive is to improve the right to information and to consultation of employees in Community-scale undertakings and Community-scale groups of undertakings.

2. To that end, a European Works Council or a procedure for informing and consulting employees shall be established in every Community-scale undertaking and every Community-scale group of undertakings, where requested in the manner laid down in Article 5(1), with the purpose of informing and consulting employees. The arrangements for informing and consulting employees shall be defined and implemented in such a way as to ensure their effectiveness and to enable the undertaking or group of undertakings to take decisions effectively.

3. Information and consultation of employees must occur at the relevant level of management and representation, according to the subject under discussion. To achieve that, the competence of the European Works Council and the scope of the information and consultation procedure for employees governed by this Directive shall be limited to transnational issues.

4. Matters shall be considered to be transnational where they concern the Community-scale undertaking or Community-scale group of undertakings as a whole, or at least two undertakings or establishments of the undertaking or group situated in two different Member States.

5. Notwithstanding paragraph 2, where a Community-scale group of undertakings within the meaning of Article 2(1)(c) comprises one or more undertakings or groups of undertakings which are Community-scale undertakings or Community-scale groups of undertakings within the meaning of Article 2(1)(a) or (c), a European Works Council shall be established at the level of the group unless the agreements referred to in Article 6 provide otherwise.

6. Unless a wider scope is provided for in the agreements referred to in Article 6, the powers and competence of European Works Councils and the scope of information and consultation procedures established to achieve the purpose specified in paragraph 1 shall, in the case of a Community-scale undertaking, cover all the establishments located within the Member States and, in the case of a Community-scale group of undertakings, all group undertakings located within the Member States.

Article 2   Definitions

1. For the purposes of this Directive:

    (a) 'Community-scale undertaking' means any undertaking with at least 1 000 employees within the Member States and at least 150 employees in each of at least two Member States;

    (b) 'group of undertakings' means a controlling undertaking and its controlled undertakings;

    (c) 'Community-scale group of undertakings' means a group of undertakings with the following characteristics:
    — at least 1 000 employees within the Member States,
    — at least two group undertakings in different Member States, and
    — at least one group undertaking with at least 150 employees in one Member State and at least one other group undertaking with at least 150 employees in another Member State;

    (d) 'employees' representatives' means the employees' representatives provided for by national law and/or practice;

    (e) 'central management' means the central management of the Community-scale undertaking or, in the case of a Community-scale group of undertakings, of the controlling undertaking;

    (f) 'information' means transmission of data by the employer to the employees' representatives in order to enable them to acquaint themselves with the subject matter and to examine it; information shall be given at such time, in such fashion and with such content as are appropriate to enable employees' representatives to undertake an in-depth assessment of the possible impact and, where appropriate, prepare for consultations with the competent organ of the Community-scale undertaking or Community-scale group of undertakings;

(g)   'consultation' means the establishment of dialogue and exchange of views between employees' representatives and central management or any more appropriate level of management, at such time, in such fashion and with such content as enables employees' representatives to express an opinion on the basis of the information provided about the proposed measures to which the consultation is related, without prejudice to the responsibilities of the management, and within a reasonable time, which may be taken into account within the Community-scale undertaking or Community-scale group of undertakings;

(h)   'European Works Council' means a council established in accordance with Article 1(2) or the provisions of Annex I, with the purpose of informing and consulting employees;

(i)   'special negotiating body' means the body established in accordance with Article 5(2) to negotiate with the central management regarding the establishment of a European Works Council or a procedure for informing and consulting employees in accordance with Article 1(2).

2.   For the purposes of this Directive, the prescribed thresholds for the size of the workforce shall be based on the average number of employees, including part-time employees, employed during the previous two years calculated according to national legislation and/or practice.

Article 3 Definition of 'controlling undertaking'

1.   For the purposes of this Directive, 'controlling undertaking' means an undertaking which can exercise a dominant influence over another undertaking (the controlled undertaking) by virtue, for example, of ownership, financial participation or the rules which govern it.

2.   The ability to exercise a dominant influence shall be presumed, without prejudice to proof to the contrary, when an undertaking, in relation to another undertaking directly or indirectly:

(a)   holds a majority of that undertaking's subscribed capital;

(b)   controls a majority of the votes attached to that undertaking's issued share capital; or

(c)   can appoint more than half of the members of that undertaking's administrative, management or supervisory body.

3.   For the purposes of paragraph 2, a controlling undertaking's rights as regards voting and appointment shall include the rights of any other controlled undertaking and those of any person or body acting in his or its own name but on behalf of the controlling undertaking or of any other controlled undertaking.

4.   Notwithstanding paragraphs 1 and 2, an undertaking shall not be deemed to be a 'controlling undertaking' with respect to another undertaking in which it has holdings where the former undertaking is a company referred to in Article 3(5)(a) or (c) of Council Regulation (EC) No 139/2004 of 20 January 2004 on the control of concentrations between undertakings.

5.   A dominant influence shall not be presumed to be exercised solely by virtue of the fact that an office holder is exercising his functions, according to the law of a Member State relating to liquidation, winding up, insolvency, cessation of payments, compositions or analogous proceedings.

6.   The law applicable in order to determine whether an undertaking is a controlling undertaking shall be the law of the Member State which governs that undertaking.
Where the law governing that undertaking is not that of a Member State, the law applicable shall be the law of the Member State within whose territory the representative of the undertaking or, in the absence of such a representative, the central management of the group undertaking which employs the greatest number of employees is situated.

7.   Where, in the case of a conflict of laws in the application of paragraph 2, two or more undertakings from a group satisfy one or more of the criteria laid down in that paragraph, the undertaking which satisfies the criterion laid down in point (c) thereof shall be regarded as the controlling undertaking, without prejudice to proof that another undertaking is able to exercise a dominant influence.

SECTION II

ESTABLISHMENT OF A EUROPEAN WORKS COUNCIL OR AN EMPLOYEE INFORMATION AND CONSULTATION PROCEDURE

Article 4   Responsibility for the establishment of a European Works Council or an employee information and consultation procedure

1. The central management shall be responsible for creating the conditions and means necessary for the setting-up of a European Works Council or an information and consultation procedure, as provided for in Article 1(2), in a Community-scale undertaking and a Community-scale group of undertakings.

2. Where the central management is not situated in a Member State, the central management's representative agent in a Member State, to be designated if necessary, shall take on the responsibility referred to in paragraph 1.

   In the absence of such a representative, the management of the establishment or group undertaking employing the greatest number of employees in any one Member State shall take on the responsibility referred to in paragraph 1.

3. For the purposes of this Directive, the representative or representatives or, in the absence of any such representatives, the management referred to in the second subparagraph of paragraph 2, shall be regarded as the central management.

4. The management of every undertaking belonging to the Community-scale group of undertakings and the central management or the deemed central management within the meaning of the second subparagraph of paragraph 2 of the Community-scale undertaking or group of undertakings shall be responsible for obtaining and transmitting to the parties concerned by the application of this Directive the information required for commencing the negotiations referred to in Article 5, and in particular the information concerning the structure of the undertaking or the group and its workforce. This obligation shall relate in particular to the information on the number of employees referred to in Article 2(1)(a) and (c).

Article 5   Special negotiating body

1. In order to achieve the objective set out in Article 1(1), the central management shall initiate negotiations for the establishment of a European Works Council or an information and consultation procedure on its own initiative or at the written request of at least 100 employees or their representatives in at least two undertakings or establishments in at least two different Member States.

2. For this purpose, a special negotiating body shall be established in accordance with the following guidelines:

   (a) The Member States shall determine the method to be used for the election or appointment of the members of the special negotiating body who are to be elected or appointed in their territories.

   Member States shall provide that employees in undertakings and/or establishments in which there are no employees' representatives through no fault of their own, have the right to elect or appoint members of the special negotiating body.

   The second subparagraph shall be without prejudice to national legislation and/or practice laying down thresholds for the establishment of employee representation bodies.

   (b) The members of the special negotiating body shall be elected or appointed in proportion to the number of employees employed in each Member State by the Community-scale undertaking or Community-scale group of undertakings, by allocating in respect of each Member State one seat per portion of employees employed in that Member State amounting to 10%, or a fraction thereof, of the number of employees employed in all the Member States taken together;

   (c) The central management and local management and the competent European workers' and employers' organisations shall be informed of the composition of the special negotiating body and of the start of the negotiations.

3. The special negotiating body shall have the task of determining, with the central management, by written agreement, the scope, composition, functions, and term

of office of the European Works Council(s) or the arrangements for implementing a procedure for the information and consultation of employees.

4.   With a view to the conclusion of an agreement in accordance with Article 6, the central management shall convene a meeting with the special negotiating body. It shall inform the local managements accordingly.

Before and after any meeting with the central management, the special negotiating body shall be entitled to meet without representatives of the central management being present, using any necessary means for communication.

For the purpose of the negotiations, the special negotiating body may request assistance from experts of its choice which can include representatives of competent recognised Community-level trade union organisations. Such experts and such trade union representatives may be present at negotiation meetings in an advisory capacity at the request of the special negotiating body.

5.   The special negotiating body may decide, by at least two-thirds of the votes, not to open negotiations in accordance with paragraph 4, or to terminate the negotiations already opened.

Such a decision shall stop the procedure to conclude the agreement referred to in Article 6. Where such a decision has been taken, the provisions in Annex I shall not apply.

A new request to convene the special negotiating body may be made at the earliest two years after the abovementioned decision unless the parties concerned lay down a shorter period.

6.   Any expenses relating to the negotiations referred to in paragraphs 3 and 4 shall be borne by the central management so as to enable the special negotiating body to carry out its task in an appropriate manner.

In compliance with this principle, Member States may lay down budgetary rules regarding the operation of the special negotiating body. They may in particular limit the funding to cover one expert only.

Article 6   Content of the agreement

1.   The central management and the special negotiating body must negotiate in a spirit of cooperation with a view to reaching an agreement on the detailed arrangements for implementing the information and consultation of employees provided for in Article 1(1).

2.   Without prejudice to the autonomy of the parties, the agreement referred to in paragraph 1 and effected in writing between the central management and the special negotiating body shall determine:

(a)   the undertakings of the Community-scale group of undertakings or the establishments of the Community-scale undertaking which are covered by the agreement;

(b)   the composition of the European Works Council, the number of members, the allocation of seats, taking into account where possible the need for balanced representation of employees with regard to their activities, category and gender, and the term of office;

(c)   the functions and the procedure for information and consultation of the European Works Council and the arrangements for linking information and consultation of the European Works Council and national employee representation bodies, in accordance with the principles set out in Article 1(3);

(d)   the venue, frequency and duration of meetings of the European Works Council;

(e)   where necessary, the composition, the appointment procedure, the functions and the procedural rules of the select committee set up within the European Works Council;

(f)   the financial and material resources to be allocated to the European Works Council;

(g)   the date of entry into force of the agreement and its duration, the arrangements for amending or terminating the agreement and the cases in which the agreement shall be renegotiated and the procedure for its renegotiation, including, where necessary, where the structure of the Community-scale undertaking or Community-scale group of undertakings changes.

3. The central management and the special negotiating body may decide, in writing, to establish one or more information and consultation procedures instead of a European Works Council.

The agreement must stipulate by what method the employees' representatives shall have the right to meet to discuss the information conveyed to them.

This information shall relate in particular to transnational questions which significantly affect workers' interests.

4. The agreements referred to in paragraphs 2 and 3 shall not, unless provision is made otherwise therein, be subject to the subsidiary requirements of Annex I.

5. For the purposes of concluding the agreements referred to in paragraphs 2 and 3, the special negotiating body shall act by a majority of its members.

Article 7 Subsidiary requirements

1. In order to achieve the objective set out in Article 1(1), the subsidiary requirements laid down by the legislation of the Member State in which the central management is situated shall apply:
   — where the central management and the special negotiating body so decide,
   — where the central management refuses to commence negotiations within six months of the request referred to in Article 5(1),
      or
   — where, after three years from the date of this request, they are unable to conclude an agreement as laid down in Article 6 and the special negotiating body has not taken the decision provided for in Article 5(5).

2. The subsidiary requirements referred to in paragraph 1 as adopted in the legislation of the Member States must satisfy the provisions set out in Annex I.

SECTION III
MISCELLANEOUS PROVISIONS

Article 8 Confidential information

1. Member States shall provide that members of special negotiating bodies or of European Works Councils and any experts who assist them are not authorised to reveal any information which has expressly been provided to them in confidence.

The same shall apply to employees' representatives in the framework of an information and consultation procedure.

That obligation shall continue to apply, wherever the persons referred to in the first and second subparagraphs are, even after the expiry of their terms of office.

2. Each Member State shall provide, in specific cases and under the conditions and limits laid down by national legislation, that the central management situated in its territory is not obliged to transmit information when its nature is such that, according to objective criteria, it would seriously harm the functioning of the undertakings concerned or would be prejudicial to them.

A Member State may make such dispensation subject to prior administrative or judicial authorisation.

3. Each Member State may lay down particular provisions for the central management of undertakings in its territory which pursue directly and essentially the aim of ideological guidance with respect to information and the expression of opinions, on condition that, at the date of adoption of this Directive such particular provisions already exist in the national legislation.

Article 9 Operation of the European Works Council and the information and consultation procedure for workers

The central management and the European Works Council shall work in a spirit of cooperation

with due regard to their reciprocal rights and obligations.

The same shall apply to cooperation between the central management and employees' representatives in the framework of an information and consultation procedure for workers.

Article 10 Role and protection of employees' representatives

1. Without prejudice to the competence of other bodies or organisations in this respect, the members of the European Works Council shall have the means required to apply the rights arising from this Directive, to represent collectively the interests of the employees of the Community-scale undertaking or Community-scale group of undertakings.

2. Without prejudice to Article 8, the members of the European Works Council shall inform the representatives of the employees of the establishments or of the undertakings of a Community-scale group of undertakings or, in the absence of representatives, the workforce as a whole, of the content and outcome of the information and consultation procedure carried out in accordance with this Directive.

3. Members of special negotiating bodies, members of European Works Councils and employees' representatives exercising their functions under the procedure referred to in Article 6(3) shall, in the exercise of their functions, enjoy protection and guarantees similar to those provided for employees' representatives by the national legislation and/or practice in force in their country of employment.

   This shall apply in particular to attendance at meetings of special negotiating bodies or European Works Councils or any other meetings within the framework of the agreement referred to in Article 6(3), and the payment of wages for members who are on the staff of the Community-scale undertaking or the Community-scale group of undertakings for the period of absence necessary for the performance of their duties.

   A member of a special negotiating body or of a European Works Council, or such a member's alternate, who is a member of the crew of a seagoing vessel, shall be entitled to participate in a meeting of the special negotiating body or of the European Works Council, or in any other meeting under any procedures established pursuant to Article 6(3), where that member or alternate is not at sea or in a port in a country other than that in which the shipping company is domiciled, when the meeting takes place. Meetings shall, where practicable, be scheduled to facilitate the participation of members or alternates, who are members of the crews of seagoing vessels.

   In cases where a member of a special negotiating body or of a European Works Council, or such a member's alternate, who is a member of the crew of a seagoing vessel, is unable to attend a meeting, the possibility of using, where possible, new information and communication technologies shall be considered.

4. In so far as this is necessary for the exercise of their representative duties in an international environment, the members of the special negotiating body and of the European Works Council shall be provided with training without loss of wages.

Article 11 Compliance with this Directive

1. Each Member State shall ensure that the management of establishments of a Community-scale undertaking and the management of undertakings which form part of a Community-scale group of undertakings which are situated within its territory and their employees' representatives or, as the case may be, employees abide by the obligations laid down by this Directive, regardless of whether or not the central management is situated within its territory.

2. Member States shall provide for appropriate measures in the event of failure to comply with this Directive; in particular, they shall ensure that adequate administrative or judicial procedures are available to enable the obligations deriving from this Directive to be enforced.

3. Where Member States apply Article 8, they shall make provision for administrative or judicial appeal procedures which the employees' representatives may initiate when the central management requires confidentiality or does not give information in accordance with that Article.

   Such procedures may include procedures designed to protect the confidentiality of the information in question.

Article 12 Relationship with other Community and national provisions

1. Information and consultation of the European Works Council shall be linked to those of the national employee representation bodies, with due regard to the competences and areas of action of each and to the principles set out in Article 1(3).

2. The arrangements for the links between the information and consultation of the European Works Council and national employee representation bodies shall be established by the agreement referred to in Article 6. That agreement shall be without prejudice to the provisions of national law and/or practice on the information and consultation of employees.

3. Where no such arrangements have been defined by agreement, the Member States shall ensure that the processes of informing and consulting are conducted in the European Works Council as well as in the national employee representation bodies in cases where decisions likely to lead to substantial changes in work organisation or contractual relations are envisaged.

4. This Directive shall be without prejudice to the information and consultation procedures referred to in Directive 2002/14/EC and to the specific procedures referred to in Article 2 of Directive 98/59/EC and Article 7 of Directive 2001/23/EC.

5. Implementation of this Directive shall not be sufficient grounds for any regression in relation to the situation which already prevails in each Member State and in relation to the general level of protection of workers in the areas to which it applies.

Article 13 Adaptation

Where the structure of the Community-scale undertaking or Community-scale group of undertakings changes significantly, and either in the absence of provisions established by the agreements in force or in the event of conflicts between the relevant provisions of two or more applicable agreements, the central management shall initiate the negotiations referred to in Article 5 on its own initiative or at the written request of at least 100 employees or their representatives in at least two undertakings or establishments in at least two different Member States.

At least three members of the existing European Works Council or of each of the existing European Works Councils shall be members of the special negotiating body, in addition to the members elected or appointed pursuant to Article 5(2).

During the negotiations, the existing European Works Council(s) shall continue to operate in accordance with any arrangements adapted by agreement between the members of the European Works Council(s) and the central management.

Article 14 Agreements in force

1. Without prejudice to Article 13, the obligations arising from this Directive shall not apply to Community-scale undertakings or Community-scale groups of undertakings in which, either

   (a) an agreement or agreements covering the entire workforce, providing for the transnational information and consultation of employees have been concluded pursuant to Article 13(1) of Directive 94/45/EC or Article 3(1) of Directive 97/74/EC, or where such agreements are adjusted because of changes in the structure of the undertakings or groups of undertakings;
   or

   (b) an agreement concluded pursuant to Article 6 of Directive 94/45/EC is signed or revised between 5 June 2009 and 5 June 2011.

   The national law applicable when the agreement is signed or revised shall continue to apply to the undertakings or groups of undertakings referred to in point (b) of the first subparagraph.

2. Upon expiry of the agreements referred to in paragraph 1, the parties to those agreements may decide jointly to renew or revise them. Where this is not the case, the provisions of this Directive shall apply.

Article 15 Report

No later than 5 June 2016, the Commission shall report to the European Parliament, the Council and the European Economic and Social Committee on the implementation of this Directive, making appropriate proposals where necessary.

Article 16 Transposition

1. Member States shall bring into force the laws, regulations and administrative provisions necessary to comply with Article 1(2), (3) and (4), Article 2(1), points (f) and (g), Articles 3(4), Article 4(4), Article 5(2), points (b) and (c), Article 5(4), Article 6(2), points (b),

(c), (e) and (g), and Articles 10, 12, 13 and 14, as well as Annex I, point 1(a), (c) and (d) and points 2 and 3, no later than 5 June 2011 or shall ensure that management and labour introduce on that date the required provisions by way of agreement, the Member States being obliged to take all necessary steps enabling them at all times to guarantee the results imposed by this Directive.

When Member States adopt those provisions, they shall contain a reference to this Directive or be accompanied by such a reference on the occasion of their official publication. They shall also include a statement that references in existing laws, regulations and administrative provisions to the directive repealed by this Directive shall be construed as references to this Directive. Member States shall determine how such reference is to be made and how that statement is to be formulated.

2.   Member States shall communicate to the Commission the text of the main provisions of national law which they adopt in the field covered by this Directive.

Article 17 Repeal

Directive 94/45/EC, as amended by the Directives listed in Annex II, Part A, is repealed with effect from 6 June 2011 without prejudice to the obligations of the Member States relating to the time limit for transposition into national law of the Directives set out in Annex II, Part B.

References to the repealed Directive shall be construed as references to this Directive and shall be read in accordance with the correlation table in Annex III.

Article 18 Entry into force

This Directive shall enter into force on the 20th day following its publication in the *Official Journal of the European Union*.

Article 1(1), (5), (6) and (7), Article 2(1), points (a) to (e), (h) and (i), Article 2(2), Articles 3(1), (2), (3), (5), (6) and (7), Article 4(1), (2) and (3), Article 5(1), (3), (5) and (6), Article 5(2), point (a), Article 6(1), Article 6(2), points (a), (d) and (f), and Article 6(3), (4) and (5), and Articles 7, 8, 9 and 11, as well as Annex I, point 1(b), (e) and (f), and points 4, 5 and 6, shall apply from 6 June 2011.

Article 19 Addressees

This Directive is addressed to the Member States.

ANNEX I

SUBSIDIARY REQUIREMENTS

(referred to in Article 7)

1.   In order to achieve the objective set out in Article 1(1) and in the cases provided for in Article 7(1), the establishment, composition and competence of a European Works Council shall be governed by the following rules:

(a)   The competence of the European Works Council shall be determined in accordance with Article 1(3).

The information of the European Works Council shall relate in particular to the structure, economic and financial situation, probable development and production and sales of the Community-scale undertaking or group of undertakings. The information and consultation of the European Works Council shall relate in particular to the situation and probable trend of employment, investments, and substantial changes concerning organisation, introduction of new working methods or production processes, transfers of production, mergers, cut-backs or closures of undertakings, establishments or important parts thereof, and collective redundancies.

The consultation shall be conducted in such a way that the employees' representatives can meet with the central management and obtain a response, and the reasons for that response, to any opinion they might express;

(b)   The European Works Council shall be composed of employees of the Community-scale undertaking or Community-scale group of undertakings elected or appointed from their number by the employees' representatives or, in the absence thereof, by the entire body of employees.

The election or appointment of members of the European Works Council shall be carried out in accordance with national legislation and/or practice;

(c)   The members of the European Works Council shall be elected or appointed in proportion to the number of employees employed in each Member State by the Community-scale undertaking or Community-scale group of undertakings, by allocating in respect of each Member State one seat per portion of employees employed in that Member State amounting to 10%, or a fraction thereof, of the number of employees employed in all the Member States taken together;

(d)   To ensure that it can coordinate its activities, the European Works Council shall elect a select committee from among its members, comprising at most five members, which must benefit from conditions enabling it to exercise its activities on a regular basis.

It shall adopt its own rules of procedure;

(e)   The central management and any other more appropriate level of management shall be informed of the composition of the European Works Council;

(f)   Four years after the European Works Council is established it shall examine whether to open negotiations for the conclusion of the agreement referred to in Article 6 or to continue to apply the subsidiary requirements adopted in accordance with this Annex.

Articles 6 and 7 shall apply, *mutatis mutandis*, if a decision has been taken to negotiate an agreement according to Article 6, in which case 'special negotiating body' shall be replaced by 'European Works Council'.

2.   The European Works Council shall have the right to meet with the central management once a year, to be informed and consulted, on the basis of a report drawn up by the central management, on the progress of the business of the Community-scale undertaking or Community-scale group of undertakings and its prospects. The local managements shall be informed accordingly.

3.   Where there are exceptional circumstances or decisions affecting the employees' interests to a considerable extent, particularly in the event of relocations, the closure of establishments or undertakings or collective redundancies, the select committee or, where no such committee exists, the European Works Council shall have the right to be informed. It shall have the right to meet, at its request, the central management, or any other more appropriate level of management within the Community-scale undertaking or group of undertakings having its own powers of decision, so as to be informed and consulted.

Those members of the European Works Council who have been elected or appointed by the establishments and/or undertakings which are directly concerned by the circumstances or decisions in question shall also have the right to participate where a meeting is organised with the select committee.

This information and consultation meeting shall take place as soon as possible on the basis of a report drawn up by the central management or any other appropriate level of management of the Community-scale undertaking or group of undertakings, on which an opinion may be delivered at the end of the meeting or within a reasonable time.

This meeting shall not affect the prerogatives of the central management.

The information and consultation procedures provided for in the above circumstances shall be carried out without prejudice to Article 1(2) and Article 8.

4.   The Member States may lay down rules on the chairing of information and consultation meetings.

Before any meeting with the central management, the European Works Council or the select committee, where necessary enlarged in accordance with the second paragraph of point 3, shall be entitled to meet without the management concerned being present.

5.   The European Works Council or the select committee may be assisted by experts of its choice, in so far as this is necessary for it to carry out its tasks.

6.   The operating expenses of the European Works Council shall be borne by the central management.

The central management concerned shall provide the members of the European Works Council with such financial and material resources as enable them to perform their duties in an appropriate manner.

In particular, the cost of organising meetings and arranging for interpretation facilities and the accommodation and travelling expenses of members of the European Works

Council and its select committee shall be met by the central management unless otherwise agreed.

In compliance with these principles, the Member States may lay down budgetary rules regarding the operation of the European Works Council. They may in particular limit funding to cover one expert only.

COUNCIL DIRECTIVE (EC) No 97/81 of 15 DECEMBER 1997
concerning the framework agreement on part-time work concluded by UNICE, CEEP and the ETUC
[1998] OJ L14/9

THE COUNCIL OF THE EUROPEAN UNION,

Having regard to the Agreement on social policy annexed to the Protocol (No. 14) on social policy, annexed to the Treaty establishing the European Community, and in particular Article 4(2) thereof,

Having regard to the proposal from the Commission,

(1)   Whereas on the basis of the Protocol on social policy annexed to the Treaty establishing the European Community, the Member States, with the exception of the United Kingdom of Great Britain and Northern Ireland (hereinafter referred to as 'the Member States'), wishing to continue along the path laid down in the 1989 Social Charter, have concluded an agreement on social policy;

(2)   Whereas management and labour (the social partners) may, in accordance with Article 4(2) of the Agreement on social policy, request jointly that agreements at Community level be implemented by a Council decision on a proposal from the Commission;

(3)   Whereas point 7 of the Community Charter of the Fundamental Social Rights of Workers provides, inter alia, that 'the completion of the internal market must lead to an improvement in the living and working conditions of workers in the European Community. This process must result from an approximation of these conditions while the improvement is being maintained, as regards in particular ... forms of employment other than open-ended contracts, such as fixed-term contracts, part-time working, temporary-work and seasonal work';

(4)   Whereas the Council has not reached a decision on the proposal for a Directive on certain employment relationships with regard to distortions of competition, as amended, nor on the proposal for a Directive on certain employment relationships with regard to working conditions;

(5)   Whereas the conclusions of the Essen European Council stressed the need to take measures to promote employment and equal opportunities for women and men, and called for measures with a view to increasing the employment-intensiveness of growth, in particular by a more flexible organisation of work in a way which fulfils both the wishes of employees and the requirements of competition;

(6)   Whereas the Commission, in accordance with Article 3(2) of the Agreement on social policy, has consulted management and labour on the possible direction of Community action with regard to flexible working time and job security;

(7)   Whereas the Commission, considering after such consultation that Community action was desirable, once again consulted management and labour at Community level on the substance of the envisaged proposal in accordance with Article 3(3) of the said Agreement;

(8)   Whereas the general cross-industry organisations, the Union of Industrial and Employer's Confederations of Europe (UNICE), the European Centre of Enterprises with Public Participation (CEEP) and the European Trade Union Confederation (ETUC) informed the Commission in their joint letter of 19 June 1996 of their desire to initiate the procedure provided for in Article 4 of the Agreement on social policy; whereas they asked the Commission, in a joint letter dated 12 March 1997, for a further three months; whereas the Commission complied with this request;

(9)   Whereas the said cross-industry organisations concluded, on 6 June 1997, a Framework Agreement on part-time work; whereas they forwarded to the Commission their joint request to implement this Framework Agreement by a Council decision on a proposal from the Commission, in accordance with Article 4(2) of the said Agreement;

(10) Whereas the Council, in its Resolution of 6 December 1994 on prospects for a European Union social policy: contribution to economic and social convergence in the Union, asked management and labour to make use of the opportunities for concluding agreements, since they are as a rule closer to social reality and to social problems;

(11) Whereas the signatory parties wished to conclude a framework agreement on part-time work setting out the general principles and minimum requirements for part-time working; whereas they have demonstrated their desire to establish a general framework for eliminating discrimination against part-time workers and to contribute to developing the potential for part-time work on a basis which is acceptable for employers and workers alike;

(12) Whereas the social partners wished to give particular attention to part-time work, while at the same time indicating that it was their intention to consider the need for similar agreements for other flexible forms of work;

(13) Whereas, in the conclusions of the Amsterdam European Council, the Heads of State and Government of the European Union strongly welcomed the agreement concluded by the social partners on part-time work;

(14) Whereas the proper instrument for implementing the Framework Agreement is a Directive within the meaning of Article 189 of the Treaty; whereas it therefore binds the Member States as to the result to be achieved, whilst leaving national authorities the choice of form and methods;

(15) Whereas, in accordance with the principles of subsidiarity and proportionality as set out in Article 3(b) of the Treaty, the objectives of this Directive cannot be sufficiently achieved by the Member States and can therefore be better achieved by the Community; whereas this Directive does not go beyond what is necessary for the attainment of those objectives;

(16) Whereas, with regard to terms used in the Framework Agreement which are not specifically defined therein, this Directive leaves Member States free to define those terms in accordance with national law and practice, as is the case for other social policy Directives using similar terms, providing that the said definitions respect the content of the Framework Agreement;

(17) Whereas the Commission has drafted its proposal for a Directive, in accordance with its Communication of 14 December 1993 concerning the application of the Protocol (No. 14) on social policy and its Communication of 18 September 1996 concerning the development of the social dialogue at Community level, taking into account the representative status of the signatory parties and the legality of each clause of the Framework Agreement;

(18) Whereas the Commission has drafted its proposal for a Directive in compliance with Article 2(2) of the Agreement on social policy which provides that Directives in the social policy domain 'shall avoid imposing administrative, financial and legal constraints in a way which would hold back the creation and development of small and medium-sized undertakings';

(19) Whereas the Commission, in accordance with its Communication of 14 December 1993 concerning the application of the Protocol (No. 14) on social policy, informed the European Parliament by sending it the text of its proposal for a Directive containing the Framework Agreement;

(20) Whereas the Commission also informed the Economic and Social Committee;

(21) Whereas Clause 6.1 of the Framework Agreement provides that Member States and/or the social partners may maintain or introduce more favourable provisions;

(22) Whereas Clause 6.2 of the Framework Agreement provides that implementation of this Directive may not serve to justify any regression in relation to the situation which already exists in each Member State;

(23) Whereas the Community Charter of the Fundamental Social Rights of Workers recognises the importance of the fight against all forms of discrimination, especially based on sex, colour, race, opinion and creed;

(24) Whereas Article F(2) of the Treaty on European Union states that the Union shall respect fundamental rights, as guaranteed by the European Convention for the Protection of Human Rights and Fundamental Freedoms and as they result from the constitutional traditions common to the Member States, as general principles of Community law;

(25) Whereas the Member States may entrust the social partners, at their joint request, with the implementation of this Directive, provided that the Member States take all the

necessary steps to ensure that they can at all times guarantee the results imposed by this Directive;

(26) Whereas the implementation of the Framework Agreement contributes to achieving the objectives under Article 1 of the Agreement on social policy,

HAS ADOPTED THIS DIRECTIVE:

Article 1

The purpose of this Directive is to implement the Framework Agreement on part-time work concluded on 6 June 1997 between the general cross-industry organisations (UNICE, CEEP and the ETUC) annexed hereto.

Article 2

1.   Member States shall bring into force the laws, regulations and administrative provisions necessary to comply with this Directive not later than 20 January 2000, or shall ensure that, by that date at the latest, the social partners have introduced the necessary measures by agreement, the Member States being required to take any necessary measures to enable them at any time to be in a position to guarantee the results imposed by this Directive. They shall forthwith inform the Commission thereof.

Member States may have a maximum of one more year, if necessary, to take account of special difficulties or implementation by a collective agreement.

They shall inform the Commission forthwith in such circumstances.

When Member States adopt the measures referred to in the first subparagraph, they shall contain a reference to this Directive or shall be accompanied by such reference on the occasion of their official publication. The methods of making such a reference shall be laid down by the Member States.

1a.   As regards the United Kingdom of Great Britain and Northern Ireland, the date of 20 January 2000 in paragraph 1 shall be replaced by the date of 7 April 2000.

2.   Member States shall communicate to the Commission the text of the main provisions of domestic law which they have adopted or which they adopt in the field governed by this Directive.

Article 3

This Directive shall enter into force on the day of its publication in the *Official Journal of the European Communities*.

Article 4

This Directive is addressed to the Member States.

ANNEX

UNION OF INDUSTRIAL AND EMPLOYERS' CONFEDERATIONS OF EUROPE, EUROPEAN TRADE UNION CONFEDERATION, EUROPEAN CENTRE OF ENTERPRISES WITH PUBLIC PARTICIPATION FRAMEWORK AGREEMENT ON PART-TIME WORK

This Framework Agreement is a contribution to the overall European strategy on employment. Part-time work has had an important impact on employment in recent years. For this reason, the parties to this agreement have given priority attention to this form of work. It is the intention of the parties to consider the need for similar agreements relating to other forms of flexible work.

Recognising the diversity of situations in Member States and acknowledging that part-time work is a feature of employment in certain sectors and activities, this Agreement sets out the general principles and minimum requirements relating to part-time work. It illustrates the willingness of the social partners to establish a general framework for the elimination of discrimination against part-time workers and to assist the development of opportunities for part-time working on a basis acceptable to employers and workers.

This Agreement relates to employment conditions of part-time workers recognising that matters concerning statutory social security are for decision by the Member States. In the context of the principle of non-discrimination, the parties to this Agreement have noted the Employment Declaration of the Dublin European Council of December 1996, wherein the Council inter alia emphasised the need to make social security systems more employment-friendly by 'developing social protection systems capable of adapting to new patterns of work and of providing appropriate protection to people engaged in such work'. The parties to this Agreement consider that effect should be given to this Declaration.

ETUC, UNICE and CEEP request the Commission to submit this Framework Agreement to the Council for a decision making these requirements binding in the Member States which are party to the Agreement on social policy annexed to the Protocol (No. 14) on social policy annexed to the Treaty establishing the European Community.

The parties to this Agreement ask the Commission, in its proposal to implement this Agreement, to request that Member States adopt the laws, regulations and administrative provisions necessary to comply with the Council decision within a period of two years from its adoption or ensure that the social partners establish the necessary measures by way of agreement by the end of this period. Member States may, if necessary to take account of particular difficulties or implementation by collective agreement, have up to a maximum of one additional year to comply with this provision.

Without prejudice to the role of national courts and the Court of Justice, the parties to this agreement request that any matter relating to the interpretation of this agreement at European level should, in the first instance, be referred by the Commission to them for an opinion.

General considerations

1. Having regard to the Agreement on social policy annexed to the Protocol (No. 14) on social policy annexed to the Treaty establishing the European Community, and in particular Articles 3(4) and 4(2) thereof;

2. Whereas Article 4(2) of the Agreement on social policy provides that agreements concluded at Community level may be implemented, at the joint request of the signatory parties, by a Council decision on a proposal from the Commission.

3. Whereas, in its second consultation document on flexibility of working time and security for workers, the Commission announced its intention to propose a legally binding Community measure;

4. Whereas the conclusions of the European Council meeting in Essen emphasised the need for measures to promote both employment and equal opportunities for women and men, and called for measures aimed at 'increasing the employment intensiveness of growth, in particular by more flexible organisation of work in a way which fulfils both the wishes of employees and the requirements of competition';

5. Whereas the parties to this agreement attach importance to measures which would facilitate access to part-time work for men and women in order to prepare for retirement, reconcile professional and family life, and take up education and training opportunities to improve their skills and career opportunities for the mutual benefit of employers and workers and in a manner which would assist the development of enterprises;

6. Whereas this Agreement refers back to Member States and social partners for the arrangements for the application of these general principles, minimum requirements and provisions, in order to take account of the situation in each Member State;

7. Whereas this Agreement takes into consideration the need to improve social policy requirements, to enhance the competitiveness of the Community economy and to avoid imposing administrative, financial and legal constraints in a way which would hold back the creation and development of small and medium-sized undertakings;

8. Whereas the social partners are best placed to find solutions that correspond to the needs of both employers and workers and must therefore be given a special role in the implementation and application of this Agreement.

THE SIGNATORY PARTIES HAVE AGREED THE FOLLOWING:

Clause 1: Purpose

The purpose of this Framework Agreement is:

(a) to provide for the removal of discrimination against part-time workers and to improve the quality of part-time work;

(b) to facilitate the development of part-time work on a voluntary basis and to contribute to the flexible organisation of working time in a manner which takes into account the needs of employers and workers.

Clause 2: Scope

1. This Agreement applies to part-time workers who have an employment contract or employment relationship as defined by the law, collective agreement or practice in force in each Member State.
2. Member States, after consultation with the social partners in accordance with national law, collective agreements or practice, and/or the social partners at the appropriate level in conformity with national industrial relations practice may, for objective reasons, exclude wholly or partly from the terms of this Agreement part-time workers who work on a casual basis. Such exclusions should be reviewed periodically to establish if the objective reasons for making them remain valid.

Clause 3: Definitions

For the purpose of this agreement:

1. The term 'part-time worker' refers to an employee whose normal hours of work, calculated on a weekly basis or on average over a period of employment of up to one year, are less than the normal hours of work of a comparable full-time worker.
2. The term 'comparable full-time worker' means a full-time worker in the same establishment having the same type of employment contract or relationship, who is engaged in the same or a similar work/occupation, due regard being given to other considerations which may include seniority and qualification/skills.
   Where there is no comparable full-time worker in the same establishment, the comparison shall be made by reference to the applicable collective agreement or, where there is no applicable collective agreement, in accordance with national law, collective agreements or practice.

Clause 4: Principle of non-discrimination

1. In respect of employment conditions, part-time workers shall not be treated in a less favourable manner than comparable full-time workers solely because they work part time unless different treatment is justified on objective grounds.
2. Where appropriate, the principle of pro rata temporis shall apply.
3. The arrangements for the application of this clause shall be defined by the Member States and/or social partners, having regard to European legislation, national law, collective agreements and practice.
4. Where justified by objective reasons, Member States after consultation of the social partners in accordance with national law, collective agreements or practice and/ or social partners may, where appropriate, make access to particular conditions of employment subject to a period of service, time worked or earnings qualification.
   Qualifications relating to access by part-time workers to particular conditions of employment should be reviewed periodically having regard to the principle of non-discrimination as expressed in Clause 4.1.

Clause 5: Opportunities for part-time work

1. In the context of Clause 1 of this Agreement and of the principle of nondiscrimination between part-time and full-time workers:
   (a) Member States, following consultations with the social partners in accordance with national law or practice, should identify and review obstacles of a legal or administrative nature which may limit the opportunities for part-time work and, where appropriate, eliminate them;
   (b) the social partners, acting within their sphere of competence and through the procedures set out in collective agreements, should identify and review obstacles which may limit opportunities for part-time work and, where appropriate, eliminate them.
2. A worker's refusal to transfer from full-time to part-time work or vice-versa should not in itself constitute a valid reason for termination of employment, without prejudice to termination in accordance with national law, collective agreements and practice, for other reasons such as may arise from the operational requirements of the establishment concerned.
3. As far as possible, employers should give consideration to:
   (a) requests by workers to transfer from full-time to part-time work that becomes available in the establishment;

(b)   requests by workers to transfer from part-time to full-time work or to increase their working time should the opportunity arise;

(c)   the provision of timely information on the availability of part-time and full-time positions in the establishment in order to facilitate transfers from full-time to part-time or vice versa;

(d)   measures to facilitate access to part-time work at all levels of the enterprise, including skilled and managerial positions, and where appropriate, to facilitate access by part-time workers to vocational training to enhance career opportunities and occupational mobility;

(e)   the provision of appropriate information to existing bodies representing workers about part-time working in the enterprise.

Clause 6: Provisions on implementation

1.   Member States and/or social partners may maintain or introduce more favourable provisions than set out in this agreement.

2.   Implementation of the provisions of this Agreement shall not constitute valid grounds for reducing the general level of protection afforded to workers in the field of this agreement. This does not prejudice the right of Member States and/or social partners to develop different legislative, regulatory or contractual provisions, in the light of changing circumstances, and does not prejudice the application of Clause 5.1 as long as the principle of non-discrimination as expressed in Clause 4.1 is complied with.

3.   This Agreement does not prejudice the right of the social partners to conclude, at the appropriate level, including European level, agreements adapting and/or complementing the provisions of this Agreement in a manner which will take account of the specific needs of the social partners concerned.

4.   This Agreement shall be without prejudice to any more specific Community provisions, and in particular Community provisions concerning equal treatment or opportunities for men and women.

5.   The prevention and settlement of disputes and grievances arising from the application of this Agreement shall be dealt with in accordance with national law, collective agreements and practice.

6.   The signatory parties shall review this Agreement, five years after the date of the Council decision, if requested by one of the parties to this Agreement.

COUNCIL DIRECTIVE (EC) No 98/59 of 20 JULY 1998
on the approximation of the laws of the Member States relating to collective redundancies
[1998] OJ L225/16

THE COUNCIL OF THE EUROPEAN UNION,

Having regard to the Treaty establishing the European Community, and in particular Article 100 thereof,

Having regard to the proposal from the Commission,

Having regard to the opinion of the European Parliament,

Having regard to the opinion of the Economic and Social Committee,

(1)   Whereas for reasons of clarity and rationality Council Directive 75/129/EEC of 17 February 1975 on the approximation of the laws of the Member States relating to collective redundancies should be consolidated;

(2)   Whereas it is important that greater protection should be afforded to workers in the event of collective redundancies while taking into account the need for balanced economic and social development within the Community;

(3)   Whereas, despite increasing convergence, differences still remain between the provisions in force in the Member States concerning the practical arrangements and procedures for such redundancies and the measures designed to alleviate the consequences of redundancy for workers;

(4)   Whereas these differences can have a direct effect on the functioning of the internal market;

(5)   Whereas the Council resolution of 21 January 1974 concerning a social action programme made provision for a directive on the approximation of Member States' legislation on collective redundancies;

(6)   Whereas the Community Charter of the fundamental social rights of workers, adopted at the European Council meeting held in Strasbourg on 9 December 1989 by the Heads of State or Government of 11 Member States, states, inter alia, in point 7, first paragraph, first sentence, and second paragraph; in point 17, first paragraph; and in point 18, third indent:

'7.   The completion of the internal market must lead to an improvement in the living and working conditions of workers in the European Community.

The improvement must cover, where necessary, the development of certain aspects of employment regulations such as procedures for collective redundancies and those regarding bankruptcies.

17.   Information, consultation and participation for workers must be developed along appropriate lines, taking account of the practices in force in the various Member States.

18.   Such information, consultation and participation must be implemented in due time, particularly in the following cases:

– in cases of collective redundancy procedures'

(7)   Whereas this approximation must therefore be promoted while the improvement is being maintained within the meaning of Article 117 of the Treaty;

(8)   Whereas, in order to calculate the number of redundancies provided for in the definition of collective redundancies within the meaning of this Directive, other forms of termination of employment contracts on the initiative of the employer should be equated to redundancies, provided that there are at least five redundancies;

(9)   Whereas it should be stipulated that this Directive applies in principle also to collective redundancies resulting where the establishment's activities are terminated as a result of a judicial decision;

(10)   Whereas the Member States should be given the option of stipulating that workers' representatives may call on experts on grounds of the technical complexity of the matters which are likely to be the subject of the informing and consulting;

(11)   Whereas it is necessary to ensure that employers' obligations as regards information, consultation and notification apply independently of whether the decision on collective redundancies emanates from the employer or from an undertaking which controls that employer;

(12)   Whereas Member States should ensure that workers' representatives and/or workers have at their disposal administrative and/or judicial procedures in order to ensure that the obligations laid down in this Directive are fulfilled;

(13)   Whereas this Directive must not affect the obligations of the Member States concerning the deadlines for transposition of the Directives set out in Annex I, Part B,

HAS ADOPTED THIS DIRECTIVE:

SECTION I
DEFINITIONS AND SCOPE

Article 1

1.   For the purposes of this Directive:

(a)   'collective redundancies' means dismissals effected by an employer for one or more reasons not related to the individual workers concerned where, according to the choice of the Member States, the number of redundancies is:

(i)   either, over a period of 30 days:

– at least 10 in establishments normally employing more than 20 and less than 100 workers,

– at least 10% of the number of workers in establishments normally employing at least 100 but less than 300 workers,

– at least 30 in establishments normally employing 300 workers or more,

(ii)   or, over a period of 90 days, at least 20, whatever the number of workers normally employed in the establishments in question;

(b)   'workers' representatives' means the workers' representatives provided for by the laws or practices of the Member States.

For the purpose of calculating the number of redundancies provided for in the first subparagraph of point (a), terminations of an employment contract which occur on the employer's initiative for one or more reasons not related to the individual workers concerned shall be assimilated to redundancies, provided that there are at least five redundancies.

2. This Directive shall not apply to:
   (a) collective redundancies effected under contracts of employment concluded for limited periods of time or for specific tasks except where such redundancies take place prior to the date of expiry or the completion of such contracts;
   (b) workers employed by public administrative bodies or by establishments governed by public law (or, in Member States where this concept is unknown, by equivalent bodies);

SECTION II
INFORMATION AND CONSULTATION

Article 2

1. Where an employer is contemplating collective redundancies, he shall begin consultations with the workers' representatives in good time with a view to reaching an agreement.

2. These consultations shall, at least, cover ways and means of avoiding collective redundancies or reducing the number of workers affected, and of mitigating the consequences by recourse to accompanying social measures aimed, inter alia, at aid for redeploying or retraining workers made redundant.

   Member States may provide that the workers' representatives may call on the services of experts in accordance with national legislation and/or practice.

3. To enable workers' representatives to make constructive proposals, the employers shall in good time during the course of the consultations:
   (a) supply them with all relevant information and
   (b) in any event notify them in writing of:
        (i)   the reasons for the projected redundancies;
        (ii) the number and categories of workers to be made redundant;
        (iii) the number and categories of workers normally employed;
        (iv) the period over which the projected redundancies are to be effected;
        (v)   the criteria proposed for the selection of the workers to be made redundant in so far as national legislation and/or practice confers the power therefore upon the employer;
        (vi) the method for calculating any redundancy payments other than those arising out of national legislation and/or practice.

   The employer shall forward to the competent public authority a copy of, at least, the elements of the written communication which are provided for in the first subparagraph, point (b), subpoints (i) to (v).

4. The obligations laid down in paragraphs 1, 2 and 3 shall apply irrespective of whether the decision regarding collective redundancies is being taken by the employer or by an undertaking controlling the employer.

   In considering alleged breaches of the information, consultation and notification requirements laid down by this Directive, account shall not be taken of any defence on the part of the employer on the ground that the necessary information has not been provided to the employer by the undertaking which took the decision leading to collective redundancies.

SECTION III
PROCEDURE FOR COLLECTIVE REDUNDANCIES

Article 3

1. Employers shall notify the competent public authority in writing of any projected collective redundancies.

   However, Member States may provide that in the case of planned collective redundancies arising from termination of the establishment's activities as a result of a judicial decision, the employer shall be obliged to notify the competent public authority in writing only if the latter so requests.

Where the projected collective redundancy concerns members of the crew of a seagoing vessel, the employer shall notify the competent authority of the State of the flag which the vessel flies.

This notification shall contain all relevant information concerning the projected collective redundancies and the consultations with workers' representatives provided for in Article 2, and particularly the reasons for the redundancies, the number of workers to be made redundant, the number of workers normally employed and the period over which the redundancies are to be effected.

2. Employers shall forward to the workers' representatives a copy of the notification provided for in paragraph 1.

The workers' representatives may send any comments they may have to the competent public authority.

Article 4

1. Projected collective redundancies notified to the competent public authority shall take effect not earlier than 30 days after the notification referred to in Article 3(1) without prejudice to any provisions governing individual rights with regard to notice of dismissal. Member States may grant the competent public authority the power to reduce the period provided for in the preceding subparagraph.

2. The period provided for in paragraph 1 shall be used by the competent public authority to seek solutions to the problems raised by the projected collective redundancies.

3. Where the initial period provided for in paragraph 1 is shorter than 60 days, Member States may grant the competent public authority the power to extend the initial period to 60 days following notification where the problems raised by the projected collective redundancies are not likely to be solved within the initial period.

Member States may grant the competent public authority wider powers of extension. The employer must be informed of the extension and the grounds for it before expiry of the initial period provided for in paragraph 1.

4. Member States need not apply this Article to collective redundancies arising from termination of the establishment's activities where this is the result of a judicial decision.

SECTION IV
FINAL PROVISIONS

Article 5

This Directive shall not affect the right of Member States to apply or to introduce laws, regulations or administrative provisions which are more favourable to workers or to promote or to allow the application of collective agreements more favourable to workers.

Article 6

Member States shall ensure that judicial and/or administrative procedures for the enforcement of obligations under this Directive are available to the workers' representatives and/or workers.

Article 7

Member States shall forward to the Commission the text of any fundamental provisions of national law already adopted or being adopted in the area governed by this Directive.

Article 8

1. The Directives listed in Annex I, Part A, are hereby repealed without prejudice to the obligations of the Member States concerning the deadlines for transposition of the said Directive set out in Annex I, Part B.

2. References to the repealed Directives shall be construed as references to this Directive and shall be read in accordance with the correlation table in Annex II.

Article 9

This Directive shall enter into force on the 20th day following its publication in the *Official Journal of the European Communities*.

Article 10

This Directive is addressed to the Member States.

ANNEX I

PART A

Repealed Directives (referred to by Article 8)
Council Directive 75/129/EEC and its following amendment: Council Directive 92/56/EEC.

PART B

DEADLINES FOR TRANSPOSITION INTO NATIONAL LAW

(referred to by Article 8)

Directive	Deadline for transposition
75/129/EEC (OJ L48, 22.2.1975, p. 29)	19 February 1977
92/56/EEC (OJ L245, 26.8.1992, p. 3)	24 June 1994

ANNEX II

CORRELATION TABLE

Directive 75/129/EEC	This Directive
Article 1(1), first subparagraph, point (a), first indent, point 1	Article 1(1),first subparagraph, point (a)(i), first indent
Article 1(1), first subparagraph, point (a), first indent, point 2	Article 1(1),first subparagraph, point (a)(i), second indent
Article 1(1), first subparagraph, point (a), first indent, point 3	Article 1(1),first subparagraph, point (a)(i), third indent
Article 1(1), first subparagraph, point (a), second indent	Article 1(1),first subparagraph, point (a)(ii)
Article 1(1), first subparagraph, point (b)	Article 1(1), first subparagraph, point (b)
Article 1(1), second subparagraph	Article 1(1), second subparagraph
Article 1(2)	Article 1(2)
Article 2	Article 2
Article 3	Article 3
Article 4	Article 4
Article 5	Article 5
Article 5a	Article 6
Article 6(1)	—
Article 6(2)	Article 7
Article 7	—
—	Article 8
—	Article 9
—	Article 10
—	Annex I
—	Annex II

COUNCIL DIRECTIVE (EC) No 1999/70 of 28 JUNE 1999
concerning the framework agreement on fixed-term work concluded by ETUC, UNICE and CEEP
[1999] OJ L175/43

THE COUNCIL OF THE EUROPEAN UNION,

Having regard to the Treaty establishing the European Community, and in particular Article 139(2) thereof,

Having regard to the proposal from the Commission,

Whereas:

(1) Following the entry into force of the Treaty of Amsterdam the provisions of the Agreement on social policy annexed to the Protocol on social policy, annexed to the Treaty establishing the European Community have been incorporated into Articles 136 to 139 of the Treaty establishing the European Community;

(2) Management and labour (the social partners) may, in accordance with Article 139(2) of the Treaty, request jointly that agreements at Community level be implemented by a Council decision on a proposal from the Commission;

(3) Point 7 of the Community Charter of the Fundamental Social Rights of Workers provides, *inter alia*, that 'the completion of the internal market must lead to an improvement in the living and working conditions of workers in the European Community. This process must result from an approximation of these conditions while the improvement is being maintained, as regards in particular forms of employment other than open-ended contracts, such as fixed-term contracts, part-time working, temporary-work and seasonal work';

(4) The Council has been unable to reach a decision on the proposal for a Directive on certain employment relationships with regard to distortions of competition, nor on the proposal for a Directive on certain employment relationships with regard to working conditions;

(5) The conclusions of the Essen European Council stressed the need to take measures with a view to 'increasing the employment-intensiveness of growth, in particular by a more flexible organisation of work in a way which fulfils both the wishes of employees and the requirements of competition';

(6) The Council Resolution of 9 February 1999 on the 1999 Employment Guidelines invites the social partners at all appropriate levels to negotiate agreements to modernise the organisation of work, including flexible working arrangements, with the aim of making under-takings productive and competitive and achieving the required balance between flexibility and security;

(7) The Commission, in accordance with Article 3(2) of the Agreement on social policy, has consulted management and labour on the possible direction of Community action with regard to flexible working time and job security;

(8) The Commission, considering after such consultation that Community action was desirable, once again consulted management and labour on the substance of the envisaged proposal in accordance with Article 3(3) of the said Agreement;

(9) The general cross-industry organisations, namely the Union of Industrial and Employers' Confederations of Europe (UNICE), the European Centre of Enterprises with Public Participation (CEEP) and the European Trade Union Confederation (ETUC), informed the Commission in a joint letter dated 23 March 1998 of their desire to initiate the procedure provided for in Article 4 of the said Agreement; they asked the Commission, in a joint letter, for a further period of three months; the Commission complied with this request extending the negotiation period to 30 March 1999;

(10) The said cross-industry organisations on 18 March 1999 concluded a framework agreement on fixed-term work; they forwarded to the Commission their joint request to implement the framework agreement by a Council Decision on a proposal from the Commission, in accordance with Article 4(2) of the Agreement on social policy;

(11) The Council, in its Resolution of 6 December 1994 on 'certain aspects for a European Union social policy: a contribution to economic and social convergence in the Union',

asked management and labour to make use of the opportunities for concluding agreements, since they are as a rule closer to social reality and to social problems;

(12) The signatory parties, in the preamble to the framework agreement on part-time work concluded on 6 June 1997, announced their intention to consider the need for similar agreements relating to other forms of flexible work;

(13) Management and labour wished to give particular attention to fixed-term work, while at the same time indicating that it was their intention to consider the need for a similar agreement relating to temporary agency work;

(14) The signatory parties wished to conclude a framework agreement on fixed-term work setting out the general principles and minimum requirements for fixed-term employment contracts and employment relationships; they have demonstrated their desire to improve the quality of fixed-term work by ensuring the application of the principle of non-discrimination, and to establish a framework to prevent abuse arising from the use of successive fixed-term employment contracts or relationships;

(15) The proper instrument for implementing the framework agreement is a directive within the meaning of Article 249 of the Treaty; it therefore binds the Member States as to the result to be achieved, whilst leaving them the choice of form and methods;

(16) In accordance with the principles of subsidiarity and proportionality as set out in Article 5 of the Treaty, the objectives of this Directive cannot be sufficiently achieved by the Member States and can therefore be better achieved by the Community; this Directive limits itself to the minimum required for the attainment of those objectives and does not go beyond what is necessary for that purpose;

(17) As regards terms used in the framework agreement but not specifically defined therein, this Directive allows Member States to define such terms in conformity with national law or practice as is the case for other Directives on social matters using similar terms, provided that the definitions in question respect the content of the framework agreement;

(18) The Commission has drafted its proposal for a Directive, in accordance with its Communication of 14 December 1993 concerning the application of the agreement on social policy and its Communication of 20 May 1998 on adapting and promoting the social dialogue at Community level, taking into account the representative status of the contracting parties, their mandate and the legality of each clause of the framework agreement; the contracting parties together have a sufficiently representative status;

(19) The Commission informed the European Parliament and the Economic and Social Committee by sending them the text of the agreement, accompanied by its proposal for a Directive and the explanatory memorandum, in accordance with its communication concerning the implementation of the Protocol on social policy;

(20) On 6 May 1999 the European Parliament adopted a Resolution on the framework agreement between the social partners;

(21) The implementation of the framework agreement contributes to achieving the objectives in Article 136 of the Treaty,

HAS ADOPTED THIS DIRECTIVE:

Article 1

The purpose of the Directive is to put into effect the frame-work agreement on fixed-term contracts concluded on 18 March 1999 between the general cross-industry organisations (ETUC, UNICE and CEEP) annexed hereto.

Article 2

Member States shall bring into force the laws, regulations and administrative provisions necessary to comply with this Directive by 10 July 2001*, or shall ensure that, by that date at the latest, management and labour have introduced the necessary measures by agreement, the Member States being required to take any necessary measures to enable them at any time to be in a position to guarantee the results imposed by this Directive. They shall forthwith inform the Commission thereof.

Member States may have a maximum of one more year, if necessary, and following consultation with management and labour, to take account of special difficulties or implementation by a collective agreement. They shall inform the Commission forthwith in such circumstances.

When Member States adopt the provisions referred to in the first paragraph, these shall contain a reference to this Directive or shall be accompanied by such reference at the time of their official publication. The procedure for such reference shall be adopted by the Member States.

Article 3

This Directive shall enter into force on the day of its publication in the *Official Journal of the European Communities*.

Article 4

This Directive is addressed to the Member States.

Note

*Corrected by Corrigendum OJ L 244, 16.9.1999, p. 64 (1999/70/EC).

ANNEX

ETUC-UNICE-CEEP

FRAMEWORK AGREEMENT ON FIXED-TERM WORK

Preamble

This framework agreement illustrates the role that the social partners can play in the European employment strategy agreed at the 1997 Luxembourg extraordinary summit and, following the framework agreement on part-time work, represents a further contribution towards achieving a better balance between 'flexibility in working time and security for workers'.

The parties to this agreement recognise that contracts of an indefinite duration are, and will continue to be, the general form of employment relationship between employers and workers. They also recognise that fixed-term employment contracts respond, in certain circumstances, to the needs of both employers and workers.

This agreement sets out the general principles and minimum requirements relating to fixed-term work, recognising that their detailed application needs to take account of the realities of specific national, sectoral and seasonal situations. It illustrates the willingness of the Social Partners to establish a general framework for ensuring equal treatment for fixed-term workers by protecting them against discrimination and for using fixed-term employment contracts on a basis acceptable to employers and workers.

This agreement applies to fixed-term workers with the exception of those placed by a temporary-work agency at the disposition of a user enterprise. It is the intention of the parties to consider the need for a similar agreement relating to temporary agency work.

This agreement relates to the employment conditions of fixed-term workers, recognising that matters relating to statutory social security are for decision by the Member States. In this respect the Social Partners note the Employment Declaration of the Dublin European Council in 1996 which emphasised inter alia, the need to develop more employment-friendly social security systems by 'developing social protection systems capable of adapting to new patterns of work and providing appropriate protection to those engaged in such work'. The parties to this agreement reiterate the view expressed in the 1997 part-time agreement that Member States should give effect to this Declaration without delay.

In addition, it is also recognised that innovations in occupational social protection systems are necessary in order to adapt them to current conditions, and in particular to provide for the transferability of rights.

The ETUC, UNICE and CEEP request the Commission to submit this framework agreement to the Council for a decision making these requirements binding in the Member States which are party to the Agreement on social policy annexed to the Protocol (No 14) on social policy annexed to the Treaty establishing the European Community.

The parties to this agreement ask the Commission, in its proposal to implement the agreement, to request Member States to adopt the laws, regulations and administrative provisions necessary to comply with the Council Decision within two years from its adoption or ensure that the social partners establish the necessary measures by way of agreement by the end of this period. Member States may, if necessary and following consultation with the social partners, and in order to take account of particular difficulties or implementation by collective agreement have up to a maximum of one additional year to comply with this provision.

The parties to this agreement request that the social partners are consulted prior to any legislative, regulatory or administrative initiative taken by a Member State to conform to the present agreement.

Without prejudice to the role of national courts and the Court of Justice, the parties to this agreement request that any matter relating to the interpretation of this agreement at European level should in the first instance be referred by the Commission to them for an opinion.

General considerations

1. Having regard to the Agreement on social policy annexed to the Protocol (No 14) on social policy annexed to the Treaty establishing the European Community, and in particular Article 3.4 and 4.2 thereof;

2. Whereas Article 4.2 of the Agreement on social policy provides that agreements concluded at Community level may be implemented, at the joint request of the signatory parties, by a Council decision on a proposal from the Commission;

3. Whereas, in its second consultation document on flexibility in working time and security for workers, the Commission announced its intention to propose a legally-binding Community measure;

4. Whereas in its opinion on the proposal for a Directive on part-time work, the European Parliament invited the Commission to submit immediately proposals for directives on other forms of flexible work, such as fixed-term work and temporary agency work;

5. Whereas in the conclusions of the extraordinary summit on employment adopted in Luxembourg, the European Council invited the social partners to negotiate agreements to 'modernise the organisation of work, including flexible working arrangements, with the aim of making undertakings productive and competitive and achieving the required balance between flexibility and security';

6. Whereas employment contracts of an indefinite duration are the general form of employment relationships and contribute to the quality of life of the workers concerned and improve performance;

7. Whereas the use of fixed-term employment contracts based on objective reasons is a way to prevent abuse;

8. Whereas fixed-term employment contracts are a feature of employment in certain sectors, occupations and activities which can suit both employers and workers;

9. Whereas more than half of fixed-term workers in the European Union are women and this agreement can therefore contribute to improving equality of opportunities between women and men;

10. Whereas this agreement refers back to Member States and social partners for the arrangements for the application of its general principles, minimum requirements and provisions, in order to take account of the situation in each Member State and the circumstances of particular sectors and occupations, including the activities of a seasonal nature;

11. Whereas this agreement takes into consideration the need to improve social policy requirements, to enhance the competitiveness of the Community economy and to avoid imposing administrative, financial and legal constraints in a way which would hold back the creation and development of small and medium-sized undertakings;

12. Whereas the social partners are best placed to find solutions that correspond to the needs of both employers and workers and shall therefore be given a special role in the implementation and application of this agreement.

THE SIGNATORY PARTIES HAVE AGREED THE FOLLOWING

Purpose (clause 1)

The purpose of this framework agreement is to:

(a) improve the quality of fixed-term work by ensuring the application of the principle of non-discrimination;

(b) establish a framework to prevent abuse arising from the use of successive fixed-term employment contracts or relationships.

Scope (clause 2)

1. This agreement applies to fixed-term workers who have an employment contract or employment relationship as defined in law, collective agreements or practice in each Member State.
2. Member States after consultation with the social partners and/or the social partners may provide that this agreement does not apply to:
   (a) initial vocational training relationships and apprenticeship schemes;
   (b) employment contracts and relationships which have been concluded within the framework of a specific public or publicly-supported training, integration and vocational retraining programme.

Definitions (clause 3)

1. For the purpose of this agreement the term 'fixed-term worker' means a person having an employment contract or relationship entered into directly between an employer and a worker where the end of the employment contract or relationship is determined by objective conditions such as reaching a specific date, completing a specific task, or the occurrence of a specific event.
2. For the purpose of this agreement, the term 'comparable permanent worker' means a worker with an employment contract or relationship of indefinite duration, in the same establishment, engaged in the same or similar work/occupation, due regard being given to qualifications/skills.
   Where there is no comparable permanent worker in the same establishment, the comparison shall be made by reference to the applicable collective agreement, or where there is no applicable collective agreement, in accordance with national law, collective agreements or practice.

Principle of non-discrimination (clause 4)

1. In respect of employment conditions, fixed-term workers shall not be treated in a less favourable manner than comparable permanent workers solely because they have a fixed-term contract or relation unless different treatment is justified on objective grounds.
2. Where appropriate, the principle of pro rata temporis shall apply.
3. The arrangements for the application of this clause shall be defined by the Member States after consultation with the social partners and/or the social partners, having regard to Community law and national law, collective agreements and practice.
4. Period of service qualifications relating to particular conditions of employment shall be the same for fixed-term workers as for permanent workers except where different length-of service qualifications are justified on objective grounds.

Measures to prevent abuse (clause 5)

1. To prevent abuse arising from the use of successive fixed-term employment contracts or relationships, Member States, after consultation with social partners in accordance with national law, collective agreements or practice, and/or the social partners, shall, where there are no equivalent legal measures to prevent abuse, introduce in a manner which takes account of the needs of specific sectors and/or categories of workers, one or more of the following measures:
   (a) objective reasons justifying the renewal of such contracts or relationships;
   (b) the maximum total duration of successive fixed-term employment contracts or relationships;
   (c) the number of renewals of such contracts or relationships.
2. Member States after consultation with the social partners and/or the social partners shall, where appropriate, determine under what conditions fixed-term employment contracts or relationships:
   (a) shall be regarded as 'successive'
   (b) shall be deemed to be contracts or relationships of indefinite duration.

Information and employment opportunities (clause 6)

1. Employers shall inform fixed-term workers about vacancies which become available in the undertaking or establishment to ensure that they have the same opportunity to secure permanent positions as other workers. Such information may be provided by way of a general announcement at a suitable place in the undertaking or establishment.

2. As far as possible, employers should facilitate access by fixed-term workers to appropriate training opportunities to enhance their skills, career development and occupational mobility.

Information and consultation (clause 7)

1. Fixed-term workers shall be taken into consideration in calculating the threshold above which workers' representative bodies provided for in national and Community law may be constituted in the undertaking as required by national provisions.
2. The arrangements for the application of clause 7.1 shall be defined by Member States after consultation with the social partners and/or the social partners in accordance with national law, collective agreements or practice and having regard to clause 4.1.
3. As far as possible, employers should give consideration to the provision of appropriate information to existing workers' representative bodies about fixed-term work in the undertaking.

Provisions on implementation (clause 8)

1. Member States and/or the social partners can maintain or introduce more favourable provisions for workers than set out in this agreement.
2. This agreement shall be without prejudice to any more specific Community provisions, and in particular Community provisions concerning equal treatment or opportunities for men and women.
3. Implementation of this agreement shall not constitute valid grounds for reducing the general level of protection afforded to workers in the field of the agreement.
4. The present agreement does not prejudice the right of the social partners to conclude at the appropriate level, including European level, agreements adapting and/or complementing the provisions of this agreement in a manner which will take note of the specific needs of the social partners concerned.
5. The prevention and settlement of disputes and grievances arising from the application of this agreement shall be dealt with in accordance with national law, collective agreements and practice.
6. The signatory parties shall review the application of this agreement five years after the date of the Council decision if requested by one of the parties to this agreement.

COUNCIL AND PARLIAMENT DIRECTIVE (EC) No 2002/14
of 11 MARCH 2002
establishing a general framework for informing and consulting employees in the European Community
[2000] OJ L80/29

THE EUROPEAN PARLIAMENT AND THE COUNCIL OF THE EUROPEAN UNION,
Having regard to the Treaty establishing the European Community, and in particular Article 137(2) thereof,
Having regard to the proposal from the Commission,
Having regard to the opinion of the Economic and Social Committee,
Having regard to the opinion of the Committee of the Regions,
Acting in accordance with the procedure referred to in Article 251, and in the light of the joint text approved by the Conciliation Committee on 23 January 2002,
Whereas:
(1) Pursuant to Article 136 of the Treaty, a particular objective of the Community and the Member States is to promote social dialogue between management and labour.
(2) Point 17 of the Community Charter of Fundamental Social Rights of Workers provides, inter alia, that information, consultation and participation for workers must be developed along appropriate lines, taking account of the practices in force in different Member States.
(3) The Commission consulted management and labour at Community level on the possible direction of Community action on the information and consultation of employees in undertakings within the Community.

(4) Following this consultation, the Commission considered that Community action was advisable and again consulted management and labour on the contents of the planned proposal; management and labour have presented their opinions to the Commission.

(5) Having completed this second stage of consultation, management and labour have not informed the Commission of their wish to initiate the process potentially leading to the conclusion of an agreement.

(6) The existence of legal frameworks at national and Community level intended to ensure that employees are involved in the affairs of the undertaking employing them and in decisions which affect them has not always prevented serious decisions affecting employees from being taken and made public without adequate procedures having been implemented beforehand to inform and consult them.

(7) There is a need to strengthen dialogue and promote mutual trust within undertakings in order to improve risk anticipation, make work organisation more flexible and facilitate employee access to training within the undertaking while maintaining security, make employees aware of adaptation needs, increase employees' availability to undertake measures and activities to increase their employability, promote employee involvement in the operation and future of the undertaking and increase its competitiveness.

(8) There is a need, in particular, to promote and enhance information and consultation on the situation and likely development of employment within the undertaking and, where the employer's evaluation suggests that employment within the undertaking may be under threat, the possible anticipatory measures envisaged, in particular in terms of employee training and skill development, with a view to offsetting the negative developments or their consequences and increasing the employability and adaptability of the employees likely to be affected.

(9) Timely information and consultation is a prerequisite for the success of the restructuring and adaptation of undertakings to the new conditions created by globalisation of the economy, particularly through the development of new forms of organisation of work.

(10) The Community has drawn up and implemented an employment strategy based on the concepts of 'anticipation', 'prevention' and 'employability', which are to be incorporated as key elements into all public policies likely to benefit employment, including the policies of individual undertakings, by strengthening the social dialogue with a view to promoting change compatible with preserving the priority objective of employment.

(11) Further development of the internal market must be properly balanced, maintaining the essential values on which our societies are based and ensuring that all citizens benefit from economic development.

(12) Entry into the third stage of economic and monetary union has extended and accelerated the competitive pressures at European level. This means that more supportive measures are needed at national level.

(13) The existing legal frameworks for employee information and consultation at Community and national level tend to adopt an excessively a posteriors approach to the process of change, neglect the economic aspects of decisions taken and do not contribute either to genuine anticipation of employment developments within the undertaking or to risk prevention.

(14) All of these political, economic, social and legal developments call for changes to the existing legal framework providing for the legal and practical instruments enabling the right to be informed and consulted to be exercised.

(15) This Directive is without prejudice to national systems regarding the exercise of this right in practice where those entitled to exercise it are required to indicate their wishes collectively.

(16) This Directive is without prejudice to those systems which provide for the direct involvement of employees, as long as they are always free to exercise the right to be informed and consulted through their representatives.

(17) Since the objectives of the proposed action, as outlined above, cannot be adequately achieved by the Member States, in that the object is to establish a framework for employee information and consultation appropriate for the new European context described above, and can therefore, in view of the scale and impact of the proposed action, be better achieved at Community level, the Community may adopt measures

in accordance with the principle of subsidiarity as set out in Article 5 of the Treaty. In accordance with the principle of proportionality, as set out in that Article, this Directive does not go beyond what is necessary in order to achieve these objectives.

(18) The purpose of this general framework is to establish minimum requirements applicable throughout the Community while not preventing Member States from laying down provisions more favourable to employees.

(19) The purpose of this general framework is also to avoid any administrative, financial or legal constraints which would hinder the creation and development of small and medium-sized undertakings. To this end, the scope of this Directive should be restricted, according to the choice made by Member States, to undertakings with at least 50 employees or establishments employing at least 20 employees.

(20) This takes into account and is without prejudice to other national measures and practices aimed at fostering social dialogue within companies not covered by this Directive and within public administrations.

(21) However, on a transitional basis, Member States in which there is no established statutory system of information and consultation of employees or employee representation should have the possibility of further restricting the scope of the Directive as regards the numbers of employees.

(22) A Community framework for informing and consulting employees should keep to a minimum the burden on undertakings or establishments while ensuring the effective exercise of the rights granted.

(23) The objective of this Directive is to be achieved through the establishment of a general framework comprising the principles, definitions and arrangements for information and consultation, which it will be for the Member States to comply with and adapt to their own national situation, ensuring, where appropriate, that management and labour have a leading role by allowing them to define freely, by agreement, the arrangements for informing and consulting employees which they consider to be best suited to their needs and wishes.

(24) Care should be taken to avoid affecting some specific rules in the field of employee information and consultation existing in some national laws, addressed to undertakings or establishments which pursue political, professional, organisational, religious, charitable, educational, scientific or artistic aims, as well as aims involving information and the expression of opinions.

(25) Undertakings and establishments should be protected against disclosure of certain particularly sensitive information.

(26) The employer should be allowed not to inform and consult where this would seriously damage the undertaking or the establishment or where he has to comply immediately with an order issued to him by a regulatory or supervisory body.

(27) Information and consultation imply both rights and obligations for management and labour at undertaking or establishment level.

(28) Administrative or judicial procedures, as well as sanctions that are effective, dissuasive and proportionate in relation to the seriousness of the offence, should be applicable in cases of infringement of the obligations based on this Directive.

(29) This Directive should not affect the provisions, where these are more specific, of Council Directive 98159/EC of 20 July 1998 on the approximation of the laws of the Member States relating to collective redundancies and of Council Directive 2001123/EC of 12 March 2001 on the approximation of the laws of the Member States relating to the safeguarding of employees' rights in the event of transfers of undertakings, businesses or parts of undertakings or businesses.

(30) Other rights of information and consultation, including those arising from Council Directive 94/45/EEC of 22 September 1994 on the establishment of a European Works Council or a procedure in Community-scale undertakings and Community-scale groups of undertakings for the purposes of informing and consulting employees, should not be affected by this Directive.

(31) Implementation of this Directive should not be sufficient grounds for a reduction in the general level of protection of workers in the areas to which it applies,

HAVE ADOPTED THIS DIRECTIVE:

Article 1 Object and principles

1. The purpose of this Directive is to establish a general framework setting out minimum requirements for the right to information and consultation of employees in undertakings or establishments within the Community.
2. The practical arrangements for information and consultation shall be defined and implemented in accordance with national law and industrial relations practices in individual Member States in such a way as to ensure their effectiveness.
3. When defining or implementing practical arrangements for information and consultation, the employer and the employees' representatives shall work in a spirit of cooperation and with due regard for their reciprocal rights and obligations, taking into account the interests both of the undertaking or establishment and of the employees.

Article 2 Definitions

For the purposes of this Directive:
(a) 'undertaking' means a public or private undertaking carrying out an economic activity, whether or not operating for gain, which is located within the territory of the Member States;
(b) 'establishment' means a unit of business defined in accordance with national law and practice, and located within the territory of a Member State, where an economic activity is carried out on an ongoing basis with human and material resources;
(c) 'employer' means the natural or legal person party to employment contracts or employment relationships with employees, in accordance with national law and practice;
(d) 'employee' means any person who, in the Member State concerned, is protected as an employee under national employment law and in accordance with national practice;
(e) 'employees' representatives' means the employees' representatives provided for by national laws and/or practices;
(f) 'information' means transmission by the employer to the employees' representatives of data in order to enable them to acquaint themselves with the subject matter and to examine it;
(g) 'consultation' means the exchange of views and establishment of dialogue between the employees' representatives and the employer.

Article 3 Scope

1. This Directive shall apply, according to the choice made by Member States, to:
(a) undertakings employing at least 50 employees in any one Member State, or
(b) establishments employing at least 20 employees in any one Member State.
Member States shall determine the method for calculating the thresholds of employees employed.
2. In conformity with the principles and objectives of this Directive, Member States may lay down particular provisions applicable to undertakings or establishments which pursue directly and essentially political, professional organisational, religious, charitable, educational, scientific or artistic aims, as well as aims involving information and the expression of opinions, on condition that, at the date of entry into force of this Directive, provisions of that nature already exist in national legislation.

Article 4 Practical arrangements for information and consultation

1. In accordance with the principles set out in Article 1 and without prejudice to any provisions and/or practices in force more favourable to employees, the Member States shall determine the practical arrangements for exercising the right to information and consultation at the appropriate level in accordance with this Article.
2. Information and consultation shall cover:
(a) information on the recent and probable development of the undertaking's or the establishment's activities and economic situation;
(b) information and consultation on the situation, structure and probable development of employment within the undertaking or establishment and on any anticipatory measures envisaged, in particular where there is a threat to employment;

(c)   information and consultation on decisions likely to lead to substantial changes in work organisation or in contractual relations, including those covered by the Community provisions referred to in Article 9(1).

3.   Information shall be given at such time, in such fashion and with such content as are appropriate to enable, in particular, employees' representatives to conduct an adequate study and, where necessary, prepare for consultation.

4.   Consultation shall take place:

    (a)   while ensuring that the timing, method and content thereof are appropriate;

    (b)   at the relevant level of management and representation, depending on the subject under discussion;

    (c)   on the basis of information supplied by the employer in accordance with Article 2(f) and of the opinion which the employees' representatives are entitled to formulate;

    (d)   in such a way as to enable employees' representatives to meet the employer and obtain a response, and the reasons for that response, to any opinion they might formulated

    (e)   with a view to reaching an agreement on decisions within the scope of the employer's powers referred to in paragraph 2(c).

Article 5   Information and consultation deriving from an agreement

Member States may entrust management and labour at the appropriate level, including at undertaking or establishment level, with defining freely and at any time through negotiated agreement the practical arrangements for informing and consulting employees. These agreements, and agreements existing on the date laid down in Article 11, as well as any subsequent renewals of such agreements, may establish, while respecting the principles set out in Article 1 and subject to conditions and limitations laid down by the Member States, provisions which are different from those referred to in Article 4.

Article 6   Confidential information

1.   Member States shall provide that, within the conditions and limits laid down by national legislation, the employees' representatives, and any experts who assist them, are not authorised to reveal to employees or to third parties, any information which, in the legitimate interest of the undertaking or establishment, has expressly been provided to them in confidence. This obligation shall continue to apply, wherever the said representatives or experts are, even after expiry of their terms of office. However, a Member State may authorise the employees' representatives and anyone assisting them to pass on confidential information to employees and to third parties bound by an obligation of confidentiality.

2.   Member States shall provide, in specific cases and within the conditions and limits laid down by national legislation, that the employer is not obliged to communicate information or under-take consultation when the nature of that information or consultation is such that, according to objective criteria, it would seriously harm the functioning of the undertaking or establishment or would be prejudicial to it.

3.   Without prejudice to existing national procedures, Member States shall provide for administrative or judicial review procedures for the case where the employer requires confidentiality or does not provide the information in accordance with paragraphs 1 and 2. They may also provide for procedures intended to safeguard the confidentiality of the information in question.

Article 7   Protection of employees' representatives

Member States shall ensure that employees' representatives, when carrying out their functions, enjoy adequate protection and guarantees to enable them to perform properly the duties which have been assigned to them.

Article 8   Protection of rights

1.   Member States shall provide for appropriate measures in the event of non-compliance with this Directive by the employer or the employees' representatives. In particular, they shall ensure that adequate administrative or judicial procedures are available to enable the obligations deriving from this Directive to be enforced.

2.   Member States shall provide for adequate sanctions to be applicable in the event of infringement of this Directive by the employer or the employees' representatives. These sanctions must be effective, proportionate and dissuasive.

Article 9 Link between this Directive and other Community and national provisions

1.   This Directive shall be without prejudice to the specific information and consultation procedures set out in Article 2 of Directive 98/59/EC and Article 7 of Directive 2001/23 EC.
2.   This Directive shall be without prejudice to provisions adopted in accordance with Directives 94/45/EC and 97/74/EC.
3.   This Directive shall be without prejudice to other rights to information, consultation and participation under national law,
4.   Implementation of this Directive shall not be sufficient grounds for any regression in relation to the situation which already prevails in each Member State and in relation to the general level of protection of workers in the areas to which it applies.

Article 10 Transitional provisions

Notwithstanding Article 3, a Member State in which there is, at the date of entry into force of this Directive, no general, permanent and statutory system of information and consultation of employees, nor a general, permanent and statutory system of employee representation at the workplace allowing employees to be represented for that purpose, may limit the application of the national provisions implementing this Directive to:
(a)   undertakings employing at least 150 employees or establishments employing at least 100 employees until 23 March 2007, and
(b)   undertakings employing at least 100 employees or establishments employing at least 50 employees during the year following the date in point (a).

Article 11 Transposition

1.   Member States shall adopt the laws, regulations and administrative provisions necessary to comply with this Directive not later than 23 March 2005 or shall ensure that management and labour introduce by that date the required provisions by way of agreement, the Member States being obliged to take all necessary steps enabling them to guarantee the results imposed by this Directive at all times. They shall forthwith inform the Commission thereof.
2.   Where Member States adopt these measures, they shall contain a reference to this Directive or shall be accompanied by such reference on the occasion of their official publication. The methods of making such reference shall be laid down by the Member States.

Article 12 Review by the Commission

Not later than 23 March 2007, the Commission shall, in consultation with the Member States and the social partners at Community level, review the application of this Directive with a view to proposing any necessary amendments.

Article 13 Entry into force

This Directive shall enter into force on the day of its publication in the *Official Journal of the European Communities*.

Article 14 Addresses

This Directive is addressed to the Member States.

COUNCIL AND PARLIAMENT DIRECTIVE (EC) No 2003/88 of 4 NOVEMBER 2003
concerning certain aspects of the organisation of working time
[2003] OJ L299/9

THE EUROPEAN PARLIAMENT AND THE COUNCIL, OF THE EUROPEAN UNION,
Having regard to the Treaty establishing the European Community, and in particular Article 137(2) thereof,
Having regard to the proposal from the Commission,

Having regard to the opinion of the European Economic and Social Committee,

Having consulted the Committee of the Regions,

Acting in accordance with the procedure referred to in Article 251 of the Treaty,

Whereas:

(1) Council Directive 93/104/EC of 23 November 1993, concerning certain aspects of the organisation of working time, which lays down minimum safety and health requirements for the organisation of working time, in respect of periods of daily rest, breaks, weekly rest, maximum weekly working time, annual leave and aspects of night work, shift work and patterns of work, has been significantly amended. In order to clarify matters, a codification of the provisions in question should be drawn up.

(2) Article 137 of the Treaty provides that the Community is to support and complement the activities of the Member States with a view to improving the working environment to protect workers' health and safety. Directives adopted on the basis of that Article are to avoid imposing administrative, financial and legal constraints in a way which would hold back the creation and development of small and medium-sized undertakings.

(3) The provisions of Council Directive 89/391/EEC of 12 June 1989 on the introduction of measures to encourage improvements in the safety and health of workers at work remain fully applicable to the areas covered by this Directive without prejudice to more stringent and/or specific provisions contained herein.

(4) The improvement of workers' safety, hygiene and health at work is an objective which should not be subordinated to purely economic considerations.

(5) All workers should have adequate rest periods. The concept of 'rest' must be expressed in units of time, i.e. in days, hours and/or fractions thereof. Community workers must be granted minimum daily, weekly and annual periods of rest and adequate breaks. It is also necessary in this context to place a maximum limit on weekly working hours.

(6) Account should be taken of the principles of the International Labour Organisation with regard to the organisation of working time, including those relating to night work.

(7) Research has shown that the human body is more sensitive at night to environmental disturbances and also to certain burdensome forms of work organisation and that long periods of night work can be detrimental to the health of workers and can endanger safety at the workplace.

(8) There is a need to limit the duration of periods of night work, including overtime, and to provide for employers who regularly use night workers to bring this information to the attention of the competent authorities if they so request.

(9) It is important that night workers should be entitled to a free health assessment prior to their assignment and thereafter at regular intervals and that whenever possible they should be transferred to day work for which they are suited if they suffer from health problems.

(10) The situation of night and shift workers requires that the level of safety and health protection should be adapted to the nature of their work and that the organisation and functioning of protection and prevention services and resources should be efficient.

(11) Specific working conditions may have detrimental effects on the safety and health of workers. The organisation of work according to a certain pattern must take account of the general principle of adapting work to the worker.

(12) A European Agreement in respect of the working time of seafarers has been put into effect by means of Council Directive 1999163/EC of 21 June 1999 concerning the Agreement on the organisation of working time of seafarers concluded by the European Community Shipowners' Association (ECSA) and the Federation of Transport Workers' Unions in the European Union (FST) based on Article 139(2) of the Treaty. Accordingly, the provisions of this Directive should not apply to seafarers.

(13) In the case of those 'share-fishermen' who are employees, it is for the Member States to determine, pursuant to this Directive, the conditions for entitlement to, and granting of, annual leave, including the arrangements for payments.

(14) Specific standards laid down in other Community instruments relating, for example, to rest periods, working time, annual leave and night work for certain categories of workers should take precedence over the provisions of this Directive.

(15) In view of the question likely to be raised by the organisation of working time within an undertaking, it appears desirable to provide for flexibility in the application of certain provisions of this Directive, whilst ensuring compliance with the principles of protecting the safety and health of workers.

(16) It is necessary to provide that certain provisions may be subject to derogations implemented, according to the case, by the Member States or the two sides of industry. As a general rule, in the event of a derogation, the workers concerned must be given equivalent compensatory rest periods.

(17) This Directive should not affect the obligations of the Member States concerning the deadlines for transposition of the Directives set out in Annex 1, part B,

HAVE ADOPTED THIS DIRECTIVE:

CHAPTER 1
SCOPE AND DEFINITIONS

Article 1   Purpose and scope

1. This Directive lays down minimum safety and health requirements for the organisation of working time.
2. This Directive applies to:
   (a)   minimum periods of daily rest, weekly rest and annual leave, to breaks and maximum weekly working time; and
   (b)   certain aspects of night work, shift work and patterns of work.
3. This Directive shall apply to all sectors of activity, both public and private, within the meaning of Article 2 of Directive 89/391/EEC, without prejudice to Articles 14, 17, 18 and 19 of this Directive.
   This Directive shall not apply to seafarers, as defined in Directive 1999/63/EC without prejudice to Article 2(8) of this Directive.
4. The provisions of Directive 89/391/EEC are fully applicable to the matters referred to in paragraph 2, without prejudice to more stringent and/or specific provisions contained in this Directive.

Article 2 Definitions

For the purposes of this Directive, the following definitions shall apply:

1. 'working time' means any period during which the worker is working, at the employer's disposal and carrying out his activity or duties, in accordance with national laws and/ or practice;
2. 'rest period' means any period which is not working time;
3. 'night time' means any period of not less than seven hours, as defined by national law, and which must include, in any case, the period between midnight and 5.00;
4. 'night worker' means:
   (a)   on the one hand, any worker, who, during night time, works at least three hours of his daily working time as a normal course; and
   (b)   on the other hand, any worker who is likely during night time to work a certain proportion of his annual working time, as defined at the choice of the Member State concerned:
      (i)   by national legislation, following consultation with the two sides of industry; or
      (ii) by collective agreements or agreements concluded between the two sides of industry at national or regional level;
5. 'shift work' means any method of organising work in shifts whereby workers succeed each other at the same work stations according to a certain pattern, including a rotating pattern, and which may be continuous or discontinuous, entailing the need for workers to work at different times over a given period of days or weeks:
6. 'shift worker' means any worker whose work schedule is part of shift work;
7. 'mobile worker' means any worker employed as a member of travelling or flying personnel by an undertaking which operates transport services for passengers or goods by road, air or inland waterway:
8. 'offshore work' means work performed mainly on or from offshore installations (including drilling rigs), directly or indirectly in connection with the exploration, extraction or exploitation of mineral resources, including hydrocarbons, and diving in connection with such activities, whether performed from an offshore installation or a vessel;

9.   'adequate rest' means that workers have regular rest periods, the duration of which is expressed in units of time and which are sufficiently long and continuous to ensure that, as a result of fatigue or other irregular working patterns, they do not cause injury to themselves, to fellow workers or to others and that they do not damage their health, either in the short term or in the longer term.

CHAPTER 2

MINIMUM REST PERIODS — OTHER ASPECTS OF THE ORGANISATION
OF WORKING TIME

Article 3   Daily rest

Member States shall take the measures necessary to ensure that every worker is entitled to a minimum daily rest period of 11 consecutive hours per 24-hour period.

Article 4   Breaks

Member States shall take the measures necessary to ensure that, where the working day is longer than six hours, every worker is entitled to a rest break, the details of which, including duration and the terms on which it is granted, shall be laid down in collective agreements or agreements between the two sides of industry or, failing that, by national legislation.

Article 5   Weekly rest period

Member States shall take the measures necessary to ensure that, per each seven-day period, every worker is entitled to a minimum uninterrupted rest period of 24 hours plus the 11 hours' daily rest referred to in Article 3.

If objective, technical or work organisation conditions so justify, a minimum rest period of 24 hours may be applied.

Article 6   Maximum weekly working time

Member States shall take the measures necessary to ensure that, in keeping with the need to protect the safety and health of workers:

(a)   the period of weekly working time is limited by means of laws, regulations or administrative provisions or by collective agreements or agreements between the two sides of industry;

(b)   the average working time for each seven-day period, including overtime, does not exceed 48 hours.

Article 7   Annual leave

1.   Member States shall take the measures necessary to ensure that every worker is entitled to paid annual leave of at least four weeks in accordance with the conditions for entitlement to, and granting of, such leave laid down by national legislation and/or practice.

2.   The minimum period of paid annual leave may not be replaced by an allowance in lieu, except where the employment relationship is terminated.

CHAPTER 3

NIGHT WORK — SHIFT WORK — PATTERNS OF WORK

Article 8   Length of night work

Member States shall take the measures necessary to ensure that:

(a)   normal hours of work for night workers do not exceed an average of eight hours in any 24-hour period;

(b)   night workers whose work involves special hazards or heavy physical or mental strain do not work more than eight hours in any period of 24 hours during which they perform night work.

For the purposes of point (b), work involving special hazards or heavy physical or mental strain shall be defined by national legislation and/or practice or by collective agreements or agreements concluded between the two sides of industry, taking account of the specific effects and hazards of night work.

Article 9 Health assessment and transfer of night workers to day work

   1.   Member States shall take the measures necessary to ensure that:

      (a)   night workers are entitled to a free health assessment before their assignment and thereafter at regular intervals;

      (b)   night workers suffering from health problems recognised as being connected with the fact that they perform night work are transferred whenever possible to day work to which they are suited.

   2.   The free health assessment referred to in paragraph 1(a) must comply with medical confidentiality.

   3.   The free health assessment referred to in paragraph 1(a) may be conducted within the national health system.

Article 10 Guarantees for night-time working

Member States may make the work of certain categories of night workers subject to certain guarantees, under conditions laid down by national legislation and/or practice, in the case of workers who incur risks to their safety or health linked to night-time working.

Article 11 Notification of regular use of night workers

Member States shall take the measures necessary to ensure that an employer who regularly uses night workers brings this information to the attention of the competent authorities if they so request.

Article 12 Safety and health protection

Member States shall take the measures necessary to ensure that:

      (a)   night workers and shift workers have safety and health protection appropriate to the nature of their work;

      (b)   appropriate protection and prevention services or facilities with regard to the safety and health of night workers and shift workers are equivalent to those applicable to other workers and are available at all times.

Article 13 Pattern of work

Member States shall take the measures necessary to ensure that an employer who intends to organise work according to a certain pattern takes account of the general principle of adapting work to the worker, with a view, in particular, to alleviating monotonous work and work at a predetermined workrate, depending on the type of activity, and of safety and health requirements, especially as regards breaks during working time.

CHAPTER 4

MISCELLANEOUS PROVISIONS

Article 14 More specific Community provisions

This Directive shall not apply where other Community instruments contain more specific requirements relating to the organisation of working time for certain occupations or occupational activities.

Article 15 More favourable provisions

This Directive shall not affect Member States' right to apply or introduce laws, regulations or administrative provisions more favourable to the protection of the safety and health of workers or to facilitate or permit the application of collective agreements or agreements concluded between the two sides of industry which are more favourable to the protection of the safety and health of workers.

Article 16 Reference periods

Member States may lay down:

      (a)   for the application of Article 5 (weekly rest period), a reference period not exceeding 14 days;

      (b)   for the application of Article 6 (maximum weekly working time), a reference period not exceeding four months,

The periods of paid annual leave, granted in accordance with Article 7, and the periods of sick leave shall not be included or shall be neutral in the calculation of the average;

(c)   for the application of Article 8 (length of night work), a reference period defined after consultation of the two sides of industry or by collective agreements or agreements concluded between the two sides of industry at national or regional level.

If the minimum weekly rest period of 24 hours required by Article 5 falls within that reference period, it shall not be included in the calculation of the average.

CHAPTER 5
DEROGATIONS AND EXCEPTIONS

Article 17 Derogations

1.   With due regard for the general principles of the protection of the safety and health of workers, Member States may derogate from Articles 3 to 6, 8 and 16 when, on account of the specific characteristics of the activity concerned, the duration of the working time is not measured and/or predetermined or can be determined by the workers themselves, and particularly in the case of.

  (a)   managing executives or other persons with autonomous decision-taking powers;
  (b)   family workers; or
  (c)   workers officiating at religious ceremonies in churches and religious communities.

2.   Derogations provided for in paragraphs 3, 4 and 5 may be adopted by means of laws, regulations or administrative provisions or by means of collective agreements or agreements between the two sides of industry provided that the workers concerned are afforded equivalent periods of compensatory rest or that, in exceptional cases in which it is not possible, for objective reasons, to grant such equivalent periods of compensatory rest, the workers concerned are afforded appropriate protection.

3.   In accordance with paragraph 2 of this Article derogations may be made from Articles 3, 4, 5, 8 and 16:

  (a)   in the case of activities where the worker's place of work and his place of residence are distant from one another, including offshore work, or where the worker's different places of work are distant from one another;
  (b)   in the case of security and surveillance activities requiring a permanent presence in order to protect property and persons, particularly security guards and caretakers or security firms;
  (c)   in the case of activities involving the need for continuity of service or production, particularly:
     (i)   services relating to the reception, treatment and/or care provided by hospitals or similar establishments, including the activities of doctors in training, residential institutions and prisons;
     (ii)   dock or airport workers;
     (iii)   press, radio, television, cinematographic production, postal and telecommunications services, ambulance, fire and civil protection services;
     (iv)   gas, water and electricity production, transmission and distribution, household refuse collection and incineration plants;
     (v)   industries in which work cannot be interrupted on technical grounds;
     (vi)   research and development activities;
     (vii) agriculture;
     (viii) workers concerned with the carriage of passengers on regular urban transport services;
  (d)   where there is a foreseeable surge of activity, particularly in:
     (i)   agriculture;
     (ii)   tourism;
     (iii)   postal services;

(e)   in the case of persons working in railway transport:
    (i)   whose activities are intermittent;
    (ii)   who spend their working time on board trains; or
    (iii) whose activities are linked to transport timetables and to ensuring the continuity and regularity of traffic;
(f)   in the circumstances described in Article 5(4) of Directive 891391/EEC;
(g)   in cases of accident or imminent risk of accident.

4.   In accordance with paragraph 2 of this Article derogations may be made from Articles 3 and 5:
(a)   in the case of shift work activities, each time the worker changes shift and cannot take daily and/or weekly rest periods between the end of one shift and the start of the next one;
(b)   in the case of activities involving periods of work split up over the day, particularly those of cleaning staff.

5.   In accordance with paragraph 2 of this Article, derogations may be made from Article 6 and Article 16(b), in the case of doctors in training, in accordance with the provisions set out in the second to the seventh subparagraphs of this paragraph.

With respect to Article 6 derogations referred to in the first subparagraph shall be permitted for a transitional period of five years from 1 August 2004.

Member States may have up to two more years, if necessary, to take account of difficulties in meeting the working time provisions with respect to their responsibilities for the organisation and delivery of health services and medical care. At least six months before the end of the transitional period, the Member State concerned shall inform the Commission giving its reasons, so that the Commission can give an opinion, after appropriate consultations, within the three months following receipt of such information. If the Member State does not follow the opinion of the Commission, it will justify its decision. The notification and justification of the Member State and the opinion of the Commission shall be published in the *Official Journal of the European Union* and forwarded to the European Parliament.

Member States may have an additional period of up to one year, if necessary, to take account of special difficulties in meeting the responsibilities referred to in the third subparagraph. They shall follow the procedure set out in that subparagraph.

Member States shall ensure that in no case will the number of weekly working hours exceed an average of 58 during the first three years of the transitional period, an average of 56 for the following two years and an average of 52 for any remaining period.

The employer shall consult the representatives of the employees in good time with a view to reaching an agreement, wherever possible, on the arrangements applying to the transitional period. Within the limits set out in the fifth subparagraph, such an agreement may cover:
(a)   the average number of weekly hours of work during the transitional period; and
(b)   the measures to be adopted to reduce weekly working hours to an average of 48 by the end of the transitional period.

With respect to Article 16(b) derogations referred to in the first subparagraph shall be permitted provided that the reference period does not exceed 12 months, during the first part of the transitional period specified in the fifth subparagraph, and six months thereafter.

Article 18 Derogations by collective agreements

Derogations may be made from Articles 3, 4, 5, 8 and 16 by means of collective agreements or agreements concluded between the two sides of industry at national or regional level or, in conformity with the rules laid down by them, by means of collective agreements or agreements concluded between the two sides of industry at a lower level.

Member States in which there is no statutory system ensuring the conclusion of collective agreements or agreements concluded between the two sides of industry at national or regional level, on the matters covered by this Directive, or those Member States in which there is a specific legislative framework for this purpose and within the limits thereof, may, in accordance with national legislation and/or practice, allow derogations from Articles 3, 4, 5, 8 and 16 by way of collective agreements or agreements concluded between the two sides of industry at the appropriate collective level.

The derogations provided for in the first and second subparagraphs shall be allowed on condition that equivalent compensating rest periods are granted to the workers concerned or, in exceptional cases where it is not possible for objective reasons to grant such periods, the workers concerned are afforded appropriate protection.

Member States may lay down rules:

(a)   for the application of this Article by the two sides of industry; and

(b)   for the extension of the provisions of collective agreements or agreements concluded in conformity with this Article to other workers in accordance with national legislation and/or practice.

Article 19 Limitations to derogations from reference periods

The option to derogate from Article 16(b), provided for in Article 17(3) and in Article 18, may not result in the establishment of a reference period exceeding six months.

However, Member States shall have the option, subject to compliance with the general principles relating to the protection of the safety and health of workers, of allowing, for objective or technical reasons or reasons concerning the organisation of work, collective agreements or agreements concluded between the two sides of industry to set reference periods in no event exceeding 12 months.

Before 23 November 2003, the Council shall, on the basis of a Commission proposal accompanied by an appraisal report, reexamine the provisions of this Article and decide what action to take.

Article 20 Mobile workers and offshore work

1.   Articles 3, 4, 5 and 8 shall not apply to mobile workers.

   Member States shall, however, take the necessary measures to ensure that such mobile workers are entitled to adequate rest, except in the circumstances laid down in Article 17(3)(f) and (g).

2.   Subject to compliance with the general principles relating to the protection of the safety and health of workers, and provided that there is consultation of representatives of the employer and employees concerned and efforts to encourage all relevant forms of social dialogue, including negotiation if the parties so wish, Member States may, for objective or technical reasons or reasons concerning the organisation of work, extend the reference period referred to in Article 16(b) to 12 months in respect of workers who mainly perform offshore work.

3.   Not later than 1 August 2005 the Commission shall, after consulting the Member States and management and labour at European level, review the operation of the provisions with regard to offshore workers from a health and safety perspective with a view to presenting, if need be, the appropriate modifications.

Article 21 Workers on board seagoing fishing vessels

1.   Articles 3 to 6 and 8 shall not apply to any worker on board a seagoing fishing vessel flying the flag of a Member State.

   Member States shall, however, take the necessary measures to ensure that any worker on board a seagoing fishing vessel flying the flag of a Member State is entitled to adequate rest and to limit the number of hours of work to 48 hours a week on average calculated over a reference period not exceeding 12 months.

2.   Within the limits set out in paragraph 1, second subparagraph, and paragraphs 3 and 4 Member States shall take the necessary measures to ensure that, in keeping with the need to protect the safety and health of such workers:

   (a)   the working hours are limited to a maximum number of hours which shall not be exceeded in a given period of time; or

   (b)   a minimum number of hours of rest are provided within a given period of time.

   The maximum number of hours of work or minimum number of hours of rest shall be specified by law, regulations, administrative provisions or by collective agreements or agreements between the two sides of the industry.

3.   The limits on hours of work or rest shall be either:
     (a)   maximum hours of work which shall not exceed:
           (i)   14 hours in any 24-hour period; and
           (ii)   72 hours in any seven-day period;
           or
     (b)   minimum hours of rest which shall not be less than:
           (i)   10 hours in any 24-hour period; and
           (ii)   77 hours in any seven-day period.
4.   Hours of rest may be divided into no more than two periods, one of which shall be at least six hours in length, and the interval between consecutive periods of rest shall not exceed 14 hours.
5.   In accordance with the general principles of the protection of the health and safety of workers, and for objective or technical reasons or reasons concerning the organisation of work, Member States may allow exceptions, including the establishment of reference periods, to the limits laid down in paragraph 1, second subparagraph, and paragraphs 3 and 4. Such exceptions shall, as far as possible, comply with the standards laid down but may take account of more frequent or longer leave periods or the granting of compensatory leave for the workers. These exceptions may be laid down by means of:
     (a)   laws, regulations or administrative provisions provided there is consultation, where possible, of the representatives of the employers and workers concerned and efforts are made to encourage all relevant forms of social dialogue; or
     (b)   collective agreements or agreements between the two sides of industry.
6.   The master of a seagoing fishing vessel shall have the right to require workers on board to perform any hours of work necessary for. the immediate safety of the vessel, persons on board or cargo, or for the purpose of giving assistance to other vessels or persons in distress at sea.
7.   Members States may provide that workers on board seagoing fishing vessels for which national legislation or practice determines that these vessels are not allowed to operate in a specific period of the calendar year exceeding one month, shall take annual leave in accordance with Article 7 within that period.

Article 22 Miscellaneous provisions

1.   A Member State shall have the option not to apply Article 6, while respecting the general principles of the protection of the safety and health of workers, and provided it takes the necessary measures to ensure that:
     (a)   no employer requires a worker to work more than 48 hours over a seven-day period, calculated as an average for the reference period referred to in Article 16(b), unless he has first obtained the worker's agreement to perform such work:
     (b)   no worker is subjected to any detriment by his employer because he is not willing to give his agreement to perform such work;
     (c)   the employer keeps up-to-date records of all workers who carry out such work;
     (d)   the records are placed at the disposal of the competent authorities, which may, for reasons connected with the safety and/or health of workers, prohibit or restrict the possibility of exceeding the maximum weekly working hours;
     (e)   the employer provides the competent authorities at their request with information on cases in which agreement has been given by workers to perform work exceeding 48 hours over a period of seven days, calculated as an average for the reference period referred to in Article 16(b).
     Before 23 November 2003, the Council shall, on the basis of a Commission proposal accompanied by an appraisal report, reexamine the provisions of this paragraph and decide on what action to take.
2.   Member States shall have the option, as regards the application of Article 7, of making use of a transitional period of not more than three years from 23 November 1996, provided that during that transitional period:
     (a)   every worker receives three weeks' paid annual leave in accordance with the conditions for the entitlement to, and granting of, such leave laid down by national legislation and/or practice: and

(b)   the three-week period of paid annual leave may not be replaced by an allowance in lieu, except where the employment relationship is terminated.

3.   If Member States avail themselves of the options provided for in this Article, they shall forthwith inform the Commission thereof.

CHAPTER 6
FINAL PROVISIONS

Article 23 Level of protection

Without prejudice to the right of Member States to develop, in the light of changing circumstances, different legislative, regulatory or contractual provisions in the field of working time, as long as the minimum requirements provided for in this Directive are complied with, implementation of this Directive shall not constitute valid grounds for reducing the general level of protection afforded to workers.

Article 24 Reports

1.   Member States shall communicate to the Commission the texts of the provisions of national law already adopted or being adopted in the field governed by this Directive.

2.   Member States shall report to the Commission every five years on the practical implementation of the provisions of this Directive, indicating the viewpoints of the two sides of industry.
The Commission shall inform the European Parliament, the Council, the European Economic and Social Committee and the Advisory Committee on Safety, Hygiene and Health Protection at Work thereof.

3.   Every five years from 23 November 1996 the Commission shall submit to the European Parliament, the Council and the European Economic and Social Committee a report on the application of this Directive taking into account Articles 22 and 23 and paragraphs 1 and 2 of this Article.

Article 25 Review of the operation of the provisions with regard to workers on board seagoing fishing vessels

Not later than 1 August 2009 the Commission shall, after consulting the Member States and management and labour at European level, review the operation of the provisions with regard to workers on board seagoing fishing vessels, and, in particular examine whether these provisions remain appropriate, in particular, as far as health and safety are concerned with a view to proposing suitable amendments, if necessary.

Article 26 Review of the operation of the provisions with regard to workers concerned with the carriage of passengers

Not later than 1 August 2005 the Commission shall, after consulting the Member States and management and labour at European level, review the operation of the provisions with regard to workers concerned with the carriage of passengers on regular urban transport services, with a view to presenting, if need be, the appropriate modifications to ensure a coherent and suitable approach in the sector.

Article 27 Repeal

1.   Directive 93/104/EC, as amended by the Directive referred to in Annex 1, part A, shall be repealed, without prejudice to the obligations of the Member States in respect of the deadlines for transposition laid down in Annex I, part B.

2.   The references made to the said repealed Directive shall be construed as references to this Directive and shall be read in accordance with the correlation table set out in Annex II.

Article 28 Entry into force

This Directive shall enter into force on 2 August 2004.

Article 29 Addressees

This Directive is addressed to the Member States.

ANNEX I
PART A

REPEALED DIRECTIVE AND ITS AMENDMENT

(Article 27)

Council Directive 93/104/EC	(OJ L 307, 13.12.1993, p. 18)
Directive 2000/34/EC of the European Parliament and of the Council	(OJ L 195, 1.8.2000, p. 41)

PART B
DEADLINES FOR TRANSPOSITION INTO NATIONAL LAW

(Article 27)

Directive	Deadline for transposition
93/104/EC	23 November 1996
2000/34/EC	1 August 2000[1]

[1] 1 August 2004 in the case of doctors in training. See Article 2 of Directive 2000/34/EC.

ANNEX II
CORRELATION TABLE

Directive 93/104/EEC	This Directive
Article 1 to 5	Article 1 to 5
Article 6, introductory words	Article 6, introductory words
Article 6(1)	Article 6(a)
Article 6(2)	Article 6(b)
Article 7	Article 7
Article 8, introductory words	Article 8, introductory words
Article 8(1)	Article 8(a)
Article 8(2)	Article 8(b)
Article 9, 10 and 11	Article 9, 10 and 11
Article 12, introductory words	Article 12, introductory words
Article 12(1)	Article 12(a)
Article 12(2)	Article 12(b)
Article 13, 14 and 15	Article 13, 14 and 15
Article 16, introductory words	Article 16, introductory words
Article 16(1)	Article 16(a)
Article 16(2)	Article 16(b)
Article 16(3)	Article 16(c)
Article 17(1)	Article 17(1)
Article 17(2), introductory words	Article 17(2)
Article 17(2)(1)	Article 17(3)(a) to (e)
Article 17(2)(2)	Article 17(3)(f) to (g)
Article 17(2)(3)	Article 17(4)
Article 17(2)(4)	Article 17(5)

Directive 93/104/EEC	This Directive
Article 17(3)	Article 18
Article 17(4)	Article 19
Article 17a(1)	Article 20(1), first subparagraph
Article 17a(2)	Article 20(1), second subparagraph
Article 17a(3)	Article 20(2)
Article 17a(4)	Article 20(3)
Article 17b(1)	Article 21(1), first subparagraph
Article 17b(2)	Article 21(1), second subparagraph
Article 17b(3)	Article 21(2)
Article 17b(4)	Article 21(3)
Article 17b(5)	Article 21(4)
Article 17b(6)	Article 21(5)
Article 17b(7)	Article 21(6)
Article 17b(8)	Article 21(7)
Article 18(1)(a)	—
Article 18(1)(b)(i)	Article 22(1)
Article 18(1)(b)(ii)	Article 22(2)
Article 18(1)(c)	Article 22(3)
Article 18(2)	—
Article 18(3)	Article 23
Article 18(4)	Article 24(1)
Article 18(5)	Article 24(2)
Article 18(6)	Article 24(3)
—	Article 25[1]
—	Article 25[2]
—	Article 27
—	Article 28
Article 19	Article 29
—	Annex I
—	Annex II

[1] Directive 2000/34/EC, Article 3.
[2] Directive 2000/34/EC, Article 4.

DIRECTIVE 2008/94/EC OF THE EUROPEAN PARLIAMENT AND OF THE COUNCIL of 22 OCTOBER 2008
on the protection of employees in the event of the insolvency of their employer
[2008] OJ L283/36

CHAPTER I

SCOPE AND DEFINITIONS

Article 1

1. This Directive shall apply to employees' claims arising from contracts of employment or employment relationships and existing against employers who are in a state of insolvency within the meaning of Article 2(1).

2. Member States may, by way of exception, exclude claims by certain categories of employee from the scope of this Directive, by virtue of the existence of other forms of guarantee if it is established that these offer the persons concerned a degree of protection equivalent to that resulting from this Directive.

3. Where such provision already applies in their national legislation, Member States may continue to exclude domestic servants employed by a natural person from the scope of this Directive.

Article 2

1. For the purposes of this Directive, an employer shall be deemed to be in a state of insolvency where a request has been made for the opening of collective proceedings based on insolvency of the employer, as provided for under the laws, regulations and administrative provisions of a Member State, and involving the partial or total divestment of the employer's assets and the appointment of a liquidator or a person performing a similar task, and the authority which is competent pursuant to the said provisions has:

   (a) either decided to open the proceedings; or

   (b) established that the employer's undertaking or business has been definitively closed down and that the available assets are insufficient to warrant the opening of the proceedings.

2. This Directive is without prejudice to national law as regards the definition of the terms 'employee', 'employer', 'pay', 'right conferring immediate entitlement' and 'right conferring prospective entitlement'.

   However, the Member States may not exclude from the scope of this Directive:

   (a) part-time employees within the meaning of Directive 97/81/EC;

   (b) employees with a fixed-term contract within the meaning of Directive 1999/70/EC;

   (c) employees with a temporary employment relationship within the meaning of Article 1(2) of Directive 91/383/EEC.

3. Member States may not set a minimum duration for the contract of employment or the employment relationship in order for employees to qualify for claims under this Directive.

4. This Directive does not prevent Member States from extending employee protection to other situations of insolvency, for example where payments have been de facto stopped on a permanent basis, established by proceedings different from those mentioned in paragraph 1 as provided for under national law.

   Such procedures shall not however create a guarantee obligation for the institutions of the other Member States in the cases referred to in Chapter IV.

CHAPTER II

PROVISIONS CONCERNING GUARANTEE INSTITUTIONS

Article 3

Member States shall take the measures necessary to ensure that guarantee institutions guarantee, subject to Article 4, payment of employees' outstanding claims resulting from contracts of employment or employment relationships, including, where provided for by national law, severance pay on termination of employment relationships.

The claims taken over by the guarantee institution shall be the outstanding pay claims relating to a period prior to and/or, as applicable, after a given date determined by the Member States.

Article 4

1. Member States shall have the option to limit the liability of the guarantee institutions referred to in Article 3.
2. If Member States exercise the option referred to in paragraph 1, they shall specify the length of the period for which outstanding claims are to be met by the guarantee institution. However, this may not be shorter than a period covering the remuneration of the last three months of the employment relationship prior to and/or after the date referred to in the second paragraph of Article 3.

   Member States may include this minimum period of three months in a reference period with a duration of not less than six months.

   Member States having a reference period of not less than 18 months may limit the period for which outstanding claims are met by the guarantee institution to eight weeks. In this case, those periods which are most favourable to the employee shall be used for the calculation of the minimum period.
3. Member States may set ceilings on the payments made by the guarantee institution. These ceilings must not fall below a level which is socially compatible with the social objective of this Directive.

   If Member States exercise this option, they shall inform the Commission of the methods used to set the ceiling.

Article 5

Member States shall lay down detailed rules for the organisation, financing and operation of the guarantee institutions, complying with the following principles in particular:

 (a) the assets of the institutions must be independent of the employers' operating capital and be inaccessible to proceedings for insolvency;

 (b) employers must contribute to financing, unless it is fully covered by the public authorities;

 (c) the institutions' liabilities must not depend on whether or not obligations to contribute to financing have been fulfilled.

CHAPTER III

PROVISIONS CONCERNING SOCIAL SECURITY

Article 6

Member States may stipulate that Articles 3, 4 and 5 shall not apply to contributions due under national statutory social security schemes or under supplementary occupational or inter-occupational pension schemes outside the national statutory social security schemes.

Article 7

Member States shall take the measures necessary to ensure that non-payment of compulsory contributions due from the employer, before the onset of his insolvency, to their insurance institutions under national statutory social security schemes does not adversely affect employees' benefit entitlement in respect of these insurance institutions in so far as the employees' contributions have been deducted at source from the remuneration paid.

Article 8

Member States shall ensure that the necessary measures are taken to protect the interests of employees and of persons having already left the employer's undertaking or business at the date of the onset of the employer's insolvency in respect of rights conferring on them immediate or prospective entitlement to old-age benefits, including survivors' benefits, under supplementary occupational or inter-occupational pension schemes outside the national statutory social security schemes.

CHAPTER IV
PROVISIONS CONCERNING TRANSNATIONAL SITUATIONS

Article 9

1. If an undertaking with activities in the territories of at least two Member States is in a state of insolvency within the meaning of Article 2(l), the institution responsible for meeting employees' outstanding claims shall be that in the Member State in whose territory they work or habitually work.
2. The extent of employees' rights shall be determined by the law governing the competent guarantee institution.
3. Member States shall take the measures necessary to ensure that, in the cases referred to in paragraph 1 of this Article, decisions taken in the context of insolvency proceedings referred to in Article 2(1), which have been requested in another Member State, are taken into account when determining the employer's state of insolvency within the meaning of this Directive.

Article 10

1. For the purposes of implementing Article 9, Member States shall make provision for the sharing of relevant information between their competent administrative authorities and/or the guarantee institutions mentioned in the first paragraph of Article 3, making it possible in particular to inform the guarantee institution responsible for meeting the employees' outstanding claims.
2. Member States shall notify the Commission and the other Member States of the contact details of their competent administrative authorities and/or guarantee institutions. The Commission shall make that information publicly accessible.

CHAPTER V
GENERAL AND FINAL PROVISIONS

Article 11

This Directive shall not affect the option of Member States to apply or introduce laws, regulations or administrative provisions which are more favourable to employees. Implementation of this Directive shall not under any circumstances be sufficient grounds for a regression in relation to the current situation in the Member States and in relation to the general level of protection of employees in the area covered by it.

Article 12

This Directive shall not affect the option of Member States:

(a) to take the measures necessary to avoid abuses;
(b) to refuse or reduce the liability referred to in the first paragraph of Article 3 or the guarantee obligation referred to in Article 7 if it appears that fulfilment of the obligation is unjustifiable because of the existence of special links between the employee and the employer and of common interests resulting in collusion between them;
(c) to refuse or reduce the liability referred to in the first paragraph of Article 3 or the guarantee obligation referred to in Article 7 in cases where the employee, on his or her own or together with his or her close relatives, was the owner of an essential part of the employer's undertaking or business and had a considerable influence on its activities.

Article 13

Member States shall notify the Commission and the other Member States of the types of national insolvency proceedings falling within the scope of this Directive, and of any amendments relating thereto.

The Commission shall publish these communications in the *Official Journal of the European Union*.

Article 14

Member States shall communicate to the Commission the text of the laws, regulations and administrative provisions which they adopt in the field covered by this Directive.

Article 15

By 8 October 2010 at the latest, the Commission shall submit to the European Parliament and to the Council a report on the implementation and application in the Member States of Articles 1 to 4, 9 and 10, Article 11, second paragraph, Article 12, point (c), and Articles 13 and 14.

Article 16

Directive 80/987/EEC, as amended by the acts listed in Annex I, is repealed, without prejudice to the obligations of the Member States relating to the time-limits for transposition into national law and application of the Directives set out in Annex I, Part C.

References to the repealed Directive shall be construed as references to this Directive and shall be read in accordance with the correlation table in Annex II.

Article 17

This Directive shall enter into force on the 20th day following its publication in the *Official Journal of the European Union*.

Article 18

This Directive is addressed to the Member States.

DIRECTIVE 2008/104/EC OF THE EUROPEAN PARLIAMENT AND OF THE COUNCIL of 19 NOVEMBER 2008
on temporary agency work
[2008] OJ L327/9

CHAPTER I
GENERAL PROVISIONS

Article 1   Scope

1.   This Directive applies to workers with a contract of employment or employment relationship with a temporary-work agency who are assigned to user undertakings to work temporarily under their supervision and direction.
2.   This Directive applies to public and private undertakings which are temporary-work agencies or user undertakings engaged in economic activities whether or not they are operating for gain.
3.   Member States may, after consulting the social partners, provide that this Directive does not apply to employment contracts or relationships concluded under a specific public or publicly supported vocational training, integration or retraining programme.

Article 2   Aim

The purpose of this Directive is to ensure the protection of temporary agency workers and to improve the quality of temporary agency work by ensuring that the principle of equal treatment, as set out in Article 5, is applied to temporary agency workers, and by recognising temporary-work agencies as employers, while taking into account the need to establish a suitable framework for the use of temporary agency work with a view to contributing effectively to the creation of jobs and to the development of flexible forms of working.

Article 3   Definitions

1.   For the purposes of this Directive:
    (a)   'worker' means any person who, in the Member State concerned, is protected as a worker under national employment law;
    (b)   'temporary-work agency' means any natural or legal person who, in compliance with national law, concludes contracts of employment or employment relationships with temporary agency workers in order to assign them to user undertakings to work there temporarily under their supervision and direction;
    (c)   'temporary agency worker' means a worker with a contract of employment or an employment relationship with a temporary-work agency with a view to being assigned to a user undertaking to work temporarily under its supervision and direction;

(d) 'user undertaking' means any natural or legal person for whom and under the supervision and direction of whom a temporary agency worker works temporarily;

(e) 'assignment' means the period during which the temporary agency worker is placed at the user undertaking to work temporarily under its supervision and direction;

(f) 'basic working and employment conditions' means working and employment conditions laid down by legislation, regulations, administrative provisions, collective agreements and/or other binding general provisions in force in the user undertaking relating to:

(i) the duration of working time, overtime, breaks, rest periods, night work, holidays and public holidays;

(ii) pay.

2. This Directive shall be without prejudice to national law as regards the definition of pay, contract of employment, employment relationship or worker.

Member States shall not exclude from the scope of this Directive workers, contracts of employment or employment relationships solely because they relate to part-time workers, fixed-term contract workers or persons with a contract of employment or employment relationship with a temporary-work agency.

Article 4 Review of restrictions or prohibitions

1. Prohibitions or restrictions on the use of temporary agency work shall be justified only on grounds of general interest relating in particular to the protection of temporary agency workers, the requirements of health and safety at work or the need to ensure that the labour market functions properly and abuses are prevented.

2. By 5 December 2011, Member States shall, after consulting the social partners in accordance with national legislation, collective agreements and practices, review any restrictions or prohibitions on the use of temporary agency work in order to verify whether they are justified on the grounds mentioned in paragraph 1.

3. If such restrictions or prohibitions are laid down by collective agreements, the review referred to in paragraph 2 may be carried out by the social partners who have negotiated the relevant agreement.

4. Paragraphs 1, 2 and 3 shall be without prejudice to national requirements with regard to registration, licensing, certification, financial guarantees or monitoring of temporary-work agencies.

5. The Member States shall inform the Commission of the results of the review referred to in paragraphs 2 and 3 by 5 December 2011.

CHAPTER II
EMPLOYMENT AND WORKING CONDITIONS

Article 5 The principle of equal treatment

1. The basic working and employment conditions of temporary agency workers shall be, for the duration of their assignment at a user undertaking, at least those that would apply if they had been recruited directly by that undertaking to occupy the same job.

For the purposes of the application of the first subparagraph, the rules in force in the user undertaking on:

(a) protection of pregnant women and nursing mothers and protection of children and young people; and

(b) equal treatment for men and women and any action to combat any discrimination based on sex, race or ethnic origin, religion, beliefs, disabilities, age or sexual orientation; must be complied with as established by legislation, regulations, administrative provisions, collective agreements and/or any other general provisions.

2. As regards pay, Member States may, after consulting the social partners, provide that an exemption be made to the principle established in paragraph 1 where temporary agency workers who have a permanent contract of employment with a temporary-work agency continue to be paid in the time between assignments.

3.   Member States may, after consulting the social partners, give them, at the appropriate level and subject to the conditions laid down by the Member States, the option of upholding or concluding collective agreements which, while respecting the overall protection of temporary agency workers, may establish arrangements concerning the working and employment conditions of temporary agency workers which may differ from those referred to in paragraph 1.

4.   Provided that an adequate level of protection is provided for temporary agency workers, Member States in which there is either no system in law for declaring collective agreements universally applicable or no such system in law or practice for extending their provisions to all similar undertakings in a certain sector or geographical area, may, after consulting the social partners at national level and on the basis of an agreement concluded by them, establish arrangements concerning the basic working and employment conditions which derogate from the principle established in paragraph 1. Such arrangements may include a qualifying period for equal treatment. The arrangements referred to in this paragraph shall be in conformity with Community legislation and shall be sufficiently precise and accessible to allow the sectors and firms concerned to identify and comply with their obligations. In particular, Member States shall specify, in application of Article 3(2), whether occupational social security schemes, including pension, sick pay or financial participation schemes are included in the basic working and employment conditions referred to in paragraph 1. Such arrangements shall also be without prejudice to agreements at national, regional, local or sectoral level that are no less favourable to workers.

5.   Member States shall take appropriate measures, in accordance with national law and/or practice, with a view to preventing misuse in the application of this Article and, in particular, to preventing successive assignments designed to circumvent the provisions of this Directive. They shall inform the Commission about such measures.

Article 6   Access to employment, collective facilities and vocational training

1.   Temporary agency workers shall be informed of any vacant posts in the user undertaking to give them the same opportunity as other workers in that undertaking to find permanent employment. Such information may be provided by a general announcement in a suitable place in the undertaking for which, and under whose supervision, temporary agency workers are engaged.

2.   Member States shall take any action required to ensure that any clauses prohibiting or having the effect of preventing the conclusion of a contract of employment or an employment relationship between the user undertaking and the temporary agency worker after his assignment are null and void or may be declared null and void.
This paragraph is without prejudice to provisions under which temporary agencies receive a reasonable level of recompense for services rendered to user undertakings for the assignment, recruitment and training of temporary agency workers.

3.   Temporary-work agencies shall not charge workers any fees in exchange for arranging for them to be recruited by a user undertaking, or for concluding a contract of employment or an employment relationship with a user undertaking after carrying out an assignment in that undertaking.

4.   Without prejudice to Article 5(1), temporary agency workers shall be given access to the amenities or collective facilities in the user undertaking, in particular any canteen, child-care facilities and transport services, under the same conditions as workers employed directly by the undertaking, unless the difference in treatment is justified by objective reasons.

5.   Member States shall take suitable measures or shall promote dialogue between the social partners, in accordance with their national traditions and practices, in order to:
     (a)   improve temporary agency workers' access to training and to child-care facilities in the temporary-work agencies, even in the periods between their assignments, in order to enhance their career development and employability;
     (b)   improve temporary agency workers' access to training for user undertakings' workers.

Article 7 Representation of temporary agency workers

1. Temporary agency workers shall count, under conditions established by the Member States, for the purposes of calculating the threshold above which bodies representing workers provided for under Community and national law and collective agreements are to be formed at the temporary-work agency.

2. Member States may provide that, under conditions that they define, temporary agency workers count for the purposes of calculating the threshold above which bodies representing workers provided for by Community and national law and collective agreements are to be formed in the user undertaking, in the same way as if they were workers employed directly for the same period of time by the user undertaking.

3. Those Member States which avail themselves of the option provided for in paragraph 2 shall not be obliged to implement the provisions of paragraph 1.

Article 8 Information of workers' representatives

Without prejudice to national and Community provisions on information and consultation which are more stringent and/or more specific and, in particular, Directive 2002/14/EC of the European Parliament and of the Council of 11 March 2002 establishing a general framework for informing and consulting employees in the European Community, the user undertaking must provide suitable information on the use of temporary agency workers when providing information on the employment situation in that undertaking to bodies representing workers set up in accordance with national and Community legislation.

CHAPTER III
FINAL PROVISIONS

Article 9 Minimum requirements

1. This Directive is without prejudice to the Member States' right to apply or introduce legislative, regulatory or administrative provisions which are more favourable to workers or to promote or permit collective agreements concluded between the social partners which are more favourable to workers.

2. The implementation of this Directive shall under no circumstances constitute sufficient grounds for justifying a reduction in the general level of protection of workers in the fields covered by this Directive. This is without prejudice to the rights of Member States and/or management and labour to lay down, in the light of changing circumstances, different legislative, regulatory or contractual arrangements to those prevailing at the time of the adoption of this Directive, provided always that the minimum requirements laid down in this Directive are respected.

Article 10 Penalties

1. Member States shall provide for appropriate measures in the event of non-compliance with this Directive by temporary-work agencies or user undertakings. In particular, they shall ensure that adequate administrative or judicial procedures are available to enable the obligations deriving from this Directive to be enforced.

2. Member States shall lay down rules on penalties applicable in the event of infringements of national provisions implementing this Directive and shall take all necessary measures to ensure that they are applied. The penalties provided for must be effective, proportionate and dissuasive. Member States shall notify these provisions to the Commission by 5 December 2011. Member States shall notify to the Commission any subsequent amendments to those provisions in good time. They shall, in particular, ensure that workers and/or their representatives have adequate means of enforcing the obligations under this Directive.

Article 11 Implementation

1. Member States shall adopt and publish the laws, regulations and administrative provisions necessary to comply with this Directive by 5 December 2011, or shall ensure that the social partners introduce the necessary provisions by way of an agreement, whereby the Member States must make all the necessary arrangements to enable them to guarantee at any time that the objectives of this Directive are being attained. They shall forthwith inform the Commission thereof.

2.   When Member States adopt these measures, they shall contain a reference to this Directive or shall be accompanied by such reference on the occasion of their official publication. The methods of making such reference shall be laid down by Member States.

Article 12 Review by the Commission

By 5 December 2013, the Commission shall, in consultation with the Member States and social partners at Community level, review the application of this Directive with a view to proposing, where appropriate, the necessary amendments.

Article 13 Entry into force

This Directive shall enter into force on the day of its publication in the *Official Journal of the European Union*.

Article 14 Addressees

This Directive is addressed to the Member States.

CONSUMER PROTECTION

COUNCIL DIRECTIVE (EEC) No 85/374 of 25 JULY 1985
on the approximation of the laws, regulations and administrative provisions of the member states concerning liability for defective products
[1985] OJ L210/29

Article 1

The producer shall be liable for damage caused by a defect in his product.

Article 2

For the purpose of this Directive 'product' means all movables even if incorporated into another movable or into an immovable. 'Product' includes electricity.

Article 3

1. 'Producer' means the manufacturer of a finished product, the producer of any raw material or the manufacturer of a component part and any person who, by putting his name, trade mark or other distinguishing feature on the product presents himself as its producer.
2. Without prejudice to the liability of the producer, any person who imports into the Community a product for sale, hire, leasing or any form of distribution in the course of his business shall be deemed to be a producer within the meaning of this Directive and shall be responsible as a producer.
3. Where the producer of the product cannot be identified, each supplier of the product shall be treated as its producer unless he informs the injured person, within a reasonable time, of the identity of the producer or of the person who supplied him with the product. The same shall apply, in the case of an imported product, if this product does not indicate the identity of the importer referred to in paragraph 2, even if the name of the producer is indicated.

Article 4

The injured person shall be required to prove the damage, the defect and the causal relationship between defect and damage.

Article 5

Where, as a result of the provisions of this Directive, two or more persons are liable for the same damage, they shall be liable jointly and severally, without prejudice to the provisions of national law concerning the rights of contribution or recourse.

Article 6

1. A product is defective when it does not provide the safety which a person is entitled to expect, taking all circumstances into account, including:
   (a) the presentation of the product;
   (b) the use to which it could reasonably be expected that the product would be put;
   (c) the time when the product was put into circulation.
2. A product shall not be considered defective for the sole reason that a better product is subsequently put into circulation.

Article 7

The producer shall not be liable as a result of this Directive if he proves:
   (a) that he did not put the product into circulation; or
   (b) that, having regard to the circumstances, it is probable that the defect which caused the damage did not exist at the time when the product was put into circulation by him or that this defect came into being afterwards; or
   (c) that the product was neither manufactured by him for sale or any form of distribution for economic purpose nor manufactured or distributed by him in the course of his business; or
   (d) that the defect is due to compliance of the product with mandatory regulations issued by the public authorities; or

(e) that the state of scientific and technical knowledge at the time when he put the product into circulation was not such as to enable the existence of the defect to be discovered; or

(f) in the case of a manufacturer of a component, that the defect is attributable to the design of the product in which the component has been fitted or to the instructions given by the manufacturer of the product.

Article 8

1. Without prejudice to the provisions of national law concerning the right of contribution or recourse, the liability of the producer shall not be reduced when the damage is caused both by a defect in product and by the act or omission of a third party.

2. The liability of the producer may be reduced or disallowed when, having regard to all the circumstances, the damage is caused both by a defect in the product and by the fault of the injured person or any person for whom the injured person is responsible.

Article 9

For the purpose of Article 1, 'damage' means:

(a) damage caused by death or by personal injuries;

(b) damage to, or destruction of, any item of property other than the defective product itself, with a lower threshold of 500 ECU, provided that the item of property:

(i) is of a type ordinarily intended for private use or consumption, and

(ii) was used by the injured person mainly for his own private use or consumption.

This Article shall be without prejudice to national provisions relating to non-material damage.

Article 10

1. Member States shall provide in their legislation that a limitation period of three years shall apply to proceedings for the recovery of damages as provided for in this Directive. The limitation period shall begin to run from the day on which the plaintiff became aware, or should reasonably have become aware, of the damage, the defect and the identity of the producer.

2. The laws of Member States regulating suspension or interruption of the limitation period shall not be affected by this Directive.

Article 11

Member States shall provide in their legislation that the rights conferred upon the injured person pursuant to this Directive shall be extinguished upon the expiry of a period of 10 years from the date on which the producer put into circulation the actual product which caused the damage, unless the injured person has in the meantime instituted proceedings against the producer.

Article 12

The liability of the producer arising from this Directive may not, in relation to the injured person, be limited or excluded by a provision limiting his liability or exempting him from liability.

Article 13

This Directive shall not affect any rights which an injured person may have according to the rules of the law of contractual or non-contractual liability or a special liability system existing at the moment when this Directive is notified.

Article 14

This Directive shall not apply to injury or damage arising from nuclear accidents and covered by international conventions ratified by the Member States.

Article 15

1. Each Member State may:

(a) ...

(b) by way of derogation from Article 7(e), maintain or, subject to the procedure set out in paragraph 2 of this Article, provide in this legislation that the producer shall be liable even if he proves that the state of scientific and technical knowledge at the time when he put the product into circulation was not such as to enable the existence of a defect to be discovered.

2. A Member State wishing to introduce the measure specified in paragraph 1(b) shall communicate the text of the proposed measure to the Commission. The Commission shall inform the other Member States thereof.

    The Member State concerned shall hold the proposed measure in abeyance for nine months after the Commission is informed and provided that in the meantime the Commission has not submitted to the Council a proposal amending this Directive on the relevant matter. However, if within three months of receiving the said information, the Commission does not advise the Member State concerned that it intends submitting such a proposal to the Council, the Member State may take the proposed measure immediately. If the Commission does submit to the Council such a proposal amending this Directive within the aforementioned nine months, the Member State concerned shall hold the proposed measure in abeyance for a further period of 18 months from the date on which the proposal is submitted.

3. Ten years after the date of notification of this Directive, the Commission shall submit to the Council a report on the effect that rulings by the courts as to the application of Article 7(e) and of paragraph 1(b) of this Article have on consumer protection and the functioning of the common market. In the light of this report the Council, acting on a proposal from the Commission and pursuant to the terms of Article 100 of the Treaty, shall decide whether to repeal Article 7(e).

Article 16

1. Any Member State may provide that a producer's total liability for damage resulting from a death or personal injury and caused by identical items with the same defect shall be limited to an amount which may not be less than 70 million ECU.

2. Ten years after the date of notification of this Directive, the Commission shall submit to the Council a report on the effect on consumer protection and the functioning of the common market of the implementation of the financial limit on liability by those Member States which have used the option provided for in paragraph 1. In the light of this report the Council, acting on a proposal from the Commission and pursuant to the terms of Article 100 of the Treaty, shall decide whether to repeal paragraph 1.

Article 17

This Directive shall not apply to products put into circulation before the date on which the provisions referred to in Article 19 enter into force.

Article 18

1. For the purposes of this Directive, the ECU shall be that defined by Regulation (EEC) No 3180/78, as amended by Regulation (EEC) No 2626/84. The equivalent in national currency shall initially be calculated at the rate obtaining on the date of adoption of this Directive.

2. Every five years the Council, acting on a proposal from the Commission, shall examine and, if need be, revise the amounts in this Directive, in the light of economic and monetary trends in the Community.

Article 19

1. Member States shall bring into force, not later than three years from the date of notification of this Directive, the laws, regulations and administrative provisions necessary to comply with this Directive. They shall forthwith inform the Commission thereof.

2. The procedure set out in Article 15(2) shall apply from the date of notification of this Directive.

Article 20

Member States shall communicate to the Commission the texts of the main provisions of national law which they subsequently adopt in the field governed by this Directive.

Article 21

Every five years the Commission shall present a report to the Council on the application of this Directive and, if necessary, shall submit appropriate proposals to it.

Article 22

This Directive is addressed to the Member States.

COUNCIL DIRECTIVE 93/13/EEC OF 5 APRIL 1993
on unfair terms in consumer contracts
[1993] OJ L95/29

Article 1

1. The purpose of this Directive is to approximate the laws, regulations and administrative provisions of the Member States relating to unfair terms in contracts concluded between a seller or supplier and a consumer.

2. The contractual terms which reflect mandatory statutory or regulatory provisions and the provisions or principles of international conventions to which the Member States or the Community are party, particularly in the transport area, shall not be subject to the provisions of this Directive.

Article 2

For the purposes of this Directive:

(a) 'unfair terms' means the contractual terms defined in Article 3;

(b) 'consumer' means any natural person who, in contracts covered by this Directive, is acting for purposes which are outside his trade, business or profession;

(c) 'seller or supplier' means any natural or legal person who, in contracts covered by this Directive, is acting for purposes relating to his trade, business or profession, whether publicly owned or privately owned.

Article 3

1. A contractual term which has not been individually negotiated shall be regarded as unfair if, contrary to the requirement of good faith, it causes a significant imbalance in the parties' rights and obligations arising under the contract, to the detriment of the consumer.

2. A term shall always be regarded as not individually negotiated where it has been drafted in advance and the consumer has therefore not been able to influence the substance of the term, particularly in the context of a pre-formulated standard contract.

   The fact that certain aspects of a term or one specific term have been individually negotiated shall not exclude the application of this Article to the rest of a contract if an overall assessment of the contract indicates that it is nevertheless a pre-formulated standard contract.

   Where any seller or supplier claims that a standard term has been individually negotiated, the burden of proof in this respect shall be incumbent on him.

3. The Annex shall contain an indicative and non-exhaustive list of the terms which may be regarded as unfair.

Article 4

1. Without prejudice to Article 7, the unfairness of a contractual term shall be assessed, taking into account the nature of the goods or services for which the contract was concluded and by referring, at the time of conclusion of the contract, to all the circumstances attending the conclusion of the contract and to all the other terms of the contract or of another contract on which it is dependent.

2. Assessment of the unfair nature of the terms shall relate neither to the definition of the main subject matter of the contract nor to the adequacy of the price and remuneration, on the one hand, as against the services or goods supplies in exchange, on the other, in so far as these terms are in plain intelligible language.

Article 5

In the case of contracts where all or certain terms offered to the consumer are in writing, these terms must always be drafted in plain, intelligible language. Where there is doubt about the meaning of a term, the interpretation most favourable to the consumer shall prevail. This rule on interpretation shall not apply in the context of the procedures laid down in Article 7 (2).

Article 6

1. Member States shall lay down that unfair terms used in a contract concluded with a consumer by a seller or supplier shall, as provided for under their national law, not be

binding on the consumer and that the contract shall continue to bind the parties upon those terms if it is capable of continuing in existence without the unfair terms.

2. Member States shall take the necessary measures to ensure that the consumer does not lose the protection granted by this Directive by virtue of the choice of the law of a non-Member country as the law applicable to the contract if the latter has a close connection with the territory of the Member States.

Article 7

1. Member States shall ensure that, in the interests of consumers and of competitors, adequate and effective means exist to prevent the continued use of unfair terms in contracts concluded with consumers by sellers or suppliers.

2. The means referred to in paragraph 1 shall include provisions whereby persons or organisations, having a legitimate interest under national law in protecting consumers, may take action according to the national law concerned before the courts or before competent administrative bodies for a decision as to whether contractual terms drawn up for general use are unfair, so that they can apply appropriate and effective means to prevent the continued use of such terms.

3. With due regard for national laws, the legal remedies referred to in paragraph 2 may be directed separately or jointly against a number of sellers or suppliers from the same economic sector or their associations which use or recommend the use of the same general contractual terms or similar terms.

Article 8

Member States may adopt or retain the most stringent provisions compatible with the Treaty in the area covered by this Directive, to ensure a maximum degree of protection for the consumer.

Article 8a

1. Where a Member State adopts provisions in accordance with Article 8, it shall inform the Commission thereof, as well as of any subsequent changes, in particular where those provisions:
   — extend the unfairness assessment to individually negotiated contractual terms or to the adequacy of the price or remuneration; or,
   — contain lists of contractual terms which shall be considered as unfair,

2. The Commission shall ensure that the information referred to in paragraph 1 is easily accessible to consumers and traders, inter alia, on a dedicated website.

3. The Commission shall forward the information referred to in paragraph 1 to the other Member States and the European Parliament. The Commission shall consult stakeholders on that information.

Article 8b

1. Member States shall lay down the rules on penalties applicable to infringements of national provisions adopted pursuant to this Directive and shall take all measures necessary to ensure that they are implemented. The penalties provided for shall be effective, proportionate and dissuasive.

2. Member States may restrict such penalties to situations where the contractual terms are expressly defined as unfair in all circumstances in national law or where a seller or supplier continues to use contractual terms that have been found to be unfair in a final decision taken in accordance with Article 7(2).

3. Member States shall ensure that the following non-exhaustive and indicative criteria are taken into account for the imposition of penalties, where appropriate:
   (a) the nature, gravity, scale and duration of the infringement;
   (b) any action taken by the seller or supplier to mitigate or remedy the damage suffered by consumers;
   (c) any previous infringements by the seller or supplier;
   (d) the financial benefits gained or losses avoided by the seller or supplier due to the infringement, if the relevant data are available;
   (e) penalties imposed on the seller or supplier for the same infringement in other Member States in cross-border cases where information about such penalties is available through the mechanism established by Regulation (EU) 2017/2394 of the European Parliament and of the Council;

(f)   any other aggravating or mitigating factors applicable to the circumstances of the case.

4.   Without prejudice to paragraph 2 of this Article, Member States shall ensure that, when penalties are to be imposed in accordance with Article 21 of Regulation (EU) 2017/2394, they include the possibility either to impose fines through administrative procedures or to initiate legal proceedings for the imposition of fines, or both, the maximum amount of such fines being at least 4 % of the seller's or supplier's annual turnover in the Member State or Member States concerned.

5.   For cases where a fine is to be imposed in accordance with paragraph 4, but information on the seller's or supplier's annual turnover is not available, Member States shall introduce the possibility to impose fines, the maximum amount of which shall be at least EUR 2 million.

6.   Member States shall, by 28 November 2021, notify the Commission of the rules and measures referred to in paragraph 1 and shall notify it, without delay, of any subsequent amendment affecting them.

Article 9

The Commission shall present a report to the European Parliament and to the Council concerning the application of this Directive five years at the latest after the date in Article 10 (1).

Article 10

1.   Member States shall bring into force the laws, regulations and administrative provisions necessary to comply with this Directive no later than 31 December 1994. They shall forthwith inform the Commission thereof.

These provisions shall be applicable to all contracts concluded after 31 December 1994.

2.   When Member States adopt these measures, they shall contain a reference to this Directive or shall be accompanied by such reference on the occasion of their official publication. The methods of making such a reference shall be laid down by the Member States.

3.   Member States shall communicate the main provisions of national law which they adopt in the field covered by this Directive to the Commission.

Article 11

This Directive is addressed to the Member States.

ANNEX
TERMS REFERRED TO IN ARTICLE 3 (3)

1.   Terms which have the object or effect of:

(a)   excluding or limiting the legal liability of a seller or supplier in the event of the death of a consumer or personal injury to the latter resulting from an act or omission of that seller or supplier;

(b)   inappropriately excluding or limiting the legal rights of the consumer vis-à-vis the seller or supplier or another party in the event of total or partial non-performance or inadequate performance by the seller or supplier of any of the contractual obligations, including the option of offsetting a debt owed to the seller or supplier against any claim which the consumer may have against him;

(c)   making an agreement binding on the consumer whereas provision of services by the seller or supplier is subject to a condition whose realisation depends on his own will alone;

(d)   permitting the seller or supplier to retain sums paid by the consumer where the latter decides not to conclude or perform the contract, without providing for the consumer to receive compensation of an equivalent amount from the seller or supplier where the latter is the party cancelling the contract;

(e)   requiring any consumer who fails to fulfil his obligation to pay a disproportionately high sum in compensation;

(f)   authorising the seller or supplier to dissolve the contract on a discretionary basis where the same facility is not granted to the consumer, or permitting the seller or supplier to retain the sums paid for services not yet supplied by him where it is the seller or supplier himself who dissolves the contract;

(g) enabling the seller or supplier to terminate a contract of indeterminate duration without reasonable notice except where there are serious grounds for doing so;

(h) automatically extending a contract of fixed duration where the consumer does not indicate otherwise, when the deadline fixed for the consumer to express this desire not to extend the contract is unreasonably early;

(i) irrevocably binding the consumer to terms with which he had no real opportunity of becoming acquainted before the conclusion of the contract;

(j) enabling the seller or supplier to alter the terms of the contract unilaterally without a valid reason which is specified in the contract;

(k) enabling the seller or supplier to alter unilaterally without a valid reason any characteristics of the product or service to be provided;

(l) providing for the price of goods to be determined at the time of delivery or allowing a seller of goods or supplier of services to increase their price without in both cases giving the consumer the corresponding right to cancel the contract if the final price is too high in relation to the price agreed when the contract was concluded;

(m) giving the seller or supplier the right to determine whether the goods or services supplied are in conformity with the contract, or giving him the exclusive right to interpret any term of the contract;

(n) limiting the seller's or supplier's obligation to respect commitments undertaken by his agents or making his commitments subject to compliance with a particular formality;

(o) obliging the consumer to fulfil all his obligations where the seller or supplier does not perform his;

(p) giving the seller or supplier the possibility of transferring his rights and obligations under the contract, where this may serve to reduce the guarantees for the consumer, without the latter's agreement;

(q) excluding or hindering the consumer's right to take legal action or exercise any other legal remedy, particularly by requiring the consumer to take disputes exclusively to arbitration not covered by legal provisions, unduly restricting the evidence available to him or imposing on him a burden of proof which, according to the applicable law, should lie with another party to the contract.

2. Scope of subparagraphs (g), (j) and (l)

(a) Subparagraph (g) is without hindrance to terms by which a supplier of financial services reserves the right to terminate unilaterally a contract of indeterminate duration without notice where there is a valid reason, provided that the supplier is required to inform the other contracting party or parties thereof immediately.

(b) Subparagraph (j) is without hindrance to terms under which a supplier of financial services reserves the right to alter the rate of interest payable by the consumer or due to the latter, or the amount of other charges for financial services without notice where there is a valid reason, provided that the supplier is required to inform the other contracting party or parties thereof at the earliest opportunity and that the latter are free to dissolve the contract immediately.

Subparagraph (j) is also without hindrance to terms under which a seller or supplier reserves the right to alter unilaterally the conditions of a contract of indeterminate duration, provided that he is required to inform the consumer with reasonable notice and that the consumer is free to dissolve the contract.

(c) Subparagraphs (g), (j) and (l) do not apply to:

— transactions in transferable securities, financial instruments and other products or services where the price is linked to fluctuations in a stock exchange quotation or index or a financial market rate that the seller or supplier does not control;

— contracts for the purchase or sale of foreign currency, traveller's cheques or international money orders denominated in foreign currency;

(d) Subparagraph (l) is without hindrance to price-indexation clauses, where lawful, provided that the method by which prices vary is explicitly described.

DIRECTIVE 2011/83/EU OF THE EUROPEAN PARLIAMENT AND OF THE COUNCIL

of 25 October 2011
on consumer rights, amending Council Directive 93/13/EEC and Directive 1999/44/EC of the European Parliament and of the Council and repealing Council Directive 85/577/EEC and Directive 97/7/EC of the European Parliament and of the Council
[2011] OJ L304/64

HAVE ADOPTED THIS DIRECTIVE:

CHAPTER I
SUBJECT MATTER, DEFINITIONS AND SCOPE

Article 1 Subject matter

The purpose of this Directive is, through the achievement of a high level of consumer protection, to contribute to the proper functioning of the internal market by approximating certain aspects of the laws, regulations and administrative provisions of the Member States concerning contracts concluded between consumers and traders.

Article 2 Definitions

For the purpose of this Directive, the following definitions shall apply:

(1) 'consumer' means any natural person who, in contracts covered by this Directive, is acting for purposes which are outside his trade, business, craft or profession;

(2) 'trader' means any natural person or any legal person, irrespective of whether privately or publicly owned, who is acting, including through any other person acting in his name or on his behalf, for purposes relating to his trade, business, craft or profession in relation to contracts covered by this Directive;

(3) 'goods' means goods as defined in point (5) of Article 2 of Directive (EU) 2019/771 of the European Parliament and of the Council;

(4) 'goods made to the consumer's specifications' means non-prefabricated goods made on the basis of an individual choice of or decision by the consumer;

(4a) 'personal data' means personal data as defined in point (1) of Article 4 of Regulation (EU) 2016/679 of the European Parliament and of the Council;

(5) 'sales contract' means any contract under which the trader transfers or undertakes to transfer ownership of goods to the consumer, including any contract having as its object both goods and services;

(6) 'service contract' means any contract other than a sales contract under which the trader supplies or undertakes to supply a service, including a digital service, to the consumer;

(7) 'distance contract' means any contract concluded between the trader and the consumer under an organised distance sales or service-provision scheme without the simultaneous physical presence of the trader and the consumer, with the exclusive use of one or more means of distance communication up to and including the time at which the contract is concluded;

(8) 'off-premises contract' means any contract between the trader and the consumer:

(a) concluded in the simultaneous physical presence of the trader and the consumer, in a place which is not the business premises of the trader;

(b) for which an offer was made by the consumer in the same circumstances as referred to in point (a);

(c) concluded on the business premises of the trader or through any means of distance communication immediately after the consumer was personally and individually addressed in a place which is not the business premises of the trader in the simultaneous physical presence of the trader and the consumer; or

(d)   concluded during an excursion organised by the trader with the aim or effect of promoting and selling goods or services to the consumer;

(9)   'business premises' means:

(a)   any immovable retail premises where the trader carries out his activity on a permanent basis; or

(b)   any movable retail premises where the trader carries out his activity on a usual basis;

(10)   'durable medium' means any instrument which enables the consumer or the trader to store information addressed personally to him in a way accessible for future reference for a period of time adequate for the purposes of the information and which allows the unchanged reproduction of the information stored;

(11)   'digital content' means digital content as defined in point (1) of Article 2 of Directive (EU) 2019/770 of the European Parliament and of the Council;

(12)   'financial service' means any service of a banking, credit, insurance, personal pension, investment or payment nature;

(13)   'public auction' means a method of sale where goods or services are offered by the trader to consumers, who attend or are given the possibility to attend the auction in person, through a transparent, competitive bidding procedure run by an auctioneer and where the successful bidder is bound to purchase the goods or services;

(14)   'commercial guarantee' means any undertaking by the trader or a producer (the guarantor) to the consumer, in addition to his legal obligation relating to the guarantee of conformity, to reimburse the price paid or to replace, repair or service goods in any way if they do not meet the specifications or any other requirements not related to conformity set out in the guarantee statement or in the relevant advertising available at the time of, or before the conclusion of the contract;

(15)   'ancillary contract' means a contract by which the consumer acquires goods or services related to a distance contract or an off-premises contract and where those goods are supplied or those services are provided by the trader or by a third party on the basis of an arrangement between that third party and the trader.

(16)   'digital service' means a digital service as defined in point (2) of Article 2 of Directive (EU) 2019/770;

(17)   'online marketplace' means a service using software, including a website, part of a website or an application, operated by or on behalf of a trader which allows consumers to conclude distance contracts with other traders or consumers;

(18)   'provider of an online marketplace' means any trader which provides an online marketplace to consumers;

(19)   'compatibility' means compatibility as defined in point (10) of Article 2 of Directive (EU) 2019/770;

(20)   'functionality' means functionality as defined in point (11) of Article 2 of Directive (EU) 2019/770;

(21)   'interoperability' means interoperability as defined in point (12) of Article 2 of Directive (EU) 2019/770.

Article 3   Scope

1.   This Directive shall apply, under the conditions and to the extent set out in its provisions, to any contract concluded between a trader and a consumer where the consumer pays or undertakes to pay the price. It shall apply to contracts for the supply of water, gas, electricity or district heating, including by public providers, to the extent that these commodities are provided on a contractual basis.

1a.   This Directive shall also apply where the trader supplies or undertakes to supply digital content which is not supplied on a tangible medium or a digital service to the consumer and the consumer provides or undertakes to provide personal data to the trader, except where the personal data provided by the consumer are exclusively processed by the trader for the purpose of supplying the digital content which is not supplied on a tangible medium or digital service in accordance with this Directive or for allowing the trader to comply with legal requirements to which the trader is subject, and the trader does not process those data for any other purpose.

2. If any provision of this Directive conflicts with a provision of another Union act governing specific sectors, the provision of that other Union act shall prevail and shall apply to those specific sectors.

3. This Directive shall not apply to contracts:

(a) for social services, including social housing, childcare and support of families and persons permanently or temporarily in need, including long-term care;

(b) for healthcare as defined in point (a) of Article 3 of Directive 2011/24/EU, whether or not they are provided via healthcare facilities;

(c) for gambling, which involves wagering a stake with pecuniary value in games of chance, including lotteries, casino games and betting transactions;

(d) for financial services;

(e) for the creation, acquisition or transfer of immovable property or of rights in immovable property;

(f) for the construction of new buildings, the substantial conversion of existing buildings and for rental of accommodation for residential purposes;

(g) on packages as defined in point 2 of Article 3 of Directive (EU) 2015/2302 of the European Parliament and of the Council.
Article 6(7), Article 8(2) and (6) and Articles 19, 21 and 22 of this Directive shall apply mutatis mutandis to packages as defined in point 2 of Article 3 of Directive (EU) 2015/2302 in relation to travellers as defined in point 6 of Article 3 of that Directive;

(h) which fall within the scope of Directive 2008/122/EC of the European Parliament and of the Council of 14 January 2009 on the protection of consumers in respect of certain aspects of timeshare, long-term holiday product, resale and exchange contracts;

(i) which, in accordance with the laws of Member States, are established by a public office-holder who has a statutory obligation to be independent and impartial and who must ensure, by providing comprehensive legal information, that the consumer only concludes the contract on the basis of careful legal consideration and with knowledge of its legal scope;

(j) for the supply of foodstuffs, beverages or other goods intended for current consumption in the household, and which are physically supplied by a trader on frequent and regular rounds to the consumer's home, residence or workplace;

(k) for passenger transport services, with the exception of Article 8(2) and Articles 19, 21 and 22;

(l) concluded by means of automatic vending machines or automated commercial premises;

(m) concluded with telecommunications operators through public payphones for their use or concluded for the use of one single connection by telephone, Internet or fax established by a consumer;

(n) for any goods sold by way of execution or otherwise by authority of law.

4. Member States may decide not to apply this Directive or not to maintain or introduce corresponding national provisions to off-premises contracts for which the payment to be made by the consumer does not exceed EUR 50. Member States may define a lower value in their national legislation.

5. This Directive shall not affect national general contract law such as the rules on the validity, formation or effect of a contract, in so far as general contract law aspects are not regulated in this Directive.

6. This Directive shall not prevent traders from offering consumers contractual arrangements which go beyond the protection provided for in this Directive.

Article 4   Level of harmonisation

Member States shall not maintain or introduce, in their national law, provisions diverging from those laid down in this Directive, including more or less stringent provisions to ensure a different level of consumer protection, unless otherwise provided for in this Directive.

CHAPTER II
CONSUMER INFORMATION FOR CONTRACTS OTHER THAN DISTANCE OR OFF-PREMISES CONTRACTS

Article 5 Information requirements for contracts other than distance or off-premises contracts

1. Before the consumer is bound by a contract other than a distance or an off-premises contract, or any corresponding offer, the trader shall provide the consumer with the following information in a clear and comprehensible manner, if that information is not already apparent from the context:

(a) the main characteristics of the goods or services, to the extent appropriate to the medium and to the goods or services;

(b) the identity of the trader, such as his trading name, the geographical address at which he is established and his telephone number;

(c) the total price of the goods or services inclusive of taxes, or where the nature of the goods or services is such that the price cannot reasonably be calculated in advance, the manner in which the price is to be calculated, as well as, where applicable, all additional freight, delivery or postal charges or, where those charges cannot reasonably be calculated in advance, the fact that such additional charges may be payable;

(d) where applicable, the arrangements for payment, delivery, performance, the time by which the trader undertakes to deliver the goods or to perform the service, and the trader's complaint handling policy;

(e) in addition to a reminder of the existence of the legal guarantee of conformity for goods, digital content and digital services, the existence and the conditions of after-sales services and commercial guarantees, where applicable;

(f) the duration of the contract, where applicable, or, if the contract is of indeterminate duration or is to be extended automatically, the conditions for terminating the contract;

(g) where applicable, the functionality, including applicable technical protection measures, of goods with digital elements, digital content and digital services;

(h) where applicable, any relevant compatibility and interoperability of goods with digital elements, digital content and digital services that the trader is aware of or can reasonably be expected to have been aware of.

2. Paragraph 1 shall also apply to contracts for the supply of water, gas or electricity, where they are not put up for sale in a limited volume or set quantity, of district heating or of digital content which is not supplied on a tangible medium.

3. Member States shall not be required to apply paragraph 1 to contracts which involve day-to-day transactions and which are performed immediately at the time of their conclusion.

4. Member States may adopt or maintain additional pre-contractual information requirements for contracts to which this Article applies.

CHAPTER III
CONSUMER INFORMATION AND RIGHT OF WITHDRAWAL FOR DISTANCE AND OFF-PREMISES CONTRACTS

Article 6 Information requirements for distance and off-premises contracts

1. Before the consumer is bound by a distance or off-premises contract, or any corresponding offer, the trader shall provide the consumer with the following information in a clear and comprehensible manner:

(a) the main characteristics of the goods or services, to the extent appropriate to the medium and to the goods or services;

(b) the identity of the trader, such as his trading name;

(c) the geographical address at which the trader is established as well as the trader's telephone number and email address; in addition, where the trader provides other means of online communication which guarantee that the consumer can keep any written correspondence, including the date and time of such correspondence, with the trader on a durable medium, the information shall also include details of those other means; all those means of communication provided by the trader shall enable the consumer to contact the trader quickly and communicate with him efficiently; where applicable, the trader shall also provide the geographical address and identity of the trader on whose behalf he is acting;

(d) if different from the address provided in accordance with point (c), the geographical address of the place of business of the trader, and, where applicable, that of the trader on whose behalf he is acting, where the consumer can address any complaints;

(e) the total price of the goods or services inclusive of taxes, or where the nature of the goods or services is such that the price cannot reasonably be calculated in advance, the manner in which the price is to be calculated, as well as, where applicable, all additional freight, delivery or postal charges and any other costs or, where those charges cannot reasonably be calculated in advance, the fact that such additional charges may be payable. In the case of a contract of indeterminate duration or a contract containing a subscription, the total price shall include the total costs per billing period. Where such contracts are charged at a fixed rate, the total price shall also mean the total monthly costs. Where the total costs cannot be reasonably calculated in advance, the manner in which the price is to be calculated shall be provided;

(ea) where applicable, that the price was personalised on the basis of automated decision-making;

(f) the cost of using the means of distance communication for the conclusion of the contract where that cost is calculated other than at the basic rate;

(g) the arrangements for payment, delivery, performance, the time by which the trader undertakes to deliver the goods or to perform the services and, where applicable, the trader's complaint handling policy;

(h) where a right of withdrawal exists, the conditions, time limit and procedures for exercising that right in accordance with Article 11(1), as well as the model withdrawal form set out in Annex I(B);

(i) where applicable, that the consumer will have to bear the cost of returning the goods in case of withdrawal and, for distance contracts, if the goods, by their nature, cannot normally be returned by post, the cost of returning the goods;

(j) that, if the consumer exercises the right of withdrawal after having made a request in accordance with Article 7(3) or Article 8(8), the consumer shall be liable to pay the trader reasonable costs in accordance with Article 14(3);

(k) where a right of withdrawal is not provided for in accordance with Article 16, the information that the consumer will not benefit from a right of withdrawal or, where applicable, the circumstances under which the consumer loses his right of withdrawal;

(l) a reminder of the existence of a legal guarantee of conformity for goods, digital content and digital services;

(m) where applicable, the existence and the conditions of after sale customer assistance, after-sales services and commercial guarantees;

(n) the existence of relevant codes of conduct, as defined in point (f) of Article 2 of Directive 2005/29/EC, and how copies of them can be obtained, where applicable;

(o) the duration of the contract, where applicable, or, if the contract is of indeterminate duration or is to be extended automatically, the conditions for terminating the contract;

(p) where applicable, the minimum duration of the consumer's obligations under the contract;

(q) where applicable, the existence and the conditions of deposits or other financial guarantees to be paid or provided by the consumer at the request of the trader;

(r) where applicable, the functionality, including applicable technical protection measures, of goods with digital elements, digital content and digital services;

(s) where applicable, any relevant compatibility and interoperability of goods with digital elements, digital content and digital services that the trader is aware of or can reasonably be expected to have been aware of;

(t) where applicable, the possibility of having recourse to an out-of-court complaint and redress mechanism, to which the trader is subject, and the methods for having access to it.

2. Paragraph 1 shall also apply to contracts for the supply of water, gas or electricity, where they are not put up for sale in a limited volume or set quantity, of district heating or of digital content which is not supplied on a tangible medium.

3. In the case of a public auction, the information referred to in points (b), (c) and (d) of paragraph 1 may be replaced by the equivalent details for the auctioneer.

4. The information referred to in points (h), (i) and (j) of paragraph 1 of this Article may be provided by means of the model instructions on withdrawal set out in Annex I(A). The trader shall have fulfilled the information requirements laid down in points (h), (i) and (j) of paragraph 1 of this Article if the trader has supplied these instructions to the consumer, correctly filled in. The references to the withdrawal period of 14 days in the model instructions on withdrawal set out in Annex I(A) shall be replaced by references to a withdrawal period of 30 days in cases where Member States have adopted rules in accordance with Article 9(1a).

5. The information referred to in paragraph 1 shall form an integral part of the distance or off-premises contract and shall not be altered unless the contracting parties expressly agree otherwise.

6. If the trader has not complied with the information requirements on additional charges or other costs as referred to in point (e) of paragraph 1, or on the costs of returning the goods as referred to in point (i) of paragraph 1, the consumer shall not bear those charges or costs.

7. Member States may maintain or introduce in their national law language requirements regarding the contractual information, so as to ensure that such information is easily understood by the consumer.

8. The information requirements laid down in this Directive are in addition to information requirements contained in Directive 2006/123/EC and Directive 2000/31/EC and do not prevent Member States from imposing additional information requirements in accordance with those Directives.

   Without prejudice to the first subparagraph, if a provision of Directive 2006/123/EC or Directive 2000/31/EC on the content and the manner in which the information is to be provided conflicts with a provision of this Directive, the provision of this Directive shall prevail.

9. As regards compliance with the information requirements laid down in this Chapter, the burden of proof shall be on the trader.

Article 6a Additional specific information requirements for contracts concluded on online marketplaces

1. Before a consumer is bound by a distance contract, or any corresponding offer, on an online marketplace, the provider of the online marketplace shall, without prejudice to Directive 2005/29/EC, provide the consumer with the following information in a clear and comprehensible manner and in a way appropriate to the means of distance communication:

   (a) general information, made available in a specific section of the online interface that is directly and easily accessible from the page where the offers are presented, on the main parameters determining ranking, as defined in point (m) of Article 2(1) of Directive 2005/29/EC, of offers presented to the consumer as a result of the search query and the relative importance of those parameters as opposed to other parameters;

   (b) whether the third party offering the goods, services or digital content is a trader or not, on the basis of the declaration of that third party to the provider of the online marketplace;

   (c) where the third party offering the goods, services or digital content is not a trader, that the consumer rights stemming from Union consumer protection law do not apply to the contract;

   (d) where applicable, how the obligations related to the contract are shared between the third party offering the goods, services or digital content and the provider of the online marketplace, such information being without prejudice to any responsibility that the provider of the online marketplace or the third-party trader has in relation to the contract under other Union or national law.

2. Without prejudice to Directive 2000/31/EC, this Article does not prevent Member States from imposing additional information requirements for providers of online marketplaces. Such provisions shall be proportionate, non-discriminatory and justified on grounds of consumer protection.

Article 7 Formal requirements for off-premises contracts

1. With respect to off-premises contracts, the trader shall give the information provided for in Article 6(1) to the consumer on paper or, if the consumer agrees, on another durable medium. That information shall be legible and in plain, intelligible language.

2. The trader shall provide the consumer with a copy of the signed contract or the confirmation of the contract on paper or, if the consumer agrees, on another durable medium, including, where applicable, the confirmation of the consumer's prior express consent and acknowledgement in accordance with point (m) of Article 16.

3. Where a consumer wants the performance of services, or the supply of water, gas or electricity, where they are not put up for sale in a limited volume or set quantity, or of district heating to begin during the withdrawal period provided for in Article 9(2), and the contract places the consumer under an obligation to pay, the trader shall require that the consumer make such an express request on a durable medium and request the consumer to acknowledge that, once the contract has been fully performed by the trader, the consumer will no longer have the right of withdrawal.

4. With respect to off-premises contracts where the consumer has explicitly requested the services of the trader for the purpose of carrying out repairs or maintenance for which the trader and the consumer immediately perform their contractual obligations and where the payment to be made by the consumer does not exceed EUR 200:

   (a) the trader shall provide the consumer with the information referred to in points (b) and (c) of Article 6(1) and information about the price or the manner in which the price is to be calculated together with an estimate of the total price, on paper or, if the consumer agrees, on another durable medium. The trader shall provide the information referred to in points (a), (h) and (k) of Article 6(1), but may choose not to provide it on paper or another durable medium if the consumer expressly agrees;

   (b) the confirmation of the contract provided in accordance with paragraph 2 of this Article shall contain the information provided for in Article 6(1).

   Member States may decide not to apply this paragraph.

5. Member States shall not impose any further formal pre-contractual information requirements for the fulfilment of the information obligations laid down in this Directive.

Article 8 Formal requirements for distance contracts

1. With respect to distance contracts, the trader shall give the information provided for in Article 6(1) or make that information available to the consumer in a way appropriate to the means of distance communication used in plain and intelligible language. In so far as that information is provided on a durable medium, it shall be legible.

2. If a distance contract to be concluded by electronic means places the consumer under an obligation to pay, the trader shall make the consumer aware in a clear and prominent manner, and directly before the consumer places his order, of the information provided for in points (a), (e), (o) and (p) of Article 6(1).

   The trader shall ensure that the consumer, when placing his order, explicitly acknowledges that the order implies an obligation to pay. If placing an order entails activating a button or a similar function, the button or similar function shall be labelled in an easily legible manner only with the words 'order with obligation to pay' or a corresponding unambiguous formulation indicating that placing the order entails an obligation to pay the trader. If the trader has not complied with this subparagraph, the consumer shall not be bound by the contract or order.

3. Trading websites shall indicate clearly and legibly at the latest at the beginning of the ordering process whether any delivery restrictions apply and which means of payment are accepted.

4. If the contract is concluded through a means of distance communication which allows limited space or time to display the information, the trader shall provide, on or through that particular means prior to the conclusion of such a contract, at least the pre-contractual information regarding the main characteristics of the goods or services,

the identity of the trader, the total price, the right of withdrawal, the duration of the contract and, if the contract is of indeterminate duration, the conditions for terminating the contract, as referred to, respectively, in points (a), (b), (e), (h) and (o) of Article 6(1) except the model withdrawal form set out in Annex I(B) referred to in point (h). The other information referred to in Article 6(1), including the model withdrawal form, shall be provided by the trader to the consumer in an appropriate way in accordance with paragraph 1 of this Article.

5. Without prejudice to paragraph 4, if the trader makes a telephone call to the consumer with a view to concluding a distance contract, he shall, at the beginning of the conversation with the consumer, disclose his identity and, where applicable, the identity of the person on whose behalf he makes that call, and the commercial purpose of the call.

6. Where a distance contract is to be concluded by telephone, Member States may provide that the trader has to confirm the offer to the consumer who is bound only once he has signed the offer or has sent his written consent. Member States may also provide that such confirmations have to be made on a durable medium.

7. The trader shall provide the consumer with the confirmation of the contract concluded, on a durable medium within a reasonable time after the conclusion of the distance contract, and at the latest at the time of the delivery of the goods or before the performance of the service begins. That confirmation shall include:
   (a) all the information referred to in Article 6(1) unless the trader has already provided that information to the consumer on a durable medium prior to the conclusion of the distance contract; and
   (b) where applicable, the confirmation of the consumer's prior express consent and acknowledgment in accordance with point (m) of Article 16.

8. Where a consumer wants the performance of services, or the supply of water, gas or electricity, where they are not put up for sale in a limited volume or set quantity, or of district heating, to begin during the withdrawal period provided for in Article 9(2), and the contract places the consumer under an obligation to pay, the trader shall require that the consumer make an express request and request the consumer to acknowledge that, once the contract has been fully performed by the trader, the consumer will no longer have the right of withdrawal.

9. This Article shall be without prejudice to the provisions on the conclusion of e-contracts and the placing of e-orders set out in Articles 9 and 11 of Directive 2000/31/EC.

10. Member States shall not impose any further formal pre-contractual information requirements for the fulfilment of the information obligations laid down in this Directive.

Article 9 Right of withdrawal

1. Save where the exceptions provided for in Article 16 apply, the consumer shall have a period of 14 days to withdraw from a distance or off-premises contract, without giving any reason, and without incurring any costs other than those provided for in Article 13(2) and Article 14.

1a. Member States may adopt rules in accordance with which the withdrawal period of 14 days referred to in paragraph 1 is extended to 30 days for contracts concluded in the context of unsolicited visits by a trader to a consumer's home or excursions organised by a trader with the aim or effect of promoting or selling products to consumers for the purpose of protecting legitimate interests of consumers with regard to aggressive or misleading marketing or selling practices. Such rules shall be proportionate, non-discriminatory and justified on grounds of consumer protection.

2. Without prejudice to Article 10, the withdrawal period referred to in paragraph 1 of this Article shall expire after 14 days or, in cases where Member States have adopted rules in accordance with paragraph 1a of this Article, 30 days from:
   (a) in the case of service contracts, the day of the conclusion of the contract;
   (b) in the case of sales contracts, the day on which the consumer or a third party other than the carrier and indicated by the consumer acquires physical possession of the goods or:
      (i) in the case of multiple goods ordered by the consumer in one order and delivered separately, the day on which the consumer or a third party other

than the carrier and indicated by the consumer acquires physical possession of the last good;

 (ii) in the case of delivery of a good consisting of multiple lots or pieces, the day on which the consumer or a third party other than the carrier and indicated by the consumer acquires physical possession of the last lot or piece;

 (iii) in the case of contracts for regular delivery of goods during defined period of time, the day on which the consumer or a third party other than the carrier and indicated by the consumer acquires physical possession of the first good;

(c) in the case of contracts for the supply of water, gas or electricity, where they are not put up for sale in a limited volume or set quantity, of district heating or of digital content which is not supplied on a tangible medium, the day of the conclusion of the contract.

3. The Member States shall not prohibit the contracting parties from performing their contractual obligations during the withdrawal period. Nevertheless, in the case of off-premises contracts, Member States may maintain existing national legislation prohibiting the trader from collecting the payment from the consumer during the given period after the conclusion of the contract.

Article 10 Omission of information on the right of withdrawal

1. If the trader has not provided the consumer with the information on the right of withdrawal as required by point (h) of Article 6(1), the withdrawal period shall expire 12 months from the end of the initial withdrawal period, as determined in accordance with Article 9(2).

2. If the trader has provided the consumer with the information provided for in paragraph 1 of this Article within 12 months from the day referred to in Article 9(2), the withdrawal period shall expire 14 days or, in cases where Member States have adopted rules in accordance with Article 9(1a), 30 days after the day upon which the consumer receives that information.

Article 11 Exercise of the right of withdrawal

1. Before the expiry of the withdrawal period, the consumer shall inform the trader of his decision to withdraw from the contract. For this purpose, the consumer may either:

(a) use the model withdrawal form as set out in Annex I(B); or

(b) make any other unequivocal statement setting out his decision to withdraw from the contract.

 Member States shall not provide for any formal requirements applicable to the model withdrawal form other than those set out in Annex I(B).

2. The consumer shall have exercised his right of withdrawal within the withdrawal period referred to in Article 9(2) and Article 10 if the communication concerning the exercise of the right of withdrawal is sent by the consumer before that period has expired.

3. The trader may, in addition to the possibilities referred to in paragraph 1, give the option to the consumer to electronically fill in and submit either the model withdrawal form set out in Annex I(B) or any other unequivocal statement on the trader's website. In those cases the trader shall communicate to the consumer an acknowledgement of receipt of such a withdrawal on a durable medium without delay.

4. The burden of proof of exercising the right of withdrawal in accordance with this Article shall be on the consumer.

Article 12 Effects of withdrawal

The exercise of the right of withdrawal shall terminate the obligations of the parties:

(a) to perform the distance or off-premises contract; or

(b) to conclude the distance or off-premises contract, in cases where an offer was made by the consumer.

Article 13 Obligations of the trader in the event of withdrawal

1. The trader shall reimburse all payments received from the consumer, including, if applicable, the costs of delivery without undue delay and in any event not later than 14 days from the day on which he is informed of the consumer's decision to withdraw from the contract in accordance with Article 11.

The trader shall carry out the reimbursement referred to in the first subparagraph using the same means of payment as the consumer used for the initial transaction, unless the consumer has expressly agreed otherwise and provided that the consumer does not incur any fees as a result of such reimbursement.

2. Notwithstanding paragraph 1, the trader shall not be required to reimburse the supplementary costs, if the consumer has expressly opted for a type of delivery other than the least expensive type of standard delivery offered by the trader.

3. Unless the trader has offered to collect the goods himself, with regard to sales contracts, the trader may withhold the reimbursement until he has received the goods back, or until the consumer has supplied evidence of having sent back the goods, whichever is the earliest.

4. In respect of personal data of the consumer, the trader shall comply with the obligations applicable under Regulation (EU) 2016/679.

5. The trader shall refrain from using any content, other than personal data, which was provided or created by the consumer when using the digital content or digital service supplied by the trader, except where such content:

    (a) has no utility outside the context of the digital content or digital service supplied by the trader;

    (b) only relates to the consumer's activity when using the digital content or digital service supplied by the trader;

    (c) has been aggregated with other data by the trader and cannot be disaggregated or only with disproportionate efforts; or

    (d) has been generated jointly by the consumer and others, and other consumers are able to continue to make use of the content.

6. Except in the situations referred to in point (a), (b) or (c) of paragraph 5, the trader shall, at the request of the consumer, make available to the consumer any content, other than personal data, which was provided or created by the consumer when using the digital content or digital service supplied by the trader.

7. The consumer shall be entitled to retrieve that digital content free of charge, without hindrance from the trader, within a reasonable time and in a commonly used and machine-readable format.

8. In the event of withdrawal from the contract, the trader may prevent any further use of the digital content or digital service by the consumer, in particular by making the digital content or digital service inaccessible to the consumer or disabling the user account of the consumer, without prejudice to paragraph 6.

Article 14 Obligations of the consumer in the event of withdrawal

1. Unless the trader has offered to collect the goods himself, the consumer shall send back the goods or hand them over to the trader or to a person authorised by the trader to receive the goods, without undue delay and in any event not later than 14 days from the day on which he has communicated his decision to withdraw from the contract to the trader in accordance with Article 11. The deadline shall be met if the consumer sends back the goods before the period of 14 days has expired.

    The consumer shall only bear the direct cost of returning the goods unless the trader has agreed to bear them or the trader failed to inform the consumer that the consumer has to bear them.

    In the case of off-premises contracts where the goods have been delivered to the consumer's home at the time of the conclusion of the contract, the trader shall at his own expense collect the goods if, by their nature, those goods cannot normally be returned by post.

2. The consumer shall only be liable for any diminished value of the goods resulting from the handling of the goods other than what is necessary to establish the nature, characteristics and functioning of the goods. The consumer shall in any event not be liable for diminished value of the goods where the trader has failed to provide notice of the right of withdrawal in accordance with point (h) of Article 6(1).

2a. In the event of withdrawal from the contract, the consumer shall refrain from using the digital content or digital service and from making it available to third parties.

3. Where a consumer exercises the right of withdrawal after having made a request in accordance with Article 7(3) or Article 8(8), the consumer shall pay to the trader an amount which is in proportion to what has been provided until the time the consumer has informed the trader of the exercise of the right of withdrawal, in comparison with the full coverage of the contract. The proportionate amount to be paid by the consumer to the trader shall be calculated on the basis of the total price agreed in the contract. If the total price is excessive, the proportionate amount shall be calculated on the basis of the market value of what has been provided.

4. The consumer shall bear no cost for:
    (a) the performance of services or the supply of water, gas or electricity, where they are not put up for sale in a limited volume or set quantity, or of district heating, in full or in part, during the withdrawal period, where:
        (i) the trader has failed to provide information in accordance with points (h) or (j) of Article 6(1); or
        (ii) the consumer has not expressly requested performance to begin during the withdrawal period in accordance with Article 7(3) and Article 8(8); or
    (b) the supply, in full or in part, of digital content which is not supplied on a tangible medium where:
        (i) the consumer has not given prior express consent to the beginning of the performance before the end of the 14-day or 30-day period referred to in Article 9;
        (ii) the consumer has not acknowledged that he loses his right of withdrawal when giving his consent; or (iii) the trader has failed to provide confirmation in accordance with Article 7(2) or Article 8(7).

5. Except as provided for in Article 13(2) and in this Article, the consumer shall not incur any liability as a consequence of the exercise of the right of withdrawal.

Article 15 Effects of the exercise of the right of withdrawal on ancillary contracts

1. Without prejudice to Article 15 of Directive 2008/48/EC of the European Parliament and of the Council of 23 April 2008 on credit agreements for consumers (20), if the consumer exercises his right of withdrawal from a distance or an off-premises contract in accordance with Articles 9 to 14 of this Directive, any ancillary contracts shall be automatically terminated, without any costs for the consumer, except as provided for in Article 13(2) and in Article 14 of this Directive.

2. The Member States shall lay down detailed rules on the termination of such contracts.

Article 16 Exceptions from the right of withdrawal

Member States shall not provide for the right of withdrawal set out in Articles 9 to 15 in respect of distance and off-premises contracts as regards the following:

(a) service contracts after the service has been fully performed but, if the contract places the consumer under an obligation to pay, only if the performance has begun with the consumer's prior express consent and acknowledgement that he will lose his right of withdrawal once the contract has been fully performed by the trader;

(b) the supply of goods or services for which the price is dependent on fluctuations in the financial market which cannot be controlled by the trader and which may occur within the withdrawal period;

(c) the supply of goods made to the consumer's specifications or clearly personalised;

(d) the supply of goods which are liable to deteriorate or expire rapidly;

(e) the supply of sealed goods which are not suitable for return due to health protection or hygiene reasons and were unsealed after delivery;

(f) the supply of goods which are, after delivery, according to their nature, inseparably mixed with other items;

(g) the supply of alcoholic beverages, the price of which has been agreed upon at the time of the conclusion of the sales contract, the delivery of which can only take place after 30 days and the actual value of which is dependent on fluctuations in the market which cannot be controlled by the trader;

(h) contracts where the consumer has specifically requested a visit from the trader for the purpose of carrying out urgent repairs or maintenance. If, on the occasion of such visit, the trader provides services in addition to those specifically requested by the consumer or goods other than replacement parts necessarily used in carrying out the maintenance or in making the repairs, the right of withdrawal shall apply to those additional services or goods;

(i)   the supply of sealed audio or sealed video recordings or sealed computer software which were unsealed after delivery;

(j)   the supply of a newspaper, periodical or magazine with the exception of subscription contracts for the supply of such publications;

(k)   contracts concluded at a public auction;

(l)   the provision of accommodation other than for residential purpose, transport of goods, car rental services, catering or services related to leisure activities if the contract provides for a specific date or period of performance;

(m)   contracts for the supply of digital content which is not supplied on a tangible medium if the performance has begun and, if the contract places the consumer under an obligation to pay, where:

    (i)   the consumer has provided prior express consent to begin the performance during the right of withdrawal period;

    (ii)   the consumer has provided acknowledgement that he thereby loses his right of withdrawal; and

    (iii) the trader has provided confirmation in accordance with Article 7(2) or Article 8(7).

Member States may derogate from the exceptions from the right of withdrawal set out in points (a), (b), (c) and (e) of the first paragraph for contracts concluded in the context of unsolicited visits by a trader to a consumer's home or excursions organised by a trader with the aim or effect of promoting or selling products to consumers for the purpose of protecting the legitimate interests of consumers with regard to aggressive or misleading marketing or selling practices. Such provisions shall be proportionate, non-discriminatory and justified on grounds of consumer protection.

In the case of service contracts which place the consumer under an obligation to pay where the consumer has specifically requested a visit from the trader for the purpose of carrying out repairs, Member States may provide that the consumer loses the right of withdrawal after the service has been fully performed provided that the performance has begun with the consumer's prior express consent.

CHAPTER IV
OTHER CONSUMER RIGHTS

Article 17 Scope

1.   Articles 18 and 20 shall apply to sales contracts. Those Articles shall not apply to contracts for the supply of water, gas or electricity, where they are not put up for sale in a limited volume or set quantity, of district heating or the supply of digital content which is not supplied on a tangible medium.

2.   Articles 19, 21 and 22 shall apply to sales and service contracts and to contracts for the supply of water, gas, electricity, district heating or digital content.

Article 18 Delivery

1.   Unless the parties have agreed otherwise on the time of delivery, the trader shall deliver the goods by transferring the physical possession or control of the goods to the consumer without undue delay, but not later than 30 days from the conclusion of the contract.

2.   Where the trader has failed to fulfil his obligation to deliver the goods at the time agreed upon with the consumer or within the time limit set out in paragraph 1, the consumer shall call upon him to make the delivery within an additional period of time appropriate to the circumstances. If the trader fails to deliver the goods within that additional period of time, the consumer shall be entitled to terminate the contract.

The first subparagraph shall not be applicable to sales contracts where the trader has refused to deliver the goods or where delivery within the agreed delivery period is essential taking into account all the circumstances attending the conclusion of the contract or where the consumer informs the trader, prior to the conclusion of the contract, that delivery by or on a specified date is essential. In those cases, if the trader fails to deliver the goods at the time agreed upon with the consumer or within the time limit set out in paragraph 1, the consumer shall be entitled to terminate the contract immediately.

3. Upon termination of the contract, the trader shall, without undue delay, reimburse all sums paid under the contract.

4. In addition to the termination of the contract in accordance with paragraph 2, the consumer may have recourse to other remedies provided for by national law.

Article 19 Fees for the use of means of payment

Member States shall prohibit traders from charging consumers, in respect of the use of a given means of payment, fees that exceed the cost borne by the trader for the use of such means.

Article 20 Passing of risk

In contracts where the trader dispatches the goods to the consumer, the risk of loss of or damage to the goods shall pass to the consumer when he or a third party indicated by the consumer and other than the carrier has acquired the physical possession of the goods. However, the risk shall pass to the consumer upon delivery to the carrier if the carrier was commissioned by the consumer to carry the goods and that choice was not offered by the trader, without prejudice to the rights of the consumer against the carrier.

Article 21 Communication by telephone

Member States shall ensure that where the trader operates a telephone line for the purpose of contacting him by telephone in relation to the contract concluded, the consumer, when contacting the trader is not bound to pay more than the basic rate.

The first subparagraph shall be without prejudice to the right of telecommunication services providers to charge for such calls.

Article 22 Additional payments

Before the consumer is bound by the contract or offer, the trader shall seek the express consent of the consumer to any extra payment in addition to the remuneration agreed upon for the trader's main contractual obligation. If the trader has not obtained the consumer's express consent but has inferred it by using default options which the consumer is required to reject in order to avoid the additional payment, the consumer shall be entitled to reimbursement of this payment.

CHAPTER V
GENERAL PROVISIONS

Article 23 Enforcement

1. Member States shall ensure that adequate and effective means exist to ensure compliance with this Directive.

2. The means referred to in paragraph 1 shall include provisions whereby one or more of the following bodies, as determined by national law, may take action under national law before the courts or before the competent administrative bodies to ensure that the national provisions transposing this Directive are applied:
   (a) public bodies or their representatives;
   (b) consumer organisations having a legitimate interest in protecting consumers;
   (c) professional organisations having a legitimate interest in acting.

Article 24 Penalties

1. Member States shall lay down the rules on penalties applicable to infringements of national provisions adopted pursuant to this Directive and shall take all measures necessary to ensure that they are implemented. The penalties provided for shall be effective, proportionate and dissuasive.

2.   Member States shall ensure that the following non-exhaustive and indicative criteria are taken into account for the imposition of penalties, where appropriate:
  (a)   the nature, gravity, scale and duration of the infringement;
  (b)   any action taken by the trader to mitigate or remedy the damage suffered by consumers;
  (c)   any previous infringements by the trader;
  (d)   the financial benefits gained or losses avoided by the trader due to the infringement, if the relevant data are available;
  (e)   penalties imposed on the trader for the same infringement in other Member States in cross-border cases where information about such penalties is available through the mechanism established by Regulation (EU) 2017/2394 of the European Parliament and of the Council;
  (f)   any other aggravating or mitigating factors applicable to the circumstances of the case.
3.   Member States shall ensure that when penalties are to be imposed in accordance with Article 21 of Regulation (EU) 2017/2394, they include the possibility either to impose fines through administrative procedures or to initiate legal proceedings for the imposition of fines, or both, the maximum amount of such fines being at least 4 % of the trader's annual turnover in the Member State or Member States concerned.
4.   For cases where a fine is to be imposed in accordance with paragraph 3, but information on the trader's annual turnover is not available, Member States shall introduce the possibility to impose fines, the maximum amount of which shall be at least EUR 2 million.
5.   Member States shall, by 28 November 2021, notify the Commission of the rules and measures referred to in paragraph 1 and shall notify it, without delay, of any subsequent amendment affecting them.

Article 25 Imperative nature of the Directive

If the law applicable to the contract is the law of a Member State, consumers may not waive the rights conferred on them by the national measures transposing this Directive.

Any contractual terms which directly or indirectly waive or restrict the rights resulting from this Directive shall not be binding on the consumer.

Article 26 Information

Member States shall take appropriate measures to inform consumers and traders of the national provisions transposing this Directive and shall, where appropriate, encourage traders and code owners as defined in point (g) of Article 2 of Directive 2005/29/EC, to inform consumers of their codes of conduct.

Article 27 Inertia selling

The consumer shall be exempted from the obligation to provide any consideration in cases of unsolicited supply of goods, water, gas, electricity, district heating or digital content or unsolicited provision of services, prohibited by Article 5(5) and point 29 of Annex I to Directive 2005/29/EC. In such cases, the absence of a response from the consumer following such an unsolicited supply or provision shall not constitute consent.

Article 28 Transposition

1.   Member States shall adopt and publish, by 13 December 2013, the laws, regulations and administrative provisions necessary to comply with this Directive. They shall forthwith communicate to the Commission the text of these measures in the form of documents. The Commission shall make use of these documents for the purposes of the report referred to in Article 30.
  They shall apply those measures from 13 June 2014.
  When Member States adopt those measures, they shall contain a reference to this Directive or be accompanied by such a reference on the occasion of their official publication. Member States shall determine how such reference is to be made.
2.   The provisions of this Directive shall apply to contracts concluded after 13 June 2014.

Article 29 Reporting requirements

1. Where a Member State makes use of any of the regulatory choices referred to in Article 3(4), Article 6(7), Article 6(8), Article 7(4), Article 8(6), Article 9(1a), Article 9(3) and the second and third paragraphs of Article 16, it shall inform the Commission thereof by 28 November 2021, as well as of any subsequent changes.
2. The Commission shall ensure that the information referred to in paragraph 1 is easily accessible to consumers and traders, inter alia, on a dedicated website.
3. The Commission shall forward the information referred to in paragraph 1 to the other Member States and the European Parliament. The Commission shall consult stakeholders on that information.

Article 30 Reporting by the Commission and review

By 13 December 2016, the Commission shall submit a report on the application of this Directive to the European Parliament and the Council. That report shall include in particular an evaluation of the provisions of this Directive regarding digital content including the right of withdrawal. The report shall be accompanied, where necessary, by legislative proposals to adapt this Directive to developments in the field of consumer rights.

CHAPTER VI
FINAL PROVISIONS

Article 31 Repeals

Directive 85/577/EEC and Directive 97/7/EC, as amended by Directive 2002/65/EC of the European Parliament and of the Council of 23 September 2002 concerning the distance marketing of consumer financial services (21) and by Directives 2005/29/EC and 2007/64/EC, are repealed as of 13 June 2014.

References to the repealed Directives shall be construed as references to this Directive and shall be read in accordance with the correlation table set out in Annex II.

Article 32 Amendment to Directive 93/13/EEC

In Directive 93/13/EEC, the following Article is inserted:

'Article 8a

1. Where a Member State adopts provisions in accordance with Article 8, it shall inform the Commission thereof, as well as of any subsequent changes, in particular where those provisions:
   — extend the unfairness assessment to individually negotiated contractual terms or to the adequacy of the price or remuneration; or,
   — contain lists of contractual terms which shall be considered as unfair,
2. The Commission shall ensure that the information referred to in paragraph 1 is easily accessible to consumers and traders, inter alia, on a dedicated website.
3. The Commission shall forward the information referred to in paragraph 1 to the other Member States and the European Parliament. The Commission shall consult stakeholders on that information.'

Article 33 Amendment to Directive 1999/44/EC

In Directive 1999/44/EC, the following Article is inserted:

'Article 8a

Reporting requirements

1. Where, in accordance with Article 8(2), a Member State adopts more stringent consumer protection provisions than those provided for in Article 5(1) to (3) and in Article 7(1), it shall inform the Commission thereof, as well as of any subsequent changes.
2. The Commission shall ensure that the information referred to in paragraph 1 is easily accessible to consumers and traders, inter alia, on a dedicated website.
3. The Commission shall forward the information referred to in paragraph 1 to the other Member States and the European Parliament. The Commission shall consult stakeholders on that information.'

Article 34 Entry into force

This Directive shall enter into force on the 20th day following its publication in the *Official Journal of the European Union*.

Article 35 Addressees

This Directive is addressed to the Member States.

Done at Strasbourg, 25 October 2011.

ANNEX I

INFORMATION CONCERNING THE EXERCISE OF THE RIGHT OF WITHDRAWAL

A.   **Model instructions on withdrawal**

Right of withdrawal

You have the right to withdraw from this contract within 14 days without giving any reason.

The withdrawal period will expire after 14 days from the day. [1]

To exercise the right of withdrawal, you must inform us [2] of your decision to withdraw from this contract by an unequivocal statement (e.g. a letter sent by post or email). You may use the attached model withdrawal form, but it is not obligatory. [3]

To meet the withdrawal deadline, it is sufficient for you to send your communication concerning your exercise of the right of withdrawal before the withdrawal period has expired.

Effects of withdrawal

If you withdraw from this contract, we shall reimburse to you all payments received from you, including the costs of delivery (with the exception of the supplementary costs resulting from your choice of a type of delivery other than the least expensive type of standard delivery offered by us), without undue delay and in any event not later than 14 days from the day on which we are informed about your decision to withdraw from this contract. We will carry out such reimbursement using the same means of payment as you used for the initial transaction, unless you have expressly agreed otherwise; in any event, you will not incur any fees as a result of such reimbursement. [4]

Instructions for completion:

[1]   Insert one of the following texts between inverted commas:

(a)   in the case of a service contract or a contract for the supply of water, gas or electricity, where they are not put up for sale in a limited volume or set quantity, of district heating or of digital content which is not supplied on a tangible medium: 'of the conclusion of the contract.';

(b)   in the case of a sales contract: 'on which you acquire, or a third party other than the carrier and indicated by you acquires, physical possession of the goods.';

(c)   in the case of a contract relating to multiple goods ordered by the consumer in one order and delivered separately: 'on which you acquire, or a third party other than the carrier and indicated by you acquires, physical possession of the last good.';

(d)   in the case of a contract relating to delivery of a good consisting of multiple lots or pieces: 'on which you acquire, or a third party other than the carrier and indicated by you acquires, physical possession of the last lot or piece.';

(e)   in the case of a contract for regular delivery of goods during a defined period of time: 'on which you acquire, or a third party other than the carrier and indicated by you acquires, physical possession of the first good.'.

[2]   Insert your name, geographical address, telephone number and email address.

[3]   If you give the option to the consumer to electronically fill in and submit information about his withdrawal from the contract on your website, insert the following: 'You can also electronically fill in and submit the model withdrawal form or any other unequivocal statement on our website [insert Internet address]. If you use this

option, we will communicate to you an acknowledgement of receipt of such a withdrawal on a durable medium (e.g. by e-mail) without delay.'.

[4]   In the case of sales contracts in which you have not offered to collect the goods in the event of withdrawal insert the following: 'We may withhold reimbursement until we have received the goods back or you have supplied evidence of having sent back the goods, whichever is the earliest.'.

[5]   If the consumer has received goods in connection with the contract:

(a)   insert:
  — 'We will collect the goods.'; or,
  — 'You shall send back the goods or hand them over to us or ... [insert the name and geographical address, where applicable, of the person authorised by you to receive the goods], without undue delay and in any event not later than 14 days from the day on which you communicate your withdrawal from this contract to us. The deadline is met if you send back the goods before the period of 14 days has expired.'

(b)   insert:
  — 'We will bear the cost of returning the goods.',
  — 'You will have to bear the direct cost of returning the goods.',
  — If, in a distance contract, you do not offer to bear the cost of returning the goods and the goods, by their nature, cannot normally be returned by post: 'You will have to bear the direct cost of returning the goods, ... EUR [insert the amount].'; or if the cost of returning the goods cannot reasonably be calculated in advance: 'You will have to bear the direct cost of returning the goods. The cost is estimated at a maximum of approximately ... EUR [insert the amount].'; or
  — If, in an off-premises contract, the goods, by their nature, cannot normally be returned by post and have been delivered to the consumer's home at the time of the conclusion of the contract: 'We will collect the goods at our own expense.'; and,

(c)   insert 'You are only liable for any diminished value of the goods resulting from the handling other than what is necessary to establish the nature, characteristics and functioning of the goods.'

[6]   In the case of a contract for the provision of services or the supply of water, gas or electricity, where they are not put up for sale in a limited volume or set qu antity, or of district heating, insert the following: 'If you requested to begin the performance of services or the supply of water/gas/electricity/district heating [delete where inapplicable] during the withdrawal period, you shall pay us an amount which is in proportion to what has been provided until you have communicated us your withdrawal from this contract, in comparison with the full coverage of the contract.'.

B.   **Model withdrawal form**

— To [here the trader's name, geographical address and email address are to be inserted by the trader]:
— I/We (*) hereby give notice that I/We (*) withdraw from my/our (*) contract of sale of the following goods (*)/for the provision of the following service (*),
— Ordered on (*)/received on (*),
— Name of consumer(s),
— Address of consumer(s),
— Signature of consumer(s) (only if this form is notified on paper),
— Date
  (*) Delete as appropriate.

DIGITAL SINGLE MARKET

REGULATION (EU) 2016/679 OF THE EUROPEAN PARLIAMENT AND OF THE COUNCIL
of 27 April 2016
on the protection of natural persons with regard to the processing of personal data and on the free movement of such data, and repealing Directive 95/46/EC (General Data Protection Regulation)
(Text with EEA relevance)

CHAPTER I
GENERAL PROVISIONS

Article 1   Subject-matter and objectives

1. This Regulation lays down rules relating to the protection of natural persons with regard to the processing of personal data and rules relating to the free movement of personal data.
2. This Regulation protects fundamental rights and freedoms of natural persons and in particular their right to the protection of personal data.
3. The free movement of personal data within the Union shall be neither restricted nor prohibited for reasons connected with the protection of natural persons with regard to the processing of personal data.

Article 2   Material scope

1. This Regulation applies to the processing of personal data wholly or partly by automated means and to the processing other than by automated means of personal data which form part of a filing system or are intended to form part of a filing system.
2. This Regulation does not apply to the processing of personal data:
   (a)   in the course of an activity which falls outside the scope of Union law;
   (b)   by the Member States when carrying out activities which fall within the scope of Chapter 2 of Title V of the TEU;
   (c)   by a natural person in the course of a purely personal or household activity;
   (d)   by competent authorities for the purposes of the prevention, investigation, detection or prosecution of criminal offences or the execution of criminal penalties, including the safeguarding against and the prevention of threats to public security.
3. For the processing of personal data by the Union institutions, bodies, offices and agencies, Regulation (EC) No 45/2001 applies. Regulation (EC) No 45/2001 and other Union legal acts applicable to such processing of personal data shall be adapted to the principles and rules of this Regulation in accordance with Article 98.
4. This Regulation shall be without prejudice to the application of Directive 2000/31/EC, in particular of the liability rules of intermediary service providers in Articles 12 to 15 of that Directive.

Article 3   Territorial scope

1. This Regulation applies to the processing of personal data in the context of the activities of an establishment of a controller or a processor in the Union, regardless of whether the processing takes place in the Union or not.
2. This Regulation applies to the processing of personal data of data subjects who are in the Union by a controller or processor not established in the Union, where the processing activities are related to:
   (a)   the offering of goods or services, irrespective of whether a payment of the data subject is required, to such data subjects in the Union; or
   (b)   the monitoring of their behaviour as far as their behaviour takes place within the Union.

3. This Regulation applies to the processing of personal data by a controller not established in the Union, but in a place where Member State law applies by virtue of public international law.

Article 4   Definitions

For the purposes of this Regulation:

(1) 'personal data' means any information relating to an identified or identifiable natural person ('data subject'); an identifiable natural person is one who can be identified, directly or indirectly, in particular by reference to an identifier such as a name, an identification number, location data, an online identifier or to one or more factors specific to the physical, physiological, genetic, mental, economic, cultural or social identity of that natural person;

(2) 'processing' means any operation or set of operations which is performed on personal data or on sets of personal data, whether or not by automated means, such as collection, recording, organisation, structuring, storage, adaptation or alteration, retrieval, consultation, use, disclosure by transmission, dissemination or otherwise making available, alignment or combination, restriction, erasure or destruction;

(3) 'restriction of processing' means the marking of stored personal data with the aim of limiting their processing in the future;

(4) 'profiling' means any form of automated processing of personal data consisting of the use of personal data to evaluate certain personal aspects relating to a natural person, in particular to analyse or predict aspects concerning that natural person's performance at work, economic situation, health, personal preferences, interests, reliability, behaviour, location or movements;

(5) 'pseudonymisation' means the processing of personal data in such a manner that the personal data can no longer be attributed to a specific data subject without the use of additional information, provided that such additional information is kept separately and is subject to technical and organisational measures to ensure that the personal data are not attributed to an identified or identifiable natural person;

(6) 'filing system' means any structured set of personal data which are accessible according to specific criteria, whether centralised, decentralised or dispersed on a functional or geographical basis;

(7) 'controller' means the natural or legal person, public authority, agency or other body which, alone or jointly with others, determines the purposes and means of the processing of personal data; where the purposes and means of such processing are determined by Union or Member State law, the controller or the specific criteria for its nomination may be provided for by Union or Member State law;

(8) 'processor' means a natural or legal person, public authority, agency or other body which processes personal data on behalf of the controller;

(9) 'recipient' means a natural or legal person, public authority, agency or another body, to which the personal data are disclosed, whether a third party or not. However, public authorities which may receive personal data in the framework of a particular inquiry in accordance with Union or Member State law shall not be regarded as recipients; the processing of those data by those public authorities shall be in compliance with the applicable data protection rules according to the purposes of the processing;

(10) 'third party' means a natural or legal person, public authority, agency or body other than the data subject, controller, processor and persons who, under the direct authority of the controller or processor, are authorised to process personal data;

(11) 'consent' of the data subject means any freely given, specific, informed and unambiguous indication of the data subject's wishes by which he or she, by a statement or by a clear affirmative action, signifies agreement to the processing of personal data relating to him or her;

(12) 'personal data breach' means a breach of security leading to the accidental or unlawful destruction, loss, alteration, unauthorised disclosure of, or access to, personal data transmitted, stored or otherwise processed;

(13) 'genetic data' means personal data relating to the inherited or acquired genetic characteristics of a natural person which give unique information about the physiology

or the health of that natural person and which result, in particular, from an analysis of a biological sample from the natural person in question;

(14) 'biometric data' means personal data resulting from specific technical processing relating to the physical, physiological or behavioural characteristics of a natural person, which allow or confirm the unique identification of that natural person, such as facial images or dactyloscopic data;

(15) 'data concerning health' means personal data related to the physical or mental health of a natural person, including the provision of health care services, which reveal information about his or her health status;

(16) 'main establishment' means:

(a)   as regards a controller with establishments in more than one Member State, the place of its central administration in the Union, unless the decisions on the purposes and means of the processing of personal data are taken in another establishment of the controller in the Union and the latter establishment has the power to have such decisions implemented, in which case the establishment having taken such decisions is to be considered to be the main establishment;

(b)   as regards a processor with establishments in more than one Member State, the place of its central administration in the Union, or, if the processor has no central administration in the Union, the establishment of the processor in the Union where the main processing activities in the context of the activities of an establishment of the processor take place to the extent that the processor is subject to specific obligations under this Regulation;

(17) 'representative' means a natural or legal person established in the Union who, designated by the controller or processor in writing pursuant to Article 27, represents the controller or processor with regard to their respective obligations under this Regulation;

(18) 'enterprise' means a natural or legal person engaged in an economic activity, irrespective of its legal form, including partnerships or associations regularly engaged in an economic activity;

(19) 'group of undertakings' means a controlling undertaking and its controlled undertakings;

(20) 'binding corporate rules' means personal data protection policies which are adhered to by a controller or processor established on the territory of a Member State for transfers or a set of transfers of personal data to a controller or processor in one or more third countries within a group of undertakings, or group of enterprises engaged in a joint economic activity;

(21) 'supervisory authority' means an independent public authority which is established by a Member State pursuant to Article 51;

(22) 'supervisory authority concerned' means a supervisory authority which is concerned by the processing of personal data because:

(a)   the controller or processor is established on the territory of the Member State of that supervisory authority;

(b)   data subjects residing in the Member State of that supervisory authority are substantially affected or likely to be substantially affected by the processing; or

(c)   a complaint has been lodged with that supervisory authority;

(23) 'cross-border processing' means either:

(a)   processing of personal data which takes place in the context of the activities of establishments in more than one Member State of a controller or processor in the Union where the controller or processor is established in more than one Member State; or

(b)   processing of personal data which takes place in the context of the activities of a single establishment of a controller or processor in the Union but which substantially affects or is likely to substantially affect data subjects in more than one Member State.

(24) 'relevant and reasoned objection' means an objection to a draft decision as to whether there is an infringement of this Regulation, or whether envisaged action in relation to the controller or processor complies with this Regulation, which clearly demonstrates the significance of the risks posed by the draft decision as regards the fundamental rights and freedoms of data subjects and, where applicable, the free flow of personal data within the Union;

(25) 'information society service' means a service as defined in point (b) of Article 1(1) of Directive (EU) 2015/1535 of the European Parliament and of the Council;

(26) 'international organisation' means an organisation and its subordinate bodies governed by public international law, or any other body which is set up by, or on the basis of, an agreement between two or more countries.

CHAPTER II
PRINCIPLES

Article 5 Principles relating to processing of personal data

1. Personal data shall be:
   (a) processed lawfully, fairly and in a transparent manner in relation to the data subject ('lawfulness, fairness and transparency');
   (b) collected for specified, explicit and legitimate purposes and not further processed in a manner that is incompatible with those purposes; further processing for archiving purposes in the public interest, scientific or historical research purposes or statistical purposes shall, in accordance with Article 89(1), not be considered to be incompatible with the initial purposes ('purpose limitation');
   (c) adequate, relevant and limited to what is necessary in relation to the purposes for which they are processed ('data minimisation');
   (d) accurate and, where necessary, kept up to date; every reasonable step must be taken to ensure that personal data that are inaccurate, having regard to the purposes for which they are processed, are erased or rectified without delay ('accuracy');
   (e) kept in a form which permits identification of data subjects for no longer than is necessary for the purposes for which the personal data are processed; personal data may be stored for longer periods insofar as the personal data will be processed solely for archiving purposes in the public interest, scientific or historical research purposes or statistical purposes in accordance with Article 89(1) subject to implementation of the appropriate technical and organisational measures required by this Regulation in order to safeguard the rights and freedoms of the data subject ('storage limitation');
   (f) processed in a manner that ensures appropriate security of the personal data, including protection against unauthorised or unlawful processing and against accidental loss, destruction or damage, using appropriate technical or organisational measures ('integrity and confidentiality').
2. The controller shall be responsible for, and be able to demonstrate compliance with, paragraph 1 ('accountability').

Article 6 Lawfulness of processing

1. Processing shall be lawful only if and to the extent that at least one of the following applies:
   (a) the data subject has given consent to the processing of his or her personal data for one or more specific purposes;
   (b) processing is necessary for the performance of a contract to which the data subject is party or in order to take steps at the request of the data subject prior to entering into a contract;
   (c) processing is necessary for compliance with a legal obligation to which the controller is subject;
   (d) processing is necessary in order to protect the vital interests of the data subject or of another natural person;
   (e) processing is necessary for the performance of a task carried out in the public interest or in the exercise of official authority vested in the controller;
   (f) processing is necessary for the purposes of the legitimate interests pursued by the controller or by a third party, except where such interests are overridden by the interests or fundamental rights and freedoms of the data subject which require protection of personal data, in particular where the data subject is a child.

Point (f) of the first subparagraph shall not apply to processing carried out by public authorities in the performance of their tasks.

2. Member States may maintain or introduce more specific provisions to adapt the application of the rules of this Regulation with regard to processing for compliance with points (c) and (e) of paragraph 1 by determining more precisely specific requirements for the processing and other measures to ensure lawful and fair processing including for other specific processing situations as provided for in Chapter IX.

3. The basis for the processing referred to in point (c) and (e) of paragraph 1 shall be laid down by:

    (a)   Union law; or
    (b)   Member State law to which the controller is subject.

    The purpose of the processing shall be determined in that legal basis or, as regards the processing referred to in point (e) of paragraph 1, shall be necessary for the performance of a task carried out in the public interest or in the exercise of official authority vested in the controller. That legal basis may contain specific provisions to adapt the application of rules of this Regulation, inter alia: the general conditions governing the lawfulness of processing by the controller; the types of data which are subject to the processing; the data subjects concerned; the entities to, and the purposes for which, the personal data may be disclosed; the purpose limitation; storage periods; and processing operations and processing procedures, including measures to ensure lawful and fair processing such as those for other specific processing situations as provided for in Chapter IX. The Union or the Member State law shall meet an objective of public interest and be proportionate to the legitimate aim pursued.

4. Where the processing for a purpose other than that for which the personal data have been collected is not based on the data subject's consent or on a Union or Member State law which constitutes a necessary and proportionate measure in a democratic society to safeguard the objectives referred to in Article 23(1), the controller shall, in order to ascertain whether processing for another purpose is compatible with the purpose for which the personal data are initially collected, take into account, inter alia:

    (a)   any link between the purposes for which the personal data have been collected and the purposes of the intended further processing;
    (b)   the context in which the personal data have been collected, in particular regarding the relationship between data subjects and the controller;
    (c)   the nature of the personal data, in particular whether special categories of personal data are processed, pursuant to Article 9, or whether personal data related to criminal convictions and offences are processed, pursuant to Article 10;
    (d)   the possible consequences of the intended further processing for data subjects;
    (e)   the existence of appropriate safeguards, which may include encryption or pseudonymisation.

Article 7   Conditions for consent

1. Where processing is based on consent, the controller shall be able to demonstrate that the data subject has consented to processing of his or her personal data.

2. If the data subject's consent is given in the context of a written declaration which also concerns other matters, the request for consent shall be presented in a manner which is clearly distinguishable from the other matters, in an intelligible and easily accessible form, using clear and plain language. Any part of such a declaration which constitutes an infringement of this Regulation shall not be binding.

3. The data subject shall have the right to withdraw his or her consent at any time. The withdrawal of consent shall not affect the lawfulness of processing based on consent before its withdrawal. Prior to giving consent, the data subject shall be informed thereof. It shall be as easy to withdraw as to give consent.

4. When assessing whether consent is freely given, utmost account shall be taken of whether, *inter alia*, the performance of a contract, including the provision of a service, is conditional on consent to the processing of personal data that is not necessary for the performance of that contract.

Article 8 Conditions applicable to child's consent in relation to information society services

1. Where point (a) of Article 6(1) applies, in relation to the offer of information society services directly to a child, the processing of the personal data of a child shall be lawful where the child is at least 16 years old. Where the child is below the age of 16 years, such processing shall be lawful only if and to the extent that consent is given or authorised by the holder of parental responsibility over the child.

 Member States may provide by law for a lower age for those purposes provided that such lower age is not below 13 years.

2. The controller shall make reasonable efforts to verify in such cases that consent is given or authorised by the holder of parental responsibility over the child, taking into consideration available technology.

3. Paragraph 1 shall not affect the general contract law of Member States such as the rules on the validity, formation or effect of a contract in relation to a child.

Article 9 Processing of special categories of personal data

1. Processing of personal data revealing racial or ethnic origin, political opinions, religious or philosophical beliefs, or trade union membership, and the processing of genetic data, biometric data for the purpose of uniquely identifying a natural person, data concerning health or data concerning a natural person's sex life or sexual orientation shall be prohibited.

2. Paragraph 1 shall not apply if one of the following applies:

 (a) the data subject has given explicit consent to the processing of those personal data for one or more specified purposes, except where Union or Member State law provide that the prohibition referred to in paragraph 1 may not be lifted by the data subject;

 (b) processing is necessary for the purposes of carrying out the obligations and exercising specific rights of the controller or of the data subject in the field of employment and social security and social protection law in so far as it is authorised by Union or Member State law or a collective agreement pursuant to Member State law providing for appropriate safeguards for the fundamental rights and the interests of the data subject;

 (c) processing is necessary to protect the vital interests of the data subject or of another natural person where the data subject is physically or legally incapable of giving consent;

 (d) processing is carried out in the course of its legitimate activities with appropriate safeguards by a foundation, association or any other not-for-profit body with a political, philosophical, religious or trade union aim and on condition that the processing relates solely to the members or to former members of the body or to persons who have regular contact with it in connection with its purposes and that the personal data are not disclosed outside that body without the consent of the data subjects;

 (e) processing relates to personal data which are manifestly made public by the data subject;

 (f) processing is necessary for the establishment, exercise or defence of legal claims or whenever courts are acting in their judicial capacity;

 (g) processing is necessary for reasons of substantial public interest, on the basis of Union or Member State law which shall be proportionate to the aim pursued, respect the essence of the right to data protection and provide for suitable and specific measures to safeguard the fundamental rights and the interests of the data subject;

 (h) processing is necessary for the purposes of preventive or occupational medicine, for the assessment of the working capacity of the employee, medical diagnosis, the provision of health or social care or treatment or the management of health or social care systems and services on the basis of Union or Member State law or pursuant to contract with a health professional and subject to the conditions and safeguards referred to in paragraph 3;

 (i) processing is necessary for reasons of public interest in the area of public health, such as protecting against serious cross-border threats to health or ensuring high standards of quality and safety of health care and of medicinal products or medical devices, on the basis of Union or Member State law which provides for suitable and specific measures to safeguard the rights and freedoms of the data subject, in particular professional secrecy;

(j)   processing is necessary for archiving purposes in the public interest, scientific or historical research purposes or statistical purposes in accordance with Article 89(1) based on Union or Member State law which shall be proportionate to the aim pursued, respect the essence of the right to data protection and provide for suitable and specific measures to safeguard the fundamental rights and the interests of the data subject.

3.   Personal data referred to in paragraph 1 may be processed for the purposes referred to in point (h) of paragraph 2 when those data are processed by or under the responsibility of a professional subject to the obligation of professional secrecy under Union or Member State law or rules established by national competent bodies or by another person also subject to an obligation of secrecy under Union or Member State law or rules established by national competent bodies.

4.   Member States may maintain or introduce further conditions, including limitations, with regard to the processing of genetic data, biometric data or data concerning health.

Article 10 Processing of personal data relating to criminal convictions and offences

Processing of personal data relating to criminal convictions and offences or related security measures based on Article 6(1) shall be carried out only under the control of official authority or when the processing is authorised by Union or Member State law providing for appropriate safeguards for the rights and freedoms of data subjects. Any comprehensive register of criminal convictions shall be kept only under the control of official authority.

Article 11 Processing which does not require identification

1.   If the purposes for which a controller processes personal data do not or do no longer require the identification of a data subject by the controller, the controller shall not be obliged to maintain, acquire or process additional information in order to identify the data subject for the sole purpose of complying with this Regulation.

2.   Where, in cases referred to in paragraph 1 of this Article, the controller is able to demonstrate that it is not in a position to identify the data subject, the controller shall inform the data subject accordingly, if possible. In such cases, Articles 15 to 20 shall not apply except where the data subject, for the purpose of exercising his or her rights under those articles, provides additional information enabling his or her identification.

CHAPTER III
RIGHTS OF THE DATA SUBJECT

SECTION 1
TRANSPARENCY AND MODALITIES

Article 12 Transparent information, communication and modalities for the exercise of the rights of the data subject

1.   The controller shall take appropriate measures to provide any information referred to in Articles 13 and 14 and any communication under Articles 15 to 22 and 34 relating to processing to the data subject in a concise, transparent, intelligible and easily accessible form, using clear and plain language, in particular for any information addressed specifically to a child. The information shall be provided in writing, or by other means, including, where appropriate, by electronic means. When requested by the data subject, the information may be provided orally, provided that the identity of the data subject is proven by other means.

2.   The controller shall facilitate the exercise of data subject rights under Articles 15 to 22. In the cases referred to in Article 11(2), the controller shall not refuse to act on

the request of the data subject for exercising his or her rights under Articles 15 to 22, unless the controller demonstrates that it is not in a position to identify the data subject.

3. The controller shall provide information on action taken on a request under Articles 15 to 22 to the data subject without undue delay and in any event within one month of receipt of the request. That period may be extended by two further months where necessary, taking into account the complexity and number of the requests. The controller shall inform the data subject of any such extension within one month of receipt of the request, together with the reasons for the delay. Where the data subject makes the request by electronic form means, the information shall be provided by electronic means where possible, unless otherwise requested by the data subject.

4. If the controller does not take action on the request of the data subject, the controller shall inform the data subject without delay and at the latest within one month of receipt of the request of the reasons for not taking action and on the possibility of lodging a complaint with a supervisory authority and seeking a judicial remedy.

5. Information provided under Articles 13 and 14 and any communication and any actions taken under Articles 15 to 22 and 34 shall be provided free of charge. Where requests from a data subject are manifestly unfounded or excessive, in particular because of their repetitive character, the controller may either:

(a) charge a reasonable fee taking into account the administrative costs of providing the information or communication or taking the action requested; or

(b) refuse to act on the request.

The controller shall bear the burden of demonstrating the manifestly unfounded or excessive character of the request.

6. Without prejudice to Article 11, where the controller has reasonable doubts concerning the identity of the natural person making the request referred to in Articles 15 to 21, the controller may request the provision of additional information necessary to confirm the identity of the data subject.

7. The information to be provided to data subjects pursuant to Articles 13 and 14 may be provided in combination with standardised icons in order to give in an easily visible, intelligible and clearly legible manner a meaningful overview of the intended processing. Where the icons are presented electronically they shall be machine-readable.

8. The Commission shall be empowered to adopt delegated acts in accordance with Article 92 for the purpose of determining the information to be presented by the icons and the procedures for providing standardised icons.

SECTION 2
INFORMATION AND ACCESS TO PERSONAL DATA

Article 13 Information to be provided where personal data are collected from the data subject

1. Where personal data relating to a data subject are collected from the data subject, the controller shall, at the time when personal data are obtained, provide the data subject with all of the following information:

(a) the identity and the contact details of the controller and, where applicable, of the controller's representative;

(b) the contact details of the data protection officer, where applicable;

(c) the purposes of the processing for which the personal data are intended as well as the legal basis for the processing;

(d) where the processing is based on point (f) of Article 6(1), the legitimate interests pursued by the controller or by a third party;

(e) the recipients or categories of recipients of the personal data, if any;

(f) where applicable, the fact that the controller intends to transfer personal data to a third country or international organisation and the existence or absence of an adequacy decision by the Commission, or in the case of transfers referred to in Article 46 or 47, or the second subparagraph of Article 49(1), reference to the appropriate or suitable safeguards and the means by which to obtain a copy of them or where they have been made available.

2.   In addition to the information referred to in paragraph 1, the controller shall, at the time when personal data are obtained, provide the data subject with the following further information necessary to ensure fair and transparent processing:
   (a)   the period for which the personal data will be stored, or if that is not possible, the criteria used to determine that period;
   (b)   the existence of the right to request from the controller access to and rectification or erasure of personal data or restriction of processing concerning the data subject or to object to processing as well as the right to data portability;
   (c)   where the processing is based on point (a) of Article 6(1) or point (a) of Article 9(2), the existence of the right to withdraw consent at any time, without affecting the lawfulness of processing based on consent before its withdrawal;
   (d)   the right to lodge a complaint with a supervisory authority;
   (e)   whether the provision of personal data is a statutory or contractual requirement, or a requirement necessary to enter into a contract, as well as whether the data subject is obliged to provide the personal data and of the possible consequences of failure to provide such data;
   (f)   the existence of automated decision-making, including profiling, referred to in Article 22(1) and (4) and, at least in those cases, meaningful information about the logic involved, as well as the significance and the envisaged consequences of such processing for the data subject.
3.   Where the controller intends to further process the personal data for a purpose other than that for which the personal data were collected, the controller shall provide the data subject prior to that further processing with information on that other purpose and with any relevant further information as referred to in paragraph 2.
4.   Paragraphs 1, 2 and 3 shall not apply where and insofar as the data subject already has the information.

Article 14 Information to be provided where personal data have not been obtained from the data subject

1.   Where personal data have not been obtained from the data subject, the controller shall provide the data subject with the following information:
   (a)   the identity and the contact details of the controller and, where applicable, of the controller's representative;
   (b)   the contact details of the data protection officer, where applicable;
   (c)   the purposes of the processing for which the personal data are intended as well as the legal basis for the processing;
   (d)   the categories of personal data concerned;
   (e)   the recipients or categories of recipients of the personal data, if any;
   (f)   where applicable, that the controller intends to transfer personal data to a recipient in a third country or international organisation and the existence or absence of an adequacy decision by the Commission, or in the case of transfers referred to in Article 46 or 47, or the second subparagraph of Article 49(1), reference to the appropriate or suitable safeguards and the means to obtain a copy of them or where they have been made available.
2.   In addition to the information referred to in paragraph 1, the controller shall provide the data subject with the following information necessary to ensure fair and transparent processing in respect of the data subject:
   (a)   the period for which the personal data will be stored, or if that is not possible, the criteria used to determine that period;
   (b)   where the processing is based on point (f) of Article 6(1), the legitimate interests pursued by the controller or by a third party;
   (c)   the existence of the right to request from the controller access to and rectification or erasure of personal data or restriction of processing concerning the data subject and to object to processing as well as the right to data portability;
   (d)   where processing is based on point (a) of Article 6(1) or point (a) of Article 9(2), the existence of the right to withdraw consent at any time, without affecting the lawfulness of processing based on consent before its withdrawal;
   (e)   the right to lodge a complaint with a supervisory authority;

     (f)   from which source the personal data originate, and if applicable, whether it came from publicly accessible sources;

     (g)   the existence of automated decision-making, including profiling, referred to in Article 22(1) and (4) and, at least in those cases, meaningful information about the logic involved, as well as the significance and the envisaged consequences of such processing for the data subject.

3.   The controller shall provide the information referred to in paragraphs 1 and 2:

     (a)   within a reasonable period after obtaining the personal data, but at the latest within one month, having regard to the specific circumstances in which the personal data are processed;

     (b)   if the personal data are to be used for communication with the data subject, at the latest at the time of the first communication to that data subject; or

     (c)   if a disclosure to another recipient is envisaged, at the latest when the personal data are first disclosed.

4.   Where the controller intends to further process the personal data for a purpose other than that for which the personal data were obtained, the controller shall provide the data subject prior to that further processing with information on that other purpose and with any relevant further information as referred to in paragraph 2.

5.   Paragraphs 1 to 4 shall not apply where and insofar as:

     (a)   the data subject already has the information;

     (b)   the provision of such information proves impossible or would involve a disproportionate effort, in particular for processing for archiving purposes in the public interest, scientific or historical research purposes or statistical purposes, subject to the conditions and safeguards referred to in Article 89(1) or in so far as the obligation referred to in paragraph 1 of this Article is likely to render impossible or seriously impair the achievement of the objectives of that processing. In such cases the controller shall take appropriate measures to protect the data subject's rights and freedoms and legitimate interests, including making the information publicly available;

     (c)   obtaining or disclosure is expressly laid down by Union or Member State law to which the controller is subject and which provides appropriate measures to protect the data subject's legitimate interests; or

     (d)   where the personal data must remain confidential subject to an obligation of professional secrecy regulated by Union or Member State law, including a statutory obligation of secrecy.

Article 15 Right of access by the data subject

1.   The data subject shall have the right to obtain from the controller confirmation as to whether or not personal data concerning him or her are being processed, and, where that is the case, access to the personal data and the following information:

     (a)   the purposes of the processing;

     (b)   the categories of personal data concerned;

     (c)   the recipients or categories of recipient to whom the personal data have been or will be disclosed, in particular recipients in third countries or international organisations;

     (d)   where possible, the envisaged period for which the personal data will be stored, or, if not possible, the criteria used to determine that period;

     (e)   the existence of the right to request from the controller rectification or erasure of personal data or restriction of processing of personal data concerning the data subject or to object to such processing;

     (f)   the right to lodge a complaint with a supervisory authority;

     (g)   where the personal data are not collected from the data subject, any available information as to their source;

     (h)   the existence of automated decision-making, including profiling, referred to in Article 22(1) and (4) and, at least in those cases, meaningful information about the logic involved, as well as the significance and the envisaged consequences of such processing for the data subject.

2.   Where personal data are transferred to a third country or to an international organisation, the data subject shall have the right to be informed of the appropriate safeguards pursuant to Article 46 relating to the transfer.

3.   The controller shall provide a copy of the personal data undergoing processing. For any further copies requested by the data subject, the controller may charge a reasonable fee based on administrative costs. Where the data subject makes the request by electronic means, and unless otherwise requested by the data subject, the information shall be provided in a commonly used electronic form.

4.   The right to obtain a copy referred to in paragraph 3 shall not adversely affect the rights and freedoms of others.

SECTION 3
RECTIFICATION AND ERASURE

Article 16 Right to rectification

The data subject shall have the right to obtain from the controller without undue delay the rectification of inaccurate personal data concerning him or her. Taking into account the purposes of the processing, the data subject shall have the right to have incomplete personal data completed, including by means of providing a supplementary statement.

Article 17 Right to erasure ('right to be forgotten')

1.   The data subject shall have the right to obtain from the controller the erasure of personal data concerning him or her without undue delay and the controller shall have the obligation to erase personal data without undue delay where one of the following grounds applies:
   (a)   the personal data are no longer necessary in relation to the purposes for which they were collected or otherwise processed;
   (b)   the data subject withdraws consent on which the processing is based according to point (a) of Article 6(1), or point (a) of Article 9(2), and where there is no other legal ground for the processing;
   (c)   the data subject objects to the processing pursuant to Article 21(1) and there are no overriding legitimate grounds for the processing, or the data subject objects to the processing pursuant to Article 21(2);
   (d)   the personal data have been unlawfully processed;
   (e)   the personal data have to be erased for compliance with a legal obligation in Union or Member State law to which the controller is subject;
   (f)   the personal data have been collected in relation to the offer of information society services referred to in Article 8(1).

2.   Where the controller has made the personal data public and is obliged pursuant to paragraph 1 to erase the personal data, the controller, taking account of available technology and the cost of implementation, shall take reasonable steps, including technical measures, to inform controllers which are processing the personal data that the data subject has requested the erasure by such controllers of any links to, or copy or replication of, those personal data.

3.   Paragraphs 1 and 2 shall not apply to the extent that processing is necessary:
   (a)   for exercising the right of freedom of expression and information;
   (b)   for compliance with a legal obligation which requires processing by Union or Member State law to which the controller is subject or for the performance of a task carried out in the public interest or in the exercise of official authority vested in the controller;
   (c)   for reasons of public interest in the area of public health in accordance with points (h) and (i) of Article 9(2) as well as Article 9(3);
   (d)   for archiving purposes in the public interest, scientific or historical research purposes or statistical purposes in accordance with Article 89(1) in so far as the right referred to in paragraph 1 is likely to render impossible or seriously impair the achievement of the objectives of that processing; or
   (e)   for the establishment, exercise or defence of legal claims.

Article 18 Right to restriction of processing

1. The data subject shall have the right to obtain from the controller restriction of processing where one of the following applies:

   (a) the accuracy of the personal data is contested by the data subject, for a period enabling the controller to verify the accuracy of the personal data;

   (b) the processing is unlawful and the data subject opposes the erasure of the personal data and requests the restriction of their use instead;

   (c) the controller no longer needs the personal data for the purposes of the processing, but they are required by the data subject for the establishment, exercise or defence of legal claims;

   (d) the data subject has objected to processing pursuant to Article 21(1) pending the verification whether the legitimate grounds of the controller override those of the data subject.

2. Where processing has been restricted under paragraph 1, such personal data shall, with the exception of storage, only be processed with the data subject's consent or for the establishment, exercise or defence of legal claims or for the protection of the rights of another natural or legal person or for reasons of important public interest of the Union or of a Member State.

3. A data subject who has obtained restriction of processing pursuant to paragraph 1 shall be informed by the controller before the restriction of processing is lifted.

Article 19 Notification obligation regarding rectification or erasure of personal data or restriction of processing

The controller shall communicate any rectification or erasure of personal data or restriction of processing carried out in accordance with Article 16, Article 17(1) and Article 18 to each recipient to whom the personal data have been disclosed, unless this proves impossible or involves disproportionate effort. The controller shall inform the data subject about those recipients if the data subject requests it.

Article 20 Right to data portability

1. The data subject shall have the right to receive the personal data concerning him or her, which he or she has provided to a controller, in a structured, commonly used and machine-readable format and have the right to transmit those data to another controller without hindrance from the controller to which the personal data have been provided, where:

   (a) the processing is based on consent pursuant to point (a) of Article 6(1) or point (a) of Article 9(2) or on a contract pursuant to point (b) of Article 6(1); and

   (b) the processing is carried out by automated means.

2. In exercising his or her right to data portability pursuant to paragraph 1, the data subject shall have the right to have the personal data transmitted directly from one controller to another, where technically feasible.

3. The exercise of the right referred to in paragraph 1 of this Article shall be without prejudice to Article 17. That right shall not apply to processing necessary for the performance of a task carried out in the public interest or in the exercise of official authority vested in the controller.

4. The right referred to in paragraph 1 shall not adversely affect the rights and freedoms of others.

SECTION 4

RIGHT TO OBJECT AND AUTOMATED INDIVIDUAL DECISION-MAKING

Article 21 Right to object

1. The data subject shall have the right to object, on grounds relating to his or her particular situation, at any time to processing of personal data concerning him or her which is based on point (e) or (f) of Article 6(1), including profiling based on those provisions. The controller shall no longer process the personal data unless the controller demonstrates compelling legitimate grounds for the processing which override the interests, rights and freedoms of the data subject or for the establishment, exercise or defence of legal claims.

2. Where personal data are processed for direct marketing purposes, the data subject shall have the right to object at any time to processing of personal data concerning him or her for such marketing, which includes profiling to the extent that it is related to such direct marketing.

3. Where the data subject objects to processing for direct marketing purposes, the personal data shall no longer be processed for such purposes.

4. At the latest at the time of the first communication with the data subject, the right referred to in paragraphs 1 and 2 shall be explicitly brought to the attention of the data subject and shall be presented clearly and separately from any other information.

5. In the context of the use of information society services, and notwithstanding Directive 2002/58/EC, the data subject may exercise his or her right to object by automated means using technical specifications.

6. Where personal data are processed for scientific or historical research purposes or statistical purposes pursuant to Article 89(1), the data subject, on grounds relating to his or her particular situation, shall have the right to object to processing of personal data concerning him or her, unless the processing is necessary for the performance of a task carried out for reasons of public interest.

Article 22 Automated individual decision-making, including profiling

1. The data subject shall have the right not to be subject to a decision based solely on automated processing, including profiling, which produces legal effects concerning him or her or similarly significantly affects him or her.

2. Paragraph 1 shall not apply if the decision:
    (a) is necessary for entering into, or performance of, a contract between the data subject and a data controller;
    (b) is authorised by Union or Member State law to which the controller is subject and which also lays down suitable measures to safeguard the data subject's rights and freedoms and legitimate interests; or
    (c) is based on the data subject's explicit consent.

3. In the cases referred to in points (a) and (c) of paragraph 2, the data controller shall implement suitable measures to safeguard the data subject's rights and freedoms and legitimate interests, at least the right to obtain human intervention on the part of the controller, to express his or her point of view and to contest the decision.

4. Decisions referred to in paragraph 2 shall not be based on special categories of personal data referred to in Article 9(1), unless point (a) or (g) of Article 9(2) applies and suitable measures to safeguard the data subject's rights and freedoms and legitimate interests are in place.

SECTION 5
RESTRICTIONS

Article 23 Restrictions

1. Union or Member State law to which the data controller or processor is subject may restrict by way of a legislative measure the scope of the obligations and rights provided for in Articles 12 to 22 and Article 34, as well as Article 5 in so far as its provisions correspond to the rights and obligations provided for in Articles 12 to 22, when such a restriction respects the essence of the fundamental rights and freedoms and is a necessary and proportionate measure in a democratic society to safeguard:
    (a) national security;
    (b) defence;
    (c) public security;
    (d) the prevention, investigation, detection or prosecution of criminal offences or the execution of criminal penalties, including the safeguarding against and the prevention of threats to public security;
    (e) other important objectives of general public interest of the Union or of a Member State, in particular an important economic or financial interest of the Union or of a Member State, including monetary, budgetary and taxation a matters, public health and social security;
    (f) the protection of judicial independence and judicial proceedings;

(g)   the prevention, investigation, detection and prosecution of breaches of ethics for regulated professions;

(h)   a monitoring, inspection or regulatory function connected, even occasionally, to the exercise of official authority in the cases referred to in points (a) to (e) and (g);

(i)   the protection of the data subject or the rights and freedoms of others;

(j)   the enforcement of civil law claims.

2.   In particular, any legislative measure referred to in paragraph 1 shall contain specific provisions at least, where relevant, as to:

(a)   the purposes of the processing or categories of processing;

(b)   the categories of personal data;

(c)   the scope of the restrictions introduced;

(d)   the safeguards to prevent abuse or unlawful access or transfer;

(e)   the specification of the controller or categories of controllers;

(f)   the storage periods and the applicable safeguards taking into account the nature, scope and purposes of the processing or categories of processing;

(g)   the risks to the rights and freedoms of data subjects; and

(h)   the right of data subjects to be informed about the restriction, unless that may be prejudicial to the purpose of the restriction.

CHAPTER IV
CONTROLLER AND PROCESSOR

SECTION 1
GENERAL OBLIGATIONS

Article 24 Responsibility of the controller

1.   Taking into account the nature, scope, context and purposes of processing as well as the risks of varying likelihood and severity for the rights and freedoms of natural persons, the controller shall implement appropriate technical and organisational measures to ensure and to be able to demonstrate that processing is performed in accordance with this Regulation. Those measures shall be reviewed and updated where necessary.

2.   Where proportionate in relation to processing activities, the measures referred to in paragraph 1 shall include the implementation of appropriate data protection policies by the controller.

3.   Adherence to approved codes of conduct as referred to in Article 40 or approved certification mechanisms as referred to in Article 42 may be used as an element by which to demonstrate compliance with the obligations of the controller.

Article 25 Data protection by design and by default

1.   Taking into account the state of the art, the cost of implementation and the nature, scope, context and purposes of processing as well as the risks of varying likelihood and severity for rights and freedoms of natural persons posed by the processing, the controller shall, both at the time of the determination of the means for processing and at the time of the processing itself, implement appropriate technical and organisational measures, such as pseudonymisation, which are designed to implement data-protection principles, such as data minimisation, in an effective manner and to integrate the necessary safeguards into the processing in order to meet the requirements of this Regulation and protect the rights of data subjects.

2.   The controller shall implement appropriate technical and organisational measures for ensuring that, by default, only personal data which are necessary for each specific purpose of the processing are processed. That obligation applies to the amount of personal data collected, the extent of their processing, the period of their storage and their accessibility. In particular, such measures shall ensure that by default personal data are not made accessible without the individual's intervention to an indefinite number of natural persons.

3.   An approved certification mechanism pursuant to Article 42 may be used as an element to demonstrate compliance with the requirements set out in paragraphs 1 and 2 of this Article.

Article 26 Joint controllers

1. Where two or more controllers jointly determine the purposes and means of processing, they shall be joint controllers. They shall in a transparent manner determine their respective responsibilities for compliance with the obligations under this Regulation, in particular as regards the exercising of the rights of the data subject and their respective duties to provide the information referred to in Articles 13 and 14, by means of an arrangement between them unless, and in so far as, the respective responsibilities of the controllers are determined by Union or Member State law to which the controllers are subject. The arrangement may designate a contact point for data subjects.

2. The arrangement referred to in paragraph 1 shall duly reflect the respective roles and relationships of the joint controllers *vis-à-vis* the data subjects. The essence of the arrangement shall be made available to the data subject.

3. Irrespective of the terms of the arrangement referred to in paragraph 1, the data subject may exercise his or her rights under this Regulation in respect of and against each of the controllers.

Article 27 Representatives of controllers or processors not established in the Union

1. Where Article 3(2) applies, the controller or the processor shall designate in writing a representative in the Union.

2. The obligation laid down in paragraph 1 of this Article shall not apply to:

    (a) processing which is occasional, does not include, on a large scale, processing of special categories of data as referred to in Article 9(1) or processing of personal data relating to criminal convictions and offences referred to in Article 10, and is unlikely to result in a risk to the rights and freedoms of natural persons, taking into account the nature, context, scope and purposes of the processing; or

    (b) a public authority or body.

3. The representative shall be established in one of the Member States where the data subjects, whose personal data are processed in relation to the offering of goods or services to them, or whose behaviour is monitored, are.

4. The representative shall be mandated by the controller or processor to be addressed in addition to or instead of the controller or the processor by, in particular, supervisory authorities and data subjects, on all issues related to processing, for the purposes of ensuring compliance with this Regulation.

5. The designation of a representative by the controller or processor shall be without prejudice to legal actions which could be initiated against the controller or the processor themselves.

Article 28 Processor

1. Where processing is to be carried out on behalf of a controller, the controller shall use only processors providing sufficient guarantees to implement appropriate technical and organisational measures in such a manner that processing will meet the requirements of this Regulation and ensure the protection of the rights of the data subject.

2. The processor shall not engage another processor without prior specific or general written authorisation of the controller. In the case of general written authorisation, the processor shall inform the controller of any intended changes concerning the addition or replacement of other processors, thereby giving the controller the opportunity to object to such changes.

3. Processing by a processor shall be governed by a contract or other legal act under Union or Member State law, that is binding on the processor with regard to the controller and that sets out the subject-matter and duration of the processing, the nature and purpose of the processing, the type of personal data and categories of data subjects and the obligations and rights of the controller. That contract or other legal act shall stipulate, in particular, that the processor:

    (a) processes the personal data only on documented instructions from the controller, including with regard to transfers of personal data to a third country or an international organisation, unless required to do so by Union or Member State law to which the processor is subject; in such a case, the processor shall inform the controller of that legal requirement before processing, unless that law prohibits such information on important grounds of public interest;

(b)   ensures that persons authorised to process the personal data have committed themselves to confidentiality or are under an appropriate statutory obligation of confidentiality;

(c)   takes all measures required pursuant to Article 32;

(d)   respects the conditions referred to in paragraphs 2 and 4 for engaging another processor;

(e)   taking into account the nature of the processing, assists the controller by appropriate technical and organisational measures, insofar as this is possible, for the fulfilment of the controller's obligation to respond to requests for exercising the data subject's rights laid down in Chapter III;

(f)   assists the controller in ensuring compliance with the obligations pursuant to Articles 32 to 36 taking into account the nature of processing and the information available to the processor;

(g)   at the choice of the controller, deletes or returns all the personal data to the controller after the end of the provision of services relating to processing, and deletes existing copies unless Union or Member State law requires storage of the personal data;

(h)   makes available to the controller all information necessary to demonstrate compliance with the obligations laid down in this Article and allow for and contribute to audits, including inspections, conducted by the controller or another auditor mandated by the controller.

With regard to point (h) of the first subparagraph, the processor shall immediately inform the controller if, in its opinion, an instruction infringes this Regulation or other Union or Member State data protection provisions.

4.   Where a processor engages another processor for carrying out specific processing activities on behalf of the controller, the same data protection obligations as set out in the contract or other legal act between the controller and the processor as referred to in paragraph 3 shall be imposed on that other processor by way of a contract or other legal act under Union or Member State law, in particular providing sufficient guarantees to implement appropriate technical and organisational measures in such a manner that the processing will meet the requirements of this Regulation. Where that other processor fails to fulfil its data protection obligations, the initial processor shall remain fully liable to the controller for the performance of that other processor's obligations.

5.   Adherence of a processor to an approved code of conduct as referred to in Article 40 or an approved certification mechanism as referred to in Article 42 may be used as an element by which to demonstrate sufficient guarantees as referred to in paragraphs 1 and 4 of this Article.

6.   Without prejudice to an individual contract between the controller and the processor, the contract or the other legal act referred to in paragraphs 3 and 4 of this Article may be based, in whole or in part, on standard contractual clauses referred to in paragraphs 7 and 8 of this Article, including when they are part of a certification granted to the controller or processor pursuant to Articles 42 and 43.

7.   The Commission may lay down standard contractual clauses for the matters referred to in paragraph 3 and 4 of this Article and in accordance with the examination procedure referred to in Article 93(2).

8.   A supervisory authority may adopt standard contractual clauses for the matters referred to in paragraph 3 and 4 of this Article and in accordance with the consistency mechanism referred to in Article 63.

9.   The contract or the other legal act referred to in paragraphs 3 and 4 shall be in writing, including in electronic form.

10. Without prejudice to Articles 82, 83 and 84, if a processor infringes this Regulation by determining the purposes and means of processing, the processor shall be considered to be a controller in respect of that processing.

Article 29 Processing under the authority of the controller or processor

The processor and any person acting under the authority of the controller or of the processor, who has access to personal data, shall not process those data except on instructions from the controller, unless required to do so by Union or Member State law.

Article 30 Records of processing activities

1. Each controller and, where applicable, the controller's representative, shall maintain a record of processing activities under its responsibility. That record shall contain all of the following information:
   (a) the name and contact details of the controller and, where applicable, the joint controller, the controller's representative and the data protection officer;
   (b) the purposes of the processing;
   (c) a description of the categories of data subjects and of the categories of personal data;
   (d) the categories of recipients to whom the personal data have been or will be disclosed including recipients in third countries or international organisations;
   (e) where applicable, transfers of personal data to a third country or an international organisation, including the identification of that third country or international organisation and, in the case of transfers referred to in the second subparagraph of Article 49(1), the documentation of suitable safeguards;
   (f) where possible, the envisaged time limits for erasure of the different categories of data;
   (g) where possible, a general description of the technical and organisational security measures referred to in Article 32(1).
2. Each processor and, where applicable, the processor's representative shall maintain a record of all categories of processing activities carried out on behalf of a controller, containing:
   (a) the name and contact details of the processor or processors and of each controller on behalf of which the processor is acting, and, where applicable, of the controller's or the processor's representative, and the data protection officer;
   (b) the categories of processing carried out on behalf of each controller;
   (c) where applicable, transfers of personal data to a third country or an international organisation, including the identification of that third country or international organisation and, in the case of transfers referred to in the second subparagraph of Article 49(1), the documentation of suitable safeguards;
   (d) where possible, a general description of the technical and organisational security measures referred to in Article 32(1).
3. The records referred to in paragraphs 1 and 2 shall be in writing, including in electronic form.
4. The controller or the processor and, where applicable, the controller's or the processor's representative, shall make the record available to the supervisory authority on request.
5. The obligations referred to in paragraphs 1 and 2 shall not apply to an enterprise or an organisation employing fewer than 250 persons unless the processing it carries out is likely to result in a risk to the rights and freedoms of data subjects, the processing is not occasional, or the processing includes special categories of data as referred to in Article 9(1) or personal data relating to criminal convictions and offences referred to in Article 10.

Article 31 Cooperation with the supervisory authority

The controller and the processor and, where applicable, their representatives, shall cooperate, on request, with the supervisory authority in the performance of its tasks.

SECTION 2
SECURITY OF PERSONAL DATA

Article 32 Security of processing

1. Taking into account the state of the art, the costs of implementation and the nature, scope, context and purposes of processing as well as the risk of varying likelihood and severity for the rights and freedoms of natural persons, the controller and the processor shall implement appropriate technical and organisational measures to ensure a level of security appropriate to the risk, including inter alia as appropriate:
   (a) the pseudonymisation and encryption of personal data;

    (b)   the ability to ensure the ongoing confidentiality, integrity, availability and resilience of processing systems and services;

    (c)   the ability to restore the availability and access to personal data in a timely manner in the event of a physical or technical incident;

    (d)   a process for regularly testing, assessing and evaluating the effectiveness of technical and organisational measures for ensuring the security of the processing.

2. In assessing the appropriate level of security account shall be taken in particular of the risks that are presented by processing, in particular from accidental or unlawful destruction, loss, alteration, unauthorised disclosure of, or access to personal data transmitted, stored or otherwise processed.

3. Adherence to an approved code of conduct as referred to in Article 40 or an approved certification mechanism as referred to in Article 42 may be used as an element by which to demonstrate compliance with the requirements set out in paragraph 1 of this Article.

4. The controller and processor shall take steps to ensure that any natural person acting under the authority of the controller or the processor who has access to personal data does not process them except on instructions from the controller, unless he or she is required to do so by Union or Member State law.

Article 33 Notification of a personal data breach to the supervisory authority

1. In the case of a personal data breach, the controller shall without undue delay and, where feasible, not later than 72 hours after having become aware of it, notify the personal data breach to the supervisory authority competent in accordance with Article 55, unless the personal data breach is unlikely to result in a risk to the rights and freedoms of natural persons. Where the notification to the supervisory authority is not made within 72 hours, it shall be accompanied by reasons for the delay.

2. The processor shall notify the controller without undue delay after becoming aware of a personal data breach.

3. The notification referred to in paragraph 1 shall at least:

    (a)   describe the nature of the personal data breach including where possible, the categories and approximate number of data subjects concerned and the categories and approximate number of personal data records concerned;

    (b)   communicate the name and contact details of the data protection officer or other contact point where more information can be obtained;

    (c)   describe the likely consequences of the personal data breach;

    (d)   describe the measures taken or proposed to be taken by the controller to address the personal data breach, including, where appropriate, measures to mitigate its possible adverse effects.

4. Where, and in so far as, it is not possible to provide the information at the same time, the information may be provided in phases without undue further delay.

5. The controller shall document any personal data breaches, comprising the facts relating to the personal data breach, its effects and the remedial action taken. That documentation shall enable the supervisory authority to verify compliance with this Article.

Article 34 Communication of a personal data breach to the data subject

1. When the personal data breach is likely to result in a high risk to the rights and freedoms of natural persons, the controller shall communicate the personal data breach to the data subject without undue delay.

2. The communication to the data subject referred to in paragraph 1 of this Article shall describe in clear and plain language the nature of the personal data breach and contain at least the information and measures referred to in points (b), (c) and (d) of Article 33(3).

3. The communication to the data subject referred to in paragraph 1 shall not be required if any of the following conditions are met:

    (a)   the controller has implemented appropriate technical and organisational protection measures, and those measures were applied to the personal data affected by the personal data breach, in particular those that render the personal data unintelligible to any person who is not authorised to access it, such as encryption;

   (b) the controller has taken subsequent measures which ensure that the high risk to the rights and freedoms of data subjects referred to in paragraph 1 is no longer likely to materialise;

   (c) it would involve disproportionate effort. In such a case, there shall instead be a public communication or similar measure whereby the data subjects are informed in an equally effective manner.

4. If the controller has not already communicated the personal data breach to the data subject, the supervisory authority, having considered the likelihood of the personal data breach resulting in a high risk, may require it to do so or may decide that any of the conditions referred to in paragraph 3 are met.

SECTION 3

DATA PROTECTION IMPACT ASSESSMENT AND PRIOR CONSULTATION

Article 35 Data protection impact assessment

1. Where a type of processing in particular using new technologies, and taking into account the nature, scope, context and purposes of the processing, is likely to result in a high risk to the rights and freedoms of natural persons, the controller shall, prior to the processing, carry out an assessment of the impact of the envisaged processing operations on the protection of personal data. A single assessment may address a set of similar processing operations that present similar high risks.

2. The controller shall seek the advice of the data protection officer, where designated, when carrying out a data protection impact assessment.

3. A data protection impact assessment referred to in paragraph 1 shall in particular be required in the case of:

   (a) a systematic and extensive evaluation of personal aspects relating to natural persons which is based on automated processing, including profiling, and on which decisions are based that produce legal effects concerning the natural person or similarly significantly affect the natural person;

   (b) processing on a large scale of special categories of data referred to in Article 9(1), or of personal data relating to criminal convictions and offences referred to in Article 10; or

   (c) a systematic monitoring of a publicly accessible area on a large scale.

4. The supervisory authority shall establish and make public a list of the kind of processing operations which are subject to the requirement for a data protection impact assessment pursuant to paragraph 1. The supervisory authority shall communicate those lists to the Board referred to in Article 68.

5. The supervisory authority may also establish and make public a list of the kind of processing operations for which no data protection impact assessment is required. The supervisory authority shall communicate those lists to the Board.

6. Prior to the adoption of the lists referred to in paragraphs 4 and 5, the competent supervisory authority shall apply the consistency mechanism referred to in Article 63 where such lists involve processing activities which are related to the offering of goods or services to data subjects or to the monitoring of their behaviour in several Member States, or may substantially affect the free movement of personal data within the Union.

7. The assessment shall contain at least:

   (a) a systematic description of the envisaged processing operations and the purposes of the processing, including, where applicable, the legitimate interest pursued by the controller;

   (b) an assessment of the necessity and proportionality of the processing operations in relation to the purposes;

   (c) an assessment of the risks to the rights and freedoms of data subjects referred to in paragraph 1; and

(d)   the measures envisaged to address the risks, including safeguards, security measures and mechanisms to ensure the protection of personal data and to demonstrate compliance with this Regulation taking into account the rights and legitimate interests of data subjects and other persons concerned.

8.   Compliance with approved codes of conduct referred to in Article 40 by the relevant controllers or processors shall be taken into due account in assessing the impact of the processing operations performed by such controllers or processors, in particular for the purposes of a data protection impact assessment.

9.   Where appropriate, the controller shall seek the views of data subjects or their representatives on the intended processing, without prejudice to the protection of commercial or public interests or the security of processing operations.

10. Where processing pursuant to point (c) or (e) of Article 6(1) has a legal basis in Union law or in the law of the Member State to which the controller is subject, that law regulates the specific processing operation or set of operations in question, and a data protection impact assessment has already been carried out as part of a general impact assessment in the context of the adoption of that legal basis, paragraphs 1 to 7 shall not apply unless Member States deem it to be necessary to carry out such an assessment prior to processing activities.

11. Where necessary, the controller shall carry out a review to assess if processing is performed in accordance with the data protection impact assessment at least when there is a change of the risk represented by processing operations.

Article 36 Prior consultation

1.   The controller shall consult the supervisory authority prior to processing where a data protection impact assessment under Article 35 indicates that the processing would result in a high risk in the absence of measures taken by the controller to mitigate the risk.

2.   Where the supervisory authority is of the opinion that the intended processing referred to in paragraph 1 would infringe this Regulation, in particular where the controller has insufficiently identified or mitigated the risk, the supervisory authority shall, within period of up to eight weeks of receipt of the request for consultation, provide written advice to the controller and, where applicable to the processor, and may use any of its powers referred to in Article 58. That period may be extended by six weeks, taking into account the complexity of the intended processing. The supervisory authority shall inform the controller and, where applicable, the processor, of any such extension within one month of receipt of the request for consultation together with the reasons for the delay. Those periods may be suspended until the supervisory authority has obtained information it has requested for the purposes of the consultation.

3.   When consulting the supervisory authority pursuant to paragraph 1, the controller shall provide the supervisory authority with:

(a)   where applicable, the respective responsibilities of the controller, joint controllers and processors involved in the processing, in particular for processing within a group of undertakings;

(b)   the purposes and means of the intended processing;

(c)   the measures and safeguards provided to protect the rights and freedoms of data subjects pursuant to this Regulation;

(d)   where applicable, the contact details of the data protection officer;

(e)   the data protection impact assessment provided for in Article 35; and

(f)   any other information requested by the supervisory authority.

4.   Member States shall consult the supervisory authority during the preparation of a proposal for a legislative measure to be adopted by a national parliament, or of a regulatory measure based on such a legislative measure, which relates to processing.

5.   Notwithstanding paragraph 1, Member State law may require controllers to consult with, and obtain prior authorisation from, the supervisory authority in relation to processing by a controller for the performance of a task carried out by the controller in the public interest, including processing in relation to social protection and public health.

SECTION 4
DATA PROTECTION OFFICER

Article 37 Designation of the data protection officer

1. The controller and the processor shall designate a data protection officer in any case where:
   (a) the processing is carried out by a public authority or body, except for courts acting in their judicial capacity;
   (b) the core activities of the controller or the processor consist of processing operations which, by virtue of their nature, their scope and/or their purposes, require regular and systematic monitoring of data subjects on a large scale; or
   (c) the core activities of the controller or the processor consist of processing on a large scale of special categories of data pursuant to Article 9 and personal data relating to criminal convictions and offences referred to in Article 10.
2. A group of undertakings may appoint a single data protection officer provided that a data protection officer is easily accessible from each establishment.
3. Where the controller or the processor is a public authority or body, a single data protection officer may be designated for several such authorities or bodies, taking account of their organisational structure and size.
4. In cases other than those referred to in paragraph 1, the controller or processor or associations and other bodies representing categories of controllers or processors may or, where required by Union or Member State law shall, designate a data protection officer. The data protection officer may act for such associations and other bodies representing controllers or processors.
5. The data protection officer shall be designated on the basis of professional qualities and, in particular, expert knowledge of data protection law and practices and the ability to fulfil the tasks referred to in Article 39.
6. The data protection officer may be a staff member of the controller or processor, or fulfil the tasks on the basis of a service contract.
7. The controller or the processor shall publish the contact details of the data protection officer and communicate them to the supervisory authority.

Article 38 Position of the data protection officer

1. The controller and the processor shall ensure that the data protection officer is involved, properly and in a timely manner, in all issues which relate to the protection of personal data.
2. The controller and processor shall support the data protection officer in performing the tasks referred to in Article 39 by providing resources necessary to carry out those tasks and access to personal data and processing operations, and to maintain his or her expert knowledge.
3. The controller and processor shall ensure that the data protection officer does not receive any instructions regarding the exercise of those tasks. He or she shall not be dismissed or penalised by the controller or the processor for performing his tasks. The data protection officer shall directly report to the highest management level of the controller or the processor.
4. Data subjects may contact the data protection officer with regard to all issues related to processing of their personal data and to the exercise of their rights under this Regulation.
5. The data protection officer shall be bound by secrecy or confidentiality concerning the performance of his or her tasks, in accordance with Union or Member State law.
6. The data protection officer may fulfil other tasks and duties. The controller or processor shall ensure that any such tasks and duties do not result in a conflict of interests.

Article 39 Tasks of the data protection officer

1. The data protection officer shall have at least the following tasks:
   (a) to inform and advise the controller or the processor and the employees who carry out processing of their obligations pursuant to this Regulation and to other Union or Member State data protection provisions;
   (b) to monitor compliance with this Regulation, with other Union or Member State data protection provisions and with the policies of the controller or processor

in relation to the protection of personal data, including the assignment of responsibilities, awareness-raising and training of staff involved in processing operations, and the related audits;

(c)   to provide advice where requested as regards the data protection impact assessment and monitor its performance pursuant to Article 35;

(d)   to cooperate with the supervisory authority;

(e)   to act as the contact point for the supervisory authority on issues relating to processing, including the prior consultation referred to in Article 36, and to consult, where appropriate, with regard to any other matter.

2.   The data protection officer shall in the performance of his or her tasks have due regard to the risk associated with processing operations, taking into account the nature, scope, context and purposes of processing.

SECTION 5
CODES OF CONDUCT AND CERTIFICATION

Article 40 Codes of conduct

1.   The Member States, the supervisory authorities, the Board and the Commission shall encourage the drawing up of codes of conduct intended to contribute to the proper application of this Regulation, taking account of the specific features of the various processing sectors and the specific needs of micro, small and medium-sized enterprises.

2.   Associations and other bodies representing categories of controllers or processors may prepare codes of conduct, or amend or extend such codes, for the purpose of specifying the application of this Regulation, such as with regard to:

(a)   fair and transparent processing;

(b)   the legitimate interests pursued by controllers in specific contexts;

(c)   the collection of personal data;

(d)   the pseudonymisation of personal data;

(e)   the information provided to the public and to data subjects;

(f)   the exercise of the rights of data subjects;

(g)   the information provided to, and the protection of, children, and the manner in which the consent of the holders of parental responsibility over children is to be obtained;

(h)   the measures and procedures referred to in Articles 24 and 25 and the measures to ensure security of processing referred to in Article 32;

(i)   the notification of personal data breaches to supervisory authorities and the communication of such personal data breaches to data subjects;

(j)   the transfer of personal data to third countries or international organisations; or

(k)   out-of-court proceedings and other dispute resolution procedures for resolving disputes between controllers and data subjects with regard to processing, without prejudice to the rights of data subjects pursuant to Articles 77 and 79.

3.   In addition to adherence by controllers or processors subject to this Regulation, codes of conduct approved pursuant to paragraph 5 of this Article and having general validity pursuant to paragraph 9 of this Article may also be adhered to by controllers or processors that are not subject to this Regulation pursuant to Article 3 in order to provide appropriate safeguards within the framework of personal data transfers to third countries or international organisations under the terms referred to in point (e) of Article 46(2). Such controllers or processors shall make binding and enforceable commitments, via contractual or other legally binding instruments, to apply those appropriate safeguards including with regard to the rights of data subjects.

4.   A code of conduct referred to in paragraph 2 of this Article shall contain mechanisms which enable the body referred to in Article 41(1) to carry out the mandatory monitoring of compliance with its provisions by the controllers or processors which undertake to apply it, without prejudice to the tasks and powers of supervisory authorities competent pursuant to Article 55 or 56.

5.   Associations and other bodies referred to in paragraph 2 of this Article which intend to prepare a code of conduct or to amend or extend an existing code shall submit the draft code, amendment or extension to the supervisory authority which is competent

pursuant to Article 55. The supervisory authority shall provide an opinion on whether the draft code, amendment or extension complies with this Regulation and shall approve that draft code, amendment or extension if it finds that it provides sufficient appropriate safeguards.

6.   Where the draft code, or amendment or extension is approved in accordance with paragraph 5, and where the code of conduct concerned does not relate to processing activities in several Member States, the supervisory authority shall register and publish the code.

7.   Where a draft code of conduct relates to processing activities in several Member States, the supervisory authority which is competent pursuant to Article 55 shall, before approving the draft code, amendment or extension, submit it in the procedure referred to in Article 63 to the Board which shall provide an opinion on whether the draft code, amendment or extension complies with this Regulation or, in the situation referred to in paragraph 3 of this Article, provides appropriate safeguards.

8.   Where the opinion referred to in paragraph 7 confirms that the draft code, amendment or extension complies with this Regulation, or, in the situation referred to in paragraph 3, provides appropriate safeguards, the Board shall submit its opinion to the Commission.

9.   The Commission may, by way of implementing acts, decide that the approved code of conduct, amendment or extension submitted to it pursuant to paragraph 8 of this Article have general validity within the Union. Those implementing acts shall be adopted in accordance with the examination procedure set out in Article 93(2).

10.   The Commission shall ensure appropriate publicity for the approved codes which have been decided as having general validity in accordance with paragraph 9.

11.   The Board shall collate all approved codes of conduct, amendments and extensions in a register and shall make them publicly available by way of appropriate means.

Article 41 Monitoring of approved codes of conduct

1.   Without prejudice to the tasks and powers of the competent supervisory authority under Articles 57 and 58, the monitoring of compliance with a code of conduct pursuant to Article 40 may be carried out by a body which has an appropriate level of expertise in relation to the subject-matter of the code and is accredited for that purpose by the competent supervisory authority.

2.   A body as referred to in paragraph 1 may be accredited to monitor compliance with a code of conduct where that body has:

(a)   demonstrated its independence and expertise in relation to the subject-matter of the code to the satisfaction of the competent supervisory authority;

(b)   established procedures which allow it to assess the eligibility of controllers and processors concerned to apply the code, to monitor their compliance with its provisions and to periodically review its operation;

(c)   established procedures and structures to handle complaints about infringements of the code or the manner in which the code has been, or is being, implemented by a controller or processor, and to make those procedures and structures transparent to data subjects and the public; and

(d)   demonstrated to the satisfaction of the competent supervisory authority that its tasks and duties do not result in a conflict of interests.

3.   The competent supervisory authority shall submit the draft criteria for accreditation of a body as referred to in paragraph 1 of this Article to the Board pursuant to the consistency mechanism referred to in Article 63.

4.   Without prejudice to the tasks and powers of the competent supervisory authority and the provisions of Chapter VIII, a body as referred to in paragraph 1 of this Article shall, subject to appropriate safeguards, take appropriate action in cases of infringement of the code by a controller or processor, including suspension or exclusion of the controller or processor concerned from the code. It shall inform the competent supervisory authority of such actions and the reasons for taking them.

5.   The competent supervisory authority shall revoke the accreditation of a body as referred to in paragraph 1 if the conditions for accreditation are not, or are no longer, met or where actions taken by the body infringe this Regulation.

6.   This Article shall not apply to processing carried out by public authorities and bodies.

Article 42 Certification

1. The Member States, the supervisory authorities, the Board and the Commission shall encourage, in particular at Union level, the establishment of data protection certification mechanisms and of data protection seals and marks, for the purpose of demonstrating compliance with this Regulation of processing operations by controllers and processors. The specific needs of micro, small and medium-sized enterprises shall be taken into account.

2. In addition to adherence by controllers or processors subject to this Regulation, data protection certification mechanisms, seals or marks approved pursuant to paragraph 5 of this Article may be established for the purpose of demonstrating the existence of appropriate safeguards provided by controllers or processors that are not subject to this Regulation pursuant to Article 3 within the framework of personal data transfers to third countries or international organisations under the terms referred to in point (f) of Article 46(2). Such controllers or processors shall make binding and enforceable commitments, via contractual or other legally binding instruments, to apply those appropriate safeguards, including with regard to the rights of data subjects.

3. The certification shall be voluntary and available via a process that is transparent.

4. A certification pursuant to this Article does not reduce the responsibility of the controller or the processor for compliance with this Regulation and is without prejudice to the tasks and powers of the supervisory authorities which are competent pursuant to Article 55 or 56.

5. A certification pursuant to this Article shall be issued by the certification bodies referred to in Article 43 or by the competent supervisory authority, on the basis of criteria approved by that competent supervisory authority pursuant to Article 58(3) or by the Board pursuant to Article 63. Where the criteria are approved by the Board, this may result in a common certification, the European Data Protection Seal.

6. The controller or processor which submits its processing to the certification mechanism shall provide the certification body referred to in Article 43, or where applicable, the competent supervisory authority, with all information and access to its processing activities which are necessary to conduct the certification procedure.

7. Certification shall be issued to a controller or processor for a maximum period of three years and may be renewed, under the same conditions, provided that the relevant requirements continue to be met. Certification shall be withdrawn, as applicable, by the certification bodies referred to in Article 43 or by the competent supervisory authority where the requirements for the certification are not or are no longer met.

8. The Board shall collate all certification mechanisms and data protection seals and marks in a register and shall make them publicly available by any appropriate means.

Article 43 Certification bodies

1. Without prejudice to the tasks and powers of the competent supervisory authority under Articles 57 and 58, certification bodies which have an appropriate level of expertise in relation to data protection shall, after informing the supervisory authority in order to allow it to exercise its powers pursuant to point (h) of Article 58(2) where necessary, issue and renew certification. Member States shall ensure that those certification bodies are accredited by one or both of the following:

    (a) the supervisory authority which is competent pursuant to Article 55 or 56;

    (b) the national accreditation body named in accordance with Regulation (EC) No 765/2008 of the European Parliament and of the Council (¹) in accordance with EN-ISO/IEC 17065/2012 and with the additional requirements established by the supervisory authority which is competent pursuant to Article 55 or 56.

2. Certification bodies referred to in paragraph 1 shall be accredited in accordance with that paragraph only where they have:

    (a) demonstrated their independence and expertise in relation to the subject-matter of the certification to the satisfaction of the competent supervisory authority;

(¹)   Regulation (EC) No 765/2008 of the European Parliament and of the Council of 9 July 2008 setting out the requirements for accreditation and market surveillance relating to the marketing of products and repealing Regulation (EEC) No 339/93 (OJ L 218, 13.8.2008, p. 30).

(b)   undertaken to respect the criteria referred to in Article 42(5) and approved by the supervisory authority which is competent pursuant to Article 55 or 56 or by the Board pursuant to Article 63;

(c)   established procedures for the issuing, periodic review and withdrawal of data protection certification, seals and marks;

(d)   established procedures and structures to handle complaints about infringements of the certification or the manner in which the certification has been, or is being, implemented by the controller or processor, and to make those procedures and structures transparent to data subjects and the public; and

(e)   demonstrated, to the satisfaction of the competent supervisory authority, that their tasks and duties do not result in a conflict of interests.

3.   The accreditation of certification bodies as referred to in paragraphs 1 and 2 of this Article shall take place on the basis of criteria approved by the supervisory authority which is competent pursuant to Article 55 or 56 or by the Board pursuant to Article 63. In the case of accreditation pursuant to point (b) of paragraph 1 of this Article, those requirements shall complement those envisaged in Regulation (EC) No 765/2008 and the technical rules that describe the methods and procedures of the certification bodies.

4.   The certification bodies referred to in paragraph 1 shall be responsible for the proper assessment leading to the certification or the withdrawal of such certification without prejudice to the responsibility of the controller or processor for compliance with this Regulation. The accreditation shall be issued for a maximum period of five years and may be renewed on the same conditions provided that the certification body meets the requirements set out in this Article.

5.   The certification bodies referred to in paragraph 1 shall provide the competent supervisory authorities with the reasons for granting or withdrawing the requested certification.

6.   The requirements referred to in paragraph 3 of this Article and the criteria referred to in Article 42(5) shall be made public by the supervisory authority in an easily accessible form. The supervisory authorities shall also transmit those requirements and criteria to the Board. The Board shall collate all certification mechanisms and data protection seals in a register and shall make them publicly available by any appropriate means.

7.   Without prejudice to Chapter VIII, the competent supervisory authority or the national accreditation body shall revoke an accreditation of a certification body pursuant to paragraph 1 of this Article where the conditions for the accreditation are not, or are no longer, met or where actions taken by a certification body infringe this Regulation.

8.   The Commission shall be empowered to adopt delegated acts in accordance with Article 92 for the purpose of specifying the requirements to be taken into account for the data protection certification mechanisms referred to in Article 42(1).

9.   The Commission may adopt implementing acts laying down technical standards for certification mechanisms and data protection seals and marks, and mechanisms to promote and recognise those certification mechanisms, seals and marks. Those implementing acts shall be adopted in accordance with the examination procedure referred to in Article 93(2).

CHAPTER V
TRANSFERS OF PERSONAL DATA TO THIRD COUNTRIES OR INTERNATIONAL ORGANISATIONS

Article 44 General principle for transfers

Any transfer of personal data which are undergoing processing or are intended for processing after transfer to a third country or to an international organisation shall take place only if, subject to the other provisions of this Regulation, the conditions laid down in this Chapter are complied with by the controller and processor, including for onward transfers of personal data from the third country or an international organisation to another third country or to another international organisation. All provisions in this Chapter shall be applied in order to ensure that the level of protection of natural persons guaranteed by this Regulation is not undermined.

Article 45 Transfers on the basis of an adequacy decision

1. A transfer of personal data to a third country or an international organisation may take place where the Commission has decided that the third country, a territory or one or more specified sectors within that third country, or the international organisation in question ensures an adequate level of protection. Such a transfer shall not require any specific authorisation.

2. When assessing the adequacy of the level of protection, the Commission shall, in particular, take account of the following elements:

   (a) the rule of law, respect for human rights and fundamental freedoms, relevant legislation, both general and sectoral, including concerning public security, defence, national security and criminal law and the access of public authorities to personal data, as well as the implementation of such legislation, data protection rules, professional rules and security measures, including rules for the onward transfer of personal data to another third country or international organisation which are complied with in that country or international organisation, case-law, as well as effective and enforceable data subject rights and effective administrative and judicial redress for the data subjects whose personal data are being transferred;

   (b) the existence and effective functioning of one or more independent supervisory authorities in the third country or to which an international organisation is subject, with responsibility for ensuring and enforcing compliance with the data protection rules, including adequate enforcement powers, for assisting and advising the data subjects in exercising their rights and for cooperation with the supervisory authorities of the Member States; and

   (c) the international commitments the third country or international organisation concerned has entered into, or other obligations arising from legally binding conventions or instruments as well as from its participation in multilateral or regional systems, in particular in relation to the protection of personal data.

3. The Commission, after assessing the adequacy of the level of protection, may decide, by means of implementing act, that a third country, a territory or one or more specified sectors within a third country, or an international organisation ensures an adequate level of protection within the meaning of paragraph 2 of this Article. The implementing act shall provide for a mechanism for a periodic review, at least every four years, which shall take into account all relevant developments in the third country or international organisation. The implementing act shall specify its territorial and sectoral application and, where applicable, identify the supervisory authority or authorities referred to in point (b) of paragraph 2 of this Article. The implementing act shall be adopted in accordance with the examination procedure referred to in Article 93(2).

4. The Commission shall, on an ongoing basis, monitor developments in third countries and international organisations that could affect the functioning of decisions adopted pursuant to paragraph 3 of this Article and decisions adopted on the basis of Article 25(6) of Directive 95/46/EC.

5. The Commission shall, where available information reveals, in particular following the review referred to in paragraph 3 of this Article, that a third country, a territory or one or more specified sectors within a third country, or an international organisation no longer ensures an adequate level of protection within the meaning of paragraph 2 of this Article, to the extent necessary, repeal, amend or suspend the decision referred to in paragraph 3 of this Article by means of implementing acts without retro-active effect. Those implementing acts shall be adopted in accordance with the examination procedure referred to in Article 93(2).

   On duly justified imperative grounds of urgency, the Commission shall adopt immediately applicable implementing acts in accordance with the procedure referred to in Article 93(3).

6. The Commission shall enter into consultations with the third country or international organisation with a view to remedying the situation giving rise to the decision made pursuant to paragraph 5.

7. A decision pursuant to paragraph 5 of this Article is without prejudice to transfers of personal data to the third country, a territory or one or more specified sectors within that third country, or the international organisation in question pursuant to Articles 46 to 49.

8. The Commission shall publish in the *Official Journal of the European Union* and on its website a list of the third countries, territories and specified sectors within a third country and international organisations for which it has decided that an adequate level of protection is or is no longer ensured.

9. Decisions adopted by the Commission on the basis of Article 25(6) of Directive 95/46/EC shall remain in force until amended, replaced or repealed by a Commission Decision adopted in accordance with paragraph 3 or 5 of this Article.

Article 46 Transfers subject to appropriate safeguards

1. In the absence of a decision pursuant to Article 45(3), a controller or processor may transfer personal data to a third country or an international organisation only if the controller or processor has provided appropriate safeguards, and on condition that enforceable data subject rights and effective legal remedies for data subjects are available.

2. The appropriate safeguards referred to in paragraph 1 may be provided for, without requiring any specific authorisation from a supervisory authority, by:
   (a)   a legally binding and enforceable instrument between public authorities or bodies;
   (b)   binding corporate rules in accordance with Article 47;
   (c)   standard data protection clauses adopted by the Commission in accordance with the examination procedure referred to in Article 93(2);
   (d)   standard data protection clauses adopted by a supervisory authority and approved by the Commission pursuant to the examination procedure referred to in Article 93(2);
   (e)   an approved code of conduct pursuant to Article 40 together with binding and enforceable commitments of the controller or processor in the third country to apply the appropriate safeguards, including as regards data subjects' rights; or
   (f)   an approved certification mechanism pursuant to Article 42 together with binding and enforceable commitments of the controller or processor in the third country to apply the appropriate safeguards, including as regards data subjects' rights.

3. Subject to the authorisation from the competent supervisory authority, the appropriate safeguards referred to in paragraph 1 may also be provided for, in particular, by:
   (a)   contractual clauses between the controller or processor and the controller, processor or the recipient of the personal data in the third country or international organisation; or
   (b)   provisions to be inserted into administrative arrangements between public authorities or bodies which include enforceable and effective data subject rights.

4. The supervisory authority shall apply the consistency mechanism referred to in Article 63 in the cases referred to in paragraph 3 of this Article.

5. Authorisations by a Member State or supervisory authority on the basis of Article 26(2) of Directive 95/46/EC shall remain valid until amended, replaced or repealed, if necessary, by that supervisory authority. Decisions adopted by the Commission on the basis of Article 26(4) of Directive 95/46/EC shall remain in force until amended, replaced or repealed, if necessary, by a Commission Decision adopted in accordance with paragraph 2 of this Article.

Article 47 Binding corporate rules

1. The competent supervisory authority shall approve binding corporate rules in accordance with the consistency mechanism set out in Article 63, provided that they:
   (a)   are legally binding and apply to and are enforced by every member concerned of the group of undertakings, or group of enterprises engaged in a joint economic activity, including their employees;
   (b)   expressly confer enforceable rights on data subjects with regard to the processing of their personal data; and
   (c)   fulfil the requirements laid down in paragraph 2.

2. The binding corporate rules referred to in paragraph 1 shall specify at least:
   (a)   the structure and contact details of the group of undertakings, or group of enterprises engaged in a joint economic activity and of each of its members;

(b)   the data transfers or set of transfers, including the categories of personal data, the type of processing and its purposes, the type of data subjects affected and the identification of the third country or countries in question;

(c)   their legally binding nature, both internally and externally;

(d)   the application of the general data protection principles, in particular purpose limitation, data minimisation, limited storage periods, data quality, data protection by design and by default, legal basis for processing, processing of special categories of personal data, measures to ensure data security, and the requirements in respect of onward transfers to bodies not bound by the binding corporate rules;

(e)   the rights of data subjects in regard to processing and the means to exercise those rights, including the right not to be subject to decisions based solely on automated processing, including profiling in accordance with Article 22, the right to lodge a complaint with the competent supervisory authority and before the competent courts of the Member States in accordance with Article 79, and to obtain redress and, where appropriate, compensation for a breach of the binding corporate rules;

(f)   the acceptance by the controller or processor established on the territory of a Member State of liability for any breaches of the binding corporate rules by any member concerned not established in the Union; the controller or the processor shall be exempt from that liability, in whole or in part, only if it proves that that member is not responsible for the event giving rise to the damage;

(g)   how the information on the binding corporate rules, in particular on the provisions referred to in points (d), (e) and (f) of this paragraph is provided to the data subjects in addition to Articles 13 and 14;

(h)   the tasks of any data protection officer designated in accordance with Article 37 or any other person or entity in charge of the monitoring compliance with the binding corporate rules within the group of undertakings, or group of enterprises engaged in a joint economic activity, as well as monitoring training and complaint-handling;

(i)   the complaint procedures;

(j)   the mechanisms within the group of undertakings, or group of enterprises engaged in a joint economic activity for ensuring the verification of compliance with the binding corporate rules. Such mechanisms shall include data protection audits and methods for ensuring corrective actions to protect the rights of the data subject. Results of such verification should be communicated to the person or entity referred to in point (h) and to the board of the controlling undertaking of a group of undertakings, or of the group of enterprises engaged in a joint economic activity, and should be available upon request to the competent supervisory authority;

(k)   the mechanisms for reporting and recording changes to the rules and reporting those changes to the supervisory authority;

(l)   the cooperation mechanism with the supervisory authority to ensure compliance by any member of the group of undertakings, or group of enterprises engaged in a joint economic activity, in particular by making available to the supervisory authority the results of verifications of the measures referred to in point (j);

(m)   the mechanisms for reporting to the competent supervisory authority any legal requirements to which a member of the group of undertakings, or group of enterprises engaged in a joint economic activity is subject in a third country which are likely to have a substantial adverse effect on the guarantees provided by the binding corporate rules; and

(n)   the appropriate data protection training to personnel having permanent or regular access to personal data.

3.   The Commission may specify the format and procedures for the exchange of information between controllers, processors and supervisory authorities for binding corporate rules within the meaning of this Article. Those implementing acts shall be adopted in accordance with the examination procedure set out in Article 93(2).

Article 48 Transfers or disclosures not authorised by Union law

Any judgment of a court or tribunal and any decision of an administrative authority of a third country requiring a controller or processor to transfer or disclose personal data may only be recognised or enforceable in any manner if based on an international agreement, such as a mutual legal assistance treaty, in force between the requesting third country and the Union or a Member State, without prejudice to other grounds for transfer pursuant to this Chapter.

Article 49 Derogations for specific situations

1.   In the absence of an adequacy decision pursuant to Article 45(3), or of appropriate safeguards pursuant to Article 46, including binding corporate rules, a transfer or a set of transfers of personal data to a third country or an international organisation shall take place only on one of the following conditions:
     (a)   the data subject has explicitly consented to the proposed transfer, after having been informed of the possible risks of such transfers for the data subject due to the absence of an adequacy decision and appropriate safeguards;
     (b)   the transfer is necessary for the performance of a contract between the data subject and the controller or the implementation of pre-contractual measures taken at the data subject's request;
     (c)   the transfer is necessary for the conclusion or performance of a contract concluded in the interest of the data subject between the controller and another natural or legal person;
     (d)   the transfer is necessary for important reasons of public interest;
     (e)   the transfer is necessary for the establishment, exercise or defence of legal claims;
     (f)   the transfer is necessary in order to protect the vital interests of the data subject or of other persons, where the data subject is physically or legally incapable of giving consent;
     (g)   the transfer is made from a register which according to Union or Member State law is intended to provide information to the public and which is open to consultation either by the public in general or by any person who can demonstrate a legitimate interest, but only to the extent that the   conditions laid   down by Union   or Member State law for consultation are fulfilled in the particular case.
     Where a transfer could not be based on a provision in Article 45 or 46, including the provisions on binding corporate rules, and none of the derogations for a specific situation referred to in the first subparagraph of this paragraph is applicable, a transfer to a third country or an international organisation may take place only if the transfer is not repetitive, concerns only a limited number of data subjects, is necessary for the purposes of compelling legitimate interests pursued by the controller which are not overridden by the interests or rights and freedoms of the data subject, and the controller has assessed all the circumstances surrounding the data transfer and has on the basis of that assessment provided suitable safeguards with regard to the protection of personal data. The controller shall inform the supervisory authority of the transfer. The controller shall, in addition to providing the information referred to in Articles 13 and 14, inform the data subject of the transfer and on the compelling legitimate interests pursued.

2.   A transfer pursuant to point (g) of the first subparagraph of paragraph 1 shall not involve the entirety of the personal data or entire categories of the personal data contained in the register. Where the register is intended for consultation by persons having a legitimate interest, the transfer shall be made only at the request of those persons or if they are to be the recipients.

3.   Points (a), (b) and (c) of the first subparagraph of paragraph 1 and the second subparagraph thereof shall not apply to activities carried out by public authorities in the exercise of their public powers.

4.   The public interest referred to in point (d) of the first subparagraph of paragraph 1 shall be recognised in Union law or in the law of the Member State to which the controller is subject.

5.   In the absence of an adequacy decision, Union or Member State law may, for important reasons of public interest, expressly set limits to the transfer of specific categories of

personal data to a third country or an international organisation. Member States shall notify such provisions to the Commission.

6. The controller or processor shall document the assessment as well as the suitable safeguards referred to in the second subparagraph of paragraph 1 of this Article in the records referred to in Article 30.

Article 50 International cooperation for the protection of personal data

In relation to third countries and international organisations, the Commission and supervisory authorities shall take appropriate steps to:

(a) develop international cooperation mechanisms to facilitate the effective enforcement of legislation for the protection of personal data;

(b) provide international mutual assistance in the enforcement of legislation for the protection of personal data, including through notification, complaint referral, investigative assistance and information exchange, subject to appropriate safeguards for the protection of personal data and other fundamental rights and freedoms;

(c) engage relevant stakeholders in discussion and activities aimed at furthering international cooperation in the enforcement of legislation for the protection of personal data;

(d) promote the exchange and documentation of personal data protection legislation and practice, including on jurisdictional conflicts with third countries.

CHAPTER VI
INDEPENDENT SUPERVISORY AUTHORITIES

SECTION 1
INDEPENDENT STATUS

Article 51 Supervisory authority

1. Each Member State shall provide for one or more independent public authorities to be responsible for monitoring the application of this Regulation, in order to protect the fundamental rights and freedoms of natural persons in relation to processing and to facilitate the free flow of personal data within the Union ('supervisory authority').

2. Each supervisory authority shall contribute to the consistent application of this Regulation throughout the Union. For that purpose, the supervisory authorities shall cooperate with each other and the Commission in accordance with Chapter VII.

3. Where more than one supervisory authority is established in a Member State, that Member State shall designate the supervisory authority which is to represent those authorities in the Board and shall set out the mechanism to ensure compliance by the other authorities with the rules relating to the consistency mechanism referred to in Article 63.

4. Each Member State shall notify to the Commission the provisions of its law which it adopts pursuant to this Chapter, by 25 May 2018 and, without delay, any subsequent amendment affecting them.

Article 52 Independence

1. Each supervisory authority shall act with complete independence in performing its tasks and exercising its powers in accordance with this Regulation.

2. The member or members of each supervisory authority shall, in the performance of their tasks and exercise of their powers in accordance with this Regulation, remain free from external influence, whether direct or indirect, and shall neither seek nor take instructions from anybody.

3. Member or members of each supervisory authority shall refrain from any action incompatible with their duties and shall not, during their term of office, engage in any incompatible occupation, whether gainful or not.

4. Each Member State shall ensure that each supervisory authority is provided with the human, technical and financial resources, premises and infrastructure necessary for

the effective performance of its tasks and exercise of its powers, including those to be carried out in the context of mutual assistance, cooperation and participation in the Board.

5. Each Member State shall ensure that each supervisory authority chooses and has its own staff which shall be subject to the exclusive direction of the member or members of the supervisory authority concerned.

6. Each Member State shall ensure that each supervisory authority is subject to financial control which does not affect its independence and that it has separate, public annual budgets, which may be part of the overall state or national budget.

Article 53 General conditions for the members of the supervisory authority

1. Member States shall provide for each member of their supervisory authorities to be appointed by means of a transparent procedure by:
    — their parliament;
    — their government;
    — their head of State; or
    — an independent body entrusted with the appointment under Member State law.

2. Each member shall have the qualifications, experience and skills, in particular in the area of the protection of personal data, required to perform its duties and exercise its powers.

3. The duties of a member shall end in the event of the expiry of the term of office, resignation or compulsory retirement, in accordance with the law of the Member State concerned.

4. A member shall be dismissed only in cases of serious misconduct or if the member no longer fulfils the conditions required for the performance of the duties.

Article 54 Rules on the establishment of the supervisory authority

1. Each Member State shall provide by law for all of the following:
    (a) the establishment of each supervisory authority;
    (b) the qualifications and eligibility conditions required to be appointed as member of each supervisory authority;
    (c) the rules and procedures for the appointment of the member or members of each supervisory authority;
    (d) the duration of the term of the member or members of each supervisory authority of no less than four years, except for the first appointment after 24 May 2016, part of which may take place for a shorter period where that is necessary to protect the independence of the supervisory authority by means of a staggered appointment procedure;
    (e) whether and, if so, for how many terms the member or members of each supervisory authority is eligible for reappointment;
    (f) the conditions governing the obligations of the member or members and staff of each supervisory authority, prohibitions on actions, occupations and benefits incompatible therewith during and after the term of office and rules governing the cessation of employment.

2. The member or members and the staff of each supervisory authority shall, in accordance with Union or Member State law, be subject to a duty of professional secrecy both during and after their term of office, with regard to any confidential information which has come to their knowledge in the course of the performance of their tasks or exercise of their powers. During their term of office, that duty of professional secrecy shall in particular apply to reporting by natural persons of infringements of this Regulation.

SECTION 2
COMPETENCE, TASKS AND POWERS

Article 55 Competence

1. Each supervisory authority shall be competent for the performance of the tasks assigned to and the exercise of the powers conferred on it in accordance with this Regulation on the territory of its own Member State.

2. Where processing is carried out by public authorities or private bodies acting on the basis of point (c) or (e) of Article 6(1), the supervisory authority of the Member State concerned shall be competent. In such cases Article 56 does not apply.

3. Supervisory authorities shall not be competent to supervise processing operations of courts acting in their judicial capacity.

Article 56 Competence of the lead supervisory authority

1. Without prejudice to Article 55, the supervisory authority of the main establishment or of the single establishment of the controller or processor shall be competent to act as lead supervisory authority for the cross-border processing carried out by that controller or processor in accordance with the procedure provided in Article 60.

2. By derogation from paragraph 1, each supervisory authority shall be competent to handle a complaint lodged with it or a possible infringement of this Regulation, if the subject matter relates only to an establishment in its Member State or substantially affects data subjects only in its Member State.

3. In the cases referred to in paragraph 2 of this Article, the supervisory authority shall inform the lead supervisory authority without delay on that matter. Within a period of three weeks after being informed the lead supervisory authority shall decide whether or not it will handle the case in accordance with the procedure provided in Article 60, taking into account whether or not there is an establishment of the controller or processor in the Member State of which the supervisory authority informed it.

4. Where the lead supervisory authority decides to handle the case, the procedure provided in Article 60 shall apply. The supervisory authority which informed the lead supervisory authority may submit to the lead supervisory authority a draft for a decision. The lead supervisory authority shall take utmost account of that draft when preparing the draft decision referred to in Article 60(3).

5. Where the lead supervisory authority decides not to handle the case, the supervisory authority which informed the lead supervisory authority shall handle it according to Articles 61 and 62.

6. The lead supervisory authority shall be the sole interlocutor of the controller or processor for the cross-border processing carried out by that controller or processor.

Article 57 Tasks

1. Without prejudice to other tasks set out under this Regulation, each supervisory authority shall on its territory:

   (a) monitor and enforce the application of this Regulation;

   (b) promote public awareness and understanding of the risks, rules, safeguards and rights in relation to processing. Activities addressed specifically to children shall receive specific attention;

   (c) advise, in accordance with Member State law, the national parliament, the government, and other institutions and bodies on legislative and administrative measures relating to the protection of natural persons' rights and freedoms with regard to processing;

   (d) promote the awareness of controllers and processors of their obligations under this Regulation;

   (e) upon request, provide information to any data subject concerning the exercise of their rights under this Regulation and, if appropriate, cooperate with the supervisory authorities in other Member States to that end;

   (f) handle complaints lodged by a data subject, or by a body, organisation or association in accordance with Article 80, and investigate, to the extent appropriate, the subject matter of the complaint and inform the complainant of the progress and the outcome of the investigation within a reasonable period, in particular if further investigation or coordination with another supervisory authority is necessary;

   (g) cooperate with, including sharing information and provide mutual assistance to, other supervisory authorities with a view to ensuring the consistency of application and enforcement of this Regulation;

(h)   conduct investigations on the application of this Regulation, including on the basis of information received from another supervisory authority or other public authority;

(i)   monitor relevant developments, insofar as they have an impact on the protection of personal data, in particular the development of information and communication technologies and commercial practices;

(j)   adopt standard contractual clauses referred to in Article 28(8) and in point (d) of Article 46(2);

(k)   establish and maintain a list in relation to the requirement for data protection impact assessment pursuant to Article 35(4);

(l)   give advice on the processing operations referred to in Article 36(2);

(m)   encourage the drawing up of codes of conduct pursuant to Article 40(1) and provide an opinion and approve such codes of conduct which provide sufficient safeguards, pursuant to Article 40(5);

(n)   encourage the establishment of data protection certification mechanisms and of data protection seals and marks pursuant to Article 42(1), and approve the criteria of certification pursuant to Article 42(5);

(o)   where applicable, carry out a periodic review of certifications issued in accordance with Article 42(7);

(p)   draft and publish the criteria for accreditation of a body for monitoring codes of conduct pursuant to Article 41 and of a certification body pursuant to Article 43;

(q)   conduct the accreditation of a body for monitoring codes of conduct pursuant to Article 41 and of a certification body pursuant to Article 43;

(r)   authorise contractual clauses and provisions referred to in Article 46(3);

(s)   approve binding corporate rules pursuant to Article 47;

(t)   contribute to the activities of the Board;

(u)   keep internal records of infringements of this Regulation and of measures taken in accordance with Article 58(2); and

(v)   fulfil any other tasks related to the protection of personal data.

2.   Each supervisory authority shall facilitate the submission of complaints referred to in point (f) of paragraph 1 by measures such as a complaint submission form which can also be completed electronically, without excluding other means of communication.

3.   The performance of the tasks of each supervisory authority shall be free of charge for the data subject and, where applicable, for the data protection officer.

4.   Where requests are manifestly unfounded or excessive, in particular because of their repetitive character, the supervisory authority may charge a reasonable fee based on administrative costs, or refuse to act on the request. The supervisory authority shall bear the burden of demonstrating the manifestly unfounded or excessive character of the request.

Article 58 Powers

1.   Each supervisory authority shall have all of the following investigative powers:

(a)   to order the controller and the processor, and, where applicable, the controller's or the processor's representative to provide any information it requires for the performance of its tasks;

(b)   to carry out investigations in the form of data protection audits;

(c)   to carry out a review on certifications issued pursuant to Article 42(7);

(d)   to notify the controller or the processor of an alleged infringement of this Regulation;

(e)   to obtain, from the controller and the processor, access to all personal data and to all information necessary for the performance of its tasks;

(f)   to obtain access to any premises of the controller and the processor, including to any data processing equipment and means, in accordance with Union or Member State procedural law.

2.   Each supervisory authority shall have all of the following corrective powers:

(a)   to issue warnings to a controller or processor that intended processing operations are likely to infringe provisions of this Regulation;

(b)   to issue reprimands to a controller or a processor where processing operations have infringed provisions of this Regulation;

(c) to order the controller or the processor to comply with the data subject's requests to exercise his or her rights pursuant to this Regulation;

(d) to order the controller or processor to bring processing operations into compliance with the provisions of this Regulation, where appropriate, in a specified manner and within a specified period;

(e) to order the controller to communicate a personal data breach to the data subject;

(f) to impose a temporary or definitive limitation including a ban on processing;

(g) to order the rectification or erasure of personal data or restriction of processing pursuant to Articles 16, 17 and 18 and the notification of such actions to recipients to whom the personal data have been disclosed pursuant to Article 17(2) and Article 19;

(h) to withdraw a certification or to order the certification body to withdraw a certification issued pursuant to Articles 42 and 43, or to order the certification body not to issue certification if the requirements for the certification are not or are no longer met;

(i) to impose an administrative fine pursuant to Article 83, in addition to, or instead of measures referred to in this paragraph, depending on the circumstances of each individual case;

(j) to order the suspension of data flows to a recipient in a third country or to an international organisation.

3. Each supervisory authority shall have all of the following authorisation and advisory powers:

(a) to advise the controller in accordance with the prior consultation procedure referred to in Article 36;

(b) to issue, on its own initiative or on request, opinions to the national parliament, the Member State government or, in accordance with Member State law, to other institutions and bodies as well as to the public on any issue related to the protection of personal data;

(c) to authorise processing referred to in Article 36(5), if the law of the Member State requires such prior authorisation;

(d) to issue an opinion and approve draft codes of conduct pursuant to Article 40(5);

(e) to accredit certification bodies pursuant to Article 43;

(f) to issue certifications and approve criteria of certification in accordance with Article 42(5);

(g) to adopt standard data protection clauses referred to in Article 28(8) and in point (d) of Article 46(2);

(h) to authorise contractual clauses referred to in point (a) of Article 46(3);

(i) to authorise administrative arrangements referred to in point (b) of Article 46(3);

(j) to approve binding corporate rules pursuant to Article 47.

4. The exercise of the powers conferred on the supervisory authority pursuant to this Article shall be subject to appropriate safeguards, including effective judicial remedy and due process, set out in Union and Member State law in accordance with the Charter.

5. Each Member State shall provide by law that its supervisory authority shall have the power to bring infringements of this Regulation to the attention of the judicial authorities and where appropriate, to commence or engage otherwise in legal proceedings, in order to enforce the provisions of this Regulation.

6. Each Member State may provide by law that its supervisory authority shall have additional powers to those referred to in paragraphs 1, 2 and 3. The exercise of those powers shall not impair the effective operation of Chapter VII.

Article 59 Activity reports

Each supervisory authority shall draw up an annual report on its activities, which may include a list of types of infringement notified and types of measures taken in accordance with Article 58(2). Those reports shall be transmitted to the national parliament, the government and other authorities as designated by Member State law. They shall be made available to the public, to the Commission and to the Board.

CHAPTER VII
COOPERATION AND CONSISTENCY

SECTION 1
COOPERATION

Article 60 Cooperation between the lead supervisory authority and the other supervisory authorities concerned

1. The lead supervisory authority shall cooperate with the other supervisory authorities concerned in accordance with this Article in an endeavour to reach consensus. The lead supervisory authority and the supervisory authorities concerned shall exchange all relevant information with each other.
2. The lead supervisory authority may request at any time other supervisory authorities concerned to provide mutual assistance pursuant to Article 61 and may conduct joint operations pursuant to Article 62, in particular for carrying out investigations or for monitoring the implementation of a measure concerning a controller or processor established in another Member State.
3. The lead supervisory authority shall, without delay, communicate the relevant information on the matter to the other supervisory authorities concerned. It shall without delay submit a draft decision to the other supervisory authorities concerned for their opinion and take due account of their views.
4. Where any of the other supervisory authorities concerned within a period of four weeks after having been consulted in accordance with paragraph 3 of this Article, expresses a relevant and reasoned objection to the draft decision, the lead supervisory authority shall, if it does not follow the relevant and reasoned objection or is of the opinion that the objection is not relevant or reasoned, submit the matter to the consistency mechanism referred to in Article 63.
5. Where the lead supervisory authority intends to follow the relevant and reasoned objection made, it shall submit to the other supervisory authorities concerned a revised draft decision for their opinion. That revised draft decision shall be subject to the procedure referred to in paragraph 4 within a period of two weeks.
6. Where none of the other supervisory authorities concerned has objected to the draft decision submitted by the lead supervisory authority within the period referred to in paragraphs 4 and 5, the lead supervisory authority and the supervisory authorities concerned shall be deemed to be in agreement with that draft decision and shall be bound by it.
7. The lead supervisory authority shall adopt and notify the decision to the main establishment or single establishment of the controller or processor, as the case may be and inform the other supervisory authorities concerned and the Board of the decision in question, including a summary of the relevant facts and grounds. The supervisory authority with which a complaint has been lodged shall inform the complainant on the decision.
8. By derogation from paragraph 7, where a complaint is dismissed or rejected, the supervisory authority with which the complaint was lodged shall adopt the decision and notify it to the complainant and shall inform the controller thereof.
9. Where the lead supervisory authority and the supervisory authorities concerned agree to dismiss or reject parts of a complaint and to act on other parts of that complaint, a separate decision shall be adopted for each of those parts of the matter. The lead supervisory authority shall adopt the decision for the part concerning actions in relation to the controller, shall notify it to the main establishment or single establishment of the controller or processor on the territory of its Member State and shall inform the complainant thereof, while the supervisory authority of the complainant shall adopt the decision for the part concerning dismissal or rejection of that complaint, and shall notify it to that complainant and shall inform the controller or processor thereof.
10. After being notified of the decision of the lead supervisory authority pursuant to paragraphs 7 and 9, the controller or processor shall take the necessary measures to

ensure compliance with the decision as regards processing activities in the context of all its establishments in the Union. The controller or processor shall notify the measures taken for complying with the decision to the lead supervisory authority, which shall inform the other supervisory authorities concerned.

11. Where, in exceptional circumstances, a supervisory authority concerned has reasons to consider that there is an urgent need to act in order to protect the interests of data subjects, the urgency procedure referred to in Article 66 shall apply.

12. The lead supervisory authority and the other supervisory authorities concerned shall supply the information required under this Article to each other by electronic means, using a standardised format.

Article 61 Mutual assistance

1. Supervisory authorities shall provide each other with relevant information and mutual assistance in order to implement and apply this Regulation in a consistent manner, and shall put in place measures for effective cooperation with one another. Mutual assistance shall cover, in particular, information requests and supervisory measures, such as requests to carry out prior authorisations and consultations, inspections and investigations.

2. Each supervisory authority shall take all appropriate measures required to reply to a request of another supervisory authority without undue delay and no later than one month after receiving the request. Such measures may include, in particular, the transmission of relevant information on the conduct of an investigation.

3. Requests for assistance shall contain all the necessary information, including the purpose of and reasons for the request. Information exchanged shall be used only for the purpose for which it was requested.

4. The requested supervisory authority shall not refuse to comply with the request unless:
   (a) it is not competent for the subject-matter of the request or for the measures it is requested to execute; or
   (b) compliance with the request would infringe this Regulation or Union or Member State law to which the supervisory authority receiving the request is subject.

5. The requested supervisory authority shall inform the requesting supervisory authority of the results or, as the case may be, of the progress of the measures taken in order to respond to the request. The requested supervisory authority shall provide reasons for any refusal to comply with a request pursuant to paragraph 4.

6. Requested supervisory authorities shall, as a rule, supply the information requested by other supervisory authorities by electronic means, using a standardised format.

7. Requested supervisory authorities shall not charge a fee for any action taken by them pursuant to a request for mutual assistance. Supervisory authorities may agree on rules to indemnify each other for specific expenditure arising from the provision of mutual assistance in exceptional circumstances.

8. Where a supervisory authority does not provide the information referred to in paragraph 5 of this Article within one month of receiving the request of another supervisory authority, the requesting supervisory authority may adopt a provisional measure on the territory of its Member State in accordance with Article 55(1). In that case, the urgent need to act under Article 66(1) shall be presumed to be met and require an urgent binding decision from the Board pursuant to Article 66(2).

9. The Commission may, by means of implementing acts, specify the format and procedures for mutual assistance referred to in this Article and the arrangements for the exchange of information by electronic means between supervisory authorities, and between supervisory authorities and the Board, in particular the standardised format referred to in paragraph 6 of this Article. Those implementing acts shall be adopted in accordance with the examination procedure referred to in Article 93(2).

Article 62 Joint operations of supervisory authorities

1. The supervisory authorities shall, where appropriate, conduct joint operations including joint investigations and joint enforcement measures in which members or staff of the supervisory authorities of other Member States are involved.

2.   Where the controller or processor has establishments in several Member States or where a significant number of data subjects in more than one Member State are likely to be substantially affected by processing operations, a supervisory authority of each of those Member States shall have the right to participate in joint operations. The supervisory authority which is competent pursuant to Article 56(1) or (4) shall invite the supervisory authority of each of those Member States to take part in the joint operations and shall respond without delay to the request of a supervisory authority to participate.

3.   A supervisory authority may, in accordance with Member State law, and with the seconding supervisory authority's authorisation, confer powers, including investigative powers on the seconding supervisory authority's members or staff involved in joint operations or, in so far as the law of the Member State of the host supervisory authority permits, allow the seconding supervisory authority's members or staff to exercise their investigative powers in accordance with the law of the Member State of the seconding supervisory authority. Such investigative powers may be exercised only under the guidance and in the presence of members or staff of the host supervisory authority. The seconding supervisory authority's members or staff shall be subject to the Member State law of the host supervisory authority.

4.   Where, in accordance with paragraph 1, staff of a seconding supervisory authority operate in another Member State, the Member State of the host supervisory authority shall assume responsibility for their actions, including liability, for any damage caused by them during their operations, in accordance with the law of the Member State in whose territory they are operating.

5.   The Member State in whose territory the damage was caused shall make good such damage under the conditions applicable to damage caused by its own staff. The Member State of the seconding supervisory authority whose staff has caused damage to any person in the territory of another Member State shall reimburse that other Member State in full any sums it has paid to the persons entitled on their behalf.

6.   Without prejudice to the exercise of its rights *vis-à-vis* third parties and with the exception of paragraph 5, each Member State shall refrain, in the case provided for in paragraph 1, from requesting reimbursement from another Member State in relation to damage referred to in paragraph 4.

7.   Where a joint operation is intended and a supervisory authority does not, within one month, comply with the obligation laid down in the second sentence of paragraph 2 of this Article, the other supervisory authorities may adopt a provisional measure on the territory of its Member State in accordance with Article 55. In that case, the urgent need to act under Article 66(1) shall be presumed to be met and require an opinion or an urgent binding decision from the Board pursuant to Article 66(2).

SECTION 2
CONSISTENCY

Article 63 Consistency mechanism

In order to contribute to the consistent application of this Regulation throughout the Union, the supervisory authorities shall cooperate with each other and, where relevant, with the Commission, through the consistency mechanism as set out in this Section.

Article 64 Opinion of the Board

1.   The Board shall issue an opinion where a competent supervisory authority intends to adopt any of the measures below. To that end, the competent supervisory authority shall communicate the draft decision to the Board, when it:

(a)   aims to adopt a list of the processing operations subject to the requirement for a data protection impact assessment pursuant to Article 35(4);

(b)   concerns a matter pursuant to Article 40(7) whether a draft code of conduct or an amendment or extension to a code of conduct complies with this Regulation;

(c)   aims to approve the criteria for accreditation of a body pursuant to Article 41(3) or a certification body pursuant to Article 43(3);

(d)   aims to determine standard data protection clauses referred to in point (d) of Article 46(2) and in Article 28(8);

(e)   aims to authorise contractual clauses referred to in point (a) of Article 46(3); or

(f)   aims to approve binding corporate rules within the meaning of Article 47.

2.   Any supervisory authority, the Chair of the Board or the Commission may request that any matter of general application or producing effects in more than one Member State be examined by the Board with a view to obtaining an opinion, in particular where a competent supervisory authority does not comply with the obligations for mutual assistance in accordance with Article 61 or for joint operations in accordance with Article 62.

3.   In the cases referred to in paragraphs 1 and 2, the Board shall issue an opinion on the matter submitted to it provided that it has not already issued an opinion on the same matter. That opinion shall be adopted within eight weeks by simple majority of the members of the Board. That period may be extended by a further six weeks, taking into account the complexity of the subject matter. Regarding the draft decision referred to in paragraph 1 circulated to the members of the Board in accordance with paragraph 5, a member which has not objected within a reasonable period indicated by the Chair, shall be deemed to be in agreement with the draft decision.

4.   Supervisory authorities and the Commission shall, without undue delay, communicate by electronic means to the Board, using a standardised format any relevant information, including as the case may be a summary of the facts, the draft decision, the grounds which make the enactment of such measure necessary, and the views of other supervisory authorities concerned.

5.   The Chair of the Board shall, without undue, delay inform by electronic means:

(a)   the members of the Board and the Commission of any relevant information which has been communicated to it using a standardised format. The secretariat of the Board shall, where necessary, provide translations of relevant information; and

(b)   the supervisory authority referred to, as the case may be, in paragraphs 1 and 2, and the Commission of the opinion and make it public.

6.   The competent supervisory authority shall not adopt its draft decision referred to in paragraph 1 within the period referred to in paragraph 3.

7.   The supervisory authority referred to in paragraph 1 shall take utmost account of the opinion of the Board and shall, within two weeks after receiving the opinion, communicate to the Chair of the Board by electronic means whether it will maintain or amend its draft decision and, if any, the amended draft decision, using a standardised format.

8.   Where the supervisory authority concerned informs the Chair of the Board within the period referred to in paragraph 7 of this Article that it does not intend to follow the opinion of the Board, in whole or in part, providing the relevant grounds, Article 65(1) shall apply.

Article 65 Dispute resolution by the Board

1.   In order to ensure the correct and consistent application of this Regulation in individual cases, the Board shall adopt a binding decision in the following cases:

(a)   where, in a case referred to in Article 60(4), a supervisory authority concerned has raised a relevant and reasoned objection to a draft decision of the lead authority or the lead authority has rejected such an objection as being not relevant or reasoned. The binding decision shall concern all the matters which are the subject of the relevant and reasoned objection, in particular whether there is an infringement of this Regulation;

(b)   where there are conflicting views on which of the supervisory authorities concerned is competent for the main establishment;

(c)   where a competent supervisory authority does not request the opinion of the Board in the cases referred to in Article 64(1), or does not follow the opinion of the Board issued under Article 64. In that case, any supervisory authority concerned or the Commission may communicate the matter to the Board.

2.   The decision referred to in paragraph 1 shall be adopted within one month from the referral of the subject-matter by a two-thirds majority of the members of the Board.

That period may be extended by a further month on account of the complexity of the subject-matter. The decision referred to in paragraph 1 shall be reasoned and addressed to the lead supervisory authority and all the supervisory authorities concerned and binding on them.

3. Where the Board has been unable to adopt a decision within the periods referred to in paragraph 2, it shall adopt its decision within two weeks following the expiration of the second month referred to in paragraph 2 by a simple majority of the members of the Board. Where the members of the Board are split, the decision shall by adopted by the vote of its Chair.

4. The supervisory authorities concerned shall not adopt a decision on the subject matter submitted to the Board under paragraph 1 during the periods referred to in paragraphs 2 and 3.

5. The Chair of the Board shall notify, without undue delay, the decision referred to in paragraph 1 to the supervisory authorities concerned. It shall inform the Commission thereof. The decision shall be published on the website of the Board without delay after the supervisory authority has notified the final decision referred to in paragraph 6.

6. The lead supervisory authority or, as the case may be, the supervisory authority with which the complaint has been lodged shall adopt its final decision on the basis of the decision referred to in paragraph 1 of this Article, without undue delay and at the latest by one month after the Board has notified its decision. The lead supervisory authority or, as the case may be, the supervisory authority with which the complaint has been lodged, shall inform the Board of the date when its final decision is notified respectively to the controller or the processor and to the data subject. The final decision of the supervisory authorities concerned shall be adopted under the terms of Article 60(7), (8) and (9). The final decision shall refer to the decision referred to in paragraph 1 of this Article and shall specify that the decision referred to in that paragraph will be published on the website of the Board in accordance with paragraph 5 of this Article. The final decision shall attach the decision referred to in paragraph 1 of this Article.

Article 66 Urgency procedure

1. In exceptional circumstances, where a supervisory authority concerned considers that there is an urgent need to act in order to protect the rights and freedoms of data subjects, it may, by way of derogation from the consistency mechanism referred to in Articles 63, 64 and 65 or the procedure referred to in Article 60, immediately adopt provisional measures intended to produce legal effects on its own territory with a specified period of validity which shall not exceed three months. The supervisory authority shall, without delay, communicate those measures and the reasons for adopting them to the other supervisory authorities concerned, to the Board and to the Commission.

2. Where a supervisory authority has taken a measure pursuant to paragraph 1 and considers that final measures need urgently be adopted, it may request an urgent opinion or an urgent binding decision from the Board, giving reasons for requesting such opinion or decision.

3. Any supervisory authority may request an urgent opinion or an urgent binding decision, as the case may be, from the Board where a competent supervisory authority has not taken an appropriate measure in a situation where there is an urgent need to act, in order to protect the rights and freedoms of data subjects, giving reasons for requesting such opinion or decision, including for the urgent need to act.

4. By derogation from Article 64(3) and Article 65(2), an urgent opinion or an urgent binding decision referred to in paragraphs 2 and 3 of this Article shall be adopted within two weeks by simple majority of the members of the Board.

Article 67 Exchange of information

The Commission may adopt implementing acts of general scope in order to specify the arrangements for the exchange of information by electronic means between supervisory authorities, and between supervisory authorities and the Board, in particular the standardised format referred to in Article 64.

Those implementing acts shall be adopted in accordance with the examination procedure referred to in Article 93(2).

SECTION 3
EUROPEAN DATA PROTECTION BOARD

Article 68 European Data Protection Board

1. The European Data Protection Board (the 'Board') is hereby established as a body of the Union and shall have legal personality.
2. The Board shall be represented by its Chair.
3. The Board shall be composed of the head of one supervisory authority of each Member State and of the European Data Protection Supervisor, or their respective representatives.
4. Where in a Member State more than one supervisory authority is responsible for monitoring the application of the provisions pursuant to this Regulation, a joint representative shall be appointed in accordance with that Member State's law.
5. The Commission shall have the right to participate in the activities and meetings of the Board without voting right. The Commission shall designate a representative. The Chair of the Board shall communicate to the Commission the activities of the Board.
6. In the cases referred to in Article 65, the European Data Protection Supervisor shall have voting rights only on decisions which concern principles and rules applicable to the Union institutions, bodies, offices and agencies which correspond in substance to those of this Regulation.

Article 69 Independence

1. The Board shall act independently when performing its tasks or exercising its powers pursuant to Articles 70 and 71.
2. Without prejudice to requests by the Commission referred to in point (b) of Article 70(1) and in Article 70(2), the Board shall, in the performance of its tasks or the exercise of its powers, neither seek nor take instructions from anybody.

Article 70 Tasks of the Board

1. The Board shall ensure the consistent application of this Regulation. To that end, the Board shall, on its own initiative or, where relevant, at the request of the Commission, in particular:
   (a) monitor and ensure the correct application of this Regulation in the cases provided for in Articles 64 and 65 without prejudice to the tasks of national supervisory authorities;
   (b) advise the Commission on any issue related to the protection of personal data in the Union, including on any proposed amendment of this Regulation;
   (c) advise the Commission on the format and procedures for the exchange of information between controllers, processors and supervisory authorities for binding corporate rules;
   (d) issue guidelines, recommendations, and best practices on procedures for erasing links, copies or replications of personal data from publicly available communication services as referred to in Article 17(2);
   (e) examine, on its own initiative, on request of one of its members or on request of the Commission, any question covering the application of this Regulation and issue guidelines, recommendations and best practices in order to encourage consistent application of this Regulation;
   (f) issue guidelines, recommendations and best practices in accordance with point (e) of this paragraph for further specifying the criteria and conditions for decisions based on profiling pursuant to Article 22(2);
   (g) issue guidelines, recommendations and best practices in accordance with point (e) of this paragraph for establishing the personal data breaches and determining the undue delay referred to in Article 33(1) and (2) and for the particular circumstances in which a controller or a processor is required to notify the personal data breach;
   (h) issue guidelines, recommendations and best practices in accordance with point (e) of this paragraph as to the circumstances in which a personal data breach is likely to result in a high risk to the rights and freedoms of the natural persons referred to in Article 34(1).

(i)   issue guidelines, recommendations and best practices in accordance with point (e) of this paragraph for the purpose of further specifying the criteria and requirements for personal data transfers based on binding corporate rules adhered to by controllers and binding corporate rules adhered to by processors and on further necessary requirements to ensure the protection of personal data of the data subjects concerned referred to in Article 47;

(j)   issue guidelines, recommendations and best practices in accordance with point (e) of this paragraph for the purpose of further specifying the criteria and requirements for the personal data transfers on the basis of Article 49(1);

(k)   draw up guidelines for supervisory authorities concerning the application of measures referred to in Article 58(1),

        (2) and (3) and the setting of administrative fines pursuant to Article 83;

(l)   review the practical application of the guidelines, recommendations and best practices referred to in points (e) and (f);

(m)   issue guidelines, recommendations and best practices in accordance with point (e) of this paragraph for establishing common procedures for reporting by natural persons of infringements of this Regulation pursuant to Article 54(2);

(n)   encourage the drawing-up of codes of conduct and the establishment of data protection certification mechanisms and data protection seals and marks pursuant to Articles 40 and 42;

(o)   carry out the accreditation of certification bodies and its periodic review pursuant to Article 43 and maintain a public register of accredited bodies pursuant to Article 43(6) and of the accredited controllers or processors established in third countries pursuant to Article 42(7);

(p)   specify the requirements referred to in Article 43(3) with a view to the accreditation of certification bodies under Article 42;

(q)   provide the Commission with an opinion on the certification requirements referred to in Article 43(8);

(r)   provide the Commission with an opinion on the icons referred to in Article 12(7);

(s)   provide the Commission with an opinion for the assessment of the adequacy of the level of protection in a third country or international organisation, including for the assessment whether a third country, a territory or one or more specified sectors within that third country, or an international organisation no longer ensures an adequate level of protection. To that end, the Commission shall provide the Board with all necessary documentation, including correspondence with the government of the third country, with regard to that third country, territory or specified sector, or with the international organisation.

(t)   issue opinions on draft decisions of supervisory authorities pursuant to the consistency mechanism referred to in Article 64(1), on matters submitted pursuant to Article 64(2) and to issue binding decisions pursuant to Article 65, including in cases referred to in Article 66;

(u)   promote the cooperation and the effective bilateral and multilateral exchange of information and best practices between the supervisory authorities;

(v)   promote common training programmes and facilitate personnel exchanges between the supervisory authorities and, where appropriate, with the supervisory authorities of third countries or with international organisations;

(w)   promote the exchange of knowledge and documentation on data protection legislation and practice with data protection supervisory authorities worldwide.

(x)   issue opinions on codes of conduct drawn up at Union level pursuant to Article 40(9); and

(y)   maintain a publicly accessible electronic register of decisions taken by supervisory authorities and courts on issues handled in the consistency mechanism.

2. Where the Commission requests advice from the Board, it may indicate a time limit, taking into account the urgency of the matter.

3. The Board shall forward its opinions, guidelines, recommendations, and best practices to the Commission and to the committee referred to in Article 93 and make them public.

4. The Board shall, where appropriate, consult interested parties and give them the opportunity to comment within a reasonable period. The Board shall, without prejudice to Article 76, make the results of the consultation procedure publicly available.

Article 71 Reports

1. The Board shall draw up an annual report regarding the protection of natural persons with regard to processing in the Union and, where relevant, in third countries and international organisations. The report shall be made public and be transmitted to the European Parliament, to the Council and to the Commission.
2. The annual report shall include a review of the practical application of the guidelines, recommendations and best practices referred to in point (l) of Article 70(1) as well as of the binding decisions referred to in Article 65.

Article 72 Procedure

1. The Board shall take decisions by a simple majority of its members, unless otherwise provided for in this Regulation.
2. The Board shall adopt its own rules of procedure by a two-thirds majority of its members and organise its own operational arrangements.

Article 73 Chair

1. The Board shall elect a chair and two deputy chairs from amongst its members by simple majority.
2. The term of office of the Chair and of the deputy chairs shall be five years and be renewable once.

Article 74 Tasks of the Chair

1. The Chair shall have the following tasks:
   (a) to convene the meetings of the Board and prepare its agenda;
   (b) to notify decisions adopted by the Board pursuant to Article 65 to the lead supervisory authority and the supervisory authorities concerned;
   (c) to ensure the timely performance of the tasks of the Board, in particular in relation to the consistency mechanism referred to in Article 63.
2. The Board shall lay down the allocation of tasks between the Chair and the deputy chairs in its rules of procedure.

Article 75 Secretariat

1. The Board shall have a secretariat, which shall be provided by the European Data Protection Supervisor.
2. The secretariat shall perform its tasks exclusively under the instructions of the Chair of the Board.
3. The staff of the European Data Protection Supervisor involved in carrying out the tasks conferred on the Board by this Regulation shall be subject to separate reporting lines from the staff involved in carrying out tasks conferred on the European Data Protection Supervisor.
4. Where appropriate, the Board and the European Data Protection Supervisor shall establish and publish a Memorandum of Understanding implementing this Article, determining the terms of their cooperation, and applicable to the staff of the European Data Protection Supervisor involved in carrying out the tasks conferred on the Board by this Regulation.
5. The secretariat shall provide analytical, administrative and logistical support to the Board.
6. The secretariat shall be responsible in particular for:
   (a) the day-to-day business of the Board;
   (b) communication between the members of the Board, its Chair and the Commission;
   (c) communication with other institutions and the public;
   (d) the use of electronic means for the internal and external communication;
   (e) the translation of relevant information;
   (f) the preparation and follow-up of the meetings of the Board;
   (g) the preparation, drafting and publication of opinions, decisions on the settlement of disputes between supervisory authorities and other texts adopted by the Board.

Article 76 Confidentiality

1. The discussions of the Board shall be confidential where the Board deems it necessary, as provided for in its rules of procedure.
2. Access to documents submitted to members of the Board, experts and representatives of third parties shall be governed by Regulation (EC) No 1049/2001 of the European Parliament and of the Council (¹).

CHAPTER VIII
REMEDIES, LIABILITY AND PENALTIES

Article 77 Right to lodge a complaint with a supervisory authority

1. Without prejudice to any other administrative or judicial remedy, every data subject shall have the right to lodge a complaint with a supervisory authority, in particular in the Member State of his or her habitual residence, place of work or place of the alleged infringement if the data subject considers that the processing of personal data relating to him or her infringes this Regulation.
2. The supervisory authority with which the complaint has been lodged shall inform the complainant on the progress and the outcome of the complaint including the possibility of a judicial remedy pursuant to Article 78.

Article 78 Right to an effective judicial remedy against a supervisory authority

1. Without prejudice to any other administrative or non-judicial remedy, each natural or legal person shall have the right to an effective judicial remedy against a legally binding decision of a supervisory authority concerning them.
2. Without prejudice to any other administrative or non-judicial remedy, each data subject shall have the right to a an effective judicial remedy where the supervisory authority which is competent pursuant to Articles 55 and 56 does not handle a complaint or does not inform the data subject within three months on the progress or outcome of the complaint lodged pursuant to Article 77.
3. Proceedings against a supervisory authority shall be brought before the courts of the Member State where the supervisory authority is established.
4. Where proceedings are brought against a decision of a supervisory authority which was preceded by an opinion or a decision of the Board in the consistency mechanism, the supervisory authority shall forward that opinion or decision to the court.

Article 79 Right to an effective judicial remedy against a controller or processor

1. Without prejudice to any available administrative or non-judicial remedy, including the right to lodge a complaint with a supervisory authority pursuant to Article 77, each data subject shall have the right to an effective judicial remedy where he or she considers that his or her rights under this Regulation have been infringed as a result of the processing of his or her personal data in non-compliance with this Regulation.
2. Proceedings against a controller or a processor shall be brought before the courts of the Member State where the controller or processor has an establishment. Alternatively, such proceedings may be brought before the courts of the Member State where the data subject has his or her habitual residence, unless the controller or processor is a public authority of a Member State acting in the exercise of its public powers.

Article 80 Representation of data subjects

1. The data subject shall have the right to mandate a not-for-profit body, organisation or association which has been properly constituted in accordance with the law of a Member State, has statutory objectives which are in the public interest, and is active in the field of the protection of data subjects' rights and freedoms with regard to the protection of their personal data to lodge the complaint on his or her behalf, to exercise the rights referred to in Articles 77, 78 and 79 on his or her behalf, and to exercise the right to receive compensation referred to in Article 82 on his or her behalf where provided for by Member State law.

(¹)   Regulation (EC) No 1049/2001 of the European Parliament and of the Council of 30 May 2001 regarding public access to European Parliament, Council and Commission documents (OJ L 145, 31.5.2001, p. 43).

2. Member States may provide that any body, organisation or association referred to in paragraph 1 of this Article, independently of a data subject's mandate, has the right to lodge, in that Member State, a complaint with the supervisory authority which is competent pursuant to Article 77 and to exercise the rights referred to in Articles 78 and 79 if it considers that the rights of a data subject under this Regulation have been infringed as a result of the processing.

Article 81 Suspension of proceedings

1. Where a competent court of a Member State has information on proceedings, concerning the same subject matter as regards processing by the same controller or processor, that are pending in a court in another Member State, it shall contact that court in the other Member State to confirm the existence of such proceedings.
2. Where proceedings concerning the same subject matter as regards processing of the same controller or processor are pending in a court in another Member State, any competent court other than the court first seized may suspend its proceedings.
3. Where those proceedings are pending at first instance, any court other than the court first seized may also, on the application of one of the parties, decline jurisdiction if the court first seized has jurisdiction over the actions in question and its law permits the consolidation thereof.

Article 82 Right to compensation and liability

1. Any person who has suffered material or non-material damage as a result of an infringement of this Regulation shall have the right to receive compensation from the controller or processor for the damage suffered.
2. Any controller involved in processing shall be liable for the damage caused by processing which infringes this Regulation. A processor shall be liable for the damage caused by processing only where it has not complied with obligations of this Regulation specifically directed to processors or where it has acted outside or contrary to lawful instructions of the controller.
3. A controller or processor shall be exempt from liability under paragraph 2 if it proves that it is not in any way responsible for the event giving rise to the damage.
4. Where more than one controller or processor, or both a controller and a processor, are involved in the same processing and where they are, under paragraphs 2 and 3, responsible for any damage caused by processing, each controller or processor shall be held liable for the entire damage in order to ensure effective compensation of the data subject.
5. Where a controller or processor has, in accordance with paragraph 4, paid full compensation for the damage suffered, that controller or processor shall be entitled to claim back from the other controllers or processors involved in the same processing that part of the compensation corresponding to their part of responsibility for the damage, in accordance with the conditions set out in paragraph 2.
6. Court proceedings for exercising the right to receive compensation shall be brought before the courts competent under the law of the Member State referred to in Article 79(2).

Article 83 General conditions for imposing administrative fines

1. Each supervisory authority shall ensure that the imposition of administrative fines pursuant to this Article in respect of infringements of this Regulation referred to in paragraphs 4, 5 and 6 shall in each individual case be effective, proportionate and dissuasive.
2. Administrative fines shall, depending on the circumstances of each individual case, be imposed in addition to, or instead of, measures referred to in points (a) to (h) and (j) of Article 58(2). When deciding whether to impose an administrative fine and deciding on the amount of the administrative fine in each individual case due regard shall be given to the following:
   (a) the nature, gravity and duration of the infringement taking into account the nature scope or purpose of the processing concerned as well as the number of data subjects affected and the level of damage suffered by them;
   (b) the intentional or negligent character of the infringement;

(c)   any action taken by the controller or processor to mitigate the damage suffered by data subjects;

(d)   the degree of responsibility of the controller or processor taking into account technical and organisational measures implemented by them pursuant to Articles 25 and 32;

(e)   any relevant previous infringements by the controller or processor;

(f)   the degree of cooperation with the supervisory authority, in order to remedy the infringement and mitigate the possible adverse effects of the infringement;

(g)   the categories of personal data affected by the infringement;

(h)   the manner in which the infringement became known to the supervisory authority, in particular whether, and if so to what extent, the controller or processor notified the infringement;

(i)   where measures referred to in Article 58(2) have previously been ordered against the controller or processor concerned with regard to the same subject-matter, compliance with those measures;

(j)   adherence to approved codes of conduct pursuant to Article 40 or approved certification mechanisms pursuant to Article 42; and

(k)   any other aggravating or mitigating factor applicable to the circumstances of the case, such as financial benefits gained, or losses avoided, directly or indirectly, from the infringement.

3.   If a controller or processor intentionally or negligently, for the same or linked processing operations, infringes several provisions of this Regulation, the total amount of the administrative fine shall not exceed the amount specified for the gravest infringement.

4.   Infringements of the following provisions shall, in accordance with paragraph 2, be subject to administrative fines up to 10 000 000 EUR, or in the case of an undertaking, up to 2 % of the total worldwide annual turnover of the preceding financial year, whichever is higher:

(a)   the obligations of the controller and the processor pursuant to Articles 8, 11, 25 to 39 and 42 and 43;

(b)   the obligations of the certification body pursuant to Articles 42 and 43;

(c)   the obligations of the monitoring body pursuant to Article 41(4).

5.   Infringements of the following provisions shall, in accordance with paragraph 2, be subject to administrative fines up to 20 000 000 EUR, or in the case of an undertaking, up to 4 % of the total worldwide annual turnover of the preceding financial year, whichever is higher:

(a)   the basic principles for processing, including conditions for consent, pursuant to Articles 5, 6, 7 and 9;

(b)   the data subjects' rights pursuant to Articles 12 to 22;

(c)   the transfers of personal data to a recipient in a third country or an international organisation pursuant to Articles 44 to 49;

(d)   any obligations pursuant to Member State law adopted under Chapter IX;

(e)   non-compliance with an order or a temporary or definitive limitation on processing or the suspension of data flows by the supervisory authority pursuant to Article 58(2) or failure to provide access in violation of Article 58(1).

6.   Non-compliance with an order by the supervisory authority as referred to in Article 58(2) shall, in accordance with paragraph 2 of this Article, be subject to administrative fines up to 20 000 000 EUR, or in the case of an undertaking, up to 4 % of the total worldwide annual turnover of the preceding financial year, whichever is higher.

7.   Without prejudice to the corrective powers of supervisory authorities pursuant to Article 58(2), each Member State may lay down the rules on whether and to what extent administrative fines may be imposed on public authorities and bodies established in that Member State.

8.   The exercise by the supervisory authority of its powers under this Article shall be subject to appropriate procedural safeguards in accordance with Union and Member State law, including effective judicial remedy and due process.

9.   Where the legal system of the Member State does not provide for administrative fines, this Article may be applied in such a manner that the fine is initiated by the competent supervisory authority and imposed by competent national courts, while ensuring that

those legal remedies are effective and have an equivalent effect to the administrative fines imposed by supervisory authorities. In any event, the fines imposed shall be effective, proportionate and dissuasive. Those Member States shall notify to the Commission the provisions of their laws which they adopt pursuant to this paragraph by 25 May 2018 and, without delay, any subsequent amendment law or amendment affecting them.

Article 84 Penalties

1. Member States shall lay down the rules on other penalties applicable to infringements of this Regulation in particular for infringements which are not subject to administrative fines pursuant to Article 83, and shall take all measures necessary to ensure that they are implemented. Such penalties shall be effective, proportionate and dissuasive.

2. Each Member State shall notify to the Commission the provisions of its law which it adopts pursuant to paragraph 1, by 25 May 2018 and, without delay, any subsequent amendment affecting them.

CHAPTER IX
PROVISIONS RELATING TO SPECIFIC PROCESSING SITUATIONS

Article 85 Processing and freedom of expression and information

1. Member States shall by law reconcile the right to the protection of personal data pursuant to this Regulation with the right to freedom of expression and information, including processing for journalistic purposes and the purposes of academic, artistic or literary expression.

2. For processing carried out for journalistic purposes or the purpose of academic artistic or literary expression, Member States shall provide for exemptions or derogations from Chapter II (principles), Chapter III (rights of the data subject), Chapter IV (controller and processor), Chapter V (transfer of personal data to third countries or international organisations), Chapter VI (independent supervisory authorities), Chapter VII (cooperation and consistency) and Chapter IX (specific data processing situations) if they are necessary to reconcile the right to the protection of personal data with the freedom of expression and information.

3. Each Member State shall notify to the Commission the provisions of its law which it has adopted pursuant to paragraph 2 and, without delay, any subsequent amendment law or amendment affecting them.

Article 86 Processing and public access to official documents

Personal data in official documents held by a public authority or a public body or a private body for the performance of a task carried out in the public interest may be disclosed by the authority or body in accordance with Union or Member State law to which the public authority or body is subject in order to reconcile public access to official documents with the right to the protection of personal data pursuant to this Regulation.

Article 87 Processing of the national identification number

Member States may further determine the specific conditions for the processing of a national identification number or any other identifier of general application. In that case the national identification number or any other identifier of general application shall be used only under appropriate safeguards for the rights and freedoms of the data subject pursuant to this Regulation.

Article 88 Processing in the context of employment

1. Member States may, by law or by collective agreements, provide for more specific rules to ensure the protection of the rights and freedoms in respect of the processing of employees' personal data in the employment context, in particular for the purposes of the recruitment, the performance of the contract of employment, including discharge of obligations laid down by law or by collective agreements, management, planning and organisation of work, equality and diversity in the workplace, health and safety at work, protection of employer's or customer's property and for the purposes of the

exercise and enjoyment, on an individual or collective basis, of rights and benefits related to employment, and for the purpose of the termination of the employment relationship.

2. Those rules shall include suitable and specific measures to safeguard the data subject's human dignity, legitimate interests and fundamental rights, with particular regard to the transparency of processing, the transfer of personal data within a group of undertakings, or a group of enterprises engaged in a joint economic activity and monitoring systems at the work place.

3. Each Member State shall notify to the Commission those provisions of its law which it adopts pursuant to paragraph 1, by 25 May 2018 and, without delay, any subsequent amendment affecting them.

Article 89 Safeguards and derogations relating to processing for archiving purposes in the public interest, scientific or historical research purposes or statistical purposes

1. Processing for archiving purposes in the public interest, scientific or historical research purposes or statistical purposes, shall be subject to appropriate safeguards, in accordance with this Regulation, for the rights and freedoms of the data subject. Those safeguards shall ensure that technical and organisational measures are in place in particular in order to ensure respect for the principle of data minimisation. Those measures may include pseudonymisation provided that those purposes can be fulfilled in that manner. Where those purposes can be fulfilled by further processing which does not permit or no longer permits the identification of data subjects, those purposes shall be fulfilled in that manner.

2. Where personal data are processed for scientific or historical research purposes or statistical purposes, Union or Member State law may provide for derogations from the rights referred to in Articles 15, 16, 18 and 21 subject to the conditions and safeguards referred to in paragraph 1 of this Article in so far as such rights are likely to render impossible or seriously impair the achievement of the specific purposes, and such derogations are necessary for the fulfilment of those purposes.

3. Where personal data are processed for archiving purposes in the public interest, Union or Member State law may provide for derogations from the rights referred to in Articles 15, 16, 18, 19, 20 and 21 subject to the conditions and safeguards referred to in paragraph 1 of this Article in so far as such rights are likely to render impossible or seriously impair the achievement of the specific purposes, and such derogations are necessary for the fulfilment of those purposes.

4. Where processing referred to in paragraphs 2 and 3 serves at the same time another purpose, the derogations shall apply only to processing for the purposes referred to in those paragraphs.

Article 90 Obligations of secrecy

1. Member States may adopt specific rules to set out the powers of the supervisory authorities laid down in points (e) and (f) of Article 58(1) in relation to controllers or processors that are subject, under Union or Member State law or rules established by national competent bodies, to an obligation of professional secrecy or other equivalent obligations of secrecy where this is necessary and proportionate to reconcile the right of the protection of personal data with the obligation of secrecy. Those rules shall apply only with regard to personal data which the controller or processor has received as a result of or has obtained in an activity covered by that obligation of secrecy.

2. Each Member State shall notify to the Commission the rules adopted pursuant to paragraph 1, by 25 May 2018 and, without delay, any subsequent amendment affecting them.

Article 91 Existing data protection rules of churches and religious associations

1. Where in a Member State, churches and religious associations or communities apply, at the time of entry into force of this Regulation, comprehensive rules relating to the protection of natural persons with regard to processing, such rules may continue to apply, provided that they are brought into line with this Regulation.

2.   Churches and religious associations which apply comprehensive rules in accordance with paragraph 1 of this Article shall be subject to the supervision of an independent supervisory authority, which may be specific, provided that it fulfils the conditions laid down in Chapter VI of this Regulation.

CHAPTER X
DELEGATED ACTS AND IMPLEMENTING ACTS

Article 92 Exercise of the delegation

1.   The power to adopt delegated acts is conferred on the Commission subject to the conditions laid down in this Article.
2.   The delegation of power referred to in Article 12(8) and Article 43(8) shall be conferred on the Commission for an indeterminate period of time from 24 May 2016.
3.   The delegation of power referred to in Article 12(8) and Article 43(8) may be revoked at any time by the European Parliament or by the Council. A decision of revocation shall put an end to the delegation of power specified in that decision. It shall take effect the day following that of its publication in the *Official Journal of the European Union* or at a later date specified therein. It shall not affect the validity of any delegated acts already in force.
4.   As soon as it adopts a delegated act, the Commission shall notify it simultaneously to the European Parliament and to the Council.
5.   A delegated act adopted pursuant to Article 12(8) and Article 43(8) shall enter into force only if no objection has been expressed by either the European Parliament or the Council within a period of three months of notification of that act to the European Parliament and the Council or if, before the expiry of that period, the European Parliament and the Council have both informed the Commission that they will not object. That period shall be extended by three months at the initiative of the European Parliament or of the Council.

Article 93 Committee procedure

1.   The Commission shall be assisted by a committee. That committee shall be a committee within the meaning of Regulation (EU) No 182/2011.
2.   Where reference is made to this paragraph, Article 5 of Regulation (EU) No 182/2011 shall apply.
3.   Where reference is made to this paragraph, Article 8 of Regulation (EU) No 182/2011, in conjunction with Article 5 thereof, shall apply.

CHAPTER XI
FINAL PROVISIONS

Article 94 Repeal of Directive 95/46/EC

1.   Directive 95/46/EC is repealed with effect from 25 May 2018.
2.   References to the repealed Directive shall be construed as references to this Regulation. References to the Working Party on the Protection of Individuals with regard to the Processing of Personal Data established by Article 29 of Directive 95/46/EC shall be construed as references to the European Data Protection Board established by this Regulation.

Article 95 Relationship with Directive 2002/58/EC

This Regulation shall not impose additional obligations on natural or legal persons in relation to processing in connection with the provision of publicly available electronic communications services in public communication networks in the Union in relation to matters for which they are subject to specific obligations with the same objective set out in Directive 2002/58/EC.

Article 96 Relationship with previously concluded Agreements

International agreements involving the transfer of personal data to third countries or international organisations which were concluded by Member States prior to 24 May 2016, and which comply with Union law as applicable prior to that date, shall remain in force until amended, replaced or revoked.

Article 97 Commission reports

1. By 25 May 2020 and every four years thereafter, the Commission shall submit a report on the evaluation and review of this Regulation to the European Parliament and to the Council. The reports shall be made public.
2. In the context of the evaluations and reviews referred to in paragraph 1, the Commission shall examine, in particular, the application and functioning of:
    (a) Chapter V on the transfer of personal data to third countries or international organisations with particular regard to decisions adopted pursuant to Article 45(3) of this Regulation and decisions adopted on the basis of Article 25(6) of Directive 95/46/EC;
    (b) Chapter VII on cooperation and consistency.
3. For the purpose of paragraph 1, the Commission may request information from Member States and supervisory authorities.
4. In carrying out the evaluations and reviews referred to in paragraphs 1 and 2, the Commission shall take into account the positions and findings of the European Parliament, of the Council, and of other relevant bodies or sources.
5. The Commission shall, if necessary, submit appropriate proposals to amend this Regulation, in particular taking into account of developments in information technology and in the light of the state of progress in the information society.

Article 98 Review of other Union legal acts on data protection

The Commission shall, if appropriate, submit legislative proposals with a view to amending other Union legal acts on the protection of personal data, in order to ensure uniform and consistent protection of natural persons with regard to processing. This shall in particular concern the rules relating to the protection of natural persons with regard to processing by Union institutions, bodies, offices and agencies and on the free movement of such data.

Article 99 Entry into force and application

1. This Regulation shall enter into force on the twentieth day following that of its publication in the *Official Journal of the European Union*.
2. It shall apply from 25 May 2018.

EUROPEAN COMMUNITIES ACT 1972
(1972, c. 68)

PART 1
GENERAL PROVISIONS

1 **Short title and interpretation**

(1) This Act may be cited as the European Communities Act 1972.

(2) In this Act ...

"the Communities" means the European Economic Community, the European Coal and Steel Community and the European Atomic Energy Community;

"the Treaties" or "the EU Treaties" means, subject to subsection (3) below, the pre-accession treaties, that is to say, those described in Part 1 of Schedule 1 to this Act, taken with—

(a) the treaty relating to the accession of the United Kingdom to the European Economic Community and to the European Atomic Energy Community, signed at Brussels on the 22nd January 1972; and

(b) the decision, of the same date, of the Council of the European Communities relating to the accession of the United Kingdom to the European Coal and Steel Community; and

...

(j) the following provisions of the Single European Act signed at Luxembourg and The Hague on 17th and 28th February 1986, namely Title II (amendment of the treaties establishing the Communities) and, so far as they relate to any of the Communities or any Community institution, the preamble and Titles I (common provisions) and IV (general and final provisions); and

(k) Titles II, III and IV of the Treaty on European Union signed at Maastricht on 7th February 1992, together with the other provisions of the Treaty so far as they relate to those Titles, and the Protocols adopted at Maastricht on that date and annexed to the Treaty establishing the European Community with the exception of the Protocol on Social Policy on page 117 of Cm 1934; and

(l) the decision, of 1st February 1993, of the Council amending the Act concerning the election of the representatives of the European Parliament by direct universal suffrage annexed to Council Decision 76/787/ECSC, EEC, Euratom of 20th September 1976; and

(m) the Agreement on the European Economic Area signed at Oporto on 2nd May 1992 together with the Protocol adjusting that Agreement signed at Brussels on 17th March 1993; and

...

(o) the following provisions of the Treaty signed at Amsterdam on 2nd October 1997 amending the Treaty on European Union, the Treaties establishing the European Communities and certain related Acts

(i) Articles 2 to 9,

(ii) Article 12, and

(iii) the other provisions of the Treaty so far as they relate to those Articles, and the Protocols adopted on that occasion other than the Protocol on Article J.7 of the Treaty on European Union; and

(p) the following provisions of the Treaty signed at Nice on 26th February 2001 amending the Treaty on European Union, the Treaties establishing the European Communities and certain related Acts

(i) Articles 2 to 10, and

(ii) the other provisions of the Treaty so far as they relate to those Articles, and the Protocols adopted on that occasion;

...
(s)   the Treaty of Lisbon Amending the Treaty on European Union and the Treaty Establishing the European Community signed at Lisbon on 13th December 2007 (together with its Annex and protocols), excluding any provision that relates to, or in so far as it relates to or could be applied in relation to, the Common Foreign and Security Policy;

...
and any other treaty entered into by the EU (except in so far as it relates to, or could be applied in relation to, the Common Foreign and Security Policy), with or without any of the member States, or entered into, as a treaty ancillary to any of the Treaties, by the United Kingdom;

and any expression defined in Schedule 1 to this Act has the meaning there given to it.

(3)   If Her Majesty by Order in Council declares that a treaty specified in the Order is to be regarded as one of the EU Treaties as herein defined, the Order shall be conclusive that it is to be so regarded; but a treaty entered into by the United Kingdom after the 22nd January 1972, other than a pre-accession treaty to which the United Kingdom accedes on terms settled on or before that date, shall not be so regarded unless it is so specified, nor be so specified unless a draft of the Order in Council has been approved by resolution of each House of Parliament.

(4)   For purposes of subsections (2) and (3) above, "treaty" includes any international agreement, and any protocol or annex to a treaty or international agreement.

2   General implementation of Treaties

(1)   All such rights, powers, liabilities, obligations and restrictions from time to time created or arising by or under the Treaties, and all such remedies and procedures from time to time provided for by or under the Treaties, as in accordance with the Treaties are without further enactment to be given legal effect or used in the United Kingdom shall be recognised and available in law, and be enforced, allowed and followed accordingly; and the expression "enforceable EU right" and similar expressions shall be read as referring to one to which this subsection applies.

(2)   Subject to Schedule 2 to this Act, at any time after its passing Her Majesty may by Order in Council, and any designated Minister or department may by order, rules, regulations or scheme, make provision—
(a)   for the purpose of implementing any EU obligation of the United Kingdom, or enabling any such obligation to be implemented, or of enabling any rights enjoyed or to be enjoyed by the United Kingdom under or by virtue of the Treaties to be exercised; or
(b)   for the purpose of dealing with matters arising out of or related to any such obligation or rights or the coming into force, or the operation from time to time, of subsection (1) above;

and in the exercise of any statutory power or duty, including any power to give directions or to legislate by means of orders, rules, regulations or other subordinate instrument, the person entrusted with the power or duty may have regard to the objects of the EU and to any such obligation or rights as aforesaid.

In this subsection "designated Minister or department" means such Minister of the Crown or government department as may from time to time be designated by Order in Council in relation to any matter or for any purpose, but subject to such restrictions or conditions (if any) as may be specified by the Order in Council.

(3)   There shall be charged on and issued out of the Consolidated Fund or, if so determined by the Treasury, the National Loans Fund the amounts required to meet any EU obligation to make payments to the EU or a member State, or any EU obligation in respect of contributions to the capital or reserves of the European Investment Bank or in respect of loans to the Bank, or to redeem any notes or obligations issued or created in respect of any such EU obligation; and, except as otherwise provided by or under any enactment,
(a)   any other expenses incurred under or by virtue of the Treaties or this Act by any Minister of the Crown or government department may be paid out of moneys provided by Parliament; and
(b)   any sums received under or by virtue of the Treaties or this Act by any Minister of the Crown or government department, save for such sums as may be required

for disbursements permitted by any other enactment, shall be paid into the Consolidated Fund or, if so determined by the Treasury, the National Loans Fund.

(4) The provision that may be made under subsection (2) above includes, subject to Schedule 2 to this Act, any such provision (of any such extent) as might be made by Act of Parliament, and any enactment passed or to be passed, other than one contained in this Part of this Act, shall be construed and have effect subject to the foregoing provisions of this section; but, except as may be provided by any Act passed after this Act, Schedule 2

shall have effect in connection with the powers conferred by this and the following sections of this Act to make Orders in Council or orders, rules, regulations or schemes.

...

3 Decisions on, and proof of, Treaties and EU instruments, etc.

(1) For the purposes of all legal proceedings any question as to the meaning or effect of any of the Treaties, or as to the validity, meaning or effect of any EU instrument, shall be treated as a question of law (and, if not referred to the European Court, be for determination as such in accordance with the principles laid down by and any relevant decision of the European Court).

(2) Judicial notice shall be taken of the Treaties, of the *Official Journal of the European Union* and of any decision of, or expression of opinion by, the European Court on any such question as aforesaid; and the Official Journal shall be admissible as evidence of any instrument or other act thereby communicated of the EU or of any EU institution.

...

EUROPEAN UNION (WITHDRAWAL) ACT 2018

(2018, c. 16)

An Act to repeal the European Communities Act 1972 and make other provision in connection with the withdrawal of the United Kingdom from the EU.

[26th June 2018]

Be it enacted by the Queen's most Excellent Majesty, by and with the advice and consent of the Lords Spiritual and Temporal, and Commons, in this present Parliament assembled, and by the authority of the same, as follows:—

Repeal of the ECA

1   Repeal of the European Communities Act 1972

The European Communities Act 1972 is repealed on exit day.

Savings for implementation period

1A   Saving for ECA for implementation period

(1) Subsections (2) to (4) have effect despite the repeal of the European Communities Act 1972 on exit day by section 1.

(2) The European Communities Act 1972, as it has effect in domestic law or the law of a relevant territory immediately before exit day, continues to have effect in domestic law or the law of the relevant territory on and after exit day so far as provided by subsections (3) to (5).

(3) The Act of 1972 has effect on and after exit day as if —

  (a) the definitions of "the Treaties" and "the EU Treaties" given by section 1(2) to (4) (interpretation)—

    (i) included Part 4 of the withdrawal agreement (implementation period), other than that Part so far as it relates to, or could be applied in relation to, the Common Foreign and Security Policy, but

    (ii) were otherwise limited to anything which falls within those definitions as at immediately before exit day so far as it is not excluded by regulations made on or after exit day by a Minister of the Crown under this sub-paragraph,

  (b) the reference in section 2(2) to the objects of the EU were a reference to those objects so far as they are applicable to and in the United Kingdom by virtue of Part 4 of the withdrawal agreement,

  (c) section 2(3) (payment of EU costs etc.) were omitted,

  (d) in section 3 (decisions on, and proof of, EU Treaties and EU instruments etc.)—

    (i) the references to the Treaties in subsections (1) and (2) included the withdrawal agreement, and

    (ii) the words in brackets in subsection (1) only applied so far as they are in accordance with Part 4 of the withdrawal agreement,

  (e) references in sections 5 and 6 (customs duties and common agricultural policy) to the common customs tariff of the EU, directly applicable EU provision, the exclusion of customs duties, EU arrangements and agricultural levies of the EU were to such things so far as they are applicable to and in the United Kingdom by virtue of Part 4 of the withdrawal agreement, and

  (f) in Part 2 of Schedule 1 (general definitions in relation to the EU)—

    (i) in the definition of "EU customs duty", the reference to directly applicable EU provision were to such provision so far as it is applicable to and in the United Kingdom by virtue of Part 4 of the withdrawal agreement, and

    (ii) in the definition of "Member" in the expression "member State", after "EU" there were inserted " and for the purposes of this expression the United Kingdom is to be treated as if it were a member of the EU during the implementation period (within the meaning given by section 1A(6) of the European Union (Withdrawal) Act 2018) ".

(4) In this section "relevant territory" means the Isle of Man, any of the Channel Islands or Gibraltar.

(5) Subsections (1) to (4) are repealed on IP completion day.

(6)   In this Act—

"the implementation period" means the transition or implementation period provided for by Part 4 of the withdrawal agreement and beginning with exit day and ending on IP completion day;

"IP completion day" (and related expressions) have the same meaning as in the European Union (Withdrawal Agreement) Act 2020 (see section 39(1) to (5) of that Act);

"withdrawal agreement" has the same meaning as in that Act (see section 39(1) and (6) of that Act).

(7)   In this Act—

     (a)   references to the European Communities Act 1972 are to be read, so far as the context permits or requires, as being or (as the case may be) including references to that Act as it continues to have effect by virtue of subsections (2) to (4) above, and

     (b)   references to any Part of the withdrawal agreement or the EEA EFTA separation agreement include references to any other provisions of that agreement so far as applying to that Part.

1B   Saving for EU-derived domestic legislation for implementation period

(1)   Subsections (2) to (5) have effect despite the repeal of the European Communities Act 1972 on exit day by section 1.

(2)   EU-derived domestic legislation, as it has effect in domestic law immediately before exit day, continues to have effect in domestic law on and after exit day, subject as follows.

(3)   Any enactment which continues to have effect by virtue of subsection (2) is to be read, on and after exit day and so far as the context permits or requires, as if—

     (a)   any reference to an expression which is to be read in accordance with Schedule 1 to the Interpretation Act 1978 and is an expression defined by section 1 of, or Part 2 of Schedule 1 to, the European Communities Act 1972 were a reference to that expression as defined by that section or that Part of that Schedule as it continues to have effect by virtue of section 1A(2) to (4) of this Act,

     (b)   any reference (however expressed and subject to paragraph (a) above) to—

         (i)   EU law,

         (ii)   any particular EU Treaty or any part of it,

         (iii)   any EU instrument, or other document of an EU entity or of the EU, or any part of any such instrument or document,

         (iv)   any part of EU law not falling within sub-paragraph (ii) or (iii),

         (v)   any tax, duty, levy or interests of the EU, or

         (vi)   any arrangement involving, or otherwise relating to, the EU of a kind not falling within sub-paragraph (i), (ii), (iii), (iv) or (v),

     were a reference to any such thing so far as it is applicable to and in the United Kingdom by virtue of Part 4 of the withdrawal agreement,

     (c)   any reference (however expressed and subject to paragraph (a) above) to the European Communities Act 1972 were or (as the case may be) included a reference to the Act of 1972 as it continues to have effect by virtue of section 1A(2) to (4) of this Act,

     (d)   any reference (however expressed) to the area of the EU or of the EEA included the United Kingdom,

     (e)   any reference (however expressed) to a citizen of the EU or a national of the EEA included a United Kingdom national (within the meaning given by Article 2(d) of the withdrawal agreement), and

     (f)   such other modifications were made as—

         (i)   are provided for by regulations under section 8A or Part 1A of Schedule 2, or

         (ii)   so far as not so provided, are necessary for any purpose of Part 4 of the withdrawal agreement and are capable of being ascertained from any such purpose or otherwise from that Part of that agreement.

(4)   Any EU-derived domestic legislation which is an enactment passed or made on or after exit day and before IP completion day is, unless the contrary intention appears, to be read in accordance with subsection (3) (and anything done or omitted to be done in connection with any such enactment is to be understood, and has effect, accordingly).

(5) Subsections (2) to (4) are subject to any regulations made under section 8A or 23 or Part 1A of Schedule 2 or otherwise under this Act or under the European Union (Withdrawal Agreement) Act 2020.

(6) Subsections (1) to (5) are repealed on IP completion day.

(7) In this Act "EU-derived domestic legislation" means any enactment so far as—

    (a) made under section 2(2) of, or paragraph 1A of Schedule 2 to, the European Communities Act 1972,

    (b) passed or made, or operating, for a purpose mentioned in section 2(2)(a) or (b) of that Act,

    (c) relating to—

        (i) anything which falls within paragraph (a) or (b), or

        (ii) any rights, powers, liabilities, obligations, restrictions, remedies or procedures which are recognised and available in domestic law by virtue of section 2(1) of the European Communities Act 1972, or

    (d) relating otherwise to the EU or the EEA,

but does not include any enactment contained in the European Communities Act 1972 or any enactment contained in this Act or the European Union (Withdrawal Agreement) Act 2020 or in regulations made under this Act or the Act of 2020.

Retention of existing EU law

2 Saving for EU-derived domestic legislation

(1) EU-derived domestic legislation, as it has effect in domestic law immediately before exit day, continues to have effect in domestic law on and after exit day.

(2) In this section "EU-derived domestic legislation" means any enactment so far as—

    (a) made under section 2(2) of, or paragraph 1A of Schedule 2 to, the European Communities Act 1972,

    (b) passed or made, or operating, for a purpose mentioned in section 2(2)(a) or (b) of that Act,

    (c) relating to anything—

        (i) which falls within paragraph (a) or (b), or

        (ii) to which section 3(1) or 4(1) applies, or

    (d) relating otherwise to the EU or the EEA,

but does not include any enactment contained in the European Communities Act 1972.

(3) This section is subject to section 5 and Schedule 1 (exceptions to savings and incorporation).

3 Incorporation of direct EU legislation

(1) Direct EU legislation, so far as operative immediately before exit day, forms part of domestic law on and after exit day.

(2) In this Act "direct EU legislation" means—

    (a) any EU regulation, EU decision or EU tertiary legislation, as it has effect in EU law immediately before exit day and so far as—

        (i) it is not an exempt EU instrument (for which see section 20(1) and Schedule 6),

        (ii) it is not an EU decision addressed only to a member State other than the United Kingdom, and

        (iii) its effect is not reproduced in an enactment to which section 2(1) applies,

    (b) any Annex to the EEA agreement, as it has effect in EU law immediately before exit day and so far as—

        (i) it refers to, or contains adaptations of, anything falling within paragraph (a), and

        (ii) its effect is not reproduced in an enactment to which section 2(1) applies, or

    (c) Protocol 1 to the EEA agreement (which contains horizontal adaptations that apply in relation to EU instruments referred to in the Annexes to that agreement), as it has effect in EU law immediately before exit day.

(3) For the purposes of this Act, any direct EU legislation is operative immediately before exit day if—

    (a)   in the case of anything which comes into force at a particular time and is stated to apply from a later time, it is in force and applies immediately before exit day,

    (b)   in the case of a decision which specifies to whom it is addressed, it has been notified to that person before exit day, and

    (c)   in any other case, it is in force immediately before exit day.

(4)   This section—

    (a)   brings into domestic law any direct EU legislation only in the form of the English language version of that legislation, and

    (b)   does not apply to any such legislation for which there is no such version, but paragraph (a) does not affect the use of the other language versions of that legislation for the purposes of interpreting it.

(5)   This section is subject to section 5 and Schedule 1 (exceptions to savings and incorporation).

4   Saving for rights etc. under section 2(1) of the ECA

(1)   Any rights, powers, liabilities, obligations, restrictions, remedies and procedures which, immediately before exit day—

    (a)   are recognised and available in domestic law by virtue of section 2(1) of the European Communities Act 1972, and

    (b)   are enforced, allowed and followed accordingly,

continue on and after exit day to be recognised and available in domestic law (and to be enforced, allowed and followed accordingly).

(2)   Subsection (1) does not apply to any rights, powers, liabilities, obligations, restrictions, remedies or procedures so far as they—

    (a)   form part of domestic law by virtue of section 3, or

    (b)   arise under an EU directive (including as applied by the EEA agreement) and are not of a kind recognised by the European Court or any court or tribunal in the United Kingdom in a case decided before exit day (whether or not as an essential part of the decision in the case).

(3)   This section is subject to section 5 and Schedule 1 (exceptions to savings and incorporation).

5   Exceptions to savings and incorporation

(1)   The principle of the supremacy of EU law does not apply to any enactment or rule of law passed or made on or after exit day.

(2)   Accordingly, the principle of the supremacy of EU law continues to apply on or after exit day so far as relevant to the interpretation, disapplication or quashing of any enactment or rule of law passed or made before exit day.

(3)   Subsection (1) does not prevent the principle of the supremacy of EU law from applying to a modification made on or after exit day of any enactment or rule of law passed or made before exit day if the application of the principle is consistent with the intention of the modification.

(4)   The Charter of Fundamental Rights is not part of domestic law on or after exit day.

(5)   Subsection (4) does not affect the retention in domestic law on or after exit day in accordance with this Act of any fundamental rights or principles which exist irrespective of the Charter (and references to the Charter in any case law are, so far as necessary for this purpose, to be read as if they were references to any corresponding retained fundamental rights or principles).

(6)   Schedule 1 (which makes further provision about exceptions to savings and incorporation) has effect.

(7)   Subsections (1) to (6) and Schedule 1 are subject to relevant separation agreement law (for which see section 7C).

6   Interpretation of retained EU law

(1)   A court or tribunal—

    (a)   is not bound by any principles laid down, or any decisions made, on or after IP completion day by the European Court, and

    (b)   cannot refer any matter to the European Court on or after IP completion day.

(2)   Subject to this and subsections (3) to (6), a court or tribunal may have regard to anything done on or after IP completion day by the European Court, another EU entity or the EU so far as it is relevant to any matter before the court or tribunal.

(3)   Any question as to the validity, meaning or effect of any retained EU law is to be decided, so far as that law is unmodified on or after IP completion day and so far as they are relevant to it—

  (a)   in accordance with any retained case law and any retained general principles of EU law, and

  (b)   having regard (among other things) to the limits, immediately before IP completion day, of EU competences.

(4)   But—

  (a)   the Supreme Court is not bound by any retained EU case law,

  (b)   the High Court of Justiciary is not bound by any retained EU case law when—

    (i)   sitting as a court of appeal otherwise than in relation to a compatibility issue (within the meaning given by section 288ZA(2) of the Criminal Procedure (Scotland) Act 1995) or a devolution issue (within the meaning given by paragraph 1 of Schedule 6 to the Scotland Act 1998), or

    (ii)   sitting on a reference under section 123(1) of the Criminal Procedure (Scotland) Act 1995, and

  (ba)   a relevant court or relevant tribunal is not bound by any retained EU case law so far as is provided for by regulations under subsection (5A),

  (c)   no court or tribunal is bound by any retained domestic case law that it would not otherwise be bound by.

(5)   In deciding whether to depart from any retained EU case law by virtue of subsection (4)(a) or (b), the Supreme Court or the High Court of Justiciary must apply the same test as it would apply in deciding whether to depart from its own case law.

(5A)   A Minister of the Crown may by regulations provide for—

  (a)   a court or tribunal to be a relevant court or (as the case may be) a relevant tribunal for the purposes of this section,

  (b)   the extent to which, or circumstances in which, a relevant court or relevant tribunal is not to be bound by retained EU case law,

  (c)   the test which a relevant court or relevant tribunal must apply in deciding whether to depart from any retained EU case law, or

  (d)   considerations which are to be relevant to—

    (i)   the Supreme Court or the High Court of Justiciary in applying the test mentioned in subsection (5), or

    (ii)   a relevant court or relevant tribunal in applying any test provided for by virtue of paragraph (c) above.

(5B)   Regulations under subsection (5A) may (among other things) provide for—

  (a)   the High Court of Justiciary to be a relevant court when sitting otherwise than as mentioned in subsection (4)(b)(i) and (ii),

  (b)   the extent to which, or circumstances in which, a relevant court or relevant tribunal not being bound by retained EU case law includes (or does not include) that court or tribunal not being bound by retained domestic case law which relates to retained EU case law,

  (c)   other matters arising in relation to retained domestic case law which relates to retained EU case law (including by making provision of a kind which could be made in relation to retained EU case law), or

  (d)   the test mentioned in paragraph (c) of subsection (5A) or the considerations mentioned in paragraph (d) of that subsection to be determined (whether with or without the consent of a Minister of the Crown) by a person mentioned in subsection (5C)(a) to (e) or by more than one of those persons acting jointly.

(5C)   Before making regulations under subsection (5A), a Minister of the Crown must consult—

  (a)   the President of the Supreme Court,

  (b)   the Lord Chief Justice of England and Wales,

  (c)   the Lord President of the Court of Session,

  (d)   the Lord Chief Justice of Northern Ireland,

    (e)   the Senior President of Tribunals, and

    (f)   such other persons as the Minister of the Crown considers appropriate.

(5D) No regulations may be made under subsection (5A) after IP completion day.

(6)   Subsection (3) does not prevent the validity, meaning or effect of any retained EU law which has been modified on or after IP completion day from being decided as provided for in that subsection if doing so is consistent with the intention of the modifications.

(6A) Subsections (1) to (6) are subject to relevant separation agreement law (for which see section 7C).

(7)   In this Act—

"retained case law" means—

    (a)   retained domestic case law, and

    (b)   retained EU case law;

"retained domestic case law" means any principles laid down by, and any decisions of, a court or tribunal in the United Kingdom, as they have effect immediately before IP completion day and so far as they—

    (a)   relate to anything to which section 2, 3 or 4 applies, and

    (b)   are not excluded by section 5 or Schedule 1,

(as those principles and decisions are modified by or under this Act or by other domestic law from time to time);

"retained EU case law" means any principles laid down by, and any decisions of, the European Court, as they have effect in EU law immediately before IP completion day and so far as they—

    (a)   relate to anything to which section 2, 3 or 4 applies, and

    (b)   are not excluded by section 5 or Schedule 1,

(as those principles and decisions are modified by or under this Act or by other domestic law from time to time);

"retained EU law" means anything which, on or after IP completion day, continues to be, or forms part of, domestic law by virtue of section 2, 3 or 4 or subsection (3) or (6) above (as that body of law is added to or otherwise modified by or under this Act or by other domestic law from time to time);

"retained general principles of EU law" means the general principles of EU law, as they have effect in EU law immediately before IP completion day and so far as they—

    (a)   relate to anything to which section 2, 3 or 4 applies, and

    (b)   are not excluded by section 5 or Schedule 1,

(as those principles are modified by or under this Act or by other domestic law from time to time).

7   Status of retained EU law

(1)   Anything which—

    (a)   was, immediately before exit day, primary legislation of a particular kind, subordinate legislation of a particular kind or another enactment of a particular kind, and

    (b)   continues to be domestic law on and after exit day by virtue of section 1A(2) or 1B(2),

continues to be domestic law as an enactment of the same kind.

(2)   Retained direct principal EU legislation cannot be modified by any primary or subordinate legislation other than—

    (a)   an Act of Parliament,

    (b)   any other primary legislation (so far as it has the power to make such a modification), or

    (c)   any subordinate legislation so far as it is made under a power which permits such a modification by virtue of—

        (i)   paragraph 3, 5(3)(a) or (4)(a), 8(3), 10(3)(a) or (4)(a), 11(2)(a) or 12(3) of Schedule 8,

        (ii)   any other provision made by or under this Act,

        (iii) any provision made by or under an Act of Parliament passed before, and in the same Session as, this Act, or

        (iv) any provision made on or after the passing of this Act by or under primary legislation.

(3)   Retained direct minor EU legislation cannot be modified by any primary or subordinate legislation other than—

(a)   an Act of Parliament,

(b)   any other primary legislation (so far as it has the power to make such a modification), or

(c)   any subordinate legislation so far as it is made under a power which permits such a modification by virtue of—

    (i)   paragraph 3, 5(2) or (4)(a), 8(3), 10(2) or (4)(a) or 12(3) of Schedule 8,

    (ii)   any other provision made by or under this Act,

    (iii)   any provision made by or under an Act of Parliament passed before, and in the same Session as, this Act, or

    (iv)   any provision made on or after the passing of this Act by or under primary legislation.

(4)   Anything which is retained EU law by virtue of section 4 cannot be modified by any primary or subordinate legislation other than—

(a)   an Act of Parliament,

(b)   any other primary legislation (so far as it has the power to make such a modification), or

(c)   any subordinate legislation so far as it is made under a power which permits such a modification by virtue of—

    (i)   paragraph 3, 5(3)(b) or (4)(b), 8(3), 10(3)(b) or (4)(b), 11(2)(b) or 12(3) of Schedule 8,

    (ii)   any other provision made by or under this Act,

    (iii)   any provision made by or under an Act of Parliament passed before, and in the same Session as, this Act, or

    (iv)   any provision made on or after the passing of this Act by or under primary legislation.

(5)   For other provisions about the status of retained EU law, see—

(a)   section 5(1) to (3) (status of retained EU law in relation to other enactments or rules of law),

(b)   section 6 (status of retained case law and retained general principles of EU law),

(c)   section 15(2) and Part 2 of Schedule 5 (status of retained EU law for the purposes of the rules of evidence),

(d)   paragraphs 13 to 16 of Schedule 8 (affirmative and enhanced scrutiny procedure for, and information about, instruments which amend or revoke subordinate legislation under section 2(2) of the European Communities Act 1972 including subordinate legislation implementing EU directives),

(e)   paragraphs 19 and 20 of that Schedule (status of certain retained direct EU legislation for the purposes of the Interpretation Act 1978), and

(f)   paragraph 30 of that Schedule (status of retained direct EU legislation for the purposes of the Human Rights Act 1998).

(6)   In this Act—

"retained direct minor EU legislation" means any retained direct EU legislation which is not retained direct principal EU legislation;

"retained direct principal EU legislation" means—

(a)   any EU regulation so far as it—

    (i)   forms part of domestic law on and after IP completion day by virtue of section 3, and

    (ii)   was not EU tertiary legislation immediately before IP completion day, or

(b)   any Annex to the EEA agreement so far as it—

    (i)   forms part of domestic law on and after IP completion day by virtue of section 3, and

    (ii)   refers to, or contains adaptations of, any EU regulation so far as it falls within paragraph (a),

(as modified by or under this Act or by other domestic law from time to time).

7A   General implementation of remainder of withdrawal agreement

(1)   Subsection (2) applies to—

(a)   all such rights, powers, liabilities, obligations and restrictions from time to time created or arising by or under the withdrawal agreement, and

(b)   all such remedies and procedures from time to time provided for by or under the withdrawal agreement, as in accordance with the withdrawal agreement are without further enactment to be given legal effect or used in the United Kingdom.

(2) The rights, powers, liabilities, obligations, restrictions, remedies and procedures concerned are to be—

    (a) recognised and available in domestic law, and

    (b) enforced, allowed and followed accordingly.

(3) Every enactment (including an enactment contained in this Act) is to be read and has effect subject to subsection (2).

(4) This section does not apply in relation to Part 4 of the withdrawal agreement so far as section 2(1) of the European Communities Act 1972 applies in relation to that Part.

(5) See also (among other things)—

    (a) Part 3 of the European Union (Withdrawal Agreement) Act 2020 (further provision about citizens' rights),

    (b) section 20 of that Act (financial provision),

    (c) section 7C of this Act (interpretation of law relating to withdrawal agreement etc.),

    (d) section 8B of this Act (power in connection with certain other separation issues),

    (e) section 8C of this Act (power in connection with the Protocol on Ireland/Northern Ireland in withdrawal agreement), and

    (f) Parts 1B and 1C of Schedule 2 to this Act (powers involving devolved authorities in connection with certain other separation issues and the Ireland/Northern Ireland Protocol).

7B   General implementation of EEA EFTA and Swiss agreements

(1) Subsection (2) applies to all such rights, powers, liabilities, obligations, restrictions, remedies and procedures as—

    (a) would from time to time be created or arise, or (in the case of remedies or procedures) be provided for, by or under the EEA EFTA separation agreement or the Swiss citizens' rights agreement, and

    (b) would, in accordance with Article 4(1) of the withdrawal agreement, be required to be given legal effect or used in the United Kingdom without further enactment,

if that Article were to apply in relation to the EEA EFTA separation agreement and the Swiss citizens' rights agreement, those agreements were part of EU law and the relevant EEA states and Switzerland were member States.

(2) The rights, powers, liabilities, obligations, restrictions, remedies and procedures concerned are to be—

    (a) recognised and available in domestic law, and

    (b) enforced, allowed and followed accordingly.

(3) Every enactment (other than section 7A but otherwise including an enactment contained in this Act) is to be read and has effect subject to subsection (2).

(4) See also (among other things)—

    (a) Part 3 of the European Union (Withdrawal Agreement) Act 2020 (further provision about citizens' rights),

    (b) section 7C of this Act (interpretation of law relating to the EEA EFTA separation agreement and the Swiss citizens' rights agreement etc.),

    (c) section 8B of this Act (power in connection with certain other separation issues), and

    (d) Part 1B of Schedule 2 to this Act (powers involving devolved authorities in connection with certain other separation issues).

(5) In this section "the relevant EEA states" means Norway, Iceland and Liechtenstein.

(6) In this Act "EEA EFTA separation agreement" and "Swiss citizens' rights agreement" have the same meanings as in the European Union (Withdrawal Agreement) Act 2020 (see section 39(1) of that Act).

7C   Interpretation of relevant separation agreement law

(1) Any question as to the validity, meaning or effect of any relevant separation agreement law is to be decided, so far as they are applicable—

    (a) in accordance with the withdrawal agreement, the EEA EFTA separation agreement and the Swiss citizens' rights agreement, and

    (b) having regard (among other things) to the desirability of ensuring that, where one of those agreements makes provision which corresponds to provision made by another of those agreements, the effect of relevant separation agreement law in relation to the matters dealt with by the corresponding provision in each agreement is consistent.

(2) See (among other things)—

    (a)   Article 4 of the withdrawal agreement (methods and principles relating to the effect, the implementation and the application of the agreement),

    (b)   Articles 158 and 160 of the withdrawal agreement (jurisdiction of the European Court in relation to Part 2 and certain provisions of Part 5 of the agreement),

    (c)   Articles 12 and 13 of the Protocol on Ireland/Northern Ireland in the withdrawal agreement (implementation, application, supervision and enforcement of the Protocol and common provisions),

    (d)   Article 4 of the EEA EFTA separation agreement (methods and principles relating to the effect, the implementation and the application of the agreement), and

    (e)   Article 4 of the Swiss citizens' rights agreement (methods and principles relating to the effect, the implementation and the application of the agreement).

(3) In this Act "relevant separation agreement law" means—

    (a)   any of the following provisions or anything which is domestic law by virtue of any of them—

        (i)   section 7A, 7B, 8B or 8C or Part 1B or 1C of Schedule 2 or this section, or

        (ii) Part 3, or section 20, of the European Union (Withdrawal Agreement) Act 2020 (citizens' rights and financial provision), or

    (b)   anything not falling within paragraph (a) so far as it is domestic law for the purposes of, or otherwise within the scope of—

        (i)   the withdrawal agreement (other than Part 4 of that agreement),

        (ii) the EEA EFTA separation agreement, or

        (iii) the Swiss citizens' rights agreement,

as that body of law is added to or otherwise modified by or under this Act or by other domestic law from time to time.

Main powers in connection with withdrawal

8   Dealing with deficiencies arising from withdrawal

(1) A Minister of the Crown may by regulations make such provision as the Minister considers appropriate to prevent, remedy or mitigate—

    (a)   any failure of retained EU law to operate effectively, or

    (b)   any other deficiency in retained EU law,

arising from the withdrawal of the United Kingdom from the EU.

(2) Deficiencies in retained EU law are where the Minister considers that retained EU law—

    (a)   contains anything which has no practical application in relation to the United Kingdom or any part of it or is otherwise redundant or substantially redundant,

    (b)   confers functions on, or in relation to, EU entities which no longer have functions in that respect under EU law in relation to the United Kingdom or any part of it,

    (c)   makes provision for, or in connection with, reciprocal arrangements between—

        (i)   the United Kingdom or any part of it or a public authority in the United Kingdom, and

        (ii) the EU, an EU entity, a member State or a public authority in a member State,

which no longer exist or are no longer appropriate,

    (d)   makes provision for, or in connection with, other arrangements which—

        (i)   involve the EU, an EU entity, a member State or a public authority in a member State, or

        (ii) are otherwise dependent upon the United Kingdom's membership of the EU or Part 4 of the withdrawal agreement

and which no longer exist or are no longer appropriate,

    (e)   makes provision for, or in connection with, any reciprocal or other arrangements not falling within paragraph (c) or (d) which no longer exist, or are no longer appropriate, as a result of the United Kingdom ceasing to be a party to any of the EU Treaties or as a result of either the end of the implementation period or any other effect of the withdrawal agreement.

(ea) is not clear in its effect as a result of the operation of any provision of sections 2 to 6 or Schedule 1,

(f) does not contain any functions or restrictions which—

    (i) were in an EU directive and in force immediately before IP completion day (including any power to make EU tertiary legislation), and

    (ii) it is appropriate to retain, or

(g) contains EU references which are no longer appropriate.

(3) There is also a deficiency in retained EU law where the Minister considers that there is—

    (a) anything in retained EU law which is of a similar kind to any deficiency which falls within subsection (2), or

    (b) a deficiency in retained EU law of a kind described, or provided for, in regulations made by a Minister of the Crown.

(4) But retained EU law is not deficient merely because it does not contain any modification of EU law which is adopted or notified, comes into force or only applies on or after IP completion day.

(5) Regulations under subsection (1) may make any provision that could be made by an Act of Parliament.

(6) Regulations under subsection (1) may (among other things) provide for functions of EU entities or public authorities in member States (including making an instrument of a legislative character or providing funding) to be—

    (a) exercisable instead by a public authority (whether or not established for the purpose) in the United Kingdom, or

    (b) replaced, abolished or otherwise modified.

(7) But regulations under subsection (1) may not—

    (a) impose or increase taxation or fees,

    (b) make retrospective provision,

    (c) create a relevant criminal offence,

    (d) establish a public authority,

    (e) ...

    (f) amend, repeal or revoke the Human Rights Act 1998 or any subordinate legislation made under it, or

    (g) amend or repeal the Scotland Act 1998, the Government of Wales Act 2006 or the Northern Ireland Act 1998 (unless the regulations are made by virtue of paragraph 21(b) of Schedule 7 to this Act or are amending or repealing any provision of those Acts which modifies another enactment).

(8) No regulations may be made under this section after the end of the period of two years beginning with IP completion day.

(9) The reference in subsection (1) to a failure or other deficiency arising from—

    (a) any aspect of that withdrawal, including (among other things)—

        (i) the end of the implementation period, or

        (ii) any other effect of the withdrawal agreement, or

    (b) that withdrawal, or any such aspect of it, taken together with the operation of any provision, or the interaction between any provisions, made by or under this Act or the European Union (Withdrawal Agreement) Act 2020.

8A Supplementary power in connection with implementation period

(1) A Minister of the Crown may by regulations—

    (a) provide for other modifications for the purposes of section 1B(3)(f)(i) (whether applying in all cases or particular cases or descriptions of case),

    (b) provide for subsection (3) or (4) of section 1B not to apply to any extent in particular cases or descriptions of case,

    (c) make different provision in particular cases or descriptions of case to that made by subsection (3) or (4) of that section,

    (d) modify any enactment contained in this Act in consequence of any repeal made by section 1A(5) or 1B(6), or

    (e) make such provision not falling within paragraph (a), (b), (c) or (d) as the Minister considers appropriate for any purpose of, or otherwise in connection with, Part 4 of the withdrawal agreement.

(2) The power to make regulations under subsection (1) may (among other things) be exercised by modifying any provision made by or under an enactment.

(3) In subsection (2) "enactment" does not include primary legislation passed or made after IP completion day.

(4) No regulations may be made under subsection (1) after the end of the period of two years beginning with IP completion day.

8B   Power in connection with certain other separation issues

(1) A Minister of the Crown may by regulations make such provision as the Minister considers appropriate—

    (a) to implement Part 3 of the withdrawal agreement (separation provisions),

    (b) to supplement the effect of section 7A in relation to that Part, or

    (c) otherwise for the purposes of dealing with matters arising out of, or related to, that Part (including matters arising by virtue of section 7A and that Part).

(2) A Minister of the Crown may by regulations make such provision as the Minister considers appropriate—

    (a) to implement Part 3 of the EEA EFTA separation agreement (separation provisions),

    (b) to supplement the effect of section 7B in relation to that Part, or

    (c) otherwise for the purposes of dealing with matters arising out of, or related to, that Part (including matters arising by virtue of section 7B and that Part).

(3) Regulations under this section may make any provision that could be made by an Act of Parliament.

(4) Regulations under this section may (among other things) restate, for the purposes of making the law clearer or more accessible, anything that forms part of domestic law by virtue of—

    (a) section 7A above and Part 3 of the withdrawal agreement, or

    (b) section 7B above and Part 3 of the EEA EFTA separation agreement.

(5) But regulations under this section may not—

    (a) impose or increase taxation or fees,

    (b) make retrospective provision,

    (c) create a relevant criminal offence,

    (d) establish a public authority,

    (e) amend, repeal or revoke the Human Rights Act 1998 or any subordinate legislation made under it, or

    (f) amend or repeal the Scotland Act 1998, the Government of Wales Act 2006 or the Northern Ireland Act 1998 (unless the regulations are made by virtue of paragraph 21(b) of Schedule 7 to this Act or are amending or repealing any provision of those Acts which modifies another enactment).

(6) In this section references to Part 3 of the withdrawal agreement or of the EEA EFTA separation agreement include references to any provision of EU law which is applied by, or referred to in, that Part (to the extent of the application or reference).

8C   Power in connection with Ireland/Northern Ireland Protocol in withdrawal agreement

(1) A Minister of the Crown may by regulations make such provision as the Minister considers appropriate—

    (a) to implement the Protocol on Ireland/Northern Ireland in the withdrawal agreement,

    (b) to supplement the effect of section 7A in relation to the Protocol, or

    (c) otherwise for the purposes of dealing with matters arising out of, or related to, the Protocol (including matters arising by virtue of section 7A and the Protocol).

(2) Regulations under subsection (1) may make any provision that could be made by an Act of Parliament (including modifying this Act).

(3) Regulations under subsection (1) may (among other things) make provision facilitating the access to the market within Great Britain of qualifying Northern Ireland goods.

(4) Such provision may (among other things) include provision about the recognition within Great Britain of technical regulations, assessments, registrations, certificates, approvals and authorisations issued by—

    (a) the authorities of a member State, or

    (b) bodies established in a member State, in respect of qualifying Northern Ireland goods.

(5) Regulations under subsection (1) may (among other things) restate, for the purposes of making the law clearer or more accessible, anything that forms part of domestic law by virtue of section 7A and the Protocol.

(6) A Minister of the Crown may by regulations define "qualifying Northern Ireland goods" for the purposes of this Act.

(7) In this section any reference to the Protocol on Ireland/Northern Ireland includes a reference to—

    (a) any other provision of the withdrawal agreement so far as applying to the Protocol, and

    (b) any provision of EU law which is applied by, or referred to, in the Protocol (to the extent of the application or reference), but does not include the second sentence of Article 11(1) of the Protocol (which provides that the United Kingdom and the Republic of Ireland may continue to make new arrangements that build on the provisions of the Belfast Agreement in other areas of North-South cooperation on the island of Ireland).

9 ...

Devolution

10 Continuation of North-South co-operation and the prevention of new border arrangements

(1) In exercising any of the powers under this Act, a Minister of the Crown or devolved authority must—

    (a) act in a way that is compatible with the terms of the Northern Ireland Act 1998, and

    (b) have due regard to the joint report from the negotiators of the EU and the United Kingdom Government on progress during phase 1 of negotiations under Article 50 of the Treaty on European Union.

(2) Nothing in section 8 or 23(1) or (6) of this Act authorises regulations which—

    (a) diminish any form of North-South cooperation provided for by the Belfast Agreement (as defined by section 98 of the Northern Ireland Act 1998), or

    (b) create or facilitate border arrangements between Northern Ireland and the Republic of Ireland after exit day which feature physical infrastructure, including border posts, or checks and controls, that did not exist before exit day and are not in accordance with an agreement between the United Kingdom and the EU.

11 Powers involving devolved authorities corresponding to sections 8 to 8C

Schedule 2 (which confers powers to make regulations involving devolved authorities which correspond to the powers conferred by sections 8 to 8C) has effect.

12 Retaining EU restrictions in devolution legislation etc.

(1) In section 29(2)(d) of the Scotland Act 1998 (no competence for the Scottish Parliament to legislate incompatibly with EU law) for "with EU law" substitute "in breach of the restriction in section 30A(1)".

(2) After section 30 of that Act (legislative competence: supplementary) insert—

"30A Legislative competence: restriction relating to retained EU law

(1) An Act of the Scottish Parliament cannot modify, or confer power by subordinate legislation to modify, retained EU law so far as the modification is of a description specified in regulations made by a Minister of the Crown.

(2) But subsection (1) does not apply to any modification so far as it would, immediately before exit day, have been within the legislative competence of the Parliament.

(3) A Minister of the Crown must not lay for approval before each House of the Parliament of the United Kingdom a draft of a statutory instrument containing regulations under this section unless—

    (a) the Scottish Parliament has made a consent decision in relation to the laying of the draft, or

    (b) the 40 day period has ended without the Parliament having made such a decision.

    (4)   For the purposes of subsection (3) a consent decision is—
        (a) a decision to agree a motion consenting to the laying of the draft,
        (b) a decision not to agree a motion consenting to the laying of the draft, or
        (c) a decision to agree a motion refusing to consent to the laying of the draft;
        and a consent decision is made when the Parliament first makes a decision falling within any of paragraphs (a) to (c) (whether or not it subsequently makes another such decision).

    (5)   A Minister of the Crown who is proposing to lay a draft as mentioned in subsection (3) must—
        (a) provide a copy of the draft to the Scottish Ministers, and
        (b) inform the Presiding Officer that a copy has been so provided.

    (6)   See also paragraph 6 of Schedule 7 (duty to make explanatory statement about regulations under this section including a duty to explain any decision to lay a draft without the consent of the Parliament).

    (7)   No regulations may be made under this section after the end of the period of two years beginning with exit day.

    (8)   Subsection (7) does not affect the continuation in force of regulations made under this section at or before the end of the period mentioned in that subsection.

    (9)   Any regulations under this section which are in force at the end of the period of five years beginning with the time at which they came into force are revoked in their application to any Act of the Scottish Parliament which receives Royal Assent after the end of that period.

    (10) Subsections (3) to (8) do not apply in relation to regulations which only relate to a revocation of a specification.

    (11) In this section—
        "the 40 day period" means the period of 40 days beginning with the day on which a copy of the draft instrument is provided to the Scottish Ministers,
        and, in calculating that period, no account is to be taken of any time during which the Parliament is dissolved or during which it is in recess for more than four days."

  (3)   In section 108A(2)(e) of the Government of Wales Act 2006 (no competence for the National Assembly for Wales to legislate incompatibly with EU law) for "with EU law" substitute "in breach of the restriction in section 109A(1)".

  (4)   After section 109 of that Act (legislative competence: supplementary) insert—

"109A Legislative competence: restriction relating to retained EU law

    (1)   An Act of the Assembly cannot modify, or confer power by subordinate legislation to modify, retained EU law so far as the modification is of a description specified in regulations made by a Minister of the Crown.

    (2)   But subsection (1) does not apply to any modification so far as it would, immediately before exit day, have been within the Assembly's legislative competence.

    (3)   No regulations are to be made under this section unless a draft of the statutory instrument containing them has been laid before, and approved by a resolution of, each House of Parliament.

    (4)   A Minister of the Crown must not lay a draft as mentioned in subsection (3) unless—
        (a) the Assembly has made a consent decision in relation to the laying of the draft, or
        (b) the 40 day period has ended without the Assembly having made such a decision.

    (5)   For the purposes of subsection (4) a consent decision is—
        (a) a decision to agree a motion consenting to the laying of the draft,
        (b) a decision not to agree a motion consenting to the laying of the draft, or
        (c) a decision to agree a motion refusing to consent to the laying of the draft;
        and a consent decision is made when the Assembly first makes a decision falling within any of paragraphs (a) to (c) (whether or not it subsequently makes another such decision).

(6)　A Minister of the Crown who is proposing to lay a draft as mentioned in subsection (3) must—
(a)　provide a copy of the draft to the Welsh Ministers, and
(b)　inform the Presiding Officer that a copy has been so provided.

(7)　See also section 157ZA (duty to make explanatory statement about regulations under this section including a duty to explain any decision to lay a draft without the consent of the Assembly).

(8)　No regulations may be made under this section after the end of the period of two years beginning with exit day.

(9)　Subsection (8) does not affect the continuation in force of regulations made under this section at or before the end of the period mentioned in that subsection.

(10)　Any regulations under this section which are in force at the end of the period of five years beginning with the time at which they came into force are revoked in their application to any Act of the Assembly which receives Royal Assent after the end of that period.

(11)　Subsections (4) to (9) do not apply in relation to regulations which only relate to a revocation of a specification.

(12)　In this section—
"the 40 day period" means the period of 40 days beginning with the day on which a copy of the draft instrument is provided to the Welsh Ministers,
and, in calculating that period, no account is to be taken of any time during which the Assembly is dissolved or during which it is in recess for more than four days."

(5)　In section 6(2)(d) of the Northern Ireland Act 1998 (no competence for the Northern Ireland Assembly to legislate incompatibly with EU law) for "incompatible with EU law" substitute "in breach of the restriction in section 6A(1)".

(6)　After section 6 of that Act (legislative competence) insert—

"6A   Restriction relating to retained EU law

(1)　An Act of the Assembly cannot modify, or confer power by subordinate legislation to modify, retained EU law so far as the modification is of a description specified in regulations made by a Minister of the Crown.

(2)　But subsection (1) does not apply to any modification so far as it would, immediately before exit day, have been within the legislative competence of the Assembly.

(3)　A Minister of the Crown must not lay for approval before each House of Parliament a draft of a statutory instrument containing regulations under this section unless—
(a)　the Assembly has made a consent decision in relation to the laying of the draft, or
(b)　the 40 day period has ended without the Assembly having made such a decision.

(4)　For the purposes of subsection (3) a consent decision is—
(a)　a decision to agree a motion consenting to the laying of the draft,
(b)　a decision not to agree a motion consenting to the laying of the draft, or
(c)　a decision to agree a motion refusing to consent to the laying of the draft;
and a consent decision is made when the Assembly first makes a decision falling within any of paragraphs (a) to (c) (whether or not it subsequently makes another such decision).

(5)　A Minister of the Crown who is proposing to lay a draft as mentioned in subsection (3) must—
(a)　provide a copy of the draft to the relevant Northern Ireland department, and
(b)　inform the Presiding Officer that a copy has been so provided.

(6)　See also section 96A (duty to make explanatory statement about regulations under this section including a duty to explain any decision to lay a draft without the consent of the Assembly).

(7)　No regulations may be made under this section after the end of the period of two years beginning with exit day.

(8)   Subsection (7) does not affect the continuation in force of regulations made under this section at or before the end of the period mentioned in that subsection.

(9)   Any regulations under this section which are in force at the end of the period of five years beginning with the time at which they came into force are revoked in their application to any Act of the Assembly which receives Royal Assent after the end of that period.

(10) Subsections (3) to (8) do not apply in relation to regulations which only relate to a revocation of a specification.

(11) Regulations under this section may include such supplementary, incidental, consequential, transitional, transitory or saving provision as the Minister of the Crown making them considers appropriate.

(12) In this section—

"the relevant Northern Ireland department" means such Northern Ireland department as the Minister of the Crown concerned considers appropriate;

"the 40 day period" means the period of 40 days beginning with the day on which a copy of the draft instrument is provided to the relevant Northern Ireland department,

and, in calculating that period, no account is to be taken of any time during which the Assembly is dissolved or during which it is in recess for more than four days."

(7) Part 1 of Schedule 3 (which makes corresponding provision in relation to executive competence to that made by subsections (1) to (6) in relation to legislative competence) has effect.

(8) Part 2 of Schedule 3 (which imposes reporting obligations on a Minister of the Crown in recognition of the fact that the powers to make regulations conferred by subsections (1) to (6) and Part 1 of Schedule 3, and any restrictions arising by virtue of them, are intended to be temporary) has effect.

(9) A Minister of the Crown may by regulations—

(a)   repeal any of the following provisions—

(i)   section 30A or 57(4) to (15) of the Scotland Act 1998,

(ii) section 80(8) to (8L) or 109A of the Government of Wales Act 2006, or

(iii) section 6A or 24(3) to (15) of the Northern Ireland Act 1998, or

(b)   modify any enactment in consequence of any such repeal.

(10) Until all of the provisions mentioned in subsection (9)(a) have been repealed, a Minister of the Crown must, after the end of each review period, consider whether it is appropriate—

(a)   to repeal each of those provisions so far as it has not been repealed, or

(b)   to revoke any regulations made under any of those provisions so far as they have not been revoked.

(11) In considering whether to exercise the power to make regulations under subsection (9), a Minister of the Crown must have regard (among other things) to—

(a)   the fact that the powers to make regulations conferred by the provisions mentioned in subsection (9)(a), and any restrictions arising by virtue of them, are intended to be temporary and, where appropriate, replaced with other arrangements, and

(b)   any progress which has been made in implementing those other arrangements.

(12) Part 3 of Schedule 3 (which contains amendments of devolution legislation not dealt with elsewhere) has effect.

(13) In this section—

"arrangement" means any enactment or other arrangement (whether or not legally enforceable);

"review period" means—

(a)   the period of three months beginning with the day on which subsection (10) comes into force, and

(b)   after that, each successive period of three months.

Parliamentary approval of outcome of EU negotiations

13   ...

13A   **Review of EU legislation during implementation period**

(1)   Subsection (2) applies where the European Scrutiny Select Committee of the House of Commons ("the ESC") publishes a report in respect of any EU legislation made, or which may be made, during the implementation period and the report—

    (a)   states that, in the opinion of the ESC, the EU legislation raises a matter of vital national interest to the United Kingdom,

    (b)   confirms that the ESC has taken such evidence as it considers appropriate as to the effect of the EU legislation and has consulted any Departmental Select Committee of the House of Commons which the ESC considers also has an interest in the EU legislation, and

    (c)   sets out the wording of a motion to be moved in the House of Commons in accordance with subsection (2).

(2)   A Minister of the Crown must, within the period of 14 Commons sitting days beginning with the day on which the report is published, make arrangements for the motion mentioned in subsection (1)(c) to be debated and voted on by the House of Commons.

(3)   Subsection (4) applies where the EU Select Committee of the House of Lords ("the EUC") publishes a report in respect of any EU legislation made, or which may be made, during the implementation period and the report—

    (a)   states that, in the opinion of the EUC, the EU legislation raises a matter of vital national interest to the United Kingdom,

    (b)   confirms that the EUC has taken such evidence as it considers appropriate as to the effect of the EU legislation, and

    (c)   sets out the wording of a motion to be moved in the House of Lords in accordance with subsection (4).

(4)   A Minister of the Crown must, within the period of 14 Lords sitting days beginning with the day on which the report is published, make arrangements for the motion mentioned in subsection (3)(c) to be debated and voted on by the House of Lords.

(5)   In this section—

"EU legislation" means—

    (a)   any amendment to the Treaty on European Union, the Treaty on the Functioning of the European Union, the Euratom Treaty or the EEA agreement,

    (b)   any EU directive, or

    (c)   any EU regulation or EU decision which is not EU tertiary legislation;

"the European Scrutiny Select Committee of the House of Commons" means the Select Committee of the House of Commons known as the European Scrutiny Select Committee or any successor of that committee;

"the EU Select Committee of the House of Lords" means the Select Committee of the House of Lords known as the EU Select Committee or any successor of that committee.

Financial and other matters

14   **Financial provision**

(1)   Schedule 4 (which contains powers in connection with fees and charges) has effect.

(2)   A Minister of the Crown, government department or devolved authority may incur expenditure, for the purpose of, or in connection with, preparing for anything about which provision may be made under a power to make subordinate legislation conferred or modified by or under this Act, before any such provision is made.

(3)   There is to be paid out of money provided by Parliament—

    (a)   any expenditure incurred by a Minister of the Crown, government department or other public authority by virtue of this Act, and

    (b)   any increase attributable to this Act in the sums payable by virtue of any other Act out of money so provided.

(4)   Subsection (3) is subject to any other provision made by or under this Act or any other enactment.

15   Publication and rules of evidence

(1)   Part 1 of Schedule 5 (which makes provision for the publication by the Queen's Printer of copies of retained direct EU legislation and related information) has effect.

(2)   Part 2 of Schedule 5 (which makes provision about rules of evidence) has effect.

15A   Prohibition on extending implementation period

A Minister of the Crown may not agree in the Joint Committee to an extension of the implementation period.

15B   Ministerial co-chairs of the Joint Committee

The functions of the United Kingdom's co-chair of the Joint Committee, under Annex VIII of the withdrawal agreement (rules of procedure of the Joint Committee and specialised committees), are to be exercised personally by a Minister of the Crown (and, accordingly, only a Minister of the Crown may be designated as a replacement under Rule 1(3)).

15C   No use of written procedure in the Joint Committee

(1)   The United Kingdom's co-chair of the Joint Committee may not consent to the Joint Committee using the written procedure provided for in Rule 9(1) of Annex VIII of the withdrawal agreement.

(2)   In subsection (1) the reference to the United Kingdom's co-chair of the Joint Committee includes a reference to any designee of the co-chair designated under Rule 1(3) of Annex VIII of the withdrawal agreement.

16   ...

17   Family unity for those seeking asylum or other protection in Europe

(1)   A Minister of the Crown must, within the period of two months beginning with the day on which the European Union (Withdrawal Agreement) Act 2020 is passed, lay before Parliament a statement of policy in relation to any future arrangements between the United Kingdom and the EU about—

(a)   unaccompanied children, who make an application for international protection to a member State, coming to the United Kingdom where it is in their best interests to join a relative who—

(i)   is a lawful resident of the United Kingdom, or

(ii)   has made a protection claim which has not been decided, and

(b)   unaccompanied children in the United Kingdom, who make a protection claim, going to a member State to join a relative there in equivalent circumstances.

(2)   For the purposes of subsection (1)(a)(i) a person is not a lawful resident of the United Kingdom if the person requires leave to enter or remain in the United Kingdom but does not have it.

(3)   For the purposes of subsection (1)(a)(ii), a protection claim is decided—

(a)   when the Secretary of State notifies the claimant of the Secretary of State's decision on the claim, unless the claimant appeals against the decision, or

(b)   if the claimant appeals against the Secretary of State's decision on the claim, when the appeal is disposed of.

(4)   In this section—

"application for international protection" has the meaning given by Article 2(h) of Directive 2011/95/EU of the European Parliament and of the Council on standards for the qualification of third-country nationals or stateless persons as beneficiaries of international protection, for a uniform status for refugees or for persons eligible for subsidiary protection, and for the content of the protection granted;

"protection claim" has the same meaning as in Part 5 of the Nationality, Immigration and Asylum Act 2002 (see section 82(2) of that Act);

"relative", in relation to an unaccompanied child, means—

(a)   a spouse or civil partner of the child or any person with whom the child has a durable relationship that is similar to marriage or civil partnership, or

(b)   a parent, grandparent, uncle, aunt, brother or sister of the child;

"unaccompanied child" means a person under the age of 18 ("the child") who is not in the care of a person who—

(a)   is aged 18 or over, and

(b) by law or custom of the country or territory in which the child is present, has responsibility for caring for the child.

18 ...

19 ...

General and final provision

20 Interpretation

(1) In this Act—

"Charter of Fundamental Rights" means the Charter of Fundamental Rights of the European Union of 7 December 2000, as adapted at Strasbourg on 12 December 2007;

"Commons sitting day" means a day on which the House of Commons is sitting (and a day is only a day on which the House of Commons is sitting if the House begins to sit on that day);

"devolved authority" means—

(a) the Scottish Ministers,

(b) the Welsh Ministers, or

(c) a Northern Ireland department;

"domestic law" means—

(a) in sections 3, 7A and 7B, the law of England and Wales, Scotland and Northern Ireland, and

(b) in any other case, the law of England and Wales, Scotland or Northern Ireland;

"the EEA" means the European Economic Area;

"enactment" means an enactment whenever passed or made and includes—

(a) an enactment contained in any Order in Council, order, rules, regulations, scheme, warrant, byelaw or other instrument made under an Act,

(b) an enactment contained in any Order in Council made in exercise of Her Majesty's Prerogative,

(c) an enactment contained in, or in an instrument made under, an Act of the Scottish Parliament,

(d) an enactment contained in, or in an instrument made under, a Measure or Act of the National Assembly for Wales,

(e) an enactment contained in, or in an instrument made under, Northern Ireland legislation,

(f) an enactment contained in any instrument made by a member of the Scottish Government, the Welsh Ministers, the First Minister for Wales, the Counsel General to the Welsh Government, a Northern Ireland Minister, the First Minister in Northern Ireland, the deputy First Minister in Northern Ireland or a Northern Ireland department in exercise of prerogative or other executive functions of Her Majesty which are exercisable by such a person on behalf of Her Majesty,

(g) an enactment contained in, or in an instrument made under, a Measure of the Church Assembly or of the General Synod of the Church of England, and

(h) except in sections 1B and 7 or where there is otherwise a contrary intention, any retained direct EU legislation;

"EU decision" means—

(a) a decision within the meaning of Article 288 of the Treaty on the Functioning of the European Union, or

(b) a decision under former Article 34(2)(c) of the Treaty on European Union;

"EU directive" means a directive within the meaning of Article 288 of the Treaty on the Functioning of the European Union;

"EU entity" means an EU institution or any office, body or agency of the EU;

"EU reference" means—

(a) any reference to the EU, an EU entity or a member State,

(b) any reference to an EU directive or any other EU law, or

(c) any other reference which relates to the EU;

"EU regulation" means a regulation within the meaning of Article 288 of the Treaty on the Functioning of the European Union;

"EU tertiary legislation" means—

(a)   any provision made under—
     (i)   an EU regulation,
     (ii)   a decision within the meaning of Article 288 of the Treaty on the Functioning of the European Union, or
     (iii) an EU directive,
     by virtue of Article 290 or 291(2) of the Treaty on the Functioning of the European Union or former Article 202 of the Treaty establishing the European Community, or
(b)   any measure adopted in accordance with former Article 34(2)(c) of the Treaty on European Union to implement decisions under former Article 34(2)(c),
but does not include any such provision or measure which is an EU directive;
"exempt EU instrument" means anything which is an exempt EU instrument by virtue of Schedule 6;
"exit day" means 31 January 2020 at 11.00 p.m. (and see subsections (2) to (5));
"Joint Committee" means the Joint Committee established by Article 164(1) of the withdrawal agreement;
"Lords sitting day" means a day on which the House of Lords is sitting (and a day is only a day on which the House of Lords is sitting if the House begins to sit on that day);
"member State" (except in the definitions of "direct EU legislation" and "EU reference") does not include the United Kingdom;
"Minister of the Crown" has the same meaning as in the Ministers of the Crown Act 1975 and also includes the Commissioners for Her Majesty's Revenue and Customs;
"modify" includes amend, repeal or revoke (and related expressions are to be read accordingly);
"Northern Ireland devolved authority" means the First Minister and deputy First Minister in Northern Ireland acting jointly, a Northern Ireland Minister or a Northern Ireland department;
"primary legislation" means—
(a)   an Act of Parliament,
(b)   an Act of the Scottish Parliament,
(c)   a Measure or Act of the National Assembly for Wales, or
(d)   Northern Ireland legislation;
"public authority" means a public authority within the meaning of section 6 of the Human Rights Act 1998;
"ratify", whether in relation to the withdrawal agreement or otherwise, has the same meaning as it does for the purposes of Part 2 of the Constitutional Reform and Governance Act 2010 in relation to a treaty (see section 25 of that Act);
"relevant criminal offence" means an offence for which an individual who has reached the age of 18 (or, in relation to Scotland or Northern Ireland, 21) is capable of being sentenced to imprisonment for a term of more than 2 years (ignoring any enactment prohibiting or restricting the imprisonment of individuals who have no previous convictions);
"retained direct EU legislation" means any direct EU legislation which forms part of domestic law by virtue of section 3 (as modified by or under this Act or by other domestic law from time to time, and including any instruments made under it on or after IP completion day);
"retrospective provision", in relation to provision made by regulations, means provision taking effect from a date earlier than the date on which the regulations are made;
"subordinate legislation" means—
(a)   any Order in Council, order, rules, regulations, scheme, warrant, byelaw or other instrument made under any Act, or
(b)   any instrument made under an Act of the Scottish Parliament, Northern Ireland legislation or a Measure or Act of the National Assembly for Wales,
and (except in section 7 or Schedule 2 or where there is a contrary intention) includes any Order in Council, order, rules, regulations, scheme, warrant, byelaw or other instrument made on or after exit day under any retained direct EU legislation;
"tribunal" means any tribunal in which legal proceedings may be brought;
"Wales" and "Welsh zone" have the same meaning as in the Government of Wales Act 2006 (see section 158 of that Act);

...

(2) In this Act references to before, after or on exit day, or to beginning with exit day, are to be read as references to before, after or at 11.00 p.m. on 31 January 2020 or (as the case may be) to beginning with 11.00 p.m. on that day.

(3) Subsection (4) applies if the day or time on or at which the Treaties are to cease to apply to the United Kingdom in accordance with Article 50(3) of the Treaty on European Union is different from that specified in the definition of "exit day" in subsection (1).

(4) A Minister of the Crown must by regulations—

    (a) amend the definition of "exit day" in subsection (1) to ensure that the day and time specified in the definition are the day and time that the Treaties are to cease to apply to the United Kingdom, and

    (b) amend subsection (2) in consequence of any such amendment.

(5) In subsections (3) and (4) "the Treaties" means the Treaty on European Union and the Treaty on the Functioning of the European Union.

(5A) In this Act references to anything which continues to be domestic law by virtue of section 1B(2) include—

    (a) references to anything to which section 1B(2) applies which continues to be domestic law on or after exit day (whether or not it would have done so irrespective of that provision), and

    (b) references to anything which continues to be domestic law on or after exit day by virtue of section 1B(2) (as that body of law is added to or otherwise modified by or under this Act or by other domestic law from time to time).

(6) In this Act references to anything which continues to be domestic law by virtue of section 2 include references to anything to which subsection (1) of that section applies which continues to be domestic law on or after IP completion day (whether or not it would have done so irrespective of that section).

(7) In this Act references to anything which is retained EU law by virtue of section 4 include references to any modifications, made by or under this Act or by other domestic law from time to time, of the rights, powers, liabilities, obligations, restrictions, remedies or procedures concerned.

(8) References in this Act (however expressed) to a public authority in the United Kingdom include references to a public authority in any part of the United Kingdom.

(9) References in this Act to former Article 34(2)(c) of the Treaty on European Union are references to that Article as it had effect at any time before the coming into force of the Treaty of Lisbon.

(10) Any other reference in this Act to—

    (a) an Article of the Treaty on European Union or the Treaty on the Functioning of the European Union, or

    (b) Article 10 of Title VII of Protocol 36 to those treaties,

includes a reference to that Article as applied by Article 106a of the Euratom Treaty.

21　Index of defined expressions

(1) In this Act, the expressions listed in the left-hand column have the meaning given by, or are to be interpreted in accordance with, the provisions listed in the right-hand column.

Expression	Provision
Anything which continues to be domestic law by virtue of section 1B(2)	Section 20(5A)
Anything which is retained EU law by virtue of section 4	Section 20(7)
Article (in relation to the Treaty on European Union or the Treaty on the Functioning of the European Union)	Section 20(10)
Charter of Fundamental Rights	Section 20(1)
Commons sitting day	Section 20(1)
Direct EU legislation	Section 3(2)

Expression	Provision
Domestic law	Section 20(1)
The EEA	Section 20(1)
EEA agreement	Schedule 1 to the Interpretation Act 1978
EEA EFTA separation agreement	Section 7B(6)
Enactment	Section 20(1)
The EU	Schedule 1 to the Interpretation Act 1978
EU decision	Section 20(1)
EU-derived domestic legislation	Section 1B(7)
EU directive	Section 20(1)
EU entity	Section 20(1)
EU institution	Schedule 1 to the Interpretation Act 1978
EU instrument	Schedule 1 to the Interpretation Act 1978
Euratom Treaty	Schedule 1 to the Interpretation Act 1978
EU reference	Section 20(1)
EU regulation	Section 20(1)
European Communities Act 1972	Section 1A(7)(a)
European Court	Schedule 1 to the Interpretation Act 1978
EU tertiary legislation	Section 20(1)
EU Treaties	Schedule 1 to the Interpretation Act 1978
Exempt EU instrument	Section 20(1)
Exit day (and related expressions)	Section 20(1) to (5)
Former Article 34(2)(c) of Treaty on European Union	Section 20(9)
Implementation period	Section 1A(6)
IP completion day (and related expressions)	Section 1A(6)
Joint Committee	Section 20(1)
Lords sitting day	Section 20(1)
Member State	Section 20(1) and Schedule 1 to the Interpretation Act 1978
Minister of the Crown	Section 20(1)
Modify (and related expressions)	Section 20(1)
Northern Ireland devolved authority	Section 20(1)
Operative (in relation to direct EU legislation)	Section 3(3)
Part (of withdrawal agreement or EEA EFTA separation agreement)	Section 1A(7)(b)

Expression	Provision
Primary legislation	Section 20(1)
Public authority	Section 20(1)
Public authority in the United Kingdom (however expressed)	Section 20(8)
Qualifying Northern Ireland goods	Section 8C(6)
Ratify	Section 20(1)
Relevant criminal offence	Section 20(1) (and paragraph 44 of Schedule 8)
Relevant separation agreement law	Section 7C(3)
Retained case law	Section 6(7)
Retained direct EU legislation	Section 20(1)
Retained direct minor EU legislation	Section 7(6)
Retained direct principal EU legislation	Section 7(6)
Retained domestic case law	Section 6(7)
Retained EU case law	Section 6(7)
Retained EU law	Section 6(7)
Retained general principles of EU law	Section 6(7)
Retrospective provision	Section 20(1)
Subordinate legislation	Section 20(1)
Swiss citizens' rights agreement	Section 7B(6)
Tribunal	Section 20(1)
Wales	Section 20(1)
Welsh zone	Section 20(1)
Withdrawal agreement	Section 1A(6)

(2)   See paragraph 22 of Schedule 8 for amendments made by this Act to Schedule 1 to the Interpretation Act 1978.

22   Regulations

Schedule 7 (which makes provision about the scrutiny by Parliament and the devolved legislatures of regulations under this Act and contains other general provision about such regulations) has effect.

23   Consequential and transitional provision

(1)   A Minister of the Crown may by regulations make such provision as the Minister considers appropriate in consequence of this Act.

(2)   The power to make regulations under subsection (1) may (among other things) be exercised by modifying any provision made by or under an enactment.

(3)   In subsection (2) "enactment" does not include primary legislation passed or made after IP completion day.

(4)   No regulations may be made under subsection (1) after the end of the period of 10 years beginning with IP completion day.

(5)   Parts 1 and 2 of Schedule 8 (which contain consequential provision) have effect.

(6)   A Minister of the Crown may by regulations make such transitional, transitory or saving provision as the Minister considers appropriate in connection with the coming

into force of any provision of this Act (including its operation in connection with IP completion day).

(7)   Parts 3 and 4 of Schedule 8 (which contain transitional, transitory and saving provision) have effect.

(8)   The enactments mentioned in Schedule 9 (which contains repeals not made elsewhere in this Act) are repealed to the extent specified.

24   Extent

(1)   Subject to subsections (2) and (3), this Act extends to England and Wales, Scotland and Northern Ireland.

(2)   Any provision of this Act which amends or repeals an enactment has the same extent as the enactment amended or repealed.

(3)   Regulations under section 8(1) or 23 may make provision which extends to Gibraltar—
   (a)   modifying any enactment which—
      (i)   extends to Gibraltar and relates to European Parliamentary elections, or
      (ii)   extends to Gibraltar for any purpose which is connected with Gibraltar forming part of an electoral region, under the European Parliamentary Elections Act 2002, for the purposes of such elections, or
   (b)   which is supplementary, incidental, consequential, transitional, transitory or saving provision in connection with a modification within paragraph (a).

25   Commencement and short title

(1)   The following provisions—
   (a)   sections 8 to 11 (including Schedule 2),
   (b)   paragraphs 4, 5, 21(2)(b), 48(b), 51(2)(c) and (d) and (4) of Schedule 3 (and section 12(8) and (12) so far as relating to those paragraphs),
   (c)   sections 13 and 14 (including Schedule 4),
   (d)   sections 16 to 18,
   (e)   sections 20 to 22 (including Schedules 6 and 7),
   (f)   section 23(1) to (4) and (6),
   (g)   paragraph 41(10), 43 and 44 of Schedule 8 (and section 23(7) so far as relating to those paragraphs),
   (h)   section 24, and
   (i)   this section,
come into force on the day on which this Act is passed.

(2)   In section 12—
   (a)   subsection (2) comes into force on the day on which this Act is passed for the purposes of making regulations under section 30A of the Scotland Act 1998,
   (b)   subsection (4) comes into force on that day for the purposes of making regulations under section 109A of the Government of Wales Act 2006, and
   (c)   subsection (6) comes into force on that day for the purposes of making regulations under section 6A of the Northern Ireland Act 1998.

(3)   In Schedule 3—
   (a)   paragraph 1(b) comes into force on the day on which this Act is passed for the purposes of making regulations under section 57(4) of the Scotland Act 1998,
   (b)   paragraph 2 comes into force on that day for the purposes of making regulations under section 80(8) of the Government of Wales Act 2006,
   (c)   paragraph 3(b) comes into force on that day for the purposes of making regulations under section 24(3) of the Northern Ireland Act 1998,
   (d)   paragraph 24(2) comes into force on that day for the purposes of making regulations under section 30A of the Scotland Act 1998,
   (e)   paragraph 24(3) comes into force on that day for the purposes of making regulations under section 57(4) of the Scotland Act 1998,
   (f)   paragraph 25 comes into force on that day for the purposes of making regulations under section 30A or 57(4) of the Scotland Act 1998,
   (g)   paragraph 43 comes into force on that day for the purposes of making regulations under section 80(8) or 109A of the Government of Wales Act 2006, and
   (h)   paragraphs 57 and 58 come into force on that day for the purposes of making regulations under section 6A or 24(3) of the Northern Ireland Act 1998;

and section 12(7) and (12), so far as relating to each of those paragraphs, comes into force on that day for the purposes of making the regulations mentioned above in relation to that paragraph.

(4) The provisions of this Act, so far as they are not brought into force by subsections (1) to (3), come into force on such day as a Minister of the Crown may by regulations appoint; and different days may be appointed for different purposes.

(5) This Act may be cited as the European Union (Withdrawal) Act 2018.

SCHEDULES

SCHEDULE 1   Section 5(6)
FURTHER PROVISION ABOUT EXCEPTIONS TO SAVINGS AND INCORPORATION

Challenges to validity of retained EU law

1   (1) There is no right in domestic law on or after IP completion day to challenge any retained EU law on the basis that, immediately before IP completion day, an EU instrument was invalid.

(2) Sub-paragraph (1) does not apply so far as—

(a) the European Court has decided before IP completion day that the instrument is invalid, or

(b) the challenge is of a kind described, or provided for, in regulations made by a Minister of the Crown.

(3) Regulations under sub-paragraph (2)(b) may (among other things) provide for a challenge which would otherwise have been against an EU institution to be against a public authority in the United Kingdom.

General principles of EU law

2   No general principle of EU law is part of domestic law on or after IP completion day if it was not recognised as a general principle of EU law by the European Court in a case decided before IP completion day (whether or not as an essential part of the decision in the case).

3   (1) There is no right of action in domestic law on or after IP completion day based on a failure to comply with any of the general principles of EU law.

(2) No court or tribunal or other public authority may, on or after IP completion day —

(a) disapply or quash any enactment or other rule of law, or

(b) quash any conduct or otherwise decide that it is unlawful,

because it is incompatible with any of the general principles of EU law.

Rule in Francovich

4   There is no right in domestic law on or after IP completion day to damages in accordance with the rule in *Francovich*.

Interpretation

5   (1) References in section 5 and this Schedule to the principle of the supremacy of EU law, the Charter of Fundamental Rights, any general principle of EU law or the rule in *Francovich* are to be read as references to that principle, Charter or rule so far as it would otherwise continue to be, or form part of, domestic law on or after IP completion day in accordance with this Act.

(2) Accordingly (among other things) the references to the principle of the supremacy of EU law in section 5(2) and (3) do not include anything which would bring into domestic law any modification of EU law which is adopted or notified, comes into force or only applies on or after IP completion day.

...

EUROPEAN UNION (WITHDRAWAL AGREEMENT) ACT 2020

(2020, c. 1)

An Act to implement, and make other provision in connection with, the agreement between the United Kingdom and the EU under Article 50(2) of the Treaty on European Union which sets out the arrangements for the United Kingdom's withdrawal from the EU.

[23rd January 2020]

PART 3

CITIZENS' RIGHTS

Rights in relation to entry and residence

7   Rights related to residence: application deadline and temporary protection

(1)   A Minister of the Crown may by regulations make such provision as the Minister considers appropriate for any of the following purposes—

    (a)   specifying the deadline that applies for the purposes of—

        (i)   the first sub-paragraph of Article 18(1)(b) of the withdrawal agreement (deadline for the submission of applications for the new residence status described in Article 18(1));

        (ii)   the first sub-paragraph of Article 17(1)(b) of the EEA EFTA separation agreement (deadline for the submission of applications for the new residence status described in Article 17(1));

        (iii)   the first sentence of Article 16(1)(b) of the Swiss citizens' rights agreement (deadline for the submission of applications for the new residence status described in Article 16(1));

    (b)   implementing Article 18(2) of the withdrawal agreement (protection for Union citizens etc. in the period prior to the deadline for the submission of applications for the new residence status described in Article 18(1));

    (c)   implementing Article 17(2) of the EEA EFTA separation agreement (protection for EEA EFTA nationals etc. in the period prior to the deadline for the submission of applications for the new residence status described in Article 17(1));

    (d)   implementing Article 16(2) of the Swiss citizens' rights agreement (protection for Swiss nationals etc. in the period prior to the deadline for the submission of applications for the new residence status described in Article 16(1));

    (e)   implementing Article 18(3) of the withdrawal agreement (protection for Union citizens etc. pending a final decision on an application for the new residence status described in Article 18(1));

    (f)   implementing Article 17(3) of the EEA EFTA separation agreement (protection for EEA EFTA nationals etc. pending a final decision on an application for the new residence status described in Article 17(1));

    (g)   implementing Article 16(3) of the Swiss citizens' rights agreement (protection for Swiss nationals etc. pending a final decision on an application for the new residence status described in Article 16(1)).

(2)   If the Minister considers it appropriate, regulations under subsection (1) relating to the implementation of a provision mentioned in subsection (1)(b), (c) or (d) may be made so as to apply both to—

    (a)   persons to whom the provision in question applies, and

    (b)   persons to whom that provision does not apply but who may be granted leave to enter or remain in the United Kingdom by virtue of residence scheme immigration rules (see section 17) and who do not have such leave.

(3) If the Minister considers it appropriate, regulations under subsection (1) relating to the implementation of a provision mentioned in subsection (1)(e), (f) or (g) may be made so as to apply both to—

    (a) persons to whom the provision in question applies, and

    (b) persons to whom that provision does not apply but who make an application for leave to enter or remain in the United Kingdom by virtue of residence scheme immigration rules.

(4) The power to make regulations under subsection (1) may (among other things) be exercised by modifying any provision made by or under an enactment.

8 Frontier workers

(1) A Minister of the Crown may by regulations make such provision as the Minister considers appropriate for the purpose of implementing any of the following—

    (a) Articles 24(3) and 25(3) of the withdrawal agreement (rights of employed and self-employed frontier workers) other than as regards rights enjoyed as workers (see section 14(1));

    (b) Articles 23(3) and 24(3) of the EEA EFTA separation agreement (rights of employed and self-employed frontier workers) other than as regards rights enjoyed as workers (see section 14(2));

    (c) Article 20(2) of the Swiss citizens' rights agreement (rights of frontier workers to enter and exit).

(2) A Minister of the Crown may by regulations make such provision as the Minister considers appropriate for the purpose of implementing any of the following—

    (a) Article 26 of the withdrawal agreement (issue of documents);

    (b) Article 25 of the EEA EFTA separation agreement (issue of documents);

    (c) Article 21(1)(a) and (2) of the Swiss citizens' rights agreement (issue of documents).

(3) The power to make regulations under subsection (1) or (2) may (among other things) be exercised by modifying any provision made by or under the Immigration Acts.

9 Restrictions of rights of entry and residence

(1) A Minister of the Crown may by regulations make such provision as the Minister considers appropriate for the purpose of implementing any of the following—

    (a) Article 20(1), (3) and (4) of the withdrawal agreement (restrictions of the rights of entry and residence);

    (b) Article 19(1), (3) and (4) of the EEA EFTA separation agreement (restrictions of the rights of entry and residence);

    (c) Articles 17(1) and (3) and 20(3) of the Swiss citizens' rights agreement (restrictions of the rights of entry and residence).

(2) If the Minister considers it appropriate, regulations under subsection (1) relating to the implementation of a provision mentioned in subsection (1)(a), (b) or (c) may be made so as to apply both to—

    (a) persons to whom the provision in question applies, and

    (b) persons to whom that provision does not apply but who—

        (i) have entry clearance granted by virtue of relevant entry clearance immigration rules (see section 17),

        (ii) have leave to enter or remain in the United Kingdom granted by virtue of residence scheme immigration rules (see section 17), or

        (iii) otherwise have leave to enter granted after arriving with entry clearance granted by virtue of relevant entry clearance immigration rules.

(3) In subsection (2)(b), references to a person who has entry clearance or leave to enter or remain include references to a person who would have had entry clearance or leave to enter or remain but for—

    (a) the making of a deportation order under section 5(1) of the Immigration Act 1971, or

    (b) the making of any other decision made in connection with restricting the right of the person to enter the United Kingdom.

(4)　The power to make regulations under subsection (1) may (among other things) be exercised by modifying any provision made—
    (a)　by or under the Immigration Acts, or
    (b)　under other primary legislation.

10　Retention of existing grounds for deportation

(1)　Section 3 of the Immigration Act 1971 (general provisions for regulation and control) is amended in accordance with subsections (2) to (4).

(2)　After subsection (5) insert—
    "(5A)　The Secretary of State may not deem a relevant person's deportation to be conducive to the public good under subsection (5) if the person's deportation—
        (a)　would be in breach of the obligations of the United Kingdom under Article 20 of the EU withdrawal agreement, Article 19 of the EEA EFTA separation agreement, or Article 17 or 20(3) of the Swiss citizens' rights agreement, or
        (b)　would be in breach of those obligations if the provision in question mentioned in paragraph (a) applied in relation to the person."

(3)　After subsection (6) insert—
    "(6A)　A court may not recommend under subsection (6) that a relevant person be deported if the offence for which the person was convicted consisted of or included conduct that took place before IP completion day."

(4)　After subsection (9) insert—
    "(10)　For the purposes of this section, a person is a "relevant person"—
        (a)　if the person is in the United Kingdom (whether or not they have entered within the meaning of section 11(1)) having arrived with entry clearance granted by virtue of relevant entry clearance immigration rules,
        (b)　if the person has leave to enter or remain in the United Kingdom granted by virtue of residence scheme immigration rules,
        (c)　if the person may be granted leave to enter or remain in the United Kingdom as a person who has a right to enter the United Kingdom by virtue of—
            (i)　Article 32(1)(b) of the EU withdrawal agreement,
            (ii)　Article 31(1)(b) of the EEA EFTA separation agreement, or
            (iii)　Article 26a(1)(b) of the Swiss citizens' rights agreement, whether or not the person has been granted such leave, or
        (d)　if the person may enter the United Kingdom by virtue of regulations made under section 8 of the European Union (Withdrawal Agreement) Act 2020 (frontier workers), whether or not the person has entered by virtue of those regulations.

    (11)　In this section—
        "EEA EFTA separation agreement" and "Swiss citizens' rights agreement" have the same meanings as in the European Union (Withdrawal Agreement) Act 2020 (see section 39(1) of that Act);
        "relevant entry clearance immigration rules" and "residence scheme immigration rules" have the meanings given by section 17 of the European Union (Withdrawal Agreement) Act 2020."

(5)　In section 33 of the UK Borders Act 2007 (exceptions to automatic deportation), after subsection (6A), insert—
    "(6B)　Exception 7 is where—
        (a)　the foreign criminal is a relevant person, and
        (b)　the offence for which the foreign criminal was convicted as mentioned in section 32(1)(b) consisted of or included conduct that took place before IP completion day.

    (6C)　For the purposes of subsection (6B), a foreign criminal is a "relevant person"—
        (a)　if the foreign criminal is in the United Kingdom (whether or not they have entered within the meaning of section 11(1) of the Immigration Act 1971) having arrived with entry clearance granted by virtue of relevant entry clearance immigration rules,
        (b)　if the foreign criminal has leave to enter or remain in the United Kingdom granted by virtue of residence scheme immigration rules,

(c)   if the foreign criminal may be granted leave to enter or remain in the United Kingdom as a person who has a right to enter the United Kingdom by virtue of—

       (i)   Article 32(1)(b) of the EU withdrawal agreement,

       (ii)   Article 31(1)(b) of the EEA EFTA separation agreement, or

       (iii)   Article 26a(1)(b) of the Swiss citizens' rights agreement, whether or not the foreign criminal has been granted such leave,

(d)   if the foreign criminal may enter the United Kingdom by virtue of regulations made under section 8 of the European Union (Withdrawal Agreement) Act 2020 (frontier workers), whether or not the foreign criminal has entered by virtue of those regulations.

(6D)   In this section—

"EEA EFTA separation agreement" and "Swiss citizens' rights agreement" have the same meanings as in the European Union (Withdrawal Agreement) Act 2020 (see section 39(1) of that Act);

"relevant entry clearance immigration rules" and "residence scheme immigration rules" have the meanings given by section 17 of the European Union (Withdrawal Agreement) Act 2020."

(6)   In section 3(10) of the Immigration Act 1971 and section 33(6C) of the UK Borders Act 2007 (for which see subsections (4) and (5) above), references to having leave to enter or remain in the United Kingdom granted by virtue of residence scheme immigration rules include references to having such leave granted by virtue of those rules before section 17 comes into force.

11   Appeals etc. against citizens' rights immigration decisions

(1)   A Minister of the Crown may by regulations make provision for, or in connection with, appeals against citizens' rights immigration decisions of a kind described in the regulations.

(2)   For the purposes of this section, each of the following is a "citizens' rights immigration decision"—

(a)   a decision made in connection with entry clearance by virtue of relevant entry clearance immigration rules (see section 17);

(b)   a decision made in connection with leave to enter or remain in the United Kingdom by virtue of residence scheme immigration rules (see section 17);

(c)   a decision made in connection with entry clearance for the purposes of acquiring leave to enter or remain in relation to a healthcare right of entry;

(d)   a decision made in connection with leave to enter or remain in the United Kingdom in relation to a healthcare right of entry;

(e)   a decision made in connection with a right to enter or remain in the United Kingdom by virtue of regulations made under section 8 (frontier workers);

(f)   a decision to make, or a refusal to revoke, a deportation order under section 5(1) of the Immigration Act 1971 in relation to a relevant person;

(g)   any other decision made in connection with restricting the right of a relevant person to enter the United Kingdom.

(3)   A Minister of the Crown may also by regulations make provision for, or in connection with, reviews (including judicial reviews) of decisions within subsection (2)(g).

(4)   The power to make regulations under subsection (1) or (3) may (among other things) be exercised by modifying any provision made by or under an enactment.

(5)   Such regulations may, for example, apply with or without modifications any enactment which applies in relation to appeals under section 82 of the Nationality, Immigration and Asylum Act 2002 or section 2 of the Special Immigration Appeals Commission Act 1997.

(6)   For the purposes of subsection (2), a "healthcare right of entry" is a right to enter the United Kingdom that a person has by virtue of—

(a)   Article 32(1)(b) of the withdrawal agreement,

(b)   Article 31(1)(b) of the EEA EFTA separation agreement, or

(c)   Article 26a(1)(b) of the Swiss citizens' rights agreement.

(7)   For the purposes of subsection (2)(f) and (g), a person is a "relevant person" if—

(a)   Article 20 of the withdrawal agreement, Article 19 of the EEA EFTA separation agreement or (as the case may be) Articles 17 or 20(3) of the Swiss citizens' rights agreement (restrictions of the rights of entry and residence) applies to the person, or

(b)   the person is not within paragraph (a) but—

     (i)   has entry clearance granted by virtue of relevant entry clearance immigration rules,

     (ii)   has leave to enter or remain in the United Kingdom granted by virtue of residence scheme immigration rules, or

     (iii)   otherwise has leave to enter granted after arriving with entry clearance granted by virtue of relevant entry clearance immigration rules.

(8)   In subsection (7)(b), references to a person who has entry clearance or leave to enter or remain include references to a person who would have had entry clearance or leave to enter or remain but for—

(a)   the making of a deportation order under section 5(1) of the Immigration Act 1971, or

(b)   the making of any other decision made in connection with restricting the right of the person to enter the United Kingdom.

Professional qualifications

12   Recognition of professional qualifications

(1)   An appropriate authority may by regulations make such provision as the authority considers appropriate—

(a)   to implement Chapter 3 of Title II of Part 2 of the withdrawal agreement (professional qualifications),

(b)   to supplement the effect of section 7A of the European Union (Withdrawal) Act 2018 in relation to that Chapter, or

(c)   otherwise for the purposes of dealing with matters arising out of, or related to, that Chapter (including matters arising by virtue of section 7A of that Act and that Chapter).

(2)   An appropriate authority may by regulations make such provision as the authority considers appropriate—

(a)   to implement Chapter 3 of Title II of Part 2 of the EEA EFTA separation agreement (professional qualifications),

(b)   to supplement the effect of section 7B of the European Union (Withdrawal) Act 2018 in relation to that Chapter, or

(c)   otherwise for the purposes of dealing with matters arising out of, or related to, that Chapter (including matters arising by virtue of section 7B of that Act and that Chapter).

(3)   An appropriate authority may by regulations make such provision as the authority considers appropriate—

(a)   to implement professional qualification provisions of the Swiss citizens' rights agreement,

(b)   to supplement the effect of section 7B of the European Union (Withdrawal) Act 2018 in relation to those provisions, or

(c)   otherwise for the purposes of dealing with matters arising out of, or related to, those provisions (including matters arising by virtue of section 7B of that Act and those provisions).

(4)   For the purposes of subsection (3) the following are "professional qualification provisions" of the Swiss citizens' rights agreement—

(a)   Part 4 of that agreement (mutual recognition of professional qualifications);

(b)   Article 23(4) of that agreement as regards the recognition of professional qualifications.

(5)   If an appropriate authority considers it appropriate, regulations under subsection (1) or (2) relating to the implementation of a provision of Chapter 3 of Title II of Part 2 of the withdrawal agreement or of the EEA EFTA separation agreement may be made so as to apply both to—

    (a)   persons to whom the provision in question applies, and

    (b)   persons to whom that provision does not apply but who may be granted leave to enter or remain in the United Kingdom by virtue of residence scheme immigration rules, whether or not they have been granted such leave (see section 17).

(6)   The power to make regulations under subsection (1), (2) or (3) may (among other things) be exercised by modifying any provision made by or under an enactment.

(7)   In subsection (6) "enactment" does not include primary legislation passed or made after IP completion day.

(8)   In this section, "appropriate authority" means—

    (a)   a Minister of the Crown,

    (b)   a devolved authority, or

    (c)   a Minister of the Crown acting jointly with a devolved authority.

(9)   Schedule 1 contains further provision about the power of devolved authorities to make regulations under this section.

Co-ordination of social security systems

13   Co-ordination of social security systems

(1)   An appropriate authority may by regulations make such provision as the authority considers appropriate—

    (a)   to implement Title III of Part 2 of the withdrawal agreement (coordination of social security systems),

    (b)   to supplement the effect of section 7A of the European Union (Withdrawal) Act 2018 in relation to that Title, or

    (c)   otherwise for the purposes of dealing with matters arising out of, or related to, that Title (including matters arising by virtue of section 7A of that Act and that Title).

(2)   An appropriate authority may by regulations make such provision as the authority considers appropriate—

    (a)   to implement Title III of Part 2 of the EEA EFTA separation agreement (co-ordination of social security systems),

    (b)   to supplement the effect of section 7B of the European Union (Withdrawal) Act 2018 in relation to that Title, or

    (c)   otherwise for the purposes of dealing with matters arising out of, or related to, that Title (including matters arising by virtue of section 7B of that Act and that Title).

(3)   An appropriate authority may by regulations make such provision as the authority considers appropriate—

    (a)   to implement social security co-ordination provisions of the Swiss citizens' rights agreement,

    (b)   to supplement the effect of section 7B of the European Union (Withdrawal) Act 2018 in relation to those provisions, or

    (c)   otherwise for the purposes of dealing with matters arising out of, or related to, those provisions (including matters arising by virtue of section 7B of that Act and those provisions).

(4)   For the purposes of subsection (3) the following are "social security coordination provisions" of the Swiss citizens' rights agreement—

    (a)   Part 3 of that agreement (co-ordination of social security systems);

    (b)   Article 23(4) of that agreement as regards social security co-ordination.

(5)   The power to make regulations under subsection (1), (2) or (3) may (among other things) be exercised by modifying any provision made by or under an enactment.

(6)   In this section, "appropriate authority" means—

    (a)   a Minister of the Crown,

    (b)   a devolved authority, or

    (c)   a Minister of the Crown acting jointly with a devolved authority.

(7)   Schedule 1 contains further provision about the power of devolved authorities to make regulations under this section.

Equal treatment etc.

14 Non-discrimination, equal treatment and rights of workers etc.

(1) An appropriate authority may by regulations make such provision as the authority considers appropriate for the purpose of implementing any of the following provisions of the withdrawal agreement—

(a) Article 12 (prohibition of discrimination on grounds of nationality);

(b) Article 23 (right to equal treatment);

(c) Articles 24(1) and 25(1) (rights of workers and the self-employed);

(d) Articles 24(3) and 25(3) (rights of employed or self-employed frontier workers) as regards rights enjoyed as workers.

(2) An appropriate authority may by regulations make such provision as the authority considers appropriate for the purpose of implementing any of the following provisions of the EEA EFTA separation agreement—

(a) Article 11 (prohibition of discrimination on grounds of nationality);

(b) Article 22 (right to equal treatment);

(c) Articles 23(1) and 24(1) (rights of workers and the self-employed);

(d) Articles 23(3) and 24(3) (rights of employed or self-employed frontier workers) as regards rights enjoyed as workers.

(3) An appropriate authority may by regulations make such provision as the authority considers appropriate for the purpose of implementing any of the following provisions of the Swiss citizens' rights agreement—

(a) Article 7 (prohibition of discrimination on grounds of nationality);

(b) Article 18 (right to take up employment etc.);

(c) Article 19 (rights of employed or self-employed persons etc.);

(d) Article 20(1) (rights of frontier workers);

(e) Article 23(1) (rights of persons providing services).

(4) If the appropriate authority considers it appropriate, regulations under subsection (1), (2) or (3) relating to the implementation of a provision mentioned in that subsection, may be made so as to apply both to—

(a) persons to whom the provision in question applies, and

(b) persons to whom that provision does not apply but who may be granted leave to enter or remain in the United Kingdom by virtue of residence scheme immigration rules, whether or not they have been granted such leave (see section 17).

(5) The power to make regulations under subsection (1), (2) or (3) may (among other things) be exercised by modifying any provision made by or under an enactment.

(6) In this section, "appropriate authority" means—

(a) a Minister of the Crown,

(b) a devolved authority, or

(c) a Minister of the Crown acting jointly with a devolved authority.

(7) Schedule 1 contains further provision about the power of devolved authorities to make regulations under this section.

Independent Monitoring Authority

15 Independent Monitoring Authority for the Citizens' Rights Agreements

(1) A body corporate called the Independent Monitoring Authority for the Citizens' Rights Agreements is established.

(2) In this Part that body is referred to as "the IMA".

(3) Schedule 2 contains provision relating to the IMA (including provisions about the IMA's constitution and functions).

General

16   Regulations: supplementary

(1)   In sections 7, 8, 9 and 14—

    (a)   a power to make provision for the purpose of implementing a provision of the withdrawal agreement includes power to make provision to supplement the effect of section 7A of the European Union (Withdrawal) Act 2018 in relation to that provision of the agreement,

    (b)   a power to make provision for the purpose of implementing a provision of the EEA EFTA separation agreement includes power to make provision to supplement the effect of section 7B of that Act in relation to that provision of the agreement, and

    (c)   a power to make provision for the purpose of implementing a provision of the Swiss citizens' rights agreement includes power to make provision to supplement the effect of section 7B of that Act in relation to that provision of the agreement.

(2)   The conferral of a power on a Minister of the Crown under section 7, 8, 9 or 11 does not affect the extent of any power of a devolved authority under section 12, 13 or 14 which overlaps with a power under section 7, 8, 9 or 11 by virtue of section 17(4).

(3)   Regulations under this Part may not provide for the conferral of functions (including the conferral of a discretion) on, or the delegation of functions to, a person who is not a public authority (but may so provide if the person is a public authority).

(4)   In subsection (3), "public authority" means a person who exercises functions of a public nature.

17   Interpretation: Part 3

(1)   In this Part, "residence scheme immigration rules" means—

    (a)   Appendix EU to the immigration rules except those rules, or changes to that Appendix, which are identified in the immigration rules as not having effect in connection with the residence scheme that operates in connection with the withdrawal of the United Kingdom from the EU, and

    (b)   any other immigration rules which are identified in the immigration rules as having effect in connection with the withdrawal of the United Kingdom from the EU.

(2)   In this Part, "relevant entry clearance immigration rules" means any immigration rules which are identified in the immigration rules as having effect in connection with the granting of entry clearance for the purposes of acquiring leave to enter or remain in the United Kingdom by virtue of residence scheme immigration rules.

(3)   In this Part, references to having leave to enter or remain in the United Kingdom granted by virtue of residence scheme immigration rules include references to having such leave granted by virtue of those rules before this section comes into force.

(4)   In this Part, a reference to a Chapter, Title, Part or other provision of the withdrawal agreement, EEA EFTA separation agreement or Swiss citizens' rights agreement includes a reference to—

    (a)   any other provision of the agreement in question so far as relating to that Chapter, Title, Part or other provision, and

    (b)   any provision of EU law which is applied by, or referred to in, that Chapter, Title, Part or other provision (to the extent of the application or reference).

(5)   In this Part—

"entry clearance" has the meaning given by section 33(1) of the Immigration Act 1971 (interpretation);

"immigration rules" has the same meaning as in the Immigration Act 1971.

PART 5

GENERAL AND FINAL PROVISION

Parliamentary sovereignty

38   Parliamentary sovereignty

(1)   It is recognised that the Parliament of the United Kingdom is sovereign.

(2)   In particular, its sovereignty subsists notwithstanding—

- (a)   directly applicable or directly effective EU law continuing to be recognised and available in domestic law by virtue of section 1A or 1B of the European Union (Withdrawal) Act 2018 (savings of existing law for the implementation period),
- (b)   section 7A of that Act (other directly applicable or directly effective aspects of the withdrawal agreement),
- (c)   section 7B of that Act (deemed direct applicability or direct effect in relation to the EEA EFTA separation agreement and the Swiss citizens' rights agreement), and
- (d)   section 7C of that Act (interpretation of law relating to the withdrawal agreement (other than the implementation period), the EEA EFTA separation agreement and the Swiss citizens' rights agreement).

(3)   Accordingly, nothing in this Act derogates from the sovereignty of the Parliament of the United Kingdom.

Interpretation

39   Interpretation

(1)   In this Act—

"devolved authority" means—

- (a)   the Scottish Ministers,
- (b)   the Welsh Ministers, or
- (c)   a Northern Ireland department;

"EEA EFTA separation agreement" means (as modified from time to time in accordance with any provision of it) the Agreement on arrangements between Iceland, the Principality of Liechtenstein, the Kingdom of Norway and the United Kingdom of Great Britain and Northern Ireland following the withdrawal of the United Kingdom from the European Union, the EEA Agreement and other agreements applicable between the United Kingdom and the EEA EFTA States by virtue of the United Kingdom's membership of the European Union;

"enactment" means an enactment whenever passed or made and includes—

- (a)   an enactment contained in any Order in Council, order, rules, regulations, scheme, warrant, byelaw or other instrument made under an Act of Parliament,
- (b)   an enactment contained in any Order in Council made in exercise of Her Majesty's Prerogative,
- (c)   an enactment contained in, or in an instrument made under, an Act of the Scottish Parliament,
- (d)   an enactment contained in, or in an instrument made under, a Measure or Act of the National Assembly for Wales,
- (e)   an enactment contained in, or in an instrument made under, Northern Ireland legislation,
- (f)   an enactment contained in any instrument made by a member of the Scottish Government, the Welsh Ministers, the First Minister for Wales, the Counsel General to the Welsh Government, a Northern Ireland Minister, the First Minister in Northern Ireland, the deputy First Minister in Northern Ireland or a Northern Ireland department in exercise of prerogative or other executive functions of Her Majesty which are exercisable by such a person on behalf of Her Majesty,
- (g)   an enactment contained in, or in an instrument made under, a Measure of the Church Assembly or of the General Synod of the Church of England, and

(h)　any retained direct EU legislation;

"IP completion day" means 31 December 2020 at 11.00 p.m (and see subsections (2) to (5));

"Minister of the Crown" has the same meaning as in the Ministers of the Crown Act 1975 and also includes the Commissioners for Her Majesty's Revenue and Customs;

"modify" includes amend, repeal or revoke (and related expressions are to be read accordingly);

"primary legislation" means—

(a)　an Act of Parliament,

(b)　an Act of the Scottish Parliament,

(c)　a Measure or Act of the National Assembly for Wales, or

(d)　Northern Ireland legislation;

"subordinate legislation" means any Order in Council, order, rules, regulations, scheme, warrant, byelaw or other instrument made under any primary legislation;

"Swiss citizens' rights agreement" means (as modified from time to time in accordance with any provision of it) the Agreement signed at Bern on 25 February 2019 between the United Kingdom of Great Britain and Northern Ireland and the Swiss Confederation on citizens' rights following the withdrawal of the United Kingdom from—

(a)　the European Union, and

(b)　the free movement of persons agreement,

so far as the Agreement operates for the purposes of the case where "specified date" for the purposes of that Agreement has the meaning given in Article 2(b)(ii) of that Agreement;

"withdrawal agreement" means the agreement between the United Kingdom and the EU under Article 50(2) of the Treaty on European Union which sets out the arrangements for the United Kingdom's withdrawal from the EU (as that agreement is modified from time to time in accordance with any provision of it).

(2)　In this Act references to before, after or on IP completion day, or to beginning with IP completion day, are to be read as references to before, after or at 11.00 p.m. on 31 December 2020 or (as the case may be) to beginning with 11.00 p.m. on that day.

(3)　Subsection (4) applies if, by virtue of any change to EU summer-time arrangements, the transition or implementation period provided for by Part 4 of the withdrawal agreement is to end on a day or time which is different from that specified in the definition of "IP completion day" in subsection (1).

(4)　A Minister of the Crown may by regulations—

(a)　amend the definition of "IP completion day" in subsection (1) to ensure that the day and time specified in the definition are the day and time that the transition or implementation period provided for by Part 4 of the withdrawal agreement is to end, and

(b)　amend subsection (2) in consequence of any such amendment.

(5)　In subsection (3) "EU summer-time arrangements" means the arrangements provided for by Directive 2000/84/EC of the European Parliament and of the Council of 19 January 2001 on summer-time arrangements.

(6)　In this Act any reference to an Article of the Treaty on European Union includes a reference to that Article as applied by Article 106a of the Euratom Treaty.

Supplementary and final

40　Regulations

Schedule 4 contains provision about regulations under this Act (including provision about procedure).

41　Consequential and transitional provision etc.

(1)　A Minister of the Crown may by regulations make such provision as the Minister considers appropriate in consequence of this Act.

(2)　The power to make regulations under subsection (1) may (among other things) be exercised by modifying any provision made by or under an enactment.

(3)   In subsection (2) "enactment" does not include primary legislation passed or made after IP completion day.

(4)   Parts 1 and 2 of Schedule 5 contain minor and consequential provision.

(5)   A Minister of the Crown may by regulations make such transitional, transitory or saving provision as the Minister considers appropriate in connection with the coming into force of any provision of this Act (including its operation in connection with exit day or IP completion day).

(6)   Part 3 of Schedule 5 contains transitional, transitory and saving provision.

42   Extent, commencement and short title

(1)   Subject to subsections (2) to (5), this Act extends to England and Wales, Scotland and Northern Ireland.

(2)   Any provision of this Act which amends or repeals an enactment has the same extent as the enactment amended or repealed.

(3)   Accordingly, section 1 (but not section 2) also extends to the Isle of Man, the Channel Islands and Gibraltar.

(4)   The power in section 36 of the Immigration Act 1971 or (as the case may be) section 60(4) of the UK Borders Act 2007 may be exercised so as to extend (with or without modifications) to the Isle of Man or any of the Channel Islands the modifications made to that Act by section 10 above.

(5)   Paragraphs 1 and 2 of Schedule 5, so far as they relate to the modification of any provision in subordinate legislation which extends outside England and Wales, Scotland and Northern Ireland, also extend there.

(6)   The following provisions—

   (a)   sections 3 and 4,

   (b)   sections 11, 16 and 17,

   (c)   sections 20, 29 and 31 to 40 (including Schedule 4),

   (d)   section 41(1) to (3) and (5),

   (e)   the following provisions of Schedule 5—

      (i)   paragraphs 1(3) to (6) and 2,

      (ii)   paragraph 3(2) to (8),

      (iii) paragraph 4,

      (iv)   paragraphs 5 and 7(a) and (b),

      (v)   paragraphs 8 and 12(a) and (b),

      (vi)   paragraphs 17, 20, 22, 24, 27 and 31,

      (vii) paragraphs 32, 36(a) and (b) and 37(b) and (c),

      (viii) paragraphs 38, 41(1) and (3)(a), 42, 44(1), (2)(a), (d) and (e) and (3), 47(1), (2), (4) and (6) and 50,

      (ix)   paragraphs 51 and 56(1) and (7)(b) for the purposes of making regulations under section 8A of, or Part 1A of Schedule 2 to, the European Union (Withdrawal) Act 2018,

      (x)   paragraphs 52(1) and (3) to (7) and 53(1) to (4), (6), (7)(a), (8)(a) and (9) to (13),

      (xi)   paragraph 56(1) and (6)(b) to (d), and

      (xii) paragraphs 65 to 68, (and section 41(4) and (6) so far as relating to any provision so far as it falls within any of sub-paragraphs (i) to (xii)), and

   (f)   this section,

come into force on the day on which this Act is passed.

(7)   The provisions of this Act, so far as they are not brought into force by subsection (6), come into force on such day as a Minister of the Crown may by regulations appoint; and different days may be appointed for different purposes.

(8)   This Act may be cited as the European Union (Withdrawal Agreement) Act 2020.

INDEX

Lightning Source UK Ltd.
Milton Keynes UK
UKHW030640111021
392004UK00003B/40